LITERATURE
and
NATURE

Four Centuries of Nature Writing

D1052056

Edited by

Bridget Keegan

and

James C. McKusick

Prentice
Hall

Upper Saddle River, New Jersey 07458

Library of Congress Cataloging-in-Publication Data

Literature and nature, 1600-2000: four centuries of nature writing: an anthology / edited
by Bridget Keegan and James C. McKusick.
   p. cm.
   Includes index.
   ISBN 0-13-012241-6
   1. Nature–Literary collections. 2. English literature. 3. American literature. I. Keegan,
Bridget. II. McKusick, James C.

PR1111.N3 L56 2000
820.8′036–dc21

00-034674

Editor in Chief: *Leah Jewell*
Senior Acquisitions Editor: *Carrie Brandon*
Editorial Assistant: *Sandy Hrasdzira*
VP, Director of Production and Manufacturing: *Barbara Kittle*
Managing Editor: *Mary Rottino*
Senior Production Editor: *Shelly Kupperman*
Prepress and Manufacturing Manager: *Nick Sklitsis*
Prepress and Manufacturing Buyer: *Mary Ann Gloriande*
Marketing Director: *Beth Gillett Mejia*
Marketing Manager: *Rachel Falk*
Creative Design Director: *Leslie Osher*
Interior and Cover Designer: *Ximena P. Tamvakopoulos*

Grateful acknowledgment is made to all the copyright holders for permission to use copy-
righted material on pages 1099–1102 which is hereby a continuation of this copyright page.

This book was set in 10/12 Janson by Progressive Information Technologies and printed
and bound by Courier, Westford. The cover was printed by Phoenix Company.

© 2001 by Prentice-Hall, Inc.
A Division of Pearson Education
Upper Saddle River, New Jersey 07458

Printed in the United States of America
10 9 8 7 6 5 4 3 2 1

ISBN 0-13-012241-6

Prentice-Hall International (UK) Limited, *London*
Prentice-Hall of Australia Pty. Limited, *Sydney*
Prentice-Hall Canada Inc., *Toronto*
Prentice-Hall Hispanoamerica, S.A., *Mexico*
Prentice-Hall of India Private Limited, *New Delhi*
Prentice-Hall of Japan, Inc., *Tokyo*
Pearson Education Asia Pte. Ltd., *Singapore*
Editora Prentice-Hall do Brasil, Ltda., *Rio de Janeiro*

Brief Contents

Contents

Part IV: 1900–1999
The Twentieth Century: The Web of Life   770

Acknowledgments

THE EDITORS WOULD LIKE TO EXTEND THEIR THANKS TO SEVERAL individuals who assisted at different stages and in different ways with the completion of this anthology. First, we would like to thank Chris Barker of Prentice Hall for encouraging us to make the initial proposal for the book. Literature Editor Carrie Brandon of Prentice Hall took us through the process of publication with patience and good humor. Diane Garvey Nesin proofread the manuscript meticulously and thoughtfully, and Production Editor, Shelly Kupperman, kept everyone on track and in good spirits. Gary Harrison of the University of New Mexico offered advice early on and generously thereafter. Several student research assistants have provided invaluable help. At Creighton University, John Stevens has worked on the project nearly since its inception and has proven himself the picture of calm, dependable efficiency. Amanda Gailey and Christopher Lantz also contributed their talents. At University of Maryland, Baltimore County, Kelly Rose worked diligently in preparing materials for the manuscript. Finally, Kirk McKusick and Eric Allman of Berkeley, California, offered their home and hospitality, fostering the collaborative effort.

Bridget Keegan wishes to thank foremost the students in English 381, Literature and the Environment, in the spring term of 1998. Without them and their inspiration, this anthology would never have been created. Brent Spencer of Creighton University and Nora Spencer offered unflagging friendship and emotional and practical support. Greg Zacharias, former chair of the Department of English at Creighton, was lavish with encouragement and advice, drawn from his considerable editorial expertise. Dean of the Graduate School, Barbara Braden, and former dean of the Creighton College of Arts and Sciences, Michael Proterra, S. J., generously supported travel and research that contributed to the work represented by this collection. Finally, Jeffrey L. Day recommended artwork and served as a reminder of how important it is to go "off the trail," as Gary Snyder says.

James McKusick wishes to express gratitude to the Graduate School of the University of Maryland, Baltimore County for funds in support of research travel to the British Library. He also wishes to thank Paige McKusick for support, both tangible and intangible.

Bridget Keegan
James C. McKusick

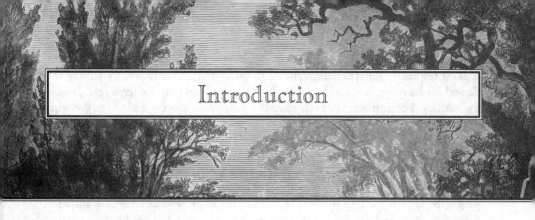

Introduction

URING THE PAST SEVERAL DECADES, ECOLOGICAL ISSUES HAVE risen to the forefront of global political and scientific agendas. Public concern for the environment is having a profound effect on the university, as student and faculty interest in environmental questions grows. This interest has gone beyond the disciplines of the natural and social sciences and is fast becoming a specialized topic in literary studies. This is not surprising, as a deep concern for the relationship between humanity and the environment has long been a topic for poets and artists. From ancient authors such as Hesiod and Virgil to postmodern writers such as Samuel Beckett and Thomas Pynchon, the natural world has been more than just a backdrop or setting. Rather, the representation of nature and the exploration of the human relationship to nature permeates all aspects of literary art from genre and form to plot and character. The relationship of literature and nature is explored not only in works that are explicitly *about* nature (e.g., James Thomson's *The Seasons* or Henry David Thoreau's *Maine Woods*), it is also present in different manners and with differing effects throughout the course of English and American literary history. It appears as the antagonist in Daniel Defoe's *Robinson Crusoe* or in Stephen Crane's "The Open Boat." It provides the metaphors for articulating otherwise ineffable philosophical and theological concepts, as in Samuel Taylor Coleridge's "Rime of the Ancient Mariner" or Wallace Stevens's "The Plain Sense of Things." It is the vehicle for human self-understanding and for the articulation of the most profound emotions of love or grief, as can be seen in John Milton's elegy "Lycidas" or in Emily Brontë's evocative lyrics. Moreover, examining nature *in* literature can also provide a helpful means of interrogating the nature *of* literature. The creative and dynamic processes of the natural world have often suggested metaphors for writers to understand their own artistic creativity, as in John Keats's "Ode to a Nightingale" or in any number of Emily Dickinson's poems.

Of course, the definition of the term "nature," and the historical shifts in the word's meaning, have helped to encourage these multiple literary manifestations. The word *nature* meant something quite different to Sir Walter Ralegh than it does to Annie Dillard. From the Latin verb meaning "to be born," its first and earliest usage denotes the inherent qualities of a thing—that which gives something its distinctive features and makes it unique. With respect to persons, this might mean their dominant disposition or what might otherwise be called their "character." It can also refer to the totality of things in the universe and to the aggregate of their respective innate characteristics. In this definition, nature is something static and unchanging. A second, more recent use specifies that the term refers not to the sum total of attributes but rather to the sum total of forces and powers at work in the universe. This definition presents nature as dynamic, subject to change and causing changes. Yet these are not the only explanations of this broad concept. Because of the scope of its various connotations, nature is often explained in relationship to its conceptual opposites: opposed, for example, to spirituality, art, or civilization. These oppositions are themselves tied to larger intellectual discourses in which the term is used. In medieval Christian theological speculation, for instance, nature intends creation and is the providential product of the omnipotent creator. Whatever changes it undergoes are the result of a divine plan, and the best way to understand nature is through a study of the Bible. For the more secular scientific discourse that arises after the Renaissance, nature becomes an abstract process best studied through direct observation and experience. As will become evident in the selections chosen for this collection, both the theological and the scientific discourses of nature, and the conflicts between them, have a profound effect on literary expressions of what nature is, where humankind fits into the natural scheme, and what our relationship to nature can or should be.

The clash between scientific and theological discourses, and the confrontation between the respective notions that nature is either static or dynamic, takes an important turn precisely at the historical moment where this anthology begins. The new usage and the new concepts of nature as motion or process derived not just from the shifts brought on by Copernicus or Bacon in the Scientific Revolution; the idea of nature was also profoundly affected by the many voyages of discovery and exploration of the New World. The use of the word *nature* is indelibly altered by the English presence in North America, which begins to flourish in the early seventeenth century. To talk about the expression of nature in British literature from 1600 forward, then, one must of necessity consider the beginning of literature written about and in America by English-speaking writers. The English opened their frontier and, coinciding with this physical and geographical expansion, a complementary intellectual, spiritual, and cultural expansion took place. The idea of America—as Paradise Regained or as hostile wilderness—shaped a great deal of British writing about nature in the seventeenth century. As America began to develop its own literary tradition, it perforce looked to the English tradition for forms and themes to adapt. This fertile cross-pollination between the two national literatures continues into the present, creating a lively ongoing dialogue about our relationship to our natural world that has included many voices over the past four centuries. Because both English and American literature participate in a mutual transatlantic language community, these two traditions cannot and should not be considered in isolation. William Shakespeare's *The Tempest* has as its source Silvester Jourdain's travel narrative. Early American author William Bartram's prose representation of the American wilderness is deeply influenced by Milton's epic image of Eden. In later centuries, John Muir must be understood in terms of his relation to the British Romantic poets. Nor should we read the poetry of Seamus Heaney without considering the influence of Robert Frost.

Given the important developments that begin around the year 1600, it is a fundamental mistake to suppose that instances of British and American literature of and about nature are either nationally specific or limited to the nineteenth and twentieth centuries. Conventional literary history claims that nature writing begins in the nineteenth century with English Romanticism and American Transcendentalism. Certainly the early nineteenth century marked a decisive turning point. However, it is our fundamental premise that broader historical and national contours are essential to full comprehension of the relationship of literature and nature in the English language. Early modern texts (such as Andrew Marvell's pastorals or John Smith's travel writing on early colonial Virginia) demonstrate that environmental awareness in literature is of much longer date, and that its expression begins to adopt more familiar contours beginning in the seventeenth century.

While we are intent upon expanding the frontiers of the notion of nature writing, we are also aware of some of the unfortunate boundaries imposed by the closed form of the book. We have opted to focus on literature primarily from the United States and from England. We have also included several authors of Irish, Scottish, and Welsh backgrounds, as well as several Native American authors whose cultures were not originally English-speaking but who themselves write in English. We have attempted to be as inclusive as possible, being certain to represent more just than the predictable canonical texts; however, because our primary focus is on the variety of literary manifestations of nature, we were not able to include textual selections from all Anglophone nations or cultures, such as Canada, the Caribbean, Australia, or New Zealand. This would be the work of a much larger anthology.

We have also worked to expand and challenge conventional notions of nature writing not only historically but also at the level of literary form, moving beyond nonfiction descriptive or meditative prose (the genre which often dominates several more popular collections). Our aim is, again, to survey the variety and multitude of modes of writing about nature produced in England and America from the early modern age to the present. We have incorporated a range of literary genres: fables, ballads, odes, epic poetry, travelogues, short stories, portions of novels and dramas, as well as the important nonfiction essay. In many cases, the broader historical scope of the anthology can allow for observing how a particular literary form for writing about nature, such as the georgic, changes over time— from Milton and John Dyer to Robert Frost and Maxine Kumin. These modes express the wealth of literary perspectives on nature, underscoring a varied and historically shifting understanding of humanity's relationship to the natural world.

Finally, we have tried to address how individual differences of expression might be connected with each author's gender, class, and racial background. In being sensitive to how these critical categories affect an author's writing about his or her environment, we hope once again to open the frontiers of the canon of nature writing, proving that the subject was of interest not only to the familiar names such as William Wordsworth, Henry David Thoreau, or John Muir. *Literature and Nature* highlights the important and longstanding contributions of women, laboring-class, African American, and Native American authors. We have tried in all circumstances to choose exemplary works, all the while remaining cognizant of the fact that choosing any selection from the rich body of work that has been recovered or is now being written by women and minority writers also means having to leave out another equally interesting or beautiful piece. We refer, wherever possible, to additional works by each author, hoping that our selections will spur further reading and reflection.

Our principles in the design and organization of this book have grown out of our own experiences as classroom teachers and have been strengthened by the input of other teachers of environmental literature and from the excellent work and inspiration of other editors of nature writing anthologies, even though their scope differed from that of the present work. Throughout, our editorial objective has been to promote accessibility by annotating as unobtrusively as possible. In order to convey the stylistic uniqueness of many of the texts from earlier historical periods, some deviations from modern conventions in punctuation and capitalization as well as older lexical forms have been retained. For greater ease in reading, however, in most circumstances, spelling has been modernized and obvious grammatical errors have been silently corrected.

The book as a whole is divided into four sections, according to century. Where an author lived and published in more than one century, we placed him or her in the century in which he or she preponderantly published or, on rare occasions, according to where the work itself seemed to fit with prevailing themes or styles. Each section begins with an overview highlighting important cultural, scientific, and political developments. To lend coherence within each century section, we have chosen a predominant theme which recurs in a number of the selections (and which might serve as a touchstone for comparison to other centuries' selections). In the presentation of texts for the seventeenth century, we highlight the theme of discovery and focus on the exploration of forests and wilderness. In the eighteenth century, the emphasis is on gardens and gardening. In the nineteenth century, we look at humankind's relationship with the birds and beasts. And finally, in the twentieth century, we draw on current theories of ecology and explore the notion of the web of life, particularly as it is manifested in the spiritual and biological significance of water. These themes are not meant to limit the reader's appreciation but instead to aid in making connections among the works in a particular century and among the selections from different centuries. In addition to these part introductions, the selections from a particular author are introduced with biographical and critical information meant to provide further context for understanding.

As we begin a new millennium and cross a significant temporal frontier, we might share some of the same excitement and wonder—as well as some of the nostalgia and anxiety—that the seventeenth-century explorers felt as they crossed over to that "brave new world." Whether that world will resemble a pastoral Arcadia or an absurdist Wasteland hinges on how well we heed the writers' lessons. For it is not unreasonable to claim that these authors were often well in advance of scientists and philosophers in expressing the complexity, diversity, and enduring mysteries of the human relationship to the natural world.

PART I: 1600–1699

The Seventeenth Century: Encompassing New Worlds

THE VAST, LARGELY UNCHARTED TERRAIN OF THE NEW WORLD, with its indigenous inhabitants, fierce beasts, and trackless forests, exercised an immense fascination upon the literary imagination of seventeenth-century British writers. English privateers such as Walter Ralegh and Francis Drake roamed the wide waters of the Atlantic and Pacific Oceans, capturing and destroying enemy vessels, exploring unknown lands, and always searching for the fabled gold and silver mines that supposedly lurked just beyond the blue horizon. Several of the most remarkable voyages of exploration were published between 1598 and 1600 by Richard Hakluyt in *The Principall Navigations, Voyages, Traffiques, and Discoveries of the English Nation,* an immense compendium of the newly emerging geographical knowledge of the New World. The English settlement of North America began in earnest during the early seventeenth century, as hardy groups of settlers arrived on the shores of Virginia, Massachusetts, and elsewhere along the Atlantic coastline. Jamestown, Virginia, was the site of the first permanent English settlement, established by a discordant group of gentlemen adventurers under the domineering leadership of Captain John Smith, whose enthusiastic commendation of the bountiful New World landscape is included in this anthology. In 1620, the *Mayflower* famously landed at Plymouth Rock, bearing on board a very different sort of English settler: an exiled band of Puritans, self-declared Pilgrims on a quest for freedom from religious persecution, seeking a suitable place to develop a "godly" community in the New World. Their leader, William Bradford, describes the main objectives of their voyage, along with their first impressions of the hideous, howling American wilderness. The captivity narrative of Mary Rowlandson, who was violently abducted by Wampanoag warriors in 1676, further exemplifies

5

the prevailing Puritan attitude toward the terrors of the New World and its "savage" inhabitants.

The unfamiliar environment of the New World inspired extremes of exuberant delight, industrious activity, reflective contemplation, and scientific inquiry among its newly arrived British inhabitants. William Shakespeare incorporated many of these perspectives in *The Tempest*, a play that draws on several New World exploration narratives of the early 1600s, particularly those published by Hakluyt, along with Silvester Jourdain's account of a shipwreck on the island of Bermuda. *The Tempest* weaves these diverse source materials into a dramatic meditation on the ultimate consequences of British colonization, taking into account the viewpoint of the indigenous inhabitants (as represented in the figure of Caliban). Many British poets of the seventeenth century, from John Milton through Andrew Marvell, incorporate the imagery of New World exploration into their description of exotic, remote, and Edenic landscapes.

"The great globe itself," as Shakespeare evoked both the name of his own theater (the Globe) and the great planet upon which it dwelled, was the object of a radically new understanding during the seventeenth century. The earth was no longer a stationary object, poised at the center of the universe, because the Copernican cosmology (describing how the earth orbits around the sun) had received empirical confirmation through the work of Galileo. Forced by the Inquisition to recant his heretical views of cosmology, Galileo whispered three defiant words: *"Eppur si muove"* (And yet it does move!). When John Milton visited the elderly, blind Galileo in 1638, he very likely heard about the astronomer's amazing discoveries: sunspots, the moons of Jupiter, the rings of Saturn, the wonders of the cosmos newly revealed by the invention of the telescope. Milton incorporated some aspects of this new cosmology into his great epic poem *Paradise Lost*, although he was careful to keep both the old and the new cosmological paradigms available, as he needed them both to fulfill his poetic purposes. Some critics have argued that the old, earth-centered cosmos is intrinsically more friendly to the human imagination. Certainly it was unsettling for many people to contemplate the earth swimming solitary in the void; indeed, the empty spaces between the stars inspired terror in Blaise Pascal. Throughout this period, English literature inhabited the discursive space between competing worldviews, and the ferment of new scientific ideas was a persistent element in the shifting intellectual currents of the seventeenth century.

The essential principles of the New Science were most perceptively laid forth in Francis Bacon's treatise *Novum Organum* (1620), which advocates a new way of generating knowledge from our experience of nature: not from dusty books, but from firsthand observation, aided by inference and experiment, using such newly invented instruments as the telescope and the microscope to extend the range and acuity of human perception. This approach to the understanding of nature, later to be known as the scientific method, had a pervasive influence on seventeenth-century English literature and culture. The Royal Society was founded in 1662 as a professional association of scientists engaged in the advancement of this new paradigm of knowledge, and the poet Margaret Cavendish was the first woman ever to visit the Society (and the only woman to do so for the next 300 years). Her lyrical engagement with contemporary science, particularly in such poems as "A Dialogue betwixt Man, and Nature," exemplifies the way that literature not only reflects scientific ideas but actually advances the discourse of science in the later seventeenth century. One of the founding members of the Royal Society was John Evelyn, whose elegantly written book on forestry, entitled *Sylva*, mingles practical advice on the planting of trees with thoughtful historical analysis of the sacredness of standing groves, indicating that even the most advanced scientific treatises of the seventeenth century could find room for the intrinsic spiritual aspects of the natural landscape.

Throughout the seventeenth century, the English language developed new forms and modes of literary expression that emerge from new ways of seeing, knowing, and experiencing the natural world. Just as Francis Bacon encouraged experimentation as a means of scientific discovery, so too the British and American writers of the seventeenth century invented an astonishing range of new literary genres. Bacon himself was the first English author to experiment with the personal essay, a newly invented prose genre. During the next two centuries, the personal essay would become the single most dominant form of nonfiction prose in the English language; and in the form of the natural history essay, as it gradually developed from Izaak Walton through Gilbert White and Henry David Thoreau, this genre would prove especially amenable to the description of flora and fauna as they are observed in their wild habitat.

Another important and pervasive literary genre during this period is the pastoral, a mode of literary expression that harks back to classical antecedents in the poetry of Theocritus and Virgil, which was rediscovered during the Elizabethan period but was more fully elaborated during the course of the seventeenth century. The pastoral mode generally involves the description of sheep and shepherds in a remote, bucolic setting, and it virtually always entails an element of nostalgia: the recollection of an earlier, more innocent and delightful way of life. Implicitly, the pastoral mode invokes a contrast between the simplicity of country life and the hectic, unhealthful environment of the city. The environmental basis of pastoral imagery is apparent in Christopher Marlowe's "The Passionate Shepherd to His Love," a lyric of seduction that offers to transport its addressee to a landscape of green valleys and waterfalls and to clothe her entirely in garments made of local fabrics and materials, if only she will "come live with me and be my love." The exquisite, idealized beauty of this setting is countered in "The Nymph's Reply to the Shepherd" by Sir Walter Ralegh; this poem questions the assumptions underlying the pastoral mode by pointing out that even such bucolic settings are subject to the ravages of time. Both pastoral and antipastoral modes are further developed during the seventeenth century, and the continuing appeal of pastoral, even in the face of ridicule, bears witness to the relevance of its message in an era of unsettling new ideas, increasing urbanization, and environmental change. The seventeenth century needed pastoral poetry because it offered its readers a gratifying vision of the green world of field and forest, now threatening to disappear into the remote past.

The pastoral mode inflects virtually all of the verse forms available to writers in the seventeenth century. Lyric poetry, in particular, frequently draws on pastoral themes and images. Thus the theme of *carpe diem* ("live for the day") is expressed in Robert Herrick's "Corinna's Going A-Maying" and in John Donne's "The Blossom" by means of the bucolic imagery of blossoms and rose petals, to which the fragile and transient beauty of the beloved is compared. Shakespeare's sonnets draw heavily on pastoral imagery, particularly in Sonnet 18, "Shall I compare thee to a summer's day?" The "Grasshopper" poems of Abraham Cowley and Richard Lovelace offer a further variation on the *carpe diem* theme, warning that the wasteful, improvident lifestyle of the grasshopper will inevitably doom it to destruction when winter comes around. These "Grasshopper" poems provide early instances of a conservation ethic, since they both implicitly advocate careful planning and wise stewardship of the earth's limited resources.

John Milton provides further evidence that a pastoral sensibility pervaded a wide range of literary genres in the seventeenth century. His poem "Lycidas" is considered the most fully realized instance of pastoral elegy in the English language, while his epic poem *Paradise Lost* relies on many pastoral conventions in its depiction of the Garden of Eden as a place of idyllic bliss, with Adam and Eve serving as shepherds to the strange beasts that wander peacefully through those green fields. Milton renders the almost unimaginable beauty of the Garden of Eden intelligible to his readers by employing the familiar imagery of pastoral poetry, and the pastoral mode is itself revised and renovated by his unexpected adaptation of it to the purposes of epic poetry. Through its depiction of a remote, primeval garden, *Paradise Lost* exemplifies the environmental ethos that is apparent in much seventeenth-century English poetry.

❧ *Christopher Marlowe* (1564–1593)

Born in Canterbury, Christopher Marlowe was educated at Cambridge University, graduating in 1584. A contemporary of Shakespeare, Marlowe invented the genre of blank-verse drama in English, and as a playwright he was remarkably precocious, composing three memorable plays while still in his twenties: Tamburlaine *(c. 1587),* Dr. Faustus *(c. 1588), and* The Jew of Malta *(c. 1589). He is also remembered for his long narrative poem* Hero and Leander *(1598) and for his lyric poetry in the pastoral mode, particularly "The Passionate Shepherd to His Love." This marvelous poem of invitation and seduction, composed in ballad stanza, is one of the finest lyrics to emerge from the English Renaissance. It evokes a green world of field and forest at the very dawn of creation, an Edenic realm of "shallow rivers, to whose falls / Melodious birds sing madrigals." In imagery of diamondlike clarity and simplicity, the poem speaks to all that the human heart has ever desired. Several English poets composed responses to it, often satirical in tone, of which the best known is by Sir Walter Ralegh (reprinted on p. 10).*

Marlowe died before the age of thirty, stabbed by a drinking companion in a tavern. His literary career ended just as that of Shakespeare was beginning. The two men very likely knew each other, and the plays of Shakespeare incorporate and build upon many aspects of Marlowe's dramaturgy, particularly in the use of blank verse as a medium of expression for the full range of human emotion, character, and situation.

The Passionate Shepherd to His Love

Come live with me, and be my love,
And we will all the pleasures prove,[1]
That valleys, groves, hills and fields,
Woods or steepy mountains yields.

And we will sit upon the rocks,   5
Seeing the shepherds feed their flocks
By shallow rivers, to whose falls
Melodious birds sing madrigals.

And I will make thee beds of roses,
And a thousand fragrant posies,   10
A cap of flowers and a kirtle[2]
Embroidered all with leaves of myrtle;

A gown made of the finest wool
Which from our pretty lambs we pull;
Fair-linèd slippers for the cold,   15
With buckles of the purest gold;

A belt of straw and ivy-buds,
With coral clasps and amber studs:
And if these pictures may thee move,
Come live with me and be my love.   20

The shepherd swains shall dance and sing
For thy delight each May morning:
If these delights thy mind may move,
Then live with me and be my love.

♫ Sir Walter Ralegh (1552–1618)

Sir Walter Ralegh epitomizes the high aspirations of the Elizabethan age, both in his literary works and in his accomplishments as a soldier, privateer, explorer, and colonist. Trained in the arts of rhetoric and logic at Oxford University, Ralegh left the university without taking a degree, turning instead to the wider world of exploration and conquest. In 1578–79 he served on an unsuccessful voyage to discover the Northwest Passage, and in 1580 he commanded a company of soldiers in Ireland, where he first met Edmund Spenser, later to become one of the leading poets of the Elizabethan era. Returning to England as a war hero, Ralegh soon became one of Queen Elizabeth's most trusted advisors, lavished with honors and privileges. He was knighted in 1585, and in 1587 he was made captain of the queen's personal guard. During his years as a courtier, Ralegh

---

[1] Find out, learn through experience.
[2] Skirt.

composed poems of courtly love, which circulated freely (and often anonymously) in man-
uscript. In 1592, however, he fell out of favor with Elizabeth, who discovered that
Ralegh had seduced, and then married, one of her ladies-in-waiting. Imprisoned in the
Tower of London, Ralegh wrote eloquent poems of lament.

Released from prison, Ralegh regained the queen's favor and embarked on a voyage of
exploration in the New World. He set forth, in 1595, in search of the fabled El Dorado,
the interior capital of Guiana, supposedly brimming with vast quantities of silver and
gold. He found no such city, but the tale of his adventures, recorded in The Discovery
of the Large, Rich, and Beautiful Empire of Guiana *(1596), is justly regarded as*
one of the greatest travel narratives ever written. Ralegh draws on pastoral conventions
in depicting the wonder of this strange land, a veritable Eden of natural beauty and un-
told mineral wealth, teeming with grassy lawns, fertile groves, and deer "that came
down feeding by the water's side as if they had been used to a keeper's call." Among the
literary descendants of this work is Shakespeare's The Tempest, *whose island likewise*
partakes of "something rich and strange."

In about 1600, Ralegh composed a reply to Christopher Marlowe's celebrated poem of
pastoral seduction, "The Passionate Shepherd to His Love." "The Nymph's Reply to the
Shepherd" offers a witty and sardonic rejoinder to the shepherd's blandishments, empha-
sizing the impermanence of earthly beauty and the destructive effects of mortality. Such
antipastoral poetry emerges from Ralegh's own experience of fierce battles, remote jun-
gles, and storm-tossed seas. It reflects his grim awareness that the world can be a cold,
bleak, and cruel place. Ralegh's own life took a turn for the worse after the death of
Elizabeth, in 1603. Imprisoned in the Tower by King James I, Ralegh remained a pris-
oner for thirteen years, writing a million-word History of the World *(1614) and*
meditating on the vanity of human ambition. Finally released from the Tower in 1617,
he embarked on a disastrous naval expedition to seek gold in Guiana. Returning empty-
handed from this voyage, Ralegh was found guilty of treason and executed in 1618.

The Nymph's Reply to the Shepherd

If all the world and love were young,
And truth in every shepherd's tongue,
These pretty pleasures might me move
To live with thee and be thy love.

Time drives the flocks from field to fold,   5
When rivers rage and rocks grow cold;
And Philomel[1] becometh dumb;
The rest complains of cares to come.

The flowers do fade, and wanton fields
To wayward winter reckoning yields;   10
A honey tongue, a heart of gall
Is fancy's spring, but sorrow's fall.

---

[1] The nightingale.

Thy gowns, thy shoes, thy beds of roses,
Thy cap, thy kirtle, and thy posies
Soon break, soon wither, soon forgotten,   15
In folly ripe, in reason rotten.

Thy belt of straw and ivy-buds,
Thy coral clasps and amber studs,
All these in me no means can move
To come to thee and be thy love.   20

But could youth last, and love still breed,
Had joys no date,[2] nor age no need,
Then these delights my mind might move
To live with thee and be thy love.

From The Discovery of the Large, Rich, and Beautiful Empire of Guiana

The great river of *Orenoque* or *Baraquan* hath nine branches which fall out on the north side of his own main mouth. On the south side it hath seven other fallings into the sea, so it disemboqueth by sixteen arms in all, between islands and broken ground; but the islands are very great, many of them as big as the *Isle of Wight*, and bigger, and many less. From the first branch on the north to the last of the south it is at least 100 leagues, so as the river's mouth is 300 miles wide at his entrance into the sea, which I take to be far bigger than that of *Amazons*. All those that inhabit in the mouth of this river upon the several north branches are these *Tivitivas*, of which there are two chief lords which have continual wars one with the other. The islands which lie on the right hand are called *Pallamos*, and the land on the left, *Hororotomaka*; and the river by which *John Douglas* returned within the land from *Amana* to *Capuri* they call *Macuri*.

These *Tivitivas* are a very goodly people and very valiant, and have the most manly speech and most deliberate that ever I heard of what nation soever. In the summer they have houses on the ground, as in other places; in the winter they dwell upon the trees, where they build very artificial towns and villages, as it is written in the Spanish story of the *West Indies* that those people do in the low lands near the gulf of *Uraba*. For between May and September the river of *Orenoque* riseth thirty foot upright, and then are those islands overflown twenty foot high above the level of the ground, saving some few raised grounds in the middle of them; and for this cause they are enforced to live in this manner. They never eat of anything that is set or sown; and as at home they use neither planting nor other manurance, so when they come abroad they refuse to feed of aught but of that which nature without labour bringeth forth. They use the tops of *palmitos* for bread, and kill deer, fish, and porks for the rest of their sustenance.

---

[2] Ending.

They have also many sorts of fruits that grow in the woods, and great variety of birds and fowls; and if to speak of them were not tedious and vulgar, surely we saw in those passages of very rare colours and forms not elsewhere to be found, for as much as I have either seen or read.

Of these people those that dwell upon the branches of *Orenoque*, called *Capuri* and *Macureo*, are for the most part carpenters of *canoas*; for they make the most and fairest *canoas*, and sell them into *Guiana* for gold and into *Trinidad* for *tabacco*, in the excessive taking whereof they exceed all nations. And notwithstanding the moistness of the air in which they live, the hardness of their diet, and the great labours they suffer to hunt, fish, and fowl for their living, in all my life, either in the *Indies* or in *Europe*, did I never behold a more goodly or better-favoured people or a more manly. They were wont to make war upon all nations, and especially on the *Cannibals*, so as none durst without a good strength trade by those rivers; but of late they are at peace with their neighbours, all holding the Spaniards for a common enemy. When their commanders die they use great lamentation; and when they think the flesh of their bodies is putrified and fallen from their bones, then they take up the carcase again and hang it in the *cacique*'s house that died, and deck his skull with feathers of all colours, and hang all his gold plates about the bones of his arms, thighs, and legs. Those nations which are called *Arwacas*, which dwell on the south of *Orenoque*, of which place and nation our Indian pilot was, are dispersed in many other places, and do use to beat the bones of their lords into powder, and their wives and friends drink it all in their several sorts of drinks.

After we departed from the port of these *Ciawani* we passed up the river with the flood and anchored the ebb, and in this sort we went onward. The third day that we entered the river, our galley came on ground; and stuck so fast as we thought that even there our discovery had ended, and that we must have left four-score and ten of our men to have inhabited, like rooks upon trees, with those nations. But the next morning, after we had cast out all her ballast, with tugging and hauling to and fro we got her afloat and went on. At four days' end we fell into as goodly a river as ever I beheld, which was called the great *Amana*, which ran more directly without windings and turnings than the other. But soon after the flood of the sea left us; and, being enforced either by main strength to row against a violent current, or to return as wise as we went out, we had then no shift but to persuade the companies that it was but two or three days' work, and therefore desired them to take pains, every gentleman and others taking their turns to row, and to spell one the other at the hour's end. Every day we passed by goodly branches of rivers, some falling from the west, others from the east, into *Amana*; but those I leave to the description in the chart of discovery, where every one shall be named with his rising and descent. When three days more were overgone, our companies began to despair, the weather being extreme hot, the river bordered with very high trees that kept away the air, and the current against us every day stronger than other. But we evermore commanded our pilots to promise an end the next day, and used it so long as we were driven to assure them from four reaches of the river to three, and so to two, and so to the next reach. But so long we laboured that many days were spent, and we driven to draw ourselves to harder allowance, our bread even at the last, and no drink at all; and our men and ourselves so wearied and scorched, and doubtful withal whether we should ever perform it or no, the heat increasing as we drew towards the line;[1] for we were now in five degrees.

The further we went on, our victual decreasing and the air breeding great faintness, we grew weaker and weaker, when we had most need of strength and ability. For hourly the river ran more violently than other against us, and the barge, wherries, and ship's boat of Captain *Gifford* and Captain *Caulfield* had spent all their provisions; so as we were brought into despair and discomfort, had we not persuaded all the company that it was but only one day's work more to attain the land where we should be relieved of all we wanted, and if we returned, that we were sure to starve by the way, and that the world would also laugh us to scorn. On the banks of these rivers were divers sorts of fruits good to eat, flowers and trees of such variety as were sufficient to make ten volumes of *Herbals*; we relieved ourselves many times with the fruits of the country, and sometimes with fowl and fish. We saw birds of all colours, some carnation, some crimson, orange-tawny, purple, watchet,[2] and of all other sorts, both simple and mixed, and it was unto us a great good-passing of the time to behold them, besides the relief we found by killing some store of them with our fowling-pieces; without which, having little or no bread, and less drink, but only the thick and troubled water of the river, we had been in a very hard case.

Our old pilot of the *Ciawani*, whom, as I said before, we took to redeem *Ferdinando*, told us, that if we would enter a branch of a river on the right hand with our barge and wherries, and leave the galley at anchor the while in the great river, he would bring us to a town of the *Arwacas*, where we should find store of bread, hens, fish, and of the country wine; and persuaded us, that departing from the galley at noon we might return ere night. I was very glad to hear this speech, and presently took my barge, with eight musketeers, Captain *Gifford's* wherry, with himself and four musketeers, and Captain *Caulfield* with his wherry, and as many; and so we entered the mouth of this river; and because we were persuaded that it was so near, we took no victual with us at all. When we had rowed three hours, we marvelled we saw no sign of any dwelling, and asked the pilot where the town was; he told us, a little further. After three hours more, the sun being almost set, we began to suspect that he led us that way to betray us; for he confessed that those Spaniards which fled from *Trinidad*, and also those that remained with *Carapana* in *Emeria*, were joined together in some village upon that river. But when it grew towards night, and we demanded where the place was, he told us but four reaches more. When we had rowed four and four, we saw no sign; and our poor watermen, even heart-broken and tired, were ready to give up the ghost; for we had now come from the galley near forty miles.

At the last we determined to hang the pilot; and if we had well known the way back again by night, he had surely gone. But our own necessities pleaded sufficiently for his safety; for it was as dark as pitch, and the river began so to narrow

[1] Equator. Ralegh's ships have approached to within five degrees latitude of the equator.
[2] Pale blue.

itself, and the trees to hang over from side to side, as we were driven with arming swords to cut a passage thorough those branches that covered the water. We were very desirous to find this town hoping of a feast, because we made but a short breakfast aboard the galley in the morning, and it was now eight o'clock at night, and our stomachs began to gnaw apace; but whether it was best to return or go on, we began to doubt, suspecting treason in the pilot more and more; but the poor old Indian ever assured us that it was but a little further, but this one turning and that turning; and at the last about one o'clock after midnight we saw a light, and rowing towards it we heard the dogs of the village. When we landed we found few people; for the lord of that place was gone with divers *canoas* above 400 miles off, upon a journey towards the head of *Orenoque*, to trade for gold, and to buy women of the *Cannibals*, who afterwards unfortunately passed by us as we rode at an anchor in the port of *Morequito* in the dark of the night, and yet came so near us as his *canoas* grated against our barges; he left one of his company at the port of *Morequito*, by whom we understood that he had brought thirty young women, divers plates of gold, and had great store of fine pieces of cotton cloth, and cotton beds. In his house we had good store of bread, fish, hens, and Indian drink, and so rested that night; and in the morning, after we had traded with such of his people as came down, we returned towards our galley, and brought with us some quantity of bread, fish, and hens.

On both sides of this river we passed the most beautiful country that ever mine eyes beheld; and whereas all that we had seen before was nothing but woods, prickles, bushes, and thorns, here we beheld plains of twenty miles in length, the grass short and green, and in divers parts groves of trees by themselves, as if they had been by all the art and labour in the world so made of purpose; and still as we rowed, the deer came down feeding by the water's side as if they had been used to a keeper's call. Upon this river there were great store of fowl, and of many sorts; we saw in it divers sorts of strange fishes, and of marvellous bigness; but for *lagartos*[3] it exceeded, for there were thousands of those ugly serpents; and the people call it, for the abundance of them, the *River of Lagartos*, in their language. I had a negro, a very proper young fellow, who leaping out of the galley to swim in the mouth of this river, was in all our sights taken and devoured with one of those *lagartos*. In the meanwhile our companies in the galley thought we had been all lost, for we promised to return before night; and sent the *Lion's Whelp*'s ship's boat with Captain *Whiddon* to follow us up the river. But the next day, after we had rowed up and down some fourscore miles, we returned, and went on our way up the great river; and when we were even at the last cast for want of victuals, Captain *Gifford* being before the galley and the rest of the boats, seeking out some place to land upon the banks to make fire, espied four *canoas* coming down the river; and with no small joy caused his men to try the uttermost of their strengths, and after a while two of the four gave over and ran themselves ashore, every man betaking himself to the fastness of the woods. The two other lesser got away, while he landed to lay hold on these; and so turned into some by-creek, we knew not whither. Those *canoas* that were taken

---

[3] Alligators and crocodiles (Spanish).

were loaden with bread, and were bound for *Margarita* in the *West Indies*, which those Indians, called *Arwacas*, proposed to carry thither for exchange; but in the lesser there were three Spaniards, who having heard of the defeat of their Governor in *Trinidad*, and that we purposed to enter *Guiana*, came away in those *canoas*; one of them was a *cavallero*,[4] as the captain of the *Arwacas* after told us, another a soldier and the third a refiner.

In the meantime, nothing on the earth could have been more welcome to us, next unto gold, than the great store of very excellent bread which we found in these *canoas*; for now our men cried, *Let us go on, we care not how far.* After that Captain *Gifford* had brought the two *canoas* to the galley, I took my barge and went to the bank's side with a dozen shot, where the *canoas* first ran themselves ashore, and landed there, sending out Captain *Gifford* and Captain *Thyn* on one hand and Captain *Caulfield* on the other, to follow those that were fled into the woods. And as I was creeping thorough the bushes, I saw an Indian basket hidden, which was the refiner's basket; for I found in it his quicksilver, saltpetre, and divers things for the trial of metals, and also the dust of such ore as he had refined; but in those *canoas* which escaped there was a good quantity of ore and gold. I then landed more men, and offered five hundred pound to what soldier soever could take one of those three Spaniards that we thought were landed. But our labours were in vain in that behalf, for they put themselves into one of the small *canoas*, and so, while the greater *canoas* were in taking, they escaped. But seeking after the Spaniards we found the *Arwacas* hidden in the woods, which were pilots for the Spaniards, and rowed their *canoas*. Of which I kept the chiefest for a pilot, and carried him with me to *Guiana*; by whom I understood where and in what countries the Spaniards had laboured for gold, though I made not the same known to all. For when the springs began to break, and the rivers to raise themselves so suddenly as by no means we could abide the digging of any mine, especially for that the richest are defended with rocks of hard stones, which we call the *white spar,* and that it required both time, men, and instruments fit for such a work, I thought it best not to hover thereabouts, lest if the same had been perceived by the company, there would have been by this time many barks and ships set out, and perchance other nations would also have gotten of ours for pilots. So as both ourselves might have been prevented, and all our care taken for good usage of the people been utterly lost, by those that only respect present profit; and such violence or insolence offered as the nations which are borderers would have changed the desire of our love and defence into hatred and violence. And for any longer stay to have brought a more quantity, which I hear hath been often objected, whosoever had seen or proved the fury of that river after it began to arise, and had been a month and odd days, as we were, from hearing aught from our ships, leaving them meanly manned 400 miles off, would perchance have turned somewhat sooner than we did, if all the mountains had been gold, or rich stones. And to say the truth, all the branches and small rivers which fell into *Orenoque* were raised with such speed, as if we waded them over the shoes in the morning outward, we were covered to the

---

[4] Gentleman (Spanish).

shoulders homeward the very same day; and to stay to dig our gold with our nails, had been *opus laboris* but not *ingenii*.[5] Such a quantity as would have served our turns we could not have had, but a discovery of the mines to our infinite disadvantage we had made, and that could have been the best profit of farther search or stay; for those mines are not easily broken, nor opened in haste, and I could have returned a good quantity of gold ready cast if I had not shot at another mark than present profit.

. . . When we were come to the tops of the first hills of the plains adjoining to the river, we beheld that wonderful breach of waters which ran down *Caroli;* and might from that mountain see the river how it ran in three parts, above twenty miles off, and there appeared some ten or twelve overfalls in sight, every one as high over the other as a church tower, which fell with that fury, that the rebound of water made it seem as if it had been all covered over with a great shower of rain; and in some places we took it at the first for a smoke that had risen over some great town. For mine own part I was well persuaded from thence to have returned, being a very ill footman; but the rest were all so desirous to go near the said strange thunder of waters, as they drew me on by little and little, till we came into the next valley, where we might better discern the same. I never saw a more beautiful country, nor more lively prospects; hills so raised here and there over the valleys; the river winding into divers branches; the plains adjoining without bush or stubble, all fair green grass; the ground of hard sand, easy to march on, either for horse or foot; the deer crossing in every path; the birds towards the evening singing on every tree with a thousand several tunes; cranes and herons of white, crimson, and carnation, perching in the river's side; the air fresh with a gentle easterly wind; and every stone that we stooped to take up promised either gold or silver by his complexion. Your Lordship shall see of many sorts, and I hope some of them cannot be bettered under the sun; and yet we had no means but with our daggers and fingers to tear them out here and there, the rocks being most hard of that mineral spar aforesaid, which is like a flint, and is altogether as hard or harder, and besides the veins lie a fathom or two deep in the rocks. But we wanted all things requisite save only our desires and good will to have performed more if it had pleased God.

Francis Bacon (1561–1626)

Born in London at the dawn of Queen Elizabeth's reign, Francis Bacon was educated at Cambridge and studied law at Gray's Inn. He resisted the traditional university curriculum, which imparted an Aristotelian system of logic and an outdated understanding of "natural philosophy," relatively untouched by the New Science that was then emerging in Europe. At the age of fifteen he accompanied the queen's ambassador to France, where he was exposed to new ideas in cosmology, meteorology, chemistry, and medicine.

[5] *Opus laboris* but not *ingenii*: "A work of great labor, but not of great cleverness" (Latin).

For the rest of his life, Bacon addressed himself to the development of a new method of scientific discovery, based on empirical research, inductive logic, and controlled experiment. Although his lifelong project for the advancement of learning contains many elements that present-day scientists would regard as archaic or even occult, Bacon nevertheless laid the intellectual foundation for the entire subsequent enterprise of Western science. His great ambition is expressed in his last published work, The New Atlantis *(1626), which declares: "The end of our foundation is the knowledge of causes, and secret motions of things; and the enlarging of the bounds of human empire, to the effecting of all things possible." Bacon's conception of scientific research is most fully articulated in his* Aphorisms Concerning the Interpretation of Nature and the Kingdom of Man, *from the* Novum Organum *(1620), in which he advocates humility before the unknown forces of the natural world: "Nature to be commanded must be obeyed."*

Bacon was the first English author to experiment with the personal essay, a new prose genre that enables its writer to explore ideas, express tentative opinions, and test various approaches to a chosen topic. Bacon adapted this genre from Michel de Montaigne, a French writer who gave the essay a personal, introspective tone. Bacon's own essays are more reticent and impersonal. The essay "Of Gardens" reveals Bacon's fascination with the abundance and diversity of Britain's indigenous plants; the essay "Of Plantations" emerges from his concern for the new English settlements in America, which (in his view) were being mismanaged for short-term gain, to the detriment of their long-term sustainability.

Bacon had a long and successful career as a civil servant, rising to become Lord Chancellor of England. But his first love was scientific inquiry, and his unquenchable curiosity was the cause of his death. In the winter of 1626, traveling by coach through frozen fields, Bacon paused to conduct an experiment on the refrigeration of meat. Leaping eagerly from the coach, he gathered up some snow and stuffed it into a chicken's carcass. He caught a chill and took shelter in a local nobleman's residence, where he died suddenly.

Of Gardens

God Almighty first planted a garden; and, indeed, it is the purest of human pleasures; it is the greatest refreshment to the spirits of man; without which buildings and palaces are but gross handiworks; and a man shall ever see, that, when ages grow to civility and elegancy, men come to build stately, sooner than to garden finely; as if gardening were the greater perfection. I do hold it in the royal ordering of gardens, there ought to be gardens for all the months in the year, in which, severally, things of beauty may be then in season. For December, and January, and the latter part of November, you must take such things as are green all winter: holly, ivy, bays, juniper, cypress-trees, yew, pineapple-trees, fir-trees, rosemary, lavender; periwinkle, the white, the purple, and the blue; germander, flag, orange-trees, lemon-trees, and myrtles, if they be stoved; and sweet marjoram, warm set. There followeth, for the latter part of January and February, the mezereon-tree, which then blossoms; crocus vernus, both the yellow and the gray; primroses, anemones, the early tulip, the hyacinthus orientalis, chamaïris fritellaria. For March, there come violets, especially the single blue, which are the earliest; the yellow daffodil, the daisy, the almond-tree in blossom, the peach-tree in blossom, the cornelian-tree in blossom, sweetbrier. In April follow the double white violet, the wall-flower, the stock-gilliflower, the cowslip, flower-de-luces, and lilies of all natures; rosemary-flowers, the tulip, the double peony, the pale daffodil, the French honeysuckle, the cherry-tree in blossom, the damascene and plum-trees in blossom, the white thorn in leaf, the lilac-tree. In May and June come pinks of all sorts, especially the slush-pink; roses of all kinds, except the musk, which comes later; honeysuckles, strawberries, bugloss, columbine, the French marigold, flos Africanus, cherry-tree in fruit, ribes, figs in fruit, rasps, vine-flowers, lavender in flowers, the sweet satyrian, with the white flower; herbs muscaria, lilium convallium, the apple-tree in blossom. In July come gilliflowers of all varieties, musk-roses, the lime-tree in blossom, early pears, and plums, in fruit, genitings, codlins. In August come plums, of all sorts in fruit, pears, apricots, barberries, filberds, muskmelons, monkshoods, of all colours. In September come grapes, apples, poppies of all colours, peaches, melocotones, nectarines, cornelians, wardens, quinces. In October and the beginning of November come services, medlars, bullaces, roses cut or removed to come late, hollyoaks, and such like. These particulars are for the climate of London; but my meaning is perceived, that you may have "ver perpetuum,"[1] as the place affords.

And because the breath of flowers is far sweeter in the air (where it comes and goes, like the warbling of music) than in the hand, therefore nothing is more fit for that delight, than to know what be the flowers and plants that do best perfume the air. Roses, damask and red, are fast flowers of their smells; so that you may walk by a whole row of them, and find nothing of their sweetness; yea, though it be in a morning's dew. Bays, likewise, yield no smell as they grow, rosemary little, nor sweet marjoram; that which, above all others, yields the sweetest smell in the air, is the violet, especially the white double violet, which comes twice a year, about the middle of April, and about Bartholomew-tide. Next to that is the musk-rose; then the strawberry-leaves dying, with a most excellent cordial smell; then the flower of the vines, it is a little dust like the dust of a bent, which grows upon the cluster in the first coming forth; then sweetbrier, then wallflowers, which are very delightful to be set under a parlour or lower chamber window; then pinks and gilliflowers, especially the matted pink and clove gilliflower; then the flowers of the lime-tree; then the honeysuckles, so they be somewhat afar off. Of bean-flowers I speak not, because they are field flowers; but those which perfume the air most delightfully, not passed by as the rest, but being trodden upon and crushed, are three, that is, burnet, wild thyme, and watermints; therefore you are to set whole alleys of them, to have the pleasure when you walk or tread.

For gardens, (speaking of those which are, indeed, prince-like, as we have done of buildings,) the contents ought not well to be under thirty acres of ground, and to be divided into three parts; a green in the entrance, a heath, or desert, in the going forth, and the main garden in the midst, besides alleys on both sides; and, I like well, that four acres of ground be assigned to the green, six

---

[1] Perpetual springtime (Latin).

to the heath, four and four to either side, and twelve to the main garden. The green hath two pleasures; the one, because nothing is more pleasant to the eye than green grass kept finely shorn, the other, because it will give you a fair alley in the midst, by which you may go in front upon a stately hedge, which is to enclose the garden: but because the alley will be long, and, in great heat of the year, or day, you ought not to buy the shade in the garden by going in the sun through the green; therefore you are, of either side the green, to plant a covert alley, upon carpenter's work, about twelve foot in height, by which you may go in shade into the garden. As for the making of knots, or figures, with divers coloured earths, that they may lie under the windows of the house on that side which the garden stands, they be but toys:[2] you may see as good sights many times in tarts. The garden is best to be square, encompassed on all the four sides with a stately arched hedge; the arches to be upon pillars of carpenter's work, of some ten foot high, and six foot broad, and the spaces between of the same dimension with the breadth of the arch. Over the arches let there be an entire hedge of some four foot high, framed also upon carpenter's work; and upon the upper hedge, over every arch, a little turret, with a belly enough to receive a cage of birds: and over every space between the arches some other little figure, with broad plates of round coloured glass gilt, for the sun to play upon: but this hedge I intend to be raised upon a bank, not steep, but gently slope, of some six foot, set all with flowers. Also I understand, that this square of the garden should not be the whole breadth of the ground, but to leave on either side ground enough for diversity of side alleys, unto which the two covert alleys of the green may deliver you; but there must be no alleys with hedges at either end of this great enclosure; not at the higher end, for letting your prospect upon this fair hedge from the green; nor at the further end, for letting your prospect from the hedge through the arches upon the heath.

For the ordering of the ground within the great hedge, I leave it to variety of device; advising, nevertheless, that whatsoever form you cast it into first, it be not too busy, or full of work; wherein I, for my part, do not like images cut out in juniper or other garden stuff; they be for children. Little low hedges, round like welts, with some pretty pyramids, I like well; and in some places fair columns, upon frames of carpenter's work. I would also have the alleys spacious and fair. You may have closer alleys upon the side grounds, but none in the main garden. I wish also, in the very middle, a fair mount, with three ascents and alleys, enough for four to walk abreast; which I would have to be perfect circles, without any bulwarks or embossments; and the whole mount to be thirty foot high, and some fine banqueting-house with some chimneys neatly cast, and without too much glass.

For fountains, they are a great beauty and refreshment; but pools mar all, and make the garden unwholesome, and full of flies and frogs. Fountains I intend to be of two natures; the one that sprinkleth or spouteth water: the other a fair receipt of water, of some thirty or forty foot square, but without fish, or slime, or mud. For the first, the ornaments of images, gilt or of marble, which are in use, do well: but the main matter is so to convey the water, as it never stay, either in

---

[2] Insignificant trifles.

the bowls or in the cistern: that the water be never by rest discoloured, green or red, or the like, or gather any mossiness or putrefaction; besides that, it is to be cleansed every day by the hand: also some steps up to it, and some fine pavement about it doth well. As for the other kind of fountain, which we may call a bathing pool, it may admit much curiosity and beauty, wherewith we will not trouble ourselves: as that the bottom be finely paved, and with images; the sides likewise; and withal embellished with coloured glass, and such things of lustre; encompassed also with fine rails of low statues: but the main point is the same which we mentioned in the former kind of fountain; which is, that the water be in perpetual motion, fed by a water higher than the pool, and delivered into it by fair spouts, and then discharged away under ground, by some equality of bores, that it stay little; and for fine devices, of arching water without spilling, and making it rise in several forms, (of feathers, drinking glasses, canopies, and the like,) they be pretty things to look on, but nothing to health and sweetness.

For the heath, which was the third part of our plot, I wished it to be framed as much as may be to a natural wildness. Trees I would have none in it, but some thickets made only of sweetbrier and honeysuckle, and some wild vine amongst; and the ground set with violets, strawberries; and primroses; for these are sweet, and prosper in the shade; and these to be in the heath here and there, not in any order. I like also little heaps, in the nature of mole hills, (such as are in wild heaths,) to be set, some with wild thyme, some with pinks, some with germander that gives a good flower to the eye; some with periwinkle, some with violets, some with strawberries, some with cowslips, some with daisies, some with red roses, some with lilium convallium, some with sweetwilliams red, some with bear's-foot, and the like low flowers, being withal sweet and sightly; part of which heaps to be with standards[3] of little bushes pricked upon their top, and part without: the standards to be roses, juniper, holly, barberries, (but here and there, because, of the smell of their blossom,) red currants, gooseberries, rosemary, bays, sweetbrier, and such like: but these standards to be kept with cutting, that they grow not out of course.

For the side-grounds, you are to fill them with variety of alleys, private, to give a full shade; some of them, wheresoever the sun be. You are to frame some of them likewise for shelter, that when the wind blows sharp, you may walk as in a gallery: and those alleys must be likewise hedged at both ends, to keep out the wind; and these closer alleys must be ever finely gravelled, and no grass, because of going wet. In many of these alleys, likewise, you are to set fruit-trees of all sorts, as well upon the walls as in ranges; and this should be generally observed, that the borders wherein you plant your fruit-trees be fair, and large, and low, and not steep; and set with fine flowers, but thin and sparingly, lest they deceive the trees. At the end of both the side-grounds I would have a mount of some pretty height, leaving the wall of the enclosure breast high, to look abroad into the fields.

For the main garden, I do not deny but there should be some fair alleys ranged on both sides, with fruit-trees, and some pretty tufts of fruit-trees and arbours with seats, set in some decent order; but these to be by no means set too

---

[3] Ornaments.

thick, but to leave the main garden so as it be not close, but the air open and free. For as for shade, I would have you rest upon the alleys of the side-grounds, there to walk, if you be disposed, in the heat of the year or day; but to make account that the main garden is for the more temperate parts of the year, and in the heat of summer, for the morning and the evening, or overcast days.

For aviaries, I like them not, except they be of that largeness as they may be turfed, and have living plants and bushes set in them; that the birds may have more scope and natural nestling, and that no foulness appear in the floor of the aviary. So I have made a platform of a princely garden, partly by precept, partly by drawing; not a model but some general lines of it; and in this I have spared for no cost; but it is nothing for great princes, that, for the most part, taking advice with workmen, with no less cost set their things together, and sometimes add statues, and such things, for state and magnificence, but nothing to the true pleasure of a garden.

Of Plantations

Plantations are amongst ancient, primitive, and heroical works. When the world was young, it begat more children; but now it is old, it begets fewer; for I may justly account new plantations to be the children of former kingdoms. I like a plantation in a pure soil; that is, where people are not displanted to the end to plant in others; for else it is rather an extirpation than a plantation. Planting of countries is like planting of woods; for you must make account to lose almost twenty years profit, and expect your recompense in the end: for the principal thing that hath been the destruction of most plantations, hath been the base and hasty drawing of profit in the first years. It is true, speedy profit is not to be neglected, as far as may stand with the good of the plantation, but no further. It is a shameful and unblessed thing to take the scum of people and wicked condemned men, to be the people with whom you plant; and not only so, but it spoileth the plantation; for they will ever live like rogues, and not fall to work, but be lazy, and do mischief, and spend victuals, and be quickly weary, and then certify over[1] to their country to the discredit of the plantation. The people wherewith you plant ought to be gardeners, ploughmen, labourers, smiths, carpenters, joiners, fishermen, fowlers, with some few apothecaries, surgeons, cooks, and bakers. In a country of plantation, first look about what kind of victual the country yields of itself to hand; as chestnuts, walnuts, pineapples, olives, dates, plums, cherries, wild honey, and the like, and make use of them. Then consider what victual, or esculent things there are which grow speedily and within the year: as parsnips, carrots, turnips, onions, radish, artichokes of Jerusalem, maize, and the like: for wheat, barley, and oats, they ask too much labour; but with pease and beans you may begin, both because they ask less labour, and because they serve for meat[2] as well as for bread; and of rice likewise cometh a great increase, and it is a kind of meat. Above all,

---

[1] *Certify over:* report back.

[2] As a main dish.

there ought to be brought store of biscuit, oatmeal, flour, meal, and the like, in the beginning, till bread may be had. For beasts, or birds, take chiefly such as are least subject to diseases, and multiply fastest; as swine, goats, cocks, hens, turkeys, geese, house-doves, and the like. The victual in plantations ought to be expended almost as in a besieged town; that is, with certain allowance: and let the main part of the ground employed to gardens or corn, be to a common stock; and to be laid in, and stored up, and then delivered out in proportion; besides some spots of ground that any particular person will manure[3] for his own private use. Consider, likewise, what commodities the soil where the plantation is doth naturally yield, that they may some way help to defray the charge of the plantation; so it be not, as was said, to the untimely prejudice of the main business, as it hath fared with tobacco in Virginia. Wood commonly aboundeth but too much: and therefore timber is fit to be one. If there be iron ore, and streams whereupon to set the mills, iron is a brave[4] commodity where wood aboundeth. Making of bay-salt, if the climate be proper for it, would be put in experience: growing silk[5] likewise, if any be, is a likely commodity: pitch and tar, where store of firs and pines are, will not fail; so drugs and sweet woods, where they are, cannot but yield great profit; soap-ashes likewise, and other things that may be thought of; but moil not too much under ground, for the hope of mines is very uncertain and useth to make the planters lazy in other things. For government, let it be in the hands of one, assisted with some counsel; and let them have commission to exercise martial laws, with some limitation; and, above all, let men make that profit of being in the wilderness, as they have God always, and his service before their eyes; let not the government of the plantation depend upon too many counsellors and undertakers[6] in the country that planteth, but upon a temperate number; and let those be rather noblemen and gentlemen, than merchants; for they look ever to the present gain: let there be freedoms from custom,[7] till the plantation be of strength; and not only freedom from custom, but freedom to carry their commodities where they may make their best of them, except there be some special cause of caution. Cram not in people, by sending too fast, company after company; but rather hearken how they waste,[8] and send supplies proportionably; but so as the number may live well in the plantation, and not by surcharge be in penury. It hath been a great endangering to the health of some plantations, that they have built along the sea and rivers in marish[9] and unwholesome grounds: therefore, though you begin there, to avoid carriage and other like discommodities, yet build still rather upwards from the stream, than along. It concerneth likewise the health of the plantation that they have good store of salt with them, that they may use it in their victuals when it shall be necessary. If you plant where savages are, do not only entertain them with trifles and gingles,

---

[3] Cultivate.

[4] Excellent, profitable.

[5] Vegetable silk.

[6] Managers.

[7] Customs duties, i.e., taxes on imports and exports.

[8] Decline in population.

[9] Marshy.

but use them justly and graciously, with sufficient guard nevertheless; and do not win their favour by helping them to invade their enemies, but for their defence it is not amiss: and send oft of them over to the country that plants, that they may see a better condition than their own, and commend it when they return. When the plantation grows to strength, then it is time to plant with women as well as with men; that the plantation may spread into generations, and not be ever pieced from without. It is the sinfullest thing in the world to forsake or destitute a plantation once in forwardness; for, besides the dishonour, it is the guiltiness of blood of many commiserable[10] persons.

From Aphorisms Concerning the Interpretation of Nature and the Kingdom of Man

Aphorism

I

Man, being the servant and interpreter of Nature, can do and understand so much and so much only as he has observed in fact or in thought of the course of nature: beyond this he neither knows anything nor can do anything.

2

Neither the naked hand nor the understanding left to itself can effect much. It is by instruments and helps that the work is done, which are as much wanted for the understanding as for the hand. And as the instruments of the hand either give motion or guide it, so the instruments of the mind supply either suggestions for the understanding or cautions.

3

Human knowledge and human power meet in one; for where the cause is not known the effect cannot be produced. Nature to be commanded must be obeyed; and that which in contemplation is as the cause is in operation as the rule.

4

Towards the effecting of works, all that man can do is to put together or put asunder natural bodies. The rest is done by nature working within.

5

The study of nature with a view to works is engaged in by the mechanic, the mathematician, the physician, the alchemist, and the magician; but by all (as things now are) with slight endeavour and scanty success.

---

[10]Worthy of compassion. Bacon probably has in mind the lost English colony of Roanoke, established by Sir Walter Ralegh in 1585. The colony vanished after being left without supplies for several years; the settlers presumably succumbed to disease and attacks from hostile Native Americans.

6

It would be an unsound fancy and self-contradictory to expect that things which have never yet been done can be done except by means which have never yet been tried.

7

The productions of the mind and hand seem very numerous in books and manufactures. But all this variety lies in an exquisite subtlety and derivations from a few things already known; not in the number of axioms.

8

Moreover the works already known are due to chance and experiment rather than to sciences; for the sciences we now possess are merely systems for the nice ordering and setting forth of things already invented; not methods of invention or directions for new works.

9

The cause and root of nearly all evils in the sciences is this—that while we falsely admire and extol the powers of the human mind we neglect to seek for its true helps.

10

The subtlety of nature is greater many times over than the subtlety of the senses and understanding; so that all those specious meditations, speculations, and glosses in which men indulge are quite from the purpose,[1] only there is no one by to observe it.

. . .

31

It is idle to expect any great advancement in science from the superinducing and engrafting of new things upon old. We must begin anew from the very foundations, unless we would revolve for ever in a circle with mean and contemptible progress.

32

The honour of the ancient authors, and indeed of all, remains untouched; since the comparison I challenge is not of wits or faculties, but of ways and methods, and the part I take upon myself is not that of a judge, but of a guide.

. . .

---

[1] Literally, "are a thing insane." Bacon is suggesting that all existing scientific theories are so inadequate that they would seem like mere madness if we could only correlate them with the actual truth of nature.

35

It was said by Borgia of the expedition of the French into Italy, that they came with chalk in their hands to mark out their lodgings, not with arms to force their way in. I in like manner would have my doctrine enter quietly into the minds that are fit and capable of receiving it; for confutations cannot be employed, when the difference is upon first principles and very notions and even upon forms of demonstration.

36

One method of delivery alone remains to us; which is simply this: we must lead men to the particulars themselves, and their series and order; while men on their side must force themselves for awhile to lay their notions by and begin to familiarise themselves with facts.

. . .

49

The human understanding is no dry light, but receives an infusion from the will and affections; whence proceed sciences which may be called "sciences as one would." For what a man had rather were true he more readily believes. Therefore he rejects difficult things from impatience of research; sober things, because they narrow hope; the deeper things of nature, from superstition; the light of experience, from arrogance and pride, lest his mind should seem to be occupied with things mean and transitory; things not commonly believed, out of deference to the opinion of the vulgar. Numberless in short are the ways, and sometimes imperceptible, in which the affections colour and infect the understanding.

50

But by far the greatest hindrance and aberration of the human understanding proceeds from the dullness, incompetency, and deceptions of the senses; in that things which strike the sense outweigh things which do not immediately strike it, though they be more important. Hence it is that speculation commonly ceases where sight ceases; insomuch that of things invisible there is little or no observation. Hence all the working of the spirits inclosed in tangible bodies lies hid and unobserved of men. So also all the more subtle changes of form in the parts of coarser substances (which they commonly call alteration, though it is in truth local motion through exceedingly small spaces) is in like manner unobserved. And yet unless these two things just mentioned be searched out and brought to light, nothing great can be achieved in nature, as far as the production of works is concerned. So again the essential nature of our common air, and of all bodies less dense than air (which are very many), is almost unknown. For the sense by itself is a thing infirm and erring; neither can instruments for enlarging or sharpening the senses do much; but all the truer kind of interpretation of nature is effected by instances and experiments fit and apposite; wherein the sense decides touching the experiment only, and the experiment touching the point in nature and the thing itself.

. . .

55

There is one principal and as it were radical distinction between different minds, in respect of philosophy and the sciences; which is this: that some minds are stronger and apter to mark the differences of things, others to mark their resemblances. The steady and acute mind can fix its contemplations and dwell and fasten on the subtlest distinctions: the lofty and discursive mind recognises and puts together the finest and most general resemblances. Both kinds however easily err in excess, by catching the one at gradations the other at shadows.

✒ Silvester Jourdain (c. 1580–1650)

Silvester Jourdain was born about 1580 at Lyme Regis, Dorset, into a Puritan family. He is known to have been a merchant, trading goods from the port city of Poole, in 1603. He accompanied Sir George Somers, who was also born in Lyme Regis, on a voyage in the Sea Venture *to Jamestown, Virginia Colony, in 1609. Also onboard were Sir Thomas Gates and Captain Christopher Newport, deputy governors of the colony, the first English settlement in North America. The ship encountered a tropical storm in the mid-Atlantic and was wrecked on the coast of Bermuda, then a virtually unknown and uninhabited island. After returning to London in 1610, Jourdain wrote an account of the storm and shipwreck, entitled* A Discovery of the Bermudas, Otherwise Called the Isle of Devils. *This pamphlet provided some significant source material for Shakespeare's* The Tempest, *in which characters are likewise shipwrecked on a remote, mysterious island. Jourdain describes how some of the sailors, exhausted by their desperate struggle against the waves, "having some good and comfortable waters in the ship, fetched them and drunk one to the other, taking their last leave one of the other." These "comfortable waters" may well have suggested to Shakespeare the cheer that Trinculo and his companions derive from their cache of liquor in* The Tempest. *Several other concrete details of Shakespeare's island, "reputed a most prodigious and enchanted place," are derived from Jourdain's pamphlet. The castaways of* The Tempest *find themselves on an island that closely resembles Bermuda, as Jourdain described it, with an abundant variety of seabirds and shellfish, fruits and nuts, pearls and precious stones.*

After his return to England, Jourdain settled in London, where he died unmarried, in 1650.

A Discovery of the Bermudas, Otherwise Called the Isle of Devils

Being in [a] ship called the "Sea Venture," with Sir Thomas Gates our governor, Sir George Somers, and Captain Newport, three most worthy, honored gentlemen (whose valor and fortitude the world must needs take notice of, and that in most honorable designs) bound for Virginia, in the height of 30 degrees of northerly latitude or thereabouts we were taken with a most sharp and cruel storm upon the five-and-twentieth day of July, anno 1609, which did not only separate us from the residue of our fleet (which were eight in number), but with the violent working of the seas our ship became so shaken, torn, and leaked that she received so much water as covered two tier of hogsheads above the ballast; that our men stood up to the middles with buckets, barricos,[1] and kettles to bail out the water and continually pumped for three days and three nights together without any intermission; and yet the water seemed rather to increase than to diminish. Insomuch that all our men, being utterly spent, tired, and disabled for longer labor, were even resolved, without any hope of their lives, to shut up the hatches and to have committed themselves to the mercy of the sea (which is said to be merciless), or rather to the mercy of their mighty God and redeemer (whose mercies exceed all His works), seeing no help nor hope in the apprehension of man's reason that any mother's child would escape that inevitable danger, which every man had proposed and digested to himself, of present sinking. So that some of them, having some good and comfortable waters[2] in the ship, fetched them and drunk one to the other, taking their last leave one of the other until their more joyful and happy meeting in a more blessed world; when it pleased God out of His most gracious and merciful providence so to direct and guide our ship (being left to the mercy of the sea) for her most advantage that Sir George Somers (sitting upon the poop of the ship, where he sate three days and three nights together, without meal's meat and [with] little or no sleep), conning[3] the ship to keep her as upright as he could (for otherwise she must needs instantly have foundered), most wishedly-happily descried land. Whereupon he most comfortably encouraged the company to follow their pumping and by no means to cease bailing out of the water with their buckets, barricos, and kettles; whereby they were so overwearied, and their spirits so spent with long fasting and continuance of their labor, that for the most part they were fallen asleep in corners and wheresoever they chanced first to sit or lie; but, hearing news of land, wherewith they grew to be somewhat revived, being carried with will and desire beyond their strength, every man bustled up and gathered his strength and feeble spirits together to perform as much as their weak force would permit him; through which weak means it pleased God to work so strongly as the water was stayed for that little time (which, as we all much feared, was the last period of our breathing) and the ship kept from present sinking, when it pleased God to send her within half an English mile of that land that Sir George Somers had not long before descried, which were the islands of the Bermudas.

And there neither did our ship sink but, more fortunately in so great a misfortune, fell in between two rocks, where she was fast lodged and locked for further budging; whereby we gained not only sufficient time, with the present help of our boat and skiff, safely to set and convey our men ashore (which were 150 in number) but afterwards had time and leisure to save some good part of our goods and provision, which the water had not spoiled, with all the tacking of the

---

[1] Kegs, small barrels.
[2] Alcoholic beverages, probably rum.
[3] Keeping a lookout and directing the steersman.

ship and much of the iron about her, which were necessaries not a little available[4] for the building and furnishing of a new ship and pinnace, which we made there for the transporting and carrying of us to Virginia. But our delivery was not more strange, in falling so opportunely and happily upon the land, as our feeding and preservation was beyond our hopes and all men's expectations most admirable.[5]

For the islands of the Bermudas, as every man knoweth that hath heard or read of them, were never inhabited by any Christian or heathen people but ever esteemed and reputed a most prodigious and enchanted place, affording nothing but gusts, storms, and foul weather, which made every navigator and mariner to avoid them as Scylla and Charybdis,[6] or as they would shun the Devil himself; and no man was ever heard to make for the place but as, against their wills, they have by storms and dangerousness of the rocks, lying seven leagues unto the sea, suffered shipwreck. Yet did we find there the air so temperate and the country so abundantly fruitful of all fit necessaries for the sustentation and preservation of man's life that, most in a manner of all our provisions of bread, beer, and victual being quite spoiled in lying long drowned in salt water, notwithstanding we were there for the space of nine months (few days over or under) not only well received, comforted, and with good satiety contented, but out of the abundance thereof provided us some reasonable quantity and proportion of provision to carry us for Virginia and to maintain ourselves and that company we found there, to the great relief of them, as it fell out, in their so great extremities and, in respect of the shortness of time, until it pleased God that by My Lord's coming thither their store was better supplied. And greater and better provisions we might have made if we had had better means for the storing and transportation thereof. Wherefore my opinion sincerely of this island is that whereas it hath been and is still accounted the most dangerous, infortunate, and most forlorn place of the world, it is in truth the richest, healthfullest, and pleasing land (the quantity and bigness thereof considered) and merely natural, as ever man set foot upon. The particular profits and benefits whereof shall be more especially inserted and hereunto annexed, which every man to his own private knowledge, that was there, can avouch and justify for a truth.

Upon the eight-and-twentieth day of July, 1609 (after the extremity of the storm was something qualified), we fell upon the shore at the Bermudas; where after our general, Sir Thomas Gates, Sir George Somers, and Captain Newport had by their provident carefulness landed all their men and so much of the goods and provisions out of the ship as was not utterly spoiled, every man disposed and applied himself to search for and to seek out such relief and sustentation as the country afforded. And Sir George Somers, a man inured to extremities (and knowing what thereunto belonged) was in this service neither idle nor backward but presently by his careful industry went and found out sufficient of many kind of fishes, and so plentiful thereof that in half an hour he took so many great

---

[4] Advantageous.

[5] Wonderful, miraculous.

[6] Mythical beasts that wreck ships and devour sailors in Homer's *Odyssey*.

fishes with hooks as did suffice the whole company one day. And fish is there so abundant that if a man step into the water they will come round about him; so that men were fain to get out for fear of biting. These fishes are very fat and sweet and of that proportion and bigness that three of them will conveniently lade two men: those we called rockfish. Besides there are such abundance of mullets that with a seine might be taken at one draught one thousand at the least; and infinite store of pilchards; with divers kinds of great fishes, the names of them unknown to me; of crayfishes very great ones and so great store as that there hath been taken in one night with making lights even sufficient to feed the whole company a day. The country affordeth great abundance of hogs, as that there hath been taken by Sir George Somers, who was the first hunted for them, to the number of two-and-thirty at one time, which he brought to the company in a boat built by his own hands.

There is fowl in great num[ber] upon the islands where they breed, that there hath been taken in two or three hours a thousand at the least, the bird being of the bigness of a good pigeon and layeth eggs as big as hen eggs upon the sand, where they come and lay them daily although men sit down amongst them, that there hath been taken up in one morning by Sir Thomas Gates's men one thousand of eggs; and Sir George Somers's men, coming a little distance of time after them, have stayed there whilst they came and laid their eggs amongst them, that they brought away as many more with them, with many young birds very fat and sweet.

Another seafowl there is that lieth in little holes in the ground, like unto a cony hole, and are in great numbers, exceeding good meat, very fat and sweet (those we had in the winter) and their eggs are white and of that bigness that they are not to be known from hen eggs. The other bird's eggs are speckled and of a different color. There are also great store and plenty of herons, and those so familiar and tame that we beat them down from the trees with stones and staves—but such were young herons—besides many white herons without so much as a black or grey feather on them; with other small birds so tame and gentle that, a man walking in the woods with a stick and whistling to them, they will come and gaze on you, so near that you may strike and kill many of them with your stick; and with singing and holloing you may do the like.

There are also great store of tortoises (which some call turtles) and those so great that I have seen a bushel of eggs in one of their bellies, which are sweeter than any hen egg; and the tortoise itself is all very good meat and yieldeth great store of oil, which is as sweet as any butter; and one of them will suffice fifty men a meal, at the least; and of these hath been taken great store, with two boats, at the least forty in one day.

The country yieldeth divers fruits, as prickled pears, great abundance, which continue green upon the trees all the year; also great plenty of mulberries, white and red, and on the same are great store of silkworms, which yield cods of silk, both white and yellow, being some coarse and some fine.

And there is a tree called a palmetto tree, which hath a very sweet berry upon which the hogs do most feed; but our men, finding the sweetness of them, did willingly share with the hogs for them, they being very pleasant and wholesome, which made them careless almost of any bread with their meat; which occasioned us to carry in a manner all that store of flour and meal we did or could save for Virginia. The head of the palmetto tree is very good meat, either raw or sodden; it yieldeth a head which weigheth about twenty pound and is far better meat than any cabbage.

There are an infinite number of cedar trees (the fairest, I think, in the world) and those bring forth a very sweet berry and wholesome to eat.

The country (forasmuch as I could find myself or hear by others) affords no venomous creature, or so much as a rat or mouse or any other thing unwholesome.

There is great store of pearl, and some of them very fair, round, and oriental,[7] and you shall find at least one hundred seed of pearl in one oyster. There hath been likewise found some good quantity of ambergris, and that of the best sort. There are also great plenty of whales, which I conceive are very easy to be killed, for they come so usually and ordinarily to the shore that we heard them oftentimes in the night abed and have seen many of them near the shore in the daytime.

There was born upon the Bermudas, at the time of our being there, two children, the one a man-child, there baptized by the name of Bermudas, and a woman-child, baptized by the name of Bermuda; as also there was a marriage between two English people upon the island. This island, I mean the main island, with all the broken islands adjacent, are made in the form of a half moon, but a little more rounder, and divided into many broken islands, and there are many good harbors in it; but we could find [only] one especial place to go in, or rather to go out from it, which was not altogether free from some danger, and that lieth on the southeast side, where there is three fathoms water at the entrance thereof, but within six, seven, or eight fathoms at the least, where you may safely be landlocked from the danger of all winds and weathers, and more to the trees. The coming into it is so narrow and strait between the rocks as that it will with small store of munition be fortified and easily defended with all advantage the place affords against the forces of the potentest king of Europe.

There are also plenty of hawks and very good tobacco, as I think, which through forgetfulness I had almost omitted.

Now, having finished and rigged our ship and pinnace, the one called the "Deliverance," the pinnace the "Patience," we prepared and made ourselves ready to ship for Virginia, having powdered[8] some store of hogs' flesh for provision thither and the company thereof for some reasonable time but were compelled to make salt there for the same purpose, for all our salt was spent and spoiled before we recovered the shore. We carried with us also a good portion of tortoise oil, which either for frying or baking did us very great pleasure, it being very sweet, nourishing, and wholesome.

The greatest defects we found there was tar and pitch for our ship and pinnace, instead whereof we were forced to make lime there of a hard kind of stone

[7] Lustrous.
[8] Salted.

and use it, which for the present occasion and necessity, with some wax we found cast up by the sea from some shipwreck, served the turn to pay[9] the seams of the pinnace Sir George Somers built, for which he had neither pitch nor tar.

So that God, in the supplying of all our wants beyond all measure, showed Himself still merciful unto us, that we might accomplish our intended voyage to Virginia, for which I confidently hope He doth yet reserve a blessing in store, and to the which I presume every honest and religious heart will readily give their Amen.

When all things were made ready and commodiously fitted, the wind coming fair, we set sail and put off from the Bermudas the tenth of May in the year 1610, and arrived at Jamestown in Virginia the four-and-twentieth day of the same month, where we found some threescore persons living. And being then some three weeks or thereabouts past, and not hearing of any supply, it was thought fitting by a general consent to use the best means for the preservation of all those people that were living, being all in number two hundred persons. And so, upon the eighth of June, 1610, we embarked at Jamestown, not having above fourteen days' victual, and so were determined to direct our course for Newfoundland, there to refresh us and supply ourselves with victual to bring us home.

But it pleased God to dispose otherwise of us and to give us better means. For being all of us shipped in four pinnaces and departed from the town, almost down half the river, we met My Lord De La Warr coming by with three ships well furnished with victual, which revived all the company and gave them great content. And after some few days My Lord, understanding of the great plenty of hogs and fish was at the Bermudas and the necessity of them in Virginia, was desirous to send thither to supply himself with those things for the better comforting of his men and the plantation of the country.

Whereupon Sir George Somers, being a man best acquainted with the place, and being willing to do service unto his prince and country without any respect of his own private gain, and being of threescore years of age at the least, out of his worthy and valiant mind offered himself to undertake to perform with God's help that dangerous voyage for the Bermudas, for the better relief and comfort of the people in Virginia and for the better plantation of it; which offer My Lord De La Warr very willingly and thankfully accepted. And so upon the nineteenth of June Sir George Somers embarked himself at Jamestown in a small barge of thirty ton or thereabout that he built at the Bermudas, wherein he labored from morning until night, as duly as any workman doth labor for wages, and built her all with cedar, with little or no ironwork at all, having in her but one bolt, which was in the kelson. Notwithstanding, thanks be to God, she brought us in safety to Virginia, and so I trust He will protect him and send him well back again, to his heart's desire and the great comfort of all the company there.[10]

The Bermudas lieth in the height of $32\frac{1}{2}$ degrees of northerly latitude, Virginia bearing directly from it, west-northwest, 230 leagues.

---

[9] Caulk.

[10] George Somers reached Bermuda safely after battling a storm, only to die there shortly afterward "of a surfeit in eating a pig."

꩜ *William Shakespeare* (1564–1616)

William Shakespeare was born in Stratford-upon-Avon, Warwickshire, in April of 1564. His father, John Shakespeare, was a leading citizen, an alderman who underwent some difficult financial times. It is believed that Shakespeare attended Stratford grammar school, where he could have acquired a knowledge of Latin. There is no evidence that he went on to university. Shakespeare married Anne Hathaway in 1582, and a daughter was born in 1583, followed by twins, a boy and a girl, in 1585. By 1592 Shakespeare was living in London, where he published the long narrative poems Venus and Adonis *and* The Rape of Lucrece. *By 1594 he was working as an actor and was already a well-known playwright. Shakespeare was part owner of the best-known theatrical company of the time, the Lord Chamberlain's Men. This group was the standard repertory company of the famous Globe theater. When James I came to power, they became known as the King's Men. It is believed that in about 1610 Shakespeare retired to Stratford to live at his house, New Place. There he continued to write plays in the hybrid (tragicomic) romance genre, including* Cymbeline *and* The Tempest. *He made his will in March of 1616, and it is generally believed that he died just a few months later. He was buried at Stratford.*

Shakespeare's nature poetry includes many of his sonnets, written in the 1590s, and several of the songs from his plays. From The Tempest, *the lyric poems "Full Fathom Five" and "Where the Bee Sucks, There Suck I" are sung by Ariel, a spirit of the enchanted isle. Throughout the unfolding of its plot,* The Tempest *reflects on the process of colonization and the encounter between "civilized" and "savage" peoples. In the excerpt printed here, the European castaways encounter Caliban, a native of the island whose name is an anagram form of "cannibal." The comic misunderstandings that emerge from this situation foreshadow the deeper and more intractable problems that the British colonizers would face as they sought to fathom, survey, and possess the New World with all its natural wonders, frightful noises, and strange beasts.*

Sonnet 18

Shall I compare thee to a summer's day?
Thou art more lovely and more temperate:
Rough winds do shake the darling buds of May,
And summer's lease hath all too short a date:
Sometime too hot the eye of heaven shines,   5
And often is his gold complexion dimmed;
And every fair from fair[1] sometime declines,
By chance or nature's changing course untrimmed;[2]
But thy eternal summer shall not fade,
Nor lose possession of that fair thou ow'st;[3]   10

---

[1] *Fair from fair:* beautiful thing from beauty.
[2] Divested of beauty.
[3] Ownest, i.e., that you do possess.

Nor shall Death brag thou wand'rest in his shade,
When in eternal lines to time thou grow'st:
  So long as men can breathe, or eyes can see,
  So long lives this, and this gives life to thee.

Sonnet 33

Full many a glorious morning have I seen
Flatter the mountain tops with sovereign eye,
Kissing with golden face the meadows green,
Gilding pale streams with heavenly alchemy;
Anon[1] permit the basest[2] clouds to ride   5
With ugly rack[3] on his celestial face,
And from the forlorn world his visage hide,
Stealing unseen to west with this disgrace:
Even so my sun one early morn did shine
With all-triumphant splendour on my brow;   10
But, out, alack! he was but one hour mine,
The region[4] cloud hath masked him from me now.
  Yet him for this my love no whit disdaineth;
  Suns of the world may stain[5] when heaven's sun staineth.

[1] Soon.
[2] Darkest.
[3] A thin mass of clouds.
[4] High-level.
[5] Darken, discolor.

Sonnet 73

That time of year thou mayst in me behold
When yellow leaves, or none, or few, do hang
Upon those boughs which shake against the cold,
Bare ruined choirs, where late the sweet birds sang.
In me thou seest the twilight of such day   5
As after sunset fadeth in the west;
Which by and by black night doth take away,
Death's second self, that seals[1] up all in rest.
In me thou seest the glowing of such fire,
That on the ashes of his youth doth lie,   10
As the death-bed whereon it must expire,
Consumed with that which it was nourished by.
  This thou perceiv'st, which makes thy love more strong,
  To love that well which thou must leave ere long.

[1] Closes.

Sonnet 98

From you have I been absent in the spring,
When proud-pied[1] April, dress'd in all his trim,[2]
Hath put a spirit of youth in every thing,
That heavy Saturn[3] laughed and leaped with him.
Yet nor the lays[4] of birds, nor the sweet smell   5
Of different flowers in odour and in hue,
Could make me any summer's story tell,
Or from their proud lap pluck them where they grew:
Nor did I wonder at the lily's white,
Nor praise the deep vermilion in the rose;   10
They were but sweet, but figures of delight,
Drawn after you, you pattern of all those.
  Yet seemed it winter still, and, you away,
  As with your shadow[5] I with these did play.

[1] Flamboyant; multicolored.
[2] Finery.
[3] The planet Saturn was traditionally regarded as sluggish and gloomy.
[4] Songs.
[5] Portrait.

Sonnet 99

The forward[1] violet thus did I chide:
"Sweet thief, whence didst thou steal thy sweet[2] that smells,
If not from my love's breath? The purple pride
Which on thy soft cheek for complexion dwells
In my love's veins thou hast too grossly[3] dyed."   5
The lily I condemnèd for thy hand,
And buds of marjoram had stol'n thy hair;
The roses fearfully on thorns did stand,
One blushing shame, another white despair;
A third, nor red nor white, had stol'n of both,   10
And to his robb'ry had annexed thy breath;
But, for his theft, in pride of all his growth
A vengeful canker eat[4] him up to death.
  More flowers I noted, yet I none could see
  But sweet or colour it had stol'n from thee.   15

[1] Early in the season; impertinent.
[2] Scent.
[3] Obviously.
[4] Was eating.

From The Tempest

FROM ACT 1, SCENE 2*
["Full Fathom Five"]
ARIEL *(Sings).*
>   Full fathom five thy father lies;
>   Of his bones are coral made;
>   Those are pearls that were his eyes:
>   Nothing of him that doth fade,
>   But doth suffer a sea-change   5
>   Into something rich and strange.
>   Sea-nymphs hourly ring his knell:
>   *(Burthen)* Ding-dong.
>   Hark! now I hear them,—Ding-dong bell.

ACT 2, SCENE 2

Another part of the island. Enter CALIBAN, *with a burden of wood. A noise of thunder heard.*

CALIBAN. All the infections that the sun sucks up
>   From bogs, fens, flats, on Prosper[1] fall, and make him
>   By inchmeal[2] a disease! His spirits hear me,
>   And yet I needs must curse. But they'll nor pinch,
>   Fright me with urchin shows,[3] pitch me i' the mire,   5
>   Nor lead me, like a firebrand,[4] in the dark
>   Out of my way, unless he bid 'em; but
>   For every trifle are they set upon me:
>   Sometime like apes, that mow[5] and chatter at me
>   And after bite me; then like hedge-hogs, which   10
>   Lie tumbling in my barefoot way and mount
>   Their pricks at my footfall; sometime am I
>   All wound with adders, who with cloven tongues
>   Do hiss me into madness.—

Enter TRINCULO.

>   Lo now! lo!
>   Here comes a spirit of his, and to torment me   15
>   For bringing wood in slowly: I'll fall flat;
>   Perchance he will not mind me.

---

* In the complete scene, this excerpt appears as lines 396 to 404; the word *Burthen* in this song means "refrain."

[1] Prospero, a magician who controls the elements and keeps Caliban enslaved on the island.

[2] *By inchmeal:* inch by inch.

[3] *Urchin shows:* magical apparitions.

[4] *Like a firebrand:* in the form of a will-o'-the-wisp.

[5] Make faces.

TRINCULO. Here's neither bush nor shrub to bear off[6] any weather at all, and another storm brewing; I hear it sing i' the wind; yond same black cloud, yond huge one, looks like a foul bombard[7] that would   20
shed his liquor. If it should thunder as it did before, I know not where to hide my head: yond same cloud cannot choose but fall by pailfuls.—What have we here? a man or a fish? Dead or alive? A fish: he smells like a fish; a very ancient and fishlike smell; a kind of not-of-the-newest Poor John.[8] A strange fish! Were I in England now,—as   25
once I was,—and had but this fish painted,[9] not a holiday fool there but would give a piece of silver: there would this monster make a man; any strange beast there makes a man. When they will not give a doit[10] to relieve a lame beggar, they will lay out ten to see a dead Indian. Legged like a man! and his fins like arms! Warm, o' my troth! I   30
do now let loose my opinion, hold it no longer; this is no fish, but an islander, that hath lately suffered by a thunderbolt. (*Thunder.*) Alas, the storm is come again: my best way is to creep under his gaberdine;[11] there is no other shelter hereabout: misery acquaints a man with strange bedfellows. I will here shroud till the dregs of the storm   35
be past.

Enter STEPHANO, *singing; a bottle in his hand.*

STEPHANO.
"I shall no more to sea, to sea,
  Here shall I die ashore:—"

This is a very scurvy tune to sing at a man's funeral:
Well, here's my comfort.   *Drinks.*   40

(*Sings.*)
"The master, the swabber, the boatswain and I,
  The gunner and his mate,
Loved Mall, Meg, and Marian and Margery,
  But none of us cared for Kate;
  For she had a tongue with a tang,   45
  Would cry to a sailor, 'Go hang!'
She loved not the savour of tar nor of pitch,
Yet a tailor might scratch her where-e'er she did itch:
  Then to sea, boys, and let her go hang."
This is a scurvy tune too: but here's my comfort.   *Drinks.*   50

---

[6] Ward off.

[7] Leather jug.

[8] *Poor John:* cheap dried fish.

[9] Painted on a sign, to attract customers at a fair.

[10] Small coin.

[11] Cloak.

CALIBAN. Do not torment me: O!

STEPHANO. What's the matter? Have we devils here? Do you put tricks upon us with savages and men of Ind?[12] Ha! I have not 'scaped drowning, to be afeard now of your four legs; for it hath been said, "As proper a man as ever went on four legs cannot make him give ground"; and it shall be said so again while Stephano breathes at 's nostrils.   55

CALIBAN. The spirit torments me: O!

STEPHANO. This is some monster of the isle with four legs, who hath got, as I take it, an ague. Where the devil should he learn our language? I will give him some relief, if it be but for that: if I can recover[13] him and keep him tame and get to Naples with him, he's a present for any emperor that ever trod on neat's leather.[14]   60

CALIBAN. Do not torment me, prithee; I'll bring my wood home faster.

STEPHANO. He's in his fit now and does not talk after the wisest. He shall taste of my bottle: if he have never drunk wine afore it will go near to remove his fit. If I can recover him, and keep him tame, I will not take too much for him: he shall pay for him that hath him, and that soundly.   65

CALIBAN. Thou dost me yet but little hurt; thou wilt anon,[15] I know it by thy trembling: now Prosper works upon thee.   70

STEPHANO. Come on your ways: open your mouth; here is that which will give language to you, cat.[16] Open your mouth: this will shake your shaking, I can tell you, and that soundly (*Gives* CALIBAN *drink.*): you cannot tell who's your friend: open your chaps[17] again.   75

TRINCULO. I should know that voice: it should be—but he is drowned; and these are devils. O! defend me.

STEPHANO. Four legs and two voices; a most delicate monster! His forward voice now is to speak well of his friend; his backward voice is to utter foul speeches, and to detract. If all the wine in my bottle will recover him, I will help his ague. Come. Amen! I will pour some in thy other mouth.   80

TRINCULO. Stephano!

STEPHANO. Doth thy other mouth call me? Mercy! mercy! This is a devil, and no monster: I will leave him; I have no long spoon.[18]   85

TRINCULO. Stephano!—if thou beest Stephano, touch me, and speak to me; for I am Trinculo:—be not afeard—thy good friend Trinculo.

---

[12] India.

[13] Cure.

[14] *Neat's leather:* cowhide, i.e., shoes.

[15] Soon.

[16] *Give language* . . . , *cat:* allusion to the proverb "Liquor will make a cat talk."

[17] Jaws.

[18] *I have no long spoon:* allusion to the proverb "He that will eat with the devil must have a long spoon."

STEPHANO. If thou beest Trinculo, come forth. I'll pull thee by the lesser legs: if any be Trinculo's legs, these are they. Thou art very Trinculo indeed! How cam'st thou to be the siege[19] of this mooncalf?[20] Can he vent Trinculos?   90

TRINCULO. I took him to be killed with a thunderstroke. But art thou not drowned, Stephano? I hope now thou art not drowned. Is the storm overblown? I hid me under the dead mooncalf's gaberdine for fear of the storm. And art thou living, Stephano? O Stephano! two Neapolitans[21] 'scaped!   95

STEPHANO. Prithee, do not turn me about: my stomach is not constant.

CALIBAN (Aside). These be fine things an if they be not sprites.
That's a brave god and bears celestial liquor:
I will kneel to him.   100

STEPHANO. How didst thou 'scape? How cam'st thou hither? Swear by this bottle, how thou cam'st hither. I escaped upon a butt of sack,[22] which the sailors heaved overboard, by this bottle! which I made of the bark of a tree with mine own hands, since I was cast ashore.

CALIBAN. I'll swear upon that bottle, to be thy true subject; for the liquor is not earthly.   105

STEPHANO. Here: swear then, how thou escapedst.

TRINCULO. Swam ashore, man, like a duck: I can swim like a duck, I'll be sworn.

STEPHANO. Here, kiss the book (Gives TRINCULO drink). Though thou canst swim like a duck, thou art made like a goose.   110

TRINCULO. O Stephano! hast any more of this?

STEPHANO. The whole butt, man: my cellar is in a rock by the seaside, where my wine is hid. How now, mooncalf! how does thine ague?

CALIBAN. Hast thou not dropped from heaven?   115

STEPHANO. Out o' the moon, I do assure thee: I was the man in the moon, when time was.

CALIBAN. I have seen thee in her, and I do adore thee; my mistress showed me thee, and thy dog, and thy bush.[23]

STEPHANO. Come, swear to that; kiss the book; I will furnish it anon with new contents; swear.   120

TRINCULO. By this good light, this is a very shallow monster.—I afeard of him!—a very weak monster.—the man i' the moon! a most poor credulous monster!—Well drawn, monster, in good sooth.[24]

---

[19] Excrement.

[20] A monstrosity.

[21] Residents of Naples, Italy, where the ship embarked upon its journey.

[22] *Butt of sack:* barrel of Spanish wine.

[23] *Thee . . . bush:* According to legend, the Man in the Moon was banished there, with his dog and his thornbush, for gathering firewood on a Sunday.

[24] *Well drawn . . . sooth:* that's a good long drink you've taken, in truth.

CALIBAN. I'll show thee every fertile inch o' the island;   125
   And I will kiss thy foot. I prithee, be my god.
TRINCULO. By this light, a most perfidious and drunken monster: when
   his god's asleep, he'll rob his bottle.
CALIBAN. I'll kiss thy foot: I'll swear myself thy subject.
STEPHANO. Come on then; down, and swear.   130
TRINCULO. I shall laugh myself to death at this puppy-headed monster.
   A most scurvy monster! I could find in my heart to beat him,—
STEPHANO. Come, kiss.
TRINCULO. But that the poor monster's in drink: an abominable mon-
   ster!   135
CALIBAN. I'll show thee the best springs; I'll pluck thee berries;
   I'll fish for thee, and get thee wood enough.
   A plague upon the tyrant that I serve!
   I'll bear him no more sticks, but follow thee,
   Thou wondrous man.   140
TRINCULO. A most ridiculous monster, to make a wonder of a poor
   drunkard!
CALIBAN. I prithee, let me bring thee where crabs[25] grow;
   And I with my long nails will dig thee pignuts;[26]
   Show thee a jay's nest and instruct thee how   145
   To snare the nimble marmozet;[27] I'll bring thee
   To clust'ring filberts, and sometimes I'll get thee
   Young scamels[28] from the rock. Wilt thou go with me?
STEPHANO. I prithee now, lead the way, without any more talking.—
   Trinculo, the king and all our company else being drowned, we will   150
   inherit here.—Here; bear my bottle.—Fellow Trinculo, we'll fill
   him by and by again.
CALIBAN. Farewell, master; farewell, farewell!   *Sings drunkenly.*
TRINCULO. A howling monster, a drunken monster.
CALIBAN.
   "No more dams I'll make for fish;   155
     Nor fetch in firing
     At requiring,
   Nor scrape trenchering,[29] nor wash dish;
     'Ban, 'Ban, Ca-Caliban,
     Has a new master—Get a new man."   160
   Freedom, high-day! high-day, freedom! freedom! high-day, freedom!
STEPHANO. O brave monster! lead the way.   *Exeunt.*

---

[25] Crab apples.
[26] Earthnuts.
[27] Marmoset (a small monkey).
[28] Meaning unknown; evidently (by context) some kind of seabirds or shellfish.
[29] Wooden plates.

FROM ACT 5, SCENE 1 (LINES 33–57):

PROSPERO. Ye elves of hills, brooks, standing lakes, and groves;
    And ye, that on the sands with printless foot
    Do chase the ebbing Neptune and do fly him
    When he comes back; you demipuppets,[1] that
    By moonshine do the green sour ringlets[2] make   5
    Whereof the ewe not bites; and you, whose pastime
    Is to make midnight mushrooms; that rejoice
    To hear the solemn curfew; by whose aid, —
    Weak masters though ye be — I have bedimmed
    The noontide sun, called forth the mutinous winds,   10
    And 'twixt the green sea and the azured vault
    Set roaring war: to the dread rattling thunder
    Have I given fire and rifted Jove's stout oak
    With his own bolt: the strong-based promontory
    Have I made shake; and by the spurs[3] plucked up   15
    The pine and cedar: graves at my command
    Have waked their sleepers, oped, and let them forth
    By my so potent art. But this rough magic
    I here abjure; and, when I have required[4]
    Some heavenly music, — which even now I do, —   20
    To work mine end upon their senses that
    This airy charm is for, I'll break my staff,
    Bury it certain fathoms in the earth,
    And, deeper than did ever plummet sound
    I'll drown my book.[5]   *Solemn music.*   25
                    . . .

["Where the Bee Sucks, There Suck I"]

ARIEL (*Sings and helps to attire* [PROSPERO]).
    Where the bee sucks, there suck I:
    In a cowslip's bell I lie;
    There I couch when owls do cry.
    On the bat's back I do fly
    After summer merrily.   5
  Merrily, merrily shall I live now
  Under the blossom that hangs on the bough.

[1] Creatures of small size.

[2] "Fairy rings," circles in the grass supposedly made by dancing fairies.

[3] Roots.

[4] Requested.

[5] Prospero's "staff" and "book" are traditional emblems of the magician's power. Prospero's farewell to his art is closely derived from a speech by Medea in Ovid's *Metamorphoses*, translated into English by Arthur Golding, in 1567.

❧ *John Donne* *(1572–1631)*

Born into a wealthy Catholic family at a time when Catholics were subject to govern-mental persecution and limited civil rights, John Donne spent his early years studying at both Oxford and Cambridge. However, because of his religion, he was barred from tak-ing university degrees. He went on to study law at Lincoln's Inn and, after renouncing his Catholicism, would most likely have had a successful civil or diplomatic career. How-ever, in 1601, his secret marriage to Ann More, the niece of his employer, Lord Egerton, put a stop to Donne's early public ambitions; in fact, his wife's powerful family disap-proved of their match, had Donne temporarily imprisoned, and disinherited his wife. For the next fourteen years, Donne and his growing family (Ann bore him twelve children) struggled financially. In 1615, King James encouraged Donne to take holy orders in the Anglican Church. Donne found greater success in his ecclesiastical career, eventually at-taining the privileged post of dean of St. Paul's Cathedral in London and the reputation of one of the foremost preachers of his day. His poetry, which he wrote largely before he became a priest, was not published until after his death in 1633. His sermons and reli-gious writings, however, were enormously popular in his own time.

Often referred to as one of the Metaphysical poets, Donne's verse frequently uses vividly concrete physical imagery to convey its complex arguments. Donne wrote both sec-ular love lyrics and religious and devotional verse; yet it is wrong to consider either type of poetry exclusively. Often Donne's amorous pieces use biblical imagery or religious rhetoric, while the devotional poetry involves sexual imagery and a language of seduc-tion. Central to the majority of Donne's poetry is his use of the conceit, an elaborately drawn-out metaphor that compares two very disparate things, so as to exhibit the aes-thetic principle of concordia discors *(the harmony of opposites) that was the foundation of Donne's poetic wit. Donne's poem "The Flea," for example, uses this tiny insect as a metaphor for the different stages of marriage and sexual reproduction. Highly original in many respects, particularly in his complex use of language and verse form, Donne also uses natural imagery to write poems that participate in the longstanding tradition of* carpe diem *(seize the day) poetry, as in "The Blossom." "The Bait" is Donne's effort to use fishing imagery as a means of seduction; it replies to similar poems by Marlowe and Ralegh. Finally, recent critics have made much of Donne's interest in and knowledge of scientific developments in his own day. While this remains a matter of some scholarly de-bate, in poems such as "The First Anniversary. An Anatomy of the World," Donne ex-hibits familiarity with many of the scientific theories of his time about the workings of the universe. "Holy Sonnet 5" ("I am a little world") could be said to employ the scien-tific notion of the microcosm, but Donne applies it to a wholly nonscientific message about sin and salvation.*

The Bait

Come live with me, and be my love,
And we will some new pleasures prove

Of golden sands, and crystal brooks:
With silken lines, and silver hooks.

There will the river whispering run   5
Warmed by thy eyes, more than the Sun.
And there the enamored fish will stay,
Begging themselves they may betray.

When thou wilt swim in that live bath,
Each fish, which every channel hath,   10
Will amorously to thee swim,
Gladder to catch thee, than thou him.

If thou, to be so seen, beest loath,
By Sun, or Moon, thou dark'nest both,
And if my self have leave to see,   15
I need not their light, having thee.

Let others freeze with angling reeds,
And cut their legs, with shells and weeds,
Or treacherously poor fish beset,
With strangling snare, or windowy net: 20

Let coarse bold hands, from slimy nest
The bedded fish in banks out-wrest,
Or curious traitors, sleave-silk flies
Bewitch poor fishes' wand'ring eyes.

For thee, thou needst no such deceit,   25
For thou thy self art thine own bait;
That fish, that is not catched thereby,
Alas, is wiser far than I.

The Flea

Mark but this flea, and mark in this,
How little that which thou deny'st me is;
It sucked me first, and now sucks thee,
And in this flea, our two bloods mingled be;
Thou know'st that this cannot be said   5
A sin, nor shame, nor loss of maidenhead,
    Yet this enjoys before it woo,
    And pampered swells with one blood made of two,
    And this, alas, is more then we would do.

Oh stay, three lives in one flea spare,   10
Where we almost, yea more then married are.
This flea is you and I, and this

Our marriage bed, and marriage temple is;
Though parents grudge, and you, we are met,
And cloistered in these living walls of Jet.   15
   Though use make you apt to kill me,
    Let not to that, self-murder added be,
    And sacrilege, three sins in killing three.

Cruel and sudden hast thou since
Purpled thy nail, in blood of innocence?   20
Wherein could this flea guilty be,
Except in that drop which it suckt from thee?
Yet thou triumph'st, and say'st that thou
Find'st not thy self, nor me the weaker now;
   'Tis true, then learn how false, fears be;   25
    Just so much honor, when thou yield'st to me,
    Will waste, as this flea's death took life from thee.

The Blossom

   Little think'st thou, poor flower,
    Whom I have watched six or seven days,
And seen thy birth, and seen what every hour
Gave to thy growth, thee to this height to raise,
And now dost laugh and triumph on this bough,   5
   Little think'st thou
That it will freeze anon, and that I shall
Tomorrow find thee fall'n, or not at all.

   Little think'st thou poor heart
    That labour'st yet to nestle thee,   10
And think'st by hovering here to get a part
In a forbidden or forbidding tree,
And hop'st her stiffness by long siege to bow:
   Little think'st thou,
That thou tomorrow, ere that Sun doth wake,   15
Must with this Sun, and me a journey take.

   But thou which lov'st to be
    Subtile to plague thy self, wilt say,
Alas, if you must go, what's that to me?
Here lies my business, and here I will stay: 20
You go to friends, whose love and means present
   Various content
To your eyes, ears, and tongue, and every part.
If then your body go, what need you a heart?

Well then, stay here; but know,   25
  When thou hast stayed and done thy most;
A naked thinking heart, that makes no show,
Is to a woman, but a kind of Ghost;
How shall she know my heart; or having none,
  Know thee for one?   30
Practise may make her know some other part,
But take my word, she doth not know a Heart.

  Meet me at London, then,
    Twenty days hence, and thou shalt see
Me fresher, and more fat, by being with men,   35
Then if I had stayed still with her and thee.
For God's sake, if you can, be you so too:
    I would give you
There, to another friend, whom we shall find
As glad to have my body, as my mind.   40

The Primrose

  Upon this Primrose hill,
    Where, if Heav'n would distill
A shower of rain, each several drop might go
To his own primrose, and grow Manna so;
And where their form, and their infinity   5
    Make a terrestrial Galaxy,
    As the small stars do in the sky:
I walk to find a true Love; and I see
That 'tis not a mere woman, that is she,
But must, or more, or less than woman be.   10

  Yet know I not, which flower
    I wish; a six, or four;
For should my true Love less than woman be,
She were scarce any thing; and then, should she
Be more than woman, she would get above   15
    All thought of sex, and think to move
    My heart to study her, and not to love;
Both these were monsters; since there must reside
Falsehood in woman, I could more abide,
She were by art, then Nature falsified.   20

  Live Primrose then, and thrive
    With thy true number five;
And women, whom this flower doth represent,
With this mysterious number be content;

Ten is the farthest number; if half ten   25
    Belong unto each woman, then
    Each woman may take half us men,
Or if this will not serve their turn, since all
Numbers are odd, or even, and they fall
First into this five, women may take us all.   30

Holy Sonnet 5

I am a little world made cunningly
Of Elements, and an Angelike spright,[1]
But black sin hath betrayed to endless night
My world's both parts, and (O) both parts must die.
You which beyond that heaven which was most high   5
Have found new spheres, and of new lands can write,
Power new seas in mine eyes, that so I might
Drown my world with my weeping earnestly,
Or wash it if it must be drowned no more:
But O it must be burnt! Alas the fire   10
Of lust and envy have burnt it heretofore,
And made it fouler; let their flames retire,
And burn me O Lord, with a fiery zeal
Of thee and thy house, which doth in eating heal.[2]

✒ *Ben Jonson* (1572–1637)

Best remembered today for his satirical comedies, Ben Jonson was a man of many talents. He worked, at various points in his life, as a bricklayer, soldier, actor, poet, critic, and songwriter; he was also England's first Poet Laureate. Of Scottish ancestry, Jonson was born in London, where he spent most of his life. He was educated at the Westminster School, where he formed the great love of classical Greek and Roman literature that was to influence his work in the many genres in which he worked: tragedy, comedy, epigrams, and verse epistles, to name only a few. Jonson first established himself in the theater in the early part of the 1600s, with plays such as Every Man in his Humour *(1598),* Volpone, or The Fox *(1606),* Epicene, or The Silent Woman *(1609), and* The Alchemist *(1610). Jonson became associated with the court of King James I, for whom he wrote masques (elaborate theatrical spectacles with allegorical or mythological plots) in collaboration with architect Inigo Jones. Jonson saw the role of the writer, as in antiquity, as that of a social and moral arbiter (although ironically, he himself had a reputa-*

---

[1] Spirit; often written as sprite.
[2] *Eating heal:* reference to the Christian Eucharist.

tion as something of an outlaw, having been imprisoned several times in his life for crimes ranging from murder to sedition). A man of great sociability, Jonson associated with many other great writers of his time, including Shakespeare, Francis Bacon, and John Donne. He served as a leader to a younger generation of poets, today called the "Cavalier School," who called themselves "the Sons of Ben" or the "Tribe of Ben." This group included Thomas Carew and Robert Herrick, among others. Jonson is buried in Westminster Abbey.

In "To Penshurst," Jonson draws upon the classical theme of rural retirement but also establishes a new poetic type in English literature: the country-house or topographical poem, which would be imitated by later poets such as Sir John Denham in "Cooper's Hill," Andrew Marvell in "Upon Appleton House," and Alexander Pope in "Windsor Forest." Written for his patrons, the Sidney family, "To Penshurst" celebrates the pleasures of country living, but it has a political and moral dimension as well. Because the English economy at the time was largely agricultural, it was in the national interest that aristocratic landowners took proper care of their estates and resisted the temptations of court life, which could not only distract them from their duties but threatened the income generated from the land around the estate. "To Penshurst" presents an idyllic and somewhat nostalgic view of the role and responsibilities of the English gentry. It expresses a hierarchical social order that parallels a presumably "natural" hierarchy. The poem "To Sir Robert Wroth" further echoes the theme of the joys of escaping from urban living, and thus it also has an important place in the long trajectory of literature contrasting the environmental and implicitly moral distinctions between country and city.

To Penshurst*

Thou art not, Penshurst, built to envious show,
    Of touch,[1] or marble; nor canst boast a row
Of polished pillars, or a roof of gold;
    Thou hast no lantern, whereof tales are told;
Or stair, or courts; but stand'st an ancient pile,   5
    And these grudged at, art reverenced the while.
Thou joy'st in better marks, of soil, of air,
    Of wood, of water; therein thou art fair.
Thou hast thy walks for health, as well as sport;
    Thy *Mount*, to which the *Dryads* do resort,   10
Where Pan, and Bacchus[2] their high feasts have made,
    Beneath the broad beech, and the chestnut shade;
That taller tree, which of a nut was set,
    At his great birth,[3] where all the *Muses* met.

---

* Home of the aristocratic Sidney family, located in Kent.

[1] Black marble.

[2] Dryads are tree nymphs; Pan and Bacchus are classical gods of nature and fertility.

[3] *At his great birth:* reference to Sir Philip Sidney (1554–1586), an English poet who excelled in the pastoral form.

There, in the writhèd bark, are cut the names;   15
 Of many a *Sylvan,* taken with his flames;
And thence, the ruddy *Satyrs* oft provoke
 The lighter *Fauns,*[4] to reach thy *Lady's Oak.*[5]
Thy copse, too, named of Gamage,[6] thou hast there,
 That never fails to serve thee seasoned deer;   20
When thou would'st feast, or exercise thy friends.
 The lower land, that to the river bends,
Thy sheep, thy bullocks, kine, and calves do feed;
 The middle grounds thy mares, and horses breed.
Each bank doth yield thee conies; and the tops   25
 Fertile of wood, Ashore, and Sydney's copse,[7]
To crown thy open table, doth provide
 The purpled pheasant, with the speckled side;
The painted partridge lies in every field,
 And, for thy mess, is willing to be killed.   30
And if the high-swoll'n *Medway*[8] fail thy dish,
 Thou hast thy ponds, that pay thee tribute fish,
Fat, agèd carps, that run into thy net.
 And pikes, now weary their own kind to eat,
As loath, the second draught, or cast to stay,   35
 Officiously, at first, themselves betray;
Bright eels, that emulate them, and leap on land
 Before the fisher, or into his hand.
Then hath thy orchard fruit, thy garden flowers,
 Fresh as the air, and new as are the hours.   40
The early cherry, with the later plum,
 Fig, grape, and quince, each in his time doth come;
The blushing apricot and woolly peach
 Hang on thy walls, that every child may reach.
And though thy walls be of the country stone,   45
 They're reared with no man's ruin, no man's groan;
There's none that dwell about them wish them down;
 But all come in, the farmer, and the clown;
And no one empty-handed, to salute
 Thy lord, and lady, though they have no suit.   50
Some bring a capon, some a rural cake,
 Some nuts, some apples; some that think they make

---

[4] A sylvan is a countryman; also, one of the forest. Satyrs and fauns are mythic woodland creatures, half animal and half human.

[5] A reference to the tree (here, an oak) under which the mother of Sir Robert Sidney, master of the house at the time of the poem's composition, went into labor for his birth.

[6] Barbara Gamage, wife of Sir Robert Sidney.

[7] Names for two woodland areas on the property.

[8] A river near the property.

The better cheeses, bring them, or else send
  By their ripe daughters, whom they would commend
This way to husbands, and whose baskets bear   55
  An emblem of themselves, in plum, or pear.
But what can this (more then express their love)
  Add to thy free provisions, far above
The need of such? whose liberal board doth flow
  With all, that hospitality doth know!   60
Where comes no guest, but is allowed to eat,
  Without his fear, and of thy lord's own meat;
Where the same beer, and bread, and self-same wine,
  That is his Lordship's, shall be also mine,
And I not fain to sit (as some, this day,   65
  At great men's tables) and yet dine away.
Here no man tells my cups;[9] nor, standing by,
  A waiter doth my gluttony envy:
But gives me what I call, and lets me eat;
  He knows, below, he shall find plenty of meat.   70
Thy tables hoard not up for the next day,
  Nor, when I take my lodging, need I pray
For fire, or lights, or livery;[10] all is there,
  As if thou, then, wert mine, or I reigned here:
There's nothing I can wish, for which I stay.   75
  That found King James, when hunting late this way,
With his brave son, the Prince, they saw thy fires
  Shine bright on every hearth as the desires
Of thy *Penates*[11] had been set on flame
  To entertain them; or the country came   80
With all their zeal, to warm their welcome here.
  What (great, I will not say, but) sudden cheer
Didst thou, then, make them! and what praise was heaped
  On thy good lady, then! who, therein, reaped
The just reward of her high housewifery;   85
  To have her linen, plate, and all things nigh,
When she was far; and not a room, but dressed,
  As if it had expected such a guest!
These, Penshurst, are thy praise, and yet not all.
  Thy lady's noble, fruitful, chaste withal.   90
His children thy great lord may call his own,
  A fortune, in this age, but rarely known.
They are, and have been taught religion; thence
  Their gentler spirits have sucked innocence.

---

[9] *Here . . . my cups:* i.e., here the host is generous and does not keep track of how much guests may be drinking.

[10] Other provisions or necessaries.

[11] The family gods sacred to ancient Roman households.

Each morn and even they are taught to pray, 95
    With the whole household, and may, every day,
Read in their virtuous parents' noble parts
    The mysteries of manners, arms, and arts.
Now, Penshurst, they that will proportion thee
    With other edifices, when they see 100
Those proud, ambitious heaps, and nothing else,
    May say, their lords have built, but thy lord dwells.

To Sir Robert Wroth*

How blest art thou, canst love the country, Wroth,
    Whether by choice, or fate, or both;
And, though so near the city, and the court,
    Art taken with neither's vice, nor sport:
That at great times, art no ambitious guest 5
    Of Sheriff's dinner, or Mayor's feast.
Nor com'st to view the better cloth of state;
    The richer hangings, or crown-plate;
Nor throng'st (when masquing is) to have a sight
    Of the short bravery of the night; 10
To view the jewels, stuffs, the pains, the wit
    There wasted, some not paid for yet!
But canst, at home, in thy securer rest,
    Live, with unbought provision blest;
Free from proud porches, or their guilded roofs, 15
    'Mongst lowing herds, and solid hooves;
Along'st the curled woods, and painted meads,
    Through which a serpent river leads
To some cool, courteous shade, which he calls his,
    And makes sleep softer than it is! 20
Or, if thou list the night in watch to break,
    A-bed canst hear the loud stag speak,
In spring, oft roused for thy master's sport,
    Who, for it, makes thy house his court;[1]
Or with thy friends, the heart of all the year, 25
    Dividest, upon the lesser Deer;
In autumn, at the Partridge makes a flight,
    And giv'st thy gladder guests the sight;

* Sir Robert Wroth (1576–1614) was married to the daughter of Sir Robert Sidney, owner of Penshurst, described in Jonson's eponymous poem.

[1] *Who . . . his court:* i.e., the king visits Sir Robert Wroth's estate to go hunting.

And, in the winter, hunt'st the flying hare,
   More for thy exercise, than fare;   30
While all, that follow, their glad ears apply
   To the full greatness of the cry;
Or hawking at the river, or the bush,
   Or shooting at the greedy thrush,
Thou dost with some delight the day out-weary,   35
   Although the coldest of the year!
The whil'st, the several seasons thou hast seen
   Of flowery fields, of copses green,
The mowed meadows, with the fleeced sheep,
   And feasts, that either shearers keep;   40
The ripened ears, yet humble in their height,
   And furrows laden with their weight;
The apple harvest, that doth longer last;
   The hogs returned home fat from mast;[2]
The trees cut out in log; and those boughs made   45
   A fire now, that lent a shade!
Thus Pan, and Sylvan, having had their rites,
   Comus[3] puts in, for new delights;
And fills thy open hall with mirth, and cheer,
   As if in Saturn's reign[4] it were;   50
Apollo's harp, and Hermes' lyre resound,
   Nor are the *Muses* strangers found;
The rout of rural folk come thronging in,
   (Their rudeness then is thought no sin)
Thy noblest spouse affords them welcome grace;   55
   And the great *Heroes*, of her race,
Sit mixed with loss of state, or reverence.
   Freedom doth with degree dispense.
The jolly wassail[5] walks the often round,
   And in their cups, their cares are drowned: 60
They think not, then, which side the cause shall leese,[6]
   Nor how to get the lawyer fees.
Such, and no other was that age, of old,
   Which boasts t' have had the head of gold.
And such since thou canst make thine own content,   65
   Strive, Wroth, to live long innocent.

---

[2] Mashed nuts fed to the hogs.

[3] In antiquity, the god of conviviality.

[4] *As if in Saturn's reign:* i.e., it seems as if it occurs in the Golden Age.

[5] A festive holiday punch.

[6] I.e., loose.

Let others watch in guilty arms, and stand
   The fury of a rash command,
Go enter breaches, meet the cannons' rage,
   That they may sleep with scars in age. 70
And show their feathers shot, and colours torn,
   And brag, that they were therefore born.
Let this man sweat, and wrangle at the bar,
   For every price, in every jar,
And change possessions, oft'ner with his breath, 75
   Then either money, war, or death:
Let him, then hardest sires, more disinherit,
   And each where boast it as his merit,
To blow up orphans, widows, and their states;[7]
   And think his power doth equal Fate's. 80
Let that go heap a mass of wretched wealth,
   Purchased by rapine, worse than stealth,
And brooding o'er it sit, with broadest eyes,
   Not doing good, scarce when he dies.
Let thousands more go flatter vice, and win, 85
   By being organs to great sin,
Get place, and honor, and be glad to keep
   The secrets, that shall break their sleep:
And, so they ride in purple, eat in plate,[8]
   Though poison, think it a great fate. 90
But thou, my Wroth, if I can truth apply,
   Shalt neither that, nor this envy:
Thy peace is made; and, when man's state is well,
   'Tis better, if he there can dwell.
God wisheth, none should wrack on a strange shelf: 95
   To him, man's dearer, than to himself.
And, howsoever we may think things sweet,
   He always gives what he knows meet;
Which who can use is happy: such be thou.
   Thy morning's and thy evening's vow 100
Be thanks to him, and earnest prayer, to find
   A body sound, with sounder mind;
To do thy country service, thy self right;
   That neither want do thee afright,
Nor death; but when thy latest sand is spent,[9] 105
   Thou mayst think life a thing but lent.

---

[7] I.e., their estates, or their possessions.

[8] Gold or silver platters.

[9] *When . . . spent:* i.e., when you die, symbolized by the last sand in an hourglass.

⮞ John Smith (1580–1631)

John Smith had an exceptionally intimate relationship with nature, one on which his survival depended. Smith helped found the precarious Jamestown colony in the Virginia wilderness and was shortly thereafter sent foraging into the forest. Although Smith's career was primarily as a publicist for British colonization and reporter to British commerce, he was forced, like the fictional Robinson Crusoe a hundred years later, into a desperate, independent fight for subsistence. Smith was well prepared for such a fight. He was only sixteen years old when he enlisted in the army, and he served in several countries throughout Europe. According to his own account, after fighting through Hungary and Transylvania, he was captured and sold into slavery in Turkey. He tells us that he killed his master before escaping back to London. Soon after his return to England, he set sail for Virginia with a company of "gentlemen adventurers," who with him established Jamestown in 1607. Despite famine, disease, turbulent politics within the colony, and his own notorious confrontation with the Indian chief Powhatan's men, Smith survived his years at Jamestown. Many of his companions did not.

Smith's first book was A True Relation of Such Occurrences and Accidents of Note as Hath Happened in Virginia Since the First Planting of That Colony. *Written in the year following the establishment of Jamestown, the manuscript of* A True Relation *sailed back to England on a supply ship and was published in the summer of 1608. Smith's second book,* A Map of Virginia, with a Description of the Country, Commodities, People, Government, and Religion, *was published in 1612, three years after his return to England.* A Description of New England, *published in 1616, was Smith's account of his return to the coast of America in 1614. That expedition took him from Maine to Cape Cod. Smith's earlier work was compiled and further developed in* The General History of Virginia, New England, and the Summer Isles *(1624). This book includes the famous story of his encounters with Powhatan (actually, Wahunsonacock, principal chief of Powhatan village) and Pocahontas, his daughter. Smith's writing shows a profound knowledge of the country, commodities, and people who would soon be exploited by his employers. His evident respect for the Native Americans he encountered was no doubt forged largely from necessity, through Smith's personal struggle for survival in an unfamiliar New World.*

From Description of Virginia and Proceedings of the Colony

Of such things which are natural in Virginia and how they use them.

Virginia doth afford many excellent vegetables and living Creatures, yet grass there is little or none but what groweth in low Marshes: for all the Country is overgrown with trees, whose droppings continually turneth their grass to weeds, by reason of the rankness of the ground; which would soon be amended by good husbandry. The wood that is most common is Oak and Walnut: many of their

Oaks are so tall and straight, that they will bear two foot and a half square of good timber for 20 yards long. Of this wood there is 2 or 3 several kinds. The Acorns of one kind, whose bark is more white than the other, is somewhat sweetish; which being boiled half a day in several waters, at last afford a sweet oil, which they keep in gourds to annoint their heads and joints. The fruit they eat, made in bread or otherwise. There is also some Elm, some black walnut tree, and some Ash: of Ash and Elm they make soap Ashes. If the trees be very great, the ashes will be good, and melt to hard lumps: but if they be small, it will be but powder, and not so good as the other. Of walnuts there is 2 or 3 kinds: there is a kind of wood we called Cypress, because both the wood, the fruit, and leaf did most resemble it; and of those trees there are some near 3 fathom about at the root, very straight, and 50, 60, or 80 foot without a branch. By the dwelling of the Savages are some great Mullbery trees; and in some parts of the Country, they are found growing naturally in pretty groves. There was an assay made to make silk, and surely the worms prospered excellent well, till the master workman fell sick: during which time, they were eaten with rats.

In some parts, were found some Chestnuts whose wild fruit equalize the best in France, Spain, Germany, or Italy, to their tastes that had tasted them all. Plums there are of 3 sorts. The red and white are like our hedge plums: but the other, which they call *Putchamins*,[1] grow as high as a Palmetto. The fruit is like a medler; it is first green, then yellow, and red when it is ripe: if it be not ripe it will draw a man's mouth awry with much torment; but when it is ripe, it is as delicious as an Apricot.

They have Cherries, and those are much like a Damson; but for their tastes and colour, we called them Cherries. We see some few Crabs,[2] but very small and bitter. Of vines, great abundance in many parts, that climb the tops of the highest trees in some places, but these bear but few grapes. But by the rivers and Savage habitations where they are not overshadowed from the sun, they are covered with fruit, though never pruned nor manured. Of those hedge grapes, we made near 20 gallons of wine, which was near as good as your French British wine, but certainly they would prove good were they well manured. There is another sort of grape near as great as a Cherry, this they call *Messaminnes;* they be fat, and the juice thick: neither doth the taste so well please when they are made in wine. They have a small fruit growing on little trees, husked like a Chestnut, but the fruit most like a very small acorn. This they call *Chechinquamins*,[3] which they esteem a great dainty. They have a berry much like our gooseberry, in greatness, colour, and taste; those they call *Rawcomenes,* and do eat them raw or boiled. Of these natural fruits they live a great part of the year, which they use in this manner. The walnuts, Chestnuts, Acorns, and *Chechinquamens* are dried to keep. When they need them, they break them between two stones, yet some part of the walnut shells will cleave to the fruit. Then do they dry them again upon a mat over a hurdle. After, they put it into a mortar of wood, and beat it very

[1] Persimmons.

[2] Crab apples.

[3] Chinquapins, the nuts of a kind of dwarf chestnut tree.

small: that done, they mix it with water, that the shells may sink to the bottom. This water will be coloured as milk; which they call *Pawcohiscora*, and keep it for their use. The fruit like medlers, they call *Putchamins*, they cast upon hurdles on a mat, and preserve them as Prunes. Of their Chestnuts and *Chechinquamens* boiled 4 hours, they make both broth and bread for their chief men, or at their greatest feasts. Besides those fruit trees, there is a white poplar, and another tree like unto it, that yieldeth a very clear and an odoriferous Gum like Turpentine, which some called Balsom. There are also Cedars and Sassafrass trees. They also yield gums in a small proportion of themselves. We tried conclusions[4] to extract it out of the wood, but nature afforded more than our arts.

In the watery valleys groweth a berry, which they call *Ocoughtanamnis*, very much like unto Capers. These they dry in summer. When they will eat them, they boil them near half a day; for otherwise they differ not much from poison. *Mattoume* groweth as our bents do in meadows. The seed is not much unlike to rye, though much smaller. This they use for a dainty bread buttered with deer suet.

During Summer there are either strawberries which ripen in April; or mulberries which ripen in May and June, Raspises, hurtes,[5] or a fruit that the Inhabitants call *Maracocks*, which is a pleasant wholesome fruit much like a lemon. Many herbs in the spring time there are commonly dispersed throughout the woods, good for broths and salads, as Violets, Purslane, Sorrel, &c. Besides many we used whose names we know not.

The chief root they have for food is called *Tockawhoughe*.[6] It groweth like a flag in low muddy freshes. In one day a Savage will gather sufficient for a week. These roots are much of the greatness and taste of Potatoes. They use to cover a great many of them with oak leaves and fern, and then cover all with earth in the manner of a coalpit; over it, on each side, they continue a great fire 24 hours before they dare eat it. Raw it is no better than poison, and being roasted, except it be tender and the heat abated, or sliced and dried in the sun, mixed with sorrel and meal or such like, it will prickle and torment the throat extremely, and yet in summer they use this ordinarily for bread.

They have an other root which they call *Wighsacan*: as the other feedeth the body, so this cureth their hurts and diseases. It is a small root which they bruise and apply to the wound. *Pocones* is a small root that groweth in the mountains, which being dried and beat in powder turneth red: and this they use for swellings, aches, annointing their joints, painting their heads and garments. They account it very precious and of much worth. *Musquaspenne*[7] is a root of the bigness of a finger, and as red as blood. In drying, it will wither almost to nothing. This they use to paint their Mats, Targets, and such like.

There is also Pellitory of Spain, Sassafrass, and divers other simples, which the Apothecaries gathered, and commended to be good and medicinable.

---

[4] Artificial methods.

[5] *Raspises* are raspberries; *hurtes* are hurtleberries (or whortleberries), similar to blueberries.

[6] Tuckahoe. This name was also given to a kind of fungus found at the roots of certain trees.

[7] Bloodroot.

In the low Marshes, grow plots of Onions containing an acre of ground or more in many places; but they are small, not past the bigness of the top of one's thumb.

Of beasts the chief are Deer, nothing differing from ours. In the deserts towards the heads of the rivers, there are many, but amongst the rivers few. There is a beast they call *Aroughcun*,[8] much like a badger, but useth to live on trees as Squirrels do. Their Squirrels some are near as great as our smallest sort of wild rabbits; some blackish or black and white, but the most are gray.

A small beast they have, they call *Assapanick*, but we call them flying squirrels, because spreading their legs, and so stretching the largeness of their skins that they have been seen to fly 30 or 40 yards. An *Opossom* hath an head like a Swine, and a tail like a Rat, and is of the bigness of a Cat. Under her belly she hath a bag, wherein she lodgeth, carrieth, and sucketh her young. *Mussascus*[9] is a beast of the form and nature of our water Rats, but many of them smell exceeding strongly of musk. Their Hares no bigger than our Conies, and few of them to be found.

Their Bears are very little in comparison of those of Muscovia and Tartaria. The Beaver is as big as an ordinary water dog, but his legs exceeding short. His forefeet like a dog's, his hinder feet like a Swan's. His tail somewhat like the form of a Racket bar without hair; which to eat, the Savages esteem a great delicate. They have many Otters, which, as the Beavers, they take with snares, and esteem the skins great ornaments; and of all those beasts they use to feed, when they catch them.

There is also a beast they call *Vetchunquoyes* in the form of a wild Cat. Their Foxes are like our silver-haired Conies, of a small proportion, and not smelling like those in England. Their Dogs of that country are like their Wolves, and cannot bark but howl; and their wolves not much bigger than our English Foxes. Martins, Polecats, Weasels and Minks we know they have, because we have seen many of their skins, though very seldom any of them alive. But one thing is strange, that we could never perceive their vermin destroy our hens, eggs, nor chickens, nor do any hurt: nor their flies nor serpents any way pernicious; where[10] in the South parts of America, they are always dangerous and often deadly.

Of birds, the Eagle is the greatest devourer. Hawks there be of diverse sorts as our Falconers called them, Sparrowhawks, Lanarets, Goshawks, Falcons and Ospreys; but they all prey most upon fish. Partridges there are little bigger than our Quails, wild Turkeys are as big as our tame. There are woosels or blackbirds with red shoulders, thrushes, and diverse sorts of small birds, some red, some blue, scarce so big as a wren, but few in Summer. In winter there are great plenty of Swans, Crains gray and white with black wings, Herons, Geese, Brants, Duck, Wigeon, Dotterell, Oxies, Parrots, and Pigeons. Of all those sorts great abundance, and some other strange kinds, to us unknown by name. But in summer not any, or a very few to be seen.

[8] Raccoon.
[9] Muskrat.
[10] Whereas.

Of fish we were best acquainted with Sturgeon, Grampus, Porpus, Seals, Stingrays whose tails are very dangerous, Brettes, Mullets, white Salmon, Trouts, Soles, Plaice, Herrings, Conyfish, Rockfish, Eels, Lampreys, Catfish, Shades, Perch of 3 sorts, Crabs, Shrimps, Crevises, Oysters, Cockles, and Mussels. But the most strange fish is a small one so like the picture of St. George his Dragon, as possible can be, except his legs and wings: and the Toadfish which will swell till it be like to burst, when it cometh into the air.

Concerning the entrails of the earth little can be said for certainty. There wanted good Refiners: for these that took upon them to have skill this way, took up the washings from the mountains and some moskered[11] shining stones and spangles which the waters brought down; flattering themselves in their own vain conceits to have been supposed that they were not, by the means of that ore, if it proved as their arts and judgments expected. Only this is certain, that many regions lying in the same latitude, afford mines very rich of diverse natures. The crust also of these rocks would easily persuade a man to believe there are other mines than iron and steel, if there were but means and men of experience that knew the mine from spar.[12]

🖎 William Bradford (1590–1657)

William Bradford was born in Yorkshire, England, and during his infancy, his father died. He was sent away from his mother to live with his grandparents, in whose care he received little formal education but was trained in farming skills, with the expectation that he would take over the family farm. As a boy in his teens, however, he heard the sermons of the Dissenting minister Richard Clyfton, the charismatic leader of a Puritan sect known as Separatists. This group wanted to become entirely separate from the established Church of England and to form an autonomous congregation of true believers. In 1606 Bradford joined a religious community of Separatists in Nottinghamshire, a group that worshiped in secret and was frequently harassed by local officials. Eventually, the Separatists moved to Holland, where Bradford joined them in 1609. He learned the trade of weaving and successfully established himself in a small business. Nevertheless, the Separatists found themselves isolated and impoverished in Holland. Hearing of the prosperous colony recently established by John Smith in Virginia, the Pilgrims (as they now called themselves) resolved to seek a new home in the New World.

The voyage of the Mayflower to the bleak shores of Massachusetts, the Pilgrims' landing—generally said to be at Plymouth Rock—in December 1620, and their desperate struggle to establish a colony of true believers, is one of the foundational narratives of American national identity. Much of what we know about these events is recorded in the journal of William Bradford, which was first published in 1856 under the title Of Plymouth Plantation. Bradford offers a vivid account of the rough voyage of the Mayflower across the stormy Atlantic, of the Pilgrims' first landing, and of their early

---

[11] Decayed; crumbled.

[12] Non-metallic ore, lacking any commercial value.

encounters with Native Americans, with whom, after some initial skirmishes, they even-
tually succeeded in forging a friendly and constructive relationship. Bradford was elected
governor of the new colony, and he served in that role until his death.

Bradford's account reveals a great deal about the early settlers' attitudes toward the
vast, uncharted American continent. In a typical passage, he writes: "What could they
see but a hideous and desolate wilderness, full of wild beasts and wild men?" The first few
months of the Plymouth colony were grim indeed; over half of the Pilgrims died in that
terrible first winter. But the fortunes of the colony gradually improved, and the Pilgrims'
dedication to the principles of self-government and religious freedom have proven influ-
ential over the subsequent course of American history. However, Americans are still deal-
ing with the consequences of a more problematic Puritan legacy, evident throughout
Bradford's account: an unshakeable antagonism toward the frightful and inscrutable
forces of nature. After four centuries, Of Plymouth Plantation still tells a quintessen-
tially American story.

From Of Plymouth Plantation

From Chapter 4
Reasons and Causes of Their Removal

The place they had thoughts on was some of those vast and unpeopled countries
of America, which are fruitful and fit for habitation, being devoid of all civil inhabitants, where there are only savage and brutish men which range up and
down, little otherwise than the wild beasts of the same. This proposition being
made public and coming to the scanning of all, it raised many variable opinions
amongst men and caused many fears and doubts amongst themselves. Some,
from their reasons and hopes conceived, laboured to stir up and encourage the
rest to undertake and prosecute the same; others again, out of their fears, objected against it and sought to divert from it; alleging many things, and those
neither unreasonable nor unprobable; as that it was a great design and subject to
many unconceivable perils and dangers; as, besides the casualties of the sea
(which none can be freed from), the length of the voyage was such as the weak
bodies of women and other persons worn out with age and travail (as many of
them were) could never be able to endure. And yet if they should, the miseries of
the land which they should be exposed unto, would be too hard to be borne and
likely, some or all of them together, to consume and utterly to ruinate them. For
there they should be liable to famine and nakedness and the want, in a manner,
of all things. The change of air, diet and drinking of water would infect their
bodies with sore sicknesses and grievous diseases. And also those which should
escape or overcome these difficulties should yet be in continual danger of the
savage people, who are cruel, barbarous and most treacherous, being most furious in their rage and merciless where they overcome; not being content only to
kill and take away life, but delight to torment men in the most bloody manner
that may be; flaying some alive with the shells of fishes, cutting off the members

and joints of others by piecemeal and broiling on the coals, eat the collops[1] of their flesh in their sight whilst they live, with other cruelties horrible to be related.

And surely it could not be thought but the very hearing of these things could not but move the very bowels of men to grate within them and make the weak to quake and tremble. It was further objected that it would require greater sums of money to furnish such a voyage and to fit them with necessaries, than their consumed estates would amount to; and yet they must as well look to be seconded with supplies as presently to be transported. Also many precedents of ill success and lamentable miseries befallen others in the like designs were easy to be found, and not forgotten to be alleged; besides their own experience, in their former troubles and hardships in their removal into Holland, and how hard a thing it was for them to live in that strange place, though it was a neighbour country and a civil and rich commonwealth.

It was answered, that all great and honourable actions are accompanied with great difficulties and must be both enterprised and overcome with answerable courages. It was granted the dangers were great, but not desperate. The difficulties were many, but not invincible. For though there were many of them likely, yet they were not certain. It might be sundry of the things feared might never befall; others by provident care and the use of good means might in a great measure be prevented; and all of them, through the help of God, by fortitude and patience, might either be borne or overcome. True it was that such attempts were not to be made and undertaken without good ground and reason, not rashly or lightly as many have done for curiosity or hope of gain, etc. But their condition was not ordinary, their ends were good and honourable, their calling lawful and urgent; and therefore they might expect the blessing of God in their proceeding. Yea, though they should lose their lives in this action, yet might they have comfort in the same and their endeavours would be honourable. They lived here but as men in exile and in a poor condition, and as great miseries might possibly befall them in this place; for the twelve years of truce were now out and there was nothing but beating of drums and preparing for war, the events whereof are always uncertain. The Spaniard might prove as cruel as the savages of America, and the famine and pestilence as sore here as there, and their liberty less to look out for remedy.

After many other particular things answered and alleged on both sides, it was fully concluded by the major part to put this design in execution and to prosecute it by the best means they could.

From Chapter 9
Their Voyage and Safe Arrival at Cape Cod

But here I cannot but stay and make a pause, and stand half amazed at this poor people's present condition; and so I think will the reader, too, when he well considers the same. Being thus passed the vast ocean, and a sea of troubles before in

---

[1] Slices.

their preparation (as may be remembered by that which went before), they had now no friends to welcome them nor inns to entertain or refresh their weather-beaten bodies; no houses or much less towns to repair to, to seek for succour. It is recorded in Scripture[1] as a mercy to the Apostle and his shipwrecked company, that the barbarians showed them no small kindness in refreshing them, but these savage barbarians, when they met with them (as after will appear) were readier to fill their sides full of arrows than otherwise. And for the season it was winter, and they that know the winters of that country know them to be sharp and violent, and subject to cruel and fierce storms, dangerous to travel to known places, much more to search an unknown coast. Besides, what could they see but a hideous and desolate wilderness, full of wild beasts and wild men—and what multitudes there might be of them they knew not. Neither could they, as it were, go up to the top of Pisgah[2] to view from this wilderness a more goodly country to feed their hopes; for which way soever they turned their eyes (save upward to the heavens) they could have little solace or content in respect of any outward objects. For summer being done, all things stand upon them with a weather-beaten face, and the whole country, full of woods and thickets, represented a wild and savage hue. If they looked behind them, there was the mighty ocean which they had passed and was now as a main bar and gulf to separate them from all the civil parts of the world. If it be said they had a ship to succour them, it is true; but what heard they daily from the master and company? But that with speed they should look out a place (with their shallop) where they would be, at some near distance; for the season was such as he would not stir from thence till a safe harbor was discovered by them, where they would be, and he might go without danger; and that victuals consumed apace but he must and would keep sufficient for themselves and their return. Yea, it was muttered by some that if they got not a place in time, they would turn them and their goods ashore and leave them. Let it also be considered what weak hopes of supply and succour they left behind them, that might bear up their minds in this sad condition and trials they were under; and they could not but be very small. It is true, indeed, the affections and love of their brethren at Leyden[3] was cordial and entire towards them, but they had little power to help them or themselves; and how the case stood between them and the merchants at their coming away hath already been declared.

What could now sustain them but the Spirit of God and His grace? May not and ought not the children of these fathers rightly say: "Our fathers were Englishmen which came over this great ocean, and were ready to perish in this wilderness; but they cried unto the Lord, and He heard their voice and looked on their adversity,"[4] etc. "Let them therefore praise the Lord, because He is good: and His mercies endure forever." "Yea, let them which have been redeemed of the Lord, shew how He hath delivered them from the hand of the oppressor. When they wandered in the desert wilderness out of the way, and found

---

[1] Acts 28.2 (noted by Bradford).

[2] Mountain from which Moses saw the Promised Land (Deuteronomy 34.1–4).

[3] A city in Holland where many of the Puritans still lived.

[4] Deuteronomy 26.6–8 (noted by Bradford).

no city to dwell in, both hungry and thirsty, their soul was overwhelmed in them. Let them confess before the Lord His lovingkindness and His wonderful works before the sons of men."[5]

[5] Psalm 107.1–5 (noted by Bradford).

From **Chapter 10**
Showing How They Sought Out a Place of Habitation; and What Befell Them Thereabout

Being thus arrived at Cape Cod the 11th of November, and necessity calling them to look out a place for habitation (as well as the master's and mariners' importunity); they having brought a large shallop with them out of England, stowed in quarters in the ship, they now got her out and set their carpenters to work to trim her up; but being much bruised and shattered in the ship with foul weather, they saw she would be long in mending. Whereupon a few of them tendered themselves to go by land and discover those nearest places, whilst the shallop was in mending; and the rather because as they went into that harbor there seemed to be an opening some two or three leagues off, which the master judged to be a river. It was conceived there might be some danger in the attempt, yet seeing them resolute, they were permitted to go, being sixteen of them well armed under the conduct of Captain Standish,[1] having such instructions given them as was thought meet.

They set forth the 15th of November; and when they had marched about the space of a mile by the seaside, they espied five or six persons with a dog coming towards them, who were savages; but they fled from them and ran up into the woods, and the English followed them, partly to see if they could speak with them, and partly to discover if there might not be more of them lying in ambush. But the Indians seeing themselves thus followed, they again forsook the woods and ran away on the sands as hard as they could, so as they could not come near them but followed them by the track of their feet sundry miles and saw that they had come the same way. So, night coming on, they made their rendezvous and set out their sentinels, and rested in quiet that night; and the next morning followed their track till they had headed a great creek and so left the sands, and turned another way into the woods. But they still followed them by guess, hoping to find their dwellings; but they soon lost both them and themselves, falling into such thickets as were ready to tear their clothes and armor in pieces; but were most distressed for want of drink. But at length they found water and refreshed themselves, being the first New England water they drunk of, and was now in great thirst as pleasant unto them as wine or beer had been in foretimes.

Afterwards they directed their course to come to the other shore, for they knew it was a neck of land they were to cross over, and so at length got to the seaside and marched to this supposed river, and by the way found a pond of clear, fresh water, and shortly after a good quantity of clear ground where the Indians

[1] Myles Standish was a professional English soldier hired by the Puritans to handle their military affairs.

had formerly set corn, and some of their graves. And proceeding further they saw new stubble where corn had been set the same year; also they found where lately a house had been, where some planks and a great kettle was remaining, and heaps of sand newly paddled with their hands. Which, they digging up, found in them divers fair Indian baskets filled with corn, and some in ears, fair and good, of divers colours, which seemed to them a very goodly sight (having never seen any such before). This was near the place of that supposed river they came to seek, unto which they went and found it to open itself into two arms with a high cliff of sand in the entrance but more like to be creeks of salt water than any fresh, for aught they saw; and that there was good harborage for their shallop, leaving it further to be discovered by their shallop, when she was ready. So, their time limited them being expired, they returned to the ship lest they should be in fear of their safety; and took with them part of the corn and buried up the rest. And so, like the men from Eshcol, carried with them of the fruits of the land and showed their brethren;[2] of which, and their return, they were marvelously glad and their hearts encouraged.

After this, the shallop being got ready, they set out again for the better discovery of this place, and the master of the ship desired to go himself. So there went some thirty men but found it to be no harbor for ships but only for boats. There was also found two of their houses covered with mats, and sundry of their implements in them, but the people were run away and could not be seen. Also there was found more of their corn and of their beans of various colours; the corn and beans they brought away, purposing to give them full satisfaction when they should meet with any of them as, about some six months afterward they did, to their good content.

And here is to be noted a special providence of God, and a great mercy to this poor people, that here they got seed to plant them corn the next year, or else they might have starved, for they had none nor any likelihood to get any till the season had been past, as the sequel did manifest. Neither is it likely they had had this, if the first voyage had not been made, for the ground was now all covered with snow and hard frozen; but the Lord is never wanting unto His in their greatest needs; let His holy name have all the praise.

The month of November being spent in these affairs, and much foul weather falling in, the 6th of December they sent out their shallop again with ten of their principal men and some seamen, upon further discovery, intending to circulate that deep bay of Cape Cod. The weather was very cold and it froze so hard as the spray of the sea lighting on their coats, they were as if they had been glazed. Yet that night betimes they got down into the bottom of the bay, and as they drew near the shore they saw some ten or twelve Indians very busy about something. They landed about a league or two from them, and had much ado to put ashore anywhere—it lay so full of flats. Being landed, it grew late and they made themselves a barricado with logs and boughs as well as they could in the time, and set out their sentinel and betook them to rest, and saw the smoke of the fire the savages made that night. When morning was come they divided their com-

---

[2] In the Book of Numbers 13.23–26, Moses' scouts return from the desert with clusters of grapes.

pany, some to coast along the shore in the boat, and the rest marched through the woods to see the land, if any fit place might be for their dwelling. They came also to the place where they saw the Indians the night before, and found they had been cutting up a great fish like a grampus, being some two inches thick of fat like a hog, some pieces whereof they had left by the way. And the shallop found two more of these fishes dead on the sands, a thing usual after storms in that place, by reason of the great flats of sand that lie off.

So they ranged up and down all that day, but found no people, nor any place they liked. When the sun grew low, they hasted out of the woods to meet with their shallop, to whom they made signs to come to them into a creek hard by, the which they did at high water; of which they were very glad, for they had not seen each other all that day since the morning. So they made them a barricado as usually they did every night, with logs, stakes and thick pine boughs, the height of a man, leaving it open to leeward, partly to shelter them from the cold and wind (making their fire in the middle and lying round about it) and partly to defend them from any sudden assaults of the savages, if they should surround them; so being very weary, they betook them to rest. But about midnight they heard a hideous and great cry, and their sentinel called "Arm! arm!" So they bestirred them and stood to their arms and shot off a couple of muskets, and then the noise ceased. They concluded it was a company of wolves or such like wild beasts, for one of the seamen told them he had often heard such a noise in Newfoundland.

So they rested till about five of the clock in the morning; for the tide, and their purpose to go from thence, made them be stirring betimes. So after prayer they prepared for breakfast, and it being day dawning it was thought best to be carrying things down to the boat. But some said it was not best to carry the arms down, others said they would be the readier, for they had lapped them up in their coats from the dew; but some three or four would not carry theirs till they went themselves. Yet as it fell out, the water being not high enough, they laid them down on the bank side and came up to breakfast.

But presently, all on the sudden, they heard a great and strange cry, which they knew to be the same voices they heard in the night, though they varied their notes; and one of their company being abroad came running in and cried, "Men, Indians! Indians!" And withal, their arrows came flying amongst them. Their men ran with all speed to recover their arms, as by the good providence of God they did. In the meantime, of those that were there ready, two muskets were discharged at them, and two more stood ready in the entrance of their rendezvous but were commanded not to shoot till they could take full aim at them. And the other two charged again with all speed, for there were only four had arms there, and defended the barricado, which was first assaulted. The cry of the Indians was dreadful, especially when they saw their men run out of the rendezvous toward the shallop to recover their arms, the Indians wheeling about upon them. But some running out with coats of mail on, and cutlasses in their hands, they soon got their arms and let fly amongst them and quickly stopped their violence. Yet there was a lusty man, and no less valiant, stood behind a tree within half a musket shot, and let his arrows fly at them; he was seen to shoot three arrows, which were all avoided. He stood three shots of a musket, till one taking full aim at him and made the bark or splinters of the tree fly about his ears, after which he gave an extraordinary shriek and away they went, all of them. They[3] left some to keep the shallop and followed them about a quarter of a mile and shouted once or twice, and shot off two or three pieces, and so returned. This they did that they might conceive that they were not afraid of them or any way discouraged.

Thus it pleased God to vanquish their enemies and give them deliverance; and by His special providence so to dispose that not any one of them were either hurt or hit, though their arrows came close by them and on every side of them; and sundry of their coats, which hung up in the barricado, were shot through and through. Afterwards they gave God solemn thanks and praise for their deliverance, and gathered up a bundle of their arrows and sent them into England afterward by the master of the ship, and called that place the First Encounter.

From hence they departed and coasted all along but discerned no place likely for harbor; and therefore hasted to a place that their pilot (one Mr. Coppin who had been in the country before) did assure them was a good harbor, which he had been in, and they might fetch it before night; of which they were glad for it began to be foul weather.

After some hours' sailing it began to snow and rain, and about the middle of the afternoon the wind increased and the sea became very rough, and they broke their rudder, and it was as much as two men could do to steer her with a couple of oars. But their pilot bade them be of good cheer for he saw the harbor; but the storm increasing, and night drawing on, they bore what sail they could to get in, while they could see. But herewith they broke their mast in three pieces and their sail fell overboard in a very grown sea, so as they had like to have been cast away. Yet by God's mercy they recovered themselves, and having the flood[4] with them, struck into the harbor. But when it came to, the pilot was deceived in the place, and said the Lord be merciful unto them for his eyes never saw that place before; and he and the master's mate would have run her ashore in a cove full of breakers before the wind. But a lusty seaman which steered bade those which rowed, if they were men, about with her or else they were all cast away; the which they did with speed. So he bid them be of good cheer and row lustily, for there was a fair sound before them, and he doubted not but they should find one place or other where they might ride in safety. And though it was very dark and rained sore, yet in the end they got under the lee of a small island and remained there all that night in safety. But they knew not this to be an island till morning, but were divided in their minds; some would keep the boat for fear they might be amongst the Indians, others were so wet and cold they could not endure but got ashore, and with much ado got fire (all things being so wet); and the rest were glad to come to them, for after midnight the wind shifted to the northwest and it froze hard.

But though this had been a day and night of much trouble and danger unto them, yet God gave them a morning of comfort and refreshing (as usually He

---

[3] I.e., the Pilgrims.

[4] I.e., the flood tide.

doth to His children) for the next day was a fair, sunshining day, and they found themselves to be on an island secure from the Indians, where they might dry their stuff, fix their pieces[5] and rest themselves; and gave God thanks for His mercies in their manifold deliverances. And this being the last day of the week, they prepared there to keep the Sabbath.

On Monday they sounded the harbor and found it fit for shipping, and marched into the land and found divers cornfields and little running brooks, a place (as they supposed) fit for situation.[6] At least it was the best they could find, and the season and their present necessity made them glad to accept of it. So they returned to their ship again with this news to the rest of their people, which did much comfort their hearts.

On the 15th of December they weighed anchor to go to the place they had discovered, and came within two leagues of it, but were fain to bear up again; but the 16th day, the wind came fair, and they arrived safe in this harbor. And afterwards took better view of the place, and resolved where to pitch their dwelling; and the 25th day began to erect the first house for common use to receive them and their goods.

✑ *Robert Herrick* (*1591–1674*)

Robert Herrick was the son of a wealthy London goldsmith. His father died, falling from the fourth floor of their home, while Herrick was still very young. Herrick was apprenticed in his father's profession in 1607, but in 1613 he obtained release to attend St. John's College, Cambridge, where he earned a B.A. degree in 1617 and an M.A. in 1620. Returning to London, Herrick took holy orders in the Anglican Church in 1623 and served for the next several years as a chaplain to various nobles. His religious career, however, did not mean he led an ascetic life. Known for his convivial temperament, Herrick enjoyed indulging himself in the finer things in life. He was closely associated with Ben Jonson and his circle and wrote a great deal of poetry, although his work did not begin to be published until 1633. In 1630 Herrick was given a living in the Devonshire countryside, which took him away from the excitement and pleasures of city life. Although he considered his assignment to a rural vicarage the equivalent of being sent into exile, his interest in rural traditions and his exploration of pastoral conventions and themes, expressed in his most well-known work, Hesperides *(1648), reveal that he was not entirely averse to country life.*

Like many other poets of his day, Herrick wrote religious verse as well. However, Hesperides *remains his most interesting effort. Comprised of 1,400 short but highly polished poems, many of which were composed as songs,* Hesperides *takes its title from the myth of the golden apples. Protected in the Garden of the Hesperides, by the Daughters of Night also called Hesperides, it was one of Hercules' twelve labors to collect this sa-*

---

[5] Guns.

[6] Samuel Eliot Morison notes that this passage is the only contemporary authority for the supposed "landing of the Pilgrims on Plymouth Rock," on December 11, 1620.

cred fruit. The poems demonstrate the strong influence of classical poets such as Horace, Catullus, and Martial, but they also incorporate imagery and details that are historically and culturally specific, even as they demonstrate more universal themes, such as the carpe diem ("live for the day") motif in "Corinna's Going A-Maying." Like his friend Ben Jonson, Herrick has a rather idealized (and implicitly moralized) view of rural life and agricultural labor, evidenced by "The Hock-Cart, or Harvest Home." These visions of the English countryside are both challenged and echoed by later poets of the rural laboring classes, such as Stephen Duck and Robert Bloomfield. Both Duck and Bloomfield depict the British tradition of the "harvest home," but do so from the perspective of those who were actually engaged in the work of the field.

From Hesperides

The Argument of His Book

I sing of *Brooks*, of *Blossoms*, *Birds*, and *Bowers*:
Of *April*, *May*, of *June*, and *July* Flowers.
I sing of *May-poles*, *Hock-carts*,[1] *Wassails*,[2] *Wakes*,
Of *Bridegrooms*, *Brides*, and of their *Bridal cakes*.
I write of *Youth*, of *Love*, and have access   5
By these, to sing of cleanly *Wantonness*.
I sing of *Dews*, of *Rains*, and piece by piece
Of *Balm*, of *Oil*, of *Spice*, and *Ambergris*.
I sing of *Times trans-shifting*; and I write
How *Roses* first came *Red*, and *Lilies White*.   10
I write of *Groves*, of *Twilights*, and I sing
The Court of *Mab*,[3] and of the *Fairy-King*.
I write of *Hell*; I sing (and ever shall)
Of *Heaven*, and hope to have it after all.

[1] The wagon which brings in the harvest.
[2] Convivial occasions for social drinking.
[3] Queen of the fairies.

Corinna's Going A-Maying

Get up, get up for shame, the Blooming Morn
Upon her wings presents the god unshorn.[1]
   See how *Aurora* throws her fair
   Fresh-quilted colours through the air:
   Get up, sweet Slug-a-bed, and see   5

[1] Apollo, the classical god identified with the sun; he was said to have long hair that shone like the rays of the sun.

The Dew-bespangling Herb and Tree.
Each Flower has wept, and bowed toward the East,
Above an hour since; yet you not dressed,
 Nay! not so much as out of bed?
 When all the Birds have Matins[2] said,
 And sung their thankful Hymns: 'tis sin,   10
 Nay, profanation to keep in,
Whenas a thousand Virgins on this day,
Spring, sooner than the Lark, to fetch in May.

Rise; and put on your Foliage, and be seen   15
To come forth, like the Spring-time, fresh and green;
 And sweet as *Flora*.[3] Take no care
 For Jewels for your Gown, or Hair:
 Fear not; the leaves will strew
 Gems in abundance upon you: 20
Besides, the childhood of the Day has kept,
Against you come, some *Orient Pearls* unwept:
 Come, and receive them while the light
 Hangs on the Dew-locks of the night:
 And *Titan* on the Eastern hill[4]   25
 Retires himself, or else stands still
Till you come forth. Wash, dress, be brief in praying:
Few Beads are best, when once we go a-Maying.

Come, my *Corinna*, come; and coming, mark
How each field turns a street; each street a Park   30
 Made green, and trimmed with trees: see how
 Devotion gives each House a Bough,
 Or Branch: Each Porch, each door, ere this,
 An Ark a Tabernacle is
Made up of white-thorn neatly interwove;   35
As if here were those cooler shades of love.
 Can such delights be in the street,
 And open fields, and we not see 't?
 Come, we'll abroad; and let's obey
 The Proclamation made for May: 40
And sin no more, as we have done, by staying;
But my *Corinna*, come, let's go a-Maying.

There's not a budding Boy, or Girl, this day,
But is got up, and gone to bring in May.
 A deal of Youth, ere this, is come   45
 Back, and with *White-thorn* laden home.

[2] Performed their morning prayer service.
[3] Goddess of spring and of flowers for the ancient Romans.
[4] *Titan . . . hill:* the rising sun.

Some have dispatched their Cakes and Cream,
    Before that we have left to dream:
And some have wept, and wooed, and plighted Troth,
And chose their Priest, ere we can cast off sloth: 50
    Many a green-gown has been given;
    Many a kiss, both odd and even:
    Many a glance too has been sent
    From out the eye, Love's Firmament:
Many a jest told of the Keys betraying   55
This night, and Locks picked, yet we are not a-Maying.

Come, let us go, while we are in our prime;
And take the harmless folly of the time.
    We shall grow old apace, and die
    Before we know our liberty.   60
    Our life is short; and our days run
    As fast away as does the Sun:
And as a vapour, or a drop of rain
Once lost, can ne'er be found again:
    So when or you or I are made   65
    A fable, song, or fleeting shade;
    All love, all liking, all delight
    Lies drowned with us in endless night.
Then while time serves, and we are but decaying;
Come, my *Corinna*, come, let's go a-Maying.   70

The Hock-Cart, *or* Harvest Home

To the Right Honourable Mildmay, Earl of Westmoreland

Come Sons of Summer, by whose toil,
We are the Lords of Wine and Oil:
By whose tough labours, and rough hands,
We rip up first, then reap our lands.
Crowned with the ears of corn, now come,   5
And, to the Pipe, sing Harvest home.
Come forth, my Lord, and see the Cart
Dressed up with all the Country Art.
See, here a *Maukin*,[1] there a sheet,
As spotless pure, as it is sweet: 10
The Horses, Mares, and frisking Fillies,
(Clad, all, in Linen, white as Lilies.)
The Harvest Swains, and Wenches bound
For joy, to see the *Hock-cart* crowned.
About the Cart hear how the Rout   15

---

[1] A scarecrow.

Of Rural Younglings raise the shout;
Pressing before, some coming after,
Those with a shout, and these with laughter.
Some bless the Cart; some kiss the sheaves;
Some prank them up with Oaken leaves: 20
Some cross the Fill-horse; some with great
Devotion, stroke the home-born wheat:
While other rustics, less attent
To Prayers, than to Merriment,
Run after with their breeches rent.   25
    Well, on, brave boys, to your Lord's Hearth,
Glitt'ring with fire; where, for your mirth,
Ye shall see first the large and chief
Foundation of your Feast, Fat Beef:
With Upper Stories, Mutton, Veal   30
And Bacon, (which makes full the meal)
With sev'ral dishes standing by,
As here a Custard, there a Pie,
And here all tempting Frumenty.[2]
And for to make the merry cheer,   35
If smirking Wine be wanting here,
There's that, which drowns all care, stout Beer;
Which freely drink to your Lord's health,
Then to the Plough, (the Common-wealth),
Next to your Flails, your Fans, your Vats;[3]   40
Then to the Maids with Wheaten Hats;
To the rough Sickle, and crooked Scythe,
Drink frolic boys, till all be blithe.
    Feed, and grow fat; and as ye eat,
Be mindful, that the lab'ring Neat[4]   45
(As you) may have their fill of meat.
And know, besides, ye must revoke
The patient Ox unto the Yoke,
And all go back unto the Plough
And Harrow, (though they're hanged up now.)   50
And, you must know, your Lord's word's true,
Feed him ye must, whose food fills you.
And that this pleasure is like rain,
Not sent ye for to drown your pain,
But for to make it spring again.

---

[2] A kind of pudding.

[3] Flails are used to thresh grain, fans to winnow it, and vats to store it in.

[4] Cattle or oxen (beasts of burden).

To Daffadills

1

Fair Daffadills, we weep to see
  You haste away so soon:
As yet the early-rising Sun
  Has not attained his Noon.
     Stay, stay,   5
    Until the hasting day
       Has run
    But to the Even-song;
And, having prayed together, we
  Will go with you along.   10

2

We have short time to stay, as you,
  We have as short a Spring;
As quick a growth to meet Decay,
  As you, or any thing.
     We die,   15
  As your hours do, and dry
       Away,
  Like to the Summer's rain;
Or as the pearls of Morning's dew
  Ne'er to be found again.   20

To Blossoms

1

Fair pledges of a fruitful Tree,
  Why do ye fall so fast?
  Your date is not so past;
But you may stay yet here a while,
  To blush and gently smile;   5
    And go at last.

2

What, were ye born to be
  An hour or half's delight;
  And so to bid goodnight?
'Twas pity Nature brought ye forth   10
  Merely to show your worth,
    And lose you quite.

3

But you are lovely Leaves, where we
   May read how soon things have
     Their end, though ne'er so brave: 15
And after they have shown their pride,
   Like you a while: They glide
     Into the Grave.

His Content in the Country

Here, here I live with what my Board,
Can with the smallest cost afford.
Though ne'er so mean the Viands be,
They well content my *Prue*[1] and me.
Or Pea, or Bean, or Wort,[2] or Beet,   5
What ever comes, content makes sweet:
Here we rejoice, because no Rent
We pay for our poor Tenement:
Wherein we rest, and never fear
The Landlord, or the Usurer.   10
The Quarter-day[3] does ne'er afright
Our Peaceful slumbers in the night.
We eat our own, and batten more,
Because we feed on no man's score:
But pity those, whose flanks grow great,   15
Swelled with the Lard of other's meat
We bless our Fortunes, when we see
Our own beloved privacy:
And like our living, where we are known
To very few, or else to none.   20

[1] Short for Prudence.
[2] A plant resembling cabbage.
[3] The time when bills come due.

Art Above Nature, to *Julia*

When I behold a Forest spread
With silken trees upon thy head;
And when I see that other Dress
Of flowers set in comeliness:
When I behold another grace   5
In the ascent of curious Lace,
Which like a Pinnacle doth show

The top, and the top-gallant[1] too.
Then, when I see thy Tresses bound
Into an Oval, square, or round;   10
And knit in knots far more than I
Can tell by tongue; or true love tie:
Next, when those Lawny Films I see
Play with a wild civility:
And all those airy silks to flow,   15
Alluring me, and tempting so:
I must confess, mine eye and heart
Dotes less on Nature, than on Art.

George Herbert (1593–1633)

Like his friend John Donne, George Herbert's lifetime is split into two succeeding phases, one devoted to secular, and the other to sacred, pursuits. A member of a prominent aristocratic family, Herbert spent the first part of his life, until around 1624, ambitiously pursuing an academic and civil career. He attended Trinity College, Cambridge, and held a variety of prestigious posts after his graduation. He was associated with the royal court and was close to other important artists and intellectuals of his age, including Francis Bacon. Herbert served in Parliament in 1624 and 1625, yet at this time he took orders in the Church of England and thereafter entered into the second stage of his life, centered on his religious vocation. He married in 1629, and he was fully ordained in 1630. Herbert gained a reputation for excellence as a priest and was genuinely committed to his work as a country parson.

Although he first published poetry in 1612, he is best known today for his posthumously published collection The Temple *(1633), from which the following selections are taken. Each of the poems in the collection is stylistically unique unto itself. They reveal Herbert's formal craft as well as his gift for song (he was known in his day as a very good musician). Though seemingly simpler in its language than Donne's poetry, Herbert's work explores equally complex issues. Like Donne, Herbert often uses physical or natural images to investigate ineffable metaphysical and theological questions. Unlike Donne, however, Herbert's verse is entirely pious and rejects the more Petrarchan language of seduction and any amorous imagery. The poems of* The Temple *closely resemble prayers, as they record Herbert's struggles with his faith, including the proper relationship of the divine to the natural and between the Creator and divine Creation. His work is witty but honest, erudite but also passionate in its exploration of the mysteries at the heart of human life in the world. Herbert's influence, particularly his expression of the providential aspect of creation, can be read in many subsequent nature writers, from Walton and Evelyn to Emerson.*

[1] Highest.

Nature

Full of rebellion, I would die,
Or fight, or travel, or deny
That thou hast ought to do with me.
     O tame my heart;
   It is thy highest art   5
To captivate strong holds to thee.

If thou shalt let this venom lurk,
And in suggestions fume and work,
My soul will turn to bubbles straight,
     And thence by kind   10
   Vanish into a wind,
Making thy workmanship deceit.

O smooth my rugged heart, and there
Engrave thy rev'rend Law and fear;
Or make a new one, since the old   15
     Is sapless grown,
   And a much fitter stone
To hide my dust, than thee to hold.

Virtue

Sweet day, so cool, so calm, so bright,
The bridal of the earth and sky:
The dew shall weep thy fall tonight;
     For thou must die.

Sweet rose, whose hue angry and brave   5
Bids the rash gazer wipe his eye:
Thy root is ever in its grave,
     And thou must die.

Sweet spring, full of sweet days and roses,
A box where sweets compacted lie;   10
My musick shows ye have your closes,
     And all must die.

Only a sweet and virtuous soul,
Like seasoned timber, never gives;
But though the whole world turn to coal,   15
     Then chiefly lives.

The Storm

If as the winds and waters here below
　　Do fly and flow,
My sighs and tears as busy were above;
　　Sure they would move
And much affect thee, as tempestuous times　　　　　5
Amaze poor mortals, and object their crimes.

Stars have their storms, ev'n in a high degree,
　　As well as we.
A throbbing conscience spurred by remorse
　　Hath a strange force:　　　　　　　　　　10
It quits the earth, and mounting more and more
Dares to assault thee, and besiege thy door.

There it stands knocking, to thy musick's wrong,
　　And drowns the song.
Glory and honour are set by, till it　　　　　　15
　　An answer get.
Poets have wronged poor storms: such days are best;
They purge the air without, within the breast.

The Pulley

　When God at first made man,
Having a glass of blessings standing by;
"Let us" (said he) "pour on him all we can:
Let the world's riches, which dispersèd lie,
　　Contract into a span."　　　　　　　　5

　So strength first made a way;
Then beauty flowed, then wisdom, honour, pleasure:
When almost all was out, God made a stay,
Perceiving that alone of all his treasure
　　Rest in the bottom lay.　　　　　　　10

　"For if I should" (said he)
"Bestow this jewel also on my creature,
He would adore my gifts instead of me,
And rest in Nature, not the God of Nature:
　　So both should losers be.　　　　　　15

　"Yet let him keep the rest,
But keep them with repining restlessness:
Let him be rich and weary, that at least,
If goodness lead him not, yet weariness
　　May toss him to my breast."　　　　　20

The Flower

How fresh, O Lord, how sweet and clean
Are thy returns! ev'n as the flowers in spring;
   To which, besides their own demesne,[1]
The late-past frosts tributes of pleasure bring.
     Grief melts away   5
     Like snow in May,
  As if there were no such cold thing.

   Who would have thought my shriveled heart
Could have recovered greenness? It was gone
   Quite underground; as flowers depart   10
To see their mother-root, when they have blown;
     Where they together
     All the hard weather,
  Dead to the world, keep house unknown.

   These are thy wonders, Lord of power,   15
Killing and quick'ning, bringing down to hell
   And up to heaven in an hour;
Making a chiming of a passing-bell.
     We say amiss,
     This or that is: 20
  Thy word is all, if we could spell.

   O that I once past changing were,
Fast in thy Paradise, where no flower can wither!
   Many a spring I shoot up fair,
Off'ring at heav'n, growing and groaning thither: 25
     Nor doth my flower
     Want a spring shower,
  My sin and I joining together.

   But while I grow in a straight line,
Still upwards bent, as if heav'n were mine own,   30
   Thy anger comes, and I decline:
What frost to that? what pole is not the zone,
     Where all things burn,
     When thou dost turn,
  And the least frown of thine is shown?   35

   And now in age I bud again,
After so many deaths I live and write;
   I once more smell the dew and rain,
And relish versing: O my only light,
     It cannot be   40
     That I am he

---

[1] domain, estate

On whom thy tempests fell all night.
These are thy wonders, Lord of love,
To make us see we are but flowers that glide:
    Which when we once can find and prove,   45
Thou hast a garden for us, where to bide.
        Who would be more,
        Swelling through store,
    Forfeit their Paradise by their pride.

🔖 *Izaak Walton* (1593–1683)

Izaak Walton grew up in the town of Stafford, England, and he received only a gram-
mar school education. Apprenticed as a child to a draper, he eventually became a success-
ful cloth merchant. Walton was fascinated by poetry from an early age; he admired the
poet Michael Drayton as an "old friend" from Stafford, and after moving to London, he
became personally acquainted with John Donne, composing an elegy, in 1633, on
Donne's death. Walton went on to invent the genre of literary biography, publishing
The Life and Death of Dr. Donne *in 1640, followed by the lives of Richard Hooker*
(1665) and George Herbert (1670). Through these works, Walton established his repu-
tation as the leading biographer of the seventeenth century.

In our own time, however, Walton is best remembered as the author of The Compleat Angler, or the Contemplative Man's Recreation *(1653). William Hazlitt de-*
scribed this book as the finest pastoral in the English language, and it is more certainly
than just a practical manual on how to catch fish. Artfully mingling the literary genres
of pastoral, georgic, and philosophical dialogue, it expresses a deep and abiding affection
for the natural world, especially for those finny creatures that inhabit the watery depths
of ponds, lakes, and streams. In Walton's elegant prose, angling becomes the occasion for
an extended meditation on the splendor of the divine Creation, and throughout The
Compleat Angler, *he evokes the delicate beauty of even the most humble creatures. Fish*
offer more than just food to the contemplative angler; the activity of fishing is an occasion
for reflection and spiritual growth. Walton's angler comes to know himself more truly
through his encounter "with all the numerous Inhabitants of that vast watery Element."

From The Compleat Angler

PISCATOR.[1]   O Sir, doubt not but that *Angling* is an Art, and an Art worth your
learning: the Question is rather whether you be capable of learning it? for
Angling is somewhat like *Poetry*, men are to be born so: I mean, with inclinations to
it, though both may be heightened by practice and experience: but he that hopes
to be a good *Angler* must not only bring an inquiring, searching, observing wit, but
he must bring a large measure of hope and patience, and a love and propensity to
the Art itself; but having once got and practiced it, then doubt not but *Angling* will
prove to be so pleasant, that it will prove like Virtue, a reward to itself.

---

[1] This passage is excerpted from *The Compleat Angler*, Chapter 1, which is written in the form of a dialogue between
Piscator (an angler) and *Venator* (a hunter), "each commending his Recreation."

VENATOR. Sir, I am now become so full of expectation that I long much to have you proceed, and in the order that you propose.

PISCATOR. Then first, for the *antiquity* of *Angling*, of which I shall not say much, but only this; Some say it is as ancient as *Deucalion's* Flood:[2] others, that *Belus*, who was the first Inventor of Godly and virtuous Recreations, was the first Inventor of *Angling*: and some others say (for former times have had their disquisitions about the Antiquity of it) that *Seth*, one of the sons of *Adam*, taught it to his Sons, and that by them it was derived to posterity: others say, that he left it engraven on those pillars which he erected, and trusted to preserve the knowledge of the *Mathematicks*, *Musick*, and the rest of that precious knowledge, and those useful Arts which by Gods appointment or allowance and his noble industry were thereby preserved from perishing in *Noah's* flood.

These, Sir, have been the opinions of several men, that have possibly endeavoured to make *Angling* more ancient than is needful, or may well be warranted; but for my part, I shall content my self in telling you that Angling is much more ancient than the Incarnation of our Saviour; for in the Prophet *Amos* mention is made of *fish-hooks*; and in the Book of *Job* (which was long before the days of *Amos*, for that book is said to be writ by *Moses*) mention is made also of Fish-hooks, which must imply Anglers in those times.

But my worthy friend, as I would rather prove my self a *Gentleman* by being *learned*, and *humble*, *valiant*, and *inoffensive*, *virtuous*, and *communicable*, than by any fond ostentation of riches, or wanting[3] these virtues myself, boast that these were in my Ancestors (and yet I grant that where a noble and ancient descent and such merits meet in any man, it is a double dignification of that person:) So if this Antiquity of *Angling* (which for my part I have not forced) shall like an ancient family, be either an honour or an ornament to this virtuous Art which I profess to love and practice, I shall be the gladder that I made an accidental mention of the antiquity of it; of which I shall say no more but proceed to that just commendation which I think it deserves.

And for that I shall tell you, that in ancient times a debate hath risen (and it remains yet unresolved) Whether the happiness of man in this world doth consist more in *Contemplation* or *action*.

Concerning which some have endeavoured to maintain their opinion of the first, by saying, *That the nearer we Mortals come to God by way of imitation, the more happy we are.* And they say, *That God enjoys himself only by a contemplation of his own infiniteness, Eternity, Power and Goodness*, and the like. And upon this ground many Cloysteral[4] men of great learning and devotion prefer *Contemplation* before *Action*. And many of the Fathers seem to approve this opinion, as may appear in their Commentaries upon the words of our Saviour to *Martha, Luke* 10.41, 42.

And on the contrary, there want not men of equal authority and credit, that prefer *action* to be the more excellent, as namely, *experiments in Physick,*[5] *and the*

---

[2] In Greek mythology, Deucalion was the son of Prometheus. When Zeus, angered by the irreverence of humankind, flooded the earth, Deucalion took refuge with his wife in an ark. With characteristically dry humor, Walton is suggesting that Deucalion went fishing from his ark during the flood.

[3] Lacking.

[4] Cloistered, secluded.

[5] Medicine.

application of it, both for the ease and prolongation of man's life; by which each man is enabled to act and do good to others; either to serve his Country, or do good to particular persons; and they say also, *That action is Doctrinal, and teaches both art and virtue, and is a maintainer of humane society;* and for these and other like reasons to be preferred before *contemplation.*

Concerning which two opinions I shall forbear to add a third, by declaring my own, and rest myself contented in telling you (my very worthy friend) that both these meet together, and do most properly belong to the most *honest, ingenuous, quiet,* and *harmless* art of *Angling.*

And first, I shall tell you what some have observed, (and I have found it to be a real truth) that the very sitting by the River's side is not only the quietest and fittest place for *contemplation,* but will invite an Angler to it: and this seems to be maintained by the learned *Pet. du Moline,*[6] who (in his Discourse of the Fulfilling of Prophecies) observes, that when God intended to reveal any future events or high notions to his Prophets, he then carried them either to the *Deserts* or the *Seashore,* that having so separated them from amidst the press of *people,* and *business,* and the cares of the world, he might settle their minds in a quiet repose, and there make them fit for Revelation.

And this seems also to be intimated by the Children of *Israel* (*Psalm* 137.) who having in a sad condition banished all mirth and music from their pensive hearts, and having hung up their then mute Harps upon the Willow-trees growing by the Rivers of *Babylon,* sate down upon those banks bemoaning the ruins of *Sion,* and contemplating their own sad condition.

And an ingenuous *Spaniard* says, *That Rivers and the Inhabitants of the wat'ry Element were made for wise men to contemplate, and fools to pass by without consideration.* And though I will not rank myself in the number of the first, yet give me leave to free myself from the last, by offering to you a short contemplation, first of *Rivers,* and then of *Fish,* concerning which I doubt not but to give you many observations that will appear very considerable: I am sure they have appeared so to me, and made many an hour pass away more pleasantly, as I have sate quietly on a flowery Bank by a calm River, and contemplated what I shall now relate to you.

And first concerning Rivers, there be divers wonders reported of them by Authors of such credit, that we need not deny them an Historical Faith.

As namely of a River in *Epirus,* that puts out any lighted Torch, and kindles any Torch that was not lighted. Some Waters being drunk cause madness, some drunkenness, and some laughter to death. The River *Selarus* in a few hours turns a rod or wand to be stone: and our *Cambden*[7] mentions the like in *England,* and the like in *Lochmere* in *Ireland.* There is also a River in *Arabia,* of which all the sheep that drink thereof have their wool turned into a Vermilion colour. And one of no less credit than *Aristotle* tells us of a merry river (the river Elusina) that dances at the noise of music, for with music it bubbles, dances and grows sandy, and so continues till the music ceases, but then it presently returns to its wonted

[6] Peter du Molin, chaplain to King Charles II and author of *The Accomplishment of Prophecies* (1613).

[7] William Camden (1551–1623), English historian, author of *Britannia* (1586).

calmness and clearness. And *Cambden* tells us of a Well near to *Kerby* in *West-moreland*, that ebbs and flows several times every day: and he tells us of a river in *Surry* (it is called *Mole*), that after it has run several miles, being opposed by hills, finds or makes itself a way underground, and breaks out again so far off, that the Inhabitants thereabout boast (as the *Spaniards* do of their River *Anus*) that they feed divers flocks of sheep upon a Bridge. And, lastly, for I would not tire your patience, one of no less authority than *Josephus* that learned Jew, tells us of a River in *Judea*, that runs swiftly all the six days of the week, and stands still and rests all their *Sabbath*. . . .

And as concerning fish, in that Psalm (*Psalm* 104) wherein for height of Poetry and Wonders the Prophet *David* seems even to exceed himself, how doth he there express himself in choice Metaphors, even to the amazement of a contemplative Reader, concerning the *Sea*, the *Rivers*, and the *Fish* therein contained? And the great Naturalist *Pliny* says, *That Nature's great and wonderful power is more demonstrated in the Sea than on the Land*. And this may appear by the numerous and various creatures, inhabiting both in and about that Element; as to the Readers of *Gesner, Randeletius, Pliny, Ausonius, Aristotle*, and others, may be demonstrated. But I will sweeten this Discourse also out of a Contemplation in Divine *Dubartas*, who says,

> God quickened in the sea and in the rivers,
> So many fishes of so many features,
> That in the waters we may see all creatures,
> Even all that on the earth is to be found,
> As if the world were in deep waters drowned.
> For seas (as well as skies) have Sun, Moon, Stars;
> (As well as air) Swallows, Rooks, and Stars;
> (As well as earth) Vines, Roses, Nettles, Melons,
> Mushrooms, Pinks, Gilliflowers, and many millions
> Of other plants, more rare, more strange than these,
> As very fishes living in the seas:
> As also Rams, Calves, Horses, Hares, and Hogs,
> Wolves, Urchins, Lions, Elephants, and Dogs;
> Yea, Men and Maids, and which I most admire,
> The mitered Bishop, and the cowled Friar.
> Of which, examples but a few years since,
> Were shown the Norway and Polonian prince.[8]

These seem to be wonders, but have had so many confirmations from men of learning and credit, that you need not doubt them; nor are the number, nor the various shapes of fishes, more strange or more fit for *contemplation*, than their different natures, inclinations and actions; concerning which I shall beg your patient ear a little longer.

The *Cuttle-fish* will cast a long gut out of her throat, which (like as an Angler doth his line) she sendeth forth and pulleth in again at her pleasure, according as

[8] Excerpted from *La sepmaine; ou, création du monde* (The Week: or, Creation of the World) (1578) by the French poet Guillaume du Bartas (1544–1590); translated into English by Joshua Sylvester in 1605.

she sees some little fish come near to her; and the *Cuttle-fish*[9] (being then hid in the gravel) lets the smaller fish nibble and bite the end of it, at which time she by little and little draws the smaller fish so near to her, that she may leap upon her, and then catches and devours her: and for this reason some have called this fish the *Sea-angler.*

And there is a fish called a *Hermit*, that at a certain age gets into a dead fish's shell, and like a Hermit dwells there alone, studying the wind and weather, and so turns her shell that she makes it defend her from the injuries that they would bring upon her.

There is also a fish called by *Elian* (in his 9. book of Living Creatures, Chap. 16.) the *Adonis*, or Darling of the Sea; so called, because it is a loving and innocent fish, a fish that hurts nothing that hath life, and is at peace with all the numerous Inhabitants of that vast watery Element: and truly I think most Anglers are so disposed to most of mankind.

🦢 *Thomas Carew* (1595–1640)

Educated at Oxford, Thomas Carew (pronounced "Carey") was among the Cavalier or court poets for whom writing poetry was a supplement to his career as a diplomat and courtier. While he produced relatively few poems in comparison to his good friends John Donne and Ben Jonson, what he did write explores similar amatory themes and is as finely wrought as the verse of his fellow authors. The strong influence of Donne and Jonson is evident in both content and style. Like Jonson, he tried his hand at a masque and also at a country-house poem, "To Saxham." Like Donne, he employs emblems from nature to express romantic desires. His collection Poems *was published posthumously, in 1640.*

The Spring

Now that the winter's gone, the earth hath lost
Her snow-white robes, and now no more the frost
Candies the grass, or castes an icy cream
Upon the silver Lake, or Crystal stream:
But the warm Sun thaws the benumbed Earth,   5
And makes it tender, gives a sacred birth
To the dead Swallow; wakes in hollow tree
The drowsy Cuckow, and the Humble Bee.
Now do a choir of chirping Minstrels bring
In triumph to the world, the youthful Spring.   10
The Valleys, hills, and woods, in rich array,
Welcome the coming of the longed for May.

---

[9] Mount, *Essays:* and others affirm this. (Note by Walton, referring to the *Essais* of Michel de Montaigne.)

Now all things smile; only my *Love* doth lour:[1]
Nor hath the scalding Noonday Sun the power,
To melt that marble ice, which still doth hold   15
Her heart congealed, and makes her pity cold.
The Ox which lately did for shelter fly
Into the stall, doth now securely lie
In open fields; and love no more is made
By the fireside; but in the cooler shade   20
Amyntas now doth with his *Cloris*[2] sleep
Under a Sycamore, and all things keep
Time with the season, only she doth carry
June in her eyes, in her heart *January*.

[1] Scowl.

[2] *Amyntas . . . Cloris:* Conventional pastoral names for a shepherd and his beloved.

To My Mistress Sitting by a River's Side. An Eddy

Mark how yon Eddy steals away,
From the rude stream into the Bay,
There locked up safe, she doth divorce
Her waters from the channel's course,
And scorns the Torrent, that did bring   5
Her headlong from her native spring.
Now doth she with her new love play,
Whilst he runs murmuring away.
Mark how she courts the banks, whilst they
As amorously their arms display,   10
T' embrace, and clip her silver waves:
See how she strokes their sides, and craves
An entrance there, which they deny;
Whereat she frowns, threat'ning to fly
Home to her stream, and begins to swim   15
Backward, but from the channel's brim,
Smiling, returns into the creek,
With thousand dimples on her cheek.
      Be thou this Eddy, and I'll make
My breast thy shore, where thou shalt take   20
Secure repose, and never dream
Of the quite forsaken stream:
Let him to the wide Ocean hast,
There lose his colour, name, and taste;
Thou shalt save all, and safe from him,   25
Within these arms forever swim.

✏ *John Milton* (1608–1674)

One of England's greatest poets, John Milton spent the first thirty years of his life train-ing himself for his poetic vocation. The son of a wealthy London businessman, he had the finest possible formal education, earning a B.A. and an M.A. from Christ's College, Cambridge, further supplementing these studies with voracious reading of his own. Mil-ton was fluent in several ancient and modern languages, and his vast erudition is evident in every line of his poetry and prose. His earlier works, such as the twin poems "L'Allegro" and "Il Penseroso" (both c.1631) and the longer poem Lycidas *(1637), reveal his bril-liance in blending classical and Christian imagery. A pastoral elegy,* Lycidas *was written to commemorate the death at sea of Milton's friend Edward King. The poem is rich in its use of water imagery: lakes, rivers, and even tears are a source of solace and spiritual nourishment. In addition,* Lycidas *deploys the pastoral conventions of the peaceful bucolic setting and the trope of poet as shepherd—both elements derived from Greek and Roman precedents—to attempt to make sense of the fact of death, in relation to the natural cycle and in terms of Christian teaching. The representation of nature is essentially idealized, yet the circumstance of death, which is the poem's point of departure, prevents the natural imagery from seeming in any way artificial, often a danger in pastoral writing.*

Political circumstances interrupted Milton's poetic development. Beginning in 1640, and lasting until the Restoration of the Stuart monarchy in 1660, he devoted his atten-tion to public activism. Passionate and radical, Milton took several controversial stands in prose works. He favored divorce and deplored government censorship. A pious man, he spoke out against corruption in the Anglican Church and advocated greater religious freedom. After the beheading of Charles I, in 1649, Milton was given the position of Latin secretary under Oliver Cromwell. Though this work was complicated by onset of blindness, in the early 1650s he wrote several pamphlets defending the Commonwealth and justifying events of the English Civil War. Such actions cost Milton dearly after Charles II returned to power in 1660. While many other public supporters of the Com-monwealth were executed, Milton was only briefly imprisoned. He had escaped with his life, but his political involvements left Milton disappointed, poor, and a virtual exile. Nonetheless, the last fourteen years of his life were his most magnificent in literary ac-complishments. His masterpiece, the epic Paradise Lost, *was published 1667. In it, Mil-ton assimilates and transforms the styles, themes, and imagery of the earlier great epics of Homer, Virgil, Dante, and Spenser. With unmatched skill,* Paradise Lost *blends the classical and the Christian to create a poem that in mythopoetic scope remains unparal-leled.*

In all of his poetry, Milton's highly visual and quite sensual use of natural imagery is all the more remarkable when one considers that the poet was completely blind after 1651. Yet nature, and Milton's representations of it, are not merely scenery. The explo-ration of nature's purpose, and humankind's relation to that purpose, serves several func-tions in the poem: it illustrates Milton's singular theology, plays a vital role in the depic-tion of the central characters (Adam, Eve, and Satan), and advances the plot of the epic. In Book 4, Satan's first view of the newly created earth in all of its prelapsarian purity underscores the enormity of his fall and the price of his infidelity, particularly compared with the harmony of Adam and Eve's life in the Garden of Eden, the archetype of liter-

ary gardens for the next four centuries. Later, in Book 7, Milton articulates the idea of stewardship. Humans are granted dominion over the rest of creation: "let them rule / Over the fish and Fowl of Sea and Air, / Beast of the Field, and over all the Earth, / And every creeping thing." This theological-ecological position assumes that man will be a responsible steward for all the rest of creation. However, when Adam and Eve eat the fruit of the forbidden tree, their fall is evidenced by the garden's decay, by the animals' hostility toward them, and by their ultimate expulsion from paradise. Their relationship to nature thenceforth becomes adversarial, suggesting perhaps that because of our selfishness, we have relinquished any right to dominion over the earth.

Sonnet 1

O nightingale, that on yon bloomy Spray
   Warbl'st at eve, when all the Woods are still,
   Thou with fresh hope the Lover's heart dost fill,
   While the jolly hours lead on propitious *May*,
Thy liquid notes that close the eye of Day,   5
   First heard before the shallow Cuckoo's bill
   Portend success in love; O if *Jove's*[1] will
   Have linked that amorous power to thy soft lay,
Now timely sing, ere the rude Bird of Hate
   Foretell my hopeless doom in some Grove nigh: 10
   As thou from year to year hast sung too late
For my relief; yet hadst no reason why,
   Whether the Muse, or Love call thee his mate,
   Both them I serve, and of their train am I.

[1] *Jove:* the king of the classical pantheon; God.

Lycidas

In this Monody, the Author bewails a learned Friend,[1] unfortunately drowned in his passage from Chester on the Irish seas, 1637; and by occasion foretells the ruin of our corrupted clergy, then in their height.

     Yet once more, O ye laurels, and once more
Ye myrtles brown, with ivy never sere,
I come to pluck your berries harsh and crude,
And with forced fingers rude,
Shatter your leaves before the mellowing year.   5

[1] Edward King, whom Milton had known at Cambridge, died in a shipwreck on August 10, 1637. His pseudonym in the poem, "Lycidas," is taken from Virgil, who used it for the name of a shepherd and poet.

Bitter constraint, and sad occasion dear,
Compels me to disturb your season due:
For Lycidas is dead, dead ere his prime,
Young Lycidas, and hath not left his peer:
Who would not sing for Lycidas? He knew   10
Himself to sing, and build the lofty rhyme.
He must not float upon his wat'ry bier
Unwept, and welter to the parching wind,
Without the meed of some melodious tear.
    Begin then, Sisters of the sacred well,[2]   15
That from beneath the seat of Jove doth spring;
Begin, and somewhat loudly sweep the string.
Hence with denial vain, and coy excuse;
So may some gentle Muse
With lucky words favour my destined urn,   20
And as he passes turn,
And bid fair peace be to my sable shroud.
For we were nursed upon the selfsame hill,
Fed the same flock by fountain, shade, and rill.
    Together both, ere the high lawns appeared   25
Under the opening eyelids of the morn,
We drove a-field, and both together heard
What time the gray-fly winds her sultry horn,
Batt'ning our flocks with the fresh dews of night,
Oft till the star that rose, at evening, bright,   30
Toward heaven's descent had sloped his west'ring wheel.
Meanwhile the rural ditties were not mute,
Tempered to the oaten flute;
Rough Satyrs danced, and Fauns[3] with cloven heel
From the glad sound would not be absent long,   35
And old Damaetus[4] loved to hear our song.
    But, O the heavy change, now thou art gone,
Now thou art gone, and never must return!
Thee, Shepherd, thee the woods, and desert caves
With wild thyme and the gadding vine o'ergrown,   40
And all their echoes mourn.
The willows, and the hazel copses green,
Shall now no more be seen,
Fanning their joyous leaves to thy soft lays.
As killing as the canker to the rose,   45
Or taint-worm to the weanling herds that graze,
Or frost to flow'rs, that their gay wardrobe wear,

---

[2] *Sisters . . . well:* i.e., the Muses.

[3] Satyrs and fauns are mythological woodland creatures, half-human and half-animal.

[4] Perhaps a reference to Milton and King's tutor at Cambridge.

When first the white-thorn blows;
Such, Lycidas, thy loss to shepherds' ear.
    Where were ye, Nymphs, when the remorseless deep   50
Closed o'er the head of your loved Lycidas?
For neither were ye playing on the steep,
Where your old Bards, the famous Druids, lie,
Nor on the shaggy top of Mona[5] high,
Nor yet where Deva[6] spreads her wizard stream.   55
Ay me! I fondly dream!
Had ye been there, for what could that have done?
What could the Muse herself that Orpheus[7] bore,
The Muse herself for her enchanting son,
Whom universal nature did lament,   60
When by the rout that made the hideous roar,
His gory visage down the stream was sent,
Down the swift Hebrus to the Lesbian shore?
    Alas! what boots it with incessant care
To tend the homely slighted shepherd's trade,   65
And strictly meditate the thankless Muse?
Were it not better done as others use,
To sport with Amaryllis in the shade,
Or with the tangles of Neaera's[8] hair?
Fame is the spur that the clear spirit doth raise   70
(That last infirmity of noble mind)
To scorn delights, and live laborious days;
But the fair guerdon[9] when we hope to find,
And think to burst out into sudden blaze;
Comes the blind Fury with th' abhorrèd shears,[10]   75
And slits the thin-spun life. "But not the praise,"
Phoebus[11] replied, and touched my trembling ears;
"Fame is no plant that grows on mortal soil,
Nor in the glist'ring foil
Set off to the world, nor in broad rumour lies;   80
But lives and spreads aloft by those pure eyes,
And perfect witness of all-judging Jove;
As he pronounces lastly on each deed,
Of so much fame in heav'n expect thy meed."

[5] The isle of Anglesey.

[6] The river Dee.

[7] Orpheus was the son of Calliope, the Muse of epic poetry. He was killed and dismembered by the frenzied followers of the god of wine, Dionysos, and his head floated down the river Hebrus to the Greek island of Lesbos.

[8] Amyrillis and Neaera are names for nymphs.

[9] A reward.

[10] *Comes . . . shears:* a reference to one of the Fates, Atropos, who cuts the thread of life.

[11] Another name for Apollo, Greek god of poetry.

O fountain Arethuse,[12] and thou honoured flood,   85
Smooth-sliding Mincius, crowned with vocal reeds!
That strain I heard was of a higher mood.
But now my oat proceeds,
And listens to the herald of the sea
That came in Neptune's[13] plea;   90
He asked the waves, and asked the felon winds,
"What hard mishap hath doomed this gentle swain?"
And questioned every gust of rugged wings
That blows from off each beakèd promontory:
They knew not of his story,   95
And sage Hippotades[14] their answer brings,
That not a blast was from his dungeon strayed;
The air was calm, and on the level brine
Sleek Panope[15] with all her sisters played.
It was that fatal and perfidious bark,   100
Built in th' eclipse, and rigged with curses dark,
That sunk so low that sacred head of thine.
  Next Camus,[16] reverend sire, went footing slow,
His mantle hairy, and his bonnet sedge,
Inwrought with figures dim, and on the edge   105
Like to that sanguine flow'r inscribed with woe.
"Ah! Who hath reft (quoth he) my dearest pledge?"
Last came, and last did go,
The pilot of the Galilean lake;[17]
Two massy keys he bore of metals twain,   110
(The golden opes, the iron shuts amain)
He shook his mitered locks, and stern bespake:
"How well could I have spared for thee, young swain,
Enow of such as for their bellies' sake
Creep, and intrude, and climb into the fold?   115
Of other care they little reckoning make;
Than how to scramble at the shearer's feast,
And shove away the worthy bidden guest.
Blind mouths! that scarce themselves know how to hold
A sheep-hook, or have learned aught else the least   120
That to the faithful herdman's art belongs!
What recks it them? What need they? They are sped;

---

[12] A nymph who was transformed into a fountain to escape the advances of the river god, Alpheus.
[13] God of the sea.
[14] God of the winds.
[15] A water nymph.
[16] Deity associated with the river Cam, which flows by the University of Cambridge.
[17] *The pilot . . . lake:* a reference to St. Peter.

And when they list, their lean and flashy songs
Grate on their scrannel[18] pipes of wretched straw;
The hungry sheep look up, and are not fed,   125
But swoln with wind, and the rank mist they draw,
Rot inwardly, and foul contagion spread.
Besides what the grim wolf[19] with privy paw
Daily devours apace, and nothing said;
But that two-handed engine at the door   130
Stands ready to smite once, and smite no more."
    Return, Alpheus, the dread voice is past,
That shrunk thy streams; return, Sicilian Muse,[20]
And call the vales, and bid them hither cast
Their bells, and flow'rets of a thousand hues.   135
Ye valleys low, where the mild whispers use
Of shades, and wanton winds, and gushing brooks,
On whose fresh lap the swart-star[21] sparely looks:
Throw hither all your quaint enameled eyes,
That on the green turf suck the honeyed showers,   140
And purple all the ground with vernal flowers.
Bring the rathe[22] primrose that forsaken dies,
The tufted crow-toe, and pale jessamine,
The white pink, and the pansy freaked with jet,
The glowing violet,   145
The musk-rose, and the well-attired woodbine,
With cowslips wan that hang the pensive head,
And every flower that sad embroidery wears:
Bid amaranthus[23] all his beauty shed,
And daffadillies fill their cups with tears,   150
To strew the laureate hearse where Lycid lies.
For so to interpose a little ease,
Let our frail thoughts dally with false surmise.
Ay me! Whilst thee the shores, and sounding seas
Wash far away, where'er thy bones are hurled,   155
Whether beyond the stormy Hebrides,
Where thou perhaps under the whelming tide
Visit'st the bottom of the monstrous world;
Or whether thou to our moist vows denied,

---

[18] Weak or feeble.

[19] A reference to a corrupt church leader or to corruption in the Anglican Church itself.

[20] *Sicilian Muse:* Theocritus, ancient Greek author and one of the first in the Western tradition to employ the pastoral form.

[21] The Dog Star, or dark star of summer.

[22] Early.

[23] A flower that is supposed to give immortality.

Sleep'st by the fable of Bellerus[24] old,   160
Where the great vision of the guarded mount
Looks toward Namancos and Bayona's[25] hold;
Look homeward Angel now, and melt with ruth:
And, O ye dolphins, waft the hapless youth.
     Weep no more, woeful Shepherds, weep no more,   165
For Lycidas your sorrow is not dead,
Sunk though he be beneath the wat'ry floor;
So sinks the day-star[26] in the ocean bed,
And yet anon repairs his drooping head,
And tricks his beams, and with new-spangled ore   170
Flames in the forehead of the morning sky;
So Lycidas sunk low, but mounted high,
Through the dear might of him[27] that walked the waves,
Where other groves, and other streams along,
With nectar pure his oozy locks he laves,   175
And hears the unexpressive nuptial song,
In the blest kingdoms meek of joy and love.
There entertain him all the saints above,
In solemn troops, and sweet societies,
That sing, and singing in their glory move,   180
And wipe the tears forever from his eyes.
Now, Lycidas, the shepherds weep no more;
Henceforth thou art the Genius of the shore,
In thy large recompense, and shalt be good
To all that wander in that perilous flood.   185
     Thus sang the uncouth swain to the oaks and rills,
While the still morn went out with sandals gray;
He touched the tender stops of various quills,
With eager thought warbling his Doric[28] lay;
And now the sun had stretched out all the hills,   190
And now was dropt into the western bay;
At last he rose, and twitched his mantle blue:
Tomorrow to fresh woods, and pastures new.

---

[24] A mythical giant supposed to have lived in Cornwall.

[25] "The guarded mount" refers to Land's End in Cornwall, England, which points toward Namancos, a mountain range, and Bayona, a city—both in Spain.

[26] I.e., the sun.

[27] Christ.

[28] I.e., pastoral.

From **Paradise Lost**

From **Book 4***

   So on he fares, and to the border comes,
Of *Eden,* where delicious Paradise,
Now nearer, Crowns with her enclosure green,
As with a rural mound the champaign head
Of a steep wilderness, whose hairy sides   5
With thicket overgrown, grotesque and wild,
Access denied; and overhead up grew
Insuperable highth of loftiest shade,
Cedar, and Pine, and Fir, and branching Palm,
A Sylvan Scene, and as the ranks ascend   10
Shade above shade, a woody Theater
Of stateliest view. Yet higher than their tops
The verdurous wall of paradise up sprung:
Which to our general Sire gave prospect large
Into his nether Empire neighbouring round.   15
And higher than that Wall a circling row
Of goodliest Trees loaden with fairest Fruit,
Blossoms and Fruits at once of golden hue
Appeared, with gay enameled colours mixed:
On which the Sun more glad impressed his beams   20
Than in fair Evening Cloud, or humid Bow,
When God hath show'red the earth; so lovely seemed
That Landscape: And of pure now purer air
Meets his approach, and to the heart inspires
Vernal delight and joy, able to drive   25
All sadness but despair: now gentle gales
Fanning their odoriferous wings dispense
Native perfumes, and whisper whence they stole
Those balmy spoils. As when to them who sail
Beyond the *Cape of Hope,* and now are past   30
Mozambic, off at Sea North-East winds blow
Sabean[1] Odours from the spicy shore
Of *Arabie* the blest, with such delay
Well pleased they slack their course, and many a League
Cheered with the grateful smell old Ocean smiles.   35
So entertained those odorous sweets the Fiend
Who came their bane, though with them better pleased
Than *Asmodeus*[2] with the fishy fume,
That drove him, though enamoured, from the Spouse

---

* Book 4 is 1,015 lines; in the original, this excerpt begins at line 131 and ends on line 749.

[1] The Cape of Good Hope and Mozambique are in Africa, and Sheba is a part of Arabia.

[2] A reference from Hebrew scripture, to the eighth chapter of Tobit; Asmodeus was an evil spirit.

Of *Tobit*'s Son, and with a vengeance sent   40
From *Media* post to *Egypt*, there fast bound.
   Now to the ascent of that steep savage Hill
Satan had journeyed on, pensive and slow;
But further way found none, so thick entwined,
As one continued brake, the undergrowth   45
Of shrubs and tangling bushes had perplext
All path of Man or Beast that passed that way:
One Gate there only was, and that looked East
On the other side: which when the arch-felon saw
Due entrance he disdained, and in contempt,   50
At one slight bound high overleaped all bound
Of Hill or highest Wall, and sheer within
Lights on his feet. As when a prowling Wolf,
Whom hunger drives to seek new haunt for prey,
Watching where Shepherds pen their Flocks at eve   55
In hurdled Cotes amid the field secure,
Leaps o'er the fence with ease into the Fold:
Or as a Thief bent to unhoard the cash
Of some rich Burgher, whose substantial doors,
Cross-barred and bolted fast, fear no assault,   60
In at the window climbs, or o'er the tiles;
So clomb this first grand Thief into God's Fold:
So since into his Church lewd Hirelings climb.
Thence up he flew, and on the Tree of Life,
The middle Tree and highest there that grew,   65
Sat like a cormorant;[3] yet not true Life
Thereby regained, but sat devising Death
To them who lived; nor on the virtue thought
Of that life-giving Plant, but only used
For prospect, what well used had been the pledge   70
Of immortality. So little knows
Any, but God alone, to value right
The good before him, but perverts best things
To worst abuse, or to their meanest use.
   Beneath him with new wonder now he views   75
To all delight of human sense exposed
In narrow room Nature's whole wealth, yea more,
A Heav'n on Earth, for blissful Paradise
Of God the Garden was, by him in the East
Of *Eden* planted; *Eden* stretched her Line   80
From *Auran* Eastward to the Royal Tow'rs
Of great *Seleucia*,[4] built by *Grecian* Kings,

---

[3] A large bird of prey that symbolizes greed.

[4] Auran was a city on the Euphrates and Seleucia was a city on the Tigris.

Or where the Sons of *Eden* long before
Dwelt in *Telassar*:[5] in this pleasant soil
His far more pleasant Garden God ordained;   85
Out of the fertile ground he caused to grow
All Trees of noblest kind for sight, smell, taste;
And all amid them stood the Tree of Life,
High eminent, blooming Ambrosial Fruit
Of vegetable Gold; and next to Life   90
Our Death the Tree of Knowledge grew fast by,
Knowledge of Good bought dear by knowing ill.
Southward through *Eden* went a River large,
Nor changed his course, but through the shaggy hill
Passed underneath engulft, for God had thrown   95
That Mountain as his Garden mold high raised
Upon the rapid current, which through veins
Of porous Earth with kindly thirst up drawn,
Rose a fresh Fountain, and with many a rill
Watered the Garden; thence united fell   100
Down the steep glade, and met the nether Flood,
Which from his darksome passage now appears,
And now divided into four main Streams,[6]
Runs diverse, wand'ring many a famous Realm
And Country whereof here needs no account,   105
But rather to tell how, if Art could tell,
How from that Sapphire Fount the crispèd Brooks,
Rolling on Orient Pearl and sands of Gold,
With mazy error under pendant shades
Ran Nectar, visiting each plant, and fed   110
Flow'rs worthy of Paradise which not nice Art
In Beds and curious Knots, but Nature boon
Powered forth profuse on Hill and Dale and Plain,
Both where the morning Sun first warmly smote
The open field, and where the unpierced shade   115
Embrowned the noontide Bow'rs: Thus was this place,
A happy rural seat of various view;
Groves whose rich Trees wept odorous Gums and Balm,
Others whose fruit burnisht with Golden Rind
Hung amiable, *Hesperian*[7] Fables true,   120
If true, here only, and of delicious taste:
Betwixt them Lawns, or level Downs, and Flocks
Grazing the tender herb, were interposed,
Or palmy hillock, or the flow'ry lap

[5] A city in Eden.
[6] *Four main Streams:* the Nile, Euphrates, Tigris, and Indus Rivers—all in the Middle East.
[7] I.e., idyllic.

Of some irriguous Valley spread her store, 125
Flow'rs of all hue, and without Thorn the Rose:
Another side, umbrageous Grots and Caves
Of cool recess, o'er which the mantling vine
Lays forth her purple Grape, and gently creeps
Luxuriant; meanwhile murmuring waters fall 130
Down the slope hills, disperst, or in a Lake,
That to the fringèd Bank with Myrtle crowned,
Her crystal mirror holds, unite their streams.
The Birds their choir apply; airs, vernal airs,
Breathing the smell of field and grove, attune 135
The trembling leaves, while Universal *Pan*
Knit with the *Graces* and the *Hours*[8] in dance
Led on the Eternal Spring. Not that fair field
Of *Enna*, where *Proserpine* gathering flow'rs
Herself a fairer Flow'r by gloomy *Dis* 140
Was gathered, which cost *Ceres*[9] all that pain
To seek her through the world; nor that sweet Grove
Of *Daphne* by *Orontes*, and the inspired
Castalian Spring,[10] might with this Paradise
Of *Eden* strive; nor that *Nyseian* Isle[11] 145
Girt with the River *Triton*, where old *Cham*,
Whom Gentiles *Ammon* call and *Lybian Jove*,
Hid *Amalthea* and her Florid Son
Young *Bacchus* from his Stepdame *Rhea's* eye;[12]
Nor where *Abassin*[13] Kings their issue Guard, 150
Mount *Amara*, though this by some supposed
True Paradise under the *Ethiop* Line[14]
By *Nilus'*[15] head, enclosed with shining Rock,
A whole day's journey high, but wide remote
From this *Assyrian* Garden, where the Fiend 155
Saw undelighted all delight, all kind
Of living Creatures new to sight and strange:
    Two of far nobler shape erect and tall,
God-like erect, with native Honour clad
In naked Majesty seemed Lords of all, 160

---

[8] Pan was the god of the woodland; the Graces and the Hours are goddesses.

[9] Ceres, goddess of the harvest, was the mother of Proserine, who was kidnapped by Dis, god of the underworld, at Enna.

[10] Orontes is located in Syria, near the site of a temple to Apollo, god of intelligence and of poetry; the Castalian spring is located on Mount Parnassus and was said to provide inspiration to poets.

[11, 12] *Nyseian Isle . . . Rhea's eye:* After fathering Bacchus with Amalthea, Jove (in Milton's passage also known as Ham and identified, too, with the Egyptian god Ammon) transported his son to Nysa, in North Africa, in order to escape the notice of his wife, Rhea.

[13] Abyssinian.

[14] I.e., the equator.

[15] The Nile.

And worthy seemed, for in their looks Divine
The image of their glorious Maker shone,
Truth, wisdom, Sanctitude severe and pure,
Severe but in true filial freedom placed;
Whence true authority in men; though both   165
Not equal, as their sex not equal seemed;
For contemplation he and valour formed,
For softness she and sweet attractive Grace,
He for God only, she for God in him:
His fair large Front and Eye sublime declared   170
Absolute rule; and Hyacinthine Locks
Round from his parted forelock manly hung
Clust'ring, but not beneath his shoulders broad:
She as a veil down to the slender waist
Her unadorned golden tresses wore   175
Disheveled, but in wanton ringlets waved
As the Vine curls her tendrils, which implied
Subjection, but required with gentle sway,
And by her yielded, by him best received,
Yielded with coy submission, modest pride,   180
And sweet reluctant amorous delay.
Nor those mysterious parts were then concealed,
Then was not guilty shame, dishonest shame
Of nature's works, honor dishonorable,
Sin-bred, how have ye troubled all mankind   185
With shows instead, mere shows of seeming pure,
And banisht from man's life his happiest life,
Simplicity and spotless innocence.
So passed they naked on, nor shunned the sight
Of God or Angel, for they thought no ill: 190
So hand in hand they passed, the loveliest pair
That ever since in love's embraces met,
Adam the goodliest man of men since born
His Sons, the fairest of her Daughters *Eve.*
Under a tuft of shade that on a green   195
Stood whispering soft, by a fresh Fountain side
They sat them down, and after no more toil
Of their sweet Gard'ning labour then sufficed
To recommend cool *Zephyr*,[16] and made ease
More easy, wholesome thirst and appetite   200
More grateful, to their Supper Fruits they fell,
Nectarine Fruits which the compliant boughs
Yielded them, sidelong as they sat recline
On the soft downy Bank damaskt with flow'rs:

[16] The west wind.

The savoury pulp they chew, and in the rind   205
Still as they thirsted scoop the brimming stream;
Nor gentle purpose, nor endearing smiles
Wanted, nor youthful dalliance as beseems
Fair couple, linkt in happy nuptial League,
Alone as they. About them frisking played   210
All Beasts of the Earth, since wild, and of all chase
In Wood or Wilderness, Forest or Den;
Sporting the Lion ramped, and in his paw
Dandled the Kid; Bears, Tigers, Ounces, Pards,
Gamboled before them, the unwieldy Elephant   215
To make them mirth used all his might, and wreathed
His Lithe Proboscis; close the Serpent sly
Insinuating, wove with Gordian twine
His breaded train, and of his fatal guile
Gave proof unheeded; others on the grass   220
Coucht, and now filled with pasture gazing sat,
Or Bedward ruminating: for the Sun
Declined was hasting now with prone career
To the Ocean Isles, and in the ascending Scale
Of Heav'n the Stars that usher Evening rose: 225
When *Satan* still in gaze, as first he stood,
Scarce thus at length failed speech recovered sad.
    O Hell! what do mine eyes with grief behold,
Into our room of bliss thus high advanced
Creatures of other mold, earth-born perhaps,   230
Not Spirits, yet to heav'nly Spirits bright
Little inferior; whom my thoughts pursue
With wonder, and could love, so lively shines
In them Divine resemblance, and such grace
The hand that formed them on their shape hath poured.   235
Ah gentle pair, ye little think how nigh
Your change approaches, when all these delights
Will vanish and deliver ye to woe,
More woe, the more your taste is now of joy;
Happy, but for so happy ill secured   240
Long to continue, and this high seat your Heav'n
Ill fenced for Heav'n to keep out such a foe
As now is entered; yet no purposed foe
To you whom I could pity thus forlorn
Though I unpitied: League with you I seek,   245
And mutual amity so strait, so close,
That I with you must dwell, or you with me
Henceforth; my dwelling haply may not please
Like this fair Paradise, your sense, yet such
Accept your Maker's work; he gave it me,   250

Which I as freely give; Hell shall unfold,
To entertain you two, her widest Gates,
And send forth all her Kings; there will be room,
Not like these narrow limits, to receive
Your numerous offspring; if no better place,   255
Thank him who puts me loath to this revenge
On you who wrong me not for him who wronged.
And should I at your harmless innocence
Melt, as I do, yet public reason just,
Honour and Empire with revenge enlarged,   260
By conquering this new World, compels me now
To do what else though damned I should abhor.
   So spake the Fiend, and with necessity,
The Tyrant's plea, excused his devilish deeds.
Then from his lofty stand on that high Tree   265
Down he alights among the sportful Herd
Of those four-footed kinds, himself now one,
Now other, as their shape served best his end
Nearer to view his prey, and unespied
To mark what of their state he more might learn   270
By word or action markt: about them round
A Lion now he stalks with fiery glare,
Then as a Tiger, who by chance hath spied
In some Purlieu[17] two gentle Fawns at play,
Straight couches close, then rising changes oft   275
His couchant watch, as one who chose his ground
Whence rushing he might surest seize them both
Gripped in each paw: when *Adam* first of men
To first of women *Eve* thus moving speech,
Turned him all ear to hear new utterance flow.   280
   Sole partner and sole part of all these joys,
Dearer thyself than all; needs must the Power
That made us, and for us this ample World
Be infinitly good, and of his good
As liberal and free as infinite,   285
That raised us from the dust and placed us here
In all this happiness, who at his hand
Have nothing merited, nor can perform
Aught whereof he hath need, he who requires
From us no other service than to keep   290
This one, this easy charge, of all the Trees
In Paradise that bear delicious fruit
So various, not to taste that only Tree
Of Knowledge, planted by the Tree of Life,

---

[17] The outskirts of a forest.

So near grows Death to Life, whate'er Death is,   295
Some dreadful thing no doubt; for well thou know'st
God hath pronounced it death to taste that Tree,
The only sign of our obedience left
Among so many signs of power and rule
Conferred upon us, and Dominion given   300
Over all other Creatures that possess
Earth, Air, and Sea. Then let us not think hard
One easy prohibition, who enjoy
Free leave so large to all things else, and choice
Unlimited of manifold delights: 305
But let us ever praise him, and extol
His bounty, following our delightful task
To prune these growing Plants, and tend these Flow'rs,
Which were it toilsome, yet with thee were sweet.
    To whom thus *Eve* replied. O thou for whom   310
And from whom I was formed flesh of thy flesh,
And without whom am to no end, my Guide
And Head, what thou hast said is just and right.
For we to him indeed all praises owe,
And daily thanks, I chiefly who enjoy   315
So far the happier Lot, enjoying thee
Preeminent by so much odds, while thou
Like consort to thyself canst nowhere find.
That day I oft remember, when from sleep
I first awaked, and found myself reposed   320
Under a shade of flow'rs, much wondering where
And what I was, whence thither brought, and how.
Not distant far from thence a murmuring sound
Of waters issued from a Cave and spread
Into a liquid Plain, then stood unmoved   325
Pure as the expanse of Heav'n; I thither went
With unexperienced thought, and laid me down
On the green bank, to look into the clear
Smooth Lake, that to me seemed another Sky.
As I bent down to look, just opposite,   330
A Shape within the wat'ry gleam appeared
Bending to look on me, I started back,
It started back, but pleased I soon returned,
Pleased it returned as soon with answering looks
Of sympathy and love; there I had fixt   335
Mine eyes till now, and pined with vain desire,
Had not a voice thus warned me, What thou seest,
What there thou seest fair Creature is thyself,
With thee it came and goes: but follow me,
And I will bring thee where no shadow stays   340

Thy coming, and thy soft embraces, he
Whose image thou art, him thou shall enjoy
Inseparably thine, to him shalt bear
Multitudes like thyself, and thence be called
Mother of human Race: what could I do,   345
But follow straight, invisibly thus led?
Till I espied thee, fair indeed and tall,
Under a Platan, yet methought less fair,
Less winning soft, less amiably mild.
Than that smooth wat'ry image; back I turned,   350
Thou following cried'st aloud, Return fair *Eve*,
Whom fly'st thou? whom thou fly'st, of him thou art,
His flesh, his bone; to give thee being I lent
Out of my side to thee, nearest my heart
Substantial Life, to have thee by my side   355
Henceforth an individual solace dear;
Part of my Soul I seek thee, and thee claim
My other half: with that thy gentle hand
Seized mine, I yielded, and from that time see
How beauty is excelled by manly grace   360
And wisdom, which alone is truly fair.
   So spake our general Mother, and with eyes
Of conjugal attraction unreproved,
And meek surrender, half embracing leaned
On our first Father, half her swelling Breast   365
Naked met his under the flowing Gold
Of her loose tresses hid: he in delight
Both of her Beauty and submissive Charms
Smiled with superior Love, as *Jupiter*
On *Juno*[18] smiles, when he impregns the Clouds   370
That shed *May* Flowers; and pressed her Matron lip
With kisses pure: aside the Devil turned
For envy, yet with jealous leer malign
Eyed them askance, and to himself thus plained.
   Sight hateful, sight tormenting! thus these two   375
Imparadised in one another's arms
The happier *Eden*, shall enjoy their fill
Of bliss on bliss, while I to Hell am thrust,
Where neither joy nor love, but fierce desire,
Among our other torments not the least,   380
Still unfulfilled with pain of longing pines;
Yet let me not forget what I have gained
From their own mouths; all is not theirs it seems:
One fatal Tree there stands of Knowledge called,

---

[18] The queen of the classical pantheon, wife of Jupiter and goddess of marriage.

Forbidden them to taste: Knowledge forbidden?   385
Suspicious, reasonless. Why should their Lord
Envy them that? can it be sin to know,
Can it be death? and do they only stand
By Ignorance, is that their happy state,
The proof of their obedience and their faith?   390
O fair foundation laid whereon to build
Their ruin! Hence I will excite their minds
With more desire to know, and to reject
Envious commands, invented with design
To keep them low whom knowledge might exalt   395
Equal with Gods; aspiring to be such,
They taste and die: what likelier can ensue?
But first with narrow search I must walk round
This Garden, and no corner leave unspied;
A chance but chance may lead where I may meet   400
Some wand'ring Spirit of Heav'n, by Fountain side,
Or in thick shade retired, from him to draw
What further would be learnt. Live while ye may,
Yet happy pair; enjoy, till I return,
Short pleasures, for long woes are to succeed.   405
  So saying, his proud step he scornful turned,
But with sly circumspection, and began
Through wood, through waste, o'er hill, o'er dale his roam.
Meanwhile in utmost Longitude, where Heav'n
With Earth and Ocean meets, the setting Sun   410
Slowly descended, and with right aspect
Against the eastern Gate of Paradise
Leveled his eyening Rays: it was a Rock
Of Alablaster, piled up to the Clouds,
Conspicuous far, winding with one ascent   415
Accessible from Earth, one entrance high;
The rest was craggy cliff, that overhung
Still as it rose, impossible to climb.
Betwixt these rocky Pillars *Gabriel*[19] sat
Chief of the Angelic Guards, awaiting night;   420
About him exercised Heroic Games
The unarmèd Youth of Heav'n, but nigh at hand
Celestial Armory, Shields, Helms, and Spears,
Hung high with Diamond flaming, and with Gold.
Thither came *Uriel*,[20] gliding through the Even   425
On a Sunbeam, swift as a shooting Star
In *Autumn* thwarts the night, when vapors fired

---

[19] Chief among the archangels sent to protect Adam and Eve in the garden.

[20] Another of the archangel guards.

Impress the Air, and shows the Mariner
From what point of his Compass to beware
Impetuous winds: he thus began in haste.   430
    Gabriel, to thee thy course by Lot hath giv'n
Charge and strict watch that to this happy Place
No evil thing approach or enter in;
This day at highth of Noon came to my Sphere
A Spirit, zealous, as he seemed, to know   435
More of the Almighty's works, and chiefly Man
God's latest Image: I described his way
Bent all on speed, and markt his Airy Gate;
But in the Mount that lies from Eden North,
Where he first lighted, soon discerned his looks   440
Alien from Heav'n, with passions foul obscured:
Mine eye pursued him still, but under shade
Lost sight of him; one of the banisht crew
I fear, hath ventured from the deep, to raise
New troubles; him thy care must be to find: 445
    To whom the wingèd Warrior thus returned:
Uriel, no wonder if thy perfect sight,
Amid the Sun's bright circle where thou sitt'st,
See far and wide: in at this Gate none pass
The vigilance here placed, but such as come   450
Well known from Heav'n; and since Meridian hour
No Creature thence: if Spirit of other sort,
So minded, have o'erleapt these earthy bounds
On purpose, hard thou know'st it to exclude
Spiritual substance with corporeal bar.   455
But if within the circuit of these walks,
In whatsoever shape he lurk, of whom
Thou tell'st, by morrow dawning I shall know.
    So promised he, and *Uriel* to his charge
Returned on that bright beam, whose point now raised   460
Bore him slope downward to the Sun now fall'n
Beneath the *Azorès;* whither the prime Orb,
Incredible how swift, had thither rolled
Diurnal, or this less volúble Earth
By shorter flight to the East, had left him there   465
Arraying with reflected Purple and Gold
The Clouds that on his Western Throne attend:
Now came still Evening on, and Twilight gray
Had in her sober Livery all things clad;
Silence accompanied, for Beast and Bird,   470
They to their grassy Couch, these to their Nests
Were slunk, all but the wakeful Nightingale;
She all night long her amorous descant sung;

Silence was pleased: now glowed the Firmament
With living Sapphires: *Hesperus*[21] that led   475
The starry Host, rode brightest, till the Moon
Rising in clouded Majesty, at length
Apparent Queen unveiled her peerless light,
And o'er the dark her Silver Mantle threw.
　　　When *Adam* thus to *Eve*: Fair Consort, the hour   480
Of night, and all things now retired to rest
Mind us of like repose, since God hath set
Labour and rest, as day and night to men
Successive, and the timely dew of sleep
Now falling with soft slumbrous weight inclines   485
Our eye-lids; other Creatures all day long
Rove idle unemployed, and less need rest;
Man hath his daily work of body or mind
Appointed, which declares his Dignity,
And the regard of Heav'n on all his ways;   490
While other Animals unactive range,
And of their doings God takes no account.
Tomorrow ere fresh Morning streak the East
With first approach of light, we must be ris'n,
And at our pleasant labour, to reform   495
Yon flow'ry Arbors, yonder Alleys green,
Our walk at noon, with branches overgrown,
That mock our scant manuring, and require
More hands than ours to lop their wanton growth:
Those Blossoms also, and those dropping Gums,   500
That lie bestrown unsightly and unsmooth,
Ask riddance, if we mean to tread with ease;
Meanwhile, as Nature wills, Night bids us rest.
　　　To whom thus *Eve* with perfect beauty adorned.
My Author and Disposer, what thou bidd'st   505
Unargued I obey; so God ordains,
God is thy Law, thou mine: to know no more
Is woman's happiest knowledge and her praise.
With thee conversing I forget all time,
All seasons and their change, all please alike.   510
Sweet is the breath of morn, her rising sweet,
With charm of earliest Birds; pleasant the Sun
When first on this delightful Land he spreads
His orient Beams, on herb, tree, fruit, and flow'r,
Glist'ring with dew; fragrant the fertile earth   515
After soft showers; and sweet the coming on
Of grateful Evening mild, then silent Night

---

[21] A star.

With this her solemn Bird and this fair Moon,
And these the Gems of Heav'n, her starry train:
But neither breath of Morn when she ascends   520
With charm of earliest Birds, nor rising Sun,
On this delightful land, nor herb, fruit, flow'r,
Glist'ring with dew, nor fragrance after showers,
Nor grateful Evening mild, nor silent Night
With this her solemn Bird, nor walk by Moon,   525
Or glittering Starlight without thee is sweet.
But wherefore all night long shine these, for whom
This glorious sight, when sleep hath shut all eyes?
    To whom our general Ancestor replied.
Daughter of God and Man, accomplisht *Eve*,   530
Those have their course to finish, round the Earth,
By morrow Evening, and from Land to Land
In order, though to Nations yet unborn,
Minist'ring light prepared, they set and rise;
Lest total darkness should by Night regain   535
Her old possession, and extinguish life
In Nature and all things, which these soft fires
Not only enlighten, but with kindly heat
Of various influence foment and warm,
Temper or nourish, or in part shed down   540
Their stellar virtue on all kinds that grow
On Earth, made hereby apter to receive
Perfection from the Sun's more potent Ray.
These then, though unbeheld in deep of night,
Shine not in vain, nor think, though men were none,   545
That Heav'n would want spectators, God want praise;
Millions of spiritual Creatures walk the Earth
Unseen, both when we wake, and when we sleep:
All these with ceaseless praise his works behold
Both day and night: how often from the steep   550
Of echoing Hill or Thicket have we heard
Celestial voices to the midnight air,
Sole, or responsive each to other's note
Singing their great Creator: oft in bands
While they keep watch, or nightly rounding walk   555
With Heav'nly touch of instrumental sounds
In full harmonic number joined, their songs
Divide the night, and lift our thoughts to Heaven.
    Thus talking hand in hand alone they passed
On to their blissful Bower; it was a place   560
Chos'n by the sovran Planter, when he framed
All things to man's delightful use; the roof
Of thickest covert was inwoven shade

Laurel and Mirtle, and what higher grew
Of firm and fragrant leaf; on either side   565
Acanthus, and each odorous bushy shrub
Fenced up the verdant wall; each beauteous flow'r,
Iris all hues, Roses, and Jessamin
Reared high their flourished heads between, and wrought
Mosaic; underfoot the Violet,   570
Crocus, and Hyacinth with rich inlay
Broidered the ground, more coloured than with stone
Of costliest Emblem: other Creature here
Beast, Bird, Insect, or Worm durst enter none;
Such was their awe of Man. In shady Bower   575
More sacred and sequestered, though but feigned,
Pan or *Silvanus* never slept, nor Nymph,
Nor *Faunus*[22] haunted. Here in close recess
With Flowers, Garlands, and sweet-smelling Herbs
Espousèd *Eve* deckt first her nuptial Bed,   580
And heav'nly Choirs the Hymenaean[23] sung,
What day the genial Angel to our Sire
Brought her in naked beauty more adorned,
More lovely than *Pandora,*[24] whom the Gods
Endowed with all their gifts, and O too like   585
In sad event, when to the unwiser Son
Of *Japhet* brought by *Hermes,* she ensnared
Mankind with her fair looks, to be avenged
On him who had stole *Jove's* authentic fire.
   Thus at their shady Lodge arrived, both stood   590
Both turned, and under op'n Sky adored
The God that made both Sky, Air, Earth and Heav'n
Which they beheld, the Moon's resplendent Globe
And starry Pole: Thou also mad'st the Night,
Maker Omnipotent, and thou the Day,   595
Which we in our appointed work employed
Have finisht happy in our mutual help
And mutual love, the Crown of all our bliss
Ordained by thee, and this delicious place
For us too large, where thy abundance wants   600
Partakers, and uncropt falls to the ground.
But thou hast promised from us two a Race
To fill the Earth, who shall with us extol

[22] Pan, Silvanus, the nymphs, and Faunus are all classical woodland deities.

[23] Song of marriage.

[24] Pandora was the woman who, according to Greek myth, succumbed to her curiosity and opened a magic box that released evil into the world. Her husband was the Titan Epimetheus, the brother of Prometheus (who had stolen fire from the gods to bring light to humankind in the first days of creation), and the son of Japetus. Milton identifies the Greek god as the same as Noah's son Japeth.

Thy goodness infinite, both when we wake,
And when we seek, as now, thy gift of sleep.   605
    This said unanimous, and other Rites
Observing none, but adoration pure
Which God likes best, into their inmost bow'r
Handed they went; and eased the putting off
These troublesome disguises which we wear,   610
Straight side by side were laid, nor turned I ween
Adam from his fair Spouse, nor *Eve* the Rites
Mysterious of connubial Love refused:
Whatever Hypocrites austerely talk
Of purity and place and innocence,   615
Defaming as impure what God declares
Pure, and commands to some, leaves free to all.
Our Maker bids increase, who bids abstain
But our destroyer, foe to God and Man?

➤ Sir John Denham (1615–1669)

Born in Dublin but raised in London, John Denham attended Trinity College, Oxford and later studied law at Lincoln's Inn. In 1639, he inherited his father's vast estate, including the lands from and about which his best-known poem, "Cooper's Hill," is written. A Royalist, Denham's property was confiscated in the early years of the Civil War, and he later went into exile in Europe with the future Charles II. After the Restoration of 1660, Denham was amply rewarded for his loyalty. He was knighted and given an important government sinecure. In the last years of his life, he married a very young woman, apparently went insane for a time, and was suspected of having poisoned his wife. He is buried in Westminster Abbey.

Although he wrote a variety of other prose and verse, "Cooper's Hill" is Denham's major work, and it exerted a profound influence on later eighteenth-century poetic style. He began work on the poem in 1641, and a pirated first edition appeared in 1642. "Cooper's Hill" is variously classified as a topographical–reflective poem, a descriptive–meditative poem, or a prospect poem. Its precedents include Jonson's "To Penshurst," and its influence is widespread, encompassing Richard Jago's "Edge-hill" and Alexander Pope's "Windsor Forest." The premise of the poem is simple: The poet surveys the landscape surrounding his elevated position on a hill near his family's estate. Looking down upon the Thames Valley, the poet is inspired with a variety of thoughts. However, these thoughts are almost entirely political and historical. Unlike later Romantic poets who would look to the landscape to find a reflection of their inner emotions, there is almost nothing personal in Denham's view of his environment. Stylistically, Denham's use of rhymed couplets was an important innovation in the history of British poetry. The ordered form of the couplets parallels the desire to see harmony in the landscape. Denham's goal is to have his poetry follow the natural order of the world he sees around him, as he says in the famous address in the poem to the river Thames, "O, could I flow like thee."

Cooper's Hill

Sure there are Poets which did never dream
Upon *Parnassus*, nor did taste the stream
Of *Helicon*,[1] we therefore may suppose
Those made not Poets, but the Poets those.
And as Courts make not Kings, but Kings the Court,   5
So where the Muses and their train resort,
Parnassus stands; if I can be to thee
A Poet, thou *Parnassus* art to me.
Nor wonder, if (advantaged in my flight,
By taking wing from thy auspicious height)   10
Through untraced ways, and airy paths I fly,
More boundless in my Fancy than my eye:
My eye, which swift as thought contracts the space
That lies between, and first salutes the place
Crowned with that sacred pile, so vast, so high,   15
That whether 'tis a part of Earth, or sky,
Uncertain seems, and may be thought a proud
Aspiring mountain, or descending cloud,
Paul's, the late theme of such a Muse whose flight
Has bravely reached and soared above thy height:[2]   20
Now shalt thou stand though sword, or time, or fire,
Or zeal more fierce than they, thy fall conspire,
Secure, whilst thee the best of Poets sings,
Preserved from ruin by the best of Kings.
Under his proud survey the City lies,   25
And like a mist beneath a hill doth rise;
Whose state and wealth the business and the crowd,
Seems at this distance but a darker cloud:
And is to him who rightly things esteems,
No other in effect than what it seems: 30
Where, with like hast, though several ways, they run
Some to undo, and some to be undone;
While luxury, and wealth, like war and peace,
Are each the other's ruin, and increase;
As Rivers lost in Seas some secret vein   35
Thence reconveys, there to be lost again.
Oh happiness of sweet retired content!
To be at once secure, and innocent.
Windsor[3] the next (where *Mars* with *Venus* dwells.

---

[1] Parnassus and Helicon are mountains in Greece that were thought in ancient times to be sacred to Apollo and the Muses, the deities of poetry.

[2] These last two lines allude to Edmund Waller's poem "Upon His Majesty's Repairing of Paul's" (1640).

[3] Windsor Castle, the home of the king, Charles I (here called "Mars"), and his queen, Henrietta Maria ("Venus"), is to the west of Cooper's Hill.

Beauty with strength) above the Valley swells   40
Into my eye, and doth itself present
With such an easy and unforced ascent,
That no stupendious precipice denies
Access, no horror turns away our eyes:
But such a Rise, as doth at once invite   45
A pleasure, and a reverence from the sight.
Thy mighty Master's Emblem, in whose face
Sate meekness, height'ned with Majestick Grace
Such seems thy gentle height, made only proud
To be the basis of that pompous load,   50
Than which, a nobler weight no Mountain bears,
But *Atlas*[4] only that supports the Spheres.
When Nature's hand this ground did thus advance,
'Twas guided by a wiser power than Chance;
Marked out for such a use, as if 'twere meant   55
T' invite the builder, and his choice prevent.
Nor can we call it choice, when what we choose,
Folly, or blindness only could refuse.
A Crown of such Majestick tow'rs doth Grace
The Gods' great Mother,[5] when her heavenly race   60
Do homage to her, yet she cannot boast
Amongst that numerous, and Celestial host,
More Heroes than can *Windsor*, nor doth Fame's
Immortal book record more noble names.
Not to look back so far, to whom this Isle   65
Owes the first Glory of so brave a pile,
Whether to *Caesar*, *Albanact*, or *Brute*,[6]
The British *Arthur*, or the Danish *Knute*,[7]
(Though this of old no less contest did move,
Then when for *Homer*'s birth seven Cities strove)[8]   70
(Like him in birth, thou should'st be like in fame,
As thine his fate, if mine had been his Flame)
But whosoere it was, Nature designed
First a brave place, and then as brave a mind.
Not to recount those several Kings, to whom   75
It gave a Cradle, or to whom a Tomb,
But thee (great *Edward*) and thy greater son.[9]

---

[4] Atlas was a classical Greek god who was punished by Zeus and condemned to carry the earth on his back.

[5] The goddess Rhea was mother to the Greek gods of Olympus; in Asia she was called Cybele.

[6] All three are historical or legendary Roman conquerors: Brute was the grandson of Rome's mythic founder, Aeneas. He is said to be the first Roman to come to England. Albanact was his son, who with his brothers conquered all of England, Scotland, and Wales.

[7] Knute was the king of England from 1018 to 1035.

[8] Seven different Greek cities claim to be the birthplace of the great epic poet.

[9] King Edward III.

(The lilies which his Father wore, he won)
And thy *Bellona*,[10] who the Consort came
Not only to thy Bed, but to thy Fame,   80
She to thy Triumph led one Captive King,[11]
And brought that son, which did the second[12] bring.
Then didst thou found that Order[13] (whither love
Or victory thy Royal thoughts did move)
Each was a noble cause, and nothing less,   85
Than the design, has been the great success:
Which foreign Kings, and Emperors esteem
The second honour to their Diadem.
Had thy great Destiny but given thee skill,
To know as well, as power to act her will,   90
That from those Kings, who then thy captives were,
In after-times should spring a Royal pair[14]
Who should possess all that thy mighty power,
Or thy desires more mighty, did devour;
To whom their better Fate reserves whate'er   95
The Victor hopes for, or the Vanquisht fear;
That blood, which thou and thy great Grandsire shed,
And all that since these sister Nations bled,
Had been unspilt, had happy *Edward* known
That all the blood he spilt, had been his own.   100
When he that Patron chose,[15] in whom are joined
Soldier and Martyr, and his arms confined
Within the Azure Circle, he did seem
But to foretell, and prophesy of him,[16]
Who to his Realms that Azure round hath joined,   105
Which Nature for their bound at first designed.
That bound, which to the World's extremest ends,
Endless itself, its liquid arms extends;
Nor doth he need those Emblems which we paint,
But is himself the Soldier and the Saint.   110
Here should my wonder dwell, and here my praise,
But my fixt thoughts my wand'ring eye betrays,
Viewing a neighbouring hill, whose top of late
A Chapel crowned, till in the Common Fate,

[10] A reference to Queen Philippa; Bellona was a Roman war goddess.
[11] King Edward captured King David II of Scotland in 1346.
[12] King Edward captured King John II of France at Poitiers.
[13] In about 1349, King Edward III founded the Order of the Garter, the highest order of British knighthood.
[14] A reference to King Charles I and Queen Henrietta Maria.
[15] *Patron chose:* St. George.
[16] Another reference to King Charles. I

The adjoining Abbey[17] fell: (may no such storm   115
Fall on our times, where ruin must reform.)
Tell me (my Muse) what monstrous dire offence,
What crime could any Christian King incense
To such a rage? Was 't Luxury, or Lust?
Was he so temperate, so chaste, so just?   120
Were these their crimes? They were his own much more:
But wealth is Crime enough to him that's poor,
Who having spent the Treasures of his Crown,
Condemns their Luxury to feed his own.
And yet this Act, to varnish o'er the shame   125
Of sacrilege, must bear devotion's name.
No Crime so bold, but would be understood
A real, or at least a seeming good.
Who fears not to do ill, yet fears the Name,
And free from Conscience, is a slave to Fame.   130
Thus he the Church at once protects and spoils:
But Princes' swords are sharper than their stiles.
And thus to th' ages past he makes amends,
Their Charity destroys, their Faith defends.
Then did Religion in a lazy Cell,   135
In empty, airy contemplations dwell;
And like the block, unmoved lay: but ours,
As much too active, like the stork devours.
Is there no temperate Region can be known,
Betwixt their Frigid, and our Torrid Zone?   140
Could we not wake from that Lethargick dream,
But to be restless in a worse extreme?
And for that Lethargy was there no cure,
But to be cast into a Calenture?
Can knowledge have no bound, but must advance   145
So far, to make us wish for ignorance?
And rather in the dark to grope our way,
Than led by a false guide to err by day?
Who sees these dismal heaps, but would demand
What barbarous Invader sackt the land?   150
But when he hears, no Goth, no Turk did bring
This desolation, but a Christian King;
When nothing, but the Name of Zeal, appears
'Twixt our best actions and the worst of theirs,
What does he think our Sacrilege would spare,   155
When such th' effects of our devotions are?

---

[17] Chertsey Abbey was seized when, during the reign of Henry VIII, the Catholic monasteries were dissolved. The lines that follow offer a criticism of the actions of Henry VIII.

Parting from thence 'twixt anger, shame, and fear,
Those for what's passed, and this for what's too near:
My eye descending from the Hill, surveys
Where *Thames* amongst the wanton valleys strays.   160
Thames, the most loved of all the Ocean's sons,
By his old Sire to his embraces runs,
Hasting to pay his tribute to the Sea,
Like mortal life to meet Eternity.
Though with those streams he no resemblance hold,   165
Whose foam is Amber, and their Gravel Gold;
His genuine, and less guilty wealth t' explore,
Search not his bottom, but survey his shore;
O'er which he kindly spreads his spacious wing,
And hatches plenty for th' ensuing Spring.   170
Nor then destroys it with too fond a stay,
Like Mothers which their Infants overlay.
Nor with a sudden and impetuous wave,
Like profuse King, resumes the wealth he gave.
No unexpected inundations spoil   175
The mower's hopes, nor mock the plowman's toil:
But God-like his unwearied Bounty flows;
First loves to do, then loves the Good he does.
Nor are his Blessings to his banks confined,
But free, and common, as the Sea or Wind;   180
When he to boast, or to disperse his stores
Full of the tributes of his grateful shores,
Visits the world, and in his flying towers
Brings home to us, and makes both *Indies* ours;
Finds wealth where 'tis, bestows it where it wants   185
Cities in deserts, woods in Cities plants.
So that to us no thing, no place is strange,
While his fair bosom is the world's exchange.
O could I flow like thee, and make thy stream
My great example, as it is my theme!   190
Though deep, yet clear, though gentle, yet not dull,
Strong without rage, without o'er-flowing full.
Heaven her *Eridanus*[18] no more shall boast,
Whose Fame in thine, like lesser Currents lost,   195
Thy Nobler streams shall visit *Jove*'s[19] abodes,
To shine amongst the Stars, and bathe the Gods.
Here Nature, whether more intent to please
Us or herself, with strange varieties,

[18] The Milky Way (a "river" of stars).
[19] Jupiter, chief Roman god.

(For things of wonder give no less delight
To the wise Maker's, than beholder's sight. 200
Though these delights from several causes move
For so our children, thus our friends we love)
Wisely she knew, the harmony of things,
As well as that of sounds, from discords springs.
Such was the discord, which did first disperse 205
Form, order, beauty through the Universe;
While dryness moisture, coldness heat resists,
All that we have, and that we are, subsists.
While the steep horrid roughness of the Wood
Strives with the gentle calmness of the flood. 210
Such huge extremes when Nature doth unite,
Wonder from thence results, from thence delight.
The stream is so transparent, pure, and clear,
That had the self-enamoured youth[20] gazed here,
So fatally deceived he had not been, 215
While he the bottom, not his face had seen.
But his proud head the airy Mountain hides
Among the Clouds; his shoulders, and his sides
A shady mantle clothes; his curled brows
Frown on the gentle stream, which calmly flows, 220
While winds and storms his lofty forehead beat:
The common fate of all that's high or great.
Low at his foot a spacious plain is placed,
Between the mountain and the stream embraced:
Which shade and shelter from the Hill derives, 225
While the kind river wealth and beauty gives;
And in the mixture of all these appears
Variety, which all the rest endears.
This scene had some bold Greek, or British Bard
Beheld of old, what stories had we heard, 230
Of Fairies, Satyrs, and the Nymphs their Dames,
Their feasts, their revels, and their amorous flames:
'Tis still the same, although their airy shape
All but a quick Poetick sight escape.
There *Faunus* and *Sylvanus*[21] keep their Courts, 235
And thither all the horned host resorts,
To graze the ranker mead, that noble herd
On whose sublime and shady fronts is reared
Nature's great Masterpiece; to show how soon
Great things are made, but sooner are undone. 240
Here have I seen the King, when great affairs

---

[20] A reference to the myth of Narcissus.
[21] *Faunus and Sylvanus:* woodland dieties.

Give leave to slacken, and unbend his cares,
Attended to the Chase by all the flower
Of youth, whose hopes a Nobler prey devour:
Pleasure with Praise, and danger, they would buy,   245
And wish a foe that would not only fly.
The stag now conscious of his fatal Growth,
At once indulgent to his fear and sloth,
To some dark covert his retreat had made,
Where nor man's eye, nor heaven's should invade   250
His soft repose; when th' unexpected sound
Of dogs, and men, his wakeful ear doth wound.
Roused with the noise, he scarce believes his ear,
Willing to think th' illusions of his fear
Had given this false Alarm, but straight his view   255
Confirms, that more than all he fears is true.
Betrayed in all his strengths, the wood beset,
All instruments, all Arts of ruin met;
He calls to mind his strength, and then his speed,
His winged heels, and then his armed head;   260
With these t' avoid, with that his Fate to meet:
But fear prevails, and bids him trust his feet.
So fast he flies, that his reviewing eye
Has lost the chasers, and his ear the cry;
Exulting, till he finds, their Nobler sense   265
Their disproportioned speed does recompense.
Then curses his conspiring feet, whose scent
Betrays that safety which their swiftness lent.
Then tries his friends, among the baser herd,
Where he so lately was obeyed, and feared,   270
His safety seeks: the herd, unkindly wise,
Or chases him from thence, or from him flies.
Like a declining Statesman, left forlorn
To his friends' pity, and pursuers' scorn,   275
With shame remembers, while himself was one
Of the same herd, himself the same had done.
Thence to the coverts, and the conscious Groves,
The scenes of his past triumphs, and his loves;
Sadly surveying where he ranged alone
Prince of the soil, and all the herd his own;   280
And like a bold Knight Errant did proclaim
Combat to all, and bore away the Dame;
And taught the woods to echo to the stream
His dreadful challenge, and his clashing beam.
Yet faintly now declines the fatal strife;   285
So much his love was dearer than his life.
Now every leaf, and every moving breath

Presents a foe, and every foe a death.
Wearied, forsaken, and pursued, at last
All safety in despair of safety placed,   290
Courage he thence resumes, resolved to bear
All their assaults, since 'tis in vain to fear.
And now too late he wishes for the fight
That strength he wasted in Ignoble flight:
But when he sees the eager chase renewed,   295
Himself by dogs, the dogs by men pursued:
He straight revokes his bold resolve, and more
Repents his courage, than his fear before;
Finds that uncertain ways unsafest are,
And Doubt a greater mischief than Despair.   300
Then to the stream, when neither friends, nor force,
Nor speed, nor Art avail, he shapes his course;
Thinks not their rage so desperate t' assay
An Element more merciless than they.
But fearless they pursue, nor can the flood   305
Quench their dire thirst; alas, they thirst for blood.
So towards a Ship the oar-finned Galleys ply,
Which wanting Sea to ride, or wind to fly,
Stands but to fall revenged on those that dare
Tempt the last fury of extreme despair.   310
So fares the Stag among th' enraged Hounds,
Repels their force, and wounds returns for wounds.
And as a Hero, whom his baser foes
In troops surround, now these assails, now those,
Though prodigal of life, disdains to die   315
By common hands; but if he can descry
Some nobler foes approach, to him he calls,
And begs his Fate, and then contented falls.
So when the King a mortal shaft lets fly
From his unerring hand, then glad to die,   320
Proud of the wound, to it resigns his blood,
And stains the Crystal with a Purple flood.
This a more Innocent, and happy chase,
Than when of old, but in the self-same place,
Fair liberty pursued, and meant a Prey   325
To lawless power, here turned, and stood at bay.
When in that remedy all hope was placed
Which was, or should have been at least, the last.
Here was that Charter[22] sealed, wherein the Crown
All marks of Arbitrary power lays down: 330
Tyrant and slave; those names of hate and fear,

[22] The Magna Carta.

The happier style of King and Subject bear:
Happy, when both to the same Center move,
When Kings give liberty, and Subjects love.
Therefore not long in force this Charter stood; 335
Wanting that seal, it must be sealed in blood.
The Subjects armed, the more their Princes gave,
Th' advantage only took the more to crave.
Till Kings by giving, give themselves away,
And even that power, that should deny, betray. 340
"Who gives constrained, but his own fear reviles
Not thanked, but scorned; nor are they gifts, but spoils."[23]
Thus Kings, by grasping more than they could hold,
First made their Subjects by oppression bold:
And popular sway, by forcing Kings to give 345
More than was fit for Subjects to receive,
Ran to the same extremes; and one excess
Made both, by striving to be greater, less.
When a calm River raised with sudden rains,
Or Snows dissolved, o'erflows th' adjoining Plains, 350
The Husbandmen with high-raised banks secure
Their greedy hopes, and this he can endure.
But if with Bays and Dams they strive to force
His channel to a new, or narrow course;
No longer then within his banks he dwells, 355
First to a Torrent, then a Deluge swells:
Stronger, and fiercer by restraint he roars,
And knows no bound, but makes his power his shores.

❧ *Abraham Cowley* (1618–1667)

Something of a child prodigy, Abraham Cowley (pronounced "Cooley") wrote his first verse at age ten, and had published his first collection, Poetic Blossoms *(1633), by the age of fifteen. He received B.A. and M.A. degrees from Cambridge, and with the start of the English Civil War, joined the royalist cause. Along with writing political prose and poetry in support of the king, like Sir John Denham, he also served the court in exile and was (for a time) a spy in its cause. Unlike Denham, however, he was not very well rewarded for his support, and he spent the remaining years of his life in rural retirement. Although Cowley wrote in a variety of genres, including dramatic and epic modes, his lyrics are the only works that have found a more enduring readership. Cowley's style is modeled on Donne; this is in evidence, for example, in "The Grasshopper," in which he wittily and surprisingly depicts the common insect as the embodiment of the*

---

[23] The speaker of these lines is unidentified.

*possibilities of true happiness. The poem is comparable to Lovelace's "The Grasshopper,"
both of which are modeled on the work of the classical poet Anacreon. Cowley's poem
on spring resembles Carew's poem of the same title, developing similar themes with
similar images.*

The Grasshopper

Happy *Insect*, what can be
In happiness compared to Thee?
Fed with nourishment divine,
The dewy *Mornings* gentle *Wine!*
Nature waits upon thee still,   5
And thy verdant Cup does fill,
'Tis filled where ever thou dost tread,
Nature self's *thy Ganimed.*[1]
Thou dost drink, and dance, and sing;
Happier than the happiest *King!*   10
All the *Fields* which thou dost see,
All the *Plants* belong to *Thee*,
All that *Summer Hours* produce,
Fertile made with early juice.
Man for thee does sow and plow;   15
Farmer He, and *Landlord Thou!*
Thou dost innocently joy;
Nor does thy *Luxury* destroy;
The *Shepherd* gladly heareth thee,
More *Harmonious* than *He*.   20
Thee Country Hinds with gladness hear,
Prophet of the ripened year!
Thee *Phoebus*[2] loves, and does inspire;
Phoebus is himself thy *Sire*.
To thee of all things upon earth,   25
Life is no longer then thy *Mirth*.
Happy *Insect*, happy Thou,
Dost neither *Age*, nor *Winter* know.
But when thou'st drunk, and danced, and sung,
Thy fill, the flow'ry Leaves among   30
(*Voluptuous*, and *Wise* with all,
Epicuraean Animal!)
Sated with thy *Summer Feast*,
Thou retirest to endless *Rest*.

---

[1] Also spelled Ganymede; a Trojan youth so beautiful that Zeus abducted him and made him cupbearer to the gods of Olympus.

[2] Epithet (meaning "shining") for Apollo, the ancient Greco-Roman god of poetry.

The Spring

1

Though you be absent here, I needs must say
The *Trees* as beauteous are, and *flowers* as gay,
    As ever they were wont to be;
    Nay the *Birds* rural musick too
    Is as melodious and free,   5
    As if they sung to pleasure you:
I saw a *Rose-Bud* ope this morn; I'll swear
The blushing *Morning* opened not more fair.

2

How could it be so fair, and you away?
How could the *Trees* be beauteous, *Flowers* so gay?   10
    Could they remember but last year,
    How *you* did *Them*, *They you* delight,
    The sprouting leaves which saw you here,
    And called their *Fellows* to the sight,
Would, looking round for the same sight in vain,   15
Creep back into their silent *Barks* again.

3

Where e'er you walked trees were as reverend made,
As when of old *Gods* dwelt in every shade.
    Is 't possible they should not know,
    What loss of honor they sustain,   20
    That thus they smile and flourish now,
    And still their former pride retain?
Dull *Creatures!* 'tis not without *Cause* that she,
Who fled the *God of wit*, was made a *Tree*.

4

In ancient times sure they much wiser were,   25
When they rejoiced the *Thracian* verse to hear;
    In vain did *Nature* bid them stay,
    When *Orpheus*[1] had his song begun,
    They called their wondring *roots* away,
    And bad them silent to him run.   30
How would those learned trees have followed you?
You would have drawn *Them*, and their *Poet* too.

---

[1] Thrace is region of ancient Greece; in Greek mythology, Orpheus, son of Apollo and Calliope, was a master musician and lyre-player whose music had magical properties.

5

But who can blame them now? for, since you're gone,
They're here the *only Fair*, and *Shine alone*.
    You did their *Natural Rights* invade;   35
    Where ever you did walk or sit,
    The thickest Boughs could make no *shade*,
    Although the Sun had granted it:
The fairest *Flowers* could please no more, near you,
Than *Painted Flowers*, set next to them, could do.   40

6

When e'er then you come hither, that shall be
The time, which this to others is, to *Me*.
    The little joys which here are now,
    The name of Punishments do bear;
    When by their sight they let us know   45
    How we deprived of greater are.
'Tis you the best of *Seasons* with you bring;
This is for *Beasts*, and that for *Men* the *Spring*.

Richard Lovelace (1618–1657)

Richard Lovelace was by all accounts a handsome, chivalrous, and dashing figure, which has led to his continuing reputation as the prototypical Cavalier, or courtly, poet of his age. Educated for a time at Oxford, he entered military service in support of the king and was among the Royalists during the English Civil War. His loyalty, however, landed him in prison twice, first in 1642 and again in 1648. During the latter stint, he prepared his collection of poems, Lucasta; Epodes, Odes, Sonnets, Songs etc., *which contains many of his best-known lyrics. Released from prison, and having sold all of his possessions in support of the royalist cause, Lovelace died in penury, before he could reap the potential rewards for his service that likely would have come after the Restoration. Like many of his contemporaries, Lovelace uses nature—and most particularly, animals—as emblems. His poems on the grasshopper, the snail, or the ant are less about nature itself than about turning to nature and nature's creatures to illustrate or argue moral and political positions. Like Cowley's, Lovelace's poem on the grasshopper is modeled on that of the Greek poet Anacreon. According to Anacreon, and also in Aesop's fables, the grasshopper is a symbol of carefree enjoyment of life, given to the indulgences of drinking and song. In many respects, then, the grasshopper represents a figure for Cavalier ideas of the good life—a life that was irrevocably lost during the period of the Puritan Commonwealth.*

The Grasshopper

To My Noble Friend, Mr. Charles Cotton[1]

Ode

1

Oh thou that swing'st upon the waving hair
    Of some well-fillèd Oaten Beard,
Drunk every night with a Delicious tear
    Dropt thee from Heaven, where now th' art reared.

2

The Joys of Earth and Air are thine entire,   5
    That with thy feet and wings dost hop and fly;
And when thy Poppy works thou dost retire
    To thy Carved Acorn-bed to lie.

3

Up with the Day, the Sun thou welcom'st then,
    Sport'st in the gilt-plats[2] of his Beams,   10
And all these merry days mak'st merry men,
    Thyself, and Melancholy streams.

4

But ah the Sickle! Golden Ears are Cropped;
    Ceres and *Bacchus*[3] bid goodnight;
Sharp frosty fingers all your Flow'rs have topt,   15
    And what scythes spared, Winds shave off quite.

5

Poor verdant fool! and now green Ice! thy Joys
    Large and as lasting, as thy Perch of Grass,
Bid us lay in 'gainst Winter, Rain, and poise[4]
    Their floods with an o'erflowing glass.   20

---

[1] The father of the poet Charles Cotton (1630–1687).

[2] Gilt, or golden braids, a symbol of sunbeams.

[3] Both are classical fertility dieties: Ceres is the goddess of the grain harvest, and Bacchus is the god of the grape harvest.

[4] Balance, or counterpoise.

6

Thou best of *Men* and *Friends!* we will create
  A Genuine Summer in each other's breast;
And spite of this cold Time and frozen Fate
  Thaw us a warm seat to our rest.

7

Our sacred hearths shall burn eternally   25
  As Vestal Flames,[5] the North Wind, he
Shall strike his frost-stretched Wings, dissolve, and fly
  This *Etna* in Epitome.

8

Dropping *December* shall come weeping in,
  Bewail th' usurping of his Reign;   30
But when in showers of old Greek we begin,
  Shall cry, he hath his Crown again!

9

Night as clear *Hesper*[6] shall our Tapers whip
  From the light Casements where we play,
And the dark Hag from her black mantle strip,   35
  And stick there everlasting Day.

10

Thus richer than untempted Kings are we,
  That asking nothing, nothing need:
Though Lord of all that Seas embrace; yet he
  That wants himself, is poor indeed.   40

[5] A reference to the flames at the ancient temple of Vesta, Roman goddess of the hearth and home.
[6] The evening star.

The Ant

1

Forbear thou great good Husband, little Ant;
  A little respite from thy flood of sweat;
Thou, thine own Horse and Cart, under this Plant

Thy spacious tent, fan thy prodigious heat;
Down with thy double load of that one grain;   5
It is a Granary for all thy Train.

2

Cease large example of wise thrift a while,
   (For thy example is become our Law)
And teach thy frowns a seasonable smile:
   So *Cato*[1] sometimes the naked Florals saw.   10
And thou almighty foe, lay by thy sting,
Whil'st thy unpayed Musicians, Crickets, sing.

3

Lucasta,[2] She that holy makes the Day,
   And 'stills new Life in fields of Fueillemort:[3]
Hath back restored their Verdure with one Ray,   15
   And with her Eye bid all to play and sport.
Ant to work still; Age will Thee Truant call;
And to save now, th' art worse than prodigal.

4

Austere and *Cynic!* not one hour t' allow,
   To lose with pleasure what thou got'st with pain: 20
But drive on sacred Festivals, thy Plow;
   Tearing high-ways with thy o'recharged Wain.
Not all thy lifetime one poor Minute live,
And thy o'er laboured Bulk with mirth relieve?

5

Look up then miserable Ant, and spy   25
   Thy fatal foes, for breaking of her Law,
Hov'ring above thee, Madam, *Margaret Pie*,
   And her fierce Servant, Meagre, Sir *John Daw*:[4]
Thy Self and Storehouse now they do store up,
And thy whole Harvest too within their Crop.   30

[1] Roman philosopher.

[2] Lucasta is the addressee of many of Lovelace's poem. Her true identity remains unknown.

[3] French for "dead leaves."

[4] Formal names for the common birds, the magpie and the jackdaw.

6

Thus we unthrifty thrive within Earth's Tomb,
   For some more rav'nous and ambitious Jaw:
The *Grain* in th' *Ant*'s, the *Ant*'s in the *Pie*'s womb,
   The *Pie* in th' *Hawk*'s, the *Hawk*'s in th' *Eagle*'s maw:
So scattering to hoard 'gainst a long Day,   35
Thinking to save all, we cast all away.

The Snail

Wise Emblem of our Politic World,
Sage Snail, within thine own self curled;
Instruct me softly to make hast,
Whil'st these my Feet go slowly fast.
   Compendious Snail! thou seem'st to me,   5
Large *Euclid*'s[1] strict Epitome;
And in each Diagram, dost Fling
Thee from the point unto the Ring.
A Figure now Triangular,
An Oval now, and now a Square;   10
And then a Serpentine dost crawl
Now a straight Line, now crooked, now all.
   Preventing Rival of the Day,
Th' art up and openest thy Ray,
And ere the Morn cradles the Moon,   15
Th' art broke into a Beauteous Noon.
Then when the Sun sups in the Deep,
Thy Silver Horns ere *Cynthia*'s[2] peep;
And thou from thine own liquid Bed
New *Phoebus* heav'st thy pleasant Head.   20
   Who shall a Name for thee create,
Deep Riddle of Mysterious State?
Bold Nature that gives common Birth
To all products of Seas and Earth,
Of thee, as Earthquakes, is afraid,   25
Nor will thy dire Delivery aid.
   Thou thine own daughter then, and Sire,

---

[1] Euclid founded the discipline of geometry in the third century B.C.

[2] Cynthia (or Artemis) was the classical Greek goddess of the moon; her twin brother, Phoebus Apollo, was god of the sun.

That Son and Mother art entire,
That big still with thyself dost go,
And liv'st an aged Embryo;   30
That like the Cubs of *India*,
Thou from thyself a while dost play:
But frighted with a Dog or Gun,
In thine own Belly thou dost run,
And as thy House was thine own womb,   35
So thine own womb, concludes thy tomb.
    But now I must (analysed King)
Thy Economic Virtues sing;
Thou great stayed Husband still within,
Thou, thee, that's thine dost Discipline;   40
And when thou art to progress bent,
Thou mov'st thyself and tenement,
As Warlike *Scythians*[3] travailed, you
Remove your Men and City too;
Then after a sad Dearth and Rain,   45
Thou scatterest thy Silver Train;
And when the Trees grow naked and old,
Thou clothest them with Cloth of Gold,
Which from thy Bowels thou dost spin,
And draw from the rich Mines within.   50
    Now hast thou changed thee Saint; and made
Thyself a Fane[4] that's cupola'd;
And in thy wreathed Cloister thou
Walkest thine own Gray friar too;
Strickt, and locked up, th' art Hood all o'er   55
And ne'er Eliminat'st thy Door.
On Salads thou dost feed severe,
And 'stead of Beads thou drop'st a tear,
And when to rest, each calls the Bell,
Thou sleep'st within thy Marble Cell;   60
Where in dark contemplation placed,
The sweets of Nature thou dost taste;
Who now with Time thy days resolve,
And in a Jelly thee dissolve.
Like a shot Star, which doth repair   65
Upward, and Rarify the Air.

---

[3] An ancient people known for their fierceness in battle.
[4] A temple.

⮑ *John Evelyn* (1620–1706)

John Evelyn was the son of a wealthy landowner in the county of Surrey, England. He was educated at Oxford and the Middle Temple, London. Starting at age eleven, and continuing for the next fifty years, he kept a personal diary. First published in 1818, Evelyn's Diary *provides a fascinating record of people, places, and events that he witnessed during a turbulent period of English history. Evelyn also published over thirty books on fine arts, forestry, numismatics, and religion.*

In political outlook, Evelyn was a staunch Royalist. However, he decided not to join the royalist cause during the English Civil War, choosing instead to travel extensively through France and Italy. In 1647, during a sojourn in Paris, he married Mary Browne, the daughter of Charles I's diplomatic representative to France. Evelyn returned to England in 1652, acquiring his father-in-law's estate and settling into the life of a country gentleman. After the Restoration in 1660, Evelyn played a more active role in public affairs, serving on several royal commissions. He was appointed a founding member of the Royal Society in 1662, and in this capacity he published Sylva, or a Discourse of Forest-trees, and the Propagation of Timber *(1664). In this treatise, Evelyn advocated the replanting of woodlands devastated during the Civil Wars as a means of restoring the nation's defenses, particularly its navy and merchant marine. The book describes the various kinds of trees, their cultivation, and the best use for each kind of timber. Although it is mainly utilitarian in its purposes,* Sylva *also presents a philosophical and aesthetic justification for the reforestation of England, particularly in its fourth and final book, entitled* Dendrologia. An Historical Account of the Sacredness and Use of Standing Groves, *which first appeared in the second edition of 1670 and was greatly expanded in subsequent editions. In its final form,* Dendrologia *delves deeply into the ancient traditions of sacred groves, and it provides a classic argument for the creation of large open estates with parklike groves and tree-lined scenic vistas.* Sylva *provided a crucial impetus for the eighteenth-century shift in English taste away from walled formal gardens and toward a more open style of landscape design that involved the extensive planting of trees. Almost single-handedly, Evelyn's popular treatise created a vogue for forestry among the English gentry. It advocated a new way of seeing forests: not merely as game-hunting preserves or as sources of raw material but as places that have an intangible aesthetic value and an intrinsic sacred character, worthy of nurturance and preservation. Evelyn's* Sylva *foreshadows the development of a conservationist ethic in the management of forests and wildlands throughout the English-speaking world.*

From Sylva, or a Discourse of Forest-trees, and the Propagation of Timber

From Dendrologia. Book the Fourth. An Historical Account of the Sacredness and Use of Standing Groves

And thus have we finished what we esteemed necessary for the direction of planting, and the culture of trees and woods in general; whether for the raising of new, or preservation of the more antient and venerable shades, crowning the brows of lofty hills, or furnishing and adorning the more fruitful and humble plains, groves, and forests, such as were never prophaned by the inhumanity of edge-tools: Woods, whose original are as unknown as the Arcadians; like the goodly Cedars of Libanus, Psalm 104, *Arbores Dei*,[1] according to the Hebrew, for something doubtless which they noted in the genius of those venerable plants, besides their mere bulk and stature: And, verily, I cannot think to have well acquitted myself of this useful subject, till I shall have in some sort vindicated the honour of trees and woods, by showing my reader of what estimation they were of old for their divine, as well as civil uses; or at least refreshed both him and myself with what occurs of historical and instructive amongst the learned concerning them. And first, standing woods and forests were not only the original habitations of men, for defence and fortresses, but the first occasion of that speech, polity, and society which made them differ from beasts. This, the Architect Vitruvius ingeniously describes, where he tells us, that the violent percussion of one tree against another, forced by an impetuous wind, setting them on fire, the flame did not so much surprise and affright the salvage foresters as the warmth, which (after a little gazing at the unusual accident) they found so comfortable: This (says he) invited them to approach it nearer, and, as it spent and consumed, by signs and barbarous tones (which in process of time were formed into significant words) to encourage one another to supply it with fresh combustibles: By this accident the wild people, who before were afraid of one another, and dwelt asunder, began to find the benefit and sweetness of society, mutual assistance, and conversation; which they afterwards improved, by building houses with those trees, and dwelling nearer together. From these mean and imperfect beginnings they arrived in time to be authors of the most polished arts; they established laws, peopled nations, planted countries, and laid the foundation of all that order and magnificence which the succeeding ages have enjoyed. No more then let us admire the enormous moles and bridges of Caligula across to Baiae; or that of Trajan over the Danubius (stupendous work of stone and marble!) to the adverse shores; whilst our timber and our trees making us bridges to the furthest Indies and Antipodes, land us into new worlds. In a word, (and to speak a bold and noble truth) trees and woods have twice saved the whole world; first by the Ark, then by the Cross; making full amends for the evil fruit of the tree in Paradise, by that which was borne on the tree in Golgotha. But that we may give an account of the sacred and other uses of these venerable retirements, we will next proceed to describe what those places were. . . .

One thing more I think not impertinent to hint, before I take my leave of this Book, concerning the Use of Standing Groves: That in some places of the world they have no other water to drink than what their trees afford them; not only of their proper juice, (as we have noted) but from their attraction of the Evening Moisture, which impends in the shape of a cloud over them: Such a tuft of trees is in the island of Ferro; of which consult the learned Isaac Vossius upon Pomponius Mela, and Magnenus de Manna: The same likewise happeneth in the Indies;

---

[1] Trees of God (Latin).

so that if their woods were once destroyed, they might perish for want of rains; upon which account Barbados grows every year more torrid, and has not near the rain it formerly enjoyed when it was better furnished with trees; and so in Jamaica, at Gunaboa, the rains are observed to diminish as their plantations extend: The like I could tell you of some parts of England not far from hence.

And now, lastly, to encourage those to plant that have opportunity, and those who innocently and with reluctancy are forced to cut down, and endeavour to supply the waste with their utmost industry: It is observed, that such planters are often blessed with health and old age, according to that of the prophet Isaiah, 60.22, "The days of a tree are the days of my people." Of their extraordinary longevity we have given abundant instances in this Discourse; and it seems to be so universally remarked, that as Paulus Venetus (that great traveler) reports, the Tartarian Astrologers affirm, nothing contributes more to men's long lives than the planting of many trees. *Haec scripsi octogenarius,*[2] and shall, if God protract my years, and continue my health, be continually planting, till it shall please him to *transplant* me into those glorious regions above, the celestial paradise, planted with Perennial Groves and Trees, bearing immortal fruit; for such is the tree of life, which they who do his commandments have right to, Apoc. 22.2, 14, 20.

Thus my reader sees, and I acknowledge, how easy it is to be lost in the wood, and that I have hardly power to take off my pen whilst I am on this delightful subject; for what more august, more charming, and useful, than the culture and preservation of such goodly plantations:

> That shade to our grand-children give.

> Virgil

What affords so sweet and so agreeable refreshment to our industrious Woodman,

> When he his wearied limbs has laid
> Under a florid Platan's shade

> Claudian

or some other goodly-spreading tree, such as we told you stopt the legions of a proud Conqueror, and that the wise Socrates swear by?

But whilst we condemn this excess in them, Christians and true Philosophers may be instructed to make use of their enjoyments to better purposes, by contemplating the miracles of their production and structure. And what Mortal is there so perfect an Atomist, who will undertake to detect the thousandth part, or point, of so exile a grain, as that insensible rudiment, or rather halituous[3] spirit, which brings forth the lofty Fir-tree, and the spreading Oak? That trees of so enormous an height and magnitude, as we find some Elms, Planes, and Cypresses; that others hard as iron, and solid as marble, (for such the Indies furnish) should be swaddled and involved within so small a dimension, (if a point may be

---

[2] Latin: "I, an octogenarian, have written this [book]."
[3] Vaporous, charged with moist vapor.

said to have any) and in so weak and feeble a substance, without the least luxation,[4] confusion, or disorder of parts! That when they are buried in the moist womb of the earth, which so easily dissolves and corrupts substances so much harder, yet this, which is at first but a kind of tender mucilage, or rather rottenness, should be able in time to displace and rend asunder whole rocks of stone, and sometimes to cleave them beyond the force iron wedges, so as even to remove mountains! That our tree, like man, (whose inverted symbol he is) being sown in corruption, rises in glory; and by little and little ascending into an hard erect stem of comely dimensions, becometh a solid tower, as it were! And that this which but lately a single ant would easily have borne to his little cavern, should now become capable of resisting the fury, and braving the rage of the most impetuous storms. . . .

For is it not plainly astonishing, how these minute atoms, rather than visible eggs, should contain the fetus exquisitely formed, (even while yet wrapped in their fecundines, like infants in the animal womb) till growing too big for their dark confinements, they break forth, and after a while more distinctly display every limb and member compleatly perfect, with all their apparel, tire, and trim of beautiful and flourishing vegetables, endowed with all the qualities of the species?

Contemplate we again what it is which begins the motion, and kindles the flame of these *Automata*,[5] causing them first to radiate in the earth, and then to display their top in the air (so different poles, as I may call them, in such different mediums); what it is which imparts these elastic, peristaltic, and other motions, so very like to the sensible and perfectest animal, how they elect, and then introsume[6] their proper food, and give suck, as it were, to the yet tender infant, till it have strength and force to prey on, and digest the more solid juices of the earth; for then, and not till then, do the roots begin to harden. Consider we how they assimilate, separate, and distribute these several supplies; how they concoct, transmute, augment, produce, and nourish without separation of excrements (at least to us visible); how without violation of virginity they generate their like; whilst furnished with tubes, ovaries, umbilical, and other vessels, the principle of any species, they are safely reserved and nourished till delivered: By what exquisite percolations and fermentations they proceed; how for the heart, fibres, veins, nerves, valves, and anastomotas,[7] they are furnished with rind, branches, leaves, blossoms, and fruit; how their colour, taste, odour, and other stupendous qualities and distinct faculties, some of them so repugnant and contrary to others, yet in so uniform and successive a series, are elaborated, and all this performed in the dark, and secret recesses of nature. It is astonishing with what analogy the solider and inflexible parts of trees agree with the bones, ribs, vertebrae, &c. nay, how the more pliables fitted to such various motions accord with the very brains and marrow. This has induced some to allow them place amongst the class of animals.

[4] Dislocation.

[5] I.e., seeds, regarded as independent living things.

[6] Consume.

[7] Pores, outlets.

For their preservation, nature has invested the whole tribe and nation (as we may say) of vegetables, with garments suitable to their naked and exposed bodies, temper, and climate: Thus some are clad with a coarser, and resist all extremes of weather; others with more tender and delicate skins and scarfs, as it were, and thinner raiment . . . What shall we say of the mysterious forms, variety, and variegation of the leaves and flowers, contrived with such art, yet without art; some round, others long, oval, multiangular, indented, crisped, rough, smooth and polished, soft and flexible; at every tremulous blast, as if it would drop in a moment, and yet so obstinately adhering, as to be able to contest against the fiercest winds that prostrate mighty structures!—— There it abides till God bids it fall: For so the wise Disposer of things has placed it, not only for ornament, but use and protection both of body and fruit, from the excessive heat of summer, and colds of the sharpest winters, and their immediate impressions; as we find it in all such places and trees, as, like the blessed and good man, have always fruit upon them ripe, or preparing to mature, such as the Pine, Fir, Arbutus, Orange, and most of those which the Indies and more southern tracts plentifully abound in, where Nature provides this continual shelter, and clothes them with perennial garments.

But with what amazement do we consider what may be demonstrated of their innumerable (and next to infinite) number of seeds, which, in an Elm, for instance, of but one hundred years standing, which suppose to be the ordinary age of that species, would amount to 15,480,000,000. —Suppose then the tree to grow and multiply as many times, and every individual grain contain a second tree, including the like number, and so on by geometrical progression in squares and cubes. At what a loss must the most enlarged human capacity be at so stupendous a consideration!

Let us examine with what care the seeds, those little souls of plants, . . . in which the whole and complete tree, tho' invisible to our dull sense, is yet perfectly and entirely wrapped up, exposed, as they seem to be, to all those accidents of weather, storms, and rapacious birds, are yet preserved from avolation,[8] diminution, and detriment within their spiny, armed, and compacted receptacles; where they sleep as in their causes, till their prisons let them gently fall into the embraces of the earth, now made pregnant with the season, and ready for another burden: for at the time of year she fails not to bring them forth. With what delight have I beheld this tender and innumerable offspring repullulating[9] at the feet of an aged tree! from whence the suckers are drawn, transplanted, and educated by human industry, and, forgetting the ferity[10] of their nature, become civilized to all this employments.

Can we look on the prodigious quantity of liquor, which one poor wounded Birch will produce in a few hours, and not be astonished how some trees should, in so short a space, weep more than they weigh? And that so dry, so feeble, and wretched a branch, as that which bears the grape, should yield a juice that chears both God and Man? That the Pine, Fir, Larch, and other resinous trees, planted

---

[8] Dispersal (onto infertile ground); wastage.

[9] Budding, sprouting.

[10] Wildness.

in such rude and uncultivated places, amongst rocks and dry pumices, should transude[11] into turpentine, and pearl out into gums and precious balms?

In a word, so astonishing and wonderful is the organism, parts, and functions of plants and trees, that some have, as we said, attributed animal life to them, and conceived that they were living creatures; for so did Anaxagoras, Empedocles, and even Plato himself.

I am sure Plants and Trees afford more matter for Medicine, and the use of Man, than either Animals or Minerals, are more familiar at hand, and safe; and within this late age being wonderfully improved, increased and searched into, they seem, by the Divine Wisdom, an inexhaustible subject for our disquisition and admiration.

There are ten thousand considerations more, besides that of their medicinal and sanative[12] properties, and the mechanical uses mentioned in this Treatise, which a contemplative person may derive from the Groves and Woods; all of them the subject of wonder. And though he had only the Palm (which Strabo affirms is fit for three hundred and sixty uses) or the Coco, (which yields wine, bread, milk, oil, sugar, salt, vinegar, tinctures, tans, spices, thread, needles, linen, cloth, cups, dishes, spoons, and other vessels and utensils; baskets, mats, umbrellas, paper, brooms, ropes, sails, and almost all that belongs to the rigging of ships; in short, this single tree furnishing a great part of the world with all that even a voluptuous man can need, or almost desire) it were sufficient to employ his meditations and his hands, as long as he were to live, though his years were as many as the most aged Oak: So as *Fr. Hernandes, Gracilasco de la Vega*, and other Travellers speaking of the Coco, Aloes, Wild Pine of Jamaica, &c. affirm there is nothing necessary for life . . . which these Polychrests[13] afford not.

What may we say then of innumerable other trees, fitted for the uses nature has designed them, especially for timber, and all other fabrile[14] employments? ——But I cease to expatiate farther on these wonders, that I may not anticipate the pleasures with which the serious Contemplator on those stupendous works of Nature, or rather God of Nature, will find himself even rapt and transported, were his contemplations only applied to the production of a single *Wood*.

🕊 *Andrew Marvell* (1621–1678)

It is largely thanks to the greed of his former housekeeper (who claimed to be his wife), that many of Andrew Marvell's lyric poems saw their way into the literary canon. Better known as a social satirist in his own time, Marvell's magnificent and often complex lyric poetry was first published in 1681, when "Mrs. Marvell" saw an opportunity to make money from her association with her dead employer. A good portion of Marvell's biography

[11] Seep out through pores.
[12] Healthful.
[13] Plants suitable for many different uses.
[14] Artisanal: belonging to a skilled craftsman.

is obscure, for while he spent his career in public service of one kind or another, he managed also to keep his private life private. He came from a Calvinist family, though he is reputed to have experimented briefly with Roman Catholicism while a student at Cambridge. He was spared much of the early turmoil of the first years of the English Civil War because he was in Europe studying languages. On returning to England, he held a variety of positions, first as tutor to the daughter of the high-ranking Commonwealth general, who was the owner of Appleton House, and later to Oliver Cromwell's son-in-law. He became assistant Latin secretary to the Council of State (Milton had been the Latin secretary from the beginning of Cromwell's government but was blind) and took on the responsibilities in full in 1658. In 1659, he began serving as a member of Parliament, and later held a variety of diplomatic positions.

It is presumed that most of his lyric poetry dates from the period of the early 1650s, since Marvell's writing from the 1660s forward was of a more political nature. Despite his association with Cromwell, Marvell was spared punishment during the Restoration, although he continued to write satirically and critically about the monarchy. The lyric poetry included here employs a variety of styles and traditions and demonstrates Marvell's wit and versatility. "Nymph Complaining for the Death of Her Faun" belongs to a tradition, dating back to Ovid and Catullus, of poems mourning the loss of a pet. Yet the imagery of the poem, drawing upon the Old Testament Song of Songs and ancient mythology, prevents the poem from seeming maudlin and suggests deeper allegorical readings. Several of Marvell's poems seem to present different perspectives on the idea of the Garden as a place with a variety of possible allegorical significations. "The Mower Against Gardens" examines the possible moral corruption inherent in using art to improve on nature. The image of the garden in the poem "The Garden" resembles the prelapsarian Eden depicted by Milton, although here it is a place to be enjoyed in seclusion, without female companionship. In this garden, the poet can meditate upon the Creator by observing the beauty of the Creation. "Bermudas," though not explicitly about a garden, makes use of garden imagery to participate in a common Renaissance trope of viewing the New World as a Paradise Regained. The other Mower poems are more conventionally pastoral, using natural imagery in the service of their amatory themes. "Upon Appleton House" represents Marvell's contribution to the lineage of English country-house poetry (such as "To Penshurst") as well as topographical and locodescriptive poetry. The poem is comprised of several different tableaux, depicting not just the house but its history, its natural surroundings (woods, river, and fields), and its inhabitants. As with "Cooper's Hill," natural scenery often gives rise to historical or moral reflection, not personal introspection, as would later be the case in the Romantic era.

Bermudas

Where the remote *Bermudas* ride
In th' Ocean's bosom unespied,
From a small Boat, that rowed along,
The listening Winds received this Song.

"What should we do but sing his Praise   5
That led us through the watery Maze,

Unto an Isle so long unknown,
And yet far kinder than our own?
Where he the huge Sea-Monsters wracks,
That lift the Deep upon their Backs.   10
He lands us on a grassy Stage;
Safe from the Storms, and Prelate's[1] rage.
He gave us this eternal Spring,
Which here enamels every thing;
And sends the Fowls to us in care,   15
On daily Visits through the Air.
He hangs in shades the Orange bright,
Like golden Lamps in a green Night.
And does in the Pomgranates close,
Jewels more rich than *Ormus*[2] shows.   20
He makes the Figs our mouths to meet;
And throws the Melons at our feet.
But Apples plants of such a price,
No Tree could ever bear them twice.
With Cedars, chosen by his hand,   25
From *Lebanon*, he stores the Land.
And makes the hollow Seas, that roar,
Proclaim the Ambergris[3] on shore.
He cast (of which we rather boast)
The Gospel's Pearl upon our Coast.   30
And in these Rocks for us did frame
A Temple, where to sound his Name.
Oh let our Voice his Praise exalt,
Till it arrive at Heaven's Vault:
Which thence (perhaps) rebounding, may   35
Echo beyond the *Mexique Bay*."

    Thus sung they, in the *English* boat,
An holy and a cheerful Note,
And all the way, to guide their Chime,
With falling Oars they kept the time.   40

[1] Official of the Anglican Church, with which the speaker has broken.
[2] A Persian Gulf city known for its luxuries.
[3] Substance used to make perfumes.

Nymph Complaining for the Death of Her Faun

The wanton Troopers[1] riding by
Have shot my Faun and it will die.

[1] *The wanton Troopers:* soldiers who, during the English Civil War of 1642–47, fought against the king.

Ungentle men! They cannot thrive
To kill thee. Thou ne'er didst alive
Them any harm: alas nor could   5
Thy death yet do them any good.
I'm sure I never wisht them ill;
Nor do I for all this; nor will:
But, if my simple Pray'rs may yet
Prevail with Heaven to forget   10
Thy murder, I will join my Tears
Rather than fail. But, O my fears!
It cannot die so. Heaven's King
Keeps register of every thing:
And nothing may we use in vain.   15
Ev'n Beasts must be with justice slain;
Else Men are made their *Deodands*.[2]
Though they should wash their guilty hands
In this warm lifeblood, which doth part
From thine, and wound me to the Heart,   20
Yet could they not be clean: their Stain
Is dyed in such a Purple Grain.
There is not such another in
The World, to offer for their Sin.
    Unconstant *Sylvio*, when yet   25
I had not found him counterfeit,
One morning (I remember well)
Tied in this silver Chain and Bell,
Gave it to me: nay and I know
What he said then; I'm sure I do.   30
Said he, Look how your Huntsman here
Hath taught a Faun to hunt his *Dear*.
But *Sylvio* soon had me beguiled.
This waxéd tame, while he grew wild,
And quite regardless of my Smart,   35
Left me his Faun, but took his Heart.
    Thenceforth I set myself to play
My solitary time away,
With this: and very well content,
Could so mine idle Life have spent.   40
For it was full of sport; and light
Of foot, and heart; and did invite,
Me to its game: it seemed to bless
Itself in me. How could I less

---

[2] According to English law, if any animal caused a person's death, that animal was handed over to the king to be used for charitable purposes.

Than love it? O I cannot be   45
Unkind, t' a Beast that loveth me.
   Had it lived long, I do not know
Whether it too might have done so
As *Sylvio* did: his Gifts might be
Perhaps as false or more than he.   50
But I am sure, for ought that I
Could in so short a time espy,
Thy Love was far more better than
The love of false and cruel men.
   With sweetest milk, and sugar, first   55
I it at mine own fingers nurst.
And as it grew, so every day
It waxed more white and sweet than they.
It had so sweet a Breath! And oft
I blusht to see its foot more soft,   60
And white, (shall I say than my hand?)
Nay, any Lady's of the Land.
   It is a wond'rous thing, how fleet
'Twas on those little silver feet.
With what a pretty skipping grace,   65
It oft would challenge me the Race:
And when 't had left me far away,
'T would stay, and run again, and stay.
For it was nimbler much than Hinds;
And trod, as on the four Winds.   70
   I have a Garden of my own,
But so with Roses overgrown,
And Lilies, that you would it guess
To be a little Wilderness.
And all the Springtime of the year   75
It only lovèd to be there.
Among the beds of Lilies, I
Have sought it oft, where it should lie;
Yet could not, till itself would rise,
Find it, although before mine Eyes.   80
For, in the flaxen Lilies' shade,
It like a bank of Lilies laid.
Upon the Roses it would feed,
Until its Lips ev'n seemed to bleed:
And then to me 'twould boldly trip,   85
And print those Roses on my Lip.
But all its chief delight was still
On Roses thus itself to fill:
And its pure virgin Limbs to fold

In whitest sheets of Lilies cold.   90
Had it lived long, it would have been
Lilies without, Roses within.
    O help! O help! I see it faint:
And die as calmly as a Saint.
See how it weeps. The Tears do come   95
Sad, slowly dropping like a Gum.
So weeps the wounded Balsom: so
The holy Frankincense doth flow.
The brotherless *Heliades*[3]
Melt in such Amber Tears as these.   100
    I in a golden Vial will
Keep these two crystal Tears; and fill
It till it do o'erflow with mine;
Then place it in *Diana's*[4] Shrine.
    Now my Sweet Faun is vanished to   105
Whither the Swans and Turtles go:
In fair *Elisium* to endure,
With milk-white Lambs, and Ermines pure.
O do not run too fast: for I
Will but bespeak thy Grave, and die.   110
    First my unhappy Statue shall
Be cut in Marble; and withal,
Let it be weeping too: but there
Th' Engraver sure his Art may spare;
For I so truly thee bemoan,   115
That I shall weep though I be Stone:
Until my Tears, still dropping, wear
My breast, themselves engraving there.
There at my feet shalt thou be laid,
Of purest Alabaster made: 120
For I would have thine Image be
White as I can, though not as Thee.

[3] The daughters of the sun god, Helios, who were transformed into amber-dropping trees because of the tears they shed over the death of their brother Phaëthon.
[4] Roman goddess of the hunt.

The Mower Against Gardens

Luxurious Man, to bring his Vice in use,
    Did after him the World seduce:
And from the fields the Flow'rs and Plants allure,
    Where Nature was most plain and pure.

He first enclosed within the Garden's square   5
   A dead and standing pool of Air:
And a more luscious Earth for them did knead,
   Which stupified them while it fed.
The Pink grew then as double as his Mind;
   The nutriment did change the kind.   10
With strange perfumes he did the Roses taint.
   And Flow'rs themselves were taught to paint.[1]
The Tulip, white, did for complexion seek;
   And learned to interline its cheek:
Its Onion root they then so high did hold,   15
   That one was for a Meadow sold.
Another World was searched, through Oceans new,
   To find the *Marvel of Peru*.[2]
And yet these Rarities might be allowed,
   To Man, that sov'reign thing and proud;   20
Had he not dealt between the Bark and Tree,
   Forbidden mixtures there to see.
No Plant now knew the Stock from which it came;
   He grafts upon the Wild the Tame:
That the uncertain and adult'rate fruit   25
   Might put the Palate in dispute.
His green *Seraglio* has its Eunuchs too;
   Lest any Tyrant him outdo.
And in the Cherry he does Nature vex,
   To procreate without a Sex.   30
'Tis all enforced; the Fountain and the Grot;
   While the sweet Fields do lie forgot:
Where willing Nature does to all dispense
   A wild and fragrant Innocence:
And *Fauns* and *Fairies* do the Meadows till,   35
   More by their presence then their skill.
Their Statues polished by some ancient hand,
   May to adorn the Gardens stand:
But howsoe'er the Figures do excel,
   The *Gods* themselves with us do dwell.   40

[1] I.e., to put on makeup.

[2] An exotic and rare flower.

The Mower's Song

I

My Mind was once the true survey
Of all these Meadows fresh and gay;
And in the greenness of the Grass
Did see its Hopes as in a Glass;
When *Juliana* came, and She   5
What I do to the Grass, does to my Thoughts and Me.

2

But these, while I with Sorrow pine,
Grew more luxuriant still and fine;
That not one Blade of Grass you spied,
But had a Flower on either side;   10
When *Juliana* came, and She
What I do to the Grass, does to my Thoughts and Me.

3

Unthankful Meadows, could you so
A fellowship so true forego,
And in your gaudy May-games meet,   15
While I lay trodden under feet?
When *Juliana* came, and She
What I do to the Grass, does to my Thoughts and Me.

4

But what you in Compassion ought,
Shall now by my Revenge be wrought: 20
And Flow'rs, and Grass, and I and all,
Will in one common Ruin fall.
For *Juliana* comes, and She
What I do to the Grass, does to my Thoughts and Me.

5

And thus, ye Meadows, which have been   25
Companions of my thoughts more green,
Shall now the Heraldry become
With which I shall adorn my Tomb;
For *Juliana* comes, and She
What I do to the Grass, does to my Thoughts and Me.   30

The Garden

1

How vainly men themselves amaze
To win the Palm, the Oak, or Bays;[1]
And their uncessant Labours see
Crowned from some single Herb or Tree.
Whose short and narrow-vergèd Shade   5
Does prudently their Toils upbraid;
While all Flow'rs and all Trees do close
To weave the Garlands of repose.

2

Fair Quiet, have I found thee here,
And Innocence thy Sister dear!   10
Mistaken long, I sought you then
In busy Companies of Men.
Your sacred Plants, if here below,
Only among the Plants will grow.
Society is all but rude,   15
To this delicious Solitude.

3

No white nor red was ever seen
So am'rous as this lovely green.
Fond Lovers, cruel as their Flame,
Cut in these Trees their Mistress' name.   20
Little, Alas, they know, or heed,
How far these Beauties Hers exceed!
Fair Trees! wheresoe'er your barks I wound,
No Name shall but your own be found.

4

When we have run our Passion's heat,   25
Love hither makes his best retreat.
The *Gods*, that mortal Beauty chase,
Still in a Tree did end their race.

---

[1] In ancient times, crowns of one kind of these leaves were given to high achievers in war, diplomacy, and poetry, respectively.

Apollo hunted *Daphne*[2] so,
Only that She might Laurel grow.
And *Pan* did after *Syrinx*[3] speed,   30
Not as a Nymph, but for a Reed.

5

What wondrous Life in this I lead!
Ripe Apples drop about my head;
The Luscious Clusters of the Vine   35
Upon my Mouth do crush their Wine;
The Nectarine, and curious Peach,
Into my hands themselves do reach;
Stumbling on Melons, as I pass,
Insnared with Flow'rs, I fall on Grass.   40

6

Meanwhile the Mind, from pleasure less,
Withdraws into its happiness:
The Mind, that Ocean where each kind
Does straight its own resemblance find;
Yet it creates, transcending these,   45
Far other Worlds, and other Seas;
Annihilating all that's made
To a green Thought in a green Shade.

7

Here at the Fountain's sliding foot,
Or at some Fruit tree's mossy root,   50
Casting the Body's Vest aside,
My Soul into the boughs does glide:
There like a Bird it sits, and sings,
Then whets, and combs its silver Wings;
And, till prepared for longer flight,   55
Waves in its Plumes the various Light.

---

[2] In myth, Daphne is transformed into a tree to escape the advances of the god. The poem reverses the story, implying that the transformation was Apollo's intention.

[3] As in the myth of Daphne, Syrinx escaped from the amorous clutches of the god Pan and changed into a reed; the causality is again reversed.

8

Such was that happy Garden-state,
While Man there walked without a Mate:[4]
After a Place so pure, and sweet,
What other Help could yet be meet!   60
But 'twas beyond a Mortal's share
To wander solitary there:
Two Paradises 'twere in one
To live in Paradise alone.

9

How well the skillful Gardner drew   65
Of flow'rs and herbs this Dial[5] new;
Where from above the milder Sun
Does through a fragrant Zodiac run;
And, as it works, th' industrious Bee
Computes its time as well as we.   70
How could such sweet and wholesome Hours
Be reckoned but with herbs and flow'rs!

[4] I.e., the garden of Eden when Adam alone dwelt there.
[5] I.e., sundial.

From Upon Appleton House

To My Lord Fairfax

1

Within this sober Frame expect
Work of no Foreign *Architect*;
That unto Caves the Quarries drew,
And Forrests did to Pastures hew;
Who of his great Design in pain   5
Did for a Model vault his Brain,
Whose Columns should so high be raised
To arch the Brows that on them gazed.

2

Why should of all things Man unruled
Such unproportioned dwellings build?   10

The Beasts are by their Dens exprest:
And Birds contrive an equal Nest;
The low roofed Tortoises do dwell
In cases fit of Tortoise-shell:
No Creature loves an empty space;   15
Their Bodies measure out their Place.

3

But He, superfluously spread,
Demands more room alive than dead.
And in his hollow Palace goes
Where Winds as he themselves may lose.   20
What need of all this Marble Crust
T' impark the wanton Mote of Dust,
That thinks by Breadth the World t' unite
Though the first Builders failed in Height?[1]

4

But all things are composed here   25
Like Nature, orderly and near:
In which we the Dimensions find
Of that more sober Age and Mind,
When larger sized Men did stoop
To enter at a narrow loop;   30
As practicing, in doors so strait,
To strain themselves through *Heaven's Gate*.

5

And surely when the after Age
Shall hither come in Pilgrimage,
These sacred Places to adore,   35
By *Vere*[2] and *Fairfax* trod before,
Men will dispute how their Extent
Within such dwarfish Confines went:
And some will smile at this, as well
As *Romulus*[3] his Bee-like Cell.   40

[1] A reference to the biblical Tower of Babel.

[2] Ann Vere is Lady Fairfax, the mistress of the house.

[3] According to legend, one of the mythical twins who founded Rome.

6

Humility alone designs
Those short but admirable Lines,
By which, ungirt and unconstrained,
Things greater are in less contained,
Let others vainly strive t' immure   45
The *Circle* in the *Quadrature!*
These *holy Mathematicks* can
In ev'ry Figure equal Man.

7

Yet thus the laden House does sweat,
And scarce endures the *Master* great: 50
But where he comes the swelling Hall
Stirs, and the *Square* grows *Spherical;*[4]
More by his *Magnitude* distrest,
Than he is by its straitness prest:
And too officiously it slights   55
That in it self which him delights.

8

So Honour better Lowness bears,
Than That unwonted Greatness wears.
Height with a certain Grace does bend,
But low Things clownishly ascend.   60
And yet what needs there here Excuse,
Where ev'ry Thing does answer Use?
Where neatness nothing can condemn,
Nor Pride invent what to contemn?

9

A Stately *Frontispice of Poor*   65
Adorns without the open Door:
Nor less the Rooms within commends
Daily new *Furniture of Friends.*
The House was built upon the Place
Only as for *a Mark of Grace;*   70

---

[4] A circle symbolizes perfection, and a square symbolizes justice and rectitude.

And for an *Inn* to entertain
Its *Lord* a while, but not remain.

10

Him *Bishops-Hill*, or *Denton* may,
Or *Bilbrough*, better hold than they:
But Nature here hath been so free   75
As if she said leave this to me.
Art would more neatly have defaced
What she had laid so sweetly waste;
In fragrant Gardens, shady Woods,
Deep Meadows, and transparent Floods.   80

• • •

61

But I, retiring from the Flood,
Take Sanctuary in the Wood;
And, while it lasts, my self embark
In this yet green, yet growing Ark;
Where the first Carpenter[5] might best   485
Fit Timber for his Keel have Pressed.
And where all Creatures might have shares,
Although in Armies, not in Pairs.

62

The double Wood of ancient Stocks
Linked in so thick, an Union locks,   490
It like two *Pedigrees* appears,
On one hand *Fairfax*, th' other *Veres*:
Of whom though many fell in War,
Yet more to Heaven shooting are:
And, as they Nature's Cradle deckt,   495
Will in green Age her Hearse expect.

63

When first the Eye this Forrest sees
It seems indeed as *Wood* not *Trees*:

---

[5] Noah.

As if their Neighbourhood so old
To one great Trunk them all did mold.   500
There the huge Bulk takes place, as meant
To thrust up a *Fifth Element*;[6]
And stretches still so closely wedged
As if the Night within were hedged.

64

Dark all without it knits; within   505
It opens passable and thin;
And in as loose an order grows,
As the *Corinthean*[7] *Porticoes*.
The arching Boughs unite between
The Columns of the Temple green;   510
And underneath the winged Choirs
Echo about their tuned Fires.

65

The *Nightingale* does here make choice
To sing the Trials of her Voice.
Low Shrubs she sits in, and adorns   515
With Musick high the squatted Thorns.
But highest Oaks stoop down to hear,
And list'ning Elders prick the Ear.
The Thorn, lest it should hurt her, draws
Within the Skin its shrunken claws.   520

66

But I have for my Musick found
A Sadder, yet more pleasing Sound:
The *Stock doves*, whose fair necks are graced
With Nuptial Rings their Ensigns chaste;
Yet always, for some Cause unknown,   525
Sad pair unto the Elms they moan.
O why should such a Couple mourn,
That in so equal Flames do burn!

---

[6] Made of something unique and thus not of what were believed to be the four elements of created matter: earth, air, water, and fire.

[7] The most elaborate of the three styles or orders of classical architecture.

67

Then as I careless on the Bed
Of gelid *Strawberries* do tread,   530
And through the Hazels thick espy
The hatching *Throstle*'s shining Eye,
The *Heron* from the Ashe's top,
The eldest of its young lets drop,
As if it Stork-like did pretend   535
That *Tribute* to *its Lord* to send.

68

But most the *Hewel*'s[8] wonders are,
Who here has the *Holt-felster*'s[9] care.
He walks still upright from the Root,
Meas'ring the Timber with his Foot;   540
And all the way, to keep it clean,
Doth from the Bark the Wood-moths glean.
He, with his Beak, examines well
Which fit to stand and which to fell.

69

The good he numbers up, and hacks;   545
As if he marked them with the Ax.
But where he, tinkling with his Beak,
Does find the hollow Oak to speak,
That for his building he designs,
And through the tainted Side he mines.   550
Who could have thought the *tallest Oak*
Should fall by such a *feeble Stroke!*

70

Nor would it, had the Tree not fed
A *Traitor-worm*, within it bred.
(As first our *Flesh* corrupt within   555
Tempts impotent and bashful *Sin.*
And yet that *Worm* triumphs not long,
But serves to feed the *Hewel's young.*

---

[8] A green woodpecker.
[9] A woodcutter.

While the Oak seems to fall content,
Viewing the Treason's Punishment.   560

71

Thus I, *easy Philosopher,*
Among the *Birds* and *Trees* confer:
And little now to make me, wants
Or of the *Fowls,* or of the *Plants.*
Give me but Wings as they, and I   565
Straight floating on the Air shall fly:
Or turn me but, and you shall see
I was but an inverted Tree.

72

Already I begin to call
In their most learned Original: 570
And where I Language want, my Signs
The Bird upon the Bough divines;
And more attentive there doth sit
Then if She were with Lime-twigs knit.
No Leaf does tremble in the Wind   575
Which I returning cannot find.

73

Out of these scattered *Sibyl's*[10] Leaves
Strange *Prophecies* my Fancy weaves:
And in one History consumes,
Like *Mexique Paintings,* all the *Plumes.*   580
What *Rome, Greece, Palestine,* ere said
I in this light *Mosaick* read.
Thrice happy he who, not mistook,
Hath read in *Nature's mystick Book.*

74

And see how Chance's better Wit   585
Could with a Mask my studies hit!
The Oak-Leaves me embroider all,
Between which Caterpillar's crawl:

---

[10] An ancient prophetess who would inscribe her visions on leaves.

And Ivy, with familiar trails,
Me licks, and clasps, and curls, and hales.   590
Under this *antick Cope* I move
Like some great *Prelate*[11] *of the Grove,*

75

Then, languishing with ease, I toss
On Pallets swoln of Velvet Moss;
While the Wind, cooling through the Boughs,   595
Flatters with Air my panting Brows.
Thanks for my Rest ye *Mossy Banks,*
And unto you *cool Zephyrs,*[12] Thanks,
Who, as my Hair, my Thoughts too shed,
And winnow from the Chaff my Head.   600

76

How safe, methinks, and strong, behind
These Trees have I encamped my Mind;
Where Beauty, aiming at the Heart,
Bends in some Tree its useless Dart;
And where the World no certain Shot   605
Can make, or me it toucheth not.
But I on it securely play,
And gall its Horsemen all the Day.

77

Bind me ye *Woodbines* in your 'twines,
Curl me about ye gadding *Vines,*   610
And, Oh, so close your Circles lace,
That I may never leave this Place:
But, lest your Fetters prove too weak,
Ere I your Silken Bondage break,
Do you, *O Brambles,* chain me too,   615
And courteous *Briars* nail me through.

78

Here in the Morning tie my Chain,
Where the two Woods have made a Lane;

[11] A high church official.
[12] The west wind.

While, like a *Guard* on either side,
The Trees before their *Lord* divide;   620
This, like a long and equal Thread,
Betwixt two *Labyrinths* does lead.
But, where the Floods did lately drown,
There at the Ev'ning stake me down.

79

For now the Waves are fall'n and dried,   625
And now the Meadows fresher dyed;
Whose Grass, with moister colour dasht,
Seems as green Silks but newly washt.
No *Serpent* new nor *Crocodile*
Remains behind our little *Nile;*   630
Unless it self you will mistake,
Among these Meads the only Snake.

80

See in what wanton harmless folds
It ev'ry where the Meadow holds;
And its yet muddy back doth lick,   635
Till as a *Crystal Mirror* slick;
Where all things gaze themselves, and doubt
If they be in it or without.
And for his shade which therein shines,
Narcissus[13] like, the *Sun* too pines.   640

81

Oh what a Pleasure 'tis to hedge
My Temples here with heavy sedge;
Abandoning my lazy Side,
Stretcht as a Bank unto the Tide;
Or to suspend my sliding Foot   645
On the Osier's[14] undermined Root,
And in its Branches tough to hang,
While at my Lines the Fishes twang!

---

[13] According to myth, Narcissus fell in love with his own image reflected in a pool of water; pining away for himself, he was transformed into a flower.

[14] Ie., the willow's.

82

But now away my Hooks, my Quills,
And Angles, idle Utensils.   650
The *young Maria*[15] walks tonight:
Hide trifling Youth thy Pleasures slight.
'Twere shame that such judicious Eyes
Should with such Toys a Man surprise;
She that already is the *Law*   655
Of all her *Sex*, her *Age's Awe*.

83

See how loose Nature, in respect
To her, it self doth recollect;
And every thing so wisht[16] and fine,
Starts forth with to its *Bonne Mine*.[17]   660
The *Sun* himself, of *Her* aware,
Seems to descend with greater Care;
And lest *She* see him go to Bed;
In blushing Clouds conceals his Head.

84

So when the Shadows laid asleep   665
From underneath these Banks do creep,
And on the River as it flows
With *Ebon Shuts*[18] begin to close;
The modest *Halcyon*[19] comes in sight,
Flying betwixt the Day and Night;   670
And such an horror calm and dumb,
Admiring Nature does benumb.

85

The viscous Air, wheresoe'er She fly,
Follows and sucks her Azure dye;
The jellying Stream compacts below,   675
If it might fix her shadow so;

[15] *The young Maria:* Mary Fairfax, Marvell's pupil and daughter of Lord and Lady Fairfax, the owners of the estate.
[16] Silent.
[17] French for "good appearance."
[18] *Ebon shuts:* black window shutters.
[19] The kingfisher.

The stupid Fishes hang, as plain
As *Flies* in *Crystal* overta'en;
And Men the silent *Scene* assist,
Charmed with the *Sapphire-winged Mist.*   680

86

Maria such, and so doth hush
The *World*, and through the *Ev'ning* rush.
No new-born *Comet* such a Train
Draws through the Sky, nor Star new-slain.
For straight those giddy Rockets fail,   685
Which from the putrid Earth exhale,
But by her *Flames,* in *Heaven* tried,
Nature is wholly *vitrified.*[20]

87

'Tis *She* that to these Gardens gave
That wondrous Beauty which they have;   690
She straightness on the Woods bestows;
To *Her* the Meadow sweetness owes;
Nothing could make the River be
So Crystal-pure but only *She;*
She yet more Pure, Sweet, Straight, and Fair,   695
Than Gardens, Woods, Meads, Rivers are.

88

Therefore what first *She* on them spent,
They gratefully again present.
The Meadow Carpets where to tread;
The Garden Flow'rs to Crown *Her* Head;   700
And for a Glass the limpid Brook,
Where *She* may all *her* Beauties look;
But, since *She* would not have them seen,
The Wood about *her* draws a Screen.

89

For *She*, to higher Beauties raised,   705
Disdains to be for lesser praised.
She counts her Beauty to converse

---

[20] Transformed into glass.

In all the Languages as *hers;*
Nor yet in those *herself* employs
But for the *Wisdom*, not the *Noise;*   710
Nor yet that *Wisdom* would affect,
But as 'tis *Heaven's Dialect*.

90

Blest Nymph! that couldst so soon prevent
Those *Trains* by Youth against thee meant;
Tears (wat'ry Shot that pierce the Mind;)   715
And *Sighs* (Love's Cannon charged with Wind;)
True Praise (that breaks through all defense;)
And *feigned complying Innocence;*
But knowing where this *Ambush* lay,
She scaped the safe, but roughest Way.   720

91

This 'tis to have been from the first
In a *Domestick Heaven* nurst,
Under the *Discipline* severe
Of *Fairfax*, and the starry *Vere;*
Where not one object can come nigh   725
But pure, and spotless as the Eye;
And *Goodness* doth it self entail
On *Females*, if there want a *Male.*

92

Go now fond Sex that on your Face
Do all your useless Study place,   730
Nor once at Vice your Brows dare knit
Lest the smooth Forehead wrinkled sit:
Yet your own Face shall at you grin,
Thorough the Black-bag of your Skin;
When *knowledge* only could have filled   735
And *Virtue* all those *Furrows tilled.*

93

Hence *She* with Graces more divine
Supplies beyond her *Sex* the *Line;*
And, like a *sprig of Mistletoe*,

On the *Fairfacian Oak* does grow; 740
Whence, for some universal good,
The *Priest* shall cut the sacred Bud;
While her *glad Parents* most rejoice,
And make their *Destiny* their *Choice*.

94

Meantime ye Fields, Springs, Bushes, Flow'rs, 745
Where yet She leads her studious Hours,
(Till Fate her worthily translates,
And find a *Fairfax* for our *Thwaites*)[21]
Employ the means you have by Her,
And in your kind yourselves prefer; 750
That, as all *Virgins* She precedes,
So you all *Woods, Streams, Gardens, Meads*.

95

For you *Thessalian Tempe's*[22] Seat
Shall now be scorned as obsolete;
Aranjuez, as less, disdained; 755
The *Bel-Retiro*[23] as constrained;
But name not the *Idalian Grove*,[24]
For 'twas the Seat of wanton Love;
Much less the Dead's *Elysian Fields*,
Yet nor to them your Beauty yields. 760

96

'Tis not, what once it was, the *World*;
But a rude heap together hurled;
All negligently overthrown,
Gulfs, Deserts, Precipices, Stone.
Your lesser *World* contains the same. 765
But in more decent Order tame;
You Heaven's Center, Nature's Lap.
And Paradise's only Map.

---

[21] A clearing in a forest.

[22] In Thessaly, in Greece, the Vale of Tempe was an arcadian landscape.

[23] Aranjuez and Bel-Retiro were two well-known Spanish palaces with beautiful gardens.

[24] A grove in Cyprus, the island sacred to Venus, goddess of love.

97

But now the *Salmon-Fishers* moist
Their *Leathern Boats* begin to hoist;   770
And, like *Antipodes*[25] in Shoes,
Have shod their *Heads* in their *Canoes*.
How *Tortoise-like*, but not so slow,
These rational *Amphibii* go?
Let's in: for the dark *Hemisphere*   775
Does now like one of them appear.

✣ *Margaret Lucas Cavendish, Duchess of Newcastle* (1623–1673)

The first woman in English history to write about science, Margaret Lucas Cavendish published prolifically and in a variety of genres, in a time when it was rare for women to publish their writings. Cavendish grew up in relative seclusion, without any formal education. She served as a maid of honor to Queen Henrietta Maria and followed the royal family into exile in France during the English Civil War. In 1645, she married the duke of Newcastle, a wealthy royalist general who was thirty years her senior. During her time in Paris, she and her husband entertained many of the leading scientists and intellectuals of the day, including René Descartes and Thomas Hobbes. These salons marked the beginning of her interest in matters of science. The duchess and her husband spent the first seventeen years of their marriage on the Continent; they returned to England after the Restoration and continued their intellectual pursuits at their estate in the countryside. From 1653 until her death, Cavendish published fourteen books, ranging from collections of poetry to plays, biography and autobiography, and speculations on chemistry and natural history. While some of Cavendish's scientific ideas may seem outlandish to twentieth-century readers, her theories of atomism, in particular, are very much in keeping with popular scientific notions of the mid-seventeenth century. Though she was opposed to Baconian empiricism, she was the first woman ever permitted to visit the Baconian Royal Society. No other woman would be invited to attend their meetings for another three hundred years.

The selections included below are taken from Cavendish's first published book, Poems and Fancies *(1653). These poems do not give a sense of the more technical dimensions of Cavendish's scientific notions (as expounded in her prose treatises on science, such as* Philosophical and Physical Opinions, *1663, or* Observations Upon Experimental Philosophy, *1665), but they do reveal an author deeply concerned with the relationship between the human and the natural world and the ways in which humans can and should know their environment. The dialogue format employed in many of the poems is an innovative stylistic feature, and demonstrates Cavendish's imaginative sympathies for her subject matter, whether it be Nature in general, a tree under the ax, or hunted*

---

[25] The two opposite sides of the earth.

beasts. These poems are critical of scientific minds that, as Wordsworth would later say, "murder to dissect." Throughout her work, Cavendish demonstrates a great deal of compassion, giving a poetic voice to inarticulate nature in its different manifestations. Alternately ridiculed and respected in her own time, Cavendish is indisputably important, not only to literary history but to the history of science. She was a trailblazer for other women writers and women scientists.

A Dialogue Betwixt Man and Nature

Man.   'Tis strange,
  How we do change.
  First to live, and then to die,
  Is a great misery.
  To give us sense, great pains to feel,   5
  To make our lives to be *Death's wheel;*
  To give us *Sense,* and *Reason* too,
  Yet know not what we're made to do.
  Whether to *Atoms* turn, or *Heaven* up fly,
  Or into new *Forms* change, and never die.   10
  Or else to *Matter Prime* to fall again,
  From thence to take new *Forms,* and so remain.
  Nature gives no such *Knowledge* to *Mankind,*
  But *Strong Desires* to torment the *Mind:*
  And *Senses,* which like *Hounds* do run about, 15
  Yet never can the *perfect Truth* find out.
  O *Nature! Nature!* cruel to *Mankind,*
  Gives *Knowledge* none, but *Misery* to find.
Nature. Why doth *Mankind* complain, and make such Moan?
  May not *I* work my *will* with what's my own? 20
  But *Men* among themselves contract, and make
  A *Bargain* for my *Tree;* that *Tree* will take:
  Most cruelly do chop in pieces small,
  And forms it as he please, then builds withal.
  Although that *Tree* by me was made to stand, 25
  Just as it grows, not to be cut by *Man.*
Man. O *Nature, Trees* are dull, and have no *Sense,*
  And therefore feel not pain, nor take offense.
  But *Beasts* have *life* and *Sense,* and *passion* strong,
  Yet *cruel man* doth kill, and doth them wrong. 30
  To take that *life,* I *gave,* before the time
  I did ordain, the *injury is mine.*
  What *Ill* man doth, *Nature* did make him do,
  For he by *Nature* is prompt thereunto.
  For it was in great *Nature's power,* and *Will,* 35

To make him as *she* pleas'd, either *good*, or *ill*.
Though *Beast* hath *Sense*, feels pain, yet whilst they live,
They *Reason* want, for to dispute, or grieve.
Beast hath no pain, but what in *Sense* doth lie,
Nor troubled *Thoughts*, to think how they shall die.   40
Reason doth stretch *Man's mind* upon the Rack,
With *Hopes*, with *Joys*, pulled up, with *Fear* pulled back.
Desire whips him forward, makes him run,
Despair doth wound, and pulls him back again.
For *Nature*, thou mad'st *Man* betwixt *Extremes*,   45
Wants *perfect Knowledge*, yet thereof he dreams.
For had he been like to a *Stock*, or *Stone*,
Or like a *Beast*, to live with *Sense* alone.
Then might he eat, or drink, or lie *stone*-still,
Ne'er troubled be, either for *Heaven*, or *Hell*.   50
Man knowledge hath enough for to inquire,
Ambition great enough for to aspire:
And *Knowledge* hath, that yet he knows not all,
And that himself he knoweth least of all:
Which makes him wonder, and thinks there is mixt   55
Two several *Qualities* in *Nature* fixt.
The one like *Love*, the other like to *Hate*,
By striving both hinders *Predestinate*.
And then sometimes, *Man* thinks, as *one* they be,
Which makes *Contrariety* so well agree;   60
That though the *World* were made by *Love and hate*,
Yet all is ruled, and governed by *Fate*.
These are *Man's fears*; man's *hopes* run smooth, and high,
Which thinks his *Mind* is some *great Deity*.
For though the body is of *low* degree,   65
In *Sense* like *Beasts*, their *Souls* like *Gods* shall be.
Says *Nature*, Why doth *Man* complain, and cry,
If he believes his *Soul* shall never die?

A Dialogue Between an Oak, and a Man Cutting Him Down

Oak.   Why cut you off my *Boughs*, both large, and long,
That keep you from the *heat*, and *scorching Sun*;
And did refresh your *fainting Limbs* from sweat?
From *thund'ring Rains I* keep you free, from *Wet*;
When on my *Bark* your weary head would lay,   5
Where *quiet sleep* did take all *Cares* away.
The whilst my *Leaves* a gentle noise did make,

And blew *cool Winds*, that you *fresh Air* might take.
Besides, *I* did invite the *Birds* to sing,
That their sweet voice might you some pleasure bring.　　　　10
Where every one did strive to do their best,
Oft changed their *Notes*, and strained their tender *Breast*.
In *Winter time*, my *Shoulders* broad did hold
Off *blustring Storms*, that wounded with *sharp Cold*.
And on my *Head* the *Flakes* of *Snow* did fall,　　　　15
Whilst you under my *Boughs* sate free from all.
And will you thus requite my *Love, Good Will*,
To take away my *Life*, and *Body* kill?
For all my *Care*, and *Service I* have past,
Must *I* be cut, and laid on *Fire* at last?　　　　20
And thus true *Love* you cruelly have *slain*,
Invent always to torture me with *pain*.
First you do peel my *Bark*, and slay my *Skin*,
Hew down my *Boughs*, so chops off every *Limb*.
With *Wedges* you do pierce my *Sides* to wound,　　　　25
And with your *Hatchet* knock me to the ground.
I minced shall be in *Chips*, and *pieces* small,
And thus doth *Man* reward *good Deeds* withal.
Man.　　Why grumblest thou, *old Oak*, when thou hast stood
This hundred years, as *King* of all the *Wood*.　　　　30
Would you forever live, and not resign
Your *Place* to one that is of your own *Line*?
Your *Acorn's young*, when they grow big, and tall,
Long for your *Crown*, and wish to see your fall;
Think every minute lost, whilst you do live,　　　　35
And grumble at each *Office* you do give.
Ambition flyeth high, and is above
All sorts of *Friendship* strong, or *Natural Love*.
Besides, all *Subjects* they in *Change* delight,
When *Kings* grow *Old*, their *Government* they slight:　　　　40
Although in *ease*, and *peace*, and *wealth* do live,
Yet all those *happy times* for *Change* will give.
Grows *discontent*, and *Factions* still do make;
What *Good* so ere *he* doth, as *Evil* take.
Were *he* as *wife*, as ever *Nature* made,　　　　45
As *picus*, *good*, as ever *Heaven* saved:
Yet when *they* die, such *Joy* is in their *Face*,
As if the *Devil* had gone from that place.
With *Shouts* of *Joy* they run anew to *Crown*,
Although *next day* they strive to pull *him* down.　　　　50
Oak.　　Why, said the *Oak*, because that *they* are mad,
Shall *I* rejoice, for my own *Death* be glad?
Because my *Subjects* all ingrateful are,

Shall *I* therefore my *health*, and *life* impair.
Good Kings govern justly, as they ought,   55
Examine not their Humours, but their Fault.
For when their *Crimes* appear, 'tis *time to strike,*
Not to examine Thoughts how they do like.
If *Kings* are never *loved*, till they do die,
Nor *wisht* to *live*, till in the *Grave* they lie: 60
Yet he that loves *himself* the less, because
He cannot get every man's *high applause:*
Shall by my *Judgment* be condemned to wear,
The *Asses' Ears*, and *Burdens* for to bear.
But let me live the *Life* that *Nature* gave,   65
And not to please my *Subjects*, dig my *Grave*.

Man.   But here, *Poor Oak*, thou liv'st in *Ignorance*,
And never seek'st thy *Knowledge* to advance.
I'll cut thee down, 'cause *Knowledge* thou may'st gain,
Shalt be a *Ship*, to traffick on the *Maine:*   70
There shalt thou *swim*, and cut the *Seas* in two,
And trample down each *Wave*, as thou dost go.
Though they rise high, and big are swelled with *pride,*
Thou on their *Shoulders broad*, and *Back*, shalt ride:
Their *lofty Heads* shalt *bow*, and make them *stoop,*   75
And on their *Necks* shalt set thy *steady Foot:*
And on their *Breast* thy *Stately Ship* shalt bear,
Till thy *Sharp Keel* the *wat'ry Womb* doth tear.
Thus shalt thou round the *World*, new *Land* to find,
That from the rest is of *another kind.*   80

Oak.   O, said the *Oak*, I am contented well,
Without that *Knowledge*, in my *Wood* to dwell.
For *I* had rather live, and simple be,
Then dangers run, some new strange *Sight* to see.
Perchance my *Ship* against a *Rock* may hit;   85
Then were *I* straight in sundry pieces split.
Besides, no rest, nor quiet *I* should have,
The *Winds* would toss me on each *troubled Wave.*
The *Billows rough* will beat on every side,
My *Breast* will *ache* to swim against the *Tide.*   90
And *greedy Merchants* may me overfreight,
So should *I* drowned be with my own weight.
Besides with *Sails*, and *Ropes* my *Body* tie,
Just like a *Prisoner*, have no *Liberty.*
And being always *wet*, shall take such *Colds.*   95
My *Ship* may get a *Pose*,[1] and leak through holes.
Which they to mend, will put me to great pain,

---

[1] An obsolete term for a head cold.

Besides, all *patched*, and *pieced*, I shall remain.
I care not for that *Wealth*, wherein the *pains*,
And *trouble*, is far greater then the *Gains*.   100
I am contented with what *Nature* gave,
I not Repine, but one *poor wish* would have,
Which is, that you my *aged Life* would save.

Man.　　To build a *Stately House I'll* cut thee down,
Wherein shall *Princes* live of great renown.   105
There shalt *thou* live with the best Company,
All their delight, and pastime *thou* shalt see.
Where *Plays*, and *Masques*, and *Beauties* bright will shine,
Thy *Wood* all oiled with Smoke of *Meat*, and *Wine*.
There thou shalt hear both *Men*, and *Women* sing,   110
Far pleasanter than *Nightingales* in Spring.
Like to a *Ball*, their *Echoes* shall rebound
Against the *Wall*, yet can no *Voice* be found.

Oak.　　Alas, what *Musick* shall I care to hear,
When on my *Shoulders* I such burthens bear?   115
Both *Brick*, and *Tiles*, upon my *Head* are laid,
Of this *Preferment* I am sore afraid.
And many times with *Nails*, and *Hammers* strong,
They pierce my *Sides*, to hang their *Pictures* on.
My *Face* is smutched with Smoke of *Candle Lights*,   120
In danger to be burnt in *Winter Nights*.
No, let me here a poor *Old Oak* still grow;
I care not for these vain *Delights* to know.
For *fruitless Promises* I do not care,
More *Honour* 'tis, my own *green Leaves* to bear.   125
More *Honour* 'tis, to be in *Nature's* dress,
Than any *Shape*, that *Men* by *Art* express.
I am not like to *Man*, would Praises have,
And for *Opinion* make my self a *Slave*.

Man.　　Why do you wish to live, and not to die,   130
Since you no *Pleasure* have, but *Misery?*
For here you stand against the *scorching Sun:*
By's *Fiery Beams*, your *fresh green Leaves* become
Withered; with *Winter's* cold you quake, and shake:
Thus in no *time*, or *season*, rest can take.   135

Oak.　　Yet I am happier, said the *Oak*, than *Man;*
With my condition I contented am.
He nothing loves, but what he cannot get,
And soon doth surfeit of one dish of meat:
Dislikes all Company, displeased alone,   140
Makes *Grief* himself, if *Fortune* gives him none.
And as his *Mind* is restless, never pleased;
So is his *Body* sick, and oft diseased.

His *Gouts*, and *Pains*, do make him sigh, and cry,
Yet in the midst of *Pains* would live, not die.   145
Man.   Alas, *poor Oak*, thou understandst, nor can
Imagine half the misery of *Man*.
All other *Creatures* only in *Sense* join,
But *Man* hath something more, which is *divine*.
He hath a *Mind*, doth to the *Heavens* aspire,   150
A *Curiosity* for to inquire:
A *Wit* that nimble is, which runs about
In every *Corner*, to seek *Nature* out.
For *She* doth hide her self, as feared to show
Man all *her works*, least *he* too powerful grow.   155
Like to a *King*, his *Favourite* makes so great,
That at the last, *he* fears his *Power* he'll get.
And what creates *desire* in *Man's Breast*,
A *Nature* is *divine*, which seeks the best:
And never can be satisfied, until   160
He, like a *God*, doth in *Perfection* dwell.
If you, as *Man*, desire like *Gods* to be,
I'll spare your *Life*, and not cut down your *Tree*.

A Dialogue of Birds

As *I* abroad in *Fields*, and *Woods* did walk,
I heard the *Birds* of several things did talk:
And on the *Boughs* would *Gossip*, *prate*, and *chat*,
And every one discourse of *this*, and *that*.
I, said the *Lark*, before the *Sun* do rise,   5
And take my flight up to the *highest Skies:*
There sing some *Notes*, to raise *Apollo's head*,
For fear that *he* might lie too long a-*Bed*.
And as *I* mount, or if descend down low,
Still do *I* sing, which way so ere *I* go.   10
Winding my *Body* up, just like a *Screw*,
So doth my *Voice* wind up a *Trillo* too.
What *Bird*, besides my self, both flies and sings,
Just tune my *Trilloes* keeps to my *flutt'ring Wings*.
I, said the *Nightingale*, all night do watch,   15
For fear a *Serpent* should my *young Ones catch:*
To keep back sleep, *I* several *Tunes* do sing,
Which Tunes so pleasant are, they *Lovers* bring
Into the *Woods;* who list'ning sit, and mark:
When *I* begin to sing, they cry, *hark*, *hark*.   20
Stretching my *Throat*, to raise my *Trilloes* high,

To gain their praises, makes me almost die.
    Then comes the *Owl*, which says, here's such a do
With your sweet *Voices;* through spite cries *Wit-a-woo.*
    In *Winter,* said the *Robin, I* should die,   25
But that *I* in a good warm house do fly:
And there do pick up *Crumbs,* which make me fat,
But oft am scared away with the *Puss-cat.*
If they molest me not, then *I* grow bold,
And stay so long, whilst *Winter Tales* are told.   30
Man superstitiously dares not hurt me,
For if *I* am killed, or hurt, *ill Luck* shall be.
    The *Sparrow* said, were our *Condition* such,
But *Men* do strive with *Nets* us for to catch:
With *Guns,* and *Bows* they shoot us from the *Trees,*   35
And by small *shot,* we oft our *Lives* do loose,
Because we pick a *Cherry* here, and there,
When, *God* he knows, we eat them in great fear.
But *Men* will *eat,* until their *Belly* burst,
And *surfeits* take: if we eat, we are *curst.*   40
Yet we by *Nature* are revenged still,
For eating overmuch themselves they kill.
And if a *Child* do chance to *cry,* or *brawl,*
They strive to catch us, to please that *Child* withal:
With *Threads* they tie our *legs* almost to crack,   45
That when we *hop* away, they pull us back:
And when they cry *Fip, Fip,* strait we must come,
And for our pains they'll give us one *small Crumb.*
    I wonder, said *Mag-pie,* you grumble so,
Dame Sparrow, we are used much worse *I* trow.   50
For they our *Tongues* do slit, their *words* to learn,
And with the *pain,* our food we dearly earn.
    Why, say the *Finches,* and the *Linnets* all,
Do you so prate *Mag-pie,* and so much bawl?
As if no *Birds* besides were wronged but you,   55
When we by *cruel Man* are injured to.
For we, to learn their *Tunes,* are kept awake,
That with their *whistling* we no rest can take.
In *darkness* we are kept, no *Light* must see,
Till we have learnt their *Tunes* most perfectly.   60
But *Jack-dawes,* they may dwell their houses nigh,
And build their *Nests* in *Elms* that do grow high:
And there may *prate,* and fly from place to place;
For why, they think they give their *House a grace.*
    Lord! said the *Partridge, Cock, Pewit, Snite,* and *Quail,*   65
Pigeons, Larks, my *Masters,* why d' ye rail?
You're kept from *Winter's Cold,* and *Summer's heat,*

Are taught new *Tunes*, and have good store of meat.
Having a *Servant* you to wait upon,
To make your *Cages* clean from *filth*, and *Dung*:   70
When we *poor Birds* are by the dozens killed,
And luxuriously us eat, till they be filled:
And of our *Flesh* they make such cruel waste,
That but some of our *Limbs* will please their taste.
In *Wood-cocks thighs* they only take delight,   75
And *Partridge wings*, which swift were in their flight.
The smaller *Lark* they eat all at one bite,
But every part is good of *Quail*, and *Snite*.
The *Murtherous Hawk* they keep, us for to catch,
And learn their *Dogs*, to *crouch*, and *creep*, and *watch*:   80
Until they have *sprung* us to *Nets*, and *Toils*,
And thus *poor Creatures* we are made *Man's* spoiles.
Cruel Nature! to make us *Gentle, Mild*:
They *happy* are, which are more *fierce*, and *wild*.
O would our *flesh* had been like *Carrion, course*,   85
To eat us only *Famine* might enforce.
But when they eat us, may they surfeits take,
May they be *poor*, when they a *Feast* us make.
The more they eat, the *leaner* may they grow,
Or else so *fat*, they cannot stir, nor go.   90
     O, said the *Swallow*, let me mourn in *black*,
For, of *Man's cruelty I* do not lack:
I am the *Messenger* of *Summer warm*,
Do neither pick their *Fruit*, nor eat their *Corn*;
Yet they will take us, when alive we be,   95
I shake to tell, *O horrid Cruelty!*
Beat us alive, till we an *Oil* become.
Can there to *Birds* be a worse *Martyrdom?*
O Man, O Man, if we should serve you so,
You would against us your *great Curses* throw.   100
But *Nature, she* is good, do not her blame:
We ought to give her thanks, and not exclaim.
For *Love* is *Nature's* chiefest *Law* in *Mind*,
Hate but an *Accident* from *Love* we find.
'Tis true, *Self-Preservation* is the chief,   105
But *Luxury* to *Nature* is a *Thief*.
Corrupted manners always do breed *Vice*,
Which by *Persuasion* doth the *Mind* entice.
No *Creature* doth usurp so much as *Man*,
Who thinks himself like *God*, because he can   110
Rule other *Creatures*, makes them to obey:
We *Souls* have, *Nature* never made, say they.
What ever comes from *Nature's Stock*, and *Treasure*,

Created is only to serve their pleasure.
Although the *Life* of *Bodies* comes from *Nature,*   115
Yet still the *Souls* come from the great *Creator.*
And they shall live, though *we* to *dust* do turn,
Either in *Bliss,* or in *hot flames* to burn.
    Then came the *Parrot* with her *painted wing;*
Spake like an *Orator* in everything.   120
Sister Jay, Neighbour Daw, Gossip Pie,
We taken are, not like the rest, to die:
Only to talk, and prate, the best we can,
To Imitate to th' *Life,* the *Speech,* of *Man.*
And just like *men,* we pass our time away,   125
With many *words,* not one wise *Speech* can say:
And *speak* as *gravely Nonsense* as the best,
As full of *empty words* as all the rest.
Then *Nature* we will praise, because *she* have
Given us such *Tongues,* as *Men* our *Lives* to save.   130
Mourn not my *Friends,* but sing in Sunshine gay,
And while you 'ave time, joy in your selves you may.
What though your lives be short, yet merry be,
And not complain, but in delights agree.
    Straight came the *Titmouse* with a *frowning face,*   135
And hopt about, as in an *angry pace.*
My *Masters* all, what are you mad,
Is no regard unto the *publick* had?
Are private *Home-Affairs* cast all aside?
Your *young Ones* cry for meat, tis time to chide.   140
For shame disperse yourselves, and some pains take,
Both for the *Common good,* and *young Chicks* sake:
And not sit murmuring here against great *Man,*
Unless for to revenge ourselves we can.
Alas, alas, we want their *Shape,* which they   145
By it have power to make all obey.
For they can *Lift, bear, strike, turn,* and *wind,*
What ways they will, which makes them new *Arts* find
'Tis not their *Wit,* which new *Inventions* make,
But 'tis their *Shapes,* which *heighth, breadth, depth,* can take.   150
Thus they can measure the *great worldly Ball,*
And Numbers set, to prove the *Truth* of all.
What *Creature* else hath *Arms,* or goeth upright,
Or have all sorts of *Motions* so unite?
Man by his *Shape* can *Nature* imitate,   155
Can *govern, rule,* and new *Arts* can create.
Then come away, since *talk* no good can do,
And what we cannot help, submit unto.
Then some their *Wives,* others their *Husbands* call,

To gather *Sticks*, to build their *Nests* withal.   160
Some that were *Shrews*, did chide, and scold, and fret,
The *Wind* blew down their *Nest* where they should sit
For all they *gathered*, with *pains*, and *care*,
Those *Sticks*, and *Straws* were blown they knew not where
But none did labour like the *little Wren*,   165
To build her *Nest*, to hatch her *young Ones* in.
She lays more *Eggs* than all the rest,
And with much *Art* doth build her *Nest*.
The *younger sort* made love, and kissed each other's *Bill*,
The *Cock* would catch some *Flies* to give his *Mistress* still.   170
The *Yellowhammer* cried, tis *wet*, tis *wet*,
For it will rain before the *Sun* doth set.
Taking their *Flight*, as each *Mind* thought it best,
Some flew *abroad*, and some home to their *Nest*.
Some went to gather *Corn* from *Sheaves* outstrewed,   175
And some to *pick* up *Seed* that's newly sowed.
Some had *Courage* a *Cherry ripe* to take,
Others catcht *Flies*, when they a *Feast* did make.
And some did pick up *Ants*, and *Eggs*, though small,
To carry home, to feed their *young* withal.   180
When every *Crop* was filled, and *Night* came on,
Then did they stretch their *Wings* to fly fast home.
And as like *Men*, from *Market* home they come,
Set out alone, but every *Mile* adds some:
Until a *Troop* of *Neighbours* get together,   185
So do a *flight* of *Birds* in *Sunshine weather*.
When to their *Nests* they get, *Lord* how they bawl,
And every *one* doth to his *Neighbour* call:
Asking each other if they weary were,
Rejoicing at *past dangers*, and *great fear*.   190
When they their *wings* had *pruned*, and *young ones* fed,
Sate *gossipping*, before they went to *Bed*.
Let us a *Carol*, said the *Black-bird*, sing,
Before we go to *Bed* this *fine Evening*.
The *Thrushes*, *Linnets*, *Finches*, all took parts,   195
A *Harmony* by *Nature*, not by *Arts*.
But all their *Songs* were *Hymns* to *God* on *high*,
Praising his *Name*, blessing his *Majesty*.
And when they askt for *Gifts*, to *God* did pray,
He would be pleased to give them a *fair day*.   200
At last they *drowsy* grew, and heavy were to *sleep*,
And then instead of singing, cried, *Peep*, *Peep*.
Just as the *Eye*, when *Sense* is locking up,
Is neither open wide, nor yet quite shut:
So doth a *Voice* still by degrees fall down,   205

And as a *Shadow*, waft so doth a *Sound*.
Thus went to rest each *Head*, under each *wing*,
For *Sleep* brings *Peace* to every *living thing*.

A Moral Discourse Betwixt Man and Beast

Man is a *Creature* like himself alone,
In him all *qualities* do join as one.
When *Man* is injured, and his *Honour* stung,
He seems a *Lion*, furious, fierce, and strong.
With greedy *Covetousness*, like to *Wolves*, and *Bears*,   5
Devours *Right*, and *Truth* in pieces tears.
Or like as crafty *Foxes* lie in wait,
To catch young *Novice Kids* by their deceit;
So *subtle Knaves* do watch, who *Errors* make,
That they thereby *Advantages* might take.   10
Not for *Examples* them to rectify,
But that much *Mischief* they can make thereby.
Others, like *Crouching Spaniels*, close will set,
Creeping about the *Partridge* too in *Net*.
Some humble seem, and *lowly* bend the *Knee*,   15
To those which have *Power*, and *Authority*:
Not out of *Love* to *Honour*, or *Renown*,
But to insnare, and so to pull them down.
Or as a *Mastiff* flies at every *Throat*,
So *Spite* will fly at all, that is of note.   20
With *Slanderous words*, as *Teeth*, good *Deeds* out tear,
Which neither *Power*, nor *Strength*, nor *Greatness* spare.
And are so *mischievous*, love not to see
Any to live without an *Infamy*.
Most like to ravenous *Beasts* in *blood* delight,   25
And only to do *mischief*, love to fight.
But some are like to *Horses*, *strong*, and *free*,
Will gallop over *Wrong*, and *Injury*.
Who fear no *Foe*, nor *Enemies* do dread,
Will fight in *Battles* till they fall down dead.   30
Their *Heart* with noble rage so hot will grow,
As from their *Nostrils Clouds* of *Smoke* do blow.
And with their *Hooves* the *firm hard ground* will strike,
In *anger*, that they cannot go to fight.
Their *Eyes* (like *Flints*) will beat out *Sparks* of *Fire*,   35
Will *neigh* out loud, when *Combats* they desire.
So *valiant Men* their *Foe* aloud will call,
To try their *Strength*, and grapple *Arms* withal.

And in their *Eyes* such *Courage* doth appear,
As if that *Mars* did rule that *Hemisphear.*   40
Some like to *slow, dull Asses,* full of *Fear,*
Contented are great *Burthens* for to bear.
And every *Clown* doth beat his *Back,* and *Side,*
Because he's *slow,* when *fast* that he would ride.
Then will he *bray* out loud, but dare not bite;   45
For why, he hath not *Courage* for to fight.
Base Minds will yield their *Heads* under the *Yoke,*
Offer their *Backs* to every *Tyrant*'s stroke.
Like *Fools* will grumble, but they dare not speak,
Nor strive for *Liberty,* their *Bonds* to break.   50
Those that in *Slavery* live, so dull will grow,
Dejected Spirits make the *Body* slow.
Others as *Swine* lie *groveling* in the *Mire,*
Have no *Heroick Thoughts* to rise up higher:
They from their *Birth,* do never *sport,* nor *play,*   55
But *eat,* and *drink,* and *grunting,* run away:
Of *grumbling Natures,* never doing good,
And cruel are, as of a *Boorish Brood.*
So *Gluttons, Sluggards* care for nought but ease,
In *Conversations* will not any please: 60
Ambition none, to make their *Name* to live;
Nor have they *Generosity* to give:
And are so *Churlish,* that if any pray
To help their *Wants,* will cursing go away.
So cruel are, so far from *death* to save,   65
That they will take away the *Life* they have.
Some like to *fearful Hart,* or *frighted Hare,*
Shun every noise, and their own *Shadows* Fear.
So *Cowards,* that are sent in *Wars* to fight,
Think not to beat, but how to make their flight.   70
When *Trumpet* sounds to charge the *Foe,* it calls,
And with that noise, the *Heart* o' th' *Coward* falls.
Others as harmless *Sheep* in peace do live,
Contented are, no *Injury* will give:
But on the tender *Grass* they gently feed,   75
Which do no *Spite,* nor *rankled Malice* breed.
They never in the ways of *mischief* stood,
To set their *Teeth* in *flesh,* or drink up *blood.*
They grieve to walk alone, will pine a way,
Grow fat in *Flocks,* will with each other play.   80
The naked they do clothe with their soft *Wool,*
The *Ewes* do feed the hungry Stomack full.
So gentle *Nature's Disposition* sweet
Shuns foolish *Quarrels,* loves the *Peace* to keep.

Full of *Compassion*, pitying the distrest,   85
And with their *Bounty* help they the opprest.
They swell not with the *Pride* of *self-conceit*,
Nor for their *Neighbour's life* do lie in wait.
Nor *Innocence* by their *Extortions* tear,
Nor fill the *Widow's Heart* with *Grief*, or *Care:*   90
Nor *Bribes* will take with covetous hands,
Nor set they back the *Mark* of th' Owner's *Lands.*
But with a grateful *Heart* do still return
The *Curtesies* that have for them been done.
And in their *Conversation*, meek, and mild,   95
Without *Lascivious words*, or *Actions* wild.
Those *Men* are *Fathers* to a *Common-wealth*,
Where *Justice* lives, and *Truth* may show her self.
Others as *Apes* do imitate the rest,
And when they *mischief* do, seem but to jest.   100
So are *Buffoons*, that seem for *Mirth* to sport,
Whose liberty fills *Factions* in a *Court.*
Those that delight in *Fools*, must in good part
Take what they say, although the words are *smart.*
But many times such *rankled Thoughts* beget   105
In *Hearts* of *Princes*, and much *Envy* set,
By praising *Rivals;* or else do reveal
Those *Faults*, most fit for privacy to conceal.
For though a *Fool*, if he an ill truth tells,
Or be it false, if like a *Truth* it smells;   110
It gets such hold, though in a wise man's *Brain*,
That hardly it will ever out again.
And so like *Worms*, some will be trod to *Earth*,
Others as *venomous Vipers* stung to *death.*
Some like to subtle *Serpents* wind about,   115
To compass their *designs* crawl in, and out:
And never leave until some *Nest* they find,
Suck out the *Eggs*, and leave the *Shells* behind.
So *Flatterers* with *Praises* wind about
A *Noble Mind*, to get a Secret out.   120
For *Flattery* through every *Ear* will glide,
Down to the *Heart*, and there some time abide;
And in the *Breast* with feigned *Friendship* lie,
Till to the *Death* he stings him cruelly.
Thus some as *Birds*, and *Beasts*, and *Flies*, are such: 125
To every *Creature* men resemble much.
Some, like to soaring *Eagle*, mount up high:
Wings of *Ambition* bear them to the *Sky.*
Or, like to *Hawks*, fly round to catch their *Prey*,
Or like to *Puttocks*, bear the *Chick* away.   130

Some like to *Ravens*, which on *Carrion* feed,
And some their spite feed on, what slanders breed.
Some like to *Peacock* proud, his tail to show:
So men, that *Followers* have, will haughty grow.
Some *Melancholy Owls*, that hate the *Light*,   135
And as the *Bat* flies in the *Shades* of *Night:*
So *Envious Men* their *Neighbour* hate to see,
When that he *Shines* in great *Prosperity:*
Keep home in discontent, repine at all,
Until some *Mischief* on the *Good* do fall.   140
Others, as cheerful *Larks*, sing as they fly.
So men are merry, which have no *Envy.*
And some as *Nightingales* do sweetly sing,
As *Messengers*, when they good *News* do bring.
Thus *Men, Birds, Beasts*, in *Humours* much agree,   145
But several *Properties* in these there be.
'Tis proper for a lively *Horse* to *neigh*,
And for a slow, dull foolish *Ass* to *bray.*
For *Dogs* to bark, *Bulls* roar, *Wolves* howl, *Pigs* squeak,
For *Men* to *frown*, to *weep*, to *laugh*, to *speak.*   150
Proper for *Flies* to buzz, *Birds* sing, and chatter,
Only for *Men* to *promise, swear,* and *flatter:*
So *Men* these *Properties* can imitate,
But not their *Faculties* that *Nature* made.
Men have no *Wings* to fly up to the *Sky*,   155
Nor can they like to *Fish* in *waters* lie.
What *Man* like *Roes* can run so swift, and long?
Nor are they like to *Horse*, or *Lions* strong.
Nor have they *Sent*, like *Dogs*, a *Hare* to find,
Or *Sight* like *Swine* to see the subtle *wind.*   160
Thus several *Creatures*, by several *Sense*,
Have better far (than *Man*) *Intelligence.*
   These several *Creatures*, several *Arts* do well,
But *Man* in general, doth them far excel.
For *Arts* in *Men* as well did *Nature* give,   165
As other *qualities* in *Beast* to live.
And from *Men's Brains* such fine *Inventions* flow,
As in his *Head* all other *heads* do grow.
What *Creature* builds like *Man* such *Stately Towers*,
And make such things, as *Time* cannot devour?   170
What *Creature* makes such *Engines* as *Man* can?
To traffick, and to use at *Sea*, and *Land.*
To *kill*, to *spoil*, or else alive to *take*,
Destroying all that other *Creatures* make.
This makes *Man* seem of all the *World* a *King*,   175

Because *he* power hath of every *thing*.
He'll teach *Birds* words, in measure *Beast* to go,
Makes *Passions* in the *Mind*, to ebb, and *flow*.
And though he cannot fly as *Birds*, with *wings*,
Yet he can take the height, and breadth of things. 180
He knows the course and number of the *Stars*,
But *Birds*, and *Beasts* are no *Astrologers*.
And though he cannot like to *Fishes* swim,
Yet *Nets He* makes, to catch those *Fishes* in.
And with his *Ships* he'll circle the *World* round. 185
What *Beast*, or *Bird* that can do so, is found?
He'll fell down *Woods*, with *Axes* sharp will strike;
Whole *Heards* of *Beasts* can never do the like.
What *Beast* can plead, to save another's *Life*,
Or by his *Eloquence* can end a *Strife?* 190
Or *Counsels* give, great *Dangers* for to shun,
Or tell the *Cause*, or how *Eclipses* come?
He'll turn the *Current* of the *Water* clear,
And make them like new *Seas* for to appear.
Where *Fishes* only in old *waters* glide. 195
Can cut new *Rivers* out on any side.
He *Mountains* makes so high, the *Clouds* will touch,
Mountains of *Moles*, or *Ants*, scarce do so much.
What *Creature* like to *Man* can *Reasons* show,
Which makes him know, that he thereby doth know? 200
And who, but *Man*, makes use of every thing,
As *Goodness* out of *Poison He* can bring?
Thus *Man* is filled a with strong Desire,
And by his *Rhet'rick* sets the *Soul* on *Fire*.
Beasts no *Ambition* have to get a *Fame*, 205
Nor build they *Tombs*, thereon to write their *Name*.
They never war, *high Honour* for to get,
But to secure themselves, or *Meat* to eat.
But *Men* are like to *Gods*, they live for ever shall;
And *Beasts* are like themselves, to *Dust* shall fall. 210

Earth's Complaint

O *Nature, Nature*, hearken to my *Cry*,
Each *Minute* wounded am, but cannot die.
My *Children* which *I* from my *Womb* did bear,
Do dig my *Sides*, and all my *Bowels* tear:
Do plow deep *Furrows* in my very *Face*, 5
From *Torment*, *I* have neither time, nor place.

No other *Element* is so abused,
Nor by *Mankind* so cruelly is used.
Man cannot reach the *Skies* to plow, and sow,
Nor can they set, or mark the *Stars* to grow.   10
But they are still as *Nature* first did plant,
Neither *Maturity*, nor *Growth* they want.
They never die, nor do they yield their place
To *younger Stars*, but still run their own *Race*.
The *Sun* doth never groan *young Suns* to bear,   15
For he himself is his own *Son*, and *Heir*.
The *Sun* just in the *Center* sits, as *King*,
The *Planets* round about encircle him.
The slowest *Orbs* over his *Head* turn slow,
And underneath, the *swiftest Planets* go.   20
Each several *Planet*, several measures take,
And with their *Motions* they sweet *Musick* make.
Thus all the *Planets* round about him move,
And he returns them *Light* for their kind *Love*.

The Hunting of the Hare

Betwixt two *Ridges* of *Plowed land*, lay *Wat*,
Pressing his *Body* close to *Earth* lay squat.
His *Nose* upon his two *Forefeet* close lies,
Glaring obliquely with his *great gray Eyes*.
His *Head* he always sets against the *Wind*;   5
If turn his *Tail*, his *Hairs* blow up behind:
Which *he* too cold will grow, but *he* is wise,
And keeps his *Coat* still down, so warm *he* lies.
Thus resting all the *day*, till *Sun* doth set,
Then riseth up, his *Relief* for to get.   10
Walking about until the *Sun* doth rise,
Then back returns, down in his *Form he* lies.
At last, *Poor Wat* was found, as *he* there lay,
By *Huntsmen*, with their *Dogs* which came that way.
Seeing, gets up, and fast begins to run,   15
Hoping some ways the *Cruel Dogs* to shun.
But they by *Nature* have so quick a *Scent*,
That by their *Nose* they trace what way *he* went.
And with their deep, wide *Mouths* set forth a *Cry*,
Which answered was by *Echoes* in the *Sky*.   20
Then *Wat* was struck with *Terror*, and with *Fear*,
Thinks every *Shadow* still the *Dogs* they were.
And running out some distance from the *noise*,
To hide himself, his *Thoughts* he now employs.

Under a *Clod* of *Earth* in *Sand pit* wide,   25
Poor *Wat* sat close, hoping himself to hide.
There long he had not sat, but straight his *Ears*
The *Winding Horns*, and crying *Dogs* he hears:
Starting with *Fear*, up leaps, then doth he run,
And with such speed, the *Ground* scarce treads upon.   30
Into a great thick *Wood he* straightway gets,
Where underneath a *broken Bough he* sits.
At every *Leaf* that with the *wind* did shake,
Did bring such *Terror*, made his *Heart* to ache.
That *Place he* left, to *Champaign Plains he* went,   35
Winding about, for to deceive their *Scent*.
And while they *snuffling* were, to find his *Track*,
Poor *Wat*, being weary, his swift pace did slack.
On his two *hinder legs* for ease did sit,
His *Forefeet* rubbed his *Face* from *Dust*, and *Sweat*.   40
Licking his *Feet*, he wiped his *Ears* so clean,
That none could tell that *Wat* had hunted been.
But casting round about his *fair great Eyes*,
The *Hounds* in full *Career he* near him 'spies:
To *Wat* it was so terrible a *Sight*,   45
Fear gave him *Wings*, and made his *Body* light.
Though weary was before, by running long,
Yet now his *Breath* he never felt more strong.
Like those that *dying* are, think *Health* returns,
When tis but a *faint Blast*, which *Life* out burns.   50
For *Spirits* seek to guard the *Heart* about,
Striving with *Death*, but *Death* doth quench them out.
Thus they so fast came on, with such loud *Cries*,
That *he* no hopes hath left, nor *help* espies.
With that the *Winds* did pity *poor Wat*'s case,   55
And with their *Breath* the *Scent* blew from the *Place*.
Then every *Nose* is busily employed,
And every *Nostril* is set open, wide:
And every *Head* doth seek a several way,
To find what *Grass*, or *Track*, the *Scent* on lay.   60
Thus quick Industry, that is not slack,
Is like to Witchery, brings lost things back.
For though the *Wind* had tied the *Scent* up close,
A *Busy Dog* thrust in his *Snuffling Nose*:
And drew it out, with it did foremost run,   65
Then *Horns* blew loud, for th' *rest* to follow on.
The *great slow Hounds*, their throats did set a *Base*,
The *Fleet swift Hounds*, as *Tenors* next in place;
The little *Beagles* they a *Treble* sing,
And through the *Air* their *Voice* a round did ring?   70

Which made a *Consort*, as they ran along;
If they but *words* could speak, might sing a *Song*,
The *Horns* kept time, the *Hunters* shout for *Joy*,
And valiant seem, *poor Wat* for to destroy:
Spurring their *Horses* to a full *Career*,   75
Swim Rivers deep, leap Ditches without fear;
Endanger *Life*, and *Limbs*, so fast will ride,
Only to see how patiently *Wat* died.
For why, the *Dogs* so near his *Heels* did get,
That they their sharp *Teeth* in his *Breech* did set.   80
Then tumbling down, did fall with *weeping Eyes*,
Gives up his *Ghost*, and thus poor *Wat he* dies.
Men hooping loud, such *Acclamations* make,
As if the *Devil* they did *Prisoner* take.
When they do but a *shiftless Creature* kill;   85
To hunt, there needs no *Valiant Soldier*'s skill.
But *Man* doth think that *Exercise*, and *Toil*,
To keep their *Health*, is best, which makes most spoil.
Thinking that *Food*, and *Nourishment* so good,
And *Appetite*, that feeds on *Flesh*, and *Blood*.   90
When they do *Lions, Wolves, Bears, Tigers* see,
To kill poor *Sheep*, straight say, they cruel be.
But for themselves all *Creatures* think too few,
For *Luxury*, wish *God* would make them new.
As if that *God* made *Creatures* for *Man's meat*,   95
To give them *Life*, and *Sense*, for *Man* to eat;
Or else for *Sport*, or *Recreation*'s sake,
Destroy those *Lives* that *God* saw good to make:
Making their *Stomacks*, *Graves*, which full they fill
With *Murthered Bodies*, that in sport they kill.   100
Yet *Man* doth think himself so gentle, mild,
When *he* of *Creatures* is most cruel wild.
And is so *Proud*, thinks only he shall live,
That *God* a *God*-like *Nature* did him give.
And that all *Creatures* for his sake alone,   105
Was made for him, to *Tyrannize* upon.

🖉 Mary Rowlandson (c. 1636–1711)

The Puritans who founded Massachusetts Bay Colony in 1620 initially established good relations with the Native Americans, but eventually conflict developed, as the growing population of English settlers expanded into the surrounding wilderness, took possession of tribal lands, and imposed English courts and property rights. In June 1675, these tensions erupted into warfare, sparked by the trial and execution of three Wampanoag

Indians for an alleged crime in Plymouth, Massachusetts. Seeking revenge, the tribal leader Metacom (called King Philip by the colonists) led a series of Wampanoag attacks on outlying British settlements. One of the most lethal wars in American history, King Philip's War, though not long, resulted in thousands of deaths on both sides. The Native American forces had the advantage of the wilderness but nevertheless were soon defeated by the numerically superior British army.

When Metacom's warriors arrived at the small town of Lancaster, Massachusetts, early in the morning of February 10, 1676, they attacked with incredible speed and ferocity, killing all adult males and capturing just a few women and children, evidently in the expectation that they could later be ransomed. Mary Rowlandson describes this attack in chilling detail, and her account of three months' captivity among the Wampanoag is one of the great classics of American literature. A Narrative of the Captivity and Restauration of Mrs. Mary Rowlandson (1682) provides fascinating insights into the early period of contact between the Puritan settlers and the indigenous people of North America. Rowlandson's description of her struggle for survival in the bleak winter landscape of New England, suffused by violence, terror, and imminent starvation, is one of the most powerful and evocative narratives to emerge from any American writer during the seventeenth century. As she wanders with her often cruel captors through the harsh and terrible wilderness, she offers a distinctively female perspective on the environment of New England in the early Colonial period.

Aside from her famous narrative, which was widely read both in Britain and America, very little is known about the life of Mary Rowlandson. She is thought to have been born in England in about 1636. It is known that she was brought to America at an early age by her father, John White, who became a prosperous landowner in Massachusetts Bay Colony. In about 1656, she married John Rowlandson, a graduate of Harvard College who served as minister to the Puritan congregation in the remote, rapidly growing town of Lancaster. For the next twenty years, Mary Rowlandson was a wife, mother, and devoted member of the local Puritan church. The eloquence, piety, and thoughtful use of biblical allusion in Rowlandson's Narrative bespeak her evident ability and self-confidence as a public speaker. Mary Rowlandson's husband died in 1678, just two years after her return from captivity. She remarried in the following year, and lived with her second husband, Captain Samuel Talcott, until her death in 1711.

From A Narrative of the Captivity and Restauration of Mrs. Mary Rowlandson

On the tenth of February 1675, Came the *Indians* with great numbers upon *Lancaster:*[1] Their first coming was about Sun-rising; hearing the noise of some Guns, we looked out; several Houses were burning, and the Smoke ascending to Heaven. There were five persons taken in one house, the Father, and the Mother and a sucking Child, they knockt on the head; the other two they took and carried away alive. There were two others, who being out of their Garison[2] upon

---

[1] Lancaster, Massachusetts, was a frontier village of about fifty families, located thirty miles to the west of Boston.

[2] Also *garrison*, a fortified house used as a place of refuge from attack.

some occasion were set upon; one was knockt on the head, the other escaped: Another there was who running along was shot and wounded, and fell down; he begged of them his life, promising them Money (as they told me) but they would not hearken to him but knockt him in head, and stript him naked, and split open his Bowels. Another seeing many of the *Indians* about his Barn, ventured and went out, but was quickly shot down. There were three others belonging to the same Garison who were killed; the *Indians* getting up upon the roof of the Barn, had advantage to shoot down upon them over their Fortification. Thus these murtherous wretches went on, burning, and destroying before them.

At length they came and beset our own house, and quickly it was the dolefulest day that ever mine eyes saw. The House stood upon the edge of a hill; some of the *Indians* got behind the hill, others into the Barn, and others behind any thing that could shelter them; from all which places they shot against the House, so that the Bullets seemed to fly like hail; and quickly they wounded one man among us, then another, and then a third. About two hours (according to my observation, in that amazing time) they had been about the house before they prevailed to fire it (which they did with Flax and Hemp, which they brought out of the Barn, and there being no defence about the House, only two Flankers[3] at two opposite corners, and one of them not finished) they fired it once and one ventured out and quenched it, but they quickly fired again, and that took. Now is that dreadful hour come, that I have often heard of (in time of War, as it was the case of others) but now mine eyes see it. Some in our house were fighting for their lives, others wallowing in their blood, the House on fire over our heads, and the bloody Heathen ready to knock us on the head, if we stirred out. Now might we hear Mothers and Children crying out for themselves, and one another, *Lord, What shall we do?* Then I took my Children[4] (and one of my sisters, hers) to go forth and leave the house: but as soon as we came to the door and appeared, the *Indians* shot so thick that the bullets rattled against the House, as if one had taken an handful of stones and threw them, so that we were fain to give back. We had six stout Dogs belonging to our Garrison, but none of them wou'd stir, though another time, if any *Indian* had come to the door, they were ready to fly upon him and tear him down. The Lord hereby would make us the more to acknowledge his hand, and to see that our help is always in him. But out we must go, the fire increasing, and coming along behind us, roaring, and the Indians gaping before us with their Guns, Spears and Hatchets to devour us. No sooner were we out of the House, but my Brother in Law (being before wounded, in defending the house, in or near the throat) fell down dead, whereat the *Indians* scornfully shouted, and hallowed, and were presently upon him, stripping off his cloaths, the bulletts flying thick, one went through my side, and the same (as would seem) through the bowels and hand of my dear Child in my arms.[5] One of my elder Sister's Children, named *William*, had then his Leg broken, which the *Indians* perceiving, they knockt him on head. Thus were we butchered by those

---

[3] Projecting fortifications.

[4] Rowlandson had three children: Joseph (age 14), Mary (age 10), and Sarah (age 6).

[5] Her youngest child, Sarah.

merciless Heathen, standing amazed, with the blood running down to our heels. My eldest Sister being yet in the House, and seeing those woeful sights, the Infidels hauling Mothers one way, and Children another, and some wallowing in their blood: and her elder Son telling her that her Son *William* was dead, and myself was wounded, she said, And, *Lord, let me die with them;* which was no sooner said, but she was struck with a Bullet, and fell down dead over the threshold. I hope she is reaping the fruit of her good labours, being faithful to the service of God in her place. In her younger years she lay under much trouble upon spiritual accounts, till it pleased God to make that precious scripture take hold of her heart, 2 *Cor.* 12.9. *And he said unto me, my grace is sufficient for thee.* More than twenty years after I have heard her tell how sweet and comfortable that place was to her. But to return: the *Indians* laid hold of us, pulling me one way, and the Children another, and said, *Come go along with us;* I told them they would kill me: they answered, *If I were willing to go along with them, they would not hurt me.*

Oh the doleful sight that now was to behold at this House! *Come, behold the works of the Lord, what desolations he has made in the Earth.*[6] Of thirty seven persons who were in this one House, none escaped either present death, or a bitter captivity, save only one, who might say as he, *Job* 1.15. *And I only am escaped alone to tell the News.* There were twelve killed, some shot, some stabbed with their Spears, some knocked down with their Hatchets. When we are in prosperity, Oh the little that we think of such dreadful sights, and to see our dear Friends, and Relations lie bleeding out their heart-blood upon the ground. There was one who was chopt into the head with a Hatchet, and stripped naked, and yet was crawling up and down. It is a solemn sight to see so many Christians lying in their blood, some here, and some there, like a company of Sheep torn by Wolves. All of them stript naked by a company of hell-hounds, roaring, singing, ranting and insulting, as if they would have torn our very hearts out; yet the Lord by his Almighty power preserved a number of us from death, for there were twenty-four of us taken alive and carried captive.

I had often before this said, that if the *Indians* should come, I should chuse rather to be killed by them than be taken alive, but when it came to the trial my mind changed; their glittering weapons so daunted my spirit, that I chose rather to go along with those (as I may say) ravenous Beasts, than that moment to end my days; and that I may the better declare what happened to me during that grievous Captivity, I shall particularly speak of the several Removes[7] we had up and down the Wilderness.

The First Remove

Now away we must go with those Barbarous Creatures, with our bodies wounded and bleeding, and our hearts no less than our bodies. About a mile we went that night, up upon a hill within sight of the Town, where they intended to lodge. There was hard by a vacant house (deserted by the English before, for fear of the

---

[6] Psalm 46.8.

[7] Departures to a different place. Rowlandson experienced a total of twenty "removes" during her captivity.

Indians). I asked them whither I might not lodge in the house that night to which they answered, What will you love *English men* still? This was the dolefulest night that ever my eyes saw. Oh the roaring, and singing and dancing, and yelling of those black creatures in the night, which made the place a lively resemblance of hell. And as miserable was the waste that was there made, of Horses, Cattle, Sheep, Swine, Calves, Lambs, Roasting Pigs, and Fowls (which they had plundered in the Town) some roasting, some lying and burning, and some boiling to feed our merciless Enemies; who were joyful enough though we were disconsolate. To add to the dolefulness of the former day, and the dismalness of the present night: my thoughts ran upon my losses and sad bereaved condition. All was gone, my Husband gone (at least separated from me, he being in the Bay,[8] and to add to my grief, the *Indians* told me they would kill him as he came homeward), my Children gone, my Relations and Friends gone, our House and home and all our comforts within door, and without, all was gone, (except my life) and I knew not but the next moment that might go too. There remained nothing to me but one poor wounded Babe, and it seemed at present worse than death that it was in such a pitiful condition, bespeaking Compassion, and I had no refreshing for it, nor suitable things to revive it. Little do many think what is the savageness and brutishness of this barbarous Enemy, aye even those that seem to profess more than others among them, when the *English* have fallen into their hands.

Those seven that were killed at *Lancaster* the summer before upon a Sabbath day, and the one that was afterward killed upon a week day, were slain and mangled in a barbarous manner, by One-ey'd *John*, and *Marlborough's* Praying *Indians*, which Capt. *Mosely* brought to *Boston*, as the *Indians* told me.[9]

The Second Remove

But now, the next morning, I must turn my back upon the Town, and travel with them into the vast and desolate Wilderness, I knew not whither. It is not my tongue, or pen can express the sorrows of my heart, and bitterness of my spirit, that I had at this departure: but God was with me, in a wonderful manner, carrying me along, and bearing up my spirit, that it did not quite fail. One of the *Indians* carried my poor wounded Babe upon a horse, it went moaning all along, I shall die, I shall die. I went on foot after it, with sorrow that cannot be exprest. At length I took it off the horse, and carried it in my arms till my strength failed, and I fell down with it: Then they set me upon a horse with my wounded Child in my lap, and there being no furniture[10] upon the horse back, as we were going down a steep hill, we both fell over the horses head, at which they like inhumane creatures laught, and rejoiced to see it, though I thought we should there have ended our days, as overcome with so many difficulties. But the Lord renewed my strength still, and carried me along, that I might see more of his Power; yea, so much that I could never have thought of, had I not experienced it.

[8] Boston, the capital of Massachusetts Bay Colony.

[9] Rowlandson refers here to an attack on Lancaster that occurred the previous August, led by an Indian known as "One-Eyed John." Some Christian Indians in the town of Marlborough were also implicated in this attack.

[10] Saddle and stirrups.

After this it quickly began to snow, and when night came on, they stopt: and now down I must sit in the snow, by a little fire, and a few boughs behind me, with my sick Child in my lap; and calling much for water, being now (through the wound) fallen into a violent Fever. My own wound also growing so stiff, that I could scarce sit down or rise up; yet so it must be, that I must sit all this cold winter night upon the cold snowy ground, with my sick Child in my arms, looking that every hour would be the last of its life; and having no Christian friend near me, either to comfort or help me. Oh, I may see the wonderful power of God, that my Spirit did not utterly sink under my affliction: still the Lord upheld me with his gracious and merciful Spirit, and we were both alive to see the light of the next morning.

The Third Remove

The morning being come, they prepared to go on their way: One of the Indians *got up upon a horse, and they set me up behind him, with my poor sick Babe in my lap.* A very wearisome and tedious day I had of it; what with my own wound, and my Child's being so exceeding sick, and in a lamentable condition with her wound. It may be easily judged what a poor feeble condition we were in, there being not the least crumb of refreshing that came within either of our mouths, from *Wednesday* night to *Saturday* night, except only a little cold water. This day in the afternoon, about an hour by Sun, we came to the place where they intended, *viz.* an Indian town called *Wenimesset*, northward of *Quabaug*. When we were come, Oh the number of Pagans (now merciless enemies) that there came about me, that I may say as *David, Psal.* 27. 13, *I had fainted, unless I had believed, &c.* The next day was the Sabbath: I then remembered how careless I had been of God's holy time: how many Sabbaths I had lost and misspent, and how evilly I had walked in God's sight; which lay so close unto my spirit, that it was easy for me to see how righteous it was with God to cut off the thread of my life, and cast me out of his presence forever. Yet the Lord still showed mercy to me, and upheld me; and as he wounded me with one hand, so he healed me with the other. This day there came to me one *Robert Pepper* (a man belonging to *Roxbury*) who was taken in Captain *Beers* his fight,[11] and had been now a considerable time with the *Indians;* and up with them almost as far as *Albany* to see king *Philip,* as he told me, and was now very lately come into these parts. Hearing, I say, that I was in this *Indian* Town, he obtained leave to come and see me. He told me, he himself was wounded in the leg at Captain *Beers* his Fight; and was not able some time to go, but as they carried him, and as he took Oaken leaves and laid to his wound, and through the blessing of God he was able to travel again. Then I took Oaken leaves and laid to my side, and with the blessing of God it cured me also; yet before the cure was wrought, I may say, as it is in *Psal.* 38. 5, 6. *My wounds stink and are corrupt, I am troubled, I am bowed down greatly, I go mourning all the day long.* I sat much alone with a poor wounded Child in my lap, which moaned night and

[11] Captain Richard Beers and his troops were attacked near Northfield, Massachusetts, in September of the previous year.

day, having nothing to revive the body, or cheer the spirits of her, but instead of that, sometimes one *Indian* would come and tell me in one hour, that your *Master* will knock your Child in the head, and then a second, and then a third, your *Master* will quickly knock your Child in the head.

This was the comfort I had from them, miserable comforters are ye all, as he said.[12] Thus nine days I sat upon my knees, with my Babe in my lap, till my flesh was raw again; my Child being even ready to depart this sorrowful world, they bade me carry it out to another Wigwam (I suppose because they would not be troubled with such spectacles), Whither I went with a very heavy heart, and down I sat with the picture of death in my lap. About two hours in the night, my sweet Babe, like a lamb departed this life, on *Feb. 18. 1675*, It being about six *years*, and *five months* old. It was *nine days* from the first wounding, in this miserable condition, without any refreshing of one nature or other, except a little cold water. I cannot but take notice, how at another time I could not bear to be in the room where any dead person was, but now the case is changed; I must and could lie down by my dead Babe, side by side all the night after. I have thought since of the wonderful goodness of God to me, in preserving me in the use of my reason and senses, in that distressed time, that I did not use wicked and violent means to end my own miserable life. In the morning, when they understood that my child was dead they sent for me home to my Master's Wigwam: (by my Master in this writing, must be understood *Quanopin*, who was a *Saggamore*,[13] and married King *Philip's* wives' Sister; not that he first took me, but I was sold to him by another *Narhaganset Indian*, who took me when first I came out of the Garison). I went to take up my dead child in my arms to carry it with me, but they bid me let it alone: there was no resisting, but go I must and leave it. When I had been at my master's *wigwam*, I took the first opportunity I could get, to go look after my dead child: when I came I askt them what they had done with it? then they told me it was upon the hill: then they went and showed me where it was, where I saw the ground was newly digged, and there they told me they had buried it: *There I left that Child in the Wilderness, and must commit it, and my self also in this Wilderness-condition, to him who is above all.* God having taken away this dear Child, I went to see my daughter *Mary*, who was at this same *Indian Town*, at a *Wigwam* not very far off, though we had little liberty or opportunity to see one another: she was about ten years old, and taken from the door at first by a *Praying Indian* and afterward sold for a gun. When I came in sight, she would fall a weeping; at which they were provoked, and would not let me come near her, but bade me be gone; which was a heart-cutting word to me. I had one Child dead, another in the Wilderness, I knew not where, the third they would not let me come near to: *Me* (as he said) *have ye bereaved of my children, Joseph is not, and Simeon is not, and ye will take Benjamin also, all these things are against me.*[14] I could not sit still in this condition, but kept, walking from *one* place to another. And as I was going along, my heart was even overwhelmed with the thoughts of

[12] Job 16.2.

[13] A sachem, or subordinate chief.

[14] Genesis 42.36.

my condition, and that I should have Children, *and a Nation which I knew not ruled over them.* Whereupon I earnestly entreated the Lord, that he would consider my low estate, and show me a token for good, and if it were his blessed will, some sign and hope of some relief. And indeed quickly the Lord answered, in some measure, my poor prayers: for as I was going up and down mourning and lamenting my condition, my Son came to me, and asked me how I did; I had not seen him before, since the destruction of the Town, and I knew not where he was, till I was informed by himself, that he was amongst a smaller parcel of *Indians,* whose place was about six miles off; with tears in his eyes, he asked me whether his sister *Sarah* was dead; and told me he had seen his sister *Mary;* and prayed me, that I would not be troubled in reference to himself. The occasion of his coming to see me at this time, was this: There was, as I said, about six miles from us, a small Plantation of *Indians,* where it seems he had been during his Captivity: and at this time, there were some Forces of the *Indians* gathered out of our company, and some also from them (among whom was my Son's master) to go to assault and burn *Medfield:* In this time of the absence of his master, his dame brought him to see me. I took this to be some gracious answer to my earnest and unfeigned desire. The next day, *viz.* to this, the *Indians* returned from *Medfield,* all the company, for those that belonged to the other small company, came through the Town that now we were at. But before they came to us, Oh! the outrageous roaring and hooping that there was: They began their din about a mile before they came to us. By their noise and hooping they signified how many they had destroyed (which was at that time twenty three). Those that were with us at home, were gathered together as soon as they heard the hooping, and every time that the other went over their number, these at home gave a shout, that the very Earth rung again: And thus they continued till those that had been upon the expedition were come up to the *Sagamore's Wigwam;* and then, Oh, the hideous insulting and triumphing that there was over some *Englishmen's* scalps that they had taken (as their manner) and brought with them. I cannot but take notice of the wonderful mercy of God to me in those afflictions, in sending me a Bible. One of the *Indians* that came from *Medfield* fight, had brought some plunder, came to me, and asked me, if I wou'd have a Bible, he had got one in his basket. I was glad of it, and asked him, whether he thought the *Indians* would let me read? He answered, yes: So I took the Bible, and in that melancholy time, it came into my mind to read first the 28. *Chap.* of *Deut.* which I did, and when I had read it, my dark heart wrought on this manner, *That there was no mercy for me, that the blessings were gone, and the curses come in their room, and that I had lost my opportunity.* But the Lord helped me still to go on reading till I came to *Chap.* 30 the seven first verses, where I found, *There was mercy promised again, if we would return to him by repentance; and though we were scattered from one end of the Earth to the other, yet the Lord would gather us together, and turn all those curses upon our Enemies.* I do not desire to live to forget this Scripture, and what comfort it was to me.

Now the *Indians* began to talk of removing from this place, some one way, and some another. There were now besides my self nine *English* Captives in this place (all of them Children, except one Woman). I got an opportunity to go and take my leave of them; they being to go one way, and I another, *I asked them whether they were earnest with God for deliverance;* they told me, they did as they were able, and it was some comfort to me, that the Lord stirred up *Children to look to him.* The Woman *viz.* Goodwife *Joslin*[15] told me, she should never see me again, and that she could find in her heart to run away; I wisht her not to run away by any means, for we were near *thirty miles* from any *English Town,* and she very big with Child, and had but one week to reckon; and another Child in her Arms, two years old, and bad Rivers there were to go over, and we were feeble, with our poor and coarse entertainment. I had my Bible with me, I pulled it out, and asked her whether she would read; we opened the Bible and lighted on *Psal.* 27. in which Psalm we especially took notice of that, *ver. ult.,*[16] *Wait on the Lord, Be of good courage, and he shall strengthen thine heart, wait I say on the Lord.*

The Fourth Remove

And now I must part with that little company I had. Here I parted from my daughter *Mary,* (whom I never saw again till I saw her in *Dorchester,* returned from Captivity), and from four little Cousins and Neighbours, some of which I never saw afterward: the Lord only knows the end of them. Amongst them also was that poor Woman before mentioned, who came to a sad end, as some of the company told me in my travel: She having much grief upon her Spirit, about her miserable condition, being so near her time, she would be often asking the Indians to let her go home; they not being willing to that, and yet vexed with her importunity, gathered a great company together about her, and stript her naked, and set her in the midst of them; and when they had sung and danced about her (in their hellish manner) as long as they pleased, they knockt her on head, and the child in her arms with her: when they had done that, they made a fire and put them both into it, and told the other Children that were with them, that if they attempted to go home, they would serve them in like manner: The Children said, she did not shed one tear, but prayed all the while. But to return to my own Journey; we travelled about half a day or little more, and came to a desolate place in the Wilderness, where there were no *Wigwams* or *Inhabitants* before; we came about the middle of the afternoon to this place; cold and wet, and snowy, and hungry, and weary, and no refreshing, for man, but the cold ground to sit on, and our poor *Indian cheer.*

Heart-aching thoughts here I had about my poor Children, who were scattered up and down among the wild beasts of the forrest: My head was light and dizzy (either through hunger or hard lodging, or trouble or all together), my knees feeble, my body raw by sitting double night and day, that I cannot express to man the affliction that lay upon my Spirit, but the Lord helped me at that time to express it to himself. I opened my Bible to read, and the Lord brought that precious scripture to me, *Jer.* 31.16. *Thus saith the Lord, refrain thy voice from weeping, and thine eyes from tears, for thy work shall be rewarded, and they shall come*

---

[15] Ann Joslin, also captured from the Rowlandson garrison. "Goodwife" is a title of courtesy for the female head of a household.

[16] Abbreviation means "last verse."

again from the land of the Enemy. This was a sweet Cordial to me, when I was ready to faint, many and many a time have I sat down, and wept sweetly over this Scripture. At this place we continued about four days. . . .

From The Twentieth Remove

But to return again to my going home, where we may see a remarkable change of Providence: At first they were all against it, except my Husband would come for me; but afterwards they assented to it, and seemed much to rejoice in it; some askt me to send them some Bread, others some Tobacco, others shaking me by the hand, offering me a Hood and Scarf to ride in; not one moving hand or tongue against it. Thus hath the Lord answered my poor desire, and the many earnest requests of others put up unto God for me. In my travels an *Indian* came to me, and told me, if I were willing, he and his *Squaw* would run away, and go home along with me: I told him *No:* I was not willing to run away, but desired to wait God's time, that I might go home quietly, and without fear. And now God hath granted me my desire. O the wonderful power of God that I have seen, and the experience that I have had: *I have been in the midst of those roaring Lions, and Salvage Bears, that feared neither God, nor Man, nor the Devil, by night and day, alone and in company: sleeping all sorts together, and yet not one of them ever offered me the least abuse of unchastity to me, in word or action.* Though some are ready to say, I speak it for my own credit; *But I speak it in the presence of God, and to His glory.* God's power is as great now, and as sufficient to save, as when he preserved *Daniel* in the Lion's den; or the three *Children* in the fiery Furnace. I may well say as his *Psal.* 107. 1, 2, *Oh give thanks unto the Lord for He is good, for his mercy endureth for ever.* Let the Redeemed of the Lord say so, whom He hath redeemed from the hand of the Enemy, especially that I should come away in the midst of so many hundreds of Enemies quietly and peaceably, and not a Dog moving his tongue. So I took my leave of them, and in coming along my heart melted into tears, more than all the while I was with them, and I was almost swallowed up with the thoughts that ever I should go home again. About the Sun going down, Mr. *Hoar,* and my self, and the two *Indians* came to *Lancaster;* and a solemn sight it was to me. There had I lived many comfortable years amongst my Relations and Neighbours, and now not one *Christian* to be seen, nor one house left standing. We went on to a Farm house that was yet standing, where we lay all night: and a comfortable lodging we had, though nothing but straw to lie on. The Lord preserved us in safety that night, and raised us up again in the morning, and carried us along, that before noon, we came to *Concord.* Now was I full of joy, and yet not without sorrow: joy to see such a lovely sight, so many *Christians* together, and some of them my Neighbours: There I met with my Brother, and my Brother in Law, who asked me, if I knew where his Wife was? Poor heart! he had helped to bury her, and knew it not; she being shot down by the house was partly burnt: so that those who were at *Boston* at the desolation of the *Town,* and came back afterward, and buried the dead, did not know her. Yet I was not without sorrow, to think how many were looking and longing, and my own Children amongst the rest, to enjoy that deliverance that I had now received, and I did not know whither ever I should see them again. Being recruited[17] with food and raiment we went to *Boston* that day, where I met with my dear Husband, but the thoughts of our dear Children, one being dead, and the other we could not tell where, abated our comfort each to other. I was not before so much hemmed in with the merciless and cruel Heathen, but now as much with pitiful, tender-hearted and compassionate Christians. In that poor, and destressed, and beggerly condition I was received in, I was kindly entertained in several Houses: so much love I received from several (some of whom I knew, and others I knew not) that I am not capable to declare it. But the Lord knows them all by name: *The Lord reward them sevenfold into their bosoms of his spirituals, for their temporals!*[18] The *twenty pounds* the price of my redemption was raised by some *Boston* Gentlemen, and Mrs. *Usher,* whose bounty and religious charity, I would not forget to make mention of. Then Mr. *Thomas Shepard* of *Charlestown* received us into his House, where we continued eleven weeks; and a Father and Mother they were to us. And many more tender-hearted Friends we met with in that place. We were now in the midst of love, yet not without much and frequent heaviness of heart for our poor Children, and other Relations, who were still in affliction. The week following, after my coming in, the Governour and Council sent forth to the *Indians* again; and that not without success; for they brought in my Sister, and Good-wife Kettle: Their not knowing where our Children were, was a sore trial to us still, and yet we were not without secret hopes that we should see them again. That which was dead lay heavier upon my spirit, than those which were alive and amongst the Heathen; thinking how it suffered with its wounds, and I was in no way able to relieve it; and how it was buried by the Heathen in the *Wilderness* from among all Christians. . . .

[17] Supplied.
[18] *Temporals:* charitable gifts.

PART II: 1700-1799

The Eighteenth Century: Cultivating the Garden

LTHOUGH THE MOST CELEBRATED GARDEN IN ENGLISH LITERATURE—
John Milton's Eden—was a product of the previous century, the image
of the garden and the impulse to cultivate—whether it be the cornfields,
the flower patch, or the human mind—predominated in the eighteenth century.
Often labeled the Age of Reason, the early eighteenth century produced writers
who expressed an optimism, encouraged by the promises of the New Science,
about our ability to understand and explain the world around us through empiri-
cally verifiable and universal laws. According to eighteenth-century deism, the
logic and consistent patterns in nature offered proof of God's existence. Nature's
beauty, as the philosopher Edmund Burke would later formulate it, was found in
its orderliness and regularity. Scientists such as Sir Isaac Newton, who according
to legend discovered the law of gravity while sitting in an orchard, confirmed the
general sense of optimism that the natural world was knowable and, once known,
would reveal rational patterns of organization and operation. In 1737, the
Swedish scientist Carolus Linnaeus invented a methodical system of naming the
natural world, thereby imposing *linguistic* order upon it. Linnaeus's two-part
Latin nomenclature, which identifies a plant or animal by its genus and species
names, was devised as a more universal system of designation to thereby facilitate
the transmission of scientific knowledge across national linguistic boundaries.
Knowledge of the laws of nature's processes and a logical system of naming nature's creations would serve humanity's efforts to impose further order, improving on nature, or, as French scientist Count Georges Buffon described it in his
groundbreaking treatise on natural history, *The Epochs of Nature* (1779; one of 36
volumes published in his *Histoire naturelle, générale et particulière*, 1749–88), "seconding" the work of nature. Although the established church considered deism

heretical, many Enlightenment intellectuals give evidence of subscribing to the notion that likened the Creator to a master watchmaker, producer of the gorgeously rational machine called the Earth, and its extension, that humanity best fulfills its divine purpose by ensuring that the world is kept polished and in neat working order. Thus the actions of humanity, equipped with scientific knowledge, would only increase nature's fruitfulness, productivity, orderliness, and overall beauty.

How this "seconding" of nature might occur is explored in numerous literary works of the century, both in more predictable genres such as locodescriptive and georgic poetry and poetry praising the virtues of rural retirement, and in the development of newer prose forms, including the novel and the natural-history essay. Poems concerning what has come to be known as the English Garden give perhaps the most concise account of the proper way for humanity to fulfill its duty of seconding or improving upon nature. Humanity's role is not to dramatically alter nature by a random imposition of artificial design but instead to better bring forward what is already intrinsically there—that is, to cultivate, not to recreate or rebuild—bringing forth and consulting what Alexander Pope called "the genius of the place." Pope's "Epistle to Burlington," William Shenstone's "Rural Elegance," and William Mason's extensive *The English Garden* are each similarly prescriptive about how best to sculpt the landscape. Pope reminds the gardener, "In all, let nature never be forgot. / But treat the goddess like a modest fair, / Nor overdress, nor leave her wholly bare." Not all locodescriptive nature poetry focused on such enclosed spaces as gardens. The century is also known for its more expansive topographic verse, poetry which displayed a more widely ranging use of description, as it attempted to cover more ground than a single piece of land, and which often traveled in time as well as space to illustrate both the variety and the temporal mutability of the environment. The definitive poem in this genre is James Thomson's masterpiece, *The Seasons*, comprised of various touristic vignettes collected as the poem's speaker travels across the globe, offering an eagle's-eye view of the scenery below. The speaker's elevated vantage point is standardized in the development of the prospect poem, several of which are named for the hills from which the vista is described: John Dyer's "Grongar Hill" and Richard Jago's *Edge-hill* are notable examples. Locodescriptive poetry, whether about gardens or hilltop views, is closely related with developments in the visual arts and contemporary landscape painting, which had derived from the European models of Claude Lorrain, Salvator Rosa, and Nicholas Poussin (artists who are often explicitly cited by the poets).

Locodescriptive poetry, however, was never purely descriptive. Instead, the scenery was meant to provoke more than a simple aesthetic appreciation. It was to have a morally instructive purpose, namely, to teach us lessons about ourselves or about national history. Such landscapes were frequently dotted with ruins, an indication of the past and a reminder of the transience and vanity of human accomplishments. In some circumstances, as in the case of the georgic, for example, the didactic qualities of the description are at the forefront, as the poets provide detailed and factually accurate information, derived from the latest scientific research, and observations about agriculture, animal husbandry, or proper techniques for fishing or hunting. Christopher Smart's "The Hop-Garden," Dyer's poem on raising sheep, *The Fleece*, or John Gay's "Rural Sports" are all significant examples of the georgic mode, a mode influenced by the renewed interest—in this neoclassical era—in classical Greek and Roman authors such as Theocritus and Virgil. Unlike its cousin the pastoral, the georgic presents the natural world as a place requiring the active intervention of human labor. It is a world that is not perfect (as is the idealized Arcadia of pastoral) and hence calls for the imposition of order. Many poets went so far as to overlay stylistic as well as thematic order upon their georgic poems, writing in the favored form of the regular and predictable heroic couplet. But the georgic mode also found its way into prose. Daniel Defoe's groundbreaking novel *Robinson Crusoe* is a virtual how-to book on transforming a barren island into a productive plantation. Hector St. John de Crèvecoeur and Thomas Jefferson transplanted the genre into the tradition of American prose. The georgic might be seen as a continuation of the more traditional Christian ideology of stewardship—only now the justifications of religion were presumably proven by the discoveries of science. These cultivated spots, be they farms or pleasure gardens, furthered the popular theme of the moral virtues of rural retirement (begun in such country-house poems of the previous century as Ben Jonson's "To Penshurst"). With the seeds of increased urbanization and industrialization being sown throughout both nations, new dimensions were added to the conventional literary contrast of the country and the city.

It would be wrong, however, to characterize the entire century as one of unwavering optimism in the human intellectual ability to know and to "second" nature. A good number of works throughout the century, including Erasmus Darwin's scientific verse *The Botanic Garden* (1791) or Gilbert White's groundbreaking work *The Natural History and Antiquities of Selbourne* (1789), continued to catalogue increasing knowledge about nature and package it in pleasurable and popularly accessible forms. Nevertheless, simultaneously, a strong strain of pessimism was gathering momentum. In satires such as Jonathan Swift's *Gulliver's Travels*, the notion of the perfectibility of creation—human or otherwise—is roundly attacked. In particular, the poetry of the later part of the century, generally known as the Literature of Sensibility, expresses a much more emotional and melancholic perspective on our ability to alter or affect our environment. Often describing sublime landscapes or natural phenomena—scenes or events, such as the hurricane of Charlotte Smith's ode—these poems reveal nature as a powerful and still-mysterious adversary, one which inspires fear and reminds us of our ultimate impotence. Other poems, such as Goldsmith's watershed elegy "The Deserted Village," demonstrate that human intervention does not allow paradise to be regained but causes irremediable environmental degradation. Goldsmith, like later nineteenth-century nature writers, saw urban industrial capitalism as a blight upon the more traditional rural agricultural community. By the end of the century, in 1798, Thomas Malthus would use the same principles of reason toward a purpose that would have been difficult to imagine in 1698. Employing the logic of mathematics and the new (and "dismal") social science of economics, Malthus made apocalyptic predictions about the impact of human population on nature. In the face of these dire prognostications, Romantic and Transcendentalist writers of the next century were compelled to search for new ways to express what precisely could or should be humankind's relationship and responsibilities to the world around us.

✍ *Daniel Defoe* (*1660–1731*)

Daniel Defoe was nearly sixty years old when he created one of the most enduring of modern myths in his novel Robinson Crusoe. *Like his hero, Defoe's life was a rollercoaster of success and failure, glory and despair. His family belonged to the Dissenters, a Nonconformist urban merchant class whose economic and political power was on the rise during the latter part of the seventeenth century. His religion prevented Defoe (whose original family name was "Foe") from attending university, but he was educated in a Dissenting academy where he was exposed to the New Science as well as to the classics. Defoe's main concern in life seems to have been financial. Although he was active politically and maintained strong religious beliefs, all that he did seemed to be motivated by a desire to earn money. Instead of entering the ministry after finishing his schooling (the usual course for those who attended the academies), he became a tradesman and traveled throughout Europe and would continue to travel avidly for the rest of his life. Defoe became involved in numerous commercial affairs, though none of them were ever ultimately successful. Defoe's writing, which can be seen as yet another dimension of his entrepreneurial activities, is varied and speaks about controversial current political and religious events with a popular audience in mind. His output was prodigious: Scholars estimate that he wrote between 500 and 650 pamphlets, journals, poems, and other pieces. The total number is difficult to ascertain; this is because Defoe published many anonymously or under a pseudonym (not a bad idea, as he was twice imprisoned for libelous or scandalous writing). Besides* Robinson Crusoe, *Defoe published several popular novels, including* Captain Singleton *(1720),* Moll Flanders *(1722),* Colonel Jack *(1722), and* Roxana *(1724). His* Journal of the Plague Year *(1722) reports on the devastating effects of the disease in the year 1665 in London. Defoe was not only a writer and a businessman but also, interestingly, a government agent, working as a secret agent in some capacity during most of his life, presumably gathering information as he traveled the English countryside. He died while in hiding from his creditors.*

With The Life and Strange and Surprising Adventures of Robinson Crusoe, of York, Mariner *(1719), the first modern English novel, Defoe created a story that was enormously popular in its own time and remains so today. The novel has been through countless editions in the past three hundred years, and the protagonist has entered popular culture as a household name. In popular mythology, Robinson Crusoe is the archetypal castaway, fighting the battle of man against nature. This notion does have firm grounding in the story: Shipwrecked on a deserted island, Crusoe must fend for himself against the elements to survive. He is alone against the forces of an often hostile nature, which retains powers that seem at once arbitrary and inexorable. Through these circumstances, Defoe is able to comment on the modern European's alienation from nature by showing the hero's difficulties in adapting to life without the trappings of civilization and its luxuries. What is surprising, however, especially to first-time readers of the novel, is that Crusoe is not just a stranded adventurer, but a venture capitalist of the first order. Although a good portion of the novel depicts Crusoe's attempt simply to survive in his natural surroundings, what the story really narrates is the gradual process by which he conquers nature, opportunistically transforming it from enemy to raw material. Crusoe's relationship to nature, however, is not only entrepreneurial. Throughout the novel, the hero reads his relation to nature as a way of understanding his relation to God, for* Robinson Crusoe *is a Puritan conversion story as much as it is an adventure tale. In the protagonist's view at least, God uses nature to both punish and reward Crusoe for his actions. The fact that by the end of the novel Crusoe has turned the desolate island into a booming plantation is to be seen as a sign that the hero is one of God's "elect"—predestined for success in this world and the next. The selection offered below narrates the period during which Crusoe begins to tame his environment and exploit its resources. The apparently careless prose style is meant to mimic the form of a personal diary. The influence of Defoe's journalistic experience is evident in the novel's easy tone of reportage as well as in the detailed attention paid to physical surroundings and material objects.*

From The Life and Strange and Surprising Adventures of Robinson Crusoe, of York, Mariner

I had been now on this unhappy island above ten months; all possibility of deliverance from this condition seemed to be entirely taken from me; and I firmly believed that no human shape had ever set foot upon that place. Having now secured my habitation, as I thought, fully to my mind, I had a great desire to make a more perfect discovery of the island, and to see what other productions I might find, which I yet knew nothing of.

It was the 15th of July that I began to take a more particular survey of the island itself. I went up the creek first, where, as I hinted, I brought my rafts on shore. I found, after I came about two miles up, that the tide did not flow any higher, and that it was no more than a little brook of running water, and very fresh and good; but this being the dry season, there was hardly any water in some parts of it, at least, not enough to run in any stream, so as it could be perceived.

On the bank of this brook I found many pleasant savannas or meadows, plain, smooth, and covered with grass; and on the rising parts of them, next to the higher grounds, where the water, as might be supposed, never overflowed, I found a great deal of tobacco, green, and growing to a great and very strong stalk. There were divers other plants, which I had no notion of, or understanding about, and might, perhaps, have virtues of their own which I could not find out.

I searched for the cassava root, which the Indians, in all that climate, make their bread of, but I could find none. I saw large plants of aloes, but did not then understand them. I saw several sugar-canes, but wild, and, for want of cultivation, imperfect. I contented myself with these discoveries for this time, and came back, musing with myself what course I might take to know the virtue and goodness of any of the fruits or plants which I should discover; but could bring it to no conclusion; for, in short, I had made so little observation while I was in the Brazils, that I knew little of the plants in the field, at least very little that might serve me to any purpose now in my distress.

The next day, the 16th, I went up the same way again; and after going something farther than I had gone the day before, I found the brook and the savannas began to cease, and the country became more woody than before. In this part I found different fruits, and particularly I found melons upon the ground in great abundance, and grapes upon the trees. The vines had spread indeed over the trees, and the clusters of grapes were just now in their prime, very ripe and rich. This was a surprising discovery, and I was exceeding glad of them; but I was warned by my experience to eat sparingly of them, remembering that when I was ashore in Barbary the eating of grapes killed several of our Englishmen, who were slaves there, by throwing them into fluxes and fevers. But I found an excellent use for these grapes; and that was, to cure or dry them in the sun, and keep them as dried grapes or raisins are kept, which I thought would be, as indeed they were, as wholesome as agreeable to eat, when no grapes might be to be had.

I spent all that evening there, and went not back to my habitation; which, by the way, was the first night, as I might say, I had lain from home. In the night, I took my first contrivance, and got up into a tree, where I slept well; and the next morning proceeded upon my discovery, travelling near four miles, as I might judge by the length of the valley, keeping still due north, with a ridge of hills on the south and north side of me.

At the end of this march I came to an opening, where the country seemed to descend to the west; and a little spring of fresh water, which issued out of the side of the hill by me, ran the other way, that is, due east; and the country appeared so fresh, so green, so flourishing, everything being in a constant verdure or flourish of spring, that it looked like a planted garden.

I descended a little on the side of that delicious vale, surveying it with a secret kind of pleasure, though mixed with my other afflicting thoughts, to think that this was all my own; that I was king and lord of all this country indefeasibly, and had a right of possession; and, if I could convey it, I might have it in inheritance as completely as any lord of a manor in England. I saw here abundance of cocoa trees, orange, and lemon, and citron trees; but all wild, and very few bearing any fruit, at least not then. However, the green limes that I gathered were not only pleasant to eat, but very wholesome; and I mixed their juice afterwards with water, which made it very wholesome, and very cool and refreshing.

I found now I had business enough to gather and carry home; and I resolved to lay up a store, as well of grapes as limes and lemons to furnish myself for the wet season, which I knew was approaching.

In order to this, I gathered a great heap of grapes in one place, and a lesser heap in another place, and a great parcel of limes and lemons in another place; and taking a few of each with me, I travelled homeward; and resolved to come again, and bring a bag or sack, or what I could make, to carry the rest home.

Accordingly, having spent three days in this journey, I came home (so I must now call my tent and my cave); but before I got thither, the grapes were spoiled;

the richness of the fruits, and the weight of the juice, having broken them and bruised them, they were good for little or nothing: as to the limes, they were good, but I could bring but a few.

The next day, being the 19th, I went back, having made me two small bags to bring home my harvest; but I was surprised, when, coming to my heap of grapes, which were so rich and fine when I gathered them, I found them all spread about, trod to pieces, and dragged about, some here, some there, and abundance eaten and devoured. By this I concluded there were some wild creatures thereabouts, which had done this; but what they were, I knew not.

However, as I found that there was no laying them up on heaps, and no carrying them away in a sack, but that one way they would be destroyed, and the other way they would be crushed with their own weight, I took another course; for I gathered a large quantity of the grapes, and hung them up upon the out-branches of the trees, that they might cure and dry in the sun; and as for the limes and lemons, I carried as many back as I could well stand under.

When I came home from this journey, I contemplated with great pleasure the fruitfulness of that valley, and the pleasantness of the situation; the security from storms on that side the water and the wood; and concluded that I had pitched upon a place to fix my abode, which was by far the worst part of the country. Upon the whole, I began to consider of removing my habitation, and to look out for a place equally safe as where I now was situate, if possible, in that pleasant fruitful part of the island.

This thought ran long in my head, and I was exceeding fond of it for some time, the pleasantness of the place tempting me; but when I came to a nearer view of it, and to consider that I was now by the seaside, where it was at least possible that something might happen to my advantage, and, by the same ill fate that brought me hither, might bring some other unhappy wretches to the same place; and though it was scarce probable that any such thing should ever happen, yet to enclose myself among the hills and woods in the centre of the island, was to anticipate my bondage, and to render such an affair not only improbable, but impossible; and that therefore I ought not by any means to remove.

However, I was so enamored of this place that I spent much of my time there for the whole remaining part of the month of July; and though, upon second thoughts, I resolved as above, not to remove, yet I built me a little kind of a bower, and surrounded it at a distance with a strong fence, being a double hedge as high as I could reach, well staked, and filled between with brushwood. And here I lay very secure, sometimes two or three nights together, always going over it with a ladder, as before; so that I fancied now I had my country-house and my sea-coast house; and this work took me up to the beginning of August.

I had but newly finished my fence, and began to enjoy my labor, but the rains came on, and made me stick close to my first habitation; for though I had made me a tent like the other, with a piece of a sail, and spread it very well, yet I had not the shelter of a hill to keep me from storms, nor a cave behind me to retreat into when the rains were extraordinary.

About the beginning of August, as I said, I had finished my bower, and began to enjoy myself. The 3d of August I found the grapes I had hung up were perfectly dried, and indeed were excellent good raisins of the sun; so I began to take them down from the trees. And it was very happy that I did so, for the rains which followed would have spoiled them, and I had lost the best part of my winter food; for I had above two hundred large bunches of them.

.   .   .

The rainy season and the dry season began now to appear regular to me, and I learned to divide them so as to provide for them accordingly; but I bought all my experience before I had it, and this I am going to relate was one of the most discouraging experiments that I made at all. I have mentioned that I had saved the few ears of barley and rice, which I had so surprisingly found spring up, as I thought, of themselves, and believe there were about thirty stalks of rice, and about twenty of barley; and now I thought it a proper time to sow it after the rains, the sun being in its southern position, going from me.

Accordingly I dug up a piece of ground as well as I could with my wooden spade, and dividing it into two parts, I sowed my grain; but as I was sowing, it casually occurred to my thoughts that I would not sow it all at first, because I did not know when was the proper time for it, so I sowed about two-thirds of the seed, leaving about a handful of each.

It was a great comfort to me afterwards that I did so, for not one grain of that I sowed this time came to anything, for the dry months following, the earth having had no rain after the seed was sown, it had no moisture to assist its growth, and never came up at all till the wet season had come again, and then it grew as if it had been but newly sown.

Finding my first seed did not grow, which I easily imagined was by the drought, I sought for a moister piece of ground to make another trial in, and I dug up a piece of ground near my new bower, and sowed the rest of my seed in February, a little before the vernal equinox. And this having the rainy months of March and April to water it, sprung up very pleasantly, and yielded a very good crop; but having part of the seed left only, and not daring to sow all that I had, I had but a small quantity at last, my whole crop not amounting to above half a peck of each kind. But by this experiment I was made master of my business, and knew exactly when the proper season was to sow, and that I might expect two seed-times and two harvests every year.

While this corn was growing, I made a little discovery, which was of use to me afterwards. As soon as the rains were over, and the weather began to settle, which was about the month of November, I made a visit up the country to my bower, where, though I had not been some months, yet I found all things just as I left them. The circle or double hedge that I had made was not only firm and entire, but the stakes which I had cut out of some trees that grew thereabouts were all shot out, and grown with long branches, as much as a willow-tree usually shoots the first year after lopping its head. I could not tell what tree to call it that these stakes were cut from. I was surprised, and yet very well pleased to see the young trees grow, and I pruned them, and led them up to grow as much alike as I could. And it is scarce credible how beautiful a figure they grew into in three years; so that though the hedge made a circle of about twenty-five yards in diameter, yet the trees, for such I might now call them, soon covered it, and it was a complete shade, sufficient to lodge under all the dry season.

This made me resolve to cut some more stakes, and make me a hedge like this, in a semicircle round my wall (I mean that of my first dwelling), which I did; and placing the trees or stakes in a double row, at about eight yards distance from my first fence, they grew presently, and were at first a fine cover to my habitation, and afterward served for a defence also, as I shall observe in its order.

I found now that the seasons of the year might generally be divided, not into summer and winter, as in Europe, but into the rainy seasons and the dry seasons; which were generally thus:

Half	February,	
	March,	Rainy, the sun being then on, or near the equinox.
Half	April,	
Half	April,	
	May,	
	June,	Dry, the sun being then to the north of the line.
	July,	
Half	August,	
Half	August,	
	September,	Rainy, the sun being then come back.
Half	October,	
Half	October,	
	November,	
	December,	Dry, the sun being then to the south of the line.
	January,	
Half	February,	

The rainy season sometimes held longer or shorter as the winds happened to blow, but this was the general observation I made. After I had found by experience the ill consequence of being abroad in the rain, I took care to furnish myself with provisions beforehand, that I might not be obliged to go out; and I sat within doors as much as possible during the wet months.

In this time I found much employment, and very suitable also to the time, for I found great occasion of many things which I had no way to furnish myself with but by hard labor and constant application; particularly, I tried many ways to make myself a basket; but all the twigs I could get for the purpose proved so brittle, that they would do nothing. It proved of excellent advantage to me now, that when I was a boy I used to take great delight in standing at a basket maker's in the town where my father lived, to see them make their wicker-ware; and being, as boys usually are, very officious to help, and a great observer of the manner how they work those things, and sometimes lending a hand, I had by this means full knowledge of the methods of it, that I wanted nothing but the materials; when it came into my mind that the twigs of that tree from whence I cut my stakes that grew might possibly be as tough as the sallows, and willows, and osiers in England, and I resolved to try.

Accordingly, the next day, I went to my country-house, as I called it; and cutting some of the smaller twigs, I found them to my purpose as much as I could desire; whereupon I came the next time prepared with a hatchet to cut down a quantity, which I soon found, for there was great plenty of them. These I set up to dry within my circle or hedge, and when they were fit for use, I carried them to my cave; and here during the next season I employed myself in making, as well as I could, a great many baskets, both to carry earth, or to carry or lay up anything as I had occasion. And though I did not finish them very handsomely, yet I made them sufficiently servicable for my purpose. And thus, afterwards, I took care never to be without them; and as my wicker-ware decayed, I made no more; especially I made strong deep baskets to place my corn in, instead of sacks, when I should come to have any quantity of it.

Having mastered this difficulty, and employed a world of time about it, I bestirred myself to see, if possible, how to supply two wants. I had no vessels to hold anything that was liquid, except two runlets, which were almost full of rum, and some glass bottles, some of the common size, and others which were case-bottles square, for the holding of waters, spirits, etc. I had not so much as a pot to boil anything except a great kettle, which I saved out of the ship, and which was too big for such use as I desired it, viz., to make broth, and stew a bit of meat by itself. The second thing I would fain have had was a tobacco-pipe; but it was impossible to me to make one. However, I found a contrivance for that, too, at last.

I employed myself in planting my second rows of stakes or piles, and in this wicker-working all the summer or dry season, when another business took me up more time than it could be imagined I could spare.

I mentioned before that I had a great mind to see the whole island, and that I had travelled up the brook, and so on to where I built my bower, and where I had an opening quite to the sea, on the other side of the island. I now resolved to travel quite across to the seashore on that side; so taking my gun, a hatchet, and my dog, and a larger quantity of powder and shot than usual, with two biscuit-cakes and a great bunch of raisins in my pouch for my store, I began my journey. When I had passsed the vale where my bower stood, as above, I came within view of the sea to the west; and it being a very clear day, I fairly descried land, whether an island or a continent I could not tell; but it lay very high, extending from the west to the WSW. at a very great distance; by my guess, it could not be less than fifteen or twenty leagues off.

I could not tell what part of the world this might be, otherwise than that I know it must be part of America, and, as I concluded, by all my observations, must be near the Spanish dominions, and perhaps was all inhabited by savages, where, if I should have landed, I had been in a worse condition than I was now; and therefore I acquiesced in the dispositions of Providence which I began now to own and to believe ordered everything for the best. I say, I quieted my mind with this, and left afflicting myself with fruitless wishes of being there.

Besides, after some pause upon this affair, I considered that if this land was the Spanish coast I should certainly, one time or other, see some vessel pass or repass one way or other; but if not, then it was the savage coast between the

Spanish country and Brazils, which are indeed the worst of savages; for they are cannibals or men-eaters, and fail not to murder and devour all the human bodies that fall into their hands.

With these considerations I walked very leisurely forward. I found that side of the island, where I now was, much pleasanter than mine, the open or savanna fields sweet, adorned with flowers and grass, and full of very fine woods.

I saw abundance of parrots, and fain I would have caught one, if possible, to have kept it to be tame, and taught it to speak to me. I did, after some painstaking, catch a young parrot, for I knocked it down with a stick, and having recovered it, I brought it home; but it was some years before I could make him speak. However, at last I taught him to call me by my name very familiarly. But the accident that followed, though it be a trifle, will be very diverting in its place.

I was exceedingly diverted with this journey. I found in the low grounds hares, as I thought them to be, and foxes; but they differed greatly from all the other kinds I had met with, nor could I satisfy myself to eat them, though I killed several. But I had no need to be venturous, for I had no want of food, and of that which was very good too; especially these three sorts, viz., goats, pigeons, and turtle, or tortoise; which, added to my grapes, Leadenhall Market could not have furnished a table better than I, in proportion to the company. And though my case was deplorable enough, yet I had great cause for thankfulness, and that I was not driven to any extremities for food, but rather plenty, even to dainties.

I never travelled in this journey above two miles outright in a day, or thereabouts; but I took so many turns and returns, to see what discoveries I could make, that I came weary enough to the place where I resolved to sit down for all night; and then I either reposed myself in a tree, or surrounded myself with a row of stakes, set upright in the ground, either from one tree to another, or so as no wild creature could come at me without waking me.

As soon as I came to the seashore, I was surprised to see that I had taken up my lot on the worst side of the island, for here indeed the shore was covered with innumerable turtles; whereas, on the other side, I had found but three in a year and a half. Here was also an infinite number of fowls of many kinds, some which I had seen, and some which I had not seen of before, and many of them very good meat, but such as I knew not the names of, except those called penguins.

I could have shot as many as I pleased, but was very sparing of my powder and shot, and therefore had more mind to kill a she-goat, if I could, which I could better feed on; and though there were many goats here, more than on my side the island, yet it was with much more difficulty that I could come near them, the country being flat and even, and they saw me much sooner than when I was on the hill.

I confess this side of the country was much pleasanter than mine; but yet I had not the least inclination to remove, for as I was fixed in my habitation, it became natural to me, and I seemed all the while I was here to be as it were upon a journey, and from home. However, I travelled along the shore of the sea towards the east, I suppose about twelve miles, and then setting up a great pole upon the shore for a mark, I concluded I would go home again; and that the next journey I took should be on the other side of the island, east from my dwelling, and so round till I came to my post again; of which in its place.

I took another way to come back than that I went, thinking I could easily keep all the island so much in my view that I could not miss finding my first dwelling by viewing the country. But I found myself mistaken; for being come about two or three miles, I found myself descended into a very large valley, but so surrounded with hills, and those hills covered with wood, that I could not see which was my way by any direction but that of the sun, nor even then, unless I knew very well the position of the sun at that time of the day.

It happened to my farther misfortune that the weather proved hazy for three or four days while I was in this valley; and not being able to see the sun, I wandered about very uncomfortably, and at last was obliged to find out the seaside, look for my post, and come back the same way I went; and then by easy journeys I turned homeward, the weather being exceeding hot, and my gun, ammunition, hatchet, and other things very heavy.

In this journey my dog surprised a young kid, and seized upon it, and I running in to take hold of it, caught it, and saved it alive from the dog. I had a great mind to bring it home if I could, for I had often been musing whether it might not be possible to get a kid or two, and so raise a breed of tame goats, which might supply me when my powder and shot should be all spent.

I made a collar to this little creature, and with a string, which I made of some rope-yarn, which I always carried about me, I led him along, though with some difficulty, till I came to my bower, and there I enclosed him and left him, for I was very impatient to be at home, from whence I had been absent above a month.

I cannot express what a satisfaction it was to me to come into my old hutch, and lie down in my hammock-bed. This little wandering journey, without settled place of abode, had been so unpleasant to me, that my own house, as I called it to myself, was a perfect settlement to me compared to that; and it rendered everything about me so comfortable, that I resolved I would never go a great way from it again, while it should be my lot to stay on the island.

I reposed myself here a week, to rest and regale myself after my long journey; during which most of the time was taken up in the weighty affair of making a cage for my Poll, who began now to be a mere domestic, and to be mighty well acquainted with me. Then I began to think of the poor kid which I had penned in within my little circle, and resolved to go and fetch it home, or give it some food. Accordingly I went, and found it where I left it, for indeed it could not get out, but almost starved for want of food. I went and cut boughs of trees, and branches of such shrubs as I could find, and threw it over, and having fed it, I tied it as I did before, to lead it away; but it was so tame with being hungry, that I had no need to have tied it, for it followed me like a dog. And as I continually fed it, the creature became so loving, so gentle, and so fond, that it became from that time one of my domestics also, and would never leave me afterwards.

The rainy season of the autumnal equinox was now come, and I kept the 30th of September in the same solemn manner as before, being the anniversary of my landing on the island, having now been there two years, and no more prospect of being delivered than the first day I came there. I spent the whole day in humble and thankful acknowledgments of the many wonderful mercies which my solitary condition was attended with, and without which it might have been infinitely more miserable. I gave humble and hearty thanks that God had been pleased to discover to me even that it was possible I might be more happy in this solitary condition, than I should have been in a liberty of society, and in all the pleasures of the world; that He could fully make up to me the deficiencies of my solitary state, and the want of human society, by His presence, and the communications of His grace to my soul, supporting, comforting, and encouraging me to depend upon His providence here, and hope for His eternal presence hereafter.

It was now that I began sensibly to feel how much more happy this life I now led was, with all its miserable circumstances, than the wicked, cursed, abominable life I led all the past part of my days. And now I changed both my sorrows and my joys; my very desires altered, my affections changed their gusts, and my delights were perfectly new from what they were at my first coming, or indeed for the two years past.

Before, as I walked about, either on my hunting, or for viewing the country, the anguish of my soul at my condition would break out upon me on a sudden, and my very heart would die within me, to think of the woods, the mountains, the deserts I was in, and how I was a prisoner, locked up with the eternal bars and bolts of the ocean, in an uninhabited wilderness, without redemption. In the midst of the greatest composures of my mind, this would break out upon me like a storm, and make me wring my hands and weep like a child. Sometimes it would take me in the middle of my work, and I would immediately sit down and sigh, and look upon the ground for an hour or two together; and this was still worse to me, for if I could burst out into tears, or vent myself by words, it would go off, and the grief, having exhausted itself, would abate.

But now I began to exercise myself with new thoughts. I daily read the Word of God, and applied all the comforts of it to my present state. One morning, being very sad, I opened the Bible upon these words, "I will never, never leave thee, nor forsake thee." Immediately it occurred that these words were to me; why else should they be directed in such a manner, just at the moment when I was mourning over my condition, as one forsaken of God and man? "Well, then," said I, "if God does not forsake me, of what ill consequence can it be, or what matters it, though the world should all forsake me, seeing on the other hand if I had all the world, and should lose the favor and blessing of God, there would be no comparison in the loss?"

From this moment I began to conclude in my mind that it was possible for me to be more happy in this forsaken solitary condition, than it was probable I should ever have been in any other particular state in the world, and with this thought I was going to give thanks to God for bringing me to this place.

I know not what it was, but something shocked my mind at that thought, and I durst not speak the words. "How canst thou be such a hypocrite," said I, even audibly, "to pretend to be thankful for a condition which, however thou mayest endeavor to be contented with, thou wouldest rather pray heartily to be delivered from?" So I stopped there; but though I could not say I thanked God for being there, yet I sincerely gave thanks to God for opening my eyes, by whatever afflicting providences, to see the former condition of my life, and to mourn for my wickedness, and repent. I never opened the Bible, or shut it, but my very soul within me blessed God for directing my friend in England, without any order of mine, to pack it up among my goods, and for assisting me afterwards to save it out of the wreck of the ship.

. . .

In the middle of this work I finished my fourth year in this place, and kept my anniversary with the same devotion, and with as much comfort as ever before; for, by a constant study and serious application of the Word of God, and by the assistance of His grace, I gained a different knowledge from what I had before. I entertained different notions of things. I looked now upon the world as a thing remote, which I had nothing to do with, no expectation from, and, indeed, no desires about. In a word, I had nothing indeed to do with it, nor was ever like to have; so I thought it looked, as we may perhaps look upon it hereafter, viz., as a place I had lived in, but was come out of it; and well might I say, as father Abraham to Dives, "Between me and thee is a great gulf fixed."

In the first place, I was removed from all the wickedness of the world here. I had neither the lust of the flesh, the lust of the eye, or the pride of life. I had nothing to covet, for I had all that I was now capable of enjoying. I was lord of the whole manor; or, if I pleased, I might call myself king or emperor over the whole country which I had possession of. There were no rivals: I had no competitor, none to dispute sovereignty or command with me. I might have raised ship-loadings of corn, but I had no use for it; so I let as little grow as I thought enough for my occasion. I had tortoise or turtles enough, but now and then one was as much as I could put to any use. I had timber enough to have built a fleet of ships. I had grapes enough to have made wine, or to have cured into raisins, to have loaded that fleet when they had been built.

But all I could make use of was all that was valuable. I had enough to eat and to supply my wants, and what was all the rest to me? If I killed more flesh than I could eat, the dog must eat it, or the vermin. If I sowed more corn than I could eat, it must be spoiled. The trees that I cut down were lying to rot on the ground; I could make no more use of them than for fuel, and that I had no occasion for but to dress my food.

In a word, the nature and experience of things dictated to me, upon just reflection, that all the good things of this world are no farther good to us than they are for our use; and that whatever we may heap up indeed to give others, we enjoy just as much as we can use, and no more. The most covetous griping miser in the world would have been cured of the vice of covetousness, if he had been in my case; for I possessed infinitely more than I knew what to do with. I had no room for desire, except it was of things which I had not, and they were but trifles, though indeed of great use to me. I had, as I hinted before, a parcel of money, as well gold as silver, about thirty-six pounds sterling. Alas! there the nasty, sorry, useless stuff lay; I had no manner of business for it; and I often thought with myself, that I would have given a handful of it for a gross of tobacco-pipes, or for a hand-mill to grind my corn; nay, I would have given it all for sixpenny-worth of turnip and carrot seed out of England, or for a handful of peas and beans, and a bottle of ink. As it was, I had not the least advantage by it, or benefit from it; but there it lay in a drawer, and grew mouldy with the damp of the cave in the wet season; and if I had had the drawer full of diamonds, it had been the same case, and they had been of no manner of value to me because of no use.

I had now brought my state of life to be much easier in itself than it was at first, and much easier to my mind, as well as to my body. I frequently sat down to my meat with thankfulness, and admired the hand of God's providence, which had thus spread my table in the wilderness. I learned to look more upon the bright side of my condition, and less upon the dark side, and to consider what I enjoyed, rather than what I wanted; and this gave me sometimes such secret comforts, that I cannot express them; and which I take notice of here, to put those discontented people in mind of it, who cannot enjoy comfortably what God has given them, because they see and covet something that He has not given them. All our discontents about what we want, appeared to me to spring from the want of thankfulness for what we have.

Anne Kingsmill Finch, Countess of Winchilsea
(1661–1720)

Born in the year following the Restoration, Anne Kingsmill served as a maid of honor to Mary of Modena, the wife of James II. In 1684, she married Heneage Finch, who was also attached to the royal court. Four years later, the Finches refused to swear allegiance to the new king, William of Orange, and were exiled from court. They took up residence in their beautiful family estate in Kent, a place that Anne Finch referred to as her Arcadia. This rural retirement inspired Finch's poetry, having given her time for reading and study and the countryside for her subject matter. Despite her removal from literary London, she was closely associated with some of the most important writers of the early eighteenth century, including Jonathan Swift, Alexander Pope, and John Gay. All of them were known to have admired Finch's poetry, which she circulated among friends and other writers in manuscript. Perhaps because she was an aristocrat and a woman, Finch resisted publishing her verse (unlike her near contemporary Margaret Cavendish), although her husband and her other admirers strongly encouraged her writing and supported her efforts. Thus, in 1713, she did bring out a collection of some of her works, Miscellany Poems on Several Occasions, Written by a Lady. *These poems won her the admiration of later generations of poets, most notably William Wordsworth, who had high praise for Finch and her descriptions of the natural world.*

The poems selected here represent some of the range of Finch's accomplishment, from Aesopian fable-poems with playful animal characters to poems that meditate on the beauty of nature as well as its awesome and sublime powers of destruction. Her poem "Upon the Hurricane" responds to a terrible storm that devastated the southern part of England (where her estate was located) in November 1703. There are some implications in the poem that the storm may be a sign of divine retribution, as the poem blends nat-

ural description with meditation on historical and political events. "A Nocturnal Reverie" is one of Finch's most anthologized poems. It represents well her sensitive and emotional description of nature, and it illustrates why she would become popular among the Romantic poets. Her poem "To the Nightingale" brings to mind Keats's later ode on the same bird.

The Bird and the Arras

By near resemblance see that Bird betrayed
Who takes the well wrought Arras[1] for a shade
There hopes to pearch and with a cheerful Tune
O'er-pass the scorchings of the sultry Noon.
But soon repulsed by the obdurate scene   5
How swift she turns but turns alas in vain
That piece a Grove, this shows an ambient sky
Where imitated Fowl their pinnions ply
Seeming to mount in flight and aiming still more high.
All she outstrips and with a moment's pride   10
Their understation silent does deride
Till the dashed Ceiling strikes her to the ground
No intercepting shrub to break the fall is found
Recovering breath the window next she gains
Nor fears a stop from the transparent Panes.   15

.   .   .   .

But we digress and leave th' imprisoned wretch
Now sinking low now on a loftier stretch
Fluttering in endless circles of dismay
Till some kind hand directs the certain way
Which through the casement an escape affords   20
And leads to ample space the only Heaven of Birds.

A Pindarick Poem

Upon the Hurricane in November 1703, referring to this Text in Psalm 148. ver. 8. Winds and Storms fulfilling his Word. With a Hymn composed of the 148th Psalm Paraphrased

You have obeyed, you Winds, that must fulfill
    The Great Disposer's righteous Will;
Throughout the Land, unlimited you flew,
Nor sought, as heretofore, with Friendly Aid

---

[1] A decorative tapestry, or wall hanging.

Only, new Motion to bestow　　　　　　　　　　　5
Upon the sluggish Vapours, bred below,
Condensing into Mists, and melancholy Shade.
　　No more such gentle Methods you pursue,
　　But marching now in terrible Array,
　　　　Undistinguished was your Prey:　　　　　10
In vain the *Shrubs*, with lowly Bent,
Sought their Destruction to prevent;
The *Beech* in vain, with outstretched Arms,
Deprecates th' approaching Harms;
In vain the *Oak* (so often stormed)　　　　　　15
Relied upon that native Force,
By which already was performed
So much of his appointed Course,
As made him, fearless of Decay,
　　Wait but the accomplished Time　　　　　　20
Of his long-wished and useful Prime,
To be removed, with Honor, to the Sea.
　The strait and ornamental *Pine*
　Did in the like Ambition join,
　And thought his Fame should ever last,　　　　25
When in some Royal Ship he stood the planted Mast;
　And should again his Length of Timber rear,
　And new engrafted Branches wear
　Of fibrous Cordage and impending Shrouds,
Still trimmed with human Care, and watered by the Clouds.　30
　But oh, you *Trees!* who solitary stood;
　　Or you, whose Numbers formed a Wood;
　　You, who on Mountains chose to rise,
　　And drew them nearer to the Skies;
　　Or you, whom Valleys late did hold　　　　　35
　　In flexible and lighter Mold;
You numerous Brethren of the Leafy Kind,
　　To whatsoever Use designed,
　　Now, vain you found it to contend
With not, alas! one Element; your Friend　　　　40
Your Mother Earth, through long preceding Rains,
　　(Which undermining sink below)
No more her wonted Strength retains;
Nor you so fixed within her Bosom grow,
That for your sakes she can resolve to bear　　　45
　　These furious Shocks of hurrying Air;
　But finding All your Ruin did conspire,
　She soon her beauteous Progeny resigned
　To this destructive, this imperious Wind,
That checked your nobler Aims, and gives you to the Fire.　50

Thus! have thy Cedars, *Libanus*,[2] been struck
    As the lithe Osiers twisted round;
Thus! *Cadiz*,[3] has thy Wilderness been shook,
When the appalling, and tremendous Sound
    Of rattling Tempests o'er you broke,   55
    And made your stubborn Glories bow,
When in such Whirlwinds the *Almighty* spoke,
Warning *Judea* then, as our *Britannia* now.
    Yet these were the remoter Harms,
Foreign the Care, and distant the Alarms: 60
    Whilst but sheltering Trees alone,
    Mastered soon, and soon o'erthrown,
    Felt those Gusts, which since prevail,
    And loftier Palaces assail;
    Whose shaken Turrets now give way,   65
With vain Inscriptions, which the Frieze has borne
Through Ages past, t' extol and to adorn,
    And to our latter Times convey;
Who did the Structure's deep Foundation lay,
Forcing his Praise upon the gazing Crowd,   70
And, whilst he moulders in a scanty Shroud,
Telling both Earth and Skies, he when alive was proud.
    Now down at once comes the superfluous Load,
    The costly Fret-work with it yields,
    Whose imitated Fruits and Flowers are strewed,   75
Like those of real Growth o'er the Autumnal Fields.
    The present Owner lifts his Eyes,
And the swift Change with sad Affrightment spies:
The Ceiling gone, that late the Roof concealed;
The Roof untiled, through which the Heavens revealed,   80
Exposes now his Head, when all Defence has failed.

      What alas, is to be done!
Those, who in Cities would from Dangers run,
    Do but increasing Dangers meet,
And Death, in various shapes, attending in the Street;   85
    While some, too tardy in their Flight,
    O'ertaken by a worse Mischance,
    Their upward Parts do scarce advance,
When on their following Limbs th' extending Ruins light.
    One half's interred, the other yet survives,   90
    And for Release with fainting Vigour strives;
    Implores the Aid of absent Friends in vain;
    With faultering Speech, and dying Wishes calls

[2] Lebanon.
[3] Picturesque region of southwestern Spain.

Those, whom perhaps, their own Domestic Walls
By parallel Distress, or swifter Death retains.   95

       O *Wells!* thy Bishop's Mansion we lament,
  So tragical the Fall, so dire th' Event!
    But let no daring Thought presume
  To point a Cause for that oppressive Doom.
Yet strictly pious Ken! had'st Thou been there,   100
This Fate, we think, had not become thy share;
    Nor had that awful Fabric bowed,
    Sliding from its loosened Bands;
    Nor yielding Timbers been allowed
    To crush thy everlifted Hands,   105
      Or interrupt thy Prayer.
Those Orisons, that nightly Watches keep,
Had called thee from thy Bed, or there secured thy Sleep.
    Whilst you, bold Winds and Storms! his Word obeyed,
    Whilst you his Scourge the Great *Jehovah* made,   110
And into ruined Heaps our Edifices laid.
You *South* and *West* the Tragedy began,
As, with disordered haste, you o'er the Surface ran;
    Forgetting, that you were designed
  (Chiefly thou *Zephyrus*, thou softest Wind!)   115
Only our Heats, when sultry, to allay,
And chase the odourous Gums by your dispersing Play.
    Now, by new Orders and Decrees,
    For our Chastisement issued forth,
You on his Confines the alarmed *North*   120
      With equal Fury sees,
    And summons swiftly to his Aid
    Eurus, his Confederate made,
His eager Second in th' opposing Fight,
That even the Winds may keep the Balance right,   125
Nor yield increase of Sway to arbitrary Might.
    Meeting now, they all contend,
    Those assail, while these defend;
    Fierce and turbulent the War,
    And in the loud tumultuous Jar   130
    Winds their own Fifes, and Clarions are.
Each Cavity, which Art or Nature leaves,
Their Inspiration hastily receives;
    Whence, from their various Forms and Size,
    As various Symphonies arise,   135
Their Trumpet every hollow Tube is made,
And, when more solid Bodies they invade
    Enraged, they can no farther come,

The beaten Flat, whilst it repels the Noise,
Resembles but with more outrageous Voice   140
  The Soldier's threatening Drum:
And when they compass thus our World around,
  When they our Rocks and Mountains rend,
When they our Sacred Piles to their Foundations send,
  No wonder if our echoing Caves rebound;   145
  No wonder if our listening Sense they wound,
When armed with so much Force, and ushered with such Sound.

Nor scarce, amidst the Terrors of that Night,
  When you, fierce Winds, such Desolations wrought,
When you from out his Stores the Great Commander brought,   150
  Could the most Righteous stand upright;
  Scarcely the Holiest Man performs
  The Service, that becomes it best,
By ardent Vows, or solemn Prayers addrest;
  Nor finds the Calm, so usual to his Breast,   155
  Full Proof against such Storms.
  How should the Guilty then be found,
The Men in Wine, or looser Pleasures drowned,
To fix a steadfast Hope, or to maintain their Ground!
  When at his Glass the late Companion feels,   160
That Giddy, like himself, the tottering Mansion reels!
  The Miser, who with many a Chest
  His gloomy Tenement oppressed,
  Now fears the overburthened Floor,
And trembles for his Life, but for his Treasure more.   165
  What shall he do, or to what Powers apply?
  To those, which threaten from on High,
  By him ne'er called upon before,
Who also will suggest th' impossible Restore?
  No; *Mammon*, to thy Laws he will be true,   170
And, rather than his Wealth, will bid the World adieu.
  The Rafters sink, and buried with his Coin
  That Fate does with his living Thoughts combine;
For still his Heart's enclosed within a Golden Mine.

  Contention with its angry Brawls   175
  By Storms o'erclamoured, shrinks and falls;
Nor Whig, nor Tory now the rash Contender calls.
  Those, who but Vanity allowed,
  Nor thought, it reached the Name of Sin,
  To be of their Perfections proud,   180
Too much adorned without, or too much raised within,
  Now find, that even the lightest Things,
  As the minuter parts of Air,

When Number to their Weight addition brings,
  Can, like the small, but numerous Insects Stings,   185
Can, like th' assembled Winds, urge Ruin and Despair.

Thus You've obeyed, you Winds, that must fulfill
  The Great disposer's Righteous Will:
Thus did your Breath a strict Enquiry make,
Thus did you our most secret Sins awake,   190
  And thus chastised their Ill.

Whilst vainly Those, of a rapacious Mind,
  Fields to other Fields had laid,
By Force, or by injurious Bargains joined,
With Fences for their Guard impenetrable made;   195
  The juster Tempest mocks the wrong,
  And sweeps, in its directed Flight,
  Th' Enclosures of another's Right,
Driving at once the Bounds, and licensed Herds along.
  The Earth again one general Scene appears;   200
  No regular distinction now,
Betwixt the Grounds for Pasture, or the Plough,
  The Face of Nature wears.

Free as the Men, who wild Confusion love,
  And lawless Liberty approve,   205
  Their Fellow-Brutes pursue their way,
To their own Loss, and disadvantage stray,
As wretched in their Choice, as unadvised as They.
  The timorous *Deer*, whilst he forsakes the Park,
And wanders on, in the misguiding Dark,   210
Believes, a Foe from every unknown Bush
  Will on his trembling Body rush,
Taking the Winds, that vary in their Notes,
For hot pursuing Hounds with deeply bellowing Throats.
  Th' awakened *Birds*, shook from their nightly Seats,   215
  Their unavailing Pinions ply,
  Repulsed, as they attempt to fly
In hopes they might attain to more secure Retreats.
  But, Where ye wildered Fowls would You repair?
  When this your happy Portion given,   220
Your upward Lot, your Firmament of Heaven,
Your unentailed, your undivided Air,
Where no Proprietor was ever known,
Where no litigious Suits have ever grown,
Whilst none from Star to Star could call the space his Own;   225
  When this no more your middle Flights can bear,
  But some rough Blast too far above conveys,
Or to unquitted Earth confines your weak Essays.

Nor You, nor wiser Man could find Repose,
   Nor could our Industry produce   230
   Expedients of the smallest Use,
To ward our greater Cares, or mitigate your Woes.
  Ye *Clouds!* that pitied our Distress,
    And by your pacifying Showers
  (The soft and usual methods of Success)   235
  Kindly assayed to make this Tempest less;
  Vainly your Aid was now alas! employed,
In vain you wept o'er those destructive Hours,
  In which the Winds full Tyranny enjoyed,
    Nor would allow you to prevail,   240
But drove your scorned, and scattered Tears to wail
    The Land that lay destroyed.

  Whilst You obeyed, you Winds! that must fulfill
    The just Disposer's Righteous Will;
  Whilst not the Earth alone, you disarray,   245
But to more ruined Seas winged your impetuous Way.

  Which to foreshow, the still portentous *Sun*
  Beamless, and pale of late, his Race begun,
  Quenching the Rays, he had no Joy to keep,
  In the obscure, and sadly threatened Deep.   250
  Farther than we, that Eye of Heaven discerns,
  And nearer placed to our malignant Stars,
Our brooding Tempests, and approaching Wars
    Anticipating learns.
    When now, too soon the dark Event   255
    Shows what that faded Planet meant;
  Whilst more the liquid Empire undergoes,
  More she resigns of her entrusted Stores,
  The Wealth, the Strength, the Pride of different Shores
  In one Devoted, one Recorded Night,   260
  Than Years had known destroyed by generous Fight,
    Or Privateering Foes.
    All Rules of Conduct laid aside,
    No more the baffled *Pilot* steers,
  Or knows an Art, when it each moment veers,   265
To vary with the Winds, or stem th' unusual Tide.
  Dispersed and loose, the shattered Vessels stray,
    Some perish within sight of Shore,
  Some, happier thought, obtain a wider Sea,
But never to return, or cast an Anchor more!   270
    Some on the *Northern* Coasts are thrown,
And by congealing Surges compassed round,
    To fixed and certain Ruin bound,

       Immoveable are grown:
The fatal *Goodwin*[4] swallows All that come   275
Within the Limits of that dangerous Sand,
Amphibious in its kind, nor Sea nor Land;
Yet kin to both, a false and faithless Strand,
Known only to our Coast for a devouring Tomb.
       Nor seemed the Hurricane content,   280
Whilst only Ships were wreckt, and Tackle rent;
    The Sailors too must fall a Prey,
Those that Command, with those that did Obey;
The best Supporters of thy pompous Style,
Thou far Renowned, thou powerful British Isle!   285
Foremost in Naval Strength, and Sovereign of the Sea!
These from thy Aid that wrathful Night divides,
Plunged in those Waves, o'er which this Title rides.
What art Thou, envied *Greatness*, at the best,
    In thy deluding Splendors dressed?   290
What are thy glorious Titles, and thy Forms?
Which cannot give Security, or Rest
To favoured Men, or Kingdoms that contest
With Popular Assaults, or Providential Storms!
Whilst on th' Omnipotent our Fate depends,   295
And They are only safe, whom He alone defends.
    Then let to Heaven our general Praise be sent,
Which did our farther Loss, our total Wreck prevent.
And as our Aspirations do ascend,
Let every Thing be summoned to attend;   300
And let the Poet *after God's own Heart*
Direct our Skill in that sublimer part,
    And our weak Numbers mend!

The Hymn

To the Almighty on his radiant Throne,
    Let endless Hallelujas rise!
Praise Him, ye wondrous Heights to us unknown,
Praise Him, ye Heavens unreached by mortal Eyes,
Praise Him, in your degree, ye sublunary Skies!   5

Praise Him, you Angels that before him bow,
    You Creatures of Celestial frame,
Our Guests of old, our wakeful Guardians now,
Praise Him, and with like Zeal our Hearts inflame,
Transporting then our Praise to Seats from whence you came!   10

---

[4] Goodwin Sands is a ten-mile-long stretch of sand bars off of the east coast of Kent; it was frequently the site of shipwrecks.

Praise Him, thou Sun in thy Meridian Force;
　　Exalt Him, all ye Stars and Light!
Praise Him, thou Moon in thy revolving Course,
Praise Him, thou gentler Guide of silent Night,
Which does to solemn Praise, and serious Thoughts invite.　　15

Praise Him, ye humid Vapours, which remain
　　Unfrozen by the sharper Air;
Praise Him, as you return in Showers again,
To bless the Earth and make her Pastures fair:
Praise Him, ye climbing Fires, the Emblems of our Prayer.　　20

Praise Him, ye Waters petrified above,
　　Ye shredded Clouds that fall in Snow,
Praise Him, for that you so divided move;
Ye Hailstones, that you do no larger grow,
Nor, in one solid Mass, oppress the World below.　　25

Praise Him, ye soaring Fowls, still as you fly,
　　And on gay Plumes your Bodies raise;
You Insects. which in dark Recesses lie,
Although th' extremest Distances you try,
Be reconciled in this, to offer mutual Praise.　　30

Praise Him, thou Earth, with thy unbounded Store;
　　Ye Depths which to the Center tend:
Praise Him ye Beasts which in the Forests roar;
Praise Him ye Serpents, though you downwards bend,
Who made your bruised Head our Ladder to ascend.　　35

Praise Him, ye Men whom youthful Vigour warms;
　　Ye Children, hastening to your Prime;
Praise Him, ye Virgins of unsullied Charms,
With beauteous Lips becoming sacred Rhyme:
You Aged, give Him Praise for your increase of Time.　　40

Praise Him, ye Monarchs in supreme Command,
　　By Anthems, like the *Hebrew* Kings;
Then with enlarged Zeal throughout the Land
Reform the Numbers, and reclaim the Strings,
Converting to His Praise, the most Harmonious Things.　　45

Ye Senators presiding by our Choice,
　　And You Hereditary Peers!
Praise Him by Union, both in Heart and Voice;
Praise Him, who your agreeing Council steers,
Producing sweeter Sounds than the according Spheres.　　50

Praise Him, ye native Altars of the Earth!
　　Ye Mountains of stupendious size!

Praise Him, ye Trees and Fruits which there have birth,
Praise Him, ye Flames that from their Bowels rise,
All fitted for the use of grateful Sacrifice.   55

He spake the Word; and from the Chaos rose
    The Forms and Species of each Kind:
He spake the Word, which did their Law compose,
    And all, with never ceasing Order joined,
Till ruffled for our Sins by his chastising Wind.   60

But now, you Storms, that have your Fury spent,
    As you his Dictates did obey,
Let now your loud and threatening Notes relent,
    Tune all your Murmurs to a softer Key,
And bless that Gracious Hand, that did your Progress stay.   65

From my contemned Retreat, obscure and low,
    As Grots from whence the Winds disperse,
May this His Praise as far extended flow;
    And if that future Times shall read my Verse,
Though worthless in itself, let them his Praise rehearse.   70

To the Nightingale

Exert thy Voice, sweet Harbinger of Spring!
    This Moment is thy Time to sing,
    This Moment I attend to Praise,
And set my Numbers to thy Lays.
    Free as thine shall be my Song;   5
    As thy Music, short, or long.
Poets, wild as thee, were born,
    Pleasing best when unconfined,
    When to Please is least designed,
Soothing but their Cares to rest;   10
    Cares do still their Thoughts molest,
    And still th' unhappy Poet's Breast,
Like thine, when best he sings, is placed against a Thorn.
She begins, Let all be still!
    Muse, thy Promise now fulfill!   15
Sweet, oh! sweet, still sweeter yet
Can thy Words such Accents fit,
Canst thou Syllables refine,
Melt a Sense that shall retain
Still some Spirit of the Brain,   20
Till with Sounds like these it join.
    'Twill not be! then change thy Note;

Let division shake thy Throat.
Hark! Division now she tries;
Yet as far the Muse outflies.   25
    Cease then, prithee, cease thy Tune;
    Trifler, wilt thou sing till *June?*
Till thy Business all lies waste,
And the Time of Building's past!
    Thus we Poets that have Speech,   30
Unlike what thy Forests teach,
    If a fluent Vein be shown
    That's transcendent to our own,
Criticize, reform, or preach,
Or censure what we cannot reach.   35

A Nocturnal Reverie

In such a *Night*, when every louder Wind
Is to its distant Cavern safe confined;
And only gentle *Zephyr* fans his Wings,
And lonely *Philomel*,[1] still waking, sings;
Or from some Tree, famed for the *Owl*'s delight,   5
She, hollowing clear, directs the Wanderer right:
In such a *Night*, when passing Clouds give place,
Or thinly veil the Heavens mysterious Face;
When in some River, overhung with Green,
The waving Moon and trembling Leaves are seen;   10
When freshened Grass now bears itself upright,
And makes cool Banks to pleasing Rest invite,
Whence springs the *Woodbind*, and the *Bramble*-Rose,
And where the sleepy *Cowslip* sheltered grows;
Whilst now a paler Hue the *Foxglove* takes,   15
Yet checkers still with Red the dusky brakes
When scattered *Glow-worms*, but in Twilight fine,
Show trivial Beauties watch their Hour to shine;
Whilst *Salisbury*[2] stands the Test of every Light,
In perfect Charms, and perfect Virtue bright: 20
When Odours, which declined repelling Day,
Through temperate Air uninterrupted stray;
When darkened Groves their softest Shadows wear,
And falling Waters we distinctly hear;
When through the Gloom more venerable shows   25
Some ancient Fabric, awful in Repose,

[1] Poetic name for a nightingale.

[2] A cathedral town in Wiltshire, England.

Claude Lorrain, (Claude Gellee) 1600-1682, *Pastoral Landscape*, 1645.

Oil on canvas. The Barber Institute of Fine Arts, University of Bimingham.
The Bridgeman Art Library International Ltd.

Thomas Gainsborough, 1727-1788, *Mr. and Mrs. Andrews.*

National Gallery, London, Great Britain.
Art Resource, New York.

John James Audubon, *The Birds of America*, *Virginian Opossum*,
published (1827-1836).

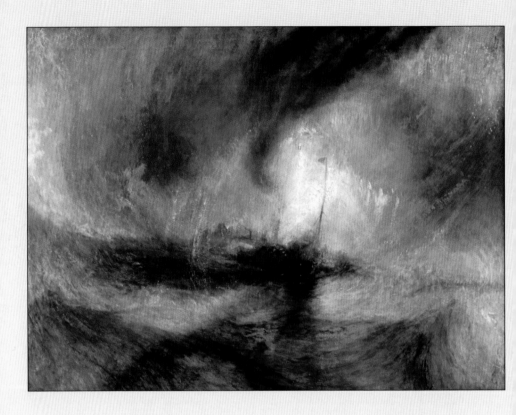

Joseph Mallord William Turner, *Snowstorm: Steamboat Off Harbor's Mouth.*

Exhibited 1842. Clore Collection, Tate Gallery, London.
Art Resource, New York.

While Sunburnt Hills their swarthy Looks conceal,
And swelling Haycocks thicken up the Vale:
When the loosed *Horse* now, as his Pasture leads,
Comes slowly grazing through th' adjoining Meads,   30
Whose stealing Pace, and lengthened Shade we fear,
Till torn up Forage in his Teeth we hear:
When nibbling *Sheep* at large pursue their Food,
And unmolested Kine rechew the Cud;
When *Curlews* cry beneath the Village walls,   35
And to her straggling Brood the *Partridge* calls;
Their shortlived Jubilee the Creatures keep,
Which but endures, whilst Tyrant-*Man* does sleep;
When a sedate Content the Spirit feels,
And no fierce Light disturb, whilst it reveals;   40
But silent Musings urge the Mind to seek
Something, too high for Syllables to speak;
Till the free Soul to a composedness charmed,
Finding the Elements of Rage disarmed,
O'er all below a solemn Quiet grown,   45
Joys in th' inferior World, and thinks it like her Own:
In such a *Night* let Me abroad remain,
Till Morning breaks, and All's confused again;
Our Cares, our Toils, our Clamours are renewed,
Or Pleasures, seldom reached, again pursued.   50

🐦 *Jonathan Swift* (1667–1745)

Satire was the predominant literary mode of the early eighteenth century, and Jonathan Swift remains the greatest satirist of his age. Swift's constant purpose in his verse and prose was to use humor and irony to teach his readers about their flaws and shortcomings, and the central target of Swift's criticism was human pride. Born of English parents in Ireland, Swift maintained an ambivalent relationship to the land of his birth. Although he would have preferred to find a career that allowed him to stay in England, he was a tireless defender of Irish economic and political freedom, as is evidenced by his most infamous satire, "A Modest Proposal" (1729). He received a degree from Trinity College, Dublin, and later a degree from Oxford. In 1695, he was ordained in the Anglican Church of Ireland, and his first position was in a remote Irish parish, a great disappointment to such an ambitious man. He received a Doctor of Divinity degree from Trinity (in 1702), and in 1704 he published his first major satirical work, A Tale of a Tub, *which took aim at corruption in religion and learning. Outspoken on matters of church and state, Swift also wrote more straightforward political polemics and religious pamphlets, in which he was, as in his literary works, consistently a champion of social justice. Though his opinions frequently impeded his career, he was eventually made*

dean of St. Patrick's Cathedral, Dublin, in 1713. He was associated, as a member of the Scriblerus Club, with other leading writers of his day, including Alexander Pope and John Gay, and their common love of poking fun at human foibles is apparent throughout Gulliver's Travels.

First published in 1726, this satirical novel which is at once an adventure tale and a moral allegory, achieved nearly instantaneous popularity. Divided into four parts, telling the story of four separate journeys and commenting on all dimensions of the human condition, perhaps the most well known of the voyages is the first, to the island of Lilliput. This kingdom in miniature, with its court intrigues and absurd religious disputes, reveals the triviality of worldly concerns and the pervasive human tendency for smallmindedness. Subsequent voyages underscore different vices and the corruption that Swift observed in European society, and all the voyages resoundingly criticize the vanity of human existence. Swift's satire reaches an extreme level of pessimism in the fourth and final voyage, to Houyhnhnm-land (pronounced "Whinnum-land," to mimic a horse's whinney). Here we find a utopian society of rational horses coexisting with the repulsive Yahoos, a race of ugly, savage, inarticulate, greedy, irrational creatures whom Gulliver gradually recognizes as his own species. Disgusted with himself, Gulliver aspires (with ridiculous results) to imitate the Houyhnhnms. While this part of the novel might not be considered explicit nature writing, we see Swift following a tradition, which dates back to Aesop, of using animals to illustrate moral virtues and vices. Perhaps more significantly, in depicting humans in their natural condition, Swift reveals himself to have a Hobbesian perspective on the State of Nature. Such a perspective serves as a counterpoint to the idealized notion of the noble savage, an idea manifest in earlier narratives of travel and exploration and further popularized through the followers of Rousseau later in the eighteenth century. Finally, one might trace an environmental agenda in the way that Swift depicts how both races interact with their natural environment. The Houyhnhnms are an agricultural society and they cultivate only what they need from the land, practicing an early version of sustainable agriculture. The Yahoos, by contrast, when not indulging their animal urges, greedily mine for diamonds, tearing at the earth to gather shiny objects, the value of which eludes the rational Houyhnhnms. Scholars have debated whether Swift's depiction of humankind as utterly depraved Yahoos moves his critique beyond satire—the aim of which is to correct and improve—toward a more despairing statement about the hopelessness of the human condition and an assertion that humans are a blight upon the rest of the natural world.

From Gulliver's Travels

Part 4: A Voyage to the Country of the Houyhnhnms

Chapter 1

The Author sets out as Captain of a ship. His men conspire against him, confine him a long time to his cabin, set him on shore in an unknown land. He travels up into the country. The Yahoos, *a strange sort of animal, described. The Author meets two* Houyhnhnms.

I continued at home with my wife and children about five months in a very happy condition, if I could have learned the lesson of knowing when I was well. I left my poor wife big with child, and accepted an advantageous offer made me to be Captain of the *Adventurer*, a stout merchantman of 350 tons: for I understood navigation well, and being grown weary of a surgeon's employment at sea, which however I could exercise upon occasion, I took a skillful young man of that calling, one Robert Purefoy, into my ship. We set sail from Portsmouth upon the seventh day of September, 1710; on the fourteenth we met with Captain Pocock of Bristol, at Tenerife, who was going to the bay of Campeche, to cut logwood. On the sixteenth, he was parted from us by a storm; I heard since my return, that his ship foundered, and none escaped but one cabin boy. He was an honest man, and a good sailor, but a little too positive in his own opinions, which was the cause of his destruction, as it hath been of several others. For if he had followed my advice, he might have been safe at home with his family at this time, as well as myself.

I had several men died in my ship of calentures,[1] so that I was forced to get recruits out of Barbados, and the Leeward Islands, where I touched by the direction of the merchants who employed me, which I had soon too much cause to repent: for I found afterwards that most of them had been buccaneers. I had fifty hands on board, and my orders were, that I should trade with the Indians in the South-Sea, and make what discoveries I could. These rogues whom I had picked up debauched my other men, and they all formed a conspiracy to seize the ship and secure me; which they did one morning, rushing into my cabin, and binding me hand and foot, threatening to throw me overboard, if I offered to stir. I told them, I was their prisoner, and would submit. This they made me swear to do, and then they unbound me, only fastening one of my legs with a chain near my bed, and placed a sentry at my door with his piece charged, who was commanded to shoot me dead, if I attempted my liberty. They sent me down victuals and drink, and took the government of the ship to themselves. Their design was to turn pirates, and plunder the Spaniards, which they could not do, till they got more men. But first they resolved to sell the goods in the ship, and then go to Madagascar for recruits, several among them having died since my confinement. They sailed many weeks, and traded with the Indians, but I knew not what course they took, being kept a close prisoner in my cabin, and expecting nothing less than to be murdered, as they often threatened me.

Upon the ninth day of May, 1711, one James Welch came down to my cabin; and said he had orders from the Captain to set me ashore. I expostulated with him, but in vain; neither would he so much as tell me who their new Captain was. They forced me into the long-boat, letting me put on my best suit of clothes, which were as good as new, and a small bundle of linen, but no arms except my hanger;[2] and they were so civil as not to search my pockets, into which I conveyed what money I had, with some other little necessaries. They rowed about a league, and then set me down on a strand. I desired them to tell me what

---

[1] A delirium caused in the Tropics by exposure to excessive heat.
[2] A type of short sword.

country it was. They all swore, they knew no more than myself, but said, that the Captain (as they called him) was resolved, after they had sold the lading, to get rid of me in the first place where they could discover land. They pushed off immediately, advising me to make haste, for fear of being overtaken by the tide, and so bade me farewell.

In this desolate condition I advanced forward, and soon got upon firm ground, where I sat down on a bank to rest myself, and consider what I had best to do. When I was a little refreshed, I went up into the country, resolving to deliver myself to the first savages I should meet, and purchase my life from them by some bracelets, glass rings, and other toys which sailors usually provide themselves with in those voyages, and whereof I had some about me. The land was divided by long rows of trees, not regularly planted, but naturally growing; there was great plenty of grass, and several fields of oats. I walked very circumspectly for fear of being surprised, or suddenly shot with an arrow from behind or on either side. I fell into a beaten road, where I saw many tracks of human feet, and some of cows, but most of horses. At last I beheld several animals in a field, and one or two of the same kind sitting in trees. Their shape was very singular, and deformed, which a little discomposed me, so that I lay down behind a thicket to observe them better. Some of them coming forward near the place where I lay, gave me an opportunity of distinctly marking their form. Their heads and breasts were covered with a thick hair, some frizzled and others lank; they had beards like goats, and a long ridge of hair down their backs and the fore parts of their legs and feet, but the rest of their bodies were bare, so that I might see their skins, which were of a brown buff colour. They had no tails, nor any hair at all on their buttocks, except about the anus; which, I presume, nature had placed there to defend them as they sat on the ground; for this posture they used, as well as lying down, and often stood on their hind feet. They climbed high trees, as nimbly as a squirrel, for they had strong extended claws before and behind, terminating in sharp points, and hooked. They would often spring, and bound, and leap with prodigious agility. The females were not so large as the males; they had long lank hair on their heads, but none on their faces, nor any thing more than a sort of down on the rest of their bodies, except about the anus, and pudenda. Their dugs hung between their fore-feet, and often reached almost to the ground as they walked. The hair of both sexes was of several colours, brown, red, black, and yellow. Upon the whole, I never beheld in all my travels so disagreeable an animal, nor one against which I naturally conceived so strong an antipathy. So that thinking I had seen enough, full of contempt and aversion, I got up and pursued the beaten road, hoping it might direct me to the cabin of some Indian. I had not got far when I met one of these creatures full in my way, and coming up directly to me. The ugly monster, when he saw me, distorted several ways every feature of his visage, and stared as at an object he had never seen before; then approaching nearer, lifted up his fore-paw, whether out of curiosity or mischief, I could not tell. But I drew my hanger, and gave him a good blow with the flat side of it, for I durst not strike with the edge, fearing the inhabitants might be provoked against me, if they should come to know, that I had killed or maimed any of their cattle. When the beast felt the smart, he drew back, and roared so loud, that a herd of at least forty came flocking about me from the next field, howling and making odious faces; but I ran to the body of a tree, and leaning my back against it, kept them off by waving my hanger. Several of this cursed brood getting hold of the branches behind, leapt up into the tree, from whence they began to discharge their excrements on my head; however, I escaped pretty well, by sticking close to the stem of the tree, but was almost stifled with the filth, which fell about me on every side.

In the midst of this distress, I observed them all to run away on a sudden as fast as they could, at which I ventured to leave the tree, and pursue the road, wondering what it was that could put them into this fright. But looking on my left hand, I saw a horse walking softly in the field; which my persecutors having sooner discovered, was the cause of their flight. The horse started a little when he came near me, but soon recovering himself, looked full in my face with manifest tokens of wonder: he viewed my hands and feet, walking round me several times. I would have pursued my journey, but he placed himself directly in the way, yet looking with a very mild aspect, never offering the least violence. We stood gazing at each other for some time; at last I took the boldness to reach my hands towards his neck, with a design to stroke it, using the common style and whistle of jockeys when they are going to handle a strange horse. But this animal seeming to receive my civilities with disdain, shook his head, and bent his brows, softly raising up his right fore-foot to remove my hand. Then he neighed three or four times, but in so different a cadence, that I almost began to think he was speaking to himself in some language of his own.

While he and I were thus employed, another horse came up; who applying himself to the first in a very formal manner, they gently struck each other's right hoof before, neighing several times by turns, and varying the sound, which seemed to be almost articulate. They went some paces off, as if it were to confer together, walking side by side, backward and forward, like persons deliberating upon some affair of weight, but often turning their eyes towards me, as if it were to watch that I might not escape. I was amazed to see such actions and behaviour in brute beasts, and concluded with myself, that if the inhabitants of this country were endued with a proportionable degree of reason, they must needs be the wisest people upon earth. This thought gave me so much comfort, that I resolved to go forward until I could discover some house or village, or meet with any of the natives, leaving the two horses to discourse together as they pleased. But the first, who was a dapple gray, observing me to steal off, neighed after me in so expressive a tone, that I fancied myself to understand what he meant; whereupon I turned back, and came near him, to expect his farther commands: but concealing my fear as much as I could, for I began to be in some pain, how this adventure might terminate; and the reader will easily believe I did not much like my present situation.

The two horses came up close to me, looking with great earnestness upon my face and hands. The gray steed rubbed my hat all round with his right fore-hoof, and discomposed it so much that I was forced to adjust it better, by taking it off, and settling it again; whereat both he and his companion (who was a brown bay) appeared to be much surprised: the latter felt the lappet of my coat, and finding it to hang loose about me, they both looked with new signs of wonder. He stroked my right hand, seeming to admire the softness and colour; but he squeezed it so hard between his hoof and his pastern, that I was forced to roar; after which they both touched me with all possible tenderness. They were under great perplexity about my shoes and stockings, which they felt very often, neighing to each other, and using various gestures, not unlike those of a philosopher, when he would attempt to solve some new and difficult phenomenon.

Upon the whole, the behaviour of these animals was so orderly and rational, so acute and judicious, that I at last concluded, they must needs be magicians, who had thus metamorphosed themselves upon some design, and seeing a stranger in the way, were resolved to divert themselves with him; or perhaps were really amazed at the sight of a man so very different in habit, feature, and complexion from those who might probably live in so remote a climate. Upon the strength of this reasoning, I ventured to address them in the following manner: "Gentlemen, if you be conjurers, as I have good cause to believe, you can understand any language; therefore I make bold to let your worships know, that I am a poor distressed Englishman, driven by his misfortunes upon your coast, and I entreat one of you, to let me ride upon his back, as if he were a real horse, to some house or village, where I can be relieved. In return of which favour, I will make you a present of this knife and bracelet," (taking them out of my pocket). The two creatures stood silent while I spoke, seeming to listen with great attention; and when I had ended, they neighed frequently towards each other, as if they were engaged in serious conversation. I plainly observed, that their language expressed the passions very well, and the words might with little pains be resolved into an alphabet more easily than the Chinese.

I could frequently distinguish the word *Yahoo*, which was repeated by each of them several times; and although it was impossible for me to conjecture what it meant, yet while the two horses were busy in conversation, I endeavoured to practise this word upon my tongue; and as soon as they were silent, I boldly pronounced *"Yahoo"* in a loud voice, imitating, at the same time, as near as I could, the neighing of a horse; at which they were both visibly surprised, and the gray repeated the same word twice, as if he meant to teach me the right accent, wherein I spoke after him as well as I could, and found myself perceivably to improve every time, though very far from any degree of perfection. Then the bay tried me with a second word, much harder to be pronounced; but reducing it to the English orthography, may be spelt thus, *Houyhnhnm*.[3] I did not succeed in this so well as the former, but after two or three farther trials, I had better fortune; and they both appeared amazed at my capacity.

After some further discourse, which I then conjectured might relate to me, the two friends took their leaves, with the same compliment of striking each other's hoof; and the gray made me signs that I should walk before him, wherein I thought it prudent to comply, till I could find a better director. When I offered to slacken my pace, he would cry *Hhuun, Hhuun*; I guessed his meaning, and gave him to understand, as well as I could, that I was weary, and not able to walk faster; upon which, he would stand a while to let me rest.

· · ·

---

[3] Pronounced "whinnim" to imitate a horse's whinney.

Chapter 3

The Author studious to learn the language, the Houyhnhnm *his master assists in teaching him. The language described. Several* Houyhnhnms *of quality come out of curiosity to see the Author. He gives his master a short account of his voyage.*

My principal endeavour was to learn the language, which my master (for so I shall henceforth call him), and his children, and every servant of his house, were desirous to teach me. For they looked upon it as a prodigy that a brute animal should discover such marks of a rational creature. I pointed to every thing, and enquired the name of it, which I wrote down in my journal-book when I was alone, and corrected my bad accent by desiring those of the family to pronounce it often. In this employment, a sorrel nag, one of the under servants, was very ready to assist me.

In speaking, they pronounce through the nose and throat, and their language approaches nearest to the High-Dutch, or German, of any I know in Europe; but is much more graceful and significant. The Emperor Charles V. made almost the same observation, when he said, that if he were to speak to his horse, it should be in High-Dutch.

The curiosity and impatience of my master were so great, that he spent many hours of his leisure to instruct me. He was convinced (as he afterwards told me) that I must be a *Yahoo*, but my teachableness, civility, and cleanliness, astonished him; which were qualities altogether so opposite to those animals. He was most perplexed about my clothes, reasoning sometimes with himself, whether they were a part of my body: for I never pulled them off till the family were asleep, and got them on before they waked in the morning. My master was eager to learn from whence I came, how I acquired those appearances of reason, which I discovered in all my actions, and to know my story from my own mouth, which he hoped he should soon do by the great proficiency I made in learning and pronouncing their words and sentences. To help my memory, I formed all I learned into the English alphabet, and writ the words down with the translations. This last, after some time, I ventured to do in my master's presence. It cost me much trouble to explain to him what I was doing; for the inhabitants have not the least idea of books or literature.

In about ten weeks time I was able to understand most of his questions, and in three months could give him some tolerable answers. He was extremely curious to know from what part of the country I came, and how I was taught to imitate a rational creature, because the *Yahoos* (whom he saw I exactly resembled in my head, hands, and face, that were only visible), with some appearance of cunning, and the strongest disposition to mischief, were observed to be the most unteachable of all brutes. I answered, that I came over the sea from a far place, with many others of my own kind, in a great hollow vessel made of the bodies of trees. That my companions forced me to land on this coast, and then left me to shift for myself. It was with some difficulty, and by the help of many signs, that I brought him to understand me. He replied, that I must needs be mistaken, or that I *said the thing which was not*. (For they have no word in their language to express lying or falsehood.) He knew it was impossible that there could be a country beyond the sea, or that a parcel of brutes could move a wooden vessel whither they pleased upon water. He was sure no *Houyhnhnm* alive could make such a vessel, nor would trust *Yahoos* to manage it.

The word *Houyhnhnm*, in their tongue, signifies a *horse*, and in its etymology, *the perfection of nature*. I told my master, that I was at a loss for expression, but could improve as fast as I could; and hoped in a short time I should be able to tell him wonders: he was pleased to direct his own mare, his colt and foal, and the servants of the family, to take all opportunities of instructing me, and every day for two or three hours, he was at the same pains himself. Several horses and mares of quality in the neighbourhood came often to our house upon the report spread of a wonderful *Yahoo*, that could speak like a *Houyhnhnm*, and seemed in his words and actions to discover some glimmerings of reason. These delighted to converse with me: they put many questions, and received such answers, as I was able to return. By all these advantages, I made so great a progress, that in five months from my arrival, I understood whatever was spoke, and could express myself tolerably well.

The *Houyhnhnms* who came to visit my master, out of a design of seeing and talking with me, could hardly believe me to be a right *Yahoo*, because my body had a different covering from others of my kind. They were astonished to observe me without the usual hair or skin, except on my head, face, and hands; but I discovered that secret to my master, upon an accident, which happened about a fortnight before.

I have already told the reader, that every night when the family were gone to bed, it was my custom to strip and cover myself with my clothes: it happened one morning early, that my master sent for me, by the sorrel nag, who was his valet; when he came, I was fast asleep, my clothes fallen off on one side, and my shirt above my waist. I awakened at the noise he made, and observed him to deliver his message in some disorder; after which he went to my master, and in a great fright gave him a very confused account of what he had seen. This I presently discovered; for going as soon as I was dressed, to pay my attendance upon his Honour, he asked me the meaning of what his servant had reported, that I was not the same thing when I slept as I appeared to be at other times; that his valet assured him, some part of me was white, some yellow, at least not so white, and some brown.

I had hitherto concealed the secret of my dress, in order to distinguish myself, as much as possible, from that cursed race of *Yahoos;* but now I found it in vain to do so any longer. Besides, I considered that my clothes and shoes would soon wear out, which already were in a declining condition, and must be supplied by some contrivance from the hides of *Yahoos* or other brutes; whereby the whole secret would be known. I therefore told my master, that in the country from whence I came, those of my kind always covered their bodies with the hairs of certain animals prepared by art, as well for decency, as to avoid the inclemencies of air, both hot and cold; of which, as to my own person, I would give him immediate conviction, if he pleased to command me: only desiring his excuse, if I did not expose those parts, that nature taught us to conceal. He said my discourse was all very strange, but especially the last part; for he could not understand, why nature should teach us to conceal what nature had given. That neither himself nor family were ashamed of any parts of their bodies; but however I might do as I pleased. Whereupon, I first unbuttoned my coat, and pulled it off. I did the same with my waistcoat; I drew off my shoes, stockings, and breeches. I let my shirt down to my waist, and drew up the bottom, fastening it like a girdle about my middle to hide my nakedness.

My master observed the whole performance with great signs of curiosity and admiration. He took up all my clothes in his pastern, one piece after another, and examined them diligently; he then stroked my body very gently, and looked round me several times, after which he said, it was plain I must be a perfect *Yahoo*; but that I differed very much from the rest of my species, in the softness, and whiteness, and smoothness of my skin, my want of hair in several parts of my body, the shape and shortness of my claws behind and before, and my affectation of walking continually on my two hinder feet. He desired to see no more, and gave me leave to put on my clothes again, for I was shuddering with cold.

I expressed my uneasiness at his giving me so often the appellation of *Yahoo*, an odious animal, for which I had so utter a hatred and contempt. I begged he would forbear applying that word to me, and take the same order in his family, and among his friends whom he suffered to see me. I requested likewise, that the secret of my having a false covering to my body might be known to none but himself, at least as long as my present clothing should last; for as to what the sorrel nag his valet had observed, his Honour might command him to conceal it.

All this my master very graciously consented to, and thus the secret was kept till my clothes began to wear out, which I was forced to supply by several contrivances, that shall hereafter be mentioned. In the meantime, he desired I would go on with my utmost diligence to learn their language, because he was more astonished at my capacity for speech and reason, than at the figure of my body, whether it were covered or no; adding, that he waited with some impatience to hear the wonder which I promised to tell him.

From thenceforward he doubled the pains he had been at to instruct me; he brought me into all company, and made them treat me with civility, because, as he told them, privately, this would put me into good humour, and make me more diverting.

Every day when I waited on him, beside the trouble he was at in teaching, he would ask me several questions concerning myself, which I answered as well as I could; and by these means he had already received some general ideas, though very imperfect. It would be tedious to relate the several steps by which I advanced to a more regular conversation: but the first account I gave of myself in any order and length, was to this purpose:

That I came from a very far country, as I already had attempted to tell him, with about fifty more of my own species; that we travelled upon the seas, in a great hollow vessel made of wood, and larger than his Honour's house. I described the ship to him in the best terms I could, and explained by the help of my handkerchief displayed how it was driven forward by the wind. That upon a quarrel among us, I was set on shore on this coast, where I walked forward without knowing whither, till he delivered me from the persecution of those execrable *Yahoos*. He asked me, who made the ship, and how it was possible that the *Houyhnhnms* of my country would leave it to the management of brutes? My answer was, that I durst proceed no further in my relation, unless he would give me his word and honour that he would not be offended, and then I would tell him the wonders I had so often promised. He agreed; and I went on by assuring him, that the ship was made by creatures like myself, who in all the countries I had travelled, as well as in my own, were the only governing, rational animals; and that upon my arrival hither, I was as much astonished to see the *Houyhnhnms* act like rational beings, as he or his friends could be in finding some marks of reason in a creature he was pleased to call a *Yahoo*, to which I owned my resemblance in every part, but could not account for their degenerate and brutal nature. I said farther, that if good fortune ever restored me to my native country, to relate my travels hither, as I resolved to do, every body would believe that I *said the thing which was not*; that I invented the story out of my own head; and with all possible respect to himself, his family and friends, and under his promise of not being offended, our countrymen would hardly think it probable, that a *Houyhnhnm* should be the presiding creature of a nation, and a *Yahoo* the brute.

◈ William Byrd (1674–1744)

William Byrd was the son of a wealthy Virginia planter and Indian trader. Born in America and educated in England, Byrd was trained as a lawyer and moved in the most elite circles of London social and intellectual life. He was acquainted with the chemist Robert Boyle, and he was elected to the Royal Society in 1696. He also explored the many dissipations that London offered to wealthy young aristocrats: he frequented whorehouses and gambling dens, recording intimate details of these escapades in his private journal. Upon his return to Virginia, Byrd found great satisfaction in rambling about his estate and in managing the resources of his vast plantation. After the death of his father in 1704, Byrd became a leading figure in Virginia's colonial aristocracy; he was elected to the House of Burgesses and was sometimes called on to assist in resolving public disputes. In 1728, he embarked on an expedition to survey the boundary between Virginia and North Carolina, seeking to resolve a long-standing dispute about the dividing line between these two neighboring colonies. During this expedition he kept a daily journal, which he later reworked into a book-length manuscript, The History of the Dividing Line, *first published in 1841. In the excerpt included below, Byrd recounts the most difficult and dangerous part of the expedition: a crossing of the Great Dismal Swamp, an uncharted wetland several miles in extent, regarded by the local inhabitants as utterly impassable. Byrd approaches this adventure with high spirits, determination, and contagious good humor; he finds much to appreciate in the beauty of the deep woods and in the darkness of the night sky, even as his men struggle to survey the great American wilderness.*

From The History of the Dividing Line

13. Early this morning our chaplain repaired to us with the men we had left at Mr. Wilson's. We had sent for them the evening before to relieve those who had the labor oar from Currituck Inlet. But to our great surprise, they petitioned not to be relieved, hoping to gain immortal reputation by being the first of mankind that ventured through the Great Dismal. But the rest being equally ambitious of the same honor, it was but fair to decide their pretensions by lot. After Fortune had declared herself, those which she had excluded offered money to the happy persons to go in their stead. But Hercules would have as soon sold the glory of cleansing the Augean stables, which was pretty near the same sort of work.[1] No sooner was the controversy at an end but we sent those unfortunate fellows back to their quarters whom chance had condemned to remain upon firm land and sleep in a whole skin. In the meanwhile, the surveyors carried the line three miles, which was no contemptible day's work, considering how cruelly they were entangled with briers and gallbushes. The leaf of this last shrub bespeaks it to be of the alaternus family.

Our work ended within a quarter of a mile of the Dismal above-mentioned, where the ground began to be already full of sunken holes and slashes, which had, here and there, some few reeds growing in them. 'Tis hardly credible how little the bordering inhabitants were acquainted with this mighty swamp, notwithstanding they had lived their whole lives within smell of it. Yet, as great strangers as they were to it, they pretended to be very exact in their account of its dimensions and were positive it could not be above seven or eight miles wide, but knew no more of the matter than stargazers know of the distance of the fixed stars. At the same time, they were simple enough to amuse our men with idle stories of the lions, panthers, and alligators they were likely to encounter in that dreadful place. In short, we saw plainly there was no intelligence of this *Terra Incognita*[2] to be got but from our own experience. For that reason it was resolved to make the requisite dispositions to enter it next morning. We allotted every one of the surveyors for this painful enterprise, with twelve men to attend them. Fewer than that could not be employed in clearing the way, carrying the chain, marking the trees, and bearing the necessary bedding and provisions. Nor would the commissioners themselves have spared their persons on this occasion but for fear of adding to the poor men's burden, while they were certain they could add nothing to their resolution. . . .

14. Before nine of the clock this morning the provisions, bedding, and other necessaries were made up into packs for the men to carry on their shoulders into the Dismal. They were victualed for eight days at full allowance, nobody doubting but that would be abundantly sufficient to carry them through that inhospitable place; nor indeed was it possible for the poor fellows to stagger under

---

[1] In Greek mythology, the sixth labor of Hercules was the cleaning of the Augean Stables, fouled by the droppings of a huge herd of cattle.

[2] Unknown Territory (Latin), a phrase frequently employed by mapmakers of the seventeenth and eighteenth centuries.

more. As it was, their loads weighed from sixty to seventy pounds, in just proportion to the strength of those who were to bear them. 'Twould have been unconscionable to have saddled them with burdens heavier than that, when they were to lug them through a filthy bog which was hardly practicable with no burden at all. Besides this luggage at their backs, they were obliged to measure the distance, mark the trees, and clear the way for the surveyors every step they went. It was really a pleasure to see with how much cheerfulness they undertook and with how much spirit they went through all this drudgery. For their greater safety, the commissioners took care to furnish them with Peruvian bark,[3] rhubarb, and ipecacuanha, in case they might happen, in that wet journey, to be taken with fevers or fluxes.

Although there was no need of example to inflame persons already so cheerful, yet to enter the people with the better grace, the author and two more of the commissioners[4] accompanied them half a mile into the Dismal. The skirts of it were thinly planted with dwarf reeds and gallbushes, but when we got into the Dismal itself we found the reeds grew there much taller and closer and, to mend the matter, were so interlaced with bamboo briers that there was no scuffling through them without the help of pioneers. At the same time we found the ground moist and trembling under our feet like a quagmire, insomuch that it was an easy matter to run a ten-foot pole up to the head in it without exerting any uncommon strength to do it. Two of the men whose burdens were the least cumbersome had orders to march before with their tomahawks and clear the way in order to make an opening for the surveyors. By their assistance we made a shift to push the line half a mile in three hours and then reached a small piece of firm land about a hundred yards wide, standing up above the rest like an island. Here the people were glad to lay down their loads and take a little refreshment, while the happy man whose lot it was to carry the jug of rum began already, like Aesop's bread carriers, to find it grow a good deal lighter.

After reposing about an hour, the commissioners recommended vigor and constancy to their fellow travelers, by whom they were answered with three cheerful huzzas, in token of obedience. This ceremony was no sooner over but they took up their burdens and attended the motion of the surveyors, who, though they worked with all their might, could reach but one mile farther, the same obstacles still attending them which they had met with in the morning. However small this distance may seem to such as are used to travel at their ease, yet our poor men, who were obliged to work with an unwieldy load at their backs, had reason to think it a long way; especially in a bog where they had no firm footing but every step made a deep impression which was instantly filled with water. At the same time they were laboring with their hands to cut down the reeds, which were ten feet high, their legs were hampered with briers. Besides, the weather happened to be warm, and the tallness of the reeds kept off

---

[3] Cinchona bark, used as a preventive treatment for malaria and other tropical diseases.

[4] Byrd was one of three commissioners appointed to survey the boundary between Virginia and North Carolina. These commissioners supervised the work, but they did not accompany the surveyors all the way into the Great Dismal Swamp.

every friendly breeze from coming to refresh them. And indeed it was a little provoking to hear the wind whistling among the branches of the white cedars, which grew here and there amongst the reeds, and at the same time not to have the comfort to feel the least breath of it.

In the meantime the three commissioners returned out of the Dismal the same way they went in and, having joined their brethren, proceeded that night as far as Mr. Wilson's. This worthy person lives within sight of the Dismal, in the skirts whereof his stocks range and maintain themselves all the winter, and yet he knew as little of it as he did of *Terra Australis Incognita.*[5] He told us a Canterbury tale[6] of a North Briton whose curiosity spurred him a long way into this great desert, as he called it, near twenty years ago, but he, having no compass nor seeing the sun for several days together, wandered about till he was almost famished; but at last he bethought himself of a secret his countrymen make use of to pilot themselves in a dark day. He took a fat louse out of his collar and exposed it to the open day on a piece of white paper, which he brought along with him for his journal. The poor insect, having no eyelids, turned himself about till he found the darkest part of the heavens and so made the best of his way toward the North. By this direction he steered himself safe out and gave such a frightful account of the monsters he saw and the distresses he underwent that no mortal since has been hardy enough to go upon the like dangerous discovery.

15. The surveyors pursued their work with all diligence but still found the soil of the Dismal so spongy that the water oozed up into every footstep they took. To their sorrow, too, they found the reeds and briers more firmly interwoven than they did the day before. But the greatest grievance was from large cypresses which the wind had blown down and heaped upon one another. On the limbs of most of them grew sharp snags, pointing every way like so many pikes, that required much pains and caution to avoid. These trees, being evergreens and shooting their large tops very high, are easily overset by every gust of wind, because there is no firm earth to steady their roots. Thus many of them were laid prostrate, to the great encumbrance of the way. Such variety of difficulties made the business go on heavily, insomuch that from morning till night the line could advance no farther than one mile and thirty-one poles.

Never was rum, that cordial of life, found more necessary than it was in this dirty place. It did not only recruit the people's spirits, now almost jaded with fatigue, but served to correct the badness of the water and at the same time to resist the malignity of the air. Whenever the men wanted to drink, which was very often, they had nothing more to do but make a hole and the water bubbled up in a moment. But it was far from being either clear or well tasted and had, besides, a physical effect from the tincture it received from the roots of the shrubs and trees that grew in the neighborhood. . . .

16. The line was this day carried one mile and an half and sixteen poles. The soil continued soft and miry but fuller of trees, especially white cedars. Many of

---

[5] Unknown Southern Continent (Latin). The mapmakers' name for a hypothetical southern continent, supposed to exist somewhere in the unexplored Pacific Ocean.

[6] A tall tale, alluding to the *Canterbury Tales* of Geoffrey Chaucer (c. 1340–1400).

these, too, were thrown down and piled in heaps, high enough for a good Muscovite fortification. The worst of it was, the poor fellows began now to be troubled with fluxes, occasioned by bad water and moist lodging, but chewing of rhubarb kept that malady within bounds.

In the meantime, the commissioners decamped early in the morning and made a march of twenty-five miles, as far as Mr. Andrew Meade's, who lives upon Nansemond River. They were no sooner got under the shelter of that hospitable roof but it began to rain hard and continued so to do great part of the night. This gave them much pain for their friends in the Dismal, whose sufferings spoiled their taste for the good cheer wherewith they were entertained themselves. However, late that evening these poor men had the fortune to come upon another terra firma, which was the luckier for them because the lower ground, by the rain that fell, was made a fitter lodging for tadpoles than men. In our journey we remarked that the north side of this great swamp lies higher than either the east or the west, nor were the approaches to it so full of sunken grounds. . . .

There fell a great deal of rain in the night, accompanied with a strong wind. The fellow feeling we had for the poor Dismalites, on account of this unkind weather, rendered the down we laid upon uneasy. We fancied them half-drowned in their wet lodging, with the trees blowing down about their ears. These were the gloomy images our fears suggested, though 'twas so much uneasiness clear gains. They happened to come off much better, by being luckily encamped on the dry piece of ground afore-mentioned.

17. They were, however, forced to keep the Sabbath in spite of their teeth, contrary to the dispensation our good chaplain had given them. Indeed, their short allowance of provision would have justified their making the best of their way without distinction of days. 'Twas certainly a work both of necessity and self-preservation to save themselves from starving. Nevertheless, the hard rain had made everything so thoroughly wet that it was quite impossible to do any business. They therefore made a virtue of what they could not help and contentedly rested in their dry situation.

Since the surveyors had entered the Dismal, they had laid eyes on no living creature: neither bird nor beast, insect nor reptile came in view. Doubtless the eternal shade that broods over this mighty bog and hinders the sunbeams from blessing the ground makes it an uncomfortable habitation for anything that has life. Not so much as a Zeeland[7] frog could endure so aguish a situation. It had one beauty, however, that delighted the eye, though at the expense of all the other senses: the moisture of the soil preserves a continual verdure and makes every plant an evergreen; but at the same time the foul damps ascend without ceasing, corrupt the air, and render it unfit for respiration. Not even a turkey buzzard will venture to fly over it, no more than the Italian vultures will over the filthy Lake Avernus,[8] or the birds in the Holy Land over the Salt Sea where Sodom and Gomorrah formerly stood.

---

[7] A southwestern region of the Netherlands, known for its boggy (and froggy) topography.

[8] A small crater lake in southern Italy known for its sulphurous vapors; it was regarded by the ancient Romans as the entrance to the underworld.

In these sad circumstances the kindest thing we could do for our suffering friends was to give them a place in The Litany. Our chaplain, for his part, did his office and rubbed us up with a seasonable sermon. This was quite a new thing to our brethren of North Carolina, who live in a climate where no clergyman can breathe, any more than spiders in Ireland. . . .

18. It was with some difficulty we could make our people quit the good cheer they met with at this house, so it was late before we took our departure; but to make us amends our landlord was so good as to conduct us ten miles on our way, as far as the Cypress Swamp, which drains itself into the Dismal. Eight miles beyond that we forded the waters of Corapeake, which tend the same way as do many others on that side. In six miles more we reached the plantation of Mr. Thomas Speight, a grandee of North Carolina. We found the good man upon his crutches, being crippled with the gout in both his knees. Here we flattered ourselves we should by this time meet with good tidings of the surveyors but had reckoned, alas! without our host: on the contrary, we were told the Dismal was at least thirty miles wide in that place. However, as nobody could say this on his own knowledge, we ordered guns to be fired and a drum to be beaten, but received no answer, unless it was from that prating nymph, Echo, who, like a loquacious wife, will always have the last word and sometimes return three for one. It was indeed no wonder our signal was not heard at that time by the people in the Dismal, because, in truth, they had then not penetrated one third of their way. They had that morning fallen to work with great vigor and, finding the ground better than ordinary, drove on the line two miles and thirty-eight poles. This was reckoned an Herculean day's work, and yet they would not have stopped there had not an impenetrable cedar thicket checked their industry.

Our landlord had seated himself on the borders of this Dismal for the advantage of the green food his cattle find there all winter and for the rooting that supports his hogs. This, I own, is some convenience to his purse, for which his whole family pay dear in their persons, for they are devoured by mosquitoes all the summer and have agues every spring and fall, which corrupt all the juices of their bodies, give them a cadaverous complexion and, besides, a lazy, creeping habit, which they never get rid of.

19. We ordered several men to patrol on the edge of the Dismal, both toward the north and toward the south, and to fire guns at proper distances. This they performed very punctually but could hear nothing in return nor gain any sort of intelligence. In the meantime, whole flocks of women and children flew hither to stare at us with as much curiosity as if we had lately landed from Bantam or Morocco. Some borderers, too, had a great mind to know where the line would come out, being for the most part apprehensive lest their lands should be taken into Virginia. In that case they must have submitted to some sort of order and government; whereas, in North Carolina, everyone does what seems best in his own eyes. There were some good women that brought their children to be baptized, but brought no capons along with them to make the solemnity cheerful. In the meantime, it was strange that none came to be married in such a multitude, if it had only been for the novelty of having their hands joined by one in holy orders. Yet so it was that though our chaplain christened above an hundred, he did

not marry so much as one couple during the whole expedition. But marriage is reckoned a lay contract in Carolina, as I said before, and a country justice can tie the fatal knot there as fast as an archbishop.

None of our visitors could, however, tell us any news of the surveyors, nor indeed was it possible any of them should at that time, they being still laboring in the midst of the Dismal. It seems they were able to carry the line this day no farther than one mile and sixty-one poles, and that whole distance was through a miry cedar bog, where the ground trembled under their feet most frightfully. In many places, too, their passage was retarded by a great number of fallen trees that lay horsing upon one another.

Though many circumstances concurred to make this an unwholesome situation, yet the poor men had no time to be sick, nor can one conceive a more calamitous case than it would have been to be laid up in that uncomfortable quagmire. Never were patients more tractable or willing to take physic than these honest fellows, but it was from a dread of laying their bones in a bog that would soon spew them up again. That consideration also put them upon more caution about their lodging. They first covered the ground with square pieces of cypress bark, which now, in the spring, they could easily slip off the tree for that purpose. On this they spread their bedding, but, unhappily, the weight and warmth of their bodies made the water rise up betwixt the joints of the bark, to their great inconvenience. Thus they lay not only moist but also exceedingly cold, because their fires were continually going out. For no sooner was the trash upon the surface burnt away but immediately the fire was extinguished by the moisture of the soil, insomuch that it was great part of the sentinel's business to rekindle it again in a fresh place every quarter of an hour. Nor could they indeed do their duty better, because cold was the only enemy they had to guard against in a miserable morass where nothing can inhabit.

20. We could get no tidings yet of our brave adventurers, notwithstanding we dispatched men to the likeliest stations to inquire after them. They were still scuffling in the mire and could not possibly forward the line this whole day more than one mile and sixty-four chains. Every step of this day's work was through a cedar bog, where the trees were somewhat smaller and grew more into a thicket. It was now a great misfortune to the men to find their provisions grow less as their labor grew greater; they were all forced to come to short allowance and consequently to work hard without filling their bellies. Though this was very severe upon English stomachs, yet the people were so far from being discomfited at it that they still kept up their good humor and merrily told a young fellow in the company, who looked very plump and wholesome, that he must expect to go first to pot if matters should come to extremity. This was only said by way of jest, yet it made him thoughtful in earnest. However, for the present he returned them a very civil answer, letting them know that, dead or alive, he should be glad to be useful to such worthy good friends. But, after all, this humorous saying had one very good effect, for that younker,[9] who before was a little inclined by his constitution to be lazy, grew on a sudden extremely indus-

---

[9] Young person.

trious, that so there might be less occasion to carbonade[10] him for the good of his fellow travelers.

While our friends were thus embarrassed in the Dismal, the commissioners began to lie under great uneasiness for them. They knew very well their provisions must by this time begin to fall short, nor could they conceive any likely means of a supply. At this time of the year both cattle and hogs had forsaken the skirts of the Dismal, invited by the springing grass on the firm land. All our hopes were that Providence would cause some wild game to fall in their way or else direct them to a wholesome vegetable for subsistence. In short, they were haunted with so many frights on this occasion that they were in truth more uneasy than the persons whose case they lamented. . . .

21. The surveyors and their attendants began now in good earnest to be alarmed with apprehensions of famine, nor could they forbear looking with some sort of appetite upon a dog which had been the faithful companion of their travels. Their provisions were now near exhausted. They had this morning made the last distribution, that so each might husband his small pittance as he pleased. Now it was that the fresh-colored young man began to tremble every joint of him, having dreamt the night before that the Indians were about to barbecue him over live coals. The prospect of famine determined the people at last, with one consent, to abandon the line for the present, which advanced but slowly, and make the best of their way to firm land. Accordingly they set off very early and, by the help of the compass which they carried along with them, steered a direct westerly course. They marched from morning till night and computed their journey to amount to about four miles, which was a great way, considering the difficulties of the ground. It was all along a cedar swamp, so dirty and perplexed that if they had not traveled for their lives they could not have reached so far. On their way they espied a turkey buzzard that flew prodigiously high to get above the noisome exhalations that ascend from that filthy place. This they were willing to understand as a good omen, according to the superstition of the ancients, who had great faith in the flight of vultures. However, after all this tedious journey they could yet discover no end of their toil, which made them very pensive, especially after they had eat the last morsel of their provisions. But to their unspeakable comfort, when all was hushed in the evening, they heard the cattle low and the dogs bark very distinctly, which, to men in that distress, was more delightful music than Faustina or Farinelli[11] could have made. . . .

22. Our patrol happened not to go far enough to the northward this morning; if they had, the people in the Dismal might have heard the report of their guns. For this reason they returned without any tidings, which threw us into a great though unnecessary perplexity. This was now the ninth day since they entered into that inhospitable swamp, and consequently we had reason to believe their provisions were quite spent. We knew they worked hard and therefore would eat heartily so long as they had wherewithal to recruit their spirits, not imagining the swamp so wide as they found it. Had we been able to guess where

[10] Broiled over charcoal.

[11] Faustina Bordoni (1693–1783) and Carlo Broschi Farinelli (1705–1782), famous Italian opera singers.

the line would come out, we would have sent men to meet them with a fresh supply; but as we could know nothing of that, and as we had neither compass nor surveyor to guide a messenger on such an errand, we were unwilling to expose him to no purpose; therefore, all we were able to do for them, in so great an extremity, was to recommend them to a merciful Providence.

However long we might think the time, yet we were cautious of showing our uneasiness for fear of mortifying our landlord. He had done his best for us, and therefore we were unwilling he should think us dissatisfied with our entertainment. In the midst of our concern, we were most agreeably surprised, just after dinner, with the news that the Dismalites were all safe. These blessed tidings were brought us by Mr. Swann, the Carolina surveyor, who came to us in a very tattered condition. After very short salutations, we got about him as if he had been a Hottentot and began to inquire into his adventures. He gave us a detail of their uncomfortable voyage through the Dismal and told us particularly they had pursued their journey early that morning, encouraged by the good omen of seeing the crows fly over their heads; that after an hour's march over very rotten ground they on a sudden began to find themselves among tall pines that grew in the water, which in many places was knee deep. This pine swamp, into which that of Corapeake drained itself, extended near a mile in breadth; and though it was exceedingly wet, yet was much harder at bottom than the rest of the swamp; that about ten in the morning they recovered firm land, which they embraced with as much pleasure as shipwrecked wretches do the shore.

After these honest adventurers had congratulated each other's deliverance, their first inquiry was for a good house where they might satisfy the importunity of their stomachs. Their good genius directed them to Mr. Brinkley's, who dwells a little to the southward of the line. This man began immediately to be very inquisitive, but they declared they had no spirits to answer questions till after dinner. "But pray, gentlemen," said he, "answer me one question at least: what shall we get for your dinner?" To which they replied, "No matter what, provided it be but enough." He kindly supplied their wants as soon as possible, and by the strength of that refreshment they made a shift to come to us in the evening, to tell their own story. They all looked very thin and as ragged as the Gibeonite ambassadors[12] did in the days of yore.

Our surveyors told us they had measured ten miles in the Dismal and computed the distance they had marched since to amount to about five more, so they made the whole breadth to be fifteen miles in all.

23. It was very reasonable that the surveyors and the men who had been sharers in their fatigue should now have a little rest. They were all, except one, in good health and good heart, blessed be God! notwithstanding the dreadful hardships they had gone through. It was really a pleasure to see the cheerfulness wherewith they received the order to prepare to re-enter the Dismal on the Monday following in order to continue the line from the place where they had

---

[12] Gibeon was an ancient village of Palestine, near Jerusalem. According to Joshua 9.3-15, the people of Gibeon disguised themselves as travelers from a distant land in order to seek the protection of Israel; thus the "Gibeonite ambassadors" wore ragged clothing.

left off measuring, that so we might have the exact breadth of that dirty place. There were no more than two of them that could be persuaded to be relieved on this occasion or suffer the other men to share the credit of that bold undertaking; neither would these have suffered it had not one of them been very lame and the other much indisposed.

By the description the surveyors gave of the Dismal, we were convinced that nothing but the exceeding dry season we had been blessed with could have made the passing of it practicable. It is the source of no less than five several rivers which discharge themselves southward into Albemarle Sound and of two that run northerly into Virginia. From thence 'tis easy to imagine that the soil must be thoroughly soaked with water or else there must be plentiful stores of it underground to supply so many rivers, especially since there is no lake or any considerable body of that element to be seen on the surface. The rivers that head in it from Virginia are the south branch of Nansemond and the west branch of Elizabeth, and those from Carolina are Northwest River, North River, Pasquotank, Little River, and Perquimans.

There is one remarkable part of the Dismal, lying to the south of the line, that has few or no trees growing on it but contains a large tract of tall reeds. These, being green all the year round and waving with every wind, have procured it the name of the Green Sea. We are not yet acquainted with the precise extent of the Dismal, the whole having never been surveyed; but it may be computed at a medium to be about thirty miles long and ten miles broad, though where the line crossed it, 'twas completely fifteen miles wide. But it seems to grow narrower toward the north, or at least does so in many places.

The exhalations that continually rise from this vast body of mire and nastiness infect the air for many miles round and render it very unwholesome for the bordering inhabitants. It makes them liable to agues, pleurisies, and many other distempers that kill abundance of people and make the rest look no better than ghosts. It would require a great sum of money to drain it, but the public treasury could not be better bestowed than to preserve the lives of His Majesty's liege people and at the same time render so great a tract of swamp very profitable, besides the advantage of making a channel to transport by water carriage goods from Albemarle Sound into Nansemond and Elizabeth rivers in Virginia.

✍ *John Gay* (*1685–1732*)

John Gay's playful attitude, seen in much of his writing, is summed up in the epitaph he wrote for himself: "Life is a jest, and all things show it; / I thought so once, but now I know it." Like his good friends in the Scriblerus Club, Jonathan Swift and Alexander Pope, Gay's writing aims largely to poke fun at pretension of any kind. He grew up in the Devon countryside and then came to London and was apprenticed to a silk merchant. Although his work is almost entirely parodic, it nevertheless demonstrates his keen sensitivity to the growing disparity between country and city life that was developing in the early eighteenth century. The question of the proper representation of rural life is at the heart of a good portion of Gay's writing. Although poems such as "Rural Sports" seem to participate in a more conventional idealization of the pleasures of country living, other poems, such as The Shepherd's Week, *simultaneously ridicule pastoral conventions, even as they would warn against abandoning these artificial trappings. By representing the traditional pastoral nymphs and swains as silly rustic clods and bumpkinish women, Gay participates in enduring stereotypes about the backwardness of countryfolk. Yet, at the same time, his depiction of these figures is not cruel or without sympathy, making it difficult to state with any certainty what Gay finally thought about country living. Gay's parody of pastoral is further seen in what is perhaps his best-known work,* The Beggar's Opera. *Known as a "Newgate pastoral" (Newgate was the main London prison), this founding work of musical comedy transforms the pastoral's Arcadian shepherds and maids into the highwaymen and prostitutes of London's criminal underworld.*

The Shepherd and the Philosopher

Remote from cities lived a Swain,
Unvexed with all the cares of gain;
His head was silvered o'er with age,
And long experience made him sage;
In summer's heat and winter's cold   5
He fed his flock and penned the fold:
His hours in cheerful labour flew,
Nor envy nor ambition knew:
His wisdom and his honest fame
Through all the country raised his name.   10
    A deep Philosopher (whose rules
Of moral life were drawn from schools)
The Shepherd's homely cottage sought,
And thus explored his reach of thought:
    "Whence is thy learning? hath thy toil   15
O'er books consumed the midnight oil?
Hast thou old Greece and Rome surveyed,
And the vast sense of Plato weighed?
Hath Socrates thy soul refined,
And hast thou fathomed Tully's mind?   20
Or, like the wise Ulysses, thrown,
By various fates, on realms unknown,
Hast thou through many cities strayed,
Their customs, laws, and manners weighed":
    The Shepherd modestly replied, —   25
"I ne'er the paths of learning tried;
Nor have I roamed in foreign parts
To read mankind, their laws and arts;
For man is practised in disguise,

He cheats the most discerning eyes: 30
Who by that search shall wiser grow,
When we ourselves can never know?
The little knowledge I have gained,
Was all from simple Nature drained;
Hence my life's maxims took their rise,   35
Hence grew my settled hate to vice.
    "The daily labours of the bee
Awake my soul to industry:
Who can observe the careful ant,
And not provide for future want?   40
My dog (the trustiest of his kind)
With gratitude inflames my mind:
I mark his true, his faithful way,
And in my service copy Tray.
In constancy and nuptial love,   45
I learn my duty from the dove.
The hen, who from the chilly air,
With pious wing, protects her care,
And every fowl that flies at large,
Instructs me in a parent's charge.   50
    "From Nature, too, I take my rule,
To shun contempt and ridicule.
I never, with important air,
In conversation overbear.
Can grave and formal pass for wise,   55
When men the solemn owl despise?
My tongue within my lips I rein;
For who talks much must talk in vain.
We from the wordy torrent fly:
Who listens to the chattering pye?[1]   60
Nor would I, with felonious slight,
By stealth invade my neighbour's right.
Rapacious animals we hate:
Kites, hawks, and wolves, deserve their fate.
Do not we just abhorrence find   65
Against the toad and serpent kind?
But Envy, Calumny, and Spite,
Bear stronger venom in their bite.
Thus every object of creation
Can furnish hints to contemplation;   70
And from the most minute and mean,
A virtuous mind can morals glean."
    "Thy fame is just," (the Sage replies)

---

[1] A magpie, or noisy bird.

"Thy virtue proves thee truly wise.
Pride often guides the author's pen;   75
Books as affected are as men:
But he who studies Nature's laws,
From certain truth his maxims draws;
And those, without our schools, suffice
To make men moral, good, and wise."   80

From Rural Sports

Inscribed to Mr. Pope

From Canto 1

You, who the sweets of rural life have known,
Despise th' ungrateful hurry of the Town;
In Windsor groves your easy hours employ,
And undisturbed, yourself and Muse enjoy:
Thames listens to thy strains, and silent flows,   5
And no rude wind through rustling osiers blows,
While all his wondering nymphs around thee throng,
To hear the Sirens[1] warble in thy song.
    But I, who ne'er was blessed by Fortune's hand,
Nor brightened ploughshares in paternal land;[2]   10
Long in the noisy Town have been immured,
Respired its smoke, and all its cares endured;
Where news and politics divide mankind,
And schemes of state involve th' uneasy mind;
Faction embroils the world, and every tongue   15
Is moved by flattery, or with scandal hung:
Friendship, for sylvan shades, the palace flies,
Where all must yield to interest's dearer ties;
Each rival Machiavel[3] with envy burns,
And honesty forsakes them all by turns;   20
While calumny upon each party 's thrown,
Which both promote, and both alike disown.
Fatigued at last, a calm retreat I chose,
And soothed my harassed mind with sweet repose,
Where fields, and shades, and the refreshing clime,   25

---

[1] Mythological creatures from Homer's *Odyssey* who were said to lure sailors to shipwreck by the beauty of their song. Used in a general sense to represent the dangers of succumbing to the temptations of pleasure.

[2] I.e., did not inherit property.

[3] Niccolo Machiavelli (1469–1527) was the Italian Renaissance author of *The Prince*, a conduct book for aspiring politicians known for its emphasis on ruthlessness.

Inspire the sylvan song, and prompt my rhyme.
My Muse shall rove through flowery meads and plains,
And deck with Rural Sports her native strains,
And the same road ambitiously pursue,
Frequented by the Mantuan swain[4] and you.   30

. . . .

    As in successive course the seasons roll,*
So circling pleasures recreate the soul.
When genial Spring a living warmth bestows,
And o'er the year her verdant mantle throws,
No swelling inundation hides the grounds,   125
But crystal currents glide within their bounds;
The finny brood their wonted haunts forsake,
Float in the sun, and skim along the lake;
With frequent leap they range the shallow streams,
Their silver coats reflect the dazzling beams: 130
Now let the fisherman his toils prepare,
And arm himself with every watery snare;
His hooks, his lines, peruse with careful eye,
Increase his tackle, and his rod re-tie.
    When floating clouds their spongy fleeces drain,   135
Troubling the streams with swift-descending rain,
And waters tumbling down the mountain's side,
Bear the loose soil into the swelling tide,
Then, soon as vernal gales begin to rise,
And drive the liquid burden through the skies,   140
The fisher to the neighbouring current speeds;
Whose rapid surface purls, unknown to weeds;
Upon a rising border of the brook
He sits him down, and ties the treacherous hook;
Now expectation cheers his eager thought,   145
His bosom glows with treasures yet uncaught;
Before his eyes a banquet seems to stand,
Where every guest applauds his skilful hand.
    Far up the stream the twisted hair he throws,
Which down the murmuring current gently flows   150
When if or chance or hunger's powerful sway
Directs the roving trout this fatal way,
He greedily sucks in the twining bait,
And tugs and nibbles the fallacious meat:
Now, happy fisherman; now twitch the line!   155

---

[4] Virgil (70–19 B.C.), the greatest poet in Latin (Roman) literature, was born near Mantua of the farmer class. He was the author of the *Georgics*, on the art of farming; the epic poem the *Aeneid* is his masterpiece.

* Lines 31 to 120 have been omitted.—Editors' note.

How thy rod bends! behold, the prize is thine!
Cast on the bank, he dies, with gasping pains,
And trickling blood his silver mail[5] distains.
    You must not every worm promiscuous use:
Judgment will tell thee proper bait to choose;   160
The worm that draws a long immoderate size
The trout abhors, and the rank morsel flies;
And if too small, the naked fraud's in sight,
And fear forbids, while hunger does invite.
Those baits will best reward the fisher's pains,   165
Whose polished tails a shining yellow stains;
Cleanse them from filth, to give a tempting gloss,
Cherish the sullied reptile race with moss;
Amid the verdant bed they twine, they toil,
And from their bodies wipe their native soil.   170
    But when the sun displays his glorious beams,
And shallow rivers flow with silver streams,
Then the deceit the scaly breed survey,
Bask in the sun, and look into the day:
You now a more delusive art must try,   175
And tempt their hunger with the curious fly.
    To frame the little animal, provide
All the gay hues that wait on female pride:
Let Nature guide thee; sometimes golden wire
The shining bellies of the fly require;   180
The peacock's plumes thy tackle must not fail,
Nor the dear purchase of the sable's tail.
Each gaudy bird some slender tribute brings,
And lends the growing insect proper wings:
Silks of all colours must their aid impart,   185
And every fur promote the fisher's art.
So the gay lady, with expensive care,
Borrows the pride of land, of sea, and air;
Furs, pearls, and plumes, the glittering thing displays,
Dazzles our eyes, and easy hearts betrays.   190
    Mark well the various seasons of the year,
How the succeeding insect-race appear;
In this revolving moon one colour reigns,
Which in the next the fickle trout disdains.
Oft have I seen a skilful angler try   195
The various colours of the treacherous fly;
When he with fruitless pain hath skimmed the brook,
And the coy fish rejects the skipping hook,
He shakes the boughs that on the margin grow,

---

[5] Armor or protective external covering, here referring to the fish's fins.

Which o'er the stream a waving forest throw,   200
When if an insect fall, (his certain guide)
He gently takes him from the whirling tide,
Examines well his form with curious eyes,
His gaudy vest, his wings, his horns, and size;
Then round his hook the chosen fur he winds,   205
And on the back a speckled feather binds;
So just the colours shine through every part,
That Nature seems to live again in Art.
Let not thy wary step advance too near,
While all thy hope hangs on a single hair;   210
The new-formed insect on the water moves,
The speckled trout the curious snare approves;
Upon the curling surface let it glide,
With natural motion from thy hand supplied,
Against the stream now let it gently play,   215
Now in the rapid eddy roll away:
The scaly shoals float by, and, seized with fear,
Behold their fellows tost in thinner air;
But soon they leap, and catch the swimming bait,
Plunge on the hook, and share an equal fate.   220
    When a brisk gale against the current blows,
And all the watery plain in wrinkles flows,
Then let the fisherman his art repeat,
Where bubbling eddies favour the deceit.
If an enormous salmon chance to spy,   225
The wanton errors of the floating fly,
He lifts his silver gills above the flood,
And greedily sucks in the unfaithful food,
Then downward plunges with the fraudful prey,
And bears with joy the little spoil away: 230
Soon in smart pain he feels the dire mistake,
Lashes the wave, and beats the foamy lake;
With sudden rage he now aloft appears,
And in his eye convulsive anguish bears;
And now again, impatient of the wound,   235
He rolls and wreathes his shining body round;
Then headlong shoots beneath the dashing tide,
The trembling fins the boiling wave divide:
Now hope exalts the fisher's beating heart,
Now he turns pale, and fears his dubious art;   240
He views the tumbling fish with longing eyes,
While the line stretches with the unwieldy prize;
Each motion humours with his steady hands,
And one slight hair the mighty bulk commands;
Till tired at last, despoiled of all his strength,   245

The game athwart the stream unfolds his length.
He now, with pleasure, views the gasping prize
Gnash his sharp teeth, and roll his bloodshot eyes
Then draws him to the shore, with artful care,
And lifts his nostrils in the sickening air: 250
Upon the burdened stream he floating lies,
Stretches his quivering fins, and gasping dies.
    Would you preserve a numerous finny race?
Let your fierce dogs the ravenous otter chase:
The amphibious monster ranges all the shores,   255
Darts through the waves, and every haunt explores:
Or let the gin[6] his roving steps betray,
And save from hostile jaws the scaly prey.
    I never wander where the bordering reeds
O'erlook the muddy stream, whose tangling weeds   260
Perplex the fisher; I nor choose to bear
The thievish nightly net nor barbed spear;
Nor drain I ponds, the golden carp to take,
Nor troll for pikes, dispeoplers of the lake.
Around the steel no tortured worm shall twine,   265
No blood of living insect stain my line:
Let me, less cruel, cast the feathered hook
With pliant rod athwart the pebbled brook,
Silent along the mazy margin stray,
And with the fur-wrought fly delude the prey.   270

🦢 Alexander Pope (1688–1744)

"First follow Nature," Alexander Pope instructs poets in his early poem An Essay on Criticism *(1711). What Pope means by this injunction is not as simple as it sounds, for Pope's notion of nature is complex, as close reading of the following selections will reveal. Pope's representation of nature in his poetry favors the orderly, the harmonious, and, importantly, the traditional, as he writes later in the same poem: "Learn hence for ancient rules a just esteem; / To copy Nature is to copy them." There is much in Pope's work that draws on classical models: His images of nature are taken from Homer, Virgil, and Horace, to name a few. But like all great poets, Pope transforms these models to make them seem both timelessly original and appropriate to his own age. His unique style (most distinguishable for its heroic couplets) and aesthetic sensibility inspired poets for most of the eighteenth century, and it is difficult to read any English landscape poetry written after Pope's that does not in some way reveal his influence.*

*   Pope's love of the natural world and the countryside is indisputable. Because his family was Catholic, they were forced to live at least ten miles outside London. This suburban*

---

[6] A snare or trap.

existence turned out to be a boon for the young Pope, whose father bought property in Windsor Forest. Sickly from his early childhood—he was a victim of tuberculosis of the spine, which left him hunchbacked and small in stature—Pope was nourished physically and artistically by the forest environment in which he grew up. His love of the outdoors would endure into adulthood, when financial success from his translations of the Iliad *and the* Odyssey *enabled him to purchase property in Twickenham, where he devoted himself to employing his influential notions about landscape gardening. Again, because of his religion, Pope was barred from attending university and from pursuing a public career. The poet turned these disabilities to advantages. He pursued his own course of study, reading with enormous range and depth, and becoming one of the most erudite scholars of his age. His freedom from having to pursue any other profession but poetry allowed him to devote himself entirely to his art. Pope was not, however, completely outside of public life. His early poetic success inevitably brought him in contact with the great and powerful, and he often used his popularity to comment on contemporary developments in politics and culture. The poet, for Pope, had a social and civic as well as an artistic responsibility. Pope's poetical opinions won him devoted friends and equally committed enemies.*

Windsor Forest is one of Pope's earliest compositions. First written in 1707 and then revised in 1713 to help commemorate the Peace of Utrecht (which ended Britain's long involvement in the War of the Spanish Succession), the poem is deeply indebted to Virgil's Georgics, *but it transposes the setting of Virgil's didactic poem to England and, specifically, to the area where Pope grew up. Windsor Forest, the traditional seat of the British monarchy, and still used in Pope's day as the royal hunting ground, provides the setting for meditative description that allows the wandering poet to use the landscape (much as Denham had in "Cooper's Hill") as a starting point from which to engage in patriotic reflections on English history and contemporary politics. The description of hunting engages a theme that frequently recurs in English and American nature writing.*

Pope's other significant classical influence was the Roman poet and satirist Horace. The Horatian mode is seen in Pope's verse epistles, such as the Essay on Man *(1733–4) and* Epistle to Burlington. *The* Essay on Man *is one of the most elegant articulations of the theory of the Great Chain of Being. According to this model, God's creation exists in a hierarchy, with Man (and here again, it is just man), placed above the animals, plants, and inanimate nature. Pope points out that, while Man's position in the chain may be superior, it also threatens to do the most harm to all the other "links." For in Pope's view, if any part of the chain is broken, the entire system suffers. Man is the only creature who might attempt to step out of this natural and divinely ordained system. While Pope could scarcely be called an environmentalist, particularly because of his emphasis on hierarchy, his ultimate message—that Man should humbly submit to his place in a greater order, which he cannot and should not control, and that he should respect the systemic holism of that order—could resonate with our more modern ideas of the ecosystem.*

The Epistle to Burlington, *subtitled "On Taste," contains one of Pope's more direct statements on landscape gardens. Pope advocates what would come to be called the English Garden, as opposed to the French or Continental model. While all gardening involves the imposition of an artificial human order upon the natural world, the English style sought to build on what was already present in the landscape, instead of imposing*

*highly regularized formal designs upon it. English gardens were supposed to look more
"wild," although such a semblance of natural "wildness" took a great deal of human effort to create. Here again, Pope advocates following nature, but following her with a
good deal of art.*

From Windsor Forest*

To the Right Honourable George Lord Lansdown

Thy forest, Windsor, and thy green retreats,
At once the monarch's and the Muses' seats,
Invite my lays. Be present, sylvan maids!
Unlock your springs, and open all your shades.
Granville[1] commands; your aid, O Muses, bring!   5
What muse for Granville can refuse to sing?
   The groves of Eden, vanished now so long,
Live in description, and look green in song;
These, were my breast inspired with equal flame,
Like them in beauty, should be like in fame.   10
Here hills and vales, the woodland and the plain
Here earth and water seem to strive again;
Not chaos-like, together crushed and bruised,
But, as the world, harmoniously confused;
Where order in variety we see,   15
And where, though all things differ, all agree.
Here waving groves a chequered scene display,
And part admit, and part exclude the day;
As some coy nymph her lover's warm address
Nor quite indulges, nor can quite repress.   20
There, interspersed in lawns and opening glades,
Thin trees arise that shun each other's shades.
Here in full light the russet plains extend;
There, wrapt in clouds, the bluish hills ascend.
Even the wild heath displays her purple dyes,   25
And 'midst the desert fruitful fields arise,
That crowned with tufted trees and springing corn.
Like verdant isles the sable waste adorn.

---

* This excerpt is 221 lines from the original 434-line poem. Lines 1–165 and lines 233–288 are included. —Editors' note.

[1] John Carteret, first earl of Granville (1690–1793), English statesman and ambassador to Sweden who helped
bring about the Treaty of Utrecht (which brought an end to what was often called the Northern War) in 1713 that
is celebrated in the poem.

Let India boast her plants, nor envy we
The weeping amber, or the balmy tree, 30
While by our oaks the precious loads are borne,
And realms commanded which those trees adorn.
Not proud Olympus[2] yields a nobler sight,
Though gods assembled grace his towering height,
Than what more humble mountains offer here, 35
Where, in their blessings, all those gods, appear.
See Pan with flocks, with fruits Pomona crowned,
Here blushing Flora paints, the enamelled ground,
Here Ceres'[3] gifts in waving prospect stand,
And, nodding, tempt the joyful reaper's hand; 40
Rich Industry sits smiling on the plains,
And peace and plenty tell, a Stuart[4] reigns.
　　Not thus the land appeared in ages past,
A dreary desert, and a gloomy waste,
To savage beasts and savage laws a prey, 45
And kings more furious and severe than they;
Who claimed the skies, dispeopled air and floods,
The lonely lords of empty wilds and woods:
Cities laid waste, they stormed the dens and caves,
(For wiser brutes were backward to be slaves); 50
What could be free when lawless beasts obeyed,
And even the elements a tyrant swayed?
In vain kind seasons swelled the teeming grain,
Soft showers distilled, and suns grew warm in vain;
The swain with tears his frustrate labour yields, 55
And famished dies amidst his ripened fields.
What wonder then, a beast or subject slain
Were equal crimes in a despotic reign?
Both doomed alike, for sportive tyrants bled,
But while the subject starved, the beast was fed. 60
Proud Nimrod[5] first the bloody chase began,
A mighty hunter, and his prey was man:
Our haughty Norman boasts that barbarous name,
And makes his trembling slaves the royal game.
The fields are ravished from the industrious swains, 65
From men their cities, and from gods their fanes

[2] A mountain in Greece, presumed home of the ancient Greek pantheon.

[3] Pan, Pomona, Flora, and Ceres are classical deities of nature. Pan is the half-human, half-goat patron of shepherds; Pomona the goddess of fruit-bearing trees; Flora, obviously, the goddess of the flowers; and Ceres, the goddess of the harvest.

[4] Queen Anne (1702–14), British monarch while Pope was composing the poem.

[5] A famous hunter described in the Old Testament, used generically to refer to any powerful or skilled hunter.

The levelled towns with weeds lie covered o'er;
The hollow winds through naked temples roar;
Round broken columns clasping ivy twined;
O'er heaps of ruin stalked the stately hind; 70
The fox obscene to gaping tombs retires,
And savage howlings fill the sacred choirs.
Awed by his nobles, by his commons curst,
The oppressor ruled tyrannic where he durst,
Stretched o'er the poor and church his iron rod, 75
And served alike his vassals and his God.
Whom even the Saxon spared, and bloody Dane,
The wanton victims of his sport remain.
But see, the man, who spacious regions gave
A waste for beasts, himself denied a grave! 80
Stretched on the lawn his second hope survey,
At once the chaser, and at once the prey:
Lo, Rufus,[6] tugging at the deadly dart,
Bleeds in the forest like a wounded hart.
Succeeding monarchs heard the subjects' cries, 85
Nor saw displeased the peaceful cottage rise:
Then gathering flocks on unknown mountains fed,
O'er sandy wilds were yellow harvests spread,
The forest wondered at the unusual grain,
And secret transports touched the conscious swain. 90
Fair Liberty, Britannia's goddess, rears
Her cheerful head, and leads the golden years.
    Ye vigorous swains! while youth ferments your blood
And purer spirits swell the sprightly flood,
Now range the hills, the gameful woods beset, 95
Wind the shrill horn, or spread the waving net.
When milder autumn summer's heat succeeds,
And in the new-shorn field the partridge feeds,
Before his lord the ready spaniel bounds,
Panting with hope, he tries the furrowed grounds; 100
But when the tainted gales the game betray,
Couched close he lies, and meditates the prey;
Secure they trust the unfaithful field beset,
Till hovering o'er them sweeps the swelling net.
Thus (if small things we may with great compare) 105
When Albion[7] sends her eager sons to war,
Some thoughtless town, with ease end plenty blest,

[6] An early Christian martyred by the Romans.
[7] England.

Near, and more near, the closing lines invest;
Sudden they seize the amazed, defenceless prize,
And high in air Britannia's standard flies. 110
    See from the brake the whirring pheasant springs,
And mounts exulting on triumphant wings:
Short is his joy; he feels the fiery wound,
Flutters in blood, and panting beats the ground.
Ah! what avail his glossy, varying dyes, 115
His purple crest, and scarlet-circled eyes,
The vivid green his shining plumes unfold,
His painted wings, and breast that flames with gold?
    Nor yet, when moist Arcturus[8] clouds the sky,
The woods and fields their pleasing toils deny. 120
To plains with well-breathed beagles we repair,
And trace the mazes of the circling hare:
(Beasts, urged by us, their fellow beasts pursue,
And learn of man each other to undo.)
With slaughtering guns the unwearied fowler roves, 125
When frosts have whitened all the naked groves;
Where doves in flocks the leafless trees o'ershade,
And lonely woodcocks haunt the watery glade,
He lifts the tube, and levels with his eye;
Straight a short thunder breaks the frozen sky: 130
Oft, as in airy rings they skim the heath,
The clamorous lapwings feel the leaden death:
Oft, as the mounting larks their notes prepare,
They fall, and leave their little lives in air.
    In genial spring, beneath the quivering shade, 135
Where cooling vapours breathe along the mead,
The patient fisher takes his silent stand,
Intent, his angle trembling in his hand;
With looks unmoved, he hopes the scaly breed,
And eyes the dancing cork and bending reed. 140
Our plenteous streams a various race supply,
The bright-eyed perch, with fins of Tyrian dye,
The silver eel, in shining volumes rolled,
The yellow carp, in scales bedropped with gold,
Swift trouts, diversified with crimson stains, 145
And pikes, the tyrants of the watery plains.
    Now Cancer glows with Phoebus' fiery car:[9]
The youth rush eager to the sylvan war,

---

[8] One of the stars of the sky above the Northern Hemisphere, thought to shine brightest in winter.

[9] The sun is in the constellation of Cancer, i.e., it is the summer.

Swarm o'er the lawns, the forest walks surround,
Rouse the fleet hart, and cheer the opening hound.   150
The impatient courser pants in every vein,
And pawing, seems to beat the distant plain:
Hills, vales, and floods appear already crossed,
And ere he starts, a thousand steps are lost.
See the bold youth strain up the threatening steep,   155
Rush through the thickets, down the valleys sweep,
Hang o'er their coursers' heads with eager speed,
And earth rolls back beneath the flying steed.
Let old Arcadia boast her ample plain,
The immortal huntress, and her virgin-train;   160
Nor envy, Windsor, since thy shades have seen
As bright a goddess, and as chaste a queen;
Whose care, like hers, protects the sylvan reign,
The earth's fair light, and empress of the main.
    Here, too, 'tis sung, of old Diana[10] strayed,   165
And Cynthus' top forsook for Windsor shade;
Here was she seen o'er airy wastes to rove,
Seek the clear spring, or haunt the pathless grove;
Here armed with silver bows, in early dawn,
Her buskined virgins traced the dewy lawn.   170

.   .   .

    Happy the man whom this bright court approves,*
His sovereign favours, and his country loves:
Happy next him, who to these shades retires,   235
Whom nature charms, and whom the Muse inspires:
Whom humbler joys of homefelt quiet please,
Successive study, exercise, and ease.
He gathers health from herbs the forest yields,
And of their fragrant physic spoils the fields: 240
With chemic art exalts the mineral powers,
And draws the aromatic souls of flowers:
Now marks the course of rolling orbs on high;
O'er figured worlds now travels with his eye;
Of ancient writ unlocks the learned store,   245
Consults the dead, and lives past ages o'er:
Or wandering thoughtful in the silent wood,
Attends the duties of the wise and good,
To observe a mean, be to himself a friend,
To follow nature, and regard his end;   250
Or looks on heaven with more than mortal eyes,

---

[10] Roman goddess of the hunt. Cynthus refers to a mountain where she is said to have dwelt.

* Lines 171 to 232 have been omitted.—Editors' note.

Bids his free soul expatiate in the skies,
Amid her kindred stars familiar roam,
Survey the region, and confess her home!
Such was the life great Scipio[11] once admired,   255
Thus Atticus and Trumball[12] thus retired.
    Ye sacred Nine! that all my soul possess,
Whose raptures fire me, and whose visions bless,
Bear me, oh bear me to sequestered scenes,
The bowery mazes, and surrounding greens;   260
To Thames's banks which fragrant breezes fill,
Or where ye Muses sport on Cooper's Hill.
(On Cooper's Hill eternal wreaths shall grow
While lasts the mountain, or while Thames shall flow.)
I seem through consecrated walks to rove,   265
I hear soft music die along the grove:
Led by the sound, I roam from shade to shade,
By godlike poets venerable made;
Here his first lays majestic Denham[13] sung;   270
There the last numbers flowed from Cowley's[14] tongue.
O early lost! what tears the river shed,
When the sad pomp along his banks was led!
His drooping swans on every note expire,
And on his willows hung each Muse's lyre.
    Since fate relentless stopped their heavenly voice,   275
No more the forests ring, or groves rejoice;
Who now shall charm the shades, where Cowley strung
His living harp, and lofty Denham sung?
But hark! the groves rejoice, the forest rings!
Are these revived? or is it Granville sings?   280
'Tis yours, my Lord, to bless our soft retreats,
And call the Muses to their ancient seats;
To paint anew the flowery sylvan scenes,
To crown the forest with immortal greens.
Make Windsor-hills in lofty numbers rise,   285
And lift her turrets nearer to the skies;
To sing those honours you deserve to wear,
And add new lustre to her silver star.

.   .   .

---

[11] Publius Cornelius Scipio Africanus (c. 234–183 B.C.) was a great Roman general who retired from public life after a successful military career.

[12] Titus Pomponius Atticus (109–32 B.C.) was a Roman philosopher; Sir William Trumball (1639–1716) was an English secretary of state and friend of Pope.

[13] John Denham, seventeenth-century author of the locodescriptive poem "Cooper's Hill," included in this anthology.

[14] Seventeenth-century English poet, whose works are also included in this anthology.

From An Essay on Man
In Four Epistles

To H. St. John, Lord Bolingbroke

Epistle 1. Of the Nature and State of Man, with Respect to the Universe

Awake, my St. John! leave all meaner things
To low ambition, and the pride of kings.
Let us (since life can little more supply
Than just to look about us and to die)
Expatiate free o'er all this scene of man;   5
A mighty maze! but not without a plan;
A wild, where weeds and flowers promiscuous shoot,
Or garden tempting with forbidden fruit.
Together let us beat this ample field,
Try what the open, what the covert yield;   10
The latent tracts, the giddy heights, explore
Of all who blindly creep, or sightless soar;
Eye nature's walks, shoot folly as it flies,
And catch the manners living as they rise;
Laugh where we must, be candid where we can;   15
But vindicate the ways of God to Man.

    1. Say first, of God above, or man below,
What can we reason, but from what we know?
Of man, what see we but his station here,
From which to reason or to which refer?   20
Through worlds unnumbered though the God be known,
'Tis ours to trace him only in our own.
He, who through vast immensity can pierce,
See worlds on worlds compose one universe,
Observe how system into system runs,   25
What other planets circle other suns,
What varied Being peoples every star,
May tell why Heaven has made us as we are.
But of this frame, the bearings and the ties,
The strong connections, nice dependencies,   30
Gradations just, has thy pervading soul
Looked through? or can a part contain the whole?
Is the great chain, that draws all to agree,
And drawn supports, upheld by God, or thee?

2. Presumptuous Man! the reason wouldst thou find   35
Why formed so weak, so little, and so blind?
First, if thou canst, the harder reason guess,
Why formed no weaker, blinder, and no less?
Ask of thy mother Earth, why oaks are made
Taller or stronger than the weeds they shade?   40
Or ask of yonder argent fields above;
Why Jove's[1] satellites are less than Jove?
Of systems possible, if 'tis confessed
That Wisdom infinite must form the best,
Where all must full or not coherent be,   45
And all that rises, rise in due degree;
Then, in the scale of reasoning life, 'tis plain,
There must be, somewhere, such a rank as Man:
And all the question (wrangle e'er so long)
Is only this, if God has placed him wrong?   50
    Respecting Man, whatever wrong we call,
May, must be right, as relative to all.
In human works, though laboured on with pain,
A thousand movements scarce one purpose gain;
In God's, one single can its end produce;   55
Yet serves to second, too, some other use.
So Man, who here seems principal alone,
Perhaps acts second to some sphere unknown,
Touches some wheel, or verges to some goal;
'Tis but a part we see, and not a whole.   60
    When the proud steed shall know why Man restrains
His fiery course, or drives him o'er the plains;
When the dull ox, why now he breaks the clod,
Is now a victim, and now Egypt's god:
Then shall man's pride and dulness comprehend.   65
His actions', passions', being's, use and end;
Why doing, suffering; checked, impelled; and why
This hour a slave, the next a deity.
    Then say not Man's imperfect, Heaven in fault;
Say rather Man's as perfect as he ought: 70
His knowledge measured to his state and place;
His time a moment, and a point his space.
If to be perfect in a certain sphere,
What matter, soon or late, or here or there?
The blest today is as completely so,   75
As who began a thousand years ago.

---

[1] The ancient god Jupiter, symbolized by the planet of the same name.

3. Heaven from all creatures hides the book of fate,
All but the page prescribed, their present state:
From brutes what men, from men what spirits know:
Or who could suffer being here below?   80
The lamb thy riot dooms to bleed today,
Had he thy reason, would he skip and play?
Pleased to the last, he crops the flowery food,
And licks the hand just raised to shed his blood.
Oh blindness to the future! kindly given,   85
That each may fill the circle marked by Heaven:
Who sees with equal eye, as God of all,
A hero perish, or a sparrow fall,
Atoms or systems into ruin hurled,
And now a bubble burst, and now a world.   90
    Hope humbly then; with trembling pinions soar;
Wait the great teacher Death; and God adore.
What future bliss, he gives not thee to know,
But gives that hope to be thy blessing now.
Hope springs eternal in the human breast: 95
Man never is, but always to be blest.
The soul, uneasy and confined, from home,
Rests and expatiates in a life to come.
Lo, the poor Indian! whose untutored mind
Sees God in clouds, or hears him in the wind;   100
His soul, proud science never taught to stray
Far as the solar walk, or milky way;
Yet simple nature to his hope has given,
Behind the cloud-topped hill, an humbler heaven;
Some safer world, in depth of woods embraced,   105
Some happier island in the watery waste,
Where slaves once more their native land behold,
No fiends torment, no Christians thirst for gold:
To be, contents his natural desire,
He asks no angel's wing, no seraph's fire;   110
But thinks, admitted to that equal sky,
His faithful dog shall bear him company.

    4. Go, wiser thou! and, in thy scale of sense,
Weigh thy opinion against Providence;
Call imperfection what thou fanciest such,   115
Say, here he gives too little, there too much:
Destroy all creatures for thy sport or gust,
Yet cry, if Man's unhappy, God's unjust;
If Man alone engross not Heaven's high care,
Alone made perfect here, immortal there: 120
Snatch from his hand the balance and the rod,

Rejudge his justice, be the God of God.
In pride, in reasoning pride, our error lies;
All quit their sphere, and rush into the skies.
Pride still is aiming at the blest abodes,   125
Men would be angels, angels would be gods.
Aspiring to be gods, if angels fell,
Aspiring to be angels, men rebel:
And who but wishes to invert the laws
Of Order, sins against the eternal Cause.   130

    5. Ask for what end the heavenly bodies shine,
Earth for whose use? Pride answers, "'Tis for mine
For me kind Nature wakes her genial power,
Suckles each herb, and spreads out every flower;
Annual for me, the grape, the rose renew   135
The juice nectareous, and the balmy dew;
For me, the mine a thousand treasures brings;
For me health gushes from a thousand springs;
Seas roll to waft me, suns to light me rise;
My footstool earth, my canopy the skies."   140
    But errs not Nature from this gracious end,
From burning suns when livid deaths descend,
When earthquakes swallow, or when tempests sweep
Towns to one grave, whole nations to the deep?
"No ('tis replied), the first almighty Cause   145
Acts not by partial, but by general laws;
The exceptions few; some change since all began:
And what created perfect?"—Why then Man?
If the great end be human happiness,
Then Nature deviates; and can man do less?   150
As much that end a constant course requires
Of showers and sunshine, as of Man's desires;
    As much eternal springs and cloudless skies,
As men for ever temperate, calm, and wise.
If plagues or earthquakes break not Heaven's design,   155
Why then a Borgia, or a Catiline?[2]
Who knows but He, whose hand the lightning forms,
Who heaves old ocean, and who wings the storms:
Pours fierce ambition in a Caesar's mind,
Or turns young Ammon[3] loose to scourge mankind?   160

[2] Cesare Borgia (1476–1507) was an Italian politician known for his cruelty and unscrupulousness. He is thought to be the model for Machiavelli's *The Prince.* Lucius Sergius Catiline (c. 108–62 B.C.) was an ancient Roman politician who was also known for his abject pursuit of power.

[3] The marauding son of Lot in Hebrew Scripture. Also, an allusion to Alexander the Great.

From pride, from pride, our very reasoning springs
Account for moral, as for natural things:
Why charge we Heaven in those, in these acquit?
In both, to reason right, is to submit.
    Better for us, perhaps it might appear,   165
Were there all harmony, all virtue here:
That never air or ocean felt the wind;
That never passion discomposed the mind.
But all subsists by elemental strife;
And passions are the elements of life.   170
The general order since the whole began,
Is kept in Nature, and is kept in Man.

    6. What would this Man? Now upward will he soar,
And little less than angels, would be more;
Now looking downwards, just as grieved appears   175
To want the strength of bulls, the fur of bears.
Made for his use all creatures if he call,
Say, what their use, had he the powers of all;
Nature to these, without profusion, kind,
The proper organs, proper powers assigned;   180
Each seeming want compensated of course,
Here with degrees of swiftness, there of force;
All in exact proportion to the state;
Nothing to add, and nothing to abate.
Each beast, each insect, happy in its own: 185
Is Heaven unkind to Man, and Man alone?
Shall he alone, whom rational we call,
Be pleased with nothing, if not blessed with all?
    The bliss of Man (could pride that blessing find),
Is not to act or think beyond mankind;   190
No powers of body or of soul to share,
But what his nature and his state can bear.
Why has not Man a microscopic eye?
For this plain reason, Man is not a fly.
Say what the use, were finer optics given,   195
To inspect a mite, not comprehend the heaven?
Or touch if tremblingly alive all o'er,
To smart and agonise at every pore?
Or quick effluvia darting through the brain,
Die of a rose in aromatic pain?   200
If Nature thundered in his opening ears,
And stunned him with the music of the spheres,
How would he wish that Heaven had left him still,
The whispering zephyr, and the purling rill?

Who finds not Providence all good and wise,   205
Alike in what it gives, and what denies?

    7. Far as creation's ample range extends
The scale of sensual, mental powers ascends:
Mark how it mounts, to Man's imperial race,
From the green myriads in the peopled grass;   210
What modes of sight betwixt each wide extreme,
The mole's dim curtain, and the lynx's beam;
Of smell, the headlong lioness between,
And hound sagacious on the tainted green;
Of hearing, from the life that fills the flood,   215
To that which warbles through the vernal wood!
The spider's touch, how exquisitely fine!
Feels at each thread, and lives along the line:
In the nice bee, what sense so subtly true
From poisonous herbs extracts the healing dew?   220
How instinct varies in the grovelling swine,
Compared, half-reasoning elephant, with thine!
'Twixt that, and reason, what a nice barrier!
For ever separate, yet forever near!
Remembrance and reflection, how allied;   225
What thin partitions sense from thought divide!
And middle natures, how they long to join,
Yet never pass the insuperable line!
Without this just gradation, could they be
Subjected, these to those, or all to thee?   230
The powers of all subdued by thee alone,
Is not thy reason all these powers in one?

    8. See, through this air, this ocean, and this earth,
All matters quick, and bursting into birth.
Above, how high progressive life may go!   235
Around, how wide, how deep extend below!
Vast chain of being! which from God began,
Natures ethereal, human, angel, man,
Beast, bird, fish, insect, what no eye can see,
No glass can reach; from Infinite to thee,   240
From thee to Nothing.—On superior powers,
Were we to press, inferior might on ours:
Or in the full creation leave a void,
Where, one step broken, the great scale's destroyed
From Nature's chain whatever link you strike,   245
Tenth, or ten thousandth, breaks the chain alike.
    And, if each system in gradation roll

Alike essential to the amazing whole,
The least confusion but in one, not all
That system only, but the whole must fall.   250
Let earth unbalanced from her orbit fly,
Planets and stars, run lawless through the sky:
Let ruling angels from their sphere be hurled,
Being on being wrecked, and world on world;
Heaven's whole foundations to their centre nod,   255
And Nature trembles to the throne of God.
All this dread order break—for whom? for thee!
Vile worm!—oh madness! pride! impiety!

9. What if the foot, ordained the dust to tread,
Or hand, to toil, aspired to be the head?   260
What if the head, the eye, or ear repined
To serve mere engines to the ruling mind?
Just as absurd for any part to claim
To be another, in this general frame:
Just as absurd, to mourn the tasks or pains,   265
The great directing MIND OF ALL ordains.
All are but parts of one stupendous whole,
Whose body Nature is, and God the soul;
That, changed through all, and yet in all the same;
Great in the earth, as in the ethereal frame;   270
Warms in the sun, refreshes in the breeze,
Glows in the stars, and blossoms in the trees,
Lives through all life, extends through all extent,
Spreads undivided, operates unspent;
Breathes in our soul, informs our mortal part,   275
As full, as perfect, in a hair as heart;
As full, as perfect, in vile man that mourns,
As the rapt seraph, that adores and burns:
To Him no high, no low, no great, no small;
He fills, He bounds, connects, and equals all.   280

10. Cease then, nor order imperfection name:
Our proper bliss depends on what we blame.
Know thy own point: This kind, this due degree
Of blindness, weakness, Heaven bestows on thee.
Submit.—In this, or any other sphere,   285
Secure to be as blest as thou canst bear:
Safe in the hand of one disposing Power,
Or in the natal, or the mortal hour.
All nature is but art, unknown to thee;
All chance, direction, which thou canst not see;   290

All discord, harmony not understood;
A partial evil, universal good:
And, spite of pride, in erring reason's spite,
One truth is clear, WHATEVER IS, IS RIGHT.

From Epistle 4

To Richard Boyle, Earl of Burlington

Of the Use of Riches*

To build, to plant, whatever you intend,
To rear the column, or the arch to bend,
To swell the terrace, or to sink the grot;
In all, let nature never be forgot.
But treat the goddess like a modest fair,   5
Nor overdress, nor leave her wholly bare;
Let not each beauty everywhere be spied,
Where half the skill is decently to hide.
He gains all points who pleasingly confounds,
Surprises, varies, and conceals the bounds.   10
    Consult the genius of the place in all;
That tells the waters or to rise or fall;
Or helps the ambitious hill the heavens to scale,
Or scoops in circling theatres the vale:
Calls in the country, catches open glades,   15
Joins willing woods, and varies shades from shades;
Now breaks, or now directs, the intending lines;
Paints as you plant, and, as you work, designs.
    Still follow sense, of every art the soul,
Parts answering parts shall slide into a whole,   20
Spontaneous beauties all around advance,
Start even from difficulty, strike from chance;
Nature shall join you; Time shall make it grow
A work to wonder at—perhaps a Stowe.[1]
    Without it, proud Versailles! thy glory falls,   25
And Nero's terraces desert their walls:
The vast parterres a thousand hands shall make,
Lo! Cobham[2] comes, and floats them with a lake:

---

* This excerpt is of lines 47–126 and lines 181–204 of the 204-line verse epistle. We have numbered the lines beginning with 1 for the reader's convenience.—Editors' note.

[1] One of the great English aristocratic estates of the eighteenth century, the seat of Lord Cobham (see below).

[2] Richard Temple, Viscount Cobham (1675–1749) transformed his estate into monumental gardens, with decorative buildings and statuary that served as an allegory of his political principles.

Or cut wide views through mountains to the plain,
You'll wish your hill or sheltered seat again.   30
Even in an ornament its place remark,
Nor in an hermitage set Dr. Clarke.[3]
 Behold Villario's ten years' toil complete;
His quincunx darkens, his espaliers meet;
The wood supports the plain, the parts unite,   35
And strength of shade contends with strength of light.
A waving glow the bloomy beds display
Blushing in bright diversities of day,
With silver-quivering rills meandered o'er—
Enjoy them, you! Villario can no more;   40
Tired of the scene parterres and fountains yield,
He finds, at last, he better likes a field.
 Through his young woods how pleased Sabinus strayed
Or sat delighted in the thickening shade,
With annual joy the reddening shoots to greet,   45
Or see the stretching branches long to meet!
His son's fine taste an opening vista loves,
Foe to the dryads of his father's groves;
One boundless green, or flourished carpet views,
With all the mournful family of yews;   50
The thriving plants, ignoble broomsticks made,
Now sweep those alleys they were born to shade.
 At Timon's villa let us pass a day,
Where all cry out, "What sums are thrown away!"
So proud, so grand; of that stupendous air,   55
Soft and agreeable come never there.
Greatness, with Timon, dwells in such a draught
As brings all Brobdingnag[4] before your thought.
To compass this, his building is a town,
His pond an ocean, his parterre a down: 60
Who but must laugh, the master when he sees,
A puny insect, shivering at a breeze!
Lo, what huge heaps of littleness around!
The whole, a laboured quarry above ground.
Two cupids squirt before: a lake behind   65
Improves the keenness of the northern wind.
His gardens next your admiration call,
On every side you look, behold the wall!
No pleasing intricacies intervene,
No artful wildness to perplex the scene: 70

---

[3] Dr. Samuel Clarke (1675–1729) was a scientist whose bust was placed by the queen in the hermitage of her gardens at Richmond.

[4] The fictional island in the Jonathan Swift's novel *Gulliver's Travels*, where everything is of enormous proportions.

Grove nods at grove, each valley has a brother.
And half the platform just reflects the other
The suffering eye inverted nature sees,
Trees cut to statues, statues thick as trees;
With here a fountain, never to be played;   75
And there a summer-house, that knows no shade;
Here Amphitrite[5] sails through myrtle bowers;
There gladiators fight, or die in flowers;
Unwatered see the drooping seahorse mourn,
And swallows roost in Nilus'[6] dusty urn   80

          .   .   .   .

   His father's acres who enjoys in peace,
Or makes his neighbours glad if he increase:
Whose cheerful tenants bless their yearly toil,
Yet to their lord owe more than to the soil;
Whose ample lawns are not ashamed to feed   85
The milky heifer, and deserving steed;
Whose rising forests, not for pride or show,
But future buildings, future navies grow:
Let his plantations stretch from down to down,
First shade a country, and then raise a town.   90
   You too proceed! make falling arts your care,
Erect new wonders, and the old repair;
Jones and Palladio[7] to themselves restore,
And be whate'er Vitruvius[8] was before:
Till kings call forth the ideas of your mind,   95
(Proud to accomplish what such hands designed),
Bid harbours open, public ways extend,
Bid temples worthier of the God ascend,
Bid the broad arch the dangerous flood contain,
The mole projected break the roaring main;   100
Back to his bounds their subject sea command,
And roll obedient rivers through the land:
These honours, peace to happy Britain brings,
These are imperial works, and worthy kings.

---

[5] A mythological naiad or sea nymph.

[6] A river god.

[7] Inigo Jones (1573–1652) was a British architect who, during the seventeenth century, popularized the neoclassical building style of Italian architect Andrea Palladio (1518–1580).

[8] Marcus Vitruvius Pollio was a Roman writer on architecture of the first century A.D. His encyclopedic book on architecture was a popular resource for builders in the Renaissance.

✑ Mary Collier (c.1690–1762)

Little is known about Mary Collier beyond the fact that her life was probably very much like that of the women laborers described in her poem, "The Woman's Labour" (1739). Like Stephen Duck, whose poem her own both imitates and critiques, Collier had no formal education but had a strong penchant for reading. While Duck had characterized his fellow countrywomen as chattering and often idle gossips, Collier depicts with honesty and good humor the reality of the double or even triple shifts many women (in the eighteenth century, as today) had to balance while working both in and outside of the home. Collier herself remained unmarried, which is likely the reason she had the time and opportunity to write. Like Duck, Collier attempts to imitate neoclassical conventions, writing in couplets and making several mythological allusions to set forth the often harsh and clearly exhausting existence of rural women of the laboring class. Unlike Duck, her poem, first published in 1739, did not bring her the assistance or encouragement of wealthy patrons. Viewed in the context of the numerous other locodescriptive and georgic poems of the period, Collier's piece is unique in demonstrating that both social class and gender have an impact on one's interaction with the environment. Nature is not an object of aesthetic contemplation, in which even a male laborer like Stephen Duck might occasionally indulge, but the hostile arena for unremitting toil.

The Woman's Labour

Immortal Bard![1] thou favorite of the Nine!
Enriched by Peers, advanced by Caroline,
Deign to look down on one that's poor and low,
Remembering you yourself was lately so;
Accept these lines: alas! what can you have   5
From her, who ever was, and's still a Slave?
No Learning ever was bestowed on me;
My life was always spent in Drudgery,
And not alone; alas! with grief I find
It is the Portion of poor Womankind.   10
Oft have I thought as on my bed I lay,
Eased from the tiresome Labours of the day,
Our first Extraction from a Mass refined
Could never be for Slavery designed,
Till Time and Custom by degrees destroyed   15
That happy state our Sex at first enjoyed.
When Men had used their utmost care and toil,
Their Recompence was but a Female Smile;
When they by Arts or Arms were rendered great,

---

[1] I.e., Stephen Duck, whose "The Thresher's Labour" this poem parodies and imitates.

They laid their Trophies at a Woman's Feet.   20
They, in those days, unto our Sex did bring
Their Hearts, their All, a freewill Offering,
And as from us their Being they derive,
They back again should all due Homage give.

    Jove once descending from the clouds did drop   25
In show'rs of gold on lovely *Danaë*'s[2] lap;
The sweet-tongued Poets, in those generous days,
Unto our Shrine still offered up their Lays:
But now, alas! that Golden Age is past,
We are the objects of your Scorn at last.   30
    And you, great Duck, upon whose happy brow
The Muses seem to fix the Garland now,
In your late Poem boldly did declare
Alcides'[3] Labours can't with yours compare;
And of your annual Task have much to say,   35
Of threshing, reaping, mowing Corn and Hay,
Boasting your daily Toil and nightly Dream,
But can't conclude your never-dying Theme,
And let our hapless Sex in Silence lie
Forgotten, and in dark Oblivion die;   40
But on our abject State you throw your Scorn,
And Women wrong, your Verses to adorn.
    You of Hay-making speak a word or two,
As if our Sex but little Work could do:
This makes the honest Farmer smiling say   45
He'll seek for Women still to make his Hay;
For if his back be turned, their Work they mind
As well as Men, as far as he can find.

    For my own part, I many a Summer's day
Have spent in throwing, turning, making Hay,   50
But ne'er could see, what you have lately found,
Our Wages paid for sitting on the Ground.
'Tis true, that when our Morning's Work is done,
And all our Grass exposed unto the Sun,
While that his scorching Beams do on it shine,   55
As well as you, we have a time to dine:
I hope that since we freely toil and sweat
To earn our Bread, you'll give us time to eat.
That over, soon we must get up again,
And nimbly turn our Hay upon the plain,   60
Nay, rake and prow it in, the case is clear,

---

[2] According to myth, the god Jove impregnated Danaë, a princess of Argos, by sending down a shower of gold.
[3] Hercules.

Or how should Cocks in equal Rows appear?
But if you'd have what you have wrote believed,
I find that you to hear us talk are grieved.
In this, I hope, you do not speak your mind,   65
For none but *Turks*, that I could ever find,
Have Mutes to serve them, or did e'er deny
Their Slaves, at Work, to chat it merrily.
Since you have Liberty to speak your mind,
And are to talk, as well as we, inclined,   70
Why should you thus repine, because that we,
Like you, enjoy that pleasing Liberty?
What! would you lord it quite, and take away
The only Privilege our Sex enjoy?

    When Evening does approach we homeward hie,   75
And our domestic Toils incessant ply:
Against your coming home prepare to get
Our Work all done, our House in order set.
Bacon and Dumpling in the pot we boil,
Our Beds we make, our Swine we feed the while,   80
Then wait at Door to see you coming home,
And set the Table out against you come.
Early next morning we on you attend;
Our Children dress and feed, their clothes we mend,
And in the Field our daily Task renew,   85
Soon as the rising Sun has dried the Dew.

    When Harvest comes, into the Field we go,
And help to reap the Wheat as well as you,
Or else we go the ears of Corn to glean,
No Labour scorning, be it e'er so mean,   90
But in the Work we freely bear a part,
And what we can, perform with all our Heart.
To get a living we so willing are,
Our tender Babes into the Field we bear,
And wrap them in our clothes to keep them warm,   95
While round about we gather up the Corn,
And often unto them our course we bend,
To keep them safe, that nothing them offend.
Our Children that are able, bear a share
In gleaning Corn, such is our frugal care.   100
When Night comes on, unto our home we go,
Our Corn we carry, and our Infant too;
Weary, alas! but 'tis not worth our while
Once to complain, or *rest at every Stile*.
We must make haste, for when we Home are come,   105
Alas! we find our Work but just begun;

So many things for our Attendance call,
Had we ten hands, we could employ them all.
Our Children put to bed, with greatest care,
We all things for your coming Home prepare: 110
You sup, and go to bed without delay,
And rest yourselves till the ensuing Day,
While we, alas! but little Sleep can have,
Because our froward Children cry and rave.
Yet without fail, soon as Daylight doth spring, 115
We in the Field again our Work begin,
And there with all our Strength our Toil renew,
Till *Titan*'s golden rays[4] have dried the Dew.
Then home we go unto our Children dear,
Dress, feed, and bring them to the Field with care. 120
Were this your case, you justly might complain
That Day nor Night you are secure from Pain;
Those mighty Troubles which perplex your Mind,
(*Thistles* before, and *Females* come behind)
Would vanish soon, and quickly disappear, 125
Were you, like us, encumbered thus with Care.
What you would have of us we do not know:
We oft take up the Corn that you do mow,
We cut the Peas, and always ready are
In every Work to take our proper Share, 130
And from the time that Harvest doth begin,
Until the Corn be cut and carried in,
Our Toil and Labour's daily so extreme
That we have hardly ever *Time to dream.*
    The Harvest ended, respite none we find, 135
The hardest of our Toil is still behind:
Hard Labour we most cheerfully pursue,
And out abroad, a-charring[5] often go,
Of which I now will briefly tell in part
What fully to declare is past my Art, 140
So many Hardships daily we go through,
I boldly say, the like *you* never knew.
    When bright *Orion* glitters in the skies
In Winter nights, then early we must rise;
The Weather ne'er so bad, wind, rain or snow, 145
Our Work appointed, we must rise and go,
While you on easy beds may lie and sleep,
Till Light does through your Chamber windows peep.
When to the House we come where we should go,

---

[4] *Titan's . . . rays:* i.e., the sun.
[5] Charring refers to menial household labor.

How to get in, alas! we do not know: 150
The Maid quite tired with Work the day before,
O'ercome with sleep; we standing at the door,
Oppressed with cold, and often call in vain,
Ere to our Work we can Admittance gain.
But when from Wind and Weather we get in,   155
Briskly with Courage we our Work begin.
Heaps of find Linen we before us view,
Whereon to lay our Strength and Patience too:
Cambricks and Muslins, which our Ladies wear,
Laces and Edgings, costly, fine, and rare,   160
Which must be washed with utmost Skill and Care.
With Holland Shirts, Ruffles and Fringes too,
Fashions which our Forefathers never knew.
For several hours here we work and slave,
Before we can one glimpse of Daylight have.   165
We labour hard before the Morning's past,
Because we fear the time runs on too fast.
    At length bright *Sol*[6] illuminates the skies,
And summons drowsy Mortals to arise.
Then comes our Mistress to us without fail,   170
And in her hand, *perhaps*, a mug of Ale
To cheer our Hearts, and also to inform
Herself, what Work is done that very Morn;
Lays her Commands upon us, that we mind
Her Linen well, nor *leave the Dirt behind.*   175
Not this alone, but also to take care
We don't her Cambricks or her Ruffles tear,
And these most strictly does of us require:
To save her Soap, and sparing be of Fire;
Tells us her Charge is great, nay, furthermore,   180
Her Clothes are fewer than the time before.
Now we drive on, resolved our Strength to try,
And what we can, we do most willingly,
Until the Heat and Work, 'tis often known,
Not only Sweat but Blood runs trickling down   185
Our wrists and fingers; still our Work demands
The constant action of our lab'ring Hands.

    Now Night comes on, from whence you have Relief,
But that, alas! does but increase our Grief.
With heavy hearts we often view the Sun,   190
Fearing he'll set before our Work is done;
For either in the Morning, or at Night,
We piece the Summer's day with Candlelight.

[6] The sun.

Though we all Day with care our Work attend,
Such is our Fate, we know not when 'twill end.   195
When Evening's come you Homeward take your way;
We till our Work is done are forced to stay,
And after all our Toil and Labour past,
Sixpence or Eightpence pays us off at last.
For all our Pains, no Prospect can we see   200
Attend us, but Old Age and Poverty.

    The Washing is not all we have to do:
We oft change Work for Work as well as you.
Our Mistress of her Pewter doth complain,
And 'tis our part to make it clean again.   205
This Work, though very hard and tiresome too,
Is not the worst we hapless Females do.
When Night comes on, and we quite weary are,
We scarce can count what falls unto our Share:
Pots, kettles, saucepans, skillets we may see,   210
Skimmers and ladles and such Trumpery,
Brought in to make complete our Slavery.
Though early in the Morning 'tis begun,
'Tis often very late before we've done.
Alas! our Labours never know an end: 215
On brass and iron we our Strength must spend,
Our tender hands and fingers scratch and tear;
All this and more, with Patience we must bear.
Coloured with Dirt and Filth we now appear;
Your threshing sooty Peas will not come near.   220
All the Perfections Woman once could boast
Are quite obscured, and altogether lost.

    Once more our Mistress sends to let us know
She wants our Help, because the Beer runs low.
Then in much haste for Brewing we prepare,   225
The Vessels clean, and scald with greatest care.
Often at Midnight from our bed we rise;
At other times even that will not suffice;
Our Work at Evening oft we do begin,
And ere we've done, the Night comes on again.   230
Water we pump, the Copper we must fill,
Or tend the Fire, for if we e'er stand still,
Like you when threshing, we a Watch must keep;
Our Wort[7] boils over if we dare to sleep.

    But to rehearse all Labour is in vain   235
Of which we very justly might complain:

---

[7] Unfermented beer.

For us, you see, but little rest is found,
Our Toil increases as the Year runs round.
While you to *Sisyphus* yourselves compare,
With *Danaus'* daughters[8] we may claim a share;   240
For while *he* labours hard against the Hill,
Bottomless Tubs of Water *they* must fill.
    So the industrious Bees do hourly strive
To bring their Loads of Honey to the Hive;
Their sordid Owners always reap the Gains,   245
And poorly recompense their Toil and Pains.

⮷ *James Thomson* (1700–1748)

James Thomson's four-book poem, The Seasons, *is in many respects a watershed in the history of English writing about nature. Written in Miltonic blank verse,* The Seasons *also approaches Miltonic epic scope in its attempt to describe and represent the many dimensions of the natural world throughout the year. Highly influenced by the picturesque landscape paintings of European artists such as Claude Lorrain, Salvator Rosa, and Nicolas Poussin, Thomson plays with visual perspective, moving the reader in close and then farther away from the object of sight. The poet not only provides a variety of visual perspectives but also includes a wide range of topics, from the effects of a winter storm to wine-making, all in his effort, as he writes at the end of "Autumn" to praise "the pure pleasures of rural life." Nature as Thomson represents it can be at once sublimely destructive and beautifully nurturing. What unites the poem and its various vignettes is the singular perspective of the narrator, who guides the reader through the wealth of scenery associated with the course of the changing year.*

    Born near the Scottish border, Thomson was educated at Edinburgh University and would have been a clergyman had he not discovered his poetic gift. Though he wrote poetry from an early age, "Winter" (1726) was his first published work. Its immediate popularity encouraged him to compose "Summer" (1727), "Spring" (1728), and finally "Autumn" (1730). The immense acclaim accorded to the entire series helped Thomson gain patrons and establish his poetic career. The patriotism evident in certain segments of The Seasons *is further elaborated in later poems such as* Britannia *(1729) and* Liberty *(1735–6). Thomson also penned several tragedies, and, near the end of his life, an allegorical poem in the style of Edmund Spenser,* The Castle of Indolence *(1748).*

    As critics such as David Fairer and Christine Gerrard have noted, one of the more striking attributes of Thomson's style is the great abundance of verbs. This underscores Thomson's idea of nature as dynamically evershifting and growing, not orderly or inert.

---

[8] As punishment for murdering their husbands, these women were condemned to an eternity filling bottomless jugs of water.

Many regard Thomson's text as foundational to the later Romantic-era landscape poetry, influential on such important nature poets as William Wordsworth, who, like Thomson, used his own subjectivity as the continual point of reference for all that he saw and wrote about in the natural environment that surrounded him. "Autumn" begins with a description of shooting and hunting, condemning these sports as brutal (compare this to the same subject as it is taken up by Pope in Windsor Forest*). In keeping with the season, the main topic of the poem is the harvest. A careful reading of the poem reveals that Thomson's key poetic influences were not so much the classics of antiquity as the Bible and Milton.*

From The Seasons

From Autumn*

Crowned with the sickle and the wheaten sheaf,
While Autumn, nodding o'er the yellow plain,
Comes jovial on; the Doric[1] reed once more,
Well-pleased, I tune. Whate'er the Wintry frost
Nitrous prepared, the various-blossomed Spring   5
Put in white promise forth, and Summer-suns
Concocted strong, rush boundless now to view,
Full, perfect all, and swell my glorious theme.

.   .   .

   When the bright Virgin gives the beauteous days,
And Libra[2] weighs in equal scales the year,   10
From Heaven's high cope the fierce effulgence shook
Of parting Summer, a serener blue,
With golden light enlivened, wide invests
The happy world. Attempered suns arise,
Sweet-beamed, and shedding oft through lucid clouds   15
A pleasing calm; while, broad and brown, below
Extensive harvests hang the heavy head.
Rich, silent, deep, they stand; for not a gale
Rolls its light billows o'er the bending plain:
A calm of plenty! till the ruffled air   20
Falls from its poise, and gives the breeze to blow.
Rent is the fleecy mantle of the sky;
The clouds fly different; and the sudden sun

---

* "Autumn" is a 1,373-line poem; we have excerpted 524 lines, which we will number from 1 to 524 but showing the location of elisions for the reader's convenience.—Editors' note.

[1] The Dorians were a branch of the ancient Greek peoples. Their dialect was thought by the more civilized Athenians to sound harsh and rough. Thus a "Doric reed" refers to adopting a less lighthearted or easy tone.

[2] The seventh sign of the Zodiac, corresponding to the time of late September and October, and symbolized by the image of the scales.

By fits effulgent gilds th' illumined field,
And black by fits the shadows sweep along;— 25
A gaily checkered heart-expanding view,
Far as the circling eye can shoot around,
Unbounded, tossing in a flood of corn.
    These are thy blessings, Industry! rough Power,
Whom labour still attends, and sweat, and pain; 30
Yet the kind source of every gentler art,
And all the soft civility of life:
Raiser of human kind! by Nature cast,
Naked and helpless, out amid the woods
And wilds, to rude inclement elements; 35
With various seeds of art deep in the mind
Implanted, and profusely poured around
Materials infinite; but idle all.
Still unexerted, in th' unconscious breast
Slept the lethargic powers; Corruption still, 40
Voracious, swallowed what the liberal hand
Of Bounty scattered o'er the savage year:
And still the sad barbarian, roving, mixed
With beasts of prey; or for his acorn meal
Fought the fierce tusky boar;—a shivering wretch, 45
Aghast, and comfortless! when the bleak North,
With Winter charged, let the mixed tempest fly,
Hail, rain, and snow, and bitter-breathing frost:
Then to the shelter of the hut he fled;
And the wild season, sordid, pined away. 50
For home he had not—home is the resort
Of love, of joy, of peace and plenty, where,
Supporting and supported, polished friends
And dear relations mingle into bliss.
But this the rugged savage never felt, 55
Even desolate in crowds; and thus his days
Rolled heavy, dark, and unenjoyed along:
A waste of time! till Industry approached,
And roused him from his miserable sloth;
His faculties unfolded; pointed out 60
Where lavish Nature the directing hand
Of Art demanded; showed him how to raise
His feeble force by the mechanic powers,
To dig the mineral from the vaulted earth,
On what to turn the piercing rage of fire, 65
On what the torrent, and the gathered blast;
Gave the tall ancient forest to his axe;
Taught him to chip the wood, and hew the stone,
Till by degrees the finished fabric rose;

Tore from his limbs the blood-polluted fur,   70
And wrapt them in the woolly vestment warm,
Or bright in glossy silk and flowing lawn;
With wholesome viands filled his table; poured
The generous glass around, inspired to wake
The life-refining soul of decent wit: 75
Nor stopped at barren bare necessity;
But, still advancing bolder, led him on
To pomp, to pleasure, elegance, and grace;
And, breathing high ambition through his soul,
Set science, wisdom, glory, in his view,   80
And bade him be the lord of all below.

.   .   .

   Here the rude clamour of the sportsman's joy,
The gun fast-thundering, and the winded horn,
Would tempt the Muse to sing the rural game:
How, in his mid career, the spaniel, struck   85
Stiff by the tainted gale; with open nose,
Outstretched and finely sensible, draws full,
Fearful, and cautious, on the latent prey;
As in the sun the circling covey bask
Their varied plumes, and, watchful every way,   90
Through the rough stubble turn the secret eye.
Caught in the meshy snare, in vain they beat
Their idle wings, entangled more and more:
Nor on the surges of the boundless air,
Though borne triumphant, are they safe; the gun,   95
Glanced just and sudden from the fowler's eye,
O'ertakes their sounding pinions, and again,
Immediate, brings them from the towering wing,
Dead to the ground; or drives them, wide-dispersed,
Wounded, and wheeling various, down the wind.   100
   These are not subjects for the peaceful Muse,
Nor will she stain with such her spotless song;
Then most delighted, when she social sees
The whole mixed animal creation round
Alive and happy. 'Tis not joy to her,   105
This falsely cheerful, barbarous game of death;
This rage of pleasure, which the restless youth
Awakes, impatient, with the gleaming morn;
When beasts of prey retire, that all night long,
Urged by necessity, had ranged the dark,   110
As if their conscious ravage shunned the light,
Ashamed. Not so the steady tyrant Man,
Who, with the thoughtless insolence of power

Inflamed, beyond the most infuriate wrath
Of the worst monster that e'er roamed the waste,   115
For sport alone pursues the cruel chase,
Amid the beamings of the gentle days.
Upbraid, ye ravening tribes, our wanton rage,
For hunger kindles you, and lawless want;
But, lavish fed, in Nature's bounty rolled,   120
To joy at anguish, and delight in blood,
Is what your horrid bosoms never knew.
    Poor is the triumph o'er the timid hare!
Scared from the corn, and now to some lone seat
Retired: the rushy fen; the rugged furze,   125
Stretched o'er the stony heath; the stubble chapped;
The thistly lawn; the thick-entangled broom;
Of the same friendly hue, the withered fern;
The fallow ground laid open to the sun,
Concoctive; and the nodding sandy bank,   130
Hung o'er the mazes of the mountain brook.
Vain is her best precaution; though she sits
Concealed, with folded ears; unsleeping eyes,
By Nature raised to take th' horizon in;
And head couched close betwixt her hairy feet,   135
In act to spring away. The scented dew
Betrays her early labyrinth; and deep,
In scattered sullen openings, far behind,
With every breeze she hears the coming storm.
But nearer, and more frequent, as it loads   140
The sighing gale, she springs amazed, and all
The savage soul of game is up at once:
The pack full-opening, various; the shrill horn
Resounded from the hills; the neighing steed,
Wild for the chase; and the loud hunter's shout;   145
O'er a weak, harmless, flying creature, all
Mixed in mad tumult and discordant joy.
    The stag, too, singled from the herd, where long
He ranged the branching monarch of the shades,
Before the tempest drives. At first, in speed   150
He, sprightly, puts his faith; and, roused by fear,
Gives all his swift aerial soul to flight;
Against the breeze he darts, that way the more
To leave the lessening murderous cry behind:
Deception short! though, fleeter than the winds   155
Blown o'er the keen-aired mountain by the North,
He bursts the thickets, glances through the glades,
And plunges deep into the wildest wood;
If slow, yet sure, adhesive to the track

Hot-steaming, up behind him come again   160
Th' inhuman rout, and from the shady depth
Expel him, circling through his every shift.
He sweeps the forest oft; and sobbing sees
The glades, mild opening to the golden day,
Where, in kind contest, with his butting friends   165
He wont to struggle, or his loves enjoy.
Oft in the full-descending flood he tries
To lose the scent, and lave his burning sides:
Oft seeks the herd; the watchful herd, alarmed,
With selfish care avoid a brother's woe.   170
What shall he do? His once so vivid nerves,
So full of buoyant spirit, now no more
Inspire the course; but fainting breathless toil,
Sick, seizes on his heart: he stands at bay,
And puts his last weak refuge in despair.   175
The big round tears run down his dappled face;
He groans in anguish; while the growling pack,
Blood-happy, hang at his fair jutting chest,
And mark his beauteous checkered sides with gore.
  Of this enough. But if the sylvan youth,   180
Whose fervent blood boils into violence,
Must have the chase, behold, despising flight,
The roused-up lion, resolute and slow,
Advancing full on the protended spear,
And coward band that circling wheel aloof.   185
Slunk from the cavern, and the troubled wood,
See the grim wolf; on him his shaggy foe
Vindictive fix, and let the ruffian die:
Or, growling horrid, as the brindled boar
Grins fell destruction, to the monster's heart   190
Let the dart lighten from the nervous arm.

.   .   .

  Hence from the busy joy-resounding fields,
In cheerful error, let us tread the maze
Of Autumn, unconfined; and taste, revived,
The breath of orchard big with bending fruit.   195
Obedient to the breeze and beating ray,
From the deep-loaded bough a mellow shower
Incessant melts away. The juicy pear
Lies, in a soft profusion, scattered round.
A various sweetness swells the gentle race,   200
By Nature's all-refining hand prepared;
Of tempered sun and water, earth and air,
In ever-changing composition mixed.

Such, falling frequent through the chiller night.
The fragrant stores, the wide-projected heaps   205
Of apples, which the lusty-handed Year,
Innumerous, o'er the blushing orchard shakes.
A various spirit, fresh, delicious, keen,
Dwells in their gelid pores; and, active, points
The piercing cider for the thirsty tongue: 210
Thy native theme, and boon inspirer too,
Philips,[3] Pomona's bard; the second thou
Who nobly durst, in rhyme-unfettered verse,
With British freedom sing the British song:
How, from Silurian[4] vats, high-sparkling wines   215
Foam in transparent floods; some strong, to cheer
The wintry revels of the labouring hind;
And tasteful some, to cool the summer hours.
    In this glad season, while his sweetest beams
The Sun sheds equal o'er the meekened day;   220
Oh, lose me in the green delightful walks
Of, Dodington,[5] thy seat, serene, and plain;
Where simple Nature reigns; and every view,
Diffusive, spreads the pure Dorsetian[6] downs,
In boundless prospect; yonder shagged with wood,   225
Here rich with harvest, and there white with flocks!
Meantime the grandeur of thy lofty dome,
Far-splendid, seizes on the ravished eye.
New beauties rise with each revolving day;
New columns swell, and still the fresh Spring finds   230
New plants to quicken, and new groves to green.
Full of thy genius all! the Muses' seat:
Where, in the secret bower and winding walk,
For virtuous Young and thee they twine the bay.
Here wandering oft, fired with the restless thirst   235
Of thy applause, I solitary court
Th' inspiring breeze, and meditate the book
Of Nature ever open; aiming thence,
Warm from the heart, to learn the moral song.
Here, as I steal along the sunny wall,   240
Where Autumn basks, with fruit empurpled deep,
My pleasing theme continual prompts my thought;
Presents the downy peach; the shining plum,

[3] John Philips (1676–1709) wrote the georgic poem *Cyder* (1708) detailing the cultivation of apples and the manufacture of cider. It is modeled on Virgil's *Georgics*.

[4] The principal British counties that produce cider are to the west of the river Severn in South Wales.

[5] The country estate of Mr. Onslow, the poem's addressee.

[6] Of the countryside around Dorset, in the south of England on the English Channel.

With a fine bluish mist of animals
Clouded; the ruddy nectarine; and, dark   245
Beneath his ample leaf, the luscious fig.
The vine too here her curling tendrils shoots;
Hangs out her clusters, glowing to the South;
And scarcely wishes for a warmer sky.
    Turn we a moment Fancy's rapid flight   250
To vigorous soils, and climes of fair extent;
Where, by the potent sun elated high,
The vineyard swells refulgent on the day;
Spreads o'er the vale; or up the mountain climbs,
Profuse; and drinks, amid the sunny rocks,   255
From cliff to cliff increased, the heightened blaze.
Low bend the weighty boughs. The clusters clear,
Half through the foliage seen, or ardent flame,
Or shine transparent; while perfection breathes
White o'er the turgid film the living dew.   260
As thus they brighten with exalted juice,
Touched into flavour by the mingling ray,
The rural youth and virgins o'er the field,
Each fond for each to cull th' autumnal prime,
Exulting rove, and speak the vintage nigh.   265
Then comes the crushing swain; the country floats,
And foams unbounded with the mashy flood,
That, by degrees fermented and refined,
Round the raised nations pours the cup of joy:
The Claret smooth, red as the lip we press   270
In sparkling fancy, while we drain the bowl;
The mellow-tasted Burgundy; and quick,
As is the wit it gives, the gay Champagne.

                  .   .   .

    The pale descending year, yet pleasing still,
A gentler mood inspires; for now the leaf   275
Incessant rustles from the mournful grove,
Oft startling such as, studious, walk below,
And slowly circles through the waving air.
But should a quicker breeze amid the boughs
Sob, o'er the sky the leafy deluge streams;   280
Till, choked and matted with the dreary shower,
The forest-walks, at every rising gale,
Roll wide the withered waste, and whistle bleak.
Fled is the blasted verdure of the fields:
And, shrunk into their beds, the flowery race   285
Their sunny robes resign. Even what remained
Of stronger fruits falls from the naked tree;

And woods, fields, gardens, orchards, all around
The desolated prospect thrills the soul.
    He comes! he comes! in every breeze the Power   290
Of Philosophic Melancholy comes!
His near approach the sudden-starting tear,
The glowing cheek, the mild dejected air,
The softened feature, and the beating heart,
Pierced deep with many a virtuous pang, declare.   295
O'er all the soul his sacred influence breathes;
Inflames imagination, through the breast
Infuses every tenderness, and far
Beyond dim earth exalts the swelling thought.
Ten thousand thousand fleet ideas, such   300
As never mingled with the vulgar dream,
Crowd fast into the Mind's creative eye.
As fast the correspondent passions rise,
As varied, and as high: Devotion, raised
To rapture and divine astonishment;   305
The love of Nature unconfined, and, chief,
Of human race; the large ambitious wish
To make them blest; the sigh for suffering worth
Lost in obscurity; the noble scorn
Of tyrant-pride; the fearless great resolve;   310
The wonder which the dying patriot draws,
Inspiring glory through remotest time;
Th' awakened throb for virtue and for fame;
The sympathies of love and friendship dear;
With all the social offspring of the heart.   315
    Oh, bear me then to vast embowering shades,
To twilight groves, and visionary vales,
To weeping grottoes and prophetic glooms,
Where angel forms athwart the solemn dusk
Tremendous sweep, or seem to sweep, along;   320
And voices more than human, through the void
Deep-sounding, seize th' enthusiastic ear!

.   .   .

    Ah, see where, robbed and murdered, in that pit
Lies the still-heaving hive! at evening snatched,
Beneath the cloud of guilt-concealing night,   325
And fixed o'er sulphur; while, not dreaming ill,
The happy people, in their waxen cells,
Sat tending public cares, and planning schemes
Of temperance, for Winter poor; rejoiced
To mark, full-flowing round, their copious stores.   330
Sudden the dark oppressive steam ascends;

And, used to milder scents, the tender race,
By thousands, tumble from their honeyed domes,
Convolved, and agonizing in the dust.
And was it then for this you roamed the Spring   335
Intent from flower to flower? for this you toiled,
Ceaseless, the burning Summer-heats away?
For this in Autumn searched the blooming waste,
Nor lost one sunny gleam? for this sad fate?
O Man! tyrannic lord! how long, how long   340
Shall prostrate Nature groan beneath your rage,
Awaiting renovation? When obliged,
Must you destroy? Of their ambrosial food
Can you not borrow, and, in just return,
Afford them shelter from the wintry winds?   345
Or, as the sharp year pinches, with their own
Again regale them on some smiling day?
See where the stony bottom of their town
Looks desolate and wild; with here and there
A helpless number, who the ruined state   350
Survive, lamenting weak, cast out to death.
Thus a proud city, populous and rich.
Full of the works of peace, and high in joy,
At theatre or feast, or sunk in sleep
(As late, Palermo,[7] was thy fate), is seized   355
By some dread earthquake, and convulsive hurled
Sheer from the black foundation, stench-involved,
Into a gulf of blue sulphureous flame.
　　Hence every harsher sight! for now the day,
O'er heaven and earth diffused, grows warm and high;   360
Infinite splendour, wide-investing all!
How still the breeze! save what the filmy threads
Of dew evaporate brushes from the plain.
How clear the cloudless sky! how deeply tinged
With a peculiar blue! th' ethereal arch   365
How swelled immense! amid whose azure throned
The radiant Sun how gay! how calm below
The gilded earth! the harvest treasures all
Now gathered in, beyond the rage of storms,
Sure to the swain; the circling fence shut up,   370
And instant Winter's utmost rage defied.
While, loose to festive joy, the country round
Laughs with the loud sincerity of mirth,
Shook to the wind their cares. The toil-strung youth,
By the quick sense of music taught alone,   375

---

[7] The capital of Sicily, in Italy.

Leaps wildly graceful in the lively dance.
Her every charm abroad, the village-toast,
Young, buxom, warm, in native beauty rich,
Darts not-unmeaning looks; and, where her eye
Points an approving smile, with double force   380
The cudgel rattles, and the wrestler twines.
Age too shines out, and, garrulous, recounts
The feats of youth. Thus they rejoice, nor think
That, with tomorrow's sun, their annual toil
Begins again the never-ceasing round.   385
    Oh, knew he but his happiness, of men
The happiest he, who, far from public rage,
Deep in the vale, with a choice few retired,
Drinks the pure pleasures of the rural life!
What though the dome be wanting, whose proud gate,   390
Each morning, vomits out the sneaking crowd
Of flatterers false, and in their turn abused?
Vile intercourse! What though the glittering robe—
Of every hue reflected light can give,
Or floating loose, or stiff with mazy gold,   395
The pride and gaze of fools—oppress him not?
What though, from utmost land and sea purveyed,
For him each rarer tributary life
Bleeds not, and his insatiate table heaps
With luxury and death? What though his bowl   400
Flames not with costly juice; nor, sunk in beds
Oft of gay care, he tosses out the night,
Or melts the thoughtless hours in idle state?
What though he knows not those fantastic joys
That still amuse the wanton, still deceive;   405
A face of pleasure, but a heart of pain;
Their hollow moments undelighted all?
Sure peace is his; a solid life, estranged
To disappointment and fallacious hope:
Rich in content, in Nature's bounty rich,   410
In herbs and fruits; whatever greens the Spring
When heaven descends in showers, or bends the bough
When Summer reddens and when Autumn beams,
Or in the wintry glebe whatever lies
Concealed, and fattens with the richest sap: 415
These are not wanting; nor the milky drove,
Luxuriant, spread o'er all the lowing vale;
Nor bleating mountains; nor the chide of streams,
And hum of bees, inviting sleep sincere
Into the guiltless breast, beneath the shade,   420
Or thrown at large amid the fragrant hay;

Nor aught besides of prospect, grove, or song,
Dim grottoes, gleaming lakes, and fountain clear.
Here too dwells simple Truth; plain Innocence;
Unsullied Beauty; sound unbroken Youth,   425
Patient of labour, with a little pleased;
Health, ever-blooming; unambitious Toil;
Calm Contemplation, and poetic Ease.
    Let others brave the flood in quest of gain,
And beat, for joyless months, the gloomy wave.   430
Let such as deem it glory to destroy,
Rush into blood, the sack of cities seek,
Unpierced, exulting in the widow's wail,
The virgin's shriek, and infant's trembling cry.
Let some, far distant from their native soil,   435
Urged or by want or hardened avarice,
Find other lands beneath another sun.
Let *this* through cities work his eager way
By legal outrage and established guile,
The social sense extinct; and *that* ferment   440
Mad into tumult the seditious herd,
Or melt them down to slavery. Let *these*
Ensnare the wretched in the toils of law,
Fomenting discord, and perplexing right,
An iron race! and *those*, of fairer front,   445
But equal inhumanity, in courts,
Delusive pomp, and dark cabals, delight;
Wreathe the deep bow, diffuse the lying smile,
And tread the weary labyrinth of state:
While he, from all the stormy passions free   450
That restless men involve, hears, and but hears,
At distance safe, the human tempest roar,
Wrapt close in conscious peace. The fall of kings,
The rage of nations, and the crush of states,
Move not the man who, from the world escaped,   455
In still retreats and flowery solitudes,
To Nature's voice attends, from month to month,
And day to day, through the revolving year;
Admiring, sees her in her every shape;
Feels all her sweet emotions at his heart;   460
Takes what she liberal gives, nor thinks of more.
He, when young Spring protrudes the bursting gems,
Marks the first bud, and sucks the healthful gale
Into his freshened soul; her genial hours
He full enjoys; and not a beauty blows,   465
And not an opening blossom breathes, in vain.
In Summer he, beneath the living shade,

Such as o'er frigid Tempe[8] wont to wave,
Or Haemus cool, reads what the Muse, of these
Perhaps, has in immortal numbers sung;   470
Or what she dictates writes; and oft, an eye
Shot round, rejoices in the vigorous year.
When Autumn's yellow lustre gilds the world,
And tempts the sickled swain into the field,
Seized by the general joy, his heart distends   475
With gentle throes; and, through the tepid gleams
Deep musing, then he best exerts his song.
Even Winter wild to him is full of bliss.
The mighty tempest, and the hoary waste,
Abrupt and deep, stretched o'er the buried earth,   480
Awake to solemn thought. At night the skies,
Disclosed and kindled by refining frost,
Pour every lustre on th' exalted eye.
A friend, a book, the stealing hours secure,
And mark them down for wisdom. With swift wing,   485
O'er land and sea imagination roams;
Or truth, divinely breaking on his mind,
Elates his being, and unfolds his powers;
Or in his breast heroic virtue burns.
The touch of kindred, too, and love, he feels;   490
The modest eye, whose beams on his alone
Ecstatic shine; the little strong embrace
Of prattling children, twined around his neck,
And, emulous to please him, calling forth
The fond parental soul. Nor purpose gay,   495
Amusement, dance, or song, he sternly scorns;
For happiness and true philosophy
Are of the social still and smiling kind.
This is the life which those who fret in guilt,
And guilty cities, never knew; the life   500
Led by primeval ages, uncorrupt,
When angels dwelt, and God himself, with man!
     Oh, Nature! all-sufficient! over all!
Enrich me with the knowledge of thy works!
Snatch me to heaven; thy rolling wonders there,   505
World beyond world, in infinite extent,
Profusely scattered o'er the blue immense,
Show me; their motions, periods, and their laws,
Give me to scan; through the disclosing deep
Light my blind way: the mineral strata there;   510
Thrust, blooming, thence the vegetable world;

---

[8] A valley in Greece, sacred to Apollo, ancient god of poetry.

O'er that the rising system, more complex,
Of animals; and, higher still, the mind,
The varied scene of quick-compounded thought,
And where the mixing passions endless shift: 515
These ever open to my ravished eye;
A search, the flight of time can ne'er exhaust!
But if to that unequal, if the blood
In sluggish streams about my heart forbid
That best ambition, under closing shades, 520
Inglorious, lay me by the lowly brook,
And whisper to my dreams. From Thee begin,
Dwell all on Thee, with Thee conclude my song;
And let me never, never stray from Thee!

🐚 *John Dyer* (1699–1757)

John Dyer's two most important works are significant examples of the two dominant genres for writing about nature in English literature in the seventeenth and eighteenth centuries: the topographical or "prospect" poem, with "Grongar Hill" (1726), and the georgic, with The Fleece *(1757). Dyer wrote "Grongar Hill" based on memories of his childhood home in Wales, near the river Towy in Carmarthenshire. What differentiates Dyer's locodescriptive verse from earlier examples, such as Denham's, is that his representation of the landscape is derived from his own memory (making his poetic process more comparable to the later Romantics than to his fellow Augustans). While Grongar Hill was the site of important British ruins, the poem is less concerned with historical and political reflections prompted from the observation of nature (as was the case with Denham or Pope); instead, the poet's personal associations as well as his moral reflections on human vanity serve as the focus.*

After a trip to Italy to further his artistic education, Dyer returned to England and retired to the countryside to improve a series of farms. Dyer's personal experiences once again became the basis for his poetry, now inspiring his four-book georgic on the British wool trade, The Fleece. *While georgic poetry went out of fashion after the eighteenth century, largely because of its didacticism, it was an immensely important literary mode in the Neoclassical era. Unlike the pastoral, which represented rural life as timeless, carefree, and fully idealized, the georgic revealed the countryside as a place of hard work, and its central purpose was to teach both the practical details of rural labor as well as to reflect on the moral necessity of such labor. In* The Fleece, *Dyer's shepherds, unlike their pastoral cousins, are more concerned with preserving their sheep from hoof-rot than with composing ditties for their beloved nymphs. Indeed, like its Virgilian prototype, Dyer's poem is full of practical information on animal husbandry and clothing manufacture, some of which remains, even today, entirely factually accurate. Given the centrality of the wool trade to the British economy, the poem also provided an occasion for some patriotic meditation. The highly technical nature of much of Dyer's verse limited its popularity, and its later fame was impeded by Dyer's enthusiasm in the poem for those*

"improvements" brought on by the industrialization that would be scorned by the major-
ity of subsequent nature writers.

From The Fleece

A Poem in Four Books

From Book 1

The care of sheep, the labours of the loom,
And arts of trade, I sing. Ye rural nymphs,
Ye swains, and princely merchants, aid the verse.
And ye, high-trusted guardians of our isle,
Whom public voice approves, or lot of birth   5
To the great charge assigns: ye good, of all
Degrees, all sects, be present to my song.
So may distress, and wretchedness, and want,
The wide felicities of labour learn:
So may the proud attempts of restless Gaul[1]   10
From our strong borders, like a broken wave,
In empty foam retire. But chiefly thou,
The people's Shepherd,[2] eminently placed
Over the numerous swains of every vale,
With well-permitted power and watchful eye,   15
On each gay field to shed beneficence,
Celestial office! thou protect the song.
     On spacious airy downs, and gentle hills,
With grass and thyme o'erspread, and clover wild,
Where smiling Phoebus[3] tempers every breeze,   20
The fairest flocks rejoice: they, nor of halt,
Hydropic tumors, nor of rot,[4] complain;
Evils deformed and foul: nor with hoarse cough
Disturb the music of the pastoral pipe:
But, crowding to the note, with silence soft   25
The close woven carpet graze; where nature blends
Flowerets and herbage of minutest size,
Innoxious[5] luxury. Wide airy downs
Are health's gay walks to shepherd and to sheep.

·   ·   ·

---

[1] France, which was frequently during the eighteenth century an adversary of England.

[2] *The people's Shepherd:* the King of England.

[3] Apollo, Greek god of the sun.

[4] Halt, hydropic tumors, and rot (or hoof-rot): all common diseases of sheep.

[5] Harmless, innocuous.

    Hail noble Albion![6] where no golden mines,[7]   30
No soft perfumes, nor oils, nor myrtle bowers,
The vigorous frame and lofty heart of man
Enervate: round whose stern cerulean brows
White-wingèd snow, and cloud, and pearly rain,
Frequent attend, with solemn majesty: 35
Rich queen of mists and vapours! These thy sons
With their cool arms compress; and twist their nerves
For deeds of excellence and high renown.
Thus formed, our Edwards, Henrys, Churchills, Blakes,[8]
Our Lockes, our Newtons, and our Miltons, rose.   40
    See! the sun gleams; the living pastures rise,
After the nurture of the fallen shower,
How beautiful! How blue the ethereal vault,
How verdurous the lawns, how clear the brooks!
Such noble warlike steeds, such herds of kine,   45
So sleek, so vast; such spacious flocks of sheep,
Like flakes of gold illumining the green,
What other paradise adorn but thine,
Britannia? happy, if thy sons would know
Their happiness. To these thy naval streams,   50
Thy frequent towns superb of busy trade,
And ports magnific add, and stately ships
Innumerous. But whither strays my Muse?
Pleased, like a traveller upon the strand
Arrived of bright Augusta:[9] wild he roves   55
From deck to deck, through groves immense of masts;
'Mong crowds, bales, cars, the wealth of either Ind;[10]
Through wharfs, and squares, and palaces, and domes,
In sweet surprise; unable yet to fix
His raptured mind, or scan in ordered course   60
Each object singly; with discoveries new
His native country studious to enrich.
    Ye shepherds, if your labours hope success,
Be first your purpose to procure a breed,
To soil and clime adapted. Every soil   65
And clime, even every tree and herd, receives
Its habitant peculiar: each to each,
The Great Invisible, and each to all,
Through earth, and seas, and air, harmonious suits

---

[6] England.

[7] Verse lines 30 to 151 in the original have been omitted; this excerpt picks up at original line 152, but we have set continuous verse line numbers for the reader's convenience. — Editors' note.

[8] Famous English military heroes.

[9] London.

[10] The West Indies and the East Indies, sites of intense British trade.

Tempestuous regions, Darwent's naked peaks,[11]   70
Snowdon and blue Plynlymmon, and the wide
Aerial sides of Cader-ydris[12] huge;
These are bestowed on goat-horned sheep, of fleece
Hairy and coarse, of long and nimble shank,
Who rove o'er bog or heath, and graze or brouse   75
Alternate, to collect, with due dispatch,
O'er the bleak wild, the thinly scattered meal.
But hills of milder air, that gently rise
O'er dewy dales, a fairer species boast,
Of shorter limb, and frontlet more ornate;   80
Such the Silurian.[13] If thy farm extends
Near Cotswold downs, or the delicious groves
Of Symmonds, honoured through the sandy soil
Of elmy Ross, or Devon's[14] myrtle vales,
That drink clear rivers near the glassy sea;   85
Regard this sort, and hence thy sire of lambs
Select: his tawny fleece in ringlets curls;
Long swings his slender tail; his front is fenced
With horns Ammonian,[15] circulating twice
Around each open ear, like those fair scrolls   90
That grace the columns of th' Ionic[16] dome.
      Yet should thy fertile glebe be marly clay,[17]
Like Melton pastures, or Tripontian fields,[18]
Where ever-gliding Avon's limpid wave
Thwarts the long course of dusty Watling-street;   95
That larger sort, of head defenceless, seek,
Whose fleece is deep and clammy, close and plain:
The ram short-limbed, whose form compact describes
One level line along his spacious back;
Of full and ruddy eye, large ears, stretched head,   100
Nostrils dilated, breast and shoulders broad,
And spacious haunches, and a lofty dock.[19]
      Thus to their kindred soil and air induced,
Thy thriving herd will bless thy skilful care,
That copies nature; who, in every change,   105
In each variety, with wisdom works,
And powers diversified of air and soil,
Her rich materials. . . .

[11] The mountains of Derbyshire, in England.

[12] Snowdon, Plynlymmon, and Cader-ydris are all peaks in North Wales.

[13] A breed of sheep named for Siluria, a region of South Wales.

[14] Cotswold, Symmonds, Ross, and Devon are all towns or regions in England.

[15] The ancient Roman god Jupiter Ammon was represented by ram's horns.

[16] A style of classical Greek architecture.

[17] A *glebe* is an allotment of land; *marly clay* is soil rich in calcium carbonate, often used as fertilizer.

[18] *Like . . . fields:* the countryside between Rugby in Warwickshire and Luttenworth in Leicestershire.

[19] A tail, or the part of a tail, left after clipping.

Grongar Hill

Silent nymph, with curious eye!
Who, the purple evening, lie
On the mountain's lonely van,[1]
Beyond the noise of busy man,
Painting fair the form of things,   5
While the yellow linnet sings;
Or the tuneful nightingale
Charms the forest with her tale;
Come with all thy various hues,
Come, and aid thy sister Muse;   10
Now while Phoebus riding high
Gives lustre to the land and sky!
Grongar Hill invites my song,
Draw the landscape bright and strong;
Grongar, in whose mossy cells   15
Sweetly musing Quiet dwells;
Grongar, in whose silent shade,
For the modest Muses made,
So oft I have, the even still,
At the fountain of a rill,   20
Sate upon a flowery bed,
With my hand beneath my head;
And strayed my eyes o'er Towy's[2] flood,
Over mead and over wood,
From house to house, from hill to hill,   25
'Till contemplation had her fill.
    About his chequered sides I wind,
And leave his brooks and meads behind,
And groves, and grottos where I lay,
And vistas shooting beams of day: 30
Wider and wider spreads the vale,
As circles on a smooth canal:
The mountains round, unhappy fate!
Sooner or later, of all height,
Withdraw their summits from the skies,   35
And lessen as the others rise:
Still the prospect wider spreads,
Adds a thousand woods and meads,
Still it widens, widens still,
And sinks the newly risen hill.   40
    Now I gain the mountain's brow,

---

[1] A wing; an elevated location.
[2] A river in South Wales, where Grongar Hill is located.

What a landscape lies below!
No clouds, no vapours intervene,
But the gay, the open scene
Does the face of Nature show,   45
In all the hues of Heaven's bow!
And, swelling to embrace the light,
Spreads around beneath the sight.
    Old castles on the cliffs arise,
Proudly towering in the skies!   50
Rushing from the woods, the spires
Seem from hence ascending fires!
Half his beams Apollo sheds
On the yellow mountain-heads!
Gilds the fleeces of the flocks: 55
And glitters on the broken rocks!
    Below me trees unnumbered rise,
Beautiful in various dyes:
The gloomy pine, the poplar blue,
The yellow beech, the sable yew,   60
The slender fir that taper grows,
The sturdy oak with broad-spread boughs.
And beyond the purple grove,
Haunt of Phillis, queen of love!
Gaudy as the opening dawn,   65
Lies a long and level lawn,
On which a dark hill, steep and high,
Holds and charms the wandering eye!
Deep are his feet in Towy's flood,
His sides are clothed with waving wood,   70
And ancient towers crown his brow,
That cast an awful look below;
Whose ragged walls the ivy creeps,
And with her arms from falling keeps;
So both a safety from the wind   75
On mutual dependence find.
    'Tis now the raven's bleak abode;
'Tis now th' apartment of the toad;
And there the fox securely feeds;
And there the poisonous adder breeds,   80
Concealed in ruins, moss and weeds,
While, ever and anon, there falls
Huge heaps of hoary mouldered walls.
Yet time has seen, that lifts the low,
And level lays the lofty brow,   85
Has seen this broken pile complete,
Big with the vanity of state;

But transient is the smile of fate!
A little rule, a little sway,
A sunbeam in a winter's day,   90
Is all the proud and mighty have
Between the cradle and the grave.
    And see the rivers how they run,
Through woods and meads; in shade and sun,
Sometimes swift, sometimes slow,   95
Wave succeeding wave, they go
A various journey to the deep,
Like human life to endless sleep!
Thus is Nature's vesture[3] wrought,
To instruct our wandering thought;   100
Thus she dresses green and gay,
To disperse our cares away.
    Ever charming, ever new,
When will the landscape tire the view!
The fountain's fall, the river's flow,   105
The woody valleys, warm and low;
The windy summit, wild and high,
Roughly rushing on the sky!
The pleasant seat, the ruined tower,
The naked rock, the shady bower;   110
The town and village, dome and farm,
Each give each a double charm,
As pearls upon an Ethiop's[4] arm.
    See on the mountain's southern side,
Where the prospect opens wide,   115
Where the evening gilds the tide;
How close and small the hedges lie!
What streaks of meadows cross the eye!
A step methinks may pass the stream,
So little distant dangers seem;   120
So we mistake the future's face,
Eyed through hope's deluding glass;
As yon summits soft and fair,
Clad in colours of the air,
Which to those who journey near,   125
Barren, brown, and rough appear;
Still we tread the same coarse way,
The present's still a cloudy day.
    O may I with myself agree,
And never covet what I see: 130

---

[3] Garment, or covering.

[4] An inhabitant of Ethiopia.

Content me with an humble shade,
My passions tamed, my wishes laid;
For while our wishes wildly roll,
We banish quiet from the soul:
'Tis thus the busy beat the air;   135
And misers gather wealth and care.

    Now, even now, my joys run high,
As on the mountain-turf I lie;
While the wanton Zephyr[5] sings,
And in the vale perfumes his wings;   140
While the waters murmur deep;
While the shepherd charms his sheep;
While the birds unbounded fly,
And with music fill the sky,
Now, even now, my joys run high.   145

    Be full, ye courts, be great who will;
Search for peace with all your skill:
Open wide the lofty door,
Seek her on the marble floor,
In vain you search, she is not there;   150
In vain ye search the domes of Care!
Grass and flowers Quiet treads,
On the meads, and mountain-heads,
Along with Pleasure, close allied,
Ever by each other's side: 155
And often, by the murmuring rill,
Hears the thrush, while all is still,
Within the groves of Grongar Hill.

Richard Lewis (c. 1700–1734)

Richard Lewis was the foremost American nature poet of the Colonial era, a prolific writer whose works were well known and widely reprinted on both sides of the Atlantic. Although the details of his early life are uncertain, there is some evidence to suggest that he was born and raised in Mongomeryshire, Wales, before matriculating at Oxford in 1718. Leaving college after only thirteen weeks, Lewis embarked for Maryland, where he was married, in 1719, and pursued a career as a schoolmaster in Annapolis, the colony's capital city. He was evidently an amateur scientist, reporting to the Royal Society of London on his observation of an explosion of air at Patapsco (near present-day Baltimore) in 1725. He later served as a member of the Maryland Assembly.

    Lewis's first publication was a translation of a Latin poem, Muscipula (The Mouse Trap) (1728), with extensive annotations that displayed a remarkable degree of classical learning.

---

[5] The classical demigod of the wind.

He went on to publish several original poems in American periodicals, including three of his finest works: "A Journey from Patapsko to Annapolis" (1731), "Food for Criticks" (1731), and "Upon Prince Madoc's Expedition to the Country now called America in the Twelfth Century" (1733). All three of these poems have American settings, and all three celebrate the unspoiled natural beauty of the New World. "A Journey from Patapsko to Annapolis" portrays the lush Maryland countryside as it awakens on a beautiful April morning; the speaker evokes the "rapid Whirl" of a hummingbird's wings, and the "vivid Green" of its plumage, with an intensity and dynamism of descriptive technique that foreshadows the work of Philip Freneau and John James Audubon. At the same time, Lewis employs the standard heroic couplets of the high Augustan mode and utilizes pastoral conventions of nature writing that he derived from such British writers as Alexander Pope, adapting them to the unfamiliar flora and fauna of the American landscape. In so doing, Lewis invented a new genre, the American pastoral, a synthesis of Old World poetic forms and New World descriptive content.

A Journey from Patapsko to Annapolis, April 4, 1730*

At length the *wintry* Horrors disappear,
And *April* views with Smiles the infant Year;
The grateful Earth from frosty Chains unbound,
Pours out its *vernal* Treasures all around,
Her Face bedecked with Grass, with Buds the Trees are crowned.   5
In this soft Season, 'ere the Dawn of Day,
I mount my Horse, and lonely take my Way,
From woody Hills that shade *Patapsko*'s Head,
(In whose deep Vales he makes his stony Bed,
From whence he rushes with resistless Force,   10
Though huge rough Rocks retard his rapid Course),
Down to *Annapolis*, on that smooth Stream
Which took from fair *Anne-Arundel* its Name.
And now the *Star* that ushers in the Day,[1]
Begins to pale her ineffectual Ray.   15
The *Moon*, with blunted Horns, now shines less bright,
Her fading Face eclipsed with growing Light;
The fleecy Clouds with streaky Lustre glow,
And Day quits Heaven to view the Earth below.
O'er yon tall *Pines* the *Sun* shows half his Face,   20
And fires their floating Foliage with his Rays;
Now sheds aslant on Earth his lightsome Beams,
That trembling shine in many-coloured Streams:
Slow-rising from the Marsh, the Mist recedes,
The Trees, emerging, rear their dewy Heads;   25

---

* "Patapsko" is an early name for the city of Baltimore, derived from the name of the river that runs into its harbor. Annapolis, on the Severn River, was then (and is today) the capital of Maryland.

[1] Venus (note by Lewis).

Their dewy Heads the *Sun* with Pleasure views,
And brightens into Pearls the pendent Dews.
    The *Beasts* uprising, quit their leafy Beds,
And to the cheerful *Sun* erect their Heads;
All joyful rise, except the filthy *Swine*,   30
On obscene Litter stretched they snore supine:
In vain the Day awakes, Sleep seals their Eyes,
Till Hunger breaks the Bond and bids them rise.
Meanwhile the *Sun* with more exalted Ray,
From cloudless Skies distributes riper Day;   35
Through sylvan Scenes my Journey I pursue,
Ten thousand Beauties rising to my View;
Which kindle in my Breast poetic Flame,
And bid me my Creator's praise proclaim;
Though my low Verse ill-suits the noble Theme.   40
    Here various Flowerets grace the teeming Plains,
Adorned by Nature's Hand with beauteous Stains;
First-born of *Spring*, here the *Pacone* appears,
Whose golden Root a silver Blossom rears.
In spreading Tufts, see there the *Crowfoot* blue,   45
On whose green Leaves still shines a globous Dew;
Behold the *Cinquefoil*, with its dazzling Dye
Of flaming Yellow, wounds the tender Eye:
But there, enclosed the grassy *Wheat* is seen,
To heal the aching Sight with cheerful Green.   50
    Safe in yon Cottage dwells the *Monarch-Swain*,
His *Subject-Flocks*, close-grazing, hide the Plain;
For him they live;——and die t' uphold his Reign.
Viands unbought his well-tilled Lands afford,
And smiling *Plenty* waits upon his Board;   55
Health shines with sprightly Beams around his Head,
And *Sleep*, with downy Wings, o'ershades his Bed;
His *Sons* robust his daily Labours share,
Patient of Toil, Companions of his Care:
And all their Toils with sweet Success are crowned.   60
In graceful Ranks there *Trees* adorn the Ground,
The *Peach*, the *Plum*, the *Apple*, here are found;
Delicious Fruits!——Which from their Kernels rise,
So fruitful is the Soil—so mild the Skies.
The lowly *Quince* yon sloping Hill o'er-shades.   65
Here lofty *Cherry Trees* erect their Heads;
High in the Air each spiry Summer waves,
Whose Blooms thick-springing yield no Space for Leaves;
Evolving Odours fill the ambient Air,
The *Birds* delighted to the Grove repair: 70
On every Tree behold a tuneful Throng,

The vocal Valleys echo to their Song.
But what is *He*,[2] who perched above the rest,
Pours out such various Music from his Breast!
His Breast, whose Plumes a cheerful White display,   75
His quivering Wings are dressed in sober Grey.
Sure, all the *Muses*, this their Bird inspire!
And *He*, alone, is equal to the Choir
Of warbling Songsters who around him play,
While, Echolike, *He* answers every Lay.   80
The chirping *Lark* now sings with sprightly Note,
Responsive to her Strain *He* shapes his Throat:
Now the poor widowed *Turtle* wails her Mate,
While in soft Sounds *He* cooes to mourn his Fate.
Oh, sweet Musician, thou dost far excel   85
The soothing Song of pleasing *Philomel!*
Sweet is her Song, but in few Notes confined;
But thine, thou *Mimic* of the feathery Kind,
Runs through all Notes!——*Thou* only know'st them *All*,
At once the *Copy*,——*and th' Original*.   90
    My *Ear* thus charmed, mine *Eye* with Pleasure sees,
Hovering about the Flowers, th' industrious *Bees*.
Like them in Size, the *Hummingbird* I view,
Like them, *He* sucks his Food, the Honey-Dew,
With nimble Tongue, and Beak of jetty Hue.   95
He takes with rapid Whirl his noisy Flight,
His gemmy Plumage strikes the Gazer's Sight;
And as he moves his ever-fluttering Wings,
Ten thousand Colours he around him flings.
Now I behold the Emerald's vivid Green,   100
Now scarlet, now a purple Dye is seen;
In brightest Blue, his Breast *He* now arrays,
Then straight his Plumes emit a golden Blaze.
Thus whirring round he flies, and varying still,
He mocks the *Poet*'s and the *Painter*'s Skill;   105
Who may forever strive with fruitless Pains,
To catch and fix those beauteous changeful Stains;
While Scarlet now, and now the Purple shines,
And Gold, to Blue its transient Gloss resigns.
Each quits, and quickly each resumes its Place,   110
And ever-varying Dyes each other chase.
Smallest of Birds, what Beauties shine in thee!
A living *Rainbow* on thy Breast I see.
    Oh had that *Bard*[3] in whose heart-pleasing Lines,

[2] The Mock Bird (note by Lewis).

[3] Claudian (note by Lewis).

The *Phoenix* in a Blaze of Glory shines,   115
Beheld those Wonders which are shown in Thee,
That *Bird* had lost his Immortality!
Thou in His Verse hadst stretched thy fluttering Wing
Above all other Birds,—their beauteous King.
    But now th' enclosed Plantation I forsake   120
And onwards through the Woods my Journey take;
The level Road, the longsome Way beguiles,
A blooming Wilderness around me smiles;
Here hardy *Oak*, there fragment *Hickory* grows,
Their bursting Buds the tender Leaves disclose;   125
The tender Leaves in downy Robes appear,
Trembling, they seem to move with cautious Fear,
Yet new to Life, and Strangers to the Air.
Here stately *Pines* unite their whispering Heads,
And with a solemn Gloom embrown the Glades.   130
See there a green *Savane* opens wide,
Through which smooth Streams in wanton Mazes glide;
Thick-branching Shrubs o'erhang the silver Streams,
Which scarcely deign t' admit the solar Beams.
    While with Delight on this soft Scene I gaze,   135
The *Cattle* upward look, and cease to graze,
But into covert run through various Ways.
And now the Clouds in black Assemblage rise,
And dreary Darkness overspreads the Skies,
Through which the Sun strives to transmit his Beams,   140
"But sheds his sickly light in straggling Streams."[4]
Hushed is the Music of the woodland Choir,
Foreknowing of the Storm, the Birds retire
For Shelter, and forsake the shrubby Plains,
And dumb Horror through the Forest reigns;   145
In that lone House which opens wide its Door,
Safe may I tarry till the Storm is o'er.
    Hark how the *Thunder* rolls with solemn Sound!
And see the forceful *Lightning* dart a Wound,
On yon tall Oak!——Behold its Top laid bare!   150
Its Body rent, and scattered through the Air
The Splinters fly!——Now—now the *Winds* arise,
From different Quarters of the lowering Skies;
Forth-issuing fierce, the *West* and *South* engage,
The waving Forest bends beneath their Rage: 155
But where the winding Valley cheeks their Course,
They roar and ravage with redoubled Force;
With circling Sweep in dreadful Whirlwinds move
And from its Roots tear up the gloomy Grove,

---

[4] An allusion to John Dryden's translation of Virgil's *Georgics* I: "Or if through mists he shoots his sullen beams, / Frugal of light, in loose and straggling streams."

Down-rushing fall the Trees, and beat the Ground,   160
In Fragments fly the shattered Limbs around;
Tremble the Under-woods, the Vales resound.
    Follows, with pattering Noise, the icy *Hail*,
And *Rain*, fast falling, floods the lowly Vale.
Again the *Thunders* roll, the *Lightnings* fly,   165
And as they first disturbed, now clear the Sky;
For lo, the *Gust* decreases by Degrees,
The dying *Winds* but sob amidst the Trees;
With pleasing Softness falls the silver Rain,
Through which at first faint-gleaming o'er the Plain,   170
The Orb of Light scarce darts a watery Ray
To gild the Drops that fall from every Spray;
But soon the dusky Vapours are dispelled,
And thro' the Mist that late his Face concealed,
Bursts the broad *Sun*, triumphant in a Blaze   175
Too keen for Sight—Yon Cloud refracts his Rays,
The mingling Beams compose th' *ethereal Bow*,
How sweet, how soft, its melting Colours glow!
Gaily they shine, by heavenly Pencils laid,
Yet vanish swift,——How soon does *Beauty* fade!   180
    The *Storm* is past, my Journey I renew,
And a new Scene of Pleasure greets my View:
Washed by the copious Rain the gummy *Pine*,
Does cheerful, with unsullied Verdure shine;
The *Dogwood* Flowers assume a snowy white,   185
The *Maple* blushing gratifies the Sight:
No verdant leaves the lovely *Redbud* grace,
Cornation blossoms now supply their Place.
The *Sassafras* unfolds its fragrant Bloom,
The *Vine* affords an exquisite Perfume;   190
These grateful Scents wide-wafting through the Air
The smelling Sense with balmy Odours cheer.
And now the *Birds*, sweet singing, stretch their Throats,
And in one Choir unite their various Notes,
Nor yet unpleasing is the *Turtle*'s Voice,   195
Though he complains while other Birds rejoice.
    These vernal Joys, all restless Thoughts control,
And gently soothing calm the troubled Soul.
    While such Delights my Senses entertain,
I scarce perceive that I have left the *Plain*;   200
'Till now the Summit of a *Mount* I gain:
Low at whose sandy Base the *River* glides,
Slow-rolling near their Height his languid Tides;
Shade above Shade, the Trees in rising Ranks,
Clothe with eternal Green his steepy Banks: 205
The Flood, well pleased, reflects their verdant Gleam
From the smooth Mirror of his limpid Stream.

But see the *Hawk*, who with acute Survey,
Towering in Air predestinates his Prey
Amid the Floods!——Down dropping from on high,
He strikes the *Fish*, and bears him through the Sky.
The Stream disturbed, no longer shows the Scene
That lately stained its silver Waves with green;
In spreading Circles roll the troubled Floods,
And to the Shores bear off the pictured Woods.   215
    Now looking round I view the outstretched *Land*,
O'er which the Sight exerts a wide Command;
The fertile Valleys, and the naked Hills,
The Cattle feeding near the crystal Rills;
The Lawns wide-opening to the sunny Ray,   220
And mazy Thickets that exclude the Day.
A-while the Eye is pleased these Scenes to trace,
Then hurrying o'er the intermediate Space,
Far distant Mountains drest in Blue appear,
And all their Woods are lost in empty Air.   225
    The *Sun* near setting now arrays his Head
In milder Beams and lengthens every Shade.
The rising Clouds usurping on the Day
A bright Variety of Dyes display;
About the wide Horizon swift they fly,   230
"And chase a Change of Colours round the Sky:"[5]
And now I view but half the *flaming Sphere*,
Now one faint Glimmer shoots along the Air,
And all his golden Glories disappear.
    Onwards the *Evening* moves in Habit grey,   235
And for her Sister *Night* prepares the Way.
The plumy People seek their secret Nests,
To Rest repair the ruminating Beasts.
Now deepening Shades confess th' Approach of Night,
Imperfect Images elude the Sight: 240
From earthly Objects I remove mine Eye,
And view with Look erect the vaulted Sky;
Where dimly shining now the Stars appear,
At first thin-scattering through the misty Air;
Till Night confirmed, her jetty Throne ascends,   245
On her the *Moon* in clouded State attends,
But soon unveiled her lovely Face is seen,
And *Stars* unnumbered wait around their Queen;
Ranged by their Maker's Hand in just Array,
They march majestic thro' th' ethereal Way.   250
    Are these bright Luminaries hung on high
Only to please with twinkling Rays our Eye?

---

[5] An allusion to "Summer" in James Thomson's *Seasons:* "See, how at once the bright effulgent sun, / Rising direct, swift chases from the sky / The short-lived Twilight."

Or may we rather count each *Star* a *Sun*,
Round which *full peopled Worlds* their Courses run?
Orb above Orb harmoniously they steer   255
Their various voyages through Seas of Air.
      Snatch me some *Angel* to those high Abodes,
The Seats perhaps of *Saints* and *Demigods!*
Where such as bravely scorned the galling Yoke
Of *vulgar Error*, and her Fetters broke;   260
Where *Patriots* who fix the public Good,
In Fields of Battle sacrificed their Blood;
Where *pious Priests* who Charity proclaimed,
And *Poets* whom a *virtuous Muse* enflamed;
Philosophers who strove to mend our Hearts,   265
And such as polished Life with *useful Arts*,
Obtain a Place; when by the Hand of Death
Touched, they retire from this poor Speck of Earth;
Their *Spirits* freed from bodily Alloy
Perceive a Foretaste of that endless Joy,   270
Which from Eternity hath been prepared,
To crown their labours with a vast Reward.
While to these Orbs my wandering Thoughts aspire,
A falling *Meteor* shoots his lambent Fire;
Thrown from the heavenly Space he seeks the Earth,   275
From whence he first derived his humble Birth.
      The *Mind* advised by this instructive Sight,
Descending sudden from th' aerial Height,
Obliges me to view a different Scene,
Of more importance to myself, though mean.   280
These distant Objects I no more pursue,
But turning inward my reflective View,
My working Fancy helps me to survey,
In the just Picture of this *April Day*,
My life o'er past,——a Course of thirty *Years*   285
Blest with few Joys, perplexed with numerous Cares.
      In the dim Twilight of our *Infancy*,
Scarce can the Eye surrounding Objects see;
Then thoughtless *Childhood* leads us pleased and gay,
In Life's fair Morning through a flowery Way: 290
The *Youth* in Schools inquisitive of Good,
Science pursues through *Learning*'s mazy Wood;
Whose lofty Trees, he, to his Grief perceives,
Are often bare of *Fruit*, and only filled with *Leaves:*
Through lonely Wilds his tedious Journey lies,   295
At last a brighter Prospect cheers his Eyes;
Now the gay Fields of *Poetry* he views,
And joyous listens to the *tuneful Muse;*
Now *History* affords him vast Delight,
And opens lovely Landscapes to his Sight: 300

But ah too soon this Scene of Pleasure flies!
And o'er his Head tempestous Troubles rise.
He hears the Thunders roll, he feels the Rains,
Before a friendly Shelter he obtains;
And thence beholds with Grief the furious Storm   305
The *noon-tide* Beauties of his *Life* deform:
He views the *painted Bow* in distant Skies;
Hence, in his Heart some Gleams of Comfort rise;
He hopes the *Gust* has almost spent its Force,
And that he safely may pursue his Course.   310
    Thus far *my Life* does with the *Day* agree,
Oh may its coming Stage from Storms be free!
While passing through the World's most private Way,
With Pleasure I my Maker's Works survey;
Within my Heart let *Peace* a Dwelling find,   315
Let my *Goodwill* extend to *all Mankind:*
Freed from *Necessity,* and blest with *Health;*
Give me *Content,* let others toil for *Wealth:*
In *busy* Scenes of Life let me exert
A *careful Hand,* and wear an *honest Heart;*   320
And suffer me my *leisure* Hours to spend,
With chosen *Books,* or a well-natured *Friend.*
Thus journeying on, as I advance in Age
May I look back with Pleasure on my Stage;
And as the setting *Sun* withdrew his Light   325
To rise on other Worlds serene and bright,
Cheerful may I resign my vital Breath,
Nor anxious tremble at th' Approach of *Death;*
Which shall (I hope) but strip me of *my Clay,*
And to a better World my Soul convey.   330
    Thus musing, I my silent Moments spend,
Till to the *River's* margin I descend,
From whence I may discern my *Journey's* End:
Annapolis adorns its further Shore,
To which the *Boat* attends to bear me o'er.   335
    And now the moving *Boat* the Flood divides,
While the *Stars* "tremble on the floating Tides;"[6]
Pleased with the Sight, again I raise mine Eye
To the Bright Glories of the azure Sky;
And while these Works of God's creative Hand,   340
The *Moon* and *Stars,* that move at his Command,
Obedient through their circling Course on high,
Employ my Sight,——struck with amaze I cry,
Almighty Lord! whom Heaven and Earth proclaim,
The *Author* of their universal Frame,   345

[6] An allusion to Alexander Pope's *Rape of the Lock,* 2:48: "The sunbeams trembling on the floating tides."

Wilt thou vouchsafe to view the *Son of Man,*
Thy Creature, who but *Yesterday* began,
Through animated Clay to draw his Breath,
Tomorrow doomed a Prey to ruthless Death!
  TREMENDOUS GOD! May I not justly fear,   350
That I, unworthy Object of thy Care,
Into this World from thy bright Presence tossed,
Am in th' Immensity of *Nature* lost!
And that my Notions of the *World above,*
Are but Creations of my own *Self-Love;*   355
To feed my coward Heart, afraid to die,
With *fancied* Feasts of *Immortality!*
  These Thoughts, which thy amazing Works suggest,
Oh glorious FATHER, rack my troubled Breast.
  Yet, GRACIOUS GOD, reflecting that my Frame   360
From *Thee* derived in animating Flame,
And that whate'er I am, however mean,
By thy Command I entered on this Scene
Of Life, —— thy wretched *Creature of a Day,*
Condemned to travel through a tiresome Way;   365
Upon whose Banks (perhaps to cheer my Toil)
I see thin Verdures rise, and *Daisies* smile:
Poor Comforts these, my Pains t' alleviate!
While on my Head tempestuous Troubles beat.
And must I, when I quit this earthly Scene,   370
Sink total into *Death*, and never rise again?
  No sure, ——These *Thoughts* which in my Bosom roll
Must issue from a *never-dying Soul;*
These active *Thoughts* that penetrate the Sky,
Excursive into dark Futurity;   375
Which hope eternal Happiness to gain,
Could never be bestowed on *Man* in vain.
To *Thee*, OH FATHER, filled with fervent Zeal,
And sunk in humble Silence I appeal;
Take me, my great Creator to *Thy Care,*   380
And gracious listen to my ardent Prayer!
  Supreme of Beings, omnipresent Power!
My great Preserver from my natal Hour,
Fountain of Wisdom, boundless Deity,
OMNISCIENT GOD, my Wants are known to Thee,   385
With Mercy look on mine Infirmity!
Whatever State thou shalt for me ordain,
Whether my Lot in Life be *Joy* or *Pain;*
Patient let me sustain thy wise Decree,
And learn to *know myself,* and *honour Thee.*   390

✒ *Stephen Duck* (c. 1705–1756)

While many of the Neoclassical poets wrote about rural life and labor, usually based on information gleaned from ancient Greek and Roman authors, very few (with perhaps the exception of Dyer) had any practical experience of what it was like to work on a farm. Such was not the case with Stephen Duck. His poem "The Thresher's Labour" (1730) describes the joys and pains of rural work from the perspective of someone who actually performed it. While Duck's representation is thus more realistic, the poem is not without the requisite references to classical mythology and is written in heroic couplets in the style of Pope. For while Duck was a poor rural laborer, with only the barest minimum of formal education, he was, in fact, quite well-read. He studied Milton and had read Virgil's Georgics *in translation.*

Duck's talent for versifying brought him to the attention of local gentry. He quickly gained the reputation of a "natural genius"—presumably evidence of the authentic poetic spirit that blossomed without the artificial assistance of education in those who lived in the English countryside. Queen Caroline was so impressed by this "peasant poet" that she became his patron and, late in 1730, made him the librarian to her fanciful "Merlin's Cave"—a curiosity she had constructed in Richmond Gardens. Duck continued to write poetry, much of it occasional verse in praise of his new noble friends, furthered his education by learning Latin, and eventually took Holy Orders. While not much is known about Duck's personal circumstances after his initial discovery, his life ended tragically in suicide. Duck's life story would serve as an inspiration and a warning to future generations of authors from the laboring classes, including Mary Collier, Robert Burns, Robert Bloomfield, and John Clare. His success served as a validation that one need not have a university education or a country estate to write sensitively and thoughtfully about the natural world, a world about which rural laborers could often legitimately claim a more intimate knowledge than their aristocratic readers and patrons.

The Thresher's Labour

The grateful Tribute of these rural Lays,
Which to her Patron's hand the Muse conveys,
Deign to accept; 'tis just she Tribute bring
To him whose Bounty gives her Life to sing:
To him whose generous Favours tune her Voice,   5
And bid her 'midst her Poverty rejoice.
Inspired by these, she dares herself prepare,
To sing the Toils of each revolving Year:
Those endless Toils, which always grow anew,
And the poor Thresher's destined to pursue.   10
Even these with pleasure can the Muse rehearse,
When You, and Gratitude, command the Verse.

Soon as the Harvest hath laid bare the Plains,
And Barns well filled reward the Farmer's pains;
What Corn each sheaf will yield, intent to hear,   15
And guess from thence the Profits of the year;
Or else impending Ruin to prevent,
By paying, timely, threatening Landlord's rent,
He calls his Threshers forth. Around we stand,
With deep attention, waiting his command.   20
To each our tasks he readily divides,
And pointing, to our different stations guides.
As he directs, to different Barns we go,
Here two for Wheat, and there for Barley two.
But first, to show what he expects to find,   25
These words, or words like these, disclose his Mind:
So dry the Corn was carried from the Field,
So easily 'twill thresh, so well 'twill yield.
Sure large day's Work I well may hope for now;
Come, strip, and try, let's see what you can do.   30

Divested of our clothes, with Flail in hand,
At a just distance, front to front we stand,
And first the Threshall's gently swung, to prove
Whether with just exactness it will move.
That once secure, more quick we whirl them round,   35
From the strong planks our Crab-tree Staves rebound,
And echoing Barns return the rattling sound.
Now in the air our knotty Weapons fly,
And now with equal force descend from high.
Down one, one up, so well they keep the Time,   40
The *Cyclops'* Hammers could not truer chime,
Nor with more heavy strokes could *Aetna* groan,
When *Vulcan* forged the arms for *Thetis'* Son.[1]
In briny streams our sweat descends apace,
Drops from our locks, or trickles down our face.   45
No intermission in our Works we know;
The noisy Threshall must forever go.
Their Master absent, others safely play;
The sleeping Threshall doth itself betray.
Nor yet the tedious Labour to beguile,   50
And make the passing Minutes sweetly smile,
Can we, like Shepherds, tell a merry tale?
The voice is lost, drowned by the noisy Flail.
But we may think—alas! what pleasing thing
Here to the Mind can the dull Fancy bring?   55

---

[1] The Cyclops were mythical one-eyed beings; Aetna is a volcano in Italy. Vulcan is the Roman god of the forge and of blacksmiths. He made armor for Aeneas, who was the founder of Roman civilization.

The eye beholds no pleasant object here;
No cheerful sound diverts the listening ear.
The Shepherd well may tune his voice to sing,
Inspired by all the beauties of the Spring:
No Fountains murmur here, no Lambkins play,   60
No Linnets warble, and no Fields look gay.
'Tis all a dull and melancholy Scene,
Fit only to provoke the Muses' Spleen.

When sooty Pease we thresh, you scarce can know
Our native colour, as from Work we go;   65
The sweat, and dust, and suffocating smoke
Make us so much like *Ethiopians* look,
We scare our Wives, when Evening brings us home,
And frighted Infants think the Bug-bear come.
Week after week we this dull Task pursue,   70
Unless when winnowing days produce a new,
A new indeed, but frequently a worse;
The Threshall yields but to the Master's Curse:
He counts the Bushels, counts how much a day,
Then swears we've idled half our Time away.   75
Why look ye, Rogues! D'ye think that this will do?
Your Neighbours thresh as much again as you.
Now in our hands we wish our noisy Tools,
To drown the hated Names of Rogues and Fools;
But wanting those, we just like Schoolboys look,   80
When th' angry Master views the blotted Book:
They cry their Ink was faulty, and their Pen;
We, the Corn threshes bad, 'twas cut too green.

But now the Winter hides his hoary head,
And Nature's face is with new Beauty spread;   85
The Spring appears, and kind refreshing Showers.
New clothe the Field with Grass, and deck with Flowers.
Next her, the ripening Summer presses on,
And *Sol*² begins his longest Stage to run.
Before the door our welcome Master stands,   90
And tells us the ripe Grass requires our hands.
The long much-wished Intelligence imparts
Life to our looks, and spirit to our hearts:
We wish the happy Season may be fair,
And joyful, long to breathe in opener Air.   95
This Change of Labour seems to give much Ease;
With thoughts of happiness our Joy's complete.
There's always Bitter mingled with the Sweet.

² The sun.

When Morn does through the Eastern Windows peep,
Straight from our Beds we start, and shake off Sleep;   100
This new Employ with eager haste to prove,
This new Employ becomes so much our Love.
Alas! that human Joys should change so soon.
Even this may bear another Face at Noon!

　　The Birds salute us as to Work we go,   105
And a new Life seems in our Breasts to glow.
Across one's shoulder hangs a Scythe well steeled,
The Weapon destined to unclothe the Field;
T' other supports the Whetstone, Scrip,[3] and Beer,
That for our Scythes, and these ourselves to cheer.   110
And now the Field designed our Strength to try
Appears, and meets at last our longing eye;
The Grass and Ground each cheerfully surveys,
Willing to see which way th' Advantage lays.
As the best man, each claims the foremost place,   115
And our first work seems but a sportive Race.
With rapid force our well-whet Blades we drive,
Strain every nerve, and blow for blow we give:
Though but this Eminence the foremost gains,
Only t' excel the rest in Toil and Pains.   120
But when the scorching Sun is mounted high,
And no kind Barns with friendly Shades are nigh,
Our weary Scythes entangle in the grass,
And streams of sweat run trickling down apace;
Our sportive Labour we too late lament,   125
And wish that Strength again we vainly spent.

　　Thus in the Morn a Courser[4] I have seen,
With headlong Fury scour the level Green,
Or mount the Hills, if Hills are in his way,
As if no Labour could his fire allay,   130
Till the meridian Sun with sultry Heat
And piercing Beams hath bathed his sides in sweat;
The lengthened Chace scarce able to sustain,
He measures back the Hills and Dales with pain.

　　With Heat and Labour tired, our Scythes we quit,   135
Search out a shady tree, and down we sit;
From Scrip and Bottle hope new Strength to gain,
But Scrip and Bottle too are tried in vain.
Down our parched throats we scarce the bread can get,

---

[3] A small bag or knapsack, used to carry food or tools.
[4] A swift horse.

And quite o'erspent with Toil, but faintly eat;   140
Nor can the Bottle only answer all,
Alas! the Bottle and the Beer's too small.[5]
Our time slides on, we move from off the Grass,
And each again betakes him to his place.
Not eager now, as late, our strength to prove,   145
But all contented regular to move.
Often we whet, as often view the Sun,
To see how near his tedious race is run.
At length he vails his radiant face from sight,
And bids the weary Traveller good-night.   150
Homewards we move, but so much spent with toil,
We walk but slow, and rest at every Stile.
Our good expecting Wives, who think we stay,
Got to the door, soon eye us in the way;
Then from the pot the dumpling's catched in haste,   155
And homely by its side the bacon's placed.
Supper and sleep by Morn new strength supply,
And out we set again our works to try,
But not so early quite, nor quite so fast,
As to our cost we did the Morning past.   160

     Soon as the rising Sun hath drunk the dew
Another scene is opened to our view:
Our Master comes, and at his Heels a Throng
Of prattling Females, armed with Rake and Prong,
Prepared, whilst he is here, to make his Hay,   165
Or, if he turns his back, prepared to play.
But here, or gone, sure of this comfort still,
Here's Company, so they may chat their fill:
And were their Hands as active as their Tongues,
How nimbly then would move their Rakes and Prongs?   170
The Grass again is spread upon the Ground,
Till not a vacant place is to be found,
And while the piercing sunbeams on it shine,
The Haymakers have time allowed to dine.
That soon dispatched, they still sit on the Ground,   175
And the brisk Chat renewed, afresh goes round;
All talk at once, but seeming all to fear
That all they speak so well, the rest won't hear.
By quick degrees so high their notes they strain,
That Standers-by can naught distinguish plain.   180
So loud their Speech, and so confused their Noise,
Scarce puzzled Echo can return a Voice;
Yet spite of this, they bravely all go on,

[5] Small beer is lower in alcohol content.

Each scorns to be, or seem to be, outdone,
Till (unobserved before) a lowering Sky,   185
Fraught with black Clouds, proclaims a Shower nigh.
The tattling Crowd can scarce their garments gain,
Before descends the thick impetuous Rain;
Their noisy Prattle all at once is done,
And to the Hedge they all for Shelter run.   190

   Thus have I seen on a bright Summer's day,
On some green brake a Flock of Sparrows play.
From twig to twig, from bush to bush they fly,
And with continued chirping fill the Sky,
But on a sudden, if a Storm appears,   195
Their chirping noise no longer dins your ears;
They fly for shelter to the thickest bush,
There silent sit, and all at once is hush.
But better Fate succeeds this rainy Day,
And little Labour serves to make the Hay;   200
Fast as 'tis cut, so kindly shines the Sun,
Turned once or twice, the pleasing Work is done.
Next day the Cocks appear in equal Rows,
Which the glad Master in safe Ricks bestows.

   But now the Field we must no longer range,   205
And yet, hard Fate! still Work for Work we change.
Back to the Barns again in haste we're sent,
Where lately so much time we pensive spent;
Not pensive now, we bless the friendly Shade,
And to avoid the parching Sun are glad.   210
But few days here we're destined to remain,
Before our Master calls us forth again:
For Harvest now, says he, yourselves prepare,
The ripened Harvest now demands your Care.
Early next Morn I shall disturb your rest,   215
Get all things ready, and be quickly dressed.
Strict to his word, scarce the next dawn appears,
Before his hasty Summons fills our ears.
Obedient to his call, straight up we get,
And finding soon our Company complete,   220
With him, our Guide, we to the Wheat field go,
He to appoint and we the Work to do.
Ye Reapers, cast your eyes around the Field,
And view the scene its different Beauties yield;
Then look again with a more tender eye,   225
To think how soon it must in ruin lie.
For once set in, where'er our blows we deal,
There's no resisting of the well-whet Steel,

But here or there, where'er our Course we bend,
Sure Desolation does our steps attend.   230
Thus when *Arabia*'s sons, in hopes of prey,
To some more fertile Country take their way,
How beauteous all things in the Morn appear,
There villages, and pleasing cots are here;
So many pleasing objects meet the sight,   235
The ravished eye could willing gaze 'till Night,
But long ere then, where'er their Troops have past,
Those pleasant Prospects lie a gloomy Waste.

    The Morning past, we sweat beneath the Sun,
And but uneasily our Work goes on.   240
Before us we perplexing Thistles find,
And Corn blown adverse with the ruffling Wind.
Behind our backs the Female Gleaners wait,
Who sometimes stoop, and sometimes hold a Chat.
Each Morn we early rise, go late to bed,   245
And lab'ring hard, a painful life we lead.
For Toils, scarce ever ceasing, press us now,
Rest never does, but on the Sabbath show,
And barely that, our Master will allow.
Nor when asleep are we secure from Pain;   250
We then perform our Labours o'er again;
Our mimic Fancy always restless seems,
And what we act awake, she acts in Dreams.
Hard Fate! Our Labours even in Sleep don't cease;
Scarce *Hercules* e'er felt such Toils as these.   255
At length in rows stands up the well-dried Corn,
A grateful Scene, and ready for the Barn.
Our well-pleased Master views the sight with joy,
And we for carrying all our force employ.
Confusion soon o'er all the Field appears,   260
And stunning Clamours fill the Workmen's ears;
The Bells and clashing Whips alternate sound,
And rattling Waggons thunder o'er the Ground.
The Wheat got in, the Pease and other Grain,
Share the same Fate, and soon leave bare the plain.   265
In noisy Triumph the last load moves on.
And loud Huzzas proclaim the Harvest's done.

    Our Master joyful at the welcome sight,
Invites us all to feast with him at Night.
A Table plentifully spread we find,   270
And jugs of humming Beer to cheer the Mind,
Which he, too generous, pushes on so fast,
We think no toils to come, nor mind the past.

But the next Morning soon reveals the Cheat,
When the same toils we must again repeat,   275
To the same Barns again must back return,
To labour there for room for next year's Corn.

    Thus as the Year's revolving course goes round,
No respite from our Labour can be found.
Like Sisyphus,[6] our Work is never done;   280
Continually rolls back the restless Stone.
Now growing Labours still succeed the past,
And growing always new, must always last.

[6] In Greek mythology, Sisyphus was punished by being forced for eternity to roll a stone up a hill only to have it fall back down when he reached the summit.

🖐 *William Shenstone* (*1714–1763*)

Born of middle-class parents and educated at Oxford, William Shenstone's ambitions as both a poet and a landscape gardener were often beyond his physical and financial means. During his lifetime, he published three volumes of poetry to moderate acclaim, Poems Upon Various Occasions (*1737*), The Judgment of Hercules (*1741*), *and* The Schoolmistress (*1742*). *He was deeply involved in the literary culture of his day and shared devoted friendships with fellow poets, such as Richard Jago and publisher Robert Dodsley. A lifelong bachelor with frequently uncertain health, Shenstone's main passion was the improvement of his small estate, The Leasowes. He described his property as a* ferme ornée, *or a "decorated farm," wherein he attempted to blend the land's useful agricultural function with surprising and delightful ornamentation. Exemplifying and elaborating upon the aesthetic principles of the English Garden, Shenstone dotted the landscape with small grottoes, decorative urns, and poetic inscriptions that were intended to embellish the natural attractiveness of the site. He corresponded with and frequently visited other noted eighteenth-century garden devotees, including Lord Lyttelton, owner of the famous grounds at Hagley, and Lady Luxborough. His poem "Rural Elegance" and his prose piece "Unconnected Thoughts on Gardening" exemplify some of the principles that guided him in his own work on the land.*

Rural Elegance

An Ode to the Late Duchess of Somerset, 1750

While orient skies restore the day,
And dewdrops catch the lucid ray;
Amid the sprightly scenes of morn
    Will aught the Muse inspire?
Oh! peace to yonder clamorous horn   5
    That drowns the sacred lyre!

Ye rural Thanes![1] that o'er the mossy down
   Some panting, timorous hare pursue,
Does Nature mean your joys alone to crown?
    Say, does she smooth her lawns for you?   10
   For you does Echo bid the rocks reply,
And, urged by rude constraint, resound the jovial cry?

See from the neighbouring hill, forlorn,
   The wretched swain your sport survey;
He finds his faithful fences torn,   15
    He finds his laboured crops a prey;
He sees his flock no more in circles feed,
   Haply beneath your ravage bleed,
And with no random curses loads the deed.

Nor yet, ye Swains! conclude   20
   That Nature smiles for you alone;
Your bounded souls and your conceptions crude,
   The proud, the selfish boast disown:
    Yours be the produce of the soil;
    O may it still reward your toil!   25
   Nor ever the defenceless train
Of clinging infants ask support in vain!

But though the various harvest gild your plains,
   Does the mere landscape feast your eye?
   Or the warm hope of distant gains   30
   Far other cause of glee supply?
   Is not the red-streak's[2] future juice
   The source of your delight profound,
Where Ariconium[3] pours her gems profuse,
   Purpling a whole horizon round?   35
A thirst ye praise the limpid stream, 'tis true;
   But though the pebbled shores among
   It mimic no unpleasing song,
The limpid fountain murmurs not for you.

Unpleased ye see the thickets bloom,   40
Unpleased the spring her flowery robe resume;
   Unmoved the mountain's airy pile,
   The dappled mead without a smile
    O let a rural conscious Muse,
   For well she knows, your froward sense accuse: 45
   Forth to the solemn oak you bring the square,

---

[1] Landowners.
[2] The apple.
[3] Region known for vineyards.

And span the massy trunk, before you cry, 'Tis fair.

    Nor yet, ye Learned! nor yet, ye Courtly Train!
        If haply from your haunts ye stray
            To waste with us a summer's day,   50
        Exclude the taste of every swain,
        Nor our untutored sense disdain:
'Tis nature only gives exclusive right
        To relish her supreme delight;
        She, where she pleases, kind or coy,   55
Who furnishes the scene, and forms us to enjoy.

    Then hither bring the fair ingenuous mind,
        By her auspicious aid refined.
    Lo! not an hedgerow hawthorn blows,
        Or humble harebell paints the plain,   60
    Or valley winds, or fountain flows,
        Or purple heath is tinged in vain:
For such the rivers dash the foaming tides,
        The mountain swells, the dale subsides:
Even thriftless furze detains their wandering sight,   65
And the rough barren rock grows pregnant with delight.

    With what suspicious fearful care
        The sordid wretch secures his claim,
    If haply some luxurious heir
Should alienate the fields that wear his name!   70
    What scruples lest some future birth
        Should litigate a span of earth!
Bonds, contracts, feoffments, names unmeet for prose,
The towering Muse endures not to disclose;
        Alas! her unreversed decree,   75
        More comprehensive and more free,
Her lavish charter, taste, appropriates all we see.

    Let gondolas their painted flags unfold.
        And be the solemn day enrolled,
    When, to confirm his lofty plea,   80
        In nuptial sort, with bridal gold,
    The grave Venetian weds the sea;
Each laughing Muse derides the vow;
        Even Adria scorns the mock embrace,
To some lone hermit on the mountain's brow,   85
    Allotted, from his natal hour,
    With all her myrtle shores in dower.
    His breast, to admiration prone,
        Enjoys the smile upon her face,

Enjoys triumphant every grace,   90
  And finds her more his own.

Fatigued with Form's oppressive laws,
  When Somerset avoids the great,
When, cloyed with merited applause,
  She seeks the rural calm retreat,   95
Does she not praise each mossy cell,
And feel the truth my numbers tell?
When deafened by the loud acclaim
  Which genius graced with rank obtains,
Could she not more delighted hear   100
Yon throstle[4] chant the rising year?
Could she not spurn the wreaths of fame,
  To crop the primrose of the plains?
Does she not sweets in each fair valley find,
Lost to the sons of power, unknown to half mankind!   105
  Ah! can she covet there to see
  The splendid slaves, the reptile race,
    That oil the tongue, and bow the knee,
  That slight her merit, but adore her place?
    Far happier, if aright I deem,   110
  When from gay throngs, and gilded spires,
    To where the lonely halcyons[5] play,
  Her philosophic step retires:
  While studious of the moral theme,
  She, to some smooth sequestered stream   115
    Likens the swains' inglorious day;
Pleased from the flowery margin to survey,
How cool, serene, and clear, the current glides away.

O blind to truth, to virtue blind,
  Who slight the sweetly pensive mind!   120
On whose fair birth the Graces mild,
  And every Muse prophetic smiled.
  Not that the poet's boasted fire
Should Fame's wide-echoing trumpet swell;
  Or, on the music of his lyre   125
Each future age with rapture dwell;
The vaunted sweets of praise remove,
  Yet shall such bosoms claim a part
  In all that glads the human heart;
Yet these the spirits formed to judge and prove   130
All Nature's charms immense, and heaven's unbounded love.

[4] A song thrush.
[5] Kingfishers.

And, oh! the transport most allied to song,
    In some fair villa's peaceful bound,
To catch soft hints from Nature's tongue,
    And bid Arcadia bloom around;   135
Whether we fringe the sloping hill,
    Or smoothe below the verdant mead;
Whether we break the falling rill,
    Or through meandering mazes lead;
Or in the horrid brambles' room   140
Bid careless groups of roses bloom;
Or let some sheltered lake serene
Reflect flowers, woods, and spires, and brighten all the scene.

O sweet disposal of the rural hour!
    O beauties never known to cloy!   145
While Worth and Genius haunt the favoured bower,
    And every gentle breast partakes the joy;
While Charity at eve surveys the swain,
    Enabled by these toils to cheer
    A train of helpless infants dear,   150
    Speed whistling home across the plain;
See vagrant Luxury, her handmaid grown,
    For half her graceless deeds atone,
And hails the bounteous work, and ranks it with her own.

Why brand these pleasures with the name   155
Of soft, unsocial toils, of indolence and shame!
    Search but the garden, or the wood,
    Let yon admired carnation own,
Not all was meant for raiment, or for food,
    Not all for needful use alone;   160
There while the seeds of future blossoms dwell,
'Tis colour'd for the sight, perfumed to please the smell.

Why knows the nightingale to sing?
    Why flows the pine's nectareous juice?
Why shines with paint the linnet's wing?   165
    For sustenance alone? for use?
    For preservation? Every sphere
Shall bid fair Pleasure's rightful claim appear.
And sure there seem, of humankind,
    Some born to shun the solemn strife;   170
Some for amusive tasks designed,
    To soothe the certain ills of life;
Grace its lone vales with many a budding rose,
    New founts of bliss disclose,
Call forth refreshing shades, and decorate repose.   175

From plains and woodlands; from the view
    Of rural Nature's blooming face,
    Smit with the glare of rank and place,
To courts the sons of Fancy flew;
There long had Art ordained a rival seat,   180
    There had she lavished all her care
    To form a scene more dazzling fair,
And called them from their green retreat
    To share her proud control;
    Had given the robe with grace to flow,   185
Had taught exotic gems to glow;
    And emulous of Nature's power,
    Mimicked the plume, the leaf, the flower;
Changed the complexion's native hue,
Molded each rustic limb anew,   190
    And warped the very soul!

Awhile her magic strikes the novel eye,
    Awhile the fairy forms delight;
    And now aloof we seem to fly
On purple pinions through a purer sky,   195
    Where all is wondrous, all is bright:
    Now, landed on some spangled shore,
    Awhile each dazzled maniac roves,
    By sapphire lakes through emerald groves:
Paternal acres please no more: 200
Adieu, the simple, the sincere delight!
    The habitual scene of hill and dale,
    The rural herds, the vernal gale,
    The tangled vetch's purple bloom,
    The fragrance of the bean's perfume,   205
Be theirs alone who cultivate the soil,
And drink the cup of thirst, and eat the bread of toil.

    But soon the pageant fades away!
    'Tis Nature only bears perpetual sway.
    We pierce the counterfeit delight,   210
    Fatigued with splendour's irksome beams.
    Fancy again demands the sight
    Of native groves and wonted streams,
Pants for the scenes that charmed her youthful eyes,
Where Truth maintains her court, and banishes Disguise.   215

    Then hither oft, ye Senators! retire;
    With Nature here high converse hold;
For who like Stamford her delights admire,
    Like Stamford shall with scorn behold

The unequal bribes of pageantry and gold;   220
Beneath the British oak's majestic shade,
   Shall see fair Truth, immortal maid!
   Friendship in artless guise arrayed,
   Honour and moral beauty shine
With more attractive charms, with radiance more divine.   225

   Yes, here alone did highest Heaven ordain
     The lasting magazine of charms,
     Whatever wins, whatever warms,
     Whatever fancy seeks to share,
     The great, the various, and the fair,   230
       For ever should remain!

   Her impulse nothing may restrain —
   Or whence the joy 'mid columns, towers,
     Midst all the city's artful trim,
To rear some breathless vapid flowers   235
     Or shrubs fuliginously[6] grim?
   From rooms of silken foliage vain,
   To trace the dun far distant grove,
   Where, smit with undissembled pain,
   The woodlark mourns her absent love,   240
Borne to the dusty town from native air,
To mimic rural life, and soothe some vapoured fair?

     But how must faithless Art prevail,
   Should all who taste our joy sincere,
   To virtue, truth, or science, dear,   245
     Forego a court's alluring pale,
   For dimpled brook and leafy grove,
For that rich luxury of thought they love!
Ah, no! from these the public sphere requires
     Examples for its giddy bands;   250
   From these impartial Heaven demands
To spread the flame itself inspires;
   To sift Opinion's mingled mass,
Impress a nation's taste, and bid the sterling pass.

     Happy, thrice happy they,   255
   Whose graceful deeds have exemplary shone
   Round the gay precincts of a throne,
     With mild effective beams!
     Who bands of fair ideas bring,
     By solemn grot, or shady spring,   260
       To join their pleasing dreams!

---

[6] Sooty, or like soot; smoky.

Theirs is the rural bliss without alloy;
    They only that deserve, enjoy.
What though nor fabled Dryad haunt their grove,   265
    Nor Naiad[7] near their fountain rove?
Yet all embodied to the mental sight,
    A train of smiling Virtues bright
    Shall there the wise retreat allow,
Shall twine triumphant palms to deck the wanderer's brow.   270

    And though by faithless friends alarmed,
Art have with Nature waged presumptuous war,
    By Seymour's winning influence charmed,
    In whom their gifts united shine,
    No longer shall their councils jar.   275
'Tis hers to mediate the peace;
    Near Percy-lodge, with awe-struck mien,
    The rebel seeks her lawful queen,
And havoc and contention cease.
    I see the rival powers combine,   280
    And aid each other's fair design:
Nature exalt the mound where Art shall build;
Art shape the gay alcove, while Nature paints the field.

    Begin, ye songsters of the grove!
O warble forth your noblest lay: 285
    Where Somerset vouchsafes to rove,
Ye leverets! freely sport and play.
    —Peace to the strepent horn!
Let no harsh dissonance disturb the Morn;
    No sounds inelegant and rude   290
    Her sacred solitudes profane!
    Unless her candour not exclude
    The lowly shepherd's votive strain,
Who tunes his reed amidst his rural cheer,
Fearful, yet not averse, that Somerset should hear.   300

[7] A dryad is a tree nymph; a naiad a water nymph.

Unconnected Thoughts on Gardening

Gardening may be divided into three species—kitchen gardening—parterre gardening—and landskip, or picturesque gardening: which latter is the subject intended in the following pages—It consists in pleasing the imagination by scenes of grandeur, beauty, or variety. Convenience merely has no share here, any farther than as it pleases the imagination.

Perhaps the division of the pleasures of imagination, according as they are struck by the great, the various, and the beautiful, may be accurate enough, for my present purpose: why each of them affects us with pleasure may be traced in other authors. See Burke, Hutchinson, Gerard, the theory of agreeable sensations, &c.

There seems however to be some objects, which afford a pleasure not reducible to either of the foregoing heads. A ruin, for instance, may be neither new to us, nor majestic, nor beautiful, yet afford that pleasing melancholy which proceeds from a reflexion on decayed magnificence. For this reason, an able gardener should avail himself of objects, perhaps, not very striking; if they serve to connect ideas, that convey reflexions of the pleasing kind.

Objects should indeed be less calculated to strike the immediate eye, than the judgment or well-formed imagination; as in painting.

It is no objection to the pleasure of novelty, that it makes an ugly object more disagreeable. It is enough that it produces a superiority betwixt things in other respects equal. It seems, on some occasions, to go even further. Are there not broken rocks and rugged grounds, to which we can hardly attribute either beauty or grandeur; and yet when introduced near an extent of lawn, impart a pleasure equal to more shapely scenes? Thus a series of lawn, though ever so beautiful, may satiate and cloy, unless the eye passes to them from wilder scenes; and then they acquire the grace of novelty.

Variety appears to me to derive good part of its effect from novelty; as the eye, passing from one form or color, to a form or color of a different kind, finds a degree of novelty in its present object, which affords immediate satisfaction.

Variety however, in some instances, may be carried to such excess as to lose its whole effect. I have observed ceilings so crammed with stucco-ornaments; that, although of the most different kinds, they have produced an uniformity. A sufficient quantity of undecorated space is necessary to exhibit such decorations to advantage.

Ground should first be considered with an eye to its peculiar character: whether it be the grand, the savage, the sprightly, the melancholy, the horrid, or the beautiful. As one or other of these characters prevail, one may somewhat strengthen its effect, by allowing every part some denomination, and then supporting its title by suitable appendages—For instance, The lover's walk may have assignation seats, with proper mottoes—Urns to faithful lovers—Trophies, garlands, &c. by means of art.

What an advantage must some Italian seats derive from the circumstance of being situate on ground mentioned in the classics? And, even in England, wherever a park or garden happens to have been the scene of any event in history, one would surely avail one's self of that circumstance, to make it more interesting to the imagination. Mottoes should allude to it, columns, &c. record it; verses moralize upon it; and curiosity receive its share of pleasure.

In designing a house and gardens, it is happy when there is an opportunity of maintaining a subordination of parts; the house so luckily placed as to exhibit a view of the whole design. I have sometimes thought that there was room for it to resemble an epic or dramatic poem. It is rather to be wished than required, that the more striking scenes may succeed those which are less so.

Taste depends much upon temper. Some prefer Tibullus to Virgil, and Virgil to Homer——Hagley to Persfield, and Persfield to the Welsh mountains. This occasions the different preferences that are given to situations—A garden strikes us most, where the grand and the pleasing succeed, not intermingle with, each other.

I believe, however, the sublime has generally a deeper effect than the merely beautiful.

I use the words landskip and prospect, the former as expressive of home scenes, the latter of distant images. Prospects should take in the blue distant hills; but never so remotely, that they be not distinguishable from clouds. Yet this mere extent is what the vulgar value.

Landskip should contain variety enough to form a picture upon canvas; and this is no bad test, as I think the landskip painter is the gardener's best designer. The eye requires a sort of balance here; but not so as to encroach upon probable nature. A wood, or hill, may balance a house or obelisk; for exactness would be displeasing. We form our notions from what we have seen; and though, could we comprehend the universe, we might perhaps find it uniformly regular; yet the portions that we see of it, habituate our fancy to the contrary.

The eye should always look rather down upon water: Customary nature makes this requisite. I know nothing more sensibly displeasing than Mr. T——'s flat ground betwixt his terrace and his water.

It is not easy to account for the fondness of former times for straight-lined avenues to their houses; straight-lined walks through their woods; and, in short, every kind of straight-line; where the foot is to travel over, what the eye has done before. This circumstance, is one objection. Another, somewhat of the same kind, is the repetition of the same object, tree after tree, for a length of way together. A third is, that this identity is purchased by the loss of that variety, which the natural country supplies everywhere, in a greater or less degree. To stand still and survey such avenues, may afford some slender satisfaction, through the change derived from perspective; but to move on continually and find no change of scene in the least attendant on our change of place, must give actual pain to a person of taste. For such an one to be condemned to pass along the famous vista from Moscow to Petersburg, or that other from Agra to Lahor in India, must be as disagreeable a sentence, as to be condemned to labour at the galleys. I conceived some idea of the sensation he must feel, from walking but a few minutes, immured, betwixt Lord D——'s high-shorn yew-hedges; which run exactly parallel, at the distance of about ten feet; and are contrived perfectly to exclude all kind of objects whatsoever.

When a building, or other objects, has been once viewed from its proper point, the foot should never travel to it by the same path, which the eye has travelled over before. Lose the object, and draw nigh, obliquely.

The side trees in vistas should be so circumstanced as to afford a probability that they grew by nature.

Ruinated structures appear to derive their power of pleasing, from the irregularity of surface, which is *variety*; and the latitude they afford the imagination, to conceive an enlargement of their dimensions, or to recollect any events or circumstances appertaining to their pristine grandeur, so far as concerns grandeur and solemnity. The breaks in them should be as bold and abrupt as possible.—If mere beauty be aimed at (which however is not their chief excellence), the waving line, with more easy transitions, will become of greater importance—Events relating to them may be simulated by numberless little artifices; but it is ever to be remembered, that high hills and sudden descents are most suitable to castles; and fertile vales, near wood and water, most imitative of the usual situation for abbeys and religious houses; large oaks, in particular, are essential to these latter;

> *Whose branching arms, and reverend height,*
> *Admit a dim religious light.*

A cottage is a pleasing object, partly on account of the variety it may introduce; on account of the tranquillity that seems to reign there; and perhaps (I am somewhat afraid) on account of the pride of human nature:

> *Longi alterius spectare laborem.*[1]

In a scene presented to the eye, objects should never lie so much to the right or left, as to give it any uneasiness in the examination. Sometimes, however, it may be better to admit valuable objects even with this disadvantage. They should else never be seen beyond a certain angle. The eye must be easy, before it can be pleased.

No mere slope from one side to the other can be agreeable ground: The eye requires a balance—i.e., a degree of uniformity: but this may be otherwise effected and the rule should be understood with some limitation:

> *—Each alley has its brother,*
> *And half the plat-form just reflects the other.*

---

[1] It is characteristic of someone who is at a distance to watch the work of another (Latin).

Let us examine what may be said in favour of that regularity which Mr. Pope exposes. Might he not seemingly as well object to the disposition of an human face, because it has an eye or cheek, that is the very picture of its companion? Or does not providence, who has observed this regularity in the external structure of our bodies and disregarded it within, seem to consider it as a beauty? The arms, the limbs, and the several parts of them correspond, but it is not the same case with the thorax and the abdomen. I believe one is generally solicitous for a kind of balance in a landskip; and, if I am not mistaken, the painters generally furnish one: a building for instance on one side, contrasted by a group of trees, a large oak, or a rising hill on the other. Whence then does this taste proceed, but from the love we bear to regularity in perfection? After all, in regard to gardens, the shape of ground, the disposition of trees, and the figure of water, must be sacred to nature; and no forms must be allowed that make a discovery of art.

All trees have a character analogous to that of men: Oaks are in all respects the perfect image of the manly character: In former times I should have said, and in present times I think I am authorized to say, the British one. As a brave man is not suddenly either elated by prosperity or depressed by adversity, so the oak displays not its verdure on the sun's first approach; nor drops it, on his first departure. Add to this its majestic appearance, the rough grandeur of its bark, and the wide protection of its branches.

A large, branching, aged oak, is perhaps the most venerable of all inanimate objects.

Urns are more solemn, if large and plain; more beautiful, if less and ornamented. Solemnity is perhaps their point, and the situation of them should still cooperate with it.

By the way, I wonder that lead statues are not more in vogue in our modern gardens. Though they may not express the finer lines of an human body, yet they seem perfectly well calculated, on account of their duration, to embellish landskips, were they some degrees inferior to what we generally behold. A statue in a room challenges examination, and is to be examined critically as a statue. A statue in a garden is to be considered as one part of a scene or landskip; the minuter touches are no more essential to it, than a good landskip painter would esteem them were he to represent a statue in his picture.

Apparent art, in its proper province, is almost as important as apparent nature. They contrast agreeably; but their provinces ever should be kept distinct.

Some artificial beauties are so dexterously managed that one cannot but conceive them natural; some natural ones so extremely fortunate that one is ready to swear they are artificial.

Concerning scenes, the more uncommon they appear, the better, provided they form a picture, and include nothing that pretends to be of nature's production, and is not. The shape of ground, the site of trees, and the fall of water, nature's province. Whatever thwarts her is treason.

On the other hand, buildings and the works of art need have no other reference to nature than that they afford the ευσεμνον[2] with which the human mind is delighted.

Art should never be allowed to set a foot in the province of nature, otherwise than clandestinely and by night. Whenever she is allowed to appear here, and men begin to compromise the difference—Night, gothicism, confusion and absolute chaos, are come again.

To see one's urns, obelisks, and waterfalls laid open; the nakedness of our beloved mistresses, the Naiads and the Dryads, exposed by that ruffian Winter to universal observation; is a severity scarcely to be supported by the help of blazing hearths, cheerful companions, and a bottle of the most grateful burgundy.

The works of a person that builds, begin immediately to decay; while those of him who plants begin directly to improve. In this, planting promises a more lasting pleasure, than building; which, were it to remain in equal perfection, would at best begin to moulder and want repairs in imagination. Now trees have a circumstance that suits our taste, and that is annual variety. It is inconvenient indeed, if they cause our love of life to take root and flourish with them; whereas the very sameness of our structures will, without the help of dilapidation, serve to wean us from our attachment to them.

It is a custom in some countries to condemn the characters of those (after death) that have neither planted a tree, nor begot a child.

The taste of the citizen and of the mere peasant are in all respects the same. The former gilds his balls; paints his stonework and statues white; plants his trees in lines or circles; cuts his yew trees four-square or conic; or gives them, what he can, of the resemblance of birds, or bears, or men; squirts up his rivulets in jetteaus; in short, admires no part of nature, but her ductility; exhibits every thing that is glaring, that implies expence, or that effects a surprize because it is unnatural. The peasant is his admirer.

It is always to be remembered in gardening that sublimity or magnificence, and beauty or variety, are very different things. Every scene we see in nature is either tame and insipid; or compounded of those. It often happens that the same ground may receive from art, either certain degrees of sublimity and magnificence, or certain degrees of variety and beauty; or a mixture of each kind. In this case it remains to be considered in which light they can be rendered most remarkable, whether as objects of beauty or magnificence. Even the temper of the

---

[2] Greek for majesty or nobility.

proprietor should not perhaps be wholly disregarded: for certain complexions of soul will prefer an orange tree or a myrtle, to an oak or cedar. However, this should not induce a gardener to parcel out a lawn into knots of shrubbery; or invest a mountain with a garb of roses. This would be like dressing a giant in a sarcenet gown, or a Saracen's head in a Brussels nightcap. Indeed, the small and circular clumps of firs, which I see planted upon some fine large swells, put me often in mind of a coronet placed on an elephant or camel's back. I say, a gardener should not do this, any more than a poet should attempt to write of the king of Prussia in the style of Philips. On the other side, what would become of Lesbia's sparrow, should it be treated in the same language with the anger of Achilles?

Gardeners may be divided into three sorts, the landskip gardener, the parterre gardener, and the kitchen gardener, agreeably to our first division of gardens.

I have used the word landskip gardeners; because, in pursuance of our present taste in gardening, every good painter of landskip appears to me the most proper designer. The misfortune of it is that these painters are apt to regard the execution of their work, much more than the choice of subject.

The art of distancing and approximating, comes truly within their sphere: the former by the gradual diminution of distinctness, and of size; the latter by the reverse. A straight-lined avenue that is widened in front, and planted there with ewe trees, then firs, then with trees more and more shady, till they end in the almond willow, or silver osier; will produce a very remarkable deception of the former kind; which deception will be increased, if the nearer dark trees are proportionable and truly larger than those at the end of the avenue that are more shady.

To distance a building, plant as near as you can to it, two or three circles of different-coloured greens — Evergreens are best for all such purposes — Suppose the outer one of holly, and the next of laurel, &c. The consequence will be that the imagination immediately allows a space betwixt these circles, and another betwixt the house and them; and as the imagined space is indeterminate, if your building be dim-coloured, it will not appear inconsiderable. The imagination is a greater magnifier than a microscopic glass. And on this head, I have known some instances, where, by showing intermediate ground, the distance has appeared less, than while an hedge or grove concealed it.

Hedges, appearing as such, are universally bad. They discover art in nature's province.

Trees in hedges partake of their artificiality, and become a part of them. There is no more sudden and obvious improvement, than an hedge removed, and the trees remaining; yet not in such manner as to mark out the former hedge.

Water should ever appear, as an irregular lake, or winding stream.

Islands give beauty, if the water be adequate; but lessen grandeur through variety.

It was the wise remark of some sagacious observer, that familiarity is for the most part productive of contempt. Graceless offspring of so amiable a parent! Unfortunate beings that we are, whose enjoyments must be either checked, or prove destructive of themselves. Our passions are permitted to sip a little pleasure; but are extinguished by indulgence, like a lamp overwhelmed with oil. Hence we neglect the beauty with which we have been intimate; nor would any addition it could receive, prove an equivalent for the advantage it derived from the first impression. Thus, negligent of graces that have the merit of reality, we too often prefer imaginary ones that have only the charm of novelty: And hence we may account, in general, for the preference of art to nature, in our old-fashioned gardens.

Art, indeed, is often requisite to collect and epitomize the beauties of nature; but should never be suffered to set her mark upon them: I mean, in regard to those articles that are of nature's province; the shaping of ground, the planting of trees, and the disposition of lakes and rivulets. Many more particulars will soon occur, which, however, she is allowed to regulate, somewhat clandestinely, upon the following account—Man is not capable of comprehending the universe at one survey. Had he faculties equal to this, he might well be censured for any minute regulations of his own. It were the same, as if, in his present situation, he strove to find amusement in contriving the fabric of an ant's nest, or the partitions of a beehive. But we are placed in the corner of a sphere; endued neither with organs, nor allowed a station, proper to give us an universal view; or to exhibit to us the variety, the orderly proportions, and dispositions of the system. We perceive many breaks and blemishes, several neglected and unvariegated places in the part; which, in the whole, would appear either imperceptible, or beautiful. And we might as rationally expect a snail to be satisfied with the beauty of our parterres, slopes, and terraces—or an ant to prefer our buildings to her own orderly range of granaries, as that man should be satisfied, without a single thought that he can improve the spot that falls to his share. But, though art be necessary for collecting nature's beauties, by what reason is she authorized to thwart and to oppose her? Why fantastically endeavor to humanize those vegetables, of which nature, discreet nature, thought it proper to make trees? Why endow the vegetable bird with wings, which nature has made momentarily dependent upon the soil? Here art seems very affectedly to make a display of that industry, which it is her glory to conceal. The stone which represents an asterisk, is valued only on account of its natural production: Nor do we view with pleasure the laboured carvings and futile diligence of Gothic artists. We view with much more satisfaction some plain Grecian fabric, where art, indeed, has been equally, but less visibly, industrious. It is thus we, indeed, admire the shining texture of the silkworm; but we loath the puny author, when she thinks proper to emerge; and to disgust us with the appearance of so vile a grub.

But this is merely true in regard to the particulars of nature's province; wherein art can only appear as the most abject vassal, and had, therefore, better not appear at all. The case is different where she has the direction of buildings, useful or ornamental; or perhaps, claims as much honor from temples, as the deities to whom they are inscribed. Here then it is her interest to be seen as much as possible: And, though nature appear doubly beautiful by the contrast her structures furnish, it is not easy for her to confer a benefit which nature, on her side, will not repay.

A rural scene to me is never perfect without the addition of some kind of building: Indeed I have known a scar of rock-work, in great measure, supply the deficiency.

In gardening, it is no small point to enforce either grandeur or beauty by surprise; for instance, by abrupt transition from their contraries—but to lay a stress upon surprise only; for example, on the surprise occasioned by an aha! without including any nobler purpose; is a symptom of bad taste, and a violent fondness for mere *concetto*.[3]

Grandeur and beauty are so very opposite, that you often diminish the one as you increase the other. Variety is most akin to the latter, simplicity to the former.

Suppose a large hill varied, by art, with large patches of different-colored clumps, scars of rock, chalk quarries, villages, or farm-houses; you will have, perhaps, a more beautiful scene, but much less grand than it was before.

In many instances, it is most eligible to compound your scene of beauty and grandeur—Suppose a magnificent swell arising out of a well-variegated valley; it would be disadvantageous to increase its beauty, by means destructive to its magnificence.

There may possibly, but there seldom happens to be any occasion to fill up valleys, with trees or otherwise. It is for the most part the gardener's business to remove trees, or aught that fills up the low ground; and to give, as far as nature allows, an artificial eminence to the high.

The hedge-row apple trees in Herefordshire afford a most beautiful scenery, at the time they are in blossom: But the prospect would be really grander, did it consist of simple foliage. For the same reason, a large oak (or beech) in autumn, is a grander object than the same in spring. The sprightly green is then obfuscated.

Smoothness and easy transitions are no small ingredient in the beautiful; abrupt and rectangular breaks have more of the nature of the sublime. Thus a tapering spire is, perhaps, a more beautiful object than a tower, which is grander.

Many of the different opinions relating to the preference to be given to seats, villas, &c. are owing to want of distinction betwixt the beautiful and the magnifi-

---

[3] A witty idea or expression (Italian).

cent. Both the former and the latter please; but there are imaginations particularly adapted to the one, and to the other.

Mr. Addison thought an open uninclosed champaign country, formed the best landskip. Somewhat here is to be considered. Large, unvariegated, simple objects have the best pretensions to sublimity; a large mountain, whose sides are unvaried with objects, is grander than one with infinite variety: But then its beauty is proportionably less.

However, I think a plain space near the eye gives it a kind of liberty it loves: And then the picture, whether you choose the grand or beautiful, should be held up at its proper distance. Variety is the principal ingredient in beauty; and simplicity is essential to grandeur.

Offensive objects, at a proper distance, acquire even a degree of beauty: For instance, stubble fallow ground———

✒ Richard Jago (1715–1781)

A graduate of Oxford, Richard Jago is remembered primarily for his lengthy topographical poem Edge-hill *(1767). Subtitled "The Rural Prospect Delineated and Moralized," the four books of this long poem represent the Warwickshire landscape as seen from the prospect of the hilltop at various times of day. The site of the first battle of the English Civil War, Edge Hill and the surrounding countryside provide the poet with ample opportunity to pursue the established conventions of locodescriptive verse. The view of the landscape invites the poem's speaker to make an assortment of mythological, historical, political, nationalistic, and moral associations, much in the style of Denham ("Cooper's Hill") and Dyer ("Grongar Hill") before him. Jago also uses his poem to pay compliments to numerous aristocrats and their estates, which he can glimpse from his viewpoint. The eighteenth century tradition of the prospect poem might be said to peak with Jago. Later poets searched for more sublime vistas.*

From Edge-hill

From Book 1*

Humbly Inscribed to the Right Honourable Lord Willoughby de Broke

Britannia's rural Charms, and tranquil Scenes,
Far from the circling Ocean, where her Fleets,

---

* For the reader's convenience, we have set verse line numbers 1–145 for the Book 1 selection and 1–89 for the Book 4 selection that follows. The specific lines excerpted are, from Book 1, lines 1–69 and 414–489 and from Book 4, lines 170–258. —Editors' note.

Like Guardian Spirits, which round *Paradise*
Performed their nightly Watch, majestic ride,
I sing; from that famed Hill, whose lofty Brow   5
Salutes thy Province's contiguous Bounds,
Fair Seat of Learning![1] May the social Claim
Invite thy Muses from their cloistered Shades,
To rove with me along the sunny Ridge,
And, with their Graces, harmonize the Strain,   10
In Numbers not unpleasing to thy Ear,
O Willoughby! accustomed to their Notes!

 Nor shall they, for a Time, regret the Loss
Of their loved Isis, and their Cherwel's[2] Banks,
While, from the beauteous Terrace, they explore   15
Scenes not less fair than Tempe's,[3] or their own;
Where Avon's[4] Silver Stream delighted strays,
With crooked Path, enlarging as it flows,
Nor hastes to join Sabrina's prouder Wave.
Like a tall Rampart! here the Mountain rears   20
Its verdant Edge; and, if thy tuneful Maids
Their Presence deign, shall with Parnassus[5] vie.
Level, and smooth the Track, that leads to thee!
Its adverse Side a Precipice presents
Abrupt, and steep! Thanks, Miller![6] to thy Paths,   25
That ease our winding Steps! Thanks to the Rill,
The Banks, the Trees, the Shrubs, th' enraptured Sense
Regaling, or with Fragrance, Shape, or Sound,
And stilling every Tumult in the Breast!
And oft the stately Towers, that overtop   30
The rising Wood, and oft the broken Arch,
Or mouldering Wall, well taught to counterfeit
The Waste of Time, to solemn Thought excite,
And crown with graceful Pomp the shaggy Hill.

 So Virtue paints the steep Ascent to Fame: 35
So her aerial Residence displays.

 Still let thy Friendship, which prepared the Way,
Attend, and guide me, as my ravished Sight
O'er the bleak Hill, or sheltered Valley roves.
Teach me with just Observance to remark   40

---

[1] University of Oxford.

[2] Isis is the poetic name for the river Thames; Cherwel is another waterway.

[3] A valley in Greece, in ancient times sacred to Apollo.

[4] Avon is the name for several rivers in England; Sabrina is the poetic name for the river Severn.

[5] A mountain in Greece, in ancient times sacred to Apollo, god of poetry, and to the Muses.

[6] Sanderson Miller, Esquire of Radway [Jago's note].

Their various Charms, their storied Fame record,
And to the visual join the mental Search.

   The Summit's gained! and, from its airy Height,
The late-trod Plain looks like an inland Sea,
Viewed from some Promontory's hoary Head,   45
With distant Shores environed; not with Face
Glassy, and uniform, but when its Waves
Are gently ruffled by the Southern Gale,
And the tall Masts like waving Forests show.

   Such is the Scene! that, from the terraced Hill,   50
Whose Sides the *Dryads*, and the *Wood Nymphs* dress
With rich Embroidery, salutes the Eye,
Ample, and various; Intermixture sweet
Of Lawns, and Groves, of open, and retired.
Vales, Farms, Towns, Villas, Castles, distant Spires,   55
And Hills, on Hills, with ambient Clouds enrobed,
In long Succession court the lab'ring Sight,
Lost in the bright Confusion. Thus the Youth,
Escaped from toilsome Drudgery of Words,
Views the fair Fields of Science wide displayed: 60
Thus every Muse his roving Passion claims.
Awhile, astonished at the radiant Forms,
He stands, then quick to each with Transport turns,
O'erpowered, bewildered in the pleasing Toil:
Till some sage Mentor, whose experienced Feet   65
Have trod the mazy Path, directs his Way,
And leads him raptured to their bright Abodes.
Come then, my Friend! the wand'ring Muse recall,
And, with thy Counsel, regulate her Flight.

          .   .   .

   Thus, from the rural Landscape, learn to know   70
The various Characters of Time and Place.
To hail, from open Scenes, and cultured Fields,
Fair Liberty, and Freedom's generous Reign,
With guardian Laws, and polished Arts adorned.
While the Portcullis huge, or moated Fence   75
The sad Reverse of savage Times betray—
Distrust, Barbarity, and *Gothic* Rule.

   Would ye, with faultless Judgment, learn to plan
The rural Seat? To copy, as ye rove,
The well-formed Picture, and correct Design?   80
First shun the false Extremes of high, and low,
With watery Vapours this your fretted Walls

Will soon deface; and that, with rough Assault,
And frequent Tempest shake your tottering Roof.
Me most the gentle Eminence delights   85
Of healthy Champaign, to the sunny South
Fair-opening, and with Woods, and circling Hills,
Nor too remote, nor, with too close Embrace,
Stopping the buxom Air, behind enclosed.
But if your Lot hath fallen in Fields less fair,   90
Consult their Genius, and, with due Regard
To Nature's clear Directions, shape your Plan.
The Site too lofty shelter, and the low
With sunny Lawns, and open Areas cheer.
The marish[7] drain, and, with capacious Urns,   95
And well-conducted Streams refresh the dry.
So shall your Lawns with healthful Verdure smile,
While others, sickening at the sultry Blaze,
A russet Wild display, or the rank Blade,
And matted Tufts the careless Owner shame.   100
Seek not, with fruitless Cost, the level Plain
To raise aloft, nor sink the rising Hill.
Each has its Charms though different, each in Kind
Improve, not alter. Art with Art conceal.
Let no straight terraced Lines your Slopes deform.   105
No barbarous Walls restrain the bounded Sight.
With better Skill your chaste Designs display;
And to the distant Fields the closer Scene
Connect. The spacious Lawn with scattered Trees
Irregular, in beauteous Negligence,   110
Clothe bountiful. Your unimprisoned Eye,
With pleasing Freedom, through the lofty Maze
Shall rove, and find no dull Satiety.
The winding Stream with stiffened Line avoid
To torture, nor prefer the long Canal,   115
Or laboured Fount to Nature's easy Flow,
And artless Fall. Your gravelly winding Paths
Now to the freshening Breeze, or sunny Gleam
Directed, now with high embowering Trees,
Or fragrant Shrubs concealed, with frequent Seat,   120
And rural Structure deck. Their pleasing Form
To Fancy's Eye suggests Inhabitants
Of more than mortal Make, and their cool Shade,
And friendly Shelter to Refreshment sweet,
And wholesome Meditation shall invite.   125
        To every Structure give its proper Site.

---

[7] Low, wet ground (poetic).

Nor, on the dreary Heath, the gay Alcove,
Nor the lone Hermit's Cell, or mournful Urn
Build on the sprightly Lawn. The grassy Slope
And sheltered Border for the cool *Arcade*, 130
Or *Tuscan* Porch reserve. To the chaste Dome,
And fair Rotunda give the swelling Mount
Of freshest Green. If to the *Gothic* Scene
Your Taste incline, in the well-watered Vale,
With lofty Pines embrowned, the mimic Fane, 135
And mouldering Abbey's fretted Windows place.
The craggy Rock, or precipitious Hill,
Shall well become the Castle's massy Walls.
In royal Villas the *Palladian*[8] Arch,
And *Grecian* Portico, with Dignity, 140
Their Pride display: Ill suits their lofty Rank
The simpler Scene. If chance Historic Deeds
Your Fields distinguish, count them doubly fair,
And studious aid, with monumental Stone,
And faithful Comment, Fancy's fond Review. 145

.　　.　　.

From Book 4

.　　.　　.

Thrice happy Land! whom Nature's partial Smile
Hath robed profusely gay! thy Champaigns wide.
With plenteous Harvests wave; thy Pastures swarm
With horned Tribes, or the Sheep's gentle Race;
Whose teeming Laps with wholesome Food supply 5
The throngèd Shambles; while their woolly Vests,
Or toughened Hides, innumerous Hands employ,
And, on their Labours, build a Nation's Weal.
Nor destitute thy Woodland Scenes of Wealth,
Or Sylvan Beauty! there the Lordly Swain 10
His scantier Field improves; o'er his own Realms
Supreme, at Will to sow his well-fenced Glebe,
With Grain successive; or with juicy Herbs,
To swell his milky Kine; or feed, at Ease,
His Flock in Pastures warm. His blazing Hearth, 15
With copious Fuel heaped, defies the Cold;
And Housewife-Arts or tease the tangled Wool,
Or, from the Distaff's Hoard, the ductile Thread,
With sportive Hand entice; while to the Wheel

[8] In the style of the Italian architect, Andrea Palladio (1518–1580).

The sprightly Carol joined, or plaintive Song   20
Diffuse, and artless sooths th' untutored Ear
With Heartfelt Strains, and the slow Task beguiles.
      Nor hath the Sun, with less propitious Ray,
Shone on the Masters of the various Scene.
Witness the splendid Train! illustrious Names,   25
That claim Precedence on the Lists of Fame,
Nor fear oblivious Time! Enraptured Bards!
Or dauntless Chiefs! or Politicians wife,
Ancient or Modern! gracing, with their Fame,
Their native Soil, and my aspiring Verse.   30
My Verse! which, guiltless or of Flattery,
Or Censure, boasts that to their green Abodes
It led the youthful Train, unequal far,
Not unattentive to their high Renown.

      Say, now my dear Companions! for enough   35
Hath surely to descriptive Song been given;
Say, shall we, ere we part, with moral Eye,
The Scene review, and close the long Survey
With Observation grave, as sober Eve
Hastes now to wrap in Shades the closing Day?   40
Perhaps the moral Strain delights you not!
Perhaps you blame the Muse's quick Retreat;
Intent to wander still along the Plain,
In Coverts cool, lulled by the murmuring Stream,
And whispering Breeze; while playful Fancy skims,   45
With careless Wing, the Surfaces of Things:
For deep Research too indolent, too light
For grave Reflection. So the *Siren* Queen
Tempted Alcides, on a flowery Plain,
With amourous Blandishment, and urged to waste   50
His Prime inglorious: But fair Virtue's Form
Rescued the yielding Youth, and fired his Breast
To manly Toil, and Glory's well-earned Prize.
O! in that dang'rous Season, O! beware
Of Sloth, envenomed Weed! and plant betimes   55
The Seeds of Virtue in the tender Soil.
Rear the just Sentiment, the wise Resolve
Invigourate, and their infant Blossoms guard:
Then, like a Garden's cultivated Trees,
Their Shoots shall flourish, and the musing Mind   60
Shall banquet on their Fruits, when Youth is o'er;
When, to the smiling Day, and mirthful Scene
Night's solemn Gloom, cold Winter's chilling Blasts,
And Pain, and Sickness, and old Age succeed.

Nor slight your faithful Guide, my gentle Train!   65
But, with a curious Eye, expatiate free
O'er Nature's moral Plan. Though dark the Theme,
Though formidable to the sensual Mind;
Yet shall the Muse, with no fictitious Aid,
Inspired, still guide you with her friendly Voice,   70
And to each seeming Ill some greater Good
Oppose, and calm your lab'ring Thoughts to rest.

    Nature herself bids us be serious,
Bids us be wise; and all her Works rebuke
The ever-thoughtless, ever-tittering Tribe.   75
What, though her lovely Hills, and Valleys smile
Today, in Beauty dressed? yet, ere three Moons
Renew their Orb, and to their Wane decline,
Ere then the beauteous Landscape all will fade;
The genial Airs retire; and shivering Swains   80
Shall, from the whitened Plain, and driving Storm,
Avert the smarting Cheek, and humid Eye.

    So some fair Maid to Time's devouring Rage
Her Bloom resigns, and, with a faded Look,
Disgusts her Paramour; unless thy Charms   85
O Virtue! with more lasting Beauty grace
Her lovelier Mind, and, through declining Age,
Fair Deeds of Piety, and modest Worth,
Still flourish, and endear her still the more.

.   .   .

👁 *Thomas Gray* (*1716–1771*)

Although he only published fourteen poems during his lifetime, Thomas Gray was an immensely popular poet in his day and was even offered the laureateship in 1756 (which he refused). His famous "Elegy written in a Country Church-Yard" (1751) is the most commonly anthologized poem in all of English literature. Educated at Eton and then Cambridge, Gray is remembered primarily as a reclusive academic who spent most of his career pursuing his studies of ancient Norse and Icelandic poetry as well as botany and natural history. He wrote poetry in both Latin and English, and his work is often grouped together with that of Thomson as the "poetry of Sensibility." The term sensibility *here has a variety of implications, but with reference to landscape description, it can be said to mark a transition between the Neoclassical and the Romantic aesthetics of poetry about nature. Neither wholly objective and moralizing nor entirely subjective and emotional, the poetry of Sensibility blends these various perspectives. Gray's "Ode on the Spring" includes classical allusions and reflections on human vanity, yet these are ulti-*

*mately personalized by the poem's conclusion. Although he has a reputation for being a
scholarly poet, some of the playfulness of Gray's personality can be seen in his "Ode on the
Death of a Favourite Cat, Drowned in a Tub of Gold Fishes."*

Ode on the Spring

Lo! where the rosy-bosomed Hours,
Fair Venus'[1] train appear,
Disclose the long-expecting flowers,
And wake the purple year!
The Attic warbler[2] pours her throat,   5
Responsive to the cuckoo's note,
The untaught harmony of spring:
While whispering pleasure as they fly,
Cool Zephyrs[3] through the clear blue sky
Their gathered fragrance fling.   10

Where'er the oak's thick branches stretch
A broader browner shade;
Where'er the rude and moss-grown beech
O'er-canopies the glade,
Beside some water's rushy brink   15
With me the Muse shall sit, and think
(At ease reclined in rustic state)
How vain the ardour of the Crowd,
How low, how little are the Proud,
How indigent the Great!   20

Still is the toiling hand of Care:
The panting herds repose:
Yet hark, how through the peopled air
The busy murmur glows!
The insect youth are on the wing,   25
Eager to taste the honied spring,
And float amid the liquid noon:
Some lightly o'er the current skim,
Some shew their gayly gilded trim
Quick-glancing to the sun.   30

To Contemplation's sober eye
Such is the race of Man:
And they that creep, and they that fly,

[1] The Roman goddess of love, sex, and hence fertility.
[2] The nightingale.
[3] Westerly winds.

Shall end where they began.
Alike the Busy and the Gay   35
But flutter through life's little day,
In fortune's varying colours drest:
Brushed by the hand of rough Mischance,
Or chilled by age, their airy dance
They leave, in dust to rest.   40

Methinks I hear in accents low
The sportive kind reply:
Poor moralist! and what art thou?
A solitary fly!
Thy Joys no glittering female meets,   45
No hive hast thou of hoarded sweets,
No painted plumage to display:
On hasty wings thy youth is flown;
Thy sun is set, thy spring is gone——
We frolic, while 'tis May.   50

Ode on the Death of a Favourite Cat, Drowned in a Tub of Gold Fishes

'Twas on a lofty vase's side,
Where China's gayest art had dyed
   The azure flowers, that blow;
Demurest of the tabby kind,
The pensive Selima reclined,   5
   Gazed on the lake below.

Her conscious tail her joy declared;
The fair round face, the snowy beard,
   The velvet of her paws,
Her coat, that with the tortoise vies,   10
Her ears of jet, and emerald eyes,
   She saw; and purred applause.

Still had she gazed; but 'midst the tide
Two angel forms were seen to glide,
   The Genii of the stream: 15
Their scaly armour's Tyrian hue
Through richest purple to the view
   Betrayed a golden gleam.

The hapless Nymph with wonder saw:
A whisker first and then a claw,   20
   With many an ardent wish,

She stretched in vain to reach the prize.
What female heart can gold despise?
   What Cat's averse to fish?

Presumptuous Maid! with looks intent   25
Again she stretched, again she bent,
   Nor knew the gulf between.
(Malignant Fate sat by, and smiled)
The slippery verge her feet beguiled,
   She tumbled headlong in.   30

Eight times emerging from the flood
She mewed to every watery God,
   Some speedy aid to send.
No Dolphin came, no Nereid[1] stirred:
Nor cruel *Tom*, nor *Susan* heard.   35
   A Favourite has no friend!

From hence, ye Beauties, undeceived,
Know, one false step is ne'er retrieved,
   And be with caution bold.
Not all that tempts your wandering eyes   40
And heedless hearts, is lawful prize;
   Nor all, that glisters, gold.

⮞ *Gilbert White* (*1720–1793*)

Born in the rural parish of Selborne in Hampshire, Gilbert White spent most of his life in his native region. He was educated at Oxford, where he was elected a fellow, was made a deacon, and, within five years, became an ordained priest of the Church of England. White never married. He returned to Selborne, where he became the village curate, a position whose responsibilities left him plenty of free time to wander through the surrounding countryside, making observations of plants and animals, weather, and soil. Throughout his adult life, White collected his observations into a daily journal, and he transcribed the best of these observations into personal letters. Encouraged by his friends to publish a selection of these letters, White took twenty years to compile The Natural History and Antiquities of Selborne *(1789). Written in the form of a series of letters to the eminent zoologists Daines Barrington and Thomas Pennant, this book is a landmark in the development of ecological consciousness. White seeks to encapsulate a complete "parochial history" of the district of Selborne, providing not merely a dry taxonomic description of the local flora and fauna but a detailed account of each species' habitat, distribution, behavior, and seasonal variation or migration. White's penchant for anecdotal presentation, and his frequent use of vernacular or dialect words to supplement the official Latin nomenclature for genus and species, pioneers a new kind of nature writing.*

---

[1] A nymph of the sea.

Throughout his work, White evokes the "economy of nature" on a local scale, meticulously describing the interaction of plant and animal species. Even insects and reptiles, in his view, are essential to the cycling of resources through the food chain; for example, he asserts, "Earthworms, though in appearance a small and despicable link in the chain of Nature, yet, if lost, would make a lamentable chasm." Such attitudes mark an important step toward the idea of a biological community in which all organisms play an essential role. Especially in his later years, White questioned the value of human intervention in the natural world, mourning the loss of favorite trees to the woodcutter's axe and resisting the conversion of "waste" areas to farmland. White's intense curiosity about the habitat and behavior of birds and animals, his anecdotal mode of presentation, and his use of colloquial language would prove influential among later nature writers, including Henry David Thoreau, Charles Darwin, and Virginia Woolf.

From The Natural History and Antiquities of Selborne

Letter 2

In the court of *Norton* farmhouse, a manor farm to the north-west of the village, on the white malms, stood within these twenty years a *broad-leaved elm*, or *wych hazel, Ulmus folio latissimo scabro* of Ray,[1] which, though it had lost a considerable leading bough in the great storm in the year 1703, equal to a moderate tree, yet, when felled, contained eight loads of timber; and, being too bulky for a carriage, was sawn off at seven feet above the butt, where it measured near eight feet in the diameter. This elm I mention to show to what a bulk *planted elms* may attain; as this tree must certainly have been such from its situation.

In the centre of the village, and near the church, is a square piece of ground surrounded by houses, and vulgarly called *The Plestor.* In the midst of this spot stood, in old times, a vast oak, with a short squat body, and huge horizontal arms extending almost to the extremity of the area. This venerable tree, surrounded with stone steps, and seats above them, was the delight of old and young, and a place of much resort in summer evenings; where the former sat in grave debate, while the latter frolicked and danced before them. Long might it have stood, had not the amazing tempest in 1703 overturned it at once, to the infinite regret of the inhabitants, and the vicar, who bestowed several pounds in setting it in its place again: but all his care could not avail; the tree sprouted for a time, then withered and died. This oak I mention to show to what a bulk *planted oaks* also may arrive: and planted this tree must certainly have been, as will appear from what will be said further concerning this area, when we enter on the antiquities of *Selborne.*

On the *Blackmoor* estate there is a small wood called *Losel's,* of a few acres, that was lately furnished with a set of oaks of a peculiar growth and great value; they were tall and taper like firs, but standing near together had very small heads,

[1] John Ray (1627–1705), author of *Historia plantarum* (The Natural History of Plants) (1686–1704). He was the first naturalist to define and use the term *species* in its modern sense.

only a little brush without any large limbs. About twenty years ago the bridge at the *Toy*, near *Hampton Court*, being much decayed, some trees were wanted for the repairs, that were fifty feet long without bough, and would measure twelve inches diameter at the little end. Twenty such trees did a purveyor find in this little wood, with this advantage, that many of them answered the description at sixty feet. These trees were sold for twenty pounds apiece.

In the centre of this grove there stood an oak, which, though shapely and tall on the whole, bulged out into a large excrescence about the middle of the stem. On this a pair of ravens had fixed their residence for such a series of years, that the oak was distinguished by the title of *The Raven-tree*. Many were the attempts of the neighbouring youths to get at this *aerie*: the difficulty whetted their inclinations, and each was ambitious of surmounting the arduous task. But, when they arrived at the swelling, it jutted out so in their way, and was so far beyond their grasp, that the most daring lads were awed, and acknowledged the undertaking to be too hazardous. So the ravens built on, nest upon nest, in perfect security, till the fatal day arrived in which the wood was to be levelled. It was in the month of *February*, when those birds usually sit. The saw was applied to the butt, the wedges were inserted into the opening, the woods echoed to the heavy blows of the beetle or mallet, the tree nodded to its fall; but still the dam sat on. At last, when it gave way, the bird was flung from her nest; and, though her parental affection deserved a better fate, was whipped down by the twigs, which brought her dead to the ground.

Letter 27

Selborne, Feb. 22, 1770.

Dear Sir,

Hedgehogs abound in my gardens and fields. The manner in which they eat their roots of the plantain in my grass walks is very curious: with their upper mandible, which is much longer than their lower, they bore under the plant, and so eat the root off upwards, leaving the tuft of leaves untouched. In this respect they are serviceable, as they destroy a very troublesome weed; but they deface the walks in some measure by digging little round holes. It appears, by the dung that they drop upon the turf, that beetles are no inconsiderable part of their food. In *June* last I procured a litter of four or five young hedgehogs, which appeared to be about five or six days old: they, I find, like puppies, are born blind, and could not see when they came to my hands. No doubt their spines are soft and flexible at the time of their birth, or else the poor dam would have but a bad time of it in the critical moment of parturition: but it is plain that they soon harden; for these little pigs had such stiff prickles on their backs and sides as would easily have fetched blood, had they not been handled with caution. Their spines are quite white at this age; and they have little hanging ears, which I do not remember to be discernible in the old ones. They can, in part, at this age draw their skin down over their faces; but are not able to contract themselves into a ball, as they do, for the sake of defence, when full grown. The reason, I suppose is, because the curious muscle that enables the creature to roll itself up in a ball was not then arrived at its full tone and firmness. Hedgehogs make a deep and warm hybernaculum[2] with leaves and moss, in which they conceal themselves for the winter: but I never could find that they stored in any winter provision, as some quadrupeds certainly do.

I have discovered an anecdote with respect to the fieldfare (*Turdus pilaris*), which I think is particular enough: this bird, though it sits on trees in the day-time, and procures the greatest part of its food from white-thorn hedges; yea, moreover, builds on very high trees; as may be seen by the *fauna suecica;*[3] yet always appears with us to roost on the ground. They are seen to come in flocks just before it is dark, and to settle and nestle among the heath on our forest. And besides, the larkers, in dragging their nets by night, frequently catch them in the wheat stubbles; while the bat fowlers, who take many redwings in the hedges, never entangle any of this species. Why these birds, in the matter of roosting, should differ from all their congeners,[4] and from themselves also with respect to their proceedings by day, is a fact for which I am by no means able to account.

I have somewhat to inform you of concerning the *moose deer;* but in general foreign animals fall seldom in my way: my little intelligence is confined to the narrow sphere of my own observations at home.

Letter 13

April 12, 1772.

Dear Sir,

While I was in *Sussex* last autumn my residence was at the village near *Lewes,* from whence I had formerly the pleasure of writing to you. On the first of *November* I remarked that the old tortoise, formerly mentioned, began first to dig the ground in order to the forming its hybernaculum, which it had fixed on just beside a great turf of hepaticas. It scrapes out the ground with its forefeet, and throws it up over its back with its hind; but the motion of its legs is ridiculously slow, little exceeding the hour-hand of a clock; and suitable to the composure of an animal said to be a whole month in performing one feat of copulation. Nothing can be more assiduous than this creature night and day in scooping the earth, and forcing its great body into the cavity; but, as the noons of that season proved unusually warm and sunny, it was continually interrupted, and called forth by the heat in the middle of the day; and though I continued there till the thirteenth of *November,* yet the work remained unfinished. Harsher weather, and frosty mornings, would have quickened its operations. No part of its behaviour ever struck me more than the extreme timidity it always expresses with regard to rain; for though it has a shell that would secure it against the wheel of a loaded cart, yet does it discover as much solicitude about rain as a lady dressed in all her best attire, shuffling away on the first sprinklings, and running its head up in a corner. If attended to, it becomes an excellent weather-glass; for as sure as it walks elate,

[2] Burrow, used for hibernation.

[3] Refers to *Fauna suecica,* a treatise on Swedish fauna by Gustaf von Paykull (1757–1826).

[4] Animals belonging to the same taxonomic genus.

and as it were on tiptoe, feeding with great earnestness in a morning, so sure will it rain before night. It is totally a diurnal animal, and never pretends to stir after it becomes dark. The tortoise, like other reptiles, has an arbitrary stomach as well as lungs; and can refrain from eating as well as breathing for a great part of the year. When first awakened it eats nothing; nor again in the autumn before it retires: through the height of the summer it feeds voraciously, devouring all the food that comes in its way. I was much taken with its sagacity in discerning those that do it kind offices: for, as soon as the good old lady comes in sight who has waited on it for more than thirty years, it hobbles towards its benefactress with awkward alacrity; but remains inattentive to strangers. Thus not only "*the ox knoweth his owner, and the ass his master's crib,*"[5] but the most abject reptile and torpid of beings distinguishes the hand that feeds it, and is touched with the feelings of gratitude.

I am, &c. &c.

P.S. In about three days after I left *Sussex* the tortoise retired into the ground under the hepatica.

Letter 20

Selborne, Feb. 26, 1774.

Dear Sir,

The sand martin, or bank martin, is by much the least of any of the *British hirundines;*[6] and, as far as we have ever seen, the smallest known hirundo: though *Brisson* asserts that there is one much smaller, and that is the *Hirundo esculenta.*

But it is much to be regretted that it is scarce possible for any observer to be so full and exact as he could wish in reciting the circumstances attending the life and conversation of this little bird, since it is *fera naturâ,*[7] at least in this part of the kingdom, disclaiming all domestic attachments, and haunting wild heaths and commons where there are large lakes: while the other species, especially the swallow and house martin, are remarkably gentle and domesticated, and never seem to think themselves safe but under the protection of man.

Here are in this parish, in the sandpits and banks of the lakes of *Wolmer forest,* several colonies of these birds; and yet they are never seen in the village; nor do they at all frequent the cottages that are scattered about in that wild district. The only instance I ever remember where this species haunts any building is at the town of *Bishop's Waltham,* in this county, where many sand martins nestle and breed in the scaffold-holes of the back wall of *William* of *Wykeham's* stables: but then this wall stands in a very sequestered and retired enclosure, and faces upon a large and beautiful lake. And indeed this species seems so to delight in large waters, that no instance occurs of their abounding, but near vast pools or rivers: and in particular it has been remarked that they swarm in the banks of the *Thames* in some places below *London bridge.*

---

[5] Isaiah 1.3.

[6] Birds of the swallow family.

[7] A wild animal (Latin).

It is curious to observe with what different degrees of architectonic skill Providence has endowed birds of the same genus, and so nearly correspondent in their general mode of life! for while the swallow and the house martin discover the greatest address in raising and securely fixing crusts or shells of loam as cunabula[8] for their young, the bank martin terebrates a round and regular hole in the sand or earth, which is serpentine, horizontal, and about two feet deep. At the inner end of this burrow does this bird deposit, in a good degree of safety, her rude nest, consisting of fine grasses and feathers, usually goose feathers, very inartificially laid together.

Perseverance will accomplish any thing: though at first one would be disinclined to believe that this weak bird, with her soft and tender bill and claws, should ever be able to bore the stubborn sand bank without entirely disabling herself: yet with these feeble instruments have I seen a pair of them make great dispatch: and could remark how much they had scooped that day by the fresh sand which ran down the bank, and was of a different colour from that which lay loose and bleached in the sun.

In what space of time these little artists are able to mine and finish these cavities I have never been able to discover, for reasons given above; but it would be a matter worthy of observation, where it falls in the way of any naturalist to make his remarks. This I have often taken notice of, that several holes of different depths are left unfinished at the end of summer. To imagine that these beginnings were intentionally made in order to be in the greater forwardness for next spring, is allowing perhaps too much foresight and *rerum prudentia*[9] to a simple bird. May not the cause of these *latebrae*[10] being left unfinished arise from their meeting in those places with strata too harsh, hard, and solid, for their purpose, which they relinquish, and go to a fresh spot that works more freely? Or may they not in other places fall in with a soil as much too loose and mouldering, liable to flounder, and threatening to overwhelm them and their labours?

One thing is remarkable—that, after some years, the old holes are forsaken and new ones bored; perhaps because the old habitations grow foul and fetid from long use, or because they may so abound with fleas as to become untenantable. This species of swallow moreover is strangely annoyed with fleas: and we have seen fleas, bed fleas (*Pulex irritans*), swarming at the mouth of these holes, like bees on the stools of their hives.

The following circumstance should by no means be omitted—that these birds do *not* make use of their caverns by way of hybernacula, as might be expected; since banks so perforated have been dug out with care in the winter, when nothing was found but empty nests.

The sand martin arrives much about the same time with the swallow, and lays, as she does, from four to six white eggs. But as this species is *cryptogame*,[11] carry-

---

[8] Cradles (Latin); i.e., enclosed or sheltered nests.

[9] Common sense (Latin).

[10] Hiding places (Latin).

[11] Hidden seed (Latin); i.e., conceals the reproduction and raising of its young.

ing on the business of nidification, incubation, and the support of its young in the dark, it would not be so easy to ascertain the time of breeding, were it not for the coming forth of the broods, which appear much about the time, or rather somewhat earlier than those of the swallow. The nestlings are supported in common like those of their congeners, with gnats and other small insects; and sometimes they are fed with *libellulae* (dragonflies) almost as long as themselves. In the last week in *June* we have seen a row of these sitting on a rail near a great pool as *perchers;* and so young and helpless, as easily to be taken by hand: but whether the dams ever feed them on the wing, as swallows and house martins do, we have never yet been able to determine; nor do we know whether they pursue and attack birds of prey.

When they happen to breed near hedges and enclosures, they are dispossessed of their breeding holes by the house sparrow, which is on the same account a fell adversary to house martins.

These *hirundines*[12] are no songsters, but rather mute, making only a little harsh noise when a person approaches their nests. They seem not to be of a sociable turn, never with us congregating with their congeners in the autumn. Undoubtedly they breed a second time, like the house martin and swallow; and withdraw about *Michaelmas.*

Though in some particular districts they may happen to abound, yet on the whole, in the south of *England* at least, is this much the rarest species. For there are few towns or large villages but what abound with house martins; few churches, towers, or steeples, but what are haunted by some swifts; scarce a hamlet or single cottage chimney that has not its swallow; while the bank martins, scattered here and there, live a sequestered life among some abrupt sand hills, and in the banks of some few rivers.

These birds have a peculiar manner of flying; flitting about with odd jerks, and vacillations, not unlike the motions of a butterfly. Doubtless the flight of all *hirundines* is influenced by, and adapted to, the peculiar sort of insects which furnish their food. Hence it would be worth inquiry to examine what particular genus of insects affords the principal food of each respective species of swallow. . . .

Letter 35

Selborne, May 20, 1777.

Dear Sir,

Lands that are subject to frequent inundations are always poor; and probably the reason may be because the worms are drowned. The most insignificant insects and reptiles are of much more consequence, and have much more influence

---

[12] Swallows.

in the economy of Nature,[13] than the incurious are aware of; and are mighty in their effect, from their minuteness, which renders them less an object of attention; and from their numbers and fecundity. Earthworms, though in appearance a small and despicable link in the chain of Nature, yet, if lost, would make a lamentable chasm. For, to say nothing of half the birds, and some quadrupeds which are almost entirely supported by them, worms seem to be the great promoters of vegetation, which would proceed but lamely without them, by boring, perforating, and loosening the soil, and rendering it pervious to rains and the fibres of plants, by drawing straws and stalks of leaves and twigs into it; and, most of all, by throwing up such infinite numbers of lumps of earth called worm casts, which, being their excrement, is a fine manure for grain and grass. Worms probably provide new soil for hills and slopes where the rain washes the earth away; and they affect slopes, probably to avoid being flooded. Gardeners and farmers express their detestation of worms; the former because they render their walks unsightly, and make them much work: and the latter because, as they think, worms eat their green corn. But these men would find that the earth without worms would soon become cold, hard-bound, and void of fermentation; and consequently sterile: and besides, in favour of worms, it should be hinted that green corn, plants, and flowers, are not so much injured by them as by many species of *coleoptera* (scarabs), and *tipulae* (long-legs), in their larva, or grub state; and by unnoticed myriads of small shell-less snails, called slugs, which silently and imperceptibly make amazing havoc in the field and garden.

These hints we think proper to throw out in order to set the inquisitive and discerning to work.

A good monography of worms would afford much entertainment and information at the same time, and would open a large and new field in natural history. Worms work most in the spring; but by no means lie torpid in the dead months; are out every mild night in the winter, as any person may be convinced that will take the pains to examine his grass plots with a candle; are hermaphrodites, and much addicted to venery, and consequently very prolific.

I am, &c.

Letter 50

Selborne, April 21, 1780.

Dear Sir,

The old *Sussex* tortoise, that I have mentioned to you so often, is become my property. I dug it out of its winter dormitory in *March* last, when it was enough awakened to express its resentments by hissing; and, packing it in a box with earth, carried it eighty miles in post-chaises. The rattle and hurry of the journey so perfectly roused it that, when I turned it out on a border, it walked twice

---

[13] "The economy of Nature" denotes the interrelatedness of all living things, a vital foreshadowing of the modern concept of ecology. See Donald Worster, *Nature's Economy: A History of Ecological Ideas* (1977).

down to the bottom of my garden; however, in the evening, the weather being cold, it buried itself in the loose mould, and continues still concealed.

As it will be under my eye, I shall now have an opportunity of enlarging my observations on its mode of life, and propensities; and perceive already that, towards the time of coming forth, it opens a breathing-place in the ground near its head, requiring, I conclude, a freer respiration as it becomes more alive. This creature not only goes under the earth from the middle of *November* to the middle of *April*, but sleeps great part of the summer; for it goes to bed in the longest days at four in the afternoon, and often does not stir in the morning till late. Besides, it retires to rest for every shower; and does not move at all in wet days.

When one reflects on the state of this strange being, it is a matter of wonder to find that Providence should bestow such a profusion of days, such a seeming waste of longevity, on a reptile that appears to relish it so little as to squander more than two thirds of its existence in a joyless stupor, and be lost to all sensation for months together in the profoundest of slumbers.

While I was writing this letter, a moist and warm afternoon, with the thermometer at 50, brought forth troops of *shell snails;* and, at the same juncture, the *tortoise* heaved up the mould and put out its head; and the next morning came forth, as it were raised from the dead; and walked about till four in the afternoon. This was a curious coincidence! a very amusing occurrence! to see such a similarity of feelings between the two *Φερεοικοι!* for so the *Greeks* called both the *shell snail* and the *tortoise*.

Summer birds are, this cold and backward spring, unusually late: I have seen but one swallow yet. This conformity with the weather convinces me more and more that they sleep in the winter.

🦢 *Christopher Smart* (1722–1771)

Brilliant and versatile, in the course of his eventful life, Christopher Smart wrote and published in a wide variety of literary genres, both high and low. Although educated at Cambridge and recognized as a brilliant scholar and five-time winner of Cambridge's Seatonian prize for poetry, he also produced a great deal of literary "hackwork" and several bawdy productions for the popular London stage. His passionate religious poetry, including the Jubilate Agno *(Rejoice in the Lamb) and* A Song to David, *won him great admiration, but his personal circumstances (which included alcoholism, two commitments to the madhouse, perpetual financial indigence, and other erratic behavior) have often colored critical appreciation of his literary accomplishments. In the selection below, Smart tries his hand successfully at the georgic, one of the most popular genres of writing about nature in the eighteenth century. "The Hop-Garden," like other georgics, combines practical and accurate information on the production of hops and addresses itself to "Yeoman and countrymen," with the numerous requisite literary and classical allusions which, in the paradoxical mode of the georgic, would most likely have been beyond the ken of most country farmers. Smart provides agricultural facts in a more playful tone, leading present-day scholars to debate the seriousness of his purpose.*

From The Hop-Garden

A Georgic in Two Books

From Book the First*

The land that answers best the farmer's care,
And silvers to maturity the Hop:
When to inhume the plants; to turn the glebe;
And wed the tendrils to th' aspiring poles:
Under what sign to pluck the crop, and how   5
To cure, and in capacious sacks infold,
I teach in verse Miltonian. Smile the muse,
And meditate an honour to that land
Where first I breathed, and struggled into life,
Impatient, Cantium, to be called thy son.   10

.   .   .

Come, fair magician, sportive Fancy, come,
With thy unbounded imagery: child of thought,
From thy aerial citadel descend,
And (for thou canst) assist me. Bring with thee
Thy all-creative Talisman; with thee   15
The active spirits ideal, towering flights,
That hover o'er the muse-resounding groves,
And all thy colourings, all thy shapes display.
Thou too be here, Experience, so shall I
My rules nor in low prose jejunely *say*,   20
Nor in smooth numbers musically err;
But vain is Fancy and Experience vain,
If thou, O Hesiod! Virgil[1] of our land,
Or hear'st thou rather, Milton, bard divine,
Whose greatness who shalt imitate, save thee?   25
If thou, O Philips,[2] favouring dost not hear
Me, inexpert of verse; with gentle hand
Uprear the unpinioned Muse, high on the top
Of that immeasurable mount, that far
Exceeds thine own Plinlimmon,[3] where thou tun'st   30

---

* We have numbered the verse lines of this excerpt from 1 to 108, and indicated where elisions have been made, for the convenience of the reader. Lines 1–10 and lines 258–355 are included in this excerpt.—Editors' note.

[1] Hesiod was a Greek poet of the eighth century B.C. and author of the first Western georgic poem, *Works and Days.* Virgil (70–19 B.C.) was the great Roman georgic and epic poet.

[2] John Philips (1676–1709) wrote the georgic poem *Cyder* (1708) detailing the cultivation of apples and the manufacture of cider. It is modeled on Virgil's *Georgics.*

[3] A mountain in Wales that is the source of the Rivers Wye and Severn.

With Phoebus'[4] self thy lyre. Give me to turn
Th' unwieldy subject with thy graceful ease,
Extol its baseness with thy art; but chief
Illumine, and invigorate with my fire.
  When Phoebus looks through Aries[5] on the spring,   35
And vernal flowers promise dulcet fruit,
Autumnal pride! delay not then thy setts[6]
In Tellus'[7] facile bosom to depose
Timely: if thou art wise the bulkiest choose:
To every root three joints indulge, and form   40
The quincunx with well-regulated hills.
Soon from the dung-enriched earth, their heads
Thy young plants will uplift, their virgin arms
They'll stretch, and, marriageable, claim the pole.
Nor frustrate thou their wishes, so thou may'st   45
Expect an hopeful issue, jolly Mirth,
Sister of taleful Jocus, tuneful Song,
And fat Good-nature with her honest face.
But yet in the novitiate of their love,
And tenderness of youth suffice small shoots   50
Cut from the widowed willow, nor provide
Poles insurmountable as yet. 'Tis then
When twice bright Phoebus' vivifying ray,
Twice the cold touch of winter's icy hand,
They've felt; 'tis then we fell sublimer props.   55
'Tis then the sturdy woodman's axe from far
Resounds, resounds, and hark! with hollow groans.
Down tumble the big trees, and rushing roll
O'er the crushed crackling brake, while in his cave
Forlorn, dejected, 'midst the weeping dryads[8]   60
Laments Sylvanus[9] for his verdant care.
The ash, or willow for thy use select,
Or storm enduring chestnut; but the oak,
Unfit for this employ, for nobler ends
Reserve untouched; she when by time matured,   65
Capacious, of some British demigod,
Vernon, or Warren,[10] shall with rapid wing
Infuriate, like Jove's[11] armour-bearing bird,

---

[4] Apollo, the ancient Greek god of the sun and of poetry.

[5] *Phoebus . . . Aries:* i.e., when the sun is in the constellation of Aries, in late March and April.

[6] Growths.

[7] In Roman religion, the goddess of the Earth; also often identified as Gaia.

[8] Ancient Greek nymphs or spirits who inhabited trees.

[9] A dweller in the woods, from the Latin *sylva,* or "forest."

[10] Two eighteenth-century British military heroes.

[11] Jupiter, the chief of the Roman gods, who is represented by the eagle.

Fly on thy foes; they, like the parted waves,
Which to the brazen beak murmuring give way   70
Amazed and roaring, from the fight recede.—
In that sweet month, when to the listening swains
Fair Philomel[12] sings love, and every cot
With garlands blooms bedight,[13] with bandage meet
The tendrils bind, and to the tall poll tie,   75
Else soon, too soon their meretricious arms
Round each ignoble clod they'll fold, and leave
Averse the lordly prop. Thus, have I heard
Where there's no mutual tie, no strong connection
Of love-conspiring hearts, oft the young bride   80
Has prostituted to her slaves her charms,
While the infatuated lord admires
Fresh-budding sprouts, and issue not his own.
Now turn the glebe: soon with correcting hand,
When smiling June in jocund dance leads on   85
Long days and happy hours, from every vine
Dock the redundant branches, and once more
With the sharp spade thy numerous acres till.
The shovel next must lend its aid, enlarge
The little hillocks, and erase the weeds.   90
This in that month its title which derives
From great Augustus' ever sacred name!
Sovereign of science! master of the muse!
Neglected genius' firm ally! of worth
Best judge, and best rewarder, whose applause   95
To bards was fame and fortune! O! 'twas well,
Well did you too in this, all glorious heroes!
Ye Romans!—on Time's wing you've stamped his praise,
And time shall bear it to eternity.
　　Now are our labours crowned with their reward,   100
Now bloom the florid hops, and in the stream
Shine in their floating silver, while above
T' embowering branches culminate, and form
A walk impervious to the sun; the poles
In comely order stand; and while you cleave   105
With the small skiff the Medway's[14] lucid wave,
In comely order still their ranks preserve,
And seem to march along th' extensive plain.

·　　·　　·

---

[12] Poetic name for the nightingale.
[13] Bedecked, arrayed.
[14] A river in Southeastern England.

❧ *William Mason* *(1725–1797)*

In the opening lines and throughout his long blank-verse poem The English Garden *(1771–81), William Mason rehearses what had become, by the time of the poem's publication, the foundational principles of English landscape design: "Great Nature scorns control: she will not bear / One beauty foreign to the spot or soil / She gives thee to adorn; 'tis thine alone / To mend, not change her features." Like other landscape gardeners and poets of the landscape such as Thomson, Mason's vision owes much to the painting of Nicolas Poussin and Claude Lorrain. In addition to acknowledging his debts to the visual arts, Mason also self-consciously blends other famous poems on gardens and gardening, such as Pope's "Epistle to Burlington" and Milton's* Paradise Lost, *into his own work. The four books of the poem each mix instruction in proper gardening procedure with moral reflection and literary allusion and together can be read as a virtual compendium of all the characteristics of the English Garden style that would reach its height in the work of Capability Brown, a landscape architect whom Mason deeply admired. A clergyman, a writer of tragedies, and an amateur painter and gardener, Mason was also close friends with Thomas Gray, who is commemorated in Book 2 of the poem.*

The English Garden

A Poem in Four Books

From Book 1*

   Begin the song! and ye of Albion's[1] sons
Attend; ye freeborn, ye ingenuous few,
Who, heirs of competence, if not of wealth,
Preserve that vestal purity of soul,
Whence genuine taste proceeds. To you, blest youths,   5
I sing: whether in academic groves
Studious ye rove, or, fraught with learning's stores,
Visit the Latian plain, fond to transplant
Those arts which Greece did, with her liberty,
Resign to Rome. Yet know, the art I sing   10
Even there ye shall not learn; Rome knew it not
While Rome was free; ah! hope not then to find
In slavish superstitious Rome the fair
Remains. Meanwhile, of old and classic aid,

---

* This excerpt begins with line 50 of the original edition. Lines have been renumbered from 1–270 for the reader's convenience. —Editors' note.

[1] England.

Though fruitless be the search, your eyes entranced 15
Shall catch those glowing scenes, that taught a Claude[2]
To grace his canvas with Hesperian hues,
And scenes like these, on Memory's tablet drawn,
Bring back to Britain; there give local form
To each idea, and, if Nature lend 20
Materials fit, of torrent, rock, and shade,
Produce new Tivolis.[3] But learn to rein
Thy skill within the limit she allows.
Great Nature scorns control: she will not bear
One beauty foreign to the spot or soil 25
She gives thee to adorn; 'tis thine alone
To mend, not change her features. Does her hand
Stretch forth a level lawn? ah, hope not thou
To lift the mountain there. Do mountains frown
Around? ah, wish not there the level lawn, 30
Yet she permits thine art, discreetly used,
To smooth or scoop the rugged and the plain.
But dare with caution; else expect, bold man!
The injured Genius of the plain to rise
In self-defence, and, like some giant fiend 35
That frowns in Gothic story, swift destroy
By night, the puny labours of thy day.

What then must he attempt, whom niggard fate
Has fixed in such an inauspicious spot
As bears no trace of beauty? must he sit 40
Dull and inactive in the desert waste,
Since Nature there no happy feature wears
To wake and meet his skill? Believe the Muse,
She does not know that inauspicious spot
Where Beauty is thus niggard of her store; 45
Believe the Muse, through this terrestrial vast
The seeds of grace are sown, profusely sown,
Even where we least may hope; the desert hills
Will hear the call of Art; the valleys dank
Obey her just behests, and smile with charms 50
Congenial to the soil, and all its own.

For tell me where's the desert? there alone
Where man resides not; or if chance resides,
He is not there the man his Maker formed,
Industrious man, by heaven's first law ordained 55

---

[2] Claude Lorrain (1600–1682), French landscape painter.

[3] A beautiful Italian town, known for its ruins of ancient Roman villas, and one of the models for garden design in the eighteenth century.

To earn his food by labour. In the waste
Place thou that man with his primaeval arms,
His plough-share, and his spade, nor shalt thou long
Impatient wait a change; the waste shall smile
With yellow harvests; what was barren heath   60
Shall soon be verdant mead. Now then arise,
Now let thine art, in union with his toil,
Exert its powers, and give, with varying skill,
The soil, already tamed, its finished grace.

    Nor less obsequious to the hand of toil,   65
If Fancy guide that hand, will the dank vale
Receive improvement meet; but Fancy here
Must lead, not follow Labour; she must tell
In what peculiar place the soil shall rise,
Where sink; prescribe what form each sluice shall wear,   70
And how direct its course; whether to spread
Broad as a lake, or, as a river pent
By fringed banks, weave its irriguous way
Through lawn and shade alternate; but if she
Preside not o'er the task, the narrow drains   75
Will run in tedious parallel, or cut
Each other in sharp angles; call her then
Swift to thine aid, ere the remorseless spade
Too deeply wound the bosom of the soil.

    Yet, in this lowly site, where all that charms   80
Within itself must charm, hard is the task
Imposed on Fancy. Hence with idle fear!
Is she not Fancy? and can Fancy fail
In sweet delusions, in concealments apt,
And wild creative power? She cannot fail.   85
And yet, full oft, when her creative power,
Her apt concealments, her delusions sweet,
Have been profusely lavished; when her groves
Have shot, with vegetative vigour strong
Even to their wished maturity; when Jove   90
Has ranged the changeful seasons o'er her lawns,
And each has left a blessing as it rolled;
Even then, perchance, some vain fastidious eye
Shall rove, unmindful of surrounding charms,
And ask for prospect. Stranger! 'tis not here.   95
Go seek it on some garish turrets height,
Seek it on Richmond's, or on Windsor's brow;
There, gazing on the gorgeous vale below,
Applaud besure, with fashioned pomp of phrase
The good and bad, which, in profusion, there   100

That gorgeous vale exhibits. Here, meanwhile,
Even in the dull, unseen, unseeing dell
Thy taste contemns, shall Contemplation imp
Her eagle plumes; the Poet here shall hold
Sweet converse with his Muse; the curious sage,   105
Who comments on great Nature's ample tome,
Shall find that volume here. For here are caves,
Where rise those gurgling rills, that sing the song
Which Contemplation loves; here shadowy glades,
Where through the tremulous foliage darts the ray   110
That gilds the Poet's daydream; here the turf
Teems with the vegetating race; the air
Is peopled with the insect tribes, that float
Upon the noontide beam, and call the sage
To number and to name them. Nor if here   115
The painter comes, shall his enchanting art
Go back without a boon: for Nature here
Has, with her living colours, formed a scene
Which Ruisdale[4] best might rival. Crystal lakes,
O'er which the giant oak, himself a grove,   120
Flings his romantic branches, and beholds
His reverend image in th' expanse below.
If distant hills be wanting, yet our eye
Forgets the want, and with delighted gaze
Rests on the lovely foreground; there applauds   125
The art, which varying forms and blending hues,
Gives that harmonious force of shade and light,
Which makes the landscape perfect. Art like this
Is only art, all else abortive toil.

    Thou then, the docile pupil of my song,   130
Attend; and learn how much on Painting's aid
Thy sister art depends; learn now its laws:
Their practice may demand a future strain.

    Of Nature's various scenes the painter culls
That for his favourite theme, where the fair whole   135
Is broken into ample parts, and bold;
Where to the eye three well-marked distances
Spread their peculiar colouring. Vivid green,
Warm brown, and black opaque, the foreground bears.
Conspicuous; sober olive coldly marks   140
The second distance; thence the third declines
In softer blue, or, lessening still, is lost
In faintest purple. When thy taste is called
To adorn a scene where Nature's self presents

---

[4] Jacob van Ruisdael (1628–1682), Dutch landscape painter.

All these distinct gradations, then rejoice   145
As does the painter, and like him apply
Thy colours; plant thou on each separate part
Its proper foliage. Chief, for there thy skill
Has its chief scope, enrich with all the hues
That flowers, that shrubs, that trees can yield, the sides   150
Of that fair path, from whence our sight is led
Gradual to view the whole. Where'er thou wind'st
That path, take heed between the scene, and eye,
To vary and to mix thy chosen greens.
Here for awhile, with cedar or with larch,   155
That from the ground spread their close foliage, hide
The view entire. Then o'er some lowly tuft,
Where rose and woodbine bloom, permit its charms
To burst upon the sight; now through a copse
Of beech, that rear their smooth and stately trunks,   160
Admit it partially, and half exclude,
And half reveal its graces; in this path,
How long soe'er the wanderer roves, each step
Shall wake fresh beauties; each short point present
A different picture, new, and yet the same.   165

    Yet some there are who deem this precept vain,
And fell each tree that intercepts the scene.
O great Poussin![5] O Nature's darling, Claude!
What if some rash and sacrilegious hand
Tore from your canvas those umbrageous pines   170
That frown in front, and give each azure hill
The charm of contrast! Nature suffers here
Like outrage, and bewails a beauty lost,
Which Time with tardy hand shall late restore.
Yet here the spoiler rests not; see him rise   175
Warm from his devastation, to improve,
For so he calls it, yonder champaign wide.
There on each bolder brow in shapes acute
His fence he scatters; there the Scottish fir
In murky file lifts his inglorious head,   180
And blots the fair horizon. So should art
Improve thy pencil's savage dignity,
Salvator![6] if where, far as eye can pierce,
Rock piled on rock, thy Alpine heights retire,
She flung her random foliage, and disturbed   185
The deep repose of the majestic scene.

---

[5] Nicolas Poussin (1594–1665), French painter who frequently depicted classical figures in an orderly natural landscape.

[6] Salvator Rosa (1615–1673), Italian landscape and history painter.

This deed were impious. Ah, forgive the thought,
Thou more than painter, more than poet! He,
Alone thy equal, who was "Fancy's child."

    Does then the song forbid the planter's hand   190
To clothe the distant hills, and veil with woods
Their barren summits? No; but it forbids
All poverty of clothing. Rich the robe,
And amply let it flow, that Nature wears
On her throned eminence: where'er she takes   195
Her horizontal march, pursue her step
With sweeping train of forest, hill to hill
Unite with prodigality of shade.
There plant thy elm, thy chestnut; nourish there
Those sapling oaks, which, at Britannia's call,   200
May heave their trunks mature into the main,
And float the bulwarks of her liberty:
But if the fir, give it its station meet,
Place it an outguard to th' assailing north,
To shield the infant scions, till possessed   205
Of native strength, they learn alike to scorn
The blast and their protectors. Fostered thus,
The cradled hero gains from female care
His future vigor; but that vigor felt,
He springs indignant from his nurse's arms,   210
He nods the plumy crest, he shakes the spear,
And is that awful thing which heaven ordained
The scourge of tyrants, and his country's pride.

    If then thou still art dubious how to treat
Nature's neglected features, turn thine eye   215
To those the masters of correct design.
Who, from her vast variety, have culled
The loveliest, boldest parts, and new arranged;
Yet, as herself approved, herself inspired.
In their immortal works thou ne'er shalt find   220
Dull uniformity, contrivance quaint,
Or laboured littleness; but contrasts broad,
And careless lines, whose undulating form
Plays through the varied canvas; these transplant
Again on Nature; take thy plastic spade,   225
It is thy pencil; take thy seeds, thy plants,
They are thy colours; and by these repay
With interest every charm she lent thy art.

    But, while I thus to Imitation's realm
Direct thy steps, deem not I lead thee wrong;   230

Nor ask, why I forget great Nature's fount,
And bring thee not the bright inspiring cup
From her original spring? Yet, if thou ask'st,
Thyself shalt give the answer. Tell me why
Did Raffael[7] steal, when his creative hand   235
Imaged the Seraphim, ideal grace
And dignity supernal from that store
Of Attic sculpture, which the ruthless Goth
Spared in his headlong fury? Tell me this;
And then confess that beauty best is taught   240
By those the favored few, whom heav'n has lent
The power to seize, select, and reunite
Her loveliest features; and of these to form
One archetype complete of sovereign grace.
Here Nature sees her fairest forms more fair;   245
Owns them her own, yet owns herself excelled
By what herself produced. Here Art and she
Embrace; connubial Juno[8] smiles benign,
And from the warm embrace Perfection springs.

    Rouse, then, each latent energy of soul   250
To clasp ideal beauty. Proteus-like,[9]
Think not the changeful nymph will long elude
Thy chase, or with reluctant coyness frown.
Inspired by her, thy happy art shall learn
To melt in fluent curves whate'er is straight,   255
Acute, or parallel. For, these unchanged,
Nature and she disdain the formal scene.
'Tis their demand, that every step of Rule
Be quite erased. For know, their every charm
Springs from variety; but all the boast   260
Of Rule is irksome Uniformity.
That end to effect we own the cube, or cone,
Are well employed; but fair Variety
Lives only where she undulates and sports
In many a winding train. As Nature then   265
Avoids, disdains, abhors all equal lines,
So Mechanism pursues, admires, adores.
Hence is their enmity; and sooner hope
With hawk and dove to draw the Cyprian[10] car,
Than reconcile these jarring principles.   270

---

[7] Raphael (*Raffaello Sanzio*, 1483–1520), one of the greatest painters of the Italian Renaissance.

[8] The Roman goddess of marriage.

[9] Proteus was an ancient Greek demigod who was able to change shape at will.

[10] Pertaining to Cyprus, the birthplace of Aphrodite, the ancient Greek goddess of love.

🦢 *Edmund Burke* (1729–1797)

Edmund Burke occupies a paradoxical position in the culture and politics of the late eighteenth century. With his Irish Catholic heritage, his early career as failed lawyer and hack writer, and his lilting Irish accent that endured throughout his parliamentary career, he seems the quintessential outsider, and he often found himself in opposition to the parliamentary majority. He in fact became a spokesman for the opposition and this very status enabled him to adopt the stance of a defender of old, established values against modern innovations, thus representing himself as the bulwark or conscience of the British nation against monarchic tyranny and anarchic insurrection. Although Burke supported the American struggle for independence, he later deplored the French Revolution for its more extreme espousal of the rights of man and its violent and indiscriminate overthrow of the monarchy. Burke's Reflections on the Revolution in France *(1790) emphatically rejects French revolutionary ideology while erecting a classic defense of the British constitutional system.*

Burke was born in Dublin of mixed religious heritage: his mother was Roman Catholic and his father Anglican. He had intended, early in his adult life, to practice law. Instead, he became renowned as a writer and philosopher. He also led an active political life; he held several appointed offices for the British government, and was elected to Parliament in 1766. Burke's interest in aesthetics is represented by A Philosophical Enquiry into the Origins of Our Ideas of the Sublime and Beautiful. *Published in 1757, it is an exploration of the feelings of wonder, pleasure, and awe inspired in the spectator by nature and by art. Burke's antithetical concepts of the sublime and the beautiful were widely influential. His fascination with the power and immensity of natural phenomena, as well as his sensitivity to more subtle gradations of color and texture, did much to awaken the Romantic movement to new possibilities of artistic creativity and poetic expression.*

From A Philosophical Enquiry into the Origins of Our Ideas of the Sublime and Beautiful

Part 1, Section 7

Of the Sublime

Whatever is fitted in any sort to excite the ideas of pain and danger, that is to say, whatever is in any sort terrible, or is conversant about terrible objects, or operates in a manner analogous to terror, is a source of the *sublime;* that is, it is productive of the strongest emotion which the mind is capable of feeling. I say the strongest emotion, because I am satisfied the ideas of pain are much more powerful than those which enter on the part of pleasure. Without all doubt, the torments which we may be made to suffer are much greater in their effect on the body and mind, than any pleasures which the most learned voluptuary could suggest, or than the liveliest imagination, and the most sound and exquisitely sensible body, could enjoy. Nay, I am in great doubt whether any man could be found, who would earn a life of the most perfect satisfaction at the price of ending it in the torments, which justice inflicted in a few hours on the late unfortunate regicide in France.[1] But as pain is stronger in its operation than pleasure, so death is in general a much more affecting idea than pain; because there are very few pains, however exquisite, which are not preferred to death: nay, what generally makes pain itself, if I may say so, more painful, is, that it is considered as an emissary of this king of terrors. When danger or pain press too nearly, they are incapable of giving any delight, and are simply terrible; but at certain distances, and with certain modifications, they may be, and they are, delightful, as we every day experience. The cause of this I shall endeavor to investigate hereafter.

Part 2, Section 2

Terror

No passion so effectually robs the mind of all its powers of acting and reasoning as *fear*. For fear being an apprehension of pain or death, it operates in a manner that resembles actual pain. Whatever therefore is terrible, with regard to sight, is sublime too, whether this cause of terror be endued with greatness of dimensions or not; for it is impossible to look on anything as trifling, or contemptible, that may be dangerous. There are many animals, who, though far from being large, are yet capable of raising ideas of the sublime, because they are considered as objects of terror. As serpents and poisonous animals of almost all kinds. And to things of great dimensions, if we annex an adventitious idea of terror, they become without comparison greater. A level plain of a vast extent on land, is certainly no mean idea; the prospect of such a plain may be as extensive as a prospect of the ocean; but can it ever fill the mind with anything so great as the ocean itself? This is owing to several causes; but it is owing to none more than this, that the ocean is an object of no small terror. Indeed terror is in all cases whatsoever, either more openly or latently, the ruling principle of the sublime. . . .

Part 2, Section 7

Vastness

Greatness of dimension is a powerful cause of the sublime. This is too evident, and the observation too common, to need any illustration; it is not so common to consider in what ways greatness of dimension, vastness of extent or quantity, has the most striking effect. For, certainly, there are ways and modes wherein the same quantity of extension shall produce greater effects than it is found to do in others. Extension is either in length, height, or depth. Of these the length strikes least; a hundred yards of even ground will never work such an effect as a tower a hundred yards high, or a rock or mountain of that altitude. I am apt to imagine,

---

[1] Alludes to the execution of Robert Francis Damiens (1714–1757), who attempted to assassinate Louis XV. After harsh torture, he was executed by *écartèlement* (quartering), on March 28, 1757.

likewise, that height is less grand than depth; and that we are more struck at looking down from a precipice, than looking up at an object of equal height; but of that I am not very positive. A perpendicular has more force in forming the sublime, than an inclined plane, and the effects of a rugged and broken surface seem stronger than where it is smooth and polished. It would carry us out of our way to enter in this place into the cause of these appearances, but certain it is they afford a large and fruitful field of speculation. However, it may not be amiss to add to these remarks upon magnitude, that as the great extreme of dimension is sublime, so the last extreme of littleness is in some measure sublime likewise; when we attend to the infinite divisibility of matter, when we pursue animal life into these excessively small, and yet organized beings, that escape the nicest inquisition of the sense; when we push our discoveries yet downward, and consider those creatures so many degrees yet smaller, and the still diminishing scale of existence, in tracing which the imagination is lost as well as the sense; we become amazed and confounded at the wonders of minuteness; nor can we distinguish in its effect this extreme of littleness from the vast itself. For division must be infinite as well as addition; because the idea of a perfect unity can no more be arrived at, than that of a complete whole, to which nothing may be added.

Part 3, Section 12

The Real Cause of Beauty

Having endeavored to show what beauty is not, it remains that we should examine, at least with equal attention, in what it really consists. Beauty is a thing much too affecting not to depend upon some positive qualities. And since it is no creature of our reason, since it strikes us without any reference to use, and even where no use at all can be discerned, since the order and method of nature is generally very different from our measures and proportions, we must conclude that beauty is, for the greater part, some quality in bodies acting mechanically upon the human mind by the intervention of the senses. We ought, therefore, to consider attentively in what manner those sensible qualities are disposed, in such things as by experience we find beautiful, or which excite in us the passion of love, or some correspondent affection.

Part 3, Section 14

Smoothness

The next property constantly observable in such objects is *smoothness*; a quality so essential to beauty, that I do not now recollect anything beautiful that is not smooth. In trees and flowers, smooth leaves are beautiful; smooth slopes of earth in gardens; smooth streams in the landscape; smooth coats of birds and beasts in animal beauties; in fine women, smooth skins; and in several sorts of ornamental furniture, smooth and polished surfaces. A very considerable part of the effect of beauty is owing to this quality; indeed the most considerable. For, take any beautiful object, and give it a broken and rugged surface; and, however well formed it may be in other respects, it pleases no longer. Whereas, let it want ever so many of the other constituents, if it wants not this, it becomes more pleasing than almost all the others without it. This seems to me so evident, that I am a good deal surprised that none who have handled the subject have made any mention of the quality of smoothness in the enumeration of those that go to the forming of beauty. For, indeed, any ruggedness, any sudden projection, any sharp angle, is in the highest degree contrary to that idea.

Part 3, Section 15

Gradual Variation

But as perfectly beautiful bodies are not composed of angular parts, so their parts never continue long in the same right line. They vary their direction every moment, and they change under the eye by a deviation continually carrying on, but for whose beginning or end you will find it difficult to ascertain a point. The view of a beautiful bird will illustrate this observation. Here we see the head increasing insensibly to the middle, from whence it lessens gradually until it mixes with the neck; the neck loses itself in a larger swell, which continues to the middle of the body, when the whole decreases again to the tail; the tail takes a new direction, but it soon varies its new course, it blends again with the other parts, and the line is perpetually changing, above, below, upon every side. In this description I have before me the idea of a dove; it agrees very well with most of the conditions of beauty. It is smooth and downy; its parts are (to use that expression) melted into one another; you are presented with no sudden protuberance through the whole, and yet the whole is continually changing. Observe that part of a beautiful woman where she is perhaps the most beautiful, about the neck and breasts; the smoothness, the softness, the easy and insensible swell; the variety of the surface, which is never for the smallest space the same; the deceitful maze through which the unsteady eye slides giddily, without knowing where to fix, or whither it is carried. Is not this a demonstration of that change of surface, continual, and yet hardly perceptible at any point, which forms one of the great constituents of beauty? It gives me no small pleasure to find that I can strengthen my theory in this point by the opinion of the very ingenious Mr. Hogarth,[2] whose idea of the line of beauty I take in general to be extremely just. But the idea of variation, without attending so accurately to the *manner* of the variation, has led him to consider angular figures as beautiful; these figures, it is true, vary greatly, yet they vary in a sudden and broken manner, and I do not find any natural object which is angular, and at the same time beautiful. Indeed, few natural objects are entirely angular. But I think those which approach the most nearly to it are the ugliest. I must add, too, that so far as I could observe of nature, though the varied line is that alone in which complete beauty is found, yet there is no particular line which is always found in the most completely beautiful, and which is therefore beautiful in preference to all other lines. At least I never could observe it.

[2] William Hogarth (1697–1764), British artist and satirist, author of *Analysis of Beauty* (1753).

✌ *Oliver Goldsmith* (*1730–1774*)

Oliver Goldsmith's The Deserted Village *is a landmark in English writing about the countryside. Although many poems before it had provided a critique of the corrupt, greedy, and dissolute behavior of the wealthy gentry and celebrated the moral superiority of country farmers, Goldsmith's pastoral elegy hit a nerve when it was published in 1770. Immediately popular, the work was subsequently criticized for its sentimentalism and its idealization of rural life. Yet as Goldsmith himself notes in the dedicatory letter to his friend, painter Joshua Reynolds, the decline and depopulation of rural communities (as wealthy landowners gradually consolidated their holdings and "improved" their land), which is described in detail in the poem, was historically accurate. Goldsmith initiates a line of poems which, while nostalgically celebrating a vision of the past, also strongly protest the misappropriation of the countryside and the deracination of rural laborers. Romantic poets, such as William Wordsworth and John Clare, owed a debt to Goldsmith for his subject matter and his style. Blending emotionally charged personal reminiscences with political protests and moral critique, Goldsmith set a pattern for many subsequent nature poets, who continue to read a society's moral condition in its relationship to the environment.*

The village of Auburn, while wholly fictional, has much in common with the Irish village where Goldsmith spent a relatively happy childhood. His father was a clergyman, and sent his son to study at Trinity College, Dublin, where he was an indifferent student. As a young man, after having gambled away the money he had been given to study law, Goldsmith toyed with a variety of careers, but with little focus or success. He traveled through Europe in the early 1750s, on the pretense of preparing for a medical career, and when he returned to London in 1756, he attempted to establish himself as a physician. It was at this time that he began writing reviews for popular periodicals and discovered his gift for writing. He would go on to produce works, in a variety of genres, which were popular and acclaimed, including several histories (of ancient Rome, ancient Greece, and even one entitled A History of the Earth, and Animated Nature); *a novel,* The Vicar of Wakefield *(1766); two popular comedies,* The Good-Natured Man *(1768) and* She Stoops to Conquer *(1773); poetry, especially his most well-known poem* The Deserted Village; *and numerous essays and reviews. The topic for* The Deserted Village, *in fact, began as an essay entitled "The Revolution in Low Life," written in 1762. Goldsmith was a member of Samuel Johnson's "Club" and was thus a friend and associate to many of the leading minds of the mid-eighteenth century. Although his publications were successful, Goldsmith was never a practical man and died in debt.*

The Deserted Village

Sweet Auburn! loveliest village of the plain,
Where health and plenty cheered the labouring swain,
Where smiling spring its earliest visit paid,
And parting summer's lingering blooms delayed,
Dear lovely bowers of innocence and ease,   5

Seats of my youth, when every sport could please,
How often have I loitered o'er thy green,
Where humble happiness endeared each scene;
How often have I paused on every charm,
The sheltered cot, the cultivated farm,   10
The never-failing brook, the busy mill,
The decent church that topped the neighbouring hill,
The hawthorn bush, with seats beneath the shade,
For talking age and whispering lovers made.
How often have I blest the coming day,   15
When toil remitting lent its turn to play,
And all the village train from labour free
Led up their sports beneath the spreading tree,
While many a pastime circled in the shade,
The young contending as the old surveyed;   20
And many a gambol frolicked o'er the ground,
And slights of art and feats of strength went round.
And still as each repeated pleasure tired,
Succeeding sports the mirthful band inspired;
The dancing pair that simply sought renown   25
By holding out to tire each other down,
The swain mistrustless of his smutted face,
While secret laughter tittered round the place,
The bashful virgin's sidelong looks of love,
The matron's glance that would those looks reprove.   30
These were thy charms, sweet village; sports like these,
With sweet succession, taught even toil to please;
These round thy bowers their cheerful influence shed,
These were thy charms—But all these charms are fled.

   Sweet smiling village, loveliest of the lawn,   35
Thy sports are fled, and all thy charms withdrawn;
Amidst thy bowers the tyrant's hand is seen,
And desolation saddens all thy green:
One only master grasps the whole domain,
And half a tillage[1] stints thy smiling plain;   40
No more thy glassy brook reflects the day,
But choked with sedges, works its weedy way.
Along thy glades, a solitary guest,
The hollow-sounding bittern guards its nest;
Amidst thy desert walks the lapwing flies,   45
And tires their echoes with unvaried cries.
Sunk are thy bowers in shapeless ruin all,
And the long grass o'ertops the mouldering wall,

---

[1] I.e., only half the land is cultivated, or tilled.

And trembling, shrinking from the spoiler's hand,
Far, far away thy children leave the land.   50

Ill fares the land, to hastening ills a prey,
Where wealth accumulates, and men decay;
Princes and lords may flourish, or may fade;
A breath can make them, as a breath has made.
But a bold peasantry, their country's pride,   55
When once destroyed, can never be supplied.

A time there was, ere England's griefs began,
When every rood[2] of ground maintained its man;
For him light labour spread her wholesome store,
Just gave what life required, but gave no more.   60
His best companions, innocence and health;
And his best riches, ignorance of wealth.

But times are altered; trade's unfeeling train
Usurp the land and dispossess the swain;
Along the lawn, where scattered hamlets rose,   65
Unwieldy wealth, and cumbrous pomp repose;
And every want to luxury allied,
And every pang that folly pays to pride.
These gentle hours that plenty bade to bloom,
Those calm desires that asked but little room,   70
Those healthful sports that graced the peaceful scene,
Lived in each look, and brightened all the green;
These far departing seek a kinder shore,
And rural mirth and manners are no more.

Sweet Auburn! parent of the blissful hour,   75
Thy glades forlorn confess the tyrant's power.
Here as I take my solitary rounds,
Amidst thy tangling walks, and ruined grounds,
And, many a year elapsed, return to view
Where once the cottage stood, the hawthorn grew,   80
Here, as with doubtful, pensive steps I range,
Trace every scene, and wonder at the change,
Remembrance wakes with all her busy train,
Swells at my breast, and turns the past to pain.

In all my wanderings round this world of care,   85
In all my griefs—and God has given my share—
I still had hopes my latest hours to crown,
Amidst these humble bowers to lay me down;
My anxious day to husband near the close,

---

[2] A measure of land.

And keep life's flame from wasting by repose.   90
I still had hopes, for pride attends us still,
Amidst the swains to show my book-learned skill,
Around my fire an evening group to draw,
And tell of all I felt, and all I saw;
And, as an hare whom hounds and horns pursue,   95
Pants to the place from whence at first she flew,
I still had hopes, my long vexations past,
Here to return—and die at home at last.

    O blest retirement, friend to life's decline,
Retreats from care that never must be mine,   100
How blest is he who crowns in shades like these,
A youth of labour with an age of ease;
Who quits a world where strong temptations try,
And, since 'tis hard to combat, learns to fly.
For him no wretches, born to work and weep,   105
Explore the mine, or tempt the dangerous deep;
No surly porter stands in guilty state
To spurn imploring famine from his gate,
But on he moves to meet his latter end,
Angels around befriending virtue's friend;   110
Sinks to the grave with unperceived decay,
While resignation gently slopes the way;
And all his prospects brightening to the last,
His Heaven commences ere the world be past!

    Sweet was the sound when oft at evening's close,   115
Up yonder hill the village murmur rose;
There as I passed with careless steps and slow,
The mingling notes came softened from below;
The swain responsive as the milkmaid sung,
The sober herd that lowed to meet their young;   120
The noisy geese that gabbled o'er the pool,
The playful children just let loose from school;
The watchdog's voice that bayed the whispering wind,
And the loud laugh that spoke the vacant mind,
These all in soft confusion sought the shade,   125
And filled each pause the nightingale had made.
But now the sounds of population fail,
No cheerful murmurs fluctuate in the gale,
No busy steps the grass-grown footway tread,
But all the bloomy flush of life is fled.   130
All but yon widowed, solitary thing
That feebly bends beside the plashy spring;
She, wretched matron, forced, in age, for bread,
To strip the brook with mantling cresses spread,

To pick her wintry faggot from the thorn,   135
To seek her nightly shed, and weep till morn;
She only left of all the harmless train,
The sad historian of the pensive plain.

    Near yonder copse, where once the garden smiled,
And still where many a garden flower grows wild;   140
There, where a few torn shrubs the place disclose,
The village preacher's modest mansion rose.
A man he was, to all the country dear,
And passing rich with forty pounds a year;
Remote from towns he ran his godly race,   145
Nor e'er had changed, nor wished to change his place;
Unskillful he to fawn, or seek for power,
By doctrines fashioned to the varying hour;
Far other aims his heart had learned to prize,
More bent to raise the wretched than to rise.   150
His house was known to all the vagrant train,
He chid their wanderings, but relieved their pain;
The long-remembered beggar was his guest,
Whose beard descending swept his aged breast;
The ruined spendthrift, now no longer proud,   155
Claimed kindred there, and had his claims allowed;
The broken soldier, kindly bade to stay,
Sate by his fire, and talked the night away;
Wept o'er his wounds, or tales of sorrow done,
Shouldered his crutch, and showed how fields were won.   160
Pleased with his guests, the good man learned to glow,
And quite forgot their vices in their woe;
Careless their merits, or their faults to scan,
His pity gave ere charity began.

    Thus to relieve the wretched was his pride,   165
And even his failings leaned to Virtue's side;
But in his duty prompt at every call,
He watched and wept, he prayed and felt, for all.
And, as a bird each fond endearment tries,
To tempt its new-fledged offspring to the skies;   170
He tried each art, reproved each dull delay,
Allured to brighter worlds, and led the way.

    Beside the bed where parting life was layed,
And sorrow, guilt, and pain, by turns dismayed,
The reverend champion stood. At his control,   175
Despair and anguish fled the struggling soul;
Comfort came down the trembling wretch to raise,
And his last faltering accents whispered praise.

At church, with meek and unaffected grace,
His looks adorned the venerable place; 180
Truth from his lips prevailed with double sway,
And fools, who came to scoff, remained to pray.
The service past, around the pious man,
With ready zeal each honest rustic ran;
Even children followed with endearing wile, 185
And plucked his gown, to share the good man's smile.
His ready smile a parent's warmth expressed,
Their welfare pleased him, and their cares distressed;
To them his heart, his love, his griefs were given,
But all his serious thoughts had rest in Heaven. 190
As some tall cliff that lifts its awful form
Swells from the vale, and midway leaves the storm,
Though round its breast the rolling clouds are spread,
Eternal sunshine settles on its head.

Beside yon straggling fence that skirts the way, 195
With blossomed furze unprofitably gay,
There, in his noisy mansion, skilled to rule,
The village master taught his little school;
A man severe he was, and stern to view,
I knew him well, and every truant knew; 200
Well had the boding tremblers learned to trace
The day's disasters in his morning face;
Full well they laughed with counterfeited glee,
At all his jokes, for many a joke had he;
Full well the busy whisper circling round, 205
Conveyed the dismal tidings when he frowned;
Yet he was kind, or if severe in aught,
The love he bore to learning was in fault;
The village all declared how much he knew;
'Twas certain he could write, and cypher too; 210
Lands he could measure, terms and tides presage,
And even the story ran that he could gauge.
In arguing too, the parson owned his skill,
For e'en though vanquished, he could argue still;
While words of learned length, and thundering sound, 215
Amazed the gazing rustics ranged around,
And still they gazed, and still the wonder grew,
That one small head could carry all he knew.

But past is all his fame. The very spot
Where many a time he triumphed, is forgot. 220
Near yonder thorn, that lifts its head on high,
Where once the signpost caught the passing eye,
Low lies that house where nut-brown draughts inspired,

Where grey-beard mirth and smiling toil retired,
Where village statesmen talked with looks profound,   225
And news much older than their ale went round.
Imagination fondly stoops to trace
The parlour splendours of that festive place;
The white-washed wall, the nicely sanded floor,
The varnished clock that clicked behind the door;   230
The chest contrived a double debt to pay,
A bed by night, a chest of drawers by day;
The pictures placed for ornament and use,
The twelve good rules, the royal game of goose;
The hearth, except when winter chilled the day,   235
With aspen boughs, and flowers, and fennel gay,
While broken teacups, wisely kept for show,
Ranged o'er the chimney, glistened in a row.

   Vain transitory splendours! Could not all
Reprieve the tottering mansion from its fall!   240
Obscure it sinks, nor shall it more impart
An hour's importance to the poor man's heart;
Thither no more the peasant shall repair
To sweet oblivion of his daily care;
No more the farmer's news, the barber's tale,   245
No more the woodman's ballad shall prevail;
No more the smith his dusky brow shall clear,
Relax his ponderous strength, and lean to hear;
The host himself no longer shall be found
Careful to see the mantling bliss go round;   250
Nor the coy maid, half-willing to be pressed,
Shall kiss the cup to pass it to the rest.

   Yes! let the rich deride, the proud disdain,
These simple blessings of the lowly train,
To me more dear, congenial to my heart,   255
One native charm, than all the gloss of art;
Spontaneous joys, where Nature has its play,
The soul adopts, and owns their firstborn sway,
Lightly they frolic o'er the vacant mind,
Unenvied, unmolested, unconfined.   260
But the long pomp, the midnight masquerade,
With all the freaks of wanton wealth arrayed,
In these, ere trifflers half their wish obtain,
The toiling pleasure sickens into pain;
And, even while fashion's brightest arts decoy,   265
The heart distrusting asks, if this be joy.

   Ye friends to truth, ye statesmen who survey
The rich man's joys increase, the poor's decay,

'Tis yours to judge, how wide the limits stand
Between a splendid and an happy land.   270
Proud swells the tide with loads of freighted ore,
And shouting Folly hails them from her shore;
Hoards, even beyond the miser's wish abound,
And rich men flock from all the world around.
Yet count our gains. This wealth is but a name   275
That leaves our useful products still the same.
Not so the loss. The man of wealth and pride,
Takes up a space that many poor supplied;
Space for his lake, his park's extended bounds,
Space for his horses, equipage, and hounds;   280
The robe that wraps his limbs in silken sloth,
Has robbed the neighbouring fields of half their growth;
His feat, where solitary sports are seen,
Indignant spurns the cottage from the green;
Around the world each needful product flies,   285
For all the luxuries the world supplies.
While thus the land adorned for pleasure all
In barren splendour feebly waits the fall.

   As some fair female unadorned and plain,
Secure to please while youth confirms her reign,   290
Slights every borrowed charm that dress supplies,
Nor shares with art the triumph of her eyes.
But when those charms are past, for charms are frail,
When time advances, and when lovers fail,
She then shines forth sollicitous to bless,   295
In all the glaring impotence of dress.
Thus fares the land, by luxury betrayed,
In nature's simplest charms at first arrayed,
But verging to decline, its splendours rise,
Its vistas strike, its palaces surprise;   300
While scourged by famine from the smiling land,
The mournful peasant leads his humble band;
And while he sinks without one arm to save,
The country blooms—a garden, and a grave.

   Where then, ah, where shall poverty reside,   305
To 'scape the pressure of contiguous pride;
If to some common's senseless limits strayed,
He drives his flock to pick the scanty blade,
Those senseless fields the sons of wealth divide,
And even the bare-worn common is denied.   310

   If to the city sped—What waits him there?
To see profusion that he must not share;

To see ten thousand baneful arts combined
To pamper luxury, and thin mankind;
To see each joy the sons of pleasure know,   315
Extorted from his fellow-creature's woe.
Here, while the courtier glitters in brocade,
There the pale artist plies the sickly trade;
Here, while the proud their long-drawn pomps display,
There the black gibbet glooms beside the way.   320
The dome where pleasure holds her midnight reign,
Here richly decked admits the gorgeous train,
Tumultuous grandeur crowds the blazing square,
The rattling chariots clash, the torches glare;
Sure scenes like these no troubles e'er annoy!   325
Sure these denote one universal joy!
Are these thy serious thoughts—Ah, turn thine eyes
Where the poor houseless shivering female lies.
She once, perhaps, in village plenty blest,
Has wept at tales of innocence distressed;   330
Her modest looks the cottage might adorn,
Sweet as the primrose peeps beneath the thorn;
Now lost to all; her friends, her virtue fled,
Near her betrayer's door she lays her head,
And pinched with cold, and shrinking from the shower,   335
With heavy heart deplores that luckless hour,
When idly first, ambitious of the town,
She left her wheel and robes of country brown.

    Do thine, sweet Auburn, thine, the loveliest train,
Do thy fair tribes participate her pain?   340
Even now, perhaps, by cold and hunger led,
At proud men's doors they ask a little bread!

    Ah, no. To distant climes, a dreary scene,
Where half the convex world intrudes between,
To torrid tracts with fainting steps they go,   345
Where wild Altama[3] murmurs to their woe.
Far different there from all that charmed before,
The various terrors of that horrid shore.
Those blazing suns that dart a downward ray,
And fiercely shed intolerable day;   350
Those matted woods where birds forget to sing,
But silent bats in drowsy clusters cling,
Those poisonous fields with rank luxuriance crowned
Where the dark scorpion gathers death around;
Where at each step the stranger fears to wake   355

---

[3] Refers to the Altamaha River in Southeast Georgia. Many dispossessed rural dwellers moved to America in the hope of starting over.

The rattling terrors of the vengeful snake;
Where crouching tigers wait their hapless prey,
And savage men more murderous still than they;
While oft in whirls the mad tornado flies,
Mingling the ravaged landscape with the skies.   360
Far different these from every former scene,
The cooling brook, the grassy vested green,
The breezy covert of the warbling grove,
That only sheltered thefts of harmless love.

  Good Heaven! what sorrows gloomed that parting day,   365
That called them from their native walks away;
When the poor exiles, every pleasure past,
Hung round their bowers, and fondly looked their last,
And took a long farewell, and wished in vain
For seats like these beyond the western main;   370
And shuddering still to face the distant deep,
Returned and wept, and still returned to weep.
The good old sire, the first prepared to go
To new found worlds, and wept for others' woe.
But for himself, in conscious virtue brave,   375
He only wished for worlds beyond the grave.
His lovely daughter, lovelier in her tears,
The fond companion of his helpless years,
Silent went next, neglectful of her charms,
And left a lover's for her father's arms.   380
With louder plaints the mother spoke her woes,
And blest the cot where every pleasure rose;
And kissed her thoughtless babes with many a tear,
And clasped them close in sorrow doubly dear;
Whilst her fond husband strove to lend relief   385
In all the decent manliness of grief.

  O luxury! Thou curst by Heaven's decree,
How ill-exchanged are things like these for thee!
How do thy potions with insidious joy,
Diffuse their pleasures only to destroy!   390
Kingdoms by thee, to sickly greatness grown,
Boast of a florid vigour not their own.
At every draught more large and large they grow,
A bloated mass of rank unwieldy woe;
Till sapped their strength, and every part unsound,   395
Down, down they sink, and spread a ruin round.

  Even now the devastation is begun,
And half the business of destruction done;
Even now, methinks, as pondering here I stand,

I see the rural virtues leave the land. 400
Down where yon anchoring vessel spreads the sail.
That idly waiting flaps with every gale,
Downward they move, a melancholy band,
Pass from the shore, and darken all the strand.
Contented toil, and hospitable care, 405
And kind connubial tenderness, are there;
And piety with wishes placed above,
And steady loyalty, and faithful love.
And thou, sweet Poetry, thou loveliest maid,
Still first to fly where sensual joys invade; 410
Unfit in these degenerate times of shame,
To catch the heart, or strike for honest fame;
Dear charming nymph, neglected and decried,
My shame in crowds my solitary pride.
Thou source of all my bliss, and all my woe, 415
That found'st me poor at first, and keep'st me so;
Thou guide by which the nobler arts excel,
Thou nurse of every virtue, fare thee well.
Farewell, and O where'er thy voice be tried, 420
On Torno's cliffs, or Pambamarca's side,[4]
Whether where equinoctial[5] fervours glow,
Or winter wraps the polar world in snow,
Still let thy voice prevailing over time,
Redress the rigours of the inclement clime;
Aid slighted truth, with thy persuasive strain 425
Teach erring man to spurn the rage of gain;
Teach him that states of native strength possessed,
Though very poor, may still be very blest;
That trade's proud empire hastes to swift decay,
As ocean sweeps the laboured mole[6] away; 430
While self-dependent power can time defy,
As rocks resist the billows and the sky.

[4] The Torne is a river in Sweden, and Pambamarca is a mountain in Ecuador.
[5] Of the equator.
[6] A breakwater, or seawall.

🖎 *William Cowper* (*1731–1800*)

Cowper's major poetic achievement, The Task, *began with the most trivial of subjects: the parlor sofa. Given the task of writing a poem by a lady friend, when Cowper complained of the lack of an adequate topic, she recommended this piece of furniture. From this somewhat absurd starting point grew 5,000 lines of meditative verse that scanned not just the house but the garden, the country landscape, and the nation beyond it. Trained in the law, Cowper was an intelligent, though not an overly ambitious, young man. Yet the strain of competing for a government post early in his career brought on the first severe episode of Cowper's lifelong struggle with mental illness. He was committed to an asylum, where he underwent a conversion to evangelical Christianity. Upon his release, he moved in with a clergyman, Morley Unwin, and his wife, Mary. After Morley's death, Cowper had planned to marry his widow, but further bouts of insanity prevented their union.*

Cowper often wrote as a kind of therapy. His identification with animals, particularly persecuted ones, makes sense in light of his own sense of personal vulnerability. A writer who could be at times quite playful (as can be seen in the mock-heroic premise of The Task *or in his poem on the halibut), Cowper's great fear that he was irredeemably damned often colored his more explicitly religious writing, including his* Olney Hymns. *"A Winter Walk at Noon," the idyllic representation of rural life and retirement in Book 6 of* The Task, *shows a much more optimistic side of Cowper's poetic persona.*

From The Task, Book 6

From The Winter Walk at Noon*

The night was winter in his roughest mood;
The morning sharp and clear. But now at noon
Upon the southern side of the slant hills,
And where the woods fence off the northern blast,
The season smiles, resigning all its rage,   5
And has the warmth of May. The vault is blue
Without a cloud, and white without a speck
The dazzling splendour of the scene below.
Again the harmony comes o'er the vale;
And through the trees I view th' embattled tower   10
Whence all the music. I again perceive
The soothing influence of the wafted strains,
And settle in soft musings as I tread
The walk, still verdant, under oaks and elms,
Whose outspread branches overarch the glade.   15
The roof, though moveable through all its length
As the wind sways it, has yet well sufficed,
And, intercepting in their silent fall
The frequent flakes, has kept a path for me.

---

* The verse line numbers have been set beginning with 1 for the reader's convenience. Lines 57–478 and lines 560–631 from the original are excerpted. — Editors' note.

No noise is here, or none that hinders thought.   20
The redbreast warbles still, but is content
With slender notes, and more than half suppressed:
Pleased with his solitude, and flitting light
From spray to spray, where'er he rests he shakes
From many a twig the pendent drops of ice,   25
That tinkle in the withered leaves below.
Stillness, accompanied with sounds so soft,
Charms more than silence. Meditation here
May think down hours to moments. Here the heart
May give an useful lesson to the head,   30
And learning wiser grow without his books.
Knowledge and wisdom, far from being one,
Have oft-times no connection. Knowledge dwells
In heads replete with thoughts of other men;
Wisdom in minds attentive to their own.   35
Knowledge, a rude unprofitable mass,
The mere materials with which wisdom builds,
Till smoothed and squared and fitted to its place,
Does but encumber whom it seems t' enrich.
Knowledge is proud that he has learned so much;   40
Wisdom is humble that he knows no more.
Books are not seldom talismans and spells,
By which the magic art of shrewder wits
Holds an unthinking multitude enthralled.
Some to the fascination of a name   45
Surrender judgment, hoodwinked. Some the style
Infatuates, and through labyrinths and wilds
Of error leads them by a tune entranced.
While sloth seduces more, too weak to bear
The insupportable fatigue of thought,   50
And swallowing, therefore, without pause or choice,
The total grist unsifted, husks and all.
But trees, and rivulets whose rapid course
Defies the check of winter, haunts of deer,
And sheep-walks populous with bleating lambs,   55
And lanes in which the primrose ere her time
Peeps through the moss that clothes the hawthorn root,
Deceive no student. Wisdom there, and truth,
Not shy, as in the world, and to be won
By slow solicitation, seize at once   60
The roving thought, and fix it on themselves.
     What prodigies can power divine perform
More grand than it produces year by year,
And all in sight of inattentive man?
Familiar with th' effect we slight the cause,   65

And, in the constancy of nature's course,
The regular return of genial months,
And renovation of a faded world,
See nought to wonder at. Should God again,
As once in Gibeon,[1] interrupt the race   70
Of the undeviating and punctual sun,
How would the world admire! but speaks it less
An agency divine, to make him know
His moment when to sink and when to rise,
Age after age, than to arrest his course?   75
All we behold is miracle; but, seen
So duly, all is miracle in vain.
Where now the vital energy that moved,
While summer was, the pure and subtle lymph
Through th' imperceptible meandering veins   80
Of leaf and flower? It sleeps; and th' icy touch
Of unprolific winter has impressed
A cold stagnation on th' intestine tide.
But let the months go round, a few short months,
And all shall be restored. These naked shoots,   85
Barren as lances, among which the wind
Makes wint'ry music, sighing as it goes,
Shall put their graceful foliage on again,
And, more aspiring, and with ampler spread,
Shall boast new charms, and more than they have lost.   90
Then, each in its peculiar honours clad,
Shall publish, even to the distant eye,
Its family and tribe. Laburnum, rich
In streaming gold; syringa, ivory pure;
The scentless and the scented rose; this red   95
And of an humbler growth, the other tall,
And throwing up into the darkest gloom
Of neighbouring cypress, or more sable yew,
Her silver globes, light as the foamy surf
That the wind severs from the broken wave;   100
The lilac, various in array, now white,
Now sanguine, and her beauteous head now set
With purple spikes pyramidal, as if,
Studious of ornament, yet unresolved
Which hue she most approved, she chose them all;   105
Copious of flowers the woodbine, pale and wan,
But well compensating her sickly looks
With never-cloying odours, early and late;

---

[1] A town of ancient Israel, in Palestine, northwest of Jerusalem. Alludes to Joshua 10.12–15: "And the sun stood still, and the moon stayed, until the people had avenged themselves upon their enemies."

Hypericum, all bloom, so thick a swarm
Of flowers, like flies clothing her slender rods,   110
That scarce a leaf appears; mezerion, too,
Though leafless, well attired, and thick beset
With blushing wreaths, investing every spray;
Althaea with the purple eye; the broom,
Yellow and bright, as bullion unalloyed,   115
Her blossoms; and, luxuriant above all,
The jasmine, throwing wide her elegant sweets,
The deep dark green of whose unvarnished leaf
Makes more conspicuous, and illumines more
The bright profusion of her scattered stars. —   120
These have been, and these shall be in their day;
And all this uniform, uncoloured scene,
Shall be dismantled of its fleecy load,
And flush into variety again.
From dearth to plenty, and from death to life,   125
Is Nature's progress when she lectures man
In heavenly truth; evincing, as she makes
The grand transition, that there lives and works
A soul in all things, and that soul is God.
The beauties of the wilderness are his,   130
That make so gay the solitary place
Where no eye sees them. And the fairer forms
That cultivation glories in, are his.
He sets the bright procession on its way,
And marshals all the order of the year;   135
He marks the bounds which winter may not pass,
And blunts his pointed fury; in its case,
Russet and rude, folds up the tender germ,
Uninjured, with inimitable art;
And, ere one flowery season fades and dies,   140
Designs the blooming wonders of the next.
      Some say that, in the origin of things,
When all creation started into birth,
The infant elements received a law,
From which they swerve not since. That under force   145
Of that controlling ordinance they move,
And need not his immediate hand, who first
Prescribed their course, to regulate it now.
Thus dream they, and contrive to save a God
Th' incumbrance of his own concerns, and spare   150
The great Artificer of all that moves
The stress of a continual act, the pain
Of unremitted vigilance and care,
As too laborious and severe a task.

So man, the moth, is not afraid, it seems,   155
To span omnipotence, and measure might
That knows no measure, by the scanty rule
And standard of his own, that is today,
And is not ere tomorrow's sun go down!
But how should matter occupy a charge   160
Dull as it is, and satisfy a law
So vast in its demands, unless impelled
To ceaseless service by a ceaseless force,
And under pressure of some conscious cause?
The Lord of all, himself through all diffused,   165
Sustains, and is the life of all that lives.
Nature is but a name for an effect,
Whose cause is God. He feeds the secret fire
By which the mighty process is maintained,
Who sleeps not, is not weary; in whose sight   170
Slow circling ages are as transient days;
Whose work is without labour; whose designs
No flaw deforms, no difficulty thwarts;
And whose beneficence no charge exhausts.
Him blind antiquity profaned, not served,   175
With self-taught rites, and under various names,
Female and male, Pomona, Pales, Pan,
And Flora, and Vertumnus; peopling earth
With tutelary goddesses and gods
That were not; and commending, as they would,   180
To each some province, garden, field, or grove.
But all are under one. One spirit—His
Who wore the platted thorns with bleeding brows—
Rules universal nature. Not a flower
But shows some touch, in freckle, streak, or stain,   185
Of his unrivalled pencil. He inspires
Their balmy odours, and imparts their hues,
And bathes their eyes with nectar, and includes,
In grains as countless as the seaside sands,
The forms with which he sprinkles all the earth.   190
Happy who walks with him! whom what he finds
Of flavour or of scent in fruit or flower,
Or what he views of beautiful or grand
In nature, from the broad majestic oak
To the green blade that twinkles in the sun,   195
Prompts with remembrance of a present God!
His presence, who made all so fair, perceived,
Makes all still fairer. As with him no scene
Is dreary, so with him all seasons please.
Though winter had been none, had man been true,   200

And earth be punished for its tenant's sake,
Yet not in vengeance; as this smiling sky,
So soon succeeding such an angry night,
And these dissolving snows, and this clear stream
Recovering fast its liquid music, prove.   205
    Who then, that has a mind well strung and tuned
To contemplation, and within his reach
A scene so friendly to his favourite task,
Would waste attention at the chequered board,
His host of wooden warriors to and fro   210
Marching and counter-marching, with an eye
As fixed as marble, with a forehead ridged
And furrowed into storms, and with a hand
Trembling, as if eternity were hung
In balance on his conduct of a pin? —   215
Nor envies he aught more their idle sport,
Who pant with application misapplied
To trivial toys, and, pushing ivory balls
Across a velvet level, feel a joy
Akin to rapture when the bauble finds   220
Its destined goal, of difficult access. —
Nor deems he wiser him, who gives his noon
To miss, the mercer's[2] plague, from shop to shop
Wandering, and littering with unfolded silks
The polished counter, and approving none,   225
Or promising with smiles to call again. —
Nor him, who by his vanity seduced,
And soothed into a dream that he discerns
The difference of a Guido from a daub,[3]
Frequents the crowded auction: stationed there   230
As duly as the Langford of the show,
With glass at eye, and catalogue in hand,
And tongue accomplished in the fulsome cant
And pedantry that coxcombs learn with ease;
Oft as the price-deciding hammer falls   235
He notes it in his book, then raps his box,
Swears 'tis a bargain, rails at his hard fate
That he has let it pass — but never bids!
    Here, unmolested, through whatever sign
The sun proceeds, I wander. Neither mist,   240
Nor freezing sky nor sultry, checking me,
Nor stranger intermeddling with my joy.
Even in the spring and play-time of the year,

---

[2] A merchant who deals in textiles.

[3] I.e., the difference between a great work of art and a mere spattering of paint.

That calls th' unwonted villager abroad
With all her little ones, a sportive train,   245
To gather king-cups in the yellow mead,
And prink their hair with daisies, or to pick
A cheap but wholesome salad from the brook,
These shades are all my own. The timourous hare,
Grown so familiar with her frequent guest,   250
Scarce shuns me; and the stock dove, unalarmed,
Sits cooing in the pine tree, nor suspends
His long love ditty for my near approach.
Drawn from his refuge in some lonely elm
That age or injury has hollowed deep,   255
Where, on his bed of wool and matted leaves,
He has outslept the winter, ventures forth
To frisk awhile, and bask in the warm sun,
The squirrel, flippant, pert, and full of play:
He sees me, and at once, swift as a bird,   260
Ascends the neighbouring beech; there whisks his brush,
And perks his ears, and stamps and cries aloud,
With all the prettiness of feigned alarm,
And anger insignificantly fierce.
     The heart is hard in nature, and unfit   265
For human fellowship, as being void
Of sympathy, and therefore dead alike
To love and friendship both, that is not pleased
With sight of animals enjoying life,
Nor feels their happiness augment his own.   270
The bounding fawn, that darts across the glade
When none pursues, through mere delight of heart,
And spirits buoyant with excess of glee;
The horse as wanton, and almost as fleet,
That skims the spacious meadow at full speed,   275
Then stops and snorts, and, throwing high his heels,
Starts to the voluntary race again;
The very kine that gambol at high noon,
The total herd receiving first from one
That leads the dance a summons to be gay,   280
Though wild their strange vagaries, and uncouth
Their efforts, yet resolved with one consent
To give such act and utterance as they may
To ecstasy too big to be suppressed—
These, and a thousand images of bliss,   285
With which kind nature graces ev'ry scene
Where cruel man defeats not her design,
Impart to the benevolent, who wish
All that are capable of pleasure pleased,

A far superior happiness to theirs, 290
The comfort of a reasonable joy.
    Man scarce had risen, obedient to his call
Who formed him from the dust, his future grave,
When he was crowned as never king was since.
God set the diadem upon his head, 295
And angel choirs attended. Wondering stood
The new-made monarch, while before him passed,
All happy, and all perfect in their kind,
The creatures summoned from their various haunts
To see their sovereign, and confess his sway. 300
Vast was his empire, absolute his power,
Or bounded only by a law, whose force
'Twas his sublimest privilege to feel
And own — the law of universal love.
He ruled with meekness, they obeyed with joy; 305
No cruel purpose lurked within his heart,
And no distrust of his intent in theirs.
So Eden was a scene of harmless sport,
Where kindness on his part who ruled the whole
Begat a tranquil confidence in all, 310
And fear as yet was not, nor cause for fear.
But sin marred all; and the revolt of man,
That source of evils not exhausted yet,
Was punished with revolt of his from him.
Garden of God, how terrible the change 315
Thy groves and lawns then witnessed! Every heart,
Each animal of every name, conceived
A jealousy and an instinctive fear,
And, conscious of some danger, either fled
Precipitate the loathed abode of man, 320
Or growled defiance in such angry sort,
As taught him, too, to tremble in his turn.
Thus harmony and family accord
Were driven from Paradise; and in that hour
The seeds of cruelty, that since have swelled 325
To such gigantic and enormous growth,
Were sown in human nature's fruitful soil.
Hence date the persecution and the pain
That man inflicts on all inferior kinds,
Regardless of their plaints. To make him sport, 330
To gratify the frenzy of his wrath,
Or his base gluttony, are causes good
And just, in his account, why bird and beast
Should suffer torture, and the streams be dyed
With blood of their inhabitants impaled. 335

Earth groans beneath the burden of a war
Waged with defenceless innocence, while he,
Not satisfied to prey on all around,
Adds tenfold bitterness to death by pangs
Needless, and first torments ere he devours.   340
Now happiest they that occupy the scenes
The most remote from his abhorred resort,
Whom once, as delegate of God on earth,
They feared, and, as his perfect image, loved.
The wilderness is theirs, with all its caves,   345
Its hollow glens, its thickets, and its plains,
Unvisited by man. There they are free,
And howl and roar as likes them, uncontrolled;
Nor ask his leave to slumber or to play.
Woe to the tyrant, if he dare intrude   350
Within the confines of their wild domain!
The lion tells him — I am monarch here!
And, if he spare him, spares him on the terms
Of royal mercy, and through generous scorn
To rend a victim trembling at his foot.   355
In measure, as by force of instinct drawn,
Or by necessity constrained, they live
Dependent upon man; those in his fields,
These at his crib, and some beneath his roof.
They prove too often at how dear a rate   360
He sells protection. — Witness at his foot,
The spaniel dying, for some venial fault,
Under dissection of the knotted scourge —
Witness the patient ox, with stripes and yells
Driven to the slaughter, goaded, as he runs,   365
To madness; while the savage at his heels
Laughs at the frantic sufferer's fury, spent
Upon the guiltless passenger o'erthrown.
He, too, is witness, noblest of the train
That wait on man, the flight-performing horse: 370
With unsuspecting readiness he takes
His murderer on his back, and, pushed all day,
With bleeding sides and flanks that heave for life,
To the far-distant goal, arrives and dies.
So little mercy shows who needs so much!   375
Does law, so jealous in the cause of man,
Denounce no doom on the delinquent? — None.
He lives, and o'er his brimming beaker boasts
(As if barbarity were high desert)
Th' inglorious feat, and, clamorous in praise   380
Of the poor brute, seems wisely to suppose

The honours of his matchless horse his own!
But many a crime, deemed innocent on earth,
Is registered in heaven; and these, no doubt,
Have each their record, with a curse annexed.   385
Man may dismiss compassion from his heart,
But God will never. When he charged the Jew
T' assist his foe's down-fallen beast to rise;
And when the bush-exploring boy, that seized
The young, to let the parent bird go free;   390
Proved he not plainly that his meaner works
Are yet his care, and have an interest all,
All, in the universal Father's love?
On Noah, and in him on all mankind,
The charter was conferred, by which we hold   400
The flesh of animals in fee, and claim
O'er all we feed on power of life and death.
But read the instrument, and mark it well:
Th' oppression of a tyrannous control
Can find no warrant there. Feed then, and yield   405
Thanks for thy food. Carnivorous, through sin,
Feed on the slain, but spare the living brute!
     The Governor of all, himself to all
So bountiful in whose attentive ear
The unfledged raven and the lion's whelp   410
Plead not in vain for pity on the pangs
Of hunger unassuaged, has interposed,
Not seldom, his avenging arm, to smite
Th' injurious trampler upon nature's law,
That claims forbearance even for a brute.   415
He hates the hardness of a Balaam's heart;
And, prophet as he was, he might not strike
The blameless animal, without rebuke,
On which he rode. Her opportune offence
Saved him, or th' unrelenting seer had died.   420
He sees that human equity is slack
To interfere, though in so just a cause;
And makes the task his own. Inspiring dumb
And helpless victims with a sense so keen
Of injury, with such knowledge of their strength,   425
And such sagacity to take revenge,
That oft the beast has seemed to judge the man.

                    .   .   .

     I would not enter on my list of friends
(Tho' graced with polished manners and fine sense,
Yet wanting sensibility) the man   430

Who needlessly sets foot upon a worm.
An inadvertent step may crush the snail
That crawls at ev'ning in the public path;
But he that has humanity, forewarned,
Will tread aside, and let the reptile live.   435
The creeping vermin, loathsome to the sight,
And charged perhaps with venom, that intrudes,
A visitor unwelcome, into scenes
Sacred to neatness and repose — th' alcove,   440
The chamber, or refectory — may die:
A necessary act incurs no blame.
Not so when, held within their proper bounds,
And guiltless of offence, they range the air,
Or take their pastime in the spacious field:
There they are privileged; and he that hunts   445
Or harms them there is guilty of a wrong,
Disturbs th' economy of nature's realm,
Who, when she formed, designed them an abode.
The sum is this. — If man's convenience, health,
Or safety, interfere, his rights and claims   450
Are paramount, and must extinguish theirs.
Else they are all — the meanest things that are —
As free to live, and to enjoy that life,
As God was free to form them at the first,
Who, in his sovereign wisdom, made them all.   455
Ye, therefore, who love mercy, teach your sons
To love it too. The springtime of our years
Is soon dishonoured and defiled in most
By budding ills, that ask a prudent hand
To check them. But, alas! none sooner shoots,   460
If unrestrained, into luxuriant growth,
Than cruelty, most devilish of them all.
Mercy to him that shows it, is the rule
And righteous limitation of its act,
By which Heaven moves in pardoning guilty man;   465
And he that shows none, being ripe in years,
And conscious of the outrage he commits,
Shall seek it, and not find it, in his turn.
    Distinguished much by reason, and still more
By our capacity of grace divine,   470
From creatures that exist but for our sake,
Which, having served us, perish, we are held
Accountable; and God, some future day,
Will reckon with us roundly for th' abuse
Of what he deems no mean or trivial trust.   475
Superior as we are, they yet depend

Not more on human help than we on theirs.
Their strength, or speed, or vigilance, were given
In aid of our defects. In some are found
Such teachable and apprehensive parts,   480
That man's attainments in his own concerns,
Matched with th' expertness of the brutes in theirs,
Are oft-times vanquished and thrown far behind.
Some show that nice sagacity of smell,
And read with such discernment, in the port   485
And figure of the man, his secret aim,
That oft we owe our safety to a skill
We could not teach, and must despair to learn.
But learn we might, if not too proud to stoop
To quadrupede instructors, many a good   490
And useful quality, and virtue too,
Rarely exemplified among ourselves.
Attachment never to be weaned, or changed
By any change of fortune; proof alike
Against unkindness, absence, and neglect;   495
Fidelity, that neither bribe nor threat
Can move or warp; and gratitude for small
And trivial favours, lasting as the life,
And glistening even in the dying eye.

.   .   .

Epitaph on a Hare

Here lies, whom hound did ne'er pursue,
    Nor swifter greyhound follow,
Whose foot ne'er tainted morning dew,
    Nor ear heard huntsman's hallo',

Old Tiney, surliest of his kind,   5
    Who, nursed with tender care,
And to domestic bounds confined,
    Was still a wild Jack-hare.

Though duly from my hand he took
    His pittance every night,   10
He did it with a jealous look,
    And, when he could, would bite.

His diet was of wheaten bread,
    And milk, and oats, and straw,
Thistles, or lettuces instead,   15
    With sand to scour his maw.

On twigs of hawthorn he regaled,
    On pippins'[1] russet peel;
And, when his juicy salads failed,
    Sliced carrot pleased him well.   20

A Turkey carpet was his lawn,
    Whereon he loved to bound,
To skip and gambol like a fawn,
    And swing his rump around.

His frisking was at evening hours,   25
    For then he lost his fear;
But most before approaching showers,
    Or when a storm drew near.

Eight years and five round-rolling moons
    He thus saw steal away,   30
Dozing out all his idle noons,
    And every night at play.

I kept him for his humour's sake,
    For he would oft beguile
My heart of thoughts that made it ache,   35
    And force me to a smile.

But now, beneath this walnut-shade
    He finds his long, last home,
And waits in snug concealment laid,
    'Till gentler Puss shall come.   40

He, still more aged, feels the shocks
    From which no care can save,
And, partner once of Tiney's box,
    Must soon partake his grave.

[1] Apples.

To the Immortal Memory of the Halibut on Which I Dined This Day

Where hast thou floated, in what seas pursued
Thy pastime? when wast thou an egg new-spawned,
Lost in th' immensity of ocean's waste?
Roar as they might, the overbearing winds
That rocked the deep, thy cradle, thou wast safe —   5
And in thy minikin and embryo state,
Attached to the firm leaf of some salt weed,

Didst outlive tempests, such as wrung and racked
The joints of many a stout and gallant bark,
And whelmed them in the unexplored abyss.   10
Indebted to no magnet and no chart,
Nor under guidance of the polar fire,
Thou wast a voyager on many coasts,
Grazing at large in meadows submarine,
Where flat Batavia just emerging peeps   15
Above the brine,—where Caledonia's rocks
Beat back the surge,—and where Hibernia[1] shoots
Her wondrous causeway far into the main.
—Wherever thou hast fed, thou little thought'st,
And I not more, that I should feed on thee.   20
Peace therefore, and good health, and much good fish,
To him who sent thee! and success, as oft
As it descends into the billowy gulf,
To the same drag that caught thee!—Fare thee well!
Thy lot thy brethren of the slimy fin   25
Would envy, could they know that thou wast doomed
To feed a bard, and to be praised in verse.

[1] Batavia, Caledonia, and Hibernia are poetic names for Germany, Scotland, and Ireland, respectively.

Yardley Oak

Survivor sole, and hardly such, of all
That once lived here thy brethren, at my birth
(Since which I number three-score winters past)
A shattered veteran, hollow-trunked perhaps
As now, and with excoriate forks deform,   5
Relics of ages! Could a mind, imbued
With truth from heaven, created thing adore,
I might with reverence kneel and worship thee.
    It seems idolatry with some excuse
When our forefather Druids in their oaks   10
Imagined sanctity. The conscience yet
Unpurified by an authentic act
Of amnesty, the meed of blood divine,
Loved not the light, but gloomy into gloom
Of thickest shades, like Adam after taste   15
Of fruit proscribed, as to a refuge, fled.
    Thou wast a bauble once; a cup and ball,
Which babes might play with; and the thievish jay
Seeking her food, with ease might have purloined

The auburn nut that held thee, swallowing down   20
Thy yet close-folded latitude of boughs
And all thine embryo vastness, at a gulp.
But Fate thy growth decreed: autumnal rains
Beneath thy parent tree mellowed the soil
Designed thy cradle, and a skipping deer,   25
With pointed hoof dibbling the glebe, prepared
The soft receptacle in which secure
Thy rudiments should sleep the winter through.
    So Fancy dreams—Disprove it, if ye can,
Ye reasoners broad awake, whose busy search   30
Of argument, employed too oft amiss,
Sifts half the pleasures of short life away.
    Thou fell'st mature, and in the loamy clod
Swelling, with vegetative force instinct
Didst burst thine egg, as theirs the fabled Twins[1]   35
Now stars; two lobes, protruding, paired exact;
A leaf succeeded, and another leaf,
And all the elements thy puny growth
Fostering propitious, thou becam'st a twig.
    Who lived when thou wast such? Oh couldst thou speak,   40
As in Dodona[2] once thy kindred trees
Oracular, I would not curious ask
The future, best unknown, but at thy mouth
Inquisitive, the less ambiguous past.
    By thee I might correct, erroneous oft,   45
The clock of history, facts and events
Timing more punctual, unrecorded facts
Recovering, and misstated setting right—
Desperate attempt, till trees shall speak again!
    Time made thee what thou wast—King of the woods;   50
And Time hath made thee what thou art—a cave
For owls to roost in. Once thy spreading boughs
O'erhung the champaign; and the numerous flock
That grazed it stood beneath that ample cope
Uncrowded, yet safe-sheltered from the storm.   55
No flock frequents thee now. Thou hast outlived
Thy popularity and art become
(Unless verse rescue thee awhile) a thing
Forgotten, as the foliage of thy youth.
    While thus through all the stages thou hast pushed   60
Of treeship, first a seedling hid in grass,

---

[1] Romulus and Remus, the fabled founders of ancient Rome, for whom are named the twin stars of the constellation of Gemini.

[2] An island in Greece, where ancient priests would make prophesies based on the sound of the wind through a sacred tree.

Then twig, then sapling, and, as century rolled
Slow after century, a giant bulk
Of girth enormous, with moss-cushioned root
Upheaved above the soil, and sides imbossed   65
With prominent wens[3] globose, till at the last
The rottenness, which time is charged t' inflict
On other mighty ones, found also thee—
What exhibitions various hath the world
Witnessed of mutability in all   70
That we account most durable below!
Change is the diet, on which all subsist
Created changeable, and change at last
Destroys them.—Skies uncertain now the heat
Transmitting cloudless, and the solar beam   75
Now quenching in a boundless sea of clouds,—
Calm and alternate storm, moisture and drought,
Invigorate by turns the springs of life
In all that live, plant, animal, and man,
And in conclusion mar them. Nature's threads,   80
Fine passing thought, even in her coarsest works,
Delight in agitation, yet sustain
The force, that agitates not unimpaired,
But, worn by frequent impulse, to the cause
Of their best tone their dissolution owe.   85
    Thought cannot spend itself, comparing still
The great and little of thy lot, thy growth
From almost nullity into a state
Of matchless grandeur, and declension thence
Slow into such magnificent decay.   90
Time was, when, settling on thy leaf, a fly
Could shake thee to the root—and time has been
When tempests could not. At thy firmest age
Thou hadst within thy bole solid contents
That might have ribbed the sides or planked the deck   95
Of some flagged admiral; and tortuous arms,
The shipwright's darling treasure, didst present
To the four-quartered winds, robust and bold,
Warped into tough knee-timber,[4] many a load.
But the axe spared thee; in those thriftier days   100
Oaks fell not, hewn by thousands, to supply
The bottomless demands of contest waged
For senatorial honours. Thus to Time
The task was left to whittle thee away

---

[3] A tumor, or swelling.

[4] The part of the tree used to build angled portions of a ship, such as where the ship's deck and sides meet.

With his sly scythe, whose ever-nibbling edge   105
Noiseless, an atom and an atom more
Disjoining from the rest, has, unobserved,
Achieved a labour, which had, far and wide,
(By man performed) made all the forest ring.
    Embowelled now, and of thy ancient self   110
Possessing nought but the scooped rind, that seems
An huge throat calling to the clouds for drink,
Which it would give in rivulets to thy root,
Thou temptest none, but rather much forbid'st
The feller's toil, which thou couldst ill requite.   115
Yet is thy root sincere, sound as the rock,
A quarry of stout spurs and knotted fangs,
Which, crooked into a thousand whimsies, clasp
The stubborn soil, and hold thee still erect.
    So stands a kingdom, whose foundations yet   120
Fail not, in virtue and in wisdom laid,
Though all the superstructure, by the tooth
Pulverized of venality, a shell
Stands now, and semblance only of itself.
    Thine arms have left thee. Winds have rent them off   125
Long since, and rovers of the forest wild
With bow and shaft have burnt them. Some have left
A splintered stump bleached to a snowy white;
And some memorial none where once they grew.
Yet life still lingers in thee, and puts forth   130
Proof not contemptible of what she can,
Even where death predominates. The spring
Thee finds not less alive to her sweet force
Than yonder upstarts of the neighbour wood,
So much thy juniors, who their birth received   135
Half a millennium since the date of thine.
    But since, although well qualified by age
To teach, no spirit dwells in thee, nor voice
May be expected from thee, seated here
On thy distorted root, with hearers none   140
Or prompter, save the scene, I will perform
Myself the oracle, and will discourse
In my own ear such matter as I may.
Thou, like myself, hast stage by stage attained
Life's wintry bourn; thou, after many years,   145
I after few; but few or many prove
A span in retrospect; for I can touch
With my least finger's end my own decease
And with extended thumb my natal hour,
And hadst thou also skill in measurement   150
As I, the past would seem as short to thee.
Evil and few—said Jacob—at an age

Thrice mine, and few and evil, I may think
The Prediluvian race, whose buxom youth
Endured two centuries, accounted theirs.   155
"Shortlived as foliage is the race of man.
The wind shakes down the leaves, the budding grove
Soon teems with others, and in spring they grow.
So pass mankind. One generation meets
Its destined period, and a new succeeds."[5]   160
Such was the tender but undue complaint
Of the Maeonian in old time; for who
Would drawl out centuries in tedious strife
Severe with mental and corporeal ill
And would not rather choose a shorter race   165
To glory, a few decades here below?
     One man alone, the Father of us all,
Drew not his life from woman; never gazed,
With mute unconsciousness of what he saw
On all around him; learned not by degrees,   170
Nor owed articulation to his ear;
But, molded by his Maker into Man
At once, upstood intelligent, surveyed
All creatures, with precision understood
Their purport, uses, properties, assigned   175
To each his name significant, and, filled
With love and wisdom, rendered back to heaven
In praise harmonious the first air he drew.
He was excused the penalties of dull
Minority. No tutor charged his hand   180
With the thought-tracing quill, or tasked his mind
With problems; history, not wanted yet,
Leaned on her elbow, watching Time, whose course,
Eventful, should supply her with a theme.

🦢 *Erasmus Darwin* (*1731–1802*)

Erasmus Darwin was renowned in his own time for a wide range of accomplishments. Regarded as England's leading physician, he had a reputation for providing free medical assistance to poor patients. His medical practice was based in Lichfield, a prosperous market town in the central industrial region of England known as the Midlands. In the 1790s he gained an international poetic reputation through the publication of The Botanic Garden *(1791, illustrated with engravings by William Blake), which strongly influenced the poetry of William Wordsworth, Samuel Taylor Coleridge, and Percy*

[5] Lines 156–60: Cowper's translation of Book 6, lines 171–75 of Homer's *Iliad*.

Bysshe Shelley. He was noted for many inventions, ranging from copying machines and insecticides to ingenious designs for steam-powered carriages, seed drills, and submarines. He was a founder of the famous Lunar Society, an informal association of Midland scientists and inventors whose work laid the foundations of the Industrial Revolution. Its members included Matthew Boulton and James Watt (inventors of a more powerful and efficient steam engine), Joseph Priestley (discoverer of oxygen), and Josiah Wedgwood (who devised an industrial process for making fine pottery). Darwin was also regarded as one of the most learned biologists of his time, the author of definitive treatises on animal and plant life, Zoonomia *(1794–96) and* Phytologia *(1800).*

Today, Darwin is perhaps best remembered for other achievements, notably for his original ideas and discoveries in many different fields of science. He foreshadowed in some detail the theory of evolution later developed by his grandson Charles Darwin. In his long poem The Temple of Nature *(1803), he traces the progress of life from "its natant form in the circumfluent waves," through the development of amphibians, to its present culmination in humankind. This poem is remarkable for its presentation of evolutionary theory in neoclassical heroic couplets, with extensive footnotes detailing the scientific facts that underlie the poetic imagery. Among his other scientific discoveries, Darwin was the first to explain how clouds form (by the condensation of water vapor in moist, rising air), and he gave a speculative theory of the moon's origin as the result of a cometary collision with the earth. Darwin's theory of lunar origin was dismissed as ludicrously improbable for two centuries, but in 1998 it was substantially confirmed through gravitational mapping of the moon by the* Lunar Prospector *space probe. No other poet of the eighteenth century, or indeed of any century, has been such an erudite, prescient, and original scientific thinker.*

From The Temple of Nature; or, The Origin of Society: A Poem with Philosophic Notes

From Canto 1*

   Organic Life—beneath the shoreless waves[1]
Was born and nursed in Ocean's pearly caves;
First forms minute, unseen by spheric glass,
Move on the mud, or pierce the watery mass;
These, as successive generations bloom,   5
New powers acquire, and larger limbs assume;

---

* For the reader's convenience, verse line numbers have been set beginning with 1 for the 97 lines of this excerpt, which is from the last part of Canto 1, lines 295 to 400 of the original.—Editors' note.

[1] The earth was originally covered with water, as appears from some of its highest mountains, consisting of shells cemented together by a solution of part of them, as the limestone rocks of the Alps. (*Ferber's Travels.*) It must be therefore concluded, that animal life began beneath the sea.

   Nor is this unanalogous to what still occurs, as all quadrupeds and mankind in their embryon state are aquatic animals; and thus may be said to resemble gnats and frogs. The fetus in the uterus has an organ called the placenta, the fine extremities of the vessels of which permeate the arteries of the uterus, and the blood of the fetus becomes thus oxygenated from the passing stream of the maternal arterial blood, exactly as is done by the gills of fish from the stream of water which they occasion to pass through them. (Note by Darwin.)

Whence countless groups of vegetation spring,
And breathing realms of fin, and feet, and wing.

    Thus the tall Oak, the giant of the wood,
Which bears Britannia's thunders on the flood;   10
The Whale, unmeasured monster of the main,
The lordly Lion, monarch of the plain,
The Eagle soaring in the realms of air,
Whose eye undazzled drinks the solar glare;
Imperious man, who rules the bestial crowd,   15
Of language, reason, and reflection proud,
With brow erect, who scorns this earthy sod,
And styles himself the image of his God;
Arose from rudiments of form and sense,
An embryon point,[2] or microscopic ens!   20

    Now in vast shoals beneath the brineless tide,[3]
On earth's firm crust testaceous tribes reside;
Age after age expands the peopled plain,
The tenants perish, but their cells remain;
Whence coral walls and sparry hills ascend,   25
From pole to pole, and round the line extend.

    Next when imprisoned fires in central caves
Burst the firm earth, and drank the headlong waves;
And, as new airs with dread explosion swell,
Formed lava-isles, and continents of shell;   30
Piled rocks on rocks, on mountains mountains raised,
And high in heaven the first volcanoes blazed;
In countless swarms an insect-myriad moves[4]
From sea-fan gardens, and from coral groves;
Leaves the cold caverns of the deep, and creeps   35

---

[2] The arguments showing that all vegetables and animals arose from such a small beginning, as a living point or living fibre, are detailed in *Zoonomia*, section 39.4.8, on Generation. (Note by Darwin.)

[3] As the salt of the sea has been gradually accumulating, being washed down into it from the recrements of animal and vegetable bodies, the sea must originally have been as fresh as river water; and as it is not saturated with salt, must become annually saline. (Note by Darwin.)

[4] After islands or continents were raised above the primeval ocean, great numbers of the most simple animals would attempt to seek food at the edges or shores of the new land, and might thence gradually become amphibious; as is now seen in the frog, who changes from an aquatic animal to an amphibious one; and in the gnat, which changes from a natant to a volant state.

    At the same time new microscopic animalcules would immediately commence wherever there was warmth or moisture, and some organic matter, that might induce putridity. Those situated on dry land, and immersed in dry air, may gradually acquire new powers to preserve their existence; and by innumerable successive reproductions for some thousands of years, or perhaps millions of ages, may at length have produced many of the vegetable and animal inhabitants which now people the earth.

    As innumerable shell-fish must have existed a long time beneath the ocean, before the calcareous mountains were produced and elevated, it is also probable, that many of the insect tribes, or less complicate animals, existed long before the quadrupeds or more complicate ones, which, in some measure, accords with the theory of Linnaeus in respect to the vegetable world; who thinks, that all the plants now extant arose from the conjunction and reproduction of about sixty different vegetables, from which he constitutes his natural orders. (Note by Darwin.)

On shelving shores, or climbs on rocky steeps.
As in dry air the sea-born stranger roves,
Each muscle quickens, and each sense improves:
Cold gills aquatic form respiring lungs,
And sounds aerial flow from slimy tongues.   40

So Trapa,[5] rooted in pellucid tides,
In countless threads her breathing leaves divides,
Waves her bright tresses in the watery mass,
And drinks with gelid gills the vital gas;
Then broader leaves in shadowy files advance,   45
Spread o'er the crystal flood their green expanse;
And, as in air the adherent dew exhales,
Court the warm sun, and breathe ethereal gales.

So still the Tadpole[6] cleaves the watery vale
With balanced fins, and undulating tail;   50
New lungs and limbs proclaim his second birth,
Breathe the dry air, and bound upon the earth.
So from deep lakes the dread Mosquito springs,
Drinks the soft breeze, and dries his tender wings,
In twinkling squadrons cuts his airy way,   55
Dips his red trunk in blood, and man his prey.

So still the Diodons, amphibious tribe,
With two-fold lungs the sea or air imbibe;
Allied to fish, the lizard cleaves the flood
With one celled heart, and dark frigescent blood;   60
Half-reasoning Beavers long-unbreathing dart
Through Erie's waves with perforated heart;
With gills and lungs respiring Lampreys steer,
Kiss the rude rocks, and suck till they adhere;
The lazy Remora's inhaling lips,   65
Hung on the keel, retard the struggling ships;
With gills pulmonic breathes the enormous Whale,
And spouts aquatic columns to the gale;
Sports on the shining wave at noontide hours,
And shifting rainbows crest the rising showers.   70

. . . .

[5] The lower leaves of this plant grow under water, and are divided into minute capillary ramifications; while the upper leaves are broad and round, and have air bladders in their foot-stalks to support them above the surface of the water. As the aerial leaves of vegetables do the office of lungs, by exposing a large surface of vessels, with their contained fluids, to the influence of air; so these aquatic leaves answer a similar purpose, like the gills of fish, and perhaps gain from the water a similar material. (Note by Darwin.)

[6] The transformation of the tadpole from an aquatic animal into an aerial one is abundantly curious. When first it is hatched from the spawn by the warmth of the season, it resembles a fish; it afterwards puts forth legs, and resembles a lizard; and finally losing its tail, and acquiring lungs instead of gills, becomes an aerial quadruped. (Note by Darwin.)

Still Nature's births enclosed in egg or seed,
From the tall forest to the lowly weed,
Her beaux and beauties, butterflies and worms,
Rise from aquatic to aerial forms.   85
Thus in the womb the nascent infant laves
Its natent form in the circumfluent waves;
With perforated heart unbreathing swims,
Awakes and stretches[7] all its recent limbs;
With gills placental seeks the arterial flood,   90
And drinks pure ether from its Mother's blood.
Erewhile the landed Stranger bursts his way,
From the warm wave emerging into day;
Feels the chill blast, and piercing light, and tries
His tender lungs, and rolls his dazzled eyes;   95
Gives to the passing gale his curling hair,
And steps a dry inhabitant of air.

---

[7] During the first six months of gestation, the embryo probably sleeps, as it seems to have no use for voluntary power; it then seems to awake, and to stretch its limbs, and change its posture in some degree, which is termed quickening. (Note by Darwin.)

✒ *Hector St. John de Crèvecoeur* (1735–1813)

Hector St. John de Crèvecoeur was born in France in 1735. He moved to England at age nineteen, learning the rudiments of the English language before moving on to Canada, where he enlisted in the militia and served as a government surveyor. He was wounded, in 1759, while defending the French colonial city of Quebec against British invasion. For the next ten years, Crèvecoeur traveled widely through the American colonies as a surveyor and Indian trader. In 1769, he purchased a farm at Pine Hill in Orange County, New York, where he married a local woman and settled down into the uneventful daily routine of an American farmer. During this idyllic interlude, which lasted only five years, Crèvecoeur wrote a series of essays about American life, based on his extensive travels and experience as a farmer. Published in London in 1782, his Letters from an American Farmer *were an immediate success in both Britain and America. By 1782, the American colonies were winning the Revolutionary War against Britain, and their great democratic experiment had attracted the attention of an international readership. Crèvecoeur's* Letters *fed this insatiable demand by projecting an appealing image of the new republic as an unspoiled agrarian landscape, rich in natural resources, where class distinctions are insignificant and individual effort is richly rewarded. Certainly some readers were aware that this portrayal of America was rather idealized; George Washington said that the book was "too flattering" to be true. But Crèvecoeur's georgic vision of the American landscape has endured; his archetypal image of the strong, self-sufficient American farmer still resonates in popular conceptions of the American Dream and replicates itself in millions of "ranch houses" that line the quiet streets of American suburbia.*

Despite his advocacy of a peaceful agrarian lifestyle, Crèvecoeur grew restless on the farm, and with the advent of war in 1776, he decided to return to France. However, he was captured by British forces in the Port of New York and imprisoned as a rebel spy (an unlikely allegation in light of his Tory sympathies). He was released in 1780 and made his way to France, where he was celebrated as a famous author and authentic American revolutionary hero. In 1783, he returned to New York, only to find that his farmhouse had been burned and his wife killed in an Indian attack. Deeply affected by this tragic loss, Crèvecoeur returned permanently to France.

From Letters from an American Farmer

From On the Situation, Feelings, and Pleasures of an American Farmer

Pray do not laugh in thus seeing an artless countryman tracing himself through the simple modifications of his life; remember that you have required it, therefore with candour, though with diffidence, I endeavour to follow the thread of my feelings, but I cannot tell you all. Often when I plough my low ground, I place my little boy on a chair which screws to the beam of the plough—its motion and that of the horses please him, he is perfectly happy and begins to chat. As I lean over the handle, various are the thoughts which crowd into my mind. I am now doing for him, I say, what my father formerly did for me, may God enable him to live that he may perform the same operations for the same purposes when I am worn out and old! I relieve his mother of some trouble while I have him with me, the odoriferous furrow exhilarates his spirits, and seems to do the child a great deal of good, for he looks more blooming since I have adopted that practice; can more pleasure, more dignity be added to that primary occupation? The father thus ploughing with his child, and to feed his family, is inferior only to the emperor of China ploughing as an example to his kingdom. In the evening when I return home through my low grounds, I am astonished at the myriads of insects which I perceive dancing in the beams of the setting sun. I was before scarcely acquainted with their existence, they are so small that it is difficult to distinguish them; they are carefully improving this short evening space, not daring to expose themselves to the blaze of our meridian sun. I never see an egg brought on my table but I feel penetrated with the wonderful change it would have undergone but for my gluttony; it might have been a gentle useful hen leading her chickens with a care and vigilance which speaks shame to many women. A cock perhaps, arrayed with the most majestic plumes, tender to its mate, bold, courageous, endowed with an astonishing instinct, with thoughts, with memory, and every distinguishing characteristic of the reason of man. I never see my trees drop their leaves and their fruit in the autumn, and bud again in the spring, without wonder; the sagacity of those animals which have long been the tenants of my farm astonish me: some of them seem to surpass even men in memory and sagacity. I could tell you singular instances of that kind. What then is this instinct which we so debase, and of which we are taught to entertain so diminutive an idea? My bees, above any other tenants of my farm, attract my attention and respect; I am astonished to see that nothing exists but what has its enemy, one species pursue and live upon the other: unfortunately our kingbirds are the destroyers of those industrious insects; but on the other hand, these birds preserve our fields from the depredation of crows which they pursue on the wing with great vigilance and astonishing dexterity.

Thus divided by two interested motives, I have long resisted the desire I had to kill them, until last year, when I thought they increased too much, and my indulgence had been carried too far; it was at the time of swarming when they all came and fixed themselves on the neighbouring trees, from whence they catched those that returned loaded from the fields. This made me resolve to kill as many as I could, and I was just ready to fire, when a bunch of bees as big as my fist, issued from one of the hives, rushed on one of the birds, and probably stung him, for he instantly screamed, and flew, not as before, in an irregular manner, but in a direct line. He was followed by the same bold phalanx, at a considerable distance, which unfortunately becoming too sure of victory, quitted their military array and disbanded themselves. By this inconsiderate step they lost all that aggregate of force which had made the bird fly off. Perceiving their disorder he immediately returned and snapped as many as he wanted; nay, he had even the impudence to alight on the very twig from which the bees had drove him. I killed him and immediately opened his craw, from which I took 171 bees; I laid them all on a blanket in the sun, and to my great surprise 54 returned to life, licked themselves clean, and joyfully went back to the hive; where they probably informed their companions of such an adventure and escape, as I believe had never happened before to American bees! I draw a great fund of pleasure from the quails which inhabit my farm; they abundantly repay me, by their various notes and peculiar tameness, for the inviolable hospitality I constantly show them in the winter. Instead of perfidiously taking advantage of their great and affecting distress, when nature offers nothing but a barren universal bed of snow, when irresistible necessity forces them to my barn doors, I permit them to feed unmolested; and it is not the least agreeable spectacle which that dreary season presents, when I see those beautiful birds, tamed by hunger, intermingling with all my cattle and sheep, seeking in security for the poor scanty grain which but for them would be useless and lost. Often in the angles of the fences where the motion of the wind prevents the snow from settling, I carry them both chaff and grain; the one to feed them, the other to prevent their tender feet from freezing fast to the earth as I have frequently observed them to do.

.   .   .

It is my bees, however, which afford me the most pleasing and extensive themes; let me look at them when I will, their government, their industry, their quarrels, their passions, always present me with something new; for which reason, when weary with labour, my common place of rest is under my locust-tree, close by my bee-house. By their movements I can predict the weather, and can tell the day of their swarming; but the most difficult point is, when on the wing, to know whether they want to go to the woods or not. If they have previously pitched in some hollow trees, it is not the allurements of salt and water, of fennel, hickory leaves, etc., nor the finest box, that can induce them to stay; they will prefer those rude, rough habitations to the best polished mahogany hive. When that is the case with mine, I seldom thwart their inclinations; it is in freedom that they work: were I to confine them, they would dwindle away and quit their labour. In such excursions we only part for a while; I am generally sure to find them again the following fall. This elopement of theirs only adds to my recreations; I know how to deceive even their superlative instinct; nor do I fear losing them, though eighteen miles from my house, and lodged in the most lofty trees, in the most impervious of our forests. I once took you along with me in one of these rambles, and yet you insist on my repeating the detail of our operations: it brings back into my mind many of the useful and entertaining reflections with which you so happily beguiled our tedious hours.

After I have done sowing, by way of recreation, I prepare for a week's jaunt in the woods, not to hunt either the deer or the bears, as my neighbours do, but to catch the more harmless bees. I cannot boast that this chase is so noble, or so famous among men, but I find it less fatiguing, and full as profitable; and the last consideration is the only one that moves me. I take with me my dog, as a companion, for he is useless as to this game; my gun, for no man you know ought to enter the woods without one; my blanket, some provisions, some wax, vermilion, honey, and a small pocket compass. With these implements I proceed to such woods as are at a considerable distance from any settlements. I carefully examine whether they abound with large trees, if so, I make a small fire on some flat stones, in a convenient place; on the fire I put some wax; close by this fire, on another stone, I drop honey in distinct drops, which I surround with small quantities of vermilion, laid on the stone; and then I retire carefully to watch whether any bees appear. If there are any in that neighbourhood, I rest assured that the smell of the burnt wax will unavoidably attract them; they will soon find out the honey, for they are fond of preying on that which is not their own; and in their approach they will necessarily tinge themselves with some particles of vermilion, which will adhere long to their bodies. I next fix my compass, to find out their course, which they keep invariably straight, when they are returning home loaded. By the assistance of my watch, I observe how long those are returning which are marked with vermilion. Thus possessed of the course, and, in some measure, of the distance, which I can easily guess at, I follow the first, and seldom fail of coming to the tree where those republics are lodged. I then mark it; and thus, with patience, I have found out sometimes eleven swarms in a season; and it is inconceivable what a quantity of honey these trees will sometimes afford. It entirely depends on the size of the hollow, as the bees never rest nor swarm till it is all replenished; for like men, it is only the want of room that induces them to quit the maternal hive. Next I proceed to some of the nearest settlements, where I procure proper assistance to cut down the trees, get all my prey secured, and then return home with my prize. The first bees I ever procured were thus found in the woods, by mere accident; for at that time I had no kind of skill in this method of tracing them. The body of the tree being perfectly sound, they had lodged themselves in the hollow of one of its principal limbs, which I carefully sawed off and with a good deal of labour and industry brought it home, where I fixed it up again in the same position in which I found it growing. This was in April; I had five swarms that year, and they have been ever since very prosperous. This business generally takes up a week of my time every fall, and to me it is a week of solitary ease and relaxation.

The seed is by that time committed to the ground; there is nothing very material to do at home, and this additional quantity of honey enables me to be more generous to my home bees, and my wife to make a due quantity of mead. The reason, Sir, that you found mine better than that of others is, that she puts two gallons of brandy in each barrel, which ripens it, and takes off that sweet, luscious taste, which it is apt to retain a long time. If we find anywhere in the woods (no matter on whose land) what is called a bee-tree, we must mark it; in the fall of the year when we propose to cut it down, our duty is to inform the proprietor of the land, who is entitled to half the contents; if this is not complied with we are exposed to an action of trespass, as well as he who should go and cut down a bee-tree which he had neither found out nor marked.

We have twice a year the pleasure of catching pigeons,[1] whose numbers are sometimes so astonishing as to obscure the sun in their flight. Where is it that they hatch? for such multitudes must require an immense quantity of food. I fancy they breed toward the plains of Ohio, and those about lake Michigan, which abound in wild oats; though I have never killed any that had that grain in their craws. In one of them, last year, I found some undigested rice. Now the nearest rice fields from where I live must be at least 560 miles; and either their digestion must be suspended while they are flying, or else they must fly with the celerity of the wind. We catch them with a net extended on the ground, to which they are allured by what we call *tame wild pigeons*, made blind, and fastened to a long string; his short flights, and his repeated calls, never fail to bring them down. The greatest number I ever catched was fourteen dozen, though much larger quantities have often been trapped. I have frequently seen them at the market so cheap, that for a penny you might have as many as you could carry away; and yet from the extreme cheapness you must not conclude, that they are but an ordinary food; on the contrary, I think they are excellent. Every farmer has a tame wild pigeon in a cage at his door all the year round, in order to be ready whenever the season comes for catching them.

The pleasure I receive from the warblings of the birds in the spring, is superior to my poor description, as the continual succession of their tuneful notes is for ever new to me. I generally rise from bed about that indistinct interval, which, properly speaking, is neither night or day; for this is the moment of the most universal vocal choir. Who can listen unmoved to the sweet love tales of our robins, told from tree to tree? or to the shrill cat birds? The sublime accents of the thrush from on high always retard my steps that I may listen to the delicious music. The variegated appearances of the dew drops, as they hang to the different objects, must present even to a clownish imagination, the most volup-

---

[1] Passenger pigeons, now extinct. The last known specimen died in 1914 at the Cincinnati Zoological Garden. On the passenger pigeon, see also the selections in this anthology from James Fenimore Cooper and Aldo Leopold.

tuous ideas. The astonishing art which all birds display in the construction of their nests, ill provided as we may suppose them with proper tools, their neatness, their convenience, always make me ashamed of the slovenliness of our houses; their love to their dame, their incessant careful attention, and the peculiar songs they address to her while she tediously incubates their eggs, remind me of my duty could I ever forget it. Their affection to their helpless little ones, is a lively precept; and in short, the whole economy of what we proudly call the brute creation, is admirable in every circumstance; and vain man, though adorned with the additional gift of reason, might learn from the perfection of instinct, how to regulate the follies, and how to temper the errors which this second gift often makes him commit. This is a subject, on which I have often bestowed the most serious thoughts; I have often blushed within myself, and been greatly astonished, when I have compared the unerring path they all follow, all just, all proper, all wise, up to the necessary degree of perfection, with the coarse, the imperfect systems of men, not merely as governors and kings, but as masters, as husbands, as fathers, as citizens. But this is a sanctuary in which an ignorant farmer must not presume to enter.

.   .   .

◈ William Bartram (1739–1823)

William Bartram was born in Philadelphia, a major center of scientific learning in the mid-eighteenth century. From an early age, he received training in botany from his father, one of the leading botanists in America. The science of botany had been revolutionized around the date of Bartram's birth by Carolus Linnaeus, whose project to describe and catalogue all known species was launched in his famous Systema naturae *(1735). Bartram's father was the proprietor of Bartram's Botanical Gardens, one of the first conservatories in North America, and the young William eagerly engaged himself in the family enterprise, tending the exotic plants and learning how to produce exact drawings and descriptions of many different flora and fauna. Benjamin Franklin saw Bartram's drawings and encouraged him to become an engraver or printer; however, his father adamantly steered him into the career of a merchant, a career for which he was temperamentally unsuited.*

New vistas opened up in 1765, when Bartram accompanied his father on a trip to Florida. Abandoning his intended mercantile career, he resolved to become an explorer of the vast, uncharted swamps and forests of the south Atlantic seaboard. In the winter of 1773, he embarked on a four-year journey through the Carolinas, Georgia, Florida, and westward to the Mississippi. Bartram's journal of his travels, originally intended to be simply an inventory of plants and animals, soon blossomed into a far more elaborate account of the places he saw, the people he met, and the astonishing range of flora and fauna that he encountered. Bartram's sense of excitement and wonder in the presence of an unknown landscape, swarming with strange beasts, generates much of the appeal of his Travels Through North and South Carolina, Georgia, East and West Florida, *first published in Philadelphia in 1791. Republished in London, this book soon attracted the attention of an international audience: William Wordsworth and Samuel Taylor Coleridge were fascinated by his portrayal of the American wilderness as a New World Eden. Although Bartram depicts the southeastern landscape as a fairly hazardous place, inhabited by fierce alligators and warlike Indians, it is still, on the whole, a pleasant and cheerful realm, abounding with fruit trees and colorful fish swimming in crystal clear streams. Bartram is one of the first writers to realize the imaginative potential of America's wild places. The sheer exuberance of his writing, and his evident delight in the presence of cascading rivers and teeming wetlands, have influenced many subsequent nature writers, from Coleridge through John Muir.*

From Travels Through North and South Carolina, Georgia, East and West Florida

The evening was temperately cool and calm. The crocodiles began to roar and appear in uncommon numbers along the shores and in the river. I fixed my camp in an open plain, near the utmost projection of the promontory, under the shelter of a large live oak, which stood on the highest part of the ground, and but a few yards from my boat. From this open, high situation, I had a free prospect of the river, which was a matter of no trivial consideration to me, having good reason to dread the subtle attacks of the alligators, who were crowding about my harbour. Having collected a good quantity of wood for the purpose of keeping up a light and smoke during the night, I began to think of preparing my supper, when, upon examining my stores, I found but a scanty provision. I thereupon determined, as the most expeditious way of supplying my necessities, to take my bob and try for some trout. About one hundred yards above my harbour began a cove or bay of the river, out of which opened a large lagoon. The mouth or entrance from the river to it was narrow, but the waters soon after spread and formed a little lake, extending into the marshes: its entrance and shores within I observed to be verged with floating lawns of the pistia and nymphea and other aquatic plants; these I knew were excellent haunts for trout.

The verges and islets of the lagoon were elegantly embellished with flowering plants and shrubs; the laughing coots with wings half spread were tripping over the little coves, and hiding themselves in the tufts of grass; young broods of the painted summer teal, skimming the still surface of the waters, and following the watchful parent unconscious of danger, were frequently surprised by the voracious trout; and he, in turn, as often by the subtle greedy alligator. Behold him rushing forth from the flags and reeds. His enormous body swells. His plaited tail brandished high, floats upon the lake. The waters like a cataract descend from his opening jaws. Clouds of smoke issue from his dilated nostrils. The earth trembles with his thunder. When immediately from the opposite coast of the lagoon, emerges from the deep his rival champion. They suddenly dart upon each other. The boiling surface of the lake marks their rapid course, and a terrific conflict commences. They now sink to the bottom folded together in horrid wreaths. The water becomes thick and discoloured. Again they rise, their jaws clap together, re-echoing through the deep surrounding forests. Again they sink, when the contest ends at the muddy bottom of the lake, and the vanquished makes a hazardous escape, hiding himself in the muddy turbulent waters and sedge on a distant shore. The proud victor exulting returns to the place of action. The shores and forests resound his dreadful roar, together with the triumphing shouts of the plaited tribes around, witnesses of the horrid combat. . . .

Still keeping close along shore, on turning a point or projection of the river bank, at once I beheld a great number of hillocks or small pyramids, resembling hay-cocks, ranged like an encampment along the banks. They stood fifteen or twenty yards distant from the water, on a high marsh, about four feet perpendicular above the water. I knew them to be the nests of the crocodile, having had a description of them before; and now expected a furious and general attack, as I saw several large crocodiles swimming abreast of these buildings. These nests being so great a curiosity to me, I was determined at all events immediately to land and examine them. Accordingly, I ran my bark on shore at one of their landing-places, which was a sort of nick or little dock, from which ascended a sloping path or road up to the edge of the meadow, where their nests were; most of them were deserted, and the great thick whitish egg-shells lay broken and scattered upon the ground round about them.

The nests or hillocks are of the form of an obtuse cone, four feet high and four or five feet in diameter at their bases; they are constructed with mud, grass and herbage. At first they lay a floor of this kind of tempered mortar on the ground, upon which they deposit a layer of eggs, and upon this a stratum of mortar, seven or eight inches in thickness, and then another layer of eggs; and in this manner one stratum upon another, nearly to the top. I believe they commonly lay from one to two hundred eggs in a nest: these are hatched, I suppose, by the heat of the sun; and perhaps the vegetable substances mixed with the earth, being acted upon by the sun, may cause a small degree of fermentation, and so increase the heat in those hillocks. The ground for several acres about these nests showed evident marks of a continual resort of alligators; the grass was everywhere beaten down, hardly a blade or straw was left standing; whereas, all about, at a distance, it was five or six feet high, and as thick as it could grow together. The female, as I imagine, carefully watches her own nest of eggs until they are all hatched; or perhaps while she is attending her own brood, she takes under her care and protection as many as she can get at one time, either from her own particular nest or others; but certain it is, that the young are not left to shift for themselves; for I have had frequent opportunities of seeing the female alligator leading about the shores her train of young ones, just as a hen does her brood of chickens; and she is equally assiduous and courageous in defending the young, which are under her care, and providing for their subsistence; and when she is basking upon the warm banks, with her brood around her, you may hear the young ones continually whining and barking like young puppies. I believe but few of a brood live to the years of full growth and magnitude, as the old feed on the young as long as they can make prey of them.

The alligator when full grown is a very large and terrible creature, and of prodigious strength, activity and swiftness in the water. I have seen them twenty feet in length, and some are supposed to be twenty-two or twenty-three feet. Their body is as large as that of a horse; their shape exactly resembles that of a lizard, except their tail, which is flat or cuneiform,[1] being compressed on each side, and gradually diminishing from the abdomen to the extremity, which, with the whole body is covered with horny plates or squammae, impenetrable when on the body of the live animal, even to a rifle ball, except about their head and just behind their fore-legs or arms, where it is said they are only vulnerable. The head of a full grown one is about three feet, and the mouth opens nearly the same length; their eyes are small in proportion, and seem sunk deep in the head, by means of the prominency of the brows; the nostrils are large, inflated and prominent on the top, so that the head in the water resembles, at a distance, a great chunk of wood floating about. Only the upper jaw moves, which they raise almost perpendicular, so as to form a right angle with the lower one. In the fore-part of the upper jaw, on each side, just under the nostrils, are two very large, thick, strong teeth or tusks, not very sharp, but rather the shape of a cone: these are as white as the finest polished ivory, and are not covered by any skin or lips, and always in sight, which gives the creature a frightful appearance: in the lower jaw are holes opposite to these teeth, to receive them: when they clap their jaws together it causes a surprising noise, like that which is made by forcing a heavy plank with violence upon the ground, and may be heard at a great distance.

But what is yet more surprising to a stranger, is the incredible loud and terrifying roar, which they are capable of making, especially in the spring season, their breeding time. It most resembles very heavy distant thunder, not only shaking the air and waters, but causing the earth to tremble; and when hundreds and thousands are roaring at the same time, you can scarcely be persuaded, but that the whole globe is violently and dangerously agitated. . . .

About noon the weather became extremely sultry, not a breath of wind stirring, hazy or cloudy, with very heavy distant thunder, which was answered by the crocodiles—sure presage of a storm!

Soon after ascending this branch of the river, on the right hand presents itself to view a delightful little bluff, consisting chiefly of shells, and covered with a dark grove of red cedar, Zanthoxylon and myrtle. I could not resist the temptation to stop here, although the tremendous thunder all around the hemisphere alarmed me greatly, having a large lake to cross. From this grove appears to view an expansive and pleasing prospect. The beauteous long lake in front, about North East from me, its most distant East shores adorned with dark, high forests of stately trees; North and South almost endless green plains and meadows, embellished with islets and projecting promontories of high, dark forests, where the pyramidal magnolia grandiflora, palma elata, and shady oak, conspicuously tower.

Being heretofore so closely invested by high forests and deep swamps of the great river, I was prevented from seeing the progress and increase of the approaching tempest, the terrific appearance of which now at once confounded me. How purple and fiery appeared the tumultuous clouds, swiftly ascending or dart-

---

[1] Wedge-shaped.

ing from the horizon upwards! they seemed to oppose and dash against each other; the skies appeared streaked with blood or purple flame overhead, the flaming lightning streaming and darting about in every direction around, seemed to fill the world with fire; whilst the heavy thunder kept the earth in a constant tremor. I had yet some hopes of crossing the lake to the plantation in sight. On the opposite shore of the creek before me, and on the cape as we enter the lake, stood a large islet or grove of oaks and palms. Here I intended to seek shelter, and abide till the fury of the hurricane was overpast, if I found it too violent to permit me to cross the lake. In consequence of this precipitate determination, I stepped into my boat and pushed off. What a dreadful rushing and roaring there was every where around me! and to my utter confusion and astonishment, I could not find from what particular quarter its strongest current or direction came, whereby I might have a proper chance of taking measures for securing a harbour or running from it. The high forests behind me bent to the blast; and the sturdy limbs of the trees cracked. I had by this time got up abreast of the grove or hommock: the hurricane close by, pursuing me, I found it dangerous and imprudent in the highest degree to put in here, as the groves were already torn up, and the spreading limbs of the ancient live oaks were flying over my head, and carried about in the air as leaves and stubble. I ran by and boldly entered the lake (being hurried in by a strong current, which seemed a prodigy, the violent wind driving the stream of the creek back again into the lake), and as soon as possible took shelter under the high reedy bank of the lake, and made fast my bark to the boughs of a low shrubby Hickory, that leaned over the water. Such was the violence of the wind, that it raised the waters on the opposite shores of the lake several feet perpendicular, and there was a rapid flow of water from the creek into it, which was contrary to its natural course. Such floods of rain fell during the space of half or three quarters of an hour, that my boat was filled, and I expected every moment when I should see her sink to the bottom of the lake; and the violence of the wind kept the cable so constantly extended, that it was beyond my ability to get to her. My box, which contained my books of specimens and other collections, was floating about in her; and for a great part of the time the rain came down with such rapidity, and fell in such quantities, that every object was totally obscured, excepting the continual streams or rivers of lightning, pouring from the clouds. All seemed a frightful chaos. When the wind and rain abated, I was overjoyed to see the face of nature again appear.

It took me an hour or more to clear the water out of my bark. I then crossed the lake before a brisk and favourable breeze (it was about a mile over), and landed safely at the plantation.

When I arrived, my friend was affrighted to see me, and immediately inquired of me in what manner I came there; supposing it impossible (until I had showed him my boat) that I could have arrived by water through so tremendous a hurricane.

Indeed I saw plainly that they were greatly terrified, having suffered almost irreparable damages from the violence of the storm. All the buildings on the plantation, except his own dwelling-house, were laid almost flat to the ground, or the logs and roof rent asunder and twisted about; the mansion-house shook and reeled over their heads. He had nearly one hundred acres of the Indigo plant almost ripe for the first cutting, which were nearly ruined; and several acres of very promising sugar-cane, totally spoiled for the season. The great live oaks which had been left standing about the fields, were torn to pieces, their limbs lying scattered over the ground: and one very large one which stood near his house torn down, which could not have been done by the united strength of a thousand men. But what is incredible, in the midst of this devastation and ruin, providentially no lives were lost; although there were about sixty Negro slaves on the plantation, and most of them in their huts when the storm came on, yet they escaped with their lives, though several were badly wounded. . . .

Having agreeably diverted away the intolerable heats of sultry noon in fruitful fragrant groves, with renewed vigour I again resumed my sylvan pilgrimage. The afternoon and evening moderately warm, and exceeding pleasant views from the river and its varied shores. I passed by Battle lagoon and the bluff, without much opposition; but the crocodiles were already assembling in the pass. Before night I came to, at a charming orange grove bluff, on the East side of the little lake; and after fixing my camp on a high open situation, and collecting a plenty of dry wood for fuel, I had time to get some fine trout for supper and joyfully return to my camp.

What a most beautiful creature is this fish before me! gliding to and fro, and figuring in the still clear waters, with his orient attendants and associates: the yellow bream or sun fish. It is about eight inches in length, nearly of the shape of the trout, but rather larger in proportion over the shoulders and breast; the mouth large, and the branchiostega[2] opens wide; the whole fish is of a pale gold (or burnished brass) colour, darker on the back and upper sides; the scales are of a proportionable size, regularly placed, and every where variably powdered with red, russet, silver, blue, and green specks, so laid on the scales as to appear like real dust or opaque bodies, each apparent particle being so projected by light and shade, and the various attitudes of the fish, as to deceive the sight; for in reality nothing can be of a more plain and polished surface than the scales and whole body of the fish. The fins are of an orange colour; and, like all the species of the bream, the ultimate angle of the branchiostega terminates by a little spatula, the extreme end of which represents a crescent of the finest ultramarine blue, encircled with silver and velvet black, like the eye in the feathers of a peacock's train. He is a fish of prodigious strength and activity in the water; a warrior in a gilded coat of mail; and gives no rest or quarter to small fish, which he preys upon. They are delicious food and in great abundance.

The orange grove is but narrow, betwixt the river banks and ancient Indian fields, where there are evident traces of the habitations of the ancients, surrounded with groves of live oak, laurel magnolia, zanthoxylon, liquidambar, and others.

How harmonious and soothing is this native sylvan music now at still evening! inexpressibly tender are the responsive cooings of the innocent dove, in the fragrant zanthoxylon groves, and the variable and tuneful warblings of the nonpareil, with the more sprightly and elevated strains of the blue linnet and golden

---

[2] Membrane covering the gills.

icterus: this is indeed harmony, even amidst the incessant croaking of the frogs: the shades of silent night are made more cheerful, with the shrill voice of the whip-poor-will and active mock-bird.

My situation high and airy: a brisk and cool breeze steadily and incessantly passing over the clear waters of the lake, and fluttering over me through the surrounding groves, wings its way to the moon-light savannas, while I repose on my sweet and healthy couch of the soft tillandsia usnea-adscites, and the latter gloomy and still hours of night pass rapidly away as it were in a moment. I arose, strengthened and cheerful, in the morning. Having some repairs to make in the tackle of my vessel, I paid my first attention to them; which being accomplished, my curiosity prompted me to penetrate the grove and view the illumined plains.

✒ *Thomas Jefferson* (*1743–1826*)

As the principal author of the Declaration of Independence, successor to Benjamin Franklin as minister to France, secretary of state under George Washington, and third president of the United States for two terms beginning in 1801, Thomas Jefferson is one of the leading figures in the founding of the American republic. The Declaration of Independence, promulgated on July 4, 1776, boldly affirms that the United States of America shall ". . . assume among the powers of the earth, the separate and equal station to which the laws of Nature and of Nature's God entitle them." The new nation is thus founded upon the laws of nature, and it is from this principle that Jefferson derives his famous declaration, "that all men are created equal." The concept of "nature" at work in this document is evidently drawn from the philosophers of the French Enlightenment, who understood nature to be a rational system of laws pervading the design of the entire universe. In Jefferson's view, however, the new republic should be one of the "powers of the earth" in a more direct and immediate sense: He conceived the new nation as comprised of independent farmers, self-sufficient on their homesteads in the abundant lands of the New World. The georgic vision of Jeffersonian democracy would prove to be an influential model of nation-building throughout the early history of the United States.

Jefferson himself was born on his father's thousand-acre plantation in what is now Albermarle County, Virginia, and throughout his lifetime he dedicated himself to improving and expanding these landholdings. A skilled architect, he designed and built the splendid mansion Monticello, and he sought to create an essentially self-sufficient agrarian community on his plantation, replicating in miniature his georgic vision for America.

Jefferson's only published book, Notes on the State of Virginia (1787), *was written at a low point in his political career. He was elected governor of Virginia in 1779, but he resigned in disgrace after the British captured the state capital of Richmond in 1781. Criticized for a lack of military preparedness, Jefferson retired to Monticello, and from 1781 to 1784, he devoted himself to his private affairs. Responding to several queries sent to him by the Marquis de Barbé-Marbois, Jefferson outlined the natural history of Virginia, describing its mountains and rivers, its flora and fauna, its commodities and manufactures. Jefferson's treatise reveals his fascination with wild nature, particularly in his description of the Potomac River's passage through the Blue Ridge Mountains, and he marvels at the majestic scale of the Natural Bridge, "the most sublime of nature's works." Although he was an Enlightenment thinker in his political philosophy, Jefferson also reveals himself to be an early American Transcendentalist in his fascination with the awe-inspiring appearances of the natural world.*

From Notes on the State of Virginia

Query 4

A notice of its *Mountains?*

For the particular geography of our mountains I must refer to *Fry* and *Jefferson's* map of Virginia; and to *Evans's* analysis of his map of America, for a more philosophical view of them than is to be found in any other work. It is worthy of notice, that our mountains are not solitary and scattered confusedly over the face of the country; but that they commence at about 150 miles from the seacoast, are disposed in ridges one behind another, running nearly parallel with the seacoast, though rather approaching it as they advance north-eastwardly. To the south-west, as the tract of country between the seacoast and the Mississippi becomes narrower, the mountains converge into a single ridge, which, as it approaches the Gulf of Mexico, subsides into plain country, and gives rise to some of the waters of that gulf, and particularly to a river called the Apalachicola, probably from the Apalachies, an Indian nation formerly residing on it. Hence the mountains giving rise to that river, and seen from its various parts, were called the Appalachian mountains, being in fact the end or termination only of the great ridges passing through the continent. European geographers however extended the name northwardly as far as the mountains extended; some giving it, after their separation into different ridges, to the Blue ridge, others to the North mountain, others to the Allegheny, others to the Laurel ridge, as may be seen in their different maps. But the fact I believe is, that none of these ridges were ever known by that name to the inhabitants, either native or emigrant, but as they saw them so called in European maps. In the same direction generally are the veins of limestone, coal, and other minerals hitherto discovered: and so range the falls of our great rivers. But the courses of the great rivers are at right angles with these. James and Potomac penetrate through all the ridges of mountains eastward of the Allegheny; that is broken by no water course. It is in fact the spine of the country between the Atlantic on one side, and the Mississippi and St. Lawrence on the other. The passage of the Potomac through the Blue ridge is perhaps one of the most stupendous scenes in nature. You stand on a very high point of land. On your right comes up the Shenandoah, having ranged along the foot of the mountain an hundred miles to seek a vent. On your left approaches the Potomac, in quest of a passage also. In the moment of their junction they rush together against the mountain, rend it asunder, and pass off to the sea. The first glance of this scene hurries our senses into the opinion, that this earth has been created in time, that the mountains were formed first, that the rivers began to flow afterwards, that in this place particularly they have been dammed up by the Blue ridge of mountains, and have formed an ocean which filled the whole valley; that continuing to rise they have at length broken over at this spot, and have torn the mountain down from its summit to its base. The piles of rock on each hand, but particularly on the Shenandoah, the evident marks of their disrupture and avulsion from their beds by the most powerful agents of nature, corroborate the impression. But the distant finishing which nature has given to the picture, is of a very different character. It is a true contrast to the foreground. It is as placid and delightful, as that is wild and tremendous. For the mountain being cloven asunder, she presents to your eye, through the cleft, a small catch of smooth blue horizon, at an infinite distance in the plain country, inviting you, as it were, from the riot and tumult roaring around, to pass through the breach and participate of the calm below. Here the eye ultimately composes itself; and that way too the road happens actually to lead. You cross the Potomac above the junction, pass along its side through the base of the mountain for three miles, its terrible precipices hanging in fragments over you, and within about 20 miles reach Fredericktown, and the fine country round that. This scene is worth a voyage across the Atlantic. Yet here, as in the neighbourhood of the Natural Bridge, are people who have passed their lives within half a dozen miles, and have never been to survey these monuments of a war between rivers and mountains, which must have shaken the earth itself to its centre.

The height of our mountains has not yet been estimated with any degree of exactness. The Allegheny being the great ridge which divides the waters of the Atlantic from those of the Mississippi, its summit is doubtless more elevated above the ocean than that of any other mountain. But its relative height, compared with the base on which it stands, is not so great as that of some others, the country rising behind the successive ridges like the steps of stairs. The mountains of the Blue ridge, and of these the Peaks of Otter, are thought to be of a greater height, measured from their base, than any others in our country, and perhaps in North America. From data, which may found a tolerable conjecture, we suppose the highest peak to be about 4000 feet perpendicular, which is not a fifth part of the height of the mountains of South America, nor one third of the height which would be necessary in our latitude to preserve ice in the open air unmelted through the year. The ridge of mountains next beyond the Blue ridge, called by us the North mountain, is of the greatest extent; for which reason they were named by the Indians the Endless mountains.

A substance, supposed to be Pumice, found floating on the Mississippi, has induced a conjecture, that there is a volcano on some of its waters: and as these are mostly known to their sources, except the Missouri, our expectations of verifying the conjecture would of course be led to the mountains which divide the waters of the Mexican Gulf from those of the South Sea; but no volcano having ever yet been known at such a distance from the sea, we must rather suppose that this floating substance has been erroneously deemed Pumice.

Query 5

Its Cascades and Caverns?

The only remarkable Cascade in this country, is that of the Falling Spring in Augusta. It is a water of James' river, where it is called Jackson's river, rising in the warm spring mountains, about twenty miles south-west of the warm spring, and flowing into that valley. About three quarters of a mile from its source, it falls over a rock 200 feet into the valley below. The sheet of water is broken in its breadth by the rock, in two or three places, but not at all in its height. Between the sheet and the rock, at the bottom you may walk across dry. This cataract will bear no comparison with that of Niagara, as to the quantity of water composing it; the sheet being only 12 or 15 feet wide above, and somewhat more spread below; but it is half as high again, the latter being only 156 feet, according to the mensuration made by order of M. Vaudreuil, Governor of Canada, and 130 according to a more recent account.

In the limestone country, there are many caverns of very considerable extent. The most noted is called Madison's Cave, and is on the north side of the Blue ridge, near the intersection of the Rockingham and Augusta line with the south fork of the southern river of Shenandoah. It is in a hill of about 200 feet perpendicular height, the ascent of which, on one side, is so steep, that you may pitch a biscuit from its summit into the river which washes its base. The entrance of the cave is, in this side, about two thirds of the way up. It extends into the earth about 300 feet, branching into subordinate caverns, sometimes ascending a little, but more generally descending, and at length terminates in two different places, at basins of water of unknown extent, and which I should judge to be nearly on a level with the water of the river; however, I do not think they are formed by refluent water from that, because they are never turbid; because they do not rise and fall in correspondence with that in times of flood, or of drought; and because the water is always cool. It is probably one of the many reservoirs with which the interior parts of the earth are supposed to abound, and which yields supplies to the fountains of water, distinguished from others only by its being accessible. The vault of this cave is of solid limestone, from 20 to 40 or 50 feet high, through which water is continually percolating. This, trickling down the sides of the cave, has incrusted them over in the form of elegant drapery; and dripping from the top of the vault generates on that, and on the base below, stalactites of a conical form, some of which have met, and formed massive columns.

Another of these caves is near the North mountain, in the county of Frederick, on the lands of Mr. Zane. The entrance into this is on the top of an extensive ridge. You descend 30 or 40 feet, as into a well, from whence the cave then extends, nearly horizontally, 400 feet into the earth, preserving a breadth of from 20 to 50 feet, and a height of from 5 to 12 feet. After entering this cave a few feet, the mercury, which in the open air was at 50°, rose to 57° of Fahrenheit's thermometer, answering to 11° of Reaumur's, and it continued at that to the remotest parts of the cave. The uniform temperature of the cellars of the observatory of Paris, which are ninety feet deep, and of all subterranean cavities of any depth, where no chemical agents may be supposed to produce a factitious heat, has been found to be 10° of Reaumur, equal to $54\frac{1}{2}°$ of Fahrenheit. The temperature of the cave above mentioned so nearly corresponds with this, that the difference may be ascribed to a difference of instruments.

At the Panther gap, in the ridge which divides the waters of the Cow and the Calf pasture, is what is called the *Blowing cave*. It is in the side of a hill, is of about 100 feet diameter, and emits constantly a current of air, of such force, as to keep the weeds prostrate to the distance of twenty yards before it. This current is strongest in dry, frosty weather, and in long spells of rain weakest. Regular inspirations and expirations of air, by caverns and fissures, have been probably enough accounted for, by supposing them combined with intermitting fountains; as they must of course inhale air while their reservoirs are emptying themselves, and again emit it while they are filling. But a constant issue of air, only varying in its force as the weather is drier or damper, will require a new hypothesis. There is another blowing cave in the Cumberland mountain, about a mile from where it crosses the Carolina line. All we know of this is, that it is not constant, and that a fountain of water issues from it.

The *Natural Bridge*, the most sublime of nature's works, though not comprehended under the present head, must not be pretermitted.[1] It is on the ascent of a hill, which seems to have been cloven through its length by some great convulsion. The fissure, just at the bridge, is by some admeasurements, 270 feet deep, by others only 205. It is about 45 feet wide at the bottom, and 90 feet at the top; this of course determines the length of the bridge, and its height from the water; its breadth in the middle is about 60 feet, but more at the ends, and the thickness of the mass, at the summit of the arch, about 40 feet. A part of this thickness is constituted by a coat of earth, which gives growth to many large trees. The residue, with the hill on both sides, is one solid rock of limestone.—The arch approaches the semi-elliptical form; but the larger axis of the ellipsis, which would be the chord of the arch, is many times longer than the transverse. Though the sides of this bridge are provided in some parts with a parapet of fixed rocks, yet few men have resolution to walk to them, and look over into the abyss. You involuntarily fall on your hands and feet, creep to the parapet and peep over it. Looking down from this height about a minute, gave me a violent headache. If the view from the top be painful and intolerable, that from below is delightful in an equal extreme. It is impossible for the emotions arising from the sublime to be felt beyond what they are here: so beautiful an arch, so elevated, so light, and springing as it were, up to heaven! the rapture of the spectator is really indescribable! The fissure continuing narrow, deep and straight, for a considerable distance above and beyond the bridge, opens a short but very pleasing view of the North mountain on one side, and Blue ridge on the other, at the distance each of them of about five miles. This bridge is in the County of Rockbridge, to which it has given name, and affords a public and commodious passage over a valley, which cannot be crossed elsewhere for a considerable distance. The stream passing under it is called Cedar-creek. It is a water of James' river, and sufficient in the driest seasons to turn a grist mill, though its fountain is not more than two miles above.

---

[1] Omitted. Jefferson owned the land (near Lexington, Virginia) where the Natural Bridge stands.

🦢 *Charlotte Smith* (1749–1806)

Charlotte Smith was born in wealthy circumstances, coming of age on a country estate in Sussex that belonged to her father, Nicholas Turner. She was sent to the best schools then available to young women, and a classmate reported that as early as age twelve, Charlotte was an avid reader who was "continually composing verses." Her education also included the study of botany, which grew into a lifelong avocation. Like most women of her social class, she was encouraged to leave school and marry; thus in 1765, at the age of fifteen, she married Benjamin Smith, the son of a wealthy London merchant. Although Charlotte Smith began the marriage with great confidence in her future financial security, these hopes were soon dashed, as her new husband proved to be avaricious, dissolute, violent, and unfaithful. Yet she remained a loyal wife throughout a troubled marriage of twenty years, while her husband was thrown into debtor's prison and then fled to France to escape his creditors. Throughout these vicissitudes, it became increasingly clear to her that her miserable condition could only be ameliorated, and her growing brood of children fed, if she devised an independent source of income. Thus, with twelve children to feed, Charlotte Smith entered the literary marketplace to become a breadwinning author, publishing ten novels and three books of poetry. Although her novels were the most lucrative part of her literary production, Smith is remembered today primarily for her poetry, which was boldly innovative in its form and content.

Smith's first book of poetry, Elegaic Sonnets *(1784), was remarkable both for its revival of the Petrarchan sonnet form (virtually extinct in English poetry since the time of Milton) and for the precision and intensity of its nature imagery. In a series of sonnets addressed to the nightingale, for example, Smith evokes the actual presence of the bird: she describes the plaintive sound of its voice at nightfall as it seeks its missing mate. The nightingale is represented not merely as a traditional emblem for poetic inspiration but more specifically as an analogue for Smith's own forlorn circumstances of poverty, misery, and heartache. The pervasive tone of melancholy, and the intensely personal, introspective quality of her lyric poetry, mark a significant departure from the prevailing norms of late eighteenth-century verse. Smith's revival of the sonnet form directly affected the work of the Romantic poets, particularly Samuel Taylor Coleridge and John Keats, whose "Ode to a Nightingale" elaborates upon Smith's evocation of that bird. In her affection for all of nature's creatures, even the lowly green chafer and the humble hedgehog, Smith evokes the possibility of a new kind of nature writing, intimate in tone and deeply personal in its mode of expression.*

To a Nightingale

Poor melancholy bird—that all night long
   Tell'st to the Moon thy tale of tender woe;
   From what sad cause can such sweet sorrow flow,
And whence this mournful melody of song?

Thy poet's musing fancy would translate   5
   What mean the sounds that swell thy little breast,

When still at dewy eve thou leavest thy nest,
Thus to the listening night to sing thy fate.

Pale Sorrow's victims wert thou once among,
   Though now released in woodlands wild to rove?   10
   Say—hast thou felt from friends some cruel wrong,
Or died'st thou—martyr of disastrous love?
Ah! songstress sad! that such my lot might be,
To sigh, and sing at liberty—like thee!

The Return of the Nightingale, Written in May 1791

Borne on the warm wing of the western gale,
   How tremulously low is heard to float
Through the green budding thorns that fringe the vale,
   The early Nightingale's prelusive[1] note.

'Tis Hope's instinctive power that through the grove   5
   Tells how benignant Heaven revives the earth;
'Tis the soft voice of young and timid Love
   That calls these melting sounds of sweetness forth.

With transport, once, sweet bird! I hailed thy lay,
   And bade thee welcome to our shades again,   10
To charm the wandering poet's pensive way
   And soothe the solitary lover's pain;
But now!—such evils in my lot combine,
As shut my languid sense—to Hope's dear voice and thine!

To the Goddess of Botany

Of Folly weary, shrinking from the view
   Of Violence and Fraud, allowed to take
   All peace from humble life; I would forsake
Their haunts forever, and, sweet Nymph! with you
   Find shelter; where my tired, and tear-swollen eyes,   5
Among your silent shades of soothing hue,
   Your "bells and florets of unnumbered dyes"[2]
   Might rest—And learn the bright varieties
That from your lovely hands are fed with dew;
   And every veined leaf, that trembling sighs   10

---

[1] Serving as a prelude (to summer).

[2] An allusion to Milton, *Lycidas*, line 135: "bells and flowerets of a thousand hues."

In mead or woodland; or in wilds remote,
    Or lurk with mosses in the humid caves,
Mantle the cliffs, on dimpling rivers float,
    Or stream from coral rocks beneath the Ocean waves.

To a Green Chafer, on a White Rose

You dwell within a lovely bower,
Little chafer, gold and green,
Nestling in the fairest flower,
The rose of snow, the garden's queen.

There you drink the chrystal dew,   5
And your shards[3] as emeralds bright
And corselet, of the ruby's hue,
Hide among the petals white.

Your fringed feet may rest them there,
And there your filmy wings may close,   10
But do not wound the flower so fair
That shelters you in sweet repose.

Insect! be not like him who dares
On pity's bosom to intrude,
And then that gentle bosom tears   15
With baseness and ingratitude.

A Walk by the Water

Let us walk where reeds are growing,
    By the alders in the mead;
Where the crystal streams are flowing,
    In whose waves the fishes feed.

There the golden carp is laving,   5
    With the trout, the perch, and bream;
Mark! their flexile fins are waving,
    As they glance along the stream.

Now they sink in deeper billows,
    Now upon the surface rise;   10
Or from under roots of willows,
    Dart to catch the water-flies.

---

[3] Outer wings (a hard shell that covers the inner wings of beetles).

'Midst the reeds and pebbles hiding,
   See the minnow and the roach;
Or by water lilies gliding,   15
   Shun with fear our near approach.

Do not dread us, timid fishes,
   We have neither net nor hook;
Wanderers we, whose only wishes
   Are to read in nature's book.   20

Invitation to the Bee

Child of patient industry,
Little active busy bee,
Thou art out at early morn,
Just as the opening flowers are born,
Among the green and grassy meads   5
Where the cowslips hang their heads;
Or by hedgerows, while the dew
Glitters on the harebell blue.—

Then on eager wing art flown,
To thymy hillocks on the down;   10
Or to revel on the broom,
Or suck the clover's crimson bloom;
Murmuring still thou busy bee
Thy little ode to industry!

Go while summer suns are bright,   15
Take at large thy wandering flight;
Go and load thy tiny feet
With every rich and various sweet,
Cling around the flowring thorn,
Dive in the woodbine's honied horn,   20
Seek the wild rose that shades the dell,
Explore the foxglove's freckled bell,
Or in the heath flower's fairy cup
Drink the fragrant spirit up.

But when the meadows shall be mown,   25
And summer's garlands overblown;
Then come, thou little busy bee,
And let thy homestead be with me,
There, sheltered by thy straw-built hive,
In my garden thou shalt live,   30
And that garden shall supply

Thy delicious alchemy;[4]
There for thee, in autumn, blows
The Indian pink and latest rose,
The mignonette perfumes the air,   35
And stocks, unfading flowers, are there.

Yet fear not when the tempests come,
And drive thee to thy waxen home,
That I shall then most treacherously
For thy honey murder thee.   40

Ah, no!—throughout the winter drear
I'll feed thee, that another year
Thou may'st renew thy industry
Among the flowers, thou little busy bee.

The Hedgehog Seen in a Frequented Path

Wherefore should man or thoughtless boy
Thy quiet harmless life destroy,
Innoxious urchin?—for thy food
Is but the beetle and the fly,
And all thy harmless luxury   5
The swarming insects of the wood.

Should man to whom his God has given
Reason, the brightest ray of heaven,
Delight to hurt, in senseless mirth,
Inferior animals?—and dare   10
To use his power in waging war
Against his brethren of the earth?

Poor creature! to the woods resort,
Lest lingering here, inhuman sport
Should render vain thy thorny case;   15
And whelming water, deep and cold,
Make thee thy spiny ball[5] unfold,
And show thy simple negro[6] face!

Fly from the cruel; know than they
Less fierce are ravenous beasts of prey,   20
And should perchance these last come near thee,
And fox or martin cat assail,

---

[4] Transformation of nectar into honey.
[5] Hedgehogs protect themselves by rolling into a ball and distending their spines.
[6] Black. The hedgehog's fur, in contrast, is brown.

Thou, safe within thy coat of mail,
May cry—Ah! noli me tangere.[7]

An Evening Walk by the Seaside

'Tis pleasant to wander along on the sand,
Beneath the high cliff that is hallowed in caves;
When the fisher has put off his boat from the land,
And the prawn-catcher wades through the short rippling waves.

While fast run before us the sandling and plover,   5
Intent on the crabs and the sand-eels to feed,
And here on a rock which the tide will soon cover,
We'll find us a seat that is tapestried with weed.

Bright gleam the white sails in the slant rays of even,
And stud as with silver the broad level main,   10
While glowing clouds float on the fair face of Heaven,
And the mirror-like water reflects them again.

How various the shades of marine vegetation,
Thrown here the rough flints and the pebbles among,
The feathered conferva[8] of deepest carnation,   15
The dark purple slake and the olive sea thong.

While Flora herself unreluctantly mingles
Her garlands with those that the Nereids[9] have worn,
For the yellow horned poppy springs up on the shingles,
And convolvulas rival the rays of the morn.   20

But now to retire from the rock we have warning,
Already the water encircles our seat,
And slowly the tide of the evening returning,
The moon beam reflects in the waves at our feet.

Ah! whether as now the mild Summer sea flowing,   25
Scarce wrinkles the sands as it murmurs on shore,
Or fierce wintry whirlwinds impetuously blowing
Bid high maddening surges resistlessly roar;

That Power, which can put the wide waters in motion,
Then bid the vast billows repose at His word;   30
Fills the mind with deep reverence, while Earth, Air, and Ocean,
Alike of the universe speak him the Lord.

---

[7] Do not touch me (Latin).

[8] Of this sea weed there is great variety. Some of a deep crimson, others pale red, green, white, or purple; they resemble tufts, or are branched, and appear like small leafless trees. (Note by Smith.)

[9] Sea nymphs (in Greek mythology).

✍ *Philip Freneau* (*1752–1832*)

Philip Freneau was born in New York City and attended the College of New Jersey, now known as Princeton University. His college roommate was James Madison, a future president of the United States. During the American Revolution, Freneau served as a soldier and privateer, and in 1780, he was captured by the British and imprisoned aboard the Scorpion, *anchored in New York Harbor. Conditions aboard this prison ship were appalling, such that when Freneau finally gained his freedom, he was in terrible condition. But he regained his health and later returned to sea as a ship captain, for the periods 1785–89 and 1802–04.*

Freneau was the United States' first professional journalist, making himself a powerful propagandist and satirist for the American Revolution and a persuasive advocate for Jeffersonian democracy. He edited various newspapers, including the partisan Freeman's Journal *and the* National Gazette. *Although his journalistic writing was widely influential, none of his papers was profitable. He published numerous books of poetry during his lifetime, including* The American Village *(1772),* American Liberty *(1775),* A Voyage to Boston *(1775),* The British Prison-Ship *(1781),* The Village Merchant *(1794), and* A Collection of Poems on American Affairs *(1815). Freneau's political and satirical poems have now faded into obscurity, but his place as a historically significant American poet is assured by such poems as "The Hurricane," "The Wild Honey Suckle," and "On the Religion of Nature." His nature poetry clearly derives from the tradition of Sensibility as epitomized by James Thomson, but Freneau's work has a distinctive New World flavor, reflecting his experience on stormy seas and amidst flourishing American farmsteads. Freneau spent his final years on a farm in New Jersey, eventually dying impoverished and unknown, lost in a snowstorm.*

The Dying Elm

Sweet, lovely Elm, who here dost grow
Companion of unsocial care,
Lo! thy dejected branches die:
Amidst this torrid air —
Smit by the sun or blasting moon,   5
Like fainting *flowers*, their verdure gone.

Thy withering leaves, that drooping hang,
Presage thine end approaching nigh;
And lo! thy amber tears distill,
Attended with that last departing sigh —   10
O charming tree! no more decline,
But be thy shades and love-sick whispers mine.

Forbear to die — this weeping eve
Shall shed her little drops on you,

Shall o'er thy sad disaster grieve,   15
And wash your wounds with pearly dew,
Shall pity you, and pity me,
And heal the langour of my tree!

Short is thy life, if thou so soon must fade,
Like angry Jonah's gourd at Nineveh,[1]   20
That, in a night, its bloomy branches spread,
And perished with the day.—
    Come, then, revive, sweet lovely Elm, lest I,
Thro' vehemence of heat, like Jonah, wish to die.

[1] A Hebrew prophet who was unwilling to share his divine message, for which he was punished by God with exile into a wasteland, where the gourd plant was his only companion.

The Hurricane*

Happy the man who, safe on shore,
Now trims, at home, his evening fire;
Unmoved, he hears the tempests roar,
That on the tufted groves expire:
Alas! on us they doubly fall,   5
Our feeble barque must bear them all.

Now to their haunts the birds retreat,
The squirrel seeks his hollow tree,
Wolves in their shaded caverns meet,
All, all are blest but wretched we—   10
Foredoomed a stranger to repose,
No rest the unsettled ocean knows.

While o'er the dark abyss we roam,
Perhaps, with last departing gleam,
We saw the sun descend in gloom,   15
No more to see his morning beam;
But buried low, by far too deep,
On coral beds, unpitied, sleep!

But what a strange, uncoasted strand
Is that, where fate permits no day—   20
No charts have we to mark that land,
No compass to direct that way—
What Pilot shall explore that realm,
What new Columbus take the helm!

* Describing a storm which occurred in Jamaica in July of 1784.

While death and darkness both surround,   25
And tempests rage with lawless power,
Of friendship's voice I hear no sound,
No comfort in this dreadful hour—
What friendship can in tempests be,
What comforts on this raging sea?   30

The barque, accustomed to obey,
No more the trembling pilots guide:
Alone she gropes her trackless way,
While mountains burst on either side—
Thus, skill and science both must fall;   35
And ruin is the lot of all.

The Wild Honey Suckle

Fair flower, that dost so comely grow,
Hid in this silent, dull retreat,
Untouched thy honeyed blossoms blow,
Unseen thy little branches greet:
    No roving foot shall crush thee here,   5
    No busy hand provoke a tear.

By Nature's self in white arrayed,
She bade thee shun the vulgar eye,
And planted here the guardian shade,
And sent soft waters murmuring by;   10
    Thus quietly thy summer goes,
    Thy days declining to repose.

Smit with those charms, that must decay,
I grieve to see your future doom;
They died—nor were those flowers more gay,   15
The flowers that did in Eden bloom;
    Unpitying frosts, and Autumn's power
    Shall leave no vestige of this flower.

From morning suns and evening dews
At first thy little being came: 20
If nothing once, you nothing lose,
For when you die you are the same;
    The space between, is but an hour,
    The frail duration of a flower.

On the Sleep of Plants

When suns are set, and stars in view,
Not only *man* to slumber yields;
But Nature grants this blessing too,
To yonder *plants*, in yonder fields.

The Summer heats and lengthening days   5
(To them the same as toil and care)
Thrice welcome make the evening breeze,
That kindly does their strength repair.

At early dawn each plant survey,
And see, revived by Nature's hand,   10
With youthful vigour, fresh and gay,
Their blossoms blow, their leaves expand.

Yon garden plant, with weeds o'er-run,
Not void of *thought*, perceives its hour,
And, watchful of the parting sun,   15
Throughout the night conceals her flower.

Like us, the slave of cold and heat,
She too enjoys her little span—
With *Reason*, only less complete
Than *that* which makes the boast of *man*.   20

Thus, moulded from one common clay,
A varied life adorns the plain;
By Nature subject to decay,
By Nature meant to bloom again.

On the Religion of Nature

The power, that gives with liberal hand
  The blessings man enjoys, while here,
And scatters through a smiling land
  Abundant products of the year;
    That power of nature, ever blessed,   5
    Bestowed religion with the rest.

Born with ourselves, her early sway
  Inclines the tender mind to take
The path of right, fair virtue's way
  Its own felicity to make.   10
    This universally extends
    And leads to no mysterious ends.

Religion, such as nature taught,
  With all divine perfection suits;
Had all mankind this system sought 15
  Sophists[1] would cease their vain disputes,
    And from this source would nations know
    All that can make their heaven below.

This deals not curses on mankind,
  Or dooms them to perpetual grief, 20
If from its aid no joys they find,
  It damns them not for unbelief;
    Upon a more exalted plan
    Creatress nature dealt with man—

Joy to the day, when all agree 25
  On such grand systems to proceed,
From fraud, design, and error free,
  And which to truth and goodness lead:
    Then persecution will retreat
    And man's religion be complete. 30

✿ *William Blake* (*1757–1827*)

William Blake was the son of a London haberdasher. He grew up in modest surroundings, and he received formal education only in art. From the age of fourteen to the age of twenty-one, he served as the apprentice to an engraver, James Basire. While learning the craft of engraving, he developed his skills as a painter, and he also began to write poetry. At the age of twenty-four, he married Catherine Boucher; the couple had a rather turbulent marriage that remained childless.

In his own lifetime, Blake sought but received little public recognition. He staged a one-man show in 1809 that proved to be a disastrous failure. But as Blake passed into his sixties, he began to achieve a small measure of success as a poet and as a speaker. He attracted a warm circle of admirers and disciples, and his last years were happy ones. He died at the age of seventy.

It was not until the twentieth century that William Blake came to be viewed as a major poet. Today, when we read one of Blake's poems on the printed page, we are experiencing only a part of what the writer intended, however. Beginning with the Songs of Innocence *(1789), Blake engraved a series of "illuminated Books" that incorporate his skills as an engraver as well as the knowledge that he acquired as an art student. He engraved his poems, along with his own illustrations, on sheets of copper, and he used watercolors to complete the design. The process was so intricate and time-consuming that only five copies of his great prophetic book,* Jerusalem, *were completed.*

---

[1] Ancient Greek term for teachers of philosophy.

In his sixties, Blake gave up poetry for painting and engraving. Some of his artwork included illustrations to Chaucer's Canterbury Tales, *Dante's* Divine Comedy, *and the book of Job. Although today we often think of Blake mainly as a poet, he is also regarded as a painter and engraver whose work is strikingly original.*

Many of Blake's best-known poems are from the Songs of Innocence *and its sequel,* Songs of Experience *(1794). Several of his poems focus on aspects of the natural world, often in contrast or juxtaposition with the grim industrial landscape of London. In works such as "The Echoing Green," "The Lamb," "The Tyger," "Earth's Answer," and "The Clod and the Pebble," Blake uses imagery and metaphor to evoke the beauty of nature, along with the harshness and cruelty that lurks both in nature and in man.*

From Songs of Innocence

Introduction

Piping down the valleys wild,
Piping songs of pleasant glee,
On a cloud I saw a child,
And he laughing said to me:

"Pipe a song about a Lamb!"   5
So I piped with merry cheer.
"Piper, pipe that song again;"
So I piped: he wept to hear.

"Drop thy pipe, thy happy pipe;
Sing thy songs of happy cheer:"   10
So I sang the same again,
While he wept with joy to hear.

"Piper, sit thee down and write
In a book, that all may read."
So he vanished from my sight,   15
And I plucked a hollow reed,

And I made a rural pen,
And I stained the water clear,
And I wrote my happy songs
Every child may joy to hear.   20

The Echoing Green

The Sun does arise,
And make happy the skies;
The merry bells ring
To welcome the Spring;
The skylark and thrush,   5
The birds of the bush,
Sing louder around
To the bells' cheerful sound,
While our sports shall be seen
On the Echoing Green.   10

Old John, with white hair,
Does laugh away care,
Sitting under the oak,
Among the old folk.
They laugh at our play,   15
And soon they all say:
"Such, such were the joys
When we all, girls and boys,
In our youth time were seen
On the Echoing Green."   20

Till the little ones, weary,
No more can be merry;
The sun does descend,
And our sports have an end.
Round the laps of their mothers   25
Many sisters and brothers,
Like birds in their nest,
Are ready for rest,
And sport no more seen
On the darkening Green.   30

The Lamb

Little Lamb, who made thee?
Dost thou know who made thee?
Gave thee life, and bid thee feed,
By the stream and o'er the mead;
Gave thee clothing of delight,   5
Softest clothing, woolly, bright;
Gave thee such a tender voice,
Making all the vales rejoice?

Little Lamb, who made thee?
Dost thou know who made thee?   10

Little Lamb, I'll tell thee,
Little Lamb, I'll tell thee:
He is callèd by thy name,
For He calls Himself a Lamb.
He is meek, and He is mild;   15
He became a little child.
I a child, and thou a lamb,
We are callèd by His name.
    Little Lamb, God bless thee!
    Little Lamb, God bless thee!   20

The Blossom

Merry, merry sparrow!
Under leaves so green,
A happy blossom
Sees you, swift as arrow,
Seek your cradle narrow.   5
Near my bosom.

Pretty, pretty robin!
Under leaves so green,
A happy blossom
Hears you sobbing, sobbing,   10
Pretty, pretty robin,
Near my bosom.

From Songs of Experience

Introduction

Hear the voice of the Bard!
Who present, past, and future, sees;
Whose ears have heard
The Holy Word
That walked among the ancient trees,[1]   5

---

[1] Alludes to Genesis 3.8: "And they heard the voice of the Lord God walking in the garden . . . and Adam and his wife hid themselves . . . among the trees of the garden."

Calling the lapsèd soul,[2]
And weeping in the evening dew;
That might control
The starry pole,
And fallen, fallen light renew!   10

"O Earth, O Earth, return!
Arise from out the dewy grass;
Night is worn,
And the morn
Rises from the slumberous mass.   15

"Turn away no more;
Why wilt thou turn away?
The starry floor,
The watery shore,
Is given thee till the break of day."   20

[2] The fallen soul (referring to the Fall of Man recounted in Genesis).

Earth's Answer

Earth raised up her head
From the darkness dread and drear.
Her light fled,
Stony dread!
And her locks covered with grey despair.   5

"Prisoned on watery shore,
Starry Jealousy does keep my den:
Cold and hoar,
Weeping o'er,
I hear the Father of the Ancient Men.   10

"Selfish Father of Men!
Cruel, jealous, selfish Fear!
Can delight,
Chained in night,
The virgins of youth and morning bear?   15

"Does spring hide its joy
When buds and blossoms grow?
Does the sower
Sow by night,
Or the ploughman in darkness plough?   20

"Break this heavy chain
That does freeze my bones around.

Selfish! vain!
Eternal bane!
That free Love with bondage bound."   25

The Fly

Little Fly,
Thy summer's play
My thoughtless hand
Has brushed away.

Am not I   5
A fly like thee?
Or art not thou
A man like me?

For I dance,
And drink, and sing,   10
Till some blind hand
Shall brush my wing.

If thought is life
And strength and breath,
And the want   15
Of thought is death;

Then am I
A happy fly,
If I live
Or if I die.   20

The Tyger

Tyger! Tyger! burning bright
In the forests of the night,
What immortal hand or eye
Could frame thy fearful symmetry?

In what distant deeps or skies   5
Burnt the fire of thine eyes?
On what wings dare he aspire?
What the hand dare seize the fire?

And what shoulder, and what art,
Could twist the sinews of thy heart?   10

And when thy heart began to beat,
What dread hand? and what dread feet?

What the hammer? what the chain?
In what furnace was thy brain?
What the anvil? what dread grasp   15
Dare its deadly terrors clasp?

When the stars threw down their spears,[3]
And watered heaven with their tears,
Did he smile his work to see?
Did he who made the Lamb make thee?   20

Tyger! Tyger! burning bright
In the forests of the night,
What immortal hand or eye,
Dare frame thy fearful symmetry?

The Sick Rose

O Rose, thou art sick!
The invisible worm,
The flies in the night,
In the howling storm,

Has found out thy bed   5
Of crimson joy;
And his dark secret love
Does thy life destroy.

The Human Abstract

Pity would be no more
If we did not make somebody poor;
And Mercy no more could be
If all were as happy as we.

And mutual fear brings peace,   5
Till the selfish loves increase;
Then Cruelty knits a snare,
And spreads his baits with care.

---

[3] Possibly referring to the fall of the rebel angels recounted in Isaiah 14.12, Revelation 8.12, and Milton's *Paradise Lost*. According to this tradition, a third of the angels, tempted by Lucifer, fell from heaven. By implication, the very existence of the Tyger raises ultimate questions about the origin of evil.

He sits down with holy fears,
And waters the ground with tears;   10
Then Humility takes its root
Underneath his foot.

Soon spreads the dismal shade
Of Mystery over his head;
And the caterpillar and fly   15
Feed in the Mystery.

And it bears the fruit of Deceit,
Ruddy and sweet to eat;
And the raven his nest has made
In its thickest shade.   20

The Gods of the earth and sea
Sought through Nature to find this tree;
But their search was all in vain:
There grows one in the Human brain.

Robert Burns (1759–1796)

Regarded even today as one of Scotland's most important poets, Robert Burns's influence can be felt every New Year's Eve when English speakers of any nationality gather to sing "Auld Lang Syne," one of the many traditional Scottish ballads that Burns collected and edited. The son of a farmer, Burns received a good education given his family's struggling circumstances. He was quite familiar, both through his formal schooling and his own avid reading, with the English and the Scottish literary traditions. However, when his first collection, Poems, Chiefly in the Scottish Dialect (1786), appeared to great popular and critical acclaim, Burns made much of being an artless "natural genius" in the tradition of such poets as Stephen Duck. By adopting the persona of an uneducated poet, Burns made his already interesting poetry seem all the more intriguing to refined readers.

Due in part to his own family's difficulties, Burns was a passionate believer in the equality of all people, and he supported both the American and French Revolutions. He was also a freethinker in his religious opinions, rejecting the strict Calvinist morality of the Scottish Kirk. In his own day, he was known for his flamboyant and somewhat dissipated lifestyle as well as for his poetry. By 1788, however, Burns had married and settled down. He received a government position that allowed him to give up the arduous labor of farming by 1791. Besides writing his own poetry, Burns also dedicated himself to the project of collecting, editing, and imitating the songs of Scotland's rich oral tradition. He did this without any remuneration and published the work anonymously, considering the work his patriotic duty. He died at the age of thirty-seven from heart problems that had plagued him for most of his adult life.

The quality of song and the influence of the ballad tradition dominate in several of the selections included below, many of which retain the four-beat poetic line and the re-

frains characteristic of most orally composed and disseminated poetry. Like John Clare after him, Burns has a sympathetic relationship with often neglected animals and land-scapes, attempting to give them a voice or a compassionate literary representation, as in "To a Mouse," "To a Mountain Daisy," or "The Humble Petition of Bruar Water." These simple songs, however, belie the rich literary print tradition that also contributes to Burns's poetry — including the sentimental works of authors such as Henry Mackenzie and the older works of late Renaissance Scottish writers. Nonetheless, Burns's emphasis on folk song and the folk tradition, as well as his decision to write in the common Scots dialect, has led many scholars to identify him as a significant precursor to the Romantic aesthetic. Burns's apparent lyric simplicity, his appreciation for the beauty of common-place nature, and his democratic politics all justify his place as a forefather to much early nineteenth-century poetry.

The Death and Dying Words of Poor Mailie
The Author's Only Pet Yowe: An Unco Mournfu' Tale*

As Mailie, an' her lambs thegither,
Was ae day nibblin on the tether,
Upon her cloot she coost a hitch,
An' owre she warsled in the ditch:
There, groanin, dying, she did lie,   5
When Hughoc he cam doytin by.

   Wi' glowrin een, an' lifted han's
Poor Hughoc like a statue stan's;
He saw her days were near-hand ended,
But, wae's my heart! he could na mend it!   10
He gapèd wide, but naething spak.
At length poor Mailie silence brak:—

   O thou, whase lamentable face
Appears to mourn my woefu' case!
My dying words attentive hear,   15
An' bear them to my Master dear.

   Tell him, if e'er again he keep
As muckle gear as buy a sheep—
O, bid him never tie them mair,
Wi' wicked strings o' hemp or hair!   20
But ca' them out to park or hill,
An' let them wander at their will:

---

*In the following selections from Burns's poetry, footnotes are keyed to each poem by line number—Editors' note.
¹ **Mailie** Mollie   **thegither** together   ² **ae** one   ³ **cloot** hoof   **coost** cast   ⁴ **warsled** floundered   ⁶ **doytin** dod-
dering   ⁷ **glowrin** staring   ¹⁰ **wae** woe   ¹⁷ **keep** own   ¹⁸ **muckle gear** much money   ²¹ **ca'** drive

So may his flock increase, an' grow
To scores o' lambs, an' packs o' woo'!

    Tell him, he was a Master kin',   25
An' ay was guid to me an' mine;
An' now my dying charge I gie him,
My helpless lambs, I trust them wi' him.

    O, bid him save their harmless lives,
Frae dogs, an' tods, an' butchers' knives!   30
But gie them guid cow milk their fill,
Till they be fit to fend themsel;
An' tent them duly, e'en an' morn,
Wi' teats o' hay an' ripps o' corn.

    'An' may they never learn the gaets,   35
Of ither vile, wanrestfu' pets—
To slink through slaps, an' reave an' steal,
At stacks o' pease, or stocks o' kail!
So may they, like their great forbears,
For monie a year come through the sheers: 40
So wives will gie them bits o' bread,
An' bairns greet for them when they're dead.

    My poor toop-lamb, my son an' heir,
O, bid him breed him up wi' care!
An' if he live to be a beast,   45
To pit some havins in his breast!
An' warn him—what I winna name—
To stay content wi' yowes at hame;
An' no to rin an' wear his cloots,
Like other menseless, graceless brutes.   50

    An' niest, my yowie, silly thing;
Gude keep thee frae a tether string!
O, may thou ne'er forgather up,
Wi' onie blastit, moorland toop;
But ay keep mind to moop an' mell,   55
Wi' sheep o' credit like thysel!

    And now, my bairns, wi' my last breath,
I lea'e my blessin wi' you baith:
An' when you think upo' your mither,
Mind to be kind to ane anither.   60

---

[30] **tods** foxes   [32] **fend** look after   [33] **tent** tend   [34] **teats** small quantities   **ripps** handfuls   [35] **gaets** ways
[36] **wanrestfu'** restless   [37] **slaps** breaches   [38] **stocks** plants   [42] **greet** weep   [43] **toop** tup, ram
[46] **havins** conduct   [47] **winna** will not   [48] **yowes** ewes   [50] **menseless** unmannerly   [51] **silly** helpless
[55] **moop** nibble   **mell** meddle

Now, honest Hughoc, dinna fail,
To tell my master a' my tale;
An' bid him burn this cursed tether,
An' for thy pains thou'se get my blether."

This said, poor Mailie turned her head,   65
An' closed her een amang the dead!

⁶⁴ **blether** bladder   ⁶⁶ **een** eyes

Poor Mailie's Elegy

1

Lament in rhyme, lament in prose,
Wi' saut tears tricklin down your nose;
Our Bardie's fate is at a close,
                Past a' remead!
The last, sad cape-stane of his woes;   5
                Poor Mailie's dead!

2

It's no the loss of warl's gear,
That could sae bitter draw the tear,
Or mak our Bardie, dowie, wear
                The mourning weed:
He's lost a friend an' neebor dear   10
                In Mailie dead.

3

Through a' the toun she trotted by him;
A lang half-mile she could descry him;
Wi' kindly bleat, when she did spy him,   15
                She ran wi' speed:
A friend mair faithfu' ne'er cam nigh him,
                Than Mailie dead.

4

I wat she was a sheep o' sense,
An' could behave hersel wi' mense: 20
I'll say't, she never brak a fence,

⁴ **remead** remedy   ⁷ **warl's gear** worldly pelf   ⁹ **dowie** drooping   ¹³ **toun** farm   ¹⁹ **wat** wot   ²⁰ **mense** tact

Through thievish greed.
Our Bardie, lanely, keeps the spence
Sin' Mailie's dead.

5

Or, if he wanders up the howe,   25
Her livin image in her yowe
Comes bleatin till him, owre the knowe,
        For bits o' bread;
An' down the briny pearls rowe
        For Mailie dead.   30

6

She was nae get o' moorlan tips,
Wi' tawted ket, an' hairy hips;
For her forbears were brought in ships,
        Frae 'yont the Tweed:
A bonier fleesh ne'er crossed the clips   35
        Than Mailie's dead.

7

Wae worth the man wha first did shape
That vile, wanchancie thing—a rape!
It maks guid fellows girn an' gape,
        Wi' chokin dread;   40
An' Robin's bonnet wave wi' crape
        For Mailie dead.

8

O a' ye bards on bonie Doon!
An' wha on Ayr your chanters tune!
Come, join the melancholious croon   45
        O' Robin's reed!
His heart will never get aboon!
        His Mailie's dead!

---

[23] **spence** parlour   [25] **howe** glen   [27] **knowe** knoll   [29] **rowe** roll   [31] **get** issue   **tips** tups
[32] **tawted ket** matted fleece   **hips** rumps   [35] **fleesh** fleece   **clips** shears   [37] **Wae worth** Woe befall
[38] **wanchancie** dangerous   **rape** rope   [39] **girn** grin   [44] **chanters** bagpipes   [47] **get aboon** rejoice

To a Mouse

On Turning Her Up in Her Nest with the Plough, November, 1785

1

Wee, sleekit, cowrin, tim'rous beastie,
O, what a panic's in thy breastie!
Thou need na start awa sae hasty
        Wi' bickering brattle!
I wad be laith to rin an' chase thee,   5
        Wi' murdering pattle!

2

I'm truly sorry man's dominion
Has broken Nature's social union,
An' justifies that ill opinion
        Which makes thee startle   10
At me, thy poor, earth-born companion
        An' fellow mortal!

3

I doubt na, whyles, but thou may thieve;
What then? poor beastie, thou maun live
A daimen icker in a thrave   15
        'S a sma' request;
I'll get a blessin wi' the lave,
        An' never miss't!

4

Thy wee-bit housie, too, in ruin!
Its silly wa's the win's are strewin!   20
An' naething, now, to big a new ane,
        O' foggage green!
An' bleak December's win's ensuin,
        Baith snell an' keen!

5

Thou saw the fields laid bare an' waste,   25
An' weary winter comin fast,

---

[1] **sleekit** sleek   [4] **bickering brattle** hurrying scamper   [5] **laith** loath   [6] **pattle** plough-staff
[13] **whyles** sometimes   [15] **daimen icker** odd ear   **thrave** twenty-four sheaves   [20] **silly** feeble
[22] **foggage** coarse grass   [24] **snell** bitter

An' cozie here, beneath the blast,
        Thou thought to dwell,
Till crash! the cruel coulter past
        Out thro' thy cell.   30

6

That wee bit heap o' leaves an' stibble,
Has cost thee monie a weary nibble!
Now thou's turned out, for a' thy trouble,
        But house or hald,
To thole the winter's sleety dribble,   35
        An' cranreuch cauld!

7

But Mousie, thou art no thy lane,
In proving foresight may be vain:
The best-laid schemes o' mice an' men
        Gang aft agley,   40
An' lea'e us nought but grief an' pain,
        For promised joy!

8

Still thou art blest, compared wi' me!
The present only toucheth thee:
But och! I backward cast my e'e,   45
        On prospects drear!
An' forward, tho' I canna see,
        I guess an' fear!

[31] **stibble** stubble   [34] **But** without   **hald** holding   [35] **thole** endure   [36] **cranreuch** hoar-frost
[37] **thy lane** alone   [40] **agley** askew

To a Mountain Daisy

On Turning One Down with the Plough in April, 1786

1

Wee, modest, crimson-tippèd flower,
Thou's met me in an evil hour;
For I maun crush amang the stoure

[3] **stoure** dust

> Thy slender stem:
> To spare thee now is past my power,   5
> Thou bonie gem.

2

> Alas! it's no thy neebor sweet,
> The bonie lark, companion meet,
> Bending thee 'mang the dewy weet,
>   Wi' spreckled breast!   10
> When upward-springing, blythe, to greet
>   The purpling east.

3

> Cauld blew the bitter-biting north
> Upon thy early, humble birth;
> Yet cheerfully thou glinted forth   15
>   Amid the storm,
> Scarce reared above the parent-earth
>   Thy tender form.

4

> The flaunting flowers our gardens yield,
> High shelt'ring woods and wa's maun shield: 20
> But thou, beneath the random bield
>   O' clod or stane,
> Adorns the histie stibble-field,
>   Unseen, alane.

5

> There, in thy scanty mantle clad,   25
> Thy snawie bosom sun-ward spread,
> Thou lifts thy unassuming head
>   In humble guise;
> But now the share uptears thy bed,
>   And low thou lies!   30

6

> Such is the fate of artless maid,
> Sweet flow'ret of the rural shade!
> By love's simplicity betrayed,

---

[9] **weet** wet   [15] **glinted** sparkled   [20] **maun** must   [21] **bield** shelter   [23] **histie** bare   **stibble** stubble

And guileless trust;
Till she, like thee, all soiled, is laid   35
Low i' the dust.

7

Such is the fate of simple Bard,
On Life's rough ocean luckless starred!
Unskilful he to note the card
Of prudent lore,   40
Till billows rage, and gales blow hard,
And whelm him o'er!

8

Such fate to suffering Worth is given,
Who long with wants and woes has striven,
By human pride or cunning driven   45
To mis'ry's brink;
Till, wrenched of ev'ry stay but Heaven,
He, ruined, sink!

9

Ev'n thou who mourn'st the Daisy's fate,
That fate is thine—no distant date;   50
Stern Ruin's plough-share drives elate,
Full on thy bloom,
Till crushed beneath the furrow's weight
Shall be thy doom!

A Winter Night

Poor naked wretches, wheresoe'er you are,
That bide the pelting of this pitiless storm!
How shall your houseless heads and unfed sides,
Your looped and windowed raggedness, defend you
From seasons such as these?

Shakespeare [*King Lear*, 3.4.28–32]

1

When biting Boreas, fell and doure,
Sharp shivers through the leafless bower;

---

¹ **fell** cruel   **doure** severe

When Phoebus gies a short-lived glower,
    Far south the lift,
Dim-dark'ning through the flaky shower   5
    Or whirling drift:

2

Ae night the storm the steeples rocked;
Poor Labour sweet in sleep was locked;
While burns, wi' snawy wreaths up-choked,
    Wild-eddying swirl,   10
Or, through the mining outlet bocked,
    Down headlong hurl:

3

List'ning the doors an' winnocks rattle,
I thought me on the ourie cattle,
Or silly sheep, wha bide this brattle   15
    O' winter war,
And through the drift, deep-lairing, sprattle
    Beneath a scaur.

4

Ilk happing bird—wee, helpless thing!—
That in the merry months o' spring   20
Delighted me to hear thee sing,
    What comes o' thee?
Whare wilt thou cow'r thy chittering wing,
    An' close thy e'e?

5

Ev'n you, on murd'ring errands toiled,   25
Lone from your savage homes exiled,
The blood-stain'd roost and sheep-cote spoiled
    My heart forgets,
While pityless the tempest wild
    Sore on you beats!   30

6

Now Phoebe, in her midnight reign,
Dark-muffled, viewed the dreary plain;

---

[3] **glower** stare   [4] **lift** horizon   [7] **Ae** One   [9] **burns** brooks   [11] **bocked** vomited   [13] **winnocks** windows
[14] **ourie** shivering   [15] **silly** helpless   [17] **sprattle** scramble   [18] **scaur** jutting rock   [19] **Ilk** Each

Still crowding thoughts, a pensive train,
    Rose in my soul,
When on my ear this plaintive strain,   35
    Slow-solemn, stole:—

7

"Blow, blow, ye winds, with heavier gust!
And freeze, thou bitter-biting frost!
Descend, ye chilly, smothering snows!
Not all your rage, as now united, shows   40
  More hard unkindness unrelenting,
  Vengeful malice, unrepenting,
Than heaven-illumined Man on brother Man bestows!
  See stern Oppression's iron grip,
    Or mad Ambition's gory hand,   45
Sending, like blood-hounds from the slip,
    Woe, Want, and Murder o'er a land!
  Ev'n in the peaceful rural vale,
  Truth, weeping, tells the mournful tale:
How pampered Luxury, Flatt'ry by her side,   50
  The parasite empoisoning her ear,
  With all the servile wretches in the rear,
Looks o'er proud Property, extended wide;
  And eyes the simple, rustic hind,
  Whose toil upholds the glitt'ring show—   55
  A creature of another kind,
  Some coarser substance, unrefined—
Placed for her lordly use, thus far, thus vile, below!
  Where, where is Love's fond, tender throe,
  With lordly Honour's lofty brow,   60
    The pow'rs you proudly own?
  Is there, beneath Love's noble name,
  Can harbour, dark, the selfish aim,
    To bless himself alone?
  Mark Maiden-Innocence a prey   65
    To love-pretending snares:
  This boasted Honour turns away,
  Shunning soft Pity's rising sway,
Regardless of the tears and unavailing prayers!
  Perhaps this hour, in Misery's squalid nest,   70
  She strains your infant to her joyless breast,
And with a mother's fears shrinks at the rocking blast!

8

"O ye! who, sunk in beds of down,
  Feel not a want but what yourselves create,
    Think, for a moment, on his wretched fate,   75
  Whom friends and fortune quite disown!
    Ill-satisfied keen nature's clam'rous call,
  Stretched on his straw, he lays himself to sleep;
While through the ragged roof and chinky wall,
  Chill, o'er his slumbers piles the drifty heap!   80
    Think on the dungeon's grim confine,
    Where Guilt and poor Misfortune pine!
    Guilt, erring man, relenting view!
    But shall thy legal rage pursue
    The wretch, already crushèd low   85
    By cruel Fortune's undeservèd blow?
Affliction's sons are brothers in distress;
A brother to relieve, how exquisite the bliss!"

9

I heard nae mair, for Chanticleer
  Shook off the pouthery snaw,   90
And hailed the morning with a cheer,
  A cottage-rousing craw.

But deep this truth impressed my mind:
  Through all His works abroad,
The heart benevolent and kind   95
  The most resembles God.

⁹⁰ **pouthery** powdery

The Humble Petition of Bruar Water

To the Noble Duke of Athole

I

My lord, I know, your noble ear
  Woe ne'er assails in vain;
Emboldened thus, I beg you'll hear
  Your humble slave complain,
How saucy Phoebus' scorching beams,   5
  In flaming summer-pride,

Dry-withering, waste my foamy streams,
  And drink my crystal tide.

2

The lightly-jumping, glowrin trouts,
  That through my waters play,
If, in their random, wanton spouts,   10
  They near the margin stray;
If, hapless chance! they linger lang,
  I'm scorching up so shallow,
They're left the whitening stanes amang   15
  In gasping death to wallow.

3

Last day I grat wi' spite and teen,
  As Poet Burns came by,
That, to a Bard, I should be seen
  Wi' half my channel dry;   20
A panegyric rhyme, I ween,
  Ev'n as I was, he shored me;
But had I in my glory been,
  He, kneeling, wad adored me.

4

Here, foaming down the skelvy rocks,   25
  In twisting strength I rin;
There high my boiling torrent smokes,
  Wild-roaring o'er a linn:
Enjoying large each spring and well,
  As Nature gave them me,   30
I am, although I say't mysel,
  Worth gaun a mile to see.

5

Would, then, my noble master please
  To grant my highest wishes,
He'll shade my banks wi' tow'ring trees   35
  And bonie spreading bushes.
Delighted doubly then, my lord,
  You'll wander on my banks,

---

⁹ **glowrin** staring   ¹⁷ **grat** wept   **teen** vexation   ²² **shored** offered   ²⁴ **wad** would have   ²⁵ **skelvy** shelvy
²⁸ **linn** fall   ³² **gaun** going

And listen monie a grateful bird
   Return you tuneful thanks.   40

6

The sober laverock, warbling wild,
   Shall to the skies aspire;
The gowdspink, Music's gayest child,
   Shall sweetly join the choir;
The blackbird strong, the lintwhite clear,   45
   The mavis mild and mellow,
The robin, pensive Autumn cheer
   In all her locks of yellow.

7

This, too, a covert shall ensure
   To shield them from the storm;   50
And coward maukin sleep secure,
   Low in her grassy form:
Here shall the shepherd make his seat
   To weave his crown of flowers;
Or find a shelt'ring, safe retreat   55
   From prone-descending showers.

8

And here, by sweet, endearing stealth,
   Shall meet the loving pair,
Despising worlds with all their wealth,
   As empty idle care: 60
The flowers shall vie, in all their charms,
   The hour of heaven to grace;
And birks extend their fragrant arms
   To screen the dear embrace.

9

Here haply too, at vernal dawn,   65
   Some musing Bard may stray,
   And eye the smoking, dewy lawn
     And misty mountain grey;
Or, by the reaper's nightly beam,
   Mild-chequering through the trees,   70
Rave to my darkly dashing stream,
   Hoarse-swelling on the breeze.

[41] **laverock** lark   [43] **gowdspink** goldfinch   [45] **lintwhite** linnet   [51] **maukin** hare   [63] **birks** birches

10

Let lofty firs and ashes cool
   My lowly banks o'erspread,
And view, deep-bending in the pool,   75
   Their shadows' wat'ry bed:
Let fragrant birks, in woodbines drest,
   My craggy cliffs adorn,
And, for the little songster's nest,
   The close embow'ring thorn!   80

11

So may, old Scotia's darling hope,
   Your little angel band
Spring, like their fathers, up to prop
   Their honoured native land!
So may, through Albion's farthest ken,   85
   To social-flowing glasses,
The grace be: "Athole's honest men
   And Athole's bonie lasses!"

On Scaring Some Waterfowl in Loch Turit

A Wild Scene Among the Hills of Oughtertyre

Why, ye tenants of the lake,
For me your wat'ry haunt forsake?
Tell me, fellow creatures, why
At my presence thus you fly?
Why disturb your social joys,   5
Parent, filial, kindred ties? —
Common friend to you and me,
Nature's gifts to all are free:
Peaceful keep your dimpling wave,
Busy feed, or wanton lave;   10
Or, beneath the sheltering rock,
Bide the surging billow's shock.

   Conscious, blushing for our race,
Soon, too soon, your fears I trace.
Man, your proud, usurping foe,   15
Would be lord of all below:
Plumes himself in freedom's pride,
Tyrant stern to all beside.

The eagle, from the cliffy brow
Marking you his prey below,   20
In his breast no pity dwells,
Strong necessity compels:
But Man, to whom alone is given
A ray direct from pitying Heaven,
Glories in his heart humane—   25
And creatures for his pleasure slain!

    In these savage, liquid plains,
Only known to wand'ring swains,
Where the mossy riv'let strays
Far from human haunts and ways,   30
All on Nature you depend,
And life's poor season peaceful spend.

    Or, if Man's superior might
Dare invade your native right,
On the lofty ether borne,   35
Man with all his powers you scorn;
Swiftly seek, on clanging wings,
Other lakes, and other springs;
And the foe you cannot brave,
Scorn at least to be his slave.   40

🐚 *Mary Wollstonecraft* (1759–1797)

Known today primarily as the first modern feminist because of her book A Vindication of the Rights of Woman *(1792), such a label gives only a small indication of the range of subjects about which Mary Wollstonecraft wrote.* A Vindication of the Rights of Woman *deftly argues for the moral necessity of equal rights for women, and in particular for equal access to education. Growing up with an abusive and alcoholic father, Wollstonecraft's early years were difficult and painful. These circumstances no doubt contributed to her desire to be more independent than was typically permitted for women. She sought financial independence first through her writing, and her first book was entitled* Thoughts on the Education of Daughters *(1786). After the failure of the school for girls she had established with her sister and a friend and further difficulties serving as a private governess, Wollstonecraft turned more and more toward writing to support herself. Encouraged by the radical publisher Joseph Johnson, she published a novel,* Mary, A Fiction, *in 1788, as well as a book for children. Johnson gave her additional work as a translator and book reviewer. Wollstonecraft soon became involved in the lively debate surrounding the French Revolution, and her* A Vindication of the Rights of Men *engaged the works of Edmund Burke and Thomas Paine. Her fervor for the ideals of the Revolution inspired her to travel to France to become involved firsthand. There she had an ill-fated affair with an American, Gilbert Imlay. Wollstonecraft followed Imlay back to London and later, at his suggestion, traveled to*

Scandinavia. Although the relationship with Imlay failed, her sojourn in Northern Europe produced Letters Written During a Short Residence in Sweden, Norway, and Denmark *(1796), which includes beautiful descriptions of the bleak northern countryside.*

Upon her return to London, Wollstonecraft met and eventually married the anarchist philosopher William Godwin. She died from complications in giving birth to their daughter who would become Mary Shelley, the author of Frankenstein. *The essay below is one of Wollstonecraft's numerous essays written for the periodical press. It appeared in the* Analytical Review *in 1797. Although Wollstonecraft's philosophical positions are always grounded in a firm appeal to rationality, here she acknowledges the important effects that nature can produce on the emotions.*

On Poetry and Our Relish for the Beauties of Nature

A taste for rural scenes, in the present state of society, appears to be very often an artificial sentiment, rather inspired by poetry and romances, than a real perception of the beauties of nature. But, as it is reckoned a proof of refined taste to praise the calm pleasures which the country affords, the theme is never exhausted. Yet it may be made a question, whether this romantic kind of declamation, has much effect on the conduct of those, who leave, for a season, the crowded cities in which they were bred.

I have been led to these reflections, by observing, when I have resided for any length of time in the country, how few people seem to contemplate nature with their own eyes. I have "brushed the dew away" in the morning; but, pacing over the printless grass, I have wondered that, in such delightful situations, the sun was allowed to rise in solitary majesty, whilst my eyes alone hailed its beautifying beams. The webs of the evening have still been spread across the hedged path, unless some labouring man, trudging to work, disturbed the fairy structure; yet, in spite of this supineness, when I joined the social circle, every tongue rang changes on the pleasures of the country.

Having frequently had occasion to make the same observation, I was led to endeavour, in one of my solitary rambles, to trace the cause, and likewise to enquire why the poetry written in the infancy of society, is most natural: which, strictly speaking (for *natural* is a very indefinite expression) is merely to say, that it is the transcript of immediate sensations, in all their native wildness and simplicity, when fancy, awakened by the sight of interesting objects, was most actively at work. At such moments, sensibility quickly furnishes smiles, and the sublimated spirits combine images, which rising spontaneously, it is not necessary coldly to ransack the understanding or memory, till the laborious efforts of judgment exclude present sensations, and damp the fire of enthusiasm.

The effusions of a vigorous mind, will ever tell us how far the understanding has been enlarged by thought, and stored with knowledge. The richness of the soil even appears on the surface; and the result of profound thinking, often mixing, with playful grace, in the reveries of the poet, smoothly incorporates with the ebullitions of animal spirits, when the finely fashioned nerve vibrates acutely with rapture, or when, relaxed by soft melancholy, a pleasing languor prompts the long-drawn sigh, and feeds the slowly falling tear.

The poet, the man of strong feelings, gives us only an image of his mind, when he was actually alone, conversing with himself, and marking the impression which nature had made on his own heart.—If, at this sacred moment, the idea of some departed friend, some tender recollection when the soul was most alive to tenderness, intruded unawares into his thoughts, the sorrow which it produced is artlessly, yet poetically expressed—and who can avoid sympathizing?

Love to man leads to devotion—grand and sublime images strike the imagination—God is seen in every floating cloud, and comes from the misty mountain to receive the noblest homage of an intelligent creature—praise. How solemn is the moment, when all affections and remembrances fade before the sublime admiration which the wisdom and goodness of God inspires, when he is worshipped in a *temple not made with hands*, and the world seems to contain only the mind that formed, and the mind that contemplates it! These are not the weak responses of ceremonial devotion; nor, to express them, would the poet need another poet's aid: his heart burns within him, and he speaks the language of truth and nature with resistless energy.

Inequalities, of course, are observable in his effusions; and a less vigorous fancy, with more taste, would have produced more elegance and uniformity; but, as passages are softened or expunged during the cooler moments of reflection, the understanding is gratified at the expence of those involuntary sensations, which, like the beauteous tints of an evening sky, are so evanescent, that they melt into new forms before they can be analyzed. For however eloquently we may boast of our reason, man must often be delighted he cannot tell why, or his blunt feelings are not made to relish the beauties which nature, poetry, or any of the imitative arts, afford.

The imagery of the ancients seems naturally to have been borrowed from surrounding objects and their mythology. When a hero is to be transported from one place to another, across pathless wastes, is any vehicle so natural, as one of the fleecy clouds on which the poet has often gazed, scarcely conscious that he wished to make it his chariot? Again, when nature seems to present obstacles to his progress at almost every step, when the tangled forest and steep mountain stand as barriers, to pass over which the mind longs for supernatural aid; an interposing deity, who walks on the waves, and rules the storm, severely felt in the first attempts to cultivate a country, will receive from the impassioned fancy "a local habitation and a name."

It would be a philosophical enquiry, and throw some light on the history of the human mind, to trace, as far as our information will allow us to trace, the spontaneous feelings and ideas which have produced the images that now frequently appear unnatural, because they are remote; and disgusting, because they have been servilely copied by poets, whose habits of thinking, and views of nature must have been different; for, though the understanding seldom disturbs the current of our present feelings, without dissipating the gay clouds which fancy has been embracing, yet it silently gives the colour to the whole tenour of them, and the dream is over, when truth is grossly violated, or images introduced, selected from books, and not from local manners or popular prejudices.

In a more advanced state of civilization, a poet is rather the creature of art, than of nature. The books that he reads in his youth, become a hot-bed in which artificial fruits are produced, beautiful to the common eye, though they want the true hue and flavour. His images do not arise from sensations; they are copies; and, like the works of the painters who copy ancient statues when they draw men and women of their own times, we acknowledge that the features are fine, and the proportions just; yet they are men of stone; insipid figures, that never convey to the mind the idea of a portrait taken from life, where the soul gives spirit and homogeneity to the whole. The silken wings of fancy are shrivelled by rules; and a desire of attaining elegance of diction, occasions an attention to words, incompatible with sublime, impassioned thoughts.

A boy of abilities, who has been taught the structure of verse at school, and been roused by emulation to compose rhymes whilst he was reading works of genius, may, by practice, produce pretty verses, and even become what is often termed an elegant poet: yet his readers, without knowing what to find fault with, do not find themselves warmly interested. In the works of the poets who fasten on their affections, they see grosser faults, and the very images which shock their taste in the modern; still they do not appear as puerile or extrinsic in one as the other. — Why? — because they did not appear so to the author.

It may sound paradoxical, after observing that those productions want vigour, that are merely the work of imitation, in which the understanding has violently directed, if not extinguished, the blaze of fancy, to assert, that, though genius be only another word for exquisite sensibility, the first observers of nature, the true poets, exercised their understanding much more than their imitators. But they exercised it to discriminate things, whilst their followers were busy to borrow sentiments and arrange words.

Boys who have received a classical education, load their memory with words, and the correspondent ideas are perhaps never distinctly comprehended. As a proof of this assertion, I must observe, that I have known many young people who could write tolerably smooth verses, and string epithets prettily together, when their prose themes showed the barrenness of their minds, and how superficial the cultivation must have been, which their understanding had received.

Dr. Johnson, I know, has given a definition of genius, which would overturn my reasoning, if I were to admit it. — He imagines, that *a strong mind, accidentally led to some particular study* in which it excels, is a genius.[1] — Not to stop to investigate the causes which produced this happy *strength* of mind, experience seems to prove, that those minds have appeared most vigorous, that have pursued a study, after nature had discovered a bent; for it would be absurd to suppose, that a slight impression made on the weak faculties of a boy, is the fiat of fate, and not to be effaced by any succeeding impression, or unexpected difficulty. Dr. Johnson in fact, appears sometimes to be of the same opinion (how consistently I shall not now enquire), especially when he observes, "that Thomson looked on nature with the eye which she only gives to a poet."[2]

But, though it should be allowed that books may produce some poets, I fear they will never be the poets who charm our cares to sleep, or extort admiration.

[1] In "Abraham Cowley," *Lives of the English Poets*, Samuel Johnson wrote, "The true genius is a mind of large general powers, accidentally determined to some particular direction."

[2] A reference to Johnson's observation on James Thomson in *Lives of the English Poets*.

They may diffuse taste, and polish the language; but I am inclined to conclude that they will seldom rouse the passions, or amend the heart.

And, to return to the first subject of discussion, the reason why most people are more interested by a scene described by a poet, than by a view of nature, probably arises from the want of a lively imagination. The poet contracts the prospect, and, selecting the most picturesque part in his *camera*,[3] the judgment is directed, and the whole force of the languid faculty turned towards the objects which excited the most forcible emotions in the poet's heart; the reader consequently feels the enlivened description, though he was not able to receive a first impression from the operations of his own mind.

Besides, it may be further observed, that gross minds are only to be moved by forcible representations. To rouse the thoughtless, objects must be presented, calculated to produce tumultuous emotions; the unsubstantial, picturesque forms which a contemplative man gazes on, and often follows with ardour till he is mocked by a glimpse of unattainable excellence, appear to them the light vapours of a dreaming enthusiast, who gives up the substance for the shadow. It is not within that they seek amusement; their eyes are seldom turned on themselves; consequently their emotions, though sometimes fervid, are always transient, and the nicer perceptions which distinguish the man of genuine taste, are not felt, or make such a slight impression as scarcely to excite any pleasurable sensations. Is it surprising then that they are often overlooked, even by those who are delighted by the same images concentrated by the poet?

But even this numerous class is exceeded, by witlings, who, anxious to appear to have wit and taste, do not allow their understandings or feelings any liberty; for, instead of cultivating their faculties and reflecting on their operations, they are busy collecting prejudices; and are predetermined to admire what the suffrage of time announces as excellent, not to store up a fund of amusement for themselves, but to enable them to talk.

These hints will assist the reader to trace some of the causes why the beauties of nature are not forcibly felt, when civilization, or rather luxury, has made considerable advances—those calm sensations are not sufficiently lively to serve as a relaxation to the voluptuary, or even to the moderate pursuer of artificial pleasures. In the present state of society, the understanding must bring back the feelings to nature, or the sensibility must have such native strength, as rather to be whetted than destroyed by the strong exercises of passion.

That the most valuable things are liable to the greatest perversion, is however as trite as true:—for the same sensibility, or quickness of senses, which makes a man relish the tranquil scenes of nature, when sensation, rather than reason, imparts delight, frequently makes a libertine of him, by leading him to prefer the sensual tumult of love a little refined by sentiment, to the calm pleasures of affectionate friendship, in whose sober satisfactions, reason, mixing her tranquilizing convictions, whispers, that content, not happiness, is the reward of virtue in this world.

---

[3]The *camera obscura* was a device used by landscape artists to create a virtual image of a natural scene. Used here in a figurative sense.

PART III: 1800–1899

The Nineteenth Century:
All Creatures Great and Small

Written and published in 1798, Samuel Taylor Coleridge's poem, *The Rime of the Ancient Mariner*, marks a decisive turning point in the history of writing about nature in the English language. The haunting tale of a mariner's murder of the mythical albatross has become a parable for the devastating consequences of humanity's selfish disregard for the earth and its other inhabitants. Although the word *ecology*, according to the *Oxford English Dictionary*, did not enter the English language until 1873, English Romantic poetry consistently expresses a deep and abiding interest in the earth as the *oikos*, "dwelling place," for all living things. The most essential insights of modern ecological thought—namely, the adaptation of species to their habitats, the interrelatedness of all life forms, and the potentially catastrophic effects of human intervention in natural systems—are first fully expressed by poets such as Coleridge, William Wordsworth, Mary Shelley, and John Clare, and then more explicitly developed by subsequent American Transcendentalist writers. Coleridge, again, plays a significant role in linking the two literary movements in his later prose works, notably the *Aids to Reflection* (1825). In this work, Coleridge provides a coherent philosophical basis for regarding the natural world as driven by holistic and cyclical processes, a view that later sparked the development of American Transcendentalism. Among Coleridge's particular admirers was Ralph Waldo Emerson, who visited Coleridge in 1832, and who developed an essentially Coleridgean theory of perception in *Nature* (1836). Emerson's disciple Henry David Thoreau is less explicit in his acknowledgment of Coleridge's influence, but his description of Walden Pond as an organic community nevertheless owes a great deal to the Romantic conception of nature.

It is with the relationship between Romanticism and Transcendentalism that we see a further significant development in the transatlantic literary conversation about the environment. English and American environmental literature throughout the nineteenth century revisits common themes and modes that originate with Romantic or Transcendentalist writers. Although nineteenth-century authors, like their predecessors, continued to be awed by the sublime powers of nature—symbolized, for instance, by great mountains, be they in Wales, Switzerland, or California—this sensationalism is tempered with a more informed and consistent care for the regional, the particular, and the everyday. John Clare stoops by the roadside to appreciate the wonders of a hidden bird's nest or mourns the loss of a tree from his backyard. William Cullen Bryant wonders at a single frail violet. Emily Dickinson and Walt Whitman will praise that most neglected and most prevalent of plants: grass. Authors throughout the nineteenth century give more explicit evidence of a particular rootedness and literary indebtedness to a specific place or ecosystem, of which the poets see themselves a part. It is hard for any reader to imagine William Wordsworth without the Lake District, Thoreau without Walden, Mark Twain without the Mississippi, Thomas Hardy without Wessex, or Sarah Orne Jewett without the rugged country of the pointed firs, coastal Maine. In England and in America, the use of regional dialect became a more acceptable and even critically praised literary device, be it Clare's defiant rejection of Linnaean terms for birds and beasts in favor of the vernacular of his native Helpston, or the colorful Southern inflections of Mark Twain's characters. The literary forms for this kind of renewed provincialism varied: In England, it found its most powerful articulation in the revival of folk ballads. In America, the invention of the modern short story by Hudson River writer Washington Irving made this genre the most popular vehicle for expressing the particularities of character in the growing number of discrete regions that made up the expanding territory of the United States.

The extension of the American frontier throughout the century, and the devastating divisions of the American Civil War at mid-century, contributed to stereotypical polarizations within American culture between the civilized, citified East and the wild Wild West, between the industrial North and the rural South. These divisions yielded a heterogeneity of style and subject, making it increasingly difficult to offer generalizations about the fundamental character of American literature. In terms of nature writing, however, the geographic growth of the United States westward was undeniably the most essential development. The romance of the West predominates in writing from the second half of the century, and the image of the West as a place of freedom and wildness is a powerful archetype in American consciousness. From the early accounts recorded by the explorers Meriwether Lewis and William Clark to Whitman's exuberant lyrics, there is a continual fascination with the wonders and challenges of the frontier. The stereotype of the American character as inherent "rugged individualism" was forged on the midwestern prairies described by James Fenimore Cooper and in the great western mountain ranges where John Muir made his home. The more popular versions of these stories—still the stuff of pulp fiction—aspire to create epic narratives of a primordial battle between humanity and nature. Reading these stories today, we realize that however much these tales of Daniel Boone or Davy Crockett expound upon the triumph of the human spirit in adversity, such triumphs came at the price of entire ecosystems, with their unique flora and fauna, indigenous peoples, autonomous cultures, free-flowing waterways, and unfenced horizons, which were mapped, plowed, hunted, eradicated, exterminated, ditched, dammed, bulldozed, channelized, and utterly destroyed in the westward course of American empire. It is only near the end of the century, in the writing of John Muir, a latter-day Transcendentalist, leader of the preservationist movement, and founder of the United States national park system, that we begin to see a more systematically articulated expression of the splendors of the West and of the vulnerability of its landscape and its indigenous inhabitants to the unbounded and often unthinking enthusiasm of white America's conquest.

The widespread efforts to annihilate the "savage" Native-American populations and to dispossess them of their "wild" land in order to cultivate and civilize it has some parallels in the deracination of the rural laboring class in England. There, the agents of the nascent agribusiness worked to buy up and conglomerate the holdings of small farmers and to enclose the so-called waste areas or commons that poorer rural laborers required to graze their livestock, gather firewood, or grow small vegetable gardens. Agronomy advocated large-scale agricultural enterprises, which displaced economically vulnerable farm laborers. As poets such as Robert Bloomfield and John Clare in the Romantic era and William Morris in the Victorian age make clear, these workers were not only deprived of economic subsistence, but just as significantly, as they moved into cities and took up work in factories, they were denied the pleasures of living close to the land. The insalubrious quality of industrialized England is given its first and most formidable expression in the work of an art historian, John Ruskin, whose lecture "The Storm Cloud of the Nineteenth Century" takes examples from the contemporary visual arts to deplore the effects of air pollution.

In England and in America, industrialization and westward expansion not only displaced people but destroyed flora and fauna. The near-destruction of the buffalo as a species is a famous example of the irreparable damage that can be done by human self-centeredness. Natural history writers such as John James Audubon lovingly drew and described animals, birds, and plants unique to North America, preserving them in words and images. John Muir founded the Sierra Club, in the interest of protecting ecosystems across the United States. It was an English scientist of the nineteenth century, Charles Darwin, whose paradigm-shifting theory of evolution gave us one of the most essential frameworks for understanding the interrelatedness of creation and the ways in which any change in a given ecosystem can alter plant and animal species within it. Darwin's theory made clear that no species is immutable or eternal: Extinction is forever. Darwin represented for the nineteenth century what Galileo did for the seventeenth century. His revolutionary ideas, backed by empirical evidence, supplied a devastating challenge to prevailing religious dogma held to justify androcentrism. Even today, fundamentalist Christians fight the dissemination of Darwin's discoveries. In the late nineteenth century, the presumed disappearance of God and the increased lack of faith in the old providential narrative gave rise, for example, to the bleak determinism of Thomas Hardy's poems and to Gerard Manley Hopkins's eccentrically articulated attempts to reassert divine wisdom in the world. If God were dead, man was no longer his special executor on earth and could no longer rely on the customary rationalizations for environmental exploitation. Scientific theories in the nineteenth century revealed and critiqued the increased possibility of global apocalypse. Scientific discoveries in the twentieth century ensured that humanity had the means to bring it about. Nevertheless, despite innumerable supposed advances in technology and in knowledge, American and English poets continue, even today, to return to the formulations of the Romantic and Transcendentalist writers to recall the moral of the ancient mariner's story of the albatross. Like the wedding guest to whom the mariner tells his tale, if we can remember to heed the lessons of the poets, we might more wisely and more lovingly coexist with "All things, both great and small."

✒ Robert Bloomfield (1766–1823)

While he was still a small boy, Robert Bloomfield was sent to live on an uncle's farm, where he had the many and frequently very happy experiences that would later provide the subject matter for his first published book The Farmer's Boy: A Rural Poem *(1800). His time on the farm, however, came to an end in 1781, when he was sent to join his brothers in London and learn the trade of shoemaking. But, as he tells it in his autobiographical prose, he was often assigned the task of reading aloud to the other laborers in his workshop. As he had little formal education, this reading helped to inspire Bloomfield's desire to become a poet. By 1786, his first poem was published in a newspaper and Bloomfield had set up his own shop as a cobbler. He married in 1790.*

He began writing The Farmer's Boy *in 1796, weaving together his nostalgic memories of his uncle's farm with the literary influences of other poets of rural life and country scenery. Duck, Thomson, and Goldsmith are among the authors whose impact can be registered in Bloomfield's verse. Yet when the poem was published in 1800, and sold more copies than any English poem before it, Bloomfield was touted, like Duck or Burns, as another example of "natural genius," a poet whose inspiration and artistry owed nothing to the artifices of literary tradition. While it is certainly true that Bloomfield did have actual experiences as a rural laborer and was largely self-educated, we do his work a great disservice if we insist upon reading it as either a completely naïve or an entirely "realistic" depiction of life on the farm. Like many of the Romantic poets, such as Wordsworth, much of the imagery and narrative sequences of the poem are colored both by the poet's imagination and his memory. Moreover, Bloomfield shows the influence of eighteenth-century locodescriptive poets, such as Thomson, in the poem's structure of loosely connected scenes and vignettes.*

While no poem attained the same kind of success as The Farmer's Boy, *Bloomfield continued to publish poetry depicting and celebrating the English countryside and its inhabitants.* Rural Tales, Ballads and Songs *appeared in 1802,* Good Tidings, or News from the Farm *in 1804,* Wild Flowers, or Pastoral and Local Poetry *in 1806,* The Banks of the Wye *in 1811,* May Day with the Muses *in 1822, and* Hazelwood Hall, a Village Drama in Three Acts *in 1823. His poetry never brought him financial security, and he died in financial distress in 1823.*

From The Farmer's Boy

From Summer

2

The Farmer's life displays in every part
A moral lesson to the sensual heart.
Though in the lap of Plenty, thoughtful still,
He looks beyond the present good or ill;
Nor estimates alone one blessing's worth,   5
From changeful seasons, or capricious earth;
But views the future with the present hours,
And looks for failures as he looks for showers;
For casual as for certain want prepares,
And round his yard the reeking haystack rears;   10
Or clover, blossomed lovely to the sight,
His team's rich store through many a wint'ry night.
What though abundance round his dwelling spreads,
Though ever moist his self-improving meads
Supply his dairy with a copious flood,   15
And seem to promise unexhausted food;
That promise fails, when buried deep in snow,
And vegetative juices cease to flow.
For this, his plough turns up the destined lands,
Whence stormy Winter draws its full demands;   20
For this, the seed minutely small he sows,
Whence, sound and sweet, the hardy turnip grows.
But how unlike to April's closing days!
High climbs the Sun, and darts his powerful rays;
Whitens the fresh-drawn mold, and pierces through   25
The cumb'rous clods that tumble round the plough.
O'er heaven's bright azure hence with joyful eyes
The Farmer sees dark clouds assembling rise;
Borne o'er his fields a heavy torrent falls,
And strikes the earth in hasty driving squalls.   30
"*Right welcome down, ye precious drops,*" he cries;
But soon, too soon, the partial blessing flies.
"*Boy, bring thy harrows, try how deep the rain
Has forced its way.*" He comes, but comes in vain;
Dry dust beneath the bubbling surface lurks,   35
And mocks his pains the more, the more he works:
Still midst huge clods he plunges on forlorn,
That laugh his harrows and the shower to scorn.
E'en thus the living clod, the stubborn fool,

Resists the stormy lectures of the school,   40
Till tried with gentler means, the dunce to please,
His head imbibes right reason by degrees;
As when from eve till morning's wakeful hour,
Light, constant rain, evinces secret power,
And ere the day resume its wonted smiles,   45
Presents a cheerful easy task for *Giles*.
Down with a touch the mellowed soil is laid,
And yon tall crop next claims his timely aid;
Thither well pleased he hies, assured to find
Wild trackless haunts, and objects to his mind.   50
   Shot up from broad rank blades that droop below,
The nodding wheat-ear forms a graceful bow,
With milky kernels starting full, weighed down,
Ere yet the sun hath tinged its head with brown;
Whilst thousands in a flock, for ever gay,   55
Loud chirping *sparrows* welcome on the day,
And from the mazes of the leafy thorn
Drop one by one upon the bending corn.
Giles with a pole assails their close retreats,
And round the grass-grown dewy border beats,   60
On either side completely overspread,
Here branches bend, there corn o'ertops his head.
Green covert, hail! for through the varying year
No hours so sweet, no scene to him so dear.
Here *Wisdom*'s placid eye delighted sees   65
His frequent intervals of lonely ease,
And with one ray his infant soul inspires,
Just kindling there her never-dying fires,
Whence solitude derives peculiar charms,
And heaven-directed thought his bosom warms.   70
Just where the parting bough's light shadows play,
Scarce in the shade, nor in the scorching day,
Stretched on the turf he lies, a peopled bed,
Where swarming insects creep around his head.
The small dust-coloured beetle climbs with pain   75
O'er the smooth plantain leaf, a spacious plain!
Thence higher still, by countless steps conveyed,
He gains the summit of a shivering blade,
And flirts his filmy wings, and looks around,
Exulting in his distance from the ground.   80
The tender speckled moth here dancing seen,
The vaulting grasshopper of glossy green,
And all prolific *Summer*'s sporting train,
Their little lives by various powers sustain.
But what can unassisted vision do?   85

What, but recoil where most it would pursue;
His patient gaze but finish with a sigh,
When musing waking speaks the *skylark* nigh!
Just starting from the corn she cheerly sings,
And trusts with conscious pride her downy wings;   90
Still louder breathes, and in the face of day
Mounts up, and calls on *Giles* to mark her way.
Close to his eyes his hat he instant bends,
And forms a friendly telescope, that lends
Just aid enough to dull the glaring light,   95
And place the wandering bird before his sight;
Yet oft beneath a cloud she sweeps along,
Lost for awhile, yet pours her varied song:
He views the spot, and as the cloud moves by,
Again she stretches up the clear blue sky;   100
Her form, her motion, undistinguished quite,
Save when she wheels direct from shade to light:
The fluttering songstress a mere speck became,
Like fancy's floating bubbles in a dream;
He sees her yet, but yielding to repose,   105
Unwittingly his jaded eyelids close.
Delicious sleep! From sleep who could forbear,
With no more guilt than *Giles*, and no more care?
Peace o'er his slumbers waves her guardian wing,
Nor conscience once disturbs him with a sting;   110
He wakes refreshed from every trivial pain,
And takes his pole and brushes round again.
    Its dark-green hue, its sicklier tints all fail,
And ripening harvest rustles in the gale.
A glorious sight, if glory dwells below,   115
Where Heaven's munificence makes all the show,
O'er every field and golden prospect found,
That glads the ploughman's Sunday morning's round,
When on some eminence he takes his stand,
To judge the smiling produce of the land.   120
Here Vanity slinks back, her head to hide:
What is there here to flatter human pride?
The towering fabric, or the dome's loud roar,
And steadfast columns, may astonish more,
Where the charmed gazer long delighted stays,   125
Yet traced but to the *architect* the praise;
Whilst here, the veriest clown that treads the sod,
Without one scruple gives the praise to GOD;
And twofold joys possess his raptured mind,
From gratitude and admiration joined.   130

Here, midst the boldest triumphs of her worth,
NATURE herself invites the reapers forth;
Dares the keen sickle from its twelvemonth's rest,
And gives that ardour which in every breast
From infancy to age alike appears, 135
When the first sheaf its plumy top uprears.
No rake takes here what Heaven to all bestows—
Children of want, for you the bounty flows!
And every cottage from the plenteous store
Receives a burden nightly at its door. 140
   Hark! where the sweeping scythe now rips along:
Each sturdy Mower emulous and strong;
Whose writhing form meridian heat defies,
Bends o'er his work, and every sinew tries;
Prostrates the waving treasure at his feet, 145
But spares the rising clover, short and sweet.
Come, HEALTH! come, Jollity! light-footed, come;
Here hold your revels, and make this your home.
Each heart awaits and hails you as its own;
Each moistened brow, that scorns to wear a frown: 150
Th' unpeopled dwelling mourns its tenants strayed;
E'en the domestic laughing dairy maid
Hies to the *field*, the general toil to share.
Meanwhile the FARMER quits his elbow-chair,
His cool brick-floor, his pitcher, and his ease, 155
And braves the sultry beams, and gladly sees
His gates thrown open, and his team abroad,
The ready group attendant on his word,
To turn the swarth, the quivering load to rear,
Or ply the busy rake, the land to clear. 160
Summer's light garb itself now cumb'rous grown,
Each his thin doublet in the shade throws down;
Where oft the mastiff sculks with half-shut eye,
And rouses at the stranger passing by;
Whilst unrestrained the social converse flows, 165
And every breast Love's powerful impulse knows,
And rival wits with more than rustic grace
Confess the presence of a pretty face.
   For, lo! encircled there, the lovely MAID,
In youth's own bloom and native smiles arrayed; 170
Her hat awry, divested of her gown,
Her creaking stays of leather, stout and brown; . . .
Invidious barrier! why art thou so high,
When the slight covering of her neck slips by,
There half revealing to the eager sight 175

Her full, ripe bosom, exquisitely white?
In many a local tale of harmless mirth,
And many a jest of momentary birth,
She bears a part, and as she stops to speak,
Strokes back the ringlets from her glowing cheek.   180
     Now noon gone by, and four declining hours,
The weary limbs relax their boasted powers;
Thirst rages strong, the fainting spirits fail,
And ask the sov'reign cordial, home-brewed ale:
Beneath some sheltering heap of yellow corn   185
Rests the hooped keg, and friendly cooling horn,
That mocks alike the goblet's brittle frame,
Its costlier potions, and its nobler name.
To *Mary* first the brimming draught is given
By toil made welcome as the dews of heaven,   190
And never lip that pressed its homely edge
Had kinder blessings or a heartier pledge.
     Of wholesome viands here a banquet smiles,
A common cheer for all; . . . e'en humble *Giles*,
Who joys his trivial services to yield   195
Amidst the fragrance of the open field;
Oft doomed in suffocating heat to bear
The cobwebbed barn's impure and dusty air;
To ride in murky state the panting steed,
Destined aloft th' unloaded grain to tread,   200
Where, in his path as heaps on heaps are thrown,
He rears, and plunges the loose mountain down:
Laborious task! with what delight when done
Both horse and rider greet th' unclouded sun!
     Yet by th' unclouded sun are hourly bred   205
The bold assailants that surround thine head,
Poor patient *Ball!* and with insulting wing
Roar in thine ears, and dart the piercing sting:
In thy behalf the crest-waved boughs avail
More than thy short-clipped remnant of a tail,   210
A moving mockery, a useless name,
A living proof of cruelty and shame.
Shame to the man, whatever fame he bore,
Who took from thee what man can ne'er restore,
Thy weapon of defence, thy chiefest good,   215
When swarming flies contending suck thy blood.
Nor thine alone the suffering, thine the care,
The fretful *Ewe* bemoans an equal share;
Tormented into sores, her head she hides,
Or angry brushes from her new-shorn sides.   220
Penned in the yard, e'en now at closing day

Unruly *Cows* with marked impatience stay,
And vainly striving to escape their foes,
The pail kick down; a piteous current flows.
    Is't not enough that plagues like these molest? 225
Must still another foe annoy their rest?
He comes, the pest and terror of the yard,
His full-fledged progeny's imperious guard;
The *Gander;* . . . spiteful, insolent, and bold,
At the colt's footlock takes his daring hold: 230
There, serpent-like, escapes a dreadful blow;
And straight attacks a poor defenceless cow:
Each booby goose th' unworthy strife enjoys,
And hails his prowess with redoubled noise.
Then back he stalks, of self-importance full, 235
Seizes the shaggy foretop of the bull,
Till whirled aloft he falls; a timely check,
Enough to dislocate his worthless neck:
For lo! of old, he boasts an honoured wound;
Behold that broken wing that trails the ground! 240
Thus fools and bravoes kindred pranks pursue;
As savage quite, and oft as fatal too.
Happy the man that foils an envious elf,
Using the darts of spleen to serve himself.
As when by turns the strolling *Swine* engage 245
The utmost efforts of the bully's rage,
Whose nibbling warfare on the grunter's side
Is welcome pleasure to his bristly hide;
Gently he stoops, or stretched at ease along,
Enjoys the insults of the gabbling throng, 250
That march exulting round his fallen head,
As human victors trample on their dead.
    Still Twilight, welcome! Rest, how sweet art thou!
Now eve o'erhangs the western cloud's thick brow:
The far-stretched curtain of retiring light, 255
With fiery treasures fraught; that on the sight
Flash from its bulging sides, where darkness lours,
In Fancy's eye, a chain of mouldering towers;
Or craggy coasts just rising into view,
Midst javelins dire, and darts of streaming blue. 260
    Anon tired labourers bless their sheltering home,
When Midnight, and the frightful Tempest come.
The Farmer wakes, and sees with silent dread
The angry shafts of Heaven gleam round his bed;
The bursting cloud reiterated roars, 265
Shakes his straw roof, and jars his bolted doors:
The slow-winged storm along the troubled skies

Spreads its dark course; the wind begins to rise;
And full-leafed elms, his dwelling's shade by day,
With mimic thunder give its fury way: 270
Sounds in his chimney top a doleful peal,
Midst pouring rain, or gusts of rattling hail;
With tenfold danger low the tempest bends,
And quick and strong the sulphurous flame descends:
The frightened mastiff from his kennel flies,   275
And cringes at the door with piteous cries. . . .
    Where now's the trifler? where the child of pride?
These are the moments when the heart is tried!
Nor lives the man with conscience e'er so clear,
But feels a solemn, reverential fear;   280
Feels too a joy relieve his aching breast,
When the spent storm hath howled itself to rest.
Still, welcome beats the long continued shower,
And sleep protracted, comes with double power;
Calm dreams of bliss bring on the morning sun,   285
For every barn is filled, and HARVEST *done!*
    Now, ere sweet SUMMER bids its long adieu,
And winds blow keen where late the blossom grew,
The bustling day and jovial night must come,
The long accustomed feast of Harvest-Home.   290
No blood-stained victory, in story bright,
Can give the philosophic mind delight;
No triumph please while rage and death destroy:
Reflection sickens at the monstrous joy.
And where the joy, if rightly understood,   295
Like cheerful praise for universal good?
The soul nor check nor doubtful anguish knows,
But free and pure the grateful current flows.
    Behold the sound oak table's massy frame
Bestride the kitchen floor! the careful dame   300
And generous host invite their friends around,
While all that cleared the crop, or tilled the ground,
Are guests by right of custom: . . . old and young;
And many a neighbouring yeoman join the throng,
With artisans that lent their dext'rous aid,   305
When o'er each field the flaming sunbeams played. —
    Yet Plenty reigns, and from her boundless hoard,
Though not one jelly trembles on the board,
Supplies the feast with all that sense can crave;
With all that made our great forefathers brave,   310
Ere the cloyed palate countless flavours tried,
And cooks had Nature's judgment set aside.

With thanks to Heaven, and tales of rustic lore,
The mansion echoes when the banquet's o'er;
A wider circle spreads, and smiles abound,   315
As quick the frothing horn performs its round;
Care's mortal foe; that sprightly joys imparts
To cheer the frame and elevate their hearts.
Here, fresh and brown, the hazel's produce lies
In tempting heaps, and peals of laughter rise,   320
And crackling Music, with the frequent *Song*,
Unheeded bear the midnight hour along.
      Here once a year Distinction lowers its crest,
The master, servant, and the merry guest,
Are equal all; and round the happy ring   325
The reaper's eyes exulting glances fling,
And, warmed with gratitude, he quits his place,
With sun-burnt hands and ale-enlivened face,
Refills the jug his honoured host to tend,
To serve at once the master and the friend;   330
Proud thus to meet his smiles, to share his tale,
His nuts, his conversation, and his ale.
      Such were the days, . . . of days long past I sing,
When Pride gave place to mirth without a sting;
Ere tyrant customs strength sufficient bore   335
To violate the feelings of the poor;
To leave them distanced in the maddening race,
Where'er Refinement shows its hated face:
Nor causeless hated; . . . 'tis the peasant's curse,
That hourly makes his wretched station worse;   340
Destroys life's intercourse; the social plan
That rank to rank cements, as man to man:
Wealth flows around him, fashion lordly reigns;
Yet poverty is his, and mental pains.
      Methinks I hear the mourner thus impart   345
The stifled murmurs of his wounded heart:
"Whence comes this change, ungracious, irksome, cold?
"Whence the new grandeur that mine eyes behold?
"The widening distance which I daily see,
"Has Wealth done this? . . . then wealth's a foe to me;   350
"Foe to our rights; that leaves a powerful few
"The paths of emulation to pursue: . . .
"For emulation stoops to us no more:
"The hope of humble industry is o'er;
"The blameless hope, the cheering sweet presage   355
"Of future comforts for declining age.
"Can my sons share from this paternal hand

"The profits with the labours of the land?
"No; though indulgent Heaven its blessing deigns,
"Where's the small farm to suit my scanty means?   360
"Content, the Poet sings, with us resides;
"In lonely cots like mine the damsel hides;
"And will he then in raptured visions tell
"That sweet Content with Want can ever dwell?
"A barley loaf, 'tis true, my table crowns,   365
"That fast diminishing in lusty rounds,
"Stops Nature's cravings; yet her sighs will flow
"From knowing this, . . . that once it was not so.
"Our annual feast, when Earth her plenty yields,
"When crowned with boughs the last load quits the fields,   370
"The aspect still of ancient joy puts on;
"The aspect only, with the substance gone:
"The self-same Horn is still at our command,
"But serves none now but the plebeian hand:
"For *home-brewed Ale*, neglected and debased,   375
"Is quite discarded from the realms of taste.
"Where unaffected Freedom charmed the soul,
"The *separate* table and the costly bowl,
"Cool as the blast that checks the budding Spring,
"A mockery of gladness round them fling.   380
"For oft the Farmer, ere his heart approves,
"Yields up the custom which he dearly loves:
"Refinement forces on him like a tide;
"Bold innovations down its current ride,
"That bear no peace beneath their showy dress,   385
"Nor add one tittle to his happiness.
"His guests selected; rank's punctilios known;
"What trouble waits upon a casual frown!
"Restraint's foul manacles his pleasures maim;
"Selected guests selected phrases claim: 390
"Nor reigns that joy when hand in hand they join
"That good old Master felt in shaking mine.
"HEAVEN bless his memory! bless his honoured name!
"(The poor will speak his lasting worthy fame):
"To souls fair-purposed strength and guidance give;   395
"In pity to us still let goodness live:
"Let labour have its due! my cot shall be
"From chilling want and guilty murmurs free:
"Let labour have its due; . . . then peace is mine,
"And never, never shall my heart repine."   400

≫ *Meriwether Lewis* (1774–1809)
William Clark (1770–1838)

Meriwether Lewis served as an army captain before becoming the personal secretary to his friend, Thomas Jefferson. Selected by President Jefferson to lead an expedition across the Louisiana Territory, recently acquired from France, Lewis chose William Clark as his lieutenant. Although lower in rank, Clark was an older and more experienced soldier, an army officer who had served in many engagements with Native-American adversaries. In practice, Lewis and Clark equally shared the responsibilities of command, working effectively together in a cooperative way. Their expedition set forth in May 1804, a group of thirty men and one Shoshone woman, Sacagawea, and her infant child, traveling up the Missouri River in small boats. The main purpose of the expedition was to find a navigable water route to the Pacific, pursuing the old dream of a Northwest Passage. Along the way, they were to explore the uncharted terrain of the West, to gather scientific information about its teeming flora and fauna, and to establish friendly relations with the Native Americans they would encounter. The hardest part of the journey came in 1805, when they reached the Great Falls of the Missouri and realized that there was no easy way forward. Instead of paddling gently upstream, they would have to portage their boats for several miles over rugged terrain. With the snow-laden Rocky Mountains looming up ahead, the vast scale of the Great West was beginning to dawn upon them. Only the assistance of Sacagawea, who negotiated with her people to obtain horses, enabled Lewis and Clark to cross the Rockies and make their way to the Pacific Ocean. After spending a miserable, rainy winter on the shores of the Columbia River, they returned the following year, arriving back in St. Louis in September 1806.

The Journals of Lewis and Clark, first published in 1904–5, record the events of the journey and the details of the surrounding landscape from two very different points of view. Lewis's voice reflects his education and social class; he is literate, tasteful, and emotionally responsive to the sublime scenery around him. Trained in botany, zoology, and celestial navigation, Lewis observes the natural world from a scientific point of view. Clark's voice, in contrast, is more pragmatic, efficient, and concise; his language displays a less-educated, more vernacular mode of expression. Together these two voices, counterpointed in their journals, convey an epic narrative that epitomizes the democratic ethos of the American frontier.

After the expedition, Lewis and Clark went their separate ways. Clark was appointed superintendent of Indian affairs and governor of the Missouri Territory, where he went on to play an important role in the history of the American West. Lewis, on the other hand, found it difficult to cope with his fame and the numerous responsibilities that grew out of the great journey. In 1809, while traveling to Washington with the journals of the expedition, he died under mysterious circumstances—possibly the result of suicide—in a lonely inn on the Natchez Trace.

From The Journals of Lewis and Clark
Chapter 10, From Maria's River to the Great Falls of the Missouri

[Lewis]   Saturday June 8th 1805.

The whole of my party to a man except myself were fully persuaided that this river was the Missouri, but being fully of opinion that it was neither the main stream, nor that which it would be advisable for us to take, I determined to give it a name and in honour of Miss Maria W——d [Wood] called it Maria's River. It is true that the hue of the waters of this turbulent and troubled stream but illy comport with the pure celestial virtues and amiable qualifications of that lovely fair one; but on the other hand it is a noble river; one destined to become in my opinion an object of contention between the two great powers of America and Great Britin with respect to the adjustment of the Northwestwardly boundary of the former;   and that it will become one of the most interesting branches of the Missouri in a commercial point of view, I have but little doubt, as it abounds with animals of the fur kind, and most probably furnishes a safe and direct communication to that productive country of valuable furs exclusively enjoyed at present by the subjects of his Brittanic Majesty; in addition to which it passes through a rich fertile and one of the most beatifully picturesque countries that I ever beheld, through the wide expanse of which, innumerable herds of living animals are seen, its borders garnished with one continued garden of roses, while its lofty and open forests are the habitation of myriads of the feathered tribes who salute the ear of the passing traveler with their wild and simple, yet sweet and cheerful melody. I arrived at camp about 5 o'clock in the evening much fatigued, where I found Capt. Clark and the balance of the party waiting our return with some anxiety for our safety having been absent near two days longer than we had engaged to return. . . .

Sunday June 9th 1805.

    We determined to deposit at this place the large red perogue[1] all the heavy baggage which we could possibly do without and some provision, salt, tools powder and Lead &c; accordingly we set some hands to digging a hole or cellar for the reception of our stores. These holes in the ground or deposits are called by the engages *cashes (cachés)*; today we examined our maps, and compared the information derived as well from them as [from] the Indians and fully settled in our minds the propriety of adopting the South fork for the Missouri, as that which it would be most expedient for us to take. Those ideas as they occurred to me I endevoured to impress on the minds of the party all of whom except Capt. C. being still firm in the belief that the N. Fork was the Missouri and that which we ought to take;   they said very cheerfully that they were ready to follow us

---

[1] A large, flat-bottomed riverboat. The shallow waters of the upper Missouri River had proven impassable to large boats, so Lewis and Clark decided to cache the perogue, and some extra supplies, alongside the river until their return trip.

any where we thought proper to direct but that they still thought that the other was the river and that they were afraid that the South fork would soon terminate in the mountains and leave us at a great distance from the Columbia. Finding them so determined in this belief, and wishing that if we were in an error to be able to detect it and rectify it as soon as possible it was agreed between Capt. C. and myself that one of us should set out with a small party by land up the South fork and continue our route up it until we found the falls or reached the snowy Mountains by which means we should be enabled to determine this question pretty accurately. This expedition I preferred undertaking as Capt. C. [is the] best waterman &c and determined to set out the day after tomorrow;   I wished to make some further observations at this place, and as we had determined to leave our blacksmith's bellows and tools here it was necessary to repair some of our arms, and particularly my Airgun[2] the main spring of which was broken, before we left this place. These and some other preparations will necessarily detain us two perhaps three days. I felt myself very unwell this morning and took a portion of salts from which I feel much relief this evening. Most of the men are busily engaged dressing skins for clothing. In the evening Cruzatte gave us some music on the violin and the men passed the evening dancing singing &c and were extremely cheerful.

[Clark]   June 10th Monday 1805.

We drew up our large Perogue into the middle of a small Island in the North fork and covered her with bushes after making her fast to the trees, branded several trees to prevent the Indians injuring her,   Sahcahgagweâ our Indian woman very sick I bled her,   we determined to ascend the South fork, and Capt Lewis selects 4 men George Drewyer, Gibson, Jo. Fields and S. Gutrich to accompany him and determine to set out in the morning. The after noon or night cloudy some rain,   river rising a little.

[Lewis]   Tuesday June 11th 1805.

At 8 A.M. I swung my pack, and set forward with my little party. Proceeded to the point where Rose River a branch [of] Maria's River approaches the Missouri so nearly. From this height we discovered a herd of Elk on the Missouri just above us to which we descended and soon killed four of them. We butchered them and hung up the meat and skins in view of the river, but before the meal was prepared I was taken with such violent pain in the intestines that I was unable to partake of the feast of marrowbones. My pain still increased and towards evening was attended with a high fever; finding myself unable to march, I determined to prepare a camp of some willow boughs and remain all night. Having brought no medicine with me I resolved to try an experiment with some simples; and the Choke cherry which grew abundantly in the bottom first struck my attention; I directed a parcel of the small twigs to be gathered stripped of their

[2] The air gun was an experimental weapon that Lewis brought along to impress Native Americans and to see how well it worked under harsh conditions. It proved very unreliable.

leaves, cut into pieces of about 2 Inches in length and boiled in water until a strong black decoction of an astringent bitter taste was produced; at sunset I took a point [pint] of this decoction and about an hour after repeated the dose by 10 in the evening I was entirely relieved from pain and in fact every symptom of the disorder forsook me; my fever abated, a gentle perspiration was produced and I had a comfortable and refreshing night's rest. Goodrich who is remarkably fond of fishing caught several dozen fish of two different species.

Thursday June 13th 1805.

We again ascended the hills of the river and gained the level country. The country through which we passed for the first six miles though more rolling than that we had passed yesterday might still with propriety be deemed a level country; our course as yesterday was generally S.W. The river from the place we left it appeared to make a considerable bend to the South. From the extremity of this rolling country I overlooked a most beautiful and level plain of great extent or at least 50 or sixty miles; in this there were infinitely more buffalo than I had ever before witnessed at a view. Nearly in the direction I had been traveling or S.W. two curious mountains presented themselves of square figures, the sides rising perpendicularly to the height of 250 feet and appeared to be formed of yellow clay; their tops appeared to be level plains; fearing that the river bore to the South and that I might pass the falls if they existed between this and the snowy mountains I altered my course nearly to the South leaving those insulated hills to my right and proceeded through the plain; I sent Feels on my right and Drewyer and Gibson on my left with orders to kill some meat and join me at the river where I should halt for dinner. I had proceeded on this course about two miles with Goodrich at some distance behind me when my ears were saluted with the agreeable sound of a fall of water and advancing a little further I saw the spray arise above the plain like a column of smoke which would frequently disappear again in an instant caused I presume by the wind which blew pretty hard from the S.W. I did not however lose my direction to this point which soon began to make a roaring too tremendous to be mistaken for any cause short of the great falls of the Missouri. Here I arrived about 12 o'clock having travelled by estimate about 15 Miles.

I took my position on the top of some rocks about 20 feet high opposite the center of the falls. This chain of rocks appear once to have formed a part of those over which the waters tumbled, but in the course of time has been separated from it to the distance of 150 yards lying parallel to it and a butment against which the water after falling over the precipice beats with great fury; this barrier extends on the right to the perpendicular clift which forms that board [border] of the river, but to the distance of 120 yards next to the clift it is but a few feet above the level of the water, and here the water in very high tides appears to pass in a channel of 40 yds. next to the higher part of the ledge of rocks; on the left it extends within 80 or ninety yards of the lard clift which is also perpendicular; between this abrupt extremity of the ledge of rocks and the perpendicular bluff the whole body of water passes with incredible swiftness.

Immediately at the cascade the river is about 300 yds. wide; about ninety or a hundred yards of this next the lard. bluff is a smooth even sheet of water falling over a precipice of at least eighty feet,   the remaining part of about 200 yards on my right forms the grandest sight I ever beheld,   the height of the fall is the same of the other but the irregular and somewhat projecting rocks below receives the water in its passage down and breaks it into a perfect white foam which assumes a thousand forms in a moment sometimes flying up in jets of sparkling foam to the height of fifteen or twenty feet and are scarcely formed before large rolling bodies of the same beaten and foaming water is thrown over and conceals them. In short the rocks seem to be most happily fixed to present a sheet of the whitest beaten froth for 200 yards in length and about 80 feet perpendicular. The water after descending strikes against the butment before mentioned or that on which I stand and seems to reverberate and being met by the more impetuous courant they roll and swell into half formed billows of great height which rise and again disappear in an instant. This butment of rock defends a handsome little bottom of about three acres which is diversified and agreeably shaded with some cottonwood trees; in the lower extremity of the bottom there is a very thick grove of the same kind of trees which are small, in this wood there are several Indian lodges formed of sticks. A few small cedar grow near the ledge of rocks where I rest. Below the point of these rocks at a small distance the river is divided by a large rock which rises several feet above the water, and extends downwards with the stream for about 20 yards.

About a mile before the water arrives at the pitch it descends very rapidly, and is confined on the lard. side by a perpendicular clift of about 100 feet,   on stard. side it is also perpendicular for about three hundred yards above the pitch where it is then broken by the discharge of a small ravine, down which the buffalo have a large beaten road to the water, for it is but in very few places that these animals can obtain water near this place owing to the steep and inaccessible banks. About 300 yards below me there is another butment of solid rock with a perpendicular face and about 60 feet high which projects from the stard. side at right angles to the distance of 134 yds. and terminates the lower part nearly of the bottom before mentioned; there being a passage around the end of this butment between it and the river of about 20 yards; here the river again assumes its usual width soon spreading to near 300 yards but still continues its rapidity. From the reflection of the sun on the spray or mist which arises from these falls is a beautiful rainbow produced which adds not a little to the beauty of this majestically grand scenery.

After writing this imperfect description I again viewed the falls and was so much disgusted with the imperfect idea which it conveyed of the scene that I determined to draw my pen across it and begin again, but then reflected that I could not perhaps succeed better than penning the first impressions of the mind; I retired to the shade of a tree where I determined to fix my camp for the present and dispatch a man in the morning to inform Capt. C. and the party of my success in finding the falls and settle in their minds all further doubts as to the Missouri. The hunters now arrived loaded with excellent buffalo meat and informed me that they had killed three very fat cows about 3/4 of a mile from hence. I walked down the river about three miles to discover if possible some place to which the canoes might arrive or at which they might be drawn on shore in order to be taken by land above the falls; but returned without effecting either of these objects; the river was one continued sene of rapids and cascades which I readily perceived could not be encountered with our canoes, and the clifts still retained their perpendicular structure and were from 150 to 200 feet high; in short the river appears here to have worn a channel in the process of time through a solid rock.

My fare is really sumptuous this evening; buffalo's humps, tongues and marrowbones, fine trout parched meal pepper and salt, and a good appetite; the last is not considered the least of the luxuries.

Friday June 14th 1805.

[On this day Lewis reconnoiters the remaining four falls and the intervening rapids which compose the Great Falls, going as far as Sun River, which during the winter they had named Medicine River. He is on the way to the latter as the entry continues.[3]]

I descended the hill and directed my course to the bend of the Missouri near which there was a herd of at least a thousand buffalo; here I thought it would be well to kill a buffalo and leave him until my return from the river and if I then found that I had not time to get back to camp this evening to remain all night here there being a few sticks of drift wood lying along shore which would answer for my fire, and a few scattering cottonwood trees a few hundred yards below which would afford me at least the semblance of a shelter. Under this impression I selected a fat buffalo and shot him very well, through the lungs; while I was gazing attentively on the poor animal discharging blood in streams from his mouth and nostrils, expecting him to fall every instant, and having entirely forgotten to reload my rifle, a large white, or rather brown bear, had perceived and crept on me within 20 steps before I discovered him; in the first moment I drew up my gun to shoot, but at the same instant recollected that she was not loaded and that he was too near for me to hope to perform this operation before he reached me, as he was then briskly advancing on me; it was an open level plain, not a bush within miles nor a tree within less than three hundred yards of me; the river bank was sloping and not more than three feet above the level of the water; in short there was no place by means of which I could conceal myself from this monster until I could charge my rifle; in this situation I thought of retreating in a brisk walk as fast as he was advancing until I could reach a tree about 300 yards below me, but I had no sooner turned myself about but he pitched at me, open mouthed and full speed, I ran about 80 yards and found he gained on me fast, I then run into the water   the idea struck me to get into the water to such depth that I could stand and he would be obliged to swim, and that I could in that situation defend myself with my espontoon; accordingly I ran

[3] There are five waterfalls on a ten-mile stretch of the Missouri River. The highest one, known as the Great Falls, is the farthest upstream. Modern hydroelectric dams have entirely destroyed their beauty and spectacle.

hastily into the water about waist deep, and faced about and presented the point of my espontoon, at this instant he arrived at the edge of the water within about 20 feet of me; the moment I put myself in this attitude of defence he suddenly wheeled about as if frightened, declined to combat on such unequal grounds, and retreated with quite as great precipitation as he had just before pursued me.

As soon as I saw him run in that manner I returned to the shore and charged my gun, which I had still retained in my hand throughout this curious adventure. I saw him run through the level open plain about three miles, till he disappeared in the woods on Medicine river; during the whole of this distance he ran at full speed, sometimes appearing to look behind him as if he expected pursuit. I now began to reflect on this novel occurence and endeavoured to account for this sudden retreat of the bear. I at first thought that perhaps he had not smelt me before he arrived at the water's edge so near me, but I then reflected that he had pursued me for about 80 or 90 yards before I took the water and on examination saw the grownd torn with his talons immediately on the impression of my steps; and the cause of his alarm still remains with me mysterious and unaccountable. So it was and I felt myself not a little gratified that he had declined the combat. My gun reloaded I felt confidence once more in my strength.

In returning through the level bottom of Medicine river and about 200 yards distant from the Missouri, my direction led me directly to an animal that I at first supposed was a wolf; but on nearer approach or about sixty paces distant I discovered that it was not, its colour was a brownish yellow; it was standing near its burrow, and when I approached it thus nearly, it couched itself down like a cat looking immediately at me as if it designed to spring on me. I took aim at it and fired, it instantly disappeared in its burrow; I loaded my gun and examined the place which was dusty and saw the track from which I am still further convinced that it was of the tiger kind. Whether I struck it or not I could not determine, but I am almost confident that I did; my gun is true and I had a steady rest by means of my espontoon, which I have found very serviceable to me in this way in the open plains. It now seemed to me that all the beasts of the neighbourhood had made a league to destroy me, or that some fortune was disposed to amuse herself at my expence, for I had not proceded more than three hundred yards from the burrow of this tiger cat, before three bull buffalo, which were feeding with a large herd about half a mile from me on my left, separated from the herd and ran full speed towards me, I thought at least to give them some amusement and altered my direction to meet them; when they arrived within a hundred yards they made a halt, took a good view of me and retreated with precipitation. I then continued my route homewards passed the buffalo which I had killed, but did not think it prudent to remain all night at this place which really from the succession of curious adventures wore the impression on my mind of enchantment; at sometimes for a moment I thought it might be a dream, but the prickly pears which pierced my feet very severely once in a while, particularly after it grew dark, convinced me that I was really awake, and that it was necessary to make the best of my way to camp.

[Clark]   June 14th Friday 1805.

A fine morning   the Indian woman[4] complaining all night and excessively
bad this morning. her case is somewhat dangerous. two men with the Tooth ache
2 with Tumors, and one man with a Tumor and a slight fever   passed the camp
Capt. Lewis made the 1st night at which place he had left part of two bear their
skins &c.   three men with Tumors went on shore and stayed out all night   one
of them killed 2 buffalo, a part of which we made use of for breakfast,   the current excessively rapid more so as we ascend   we find great difficulty in getting
the Perogue and canoes up in safety, canoes take in water frequently,   at 4
o'clock this evening Jo: Fields returned from Capt. Lewis with a letter for me,
Capt Lewis dates his letter from the Great falls of the Missouri, which Fields informs me is about 20 miles in advance and about 10 miles above the place I left
the river the time I was up last week.

                                                    June the 15th Satturday 1805.

We set out at the usual time and proceeded on with great difficulty as the
river is more rapid we can hear the falls this morning very distinctly. Our Indian
woman sick and low spirited   I gave her the bark and apply it externally to her
region which revived her much. The current excessively rapid and difficult to ascend   great numbers of dangerous places, and the fatigue which we have to encounter is incretiatable   the men in the water from morning until night hauling
the cord and boats walking on sharp rocks and round slippery stones which alternately cut their feet and throw them down, notwithstanding all this difficulty
they go with great cheerfulness,   added to those difficulties the rattle snakes innumerable and require great caution to prevent being bitten.

[Lewis]   Sunday June 16th 1805.

At noon the men arrived and shortly after I set out with them to rejoin the
party,   we took with us the dried meat consisting of about 600 lbs. and several
dozen of dried trout. About 2 P.M. I reached the camp found the Indian woman
extremely ill and much reduced by her indisposition. This gave me some concern as well for the poor object herself, then with a young child in her arms, as
from the consideration of her being our only dependence for a friendly negotia-
tion with the Snake Indians on whom we depend for horses to assist us in our
portage from the Missouri to the Columbia river. I now informed Capt. C. of my
discoveries with respect to the most proper side for our portage, and of its great
length, which I could not estimate at less than 16 miles. Capt. C. had already
sent two men this morning to examine the country on the S. side of the river; he
now passed over with the party to that side and fixed a camp about a mile below
the entrance of a Creek where there was a sufficient quantity of wood for fuel, an
article which can be obtained but in few places in this neighbourhood.

[4] Sacagawea.

After discharging the loads four of the canoes were sent back to me, which by means of strong ropes we hauled above the rapid and passed over to the south side from whence the water not being rapid we can readily convey them into the creek by means of which we hope to get them on the high plain with more ease. One of the small canoes was left below this rapid in order to pass and repass the river for the purpose of hunting as well as to procure the water of the Sulphur spring, the virtues of which I now resolved to try on the Indian woman. Capt. Clark determined to set out in the morning to examine (the country) and survey the portage, and discover the best route. As the distance was too great to think of transporting the canoes and baggage on the men's shoulders, we selected six men, and ordered them to look out some timber this evening, and early in the morning to set about making a parcel of truck wheels in order to convey our canoes and baggage over the portage. We determined to leave the white perogue at this place, and substitute the Iron boat,[5] and also to make a further deposit of a part of our stores. I found that two doses of barks and opium which I had given her [Sacajawea] since my arrival had produced an alteration in her pulse for the better; they were now much fuller and more regular. I caused her to drink the mineral water altogether. She complains principally of the lower region of the abdomen, I therefore continued the cataplasms of barks and laudanum which had been previously used by my friend Capt. Clark. I believe her disorder originated principally from an obstruction of the mensis[6] in consequence of taking cold.

Monday June 17th 1805.

Capt. Clark set out early this morning with five men to examine the country and survey the river and portage as had been concerted last evening. I set six men at work to prepare four sets of truck wheels with couplings, tongues and bodies, that they might either be used without the bodies for transporting our canoes, or with them in transporting our baggage. We were fortunate enough to find one cottonwood tree just below the entrance of portage creek that was large enough to make our carriage wheels about 22 Inches in diameter; fortunate I say because I do not believe that we could find another of the same size perfectly sound within 20 miles of us. The cottonwood which we are obliged to employ in the other parts of the work is extremely illy calculated for it being soft and brittle. We have made two axeltrees of the mast of the white perogue, which I hope will answer tolerably well tho' it is rather small. The Indian woman much better today; I have still continued the same course of medicine; she is free from pain clear of fever, her pulse regular, and eats as heartily as I am willing to permit her of broiled buffalo well seasoned with pepper and salt and rich soup of the same meat; I think therefore that there is every rational hope of her recovery.

---

[5] A collapsible boat with an iron frame covered by skins. An experimental craft, it never worked very well.

[6] A menstrual disorder. Lewis's course of treatment, which included herbal remedies, bleeding, and opium, was standard medical practice for the time.

[Clark]   June 18th Tuesday 1805.

This evening, one man A. Willard going for a load of meat at 170 yards distance on an Island was attacked by a white bear and very near being caught, pursued within 40 yards of the camp where I was with one man   I collected 3 others of the party and pursued the bear (who had pursued my track from a buffalo I had killed on the Island at about 300 yards distance and chanced to meet Willard) for fear of his attacking one man Colter at the lower point of the Island. Before we had got down the bear had alarmed the man and pursued him into the water,   at our approach he retreated, and we relieved the man in the water,   I saw the bear but the bushes was so thick that I could not shoot him and it was nearly dark,

                                            June 20th Thursday 1805.

I direct stakes to be cut to stick up in the prairies to show the way for the party to transport the baggage &c. &c.   We set out early on the portage,   soon after we set out it began to rain and continued a short time   we proceeded on thro' a tolerable level plain, and found the hollow of a Deep riveen to obstruct our route   as it could not be passed with canoes and baggage for some distance above the place we struck it. I examined it for some time and finding it late determined to strike the river and take its Course and distance to camp which I accordingly did   the wind hard from the S.W.   A fair after noon,   the river on both sides cut with raveens some of which is passes through steep clifts into the river,   the country above the falls and up the Medicine river is level, with low banks,   a chain of mountains to the west some part of which particular those to the N W. & S W are covered with snow and appear very high. I saw a rattle snake in an open plain 2 miles from any creek or woods. When I arrived at camp found all well with quantities of meat,   the canoes Capt Lewis had carried up the Creek $1\frac{3}{4}$ miles to a good place to ascend the land and taken up. Not having seen the Snake Indians or knowing in fact whether to calculate on their friendship or hostility, we have conceived our party sufficiently small, and therefore have concluded not to dispatch a canoe with a part of our men to St. Louis as we have entended early in the Spring. We fear also that such a measure might also discourage those who would in such case remain, and might possibly hazard the fate of the expedition. We have never hinted to any one of the party that we had such a scheme in contemplation, and all appear perfectly to have made up their minds to Succeed in the expedition or perish in the attempt. We all believe that we are about to enter on the most perilous and difficult part of our Voyage, yet I see no one repineing; all appear ready to meet those difficulties which await us with resolution and becoming fortitude.

The Mountains to the N.W. and West of us are still entirely covered are white and glitter with the reflection of the sun. I do not believe that the clouds that prevail at this season of the year reach the summits of those lofty mountains; and if they do the probability is that they deposit snow only for there has been no perceptible diminution of the snow which they contain since we first saw them. I have thought it probable that these mountains might have derived their appellation of *Shineing Mountains*, from their glittering appearance when the sun shines in certain directions on the snow which cover them.

During the time of my being on the Plains and above the falls I as also all my party repeatedly heard a noise which proceeded from a Direction a little to the N. of West, a loud [noise] and resembling precisely the discharge of a piece of ordinance of 6 pounds at the distance of 5 or six miles. I was informed of it several times by the men J: Fields particularly before I paid any attention to it, thinking it was thunder most probably which they had mistaken. At length walking in the plains yesterday near the most extreme S. E bend of the River above the falls I heard this *noise* very distinctly, it was perfectly calm clear and not a cloud to be seen, I halted and listened attentively about two hour[s] during which time I heard two other discharges, and took the direction of the sound with my pocket compass which was as nearly West from me as I could estimate from the sound. I have no doubt but if I had leisure I could find from whence it issued. I have thought it probable that it might be caused by running water in some of the caverns of those immense mountains, on the principal of the blowing caverns; but in such case the sounds would be periodical and regular, which is not the case with this, being sometimes heard once only and at other times several discharges in quick succession. it is heard also at different times of the day and night. I am at a great loss to account for this Phenomenon. I well recollect hearing the Minitarees say that those Rocky mountains make a great noise, but they could not tell me the cause, neither could they inform me of any remarkable substance or situation in these mountains which would authorise a conjecture of a probable cause of this noise.

William Wordsworth (1770–1850)

William Wordsworth was born in Cockermouth in West Cumberland, on the outskirts of the English Lake District. After his mother's death, Wordsworth, then eight years old, was placed in Hawkshead school. There, he and his three brothers were boarded in a cottage under the care of Ann Tyson. Having limited supervision, Wordsworth was free to spend much time wandering the countryside, experiencing facets of nature that would later become an integral part of his poetry. William Taylor, his headmaster at Hawkshead, gave Wordsworth access to his personal library and encouraged him to start writing poetry. When Wordsworth was thirteen, his father died suddenly. Although he left his five children an inheritance in the form of a debt owed to him by Lord Lonsdale, that debt was not collected until many years later. Still, in 1787, Wordsworth found the means to attend Cambridge. He received his degree in 1791, though he had found little in the academic program that was challenging.

Wordsworth traveled to France in 1791–92, during the excitement and ferment of its revolutionary period. In France, he fathered a daughter out of wedlock by his mistress, Annette Vallon, but they were soon separated by the advent of the Napoleonic Wars, and they drifted irrevocably apart. Back in England, Wordsworth was reunited with his sis-

ter, Dorothy, from whom he had been separated ever since their mother's death. They soon became an inseparable pair of itinerant writers, living in a succession of rented or borrowed lodgings, as Wordsworth began to develop his latent poetic talents. In 1795, Wordsworth met Samuel Taylor Coleridge, a younger man who was already a well-established poet, radical journalist, and public speaker. The two began to collaborate, and in 1798, Lyrical Ballads, with a Few Other Poems *was published anonymously.*

In 1802, a brief interlude of peace enabled Wordsworth to travel once more to France, where he reached a financial settlement with Annette Vallon. Returning to his home in Grasmere, he married Mary Hutchinson, a friend since childhood. During these years, his communications with Coleridge became strained and sporadic. By 1810, the relationship was so damaged that it was almost twenty years until they were able to become close friends again. This was also a time when Wordsworth's national reputation as a poet was becoming firmly established. The culmination of this recognition came in 1843, when Wordsworth was appointed Poet Laureate of England. In 1850, at the age of eighty, William Wordsworth died. The Prelude, *his autobiographical poem, was posthumously published three months after his death. And even though the friend of his youth had died sixteen years earlier, Wordsworth had continued to refer to this great work as "the poem to Coleridge."*

Lines Written in Early Spring

I heard a thousand blended notes,
While in a grove I sate reclined,
In that sweet mood when pleasant thoughts
Bring sad thoughts to the mind.

To her fair works did Nature link   5
The human soul that through me ran;
And much it grieved my heart to think
What man has made of man.

Through primrose tufts, in that green bower,
The periwinkle trailed its wreaths;   10
And 'tis my faith that every flower
Enjoys the air it breathes.

The birds around me hopped and played,
Their thoughts I cannot measure:—
But the least motion which they made   15
It seemed a thrill of pleasure.

The budding twigs spread out their fan,
To catch the breezy air;
And I must think, do all I can,
That there was pleasure there.   20

If this belief from heaven be sent,
If such be Nature's holy plan,
Have I not reason to lament
What man has made of man?

Expostulation and Reply

"Why, William, on that old grey stone,
Thus for the length of half a day,
Why, William, sit you thus alone,
And dream your time away?

"Where are your books? — that light bequeathed   5
To Beings else forlorn and blind!
Up! up! and drink the spirit breathed
From dead men to their kind.

"You look round on your Mother Earth,
As if she for no purpose bore you;   10
As if you were her first-born birth,
And none had lived before you!"

One morning thus, by Esthwaite lake,
When life was sweet, I knew not why,
To me my good friend Matthew spake,   15
And thus I made reply:

"The eye — it cannot choose but see;
We cannot bid the ear be still;
Our bodies feel, where'er they be,
Against or with our will.   20

"Nor less I deem that there are Powers
Which of themselves our minds impress;
That we can feed this mind of ours
In a wise passiveness.

"Think you, 'mid all this mighty sum   25
Of things forever speaking,
That nothing of itself will come,
But we must still be seeking?

"—Then ask not wherefore, here, alone,
Conversing as I may,   30
I sit upon this old grey stone,
And dream my time away."

The Tables Turned

An Evening Scene on the Same Subject

Up! up! my Friend, and quit your books;
Or surely you'll grow double:
Up! up! my Friend, and clear your looks;
Why all this toil and trouble?

The sun, above the mountain's head,   5
A freshening lustre mellow
Through all the long green fields has spread,
His first sweet evening yellow.

Books! 'tis a dull and endless strife:
Come, hear the woodland linnet,   10
How sweet his music! on my life,
There's more of wisdom in it.

And hark! how blithe the throstle sings!
He, too, is no mean preacher:
Come forth into the light of things,   15
Let Nature be your teacher.

She has a world of ready wealth,
Our minds and hearts to bless—
Spontaneous wisdom breathed by health,
Truth breathed by cheerfulness.   20

One impulse from a vernal wood
May teach you more of man,
Of moral evil and of good,
Than all the sages can.

Sweet is the lore which Nature brings: 25
Our meddling intellect
Mis-shapes the beauteous forms of things:—
We murder to dissect.

Enough of Science and of Art;
Close up those barren leaves;   30
Come forth, and bring with you a heart
That watches and receives.

Lines

Composed a Few Miles Above Tintern Abbey, On Revisiting the Banks of the Wye During a Tour, July 13, 1798

Five years have past; five summers, with the length
Of five long winters! and again I hear
These waters, rolling from their mountain-springs
With a soft inland murmur.—Once again
Do I behold these steep and lofty cliffs,   5
That on a wild secluded scene impress
Thoughts of more deep seclusion; and connect
The landscape with the quiet of the sky.
The day is come when I again repose
Here, under this dark sycamore, and view   10
These plots of cottage-ground, these orchard-tufts,
Which at this season, with their unripe fruits,
Are clad in one green hue, and lose themselves
'Mid groves and copses. Once again I see
These hedgerows, hardly hedgerows, little lines   15
Of sportive wood run wild: these pastoral farms,
Green to the very door; and wreaths of smoke
Sent up, in silence, from among the trees!
With some uncertain notice, as might seem
Of vagrant dwellers in the houseless woods,   20
Or of some Hermit's cave, where by his fire
The Hermit sits alone.
                                        These beauteous forms,
Through a long absence, have not been to me
As is a landscape to blind man's eye:
But oft, in lonely rooms, and 'mid the din   25
Of towns and cities, I have owed to them
In hours of weariness, sensations sweet,
Felt in the blood, and felt along the heart;
And passing even into my purer mind,
With tranquil restoration:—feelings too   30
Of unremembered pleasure: such, perhaps,
As have no slight or trivial influence
On that best portion of a good man's life,
His little, nameless, unremembered, acts
Of kindness and of love. Nor less, I trust,   35
To them I may have owed another gift,
Of aspect more sublime; that blessed mood,
In which the burthen of the mystery,
In which the heavy and the weary weight
Of all this unintelligible world,   40

Is lightened:—that serene and blessed mood,
In which the affections gently lead us on,—
Until, the breath of this corporeal frame
And even the motion of our human blood
Almost suspended, we are laid asleep   45
In body, and become a living soul:
While with an eye made quiet by the power
Of harmony, and the deep power of joy,
We see into the life of things.
                                              If this
Be but a vain belief, yet, oh! how oft—   50
In darkness and amid the many shapes
Of joyless daylight; when the fretful stir
Unprofitable, and the fever of the world,
Have hung upon the beatings of my heart—
How oft, in spirit, have I turned to thee,   55
O sylvan Wye! thou wanderer through the woods,
How often has my spirit turned to thee!
      And now, with gleams of half-extinguished thought,
With many recognitions dim and faint,
And somewhat of a sad perplexity,   60
The picture of the mind revives again:
While here I stand, not only with the sense
Of present pleasure, but with pleasing thoughts
That in this moment there is life and food
For future years. And so I dare to hope,   65
Though changed, no doubt, from what I was when first
I came among these hills; when like a roe
I bounded o'er the mountains, by the sides
Of the deep rivers, and the lonely streams,
Wherever nature led: more like a man   70
Flying from something that he dreads, than one
Who sought the thing he loved. For nature then
(The coarser pleasures of my boyish days,
And their glad animal movements all gone by)
To me was all in all.—I cannot paint   75
What then I was. The sounding cataract
Haunted me like a passion: the tall rock,
The mountain, and the deep and gloomy wood,
Their colours and their forms, were then to me
An appetite; a feeling and a love,   80
That had no need of a remoter charm,
By thought supplied, nor any interest
Unborrowed from the eye.—That time is past,
And all its aching joys are now no more,
And all its dizzy raptures. Not for this   85

Faint I, nor mourn nor murmur; other gifts
Have followed; for such loss, I would believe,
Abundant recompense. For I have learned
To look on nature, not as in the hour
Of thoughtless youth; but hearing oftentimes   90
The still, sad music of humanity,
Nor harsh nor grating, though of ample power
To chasten and subdue. And I have felt
A presence that disturbs me with the joy
Of elevated thoughts; a sense sublime   95
Of something far more deeply interfused,
Whose dwelling is the light of setting suns,
And the round ocean and the living air,
And the blue sky, and in the mind of man;
A motion and a spirit, that impels   100
All thinking things, all objects of all thought,
And rolls through all things. Therefore am I still
A lover of the meadows and the woods,
And mountains; and of all that we behold
From this green earth; of all the mighty world   105
Of eye, and ear,—both what they half create,
And what perceive; well pleased to recognise
In nature and the language of the sense,
The anchor of my purest thoughts, the nurse,
The guide, the guardian of my heart, and soul   110
Of all my moral being.
                          Nor perchance,
If I were not thus taught, should I the more
Suffer my genial spirits to decay:
For thou art with me here upon the banks
Of this fair river; thou my dearest Friend,   115
My dear, dear Friend; and in thy voice I catch
The language of my former heart, and read
My former pleasures in the shooting lights
Of thy wild eyes. Oh! yet a little while
May I behold in thee what I was once,   120
My dear, dear Sister! and this prayer I make,
Knowing that Nature never did betray
The heart that loved her; 'tis her privilege,
Through all the years of this our life, to lead
From joy to joy: for she can so inform   125
The mind that is within us, so impress
With quietness and beauty, and so feed
With lofty thoughts, that neither evil tongues,
Rash judgments, nor the sneers of selfish men,
Nor greetings where no kindness is, nor all   130

The dreary intercourse of daily life,
Shall e'er prevail against us, or disturb
Our cheerful faith, that all which we behold
Is full of blessings. Therefore let the moon
Shine on thee in thy solitary walk;   135
And let the misty mountain winds be free
To blow against thee: and, in after years,
When these wild ecstasies shall be matured
Into a sober pleasure; when thy mind
Shall be a mansion for all lovely forms,   140
Thy memory be as a dwelling-place
For all sweet sounds and harmonies; oh! then,
If solitude, or fear, or pain, or grief,
Should be thy portion, with what healing thoughts
Of tender joy wilt thou remember me,   145
And these my exhortations! Nor, perchance—
If I should be where I no more can hear
Thy voice, nor catch from thy wild eyes those gleams
Of past existence—wilt thou then forget
That on the banks of this delightful stream   150
We stood together; and that I, so long
A worshipper of Nature, hither came
Unwearied in that service; rather say
With warmer love—oh! with far deeper zeal
Of holier love. Nor wilt thou then forget,   155
That after many wanderings, many years
Of absence, these steep woods and lofty cliffs,
And this green pastoral landscape, were to me
More dear, both for themselves and for thy sake!

Nutting

————It seems a day
(I speak of one from many singled out)
One of those heavenly days that cannot die;
When, in the eagerness of boyish hope,
I left our cottage threshold, sallying forth   5
With a huge wallet o'er my shoulder slung,
A nutting-crook in hand; and turned my steps
Toward some far-distant wood, a Figure quaint,
Tricked out in proud disguise of cast-off weeds[1]
Which for that service had been husbanded,   10

---

[1] Clothes.

By exhortation of my frugal Dame—
Motley accoutrement, of power to smile
At thorns, and brakes, and brambles,—and, in truth,
More ragged than need was! O'er pathless rocks,
Through beds of matted fern, and tangled thickets,   15
Forcing my way, I came to one dear nook
Unvisited, where not a broken bough
Drooped with its withered leaves, ungracious sign
Of devastation; but the hazels rose
Tall and erect, with tempting clusters hung,   20
A virgin scene!—A little while I stood,
Breathing with such suppression of the heart
As joy delights in; and, with wise restraint
Voluptuous, fearless of a rival, eyed
The banquet;—or beneath the trees I sate   25
Among the flowers, and with the flowers I played;
A temper known to those, who, after long
And weary expectation, have been blest
With sudden happiness beyond all hope.
Perhaps it was a bower beneath whose leaves   30
The violets of five seasons re-appear
And fade, unseen by any human eye;
Where fairy water-breaks do murmur on
Forever; and I saw the sparkling foam,
And—with my cheek on one of those green stones   35
That, fleeced with moss, under the shady trees,
Lay round me, scattered like a flock of sheep—
I heard the murmur and the murmuring sound,
In that sweet mood when pleasure loves to pay
Tribute to ease; and, of its joy secure,   40
The heart luxuriates with indifferent things,
Wasting its kindliness on stocks and stones,
And on the vacant air. Then up I rose,
And dragged to earth both branch and bough, with crash
And merciless ravage; and the shady nook   45
Of hazels, and the green and mossy bower,
Deformed and sullied, patiently gave up
Their quiet being; and, unless I now
Confound my present feelings with the past;
Ere from the mutilated bower I turned   50
Exulting, rich beyond the wealth of kings,
I felt a sense of pain when I beheld
The silent trees, and saw the intruding sky—
Then, dearest Maiden, move along these shades
In gentleness of heart; with gentle hand   55
Touch—for there is a spirit in the woods.

"I wandered lonely as a cloud"*

I wandered lonely as a cloud
That floats on high o'er vales and hills,
When all at once I saw a crowd,
A host, of golden daffodils;
Beside the lake, beneath the trees,   5
Fluttering and dancing in the breeze.

Continuous as the stars that shine
And twinkle on the milky way,
They stretched in never-ending line
Along the margin of a bay: 10
Ten thousand saw I at a glance,
Tossing their heads in sprightly dance.

The waves beside them danced; but they
Outdid the sparkling waves in glee:
A poet could not but be gay,   15
In such a jocund company:
I gazed—and gazed—but little thought
What wealth the show to me had brought:

For oft, when on my couch I lie,
In vacant or in pensive mood,   20
They flash upon that inward eye
Which is the bliss of solitude;
And then my heart with pleasure fills,
And dances with the daffodils.

* This poem grows out of a walk that William Wordsworth took with his sister, Dorothy Wordsworth. Her version of that experience is recorded in *The Grasmere Journal*, April 15, 1802.

"The world is too much with us"

The world is too much with us; late and soon,
Getting and spending, we lay waste our powers:
Little we see in Nature that is ours;
We have given our hearts away, a sordid boon!
The Sea that bares her bosom to the moon;   5
The winds that will be howling at all hours,
And are up-gathered now like sleeping flowers;
For this, for everything, we are out of tune;
It moves us not.—Great God! I'd rather be
A Pagan suckled in a creed outworn;   10
So might I, standing on this pleasant lea,

Have glimpses that would make me less forlorn;
Have sight of Proteus[1] rising from the sea;
Or hear old Triton[2] blow his wreathèd horn.

[1] In Greek mythology, a sea god who could change his shape at will.

[2] Another ancient Greek sea god, represented as having the torso of a man and the tail of a fish and often portrayed blowing a trumpet made from a conch shell.

From Description of the Scenery of the Lakes

From Section First, View of the Country as Formed by Nature*

It may now be proper to say a few words respecting climate, and "skiey influences,"[1] in which this region, as far as the character of its landscapes is affected by them, may, upon the whole, be considered fortunate. The country is, indeed, subject to much bad weather, and it has been ascertained that twice as much rain falls here as in many parts of the island; but the number of black drizzling days, that blot out the face of things, is by no means *proportionally* great. Nor is a continuance of thick, flagging, damp air, so common as in the West of England and Ireland. The rain here comes down heartily, and is frequently succeeded by clear, bright weather, when every brook is vocal, and every torrent sonorous; brooks and torrents, which are never muddy, even in the heaviest floods, except, after a drought, they happen to be defiled for a short time by waters that have swept along dusty roads, or have broken out into ploughed fields. Days of unsettled weather, with partial showers, are very frequent; but the showers, darkening, or brightening, as they fly from hill to hill, are not less grateful to the eye than finely interwoven passages of gay and sad music are touching to the ear. Vapours exhaling from the lakes and meadows after sunrise, in a hot season, or, in moist weather, brooding upon the heights, or descending towards the valleys with inaudible motion, give a visionary character to everything around them; and are in themselves so beautiful, as to dispose us to enter into the feelings of those simple nations (such as the Laplanders of this day) by whom they are taken for guardian deities of the mountains; or to sympathise with others who have fancied these delicate apparitions to be the spirits of their departed ancestors. Akin to these are fleecy clouds resting upon the hill-tops; they are not easily managed in picture, with their accompaniments of blue sky; but how glorious are they in nature! how pregnant with imagination for the poet! and the height of the Cumbrian mountains is sufficient to exhibit daily and hourly instances of those mysterious attachments. Such clouds, cleaving to their stations, or lifting up suddenly their glittering heads from behind rocky barriers, or hurrying out of sight with speed of the sharpest edge—will often tempt an inhabitant to congratulate himself on belonging to a country of mists and clouds and storms, and make him think of the blank sky of Egypt, and of the cerulean vacancy of Italy, as an unanimated and

* The selection provided begins several pages into the first section.—Editors' note.

[1] William Shakespeare, *Measure for Measure*, 3.1.8–9.

even a sad spectacle. The atmosphere, however, as in every country subject to much rain, is frequently unfavourable to landscape, especially when keen winds succeed the rain which are apt to produce coldness, spottiness, and an unmeaning or repulsive detail in the distance;—a sunless frost, under a canopy of leaden and shapeless clouds, is, as far as it allows things to be seen, equally disagreeable.

It has been said that in human life there are moments worth ages. In a more subdued tone of sympathy may we affirm, that in the climate of England there are, for the lover of nature, days which are worth whole months,—I might say—even years. One of these favoured days sometimes occurs in spring-time, when that soft air is breathing over the blossoms and new-born verdure, which inspired Buchanan with his beautiful Ode to the first of May;[2] the air, which, in the luxuriance of his fancy, he likens to that of the golden age,—to that which gives motion to the funereal cypresses on the banks of Lethe;[3]—to the air which is to salute beatified spirits when expiatory fires shall have consumed the earth with all her habitations. But it is in autumn that days of such affecting influence most frequently intervene;—the atmosphere seems refined, and the sky rendered more crystalline, as the vivifying heat of the year abates; the lights and shadows are more delicate; the coloring is richer and more finely harmonized; and, in this season of stillness, the ear being unoccupied, or only gently excited, the sense of vision becomes more susceptible of its appropriate enjoyments. A resident in a country like this which we are treating of, will agree with me, that the presence of a lake is indispensable to exhibit in perfection the beauty of one of these days; and he must have experienced, while looking on the unruffled waters, that the imagination, by their aid, is carried into recesses of feeling otherwise impenetrable. The reason of this is, that the heavens are not only brought down into the bosom of the earth, but that the earth is mainly looked at, and thought of, through the medium of a purer element. The happiest time is when the equinoxial gales are departed; but their fury may probably be called to mind by the sight of a few shattered boughs, whose leaves do not differ in colour from the faded foliage of the stately oaks from which these relics of the storm depend: all else speaks of tranquillity;—not a breath of air, no restlessness of insects, and not a moving object perceptible—except the clouds gliding in the depths of the lake, or the traveller passing along, an inverted image, whose motion seems governed by the quiet of a time, to which its archetype, the living person, is, perhaps, insensible:—or it may happen, that the figure of one of the larger birds, a raven or a heron, is crossing silently among the reflected clouds, while the voice of the real bird, from the element aloft, gently awakens in the spectator the recollection of appetites and instincts, pursuits and occupations, that deform and agitate the world,—yet have no power to prevent nature from putting on an aspect capable of satisfying the most intense cravings for the tranquil, the lovely, and the perfect, to which man, the noblest of her creatures, is subject.

· · ·

[2] *Ode . . . May:* alludes to a Latin poem *Calendae Maiae* ("The First of May") by George Buchanan (1506–1582), Scottish humanist and historian.

[3] In Greek mythology, the river of forgetfulness, one of five rivers in Hades.

🐚 *Dorothy Wordsworth* (*1771–1855*)

Born in Cockermouth, in the English Lake District, Dorothy Wordsworth was the only daughter in a family of five children, and from an early age she enjoyed a close, affectionate relationship with her brother William. But in 1778 their mother died, and six-year-old Dorothy was sent away to live with various relatives. She attended school until age fifteen, and she received some further tutoring in French, mathematics, and geography from her uncle. She was, however, consistently unhappy with her relatives, who treated her as little more than a servant, and in 1795 she leaped at the opportunity to set up a household with her brother William, who invited her to join him in a rented house at Racedown, in Somerset. William Wordsworth had already dedicated himself to the profession of poetry, and his sister was eager to assist him in keeping house, writing letters, and transcribing manuscripts. When the pair moved to Alfoxden House, mainly in order to be close to their new friend, Samuel Taylor Coleridge, Dorothy Wordsworth began keeping a journal of the daily events in their lives. The Alfoxden Journal was composed beginning in 1797, with only the period January to April 1798 surviving; thus it describes three eventful months in which her brother and Coleridge were collaborating on the production of Lyrical Ballads. *Dorothy Wordsworth was just then discovering her own voice as a writer, and her journal entries reveal her fascination with the precise appearances of the natural world. As she records the daily events of her household, the comings and goings of their visitors, and the progress of the seasons, she frequently pauses to examine unique details in the surrounding landscape: a single strawberry blossom, a mass of straggling clouds, and the spinning motion of insects in the sun.*

Dorothy Wordsworth continues to discover her voice in The Grasmere Journal, *actually a series of journals composed from May 1800 to January 1803. These journals, written amid the sublime scenery of the English Lake District, reveal even more of her personality, and of her deep intellectual and emotional response to the natural world, while they continue to record a rich variety of daily events. Not intended for publication, these notebooks have a relaxed informality and an emotional frankness that is unusual in the published writing of this period. Dorothy Wordsworth writes very freely of her affection for William, her anxiety over his impending marriage to Mary Hutchinson, and of their visit to William's former mistress, Annette Vallon, in Calais, France. Unpublished until 1897, the journals were unknown to any of Dorothy Wordsworth's contemporaries except her brother William and, perhaps, a few other close friends and relatives. The journals articulate new ways of perceiving and knowing the self in relation to the natural world and are now regarded as foundational texts of Romantic nature writing.*

From The Alfoxden Journal (1798)

February 3rd.   A mild morning, the windows open at breakfast, the redbreasts singing in the garden. Walked with Coleridge over the hills. The sea at first obscured by vapour; that vapour afterwards slid in one mighty mass along the seashore; the islands and one point of land clear beyond it. The distant country (which was purple in the clear dull air), overhung by straggling clouds that sailed over it, appeared like the darker clouds, which are often seen at a great distance apparently motionless, while the nearer ones pass quickly over them, driven by the lower winds. I never saw such a union of earth, sky, and sea. The clouds beneath our feet spread themselves to the water, and the clouds of the sky almost joined them. Gathered sticks in the wood; a perfect stillness. The redbreasts sang upon the leafless boughs. Of a great number of sheep in the field, only one standing. Returned to dinner at five o'clock. The moonlight still and warm as a summer's night at nine o'clock.

February 4th.   Walked a great part of the way to Stowey[1] with Coleridge. The morning warm and sunny. The young lasses seen on the hill-tops, in the villages and roads, in their summer holiday clothes—pink petticoats and blue. Mothers with their children in arms, and the little ones that could just walk, tottering by their side. Midges or small flies spinning in the sunshine; the songs of the lark and redbreast; daisies upon the turf; the hazels in blossom; honeysuckles budding. I saw one solitary strawberry flower under a hedge. The furze gay with blossom. The moss rubbed from the pailings by the sheep, that leave locks of wool, and the red marks with which they are spotted, upon the wood.

---

[1] Coleridge's cottage was in the village of Nether Stowey, three miles from Alfoxden.

From The Grasmere Journal (1802)

[*January*] *31st, Sunday.*   Wm. had slept very ill—he was tired and had a bad headache. We walked round the two lakes. Grasmere was very soft, and Rydale was extremely beautiful from the western side. Nab Scar was just topped by a cloud which, cutting it off as high as it could be cut off, made the mountain look uncommonly lofty. We sate down a long time in different places. I always love to walk that way, because it is the way I first came to Rydale and Grasmere, and because our dear Coleridge did also. When I came with Wm., $6\frac{1}{2}$ years ago, it was just at sunset. There was a rich yellow light on the waters, and the Islands were reflected there. Today it was grave and soft, but not perfectly calm. William says it was much such a day as when Coleridge came with him. The sun shone out before we reached Grasmere. We sate by the roadside at the foot of the Lake, close to Mary's dear name, which she had cut herself upon the stone. Wm. cut at it with his knife to make it plainer. We amused ourselves for a long time in watching the breezes, some as if they came from the bottom of the lake, spread in a circle, brushing along the surface of the water, and growing more delicate, as it were thinner, and of a *paler* colour till they died away. Others spread out like a peacock's tail, and some went right forward this way and that in all directions. The lake was still where these breezes were not, but they made it all alive. I found a strawberry blossom in a rock. The little slender flower had more courage than the green leaves, for *they* were but half expanded and half grown, but the blossom was spread full out. I uprooted it rashly, and I felt as if I had been committing an outrage, so I planted it again. It will have but a stormy life of it, but let it live if it can. . . .

.   .   .

[*April*] *15th, Thursday.*   It was a threatening, misty morning, but mild. We set off after dinner from Eusemere. Mrs. Clarkson went a short way with us, but turned back. The wind was furious, and we thought we must have returned. We first rested in the large boat-house, then under a furze bush opposite Mr. Clarkson's. Saw the plough going in the field. The wind seized our breath. The Lake was rough. There was a boat by itself floating in the middle of the bay below Water Millock. We rested again in the Water Millock Lane. The hawthorns are black and green, the birches here and there greenish, but there is yet more of purple to be seen on the twigs. We got over into a field to avoid some cows — people working. A few primroses by the roadside — woodsorrel flower, the anemone, scentless violets, strawberries, and the starry, yellow flower which Mrs. C. calls pile wort. When we were in the woods beyond Gowbarrow Park we saw a few daffodils[1] close to the waterside. We fancied that the lake had floated the seeds ashore, and that the little colony had so sprung up. But as we went along there were more and yet more; and at last, under the boughs of the trees, we saw that there was a long belt of them along the shore, about the breadth of a country turnpike road. I never saw daffodils so beautiful. They grew among the mossy stones about and about them; some rested their heads upon these stones as on a pillow for weariness; and the rest tossed and reeled and danced, and seemed as if they verily laughed with the wind, that blew upon them over the lake; they looked so gay, ever glancing, ever changing. This wind blew directly over the lake to them. There was here and there a little knot, and a few stragglers a few yards higher up; but they were so few as not to disturb the simplicity, unity, and life of that one busy highway. We rested again and again. The bays were stormy, and we heard the waves at different distances, and in the middle of the water, like the sea. Rain came on — we were wet when we reached Luff's, but we called in. Luckily all was cheerless and gloomy, so we faced the storm — we *must* have been wet if we had waited — put on dry clothes at Dobson's. I was very kindly treated by a young woman, the landlady looked sour, but it is her way. She gave us a goodish supper, excellent ham and potatoes. We paid 7/- when we came away. William was sitting by a bright fire when I came downstairs. He soon made his way to the library, piled up in a corner of the window. He brought out a volume of Enfield's *Speaker*, another miscellany, and an odd volume of Congreve's plays. We had a glass of warm rum and water. We enjoyed ourselves, and wished for Mary. It rained and blew, when we went to bed. N.B. Deer in Gowbarrow Park like skeletons.

.   .   .

[*April*] *29th, Thursday.*   A beautiful morning — the sun shone and all was pleasant. We sent off our parcel to Coleridge by the waggon. Mr. Simpson heard the Cuckow today. Before we went out, after I had written down *The Tinker*, which William finished this morning, Luff called — he was very lame, limped

---

[1] William Wordsworth drew upon this passage in his poem, "I wandered lonely as a cloud," composed two years after Dorothy recorded their close encounter with the daffodils.

into the kitchen. He came on a little pony. We then went to John's Grove, sate a while at first. Afterwards William lay, and I lay, in the trench under the fence—he with his eyes shut, and listening to the waterfalls and the birds. There was no one waterfall above another—it was a sound of waters in the air—the voice of the air. William heard me breathing and rustling now and then, but we both lay still, and unseen by one another; he thought that it would be as sweet thus to lie so in the grave, to hear the *peaceful* sounds of the earth, and just to know that our dear friends were near. The lake was still; there was a boat out. Silver How reflected with delicate purple and yellowish hues, as I have seen spar; lambs on the island, and running races together by the half-dozen, in the round field near us. The copses greenish, hawthorns green. Came home to dinner, then went to Mr. Simpson—we rested a long time under a wall, sheep and lambs were in the field—cottages smoking. As I lay down on the grass, I observed the glittering silver line on the ridge of the backs of the sheep, owing to their situation respecting the sun, which made them look beautiful, but with something of strangeness, like animals of another kind, as if belonging to a more splendid world. Met old Mrs. S. at the door—Mrs. S. poorly. I got mullins and pansies. I was sick and ill and obliged to come home soon. We went to bed immediately—I slept upstairs. The air coldish, where it was felt—somewhat frosty.

.   .   .

[*June 1st,*] *Tuesday.*   A very sweet day, but a sad want of rain. We went into the orchard before dinner, after I had written to M. H. Then on to Mr. Olliff's intakes. We found some torn birds' nests. The columbine was growing upon the rocks; here and there a solitary plant, sheltered and shaded by the tufts and bowers of trees. It is a graceful slender creature, a female seeking retirement, and growing freest and most graceful where it is most alone. I observed that the more shaded plants were always the tallest. A short note and gooseberries from Coleridge.

.   .   .

June 16th, Wednesday.   We walked towards Rydale for letters—met Frank Batey with the expected one from Mary. We went up into Rydale woods and read it there. We sate near an old wall, which fenced a hazel grove, which Wm. said was exactly like the filbert grove at Middleham. It is a beautiful spot, a sloping or rather steep piece of ground, with hazels growing "tall and erect"[2] in clumps at distances, almost seeming regular, as if they had been planted. We returned to dinner. I wrote to Mary[3] after dinner, while William sate in the orchard. Old Mr. Simpson drank tea with us. When Mr. S. was gone I read my letter to William, speaking to Mary about having a cat. I spoke of the little birds

---

[2] Alludes to William Wordsworth, "Nutting," line 20.

[3] Mary Hutchinson, William Wordsworth's fiancée. Dorothy had mixed feelings about the impending marriage: She was fond of Mary, but she feared the disruption of her own close relationship with William.

keeping us company, and William told me that that very morning a bird had perched upon his leg. He had been lying very still, and had watched this little creature, it had come under the bench where he was sitting, and then flew up to his leg; he thoughtlessly stirred himself to look further at it, and it flew on to the apple tree above him. It was a little young creature, that had just left its nest, equally unacquainted with man, and unaccustomed to struggle against storms and winds. While it was upon the apple tree the wind blew about the stiff boughs, and the bird seemed bemazed, and not strong enough to strive with it. The swallows come to the sitting-room window as if wishing to build, but I am afraid they will not have courage for it, but I believe they will build in my room window. They twitter, and make a bustle and a little cheerful song, hanging against the panes of glass, with their soft white bellies close to the glass, and their forked fishlike tails. They swim round and round, and again they come. . . .

.   .   .

June 25th, Friday.   Wm. had not fallen asleep till after 3 o'clock, but he slept tolerably. Miss Simpson came to colour the rooms. I began with whitewashing the ceiling. I worked with them (William was very busy) till dinner time, but after dinner I went to bed and fell asleep. When I rose I went just before tea into the garden. I looked up at my swallow's nest, and it was gone. It had fallen down. Poor little creatures, they could not themselves be more distressed than I was. I went upstairs to look at the ruins. They lay in a large heap upon the window ledge; these swallows had been ten days employed in building this nest, and it seemed to be almost finished. I had watched them early in the morning, in the day many and many a time, and in the evenings when it was almost dark. I had seen them sitting together side by side in their unfinished nest, both morning and night. When they first came about the window they used to hang against the panes, with their white bellies and their forked tails, looking like fish; but then they fluttered and sang their own little twittering song. As soon as the nest was broad enough, a sort of ledge for them, they sate both mornings and evenings, but they did not pass the night there. I watched them one morning, when William was at Eusemere, for more than an hour. Every now and then there was a feeling motion in their wings, a sort of tremulousness, and they sang a low song to one another.

.   .   .

    . . . We arrived at Calais[4] at 4 o'clock on Sunday morning, the 1st of August. We stayed in the vessel till $\frac{1}{2}$-past 7, then William went for letters, at about $\frac{1}{2}$-past 8 or 9 we found out Annette and C. chez Madame Avril dans la Rue de la Tête d'or. We lodged opposite two ladies, in tolerably decent-sized rooms, but badly

---

[4] William and Dorothy have traveled to Calais, France, to reach some kind of financial settlement with Annette Vallon, the mother of William's natural daughter, Caroline. Dorothy is evidently delighted to meet her nine-year-old niece for the first time.

furnished and with large store of bad smells and dirt in the yard, and all about. The weather was very hot. We walked by the seashore almost every evening with Annette and Caroline, or Wm. and I alone. I had a bad cold, and could not bathe at first, but William did. It was a pretty sight to see, as we walked upon the sands when the tide was low, perhaps a hundred people bathing about a quarter of a mile distant from us, and we had delightful walks after the heat of the day was passed away—seeing far off in the west the coast of England like a cloud crested with Dover Castle, which was but like the summit of the cloud—the evening star and the glory of the sky. The reflections in the water were more beautiful than the sky itself, purple waves brighter than precious stones, forever melting away upon the sands. The fort, a wooden building, at the entrance of the harbour at Calais, when the evening twilight was coming on, and we could not see anything of the building but its shape, which was far more distinct than in perfect daylight, seemed to be reared upon pillars of ebony, between which pillars the sea was seen in the most beautiful colours that can be conceived. Nothing in romance was ever half so beautiful. Now came in view, as the evening star sank down, and the colours of the west faded away, the two lights of England, lighted up by Englishmen in our country, to warn vessels off rocks or sands. These we used to see from the pier, when we could see no other distant objects but the clouds, the sky, and the sea itself: All was dark behind. The town of Calais seemed deserted of the light of heaven, but there was always light and life and joy upon the sea. One night, though, I shall never forget—the day had been very hot, and William and I walked alone together upon the pier. The sea was gloomy, for there was a blackness over all the sky, except when it was overspread with lightning, which often revealed to us a distant vessel. Near us the waves roared and broke against the pier, and they were interfused with greenish fiery light. The more distant sea always black and gloomy. It was also beautiful, on the calm hot night, to see the little boats row out of harbour with wings of fire, and the sailboats with the fiery track which they cut as they went along, and which closed up after them with a hundred thousand sparkles, balls, shootings and streams of glow-worm light. Caroline was delighted. . . .

Samuel Taylor Coleridge (1772–1834)

The youngest of ten children, Samuel Taylor Coleridge was born in the village of Ottery St. Mary in Devonshire. His father died in 1781, leaving the nine-year-old Samuel to fend for himself. He was sent to London and enrolled as a charity boy at Christ's Hospital, a preparatory school of some intellectual repute, but a cold and inhospitable place for the young and impressionable orphan. Coleridge's extraordinary intellectual talents were soon noticed by his teachers, who promoted him to the elite class of "Grecians" destined for the university. Coleridge's mathematics teacher was William Wales, a professional astronomer on Captain James Cook's second voyage, who told his students fascinating tales of his exploits in the Antarctic Ocean, where he encountered icebergs, albatrosses, and strange luminous phenomena. These tales sparked Coleridge's interest in the history

*of British maritime exploration, leading him to read voraciously in old travel books, and
eventually bearing fruit in his haunting, visionary poem, "The Rime of the Ancient
Mariner."*

*Coleridge attended Cambridge, where he became an academic prodigy, but he left
without taking a degree. Together with the poet Robert Southey, Coleridge devised a
utopian (and ultimately impractical) scheme called Pantisocracy, which aspired to create
an ideal agrarian community on the banks of the Susquehanna River in Pennsylvania.
Since only married couples were expected to embark on the Pantisocratic adventure,
Coleridge soon found himself engaged to Sara Fricker, the sister of Southey's fiancée.
Married in 1795, the couple moved into a cottage at Nether Stowey, a rural village fifty
miles southwest of Bristol in Somerset, where they shared the labor of growing vegetables
and raising their infant son, David Hartley. Coleridge's residence at Nether Stowey was
one of his happiest and most productive periods, as he began a collaboration with William
Wordsworth. In July 1797, Wordsworth and his sister Dorothy moved into Alfoxden
House, just three miles away from Coleridge's cottage. Coleridge spent much of his time
in their company, often walking out in stormy weather to discuss their literary projects.
Among these was a collaborative volume of poems,* Lyrical Ballads, *which appeared in
September 1798.*

Lyrical Ballads *marks a bold new departure in English verse, heralding the advent
of Romanticism as a literary movement. Some of its innovative features are the revival
of ballad stanza, reliance upon the language of everyday life, and extensive use of natural imagery drawn from direct personal observation. In their composition of* Lyrical
Ballads, *Wordsworth and Coleridge shared a common perception of the natural world as
a dynamic ecosystem and a passionate commitment to the preservation of wild creatures
and scenic areas. In "The Rime of the Ancient Mariner," Coleridge conveys a sense of the
sheer mystery and wonder of the natural world, and he advocates an unconditional love
for "all creatures great and small." His poem "The Eolian Harp" evokes the harmony
and interconnectedness of all living things, while "This Lime-Tree Bower My Prison"
reminds us that natural beauty can be found anywhere, even in the most humble of surroundings. Coleridge's poetry has provided inspirational models for many subsequent nature writers, particularly those of the American Transcendentalist tradition, from Ralph
Waldo Emerson through John Muir.*

The Eolian Harp*

Composed at Clevedon, Somersetshire

My pensive Sara! thy soft cheek reclined
Thus on mine arm, most soothing sweet it is
To sit beside our Cot, our Cot o'ergrown
With white-flowered Jasmine, and the broad-leaved Myrtle,

---

* Placed in a window, an aeolian harp makes soft, eerie music when the wind blows across its strings. A recurrent
image in Romantic poetry, the wind harp serves as an emblem for poetic inspiration by the forces of nature. This
poem is addressed to Sara Fricker, whom Coleridge married on October 4, 1795; for the next few months, they
lived in a cottage at Clevedon, overlooking the Bristol Channel.

(Meet emblems they of Innocence and Love!)   5
And watch the clouds, that late were rich with light,
Slow saddening round, and mark the star of eve
Serenely brilliant (such should Wisdom be)
Shine opposite! How exquisite the scents
Snatched from yon bean-field! and the world *so* hushed!   10
The stilly murmur of the distant Sea
Tells us of silence.
                 And that simplest Lute,
Placed lengthways in the clasping casement, hark!
How by the desultory breeze caressed,
Like some coy maid half yielding to her lover,   15
It pours such sweet upbraiding, as must needs
Tempt to repeat the wrongs! And now, its strings
Boldlier swept, the long sequacious notes
Over delicious surges sink and rise,
Such a soft floating witchery of sound   20
As twilight Elfins make, when they at eve
Voyage on gentle gales from Fairy-Land,
Where Melodies round honey-dropping flowers,
Footless and wild, like birds of Paradise,[1]
Nor pause, nor perch, hovering on untamed wing!   25
O! the one Life within us and abroad,
Which meets all motion and becomes its soul,
A light in sound, a sound-like power in light,
Rhythm in all thought, and joyance every where —
Methinks, it should have been impossible   30
Not to love all things in a world so filled;
Where the breeze warbles, and the mute still air
Is Music slumbering on her instrument.

And thus, my Love! as on the midway slope
Of yonder hill I stretch my limbs at noon,   35
Whilst through my half-closed eyelids I behold
The sunbeams dance, like diamonds, on the main,
And tranquil muse upon tranquillity;
Full many a thought uncalled and undetained,
And many idle flitting phantasies,   40
Traverse my indolent and passive brain,
As wild and various as the random gales
That swell and flutter on this subject Lute!
    And what if all of animated nature
Be but organic Harps diversely framed,   45

---

[1] Brightly colored birds native to New Guinea. Early specimens, sent to Europe without feet, led naturalists to speculate that the bird spent its entire life hovering in the air.

That tremble into thought, as o'er them sweeps
Plastic and vast, one intellectual breeze,
At once the Soul of each, and God of all?
    But thy more serious eye a mild reproof
Darts, O belovéd Woman! nor such thoughts   50
Dim and unhallowed dost thou not reject,
And biddest me walk humbly with my God.
Meek Daughter in the family of Christ!
Well hast thou said and holily dispraised
These shapings of the unregenerate mind;   55
Bubbles that glitter as they rise and break
On vain Philosophy's aye-babbling spring.
For never guiltless may I speak of him,
The Incomprehensible! save when with awe
I praise him, and with Faith that inly *feels*;   60
Who with his saving mercies healéd me,
A sinful and most miserable man,
Wildered and dark, and gave me to possess
Peace, and this Cot, and thee, heart-honoured Maid!

This Lime-Tree Bower My Prison

[Addressed to Charles Lamb, of the India House, London]

In the June of 1797 some long-expected friends paid a visit to the author's cottage; and on the morning of their arrival, he met with an accident, which disabled him from walking during the whole time of their stay. One evening, when they had left him for a few hours, he composed the following lines in the garden-bower.[2]

Well, they are gone, and here must I remain,
This lime-tree bower my prison! I have lost
Beauties and feelings, such as would have been
Most sweet to my remembrance even when age
Had dimmed mine eyes to blindness! They, meanwhile,   5
Friends, whom I never more may meet again,
On springy heath, along the hilltop edge,
Wander in gladness, and wind down, perchance,
To that still roaring dell, of which I told;
The roaring dell, o'erwooded, narrow, deep,   10
And only speckled by the midday sun;
Where its slim trunk the ash from rock to rock

---

[2] In a letter of July 1797, Coleridge explains that the visiting friends were William and Dorothy Wordsworth and Charles Lamb. He is unable to accompany them on the walk because "dear Sara [i.e., his wife] accidentally emptied a skillet of boiling milk on my foot."

Flings arching like a bridge; — that branchless ash,
Unsunned and damp, whose few poor yellow leaves
Ne'er tremble in the gale, yet tremble still,   15
Fanned by the waterfall! and there my friends
Behold the dark green file of long lank weeds,
That all at once (a most fantastic sight!)
Still nod and drip beneath the dripping edge
Of the blue clay-stone.
                          Now, my friends emerge   20
Beneath the wide wide Heaven — and view again
The many-steepled tract magnificent
Of hilly fields and meadows, and the sea,
With some fair bark, perhaps, whose sails light up
The slip of smooth clear blue betwixt two Isles   25
Of purple shadow! Yes! they wander on
In gladness all; but thou, methinks, most glad,
My gentle-hearted Charles! for thou hast pined
And hungered after Nature, many a year,
In the great City pent, winning thy way   30
With sad yet patient soul, through evil and pain
And strange calamity! Ah! slowly sink
Behind the western ridge, thou glorious Sun!
Shine in the slant beams of the sinking orb,
Ye purple heath flowers! richlier burn, ye clouds!   35
Live in the yellow light, ye distant groves!
And kindle, thou blue Ocean! So my friend
Struck with deep joy may stand, as I have stood,
Silent with swimming sense; yea, gazing round
On the wide landscape, gaze till all doth seem   40
Less gross than bodily; and of such hues
As veil the Almighty Spirit, when yet he makes
Spirits perceive his presence.

                          A delight
Comes sudden on my heart, and I am glad
As I myself were there! Nor in this bower,   45
This little lime-tree bower, have I not marked
Much that has soothed me. Pale beneath the blaze
Hung the transparent foliage; and I watched
Some broad and sunny leaf, and loved to see
The shadow of the leaf and stem above   50
Dappling its sunshine! And that walnut tree
Was richly tinged, and a deep radiance lay
Full on the ancient ivy, which usurps
Those fronting elms, and now, with blackest mass
Makes their dark branches gleam a lighter hue   55

Through the late twilight: and though now the bat
Wheels silent by, and not a swallow twitters,
Yet still the solitary humble-bee
Sings in the bean-flower! Henceforth I shall know
That Nature ne'er deserts the wise and pure; 60
No plot so narrow, be but Nature there,
No waste so vacant, but may well employ
Each faculty of sense, and keep the heart
Awake to Love and Beauty! and sometimes
'Tis well to be bereft of promised good, 65
That we may lift the soul, and contemplate
With lively joy the joys we cannot share.
My gentle-hearted Charles! when the last rook
Beat its straight path along the dusky air
Homewards, I blest it! deeming its black wing 70
(Now a dim speck, now vanishing in light)
Had crossed the mighty Orb's dilated glory,
While thou stood'st gazing; or, when all was still,
Flew creeking[3] o'er thy head, and had a charm
For thee, my gentle-hearted Charles, to whom 75
No sound is dissonant which tells of Life.

[3] Some months after I had written this line, it gave me great pleasure to find that [William] Bartram had observed the same circumstance of the Savannah Crane. "When these Birds move their wings in flight, their strokes are slow, moderate, and regular; and even when at a considerable distance or high above us, we plainly hear the quill-feathers: their shafts and webs upon one another creek as the joints or working of a vessel in a tempestuous sea."

The Rime of the Ancient Mariner

in seven parts

Argument

How a Ship having passed the Line was driven by storms to the cold Country towards the South Pole; and how from thence she made her course to the tropical Latitude of the Great Pacific Ocean; and of the strange things that befell; and in what manner the Ancyent Marinere came back to his own Country.

Part 1

An ancient
Mariner meeteth
three Gallants
bidden to a
wedding-feast,
and detaineth one.

It is an ancient Mariner,
And he stoppeth one of three.
"By thy long grey beard and glittering eye,
Now wherefore stopp'st thou me?

The Bridegroom's doors are opened wide,   5
And I am next of kin;
The guests are met, the feast is set:
May'st hear the merry din."

He holds him with his skinny hand,
"There was a ship," quoth he.   10
"Hold off! unhand me, grey-beard loon!"
Eftsoons[1] his hand dropt he.

*The Wedding
Guest is
spellbound by
the eye of the old
seafaring man,
and constrained
to hear his tale.*

He holds him with his glittering eye—
The Wedding Guest stood still,
And listens like a three years' child: 15
The Mariner hath his will.

The Wedding Guest sat on a stone:
He cannot choose but hear;
And thus spake on that ancient man,
The bright-eyed Mariner.   20

*The Mariner
tells how the ship
sailed southward
with a good wind
and fair weather,
till it reached the
line.*

"The ship was cheered, the harbour cleared,
Merrily did we drop
Below the kirk,[2] below the hill,
Below the lighthouse top.

The Sun came up upon the left,   25
Out of the sea came he!
And he shone bright, and on the right
Went down into the sea.

Higher and higher every day,
Till over the mast at noon—"   30
The Wedding Guest here beat his breast,
For he heard the loud bassoon.

*The Wedding
Guest heareth
the bridal music;
but the Mariner
continueth his
tale.*

The bride hath paced into the hall,
Red as a rose is she;
Nodding their heads before her goes   35
The merry minstrelsy.

The Wedding Guest he beat his breast,
Yet he cannot choose but hear;
And thus spake on that ancient man,
The bright-eyed Mariner.   40

*The ship driven
by a storm
toward the South
Pole.*

"And now the STORM-BLAST came, and he
Was tyrannous and strong:
He struck with his o'ertaking wings,
And chased us south along.

[1] Immediately.
[2] Church.

With sloping masts and dipping prow,   45
As who pursued with yell and blow
Still treads the shadow of his foe,
And forward bends his head,
The ship drove fast, loud roared the blast,
And southward aye we fled.   50

And now there came both mist and snow,
And it grew wondrous cold:
And ice, mast-high, came floating by,
As green as emerald.

The land of ice, and of fearful sounds where no living thing was to be seen.

And through the drifts the snowy clifts   55
Did send a dismal sheen:
Nor shapes of men nor beasts we ken—
The ice was all between.

The ice was here, the ice was there,
The ice was all around: 60
It cracked and growled, and roared and howled,
Like noises in a swound!³

Till a great seabird, called the Albatross, came through the snow-fog, and was received with great joy and hospitality.

At length did cross an Albatross,
Thorough the fog it came;
As if it had been a Christian soul,   65
We hailed it in God's name.

It ate the food it ne'er had eat,
And round and round it flew.
The ice did split with a thunder-fit;
The helmsman steered us through!   70

And lo! the Albatross proveth a bird of good omen, and followeth the ship as it returned northward through fog and floating ice.

And a good south wind sprung up behind;
The Albatross did follow,
And every day, for food or play,
Came to the mariner's hollo!

In mist or cloud, on mast or shroud,   75
It perched for vespers nine;
Whiles all the night, through fog-smoke white,
Glimmered the white Moon-shine."

The ancient Mariner inhospitably killeth the pious bird of good omen.

"God save thee, ancient Mariner!
From the fiends, that plague thee thus!—   80
Why look'st thou so?"—With my cross-bow
I shot the ALBATROSS.

³ Swoon, fainting spell.

Part 2

The Sun now rose upon the right:
Out of the sea came he,
Still hid in mist, and on the left   85
Went down into the sea.

And the good south wind still blew behind,
But no sweet bird did follow,
Nor any day for food or play
Came to the mariners' hollo!   90

His shipmates
cry out against
the ancient
Mariner, for
killing the bird of
good luck.

And I had done a hellish thing,
And it would work 'em woe:
For all averred, I had killed the bird
That made the breeze to blow.
Ah wretch! said they, the bird to slay,   95
That made the breeze to blow!

But when the fog
cleared off, they
justify the same,
and thus make
themselves
accomplices in
the crime.

Nor dim nor red, like God's own head,
The glorious Sun uprist:
Then all averred, I had killed the bird
That brought the fog and mist.   100
'Twas right, said they, such birds to slay,
That bring the fog and mist.

The fair breeze
continues; the
ship enters the
Pacific Ocean,
and sails north-
ward, even till it
reaches the Line.

The fair breeze blew, the white foam flew,
The furrow followed free;
We were the first that ever burst   105
Into that silent sea.[4]

The ship hath
been suddenly
becalmed.

Down dropt the breeze, the sails dropt down,
'Twas sad as sad could be;
And we did speak only to break
The silence of the sea!   110

All in a hot and copper sky,
The bloody Sun, at noon,
Right up above the mast did stand,
No bigger than the Moon.

Day after day, day after day,   115
We stuck, nor breath nor motion;

---

[4] The Pacific Ocean (so named by early explorers for its peaceful, tranquil aspect). Ferdinand Magellan was the first European explorer to reach the Pacific Ocean, in 1520. By implication, that early period of European exploration is the poem's historical setting.

As idle as a painted ship
Upon a painted ocean.

And the
Albatross begins
to be avenged.
Water, water, everywhere,
And all the boards did shrink;   120
Water, water, everywhere,
Nor any drop to drink.

The very deep did rot: O Christ!
That ever this should be!
Yea, slimy things did crawl with legs   125
Upon the slimy sea.

About, about, in reel and rout
The death-fires danced at night;
The water, like a witch's oils,
Burnt green, and blue and white.   130

A Spirit had
followed them;
one of the
invisible
inhabitants of
And some in dreams assuréd were
Of the Spirit that plagued us so;
Nine fathom deep he had followed us
From the land of mist and snow.

this planet, neither departed souls nor angels; concerning whom the learned Jew, Josephus,
and the Platonic Constantinopolitan, Michael Psellus, may be consulted. They are very
numerous, and there is no climate or element without one or more.

And every tongue, through utter drought,   135
Was withered at the root;
We could not speak, no more than if
We had been choked with soot.

The shipmates,
in their sore
distress, would
fain throw the
whole guilt on
Ah! well a-day! what evil looks
Had I from old and young!   140
Instead of the cross, the Albatross
About my neck was hung.

the ancient Mariner: in sign whereof they hang the dead seabird round his neck.

Part 3

There passed a weary time. Each throat
Was parched, and glazed each eye.
A weary time! a weary time!   145
The ancient
Mariner
beholdeth a sign
in the element
afar off.
How glazed each weary eye,
When looking westward, I beheld
A something in the sky.

At first it seemed a little speck,
And then it seemed a mist;   150
It moved and moved, and took at last
A certain shape, I wist.[5]

A speck, a mist, a shape, I wist!
And still it neared and neared:
As if it dodged a water sprite,   155
It plunged and tacked and veered.

At its nearer
approach, it
seemeth him to
be a ship; and at a
dear ransom he
freeth his speech
from the bonds
of thirst.

With throats unslaked, with black lips baked,
We could nor laugh nor wail;
Through utter drought all dumb we stood!
I bit my arm, I sucked the blood,   160
And cried, A sail! a sail!

A flash of joy;

With throats unslaked, with black lips baked,
Agape they heard me call:
Gramercy![6] they for joy did grin,
And all at once their breath drew in,   165
As they were drinking all.

And horror
follows. For can
it be a ship that
comes onward
without wind or
tide?

See! see! (I cried) she tacks no more!
Hither to work us weal;[7]
Without a breeze, without a tide,
She steadies with upright keel!   170

The western wave was all aflame.
The day was well nigh done!
Almost upon the western wave
Rested the broad bright Sun;
When that strange shape drove suddenly   175
Betwixt us and the Sun.

It seemeth him
but the skeleton
of a ship.

And straight the Sun was flecked with bars,
(Heaven's Mother send us grace!)
As if through a dungeon-grate he peered
With broad and burning face.   180

And its ribs are
seen as bars on
the face of the
setting Sun.

Alas! (thought I, and my heart beat loud)
How fast she nears and nears!
Are those *her* sails that glance in the Sun,
Like restless gossameres?

[5] Knew.

[6] Expression of surprise or gratitude.

[7] Benefit.

The Spectre-Woman and her Death-mate, and no other on board the skeleton ship.	Are those *her* ribs through which the Sun 185 Did peer, as through a grate? And is that Woman all her crew? Is that a DEATH? and are there two? Is DEATH that woman's mate?

Are those *her* ribs through which the Sun   185
Did peer, as through a grate?
And is that Woman all her crew?
Is that a DEATH? and are there two?
Is DEATH that woman's mate?

Her lips were red, *her* looks were free,   190
Her locks were yellow as gold:
Her skin was as white as leprosy,
The Nightmare LIFE-IN-DEATH was she,
Who thicks man's blood with cold.

The naked hulk alongside came,   195
And the twain were casting dice;
"The game is done! I've won! I've won!"
Quoth she, and whistles thrice.

The Sun's rim dips; the stars rush out:
At one stride comes the dark;   200
With far-heard whisper, o'er the sea,
Off shot the spectre-bark.

We listened and looked sideways up!
Fear at my heart, as at a cup,
My life-blood seemed to sip!   205
The stars were dim, and thick the night,
The steersman's face by his lamp gleamed white;
From the sails the dew did drip—
Till clomb above the eastern bar
The hornéd Moon, with one bright star   210
Within the nether tip.

One after one, by the star-dogged Moon,
Too quick for groan or sigh,
Each turned his face with a ghastly pang,
And cursed me with his eye.   215

Four times fifty living men,
(And I heard nor sigh nor groan)
With heavy thump, a lifeless lump,
They dropped down one by one.

The souls did from their bodies fly,—   220
They fled to bliss or woe!
And every soul, it passed me by,
Like the whizz of my crossbow!

Marginal glosses:

Like vessel, like crew!

Death and Life-in-Death have diced for the ship's crew, and she (the latter) winneth the ancient Mariner.

No twilight within the courts of the Sun.

At the rising of the Moon,

One after another,

His shipmates drop down dead.

But Life-in-Death begins her work on the ancient Mariner.

Part 4

The Wedding
Guest feareth
that a Spirit is
talking to him;

"I fear thee, ancient Mariner!
I fear thy skinny hand!
And thou art long, and lank, and brown,
As is the ribbed sea-sand.

225

I fear thee and thy glittering eye,
And thy skinny hand, so brown."—

But the ancient
Mariner assureth
him of his bodily
life, and
proceedeth to
relate his
horrible penance.

Fear not, fear not, thou Wedding Guest!
This body dropt not down.

230

Alone, alone, all, all alone,
Alone on a wide wide sea!
And never a saint took pity on
My soul in agony.

235

He despiseth the
creatures of the
calm,

The many men, so beautiful!
And they all dead did lie:
And a thousand thousand slimy things
Lived on; and so did I.

And envieth that
they should live,
and so many lie
dead.

I looked upon the rotting sea,
And drew my eyes away;
I looked upon the rotting deck,
And there the dead men lay.

240

I looked to heaven, and tried to pray;
But or ever a prayer had gusht,
A wicked whisper came, and made
My heart as dry as dust.

245

I closed my lids, and kept them close,
And the balls like pulses beat;
For the sky and the sea, and the sea and the sky
Lay like a load on my weary eye,
And the dead were at my feet.

250

But the curse
liveth for him in
the eye of the
dead men.

The cold sweat melted from their limbs,
Nor rot nor reek did they:
The look with which they looked on me
Had never passed away.

255

An orphan's curse would drag to hell
A spirit from on high;
But oh! more horrible than that
Is the curse in a dead man's eye!

260

Seven days, seven nights, I saw that curse,
And yet I could not die.

In his loneliness
and fixedness he
yearneth towards
the journeying
Moon, and the
stars that still
sojourn, yet still
move onward;
and every where
the blue sky
belongs to them,
and is their

The moving Moon went up the sky,
And no where did abide:
Softly she was going up,   265
And a star or two beside—

Her beams bemocked the sultry main,
Like April hoar-frost spread;
But where the ship's huge shadow lay,
The charméd water burnt alway   270
A still and awful red.

appointed rest, and their native country and their own natural homes, which they enter
unannounced, as lords that are certainly expected and yet there is a silent joy at their
arrival.

By the light of
the Moon he
beholdeth God's
creatures of the
great calm.

Beyond the shadow of the ship,
I watched the water-snakes:
They moved in tracks of shining white,
And when they reared, the elfish light   275
Fell off in hoary flakes.

Within the shadow of the ship
I watched their rich attire:
Blue, glossy green, and velvet black,
They coiled and swam; and every track   280
Was a flash of golden fire.

Their beauty and
their happiness.

O happy living things! no tongue
Their beauty might declare:
A spring of love gushed from my heart,

He blesseth them
in his heart.

And I blessed them unaware: 285
Sure my kind saint took pity on me,
And I blessed them unaware.

The spell begins
to break.

The self-same moment I could pray;
And from my neck so free
The Albatross fell off, and sank   290
Like lead into the sea.

Part 5

Oh sleep! it is a gentle thing,
Beloved from pole to pole!
To Mary Queen the praise be given!

She sent the gentle sleep from Heaven,   295
That slid into my soul.

By grace of the
holy Mother, the
ancient Mariner
is refreshed with
rain.

The silly buckets on the deck,
That had so long remained,
I dreamt that they were filled with dew;
And when I awoke, it rained.   300

My lips were wet, my throat was cold,
My garments all were dank;
Sure I had drunken in my dreams,
And still my body drank.

I moved, and could not feel my limbs: 305
I was so light—almost
I thought that I had died in sleep,
And was a blesséd ghost.

He heareth
sounds and seeth
strange sights
and commotions
in the sky and the
element.

And soon I heard a roaring wind:
It did not come anear;   310
But with its sound it shook the sails,
That were so thin and sere.

The upper air burst into life!
And a hundred fire-flags sheen,
To and fro they were hurried about!   315
And to and fro, and in and out,
The wan stars danced between.

And the coming wind did roar more loud,
And the sails did sigh like sedge;
And the rain poured down from one black cloud;   320
The Moon was at its edge.

The thick black cloud was cleft, and still
The Moon was at its side:
Like waters shot from some high crag,
The lightning fell with never a jag,   325
A river steep and wide.

The bodies of the
ship's crew are
inspired
[inspirited] and
the ship moves
on;

The loud wind never reached the ship,
Yet now the ship moved on!
Beneath the lightning and the Moon
The dead men gave a groan.   330

They groaned, they stirred, they all up-rose,
Nor spake, nor, moved their eyes;

It had been strange, even in a dream,
To have seen those dead men rise.

The helmsman steered, the ship moved on;   335
Yet never a breeze up-blew;
The mariners all 'gan work the ropes,
Where they were wont to do;
They raised their limbs like lifeless tools—
We were a ghastly crew.   340

The body of my brother's son
Stood by me, knee to knee:
The body and I pulled at one rope,
But he said nought to me.

"I fear thee, ancient Mariner!"   345
Be calm, thou Wedding-Guest!
'Twas not those souls that fled in pain,
Which to their corses[8] came again,
But a troop of spirits blest:

For when it dawned—they dropped their arms,   350
And clustered round the mast;
Sweet sounds rose slowly through their mouths,
And from their bodies passed.

Around, around, flew each sweet sound,
Then darted to the Sun;   355
Slowly the sounds came back again,
Now mixed, now one by one.

Sometimes a-dropping from the sky
I heard the skylark sing;
Sometimes all little birds that are,   360
How they seemed to fill the sea and air
With their sweet jargoning![9]

And now 'twas like all instruments,
Now like a lonely flute;
And now it is an angel's song,   365
That makes the heavens be mute.

It ceased; yet still the sails made on
A pleasant noise till noon,
A noise like of a hidden brook

But not by the souls of the men, nor by daemons of earth or middle air, but by a blessed troop of angelic spirits, sent down by the invocation of the guardian saint.

[8] Corpses.
[9] Singing; vocalizing in a strange language.

In the leafy month of June,   370
That to the sleeping woods all night
Singeth a quiet tune.

Till noon we quietly sailed on,
Yet never a breeze did breathe:
Slowly and smoothly went the ship,   375
Moved onward from beneath.

The lonesome
Spirit from the   Under the keel nine fathom deep,
South Pole   From the land of mist and snow,
carries on the   The spirit slid: and it was he
ship as far as the   That made the ship to go.   380
Line, in   The sails at noon left off their tune,
obedience to the   And the ship stood still also.
angelic troop, but
still requireth   The Sun, right up above the mast,
vengeance.   Had fixed her to the ocean:
                          But in a minute she 'gan stir,   385
                          With a short uneasy motion—
                          Backwards and forwards half her length
                          With a short uneasy motion.

                          Then like a pawing horse let go,
                          She made a sudden bound: 390
                          It flung the blood into my head,
                          And I fell down in a swound.

                          How long in that same fit I lay,
                          I have not to declare;
The Polar Spirit's   But ere my living life returned,   395
fellow daemons,   I heard and in my soul discerned
the invisible   Two voices in the air.
inhabitants of the
element, take   "Is it he?" quoth one, "Is this the man?
part in his wrong;   By him who died on cross,
and two of them   With his cruel bow he laid full low   400
relate, one to the   The harmless Albatross.
other, that
penance long and   The spirit who bideth by himself
heavy for the   In the land of mist and snow,
ancient Mariner   He loved the bird that loved the man
hath been   Who shot him with his bow."   405
accorded to the
Polar Spirit, who
returneth   The other was a softer voice,
southward.   As soft as honeydew:

Quoth he, "The man hath penance done,
And penance more will do."

Part 6

FIRST VOICE

"But tell me, tell me! speak again,   410
Thy soft response renewing—
What makes that ship drive on so fast?
What is the ocean doing?"

SECOND VOICE

"Still as a slave before his lord,
The ocean hath no blast;   415
His great bright eye most silently
Up to the Moon is cast—

If he may know which way to go;
For she guides him smooth or grim.
See, brother, see! how graciously   420
She looketh down on him."

FIRST VOICE

The Mariner
hath been cast
into a trance; for
the angelic power
causeth the
vessel to drive
northward faster
than human life
could endure.

"But why drives on that ship so fast,
Without or wave or wind?"

SECOND VOICE

"The air is cut away before,
And closes from behind.   425

Fly, brother, fly! more high, more high!
Or we shall be belated:
For slow and slow that ship will go,
When the Mariner's trance is abated."

The supernatural
motion is
retarded; the
Mariner awakes,
and his penance
begins anew.

I woke, and we were sailing on   430
As in a gentle weather:
'Twas night, calm night, the moon was high;
The dead men stood together.

All stood together on the deck,
For a charnel-dungeon fitter: 435

All fixed on me their stony eyes,
That in the Moon did glitter.

The pang, the curse, with which they died,
Had never passed away:
I could not draw my eyes from theirs,   440
Nor turn them up to pray.

The curse is
finally expiated.

And now this spell was snapt: once more
I viewed the ocean green,
And looked far forth, yet little saw
Of what had else been seen—   445

Like one, that on a lonesome road
Doth walk in fear and dread,
And having once turned round walks on,
And turns no more his head;
Because he knows, a frightful fiend   450
Doth close behind him tread.

But soon there breathed a wind on me,
Nor sound nor motion made:
Its path was not upon the sea,
In ripple or in shade.   455

It raised my hair, it fanned my cheek
Like a meadow-gale of spring—
It mingled strangely with my fears,
Yet it felt like a welcoming.

Swiftly, swiftly flew the ship,   460
Yet she sailed softly too:
Sweetly, sweetly blew the breeze—
On me alone it blew.

And the ancient
Mariner
beholdeth his
native country.

Oh! dream of joy! is this indeed
The lighthouse top I see?   465
Is this the hill? is this the kirk?
Is this mine own countree?

We drifted o'er the harbour bar,
And I with sobs did pray—
O let me be awake, my God!   470
Or let me sleep alway.

The harbour bay was clear as glass,
So smoothly it was strewn!

And on the bay the moonlight lay,
And the shadow of the Moon. 475

The rock shone bright, the kirk no less,
That stands above the rock:
The moonlight steeped in silentness
The steady weathercock.

And the bay was white with silent light, 480
Till rising from the same,
Full many shapes, that shadows were,
In crimson colours came.

A little distance from the prow
Those crimson shadows were: 485
I turned my eyes upon the deck—
Oh, Christ! what saw I there!

Each corse lay flat, lifeless and flat,
And, by the holy rood!
A man all light, a seraph-man,[10] 490
On every corse there stood.

This seraph-band, each waved his hand:
It was a heavenly sight!
They stood as signals to the land,
Each one a lovely light; 495

This seraph-band, each waved his hand,
No voice did they impart—
No voice; but oh! the silence sank
Like music on my heart.

But soon I heard the dash of oars, 500
I heard the Pilot's cheer;
My head was turned perforce away
And I saw a boat appear.

The Pilot and the Pilot's boy,
I heard them coming fast: 505
Dear Lord in Heaven! it was a joy
The dead men could not blast.

I saw a third—I heard his voice:
It is the Hermit good!

The angelic spirits leave the dead bodies,

And appear in their own forms of light.

[10] Angelic being.

He singeth loud his godly hymns   510
That he makes in the wood.
He'll shrieve my soul, he'll wash away
The Albatross's blood.

Part 7

The Hermit of   This Hermit good lives in that wood
the Wood,   Which slopes down to the sea.   515
How loudly his sweet voice he rears!
He loves to talk with marineres
That come from a far countree.

He kneels at morn, and noon, and eve —
He hath a cushion plump: 520
It is the moss that wholly hides
The rotted old oak stump.

The skiff-boat neared: I heard them talk,
"Why, this is strange, I trow!
Where are those lights so many and fair,   525
That signal made but now?"

Approacheth the   "Strange, by my faith!" the Hermit said —
ship with   "And they answered not our cheer!
wonder.   The planks looked warped! and see those sails,
How thin they are and sere!   530
I never saw aught like to them,
Unless perchance it were

Brown skeletons of leaves that lag
My forest-brook along;
When the ivy tod[11] is heavy with snow,   535
And the owlet whoops to the wolf below,
That eats the she-wolf's young."

"Dear Lord! it hath a fiendish look —
(The Pilot made reply)
I am a-feared" — "Push on, push on!"   540
Said the Hermit cheerily.

The boat came closer to the ship,
But I nor spake nor stirred;
The boat came close beneath the ship,
And straight a sound was heard.   545

---

[11] Bush or clump of ivy.

The ship
suddenly sinketh.

Under the water it rumbled on,
Still louder and more dread;
It reached the ship, it split the bay;
The ship went down like lead.

The ancient
Mariner is saved
in the Pilot's
boat.

Stunned by that loud and dreadful sound,   550
Which sky and ocean smote,
Like one that hath been seven days drowned
My body lay afloat;
But swift as dreams, myself I found
Within the Pilot's boat.   555

Upon the whirl, where sank the ship,
The boat spun round and round;
And all was still, save that the hill
Was telling of the sound.

I moved my lips—the Pilot shrieked   560
And fell down in a fit;
The holy Hermit raised his eyes,
And prayed where he did sit.

I took the oars: the Pilot's boy,
Who now doth crazy go,   565
Laughed loud and long, and all the while
His eyes went to and fro.
"Ha! ha!" quoth he, "full plain I see,
The Devil knows how to row."

And now, all in my own countree,   570
I stood on the firm land!
The Hermit stepped forth from the boat,
And scarcely he could stand.

The ancient
Mariner
earnestly
entreateth the
Hermit to
shrieve him; and
the penance of
life falls on him.

"O shrieve me, shrieve me,[12] holy man!"
The Hermit crossed his brow.   575
"Say quick," quoth he, "I bid thee say—
What manner of man art thou?"

Forthwith this frame of mine was wrenched
With a woeful agony,
Which forced me to begin my tale;   580
And then it left me free.

---

[12] Hear my confession and grant absolution (for my sins).

And ever and anon throughout his future life an agony constraineth him to travel from land to land;

Since then, at an uncertain hour,
That agony returns:
And till my ghastly tale is told,
This heart within me burns.   585

I pass, like night, from land to land;
I have strange power of speech;
That moment that his face I see,
I know the man that must hear me:
To him my tale I teach.   590

What loud uproar bursts from that door!
The wedding guests are there:
But in the garden bower the bride
And bride-maids singing are:
And hark the little vesper bell,   595
Which biddeth me to prayer!

O Wedding Guest! this soul hath been
Alone on a wide wide sea:
So lonely 'twas, that God himself
Scarce seeméd there to be.   600

O sweeter than the marriage feast,
'Tis sweeter far to me,
To walk together to the kirk
With a goodly company!—

To walk together to the kirk,   605
And all together pray,
While each to his great Father bends,
Old men, and babes, and loving friends
And youths and maidens gay!

And to teach, by his own example, love and reverence to all things that God made and loveth.

Farewell, farewell! but this I tell   610
To thee, thou Wedding Guest!
He prayeth well, who loveth well
Both man and bird and beast.

He prayeth best, who loveth best
All things both great and small;   615
For the dear God who loveth us,
He made and loveth all.

The Mariner, whose eye is bright,
Whose beard with age is hoar,

Is gone: and now the Wedding Guest   620
Turned from the bridegroom's door.

He went like one that hath been stunned,
And is of sense forlorn:
A sadder and a wiser man,
He rose the morrow morn.   625

❧ *Jane Austen* (1775–1817)

While Jane Austen's novels would seem to emphasize conversation and human relationships rather than the relationship between humans and the environment, a closer reading of works such as Emma *reveals Austen's keen but subtle understanding of the importance of natural setting. Though Austen does not dramatically foreground nature as a reflection of the inner turmoil of her characters (as her Romantic contemporaries did), the influence of eighteenth-century locodescriptive and moral poets such as Cowper and Crabbe is easy to discern. These two writers, as well as several other novelists and essayists of the previous century, notably Fielding, Johnson, and Burney, were among those whom Austen read and admired.*

Austen's life was similar to the lives of her memorable heroines, with the particular exception that Austen herself never married. Her father was a clergyman with a modest living, which was nevertheless enough to support Austen and her six brothers and one sister. Like most women of her day, Austen had little formal education, but her father was supportive of her reading and writing habits and she profited from the family's large library. She was writing stories by the age of twelve and by the age of twenty had drafted several of her later published novels. Austen was not ostentatious about her writing. She often wrote in the parlor of her home and hid her manuscripts as family or guests entered the room, not wishing to draw attention to her artistic pursuits. Throughout her life, Austen was busy with social activities, whether it was the balls or parties that her novels are famous for representing or visiting or entertaining her family members. She traveled to London and to Bath as a young woman, and when her father retired in 1800, she and her family moved with him to the resort town. After her father's death in 1805, Austen became financially dependent on her brothers, and she moved to Southampton to be nearer the two who were in the navy. By 1809, she had relocated once more to Hampshire. Although she had previously tried to bring out Northanger Abbey, *her first novel to be published was* Sense and Sensibility, *in 1811. It was published anonymously, and its favorable acclaim encouraged Austen to continue.* Pride and Prejudice *followed in 1813,* Mansfield Park *in 1814,* Emma *in 1815, and* Persuasion *and* Northanger Abbey *posthumously, in 1817. The scene from* Emma *excerpted below shows Austen in the lineage of those eighteenth-century authors for whom the landscape's significance was largely moral. In it, the heroine learns an important moral lesson in a picturesque setting.*

From Emma

Chapter 42

After being long fed with hopes of a speedy visit from Mr. and Mrs. Suckling, the Highbury world were obliged to endure the mortification of hearing that they could not possibly come till the autumn. No such importation of novelties could enrich their intellectual stores at present. In the daily interchange of news, they must be again restricted to the other topics, with which for a while the Sucklings' coming had been united, such as the last accounts of Mrs. Churchill, whose health seemed every day to supply a different report, and the situation of Mrs. Weston, whose happiness, it was to be hoped, might eventually be as much increased by the arrival of a child, as that of all her neighbours was by the approach of it.

Mrs. Elton was very much disappointed. It was the delay of a great deal of pleasure and parade. Her introductions and recommendations must all wait, and every projected party be still only talked of. So she thought at first; but a little consideration convinced her that everything need not be put off. Why should not they explore to Box Hill though the Sucklings did not come? They could go there again with them in the autumn. It was settled that they should go to Box Hill. That there was to be such a party had been long generally known; it had even given the idea of another. Emma had never been to Box Hill; she wished to see what everybody found so well worth seeing, and she and Mr. Weston had agreed to choose some fine morning and drive thither. Two or three more of the chosen only were to be admitted to join them, and it was to be done in a quiet, unpretending, elegant way, infinitely superior to the bustle and preparation, the regular eating and drinking and picnic parade of the Eltons and the Sucklings.

This was so very well understood between them that Emma could not but feel some surprise, and a little displeasure, on hearing from Mr. Weston that he had been proposing to Mrs. Elton, as her brother and sister had failed her, that the two parties should unite, and go together; and that as Mrs. Elton had very readily acceded to it, so it was to be, if she had no objection. Now, as her objection was nothing but her very great dislike of Mrs. Elton, of which Mr. Weston must already be perfectly aware, it was not worth bringing forward again: it could not be done without a reproof to him, which would be giving pain to his wife; and she found herself, therefore, obliged to consent to an arrangement which she would have done a great deal to avoid; an arrangement which would, probably, expose her even to the degradation of being said to be of Mr. Elton's party! Every feeling was offended; and the forbearance of her outward submission left a heavy arrear due of secret severity in her reflections, on the unmanageable goodwill of Mr. Weston's temper.

"I am glad you approve of what I have done," said he, very comfortably. "But I thought you would. Such schemes as these are nothing without numbers. One cannot have too large a party. A large party secures its own amusement. And she is a good-natured woman after all. One could not leave her out."

Emma denied none of it aloud, and agreed to none of it in private.

It was now the middle of June and the weather fine; and Mrs. Elton was growing impatient to name the day, and settle with Mr. Weston as to pigeon-pies and cold lamb, when a lame carriage-horse threw everything into sad uncertainty. It might be weeks, it might be only a few days, before the horse were usable; but no preparations could be ventured on, and it was all melancholy stagnation. Mrs. Elton's resources were inadequate to such an attack.

"Is not this most vexatious, Knightley?" she cried; "and such weather for exploring! These delays and disappointments are quite odious. What are we to do? The year will wear away at this rate, and nothing done. Before this time last year, I assure you, we had a delightful exploring party from Maple Grove to King's Weston."

"You had better explore to Donwell," replied Mr. Knightley. "That may be done without horses. Come and eat my strawberries; they are ripening fast."

If Mr. Knightley did not begin seriously, he was obliged to proceed so; for his proposal was caught at with delight; and the "Oh! I should like it of all things," was not plainer in words than manner. Donwell was famous for its strawberry-beds, which seemed a plea for the invitation; but no plea was necessary; cabbage-beds would have been enough to tempt the lady, who only wanted to be going somewhere. She promised him again and again to come—much oftener than he doubted—and was extremely gratified by such a proof of intimacy, such a distinguishing compliment as she chose to consider it.

"You may depend upon me," said she; "I certainly will come. Name your day, and I will come. You will allow me to bring Jane Fairfax?"

"I cannot name a day," said he, "till I have spoken to some others, whom I would wish to meet you."

"Oh, leave all that to me; only give me a *carte blanche*. I am Lady Patroness, you know. It is my party. I will bring friends with me."

"I hope you will bring Elton," said he; "but I will not trouble you to give any other invitations."

"Oh, now you are looking very sly; but consider—you need not be afraid of delegating power to *me*. I am no young lady on her preferment. Married women, you know, may be safely authorised. It is my party. Leave it all to me. I will invite your guests."

"No," he calmly replied, "there is but one married woman in the world whom I can ever allow to invite what guests she pleases to Donwell, and that one is——"

"Mrs. Weston, I suppose," interrupted Mrs. Elton, rather mortified.

"No—Mrs. Knightley; and till she is in being, I will manage such matters myself."

"Ah, you are an odd creature!" she cried, satisfied to have no one preferred to herself. "You are a humorist, and may say what you like. Quite a humorist. Well, I shall bring Jane with me—Jane and her aunt. The rest I leave to you. I have no objections at all to meeting the Hartfield family. Don't scruple, I know you are attached to them."

"You certainly will meet them, if I can prevail; and I shall call on Miss Bates in my way home."

"That's quite unnecessary; I see Jane every day; but as you like. It is to be a morning scheme, you know, Knightley; quite a simple thing. I shall wear a large bonnet, and bring one of my little baskets hanging on my arm. Here—probably this basket with pink ribbon. Nothing can be more simple, you see. And Jane will have such another. There is to be no form or parade—a sort of gypsy party. We are to walk about your gardens, and gather the strawberries ourselves, and sit under trees; and whatever else you may like to provide, it is to be all out of doors; a table spread in the shade, you know. Everything as natural and simple as possible. Is not that your idea?"

"Not quite. My idea of the simple and the natural will be to have the table spread in the dining-room. The nature and the simplicity of gentlemen and ladies, with their servants and furniture, I think is best observed by meals within doors. When you are tired of eating strawberries in the garden, there shall be cold meat in the house."

"Well, as you please; only don't have a great set-out. And, by the bye, can I or my housekeeper be of any use to you with our opinion? Pray be sincere, Knightley. If you wish me to talk to Mrs. Hodges, or to inspect anything——"

"I have not the least wish for it, I thank you."

"Well—but if any difficulties should arise, my housekeeper is extremely clever."

"I will answer for it that mine thinks herself full as clever, and would spurn anybody's assistance."

"I wish we had a donkey. The thing would be for us all to come on donkeys, Jane, Miss Bates, and me, and my *caro sposo*[1] walking by. I really must talk to him about purchasing a donkey. In a country life I conceive it to be a sort of necessary; for, let a woman have ever so many resources, it is not possible for her to be always shut up at home; and very long walks, you know—in summer there is dust, and in winter there is dirt."

"You will not find either between Donwell and Highbury. Donwell Lane is never dusty, and now it is perfectly dry. Come on a donkey, however, if you prefer it. You can borrow Mrs. Cole's. I would wish everything to be as much to your taste as possible."

"That I am sure you would. Indeed I do you justice, my good friend. Under that peculiar sort of dry, blunt manner, I know you have the warmest heart. As I tell Mr. E., you are a thorough humorist. Yes, believe me, Knightley, I am fully sensible of your attention to me in the whole of this scheme. You have hit upon the very thing to please me."

Mr. Knightley had another reason for avoiding a table in the shade. He wished to persuade Mr. Woodhouse, as well as Emma, to join the party; and he knew that to have any of them sitting down out of doors to eat would inevitably make him ill. Mr. Woodhouse must not, under the specious pretence of a morning drive, and an hour or two spent at Donwell, be tempted away to his misery.

He was invited on good faith. No lurking horrors were to upbraid him for his easy credulity. He did consent. He had not been at Donwell for two years. "Some very fine morning, he, and Emma, and Harriet could go very well; and he could sit still with Mrs. Weston while the dear girls walked about the garden. He

---

[1] Dear husband (Italian).

did not suppose they could be damp now, in the middle of the day. He should like to see the old house again exceedingly, and should be very happy to meet Mr. and Mrs. Elton, and any other of his neighbours. He could not see any objection at all to his, and Emma's and Harriet's going there some very fine morning. He thought it very well done of Mr. Knightley to invite them; very kind and sensible; much cleverer than dining out. He was not fond of dining out."

Mr. Knightley was fortunate in everybody's most ready concurrence. The invitation was everywhere so well received, that it seemed as if, like Mrs. Elton, they were all taking the scheme as a particular compliment to themselves. Emma and Harriet professed very high expectations of pleasure from it; and Mr. Weston, unasked, promised to get Frank over to join them, if possible; a proof of approbation and gratitude which could have been dispensed with. Mr. Knightley was then obliged to say that he should be glad to see him; and Mr. Weston engaged to lose no time in writing, and spare no arguments to induce him to come.

In the meanwhile the lame horse recovered so fast that the party to Box Hill was again under happy consideration; and at last Donwell was settled for one day; and Box Hill for the next, the weather appearing exactly right.

Under a bright midday sun, at almost Midsummer, Mr. Woodhouse was safely conveyed in his carriage, with one window down, to partake of this *alfresco*[2] party; and in one of the most comfortable rooms in the Abbey, especially prepared for him by a fire all the morning, he was happily placed, quite at his ease, ready to talk with pleasure of what had been achieved, and advise everybody to come and sit down, and not to heat themselves. Mrs. Weston, who seemed to have walked there on purpose to be tired, and sit all the time with him, remained, when all the others were invited or persuaded out, his patient listener and sympathizer.

It was so long since Emma had been at the Abbey, that as soon as she was satisfied of her father's comfort, she was glad to leave him and look around her; eager to refresh and correct her memory with more particular observation, more exact understanding of a house and grounds which must ever be so interesting to her and all her family.

She felt all the honest pride and complacency which her alliance with the present and future proprietor could fairly warrant, as she viewed the respectable size and style of the building, its suitable, becoming, characteristic situation, low and sheltered; its ample gardens stretching down to meadows washed by a stream, of which the Abbey, with all the old neglect of prospect, had scarcely a sight—and its abundance of timber in rows and avenues, which neither fashion nor extravagance had rooted up. The house was larger than Hartfield, and totally unlike it, covering a good deal of ground, rambling and irregular, with many comfortable, and one or two handsome rooms. It was just what it ought to be, and it looked what it was; and Emma felt an increasing respect for it, as the residence of a family of such true gentility, untainted in blood and understanding. Some faults of temper John Knightley had; but Isabella had connected herself unexceptionally. She had given them neither men, nor names, nor places, that could raise a blush. These were pleasant feelings, and she walked about and indulged them till it was

---

[2] In the open air (Italian).

necessary to do as the others did, and collect round the strawberry-beds. The whole party were assembled, excepting Frank Churchill, who was expected every moment from Richmond; and Mrs. Elton, in all her apparatus of happiness, her large bonnet and her basket, was very ready to lead the way in gathering, accepting, or talking. Strawberries, and only strawberries, could now be thought or spoken of. "The best fruit in England—everybody's favourite—always wholesome. These the finest beds and finest sorts. Delightful to gather for one's self— the only way of really enjoying them. Morning decidedly the best time—never tired—every sort good—hautboy infinitely superior—no comparison—the others hardly eatable—hautboys very scarce—Chili preferred—white wood finest flavour of all—price of strawberries in London—abundance about Bristol—Maple Grove—cultivations—beds when to be renewed—gardeners thinking exactly different—no general rule—gardeners never to be put out of their way—delicious fruit—only too rich to be eaten much of—inferior to cherries—currants more refreshing—only objections to gathering strawberries the stooping—glaring sun—tired to death—could bear it no longer—must go and sit in the shade."

Such, for half an hour, was the conversation; interrupted only once by Mrs. Weston, who came out, in her solicitude after her son-in-law, to inquire if he were come; and she was a little uneasy. She had some fears of his horse.

Seats tolerably in the shade were found; and now Emma was obliged to overhear what Mrs. Elton and Jane Fairfax were talking of. A situation, a most desirable situation, was in question. Mrs. Elton had received notice of it that morning, and was in raptures. It was not with Mrs. Suckling, it was not with Mrs. Bragge, but in felicity and splendour it fell short only of them: it was with a cousin of Mrs. Bragge, an acquaintance of Mrs. Suckling, a lady known at Maple Grove. Delightful, charming, superior, first circles, spheres, lines, ranks, everything; and Mrs. Elton was wild to have the offer closed with immediately. On her side, all was warmth, energy, and triumph; and she positively refused to take her friend's negative, though Miss Fairfax continued to assure her that she would not at present engage in anything—repeating the same motives which she had been heard to urge before. Still Mrs. Elton insisted on being authorised to write an acquiescence by the morrow's post. How Jane could bear it at all, was astonishing to Emma. She did look vexed, she did speak pointedly—and at last, with a decision of action unusual to her, proposed a removal. "Should not they walk? Would not Mr. Knightley show them the gardens—all the gardens? She wished to see the whole extent." The pertinacity of her friend seemed more than she could bear.

It was hot; and after walking some time over the gardens in a scattered, dispersed way, scarcely any three together, they insensibly followed one another to the delicious shade of a broad short avenue of limes, which stretching beyond the garden at an equal distance from the river, seemed the finish of the pleasure ground. It led to nothing; nothing but a view at the end over a low stone wall with high pillars, which seemed intended in their erection, to give the appearance of an approach to the house, which never had been there. Disputable, however, as might be the taste of such a termination, it was in itself a charming walk, and the view which closed it extremely pretty. The considerable slope, at nearly the foot of which the Abbey stood, gradually acquired a steeper form beyond its grounds, and at half a mile distant was a bank of considerable abruptness and grandeur, well-clothed with wood; and at the bottom of this bank, favourably placed and sheltered, rose the Abbey-Mill Farm, with meadows in front, and the river making a close and handsome curve around it.

It was a sweet view — sweet to the eye and the mind. English verdure, English culture, English comfort, seen under a bright sun, without being oppressive.

In this walk Emma and Mr. Weston found all the others assembled; and towards this view she immediately perceived Mr. Knightley and Harriet distinct from the rest, quietly leading the way. Mr. Knightley and Harriet! It was an odd *tête-à-tête;*[3] but she was glad to see it. There had been a time when he would have scorned her as a companion, and turned from her with little ceremony. Now they seemed in pleasant conversation. There had been a time also when Emma would have been sorry to see Harriet in a spot so favourable for the Abbey-Mill Farm; but now she feared it not. It might be safely viewed, with all its appendages of prosperity and beauty, its rich pastures, spreading flocks, orchard in blossom, and light column of smoke ascending. She joined them at the wall, and found them more engaged in talking than in looking around. He was giving Harriet information as to modes of agriculture, etc.; and Emma received a smile which seemed to say, "These are my own concerns. I have a right to talk on such subjects, without being suspected of introducing Robert Martin." She did not suspect him. It was too old a story. Robert Martin had probably ceased to think of Harriet. They took a few turns together along the walk. The shade was most refreshing, and Emma found it the pleasantest part of the day.

The next remove was to the house; they must all go in and eat; and they were all seated and busy, and still Frank Churchill did not come. Mrs. Weston looked, and looked in vain. His father would not own himself uneasy, and laughed at her fears; but she could not be cured of wishing that he would part with his black mare. He had expressed himself as to coming with more than common certainty. "His aunt was so much better, that he had not a doubt of getting over to them." Mrs. Churchill's state, however, as many were ready to remind her, was liable to such sudden variation as might disappoint her nephew in the most reasonable dependence; and Mrs. Weston was at last persuaded to believe, or to say, that it must be by some attack of Mrs. Churchill that he was prevented coming. Emma looked at Harriet while the point was under consideration; she behaved very well, and betrayed no emotion.

The cold repast was over, and the party were to go out once more to see what had not yet been seen, the old Abbey fish-ponds; perhaps get as far as the clover, which was to be begun cutting on the morrow, or, at any rate, have the pleasure of being hot, and growing cool again. Mr. Woodhouse, who had already taken his little round in the highest part of the gardens, where no damps from the river were imagined even by him, stirred no more; and his daughter resolved to remain with him, that Mrs. Weston might be persuaded away by her husband to the exercise and variety which her spirits seemed to need.

---

[3] Confidential conversation (French).

Mr. Knightley had done all in his power for Mr. Woodhouse's entertainment. Books of engravings, drawers of medals, cameos, corals, shells, and every other family collection within his cabinets, had been prepared for his old friend, to while away the morning; and the kindness had perfectly answered. Mr. Woodhouse had been exceedingly well amused. Mrs. Weston had been showing them all to him, and now he would show them all to Emma; fortunate in having no other resemblance to a child, than in a total want of taste for what he saw, for he was slow, constant, and methodical. Before this second looking over was begun, however, Emma walked into the hall for the sake of a few moments' free observation of the entrance and ground-plot of the house, and was hardly there when Jane Fairfax appeared, coming quickly in from the garden, and with a look of escape. Little expecting to meet Miss Woodhouse so soon, there was a start at first; but Miss Woodhouse was the very person she was in quest of.

"Will you be so kind," said she, "when I am missed, as to say that I am gone home! I am going this moment. My aunt is not aware how late it is, nor how long we have been absent; but I am sure we shall be wanted, and I am determined to go directly. I have said nothing about it to anybody. It would only be giving trouble and distress. Some are gone to the ponds, and some to the lime-walk. Till they all come in I shall not be missed; and when they do, will you have the goodness to say that I am gone?"

"Certainly, if you wish it; but you are not going to walk to Highbury alone?"

"Yes; what should hurt me? I walk fast. I shall be at home in twenty minutes."

"But it is too far, indeed it is, to be walking quite alone. Let my father's servant go with you. Let me order the carriage. It can be round in five minutes."

"Thank you, thank you—but on no account—I would rather walk. And for *me* to be afraid of walking alone!—I, who may so soon have to guard others!"

She spoke with great agitation; and Emma very feelingly replied: "That can be no reason for your being exposed to danger now. I must order the carriage. The heat even would be danger. You are fatigued already."

"I am," she answered, "I am fatigued; but it is not the sort of fatigue—quick walking will refresh me. Miss Woodhouse, we all know at times what it is to be wearied in spirits. Mine, I confess, are exhausted. The greatest kindness you can show me will be to let me have my own way, and only say that I am gone when it is necessary."

Emma had not another word to oppose. She saw it all; and entering into her feelings, promoted her quitting the house immediately, and watched her safely off with the zeal of a friend. Her parting look was grateful; and her parting words, "Oh! Miss Woodhouse, the comfort of being sometimes alone!" seemed to burst from an overcharged heart, and to describe somewhat of the continual endurance to be practised by her, even towards some of those who loved her best.

"Such a home, indeed! Such an aunt!" said Emma, as she turned back into the hall again. "I do pity you. And the more sensibility you betray of their just horrors, the more I shall like you."

Jane had not been gone a quarter of an hour, and they had only accomplished some views of St. Mark's Place, Venice, when Frank Churchill entered the room. Emma had not been thinking of him; she had forgotten to think of him, but she was very glad to see him. Mrs. Weston would be at ease. The black mare was blameless; *they* were right who had named Mrs. Churchill as the cause. He had been detained by a temporary increase of illness in her—a nervous seizure which had lasted some hours; and he had quite given up every thought of coming till very late; and had he known how hot a ride he should have, and how late, with all his hurry, he must be, he believed he should not have come at all. The heat was excessive; he had never suffered anything like it—almost wished he had stayed at home—nothing killed him like heat—he could bear any degree of cold, etc., but heat was intolerable; and he sat down, at the greatest possible distance from the slight remains of Mr. Woodhouse's fire, looking very deplorable.

"You will soon be cooler, if you sit still," said Emma.

"As soon as I am cooler I shall go back again. I could very ill be spared; but such a point had been made of my coming! You will all be going soon, I suppose; the whole party breaking up. I met *one* as I came. Madness in such weather—absolute madness!"

Emma listened, and looked, and soon perceived that Frank Churchill's state might be best defined by the expressive phrase of being out of humour. Some people were always cross when they were hot. Such might be his constitution; and as she knew that eating and drinking were often the cure of such incidental complaints, she recommended his taking some refreshment; he would find abundance of everything in the dining-room; and she humanely pointed out the door.

"No; he should not eat. He was not hungry; it would only make him hotter." In two minutes, however, he relented in his own favour; and muttering something about spruce-beer, walked off. Emma returned all her attention to her father, saying in secret:

"I am glad I have done being in love with him. I should not like a man who is so soon discomposed by a hot morning. Harriet's sweet easy temper will not mind it."

He was gone long enough to have had a very comfortable meal, and came back all the better—grown quite cool, and with good manners, like himself, able to draw a chair close to them, take an interest in their employment, and regret, in a reasonable way, that he should be so late. He was not in his best spirits, but seemed trying to improve them; and, at last, made himself talk nonsense very agreeably. They were looking over views in Switzerland.

"As soon as my aunt gets well I shall go abroad," said he. "I shall never be easy till I have seen some of these places. You will have my sketches, some time or other, to look at—or my tour to read—or my poem. I shall do something to expose myself."

"That may be—but not by sketches in Switzerland. You will never go to Switzerland. Your uncle and aunt will never allow you to leave England."

"They may be induced to go too. A warm climate may be prescribed for her. I have more than half an expectation of our all going abroad. I assure you, I have. I feel a strong persuasion, this morning, that I shall soon be abroad. I ought to travel. I am tired of doing nothing. I want a change. I am serious, Miss Woodhouse, whatever your penetrating eyes may fancy—I am sick of England, and would leave it tomorrow if I could."

"You are sick of prosperity and indulgence! Cannot you invent a few hardships for yourself, and be contented to stay?"

"*I* sick of prosperity and indulgence! You are quite mistaken. I do not look upon myself as either prosperous or indulged. I am thwarted in everything material. I do not consider myself at all a fortunate person."

"You are not quite so miserable, though, as when you first came. Go and eat and drink a little more, and you will do very well. Another slice of cold meat, another draught of Madeira and water, will make you nearly on a par with the rest of us."

"No—I shall not stir. I shall sit by you. You are my best cure."

"We are going to Box Hill tomorrow; you will join us. It is not Switzerland, but it will be something for a young man so much in want of a change. You will stay and go with us?"

"No; certainly not. I shall go home in the cool of the evening."

"But you may come again in the cool of tomorrow morning."

"No—it will not be worth while. If I come, I shall be cross."

"Then pray stay at Richmond."

"But if I do, I shall be crosser still. I can never bear to think of you all there without me."

"These are difficulties which you must settle for yourself. Choose your own degree of crossness. I shall press you no more."

The rest of the party were now returning, and all were soon collected. With some there was great joy at the sight of Frank Churchill; others took it very composedly; but there was a very general distress and disturbance on Miss Fairfax's disappearance being explained. That it was time for everybody to go concluded the subject; and with a short final arrangement for the next day's scheme, they parted. Frank Churchill's little inclination to exclude himself increased so much, that his last words to Emma were:

"Well; if *you* wish me to stay and join the party, I will."

She smiled her acceptance; and nothing less than a summons from Richmond was to take him back before the following evening.

Chapter 43

They had a very fine day for Box Hill; and all the other outward circumstances of arrangement, accommodation, and punctuality, were in favour of a pleasant party. Mr. Weston directed the whole, officiating safely between Hartfield and the vicarage, and everybody was in good time. Emma and Harriet went together; Miss Bates and her niece with the Eltons; the gentlemen on horseback. Mrs. Weston remained with Mr. Woodhouse. Nothing was wanting but to be happy when they got there. Seven miles were travelled in expectation of enjoyment, and everybody had a burst of admiration on first arriving; but in the general amount of the day there was deficiency. There was a languor, a want of spirits, a want of union, which could not be got over. They separated too much into parties. The Eltons walked together; Mr. Knightley took charge of Miss Bates and Jane; and Emma and Harriet belonged to Frank Churchill. And Mr. Weston tried, in vain, to make them harmonize better. It seemed at first an accidental division, but it never materially varied. Mr. and Mrs. Elton, indeed, showed no unwillingness to mix, and be as agreeable as they could; but during the two whole hours that were spent on the Hill, there seemed a principle of separation between the other parties, too strong for any fine prospects, or any cold collation, or any cheerful Mr. Weston, to remove.

At first it was downright dullness to Emma. She had never seen Frank Churchill so silent and stupid. He said nothing worth hearing—looked without seeing—admired without intelligence—listened without knowing what she said. While he was so dull, it was no wonder that Harriet should be dull likewise; and they were both insufferable.

When they all sat down it was better—to her taste a great deal better—for Frank Churchill grew talkative and gay, making her his first object. Every distinguishing attention that could be paid, was paid to her. To amuse her, and be agreeable in her eyes, seemed all that he cared for—and Emma, glad to be enlivened, not sorry to be flattered, was gay and easy too, and gave him all the friendly encouragement, the admission to be gallant, which she had ever given in the first and most animating period of their acquaintance; but which now, in her own estimation, meant nothing, though in the judgment of most people looking on, it must have had such an appearance as no English word but flirtation could very well describe. "Mr. Frank Churchill and Miss Woodhouse flirted together excessively." They were laying themselves open to that very phrase—and to having it sent off in a letter to Maple Grove by one lady, to Ireland by another. Not that Emma was gay and thoughtless from any real felicity; it was rather because she felt less happy than she had expected. She laughed because she was disappointed; and though she liked him for his attentions, and thought them all, whether in friendship, admiration, or playfulness, extremely judicious, they were not winning back her heart. She still intended him for her friend.

"How much I am obliged to you," said he, "for telling me to come today! If it had not been for you, I should certainly have lost all the happiness of this party. I had quite determined to go away again."

"Yes, you were very cross; and I do not know what about, except that you were too late for the best strawberries. I was a kinder friend than you deserved. But you were humble. You begged hard to be commanded to come."

"Don't say I was cross. I was fatigued. The heat overcame me."

"It is hotter today."

"Not to my feelings. I am perfectly comfortable today."

"You are comfortable because you are under command."

"Your command? Yes."

"Perhaps I intended you to say so, but I meant self-command. You had, somehow or other, broken bounds yesterday, and run away from your own management; but today you are got back again—and as I cannot be always with you, it is best to believe your temper under your own command rather than mine."

"It comes to the same thing. I can have no self-command without a motive. You order me, whether you speak or not. And you can be always with me. You are always with me."

"Dating from three o'clock yesterday. My perpetual influence could not begin earlier, or you would not have been so much out of humour before."

"Three o'clock yesterday! That is your date. I thought I had seen you first in February."

"Your gallantry is really unanswerable. But" (lowering her voice), "nobody speaks except ourselves, and it is rather too much to be talking nonsense for the entertainment of seven silent people."

"I say nothing of which I am ashamed," replied he, with lively impudence. "I saw you first in February. Let everybody on the Hill hear me if they can. Let my accent swell to Mickleham on one side, and Dorking on the other. I saw you first in February." And then whispering: "Our companions are excessively stupid. What shall we do to rouse them? Any nonsense will serve. They *shall* talk. Ladies and gentlemen, I am ordered by Miss Woodhouse (who, wherever she is, presides) to say, that she desires to know what you are all thinking of."

Some laughed, and answered good-humouredly. Miss Bates said a great deal; Mrs. Elton swelled at the idea of Miss Woodhouse's presiding; Mr. Knightley's answer was the most distinct.

"Is Miss Woodhouse sure that she would like to hear what we are all thinking of?"

"Oh, no, no!" cried Emma, laughing as carelessly as she could; "upon no account in the world. It is the very last thing I would stand the brunt of just now. Let me hear anything rather than what you are all thinking of. I will not say quite all. There are one or two perhaps" (glancing at Mr. Weston and Harriet), "whose thoughts I might not be afraid of knowing."

"It is a sort of thing," cried Mrs. Elton emphatically, "which *I* should not have thought myself privileged to inquire into. Though, perhaps, as the *chaperone* of the party—*I* never was in any circle—exploring parties—young ladies—married women——"

Her mutterings were chiefly to her husband; and he murmured, in reply:

"Very true, my love, very true. Exactly so, indeed—quite unheard of—but some ladies say anything. Better pass it off as a joke. Everybody knows what is due to *you*."

"It will not do," whispered Frank to Emma, "they are most of them affronted. I will attack them with more address. Ladies and gentlemen, I am ordered by Miss Woodhouse to say, that she waives her right of knowing exactly what you may all be thinking of, and only requires something very entertaining from each of you, in a general way. Here are seven of you, besides myself (who, she is pleased to say, am very entertaining already), and she only demands from each of you, either one thing very clever, be it prose or verse, original or repeated; or two things moderately clever; or three things very dull indeed; and she engages to laugh heartily at them all."

"Oh! very well," exclaimed Miss Bates; "then I need not be uneasy. 'Three things very dull indeed.' That will just do for me, you know. I shall be sure to say three dull things as soon as ever I open my mouth, shan't I?" (looking round with the most good-humoured dependence on everybody's assent). "Do not you all think I shall?"

Emma could not resist.

"Ah! ma'am but there may be a difficulty. Pardon me, but you will be limited as to number—only three at once."

Miss Bates, deceived by the mock ceremony of her manner, did not immediately catch her meaning; but, when it burst on her, it could not anger, though a slight blush showed that it could pain her.

"Ah! well—to be sure. Yes, I see what she means" (turning to Mr. Knightley), "and I will try to hold my tongue. I must make myself very disagreeable, or she would not have said such a thing to an old friend."

"I like your plan," cried Mr. Weston. "Agreed, agreed. I will do my best. I am making a conundrum. How will a conundrum reckon?"

"Low, I am afraid, sir, very low," answered his son; "but we shall be indulgent, especially to anyone who leads the way."

"No, no," said Emma, "it will not reckon low. A conundrum of Mr. Weston's shall clear him and his next neighbour. Come, sir, pray let me hear it."

"I doubt its being very clever myself," said Mr. Weston. "It is too much a matter of fact; but here it is: What two letters of the alphabet are there that express perfection?"

"What two letters—express perfection? I am sure I do not know."

"Ah! you will never guess. You" (to Emma), "I am certain, will never guess. I will tell you. M. and A. Emma. Do you understand?"

Understanding and gratification came together. It might be a very indifferent piece of wit, but Emma found a great deal to laugh at and enjoy in it: and so did Frank and Harriet. It did not seem to touch the rest of the party equally; some looked very stupid about it, and Mr. Knightley gravely said:

"This explains the sort of clever thing that is wanted, and Mr. Weston has done very well for himself; but he must have knocked up everybody else. *Perfection* should not have come quite so soon."

"Oh! for myself, I protest I must be excused," said Mrs. Elton. "*I* really cannot attempt—I am not at all fond of the sort of thing. I had an acrostic once sent to me upon my own name which I was not at all pleased with. I knew who it came from. An abominable puppy! You know who I mean" (nodding to her husband). "These kind of things are very well at Christmas, when one is sitting round the fire; but quite out of place, in my opinion, when one is exploring about the country in summer. Miss Woodhouse must excuse me. I am not one of those who have witty things at everybody's service. I do not pretend to be a wit. I have a great deal of vivacity in my own way, but I really must be allowed to judge when to speak, and when to hold my tongue. Pass us, if you please, Mr. Churchill. Pass Mr. E., Knightley, Jane, and myself. We have nothing clever to say—not one of us."

"Yes, yes, pray pass *me*," added her husband, with a sort of sneering consciousness; "*I* have nothing to say that can entertain Miss Woodhouse, or any other young lady. An old married man—quite good for nothing. Shall we walk, Augusta?"

"With all my heart. I am really tired of exploring so long on one spot. Come, Jane, take my other arm."

Jane declined it, however, and the husband and wife walked off. "Happy couple!" said Frank Churchill, as soon as they were out of hearing; "how well they suit one another! Very lucky—marrying as they did, upon an acquaintance formed only in a public place! They only knew each other, I think, a few weeks in Bath! Peculiarly lucky! For as to any real knowledge of a person's disposition that Bath, or any public place, can give—it is all nothing; there can be no knowledge. It is only by seeing women in their own homes, among their own set, just as they always are, that you can form any just judgment. Short of that, it is all guess and luck—and will generally be ill-luck. How many a man has committed himself on a short acquaintance, and rued it all the rest of his life!"

Miss Fairfax, who had seldom spoken before, except among her own confederates, spoke now.

"Such things do occur, undoubtedly." She was stopped by a cough. Frank Churchill turned towards her to listen.

"You were speaking," said he gravely. She recovered her voice.

"I was only going to observe, that though such unfortunate circumstances do sometimes occur both to men and women, I cannot imagine them to be very frequent. A hasty and imprudent attachment may arise—but there is generally time to recover from it afterwards. I would be understood to mean, that it can be only weak, irresolute characters (whose happiness must be always at the mercy of chance), who will suffer an unfortunate acquaintance to be an inconvenience, an oppression forever."

He made no answer; merely looked, and bowed in submission; and soon afterwards said, in a lively tone:

"Well, I have so little confidence in my own judgment, that whenever I marry, I hope somebody will choose my wife for me? Will you?" (turning to Emma). "Will you choose a wife for me? I am sure I should like anybody fixed on by you. You provide for the family, you know" (with a smile at his father). "Find somebody for me. I am in no hurry. Adopt her; educate her."

"And make her like myself."

"By all means, if you can."

"Very well. I undertake the commission. You shall have a charming wife."

"She must be very lively and have hazel eyes. I care for nothing else. I shall go abroad for a couple of years—and when I return, I shall come to you for my wife. Remember."

Emma was in no danger of forgetting. It was a commission to touch every favourite feeling. Would not Harriet be the very creature described? Hazel eyes excepted, two years more might make her all that he wished. He might even have Harriet in his thoughts at the moment; who could say? Referring the education to her seemed to imply it.

"Now, ma'am," said Jane to her aunt, "shall we join Mrs. Elton?"

"If you please, my dear. With all my heart. *I* am quite ready. I was ready to have gone with her, but this will do just as well. We shall soon overtake her. There she is—no, that's somebody else. That's one of the ladies in the Irish car party, not at all like her. Well, I declare——"

They walked off, followed in half a minute by Mr. Knightley. Mr. Weston, his son, Emma, and Harriet only remained; and the young man's spirits now rose to a pitch almost unpleasant. Even Emma grew tired at last of flattery and merriment, and wished herself rather walking quietly about with any of the others, or sitting almost alone, and quite unattended to, in tranquil observation of the beautiful views beneath her. The appearance of the servants looking out for them to give notice of the carriages was a joyful sight; and even the bustle of collecting and preparing to depart, and the solicitude of Mrs. Elton to have *her* carriage first, were gladly endured, in the prospect of the quiet drive home which was to close the very questionable enjoyments of this day of pleasure. Such another scheme, composed of so many ill-assorted people, she hoped never to be betrayed into again.

While waiting for the carriage, she found Mr. Knightley by her side. He looked around, as if to see that no one were near, and then said:

"Emma, I must once more speak to you as I have been used to do; a privilege rather endured than allowed, perhaps, but I must still use it. I cannot see you acting wrong, without a remonstrance. How could you be so unfeeling to Miss Bates? How could you be so insolent in your wit to a woman of her character, age, and situation? Emma, I had not thought it possible."

Emma recollected, blushed, was sorry, but tried to laugh it off.

"Nay, how could I help saying what I did? Nobody could have helped it. It was not so very bad. I dare say she did not understand me."

"I assure you she did. She felt your full meaning. She has talked of it since. I wish you could have heard how she talked of it—with what candour and generosity. I wish you could have heard her honouring your forbearance, in being able to pay her such attentions, as she was forever receiving from yourself and your father, when her society must be so irksome."

"Oh!" cried Emma, "I know there is not a better creature in the world; but you must allow, that what is good and what is ridiculous are most unfortunately blended in her."

"They are blended," said he, "I acknowledge; and, were she prosperous, I could allow much for the occasional prevalence of the ridiculous over the good. Were she a woman of fortune, I would leave every harmless absurdity to take its chance; I would not quarrel with you for any liberties of manner. Were she your equal in situation—but, Emma, consider how far this is from being the case. She is poor; she has sunk from the comforts she was born to; and if she live to old age must probably sink more. Her situation should secure your compassion. It was badly done, indeed! You, whom she had known from an infant, whom she had seen grow up from a period when her notice was an honour—to have you now, in thoughtless spirits, and the pride of the moment, laugh at her, humble her— and before her niece, too—and before others, many of whom (certainly *some*) would be entirely guided by *your* treatment of her. This is not pleasant to you, Emma—and it is very far from pleasant to me; but I must, I will—I will tell you truths while I can; satisfied with proving myself your friend by very faithful counsel and trusting that you will some time or other do me greater justice than you can do now."

While they talked they were advancing towards the carriage; it was ready;

and, before she could speak again, he had handed her in. He had misinterpreted the feelings which had kept her face averted, and her tongue motionless. They were combined only of anger against herself, mortification, and deep concern. She had not been able to speak; and, on entering the carriage, sunk back for a moment overcome; then reproaching herself for having taken no leave, making no acknowledgment, parting in apparent sullenness, she looked out with voice and hand eager to show a difference; but it was just too late. He had turned away, and the horses were in motion. She continued to look back, but in vain; and soon, with what appeared unusual speed, they were half-way down the hill, and everything left far behind. She was vexed beyond what could have been expressed—almost beyond what she could conceal. Never had she felt so agitated, mortified, grieved, at any circumstance in her life. She was most forcibly struck. The truth of his representation there was no denying. She felt it at her heart. How could she have been so brutal, so cruel to Miss Bates! How could she have exposed herself to such ill opinion in any one she valued! And how suffer him to leave her without saying one word of gratitude, of concurrence, of common kindness!

Time did not compose her. As she reflected more, she seemed but to feel it more. She never had been so depressed. Happily it was not necessary to speak. There was only Harriet, who seemed not in spirits herself, fagged, and very willing to be silent; and Emma felt the tears running down her cheeks almost all the way home, without being at any trouble to check them, extraordinary as they were.

🖐 *Washington Irving* (*1783–1859*)

Washington Irving was America's first successful professional man of letters, with exceptional talents in many genres: history, satire, short story, and nonfiction essay. He remains today one of America's most historically significant writers, both for his development of a characteristically American prose style and for his distinctive achievements as a pioneering professional writer. Born in New York City, the youngest of eleven children, Irving showed early signs of literary vocation. At age nineteen he published a series of humorous essays on the theater and New York society, modeling his youthful prose style on the Spectator *essays of Joseph Addison. In 1804, he embarked on a two-year tour of Europe, where he proved to be an acute observer of social and cultural institutions in Italy, France, Germany, and England, precisely recording his experiences in notebooks and letters. Upon his return to New York, Irving (in collaboration with his brother William) launched a satirical magazine,* Salmagundi, *which was published through 1807, with a eclectic range of essays and poems on politics, drama, and current events. His next major publication was* A History of New York, *a broadly satirical work that appeared under the pseudonym of Diedrich Knickerbocker in 1809. This comic history was Irving's first major financial and critical success, admired by such English writers as Charles Dickens and Sir Walter Scott.*

Irving's most memorable and distinctive work is The Sketch Book (*1819–20*), *a miscellaneous collection of literary essays, descriptive vignettes, and traveling reminiscences, along with two vigorous short stories set in rural upstate New York:* Rip Van Winkle *and* The Legend of Sleepy Hollow. *Both of these stories are classics of American fiction. Irving's innovative adaptation of traditional German folktales to a New World setting, along with his naturalistic depiction of rural life and his nuanced portrayal of character, is a distinctive contribution to the modern short story genre. The* Legend of Sleepy Hollow *is also notable for its affectionate description of a "lap of land, among high hills, which is one of the quietest places in the whole world." Irving depicts the rural American landscape as an Arcadian sanctuary, troubled only by the endlessly amusing foibles of humankind—most noticeably, in this story, the superstitious reveries of his gawky protagonist, Ichabod Crane. Irving's pastoral ideal is utterly unthreatened by such shenanigans; the American Eden remains unfallen.*

The Legend of Sleepy Hollow

Found Among the Papers of the Late Diedrich Knickerbocker

> A pleasing land of drowsy head it was,
> Of dreams that wave before the half-shut eye;
> And of gay castles in the clouds that pass,
> Forever flushing round a summer sky.
>
> *Castle of Indolence*[1]

In the bosom of one of those spacious coves which indent the eastern shore of the Hudson, at that broad expansion of the river denominated by the ancient Dutch navigators the Tappan Zee, and where they always prudently shortened sail, and implored the protection of St. Nicholas when they crossed, there lies a small market-town or rural port, which by some is called Greensburgh, but which is more generally and properly known by the name of Tarry Town. This name was given, we are told, in former days, by the good housewives of the adjacent country, from the inveterate propensity of their husbands to linger about the village tavern on market days. Be that as it may, I do not vouch for the fact, but merely advert to it, for the sake of being precise and authentic. Not far from this village, perhaps about two miles, there is a little valley, or rather lap of land, among high hills, which is one of the quietest places in the whole world. A small brook glides through it, with just murmur enough to lull one to repose; and the occasional whistle of a quail, or tapping of a woodpecker, is almost the only sound that ever breaks in upon the uniform tranquillity.

I recollect that, when a stripling, my first exploit in squirrel-shooting was in a grove of tall walnut trees that shades one side of the valley. I had wandered into it at noon time, when all nature is peculiarly quiet, and was startled by the roar of my own gun, as it broke the Sabbath stillness around, and was prolonged and reverberated by the angry echoes. If ever I should wish for a retreat, whither I

---

[1] From *The Castle of Indolence* (1:46–49) by James Thomson. For further information on this Scottish poet, see headnote above.

might steal from the world and its distractions, and dream quietly away the remnant of a troubled life, I know of none more promising than this little valley.

From the listless repose of the place, and the peculiar character of its inhabitants, who are descendants from the original Dutch settlers, this sequestered glen has long been known by the name of Sleepy Hollow, and its rustic lads are called the Sleepy Hollow Boys throughout all the neighboring country. A drowsy, dreamy influence seems to hang over the land, and to pervade the very atmosphere. Some say that the place was bewitched by a high German doctor, during the early days of the settlement; others, that an old Indian chief, the prophet or wizard of his tribe, held his pow-wows there before the country was discovered by Master Hendrick Hudson.[2] Certain it is, the place still continues under the sway of some witching power, that holds a spell over the minds of the good people, causing them to walk in a continual reverie. They are given to all kinds of marvellous beliefs; are subject to trances and visions; and frequently see strange sights, and hear music and voices in the air. The whole neighborhood abounds with local tales, haunted spots, and twilight superstitions; stars shoot and meteors glare oftener across the valley than in any other part of the country, and the nightmare, with her whole nine fold, seems to make it the favorite scene of her gambols.

The dominant spirit, however, that haunts this enchanted region, and seems to be commander-in-chief of all the powers of the air, is the apparition of a figure on horseback without a head. It is said by some to be the ghost of a Hessian trooper,[3] whose head had been carried away by a cannon-ball, in some nameless battle during the revolutionary war; and who is ever and anon seen by the country folk, hurrying along in the gloom of night, as if on the wings of the wind. His haunts are not confined to the valley, but extend at times to the adjacent roads, and especially to the vicinity of a church at no great distance. Indeed, certain of the most authentic historians of those parts, who have been careful in collecting and collating the floating facts concerning this spectre, allege that the body of the trooper, having been buried in the church-yard, the ghost rides forth to the scene of battle in nightly quest of his head; and that the rushing speed with which he sometimes passes along the Hollow, like a midnight blast, is owing to his being belated, and in a hurry to get back to the church-yard before daybreak.

Such is the general purport of this legendary superstition, which has furnished materials for many a wild story in that region of shadows; and the spectre is known, at all the country firesides, by the name of the Headless Horseman of Sleepy Hollow.

It is remarkable that the visionary propensity I have mentioned is not confined to the native inhabitants of the valley, but is unconsciously imbibed by every one who resides there for a time. However wide awake they may have been before they entered that sleepy region, they are sure, in a little time, to inhale the witching influence of the air, and begin to grow imaginative—to dream dreams, and see apparitions.

---

[2] Henry Hudson (d. 1611), English navigator and explorer.

[3] German mercenaries from Hesse who fought for the British during the American Revolution.

I mention this peaceful spot with all possible laud; for it is in such little retired Dutch valleys, found here and there embosomed in the great State of New-York, that population, manners, and customs, remain fixed; while the great torrent of migration and improvement, which is making such incessant changes in other parts of this restless country, sweeps by them unobserved. They are like those little nooks of still water which border a rapid stream; where we may see the straw and bubble riding quietly at anchor, or slowly revolving in their mimic harbor, undisturbed by the rush of the passing current. Though many years have elapsed since I trod the drowsy shades of Sleepy Hollow, yet I question whether I should not still find the same trees and the same families vegetating in its sheltered bosom.

In this by-place of nature, there abode, in a remote period of American history, that is to say, some thirty years since, a worthy wight of the name of Ichabod Crane; who sojourned, or, as he expressed it, "tarried," in Sleepy Hollow, for the purpose of instructing the children of the vicinity. He was a native of Connecticut; a State which supplies the Union with pioneers for the mind as well as for the forest, and sends forth yearly its legions of frontier woodsmen and country schoolmasters. The cognomen of Crane was not inapplicable to his person. He was tall, but exceedingly lank, with narrow shoulders, long arms and legs, hands that dangled a mile out of his sleeves, feet that might have served for shovels, and his whole frame most loosely hung together. His head was small, and flat at top, with huge ears, large green glassy eyes, and a long snipe nose, so that it looked like a weather-cock, perched upon his spindle neck, to tell which way the wind blew. To see him striding along the profile of a hill on a windy day, with his clothes bagging and fluttering about him, one might have mistaken him for the genius of famine descending upon the earth, or some scarecrow eloped from a cornfield.

His schoolhouse was a low building of one large room, rudely constructed of logs; the windows partly glazed, and partly patched with leaves of old copybooks. It was most ingeniously secured at vacant hours, by a withe[4] twisted in the handle of the door, and stakes set against the window shutters; so that, though a thief might get in with perfect ease, he would find some embarrassment in getting out; an idea most probably borrowed by the architect, Yost Van Houten, from the mystery of an eel-pot.[5] The schoolhouse stood in a rather lonely but pleasant situation, just at the foot of a woody hill, with a brook running close by, and a formidable birch tree growing at one end of it. From hence the low murmur of his pupils' voices, conning over their lessons, might be heard in a drowsy summer's day, like the hum of a beehive; interrupted now and then by the authoritative voice of the master, in the tone of menace or command; or, peradventure, by the appalling sound of the birch, as he urged some tardy loiterer along the flowery path of knowledge. Truth to say, he was a conscientious man, and ever bore in mind the golden maxim, "Spare the rod and spoil the child." Ichabod Crane's scholars certainly were not spoiled.

I would not have it imagined, however, that he was one of those cruel poten-

---

[4] Willow branch.

[5] Eel trap.

tates of the school, who joy in the smart of their subjects; on the contrary, he administered justice with discrimination rather than severity; taking the burthen off the backs of the weak, and laying it on those of the strong. Your mere puny stripling, that winced at the least flourish of the rod, was passed by with indulgence; but the claims of justice were satisfied by inflicting a double portion on some little, tough, wrong-headed, broad-skirted Dutch urchin, who sulked and swelled and grew dogged and sullen beneath the birch. All this he called "doing his duty by their parents;" and he never inflicted a chastisement without following it by the assurance, so consolatory to the smarting urchin, that "he would remember it, and thank him for it the longest day he had to live."

When school hours were over, he was even the companion and playmate of the larger boys; and on holiday afternoons would convoy some of the smaller ones home, who happened to have pretty sisters, or good housewives for mothers, noted for the comforts of the cupboard. Indeed it behooved him to keep on good terms with his pupils. The revenue arising from his school was small, and would have been scarcely sufficient to furnish him with daily bread, for he was a huge feeder, and though lank, had the dilating powers of an anaconda; but to help out his maintenance, he was, according to country custom in those parts, boarded and lodged at the houses of the farmers, whose children he instructed. With these he lived successively a week at a time; thus going the rounds of the neighborhood, with all his wordly effects tied up in a cotton handkerchief.

That all this might not be too onerous on the purses of his rustic patrons, who are apt to consider the costs of schooling a grievous burden, and schoolmasters as mere drones, he had various ways of rendering himself both useful and agreeable. He assisted the farmers occasionally in the lighter labors of their farms; helped to make hay; mended the fences; took the horses to water; drove the cows from pasture; and cut wood for the winter fire. He laid aside, too, all the dominant dignity and absolute sway with which he lorded it in his little empire, the school, and became wonderfully gentle and ingratiating. He found favor in the eyes of the mothers, by petting the children, particularly the youngest; and like the lion bold, which whilom so magnanimously the lamb did hold, he would sit with a child on one knee, and rock a cradle with his foot for whole hours together.

In addition to his other vocations, he was the singing-master of the neighborhood, and picked up many bright shillings by instructing the young folks in psalmody. It was a matter of no little vanity to him, on Sundays, to take his station in front of the church gallery, with a band of chosen singers; where, in his own mind, he completely carried away the palm from the parson. Certain it is, his voice resounded far above all the rest of the congregation; and there are peculiar quavers still to be heard in that church, and which may even be heard half a mile off, quite to the opposite side of the mill-pond, on a still Sunday morning, which are said to be legitimately descended from the nose of Ichabod Crane. Thus, by divers little make-shifts in that ingenious way which is commonly denominated "by hook and by crook," the worthy pedagogue got on tolerably enough, and was thought, by all who understood nothing of the labor of headwork, to have a wonderfully easy life of it.

The schoolmaster is generally a man of some importance in the female circle of a rural neighborhood; being considered a kind of idle gentlemanlike personage, of vastly superior taste and accomplishments to the rough country swains, and, indeed, inferior in learning only to the parson. His appearance, therefore, is apt to occasion some little stir at the tea-table of a farmhouse, and the addition of a supernumerary dish of cakes or sweetmeats, or, peradventure, the parade of a silver tea-pot. Our man of letters, therefore, was peculiarly happy in the smiles of all the country damsels. How he would figure among them in the church-yard, between services on Sundays! gathering grapes for them from the wild vines that overrun the surrounding trees; reciting for their amusement all the epitaphs on the tombstones; or sauntering, with a whole bevy of them, along the banks of the adjacent mill-pond; while the more bashful country bumpkins hung sheepishly back, envying his superior elegance and address.

From his half itinerant life, also, he was a kind of travelling gazette, carrying the whole budget of local gossip from house to house; so that his appearance was always greeted with satisfaction. He was, moreover, esteemed by the women as a man of great erudition, for he had read several books quite through, and was a perfect master of Cotton Mather's history of New-England Witchcraft, in which, by the way, he most firmly and potently believed.

He was, in fact, an odd mixture of small shrewdness and simple credulity. His appetite for the marvellous, and his powers of digesting it, were equally extraordinary; and both had been increased by his residence in this spellbound region. No tale was too gross or monstrous for his capacious swallow. It was often his delight, after his school was dismissed in the afternoon, to stretch himself on the rich bed of clover, bordering the little brook that whimpered by his school-house, and there con over old Mather's direful tales, until the gathering dusk of the evening made the printed page a mere mist before his eyes. Then, as he wended his way, by swamp and stream and awful woodland, to the farm-house where he happened to be quartered, every sound of nature, at that witching hour, fluttered his excited imagination: the moan of the whip-poor-will from the hillside; the boding cry of the tree toad, that harbinger of storm; the dreary hooting of the screech owl, or the sudden rustling in the thicket of birds frightened from their roost. The fireflies, too, which sparkled most vividly in the darkest places, now and then startled him, as one of uncommon brightness would stream across his path; and if, by chance, a huge blockhead of a beetle came winging his blundering flight against him, the poor varlet was ready to give up the ghost, with the idea that he was struck with a witch's token. His only resource on such occasions, either to drown thought, or drive away evil spirits, was to sing psalm tunes; and the good people of Sleepy Hollow, as they sat by their doors of an evening, were often filled with awe, at hearing his nasal melody, "in linked sweetness long drawn out," floating from the distant hill, or along the dusky road.

Another of his sources of fearful pleasure was, to pass long winter evenings with the old Dutch wives, as they sat spinning by the fire, with a row of apples roasting and spluttering along the hearth, and listen to their marvellous tales of ghosts and goblins, and haunted fields, and haunted brooks, and haunted bridges, and haunted houses, and particularly of the headless horseman, or galloping Hessian of the Hollow, as they sometimes called him. He would delight them equally by his anecdotes of witchcraft, and of the direful omens and portentous sights and sounds in the air, which prevailed in the earlier times of Connecticut; and would frighten them wofully with speculations upon comets and shooting stars; and with the alarming fact that the world did absolutely turn round, and that they were half the time topsy-turvy!

But if there was a pleasure in all this, while snugly cuddling in the chimney corner of a chamber that was all of a ruddy glow from the crackling wood fire, and where, of course, no spectre dared to show his face, it was dearly purchased by the terrors of his subsequent walk homewards. What fearful shapes and shadows beset his path amidst the dim and ghastly glare of a snowy night!—With what wistful look did he eye every trembling ray of light streaming across the waste fields from some distant window!—How often was he appalled by some shrub covered with snow, which, like a sheeted spectre, beset his very path!— How often did he shrink with curdling awe at the sound of his own steps on the frosty crust beneath his feet; and dread to look over his shoulder, lest he should behold some uncouth being tramping close behind him!—and how often was he thrown into complete dismay by some rushing blast, howling among the trees, in the idea that it was the Galloping Hessian on one of his nightly scourings!

All these, however, were mere terrors of the night, phantoms of the mind that walk in darkness; and though he had seen many spectres in his time, and been more than once beset by Satan in divers shapes, in his lonely perambulations, yet daylight put an end to all these evils; and he would have passed a pleasant life of it, in despite of the devil and all his works, if his path had not been crossed by a being that causes more perplexity to mortal man than ghosts, goblins, and the whole race of witches put together, and that was—a woman.

Among the musical disciples who assembled, one evening in each week, to receive his instructions in psalmody, was Katrina Van Tassel, the daughter and only child of a substantial Dutch farmer. She was a blooming lass of fresh eighteen; plump as a partridge; ripe and melting and rosy cheeked as one of her father's peaches, and universally famed, not merely for her beauty, but her vast expectations. She was withal a little of a coquette, as might be perceived even in her dress, which was a mixture of ancient and modern fashions, as most suited to set off her charms. She wore the ornaments of pure yellow gold, which her great-great-grandmother had brought over from Saardam; the tempting stomacher of the olden time; and withal a provokingly short petticoat, to display the prettiest foot and ankle in the country round.

Ichabod Crane had a soft and foolish heart towards the sex; and it is not to be wondered at, that so tempting a morsel soon found favor in his eyes; more especially after he had visited her in her paternal mansion. Old Baltus Van Tassel was a perfect picture of a thriving, contented, liberal-hearted farmer. He seldom, it is true, sent either his eyes or his thoughts beyond the boundaries of his own farm; but within those every thing was snug, happy, and well-conditioned. He was satisfied with his wealth, but not proud of it; and piqued himself upon the hearty abundance, rather than the style in which he lived. His stronghold was situated on the banks of the Hudson, in one of those green, sheltered, fertile nooks, in which the Dutch farmers are so fond of nestling. A great elm tree spread its broad branches over it; at the foot of which bubbled up a spring of the softest and sweetest water, in a little well, formed of a barrel; and then stole sparkling away through the grass, to a neighboring brook, that bubbled along among alders and dwarf willows. Hard by the farmhouse was a vast barn, that might have served for a church; every window and crevice of which seemed bursting forth with the treasures of the farm; the flail was busily resounding within it from morning to night; swallows and martins skimmed twittering about the eaves; and rows of pigeons, some with one eye turned up, as if watching the weather, some with their heads under their wings, or buried in their bosoms, and others swelling, and cooing, and bowing about their dames, were enjoying the sunshine on the roof. Sleek unwieldy porkers were grunting in the repose and abundance of their pens; whence sallied forth, now and then, troops of sucking pigs, as if to snuff the air. A stately squadron of snowy geese were riding in an adjoining pond, convoying whole fleets of ducks; regiments of turkeys were gobbling through the farmyard, and guinea fowls fretting about it like ill-tempered housewives, with their peevish discontented cry. Before the barn door strutted the gallant cock, that pattern of a husband, a warrior, and a fine gentleman, clapping his burnished wings, and crowing in the pride and gladness of his heart—sometimes tearing up the earth with his feet, and then generously calling his ever-hungry family of wives and children to enjoy the rich morsel which he had discovered.

The pedagogue's mouth watered, as he looked upon this sumptuous promise of luxurious winter fare. In his devouring mind's eye, he pictured to himself every roasting pig running about with a pudding in his belly, and an apple in his mouth; the pigeons were snugly put to bed in a comfortable pie, and tucked in with a coverlet of crust; the geese were swimming in their own gravy; and the ducks pairing cosily in dishes, like snug married couples, with a decent competency of onion sauce. In the porkers he saw carved out the future sleek side of bacon, and juicy relishing ham; not a turkey but he beheld daintily trussed up, with its gizzard under its wing, and, peradventure, a necklace of savory sausages; and even bright chanticleer himself lay sprawling on his back, in a side dish, with uplifted claws, as if craving that quarter which his chivalrous spirit disdained to ask while living.

As the enraptured Ichabod fancied all this, and as he rolled his great green eyes over the fat meadowlands, the rich fields of wheat, of rye, of buckwheat, and Indian corn, and the orchards burthened with ruddy fruit, which surrounded the warm tenement of Van Tassel, his heart yearned after the damsel who was to inherit these domains, and his imagination expanded with the idea, how they might be readily turned into cash, and the money invested in immense tracts of wild land, and shingle palaces in the wilderness. Nay, his busy fancy already realized his hopes, and presented to him the blooming Katrina, with a whole family of children, mounted on the top of a wagon loaded with household trumpery, with pots and kettles dangling beneath; and he beheld himself bestriding a pacing mare, with a colt at her heels, setting out for Kentucky, Tennessee, or the Lord knows where.

When he entered the house the conquest of his heart was complete. It was one of those spacious farmhouses, with high-ridged, but lowly sloping roofs, built in the style handed down from the first Dutch settlers; the low projecting eaves forming a piazza along the front, capable of being closed up in bad weather. Under this were hung flails, harness, various utensils of husbandry, and nets for fishing in the neighboring river. Benches were built along the sides for summer use; and a great spinning-wheel at one end, and a churn at the other, showed the various uses to which this important porch might be devoted. From this piazza the wondering Ichabod entered the hall, which formed the centre of the mansion and the place of usual residence. Here, rows of resplendent pewter, ranged on a long dresser, dazzled his eyes. In one corner stood a huge bag of wool ready to be spun; in another a quantity of linsey-woolsey just from the loom; ears of Indian corn, and strings of dried apples and peaches, hung in gay festoons along the walls, mingled with the gaud of red peppers; and a door left ajar gave him a peep into the best parlor, where the claw-footed chairs, and dark mahogany tables, shone like mirrors; and irons, with their accompanying shovel and tongs, glistened from their covert of asparagus tops; mock oranges and conch shells decorated the mantelpiece; strings of various colored birds' eggs were suspended above it: a great ostrich egg was hung from the center of the room, and a corner cupboard, knowingly left open, displayed immense treasures of old silver and well-mended china.

From the moment Ichabod laid his eyes upon these regions of delight, the peace of his mind was at an end, and his only study was how to gain the affections of the peerless daughter of Van Tassel. In this enterprise, however, he had more real difficulties than generally fell to the lot of a knight-errant of yore, who seldom had any thing but giants, enchanters, fiery dragons, and such like easily conquered adversaries, to contend with; and had to make his way merely through gates of iron and brass, and walls of adamant, to the castle keep, where the lady of his heart was confined; all which he achieved as easily as a man would carve his way to the center of a Christmas pie; and then the lady gave him her hand as a matter of course. Ichabod, on the contrary, had to win his way to the heart of a country coquette, beset with a labyrinth of whims and caprices, which were forever presenting new difficulties and impediments; and he had to encounter a host of fearful adversaries of real flesh and blood, the numerous rustic admirers, who beset every portal to her heart; keeping a watchful and angry eye upon each other, but ready to fly out in the common cause against any new competitor.

Among these the most formidable was a burly, roaring, roystering blade, of the name of Abraham, or, according to the Dutch abbreviation, Brom Van Brunt, the hero of the country round, which rang with his feats of strength and hardihood. He was broad-shouldered and double-jointed, with short curly black hair, and a bluff, but not unpleasant countenance, having a mingled air of fun and arrogance. From his Herculean frame and great powers of limb, he had received the nickname of Brom Bones, by which he was universally known. He was famed for great knowledge and skill in horsemanship, being as dexterous on horseback as a Tartar. He was foremost at all races and cockfights; and, with the ascendency which bodily strength acquires in rustic life, was the umpire in all disputes, setting his hat on one side, and giving his decisions with an air and tone admitting of no gainsay or appeal. He was always ready for either a fight or a frolic; but had more mischief than ill-will in his composition; and, with all his overbearing roughness, there was a strong dash of waggish good humor at bottom. He had three or four boon companions, who regarded him as their model, and at the head of whom he scoured the country, attending every scene of feud or merriment for miles round. In cold weather he was distinguished by a fur cap, surmounted with a flaunting fox's tail; and when the folks at a country gathering descried this well-known crest at a distance, whisking about among a squad of hard riders, they always stood by for a squall. Sometimes his crew would be heard dashing along past the farmhouses at midnight, with whoop and halloo, like a troop of Don Cossacks;[6] and the old dames, startled out of their sleep, would listen for a moment till the hurry-scurry had clattered by, and then exclaim, "Ay, there goes Brom Bones and his gang!" The neighbors looked upon him with a mixture of awe, admiration, and good will; and when any madcap prank, or rustic brawl, occurred in the vicinity, always shook their heads, and warranted Brom Bones was at the bottom of it.

This rantipole[7] hero had for some time singled out the blooming Katrina for the object of his uncouth gallantries, and though his amorous toyings were something like the gentle caresses and endearments of a bear, yet it was whispered that she did not altogether discourage his hopes. Certain it is, his advances were signals for rival candidates to retire, who felt no inclination to cross a lion in his amours; insomuch, that when his horse was seen tied to Van Tassel's paling,[8] on a Sunday night, a sure sign that his master was courting, or as it is termed, "sparking," within, all other suitors passed by in despair, and carried the war into other quarters.

Such was the formidable rival with whom Ichabod Crane had to contend, and, considering all things, a stouter man than he would have shrunk from the competition, and a wiser man would have despaired. He had, however, a happy mixture of pliability and perseverance in his nature; he was in form and spirit like a supple-jack[9]—yielding, but tough; though he bent, he never broke; and though he bowed beneath the slightest pressure, yet, the moment it was away—jerk! he was as erect, and carried his head as high as ever.

To have taken the field openly against his rival would have been madness; for he was not a man to be thwarted in his amours, any more than that stormy lover, Achilles.[10] Ichabod, therefore, made his advances in a quiet and gently insinuating manner. Under cover of his character of singing-master, he made frequent visits at the farmhouse; not that he had any thing to apprehend from the meddle-

---

[6] Russian cavalry.

[7] Rowdy; rambunctious.

[8] Boundary fence.

[9] Walking stick made from tough, flexible wood.

[10] The hero of Homer's *Iliad*, Achilles sulks in his tent when the captive maiden Briseis is taken from him by King Agamemnon.

some interference of parents, which is so often a stumbling block in the path of lovers. Balt Van Tassel was an easy indulgent soul; he loved his daughter better even than his pipe, and, like a reasonable man and an excellent father, let her have her way in every thing. His notable little wife, too, had enough to do to attend to her housekeeping and manage her poultry; for, as she sagely observed, ducks and geese are foolish things, and must be looked after, but girls can take care of themselves. Thus while the busy dame bustled about the house, or plied her spinning-wheel at one end of the piazza, honest Balt would sit smoking his evening pipe at the other, watching the achievements of a little wooden warrior, who, armed with a sword in each hand, was most valiantly fighting the wind on the pinnacle of the barn. In the mean time, Ichabod would carry on his suit with the daughter by the side of the spring under the great elm, or sauntering along in the twilight, that hour so favorable to the lover's eloquence.

I profess not to know how women's hearts are wooed and won. To me they have always been matters of riddle and admiration. Some seem to have but one vulnerable point, or door of access; while others have a thousand avenues, and may be captured in a thousand different ways. It is a great triumph of skill to gain the former, but a still greater proof of generalship to maintain possession of the latter, for the man must battle for his fortress at every door and window. He who wins a thousand common hearts is therefore entitled to some renown; but he who keeps undisputed sway over the heart of a coquette, is indeed a hero. Certain it is, this was not the case with the redoubtable Brom Bones; and from the moment Ichabod Crane made his advances, the interests of the former evidently declined; his horse was no longer seen tied at the palings on Sunday nights, and a deadly feud gradually arose between him and the preceptor of Sleepy Hollow.

Brom, who had a degree of rough chivalry in his nature, would fain have carried matters to open warfare, and have settled their pretensions to the lady, according to the mode of those most concise and simple reasoners, the knight-serrant of yore—by single combat; but Ichabod was too conscious of the superior might of his adversary to enter the lists against him: he had overheard a boast of Bones, that he would "double the schoolmaster up, and lay him on a shelf of his own schoolhouse;" and he was too wary to give him an opportunity. There was something extremely provoking in this obstinately pacific system; it left Brom no alternative but to draw upon the funds of rustic waggery in his disposition, and to play off boorish practical jokes upon his rival. Ichabod became the object of whimsical persecution to Bones, and his gang of rough riders. They harried his hitherto peaceful domains; smoked out his singing school, by stopping up the chimney; broke into the school-house at night, in spite of its formidable fastenings of withe and window stakes, and turned every thing topsy-turvy: so that the poor schoolmaster began to think all the witches in the country held their meetings there. But what was still more annoying, Brom took all opportunities of turning him into ridicule in presence of his mistress, and had a scoundrel dog whom he taught to whine in the most ludicrous manner, and introduced as a rival of Ichabod's to instruct her in psalmody.

In this way matters went on for some time, without producing any material

effect on the relative situation of the contending powers. On a fine autumnal afternoon, Ichabod, in pensive mood, sat enthroned on the lofty stool whence he
usually watched all the concerns of his little literary realm. In his hand he swayed
a ferule, that sceptre of despotic power; the birch of justice reposed on three
nails, behind the throne, a constant terror to evil doers; while on the desk before
him might be seen sundry contraband articles and prohibited weapons, detected
upon the persons of idle urchins; such as half-munched apples, popguns,
whirligigs, fly cages, and whole legions of rampant little paper game-cocks. Apparently there had been some appalling act of justice recently inflicted, for his
scholars were all busily intent upon their books, or slyly whispering behind them
with one eye kept upon the master; and a kind of buzzing stillness reigned
throughout the schoolroom. It was suddenly interrupted by the appearance of a
Negro, in tow-cloth jacket and trousers, a round-crowned fragment of a hat, like
the cap of Mercury,[11] and mounted on the back of a ragged, wild, half-broken
colt, which he managed with a rope by way of halter. He came clattering up to
the school door with an invitation to Ichabod to attend a merry-making or
"quilting frolic," to be held that evening at Mynheer Van Tassel's; and having delivered his message with that air of importance, and effort at fine language,
which a Negro is apt to display on petty embassies of the kind, he dashed over
the brook, and was seen scampering away up the hollow, full of the importance
and hurry of his mission.

All was now bustle and hubbub in the late quiet schoolroom. The scholars
were hurried through their lessons, without stopping at trifles; those who were
nimble skipped over half with impunity, and those who were tardy, had a smart
application now and then in the rear, to quicken their speed, or help them over a
tall word. Books were flung aside without being put away on the shelves, ink-
stands were overturned, benches thrown down, and the whole school was turned
loose an hour before the usual time, bursting forth like a legion of young imps,
yelping and racketing about the green, in joy at their early emancipation.

The gallant Ichabod now spent at least an extra half hour at his toilet, brushing and furbishing up his best, and indeed only, suit of rusty black, and arranging
his looks by a bit of broken looking-glass, that hung up in the schoolhouse. That
he might make his appearance before his mistress in the true style of a cavalier,
he borrowed a horse from the farmer with whom he was domiciliated, a choleric
old Dutchman, of the name of Hans Van Ripper, and, thus gallantly mounted, issued forth, like a knight-errant in quest of adventures. But it is meet I should, in
the true spirit of romantic story, give some account of the looks and equipments
of my hero and his steed. The animal he bestrode was a broken-down plough
horse, that had outlived almost every thing but his viciousness. He was gaunt and
shagged, with a ewe neck and a head like a hammer; his rusty mane and tail were
tangled and knotted with burrs; one eye had lost its pupil, and was glaring and
spectral; but the other had the gleam of a genuine devil in it. Still he must have
had fire and mettle in his day, if we may judge from the name he bore of Gunpowder. He had, in fact, been a favorite steed of his master's, the choleric

---

[11] A winged cap worn by Mercury, messenger to the gods.

Van Ripper, who was a furious rider, and had infused, very probably, some of his own spirit into the animal; for, old and broken-down as he looked, there was more of the lurking devil in him than in any young filly in the country.

Ichabod was a suitable figure for such a steed. He rode with short stirrups, which brought his knees nearly up to the pommel of the saddle; his sharp elbows stuck out like grasshoppers'; he carried his whip perpendicularly in his hand, like a sceptre, and, as his horse jogged on, the motion of his arms was not unlike the flapping of a pair of wings. A small wool hat rested on the top of his nose, for so his scanty strip of forehead might be called; and the skirts of his black coat fluttered out almost to the horse's tail. Such was the appearance of Ichabod and his steed, as they shambled out of the gate of Hans Van Ripper, and it was altogether such an apparition as is seldom to be met with in broad daylight.

It was, as I have said, a fine autumnal day, the sky was clear and serene, and nature wore that rich and golden livery which we always associate with the idea of abundance. The forests had put on their sober brown and yellow, while some trees of the tenderer kind had been nipped by the frosts into brilliant dyes of orange, purple, and scarlet. Streaming files of wild ducks began to make their appearance high in the air; the bark of the squirrel might be heard from the groves of beech and hickory nuts, and the pensive whistle of the quail at intervals from the neighboring stubble field.

The small birds were taking their farewell banquets. In the fulness of their revelry, they fluttered, chirping and frolicking, from bush to bush, and tree to tree, capricious from the very profusion and variety around them. There was the honest cock-robin, the favorite game of stripling sportsmen, with its loud querulous note; and the twittering blackbirds flying in sable clouds; and the golden-winged woodpecker, with his crimson crest, his broad black gorget, and splendid plumage; and the cedar bird, with its red-tipt wings and yellow-tipt tail, and its little monteiro cap of feathers; and the blue jay, that noisy coxcomb, in his gay light blue coat and white under-clothes; screaming and chattering, nodding and bobbing and bowing, and pretending to be on good terms with every songster of the grove.

As Ichabod jogged slowly on his way, his eye, ever open to every symptom of culinary abundance, ranged with delight over the treasures of jolly autumn. On all sides he beheld vast store of apples; some hanging in oppressive opulence on the trees; some gathered into baskets and barrels for the market; others heaped up in rich piles for the cider-press. Farther on he beheld great fields of Indian corn, with its golden ears peeping from their leafy coverts, and holding out the promise of cakes and hasty pudding; and the yellow pumpkins lying beneath them, turning up their fair round bellies to the sun, and giving ample prospects of the most luxurious of pies; and anon he passed the fragrant buckwheat fields, breathing the odor of the bee-hive, and as he beheld them, soft anticipations stole over his mind of dainty slapjacks, well buttered, and garnished with honey or treacle, by the delicate little dimpled hand of Katrina Van Tassel.

Thus feeding his mind with many sweet thoughts and "sugared suppositions," he journeyed along the sides of a range of hills which look out upon some of the goodliest scenes of the mighty Hudson. The sun gradually wheeled his broad disk down into the west. The wide bosom of the Tappan Zee lay motionless and glassy, excepting that here and there a gentle undulation waved and prolonged the blue shadow of the distant mountain. A few amber clouds floated in the sky, without a breath of air to move them. The horizon was of a fine golden tint, changing gradually into a pure apple green, and from that into the deep blue of the mid-heaven. A slanting ray lingered on the woody crests of the precipices that overhung some parts of the river, giving greater depth to the dark gray and purple of their rocky sides. A sloop was loitering in the distance, dropping slowly down with the tide, her sail hanging uselessly against the mast; and as the reflection of the sky gleamed along the still water, it seemed as if the vessel was suspended in the air.

It was toward evening that Ichabod arrived at the castle of the Heer Van Tassel, which he found thronged with the pride and flower of the adjacent country. Old farmers, a spare leathern-faced race, in homespun coats and breeches, blue stockings, huge shoes, and magnificent pewter buckles. Their brisk withered little dames, in close crimped caps, long-waisted short-gowns, homespun petticoats, with scissors and pincushions, and gay calico pockets hanging on the outside. Buxom lasses, almost as antiquated as their mothers, excepting where a straw hat, a fine ribbon, or perhaps a white frock, gave symptoms of city innovation. The sons, in short square-skirted coats with rows of stupendous brass buttons, and their hair generally queued in the fashion of the times, especially if they could procure an eel skin for the purpose, it being esteemed, throughout the country, as a potent nourisher and strengthener of the hair.

Brom Bones, however, was the hero of the scene, having come to the gathering on his favorite steed Daredevil, a creature, like himself, full of mettle and mischief, and which no one but himself could manage. He was, in fact, noted for preferring vicious animals, given to all kinds of tricks, which kept the rider in constant risk of his neck, for he held a tractable well-broken horse as unworthy of a lad of spirit.

Fain would I pause to dwell upon the world of charms that burst upon the enraptured gaze of my hero, as he entered the state parlor of Van Tassel's mansion. Not those of the bevy of buxom lasses, with their luxurious display of red and white; but the ample charms of a genuine Dutch country tea-table, in the sumptuous time of autumn. Such heaped-up platters of cakes of various and almost indescribable kinds, known only to experienced Dutch housewives! There was the doughty dough-nut, the tenderer oly koek,[12] and the crisp and crumbling cruller; sweet cakes and short cakes, ginger cakes and honey cakes, and the whole family of cakes. And then there were apple pies and peach pies and pumpkin pies; besides slices of ham and smoked beef; and moreover delectable dishes of preserved plums, and peaches, and pears, and quinces; not to mention broiled shad and roasted chickens; together with bowls of milk and cream, all mingled higgledy-piggledy, pretty much as I have enumerated them, with the motherly tea-pot sending up its clouds of vapor from the midst—Heaven bless the mark! I want breath and time to discuss this banquet as it deserves, and am too eager to get on

---

[12] Deep-fried shortbread (Dutch).

with my story. Happily, Ichabod Crane was not in so great a hurry as his historian, but did ample justice to every dainty.

He was a kind and thankful creature, whose heart dilated in proportion as his skin was filled with good cheer; and whose spirits rose with eating as some men's do with drink. He could not help, too, rolling his large eyes round him as he ate, and chuckling with the possibility that he might one day be lord of all this scene of almost unimaginable luxury and splendor. Then, he thought, how soon he'd turn his back upon the old school-house; snap his fingers in the face of Hans Van Ripper, and every other niggardly patron, and kick any itinerant pedagogue out of doors that should dare to call him comrade!

Old Baltus Van Tassel moved about among his guests with a face dilated with content and good humor, round and jolly as the harvest moon. His hospitable attentions were brief, but expressive, being confined to a shake of the hand, a slap on the shoulder, a loud laugh, and a pressing invitation to "fall to, and help themselves."

And now the sound of the music from the common room, or hall, summoned to the dance. The musician was an old gray-headed Negro, who had been the itinerant orchestra of the neighborhood for more than half a century. His instrument was as old and battered as himself. The greater part of the time he scraped on two or three strings, accompanying every movement of the bow with a motion of the head; bowing almost to the ground, and stamping with his foot whenever a fresh couple were to start.

Ichabod prided himself upon his dancing as much as upon his vocal powers. Not a limb, not a fibre about him was idle; and to have seen his loosely hung frame in full motion, and clattering about the room, you would have thought Saint Vitus[13] himself, that blessed patron of the dance, was figuring before you in person. He was the admiration of all the Negroes; who, having gathered, of all ages and sizes, from the farm and the neighborhood, stood forming a pyramid of shining black faces at every door and window, gazing with delight at the scene, rolling their white eyeballs, and showing grinning rows of ivory from ear to ear. How could the flogger of urchins be otherwise than animated and joyous? the lady of his heart was his partner in the dance, and smiling graciously in reply to all his amorous oglings; while Brom Bones, sorely smitten with love and jealousy, sat brooding by himself in one corner.

When the dance was at an end, Ichabod was attracted to a knot of the sager folks, who, with old Van Tassel, sat smoking at one end of the piazza, gossiping over former times, and drawing out long stories about the war.

This neighborhood, at the time of which I am speaking, was one of those highly favored places which abound with chronicle and great men. The British and American line had run near it during the war; it had, therefore, been the scene of marauding, and infested with refugees, cow-boys, and all kinds of border chivalry. Just sufficient time had elapsed to enable each story-teller to dress up his tale with a little becoming fiction, and, in the indistinctness of his recollection, to make himself the hero of every exploit.

---

[13] Fourth-century Sicilian martyr, often invoked for protection against epilepsy and other nervous disorders.

There was the story of Doffue Martling, a large blue-bearded Dutchman, who had nearly taken a British frigate with an old iron nine-pounder from a mud breastwork, only that his gun burst at the sixth discharge. And there was an old gentleman who shall be nameless, being too rich a mynheer to be lightly mentioned, who, in the battle of White-plains,[14] being an excellent master of defence, parried a musket ball with a small sword, insomuch that he absolutely felt it whiz round the blade, and glance off at the hilt: in proof of which, he was ready at any time to show the sword, with the hilt a little bent. There were several more that had been equally great in the field, not one of whom but was persuaded that he had a considerable hand in bringing the war to a happy termination.

But all these were nothing to the tales of ghosts and apparitions that succeeded. The neighborhood is rich in legendary treasures of the kind. Local tales and superstitions thrive best in these sheltered long-settled retreats; but are trampled under foot by the shifting throng that forms the population of most of our country places. Besides, there is no encouragement for ghosts in most of our villages, for they have scarcely had time to finish their first nap, and turn themselves in their graves, before their surviving friends have travelled away from the neighborhood; so that when they turn out at night to walk their rounds, they have no acquaintance left to call upon. This is perhaps the reason why we so seldom hear of ghosts except in our long-established Dutch communities.

The immediate cause, however, of the prevalence of supernatural stories in these parts, was doubtless owing to the vicinity of Sleepy Hollow. There was a contagion in the very air that blew from that haunted region; it breathed forth an atmosphere of dreams and fancies infecting all the land. Several of the Sleepy Hollow people were present at Van Tassel's, and, as usual, were doling out their wild and wonderful legends. Many dismal tales were told about funeral trains, and mourning cries and wailings heard and seen about the great tree where the unfortunate Major André[15] was taken, and which stood in the neighborhood. Some mention was made also of the woman in white, that haunted the dark glen at Raven Rock, and was often heard to shriek on winter nights before a storm, having perished there in the snow. The chief part of the stories, however, turned upon the favorite spectre of Sleepy Hollow, the headless horseman, who had been heard several times of late, patrolling the country; and, it was said, tethered his horse nightly among the graves in the church-yard.

The sequestered situation of this church seems always to have made it a favorite haunt of troubled spirits. It stands on a knoll, surrounded by locust trees and lofty elms, from among which its decent whitewashed walls shine modestly forth, like Christian purity beaming through the shades of retirement. A gentle slope descends from it to a silver sheet of water, bordered by high trees, between which, peeps may be caught at the blue hills of the Hudson. To look upon its grass-grown yard, where the sunbeams seem to sleep so quietly, one would think that there at least the dead might rest in peace. On one side of the church ex-

---

[14] George Washington's forces were defeated by the British at the battle of White Plains, north of New York City, in 1776.

[15] British spy captured and executed by American forces near Tarrytown, New York, in 1780.

tends a wide woody dell, along which raves a large brook among broken rocks and trunks of fallen trees. Over a deep black part of the stream, not far from the church, was formerly thrown a wooden bridge; the road that led to it, and the bridge itself, were thickly shaded by overhanging trees, which cast a gloom about it, even in the daytime; but occasioned a fearful darkness at night. This was one of the favorite haunts of the headless horseman; and the place where he was most frequently encountered. The tale was told of old Brouwer, a most heretical disbeliever in ghosts, how he met the horseman returning from his foray into Sleepy Hollow, and was obliged to get up behind him; how they galloped over bush and brake, over hill and swamp, until they reached the bridge; when the horseman suddenly turned into a skeleton, threw old Brouwer into the brook, and sprang away over the tree-tops with a clap of thunder.

This story was immediately matched by a thrice marvellous adventure of Brom Bones, who made light of the galloping Hessian as an arrant jockey. He affirmed that, on returning one night from the neighboring village of Sing Sing, he had been overtaken by this midnight trooper; that he had offered to race with him for a bowl of punch, and should have won it too, for Daredevil beat the goblin horse all hollow, but, just as they came to the church bridge, the Hessian bolted, and vanished in a flash of fire.

All these tales, told in that drowsy undertone with which men talk in the dark, the countenances of the listeners only now and then receiving a casual gleam from the glare of a pipe, sank deep in the mind of Ichabod. He repaid them in kind with large extracts from his invaluable author, Cotton Mather, and added many marvellous events that had taken place in his native State of Connecticut, and fearful sights which he had seen in his nightly walks about Sleepy Hollow.

The revel now gradually broke up. The old farmers gathered together their families in their wagons, and were heard for some time rattling along the hollow roads, and over the distant hills. Some of the damsels mounted on pillions behind their favorite swains, and their light-hearted laughter, mingling with the clatter of hoofs, echoed along the silent woodlands, sounding fainter and fainter until they gradually died away—and the late scene of noise and frolic was all silent and deserted. Ichabod only lingered behind, according to the custom of country lovers, to have a tête-à-tête[16] with the heiress, fully convinced that he was now on the high road to success. What passed at this interview I will not pretend to say, for in fact I do not know. Something, however, I fear me, must have gone wrong, for he certainly sallied forth, after no very great interval, with an air quite desolate and shop-fallen.—Oh these women! these women! Could that girl have been playing off any of her coquettish tricks?—Was her encouragement of the poor pedagogue all a mere sham to secure her conquest of his rival?—Heaven only knows, not I!—Let it suffice to say, Ichabod stole forth with the air of one who had been sacking a hen roost, rather than a fair lady's heart. Without looking to the right or left to notice the scene of rural wealth, on which he had so often gloated, he went straight to the stable, and with several hearty cuffs and kicks, roused his steed most uncourteously from the comfortable quar-

---

[16] Confidential conversation (French).

ters in which he was soundly sleeping, dreaming of mountains of corn and oats, and whole valleys of timothy and clover.

It was the very witching time of night that Ichabod, heavy-hearted and crest-fallen, pursued his travel homewards, along the sides of the lofty hills which rise above Tarry Town, and which he had traversed so cheerily in the afternoon. The hour was as dismal as himself. Far below him, the Tappan Zee spread its dusky and indistinct waste of waters, with here and there the tall mast of a sloop, riding quietly at anchor under the land. In the dead hush of midnight, he could even hear the barking of the watch dog from the opposite shore of the Hudson; but it was so vague and faint as only to give an idea of his distance from this faithful companion of man. Now and then, too, the long-drawn crowing of a cock, accidentally awakened, would sound far, far off, from some farm-house away among the hills—but it was like a dreaming sound in his ear. No signs of life occurred near him, but occasionally the melancholy chirp of a cricket, or perhaps the guttural twang of a bullfrog, from a neighboring marsh, as if sleeping uncomfortably, and turning suddenly in his bed.

All the stories of ghosts and goblins that he had heard in the afternoon, now came crowding upon his recollection. The night grew darker and darker; the stars seemed to sink deeper in the sky, and driving clouds occasionally hid them from his sight. He had never felt so lonely and dismal. He was, moreover, approaching the very place where many of the scenes of the ghost stories had been laid. In the center of the road stood an enormous tulip tree, which towered like a giant above all the other trees of the neighborhood, and formed a kind of landmark. Its limbs were gnarled, and fantastic, large enough to form trunks for ordinary trees, twisting down almost to the earth, and rising again into the air. It was connected with the tragical story of the unfortunate André, who had been taken prisoner hard by; and was universally known by the name of Major André's tree. The common people regarded it with a mixture of respect and superstition, partly out of sympathy for the fate of its ill-starred namesake, and partly from the tales of strange sights and doleful lamentations told concerning it.

As Ichabod approached this fearful tree, he began to whistle: he thought his whistle was answered—it was but a blast sweeping sharply through the dry branches. As he approached a little nearer, he thought he saw something white, hanging in the midst of the tree—he paused and ceased whistling; but on looking more narrowly, perceived that it was a place where the tree had been scathed by lightning, and the white wood laid bare. Suddenly he heard a groan—his teeth chattered and his knees smote against the saddle: it was but the rubbing of one huge bough upon another, as they were swayed about by the breeze. He passed the tree in safety, but new perils lay before him.

About two hundred yards from the tree a small brook crossed the road, and ran into a marshy and thickly wooded glen, known by the name of Wiley's swamp. A few rough logs, laid side by side, served for a bridge over this stream. On that side of the road where the brook entered the wood, a group of oaks and chestnuts, matted thick with wild grapevines, threw a cavernous gloom over it. To pass this bridge was the severest trial. It was at this identical spot that the unfortunate André was captured, and under the covert of those chestnuts and vines were the sturdy yeomen concealed who surprised him. This has ever since been considered a haunted stream, and fearful are the feelings of the schoolboy who has to pass it alone after dark.

As he approached the stream his heart began to thump; he summoned up, however, all his resolution, gave his horse half a score of kicks in the ribs, and attempted to dash briskly across the bridge; but instead of starting forward, the perverse old animal made a lateral movement, and ran broadside against the fence. Ichabod, whose fears increased with the delay, jerked the reins on the other side, and kicked lustily with the contrary foot: it was all in vain; his steed started, it is true, but it was only to plunge to the opposite side of the road into a thicket of brambles and alder bushes. The schoolmaster now bestowed both whip and heel upon the starveling ribs of old Gunpowder, who dashed forward, snuffling and snorting, but came to a stand just by the bridge, with a suddenness that had nearly sent his rider sprawling over his head. Just at this moment a plashy tramp by the side of the bridge caught the sensitive ear of Ichabod. In the dark shadow of the grove, on the margin of the brook, he beheld something huge, misshapen, black and towering. It stirred not, but seemed gathered up in the gloom, like some gigantic monster ready to spring upon the traveller.

The hair of the affrighted pedagogue rose upon his head with terror. What was to be done? To turn and fly was now too late; and besides, what chance was there of escaping ghost or goblin, if such it was, which could ride upon the wings of the wind? Summoning up, therefore, a show of courage, he demanded in stammering accents—"Who are you?" He received no reply. He repeated his demand in a still more agitated voice. Still there was no answer. Once more he cudgelled the sides of the inflexible Gunpowder, and, shutting his eyes, broke forth with involuntary fervor into a psalm tune. Just then the shadowy object of alarm put itself in motion, and, with a scramble and a bound, stood at once in the middle of the road. Though the night was dark and dismal, yet the form of the unknown might now in some degree be ascertained. He appeared to be a horseman of large dimensions, and mounted on a black horse of powerful frame. He made no offer of molestation or sociability, but kept aloof on one side of the road, jogging along on the blind side of old Gunpowder, who had now got over his fright and waywardness.

Ichabod, who had no relish for this strange midnight companion, and bethought himself of the adventure of Brom Bones with the Galloping Hessian, now quickened his steed, in hopes of leaving him behind. The stranger, however, quickened his horse to an equal pace. Ichabod pulled up, and fell into a walk, thinking to lag behind—the other did the same. His heart began to sink within him; he endeavored to resume his psalm tune, but his parched tongue clove to the roof of his mouth, and he could not utter a stave. There was something in the moody and dogged silence of this pertinacious companion that was mysterious and appalling. It was soon fearfully accounted for. On mounting a rising ground, which brought the figure of his fellow traveller in relief against the sky, gigantic in height, and muffled in a cloak, Ichabod was horror-struck, on perceiving that he was headless!—but his horror was still more increased, on observing that the head, which should have rested on his shoulders, was carried before him on the pommel of the saddle: his terror rose to desperation; he rained a shower of kicks and blows upon Gunpowder, hoping, by a sudden movement, to give his companion the slip—but the spectre started full jump with him. Away then they dashed, through thick and thin; stones flying, and sparks flashing at every bound. Ichabod's flimsy garments fluttered in the air, as he stretched his long lank body away over his horse's head, in the eagerness of his flight.

They had now reached the road which turns off to Sleepy Hollow; but Gunpowder, who seemed possessed with a demon, instead of keeping up it, made an opposite turn, and plunged headlong down hill to the left. This road leads through a sandy hollow, shaded by trees for about a quarter of a mile, where it crosses the bridge famous in goblin story, and just beyond swells the green knoll on which stands the whitewashed church.

As yet the panic of the steed had given his unskillful rider an apparent advantage in the chase; but just as he had got half way through the hollow, the girths of the saddle gave way, and he felt it slipping from under him. He seized it by the pommel, and endeavored to hold it firm, but in vain; and had just time to save himself by clasping old Gunpowder round the neck, when the saddle fell to the earth, and he heard it trampled under foot by his pursuer. For a moment the terror of Hans Van Ripper's wrath passed across his mind—for it was his Sunday saddle; but this was no time for petty fears; the goblin was hard on his haunches; and (unskillful rider that he was!) he had much ado to maintain his seat; sometimes slipping on one side, sometimes on another, and sometimes jolted on the high ridge of his horse's backbone, with a violence that he verily feared would cleave him asunder.

An opening in the trees now cheered him with the hopes that the church bridge was at hand. The wavering reflection of a silver star in the bosom of the brook told him that he was not mistaken. He saw the walls of the church dimly glaring under the trees beyond. He recollected the place where Brom Bones's ghostly competitor had disappeared. "If I can but reach that bridge," thought Ichabod, "I am safe." Just then he heard the black steed panting and blowing close behind him; he even fancied that he felt his hot breath. Another convulsive kick in the ribs, and old Gunpowder sprang upon the bridge; he thundered over the resounding planks; he gained the opposite side; and now Ichabod cast a look behind to see if his pursuer should vanish, according to rule, in a flash of fire and brimstone. Just then he saw the goblin rising in his stirrups, and in the very act of hurling his head at him. Ichabod endeavored to dodge the horrible missile, but too late. It encountered his cranium with a tremendous crash—he was tumbled headlong into the dust, and Gunpowder, the black steed, and the goblin rider, passed by like a whirlwind.

The next morning the old horse was found without his saddle, and with the bridle under his feet, soberly cropping the grass at his master's gate. Ichabod did not make his appearance at breakfast—dinner-hour came, but no Ichabod. The boys assembled at the schoolhouse, and strolled idly about the banks of the brook; but no schoolmaster. Hans Van Ripper now began to feel some uneasiness about the fate of poor Ichabod, and his saddle. An inquiry was set on foot, and after diligent investigation they came upon his traces. In one part of the road leading to the church was found the saddle trampled in the dirt; the tracks of horses' hoofs deeply dented in the road, and evidently at furious speed, were traced to the bridge, beyond which, on the bank of a broad part of the brook, where the water ran deep and black, was found the hat of the unfortunate Ichabod, and close beside it a shattered pumpkin.

The brook was searched, but the body of the schoolmaster was not to be discovered. Hans Van Ripper, as executor of his estate, examined the bundle which contained all his worldly effects. They consisted of two shirts and a half; two stocks for the neck; a pair or two of worsted stockings; an old pair of corduroy small-clothes; a rusty razor; a book of psalm tunes, full of dogs' ears; and a broken pitchpipe. As to the books and furniture of the schoolhouse, they belonged to the community, excepting Cotton Mather's History of Witchcraft, a New-England Almanac, and a book of dreams and fortune-telling; in which last was a sheet of foolscap much scribbled and blotted in several fruitless attempts to make a copy of verses in honor of the heiress of Van Tassel. These magic books and the poetic scrawl were forthwith consigned to the flames by Hans Van Ripper; who from that time forward determined to send his children no more to school; observing, that he never knew any good come of this same reading and writing. Whatever money the schoolmaster possessed, and he had received his quarter's pay but a day or two before, he must have had about his person at the time of his disappearance.

The mysterious event caused much speculation at the church on the following Sunday. Knots of gazers and gossips were collected in the churchyard, at the bridge, and at the spot where the hat and pumpkin had been found. The stories of Brouwer, of Bones, and a whole budget of others, were called to mind; and when they had diligently considered them all, and compared them with the symptoms of the present case, they shook their heads, and came to the conclusion that Ichabod had been carried off by the galloping Hessian. As he was a bachelor, and in nobody's debt, nobody troubled his head any more about him. The school was removed to a different quarter of the hollow, and another pedagogue reigned in his stead.

It is true, an old farmer, who had been down to New-York on a visit several years after, and from whom this account of the ghostly adventure was received, brought home the intelligence that Ichabod Crane was still alive; that he had left the neighborhood, partly through fear of the goblin and Hans Van Ripper, and partly in mortification at having been suddenly dismissed by the heiress; that he had changed his quarters to a distant part of the country; had kept school and studied law at the same time, had been admitted to the bar, turned politician, electioneered, written for the newspapers, and finally had been made a justice of the Ten Pound Court. Brom Bones too, who shortly after his rival's disappearance conducted the blooming Katrina in triumph to the altar, was observed to look exceedingly knowing whenever the story of Ichabod was related, and always burst into a hearty laugh at the mention of the pumpkin; which led some to suspect that he knew more about the matter than he chose to tell.

The old country wives, however, who are the best judges of these matters, maintain to this day that Ichabod was spirited away by supernatural means; and it is a favorite story often told about the neighborhood round the winter evening fire. The bridge became more than ever an object of superstitious awe, and that may be the reason why the road has been altered of late years, so as to approach the church by the border of the mill-pond. The schoolhouse being deserted, soon fell to decay, and was reported to be haunted by the ghost of the unfortunate pedagogue; and the ploughboy, loitering homeward of a still summer evening, has often fancied his voice at a distance, chanting a melancholy psalm tune among the tranquil solitudes of Sleepy Hollow.

John James Audubon (1785–1851)

The illegitimate son of a French slave trader, John James Audubon was born in the West Indies but brought to France at age five by his father. Restless and unruly as a schoolboy, he soon developed an interest in drawing birds. Audubon emigrated to America at age eighteen, partly to avoid the draft during the Napoleonic Wars, partly to investigate business opportunities, and especially to indulge his lifelong interest in natural history. Traveling from the swampy coast of Florida to the icy steppes of Labrador, Audubon made the first truly comprehensive scientific observations of North American birds and mammals. Audubon also tried his hand at several business ventures: he operated a mine, then he opened a general store. All of these attempts failed, and by about 1820, Audubon resorted to the handicrafts he had learned as a boy: for a time he worked as a taxidermist, then as a portraitist and drawing teacher, while his wife found work as a governess. Meanwhile, he continued to indulge his interest in natural history, and by 1824 Audubon was seeking a publisher for his extensive collection of exquisitely detailed drawings of birds.

Audubon's massive collection, The Birds of America *(1827–38), was published in four volumes, with 435 hand-colored engravings; it was known as an "elephant folio" because it was printed on the largest available sheets of paper. It was accompanied by five volumes of text,* Ornithological Biography *(1831–39), written by Audubon in collaboration with William MacGillivray. For fifteen years, Audubon worked intensively on the production of these volumes, traveling between Europe and the United States to gather material, complete illustrations, and sell subscriptions. Once his reputation had been established, Audubon settled in New York City and devoted himself to a subsequent work on mammals,* Viviparous Quadrupeds of North America *(1845–48), comprising three volumes of hand-colored plates and three volumes of accompanying text (written in collaboration with his sons and the naturalist John Bachman).*

Audubon has sometimes been criticized for shooting the birds he sought to illustrate, including such endangered species as the ivory-billed woodpecker; however, before the invention of the camera, killing the bird was generally the only way to capture its appearance in accurate detail. The enduring value of his illustrations lies not only in their astonishing precision but also in their artistic distinction; they gracefully portray the dynamic form of each creature and often situate it in a specific habitat. Audubon's "ornithological biographies" are admired for their narrative description of each species' life cycle, interspersed with keen personal observations and telling anecdotes. "The Opossum" reveals Audubon's fondness for a shy, nocturnal animal often reviled as "vermin," and "The Whooping Crane" displays his deep knowledge of a bird that has come perilously close to extinction in the twentieth century. Audubon's natural history integrates text and illustration on a scale never before attempted.

The Opossum

This singular animal is found more or less abundant in most parts of the Southern, Western, and Middle States of the Union. It is the *Didelphis virginiana* of Pennant, Harlan, and other authors who have given some accounts of its habits; but as none of them, so far as I know, have illustrated its propensity to dissimulate, and as I have had opportunities of observing its manners, I trust that a few particulars of its biography will prove amusing.

The Opossum is fond of secluding itself during the day, although it by no means confines its predatory rangings to the night. Like many other quadrupeds which feed principally on flesh, it is also both frugivorous[1] and herbivorous, and, when very hard pressed by hunger, it seizes various kinds of insects and reptiles. Its gait, while travelling, and at a time when it supposes itself unobserved, is altogether ambling; in other words, it, like a young foal, moves the two legs of one side forward at once. The Newfoundland dog manifests a similar propensity. Having a constitution as hardy as that of the most northern animals, it stands the coldest weather, and does not hibernate, although its covering of fur and hair may be said to be comparatively scanty even during winter. The defect, however, seems to be compensated by a skin of considerable thickness, and a general subcutaneous layer of fat. Its movements are usually rather slow, and as it walks or ambles along, its curious prehensile tail is carried just above the ground, its rounded ears are directed forward, and at almost every step its pointed nose is applied to the objects beneath it, in order to discover what sort of creatures may have crossed its path.

Methinks I see one at this moment slowly and cautiously trudging over the melting snows by the side of an unfrequented pond, nosing as it goes for the fare its ravenous appetite prefers. Now it has come upon the fresh track of a Grouse or Hare, and it raises its snout and snuffs the keen air. At length it has decided on its course, and it speeds onward at the rate of a man's ordinary walk. It stops and seems at a loss in what direction to go, for the object of its pursuit has either taken a considerable leap or has cut backwards before the Opossum entered its track. It raises itself up, stands for a while on its hind feet, looks around, snuffs the air again, and then proceeds; but now, at the foot of a noble tree, it comes to a full stand. It walks round the base of the huge trunk, over the snow-covered roots, and among them finds an aperture which it at once enters. Several minutes elapse, when it reappears, dragging along a Squirrel already deprived of life, with which in its mouth it begins to ascend the tree. Slowly it climbs. The first fork does not seem to suit it, for perhaps it thinks it might there be too openly exposed to the view of some wily foe; and so it proceeds, until it gains a cluster of

---

[1] Fruit-eating.

branches intertwined with grapevines, and there composing itself, it twists its tail round one of the twigs, and with its sharp teeth demolishes the unlucky Squirrel, which it holds all the while with its forepaws.

The pleasant days of spring have arrived, and the trees vigorously shoot forth their buds; but the Opossum is almost bare, and seems nearly exhausted by hunger. It visits the margins of creeks, and is pleased to see the young frogs, which afford it a tolerable repast. Gradually the poke-berry and the nettle shoot up, and on their tender and juicy stems it gladly feeds. The matin calls of the Wild Turkey Cock delight the ear of the cunning creature, for it well knows that it will soon hear the female and trace her to her nest, when it will suck the eggs with delight. Travelling through the woods, perhaps on the ground, perhaps aloft, from tree to tree, it hears a cock crow, and its heart swells as it remembers the savory food on which it regaled itself last summer in the neighboring farm-yard. With great care, however, it advances, and at last conceals itself in the very hen-house.

Honest farmer! why did you kill so many Crows last winter? ay and Ravens too? Well, you have had your own way of it; but now hie to the village and pro-cure a store of ammunition, clean your rusty gun, set your traps, and teach your lazy curs to watch the Opossum. There it comes. The sun is scarcely down, but the appetite of the prowler is keen; hear the screams of one of your best chickens that has been seized by him! The cunning beast is off with it, and nothing can now be done, unless you stand there to watch the Fox or the Owl, now exulting in the thought that you have killed their enemy and your own friend, the poor Crow. That precious hen under which you last week placed a dozen eggs or so is now deprived of them. The Opossum, notwithstanding her angry outcries and rufflings of feathers, has removed them one by one, and now look at the poor bird as she moves across your yard; if not mad, she is at least stupid, for she scratches here and there, calling to her chickens all the while. All this comes from your shooting Crows. Had you been more merciful or more prudent, the Opossum might have been kept within the woods, where it would have been sat-isfied with a Squirrel, a young Hare, the eggs of a Turkey, or the grapes that so profusely adorn the boughs of our forest trees. But I talk to you in vain.

There cannot be a better exemplification of maternal tenderness than the fe-male Opossum. Just peep into that curious sack in which the young are con-cealed, each attached to a teat. The kind mother not only nourishes them with care, but preserves them from their enemies; she moves with them as the shark does with its progeny, and now, aloft on the tulip tree, she hides among the thick foliage. By the end of two months they begin to shift for themselves; each has been taught its particular lesson, and must now practise it.

But suppose the farmer has surprised an Opossum in the act of killing one of his best fowls. His angry feelings urge him to kick the poor beast, which, con-scious of its inability to resist, rolls off like a ball. The more the farmer rages, the more reluctant is the animal to manifest resentment; at last there it lies, not dead, but exhausted, its jaws open, its tongue extended, its eye dimmed; and there it would lie until the bottle-fly should come to deposit its eggs, did not its tormentor at length walk off. "Surely," says he to himself, "the beast must be dead." But no, reader, it is only " 'possuming," and no sooner has its enemy withdrawn than it gradually gets on its legs, and once more makes for the woods.

Once, while descending the Mississippi, in a sluggish flat-bottomed boat, expressly for the purpose of studying those objects of nature more nearly connected with my favorite pursuits, I chanced to meet with two well-grown Opossums, and brought them alive to the "ark." The poor things were placed on the roof or deck, and were immediately assailed by the crew, when, following their natural instinct, they lay as if quite dead. An experiment was suggested, and both were thrown overboard. On striking water, and for a few moments after, neither evinced the least disposition to move; but finding their situation desperate, they began to swim towards our uncouth rudder, which was formed of a long slender tree, extending from the middle of the boat thirty feet beyond its stern. They both got upon it, were taken up, and afterwards let loose in their native woods.

In the year 1829, I was in a portion of lower Louisiana, where the Opossum abounds at all seasons, and having been asked by the President and the Secretary of the Zoölogical Society of London, to forward live animals of this species to them, I offered a price a little above the common, and soon found myself plentifully supplied, twenty-five having been brought to me. I found them excessively voracious, and not less cowardly. They were put into a large box, with a great quantity of food, and conveyed to a steamer bound for New Orleans. Two days afterwards, I went to that city, to see about sending them off to Europe; but, to my surprise, I found that the old males had destroyed the younger ones, and eaten off their heads, and that only sixteen remained alive. A separate box was purchased for each, and some time after they reached my friends, the Rathbones of Liverpool, who, with their usual attention, sent them off to London, where, on my return, I saw a good number of them in the Zoölogical Gardens.

This animal is fond of grapes, of which a species now bears its name. Persimmons are greedily eaten by it, and in severe weather I have observed it eating lichens. Fowls of every kind, and quadrupeds less powerful than itself, are also its habitual prey.

The flesh of the Opossum resembles that of a young pig, and would perhaps be as highly prized, were it not for the prejudice generally entertained against it. Some "very particular" persons, to my knowledge, have pronounced it excellent eating. After cleaning its body, suspend it for a whole week in the frosty air, for it is not eaten in summer; then place it on a heap of hot wood embers; sprinkle it when cooked with gunpowder; and now tell me, good reader, does it not equal the famed Canvas-back Duck? Should you visit any of our markets, you may see it there in company with the best game.

The Whooping Crane

The variegated foliage of the woods indicates that the latter days of October have arrived; gloomy clouds spread over the heavens; the fierce blasts of the north, as if glad to escape from the dreary regions of their nativity, sport in dreadful revelry among the forests and glades. Showers of sleet and snow descend at intervals, and the careful husbandman gathers his flocks, to drive them to a place of shelter. The traveller gladly accepts the welcome of the forester, and as he seats himself by the blazing fire, looks with pleasure on the spinning-wheels of the industrious inmates. The lumberer prepares to set out on his long voyage, the trapper seeks the retreats of the industrious beaver, and the red Indian is making arrangements for his winter hunts. The Ducks and Geese have already reached the waters of the western ponds; here a Swan or two is seen following in their train, and as the observer of nature stands watching the appearances and events of this season of change, he hears from on high the notes of the swiftly travelling but unseen Whooping Crane. Suddenly the turbid atmosphere clears, and now he can perceive the passing birds. Gradually they descend, dress their extended lines, and prepare to alight on the earth. With necks outstretched, and long bony legs extended behind, they proceed, supported by wings white as the snow but tipped with jet, until arriving over the great savannah they wheel their circling flight, and slowly approach the ground, on which with half-closed wings, and outstretched feet they alight, running along for a few steps to break the force of their descent.

Reader, see the majestic bird shake its feathers, and again arrange them in order. Proud of its beautiful form, and prouder still of its power of flight, it stalks over the withering grasses with all the majesty of a gallant chief. With long and measured steps he moves along, his head erect, his eye glistening with delight. His great journey is accomplished, and being well acquainted with a country which has often been visited by him, he at once commences his winter avocations.

The Whooping Crane reaches the Western Country about the middle of October, or the beginning of November, in flocks of twenty or thirty individuals, sometimes of twice or thrice that number; the young by themselves, but closely followed by their parents. They spread from Illinois over Kentucky, and all the intermediate States, until they reach the Carolinas on the southern coast, the Floridas, Louisiana, and the countries bordering on Mexico, in all of which they spend the winter, seldom returning northward until about the middle of April, or towards the beginning of May. They are seen on the edges of large ponds supplied with rank herbage, on fields or savannahs, now in swampy woods, and again on extensive marshes. The interior of the country, and the neighborhood of the seashores, suit them equally well, so long as the temperature is sufficiently high. In the Middle States, it is very seldom indeed that they are seen; and to the eastward of these countries they are unknown; for all their migrations are performed far inland, and thus they leave and return to the northern retreats where, it is said, they breed and spend the summer. While migrating they appear to travel both by night and by day, and I have frequently heard them at the former, and seen them at the latter time, as they were proceeding toward their destination. Whether the weather be calm or tempestuous, it makes no difference to them, their power of flight being such as to render them regardless of the winds. Nay, I have observed them urging their way during very heavy gales, shifting from high to low in the air with remarkable dexterity. The members of a flock sometimes arrange themselves in the form of an acute-angled triangle; sometimes they move in a long line; again they mingle together without order, or form an extended front; but in whatever manner they advance, each bird sounds his loud note in succession, and on all occasions of alarm these birds manifest the same habit.

I had, in 1810, the gratification of taking Alexander Wilson to some ponds within a few miles of Louisville, and of showing him many birds of this species, of which he had not previously seen any other than stuffed specimens. I told him that the white birds were the adults, and that the grey ones were the young. Wilson, in his article on the Whooping Crane, has alluded to this, but, as on other occasions, has not informed his readers whence the information came.

The wariness of this species is so remarkable, that it takes all the cunning and care of an Indian hunter to approach it at times, especially in the case of an old bird. The acuteness of their sight and hearing is quite wonderful. If they perceive a man approaching, even at the distance of a quarter of a mile, they are sure to take to wing. Should you accidentally tread on a stick and break it, or suddenly cock your gun, all the birds in the flock raise their heads and emit a cry. Shut the gate of a field after you, and from that moment they all watch your motions. To attempt to crawl towards them, even among long grass, after such an intimation, would be useless; and unless you lie in wait for them, and be careful to maintain a perfect silence, or may have the cover of some large trees, heaps of brushwood, or fallen logs, you may as well stay at home. They generally see you long before you perceive them, and so long as they are aware that you have not observed them, they remain silent; but the moment that, by some inadvertency, you disclose to them your sense of their presence, some of them sound an alarm. For my part, reader, I would as soon undertake to catch a deer by fair running, as to shoot a Sand-hill Crane that had observed me. Sometimes, indeed, towards the approach of spring, when they are ready to depart for their breeding grounds, the voice of one will startle and urge to flight all within a mile of the spot. When this happens, all the birds around join into a great flock, gradually rise in a spiral manner, ascend to a vast height, and sail off in a straight course.

When wounded, these birds cannot be approached without caution, as their powerful bill is capable of inflicting a severe wound. Knowing this as I do, I would counsel any sportsman not to leave his gun behind, while pursuing a wounded Crane.

While in the Floridas, I saw only a few of these birds alive, but many which had been shot by the Spaniards and Indians, for the sake of their flesh and beautiful feathers, of which latter they make fans and fly brushes.

According to circumstances, this species roosts either on the ground or on high trees. In the latter case, they leave their feeding ground about an hour before sunset, and going off in silence, proceed towards the interior of high land forests, where they alight on the largest branches of lofty trees, six or seven settling on the same branch. For half an hour or so, they usually dress their plumage, standing erect: but afterwards they crouch in the manner of Wild Turkeys. In this situation they are sometimes shot by moonlight. Those which resort to plantations, situated in the vicinity of large marshes, covered with tall grasses, cat's-tails, and other plants, spend the night on some hillock, standing on one leg, the other being drawn under the body, whilst the head is thrust beneath the broad feathers of the shoulder. In returning towards the feeding grounds, they all emit their usual note, but in a very low undertone, leaving their roost at an earlier or later hour, according to the state of the weather. When it is cold and clear, they start very early; but when warm and rainy, not until late in the morning. Their motions toward night are determined by the same circumstances. They rise easily from the ground after running a few steps, fly low for thirty or forty yards, then rise in circles, crossing each other in their windings, like Vultures, Ibises, and some other birds. If startled or shot at, they utter loud and piercing cries. These cries, which I cannot compare to the sounds of any instrument known to me, I have heard at the distance of three miles, at the approach of spring, when the males were paying their addresses to the females, or fighting among themselves. They may be in some degree represented by the syllables *kewrr, kewrr, kewrooh;* and strange and uncouth as they are, they have always sounded delightful in my ear.

From On the Dakota Prairies

August 10, Thursday. Although I have said much about Buffalo running, and butchering in general, I have not given the particular manner in which the latter is performed by the hunters of this country—I mean the white hunters—and I will now try to do so. The moment that the Buffalo is dead, three or four hunters, their faces and hands often covered with gunpowder, and with pipes lighted, place the animal on its belly, and by drawing out each fore and hind leg, fix the body so that it cannot fall down again; an incision is made near the root of the tail, immediately above the root in fact, and the skin cut to the neck, and taken off in the roughest manner imaginable, downwards and on both sides at the same time.

The knives are going in all directions, and many wounds occur to the hands and fingers, but are rarely attended to at this time. The pipe of one man has perhaps given out, and with his bloody hands he takes the one of his nearest companion, who has his own hands equally bloody. Now one breaks in the skull of the bull, and with bloody fingers draws out the hot brains and swallows them with peculiar zest; another has now reached the liver, and is gobbling down enormous pieces of it; whilst, perhaps, a third, who has come to the paunch, is feeding luxuriously on some—to me—disgusting-looking offal. But the main business proceeds. The flesh is taken off from the sides of the boss, or hump bones, from where these bones begin to the very neck, and the hump itself is thus destroyed. The hunters give the name of "hump" to the mere bones when slightly covered by flesh; and it is cooked, and very good when fat, young, and well broiled. The pieces of flesh taken from the sides of these bones are called *filets*, and are the best portion of the animal when properly cooked. The forequarters, or shoulders, are taken off, as well as the hind ones, and the sides, covered by a thin portion of flesh called the *depouille*, are taken out. Then the ribs are broken off at the vertebrae, as well as the boss bones. The marrow-bones, which are those of the fore and hind legs only, are cut out last. The feet usually remain attached to these; the paunch is stripped of its covering of layers of fat, the head and the backbone are left to the Wolves, the pipes are all emptied, the hands, faces, and clothes all bloody, and now a glass of grog is often enjoyed, as the stripping off the skins and flesh of three or four animals is truly very hard work.

In some cases when no water was near, our supper was cooked without our being washed, and it was not until we had travelled several miles the next morning that we had any opportunity of cleaning ourselves; and yet, despite everything, we are all hungry, eat heartily, and sleep soundly. When the wind is high and the Buffaloes run towards it, the hunter's guns very often snap, and it is during their exertions to replenish their pans, that the powder flies and sticks to the moisture every moment accumulating on their faces; but nothing stops these daring and usually powerful men, who the moment the chase is ended, leap from their horses, let them graze, and begin their butcher-like work.

August 11, Friday. The activity of Buffaloes is almost beyond belief; they can climb the steep defiles of the Mauvaises Terres in hundreds of places where men cannot follow them, and it is a fine sight to see a large gang of them proceeding along these defiles four or five hundred feet above the level of the bottoms, and from which pathway if one of the number makes a misstep or accidentally slips, he goes down rolling over and over, and breaks his neck ere the level ground is reached. The thing that troubles them most is crossing rivers on the ice; their hoofs slip from side to side, they become frightened, and stretch their four legs apart to support the body, and in such situations the Indians and white hunters easily approach, and stab them to the heart, or cut the hamstrings, when they become an easy prey. When in large gangs those in the center are supported by those on the outposts, and if the stream is not large, reach the shore and readily escape.

Indians of different tribes hunt the Buffalo in different ways; some hunt on horseback, and use arrows altogether; they are rarely expert in reloading the gun in the close race. Others hunt on foot, using guns, arrows, or both. Others follow with patient perseverance, and kill them also. But I will give you the manner pursued by the Mandans. Twenty to fifty men start, as the occasion suits, each provided with two horses, one of which is a pack-horse, the other fit for the chase. They have quivers with from twenty to fifty arrows, according to the wealth of the hunter. They ride the pack-horse bareback, and travel on, till they see the game, when they leave the pack-horse, and leap on the hunter, and start at full speed and soon find themselves amid the Buffaloes, on the flanks of the herd, and on both sides. When within a few yards the arrow is sent, they shoot at a Buffalo somewhat ahead of them, and send the arrow in an oblique manner, so as to pass through the lights. If the blood rushes out of the nose and mouth the animal is fatally wounded, and they shoot at it no more; if not, a second, and perhaps a third arrow, is sent before this happens.

The Buffaloes on starting carry the tail close in between the legs, but when wounded they switch it about, especially if they wish to fight, and then the hunter's horse shies off and lets the mad animal breathe awhile. If shot through the heart, they occasionally fall dead on the instant; sometimes, if not hit in the right place, a dozen arrows will not stop them. When wounded and mad they turn suddenly round upon the hunter, and rush upon him in such a quick and furious manner that if horse and rider are not both on the alert, the former is overtaken, hooked and overthrown, the hunter pitched off, trampled and gored to death. Although the Buffalo is such a large animal, and to all appearance a clumsy one, it can turn with the quickness of thought, and when once enraged, will rarely give up the chase until avenged for the wound it has received. If, however, the hunter is expert, and the horse fleet, they outrun the bull, and it returns to the herd. Usually the greater number of the gang is killed, but it very rarely happens that some of them do not escape.

This however is not the case when the animal is pounded, especially by the Gros Ventres, Black Feet, and Assiniboins. These pounds are called "parks," and the Buffaloes are made to enter them in the following manner: The park is sometimes round and sometimes square, this depending much on the ground where it is put up; at the end of the park is what is called a *precipice* of some fifteen feet or less, as may be found. It is approached by a funnel-shaped passage, which like the park itself is strongly built of logs, brushwood, and pickets, and when all is ready a young man, very swift of foot, starts at daylight covered over with a Buffalo robe and wearing a Buffalo headdress. The moment he sees the herd to be taken, he bellows like a young calf, and makes his way slowly towards the contracted part of the funnel, imitating the cry of the calf, at frequent intervals. The Buffaloes advance after the decoy; about a dozen mounted hunters are yelling and galloping behind them, and along both flanks of the herd, forcing them by these means to enter the mouth of the funnel.

Women and children are placed behind the fences of the funnel to frighten the cattle, and as soon as the young man who acts as decoy feels assured that the game is in a fair way to follow to the bank or "precipice," he runs or leaps down the bank, over the barricade, and either rests, or joins in the fray. The poor Buffaloes, usually headed by a large bull, proceed, leap down the bank in haste and confusion, the Indians all yelling and pursuing till every bull, cow, and calf is impounded. Although this is done at all seasons, it is more general in October or November, when the hides are good and salable.

Now the warriors are all assembled by the pen, calumets are lighted, and the chief smokes to the Great Spirit, the four points of the compass, and lastly to the Buffaloes. The pipe is passed from mouth to mouth in succession, and as soon as this ceremony is ended, the destruction commences. Guns shoot, arrows fly in all directions, and the hunters being on the outside of the enclosure, destroy the whole gang, before they jump over to clean and skin the murdered herd. Even the children shoot small, short arrows to assist in the destruction.

It happens sometimes however, that the leader of the herd will be restless at the sight of the precipices, and if the fence is weak will break through it, and all his fellows follow him, and escape. The same thing sometimes takes place in the pen, for so full does this become occasionally that the animals touch each other, and as they cannot move, the very weight against the fence of the pen is quite enough to break it through; the smallest aperture is sufficient, for in a few minutes it becomes wide, and all the beasts are seen scampering over the prairies, leaving the poor Indians starving and discomfited.

Mr. Kipp told me that while travelling from Lake Travers to the Mandans, in the month of August, he rode in a heavily laden cart for six successive days through masses of Buffaloes, which divided for the cart, allowing it to pass without opposition. He has seen the immense prairie back of Fort Clark look black to the tops of the hills, though the ground was covered with snow, so crowded was it with these animals; and the masses probably extended much further. In fact it is *impossible to describe or even conceive* the vast multitudes of these animals that exist even now, and feed on these ocean-like prairies.

✑ Lord Byron, George Gordon (1788–1824)

George Gordon, Lord Byron led a life much like one of the heroes from his narrative poetry—it was passionate, extreme, and always full of drama. Although he spent his early childhood in difficult financial circumstances (due to his father's dissolute lifestyle), as soon as he inherited his noble title, he began to follow the common path of male aristocrats in the Regency period. He attended Cambridge, graduating with an M.A., and then set to enjoying himself and spending his fortune in London. He published his first collection of poems, Hours of Idleness, *in 1807, and from 1809 until 1811, he went on his grand tour of Europe (expected of all young men of standing), visiting Spain, Portugal, and the Greek Isles. There he composed the first two cantos of his long poem* Childe Harold's Pilgrimage. *Publishing it upon his return to England, he gained instant fame, to which he added notoriety by his amorous liaisons, including one with his own half-sister, Augusta. An ill-fated marriage and a worsening personal reputation led Byron to exile himself to Europe in 1816, where he remained for the rest of his life. First he spent time in Switzerland, with his friends Percy and Mary Shelley, composing there the third canto of* Childe Harold *and continuing to build a reputation as someone who was "mad, bad, and dangerous to know." Next, he traveled extensively in Italy, all the while writing poetry that was more popular with a Continental audience than it was in England. A man of strong liberal and democratic ideas in politics, Byron had written about the oppression of the Greeks by the Turks and decided to join the Greeks in their resistance. He gave his money and his leadership to the Greek army, but died of fever before he could engage in battle.*

In Childe Harold, *Byron created what would come to be known as the Byronic hero—a hero who had some attributes in common with his author (though Byron would deny the autobiographical parallels). This hero was a wanderer, an exile, a person outside of common society. Driven by a guilt from a source that is rarely named, the Byronic hero at once nurtures and regrets his great unnamed sin. He is charismatic yet menacing, glamorous yet egotistical, a figure much like Milton's Satan, that prototypical literary rebel. The poem is written in Spenserian stanzas and further points back to the Renaissance tradition by addressing its protagonist with the archaic term "Childe," which was once used to refer to an aristocrat in training to become a knight. As a whole, the poem tells of Harold's travels through Spain, Portugal, and the Near East (books 1 and 2); up the Rhine and into Switzerland and the Alps (book 3); and, finally, to Italy (book 4). Comprised of often declamatory vignettes, the story is something of an emotional travelogue, recording the hero's passionate reactions to natural scenery and to the historical events and individuals associated with that scenery. The frequent association of landscape with political and historical events makes Byron's poetry distinctive, suggesting his affinity with an earlier eighteenth-century rather than the prevailing nineteenth-century nature aesthetic.*

From Childe Harold's Pilgrimage

From Canto 3

3

In my youth's summer I did sing of One,[1]
The wandering outlaw of his own dark mind;   20
Again I seize the theme, but begun,
And bear it with me, as the rushing wind
Bears the cloud onwards: in that Tale I find
The furrows of long thought, and dried-up tears,
Which, ebbing, leave a sterile track behind,   25
O'er which all heavily the journeying years
Plod the last sands of life—where not a flower appears.

4

Since my young days of passion—joy, or pain,
Perchance my heart and harp have lost a string,
And both may jar: it may be, that in vain   30
I would essay as I have sung to sing.
Yet, though a dreary strain, to this I cling,
So that it wean me from the weary dream
Of selfish grief or gladness—so it fling
Forgetfulness around me—it shall seem   35
To me, though to none else, a not ungrateful theme.

5

He who, grown aged in this world of woe,
In deeds, not years, piercing the depths of life,
So that no wonder waits him; nor below

---

[1] *One:* Childe Harold, the hero of the previous two cantos of the poem. [*Editors' Note:* Verse line numbers begin at line 19 of the original complete Canto 3.]

Can love or sorrow, fame, ambition, strife,   40
Cut to his heart again with the keen knife
Of silent, sharp endurance: he can tell
Why thought seeks refuge in lone caves, yet rife
With airy images, and shapes which dwell
Still unimpaired, though old, in the soul's haunted cell.   45

6

'Tis to create, and in creating live
A being more intense, that we endow
With form our fancy, gaining as we give
The life we image, even as I do now.
What am I? Nothing: but not so art thou,   50
Soul of my thought! with whom I traverse earth,
Invisible but gazing, as I glow
Mixed with thy spirit, blended with thy birth,
And feeling still with thee in my crushed feelings' dearth.

7

Yet must I think less wildly: I have thought   55
Too long and darkly, till my brain became,
In its own eddy boiling and o'erwrought,
A whirling gulf of phantasy and flame:
And thus, untaught in youth my heart to tame,
My springs of life were poisoned. 'Tis too late!   60
Yet am I changed; though still enough the same
In strength to bear what time can not abate,
And feed on bitter fruits without accusing Fate.

8

Something too much of this: but now 'tis past,
And the spell closes with its silent seal.   65
Long-absent Harold reappears at last;
He of the breast which fain no more would feel,
Wrung with the wounds which kill not, but ne'er heal;
Yet Time, who changes all, had altered him
In soul and aspect as in age: years steal   70
Fire from the mind as vigor from the limb:
And life's enchanted cup but sparkles near the brim.

9

His had been quaffed too quickly, and he found
The dregs were wormwood;[2] but he filled again,
And from a purer fount, on holier ground,   75

---

[2] A bitter-tasting herb; in general, something unpleasant.

And deemed its spring perpetual; but in vain!
Still round him clung invisibly a chain
Which galled for ever, fettering though unseen,
And heavy though it clanked not; worn with pain,
Which pined although it spoke not, and grew keen,   80
Entering with every step he took through many a scene.

10

Secure in guarded coldness, he had mixed
Again in fancied safety with his kind,
And deemed his spirit now so firmly fixed
And sheathed with an invulnerable mind,   85
That, if no joy, no sorrow lurked behind;
And he, as one, might 'midst the many stand
Unheeded, searching through the crowd to find
Fit speculation; such as in strange land
He found in wonder-works of God and Nature's hand.   90

11

But who can view the ripened rose, nor seek
To wear it? who can curiously behold
The smoothness and the sheen of beauty's cheek,
Nor feel the heart can never all grow old?
Who can contemplate Fame through clouds unfold   95
The star which rises o'er her steep, nor climb?
Harold, once more within the vortex rolled
On with the giddy circle, chasing Time,
Yet with a nobler aim than in his youth's fond prime.

12

But soon he knew himself the most unfit   100
Of men to herd with man; with whom he held
Little in common; untaught to submit
His thoughts to others, though his soul was quelled,
In youth by his own thoughts; still uncompelled,
He would not yield dominion of his mind   105
To spirits against whom his own rebelled;
Proud though in desolation; which could find
A life within itself, to breathe without mankind.

13

Where rose the mountains, there to him were friends;
Where rolled the ocean, thereon was his home,   110
Where a blue sky, and glowing clime, extends,
He had the passion and the power to roam;
The desert, forest, cavern, breaker's foam,

Were unto him companionship; they spake
A mutual language, clearer than the tone   115
Of his land's tongue, which he would oft forsake
For Nature's pages glassed by sunbeams on the lake.

14

Like the Chaldean,[3] he could watch the stars,
Till he had peopled them with beings bright
As their own beams; and earth, and earth-born jars,   120
And human frailties, were forgotten quite:
Could he have kept his spirit to that flight,
He had been happy; but this clay will sink
Its spark immortal, envying it the light
To which it mounts, as if to break the link   125
That keeps us from yon heaven which woos us to its brink.

15

But in Man's dwellings he became a thing
Restless and worn, and stern and wearisome,
Drooped as a wild-born falcon with clipt wing,
To whom the boundless air alone were home: 130
Then came his fit again, which to o'ercome,
As eagerly the barred-up bird will beat
His breast and beak against his wiry dome
Till the blood tinge his plumage, so the heal
Of his impeded soul would through his bosom eat.   135

16

Self-exiled Harold wanders forth again,
With naught of hope left, but with less of gloom;
The very knowledge that he lived in vain,
That all was over on this side the tomb,
Had made Despair a smilingness assume,   140
Which, though 'twere wild—as on the plundered wreck
When mariners would madly meet their doom
With draughts intemperate on the sinking deck—
Did yet inspire a cheer, which he forbore to check.

.   .   .

68

Lake Leman[4] woos me with its crystal face,
The mirror where the stars and mountains view   645

---

[3] An inhabitant of ancient Babylon; they were known for their knowledge of astrology and occult magic.
[4] A lake near Geneva, Switzerland.

The stillness of their aspect in each trace
Its clear depth yields of their far height and hue:
There is too much of man here, to look through
With a fit mind the might which I behold;
But soon in me shall Loneliness renew   650
Thoughts hid, but not less cherish'd than of old,
Ere mingling with the herd had penned me in their fold.

69

To fly from, need not be to hate, mankind;
All are not fit with them to stir and toil,
Nor is it discontent to keep the mind   655
Deep in its fountain, lest it overboil
In one hot throng, where we become the spoil
Of our infection, till too late and long
We may deplore and struggle with the coil,
In wretched interchange of wrong for wrong   660
'Midst a contentious world, striving where none are strong.

70

There, in a moment, we may plunge our years
In fatal penitence, and in the blight
Of our own soul, turn all our blood to tears,
And color things to come with hues of Night;   665
The race of life becomes a hopeless flight
To those that walk in darkness: on the sea,
The boldest steer but where their ports invite,
But there are wanderers o'er Eternity
Whose bark[5] drives on and on, and anchored ne'er shall be.   670

71

Is it not better, then, to be alone,
And love Earth only for its earthly sake?
By the blue rushing of the arrowy Rhone,[6]
Or the pure bosom of its nursing lake,
Which feeds it as a mother who doth make   675
A fair but froward infant her own care,
Kissing its cries away as these awake;—
Is it not better thus our lives to wear,
Than join the crushing crowd, doomed to inflict or bear?

72

I live not in myself, but I become   680
Portion of that around me; and to me,

---

[5] A ship.
[6] A river through Switzerland and southeastern France.

High mountains are a feeling, but the hum
Of human cities torture: I can see
Nothing to loathe in nature, save to be
A link reluctant in a fleshly chain,   685
Classed among creatures, when the soul can flee,
And with the sky, the peak, the heaving plain
Of ocean, or the stars, mingle, and not in vain.

73

And thus I am absorbed, and this is life:
I look upon the peopled desert past,   690
As on a place of agony and strife,
Where, for some sin, to Sorrow I was cast,
To act and suffer, but remount at last
With a fresh pinion;[7] which I felt to spring,
Though young, yet waxing vigorous as the blast   695
Which it would cope with, on delighted wing,
Spurning the clay-cold bonds which round our being cling.

74

And when, at length, the mind shall be all free
From what it hates in this degraded form,
Reft of its carnal life, save what shall be   700
Existent happier in the fly and worm,—
When elements to elements conform,
And dust is as it should be, shall I not
Feel all I see, less dazzling, but more warm?
The bodiless thought? the Spirit of each spot?   705
Of which, even now, I share at times the immortal lot?

75

Are not the mountains, waves, and skies a part
Of me and of my soul, as I of them?
Is not the love of these deep in my heart
With a pure passion? should I not contemn   710
All objects, if compared with these? and stem
A tide of suffering, rather than forego
Such feelings for the hard and worldly phlegm
Of those whose eyes are only turned below,
Gazing upon the ground, with thoughts which dare not glow?   715

.   .   .

---

[7] The bottom portion of a bird's wing which, when clipped or damaged, can impede its flight.

85

Clear, placid, Leman! thy contrasted lake,
With the wide world I dwelt in, is a thing
Which warns me, with its stillness, to forsake
Earth's troubled waters for a purer spring.   800
This quiet sail is as a noiseless wing
To waft me from distraction; once I loved
Torn ocean's roar, but thy soft murmuring
Sounds sweet as if a Sister's voice reproved,
That I with stern delights should e'er have been so moved.   805

86

It is the hush of night, and all between
Thy margin and the mountains, dusk, yet clear,
Mellowed and mingling, yet distinctly seen,
Save darkened Jura,[8] whose capped heights appear
Precipitously steep; and drawing near,   810
There breathes a living fragrance from the shore,
Of flowers yet fresh with childhood; on the ear
Drops the light drip of the suspended oar,
Or chirps the grasshopper one good-night carol more;

87

He is an evening reveller, who makes   815
His life an infancy, and sings his fill;
At intervals, some bird from out the brakes
Starts into voice a moment, then is still.
There seems a floating whisper on the hill,
But that is fancy, for the starlight dews   820
All silently their tears of love instill,
Weeping themselves away, till they infuse
Deep into Nature's breast the spirit of her hues.

88

Ye stars! which are the poetry of heaven,
If in your bright leaves we would read the fate   825
Of men and empires, — 'tis to be forgiven,
That in our aspirations to be great,
Our destinies o'erleap their mortal state,
And claim a kindred with you; for ye are
A beauty and a mystery, and create   830
In us such love and reverence from afar,
That fortune, fame, power, life, have named themselves a star.

---

[8] A mountain range in eastern France and western Switzerland.

89

All heaven and earth are still—though not in sleep,
But breathless, as we grow when feeling most;
And silent, as we stand in thoughts too deep:—   835
All heaven and earth are still: From the high host
Of stars, to the lulled lake and mountain-coast,
All is concentered in a life intense,
Where not a beam, nor air, nor leaf is lost,
But hath a part of being, and a sense   840
Of that which is of all Creator and defence.

90

Then stirs the feeling infinite, so felt
In solitude, where we are least alone;
A truth, which, through our being then doth melt,
And purifies from self: it is a tone,   845
The soul and source of music, which makes known
Eternal harmony, and sheds a charm,
Like to the fabled Cytherea's zone,[9]
Binding all things with beauty;—'twould disarm
The spectre Death, had he substantial power to harm.   850

.   .   .

[9] The island of Aphrodite, ancient Greek goddess of love.

Darkness

I had a dream, which was not all a dream.
The bright sun was extinguished, and the stars
Did wander darkling in the eternal space,
Rayless, and pathless, and the icy earth
Swung blind and blackening in the moonless air;   5
Morn came and went—and came, and brought no day,
And men forgot their passions in the dread
Of this their desolation; and all hearts
Were chilled into a selfish prayer for light:
And they did live by watchfires—and the thrones,   10
The palaces of crowned kings—the huts,
The habitations of all things which dwell,
Were burnt for beacons; cities were consumed,
And men were gathered round their blazing homes
To look once more into each others' face;   15
Happy were those who dwelt within the eye

Of the volcanoes, and their mountain-torch:
A fearful hope was all the world contained;
Forests were set on fire—but hour by hour
They fell and faded—and the crackling trunks   20
Extinguished with a crash—and all was black.
The brows of men by the despairing light
Wore an unearthly aspect, as by fits
The flashes fell upon them; some lay down
And hid their eyes and wept; and some did rest   25
Their chins upon their clenched hands, and smiled;
And others hurried to and fro, and fed
Their funeral piles with fuel, and looked up
With mad disquietude on the dull sky,
The pall of a past world; and then again   30
With curses cast them down upon the dust,
And gnashed their teeth and howled: the wild birds shrieked
And, terrified, did flutter on the ground,
And flap their useless wings; the wildest brutes
Came tame and tremulous; and vipers crawled   35
And twined themselves among the multitude,
Hissing but stingless—they were slain for food:
And War, which for a moment was no more,
Did glut himself again;—a meal was bought
With blood, and each sate sullenly apart   40
Gorging himself in gloom: no love was left;
All earth was but one thought—and that was death,
Immediate and inglorious; and the pang
Of famine fed upon all entrails—men
Died, and their bones were tombless as their flesh;   45
The meagre by the meagre were devoured,
Even dogs assailed their masters, all save one,
And he was faithful to a corse,[1] and kept
The birds and beasts and famished men at bay,
Till hunger clung them, or the dropping dead   50
Lured their lank jaws; himself sought out no food,
But with a piteous and perpetual moan,
And a quick desolate cry, licking the hand
Which answered not with a caress—he died.
The crowd was famished by degrees; but two   55
Of an enormous city did survive,
And they were enemies: they met beside
The dying embers of an altar-place
Where had been heaped a mass of holy things
For an unholy usage; they raked up,   60

---

[1] A corpse.

And shivering scraped with their cold skeleton hands
The feeble ashes, and their feeble breath
Blew for a little life, and made a flame
Which was a mockery; then they lifted up
Their eyes as it grew lighter, and beheld   65
Each other's aspects—saw, and shrieked, and died—
Even of their mutual hideousness they died,
Unknowing who he was upon whose brow
Famine had written Fiend. The world was void,
The populous and the powerful was a lump,   70
Seasonless, herbless, treeless, manless, lifeless—
A lump of death—a chaos of hard clay.
The rivers, lakes, and ocean all stood still,
And nothing stirred within their silent depths;   75
Ships sailorless lay rolling on the sea,
And their masts fell down piecemeal; as they dropped
They slept on the abyss without a surge—
The waves were dead; the tides were in their grave,
The Moon, their mistress had expired before;
The winds were withered in the stagnant air,   80
And the clouds perished! Darkness had no need
Of aid from them—She was the Universe!

✒ *James Fenimore Cooper* (*1789–1851*)

Born in New Jersey, James Fenimore Cooper was carried as an infant to Cooperstown, a remote village in upstate New York, where his father, William Cooper, presided as land-lord, county court judge, and representative to the U.S. Congress. He was schooled by private tutors in Cooperstown, then sent to an elite boarding school in Albany. In 1803, he enrolled at Yale University, where he showed little inclination to pursue his studies. After an incident in which he blew up a fellow student's door with gunpowder, Cooper was expelled. He served for a year in the U.S. Navy, then returned to New York State, where, upon his father's untimely death, he became the executor of a large estate. Mar-rying a wealthy socialite in 1810, Cooper settled down into a life of aristocratic leisure and proceeded to squander all of his inherited wealth. By 1820, he faced bankruptcy and, with an insouciance born of desperation, decided to become an author. His first book, Precaution (1820), was a conventional novel of manners set in English society; but his second book, The Spy (1821), was an exciting adventure tale set in the turmoil of the American Revolution. Almost by accident, Cooper had invented the genre of the American novel.

Cooper's third novel, The Pioneers (1823), is generally regarded as his best book, and it is certainly the most autobiographical of all his works. Set in a fictionalized ver-sion of Cooperstown, the novel contains recognizable portraits of Cooper's father (in Judge Marmaduke) and of his sister (in Elizabeth Temple, the story's heroine). The novel's most famous character is Natty Bumppo, nicknamed "Leather-stocking." Rough and illiterate, yet a crack shot and a skilled frontiersman, Natty is a rescuer of damsels in distress, a friend to Indians, and a sympathetic witness to the cruel extinction of the passenger pigeon, a bird whose flocks once darkened the skies of America. At the end of the novel, Natty shoulders his rifle and marches off into the sunset, answering the call of the open frontier.

Over the next two decades, Cooper wrote four more novels about Natty Bumppo: The Last of the Mohicans *(1826),* The Prairie *(1827),* The Pathfinder *(1840), and* The Deerslayer *(1841). Known collectively as* The Leather-Stocking Tales, *these five novels tell a distinctively American story that is epic in scope: the taming of wilderness, the destruction of indigenous peoples, the settling of the frontier, and the development of a new social order that we now recognize as the epitome of small-town America. As a roving adventurer in the midst of these events, Natty Bumppo remains aloof from the social order that is encroaching upon the wilderness, and this position as an outsider enables Cooper to develop a uniquely ambivalent perspective on the inexorable march of civilization across the North American continent.*

From The Pioneers

Chapter 22

> Men, boys, and girls,
> Desert th' unpeopled village; and wild crowds
> Spread o'er the plain, by the sweet phrensy driven.
>
> Somerville[1]

From this time to the close of April the weather continued to be a succession of great and rapid changes. One day, the soft airs of spring seemed to be stealing along the valley, and in unison with an invigorating sun, attempting covertly to rouse the dormant powers of the vegetable world; while on the next, the surly blasts from the north would sweep across the lake, and erase every impression left by their gentle adversaries. The snow, however, finally disappeared, and the green wheat-fields were seen in every direction, spotted with the dark and charred stumps that had, the preceding season, supported some of the proudest trees of the forest. Ploughs were in motion, wherever those useful implements could be used, and the smokes of the sugar-camps[2] were no longer seen issuing from the woods of maple. The lake had lost the beauty of a field of ice, but still a dark and gloomy covering concealed its waters, for the absence of currents left them yet hidden under a porous crust, which, saturated with the fluid, barely retained enough strength to preserve the contiguity of its parts. Large flocks of wild geese were seen passing over the country, which hovered, for a time, around the hidden sheet of water, apparently searching for a resting place; and then, on finding themselves excluded by

---

[1] From *The Chace*, 2:197–99, by the English poet William Somerville (1675–1742).

[2] Shacks where maple sap was boiled down into syrup.

the chill covering, would soar away to the north, filling the air with discordant screams, as if venting their complaints at the tardy operations of nature.

For a week, the dark covering of the Otsego was left to the undisturbed possession of two eagles, who alighted on the centre of its field, and sat eyeing their undisputed territory. During the presence of these monarchs of the air, the flocks of migrating birds avoided crossing the plain of ice, by turning into the hills, apparently seeking the protection of the forests, while the white and bald heads of the tenants of the lake were turned upward, with a look of contempt. But the time had come when even these kings of birds were to be dispossessed. An opening had been gradually increasing at the lower extremity of the lake, and around the dark spot where the current of the river prevented the formation of ice, during even the coldest weather; and the fresh southerly winds, that now breathed freely upon the valley, made an impression on the waters. Mimic waves began to curl over the margin of the frozen field, which exhibited an outline of crystallizations that slowly receded toward the north. At each step the power of the winds and the waves increased, until, after a struggle of a few hours, the turbulent little billows succeeded in setting the whole field in motion, when it was driven beyond the reach of the eye, with a rapidity that was as magical as the change produced in the scene by this expulsion of the lingering remnant of winter. Just as the last sheet of agitated ice was disappearing in the distance, the eagles rose, and soared with a wide sweep above the clouds, while the waves tossed their little caps of snow into the air, as if rioting in their release from a thraldom of five months' duration.

The following morning Elizabeth[3] was awakened by the exhilarating sounds of the martins, who were quarrelling and chattering around the little boxes suspended above her windows, and the cries of Richard, who was calling in tones animating as the signs of the season itself—

"Awake! awake! my fair lady! the gulls are hovering over the lake already, and the heavens are alive with pigeons. You may look an hour before you can find a hole through which to get a peep at the sun. Awake! awake! lazy ones! Benjamin is overhauling the ammunition, and we only wait for our breakfasts, and away for the mountains and pigeon shooting."

There was no resisting this animated appeal, and in a few minutes Miss Temple and her friend descended to the parlor. The doors of the hall were thrown open, and the mild, balmy air of a clear spring morning was ventilating the apartment where the vigilance of the ex-steward had been so long maintaining an artificial heat with such unremitted diligence. The gentlemen were impatiently waiting for their morning's repast, each equipped in the garb of a sportsman. Mr. Jones made many visits to the southern door, and would cry—

"See, cousin Bess! see, 'duke, the pigeon-roosts of the south have broken up! They are growing more thick every instant. Here is a flock that the eye cannot see the end of. There is food enough in it to keep the army of Xerxes[4] for a

---

[3] Elizabeth Temple is the daughter of Marmaduke Temple, a judge in the frontier village of Templeton (modeled after Cooperstown, New York). Several other characters in the novel are related to Marmaduke: Richard Jones (the village sheriff) is his cousin, and Benjamin Penguillan is his majordomo, or steward.

[4] Xerxes the Great, King of Persia from 486 to 465 B.C.

month, and feathers enough to make beds for the whole country. Xerxes, Mr. Edwards,[5] was a Grecian king who—no, he was a Turk, or a Persian, who wanted to conquer Greece, just the same as these rascals will overrun our wheat-fields, when they come back in the fall. Away! away! Bess; I long to pepper them."

In this wish both Marmaduke and young Edwards seemed equally to participate, for the sight was exhilarating to a sportsman; and the ladies soon dismissed the party after a hasty breakfast.

If the heavens were alive with pigeons,[6] the whole village seemed equally in motion, with men, women, and children. Every species of fire-arms, from the French ducking-gun with a barrel near six feet in length, to the common horseman's pistol, was to be seen in the hands of the men and boys; while bows and arrows, some made of the simple stick of a walnut sapling, and others in a rude imitation of the ancient cross-bows, were carried by many of the latter.

The houses and the signs of life apparent in the village, drove the alarmed birds from the direct line of their flight, toward the mountains, along the sides and near the bases of which they were glancing in dense masses, equally wonderful by the rapidity of their motion, and their incredible numbers.

We have already said, that across the inclined plane which fell from the steep ascent of the mountain to the banks of the Susquehanna, ran the highway, on either side of which a clearing of many acres had been made at a very early day. Over those clearings, and up the eastern mountain, and along the dangerous path that was cut into its side, the different individuals posted themselves, and in a few moments the attack commenced.

Among the sportsmen was the tall, gaunt form of Leather-stocking,[7] walking over the field, with his rifle hanging on his arm, his dogs at his heels; the latter now scenting the dead or wounded birds, that were beginning to tumble from the flocks, and then crouching under the legs of their master, as if they participated in his feelings at this wasteful and unsportsmanlike execution.

The reports of the fire-arms became rapid, whole volleys rising from the plain, as flocks of more than ordinary numbers darted over the opening, shadowing the field like a cloud; and then the light smoke of a single piece would issue from among the leafless bushes on the mountain, as death was hurled on the retreat of the affrighted birds, who were rising from a volley, in a vain effort to escape. Arrows, and missiles of every kind, were in the midst of the flocks; and so numerous were the birds, and so low did they take their flight, that even long poles, in the hands of those on the sides of the mountain, were used to strike them to the earth.

During all this time, Mr. Jones, who disdained the humble and ordinary means of destruction used by his companions, was busily occupied, aided by Benjamin, in making arrangements for an assault of more than ordinarily fatal character. Among the relics of the old military excursions, that occasionally are

[5] Oliver Edwards, an eligible young bachelor, who is a stranger to the village.

[6] Passenger pigeons, now extinct. On the passenger pigeon, see also the selections in this anthology from Crèvecoeur and Leopold.

[7] Natty Bumppo, known as "Leather-stocking," is over seventy years old in this novel. Six feet tall, clad in deerskin, he embodies the independent spirit of the American frontier.

discovered throughout the different districts of the western part of New York, there had been found in Templeton, at its settlement, a small swivel,[8] which would carry a ball of a pound weight. It was thought to have been deserted by a war party of the whites, in one of their inroads into the Indian settlements, when, perhaps, convenience or their necessity induced them to leave such an incumbrance behind them in the woods. This miniature cannon had been released from the rust, and being mounted on little wheels, was now in a state for actual service. For several years it was the sole organ for extraordinary rejoicings used in those mountains. On the mornings of the Fourths of July, it would be heard ringing among the hills; and even Captain Hollister, who was the highest authority in that part of the country on all such occasions, affirmed that, considering its dimensions, it was no despicable gun for a salute. It was somewhat the worse for the service it had performed, it is true, there being but a trifling difference in size between the touch-hole and the muzzle. Still, the grand conceptions of Richard had suggested the importance of such an instrument in hurling death at his nimble enemies. The swivel was dragged by a horse into a part of the open space that the Sheriff thought most eligible for planting a battery of the kind, and Mr. Pump proceeded to load it. Several handfuls of duck-shot were placed on top of the powder, and the major-domo announced that his piece was ready for service.

The sight of such an implement collected all the idle spectators to the spot, who, being mostly boys, filled the air with cries of exultation and delight. The gun was pointed high, and Richard, holding a coal of fire in a pair of tongs, patiently took his seat on a stump, awaiting the appearance of a flock worthy of his notice.

So prodigious was the number of the birds, that the scattering fire of the guns, with the hurling of missiles, and the cries of the boys, had no other effect than to break off small flocks from the immense masses that continued to dart along the valley, as if the whole of the feathered tribe were pouring through that one pass. None pretended to collect the game, which lay scattered over the fields in such profusion as to cover the very ground with the fluttering victims.

Leather-stocking was a silent, but uneasy spectator of all these proceedings, but was able to keep his sentiments to himself until he saw the introduction of the swivel into the sports.

"This comes of settling a country!" he said; "here have I known the pigeons to fly for forty long years, and, till you made your clearings, there was nobody to skear or to hurt them. I loved to see them come into the woods, for they were company to a body; hurting nothing; being, as it was, as harmless as a garter-snake. But now it gives me sore thoughts when I hear the frighty things whizzing through the air, for I know it's only a motion to bring out all the brats in the village. Well! the Lord won't see the waste of his creatures for nothing, and right will be done to the pigeons, as well as others, by and by. There's Mr. Oliver, as bad as the rest of them, firing into the flocks, as if he was shooting down nothing but Mingo warriors."

[8] A small cannon that rotates on a pivot.

Among the sportsmen was Billy Kirby, who, armed with an old musket, was loading, and without even looking into the air, was firing and shouting as his victims fell even on his own person. He heard the speech of Natty, and took upon himself to reply—

"What! old Leather-stocking," he cried, "grumbling at the loss of a few pigeons! If you had to sow your wheat twice, and three times, as I have done, you wouldn't be so massyfully[9] feeling toward the divils.—Hurrah, boys! scatter the feathers! This is better than shooting at a turkey's head and neck, old fellow."

"It's better for you, maybe, Billy Kirby," replied the indignant old hunter, "and all them that don't know how to put a ball down a rifle barrel, or how to bring it up again with a true aim; but it's wicked to be shooting into flocks in this wasty manner; and none do it, who know how to knock over a single bird. If a body has a craving for pigeon's flesh, why, it's made the same as all other creatures, for man's eating; but not to kill twenty and eat one. When I want such a thing I go into the woods till I find one to my liking, and then I shoot him off the branches, without touching the feather of another, though there might be a hundred on the same tree. You couldn't do such a thing, Billy Kirby—you couldn't do it, if you tried."

"What's that, old corn-stalk? you sapless stub!" cried the wood chopper. "You have grown wordy, since the affair of the turkey; but if you are for a single shot, here goes at that bird which comes on by himself."

The fire from the distant part of the field had driven a single pigeon below the flock to which it belonged, and, frightened with the constant reports of the muskets, it was approaching the spot where the disputants stood, darting first from one side and then to the other, cutting the air with the swiftness of lightning, and making a noise with its wings not unlike the rushing of a bullet. Unfortunately for the wood-chopper, notwithstanding his vaunt, he did not see this bird until it was too late to fire as it approached, and he pulled his trigger at the unlucky moment when it was darting immediately over his head. The bird continued its course with the usual velocity.

Natty lowered the rifle from his arm when the challenge was made, and waiting a moment, until the terrified victim had got in a line with his eye, and had dropped near the bank of the lake, he raised it again with uncommon rapidity, and fired. It might have been chance, or it might have been skill, that produced the result; it was probably a union of both; but the pigeon whirled over in the air, and fell into the lake, with a broken wing. At the sound of his rifle, both his dogs started from his feet, and in a few minutes the "slut"[10] brought out the bird, still alive.

The wonderful exploit of Leather-stocking was noised through the field with great rapidity, and the sportsmen gathered in, to learn the truth of the report.

"What!" said young Edwards, "have you really killed a pigeon on the wing, Natty, with a single ball?"

"Haven't I killed loons before now, lad, that dive at the flash?" returned the hunter. "It's much better to kill only such as you want, without wasting your

---

[9] Mercifully.

[10] Female dog.

powder and lead, than to be firing into God's creatures in this wicked manner. But I came out for a bird, and you know the reason why I like small game, Mr. Oliver, and now I have got one I will go home, for I don't relish to see these wasty ways that you are all practsing as if the least thing wasn't made for use, and not to destroy."

"Thou sayest well, Leather-stocking," cried Marmaduke, "and I begin to think it time to put an end to this work of destruction."

"Put an ind, Judge, to your clearings. An't the woods his work as well as the pigeons? Use, but don't waste. Wasn't the woods made for the beasts and birds to harbor in? and when man wanted their flesh, their skins, or their feathers, there's the place to seek them. But I'll go to the hut with my own game, for I wouldn't touch one of the harmless things that cover the ground here, looking up with their eyes on me, as if they only wanted tongues to say their thoughts."

With this sentiment in his mouth, Leather-stocking threw his rifle over his arm, and followed by his dogs, stepped across the clearing with great caution, taking care not to tread on one of the wounded birds in his path. He soon entered the bushes on the margin of the lake, and was hid from view.

Whatever impression the morality of Natty made on the Judge, it was utterly lost on Richard. He availed himself of the gathering of the sportsmen, to lay a plan for one "fell swoop" of destruction. The musket men were drawn up in battle array, in a line extending on each side of his artillery, with orders to await the signal of firing from himself.

"Stand by, my lads," said Benjamin, who acted as an aide-de-camp on this occasion; "stand by, my hearties, and when Squire Dickens heaves out the signal to begin firing, d'ye see, you may open upon them in a broadside. Take care and fire low, boys, and you'll be sure to hull the flock."

"Fire low!" shouted Kirby:—"hear the old fool! If we fire low, we may hit the stumps, but not ruffle a pigeon."

"How should you know, you lubber?" cried Benjamin, with a very unbecoming heat for an officer on the eve of battle—"how should you know, you grampus? Haven't I sailed aboard of the Boadishy[11] for five years? and wasn't it a standing order to fire low, and to hull your enemy? Keep silence at your guns, boys, and mind the order that is passed."

The loud laughs of the musket men were silenced by the more authoritative voice of Richard, who called for attention and obedience to his signals.

Some millions of pigeons were supposed to have already passed, that morning, over the valley of Templeton; but nothing like the flock that was now approaching had been seen before. It extended from mountain to mountain in one solid blue mass, and the eye looked in vain, over the southern hills, to find its termination. The front of this living column was distinctly marked by a line but very slightly indented, so regular and even was the flight. Even Marmaduke forgot the morality of Leather-stocking as it approached, and, in common with the rest, brought his musket to a poise.

---

[11] The *Boadicea*, a naval vessel named after an ancient British queen, on which Benjamin had served during his military career.

"Fire!" cried the Sheriff, clapping a coal to the priming of the cannon. As half of Benjamin's charge escaped through the touch-hole, the whole volley of the musketry preceded the report of the swivel. On receiving this united discharge of small-arms, the front of the flock darted upward, while, at the same instant, myriads of those in the rear rushed with amazing rapidity into their places, so that when the column of white smoke gushed from the mouth of the little cannon, an accumulated mass of objects was gliding over its point of direction. The roar of the gun echoed along the mountains, and died away to the north, like distant thunder, while the whole flock of alarmed birds seemed, for a moment, thrown into one disorderly and agitated mass. The air was filled with their irregular flight, layer rising above layer, far above the tops of the highest pines, none daring to advance beyond the dangerous pass; when, suddenly, some of the leaders of the feathered tribe shot across the valley, taking their flight directly over the village, and hundreds of thousands in their rear followed the example, deserting the eastern side of the plain to their persecutors and the slain.

"Victory!" shouted Richard, "victory! we have driven the enemy from the field."

"Not so, Dickon," said Marmaduke: "the field is covered with them; and, like the Leather-stocking, I see nothing but eyes, in every direction, as the innocent sufferers turn their heads in terror. Full one-half of those that have fallen are yet alive; and I think it is time to end the sport, if sport it be."

"Sport!" cried the Sheriff; "it is princely sport! There are some thousands of the blue-coated boys on the ground, so that every old woman in the village may have a pot-pie for the asking."

"Well, we have happily frightened the birds from this side of the valley," said Marmaduke, "and the carnage must of necessity end, for the present. Boys, I will give you six-pence a hundred for the pigeons' heads only: so go to work and bring them into the village."

This expedient produced the desired effect, for every urchin on the ground went industriously to work to wring the necks of the wounded birds. Judge Temple retired toward his dwelling with that kind of feeling that many a man has experienced before him, who discovers, after the excitement of the moment has passed, that he has purchased pleasure at the price of misery to others. Horses were loaded with the dead; and, after this first burst of sporting, the shooting of pigeons became a business, with a few idlers, for the remainder of the season. Richard, however, boasted for many a year, of his shot with the "cricket"; and Benjamin gravely asserted, that he thought they killed nearly as many pigeons on that day, as there were Frenchmen destroyed on the memorable occasion of Rodney's victory.[12]

---

[12] A famous naval engagement in which the British admiral George Bridges, Baron Rodney, defeated French forces off the coast of Dominica in April 1782.

✑ Percy Bysshe Shelley (1792–1822)

Like his good friend Lord Byron, Percy Bysshe Shelley was from an aristocratic family whose conservative values he did his level best to reject, rebelling against the social and moral conventions of his day. He studied for only six months at Oxford before a pamphlet that he and a friend had written, entitled The Necessity of Atheism, *led to his expulsion. Soon after, he disobeyed his father and married the sixteen-year-old daughter of the proprietor of a coffeehouse, Harriet Westbrook. The couple traveled throughout Scotland and England, with Shelley all the while engaged in writing about various radical causes, including freedom of the press, Irish rights, and vegetarianism. Shelley's radicalism was in the spirit of the principles of the French Revolution, and thus it is no surprise that when he and his wife returned to London, Shelley attached himself to radical social philosopher William Godwin. A believer in nonexclusivity in romantic relationships, Shelley fell in love with Godwin's daughter, Mary Godwin, and the two ran away to Europe together and then returned to England. Two years later, in 1816, Harriet Shelley committed suicide, and he married Mary Godwin. In England, Shelley found himself socially ostracized for his behavior and financially burdened by debts. He moved his family to Italy permanently in 1818. Despite almost continuous domestic upheavals, Shelley wrote some of his best poetry and his finest essays in this period. He drowned in a boating accident in Italy in 1822.*

Nearly all of Shelley's work demonstrates his commitment to battling injustice and oppression of any kind, although some of his work exhibits that commitment through a heavy dose of literary and philosophical abstraction. Although Shelley pledged himself to live according to his principles, he was fundamentally an idealist. Even his most beautifully sensual natural descriptions, in such poems as "Ode to the West Wind" or "Mont Blanc," develop more abstruse statements about the nature of power in general. In addition, poems such as "To a Skylark" and "Ode to the West Wind" demonstrate the important role of poetry in the process of human liberation, illustrating Shelley's famous claim in his essay "A Defence of Poetry" that "Poets are the unacknowledged legislators of the World."

Mont Blanc*

Lines Written in the Vale of Chamouni

I

The everlasting universe of things
Flows through the mind, and rolls its rapid waves,
Now dark, now glittering, now reflecting gloom,
Now lending splendor, where from secret springs
The source of human thought its tribute brings   5

---

* Mont Blanc is the tallest of the Alps.

Of waters,—with a sound but half its own,
Such as a feeble brook will oft assume
In the wild woods, among the mountains lone,
Where waterfalls around it leap forever,
Where woods and winds contend, and a vast river   10
Over its rocks ceaselessly bursts and raves.

2

Thus thou, Ravine of Arve[1]—dark, deep Ravine—
Thou many-colored, many-voicèd vale,
Over whose pines, and crags, and caverns sail
Fast cloud-shadows, and sunbeams! awful scene,   15
Where Power in likeness of the Arve comes down
From the ice-gulfs that gird his secret throne,
Bursting through these dark mountains like the flame
Of lightning through the tempest! thou dost lie,—
Thy giant brood of pines around thee clinging,   20
Children of elder time, in whose devotion
The chainless winds still come and ever came
To drink their odors, and their mighty swinging
To hear—an old and solemn harmony;
Thine earthly rainbows stretched across the sweep   25
Of the ethereal waterfall, whose veil
Robes some unsculptured image; the strange sleep
Which when the voices of the desert fail
Wraps all in its own deep eternity;
Thy caverns echoing to the Arve's commotion—   30
A loud, lone sound no other sound can tame.
Thou art pervaded with that ceaseless motion,
Thou art the path of that unresting sound,
Dizzy Ravine! and when I gaze on thee,
I seem as in a trance sublime and strange   35
To muse on my own separate fantasy,
My own, my human mind, which passively
Now renders and receives fast influencings,
Holding an unremitting interchange
With the clear universe of things around;   40
One legion of wild thoughts, whose wandering wings
Now float above thy darkness, and now rest,
Where that or thou art no unbidden guest,
In the still cave of the witch Poesy,
Seeking among the shadows that pass by—   45
Ghosts of all things that are—some shade of thee,

---

[1] The Arve River is located in the Chamounix Valley (now southeastern France), near Mont Blanc.

Some phantom, some faint image; till the breast
From which they fled recalls them, thou art there!

3

Some say that gleams of a remoter world
Visit the soul in sleep,—that death is slumber,   50
And that its shapes the busy thoughts outnumber
Of those who wake and live. I look on high;
Has some unknown Omnipotence unfurled
The veil of life and death? or do I lie
In dream, and does the mightier world of sleep   55
Spread far around and inaccessibly
Its circles? for the very spirit fails,
Driven like a homeless cloud from steep to steep
That vanishes among the viewless gales!
Far, far above, piercing the infinite sky,   60
Mont Blanc appears,—still, snowy and serene—
Its subject mountains their unearthly forms
Pile around it, ice and rock; broad vales between
Of frozen floods, unfathomable deeps,
Blue as the overhanging heaven, that spread   65
And wind among the accumulated steeps;
A desert peopled by the storms alone,
Save when the eagle brings some hunter's bone,
And the wolf tracks her there. How hideously
Its shapes are heaped around! rude, bare and high,   70
Ghastly, and scarred, and riven.—Is this the scene
Where the old Earthquake-daemon taught her young
Ruin? Were these their toys? or did a sea
Of fire envelop once this silent snow?
None can reply—all seems eternal now.   75
The wilderness has a mysterious tongue
Which teaches awful doubt, or faith so mild,
So solemn, so serene, that man may be
But for such faith with Nature reconciled;
Thou hast a voice, great Mountain, to repeal   80
Large codes of fraud and woe; not understood
By all, but which the wise, and great, and good,
Interpret, or make felt, or deeply feel.

4

The fields, the lakes, the forests and the streams,
Ocean, and all the living things that dwell   85
Within the daedal[2] earth, lightning, and rain,

---

[2] Ornate or intricately made, from the name Daedalus, the builder of the mythical labyrinth in Crete.

Earthquake, and fiery flood, and hurricane,
The torpor of the year when feeble dreams
Visit the hidden buds or dreamless sleep
Holds every future leaf and flower, the bound   90
With which from that detested trance they leap,
The works and ways of man, their death and birth,
And that of him and all that his may be, —
All things that move and breathe with toil and sound
Are born and die, revolve, subside and swell;   95
Power dwells apart in its tranquillity,
Remote, serene, and inaccessible; —
And *this*, the naked countenance of earth
On which I gaze, even these primeval mountains,
Teach the adverting mind. The glaciers creep,   100
Like snakes that watch their prey, from their far fountains,
Slow rolling on; there many a precipice
Frost and the Sun in scorn of mortal power
Have piled — dome, pyramid and pinnacle,
A city of death, distinct with many a tower   105
And wall impregnable of beaming ice;
Yet not a city, but a flood of ruin
Is there, that from the boundaries of the sky
Rolls its perpetual stream; vast pines are strewing
Its destined path, or in the mangled soil   110
Branchless and shattered stand; the rocks, drawn down
From yon remotest waste, have overthrown
The limits of the dead and living world,
Never to be reclaimed. The dwelling-place
Of insects, beasts and birds, becomes its spoil,   115
Their food and their retreat forever gone;
So much of life and joy is lost. The race
Of man flies far in dread; his work and dwelling
Vanish, like smoke before the tempest's stream,
And their place is not known. Below, vast caves   120
Shine in the rushing torrents' restless gleam,
Which from those secret chasms in tumult welling
Meet in the Vale; and one majestic River,
The breath and blood of distant lands, forever
Rolls its loud waters to the ocean waves,   125
Breathes its swift vapors to the circling air.

5

Mont Blanc yet gleams on high: the power is there,
The still and solemn power of many sights
And many sounds, and much of life and death.
In the calm darkness of the moonless nights,   130

In the lone glare of day, the snows descend
Upon that Mountain; none beholds them there,
Nor when the flakes burn in the sinking sun,
Or the star-beams dart through them; winds contend
Silently there, and heap the snow, with breath   135
Rapid and strong, but silently! Its home
The voiceless lightning in these solitudes
Keeps innocently, and like vapor broods
Over the snow. The secret strength of things,
Which governs thought, and to the infinite dome   140
Of heaven is as a law, inhabits thee!
And what were thou, and earth, and stars, and sea,
If to the human mind's imaginings
Silence and solitude were vacancy?

Ode to the West Wind

1

O wild West Wind, thou breath of Autumn's being,
Thou, from whose unseen presence the leaves dead
Are driven, like ghosts from an enchanter fleeing,

Yellow, and black, and pale, and hectic red,
Pestilence-stricken multitudes: O Thou,   5
Who chariotest to their dark wintry bed

The wingèd seeds, where they lie cold and low,
Each like a corpse within its grave, until
Thine azure sister of the Spring shall blow

Her clarion o'er the dreaming earth, and fill   10
(Driving sweet buds like flocks to feed in air)
With living hues and odors plain and hill:

Wild Spirit, which art moving everywhere;
Destroyer and preserver; hear, O hear!

2

Thou on whose stream, 'mid the steep sky's commotion,   15
Loose clouds like earth's decaying leaves are shed,
Shook from the tangled boughs of Heaven and Ocean,

Angels of rain and lightning: there are spread
On the blue surface of thine airy surge,
Like the bright hair uplifted from the head   20

Of some fierce Maenad,[1] even from the dim verge
Of the horizon to the zenith's height,
The locks of the approaching storm. Thou dirge

Of the dying year, to which this closing night
Will be the dome of a vast sepulchre,   25
Vaulted with all thy congregated might

Of vapors, from whose solid atmosphere
Black rain, and fire, and hail will burst: O hear!

3

Thou who didst waken from his summer dreams
The blue Mediterranean, where he lay,   30
Lulled by the coil of his crystalline streams,

Beside a pumice isle in Baiae's bay,[2]
And saw in sleep old palaces and towers
Quivering within the wave's intenser day,

All overgrown with azure moss and flowers   35
So sweet the sense faints picturing them! thou
For whose path the Atlantic's level powers

Cleave themselves into chasms, while far below
The sea-blooms and the oozy woods which wear
The sapless foliage of the ocean know   40

Thy voice, and suddenly grow gray with fear,
And tremble and despoil themselves: O hear!

4

If I were a dead leaf thou mightest bear;
If I were a swift cloud to fly with thee;
A wave to pant beneath thy power, and share   45

The impulse of thy strength, only less free
Than thou, O Uncontrollable! If even
I were as in my boyhood, and could be

The comrade of thy wanderings over Heaven,
As then, when to outstrip thy skyey speed   50
Scarce seemed a vision; I would ne'er have striven

As thus with thee in prayer in my sore need.
Oh, lift me as a wave, a leaf, a cloud!
I fall upon the thorns of life! I bleed!

---

[1] A female follower of Dionysus, the Greek god of wine and fertility. The Maenads were known for their frenzied and ecstatic worship.

[2] In Italy, near Naples.

A heavy weight of hours has chained and bowed   55
One too like thee: tameless, and swift, and proud.

5

Make me thy lyre, even as the forest is:
What if my leaves are falling like its own!
The tumult of thy mighty harmonies

Will take from both a deep, autumnal tone,   60
Sweet though in sadness. Be thou, Spirit fierce,
My spirit! Be thou me, impetuous one!

Drive my dead thoughts over the universe
Like withered leaves to quicken a new birth!
And, by the incantation of this verse,   65

Scatter, as from an unextinguished hearth
Ashes and sparks, my words among mankind!
Be through my lips to unawakened Earth

The trumpet of a prophecy! O Wind,
If Winter comes, can Spring be far behind?   70

The Cloud

I bring fresh showers for the thirsting flowers,
    From the seas and the streams;
I bear light shade for the leaves when laid
    In their noonday dreams.
From my wings are shaken the dews that waken   5
    The sweet buds every one,
When rocked to rest on their Mother's breast,
    As she dances about the sun.
I wield the flail of the lashing hail,
    And whiten the green plains under,   10
And then again I dissolve it in rain,
    And laugh as I pass in thunder.

I sift the snow on the mountains below,
    And their great pines groan aghast;
And all the night 'tis my pillow white,   15
    While I sleep in the arms of the Blast.
Sublime on the towers of my skyey bowers,
    Lightning my pilot sits;
In a cavern under is fettered the Thunder,
    It struggles and howls at fits;   20
Over earth and ocean with gentle motion,
    This pilot is guiding me,

Lured by the love of the Genii that move
　In the depths of the purple sea;
Over the rills, and the crags, and the hills,　　　　　　　　　25
　Over the lakes and the plains,
Wherever he dream, under mountain or stream,
　The Spirit he loves remains;
And I all the while bask in heaven's blue smile,
　Whilst he is dissolving in rains.　　　　　　　　　　　30

The sanguine Sunrise, with his meteor eyes,
　And his burning plumes outspread,
Leaps on the back of my sailing rack,
　When the morning star shines dead;
As on the jag of a mountain crag,　　　　　　　　　　　35
　Which an earthquake rocks and swings,
An eagle alit one moment may sit
　In the light of its golden wings.
And when Sunset may breathe, from the lit sea beneath,
　Its ardors of rest and of love,　　　　　　　　　　　40
And the crimson pall of eve may fall
　From the depth of heaven above,
With wings folded I rest, on mine airy nest,
　As still as a brooding dove.

That orbèd maiden, with white fire laden,　　　　　　　45
　Whom mortals call the Moon,
Glides glimmering o'er my fleece-like floor,
　By the midnight breezes strewn;
And wherever the beat of her unseen feet,
　Which only the angels hear,　　　　　　　　　　　50
May have broken the woof of my tent's thin roof,
　The stars peep behind her and peer;
And I laugh to see them whirl and flee,
　Like a swarm of golden bees,
When I widen the rent in my wind-built tent,　　　　　55
　Till the calm rivers, lakes, and seas,
Like strips of the sky fallen through me on high,
　Are each paved with the moon and these.

I bind the Sun's throne with a burning zone,
　And the Moon's with a girdle of pearl;　　　　　　　60
The Volcanoes are dim, and the Stars reel and swim,
　When the Whirlwinds my banner unfurl.
From cape to cape, with a bridge-like shape,
　Over a torrent sea,
Sunbeam-proof, I hang like a roof,—　　　　　　　　65
　The mountains its columns be.
The triumphal arch, through which I march,
　With hurricane, fire, and snow,

When the powers of the air are chained to my chair,
  Is the million-colored bow;   70
The Sphere-fire above its soft colors wove,
  While the moist Earth was laughing below.

I am the daughter of Earth and Water,
  And the nursling of the Sky;
I pass through the pores of the ocean and shores;   75
  I change, but I cannot die.
For after the rain, when with never a stain
  The pavilion of heaven is bare,
And the winds and sunbeams with their convex gleams
  Build up the blue dome of air,   80
I silently laugh at my own cenotaph,
  And out of the caverns of rain,
Like a child from the womb, like a ghost from the tomb,
  I arise and unbuild it again.

To a Skylark

Hail to thee, blithe Spirit!
  Bird thou never wert,
That from Heaven, or near it,
  Pourest thy full heart
In profuse strains of unpremeditated art.   5

Higher still and higher
  From the earth thou springest
Like a cloud of fire;
  The blue deep thou wingest,
And singing still dost soar, and soaring ever singest.   10

In the golden lightning
  Of the sunken Sun,
O'er which clouds are bright'ning,
  Thou dost float and run;
Like an unbodied joy whose race is just begun.   15

The pale purple even
  Melts around thy flight;
Like a star of Heaven
  In the broad daylight
Thou art unseen,—but yet I hear thy shrill delight,   20

Keen as are the arrows
  Of that silver sphere,
Whose intense lamp narrows

In the white dawn clear
Until we hardly see—we feel that it is there;   25

All the earth and air
With thy voice is loud,
As when Night is bare
From one lonely cloud
The moon rains out her beams,—and Heaven is overflowed.   30

What thou art we know not;
What is most like thee?
From rainbow clouds there flow not
Drops so bright to see
As from thy presence showers a rain of melody.   35

Like a Poet hidden
In the light of thought,
Singing hymns unbidden
Till the world is wrought
To sympathy with hopes and fears it heeded not: 40

Like a high-born maiden
In a palace tower,
Soothing her love-laden
Soul in secret hour
With music sweet as love,—which overflows her bower: 45

Like a glow-worm golden
In a dell of dew,
Scattering unbeholden
Its aerial hue
Among the flowers and grass which screen it from the view: 50

Like a rose embowered
In its own green leaves,
By warm winds deflowered,
Till the scent it gives
Makes faint with too much sweet those heavy-wingèd thieves.   55

Sound of vernal showers
On the twinkling grass,
Rain-awakened flowers,
All that ever was
Joyous and clear and fresh, thy music doth surpass.   60

Teach us, Sprite or Bird,
What sweet thoughts are thine;
I have never heard
Praise of love or wine
That panted forth a flood of rapture so divine: 65

Chorus Hymeneal,[1]
  Or triumphal chant,
Matched with thine, would be all
  But an empty vaunt,
A thing wherein we feel there is some hidden want.   70

What objects are the fountains
  Of thy happy strain?
What fields or waves or mountains?
  What shapes of sky or plain?
What love of thine own kind? what ignorance of pain?   75

With thy clear keen joyance
  Languor cannot be;
Shadow of annoyance
  Never came near thee;
Thou lovest—but ne'er knew love's sad satiety.   80

Waking or asleep
  Thou of death must deem
Things more true and deep
  Than we mortals dream—
Or how could thy notes flow in such a crystal stream?   85

We look before and after,
  And pine for what is not;
Our sincerest laughter
  With some pain is fraught;
Our sweetest songs are those that tell of saddest thought.   90

Yet if we could scorn
  Hate and pride and fear;
If we were things born
  Not to shed a tear,
I know not how thy joy we ever should come near.   95

Better than all measures
  Of delightful sound,
Better than all treasures
  That in books are found,
Thy skill to poet were, thou Scorner of the ground!   100

Teach me half the gladness
  That thy brain must know,
Such harmonious madness
  From my lips would flow
The world should listen then—as I am listening now.   105

---

[1] Of or pertaining to weddings or marriage.

✒ *John Clare* (1793–1864)

Despite the fact that he had only a rudimentary formal education, John Clare was one of the most prolific poets of the nineteenth century. Born in the village of Helpston in the rural southeast of England, Clare devotes much of his poetry to recording the devastating effects of agricultural enclosure and property consolidation on his native landscape. "Improvements" such as land enclosure were intended to promote the more efficient use of farmland. However, as poems such as "The Lament of Swordy Well" and "Helpston Green" poignantly reveal, enclosure not only destroyed the livelihoods of small landholders (like Clare's own parents), it also obliterated open fields and common "waste" areas and decimated innocent trees, plants, and animals in the name of increased agricultural output. Clare nostalgizes an idyllic countryside before the com- ing of enclosure, one which is associated with memories of his own childhood. He also elegizes the disappearing landscape around him and all of its endangered inhabitants, be they daisies, badgers, or rural farmers. Clare's skills as one of the first working-class natural historians are evident in the painstakingly attentive care he devotes to observ- ing and honestly describing even the smallest and seemingly least significant parts of his local ecosystem. This technique is seen in poems such as "The Pettichap's Nest." While Clare is fascinated with that which is hidden or possibly unobserved, he also realizes the trespass that his poetic description potentially commits. Clare attempts to counter any possible act of literary violation in his work through an ever-present, empathetic identification with his environment. This feature makes Clare's poems, even with their irregular spelling and punctuation (indications of Clare's self-taught status), equal to the achievement of any of his Romantic contemporaries in his writing about nature. And although Clare was influenced by the sensibility of his own age, his poetry also owes a debt to the great tradition of eighteenth-century locodescriptive poetry, in particular the work of Thomson, whose Seasons *was the first book Clare ever owned and which remained one of his particular favorites. Thomson's impact is evident in the intensely visual quality of Clare's poetry as well as in dimensions of its style, language, and imagery. He was also an admirer of fellow laboring-class poet Robert Bloomfield's work.*

Clare published four volumes during his lifetime: Poems Descriptive of Rural Life and Scenery *(1820),* The Village Minstrel *(1821),* The Shepherd's Calendar; with Village Stories and Other Poems *(1827), and* The Rural Muse *(1835). These col- lections represent only a small portion of Clare's output, as he wrote voluminously throughout his life, leaving much of his poetry and nonfiction prose unpublished at the time of his death. Although he enjoyed moderate success with his first two publications, Clare never attained financial security from his writing and, despite some well-meaning patronage, continued to work as a day laborer to support his large family, until he grad- ually succumbed to the mental illness that would necessitate his incarceration for the final twenty-seven years of his life. So attached was Clare to his local environment that many scholars feel that his family's move to a town only three miles distant from where Clare grew up was enough to precipitate his first serious breakdown. Clare continues to be a "poet's poet" and his importance has grown in the twentieth century, notably through his influence on authors such as Theodore Roethke, John Ashbery, and Seamus Heaney.*

Helpston Green

Ye injured fields ere while so gay
When nature's hand displayed
Long waving rows of Willows gray
And clumps of Hawthorn shade
But now alas your awthorn bowers   5
All desolate we see
The tyrant's hand their shade devours
And cuts down every tree

Not trees alone have felt their force
Whole Woods beneath them bowed   10
They stopt the winding runlets course
And flowrey pastures ploughed
To shrub nor tree throughout thy fields
They no compasion show
The uplifted ax no mercy yields   15
But strikes a fatal blow

When ere I muse along the plain
And mark where once they grew
Rememberance wakes her busy train
And brings past scenes to view   20
The well known brook the favorite tree
In fancy's eye appear
And next that pleasant green I see
That green for ever dear

O'er its green hills I've often strayed   25
In Childhood's happy hour
Oft sought the nest along the shade
And gathered many a flower
With fellow playmates often joined
In fresher sports to plan   30
But now increasing years have coined
This playmate into man

The green's gone too ah lovely scene
No more the king cup gay
Shall shine in yellow o'er the green   35
And add a golden ray
Nor more the herdsman's early call
Shall bring the cows to feed
Nor more the milk maids awkard brawl
Bright echo in the mead   40

Both milkmaid's shouts and herdsman's call
Have vanished with the green
The king kups yellow shades and all
Shall never more be seen
For all the cropping that does grow   45
Will so efface the scene
That after times will hardly know
It ever was a green

Farwell delightful spot farwell
Since every effort's vain   50
All I can do is still to tell
Of thy delightful plain
But that proves short—increasing years
That did my youth presage
When every new year's day appears   55
Will mellow into age

When age resumes the faultering tongue
Alas there's nought can save
Take one more step then all along
We drop into the grave   60
Reflection pierces deadly keen
While I the morral scan
As are the changes of the green
So is the life of man

Swordy Well

I've loved thee Swordy Well and love thee still
Long was I with thee tending sheep and cow
In boyhood ramping up each steepy hill
To play at "roly poly" down—and now
A man I trifle o'er thee cares to kill   5
Haunting thy mossy steeps to botanize
And hunt the orchis tribes where nature's skill
Doth like my thoughts run into phantasys
Spider and Bee all mimicking at will
Displaying powers that fools the proudly wise   10
Showing the wonders of great nature's plan
In trifles insignificant and small
Puzzling the power of that great trifle man
Who finds no reason to be proud at all

Emmonsales Heath

In thy wild garb of other times
I find thee lingering still
Furze o'er each lazy summit climbs
At nature's easy will

Grasses that never knew a scythe   5
Waves all the summer long
And wild weed blossoms waken blythe
That ploughshares never wrong

Stern industry with stubborn toil
And wants unsatisfied   10
Still leaves untouched thy maiden soil
In its unsullied pride

The birds still find their summer shade
To build their nests again
And the poor hare its rushy glade   15
To hide from savage men

Nature its family protects
In thy security
And blooms that love what man neglects
Find peaceful homes in thee   20

The wild rose scents thy summer air
And woodbines weave in bowers
To glad the swain sojourning there
And maidens gathering flowers

Creation's steps one's wandering meets   25
Untouched by those of man
Things seem the same in such retreats
As when the world began

Furze ling and brake[1] all mingling free
And grass forever green   30
All seem the same old things to be
As they have ever been

The brook o'er such neglected ground
One's weariness to soothe
Still wildly threads its lawless bounds   35
And chafes the pebble smooth

---

[1] *Furze ling and brake*: Furze is a thorny evergreen shrub. Ling is another name for heather, a common heath plant. Brake is a clump of brush or briars.

Crooked and rude as when at first
Its waters learned to stray
And from their mossy fountain burst
It washed itself a way   40

O who can pass such lovely spots
Without a wish to stray
And leave life's cares a while forgot
To muse an hour away

I've often met with places rude   45
Nor failed their sweet to share
But passed an hour with solitude
And left my blessing there

He that can meet the morning wind
And o'er such places roam   50
Nor leave a lingering wish behind
To make their peace his home—

His heart is dead to quiet hours
No love his mind employs
Poesy with him ne'er shares its flowers   55
Nor solitude its joys

O there are spots amid thy bowers
Which nature loves to find
Where spring drops round her earliest flowers
Uncheckt by winter's wind   60

Where cowslips wake the child's supprise
Sweet peeping ere their time
Ere April spreads her dappled skies
Mid morning's powdered rime

I've stretched my boyish walks to thee   65
When Mayday's paths were dry
When leaves had nearly hid each tree
And grass greened ankle-high

And mused the sunny hours away
And thought of little things   70
That children mutter o'er their play
When fancy tries its wings

Joy nursed me in her happy moods
And all life's little crowd
That haunt the waters fields and woods   75
Would sing their joys aloud

I thought how kind that mighty power
Must in his splendour be
Who spread around my boyish hour
Such gleams of harmony   80

Who did with joyous rapture fill
The low as well as high
And make the pismires round the hill
Seem full as blest as I

Hope's sun is seen of every eye   85
The halo that it gives
In nature's wide and common sky
Cheers every thing that lives

Sand Martin

Thou hermit haunter of the lonely glen
And common wild and heath—the desolate face
Of rude waste landscapes far away from men
Where frequent quarrys give thee dwelling place
With strangest taste and labour undeterred   5
Drilling small holes along the quarry's side
More like the haunts of vermin than a bird
And seldom by the nesting boy descried
I've seen thee far away from all thy tribe
Flirting about the unfrequented sky   10
And felt a feeling that I can't describe
Of lone seclusion and a hermit joy
To see thee circle round nor go beyond
That lone heath and its melancholly pond

The Yellowhammer's Nest

Just by the wooden brig a bird flew up
Frit[1] by the cowboy as he scrambled down
To reach the misty dewberry—let us stoop
And seek its nest—the brook we need not dread
'Tis scarcely deep enough a bee to drown   5
So it sings harmless o'er its pebbly bed
—Aye here it is, stuck close beside the bank
Beneath the bunch of grass that spindles rank

[1] Frightened.

Its husk-seeds tall and high — 'tis rudely planned
Of bleached stubbles and the withered fare   10
That last year's harvest left upon the land
Lined thinly with the horse's sable hair
— Five eggs pen-scribbled over lilac shells
Resembling writing, scrawls which fancy reads
As nature's poesy and pastoral spells   15
They are the yellowhammer's and she dwells
A poet like — where brooks and flowery weeds
As sweet as Castaly[2] to fancy seems
And that old molehill like as Parnass[3] hill
On which her partner haply sits and dreams   20
O'er all his joy of song — so leave it still
A happy home of sunshine flowers and streams
Yet in the sweetest places cometh ill
A noisome weed that burthens every soil
For snakes are known with chill and deadly coil   25
To watch such nests and seize the helpless young
And like as though the plague became a guest
Leaving a houseless home a ruined nest
And mournful hath the little warblers sung
When such like woes hath rent its little breast   30

---

[2] Castaly is perhaps Castalan, a spring on Mt. Parnassus that was said to bring inspiration.
[3] Parnassus, a Greek mountain; according to myth, home to Apollo, god of poetry.

The Pettichap's Nest

Well, in my many walks I rarely found
A place less likely for a bird to form
Its nest close by the rut-gulled waggon road
And on the almost bare foot-trodden ground
With scarce a clump of grass to keep it warm   5
And not a thistle spreads its spears abroad
Or prickly bush to shield it from harm's way
And yet so snugly made that none may spy
It out, save accident — and you and I
Had surely passed it on our walk today   10
Had chance not led us by it — nay e'en now
Had not the old bird heard us trampling by
And fluttered out — we had not seen it lie
Brown as the roadway side — small bits of hay
Pluckt from the old propt-haystack's pleachy brow   15
And withered leaves make up its outward walls

That from the snub-oak dotterel yearly falls
And in the old hedge bottom rot away
Built like an oven with a little hole
Hard to discover—that snug entrance wins   20
Scarcely admitting e'en two fingers in
And lined with feathers warm as silken stole
And soft as seats of down for painless ease
And full of eggs scarce bigger e'en than peas
Here's one most delicate with spots as small   25
As dust—and of a faint and pinky red
—We'll let them be and safety guard them well
For fear's rude paths around are thickly spread
And they are left to many dangers' ways
When green grasshopper's jump might break the shells   30
While lowing oxen pass them morn and night
And restless sheep around them hourly stray
And no grass springs but hungry horses bite
That trample past them twenty times a day
Yet like a miracle in safety's lap   35
They still abide unhurt and out of sight
—Stop, here's the bird. That woodman at the gap
Hath put it from the hedge—'tis olive green
Well I declare it is the pettichap
Not bigger than the wren and seldom seen   40
I've often found their nests in chance's way
When I in pathless woods did idly roam
But never did I dream untill today
A spot like this would be her chosen home

Insects

Thou tiney loiterer on the barley's beard
And happy unit of a numerous herd
Of playfellows the laughing summer brings
Mocking the sun's face in their glittering wings
How merrily they creep and run and flye   5
No kin they bear to labour's drudgery
Smoothing the velvet of the pale hedge-rose
And where they flye for dinner no one knows
The dewdrops feed them not—they love the shine
Of noon whose sun may bring them golden wine   10
All day they're playing in their Sunday dress
Till night goes sleep and they can do no less.
Then in the heath bell's silken hood they flie

And like to princes in their slumber lie
From coming night and dropping dews and all 15
In silken beds and roomy painted hall
So happily they spend their summer day
Now in the corn fields now the new mown hay
One almost fancys that such happy things
In coloured moods and richly burnished wings 20
Are fairy folk in splendid masquerade
Disguised through fear of mortal folk affraid
Keeping their merry pranks a mystery still
Lest glaring day should do their secrets ill

The Hedgehog

The hedgehog hides beneath the rotten hedge
And makes a great round nest of grass and sedge
Or in a bush or in a hollow tree
And many often stoops and say they see
Him roll and fill his prickles full of crabs 5
And creep away and where the magpie dabs
His wing at muddy dyke in aged root
He makes a nest and fills it full of fruit
On the hedge-bottom hunts for crabs and sloes
And whistles like a cricket as he goes 10
It rolls up like a ball or shapeless hog
When gipseys hunt it with their noisey dogs
I've seen it in their camps they call it sweet
Though black and bitter and unsavoury meat

But they who hunt the field for rotten meat[1] 15
And wash in muddy dyke and call it sweet
And eat what dogs refuse where e'er they dwell
Care little either for the taste or smell
They say they milk the cows and when they lye
Nibble their fleshy teats and make them dry 20
But they who've seen the small head like a hog
Rolled up to meet the savage of a dog
With mouth scarce big enough to hold a straw
Will ne'er believe what no one ever saw
But still they hunt the hedges all about 25
And shepherd dogs are trained to hunt them out
They hurl with savage force the stick and stone
And no one cares and still the strife goes on

[1] A reference to the gypsies.

The Badger

The badger grunting on his woodland track
With shaggy hide and sharp nose scrowed with black
Roots in the bushes and the woods and makes
A great hugh burrow in the ferns and brakes
With nose on ground he runs an awkward pace   5
And anything will beat him in the race
The shepherd's dog will run him to his den
Followed and hooted by the dogs and men
The woodman when the hunting comes about
Go round at night to stop the foxes out   10
And hurrying through the bushes ferns and brakes
Nor sees the many holes the badger makes
And often through the bushes to the chin
Breaks the old holes and tumbles headlong in

Some keep a baited badger tame as hog   15
And tame him till he follows like the dog
They urge him on like dogs and show fair play
He beats and scarcely wounded goes away
Lapt up as if asleep he scorns to fly
And siezes any dog that ventures nigh   20
Clapt like a dog he never bites the men
But worrys dogs and hurrys to his den
They let him out and turn a harrow down
And there he fights the host of all the town
He licks the patting hand and trys to play   25
And never trys to bite or run away
And runs away from noise in hollow trees
Burnt by the boys to get a swarm of bees

When midnight comes a host of dogs and men
Go out and track the badger to his den   30
And put a sack within the hole and lye
Till the old grunting badger passes bye
He comes and hears they let the strongest loose
The old fox hears the noise and drops the goose
The poacher shoots and hurrys from the cry   35
And the old hare half-wounded buzzes bye
They get a forked stick to bear him down
And clap the dogs and bear him to the town
And bait him all the day with many dogs
And laugh and shout and fright the scampering hogs   40
He runs along and bites at all he meets
They shout and hollo down the noisey streets

He turns about to face the loud uproar
And drives the rebels to their very doors
The frequent stone is hurled where e'er they go   45
When badgers fight and every one's a foe
The dogs are clapt and urged to join the fray
The badger turns and drives them all away
Though scarcly half as big, dimute and small,
He fights with dogs for hours and beats them all   50
The heavy mastiff savage in the fray
Lies down and licks his feet and turns away
The bull-dog knows his match and waxes cold
The badger grins and never leaves his hold
He drives the crowd and follows at their heels   55
And bites them through. The drunkard swears and reels,

The frighted women takes the boys away
The blackguard laughs and hurrys on the fray:
He tries to reach the woods, an awkard race,
But sticks and cudgels quickly stop the chace   60
He turns agen and drives the noisey crowd
And beats the many dogs in noises loud
He drives away and beats them every one
And then they loose them all and set them on
He falls as dead and kicked by boys and men   65
Then starts and grins and drives the crowd agen
Till kicked and torn and beaten out he lies
And leaves his hold and cackles groans and dies

The Eternity of Nature

Leaves from eternity are simple things
To the world's gaze—whereto a spirit clings
Sublime and lasting—trampled underfoot
The daisy lives and strikes its little root
Into the lap of time—centurys may come   5
And pass away into the silent tomb
And still the child hid in the womb of time
Shall smile and pluck them when this simple rhyme
Shall be forgotten like a churchyard-stone
Or lingering lie unnoticed and alone   10
When eighteen hundred years our common date
Grows many thousands in their marching state
Aye still the child with pleasure in his eye
Shall cry "The daisy!"—a familiar cry—
And run to pluck it—in the self-same state   15

As when time found it in his infant date
And like a child himself when all was new
Wonder might smile and make him notice too
—Its little golden bosom frilled with snow
Might win e'en Eve to stoop adown and show   20
Her partner Adam in the silky grass
This little gem that smiled where pleasure was
And loving Eve from Eden followed ill
And bloomed with sorrow and lives smiling still
As once in Eden under Heaven's breath   25
So now on blighted earth and on the lap of death
It smiles forever—cowslaps' golden blooms
That in the closen and the meadow comes
Shall come when kings and empires fade and die
And in the meadows as time's partners lie   30
As fresh two thousand years to come as now
With those five crimson spots upon its brow
And little brooks that hum a simple lay
In green unnoticed spots from praise away
Shall sing when poets in time's darkness hid   35
Shall lie like memory in a pyramid
Forgetting yet not all forgot—though lost
Like a thread's end in ravelled windings crost
And the small bumble-bee shall hum as long
As nightingales, for time protects the song   40
And nature is their soul to whom all clings
Of fair or beautiful in lasting things
The little robin in the quiet glen
Hidden from fame and all the strife of men
Sings unto time a pastoral and gives   45
A music that lives on and ever lives
Both spring and autumn, years rich bloom and fade
Longer than songs that poets ever made
And think ye these time's playthings—pass, proud skill,
Time loves them like a child and ever will   50
And so I worship them in bushy spots
And sing with them when all else notice not
And feel the music of their mirth agree
With that sooth quiet that bestirreth me
And if I touch aright that quiet tone   55
That soothing truth that shadows forth their own
Then many a year shall grow in after days
And still find hearts to love my quiet lays
Yet cheering mirth with thoughts sung not for fame

But for the joy that with their utterance came   60
That inward breath of rapture urged not loud
—Birds singing lone flie silent past the crowd
So in these pastoral spots which childish time
Makes dear to me I wander out and ryhme
What time the dewy morning's infancy   65
Hangs on each blade of grass and every tree
And sprents the red thighs of the bumble-bee
Who 'gins by times unwearied minstrelsy
Who breakfasts, dines, and most divinely sups
With every flower save golden buttercups   70
On their proud bosoms he will never go
And passes by with scarcely "How do ye do"
So in their showy gaudy shining cells
Maybe the summer's honey never dwells
—Her ways are mysterys all, yet endless youth   75
Lives in them all unchangable as truth
With the odd number five. Strange nature's laws
Plays many freaks nor once mistakes the cause
And in the cowslap-peeps this very day
Five spots appear which time ne'er wears away   80
Nor once mistakes the counting—look within
Each peep and five nor more nor less is seen
And trailing bindweed with its pinky cup
Five lines of paler hue goes streaking up
And birds a many keep the rule alive   85
And lay five eggs nor more nor less than five
And flowers how many own that mystic power
With five leaves ever making up the flower
The five-leaved grass trailing its golden cup
Of flowers—five leaves make all for which I stoop   90
And briony in the hedge that now adorns
The tree to which it clings and now the thorns
Own five star-pointed leaves of dingy white
Count which I will all make the number right
And spreading goosegrass trailing all abroad   95
In leaves of silver green about the road
Five leaves make every blossom all along
I stoop for many, none are counted wrong
'Tis nature's wonder and her maker's will
Who bade earth be and order owns him still   100
As that superior power who keeps the key
Of wisdom, power, and might through all eternity

Song's Eternity

What is song's eternity?
Come and see
Can it noise and bustle be?
Come and see
Praises sung or praises said,   5
Can it be?
Wait awhile and these are dead
Sigh sigh
Be they high or lowly bred
They die   10

What is song's eternity?
Come and see
Melodys of earth and sky
Here they be
Songs once sung to Adam's ears   15
Can it be?
—Ballads of six thousand years
Thrive thrive
Songs awakened with the spheres
Alive   20

Mighty songs that miss decay
What are they?
Crowds and citys pass away
Like a day
Books are writ and books are read   25
What are they?
Years will lay them with the dead
Sigh sigh
Trifles unto nothing wed
They die   30

Dreamers list' the honey-bee
Mark the tree
Where the blue cap, tootle tee,
Sings a glee
Sung to Adam and to Eve   35
Here they be
When floods covered every bough
Noah's ark
Heard that ballad singing now
Hark hark   40

Tootle tootle tootle tee
Can it be

Pride and fame must shadows be?
Come and see
Every season own her own   45
Bird and bee
Sing creation's music on
Nature's glee
Is in every mood and tone
Eternity   50

The eternity of song
Liveth here
Nature's universal tongue
Singeth here
Songs I've heard and felt and seen   55
Everywhere
Songs like the grass are evergreen
The giver
Said live and be, and they have been
For ever   60

Pastoral Poesy

True poesy is not in words
But images that thoughts express
By which the simplest hearts are stirred
To elevated happiness

Mere books would be but useless things   5
Where none had taste or mind to read
Like unknown lands where beauty springs
And none are there to heed

But poesy is a language meet
And fields are everyone's employ   10
The wild flower neath the shepherd's feet
Looks up and gives him joy

A language that is ever green
That feelings unto all impart
As awthorn blossoms soon as seen   15
Give May to every heart

The pictures that our summer minds
In summer's dwellings meet
The fancys that the shepherd finds
To make his leisure sweet   20

The dustmills that the cowboy delves
In banks for dust to run
Creates a summer in ourselves
He does as we have done

An image to the mind is brought   25
Where happiness enjoys
An easy thoughtlessness of thought
And meets excess of joys

The world is in that little spot
With him—and all beside   30
Is nothing. All a life forgot
In feelings satisfied

And such is poesy. Its power
May varied lights employ
Yet to all minds it gives the dower   35
Of self-creating joy

And whether it be hill or moor
I feel where e'er I go
A silence that discourses more
Than any tongue can do   40

Unruffled quietness hath made
A peace in every place
And woods are resting in their shade
Of social loneliness

The storm from which the shepherd turns   45
To pull his beaver down
While he upon the heath sojourns
Which autumn bleaches brown

Is music aye and more indeed
To those of musing mind   50
Who through the yellow woods proceed
And listen to the wind

The poet in his fitful glee
And fancy's many moods
Meets it as some strange melody   55
And poem of the woods

It sings and whistles in his mind
And then it talks aloud
While by some leaning tree reclined
He shuns a coming cloud   60

That sails its bulk against the sun
A mountain in the light
He heeds not for the storm begun
But dallys with delight

And now a harp that flings around   65
The music of the wind
The poet often hears the sound
When beauty fills the mind

The morn with saffron stripes and grey
Or blushing to the view   70
Like summer fields when run away
In weeds of crimson hue

Will simple shepherds' hearts imbue
With nature's poesy
Who inly fancy while they view   75
How grand must heaven be

With every musing mind she steals
Attendance on their way
The simplest thing her heart reveals
Is seldom thrown away   80

The old man full of leisure hours
Sits cutting at his door
Rude fancy sticks to tye his flowers
—They're sticks and nothing more

With many passing by his door,   85
But pleasure has its bent
With him 'tis happiness and more
Heart-satisfied content

Those box-edged borders that imprint
Their fragrance near his door   90
Hath been the comfort of his heart
For sixty years and more

That mossy thatch above his head
In winter's drifting showers
To him and his old partner made   95
A music many hours

It patted to their hearts a joy
That humble comfort made
A little fire to keep them dry
And shelter over head   100

And such no matter what they call
Each, all are nothing less
Then poesy's power that gives to all
A cheerful blessedness

So would I my own mind employ   105
And my own heart impress
That poesy's self's a dwelling joy
Of humble quietness

So would I for the biding joy
That to such thoughts belong   110
That I life's errand may employ
As harmless as a song

The Fallen Elm

Old elm that murmured in our chimney top
The sweetest anthem autumn ever made
And into mellow whispering calms would drop
When showers fell on thy many-coloured shade
And when dark tempests mimic thunder made   5
While darkness came as it would strangle light
With the black tempest of a winter night
That rocked thee like a cradle to thy root
How did I love to hear the winds upbraid
Thy strength without—while all within was mute   10
It seasoned comfort to our hearts' desire
We felt thy kind protection like a friend
And edged our chairs up closer to the fire
Enjoying comforts that was never penned
Old favourite tree thou'st seen time's changes lower   15
Though change till now did never injure thee
For time beheld thee as her sacred dower
And nature claimed thee her domestic tree
Storms came and shook thee many a weary hour
Yet stedfast to thy home thy roots hath been   20
Summers of thirst parched round thy homely bower
Till earth grew iron—still thy leaves was green
The children sought thee in thy summer shade
And made their play-house rings of sticks and stone
The mavis sang and felt himself alone   25
While in thy leaves his early nest was made
And I did feel his happiness mine own
Nought heeding that our friendship was betrayed

Friend not inanimate—though stocks and stones
There are and many formed of flesh and bones— 30
Thou owned a language by which hearts are stirred
Deeper than by a feeling cloathed in words
And speakest now what's known of every tongue
Language of pity and the force of wrong
What cant assumes, what hypocrites will dare 35
Speaks home to truth and shows it what they are
I see a picture which thy fate displays
And learn a lesson from thy destiny
Self-interest saw thee stand in freedom's ways
So thy old shadow must a tyrant be 40
Thou'st heard the knave abusing those in power
Bawl freedom loud and then opress the free
Thou'st sheltered hypocrites in many a shower
That when in power would never shelter thee
Thou'st heard the knave supply his canting powers 45
With wrong's illusions when he wanted friends
That bawled for shelter when he lived in showers
And when clouds vanished made thy shade amends
With axe at root he felled thee to the ground
And barked of freedom—O I hate the sound 50
Time hears its visions speak and age sublime
Had made thee a deciple unto time
—It grows the cant term of enslaving tools
To wrong another by the name of right
It grows the liscence of o'erbearing fools 55
To cheat plain honesty by force of might
Thus came enclosure—ruin was its guide
But freedom's clapping hands enjoyed the sight
Though comfort's cottage soon was thrust aside
And workhouse prisons raised upon the site 60
E'en nature's dwellings far away from men,
The common heath, became the spoilers' prey
The rabbit had not where to make his den
And labour's only cow was drove away
No matter—wrong was right and right was wrong 65
And freedom's bawl was sanction to the song
—Such was thy ruin, music-making elm
The rights of freedom was to injure thine
As thou wert served, so would they overwhelm
In freedom's name the little that is mine 70
And there are knaves that brawl for better laws
And cant of tyranny in stronger powers
Who glut their vile unsatiated maws
And freedom's birthright from the weak devours

The Mores

Far spread the moorey ground a level scene
Bespread with rush and one eternal green
That never felt the rage of blundering plough
Though centurys wreathed spring's blossoms on its brow
Still meeting plains that stretched them far away   5
In uncheckt shadows of green, brown, and grey
Unbounded freedom ruled the wandering scene
Nor fence of ownership crept in between
To hide the prospect of the following eye
Its only bondage was the circling sky   10
One mighty flat undwarfed by bush and tree
Spread its faint shadow of immensity
And lost itself, which seemed to eke its bounds
In the blue mist the horizon's edge surrounds

   Now this sweet vision of my boyish hours   15
Free as spring clouds and wild as summer flowers
Is faded all—a hope that blossomed free,
And hath been once, no more shall ever be
Inclosure came and trampled on the grave
Of labour's rights and left the poor a slave   20
And memory's pride ere want to wealth did bow
Is both the shadow and the substance now
The sheep and cows were free to range as then
Where change might prompt nor felt the bonds of men
Cows went and came, with evening morn and night,   25
To the wild pasture as their common right
And sheep, unfolded with the rising sun,
Heard the swains shout and felt their freedom won
Tracked the red fallow field and heath and plain
Then met the brook and drank and roamed again   30
The brook that dribbled on as clear as glass
Beneath the roots they hid among the grass
While the glad shepherd traced their tracks along
Free as the lark and happy as her song
But now all's fled and flats of many a dye   35
That seemed to lengthen with the following eye
Moors, loosing from the sight, far, smooth, and blea,
Where swoopt the plover in its pleasure free
Are vanished now with commons wild and gay
As poet's visions of life's early day   40
Mulberry-bushes where the boy would run

To fill his hands with fruit are grubbed and done
And hedgrow-briars—flower-lovers overjoyed
Came and got flower-pots—these are all destroyed
And sky-bound mores in mangled garbs are left   45
Like mighty giants of their limbs bereft
Fence now meets fence in owners' little bounds
Of field and meadow large as garden grounds
In little parcels little minds to please
With men and flocks imprisoned ill at ease   50
Each little path that led its pleasant way
As sweet as morning leading night astray
Where little flowers bloomed round a varied host
That travel felt delighted to be lost
Nor grudged the steps that he had ta'en as vain   55
When right roads traced his journeys and again—
Nay, on a broken tree he'd sit awhile
To see the mores and fields and meadows smile
Sometimes with cowslaps smothered—then all white
With daiseys—then the summer's splendid sight   60
Of cornfields crimson o'er the headache bloomed
Like splendid armys for the battle plumed
He gazed upon them with wild fancy's eye
As fallen landscapes from an evening sky
These paths are stopt—the rude philistine's thrall   65
Is laid upon them and destroyed them all
Each little tyrant with his little sign
Shows where man claims earth glows no more divine
But paths to freedom and to childhood dear
A board sticks up to notice "no road here"   70
And on the tree with ivy overhung
The hated sign by vulgar taste is hung[1]
As though the very birds should learn to know
When they go there they must no further go
Thus, with the poor, scared freedom bade goodbye   75
And much they feel it in the smothered sigh
And birds and trees and flowers without a name
All sighed when lawless law's enclosure came
And dreams of plunder in such rebel schemes
Have found too truly that they were but dreams   80

[1] A "No Trespassing" sign.

The Lament of Swordy Well

Petitioners are full of prayers
To fall in pity's way
But if her hand the gift forbears
They'll sooner swear than pray
They're not the worst to want who lurch   5
On plenty with complaints
No more then those who go to church
Are e'er the better saints

I hold no hat to beg a mite
Nor pick it up when thrown   10
Nor limping leg I hold in sight
But pray to keep my own
Where profit gets his clutches in
There's little he will leave
Gain stooping for a single pin   15
Will stick it on his sleeve

For passers-by I never pin
No troubles to my breast
Nor carry round some names to win
More money from the rest   20
I'm Swordy Well a piece of land
That's fell upon the town
Who worked me till I couldn't stand
And crush me now I'm down

In parish bonds I well may wail   25
Reduced to every shift
Pity may grieve at trouble's tale
But cunning shares the gift
Harvests with plenty on his brow
Leaves losses' taunts with me   30
Yet gain comes yearly with the plough
And will not let me be

Alas dependance thou'rt a brute
Want only understands
His feelings wither branch and root   35
That falls in parish hands.
The muck that clouts the ploughman's shoe
The moss that hides the stone,
Now I'm become the parish due,
Is more then I can own   40

Though I'm no man yet any wrong
Some sort of right may seek
And I am glad if e'en a song
Gives me the room to speak
I've got among such grubbling geer   45
And such a hungry pack
If I brought harvests twice a year
They'd bring me nothing back

When war their tyrant-prices got
I trembled with alarms   50
They fell and saved my little spot
Or towns had turned to farms
Let profit keep an humble place
That gentry may be known
Let pedigrees their honours trace   55
And toil enjoy its own

The silver springs grown naked dykes
Scarce own a bunch of rushes
When grain got high the tasteless tykes
Grubbed up trees, banks, and bushes   60
And me, they turned me inside out
For sand and grit and stones
And turned my old green hills about
And pickt my very bones

These things that claim my own as theirs   65
Were born by yesterday
But ere I fell to town affairs
I were as proud as they
I kept my horses, cows, and sheep
And built the town below   70
Ere they had cat or dog to keep
And then to use me so

Parish allowance gaunt and dread
Had it the earth to keep
Would even pine the bees to dead   75
To save an extra keep
Pride's workhouse is a place that yields
From poverty its gains
And mines a workhouse for the fields
A-starving the remains   80

The bees flye round in feeble rings
And find no blossom bye

Then thrum their almost weary wings
Upon the moss and die
Rabbits that find my hills turned o'er   85
Forsake my poor abode
They dread a workhouse like the poor
And nibble on the road

If with a clover bottle now
Spring dares to lift her head   90
The next day brings the hasty plough
And makes me misery's bed
The butterflyes may wir[1] and come
I cannot keep 'em now
Nor can they bear my parish home   95
That withers on my brow

No, now not e'en a stone can lie
I'm just what e'er they like
My hedges like the winter flye
And leave me but the dyke   100
My gates are thrown from off the hooks
The parish thoroughfare
Lord he that's in the parish books
Has little wealth to spare

I couldn't keep a dust of grit   105
Nor scarce a grain of sand
But bags and carts claimed every bit
And now they've got the land
I used to bring the summer's life
To many a butterflye   110
But in oppression's iron strife
Dead tussocks bow and sigh

I've scarce a nook to call my own
For things that creep or flye
The beetle hiding 'neath a stone   115
Does well to hurry bye
Stock eats my struggles every day
As bare as any road
He's sure to be in something's way
If e'er he stirs abroad   120

I am no man to whine and beg
But fond of freedom still
I hang no lies on pity's peg

---

[1] I.e., whirr.

To bring a grist to mill
On pity's back I needn't jump   125
My looks speak loud alone
My only tree they've left a stump
And nought remains my own

My mossy hills gain's greedy hand
And more than greedy mind   130
Levels into a russet land
Nor leaves a bent behind
In summers gone I bloomed in pride
Folks came for miles to prize
My flowers that bloomed nowhere beside   135
And scarce believed their eyes

Yet worried with a greedy pack
They rend and delve and tear
The very grass from off my back
I've scarce a rag to wear   140
Gain takes my freedom all away
Since its dull suit I wore
And yet scorn vows I never pay
And hurts me more and more

And should the price of grain get high—   145
Lord help and keep it low—
I shan't possess a single flye
Or get a weed to grow
I shan't possess a yard of ground
To bid a mouse to thrive   150
For gain has put me in a pound
I scarce can keep alive

I own I'm poor like many more
But then the poor mun live
And many came for miles before   155
For what I had to give
But since I fell upon the town
They pass me with a sigh
I've scarce the room to say "Sit down"
And so they wander bye   160

Though now I seem so full of clack
Yet when ye're riding bye
The very birds upon my back
Are not more fain to flye
I feel so lorn in this disgrace   165
God send the grain to fall

I am the oldest in the place
And the worst-served of all

Lord bless ye I was kind to all
And poverty in me   170
Could always find a humble stall
A rest and lodging free
Poor bodys with an hungry ass
I welcomed many a day
And gave him tether-room and grass   175
And never said him nay

There was a time my bit of ground
Made freemen of the slave
The ass no pindar'd dare to pound
When I his supper gave   180
The gipsey's camp was not affraid
I made his dwelling free
Till vile enclosure came and made
A parish slave of me

The gipseys further on sojourn   185
No parish bounds they like
No sticks I own and would earth burn
I shouldn't own a dyke
I am no friend to lawless work
Nor would a rebel be   190
And why I call a Christian turk
Is they are turks to me

And if I could but find a friend
With no deciet to sham
Who'd send me some few sheep to tend   195
And leave me as I am
To keep my hills from cart and plough
And strife of mongerel men
And as spring found me find me now
I should look up agen   200

And save his Lordship's woods, that past
The day of danger dwell,
Of all the fields I am the last
That my own face can tell
Yet what with stone pits' delving holes   205
And strife to buy and sell
My name will quickly be the whole
That's left of Swordy Well

I Am

I am—yet what I am, none cares or knows;
 My friends forsake me like a memory lost:
I am the self-consumer of my woes—
 They rise and vanish in oblivion's host
Like shadows in love-frenzied stifled throes   5
 And yet I am, and live—like vapours tost

Into the nothingness of scorn and noise,
 Into the living sea of waking dreams,
Where there is neither sense of life or joys,
 But the vast shipwreck of my life's esteems;   10
Even the dearest that I love the best
 Are strange—nay, rather, stranger than the rest.

I long for scenes where man hath never trod
 A place where woman never smiled or wept
There to abide with my Creator, God,   15
 And sleep as I in childhood sweetly slept,
Untroubling and untroubled where I lie
 The grass below—above, the vaulted sky.

The Peasant Poet

He loved the brook's soft sound
The swallow swimming by
He loved the daisy-covered ground
The cloud-bedappled sky
To him the dismal storm appeared   5
The very voice of God
And where the Evening rock was reared
Stood Moses with his rod
And every thing his eyes surveyed
The insects i' the brake   10
Were creatures God almighty made
He loved them for his sake
A silent man in life's affairs
A thinker from a Boy
A Peasant in his daily cares—   15
The Poet in his joy

✍ *William Cullen Bryant* (1794–1878)

William Cullen Bryant was born in the rural village of Cummington, Massachusetts. His father was a country doctor who possessed a good command of Latin and Greek, and the young Bryant showed precocious verbal ability, composing his first verses at age nine and publishing his first book of poetry, a political satire entitled The Embargo, *at age thirteen. Bryant entered Williams College in 1810, but he dropped out after a few months. In about 1810, Bryant acquired a copy of Wordsworth and Coleridge's* Lyrical Ballads, *a work that opened his eyes to new possibilities of writing about the natural world. Henceforth, he would emulate these English Romantic poets in his choice of metrical forms (particularly the ballad stanza and blank verse) and in his lyrical description of natural objects.*

Under pressure from his father to choose a lucrative profession, Bryant was apprenticed to study law. Admitted to the bar in 1815, he established a law practice in Great Barrington, Massachusetts. But Bryant still aspired to become a professional man of letters, and in 1821 he published a slim volume of poetry containing the extended blank verse meditation on death, "Thanatopsis," which remains his single best-known poem. Giving full rein to his literary ambition, in 1825 Bryant moved to New York City to become an editor of the New-York Review *and* Atheneum Magazine. *Although this magazine soon failed, Bryant eventually found a successful career as a journalist, and as a big-city editorial writer, he influenced the course of American politics for several decades. He advocated the development of the American West as a region free from slavery, and in 1860 he was a staunch supporter of Abraham Lincoln. Within New York City, Bryant campaigned for the creation of Central Park as oasis of greenery and fresh air.*

Bryant's fascination with the American West is apparent in his poem "The Prairies," written after a visit to Illinois in 1832 and first published in his Poems of 1834. *This lyrical depiction of the vast, fertile American plains is now regarded as his most characteristic and original work, and it clearly fulfills his ambition to create a new, distinctively American poetry. He evokes a mythic past in which the plains were inhabited by a civilized race of Mound Builders, and he imagines a future in which these silent, open spaces will be occupied by pioneering American settlers. Bryant affectionately describes the "gentle quadrupeds" that roam the prairies, and his poem ends on an elegiac note: He laments the impending devastation of the American wilderness, with all of its "startlingly beautiful" creatures.*

Thanatopsis*

    To him who in the love of Nature holds
Communion with her visible forms, she speaks
A various language; for his gayer hours
She has a voice of gladness, and a smile
And eloquence of beauty, and she glides   5

---

* Literally, "a meditation on death."

Into his darker musings, with a mild
And healing sympathy, that steals away
Their sharpness, ere he is aware. When thoughts
Of the last bitter hour come like a blight
Over thy spirit, and sad images   10
Of the stern agony, and shroud, and pall,
And breathless darkness, and the narrow house,
Make thee to shudder, and grow sick at heart;—
Go forth, under the open sky, and list
To Nature's teachings, while from all around—   15
Earth and her waters, and the depths of air,—
Comes a still voice—Yet a few days, and thee
The all-beholding sun shall see no more
In all his course; nor yet in the cold ground,
Where thy pale form was laid, with many tears,   20
Nor in the embrace of ocean, shall exist
Thy image. Earth, that nourished thee, shall claim
Thy growth, to be resolved to earth again,
And, lost each human trace, surrendering up
Thine individual being, shalt thou go   25
To mix for ever with the elements,
To be a brother to the insensible rock
And to the sluggish clod, which the rude swain
Turns with his share, and treads upon. The oak
Shall send his roots abroad, and pierce thy mould.   30

    Yet not to thine eternal resting place
Shalt thou retire alone—nor couldst thou wish
Couch more magnificent. Thou shalt lie down
With patriarchs of the infant world—with kings,
The powerful of the earth—the wise, the good,   35
Fair forms, and hoary seers of ages past,
All in one mighty sepulchre.—The hills
Rock-ribbed and ancient as the sun,—the vales
Stretching in pensive quietness between;
The venerable woods—rivers that move   40
In majesty, and the complaining brooks
That make the meadows green; and, poured round all,
Old ocean's gray and melancholy waste,—
Are but the solemn decorations all
Of the great tomb of man. The golden sun,   45
The planets, all the infinite host of heaven,
Are shining on the sad abodes of death,
Through the still lapse of ages. All that tread
The globe are but a handful to the tribes
That slumber in its bosom.—Take the wings   50

Of morning—and the Barcan desert[1] pierce,
Or lose thyself in the continuous woods
Where rolls the Oregan,[2] and hears no sound,
Save his own dashings—yet—the dead are there:
And millions in those solitudes, since first   55
The flight of years began, have laid them down
In their last sleep—the dead reign there alone.
So shalt thou rest—and what if thou withdraw
Unheeded by the living, and no friend
Take note of thy departure? All that breathe   60
Will share thy destiny. The gay will laugh
When thou art gone, the solemn brood of care
Plod on, and each one as before will chase
His favourite phantom; yet all these shall leave
Their mirth and their employments, and shall come,   65
And make their bed with thee. As the long train
Of ages glide away, the sons of men,
The youth in life's green spring, and he who goes
In the full strength of years, matron, and maid,
And the sweet babe, and the gray-headed man,—   70
Shall one by one be gathered to thy side,
By those, who in their turn shall follow them.
    So live, that when thy summons comes to join
The innumerable caravan, that moves
To that mysterious realm, where each shall take   75
His chamber in the silent halls of death,
Thou go not like the quarry-slave at night,
Scourged to his dungeon, but, sustained and soothed
By an unfaltering trust, approach thy grave,
Like one who wraps the drapery of his couch   80
About him, and lies down to pleasant dreams.

[1] A desert in north Africa.
[2] An early name for the Columbia River.

The Yellow Violet

When beechen buds begin to swell,
    And woods the blue-bird's warble know,
The yellow violet's modest bell
    Peeps from the last year's leaves below.

Ere russet fields their green resume,   5
    Sweet flower, I love, in forest bare,

To meet thee, when thy faint perfume
  Alone is in the virgin air.

Of all her train, the hands of Spring
  First plant thee in the watery mould,   10
And I have seen thee blossoming
  Beside the snow-bank's edges cold.

Thy parent sun, who bade thee view
  Pale skies, and chilling moisture sip,
Has bathed thee in his own bright hue,   15
  And streaked with jet thy glowing lip.

Yet slight thy form, and low thy seat,
  And earthward bent thy gentle eye,
Unapt the passing view to meet,
  When loftier flowers are flaunting nigh.   20

Oft, in the sunless April day,
  Thy early smile has stayed my walk;
But midst the gorgeous blooms of May,
  I passed thee on thy humble stalk.

So they, who climb to wealth, forget   25
  The friends in darker fortunes tried.
I copied them—but I regret
  That I should ape the ways of pride.

And when again the genial hour
  Awakes the painted tribes of light,   30
I'll not o'erlook the modest flower
  That made the woods of April bright.

To a Waterfowl

  Whither, 'midst failing dew,
While glow the heavens with the last steps of day,
Far, through their rosy depths, dost thou pursue
  Thy solitary way?

  Vainly the fowler's eye   5
Might mark thy distant flight to do thee wrong,
As, darkly painted on the crimson sky,
  Thy figure floats along.

  Seek'st thou the plashy brink
Of weedy lake, or marge of river wide,   10

Or where the rocking billows rise and sink
    On the chafed ocean side?

    There is a Power whose care
Teaches thy way along that pathless coast,—
The desert and illimitable air,—   15
    Lone wandering, but not lost.

    All day thy wings have fanned,
At that far height, the cold, thin atmosphere,
Yet stoop not, weary, to the welcome land,
    Though the dark night is near.   20

    And soon that toil shall end;
Soon shalt thou find a summer home, and rest,
And scream among thy fellows; reeds shall bend,
    Soon, o'er thy sheltered nest.

    Thou'rt gone, the abyss of heaven   25
Hath swallowed up thy form; yet, on my heart
Deeply hath sunk the lesson thou hast given,
    And shall not soon depart.

    He who, from zone to zone,
Guides through the boundless sky thy certain flight,   30
In the long way that I must tread alone,
    Will lead my steps aright.

To the Fringed Gentian

Thou blossom bright with autumn dew,
And coloured with the heaven's own blue,
That openest when the quiet light
Succeeds the keen and frosty night.

Thou comest not when violets lean   5
O'er wandering brooks and springs unseen,
Or columbines, in purple dressed,
Nod o'er the ground-bird's hidden nest.

Thou waitest late and com'st alone,
When woods are bare and birds are flown,   10
And frosts and shortening days portend
The aged year is near his end.

Then doth thy sweet and quiet eye
Look through its fringes to the sky,
Blue—blue—as if that sky let fall   15
A flower from its cerulean wall.

I would that thus, when I shall see
The hour of death draw near to me,
Hope, blossoming within my heart,
May look to heaven as I depart.   20

The Prairies

These are the gardens of the Desert, these
The unshorn fields, boundless and beautiful,
For which the speech of England has no name—
The Prairies. I behold them for the first,
And my heart swells, while the dilated sight   5
Takes in the encircling vastness. Lo! they stretch
In airy undulations, far away,
As if the ocean, in his gentlest swell,
Stood still, with all his rounded billows fixed,
And motionless forever.—Motionless?—   10
No—they are all unchained again. The clouds
Sweep over with their shadows, and, beneath,
The surface rolls and fluctuates to the eye;
Dark hollows seem to glide along and chase
The sunny ridges. Breezes of the South!   15
Who toss the golden and the flame-like flowers,
And pass the prairie hawk that, poised on high,
Flaps his broad wings, yet moves not—ye have played
Among the palms of Mexico and vines
Of Texas, and have crisped the limpid brooks   20
That from the fountains of Sonora glide
Into the calm Pacific—have ye fanned
A nobler or a lovelier scene than this?
Man hath no part in all this glorious work:
The hand that built the firmament hath heaved   25
And smoothed these verdant swells, and sown their slopes
With herbage, planted them with island groves,
And hedged them round with forests. Fitting floor
For this magnificent temple of the sky—
With flowers whose glory and whose multitude   30
Rival the constellations! The great heavens
Seem to stoop down upon the scene in love,—
A nearer vault, and of a tenderer blue,
Than that which bends above the eastern hills.

As o'er the verdant waste I guide my steed,   35
Among the high rank grass that sweeps his sides
The hollow beating of his footstep seems

A sacrilegious sound. I think of those
Upon whose rest he tramples. Are they here—
The dead of other days?—and did the dust   40
Of these fair solitudes once stir with life
And burn with passion? Let the mighty mounds
That overlook the rivers, or that rise
In the dim forest crowded with old oaks,
Answer. A race, that long has passed away,   45
Built them;—a disciplined and populous race
Heaped, with long toil, the earth, while yet the Greek
Was hewing the Pentelicus[1] to forms
Of symmetry, and rearing on its rock
The glittering Parthenon. These ample fields   50
Nourished their harvests, here their herds were fed,
When haply by their stalls the bison lowed,
And bowed his maned shoulder to the yoke.
All day this desert murmured with their toils,
Till twilight blushed, and lovers walked, and wooed   55
In a forgotten language, and old tunes,
From instruments of unremembered form,
Gave the soft winds a voice. The red man came—
The roaming hunter tribes, warlike and fierce,
And the mound-builders vanished from the earth.   60
The solitude of centuries untold
Has settled where they dwelt. The prairie wolf
Hunts in their meadows, and his fresh-dug den
Yawns by my path. The gopher mines the ground
Where stood their swarming cities. All is gone—   65
All—save the piles of earth that hold their bones—
The platforms where they worshipped unknown gods—
The barriers which they builded from the soil
To keep the foe at bay—till o'er the walls
The wild beleaguerers broke, and, one by one,   70
The strongholds of the plain were forced, and heaped
With corpses. The brown vultures of the wood
Flocked to those vast uncovered sepulchres,
And sat, unscared and silent, at their feast.
Haply some solitary fugitive,   75
Lurking in marsh and forest, till the sense
Of desolation and of fear became
Bitterer than death, yielded himself to die.
Man's better nature triumphed then. Kind words
Welcomed and soothed him; the rude conquerors   80

---

[1] A mountain in Greece from which the marble to build the Parthenon, a famous classical temple in Athens, was hewn.

Seated the captive with their chiefs; he chose
A bride among their maidens, and at length
Seemed to forget,—yet ne'er forgot,—the wife
Of his first love, and her sweet little ones,
Butchered, amid their shrieks, with all his race.   85

    Thus change the forms of being. Thus arise
Races of living things, glorious in strength,
And perish, as the quickening breath of God
Fills them, or is withdrawn. The red man, too,
Has left the blooming wilds he ranged so long,   90
And, nearer to the Rocky Mountains, sought
A wilder hunting ground. The beaver builds
No longer by these streams, but far away,
On waters whose blue surface ne'er gave back
The white man's face—among Missouri's springs,   95
And pools whose issues swell the Oregan,
He rears his little Venice. In these plains
The bison feeds no more. Twice twenty leagues
Beyond remotest smoke of hunter's camp,
Roams the majestic brute, in herds that shake   100
The earth with thundering steps—yet here I meet
His ancient footprints stamped beside the pool.

    Still this great solitude is quick with life.
Myriads of insects, gaudy as the flowers
They flutter over, gentle quadrupeds,   105
And birds, that scarce have learned the fear of man,
Are here, and sliding reptiles of the ground,
Startlingly beautiful. The graceful deer
Bounds to the wood at my approach. The bee,
A more adventurous colonist than man,   110
With whom he came across the eastern deep,
Fills the savannas with his murmurings,
And hides his sweets, as in the golden age,
Within the hollow oak. I listen long
To his domestic hum, and think I hear   115
The sound of that advancing multitude
Which soon shall fill these deserts. From the ground
Comes up the laugh of children, the soft voice
Of maidens, and the sweet and solemn hymn
Of Sabbath worshippers. The low of herds   120
Blends with the rustling of the heavy grain
Over the dark-brown furrows. All at once
A fresher wind sweeps by, and breaks my dream,
And I am in the wilderness alone.

☙ *John Keats* (*1795–1821*)

The majority of John Keats's most familiar masterpieces, including the two great odes included below, were produced in the period between January and September of 1819. Keats had unlikely training as a poet. His father managed a stable, but died when Keats was only eight; his mother died when he was fourteen. His guardian arranged for Keats to be apprenticed as an apothecary-surgeon, but just as he was completing his training, he abandoned a medical career for poetry. Although he had only begun to write at the age of eighteen, and despite family financial difficulties which ought to have further discouraged him in his artistic vocation, Keats believed in his abilities and published his first collection of poems in 1817. He was encouraged in his work by a circle of close friends, including his former teacher, Charles Cowden Clarke, and Leigh Hunt. While the critics gave Keats's debut volume a lukewarm reception, they were positively hostile to his second publication, the long poem Endymion, *in 1818. Nonetheless, Keats persevered despite continued family difficulties, most notably the death of his younger brother Tom, whom Keats had nursed through his difficult battle with tuberculosis. A burst of creativity in 1819 was foreshortened, in part due to Keats's own debilitation from the disease that had taken his brother. By the end of 1819, with his health rapidly failing, Keats was invited by Percy Shelley to travel to the milder climate of Italy to ease his suffering. Then, early in 1821, Keats died in Rome. His tragic fate, as well as the undeniable brilliance of the poetry he was able to produce in his short life, has given Keats enduring popularity and almost unwavering critical acclaim in the past two centuries.*

A reader of Keats's poetry is apt to notice first the poems' intense sensuality. When Keats describes an object, whether it is a cultural artifact such as a Grecian urn or a living creature such as a nightingale, he involves more than one of the senses in that description. Thus, unlike a great deal of nature poetry, the visual is not always dominant. In "Ode to a Nightingale" it is the auditory as well as the gustatory that take the forefront, offering an original perspective on the conventional equation of birds and poetry. The poem "To Autumn" demonstrates another dimension of Keats's aesthetic, according to which pleasure and pain and fruitfulness and corruption are delicately balanced in a necessary coexistence. The fruit, which has "ripeness to the core," is on the verge of becoming rotten, while the "stubble plains" that indicate a rich harvest also forebode the coming of winter. Keats took pleasure in the world around him and looked to lose himself in an identification with external nature (what he would call in a letter "negative capability"). The landscapes in Keats's poems are not mirrors for his own ego or illustrations of moral principles, but beautiful sites wherein the poet and the reader can forget themselves.

On the Grasshopper and Cricket

The poetry of earth is never dead:
　When all the birds are faint with the hot sun,
　And hide in cooling trees, a voice will run
From hedge to hedge about the new-mown mead;

That is the Grasshopper's—he takes the lead 5
   In summer luxury,—he has never done
   With his delights; for when tired out with fun,
He rests at ease beneath some pleasant weed.
The poetry of earth is ceasing never:
   On a lone winter evening, when the frost 10
      Has wrought a silence, from the stove there shrills
The Cricket's song, in warmth increasing ever,
   And seems to one, in drowsiness half lost,
      The Grasshopper's among some grassy hills.

La Belle Dame sans Merci*

1

Ah, what can ail thee, wretched wight,[1]
   Alone and palely loitering?
The sedge is withered from the lake,
   And no birds sing.

2

Ah, what can ail thee, wretched wight, 5
   So haggard and so woe-begone?
The squirrel's granary is full,
   And the harvest's done.

3

I see a lily on thy brow,
   With anguish moist and fever dew; 10
And on thy cheek a fading rose
   Fast withereth too.

4

I met a lady in the meads,
   Full beautiful—a faery's child;
Her hair was long, her foot was light, 15
   And her eyes were wild.

5

I set her on my pacing steed,
   And nothing else saw all day long,

---

* From the French meaning "The Beautiful Lady Without Pity." Keats's poem takes its title from a medieval poem so titled.

[1] In an earlier version of the poem, lines 1 and 5 read, "O what can ail thee, Knight at arms."

For sideways would she lean, and sing
    A faery's song.   20

6

I made a garland for her head,
    And bracelets too, and fragrant zone;
She looked at me as she did love,
    And made sweet moan.

7

She found me roots of relish sweet,   25
    And honey wild, and manna dew;
And sure in language strange she said—
    "I love thee true."

8

She took me to her elfin grot,
    And there she gazed, and sighed deep,   30
And there I shut her wild wild eyes
    So kissed to sleep.

9

And there we slumbered on the moss,
    And there I dreamed—Ah! woe betide!
The latest dream I ever dreamed   35
    On the cold hill side.

10

I saw pale kings, and princes too,
    Pale warriors, death pale were they all;
They cried—"La Belle Dame sans Merci
    Hath thee in thrall!"   40

11

I saw their starved lips in the gloam,
    With horrid warning gaped wide,
And I awoke, and found me here
    On the cold hill side.

12

And this is why I sojourn here,   45
    Alone and palely loitering,
Though the sedge is withered from the lake,
    And no birds sing.

Ode to a Nightingale

I

My heart aches, and a drowsy numbness pains
   My sense, as though of hemlock I had drunk,
Or emptied some dull opiate to the drains
   One minute past, and Lethe-wards[1] had sunk:
'Tis not through envy of thy happy lot,   5
   But being too happy in thine happiness,—
      That thou, light-winged Dryad[2] of the trees,
         In some melodious plot
Of beechen green, and shadows numberless,
      Singest of summer in full-throated ease.   10

2

O for a draught of vintage! that hath been
   Cooled a long age in the deep-delved earth,
Tasting of Flora[3] and the country green,
   Dance, and Provençal song, and sunburnt mirth!
O for a beaker full of the warm South,   15
   Full of the true, the blushful Hippocrene,[4]
      With beaded bubbles winking at the brim,
         And purple-stained mouth;
That I might drink, and leave the world unseen,
      And with thee fade away into the forest dim: 20

3

Fade far away, dissolve, and quite forget
   What thou among the leaves hast never known,
The weariness, the fever, and the fret
   Here, where men sit and hear each other groan;
Where palsy shakes a few, sad, last gray hairs,   25
   Where youth grows pale, and spectre-thin, and dies;
      Where but to think is to be full of sorrow
         And leaden-eyed despairs,
Where Beauty cannot keep her lustrous eyes,
      Or new Love pine at them beyond tomorrow.   30

---

[1] The Lethe is the river of forgetfulness, one of the five rivers of the classical underworld.

[2] Wood nymph.

[3] Roman goddess of flowers, symbolizes here flowers themselves.

[4] A fountain on Mt. Helicon, said to be the home of the Muses.

4

Away! away! for I will fly to thee,
  Not charioted by Bacchus[5] and his pards,
But on the viewless wings of Poesy,
  Though the dull brain perplexes and retards:
Already with thee! tender is the night,   35
  And haply the Queen-Moon is on her throne,
    Clustered around by all her starry Fays;
      But here there is no light,
  Save what from heaven is with the breezes blown
    Through verdurous glooms and winding mossy ways.   40

5

I cannot see what flowers are at my feet,
  Nor what soft incense hangs upon the boughs,
But, in embalmed darkness, guess each sweet
  Wherewith the seasonable month endows
The grass, the thicket, and the fruit-tree wild;   45
  White hawthorn, and the pastoral eglantine;.
    Fast fading violets covered up in leaves;
      And mid-May's eldest child,
  The coming musk rose, full of dewy wine,
    The murmurous haunt of flies on summer eves.   50

6

Darkling I listen; and, for many a time
  I have been half in love with easeful Death,
Called him soft names in many a mused rhyme,
  To take into the air my quiet breath;
Now more than ever seems it rich to die,   55
  To cease upon the midnight with no pain,
    While thou art pouring forth thy soul abroad
      In such an ecstasy!
  Still wouldst thou sing, and I have ears in vain—
    To thy high requiem become a sod.   60

7

Thou wast not born for death, immortal Bird!
  No hungry generations tread thee down;
The voice I hear this passing night was heard
  In ancient days by emperor and clown:
Perhaps the self-same song that found a path   65

---

[5] The Greek god of wine and fertility, whose chariot was pulled by leopards.

Through the sad heart of Ruth[6] when, sick for home,
    She stood in tears amid the alien corn;
       The same that oft-times hath
Charmed magic casements, opening on the foam
    Of perilous seas, in faery lands forlorn.   70

8

Forlorn! the very word is like a bell
    To toll me back from thee to my sole self!
Adieu! the fancy cannot cheat so well
    As she is famed to do, deceiving elf.   75
Adieu! adieu! thy plaintive anthem fades
    Past the near meadows, over the still stream,
       Up the hill-side; and now 'tis buried deep
         In the next valley glades:
    Was it a vision, or a waking dream?
       Fled is that music:—do I wake or sleep?   80

---

[6] The young widow of Hebrew Scripture in the Book of Ruth.

To Autumn

I

Season of mists and mellow fruitfulness,
    Close bosom-friend of the maturing sun;
Conspiring with him how to load and bless
    With fruit the vines that round the thatch-eaves run;
To bend with apples the mossed cottage trees,   5
    And fill all fruit with ripeness to the core;
       To swell the gourd, and plump the hazel shells
    With a sweet kernel; to set budding more,
And still more, later flowers for the bees,
Until they think warm days will never cease,   10
       For Summer has o'er-brimmed their clammy cells.

2

Who hath not seen thee oft amid thy store?
    Sometimes whoever seeks abroad may find
Thee sitting careless on a granary floor,
    Thy hair soft-lifted by the winnowing wind;   15
Or on a half-reaped furrow sound asleep,
    Drowsed with the fume of poppies, while thy hook
       Spares the next swath and all its twined flowers:
And sometimes like a gleaner thou dost keep

Steady thy laden head across a brook;   20
Or by a cider press, with patient look,
   Thou watchest the last oozings, hours by hours.

3

Where are the songs of Spring? Ay, where are they?
   Think not of them, thou hast thy music too,—
While barred clouds bloom the soft-dying day,   25
   And touch the stubble plains with rosy hue;
Then in a wailful choir the small gnats mourn
   Among the river sallows, borne aloft
     Or sinking as the light wind lives or dies;
And full-grown lambs loud bleat from hilly bourn;   30
   Hedge crickets sing; and now with treble soft
   The redbreast whistles from a garden-croft,
     And gathering swallows twitter in the skies.

Mary Wollstonecraft Shelley (1797–1851)

The daughter of anarchist philosopher William Godwin and feminist intellectual Mary Wollstonecraft, the young Mary Godwin seemed destined for literary greatness. She grew up amidst the vibrant intellectual and politically radical circle that surrounded her father, and which, by sometime in 1812, included the attractive poet Percy Shelley. Mary eloped with him (despite his being married to another woman at the time) when she was only sixteen. Her years with Percy Bysshe Shelley, spent largely traveling through Europe, were tumultuous. During their relationship, Mary Shelley had several miscarriages and gave birth to four children, only one of whom survived to adulthood. This restless lifestyle and the loss of so many children put a great strain on their relationship as well as on Mary Shelley personally; she was nonetheless able during that time to produce what has become one of the most popular and significant novels of the modern era, Frankenstein. *Inspired by a contest she entered with her husband and Lord Byron in the summer of 1816 to determine who could invent the most terrifying ghost story, Mary's literary project quickly outstripped those of her formidable opponents. The book was published anonymously. After its initial appearance, many readers felt that it was too horrifying to have been written by a woman, and most supposed the novel had been produced by the author's husband.*

The story of Victor Frankenstein, the archetypal mad scientist who would take control of the powers of nature to defeat death, has attained mythic status as a warning of the consequences that can result when humans attempt to tamper with the natural order. Popularized in movies (which have little in common with the plot of the novel), the story is heralded as an early example of science fiction writing. Twentieth-century history is rife with confirmations of Mary Shelley's fictional warning about the destructive power of scientific hubris.

When Percy Shelley died in 1822, he left his wife and their one remaining child nearly penniless. Mary Shelley returned to England where, besides editing her husband's literary remains, she continued to work on her own fiction. Her novel The Last Man *(1826), the final chapter of which is excerpted below, has recently gained increased critical attention, once again for the author's apparent prescience. In it, the earth is attacked by a mysterious and incurable plague, which spreads across the globe leaving only one man left alive to tell the story of the destruction of the human race at the hands of an invisible disease, a match for many modern readers to HIV or the Ebola virus.*

From The Last Man

Volume 3, Chapter 10

I awoke in the morning, just as the higher windows of the lofty houses received the first beams of the rising sun. The birds were chirping, perched on the windows sills and deserted thresholds of the doors. I awoke, and my first thought was, Adrian and Clara are dead. I no longer shall be hailed by their good-morrow—or pass the long day in their society. I shall never see them more. The ocean has robbed me of them—stolen their hearts of love from their breasts, and given over to corruption what was dearer to me than light, or life, or hope.

I was an untaught shepherd boy, when Adrian deigned to confer on me his friendship. The best years of my life had been passed with him. All I had possessed of this world's goods, of happiness, knowledge, or virtue—I owed to him. He had, in his person, his intellect, and rare qualities, given a glory to my life, which without him it had never known. Beyond all other beings he had taught me, that goodness, pure and single, can be an attribute of man. It was a sight for angels to congregate to behold, to view him lead, govern, and solace, the last days of the human race.

My lovely Clara also was lost to me—she who last of the daughters of man, exhibited all those feminine and maiden virtues, which poets, painters, and sculptors, have in their various languages strove to express. Yet, as far as she was concerned, could I lament that she was removed in early youth from the certain advent of misery? Pure she was of soul, and all her intents were holy. But her heart was the throne of love, and the sensibility her lovely countenance expressed, was the prophet of many woes, not the less deep and drear, because she would have for ever concealed them.

These two wondrously endowed beings had been spared from the universal wreck, to be my companions during the last year of solitude. I had felt, while they were with me, all their worth. I was conscious that every other sentiment, regret, or passion had by degrees merged into a yearning, clinging affection for them. I had not forgotten the sweet partner of my youth, mother of my children, my adored Idris; but I saw at least a part of her spirit alive again in her brother; and after, that by Evelyn's death I had lost what most dearly recalled her to me; I enshrined her memory in Adrian's form, and endeavoured to confound the two dear ideas. I sound the depths of my heart, and try in vain to draw thence the expressions that can typify my love for these remnants of my race. If regret and sorrow came athwart me, as well it might in our solitary and uncertain state, the clear tones of Adrian's voice, and his fervent look, dissipated the gloom; or I was cheered unaware by the mild content and sweet resignation Clara's cloudless brow and deep blue eyes expressed. They were all to me—the suns of my be-nighted soul—repose in my weariness—slumber in my sleepless woe. Ill, most ill, with disjointed words, bare and weak, have I expressed the feeling with which I clung to them. I would have wound myself like ivy inextricably round them, so that the same blow might destroy us. I would have entered and been a part of them—so that

> If the dull substance of my flesh were thought,[1]

even now I had accompanied them to their new and incommunicable abode.

Never shall I see them more. I am bereft of their dear converse—bereft of sight of them. I am a tree rent by lightning; never will the bark close over the bared fibres—never will their quivering life, torn by the winds, receive the opi-ate of a moment's balm. I am alone in the world—but that expression as yet was less pregnant with misery, than that Adrian and Clara are dead.

The tide of thought and feeling rolls on forever the same, though the banks and shapes around, which govern its course, and the reflection in the wave, vary. Thus the sentiment of immediate loss in some sort decayed, while that of utter, irremediable loneliness grew on me with time. Three days I wandered through Ravenna—now thinking only of the beloved beings who slept in the oozy caves of ocean—now looking forward on the dread blank before me; shuddering to make an onward step—writhing at each change that marked the progress of the hours.

For three days I wandered to and fro in this melancholy town. I passed whole hours in going from house to house, listening whether I could detect some lurk-ing sign of human existence. Sometimes I rang at a bell; it tinkled through the vaulted rooms, and silence succeeded to the sound. I called myself hopeless, yet still I hoped; and still disappointment ushered in the hours, intruding the cold, sharp steel which first pierced me, into the aching festering wound. I fed like a wild beast, which seizes its food only when stung by intolerable hunger. I did not change my garb, or seek the shelter of a roof, during all those days. Burning heats, nervous irritation, a ceaseless, but confused flow of thought, sleepless nights, and days instinct with a frenzy of agitation, possessed me during that time.

As the fever of my blood increased, a desire of wandering came upon me. I re-member, that the sun had set on the fifth day after my wreck, when, without pur-pose or aim, I quitted the town of Ravenna. I must have been very ill. Had I been possessed by more or less of delirium, that night had surely been my last; for, as I continued to walk on the banks of the Mantone, whose upward course I fol-lowed, I looked wistfully on the stream, acknowledging to myself that its pellucid waves could medicine my woes for ever, and was unable to account to myself for my tardiness in seeking their shelter from the poisoned arrows of thought, that

---

[1] Shakespeare, Sonnet 44, line 1.

were piercing me through and through. I walked a considerable part of the night, and excessive weariness at length conquered my repugnance to the availing myself of the deserted habitations of my species. The waning moon, which had just risen, showed me a cottage, whose neat entrance and trim garden reminded me of my own England. I lifted up the latch of the door and entered. A kitchen first presented itself, where, guided by the moonbeams, I found materials for striking a light. Within this was a bedroom; the couch was furnished with sheets of snowy whiteness; the wood piled on the hearth, and an array as for a meal, might almost have deceived me into the dear belief that I had here found what I had so long sought—one survivor, a companion for my loneliness, a solace to my despair. I steeled myself against the delusion; the room itself was vacant: it was only prudent, I repeated to myself, to examine the rest of the house. I fancied that I was proof against the expectation; yet my heart beat audibly, as I laid my hand on the lock of each door, and it sunk again, when I perceived in each the same vacancy. Dark and silent they were as vaults; so I returned to the first chamber, wondering what sightless host had spread the materials for my repast, and my repose. I drew a chair to the table, and examined what the viands were of which I was to partake. In truth it was a death feast! The bread was blue and mouldy; the cheese lay a heap of dust. I did not dare examine the other dishes; a troop of ants passed in a double line across the tablecloth; every utensil was covered with dust, with cobwebs, and myriads of dead flies: these were objects each and all betokening the fallaciousness of my expectations. Tears rushed into my eyes; surely this was a wanton display of the power of the destroyer. What had I done, that each sensitive nerve was thus to be anatomized? Yet why complain more now than ever? This vacant cottage revealed no new sorrow—the world was empty; mankind was dead—I knew it well—why quarrel therefore with an acknowledged and stale truth? Yet, as I said, I had hoped in the very heart of despair, so that every new impression of the hard-cut reality on my soul brought with it a fresh pang, telling me the yet unstudied lesson, that neither change of place nor time could bring alleviation to my misery, but that, as I now was, I must continue, day after day, month after month, year after year, while I lived. I hardly dared conjecture what space of time that expression implied. It is true, I was no longer in the first blush of manhood; neither had I declined far in the vale of years—men have accounted mine the prime of life: I had just entered my thirty-seventh year; every limb was as well knit, every articulation as true, as when I had acted the shepherd on the hills of Cumberland; and with these advantages I was to commence the train of solitary life. Such were the reflections that ushered in my slumber on that night.

The shelter, however, and less disturbed repose which I enjoyed, restored me the following morning to a greater portion of health and strength, than I had experienced since my fatal shipwreck. Among the stores I had discovered on searching the cottage the preceding night, was a quantity of dried grapes; these refreshed me in the morning, as I left my lodging and proceeded towards a town which I discerned at no great distance. As far as I could divine, it must have been Forli. I entered with pleasure its wide and grassy streets. All, it is true, pictured the excess of desolation; yet I loved to find myself in those spots which had been the abode of my fellow creatures. I delighted to traverse street after street, to look up at the tall houses, and repeat to myself, once they contained beings similar to myself—I was not always the wretch I am now. The wide square of Forli, the arcade around it, its light and pleasant aspect cheered me. I was pleased with the idea, that, if the earth should be again peopled, we, the lost race, would, in the relics left behind, present no contemptible exhibition of our powers to the new comers.

I entered one of the palaces, and opened the door of a magnificent saloon. I started—I looked again with renewed wonder. What wild-looking, unkempt, half-naked savage was that before me? The surprise was momentary.

I perceived that it was I myself whom I beheld in a large mirror at the end of the hall. No wonder that the lover of the princely Idris should fail to recognize himself in the miserable object there portrayed. My tattered dress was that in which I had crawled half alive from the tempestuous sea. My long and tangled hair hung in elf locks on my brow—my dark eyes, now hollow and wild, gleamed from under them—my cheeks were discoloured by the jaundice, which (the effect of misery and neglect) suffused my skin, and were half hid by a beard of many days' growth.

Yet why should I not remain thus, I thought; the world is dead, and this squalid attire is a fitter mourning garb than the foppery of a black suit. And thus, methinks, I should have remained, had not hope, without which I do not believe man could exist, whispered to me, that, in such a plight, I should be an object of fear and aversion to the being, preserved I knew not where, but I fondly trusted, at length, to be found by me. Will my readers scorn the vanity, that made me attire myself with some care, for the sake of this visionary being? Or will they forgive the freaks of a half crazed imagination? I can easily forgive myself—for hope, however vague, was so dear to me, and a sentiment of pleasure of so rare occurrence, that I yielded readily to any idea, that cherished the one, or promised any recurrence of the former to my sorrowing heart.

After such occupation, I visited every street, alley, and nook of Forli. These Italian towns presented an appearance of still greater desolation, than those of England or France. Plague had appeared here earlier—it had finished its course, and achieved its work much sooner than with us. Probably the last summer had found no human being alive, in all the track included between the shores of Calabria and the northern Alps. My search was utterly vain, yet I did not despond. Reason methought was on my side; and the chances were by no means contemptible, that there should exist in some part of Italy a survivor like myself—of a wasted, depopulate land. As therefore I rambled through the empty town, I formed my plan for future operations. I would continue to journey on towards Rome. After I should have satisfied myself, by a narrow search, that I left behind no human being in the towns through which I passed, I would write up in a conspicuous part of each, with white paint, in three languages, that "Verney, the last of the race of Englishmen, had taken up his abode in Rome."

In pursuance of this scheme, I entered a painter's shop, and procured myself the paint. It is strange that so trivial an occupation should have consoled, and even enlivened me. But grief renders one childish, despair fantastic. To this simple inscription, I merely added the adjuration, "Friend, come! I wait for thee!—*Deh, vieni! ti aspetto!*"[2]

On the following morning, with something like hope for my companion, I quitted Forli on my way to Rome. Until now, agonizing retrospect, and dreary prospects for the future, had stung me when awake, and cradled me to my repose. Many times I had delivered myself up to the tyranny of anguish—many times I resolved a speedy end to my woes; and death by my own hands was a remedy, whose practicability was even cheering to me. What could I fear in the other world? If there were an hell, and I were doomed to it, I should come an adept to the sufferance of its tortures—the act were easy, the speedy and certain end of my deplorable tragedy. But now these thoughts faded before the new born expectation. I went on my way, not as before, feeling each hour, each minute, to be an age instinct with incalculable pain.

As I wandered along the plain, at the foot of the Apennines—through their valleys, and over their bleak summits, my path led me through a country which had been trodden by heroes, visited and admired by thousands. They had, as a tide, receded, leaving me blank and bare in the midst. But why complain? Did I not hope?—so I schooled myself, even after the enlivening spirit had really deserted me, and thus I was obliged to call up all the fortitude I could command, and that was not much, to prevent a recurrence of that chaotic and intolerable despair, that had succeeded to the miserable shipwreck, that had consummated every fear, and dashed to annihilation every joy.

I rose each day with the morning sun, and left my desolate inn. As my feet strayed through the unpeopled country, my thoughts rambled through the universe, and I was least miserable when I could, absorbed in reverie, forget the passage of the hours. Each evening, in spite of weariness, I detested to enter any dwelling, there to take up my nightly abode—I have sat, hour after hour, at the door of the cottage I had selected, unable to lift the latch, and meet face to face blank desertion within. Many nights, though autumnal mists were spread around, I passed under an ilex—many times I have supped on arbutus berries and chestnuts, making a fire, gypsy-like, on the ground—because wild natural scenery reminded me less acutely of my hopeless state of loneliness. I counted the days, and bore with me a peeled willow-wand, on which, as well as I could remember, I had notched the days that had elapsed since my wreck, and each night I added another unit to the melancholy sum.

I had toiled up a hill which led to Spoleto. Around was spread a plain, encircled by the chestnut-covered Apennines. A dark ravine was on one side, spanned by an aqueduct, whose tall arches were rooted in the dell below, and attested that man had once deigned to bestow labour and thought here, to adorn and civilize nature. Savage, ungrateful nature, which in wild sport defaced his remains, protruding her easily renewed, and fragile growth of wild flowers and parasite plants around his eternal edifices. I sat on a fragment of rock, and looked round. The sun had bathed in gold the western atmosphere, and in the east the clouds caught the radiance, and budded into transient loveliness. It set on a world that

---

[2] "Pray, come! I wait for thee!"

contained me alone for its inhabitant. I took out my wand—I counted the marks. Twenty-five were already traced—twenty-five days had already elapsed, since human voice had gladdened my ears, or human countenance met my gaze. Twenty-five long, weary days, succeeded by dark and lonesome nights, had mingled with foregone years, and had become a part of the past—the never to be recalled—a real, undeniable portion of my life—twenty-five long, long days.

Why this was not a month!—Why talk of days—or weeks—or months—I must grasp years in my imagination, if I would truly picture the future to myself—three, five, ten, twenty, fifty anniversaries of that fatal epoch might elapse—every year containing twelve months, each of more numerous calculation in a diary, than the twenty-five days gone by—Can it be? Will it be?—We had been used to look forward to death tremulously—wherefore, but because its place was obscure? But more terrible, and far more obscure, was the unveiled course of my lone futurity. I broke my wand; I threw it from me. I needed no recorder of the inch and barley-corn growth of my life, while my unquiet thoughts created other divisions, than those ruled over by the planets—and, in looking back on the age that had elapsed since I had been alone, I disdained to give the name of days and hours to the throes of agony which had in truth portioned it out.

I hid my face in my hands. The twitter of the young birds going to rest, and their rustling among the trees, disturbed the still evening-air—the crickets chirped—the aziolo cooed at intervals. My thoughts had been of death—these sounds spoke to me of life. I lifted up my eyes—a bat wheeled round—the sun had sunk behind the jagged line of mountains, and the paly, crescent moon was visible, silver white, amidst the orange sunset, and accompanied by one bright star, prolonged thus the twilight. A herd of cattle passed along in the dell below, untended, towards their watering place—the grass was rustled by a gentle breeze, and the olive-woods, mellowed into soft masses by the moonlight, contrasted their sea-green with the dark chestnut foliage. Yes, this is the earth; there is no change—no ruin—no rent made in her verdurous expanse; she continues to wheel round and round, with alternate night and day, through the sky, though man is not her adorner or inhabitant. Why could I not forget myself like one of those animals, and no longer suffer the wild tumult of misery that I endure? Yet, ah! what a deadly breach yawns between their state and mine! Have not they companions? Have not they each their mate—their cherished young, their home, which, though unexpressed to us, is, I doubt not, endeared and enriched, even in their eyes, by the society which kind nature has created for them? It is I only that am alone—I, on this little hill top, gazing on plain and mountain recess—on sky, and its starry population, listening to every sound of earth, and air, and murmuring wave,—I only cannot express to any companion my many thoughts, nor lay my throbbing head on any loved bosom, nor drink from meeting eyes an intoxicating dew, that transcends the fabulous nectar of the gods. Shall I not then complain? Shall I not curse the murderous engine which has mowed down the children of men, my brethren? Shall I not bestow a malediction on every other of nature's offspring, which dares live and enjoy, while I live and suffer?

Ah, no! I will discipline my sorrowing heart to sympathy in your joys; I will be happy, because ye are so. Live on, ye innocents, nature's selected darlings; I am not much unlike to you. Nerves, pulse, brain, joint, and flesh, of such am I composed, and ye are organized by the same laws. I have something beyond this, but I will call it a defect, not an endowment, if it leads me to misery, while ye are happy. Just then, there emerged from a near copse two goats and a little kid, by the mother's side; they began to browze the herbage of the hill. I approached near to them, without their perceiving me; I gathered a handful of fresh grass, and held it out; the little one nestled close to its mother, while she timidly withdrew. The male stepped forward, fixing his eyes on me: I drew near, still holding out my lure, while he, depressing his head, rushed at me with his horns. I was a very fool; I knew it, yet I yielded to my rage. I snatched up a huge fragment of rock; it would have crushed my rash foe. I poised it—aimed it—then my heart failed me. I hurled it wide of the mark; it rolled clattering among the bushes into dell. My little visitants, all aghast, galloped back into the covert of the wood; while I, my very heart bleeding and torn, rushed down the hill, and by the violence of bodily exertion, sought to escape from my miserable self.

No, no, I will not live among the wild scenes of nature, the enemy of all that lives. I will seek the towns—Rome, the capital of the world, the crown of man's achievements. Among its storied streets, hallowed ruins, and stupendous remains of human exertion, I shall not, as here, find every thing forgetful of man; trampling on his memory, defacing his works, proclaiming from hill to hill, and vale to vale,—by the torrents freed from the boundaries which he imposed—by the vegetation liberated from the laws which he enforced—by his habitation abandoned to mildew and weeds, that his power is lost, his race annihilated for ever.

I hailed the Tiber, for that was as it were an unalienable possession of humanity. I hailed the wild Campagna, for every rood had been trod by man; and its savage uncultivation, of no recent date, only proclaimed more distinctly his power, since he had given an honourable name and sacred title to what else would have been a worthless, barren track. I entered Eternal Rome by the Porta del Popolo, and saluted with awe its time-honoured space. The wide square, the churches near, the long extent of the Corso, the near eminence of Trinita de' Monti appeared like fairy work, they were so silent, so peaceful, and so very fair. It was evening; and the population of animals which still existed in this mighty city, had gone to rest; there was no sound, save the murmur of its many fountains, whose soft monotony was harmony to my soul. The knowledge that I was in Rome, soothed me; that wondrous city, hardly more illustrious for its heroes and sages, than for the power it exercised over the imaginations of men. I went to rest that night; the eternal burning of my heart quenched,—my senses tranquil.

The next morning I eagerly began my rambles in search of oblivion. I ascended the many terraces of the garden of the Colonna Palace, under whose roof I had been sleeping; and passing out from it at its summit, I found myself on Monte Cavallo. The fountain sparkled in the sun; the obelisk above pierced the clear dark-blue air. The statues on each side, the works, as they are inscribed, of Phidias and Praxiteles, stood in undiminished grandeur, representing Castor and

Pollux, who with majestic power tamed the rearing animal at their side. If those illustrious artists had in truth chiseled these forms, how many passing generations had their giant proportions outlived! and now they were viewed by the last of the species they were sculptured to represent and deify. I had shrunk into insignificance in my own eyes, as I considered the multitudinous beings these stone demigods had outlived, but this after-thought restored me to dignity in my own conception. The sight of the poetry eternized in these statues, took the sting from the thought, arraying it only in poetic ideality.

I repeated to myself,—I am in Rome! I behold, and as it were, familiarly converse with the wonder of the world, sovereign mistress of the imagination, majestic and eternal survivor of millions of generations of extinct men. I endeavoured to quiet the sorrows of my aching heart, by even now taking an interest in what in my youth I had ardently longed to see. Every part of Rome is replete with relics of ancient times. The meanest streets are strewed with truncated columns, broken capitals—Corinthian and Ionic, and sparkling fragments of granite or porphyry. The walls of the most penurious dwellings enclose a fluted pillar or ponderous stone, which once made part of the palace of the Caesars; and the voice of dead time, in still vibrations, is breathed from these dumb things, animated and glorified as they were by man.

I embraced the vast columns of the temple of Jupiter Stator, which survives in the open space that was the Forum, and leaning my burning cheek against its cold durability, I tried to lose the sense of present misery and present desertion, by recalling to the haunted cell of my brain vivid memories of times gone by. I rejoiced at my success, as I figured Camillus, the Gracchi, Cato, and last the heroes of Tacitus, which shine meteors of surpassing brightness during the murky night of the empire;—as the verses of Horace and Virgil, or the glowing periods of Cicero thronged into the opened gates of my mind, I felt myself exalted by long forgotten enthusiasm. I was delighted to know that I beheld the scene which they beheld—the scene which their wives and mothers, and crowds of the unnamed witnessed, while at the same time they honoured, applauded, or wept for these matchless specimens of humanity. At length, then, I had found a consolation. I had not vainly sought the storied precincts of Rome—I had discovered a medicine for my many and vital wounds.

I sat at the foot of these vast columns. The Coliseum, whose naked ruin is robed by nature in a verdurous and glowing veil, lay in the sunlight on my right. Not far off, to the left, was the Tower of the Capitol. Triumphal arches, the falling walls of many temples, strewed the ground at my feet. I strove, I resolved, to force myself to see the Plebeian multitude and lofty Patrician forms congregated around; and, as the Diorama of ages passed across my subdued fancy, they were replaced by the modern Roman; the Pope, in his white stole, distributing benedictions to the kneeling worshippers; the friar in his cowl; the dark-eyed girl, veiled by her mezzera; the noisy, sun-burnt rustic, leading his heard of buffaloes and oxen to the Campo Vaccino. The romance with which, dipping our pencils in the rainbow hues of sky and transcendent nature, we to a degree gratuitously endow the Italians, replaced the solemn grandeur of antiquity. I remembered the dark monk, and floating figures of *The Italian*, and how my boyish blood had thrilled at the description. I called to mind Corinna ascending the Capitol to be crowned, and, passing from the heroine to the author, reflected how the Enchantress Spirit of Rome held sovereign sway over the minds of the imaginative, until it rested on me—sole remaining spectator of its wonders.

I was long wrapt by such ideas; but the soul wearies of a pauseless flight; and, stooping from its wheeling circuits round and round this spot, suddenly it fell ten thousand fathom deep, into the abyss of the present—into self-knowledge— into tenfold sadness. I roused myself—I cast off my waking dreams; and I, who just now could almost hear the shouts of the Roman throng, and was hustled by countless multitudes, now beheld the desert ruins of Rome sleeping under its own blue sky; the shadows lay tranquilly on the ground; sheep were grazing un- tended on the Palatine, and a buffalo stalked down the Sacred Way that led to the Capitol. I was alone in the Forum; alone in Rome; alone in the world. Would not one living man—one companion in my weary solitude, be worth all the glory and remembered power of this time-honoured city? Double sorrow—sad- ness, bred in Cimmerian caves, robed my soul in a mourning garb. The genera- tions I had conjured up to my fancy, contrasted more strongly with the end of all—the single point in which, as a pyramid, the mighty fabric of society had ended, while I, on the giddy height, saw vacant space around me.

From such vague laments I turned to the contemplation of the minutiae of my situation. So far, I had not succeeded in the sole object of my desires, the finding a companion for my desolation. Yet I did not despair. It is true that my inscrip- tions were set up for the most part, in insignificant towns and villages; yet, even without these memorials, it was possible that the person, who like me should find himself alone in a depopulate land, should, like me, come to Rome. The more slender my expectation was, the more I chose to build on it, and to accom- modate my actions to this vague possibility.

It became necessary therefore, that for a time I should domesticate myself at Rome. It became necessary, that I should look my disaster in the face—not play- ing the school-boy's part of obedience without submission; enduring life, and yet rebelling against the laws by which I lived.

Yet how could I resign myself? Without love, without sympathy, without communion with any, how could I meet the morning sun, and with it trace its oft repeated journey to the evening shades? Why did I continue to live—why not throw off the weary weight of time, and with my own hand, let out the fluttering prisoner from my agonized breast?—It was not cowardice that withheld me; for the true fortitude was to endure; and death had a soothing sound accompanying it, that would easily entice me to enter its demesne. But this I would not do. I had, from the moment I had reasoned on the subject, instituted myself the sub- ject to fate, and the servant of necessity, the visible laws of the invisible God—I believed that my obedience was the result of sound reasoning, pure feeling, and an exalted sense of the true excellence and nobility of my nature. Could I have seen in this empty earth, in the seasons and their change, the hand of a blind power only, most willingly would I have placed my head on the sod, and closed my eyes on its loveliness forever. But fate had administered life to me, when the plague had already seized on its prey—she had dragged me by the hair from out the strangling waves—By such miracles she had bought me for her own; I admitted her authority, and bowed to her decrees. If, after mature consideration, such was my resolve, it was doubly necessary that I should not lose the end of life, the improvement of my faculties, and poison its flow by repinings without end. Yet how cease to repine, since there was no hand near to extract the barbed spear that had entered my heart of hearts? I stretched out my hand, and it touched none whose sensations were responsive to mine. I was girded, walled in, vaulted over, by seven-fold barriers of loneliness. Occupation alone, if I could deliver myself up to it, would be capable of affording an opiate to my sleepless sense of woe. Having determined to make Rome my abode, at least for some months, I made arrangements for my accommodation—I selected my home. The Colonna Palace as well adapted for my purpose. Its grandeur—its treasure of paintings, its magnificent halls were objects soothing and even exhilarating.

I found the granaries of Rome well stored with grain, and particularly with Indian corn; this product requiring less art in its preparation for food, I selected as my principal support. I now found the hardships and lawlessness of my youth turn to account. A man cannot throw off the habits of sixteen years. Since that age, it is true, I had lived luxuriously, or at least surrounded by all the conveniences civilization afforded. But before that time, I had been "as uncouth a savage, as the wolf-bred founder of old Rome"—and now, in Rome itself, robber and shepherd propensities, similar to those of its founder, were of advantage to its sole inhabitant. I spent the morning riding and shooting in the Campagna—I passed long hours in the various galleries—I gazed at each statue, and lost myself in a reverie before many a fair Madonna or beauteous nymph. I haunted the Vatican, and stood surrounded by marble forms of divine beauty. Each stone deity was possessed by sacred gladness, and the eternal fruition of love. They looked on me with unsympathizing complacency, and often in wild accents I reproached them for their supreme indifference—for they were human shapes, the human form divine was manifest in each fairest limb and lineament. The perfect moulding brought with it the idea of colour and motion; often, half in bitter mockery, half in self-delusion, I clasped their icy proportions, and, coming between Cupid and his Psyche's lips, pressed the unconceiving marble.

I endeavoured to read. I visited the libraries of Rome. I selected a volume, and, choosing some sequestered, shady nook, on the banks of the Tiber, or opposite the fair temple in the Borghese Gardens, or under the old pyramid of Cestius, I endeavoured to conceal me from myself, and immerse myself in the subject traced on the pages before me. As if in the same sod you plant nightshade and a myrtle tree, they will each appropriate the mold, moisture, and air administered, for the fostering their several properties— so did my grief find sustenance, and power of existence, and growth, in what else had been divine manna, to feed radiant meditation. Ah! while I streak this paper with the tale of what my so named occupations were—while I shape the skeleton of my days—my hand trembles—my heart pants, and my brain refuses to lend expression, or phrase, or idea, by which to image forth the veil of unutterable woe that clothed these bare realities. O, worn and beating heart, may I dissect thy fibres, and tell how in each unmitigable misery, sadness dire, repinings, and despair, existed? May I record my many ravings—the wild curses I hurled at torturing nature—and how I have passed days shut out from light and food—from all except the burning hell alive in my own bosom?

I was presented, meantime, with one other occupation, the one best fitted to discipline my melancholy thoughts, which strayed backwards, over many a ruin, and through many a flowery glade, even to the mountain recess, from which in early youth I had first emerged.

During one of my rambles through the habitations of Rome, I found writing materials on a table in an author's study. Parts of a manuscript lay scattered about. It contained a learned disquisition on the Italian language; one page an unfinished dedication to posterity, for whose profit the writer had sifted and selected the niceties of this harmonious language—to whose everlasting benefit he bequeathed his labours.

I also will write a book, I cried—for whom to read?—to whom dedicated? And then with silly flourish (what so capricious and childish as despair?) I wrote,

DEDICATION

TO THE ILLUSTRIOUS DEAD.

SHADOWS, ARISE, AND READ YOUR FALL!

BEHOLD THE HISTORY OF THE

LAST MAN.

Yet, will not this world be re-peopled, and the children of a saved pair of lovers, in some to me unknown and unattainable seclusion, wandering to these prodigious relics of the ante-pestilential race, seek to learn how beings so wondrous in their achievements, with imaginations infinite, and powers godlike, had departed from their home to an unknown country?

I will write and leave in this most ancient city, this "world's sole monument," a record of these things. I will leave a monument of the existence of Verney, the Last Man. At first I thought only to speak of plague, of death, and last, of desertion; but I lingered fondly on my early years, and recorded with sacred zeal the virtues of my companions. They have been with me during the fulfilment of my task. I have brought it to an end—I lift my eyes from my paper—again they are lost to me. Again I feel that I am alone.

A year has passed since I have been thus occupied. The seasons have made their wonted round, and decked this eternal city in a changeful robe of surpassing beauty. A year has passed; and I no longer *guess* at my state or my prospects—loneliness is my familiar, sorrow my inseparable companion. I have endeavoured to brave the storm—I have endeavoured to school myself to fortitude—I have sought to imbue myself with the lessons of wisdom. It will not do. My hair has become nearly grey—my voice, unused now to utter sound, comes strangely on my ears. My person, with its human powers and features, seem to me a monstrous excrescence of nature. How express in human language a woe human being until this hour never knew! How give intelligible expression to a pang none but I could ever understand!—No one has entered Rome. None will ever come. I smile bitterly at the delusion I have so long nourished, and still more, when I reflect that I have exchanged it for another as delusive, as false, but to which I now cling with the same fond trust.

Winter has come again; and the gardens of Rome have lost their leaves—the sharp air comes over the Campagna, and has driven its brute inhabitants to take up their abode in the many dwellings of the deserted city—frost has suspended the gushing fountains—and Trevi has stilled her eternal music. I had made a rough calculation, aided by the stars, by which I endeavoured to ascertain the first day of the new year. In the old out-worn age, the Soverign Pontiff was used to go in solemn pomp, and mark the renewal of the year by driving a nail in the gate of the temple of Janus. On that day I ascended St. Peter's, and carved on its topmost stone the era 2100, last year of the world!

My only companion was a dog, a shaggy fellow, half water and half shepherd's dog, whom I found tending sheep in the Campagna. His master was dead, but nevertheless he continued fulfilling his duties in expectation of his return. If a sheep strayed from the rest, he forced it to return to the flock, and sedulously kept off every intruder. Riding in the Campagna I had come upon his sheep-walk, and for some time observed his repetition of lessons learned from man, now useless, though unforgotten. His delight was excessive when he saw me. He sprung up to my knees; he capered round and round, wagging his tail, with the short, quick bark of pleasure; he left his fold to follow me, and from that day has never neglected to watch by and attend on me, showing boisterous gratitude whenever I caressed or talked to him. His pattering steps and mine alone were heard, when we entered the magnificent extent of nave and aisle of St. Peter's. We ascended the myriad steps together, when on the summit I achieved my design, and in rough figures noted the date of the last year. I then turned to gaze on the country, and to take leave of Rome. I had long determined to quit it, and I now formed the plan I would adopt for my future career, after I had left this magnificent abode.

A solitary being is by instinct a wanderer, and that I would become. A hope of amelioration always attends on change of place, which would even lighten the burthen of my life. I had been a fool to remain in Rome all this time: Rome noted for Malaria, the famous caterer for death. But it was still possible, that, could I visit the whole extent of earth, I should find in some part of the wide extent a survivor. Methought the sea-side was the most probable retreat to be chosen by such a one. If left alone in an inland district, still they could not continue in the spot where their last hopes had been extinguished; they would journey on, like me, in search of a partner for their solitude, till the watery barrier stopped their further progress.

To that water—cause of my woes, perhaps now to be their cure, I would betake myself. Farewell, Italy!—farewell, thou ornament of the world, matchless Rome, the retreat of the solitary one during long months!—to civilized life—to the settled home and succession of monotonous days, farewell! Peril will now be mine; and I hail her as a friend—death will perpetually cross my path, and I will meet him as a benefactor; hardship, inclement weather, and dangerous tempests will be my sworn mates. Ye spirits of storm, receive me! ye powers of destruction, open wide your arms, and clasp me forever! if a kinder power have not decreed another end, so that after long endurance I may reap my reward, and again feel my heart beat near the heart of another like to me.

Tiber, the road which is spread by nature's own hand, threading her continent, was at my feet, and many a boat was tethered to the banks. I would with a few books, provisions, and my dog, embark in one of these and float down the current of the stream into the sea; and then, keeping near land, I would coast the beauteous shores and sunny promontories of the blue Mediterranean, pass Naples, along Calabria, and would dare the twin perils of Scylla and Charybdis; then, with fearless aim, (for what had I to lose?) skim ocean's surface towards Malta and the further Cyclades. I would avoid Constantinople, the sight of whose well-known towers and inlets belonged to another state of existence from my present one; I would coast Asia Minor, and Syria, and, passing the seven-mouthed Nile, steer northward again, till losing sight of forgotten Carthage and deserted Lybia, I should reach the pillars of Hercules. And then—no matter where—the oozy caves, and soundless depths of ocean may be my dwelling, before I accomplish this long-drawn voyage, or the arrow of disease find my heart as I float singly on the weltering Mediterranean; or, in some place I touch at, I may find what I seek—a companion; or if this may not be—to endless time, decrepid and grey headed—youth already in the grave with those I love—the lone wanderer will still unfurl his sail, and clasp the tiller—and, still obeying the breezes of heaven, for ever round another and another promontory, anchoring in another and another bay, still ploughing seedless ocean, leaving behind the verdant land of native Europe, adown the tawny shore of Africa, having weathered the fierce seas of the Cape, I may moor my worn skiff in a creek, shaded by spicy groves of the odorous islands of the far Indian ocean.

These are wild dreams. Yet since, now a week ago, they came on me, as I stood on the height of St. Peter's, they have ruled my imagination. I have chosen my boat, and laid in my scant stores. I have selected a few books; the principal are Homer and Shakespeare—But the libraries of the world are thrown open to me—and in any port I can renew my stock. I form no expectation of alteration for the better; but the monotonous present is intolerable to me. Neither hope nor joy are my pilots—restless despair and fierce desire of change lead me on. I long to grapple with danger, to be excited by fear, to have some task, however slight or voluntary, for each day's fulfilment. I shall witness all the variety of appearance, that the elements can assume—I shall read fair augury in the rainbow—menace in the cloud—some lesson or record dear to my heart in everything. Thus around the shores of deserted earth, while the sun is high, and the moon waxes or wanes, angels, the spirits of the dead, and the ever-open eye of the Supreme, will behold the tiny bark, freighted with Verney—the LAST MAN.

➣ *Ralph Waldo Emerson* (1803–1882)

The son of a Boston Congregationalist minister, Ralph Waldo Emerson did very little to distinguish himself in his first thirty years, and he showed every sign of following dutifully in his father's footsteps. He attended Boston Public Latin School, Harvard College, and Harvard Divinity School, he married a well-to-do merchant's daughter, and in 1829, he became junior pastor of Boston's Second Church, a Unitarian institution. Inwardly, however, Emerson was torn by doubts and dissatisfactions with orthodox Christian piety; this unrest was exacerbated by inconsolable grief at the sudden death of his wife and, in 1832, he resigned from the ministry. Henceforth, he would seek his own path, beyond the boundaries of conventional religious belief.

Emerson spent a year traveling in England, where he met with several leading literary figures of the Romantic period, including William Wordsworth, Samuel Taylor Coleridge, and Thomas Carlyle. Of these figures, Coleridge was the most directly influential in the subsequent development of Emerson's thought. Coleridge's emphasis on the intuitive ability of human reason to discover spiritual truth, as well as his evident affection for "all creatures great and small," struck resonant chords within Emerson's troubled, questing intellect.

Upon his return to America, Emerson found an ideal outlet for his eloquence in the Lyceum movement, a loose coalition of grassroots organizations that sponsored educational programs of visiting lecturers. Starting in 1833 and continuing for several decades, Emerson found a meaningful and socially prominent role for himself as a traveling speaker throughout New England, holding audiences spellbound with his thoughtful, provocative lectures. Emerson used these occasions to refine and develop his ideas on a vast range of topics, and many of his most successful lectures were subsequently published, thereby establishing him as America's leading public intellectual. His first significant publication was a slim, anonymous volume entitled Nature *(1836), a redaction of several lectures in the form of an extended manifesto. This groundbreaking essay, printed here in its entirety, is the single most influential American statement of the Transcendentalist idea of nature. Emerson argues that we need not derive our knowledge of the world only from dusty books. Rather, through our own immediate experience of the natural world, we can "enjoy an original relation to the universe." This emphasis on the primacy of individual experience, later developed in such essays as "Self-Reliance," is one of the most vital and recurrent themes in Emerson's writing, and it provided inspiration to numerous American writers in the Transcendentalist tradition, from Henry David Thoreau and Walt Whitman through John Muir and Mary Austin.*

Nature

A subtle chain of countless rings
The next unto the farthest brings;
The eye reads omens where it goes,

And speaks all languages the rose;
And, striving to be man, the worm
Mounts through all the spires of form.[1]

Introduction

Our age is retrospective. It builds the sepulchres of the fathers. It writes biographies, histories, and criticism. The foregoing generations beheld God and nature face to face; we, through their eyes. Why should not we also enjoy an original relation to the universe? Why should not we have a poetry and philosophy of insight and not of tradition, and a religion by revelation to us, and not the history of theirs? Embosomed for a season in nature, whose floods of life stream around and through us, and invite us, by the powers they supply, to action proportioned to nature, why should we grope among the dry bones of the past, or put the living generation into masquerade out of its faded wardrobe? The sun shines today also. There is more wool and flax in the fields. There are new lands, new men, new thoughts. Let us demand our own works and laws and worship.

Undoubtedly we have no questions to ask which are unanswerable. We must trust the perfection of the creation so far as to believe that whatever curiosity the order of things has awakened in our minds, the order of things can satisfy. Every man's condition is a solution in hieroglyphic to those inquiries he would put. He acts it as life, before he apprehends it as truth. In like manner, nature is already, in its forms and tendencies, describing its own design. Let us interrogate the great apparition that shines so peacefully around us. Let us inquire, to what end is nature?

All science has one aim, namely, to find a theory of nature. We have theories of races and of functions, but scarcely yet a remote approach to an idea of creation. We are now so far from the road to truth, that religious teachers dispute and hate each other, and speculative men are esteemed unsound and frivolous. But to a sound judgment, the most abstract truth is the most practical. Whenever a true theory appears, it will be its own evidence. Its test is, that it will explain all phenomena. Now many are thought not only unexplained but inexplicable; as language, sleep, madness, dreams, beasts, sex.

Philosophically considered, the universe is composed of Nature and the Soul. Strictly speaking, therefore, all that is separate from us, all which Philosophy distinguishes as the NOT ME, that is, both nature and art, all other men and my own body, must be ranked under this name, NATURE. In enumerating the values of nature and casting up their sum, I shall use the word in both senses;—in its common and in its philosophical import. In inquiries so general as our present one, the inaccuracy is not material; no confusion of thought will occur. *Nature*, in the common sense, refers to essences unchanged by man; space, the air, the river, the leaf. *Art* is applied to the mixture of his will with the same things, as in

---

[1] Verse by Emerson. These lines were added to the 1849 edition, replacing the 1836 epigraph attributed to Plotinus: "Nature is but an image or imitation of wisdom, the last thing of the soul; nature being a thing that doth only do, but not know."

a house, a canal, a statue, a picture. But his operations taken together are so insignificant, a little chipping, baking, patching, and washing, that in an impression so grand as that of the world on the human mind, they do not vary the result.

I.   Nature

To go into solitude, a man needs to retire as much from his chamber as from society. I am not solitary whilst I read and write, though nobody is with me. But if a man would be alone, let him look at the stars. The rays that come from those heavenly worlds will separate between him and what he touches. One might think the atmosphere was made transparent with this design, to give man, in the heavenly bodies, the perpetual presence of the sublime. Seen in the streets of cities, how great they are! If the stars should appear one night in a thousand years, how would men believe and adore; and preserve for many generations the remembrance of the city of God which had been shown! But every night come out these envoys of beauty, and light the universe with their admonishing smile.

  The stars awaken a certain reverence, because though always present, they are inaccessible; but all natural objects make a kindred impression, when the mind is open to their influence. Nature never wears a mean appearance. Neither does the wisest man extort her secret, and lose his curiosity by finding out all her perfection. Nature never became a toy to a wise spirit. The flowers, the animals, the mountains, reflected the wisdom of his best hour, as much as they had delighted the simplicity of his childhood.

  When we speak of nature in this manner, we have a distinct but most poetical sense in the mind. We mean the integrity of impression made by manifold natural objects. It is this which distinguishes the stick of timber of the wood-cutter from the tree of the poet. The charming landscape which I saw this morning is indubitably made up of some twenty or thirty farms. Miller owns this field, Locke that, and Manning the woodland beyond. But none of them owns the landscape. There is a property in the horizon which no man has but he whose eye can integrate all the parts, that is, the poet. This is the best part of these men's farms, yet to this their warranty deeds give no title.

  To speak truly, few adult persons can see nature. Most persons do not see the sun. At least they have a very superficial seeing. The sun illuminates only the eye of the man, but shines into the eye and the heart of the child. The lover of nature is he whose inward and outward senses are still truly adjusted to each other; who has retained the spirit of infancy even into the era of manhood.[2] His intercourse with heaven and earth becomes part of his daily food. In the presence of nature a wild delight runs through the man, in spite of real sorrows. Nature says, — he is my creature, and maugre[3] all his impertinent griefs, he shall be glad with me. Not the sun or the summer alone, but every hour and season yields its tribute of delight; for every hour and change corresponds to and authorizes a different state of the mind, from breathless noon to grimmest midnight. Nature is a

---

[2] A concept derived from Samuel Taylor Coleridge, *Biographia Literaria*, Chapter 4, where he claims that the character and privilege of genius is "to carry on the feelings of childhood into the powers of manhood."

[3] Despite.

setting that fits equally well a comic or a mourning piece. In good health, the air is a cordial of incredible virtue. Crossing a bare common, in snow puddles, at twilight, under a clouded sky, without having in my thoughts any occurrence of special good fortune, I have enjoyed a perfect exhilaration. I am glad to the brink of fear. In the woods, too, a man casts off his years, as the snake his slough, and at what period soever of life, is always a child. In the woods is perpetual youth. Within these plantations of God, a decorum and sanctity reign, a perennial festival is dressed, and the guest sees not how he should tire of them in a thousand years. In the woods, we return to reason and faith. There I feel that nothing can befall me in life,—no disgrace, no calamity (leaving me my eyes), which nature cannot repair. Standing on the bare ground,—my head bathed by the blithe air, and uplifted into infinite space,—all mean egotism vanishes. I become a transparent eyeball; I am nothing; I see all; the currents of the Universal Being circulate through me; I am part or parcel of God. The name of the nearest friend sounds then foreign and accidental: to be brothers, to be acquaintances,—master or servant, is then a trifle and a disturbance. I am the lover of uncontained and immortal beauty. In the wilderness, I find something more dear and connate than in streets or villages. In the tranquil landscape, and especially in the distant line of the horizon, man beholds somewhat as beautiful as his own nature.

The greatest delight which the fields and woods minister is the suggestion of an occult relation between man and the vegetable. I am not alone and unacknowledged. They nod to me, and I to them. The waving of the boughs in the storm is new to me and old. It takes me by surprise, and yet is not unknown. Its effect is like that of a higher thought or a better emotion coming over me, when I deemed I was thinking justly or doing right.

Yet it is certain that the power to produce this delight does not reside in nature, but in man, or in a harmony of both. It is necessary to use these pleasures with great temperance. For nature is not always tricked in holiday attire, but the same scene which yesterday breathed perfume and glittered as for the frolic of the nymphs, is overspread with melancholy today. Nature always wears the colors of the spirit. To a man laboring under calamity, the heat of his own fire hath sadness in it. Then there is a kind of contempt of the landscape felt by him who has just lost by death a dear friend. The sky is less grand as it shuts down over less worth in the population.

II. Commodity

Whoever considers the final cause of the world will discern a multitude of uses that enter as parts into that result. They all admit of being thrown into one of the following classes: Commodity; Beauty; Language; and Discipline.

Under the general name of commodity, I rank all those advantages which our senses owe to nature. This, of course, is a benefit which is temporary and mediate, not ultimate, like its service to the soul. Yet although low, it is perfect in its kind, and is the only use of nature which all men apprehend. The misery of man appears like childish petulance, when we explore the steady and prodigal provision that has been made for his support and delight on this green ball which floats him through the heavens. What angels invented these splendid ornaments, these rich conveniences, this ocean of air above, this ocean of water beneath, this firmament of earth between? this zodiac of lights, this tent of dropping clouds, this striped coat of climates, this fourfold year? Beasts, fire, water, stones, and corn serve him. The field is at once his floor, his work-yard, his play-ground, his garden, and his bed.

> "More servants wait on man
> Than he'll take notice of."——[4]

Nature, in its ministry to man, is not only the material, but is also the process and the result. All the parts incessantly work into each other's hands for the profit of man. The wind sows the seed; the sun evaporates the sea; the wind blows the vapor to the field; the ice, on the other side of the planet, condenses rain on this; the rain feeds the plant; the plant feeds the animal; and thus the endless circulations of the divine charity nourish man.

The useful arts are reproductions or new combinations by the wit of man, of the same natural benefactors. He no longer waits for favoring gales, but by means of steam, he realizes the fable of Aeolus's bag, and carries the two and thirty winds in the boiler of his boat. To diminish friction, he paves the road with iron bars, and, mounting a coach with a ship-load of men, animals, and merchandise behind him, he darts through the country, from town to town, like an eagle or a swallow through the air. By the aggregate of these aids, how is the face of the world changed, from the era of Noah to that of Napoleon! The private poor man hath cities, ships, canals, bridges, built for him. He goes to the post-office, and the human race run on his errands; to the book-shop, and the human race read and write of all that happens, for him; to the court-house, and nations repair his wrongs. He sets his house upon the road, and the human race go forth every morning, and shovel out the snow, and cut a path for him.

But there is no need of specifying particulars in this class of uses. The catalogue is endless, and the examples so obvious, that I shall leave them to the reader's reflection, with the general remark, that this mercenary benefit is one which has respect to a farther good. A man is fed, not that he may be fed, but that he may work.

III. Beauty

A nobler want of man is served by nature, namely, the love of Beauty.

The ancient Greeks called the world κόσμος,[5] beauty. Such is the constitution of all things, or such the plastic power of the human eye, that the primary forms, as the sky, the mountain, the tree, the animal, give us a delight *in and for themselves*; a pleasure arising from outline, color, motion, and grouping. This seems partly owing to the eye itself. The eye is the best of artists. By the mutual action of its structure and of the laws of light, perspective is produced, which in-

---

[4] From George Herbert, *Man.*

[5] Cosmos, i.e., order.

tegrates every mass of objects, of what character soever, into a well colored and shaded globe, so that where the particular objects are mean and unaffecting, the landscape which they compose is round and symmetrical. And as the eye is the best composer, so light is the first of painters. There is no object so foul that intense light will not make beautiful. And the stimulus it affords to the sense, and a sort of infinitude which it hath, like space and time, make all matter gay. Even the corpse has its own beauty. But besides this general grace diffused over nature, almost all the individual forms are agreeable to the eye, as is proved by our endless imitations of some of them, as the acorn, the grape, the pine cone, the wheat-ear, the egg, the wings and forms of most birds, the lion's claw, the serpent, the butterfly, sea-shells, flames, clouds, buds, leaves, and the forms of many trees, as the palm.

For better consideration, we may distribute the aspects of Beauty in a threefold manner.

1. First, the simple perception of natural forms is a delight. The influence of the forms and actions in nature is so needful to man, that, in its lowest functions, it seems to lie on the confines of commodity and beauty. To the body and mind which have been cramped by noxious work or company, nature is medicinal and restores their tone. The tradesman, the attorney comes out of the din and craft of the street and sees the sky and the woods, and is a man again. In their eternal calm, he finds himself. The health of the eye seems to demand a horizon. We are never tired, so long as we can see far enough.

But in other hours, Nature satisfies by its loveliness, and without any mixture of corporeal benefit. I see the spectacle of morning from the hilltop over against my house, from daybreak to sunrise, with emotions which an angel might share. The long slender bars of cloud float like fishes in the sea of crimson light. From the earth, as a shore, I look out into that silent sea. I seem to partake its rapid transformations; the active enchantment reaches my dust, and I dilate and conspire with the morning wind. How does Nature deify us with a few and cheap elements! Give me health and a day, and I will make the pomp of emperors ridiculous. The dawn is my Assyria; the sunset and moonrise my Paphos, and unimaginable realms of faerie; broad noon shall be my England of the senses and the understanding; the night shall be my Germany of mystic philosophy and dreams.

Not less excellent, except for our less susceptibility in the afternoon, was the charm, last evening, of a January sunset. The western clouds divided and subdivided themselves into pink flakes modulated with tints of unspeakable softness, and the air had so much life and sweetness that it was a pain to come within doors. What was it that nature would say? Was there no meaning in the live repose of the valley behind the mill, and which Homer or Shakespeare could not re-form for me in words? The leafless trees become spires of flame in the sunset, with the blue east for their background, and the stars of the dead calices of flowers, and every withered stem and stubble rimed with frost, contribute something to the mute music.

The inhabitants of cities suppose that the country landscape is pleasant only half the year. I please myself with the graces of the winter scenery, and believe that we are as much touched by it as by the genial influences of summer. To the attentive eye, each moment of the year has its own beauty, and in the same field, it beholds, every hour, a picture which was never seen before, and which shall never be seen again. The heavens change every moment, and reflect their glory or gloom on the plains beneath. The state of the crop in the surrounding farms alters the expression of the earth from week to week. The succession of native plants in the pastures and roadsides, which makes the silent clock by which time tells the summer hours, will make even the divisions of the day sensible to a keen observer. The tribes of birds and insects, like the plants punctual to their time, follow each other, and the year has room for all. By water-courses, the variety is greater. In July, the blue pontederia or pickerel-weed blooms in large beds in the shallow parts of our pleasant river, and swarms with yellow butterflies in continual motion. Art cannot rival this pomp of purple and gold. Indeed the river is a perpetual gala, and boasts each month a new ornament.

But this beauty of Nature which is seen and felt as beauty, is the least part. The shows of day, the dewy morning, the rainbow, mountains, orchards in blossom, stars, moonlight, shadows in still water, and the like, if too eagerly hunted, become shows merely, and mock us with their unreality. Go out of the house to see the moon, and 'tis mere tinsel; it will not please as when its light shines upon your necessary journey. The beauty that shimmers in the yellow afternoons of October, who ever could clutch it? Go forth to find it, and it is gone; 'tis only a mirage as you look from the windows of diligence.

2. The presence of a higher, namely, of the spiritual element is essential to its perfection. The high and divine beauty which can be loved without effeminacy, is that which is found in combination with the human will. Beauty is the mark God sets upon virtue. Every natural action is graceful. Every heroic act is also decent, and causes the place and the bystanders to shine. We are taught by great actions that the universe is the property of every individual in it. Every rational creature has all nature for his dowry and estate. It is his, if he will. He may divest himself of it; he may creep into a corner, and abdicate his kingdom, as most men do, but he is entitled to the world by his constitution. In proportion to the energy of his thought and will, he takes up the world into himself. "All those things for which men plough, build, or sail, obey virtue;" said Sallust.[6] "The winds and waves," said Gibbon, "are always on the side of the ablest navigators."[7] So are the sun and moon and all the stars of heaven. When a noble act is done,—perchance in a scene of great natural beauty; when Leonidas[8] and his three hundred martyrs consume one day in dying, and the sun and moon come each and look at them once in the steep defile of Thermopylae; when Arnold Winkelried,[9] in the high Alps, under the shadow of the avalanche, gathers in his side a sheaf of Austrian spears to break the line for his comrades; are not these heroes entitled to add the beauty of the scene to the beauty of the deed? When the bark of Colum-

---

[6] Sallust, a Roman historian of the first century A.D., in *The Conspiracy of Cataline*, Chapter 2.

[7] Edward Gibbon, *The History of Decline and Fall of the Roman Empire* (1776–88), Chapter 68.

[8] King of Sparta who died in 480 B.C. while defending the mountain pass at Thermopylae against an invading Persian army.

[9] Swiss hero who died in a battle against the Austrians at Sempach (1386).

bus nears the shore of America;—before it, the beach lined with savages, fleeing out of all their huts of cane; the sea behind; and the purple mountains of the Indian Archipelago around, can we separate the man from the living picture? Does not the New World clothe his form with her palm groves and savannahs as fit drapery? Ever does natural beauty steal in like air, and envelop great actions. When Sir Harry Vane[10] was dragged up the Tower-hill, sitting on a sled, to suffer death as the champion of the English laws, one of the multitude cried out to him, "You never sate on so glorious a seat!" Charles II, to intimidate the citizens of London, caused the patriot Lord Russell[11] to be drawn in an open coach through the principal streets of the city on his way to the scaffold. "But," his biographer says, "the multitude imagined they saw liberty and virtue sitting by his side." In private places, among sordid objects, an act of truth or heroism seems at once to draw to itself the sky as its temple, the sun as its candle. Nature stretches out her arms to embrace man, only let his thoughts be of equal greatness. Willingly does she follow his steps with the rose and the violet, and bend her lines of grandeur and grace to the decoration of her darling child. Only let his thoughts be of equal scope, and the frame will suit the picture. A virtuous man is in unison with her works, and makes the central figure of the visible sphere. Homer, Pindar, Socrates, Phocion, associate themselves fitly in our memory with the geography and climate of Greece. The visible heavens and earth sympathize with Jesus. And in common life whosoever has seen a person of powerful character and happy genius, will have remarked how easily he took all things along with him,—the persons, the opinions, and the day, and nature became ancillary to a man.

3. There is still another aspect under which the beauty of the world may be viewed, namely, as it becomes an object of the intellect. Beside the relation of things to virtue, they have a relation to thought. The intellect searches out the absolute order of things as they stand in the mind of God, and without the colors of affection. The intellectual and the active powers seem to succeed each other, and the exclusive activity of the one generates the exclusive activity of the other. There is something unfriendly in each to the other, but they are like the alternate periods of feeding and working in animals; each prepares and will be followed by the other. Therefore does beauty, which, in relation to actions, as we have seen, comes unsought, and comes because it is unsought, remain for the apprehension and pursuit of the intellect; and then again, in its turn, of the active power. Nothing divine dies. All good is eternally reproductive. The beauty of nature re-forms itself in the mind, and not for barren contemplation, but for new creation.

All men are in some degree impressed by the face of the world; some men even to delight. This love of beauty is Taste. Others have the same love in such excess, that, not content with admiring, they seek to embody it in new forms. The creation of beauty is Art.

The production of a work of art throws a light upon the mystery of humanity. A work of art is an abstract or epitome of the world. It is the result or expression

[10] Puritan statesman and colonial governor of Massachusetts, executed for treason in 1662.

[11] William Russell (born 1639) was a member of Parliament, executed for (allegedly) conspiring to assassinate Charles II in 1683.

of nature, in miniature. For although the works of nature are innumerable and all different, the result or the expression of them all is similar and single. Nature is a sea of forms radically alike and even unique. A leaf, a sunbeam, a landscape, the ocean, make an analogous impression on the mind. What is common to them all,—that perfectness and harmony, is beauty. The standard of beauty is the entire circuit of natural forms,—the totality of nature; which the Italians expressed by defining beauty "il più nell' uno."[12] Nothing is quite beautiful alone; nothing but is beautiful in the whole. A single object is only so far beautiful as it suggests this universal grace. The poet, the painter, the sculptor, the musician, the architect, seek each to concentrate this radiance of the world on one point, and each in his several work to satisfy the love of beauty which stimulates him to produce. Thus is Art a nature passed through the alembic[13] of man. Thus in art does Nature work through the will of a man filled with the beauty of her first works.

The world thus exists to the soul to satisfy the desire of beauty. This element I call an ultimate end. No reason can be asked or given why the soul seeks beauty. Beauty, in its largest and profoundest sense, is one expression for the universe. God is the all-fair. Truth, and goodness, and beauty, are but different faces of the same All. But beauty in nature is not ultimate. It is the herald of inward and eternal beauty, and is not alone a solid and satisfactory good. It must stand as a part, and not as yet the last or highest expression of the final cause of Nature.

IV. Language

Language is a third use which Nature subserves to man. Nature is the vehicle of thought, and in a simple, double, and three-fold degree.

1. Words are signs of natural facts.

2. Particular natural facts are symbols of particular spiritual facts.

3. Nature is the symbol of spirit.

1. Words are signs of natural facts. The use of natural history is to give us aid in supernatural history; the use of the outer creation, to give us language for the beings and changes of the inward creation. Every word which is used to express a moral or intellectual fact, if traced to its root, is found to be borrowed from some material appearance. *Right* means *straight*; *wrong* means *twisted*. *Spirit* primarily means *wind*; *transgression*, the crossing of a *line*; *supercilious*, the *raising of the eyebrow*. We say the *heart* to express emotion, the *head* to denote thought; and *thought* and *emotion* are words borrowed from sensible things, and now appropriated to spiritual nature. Most of the process by which this transformation is made, is hidden from us in the remote time when language was framed; but the same tendency may be daily observed in children. Children and savages use only nouns or names of things, which they convert into verbs, and apply to analogous mental acts.

[12] "The many in one" (Italian); a phrase borrowed from Coleridge, *Table Talk* (1835).
[13] Distilling flask.

2. But this origin of all words that convey a spiritual import,—so conspicuous a fact in the history of language,—is our least debt to nature. It is not words only that are emblematic; it is things which are emblematic. Every natural fact is a symbol of some spiritual fact. Every appearance in nature corresponds to some state of the mind, and that state of the mind can only be described by presenting that natural appearance as its picture. An enraged man is a lion, a cunning man is a fox, a firm man is a rock, a learned man is a torch. A lamb is innocence; a snake is subtle spite; flowers express to us the delicate affections. Light and darkness are our familiar expression for knowledge and ignorance; and heat for love. Visible distance behind and before us, is respectively our image of memory and hope.

Who looks upon a river in a meditative hour and is not reminded of the flux of all things? Throw a stone into the stream, and the circles that propagate themselves are the beautiful type of all influence. Man is conscious of a universal soul within or behind his individual life, wherein, as in a firmament, the natures of Justice, Truth, Love, Freedom, arise and shine. This universal soul he calls Reason: it is not mine, or thine, or his, but we are its; we are its property and men. And the blue sky in which the private earth is buried, the sky with its eternal calm, and full of everlasting orbs, is the type of Reason. That which intellectually considered we call Reason, considered in relation to nature, we call Spirit. Spirit is the Creator. Spirit hath life in itself. And man in all ages and countries embodies it in his language as the FATHER.

It is easily seen that there is nothing lucky or capricious in these analogies, but that they are constant, and pervade nature. These are not the dreams of a few poets, here and there, but man is an analogist, and studies relations in all objects. He is placed in the centre of beings, and a ray of relation passes from every other being to him. And neither can man be understood without these objects, nor these objects without man. All the facts in natural history taken by themselves, have no value, but are barren, like a single sex. But marry it to human history, and it is full of life. Whole floras, all Linnaeus' and Buffon's volumes,[14] are dry catalogues of facts; but the most trivial of these facts, the habit of a plant, the organs, or work, or noise of an insect, applied to the illustration of a fact in intellectual philosophy, or in any way associated to human nature, affects us in the most lively and agreeable manner. The seed of a plant,—to what affecting analogies in the nature of man is that little fruit made use of, in all discourse, up to the voice of Paul, who calls the human corpse a seed,—"It is sown a natural body; it is raised a spiritual body."[15] The motion of the earth round its axis and round the sun, makes the day and the year. These are certain amounts of brute light and heat. But is there no intent of an analogy between man's life and the seasons? And do the seasons gain no grandeur or pathos from that analogy? The instincts of the ant are very unimportant considered as the ant's; but the moment a ray of relation is seen to extend from it to man, and the little drudge is seen to be a monitor, a little body with a mighty heart, then all its habits, even that said to be recently observed, that it never sleeps, become sublime.

---

[14] Carolus Linnaeus (1707–1778) and George-Louis Leclerc, compte de Buffon (1707–1788), eminent authorities in the study of natural history.

[15] 1 Corinthians 15.44.

Because of this radical correspondence between visible things and human thoughts, savages, who have only what is necessary, converse in figures. As we go back in history, language becomes more picturesque, until its infancy, when it is all poetry; or all spiritual facts are represented by natural symbols. The same symbols are found to make the original elements of all languages. It has moreover been observed, that the idioms of all languages approach each other in passages of the greatest eloquence and power. And as this is the first language, so is it the last. This immediate dependence of language upon nature, this conversion of an outward phenomenon into a type of somewhat in human life, never loses its power to affect us. It is this which gives that piquancy to the conversation of a strong-natured farmer or backwoodsman, which all men relish.

A man's power to connect his thought with its proper symbol, and so to utter it, depends on the simplicity of his character, that is, upon his love of truth and his desire to communicate it without loss. The corruption of man is followed by the corruption of language. When simplicity of character and the sovereignty of ideas is broken up by the prevalence of secondary desires,—the desire of riches, of pleasure, of power, and of praise,—and duplicity and falsehood take place of simplicity and truth, the power over nature as an interpreter of the will is in a degree lost; new imagery ceases to be created, and old words are perverted to stand for things which are not; a paper currency is employed, when there is no bullion in the vaults. In due time the fraud is manifest, and words lose all power to stimulate the understanding or the affections. Hundreds of writers may be found in every long-civilized nation who for a short time believe and make others believe that they see and utter truths, who do not of themselves clothe one thought in its natural garment, but who feed unconsciously on the language created by the primary writers of the country, those, namely, who hold primarily on nature.

But wise men pierce this rotten diction and fasten words again to visible things; so that picturesque language is at once a commanding certificate that he who employs it is a man in alliance with truth and God. The moment our discourse rises above the ground line of familiar facts and is inflamed with passion or exalted by thought, it clothes itself in images. A man conversing in earnest, if he watch his intellectual processes, will find that a material image more or less luminous arises in his mind, contemporaneous with every thought, which furnishes the vestment of the thought. Hence, good writing and brilliant discourse are perpetual allegories. This imagery is spontaneous. It is the blending of experience with the present action of the mind. It is proper creation. It is the working of the Original Cause through the instruments he has already made.

These facts may suggest the advantage which the country-life possesses, for a powerful mind, over the artificial and curtailed life of cities. We know more from nature than we can at will communicate. Its light flows into the mind evermore, and we forget its presence. The poet, the orator, bred in the woods, whose senses have been nourished by their fair and appeasing changes, year after year, without design and without heed,—shall not lose their lesson altogether, in the roar of cities or the broil of politics. Long hereafter, amidst agitation and terror in national councils,—in the hour of revolution,—these solemn images shall reappear in their morning lustre, as fit symbols and words of the thoughts which the passing events shall awaken. At the call of a noble sentiment, again the woods wave, the pines murmur, the river rolls and shines, and the cattle low upon the mountains, as he saw and heard them in his infancy. And with these forms, the spells of persuasion, the keys of power are put into his hands.

3. We are thus assisted by natural objects in the expression of particular meanings. But how great a language to convey such pepper-corn informations! Did it need such noble races of creatures, this profusion of forms, this host of orbs in heaven, to furnish man with the dictionary and grammar of his municipal speech? Whilst we use this grand cipher to expedite the affairs of our pot and kettle, we feel that we have not yet put it to its use, neither are able. We are like travellers using the cinders of a volcano to roast their eggs. Whilst we see that it always stands ready to clothe what we would say, we cannot avoid the question whether the characters are not significant of themselves. Have mountains, and waves, and skies, no significance but what we consciously give them when we employ them as emblems of our thoughts? The world is emblematic. Parts of speech are metaphors, because the whole of nature is a metaphor of the human mind. The laws of moral nature answer to those of matter as face to face in a glass. "The visible world and the relation of its parts, is the dial plate of the invisible."[16] The axioms of physics translate the laws of ethics. Thus, "the whole is greater than its part;" "reaction is equal to action;" "the smallest weight may be made to lift the greatest, the difference of weight being compensated by time;" and many the like propositions, which have an ethical as well as physical sense. These propositions have a much more extensive and universal sense when applied to human life, than when confined to technical use.

In like manner, the memorable words of history and the proverbs of nations consist usually of a natural fact, selected as a picture or parable of a moral truth. Thus; A rolling stone gathers no moss; A bird in the hand is worth two in the bush; A cripple in the right way will beat a racer in the wrong; Make hay while the sun shines; 'Tis hard to carry a full cup even; Vinegar is the son of wine; The last ounce broke the camel's back; Long-lived trees make roots first;—and the like. In their primary sense these are trivial facts, but we repeat them for the value of their analogical import. What is true of proverbs, is true of all fables, parables, and allegories.

This relation between the mind and matter is not fancied by some poet, but stands in the will of God, and so is free to be known by all men. It appears to men, or it does not appear. When in fortunate hours we ponder this miracle, the wise man doubts if at all other times he is not blind and deaf;

> ——"Can such things be,
> And overcome us like a summer's cloud,
> Without our special wonder?"[17]

[16] Cited from Emanuel Swedenborg (1688–1772), Swedish scientist and religious philosopher.
[17] Shakespeare, *Macbeth*, 3.4.110–12.

for the universe becomes transparent, and the light of higher laws than its own shines through it. It is the standing problem which has exercised the wonder and the study of every fine genius since the world began; from the era of the Egyptians and the Brahmins to that of Pythagoras, of Plato, of Bacon, of Leibnitz, of Swedenborg. There sits the Sphinx at the roadside, and from age to age, as each prophet comes by, he tries his fortune at reading her riddle. There seems to be a necessity in spirit to manifest itself in material forms; and day and night, river and storm, beast and bird, acid and alkali, preëxist in necessary Ideas in the mind of God, and are what they are by virtue of preceding affections in the world of spirit. A Fact is the end or last issue of spirit. The visible creation is the terminus or the circumference of the invisible world. "Material objects," said a French philosopher, "are necessarily kinds of *scoriæ* of the substantial thoughts of the Creator, which must always preserve an exact relation to their first origin; in other words, visible nature must have a spiritual and moral side."[18]

This doctrine is abstruse, and though the images of "garment," "scoriae," "mirror," etc., may stimulate the fancy, we must summon the aid of subtler and more vital expositors to make it plain. "Every scripture is to be interpreted by the same spirit which gave it forth,"[19] — is the fundamental law of criticism. A life in harmony with Nature, the love of truth and of virtue, will purge the eyes to understand her text. By degrees we may come to know the primitive sense of the permanent objects of nature, so that the world shall be to us an open book, and every form significant of its hidden life and final cause.

A new interest surprises us, whilst, under the view now suggested, we contemplate the fearful extent and multitude of objects; since "every object rightly seen, unlocks a new faculty of the soul." That which was unconscious truth, becomes, when interpreted and defined in an object, a part of the domain of knowledge, — a new weapon in the magazine of power.[20]

V.   Discipline

In view of the significance of nature, we arrive at once at a new fact, that nature is a discipline. This use of the world includes the preceding uses, as parts of itself.

Space, time, society, labor, climate, food, locomotion, the animals, the mechanical forces, give us sincerest lessons, day by day, whose meaning is unlimited. They educate both the Understanding and the Reason. Every property of matter is a school for the understanding, — its solidity or resistance, its inertia, its extension, its figure, its divisibility. The understanding adds, divides, combines, measures, and finds nutriment and room for its activity in this worthy scene. Meantime, Reason transfers all these lessons into its own world of thought, by perceiving the analogy that marries Matter and Mind.

---

[18] From Guillaume Oegger, *The True Messiah* (1829). *Scoriae*: the refuse of smelted metal; slag.

[19] From George Fox (1624–1691), founder of Quakerism.

[20] Paraphrased from Coleridge's *Biographia Literaria*, chapter 4: "In energetic minds, truth soon changes by domestication into power."

1. Nature is a discipline of the understanding in intellectual truths. Our dealing with sensible objects is a constant exercise in the necessary lessons of difference, of likeness, of order, of being and seeming, of progressive arrangement; of ascent from particular to general; of combination to one end of manifold forces. Proportioned to the importance of the organ to be formed, is the extreme care with which its tuition is provided,—a care pretermitted in no single case. What tedious training, day after day, year after year, never ending, to form the common sense; what continual reproduction of annoyances, inconveniences, dilemmas; what rejoicing over us of little men; what disputing of prices, what reckonings of interest,—and all to form the Hand of the mind;—to instruct us that "good thoughts are no better than good dreams, unless they be executed!"[21]

The same good office is performed by Property and its filial systems of debt and credit. Debt, grinding debt, whose iron face the widow, the orphan, and the sons of genius fear and hate;—debt, which consumes so much time, which so cripples and disheartens a great spirit with cares that seem so base, is a preceptor whose lessons cannot be foregone, and is needed most by those who suffer from it most. Moreover, property, which has been well compared to snow,—"if it fall level to-day, it will be blown into drifts to-morrow,"—is the surface action of internal machinery, like the index on the face of a clock. Whilst now it is the gymnastics of the understanding, it is hiving, in the foresight of the spirit, experience in profounder laws.

The whole character and fortune of the individual are affected by the least inequalities in the culture of the understanding; for example, in the perception of differences. Therefore is Space, and therefore Time, that man may know that things are not huddled and lumped, but sundered and individual. A bell and a plough have each their use, and neither can do the office of the other. Water is good to drink, coal to burn, wool to wear; but wool cannot be drunk, nor water spun, nor coal eaten. The wise man shows his wisdom in separation, in gradation, and his scale of creatures and of merits is as wide as nature. The foolish have no range in their scale, but suppose every man is as every other man. What is not good they call the worst, and what is not hateful, they call the best.

In like manner, what good heed Nature forms in us! She pardons no mistakes. Her yea is yea, and her nay, nay.

The first steps in Agriculture, Astronomy, Zoölogy (those first steps which the farmer, the hunter, and the sailor take), teach that Nature's dice are always loaded; that in her heaps and rubbish are concealed sure and useful results.

How calmly and genially the mind apprehends one after another the laws of physics! What noble emotions dilate the mortal as he enters into the councils of the creation, and feels by knowledge the privilege to BE! His insight refines him. The beauty of nature shines in his own breast. Man is greater that he can see this, and the universe less, because Time and Space relations vanish as laws are known.

Here again we are impressed and even daunted by the immense Universe to be explored. "What we know is a point to what we do not know."[22] Open any re-

---

[21] From Francis Bacon's essay, *Of Great Place.*
[22] A saying ascribed to Sir Isaac Newton (1642–1727).

cent journal of science, and weigh the problems suggested concerning Light, Heat, Electricity, Magnetism, Physiology, Geology, and judge whether the interest of natural science is likely to be soon exhausted.

Passing by many particulars of the discipline of nature, we must not omit to specify two.

The exercise of the Will, or the lesson of power, is taught in every event. From the child's successive possession of his several senses up to the hour when he saith, "Thy will be done!"[23] he is learning the secret that he can reduce under his will not only particular events but great classes, nay, the whole series of events, and so conform all facts to his character. Nature is thoroughly mediate. It is made to serve. It receives the dominion of man as meekly as the ass on which the Saviour rode.[24] It offers all its kingdoms to man as the raw material which he may mould into what is useful. Man is never weary of working it up. He forges the subtile and delicate air into wise and melodious words, and gives them wing as angels of persuasion and command. One after another his victorious thought comes up with and reduces all things, until the world becomes at last only a realized will,—the double of the man.

2. Sensible objects conform to the premonitions of Reason and reflect the conscience. All things are moral; and in their boundless changes have an unceasing reference to spiritual nature. Therefore is nature glorious with form, color, and motion; that every globe in the remotest heaven, every chemical change from the rudest crystal up to the laws of life, every change of vegetation from the first principle of growth in the eye of a leaf, to the tropical forest and antediluvian coal mine, every animal function from the sponge up to Hercules, shall hint or thunder to man the laws of right and wrong, and echo the Ten Commandments. Therefore is Nature ever the ally of Religion: lends all her pomp and riches to the religious sentiment. Prophet and priest, David, Isaiah, Jesus, have drawn deeply from this source. This ethical character so penetrates the bone and marrow of nature, as to seem the end for which it was made. Whatever private purpose is answered by any member or part, this is its public and universal function, and is never omitted. Nothing in nature is exhausted in its first use. When a thing has served an end to the uttermost, it is wholly new for an ulterior service. In God, every end is converted into a new means. Thus the use of commodity, regarded by itself, is mean and squalid. But it is to the mind an education in the doctrine of Use, namely, that a thing is good only so far as it serves; that a conspiring of parts and efforts to the production of an end is essential to any being. The first and gross manifestation of this truth is our inevitable and hated training in values and wants, in corn and meat.

It has already been illustrated, that every natural process is a version of a moral sentence. The moral law lies at the centre of nature and radiates to the circumference. It is the pith and marrow of every substance, every relation, and every process. All things with which we deal, preach to us. What is a farm but a mute gospel? The chaff and the wheat, weeds and plants, blight, rain, insects,

[23] Matthew 6.10, 26.42.
[24] Matthew 21.5.

sun,—it is a sacred emblem from the first furrow of spring to the last stack which the snow of winter overtakes in the fields. But the sailor, the shepherd, the miner, the merchant, in their several resorts, have each an experience precisely parallel, and leading to the same conclusion: because all organizations are radically alike. Nor can it be doubted that this moral sentiment which thus scents the air, grows in the grain, and impregnates the waters of the world, is caught by man and sinks into his soul. The moral influence of nature upon every individual is that amount of truth which it illustrates to him. Who can estimate this? Who can guess how much firmness the sea-beaten rock has taught the fisherman? how much tranquillity has been reflected to man from the azure sky, over whose unspotted deeps the winds forevermore drive flocks of stormy clouds, and leave no wrinkle or stain? how much industry and providence and affection we have caught from the pantomime of brutes? What a searching preacher of self-command is the varying phenomenon of Health!

Herein is especially apprehended the unity of Nature,—the unity in variety,—which meets us everywhere. All the endless variety of things make an identical impression. Xenophanes[25] complained in his old age, that, look where he would, all things hastened back to Unity. He was weary of seeing the same entity in the tedious variety of forms. The fable of Proteus[26] has a cordial truth. A leaf, a drop, a crystal, a moment of time, is related to the whole, and partakes of the perfection of the whole. Each particle is a microcosm, and faithfully renders the likeness of the world.

Not only resemblances exist in things whose analogy is obvious, as when we detect the type of the human hand in the flipper of the fossil saurus, but also in objects wherein there is great superficial unlikeness. Thus architecture is called "frozen music," by De Staël and Goethe.[27] Vitruvius thought an architect should be a musician. "A Gothic church," said Coleridge, "is a petrified religion."[28] Michael Angelo maintained, that, to an architect, a knowledge of anatomy is essential. In Haydn's[29] oratorios, the notes present to the imagination not only motions, as of the snake, the stag, and the elephant, but colors also; as the green grass. The law of harmonic sound reappears in the harmonic colors. The granite is differenced in its laws only by the more or less of heat from the river that wears it away. The river, as it flows, resembles the air that flows over it; the air resembles the light which traverses it with more subtle currents; the light resembles the heat which rides with it through Space. Each creature is only a modification of the other; the likeness in them is more than the difference, and their radical law is one and the same. A rule of one art, or a law of one organization, holds true throughout nature. So intimate is this Unity, that, it is easily seen, it lies under the undermost garment of Nature, and betrays its source in Universal

---

[25] Greek philosopher (c. 580–c. 470 B.C.). He taught that there is only one god, immanent in all the appearances of nature, an early form of pantheism.

[26] In Greek mythology, a sea god who could change his shape at will.

[27] Madame de Staël (1766–1817) and Johann Wolfgang von Goethe (1749–1832).

[28] Coleridge, *Lecture on the General Character of the Gothic Mind in the Middle Ages* (1836).

[29] Franz Joseph Haydn (1732–1809), Austrian composer.

Spirit. For it pervades Thought also. Every universal truth which we express in words, implies or supposes every other truth. *Omne verum vero consonat*.[30] It is like a great circle on a sphere, comprising all possible circles; which, however, may be drawn and comprise it in like manner. Every such truth is the absolute Ens seen from one side. But it has innumerable sides.

The central Unity is still more conspicuous in actions. Words are finite organs of the infinite mind. They cannot cover the dimensions of what is in truth. They break, chop, and impoverish it. An action is the perfection and publication of thought. A right action seems to fill the eye, and to be related to all nature. "The wise man, in doing one thing, does all; or, in the one thing he does rightly, he sees the likeness of all which is done rightly."[31]

Words and actions are not the attributes of brute nature. They introduce us to the human form, of which all other organizations appear to be degradations. When this appears among so many that surround it, the spirit prefers it to all others. It says, "From such as this have I drawn joy and knowledge; in such as this have I found and beheld myself; I will speak to it; it can speak again; it can yield me thought already formed and alive." In fact, the eye,—the mind,—is always accompanied by these forms, male and female; and these are incomparably the richest informations of the power and order that lie at the heart of things. Unfortunately every one of them bears the marks as of some injury; is marred and superficially defective. Nevertheless, far different from the deaf and dumb nature around them, these all rest like fountain-pipes on the unfathomed sea of thought and virtue whereto they alone, of all organizations, are the entrances.

It were a pleasant inquiry to follow into detail their ministry to our education, but where would it stop? We are associated in adolescent and adult life with some friends, who, like skies and waters, are coextensive with our idea; who, answering each to a certain affection of the soul, satisfy our desire on that side; whom we lack power to put at such focal distance from us, that we can mend or even analyze them. We cannot choose but love them. When much intercourse with a friend has supplied us with a standard of excellence, and has increased our respect for the resources of God who thus sends a real person to outgo our ideal; when he has, moreover, become an object of thought, and, whilst his character retains all its unconscious effect, is converted in the mind into solid and sweet wisdom,—it is a sign to us that his office is closing, and he is commonly withdrawn from our sight in a short time.

VI. Idealism

Thus is the unspeakable but intelligible and practicable meaning of the world conveyed to man, the immortal pupil, in every object of sense. To this one end of Discipline, all parts of nature conspire.

A noble doubt perpetually suggests itself,—whether this end be not the Final Cause of the Universe; and whether nature outwardly exists. It is a sufficient ac-

---

[30] "Every truth agrees with every other truth" (Latin).

[31] From Goethe, *Wilhelm Meister* (1796), a classic *Bildungsroman* translated by Thomas Carlyle.

count of that Appearance we call the World, that God will teach a human mind, and so makes it the receiver of a certain number of congruent sensations, which we call sun and moon, man and woman, house and trade. In my utter impotence to test the authenticity of the report of my senses, to know whether the impressions they make on me correspond with outlying objects, what difference does it make, whether Orion is up there in heaven, or some god paints the image in the firmament of the soul? The relations of parts and the end of the whole remaining the same, what is the difference, whether land and sea interact, and worlds revolve and intermingle without number or end,—deep yawning under deep, and galaxy balancing galaxy, throughout absolute space,—or whether, without relations of time and space, the same appearances are inscribed in the constant faith of man? Whether nature enjoy a substantial existence without, or is only in the apocalypse of the mind, it is alike useful and alike venerable to me. Be it what it may, it is ideal to me so long as I cannot try the accuracy of my senses.

The frivolous make themselves merry with the Ideal theory, as if its consequences were burlesque; as if it affected the stability of nature. It surely does not. God never jests with us, and will not compromise the end of nature by permitting any inconsequence in its procession. Any distrust of the permanence of laws would paralyze the faculties of man. Their permanence is sacredly respected, and his faith therein is perfect. The wheels and springs of man are all set to the hypothesis of the permanence of nature. We are not built like a ship to be tossed, but like a house to stand. It is a natural consequence of this structure, that so long as the active powers predominate over the reflective, we resist with indignation any hint that nature is more short-lived or mutable than spirit. The broker, the wheelwright, the carpenter, the tollman, are much displeased at the intimation.

But whilst we acquiesce entirely in the permanence of natural laws, the question of the absolute existence of nature still remains open. It is the uniform effect of culture on the human mind, not to shake our faith in the stability of particular phenomena, as of heat, water, azote;[32] but to lead us to regard nature as phenomenon, not a substance; to attribute necessary existence to spirit; to esteem nature as an accident and an effect.

To the senses and the unrenewed understanding, belongs a sort of instinctive belief in the absolute existence of nature. In their view man and nature are indissolubly joined. Things are ultimates, and they never look beyond their sphere. The presence of Reason mars this faith. The first effort of thought tends to relax this despotism of the senses which binds us to nature as if we were a part of it, and shows us nature aloof, and, as it were, afloat. Until this higher agency intervened, the animal eye sees, with wonderful accuracy, sharp outlines and colored surfaces. When the eye of Reason opens, to outline and surface are at once added grace and expression. These proceed from imagination and affection, and abate somewhat of the angular distinctness of objects. If the Reason be stimulated to more earnest vision, outlines and surfaces become transparent, and are no longer seen; causes and spirits are seen through them. The best moments of

[32] Nitrogen.

life are these delicious awakenings of the higher powers, and the reverential withdrawing of nature before its God.

Let us proceed to indicate the effects of culture.

1. Our first institution in the Ideal philosophy is a hint from Nature herself.

Nature is made to conspire with spirit to emancipate us. Certain mechanical changes, a small alteration in our local position, apprises us of a dualism. We are strangely affected by seeing the shore from a moving ship, from a balloon, or through the tints of an unusual sky. The least change in our point of view gives the whole world a pictorial air. A man who seldom rides, needs only to get into a coach and traverse his own town, to turn the street into a puppet show. The men, the women,—talking, running, bartering, fighting,—the earnest mechanic, the lounger, the beggar, the boys, the dogs, are unrealized at once, or, at least, wholly detached from all relation to the observer, and seen as apparent, not substantial beings. What new thoughts are suggested by seeing a face of country quite familiar, in the rapid movement of the railroad car! Nay, the most wonted objects, (make a very slight change in the point of vision,) please us most. In a camera obscura,[33] the butcher's cart, and the figure of one of our own family amuse us. So a portrait of a well-known face gratifies us. Turn the eyes upside down, by looking at the landscape through your legs, and how agreeable is the picture, though you have seen it any time these twenty years!

In these cases, by mechanical means, is suggested the difference between the observer and the spectacle—between man and nature. Hence arises a pleasure mixed with awe; I may say, a low degree of the sublime is felt, from the fact, probably, that man is hereby apprised that whilst the world is a spectacle, something in himself is stable.

2. In a higher manner the poet communicates the same pleasure. By a few strokes he delineates, as on air, the sun, the mountain, the camp, the city, the hero, the maiden, not different from what we know them, but only lifted from the ground and afloat before the eye. He unfixes the land and the sea, makes them revolve around the axis of his primary thought, and disposes them anew. Possessed himself by a heroic passion, he uses matter as symbols of it. The sensual man conforms thoughts to things; the poet conforms things to his thoughts. The one esteems nature as rooted and fast; the other, as fluid, and impresses his being thereon. To him, the refractory world is ductile and flexible; he invests dust and stones with humanity, and makes them the words of the Reason. The Imagination may be defined to be the use which the Reason makes of the material world. Shakespeare possesses the power of subordinating nature for the purposes of expression, beyond all poets. His imperial muse tosses the creation like a bauble from hand to hand, and uses it to embody any caprice of thought that is uppermost in his mind. The remotest spaces of nature are visited, and the farthest sundered things are brought together, by a subtle spiritual connection. We are made aware that magnitude of material things is relative, and all objects shrink and expand to serve the passion of the poet. Thus in his sonnets, the lays

---

[33] A dark chamber with a lens through which images of external objects are projected.

of birds, the scents and dyes of flowers he finds to be the *shadow* of his beloved; time, which keeps her from him, is his *chest;* the suspicion she has awakened, is her *ornament;*

> The ornament of beauty is Suspect,
> A crow which flies in heaven's sweetest air.[34]

His passion is not the fruit of chance; it swells, as he speaks, to a city, or a state.

> No, it was builded far from accident;
> It suffers not in smiling pomp, nor falls
> Under the brow of thralling discontent;
> It fears not policy, that heretic,
> That works on leases of short numbered hours,
> But all alone stands hugely politic.[35]

In the strength of his constancy, the Pyramids seem to him recent and transitory. The freshness of youth and love dazzles him with its resemblance to morning;

> Take those lips away
> Which so sweetly were forsworn;
> And those eyes,—the break of day,
> Lights that do mislead the morn.[36]

The wild beauty of this hyperbole, I may say in passing, it would not be easy to match in literature.

This transfiguration which all material objects undergo through the passion of the poet,—this power which he exerts to dwarf the great, to magnify the small,—might be illustrated by a thousand examples from his Plays. I have before me the Tempest, and will cite only these few lines.

> PROSPERO. The strong based promontory
> Have I made shake, and by the spurs plucked up
> The pine and cedar.[37]

Prospero calls for music to soothe the frantic Alonzo, and his companions;

> A solemn air, and the best comforter
> To an unsettled fancy, cure my brains
> Now useless, boiled within thy skull.

[34] Shakespeare, Sonnet 70.
[35] Shakespeare, Sonnet 124.
[36] Shakespeare, *Measure for Measure*, 5.1.1–4.
[37] Shakespeare, *The Tempest*, 5.1.46–48. The three following quotations are from *The Tempest*, 5.1.58–60, 64–68, and 79–82, respectively.

Again;

> The charm dissolves apace,
> And, as the morning steals upon the night,
> Melting the darkness, so their rising senses
> Begin to chase the ignorant fumes that mantle
> Their clearer reason.

> Their understanding
> Begins to swell: and the approaching tide
> Will shortly fill the reasonable shores
> That now lie foul and muddy.

The perception of real affinities between events (that is to say, of *ideal* affinities, for those only are real), enables the poet thus to make free with the most imposing forms and phenomena of the world, and to assert the predominance of the soul.

3. Whilst thus the poet animates nature with his own thoughts, he differs from the philosopher only herein, that the one proposes Beauty as his main end; the other Truth. But the philosopher, not less than the poet, postpones the apparent order and relations of things to the empire of thought. "The problem of philosophy," according to Plato, "is, for all that exists conditionally, to find a ground unconditioned and absolute."[38] It proceeds on the faith that a law determines all phenomena, which being known, the phenomena can be predicted. That law, when in the mind, is an idea. Its beauty is infinite. The true philosopher and the true poet are one, and a beauty, which is truth, and a truth, which is beauty, is the aim of both. Is not the charm of one of Plato's or Aristotle's definitions strictly like that of the Antigone of Sophocles?[39] It is, in both cases, that a spiritual life has been imparted to nature; that the solid seeming block of matter has been pervaded and dissolved by a thought; that this feeble human being has penetrated the vast masses of nature with an informing soul, and recognized itself in their harmony, that is, seized their law. In physics, when this is attained, the memory disburthens itself of its cumbrous catalogues of particulars, and carries centuries of observation in a single formula.

Thus even in physics, the material is degraded before the spiritual. The astronomer, the geometer, rely on their irrefragable analysis, and disdain the results of observation. The sublime remark of Euler on his law of arches, "This will be found contrary to all experience, yet is true;"[40] had already transferred nature into the mind, and left matter like an outcast corpse.

4. Intellectual science has been observed to beget invariably a doubt of the existence of matter. Turgot said, "He that has never doubted the existence of matter, may be assured he has no aptitude for metaphysical inquiries."[41] It fas-

---

[38] Emerson derives this quotation from Coleridge, *The Friend* (1818).

[39] Alludes to the tragedy *Antigone* by the ancient Greek dramatist Sophocles.

[40] Leonhard Euler (1707–1783), Swiss mathematician. Emerson derives this quotation from Coleridge, *Aids to Reflection* (1825).

[41] Anne Robert Jacques Turgot (1727–1781), French economist and Enlightenment philosopher.

tens the attention upon immortal necessary uncreated natures, that is, upon Ideas; and in their presence we feel that the outward circumstance is a dream and a shade. Whilst we wait in this Olympus of gods, we think of nature as an appendix to the soul. We ascend into their region, and know that these are the thoughts of the Supreme Being. "These are they who were set up from everlasting, from the beginning, or ever the earth was. When he prepared the heavens, they were there; when he established the clouds above, when he strengthened the fountains of the deep. Then they were by him, as one brought up with him. Of them took he counsel."[42]

Their influence is proportionate. As objects of science they are accessible to few men. Yet all men are capable of being raised by piety or by passion, into their region. And no man touches these divine natures, without becoming, in some degree, himself divine. Like a new soul, they renew the body. We become physically nimble and lightsome; we tread on air; life is no longer irksome, and we think it will never be so. No man fears age or misfortune or death in their serene company, for he is transported out of the district of change. Whilst we behold unveiled the nature of Justice and Truth, we learn the difference between the absolute and the conditional or relative. We apprehend the absolute. As it were, for the first time, *we exist*. We become immortal, for we learn that time and space are relations of matter; that with a perception of truth or a virtuous will they have no affinity.

5. Finally, religion and ethics, which may be fitly called the practice of ideas, or the introduction of ideas into life, have an analogous effect with all lower culture, in degrading nature and suggesting its dependence on spirit. Ethics and religion differ herein; that the one is the system of human duties commencing from man; the other, from God. Religion includes the personality of God; Ethics does not. They are one to our present design. They both put nature under foot. The first and last lesson of religion is, "The things that are seen, are temporal; the things that are unseen, are eternal."[43] It puts an affront upon nature. It does that for the unschooled, which philosophy does for Berkeley and Viasa.[44] The uniform language that may be heard in the churches of the most ignorant sects is,—"Contemn the unsubstantial shows of the world; they are vanities, dreams, shadows, unrealities; seek the realities of religion." The devotee flouts nature. Some theosophists have arrived at a certain hostility and indignation towards matter, as the Manichean and Plotinus.[45] They distrusted in themselves any looking back to these flesh-pots of Egypt. Plotinus was ashamed of his body. In short, they might all say of matter, what Michael Angelo said of external beauty, "It is the frail and weary weed, in which God dresses the soul which he has called into time."[46]

[42] Proverbs 8.23–30.

[43] 2 Corinthians 4.18.

[44] George Berkeley (1685–1753), British idealist philosopher, and Viasa, reputed author of the Vedas (the ancient sacred texts of Hinduism).

[45] Manichaeism is a dualistic philosophy that divides the world between good and evil principles. Plotinus was a Neoplatonic philosopher of the third century A.D.

[46] Michelangelo, Sonnet 51.

It appears that motion, poetry, physical and intellectual science, and religion, all tend to affect our convictions of the reality of the external world. But I own there is something ungrateful in expanding too curiously the particulars of the general proposition, that all culture tends to imbue us with idealism. I have no hostility to nature, but a child's love to it. I expand and live in the warm day like corn and melons. Let us speak her fair. I do not wish to fling stones at my beautiful mother, nor soil my gentle nest. I only wish to indicate the true position of nature in regard to man, wherein to establish man all right education tends; as the ground which to attain is the object of human life, that is, of man's connection with nature. Culture inverts the vulgar views of nature, and brings the mind to call that apparent which it uses to call real, and that real which it uses to call visionary. Children, it is true, believe in the external world. The belief that it appears only, is an afterthought, but with culture this faith will as surely arise on the mind as did the first.

The advantage of the ideal theory over the popular faith is this, that it presents the world in precisely that view which is most desirable to the mind. It is, in fact, the view which Reason, both speculative and practical, that is, philosophy and virtue, take. For seen in the light of thought, the world always is phenomenal; and virtue subordinates it to the mind. Idealism sees the world in God. It beholds the whole circle of persons and things, of actions and events, of country and religion, not as painfully accumulated, atom after atom, act after act, in an aged creeping Past, but as one vast picture which God paints on the instant eternity for the contemplation of the soul. Therefore the soul holds itself off from a too trivial and microscopic study of the universal tablet. It respects the end too much to immerse itself in the means. It sees something more important in Christianity than the scandals of ecclesiastical history or the niceties of criticism; and, very incurious concerning persons or miracles, and not at all disturbed by chasms of historical evidence, it accepts from God the phenomenon, as it finds it, as the pure and awful form of religion in the world. It is not hot and passionate at the appearance of what it calls its own good or bad fortune, at the union or opposition of other persons. No man is its enemy. It accepts whatsoever befalls, as part of its lesson. It is a watcher more than a doer, and it is a doer, only that it may the better watch.

VII.   Spirit

It is essential to a true theory of nature and of man, that it should contain somewhat progressive. Uses that are exhausted or that may be, and facts that end in the statement, cannot be all that is true of this brave lodging wherein man is harbored, and wherein all his faculties find appropriate and endless exercise. And all the uses of nature admit of being summed in one, which yields the activity of man an infinite scope. Through all its kingdoms, to the suburbs and outskirts of things, it is faithful to the cause whence it had its origin. It always speaks of Spirit. It suggests the absolute. It is a perpetual effect. It is a great shadow pointing always to the sun behind us.

The aspect of Nature is devout. Like the figure of Jesus, she stands with bended head, and hands folded upon the breast. The happiest man is he who learns from nature the lesson of worship.

Of that ineffable essence which we call Spirit, he that thinks most, will say least. We can foresee God in the coarse, and, as it were, distant phenomena of matter; but when we try to define and describe himself, both language and thought desert us, and we are as helpless as fools and savages. That essence refuses to be recorded in propositions, but when man has worshipped him intellectually, the noblest ministry of nature is to stand as the apparition of God. It is the organ through which the universal spirit speaks to the individual, and strives to lead back the individual to it.

When we consider Spirit, we see that the views already presented do not include the whole circumference of man. We must add some related thoughts.

Three problems are put by nature to the mind: What is matter? Whence is it? and Whereto? The first of these questions only, the ideal theory answers. Idealism saith: matter is a phenomenon, not a substance. Idealism acquaints us with the total disparity between the evidence of our own being and the evidence of the world's being. The one is perfect; the other, incapable of any assurance; the mind is a part of the nature of things; the world is a divine dream, from which we may presently awake to the glories and certainties of day. Idealism is a hypothesis to account for nature by other principles than those of carpentry and chemistry. Yet, if it only deny the existence of matter, it does not satisfy the demands of the spirit. It leaves God out of me. It leaves me in the splendid labyrinth of my perceptions, to wander without end. Then the heart resists it, because it balks the affections in denying substantive being to men and women. Nature is so pervaded with human life that there is something of humanity in all and in every particular. But this theory makes nature foreign to me, and does not account for that consanguinity which we acknowledge to it.

Let it stand then, in the present state of our knowledge, merely as a useful introductory hypothesis, serving to apprise us of the eternal distinction between the soul and the world.

But when, following the invisible steps of thought, we come to inquire, Whence is matter? and Whereto? many truths arise to us out of the recesses of consciousness. We learn that the highest is present to the soul of man; that the dread universal essence, which is not wisdom, or love, or beauty, or power, but all in one, and each entirely, is that for which all things exist, and that by which they are; that spirit creates; that behind nature, throughout nature, spirit is present; one and not compound it does not act upon us from without, that is, in space and time, but spiritually, or through ourselves: therefore, that spirit, that is, the Supreme Being, does not build up nature around us, but puts it forth through us, as the life of the tree puts forth new branches and leaves through the pores of the old. As a plant upon the earth, so a man rests upon the bosom of God; he is nourished by unfailing fountains, and draws at his need inexhaustible power. Who can set bounds to the possibilities of man? Once inhale the upper air, being admitted to behold the absolute natures of justice and truth, and we learn that man has access to the entire mind of the Creator, is himself the creator in the finite. This view, which admonishes me where the sources of wisdom and power lie, and points to virtue as to

> "The golden key
> Which opes the palace of eternity."[47]

carries upon its face the highest certificate of truth, because it animates me to create my own world through the purification of my soul.

The world proceeds from the same spirit as the body of man. It is a remoter and inferior incarnation of God, a projection of God in the unconscious. But it differs from the body in one important respect. It is not, like that, now subjected to the human will. Its serene order is inviolable by us. It is, therefore, to us, the present expositor of the divine mind. It is a fixed point whereby we may measure our departure. As we degenerate, the contrast between us and our house is more evident. We are as much strangers in nature as we are aliens from God. We do not understand the notes of birds. The fox and the deer run away from us; the bear and tiger rend us. We do not know the uses of more than a few plants, as corn and the apple, the potato and the vine. Is not the landscape, every glimpse of which hath a grandeur, a face of him? Yet this may show us what discord is between man and nature, for you cannot freely admire a noble landscape if laborers are digging in the field hard by. The poet finds something ridiculous in his delight until he is out of the sight of men.

VIII. Prospects

In inquiries respecting the laws of the world and the frame of things, the highest reason is always the truest. That which seems faintly possible, it is so refined, is often faint and dim because it is deepest seated in the mind among the eternal verities. Empirical science is apt to cloud the sight, and by the very knowledge of functions and processes to bereave the student of the manly contemplation of the whole. The savant becomes unpoetic. But the best read naturalist who lends an entire and devout attention to truth, will see that there remains much to learn of his relation to the world, and that it is not to be learned by any addition or subtraction or other comparison of known quantities, but is arrived at by untaught sallies of the spirit, by a continual self-recovery, and by entire humility. He will perceive that there are far more excellent qualities in the student than preciseness and infallibility; that a guess is often more fruitful than an indisputable affirmation, and that a dream may let us deeper into the secret of nature than a hundred concerted experiments.

For the problems to be solved are precisely those which the physiologist and the naturalist omit to state. It is not so pertinent to man to know all the individuals of the animal kingdom, as it is to know whence and whereto is this tyrannizing unity in his constitution, which evermore separates and classifies things, endeavoring to reduce the most diverse to one form. When I behold a rich landscape, it

[47] John Milton, *Comus*, lines 13–14.

is less to my purpose to recite correctly the order and superposition of the strata, than to know why all thought of multitude is lost in a tranquil sense of unity. I cannot greatly honor minuteness in details, so long as there is no hint to explain the relation between things and thoughts; no ray upon the *metaphysics* of conchology, of botany, of the arts, to show the relation of the forms of flowers, shells, animals, architecture, to the mind, and build science upon ideas. In a cabinet of natural history, we become sensible of a certain occult recognition and sympathy in regard to the most unwieldy and eccentric forms of beast, fish, and insect. The American who has been confined, in his own country, to the sight of buildings designed after foreign models, is surprised on entering York Minster or St. Peter's at Rome, by the feeling that these structures are imitations also,—faint copies of an invisible archetype. Nor has science sufficient humanity, so long as the naturalist overlooks that wonderful congruity which subsists between man and the world; of which he is lord, not because he is the most subtile inhabitant, but because he is its head and heart, and finds something of himself in every great and small thing, in every mountain stratum, in every new law of color, fact of astronomy, or atmospheric influence which observation or analysis lays open. A perception of this mystery inspires the muse of George Herbert, the beautiful psalmist of the seventeenth century. The following lines are part of his little poem on Man.

> Man is all symmetry,
> Full of proportions, one limb to another,
> And all to all the world besides.
> Each part may call the farthest, brother;
> For head with foot hath private amity,
> And both with moons and tides.
>
> Nothing hath got so far
> But man hath caught and kept it as his prey;
> His eyes dismount the highest star:
> He is in little all the sphere.
> Herbs gladly cure our flesh, because that they
> Find their acquaintance there.
>
> For us, the winds do blow,
> The earth doth rest, heaven move, and fountains flow;
> Nothing we see, but means our good,
> As our delight, or as our treasure;
> The whole is either our cupboard of food,
> Or cabinet of pleasure.
>
> The stars have us to bed:
> Night draws the curtain; which the sun withdraws.
> Music and light attend our head.
> All things unto our flesh are kind,
> In their descent and being; to our mind,
> In their ascent and cause.

> More servants wait on man
> Than he'll take notice of. In every path,
>> He treads down that which doth befriend him
>> When sickness makes him pale and wan.
> Oh mighty love! Man is one world, and hath
>> Another to attend him.[48]

The perception of this class of truths makes the attraction which draws men to science, but the end is lost sight of in attention to the means. In view of this half-sight of science, we accept the sentence of Plato, that "poetry comes nearer to vital truth than history."[49] Every surmise and vaticination[50] of the mind is entitled to a certain respect, and we learn to prefer imperfect theories, and sentences which contain glimpses of truth, to digested systems which have no one valuable suggestion. A wise writer will feel that the ends of study and composition are best answered by announcing undiscovered regions of thought, and so communicating, through hope, new activity to the torpid spirit.

I shall therefore conclude this essay with some traditions of man and nature, which a certain poet sang to me;[51] and which, as they have always been in the world, and perhaps reappear to every bard, may be both history and prophecy.

"The foundations of man are not in matter, but in spirit. But the element of spirit is eternity. To it, therefore, the longest series of events, the oldest chronologies are young and recent. In the cycle of the universal man, from whom the known individuals proceed, centuries are points, and all history is but the epoch of one degradation.

"We distrust and deny inwardly our sympathy with nature. We own and disown our relation to it, by turns. We are like Nebuchadnezzar, dethroned, bereft of reason, and eating grass like an ox.[52] But who can set limits to the remedial force of spirit?

"A man is a god in ruins. When men are innocent, life shall be longer, and shall pass into the immortal as gently as we awake from dreams. Now, the world would be insane and rabid, if these disorganizations should last for hundreds of years. It is kept in check by death and infancy. Infancy is the perpetual Messiah, which comes into the arms of fallen men, and pleads with them to return to paradise.

"Man is the dwarf of himself. Once he was permeated and dissolved by spirit. He filled nature with his overflowing currents. Out from him sprang the sun and moon; from man the sun, from woman the moon. The laws of his mind, the periods of his actions externized themselves into day and night, into the year and the seasons. But, having made for himself this huge shell, his waters retired; he no longer fills the veins and veinlets; he is shrunk to a drop. He sees that the

---

[48] Stanzas excerpted from the poem by George Herbert, *Man*.

[49] Emerson misattributes this quotation to Plato; it is actually from Aristotle's *Poetics*, section 9.

[50] Foretelling; prophecy.

[51] The following four-paragraph passage, ostensibly quoted from "a certain poet," was actually written by Emerson himself.

[52] Alludes to Daniel 4.31–33.

structure still fits him, but fits him colossally. Say, rather, once it fitted him, now it corresponds to him from far and on high. He adores timidly his own work. Now is man the follower of the sun, and woman the follower of the moon. Yet sometimes he starts in his slumber, and wonders at himself and his house, and muses strangely at the resemblance betwixt him and it. He perceives that if his law is still paramount, if still he have elemental power, if his word is sterling yet in nature, it is not conscious power, it is not inferior but superior to his will. It is instinct." Thus my Orphic poet sang.

At present, man applies to nature but half his force. He works on the world with his understanding alone. He lives in it and masters it by a penny-wisdom; and he that works most in it is but a half-man, and whilst his arms are strong and his digestion good, his mind is imbruted, and he is a selfish savage. His relation to nature, his power over it, is through the understanding, as by manure; the economic use of fire, wind, water, and the mariner's needle; steam, coal, chemical agriculture; the repairs of the human body by the dentist and the surgeon. This is such a resumption of power as if a banished king should buy his territories inch by inch, instead of vaulting at once into his throne. Meantime, in the thick darkness, there are not wanting gleams of a better light,—occasional examples of the action of man upon nature with his entire force,—with reason as well as understanding. Such examples are, the traditions of miracles in the earliest antiquity of all nations; the history of Jesus Christ; the achievements of a principle, as in religious and political revolutions, and in the abolition of the slave trade; the miracles of enthusiasm, as those reported of Swedenborg, Hohenlohe, and the Shakers;[53] many obscure and yet contested facts, now arranged under the name of Animal Magnetism;[54] prayer; eloquence; self-healing; and the wisdom of children. These are examples of Reason's momentary grasp of the sceptre; the exertions of a power which exists not in time or space, but an instantaneous instreaming causing power. The difference between the actual and the ideal force of man is happily figured by the schoolmen,[55] in saying, that the knowledge of man is an evening knowledge, *vespertina cognitio*, but that of God is a morning knowledge, *matutina cognitio*.

The problem of restoring to the world original and eternal beauty is solved by the redemption of the soul. The ruin or the blank that we see when we look at nature, is in our own eye. The axis of vision is not coincident with the axis of things, and so they appear not transparent but opaque. The reason why the world lacks unity, and lies broken and in heaps, is because man is disunited with himself. He cannot be a naturalist until he satisfies all the demands of the spirit. Love is as much its demand as perception. Indeed, neither can be perfect without the other. In the uttermost meaning of the words, thought is devout, and devotion is thought. Deep calls unto deep.[56] But in actual life, the marriage is not cel-

---

[53] Prince Alexander Leopold of Hohenlohe (1794–1849) was known for his miracle cures; the Shakers, a communal Christian group, also believed in miraculous healing powers.

[54] Mesmerism, a method of hypnotic induction invented by Franz Mesmer (1734–1815).

[55] Scholastic philosophers of the Middle Ages.

[56] Psalm 42.7.

ebrated. There are innocent men who worship God after the tradition of their fathers, but their sense of duty has not yet extended to the use of all their faculties. And there are patient naturalists, but they freeze their subject under the wintry light of the understanding. Is not prayer also a study of truth,—a sally of the soul into the unfound infinite? No man ever prayed heartily without learning something. But when a faithful thinker, resolute to detach every object from personal relations and see it in the light of thought, shall, at the same time, kindle science with the fire of the holiest affections, then will God go forth anew into the creation.

It will not need, when the mind is prepared for study, to search for objects. The invariable mark of wisdom is to see the miraculous in the common. What is a day? What is a year? What is summer? What is woman? What is a child? What is sleep? To our blindness, these things seem unaffecting. We make fables to hide the baldness of the fact and conform it, as we say, to the higher law of the mind. But when the fact is seen under the light of an idea, the gaudy fable fades and shrivels. We behold the real higher law. To the wise, therefore, a fact is true poetry, and the most beautiful of fables. These wonders are brought to our own door. You also are a man. Man and woman and their social life, poverty, labor, sleep, fear, fortune, are known to you. Learn that none of these things is superficial, but that each phenomenon has its roots in the faculties and affections of the mind. Whilst the abstract question occupies your intellect, nature brings it in the concrete to be solved by your hands. It were a wise inquiry for the closet, to compare, point by point, especially at remarkable crises in life, our daily history with the rise and progress of ideas in the mind.

So shall we come to look at the world with new eyes. It shall answer the endless inquiry of the intellect,—What is truth? and of the affections,—What is good? by yielding itself passive to the educated Will. Then shall come to pass what my poet said: "Nature is not fixed but fluid. Spirit alters, molds, makes it. The immobility or bruteness of nature is the absence of spirit; to pure spirit it is fluid, it is volatile, it is obedient. Every spirit builds itself a house, and beyond its house a world, and beyond its world a heaven. Know then that the world exists for you. For you is the phenomenon perfect. What we are, that only can we see. All that Adam had, all that Caesar could, you have and can do. Adam called his house, heaven and earth; Caesar called his house, Rome; you perhaps call yours, a cobbler's trade; a hundred acres of ploughed land; or a scholar's garret. Yet line for line and point for point your dominion is as great as theirs, though without fine names. Build therefore your own world. As fast as you conform your life to the pure idea in your mind, that will unfold its great proportions. A correspondent revolution in things will attend the influx of the spirit. So fast will disagreeable appearances, swine, spiders, snakes, pests, madhouses, prisons, enemies, vanish; they are temporary and shall be no more seen. The sordor and filths of nature, the sun shall dry up and the wind exhale. As when the summer comes from the south the snowbanks melt and the face of the earth becomes green before it, so shall the advancing spirit create its ornaments along its path, and carry with it the beauty it visits and the song which enchants it; it shall draw beautiful faces, warm hearts, wise discourse, and heroic acts, around its way, until evil is no more seen. The kingdom of man over nature, which cometh not with observation,—a dominion such as now is beyond his dream of God,—he shall enter without more wonder than the blind man feels who is gradually restored to perfect sight."

✒ *Charles Darwin* (1809–1882)

Charles Darwin is renowned for his great work, On the Origin of Species by Means of Natural Selection *(1859), which established the theory of evolution as a basis for all subsequent research in the environmental and biological sciences. Highly controversial when it first appeared, this book is now regarded a classic in the history of science, and its enormous reputation has tended to overshadow Darwin's other work. In his autobiography, Darwin states that the most formative event of his life was his voyage in 1831–36 onboard the* Beagle, *a British naval vessel that explored the coast of South America and mapped the islands of the Pacific Ocean. Darwin's account of that voyage, entitled* Journal of Researches into the Geology and Natural History of the Various Countries Visited During the Voyage of the H.M.S. *Beagle* Round the World *(1839), reached a wide popular audience in its own time, and it deserves to be better known today.*

Charles Darwin was a restless and wayward young man. Born in the rural village of Shrewsbury, Shropshire, he did poorly in grammar school but revealed an ardent interest in gardening and in collecting pebbles, newts, birds' eggs, and beetles. He was encouraged to follow in the footsteps of his father (and of his grandfather, Erasmus Darwin) and become a physician; but he showed very little interest or aptitude in his medical studies at Edinburgh University. Deeply disappointed, Darwin's father sent him to Christ's College, Cambridge, where he would study to become an Anglican clergyman. While at Cambridge, Darwin displayed no talent for theology, but he became fascinated by the study of natural history, and upon completing his college degree in 1831, he eagerly accepted an invitation to accompany Captain Robert Fitzroy as a "gentleman naturalist" aboard the Beagle. *This expedition enabled Darwin to make firsthand scientific observations of people and places, plants and animals, and geological strata and fossils across a fabulously diverse array of ecosystems, from the tropical island of Tahiti to the frozen tundra of Tierra del Fuego. Although he had not yet devised his famous theory of evolution, Darwin began to realize from these observations that there was something wrong with the conventional biblical chronology of the earth's formation, and he became increasingly dissatisfied with the standard Creationist account of the origin of living things. These intellectual misgivings are particularly apparent in his chapter on the Galapagos Islands, excerpted below, in which he describes the incredible variation of species among the different islands and the striking adaptation of living things to their local environments. Intuitively, the young Darwin realizes that the Galapagos Islands bring him close to the secret heart of things, to "that mystery of mysteries—the first appearance of new beings on this earth." Darwin returns from this voyage with more questions than answers.* The Voyage of the Beagle *is a masterpiece of natural history writing, combining trenchant observation with a keen, probing intelligence.*

From Journal of Researches into the Geology and Natural History of the Various Countries Visited During the Voyage of the H.M.S. *Beagle* Round the World

In the morning (17th) we landed on Chatham Island, which, like the others, rises with a tame and rounded outline, broken here and there by scattered hillocks, the remains of former craters. Nothing could be less inviting than the first appearance. A broken field of black basaltic lava, thrown into the most rugged waves, and crossed by great fissures, is everywhere covered by stunted, sun-burnt brushwood, which shows little signs of life. The dry and parched surface, being heated by the noonday sun, gave to the air a close and sultry feeling, like that from a stove: we fancied even that the bushes smelt unpleasantly. Although I diligently tried to collect as many plants as possible, I succeeded in getting very few; and such wretched-looking little weeds would have better become an arctic than an equatorial Flora. The brushwood appears, from a short distance, as leafless as our trees during winter; and it was some time before I discovered that not only almost every plant was now in full leaf, but that the greater number were in flower. The commonest bush is one of the *Euphorbiaceae*: an acacia and a great odd-looking cactus are the only trees which afford any shade. After the season of heavy rains, the islands are said to appear for a short time partially green. The volcanic island of Fernando Noronha, placed in many respects under nearly similar conditions, is the only other country where I have seen a vegetation at all like this of the Galapagos islands.

The *Beagle* sailed round Chatham Island, and anchored in several bays. One night I slept on shore on a part of the island, where black truncated cones were extraordinarily numerous: from one small eminence I counted sixty of them, all surmounted by craters more or less perfect. The greater number consisted merely of a ring of red scoriae or slags, cemented together: and their height above the plain of lava was not more than from fifty to a hundred feet: none had been very lately active. The entire surface of this part of the island seems to have been permeated, like a sieve, by the subterranean vapours: here and there the lava, whilst soft, has been blown into great bubbles; and in other parts, the tops of caverns similarly formed have fallen in, leaving circular pits with steep sides. From the regular form of the many craters, they gave to the country an artificial appearance, which vividly reminded me of those parts of Staffordshire, where the great iron-foundries are most numerous. The day was glowing hot, and the scrambling over the rough surface and through the intricate thickets, was very fatiguing; but I was well repaid by the strange Cyclopean[1] scene. As I was walking along I met two large tortoises, each of which must have weighed at least two hundred pounds: one was eating a piece of cactus, and as I approached, it stared at me and slowly stalked away; the other gave a deep hiss, and drew in its head. These huge reptiles, surrounded by the black lava, the leafless shrubs, and large

---

[1] Gigantic, primordial.

cacti, seemed to my fancy like some antediluvian animals. The few dull-coloured birds cared no more for me, than they did for the great tortoises.

. . .

October 8th.—We arrived at James Island; this island, as well as Charles Island, were long since thus named after our kings of the Stuart line. Mr. Bynoe, myself, and our servants were left here for a week, with provisions and a tent, whilst the *Beagle* went for water. We found here a party of Spaniards, who had been sent from Charles Island to dry fish, and to salt tortoise meat. About six miles inland, and at the height of nearly 2000 feet, a hovel had been built in which two men lived, who were employed in catching tortoises, whilst the others were fishing on the coast. I paid this party two visits, and slept there one night. As in the other islands, the lower region was covered by nearly leafless bushes, but the trees were here of a larger growth than elsewhere, several being two feet and some even two feet nine inches in diameter. The upper region being kept damp by the clouds, supports a green and flourishing vegetation. So damp was the ground, that there were large beds of a coarse *Cyperus*, in which great numbers of a very small water rail lived and bred. While staying in this upper region, we lived entirely upon tortoise meat: the breast-plate roasted (as the Gauchos do *carne con cuero*[2]), with the flesh on it, is very good; and the young tortoises make excellent soup; but otherwise the meat to my taste is indifferent.

One day we accompanied a party of the Spaniards in their whaleboat to a salina, or lake from which salt is procured. After landing, we had a very rough walk over a rugged field of recent lava, which has almost surrounded a tuff crater, at the bottom of which the salt lake lies. The water is only three or four inches deep, and rests on a layer of beautifully crystallized, white salt. The lake is quite circular, and is fringed with a border of bright green succulent plants; the almost precipitous walls of the crater are clothed with wood, so that the scene was altogether both picturesque and curious. A few years since, the sailors belonging to a sealing vessel murdered their captain in this quiet spot; and we saw his skull lying among the bushes.

During the greater part of our stay of a week, the sky was cloudless, and if the trade wind failed for an hour, the heat became very oppressive. On two days, the thermometer within the tent stood for some hours at 93°; but in the open air, in the wind and sun, at only 85°. The sand was extremely hot; the thermometer placed in some of a brown colour immediately rose to 137°, and how much above that it would have risen, I do not know, for it was not graduated any higher. The black sand felt much hotter, so that even in thick boots it was quite disagreeable to walk over it.

The natural history of these islands is eminently curious, and well deserves attention. Most of the organic productions are aboriginal creations, found nowhere else; there is even a difference between the inhabitants of the different

---

[2] Meat cooked in the skin (Spanish).

islands; yet all show a marked relationship with those of America, though separated from that continent by an open space of ocean, between 500 and 600 miles in width. The archipelago is a little world within itself, or rather a satellite attached to America, whence it has derived a few stray colonists, and has received the general character of its indigenous productions. Considering the small size of these islands, we feel the more astonished at the number of their aboriginal beings, and at their confined range. Seeing every height crowned with its crater, and the boundaries of most of the lava streams still distinct, we are led to believe that within a period, geologically recent, the unbroken ocean was here spread out. Hence, both in space and time, we seem to be brought somewhat near to that great fact—that mystery of mysteries—the first appearance of new beings on this earth.

.   .   .

I will first describe the habits of the tortoise (*Testudo nigra*, formerly called *Indica*), which has been so frequently alluded to. These animals are found, I believe, on all the islands of the Archipelago; certainly on the greater number. They frequent in preference the high damp parts, but they likewise live in the lower and arid districts. I have already shown, from the numbers which have been caught in a single day, how very numerous they must be. Some grow to an immense size: Mr. Lawson, an Englishman, and vice-governor of the colony, told us that he had seen several so large, that it required six or eight men to lift them from the ground; and that some had afforded as much as two hundred pounds of meat. The old males are the largest, the females rarely growing to so great a size: the male can readily be distinguished from the female by the greater length of its tail. The tortoises which live on those islands where there is no water, or in the lower and arid parts of the others, feed chiefly on the succulent cactus. Those which frequent the higher and damp regions, eat the leaves of various trees, a kind of berry (called *guayavita*) which is acid and austere, and likewise a pale green filamentous lichen (*Usnera plicata*), that hangs in tresses from the boughs of the trees.

The tortoise is very fond of water, drinking large quantities, and wallowing in the mud. The larger islands alone possess springs, and these are always situated towards the central parts, and at a considerable height. The tortoises, therefore, which frequent the lower districts, when thirsty, are obliged to travel from a long distance. Hence broad and well-beaten paths branch off in every direction from the wells down to the seacoast; and the Spaniards by following them up, first discovered the watering places. When I landed at Chatham Island, I could not imagine what animal travelled so methodically along well-chosen tracks. Near the springs it was a curious spectacle to behold many of these huge creatures, one set eagerly travelling onwards with outstretched necks, and another set returning, after having drunk their fill. When the tortoise arrives at the spring, quite regardless of any spectator, he buries his head in the water above his eyes, and greedily swallows great mouthfuls, at the rate of about ten in a minute. The inhabitants say each animal stays three or four days in the neighbourhood of the water, and then returns to the lower country; but they differed respecting the frequency of these visits. The animal probably regulates them according to the nature of the food on which it has lived. It is, however, certain, that tortoises can subsist even on those islands, where there is no other water than what falls during a few rainy days in the year.

I believe it is well ascertained, that the bladder of the frog acts as a reservoir for the moisture necessary to its existence: such seems to be the case with the tortoise. For some time after a visit to the springs, their urinary bladders are distended with fluid, which is said gradually to decrease in volume, and to become less pure. The inhabitants, when walking in the lower district, and overcome with thirst, often take advantage of this circumstance, and drink the contents of the bladder if full: in one I saw killed, the fluid was quite limpid, and had only a very slightly bitter taste. The inhabitants, however, always first drink the water in the pericardium, which is described as being best.

The tortoises, when purposely moving towards any point, travel by night and day, and arrive at their journey's end much sooner than would be expected. The inhabitants, from observing marked individuals, consider that they travel a distance of about eight miles in two or three days. One large tortoise, which I watched, walked at the rate of sixty yards in ten minutes, that is 360 yards in the hour, or four miles a day,—allowing a little time for it to eat on the road. During the breeding season, when the male and female are together, the male utters a hoarse roar or bellowing, which, it is said, can be heard at the distance of more than a hundred yards. The female never uses her voice, and the male only at these times; so that when the people hear this noise, they know that the two are together. They were at this time (October) laying their eggs. The female, where the soil is sandy, deposits them together, and covers them up with sand; but where the ground is rocky she drops them indiscriminately in any hole: Mr. Bynoe found seven placed in a fissure. The egg is white and spherical; one which I measured was seven inches and three-eighths in circumference, and therefore larger than a hen's egg. The young tortoises, as soon as they are hatched, fall a prey in great numbers to the carrion-feeding buzzard. The old ones seem generally to die from accidents, as from falling down precipices: at least, several of the inhabitants told me, that they had never found one dead without some evident cause.

The inhabitants believe that these animals are absolutely deaf; certainly they do not overhear a person walking close behind them. I was always amused when overtaking one of these great monsters, as it was quietly pacing along, to see how suddenly, the instant I passed, it would draw in its head and legs, and uttering a deep hiss fall to the ground with a heavy sound, as if struck dead. I frequently got on their backs, and then giving a few raps on the hinder part of their shells, they would rise up and walk away;—but I found it very difficult to keep my balance. The flesh of this animal is largely employed, both fresh and salted; and a beautifully clear oil is prepared from the fat. When a tortoise is caught, the man makes a slit in the skin near its tail, so as to see inside its body, whether the fat under the dorsal plate is thick. If it is not, the animal is liberated; and it is said to recover soon from this strange operation. In order to secure the tortoises, it is not sufficient to turn them like turtle, for they are often able to get on their legs again.

There can be little doubt that this tortoise is an aboriginal inhabitant of the Galapagos; for it is found on all, or nearly all, the islands, even on some of the smaller ones where there is no water; had it been an imported species, this would hardly have been the case in a group which has been so little frequented. Moreover, the old Buccaneers found this tortoise in greater numbers even than at present: Wood and Rogers also, in 1708, say that it is the opinion of the Spaniards, that it is found nowhere else in this quarter of the world. It is now widely distributed, but it may be questioned whether it is in any other place an aboriginal. The bones of a tortoise at Mauritius, associated with those of the extinct Dodo, have generally been considered as belonging to this tortoise: if this had been so, undoubtedly it must have been there indigenous, but M. Bibron informs me that he believes that it was distinct, as the species now living there certainly is.

. . .

I have not as yet noticed by far the most remarkable feature in the natural history of this archipelago; it is, that the different islands to a considerable extent are inhabited by a different set of beings. My attention was first called to this fact by the Vice-Governor, Mr. Lawson, declaring that the tortoises differed from the different islands, and that he could with certainty tell from which island any one was brought. I did not for some time pay sufficient attention to this statement, and I had already partially mingled together the collections from two of the islands. I never dreamed that islands, about fifty or sixty miles apart, and most of them in sight of each other, formed of precisely the same rocks, placed under a quite similar climate, rising to a nearly equal height, would have been differently tenanted; but we shall soon see that this is the case. It is the fate of most voyagers, no sooner to discover what is most interesting in any locality, than they are hurried from it; but I ought, perhaps, to be thankful that I obtained sufficient material to establish this most remarkable fact in the distribution of organic beings.

. . .

The distribution of the tenants of this archipelago would not be nearly so wonderful, if, for instance, one island had a mocking-thrush, and a second island some other quite distinct genus;—if one island had its genus of lizard, and a second island another distinct genus, or none whatever;—or if the different islands were inhabited, not by representative species of the same genera of plants, but by totally different genera, as does to a certain extent hold good; for, to give one instance, a large berry-bearing tree at James Island has no representative species in Charles Island. But it is the circumstance, that several of the islands possess their own species of the tortoise, mocking-thrush, finches, and numerous plants, these species having the same general habits, occupying analogous situations, and obviously filling the same place in the natural economy of this archipelago, that strikes me with wonder. It may be suspected that some of these representative species, at least in the case of the tortoise and of some of the birds, may hereafter prove to be only well-marked races; but this would be of equally great interest to the philosophical naturalist. I have said that most of the islands are in sight of each other: I may specify that Charles Island is fifty miles from the nearest part of Chatham Island, and thirty-three miles from the nearest part of Albemarle Island. Chatham Island is sixty miles from the nearest part of James Island, but there are two intermediate islands between them which were not visited by me. James Island is only ten miles from the nearest part of Albemarle Island, but the two points where the collections were made are thirty-two miles apart. I must repeat, that neither the nature of the soil, nor height of the land, nor the climate, nor the general character of the associated beings, and therefore their action one on another, can differ much in the different islands. If there be any sensible difference in their climates, it must be between the windward group (namely Charles and Chatham Islands), and that to leeward; but there seems to be no corresponding difference in the productions of these two halves of the archipelago.

The only light which I can throw on this remarkable difference in the inhabitants of the different islands, is, that very strong currents of the sea running in a westerly and W.N.W. direction must separate, as far as transportal by the sea is concerned, the southern islands from the northern ones; and between these northern islands a strong N.W. current was observed, which must effectually separate James and Albemarle Islands. As the archipelago is free to a most remarkable degree from gales of wind, neither the birds, insects, nor lighter seeds, would be blown from island to island. And lastly, the profound depth of the ocean between the islands, and their apparently recent (in a geological sense) volcanic origin, render it highly unlikely that they were ever united; and this, probably, is a far more important consideration than any other, with respect to the geographical distribution of their inhabitants. Reviewing the facts here given, one is astonished at the amount of creative force, if such an expression may be used, displayed on these small, barren, and rocky islands; and still more so, at its diverse yet analogous action on points so near each other. I have said that the Galapagos Archipelago might be called a satellite attached to America, but it should rather be called a group of satellites, physically similar, organically distinct, yet intimately related to each other, and all related in a marked, though much lesser degree, to the great American continent.

Alfred, Lord Tennyson (1809–1883)

Alfred Tennyson's childhood was spent in the genteel poverty of a country rectory, made even more miserable by an abusive and alcoholic father. The young Tennyson found refuge in the pastoral scenery of the fields and forests of Lincolnshire, and he started to write poetry at an early age. His happiest years were spent at Trinity College, Cambridge, where he collaborated with his brother Charles on the publication of Poems by

Two Brothers *(1827), a remarkable tour de force that displayed the supple versification and prodigality of imagery that would characterize Tennyson's mature work. Although this book sold few copies, it confirmed Tennyson's determination to devote his life to poetry. In 1829 Tennyson met Arthur Henry Hallam, and they soon became inseparable companions. Their friendship grew even closer when Hallam became engaged to Tennyson's younger sister, Emily. In the summer of 1830, the two men embarked on a bizarre secret mission to assist revolutionary guerrillas in Spain. Quickly disillusioned of his revolutionary fervor, Tennyson nonetheless reveled in the sublime scenery of their journey through France to the Pyrénées. For the rest of his life, the rugged landscapes of these mountains would form a backdrop to many of his most famous poems; "The Lotos-Eaters" was inspired by a waterfall that he observed there and by the relaxed, idyllic pace of peasant life in that region.*

Arthur Hallam died of a sudden illness in 1833, and Tennyson was plunged into a deep state of grief. Struggling with depression, he continued to write poetry; in fact, Hallam's death provided the creative impetus for some of his finest poems, including "Ulysses" and "Break, break, break." Loss and bereavement are predominant themes in much of Tennyson's later poetry, both in his two-volume collection of Poems *(1842) and in his long elegy for Hallam,* In Memoriam *(1850), which earned Tennyson an appointment as Poet Laureate. Tennyson's poetry often reflects what he called "the passion of the past": an acute nostalgia for bygone days, either the heroic events of ancient history or the more immediate past of his own life, once idyllic and now riven by inconsolable grief.*

Yet Tennyson's underlying affection for the pastoral landscape of his birthplace, and his frequent evocation of the enduring beauty of nature, lend his poetry an intensity of natural imagery that is unparalleled by any other Victorian poet. As nineteenth-century England became increasingly urban and industrialized, the nation needed a poet like Tennyson to recall its rural, agricultural past. His poem "Amphion" celebrates the regenerative energies of nature, the ability of living things to transform a "wild and barren" landscape into a luxuriant green forest. Drawing on the boisterous pagan energies of ancient Greece (and specifically invoking the myth of Amphion's magical lyre), Tennyson's poem plants a sacred grove of trees in the heart of industrial England.

The Lotos-Eaters*

"Courage!" he said, and pointed toward the land,
"This mounting wave will roll us shoreward soon."
In the afternoon they came unto a land
In which it seemèd always afternoon.
All round the coast the languid air did swoon,   5
Breathing like one that hath a weary dream.
Full-faced above the valley stood the moon;
And like a downward smoke, the slender stream
Along the cliff to fall and pause and fall did seem.

---

* Based on an episode from the *Odyssey* (9.82–97), the poem depicts the sailors of Odysseus as they arrive at the land of the Lotos-eaters, who consume a sweet fruit that makes them drowsy, lethargic, and forgetful.

California Redwoods.

Christie's Images, Inc.

Georgia O'Keeffe, (1887-1986), *Ram's Head, White Hollyhock-Hills,* 1935.

Oil on canvas, 30 x 36 in. (72.2 x 91.5 cm). Brooklyn Museum of Art.
Bequest of Edith and Milton Lowenthal, 1992. 11.28

Erosion No. 2. Mother Earth Laid Bare.

The Philbrook Museum of Art, Tulsa, Oklahoma.

Rocks on a Hillside.

Photograph by Andy Goldsworthy.

A land of streams! some, like a downward smoke,   10
Slow-dropping veils of thinnest lawn, did go;
And some through wavering lights and shadows broke,
Rolling a slumbrous sheet of foam below.
They saw the gleaming river seaward flow
From the inner land: far off, three mountaintops,   15
Three silent pinnacles of aged snow,
Stood sunset-flushed: and, dewed with showery drops,
Up-clomb the shadowy pine above the woven copse.

The charmèd sunset lingered low adown
In the red West: through mountain clefts the dale   20
Was seen far inland, and the yellow down
Bordered with palm, and many a winding vale
And meadow, set with slender galingale;[1]
A land where all things always seemed the same!
And round about the keel with faces pale,   25
Dark faces pale against that rosy flame,
The mild-eyed melancholy Lotos-eaters came.

Branches they bore of that enchanted stem,
Laden with flower and fruit, whereof they gave
To each, but whoso did receive of them,   30
And taste, to him the gushing of the wave
Far far away did seem to mourn and rave
On alien shores; and if his fellow spake,
His voice was thin, as voices from the grave;
And deep-asleep he seemed, yet all awake,   35
And music in his ears his beating heart did make.

They sat them down upon the yellow sand,
Between the sun and moon upon the shore;
And sweet it was to dream of Fatherland,
Of child, and wife, and slave; but evermore   40
Most weary seemed the sea, weary the oar,
Weary the wandering fields of barren foam.
Then some one said, "We will return no more";
And all at once they sang, "Our island home
Is far beyond the wave; we will no longer roam."   45

Choric Song

I

There is sweet music here that softer falls
Than petals from blown roses on the grass,

---

[1] Sedges of the genus *Cyperus*, having rough-edged leaves and aromatic roots.

Or night-dews on still waters between walls
Of shadowy granite, in a gleaming pass;
Music that gentlier on the spirit lies,   50
Than tired eyelids upon tired eyes;
Music that brings sweet sleep down from the blissful skies.
Here are cool mosses deep,
And through the moss the ivies creep,
And in the stream the long-leaved flowers weep,   55
And from the craggy ledge the poppy hangs in sleep.

2

Why are we weighed upon with heaviness,
And utterly consumed with sharp distress,
While all things else have rest from weariness?
All things have rest: why should we toil alone,   60
We only toil, who are the first of things,
And make perpetual moan,
Still from one sorrow to another thrown:
Nor ever fold our wings,
And cease from wanderings,   65
Nor steep our brows in slumber's holy balm;
Nor harken what the inner spirit sings,
"There is no joy but calm!"
Why should we only toil, the roof and crown of things?

3

Lo! in the middle of the wood,   70
The folded leaf is wooed from out the bud
With winds upon the branch, and there
Grows green and broad, and takes no care,
Sun-steeped at noon, and in the moon
Nightly dew-fed; and turning yellow   75
Falls, and floats adown the air.
Lo! sweetened with the summer light,
The full-juiced apple, waxing over-mellow,
Drops in a silent autumn night.
All its allotted length of days,   80
The flower ripens in its place,
Ripens and fades, and falls, and hath no toil,
Fast-rooted in the fruitful soil.

4

Hateful is the dark-blue sky,
Vaulted o'er the dark-blue sea.   85
Death is the end of life; ah, why

Should life all labour be?
Let us alone. Time driveth onward fast,
And in a little while our lips are dumb.
Let us alone. What is it that will last? 90
All things are taken from us, and become
Portions and parcels of the dreadful Past.
Let us alone. What pleasure can we have
To war with evil? Is there any peace
In ever climbing up the climbing wave? 95
All things have rest, and ripen toward the grave
In silence; ripen, fall and cease:
Give us long rest or death, dark death, or dreamful ease.

5

How sweet it were, hearing the downward stream,
With half-shut eyes ever to seem 100
Falling asleep in a half-dream!
To dream and dream, like yonder amber light,
Which will not leave the myrrh-bush on the height;
To hear each other's whispered speech;
Eating the Lotos day by day, 105
To watch the crisping ripples on the beach,
And tender curving lines of creamy spray;
To lend our hearts and spirits wholly
To the influence of mild-minded melancholy;
To muse and brood and live again in memory, 110
With those old faces of our infancy
Heaped over with a mound of grass,
Two handfuls of white dust, shut in an urn of brass!

6

Dear is the memory of our wedded lives,
And dear the last embraces of our wives 115
And their warm tears: but all hath suffered change:
For surely now our household hearths are cold:
Our sons inherit us: our looks are strange:
And we should come like ghosts to trouble joy.
Or else the island princes over-bold 120
Have eat our substance, and the minstrel sings
Before them of the ten years' war in Troy,
And our great deeds, as half-forgotten things.
Is there confusion in the little isle?
Let what is broken so remain. 125
The Gods are hard to reconcile:
'Tis hard to settle order once again.

There *is* confusion worse than death,
Trouble on trouble, pain on pain,
Long labour unto aged breath,   130
Sore task to hearts worn out by many wars
And eyes grown dim with gazing on the pilot-stars.

7

But, propped on beds of amaranth and moly,[2]
How sweet (while warm airs lull us, blowing lowly)
With half-dropped eyelid still,   135
Beneath a heaven dark and holy,
To watch the long bright river drawing slowly
His waters from the purple hill—
To hear the dewy echoes calling
From cave to cave through the thick-twined vine—   140
To watch the emerald-coloured water falling
Through many a woven acanthus wreath[3] divine!
Only to hear and see the far-off sparkling brine,
Only to hear were sweet, stretched out beneath the pine.

8

The Lotos blooms below the barren peak: 145
The Lotos blows by every winding creek:
All day the wind breathes low with mellower tone:
Through every hollow cave and alley lone
Round and round the spicy downs the yellow Lotos-dust is blown.
We have had enough of action, and of motion we,   150
Rolled to starboard, rolled to larboard, when the surge was seething free,
Where the wallowing monster spouted his foam-fountains in the sea.
Let us swear an oath, and keep it with an equal mind,
In the hollow Lotos-land to live and lie reclined
On the hills like Gods together, careless of mankind.   155
For they lie beside their nectar, and the bolts are hurled
Far below them in the valleys, and the clouds are lightly curled
Round their golden houses, girdled with the gleaming world:
Where they smile in secret, looking over wasted lands,
Blight and famine, plague and earthquake, roaring deeps and fiery sands, 160
Clanging fights, and flaming towns, and sinking ships, and praying hands.
But they smile, they find a music centred in a doleful song
Steaming up, a lamentation and an ancient tale of wrong,
Like a tale of little meaning though the words are strong;
Chanted from an ill-used race of men that cleave the soil,   165

[2] *Amaranth* is a legendary flower that never fades. *Moly:* In Greek mythology, a magic herb given to Odysseus to ward off the spells of Circe.
[3] A shrub bearing broad leaves with spiny margins; used in ancient Greece as a model for Corinthian columns.

Sow the seed, and reap the harvest with enduring toil,
Storing yearly little dues of wheat, and wine and oil;
Till they perish and they suffer—some, 'tis whispered—down in hell
Suffer endless anguish, others in Elysian valleys dwell,
Resting weary limbs at last on beds of asphodel.[4]   170
Surely, surely, slumber is more sweet than toil, the shore
Than labour in the deep mid-ocean, wind and wave and oar;
Oh rest ye, brother mariners, we will not wander more.

[4] In Greek poetry, the flowers of Hades, sacred to Persephone.

Tithonus*

The woods decay, the woods decay and fall,
The vapours weep their burthen to the ground,
Man comes and tills the field and lies beneath,
And after many a summer dies the swan.
Me only cruel immortality   5
Consumes: I wither slowly in thine arms,
Here at the quiet limit of the world,
A white-haired shadow roaming like a dream
The ever-silent spaces of the East,
Far-folded mists, and gleaming halls of morn.   10

    Alas! for this gray shadow, once a man—
So glorious in his beauty and thy choice,
Who madest him thy chosen, that he seemed
To his great heart none other than a God!
I asked thee, "Give me immortality."   15
Then didst thou grant mine asking with a smile,
Like wealthy men who care not how they give.
But thy strong Hours indignant worked their wills,
And beat me down and marred and wasted me,
And though they could not end me, left me maimed   20
To dwell in presence of immortal youth,
Immortal age beside immortal youth,
And all I was, in ashes. Can thy love,
Thy beauty, make amends, though even now,
Close over us, the silver star, thy guide,   25
Shines in those tremulous eyes that fill with tears
To hear me? Let me go: take back thy gift:
Why should a man desire in any way

* According to Greek myth, Tithonus, a prince of Troy, was loved by Eos, the goddess of dawn. She obtained for him the gift of immortality; but she forgot to ask for the gift of eternal youth. He grew older and older, unable to escape his decrepit body.

To vary from the kindly race of men,
Or pass beyond the goal of ordinance   30
Where all should pause, as is most meet for all?

   A soft air fans the cloud apart; there comes
A glimpse of that dark world where I was born.
Once more the old mysterious glimmer steals
From thy pure brows, and from thy shoulders pure,   35
And bosom beating with a heart renewed.
Thy cheek begins to redden through the gloom,
Thy sweet eyes brighten slowly close to mine,
Ere yet they blind the stars, and the wild team
Which love thee, yearning for thy yoke, arise,   40
And shake the darkness from their loosened manes,
And beat the twilight into flakes of fire.

   Lo! ever thus thou growest beautiful
In silence, then before thine answer given
Departest, and thy tears are on my cheek.   45

   Why wilt thou ever scare me with thy tears,
And make me tremble lest a saying learnt,
In days far-off, on that dark earth, be true?
"The Gods themselves cannot recall their gifts."

   Ay me! ay me! with what another heart   50
In days far-off, and with what other eyes
I used to watch — if I be he that watched —
The lucid outline forming round thee; saw
The dim curls kindle into sunny rings;
Changed with thy mystic change, and felt my blood   55
Glow with the glow that slowly crimsoned all
Thy presence and thy portals, while I lay,
Mouth, forehead, eyelids, growing dewy-warm
With kisses balmier than half-opening buds
Of April, and could hear the lips that kissed   60
Whispering I knew not what of wild and sweet,
Like that strange song I heard Apollo sing,
While Ilion like a mist rose into towers.[1]

   Yet hold me not for ever in thine East:
How can my nature longer mix with thine?   65
Coldly thy rosy shadows bathe me, cold
Are all thy lights, and cold my wrinkled feet
Upon thy glimmering thresholds, when the steam
Floats up from those dim fields about the homes
Of happy men that have the power to die,   70

---

[1] Apollo played music while the walls of Troy (Ilion) were being built.

And grassy barrows of the happier dead.
Release me, and restore me to the ground;
Thou seest all things, thou wilt see my grave:
Thou wilt renew thy beauty morn by morn;
I earth in earth forget these empty courts,   75
And thee returning on thy silver wheels.

Amphion*

My father left a park to me,
 But it is wild and barren,
A garden too with scarce a tree,
 And waster than a warren:
Yet say the neighbours when they call,   5
 It is not bad but good land,
And in it is the germ of all
 That grows within the woodland.

O had I lived when song was great
 In days of old Amphion,   10
And ta'en my fiddle to the gate,
 Nor cared for seed or scion!
And had I lived when song was great,
 And legs of trees were limber,
And ta'en my fiddle to the gate,   15
 And fiddled in the timber!

'Tis said he had a tuneful tongue,
 Such happy intonation,
Wherever he sat down and sung
 He left a small plantation;   20
Wherever in a lonely grove
 He set up his forlorn pipes,
The gouty oak began to move,
 And flounder into hornpipes.

The mountain stirred its bushy crown,   25
 And, as tradition teaches,
Young ashes pirouetted down
 Coquetting with young beeches;
And bryony-vine and ivy-wreath
 Ran forward to his rhyming,   30
And from the valleys underneath
 Came little copses climbing.

* In Greek mythology, Amphion was a demigod (the son of Zeus by Antiope, princess of Thebes). He was a great singer and musician; he built a wall around Thebes with stones that were drawn into position by the magical notes of his lyre. Some ancient writers also attribute to Amphion the power to make trees approach the sound of his music.

The linden broke her ranks and rent
   The woodbine wreaths that bind her,
And down the middle, buzz! she went   35
   With all her bees behind her:
The poplars, in long order due,
   With cypress promenaded,
The shock-head willows two and two
   By rivers gallopaded.   40

Came wet-shod alder from the wave,
   Came yews, a dismal coterie;
Each plucked his one foot from the grave,
   Poussetting with a sloe-tree:
Old elms came breaking from the vine,   45
   The vine streamed out to follow,
And, sweating rosin, plumped the pine
   From many a cloudy hollow.

And wasn't it a sight to see,
   When, ere his song was ended,   50
Like some great landslip, tree by tree,
   The countryside descended;
And shepherds from the mountain-eaves
   Looked down, half-pleased, half-frightened,
As dashed about the drunken leaves   55
   The random sunshine lightened!

Oh, nature first was fresh to men,
   And wanton without measure;
So youthful and so flexile then,
   You moved her at your pleasure.   60
Twang out, my fiddle! shake the twigs!
   And make her dance attendance;
Blow, flute, and stir the stiff-set sprigs,
   And scirrhous roots and tendons.

'Tis vain! in such a brassy age   65
   I could not move a thistle;
The very sparrows in the hedge
   Scarce answer to my whistle;
Or at the most, when three-parts-sick
   With strumming and with scraping,   70
A jackass heehaws from the rick,
   The passive oxen gaping.

But what is that I hear? a sound
   Like sleepy counsel pleading;
O Lord!—'tis in my neighbour's ground,   75

The modern Muses reading.
They read Botanic Treatises,
    And Works on Gardening through there,
And Methods of transplanting trees
    To look as if they grew there.   80

The withered Misses! how they prose
    O'er books of travelled seamen,
And show you slips of all that grows
    From England to Van Diemen.[1]
They read in arbours clipped and cut,   85
    And alleys, faded places,
By squares of tropic summer shut
    And warmed in crystal cases.

But these, though fed with careful dirt,
    Are neither green nor sappy;   90
Half-conscious of the garden-squirt,
    The spindlings look unhappy.
Better to me the meanest weed
    That blows upon its mountain,
The vilest herb that runs to seed   95
    Beside its native fountain.

And I must work through months of toil,
    And years of cultivation,
Upon my proper patch of soil
    To grow my own plantation.   100
I'll take the showers as they fall,
    I will not vex my bosom:
Enough if at the end of all
    A little garden blossom.

Break, break, break

Break, break, break,
    On thy cold gray stones, O Sea!
And I would that my tongue could utter
    The thoughts that arise in me.

O well for the fisherman's boy,   5
    That he shouts with his sister at play!
O well for the sailor lad,
    That he sings in his boat on the bay!

---

[1] Van Diemen's Land (now called Tasmania), an island south of Australia. Formerly a penal colony, it was thought to be the most remote and godforsaken part of the British Empire.

And the stately ships go on
  To their haven under the hill;   10
But O for the touch of a vanished hand,
  And the sound of a voice that is still!

Break, break, break
  At the foot of thy crags, O Sea!
But the tender grace of a day that is dead   15
  Will never come back to me.

☙ Henry David Thoreau (1817–1862)

*Born in Concord, Massachusetts, Henry David Thoreau came of age in an era of flour-
ishing national self-confidence and booming commercial prosperity. His father was the
proprietor of a pencil factory, a moderately successful enterprise that provided the means
for his son to attend the prestigious Concord Academy and Harvard College. An above-
average student, Thoreau was invited at his graduation from Harvard in 1837 to give
a commencement address on the "Commercial Spirit." He shocked his audience by de-
nouncing the mindless pursuit of affluence, advocating instead a lifelong "Sabbath of the
affections and the soul, — in which to range this widespread garden, and drink in the soft
influences and sublime revelations of nature." Thoreau heeded his own advice: He never
undertook a professional career or held a steady job, opting instead to earn what little he
needed to support himself through occasional odd jobs, which included land surveying,
carpentry, gardening, and house-sitting for his closest friend, Ralph Waldo Emerson.*

*Thoreau did aspire to become a published author, and his reluctance to pursue a con-
ventional career stemmed in part from his need to create time and space for his writing.
His ultimate retreat from the world occurred in the period 1845–47, when he persuaded Emerson to let him build a cabin on some land that he owned on the shores of
Walden Pond, a deep, clear, spring-fed lake just two miles south of Concord. During the
two years that Thoreau spent at Walden Pond, he wrote the two books that were published in his lifetime:* A Week on the Concord and Merrimack Rivers *(1849), a tedious, digressive travelogue that sold only about two hundred copies, and* Walden; or,
Life in the Woods *(1854), justly regarded as a classic of American nature writing.
More than just a factual account of life in the woods,* Walden *has a much deeper and
broader appeal. As a parable of human experience, it offers an extended meditation on
the value of a simple lifestyle, along with profoundly insightful observations of the natural world that foreshadow many aspects of modern ecological thought.* Walden *also
marks Thoreau's discovery of his own personal voice: pithy and concise, sometimes playful
and ironic, yet always as pellucid as the waters of Walden Pond. Utilizing the vigorous,
bantering, telegraphic rhythms of the American vernacular, Thoreau provided a robust
model of prose style for future generations of American writers.*

*While living at Walden Pond in 1846, Thoreau took a long trip by canoe through the
Maine woods with his cousin, George Thatcher, and a local Native American guide. He
later recounted his adventures in a series of lectures that he presented at the Concord*

Lyceum, first published as "Ktaadn, and the Maine Woods" in Union *Magazine (1848) and also published posthumously as* The Maine Woods *(1864). In the passage excerpted here, Thoreau tells how he climbed to the summit of Katahdin, Maine's highest mountain, where he confronted an utterly inhuman wilderness, startlingly different from the tranquil fields and forests of Concord: "Nature was here something savage and awful, though beautiful." In this elemental encounter with the wild, Thoreau calls into question all that he knows about the relationship between humankind and the natural world.*

From The Maine Woods

In the night I dreamed of trout fishing; and, when at length I awoke, it seemed a fable that this painted fish swam there so near my couch, and rose to our hooks the last evening, and I doubted if I had not dreamed it all. So I arose before dawn to test its truth, while my companions were still sleeping. There stood Ktaadn[1] with distinct and cloudless outline in the moonlight; and the rippling of the rapids was the only sound to break the stillness. Standing on the shore, I once more cast my line into the stream, and found the dream to be real and the fable true. The speckled trout and silvery roach, like flying fish, sped swiftly through the moonlight air, describing bright arcs on the dark side of Ktaadn, until moonlight, now fading into daylight, brought satiety to my mind, and the minds of my companions, who had joined me.

By six o'clock, having mounted our packs and a good blanketful of trout, ready dressed, and swung up such baggage and provision as we wished to leave behind upon the tops of saplings, to be out of the reach of bears, we started for the summit of the mountain, distant, as Uncle George said the boatmen called it, about four miles, but as I judged, and as it proved, nearer fourteen. He had never been any nearer the mountain than this, and there was not the slightest trace of man to guide us farther in this direction. At first, pushing a few rods up the Aboljacknagesic, or "open-land stream," we fastened our batteau to a tree, and traveled up the north side, through burnt lands, now partially overgrown with young aspens and other shrubbery; but soon, recrossing this stream, where it was about fifty or sixty feet wide, upon a jam of logs and rocks—and you could cross it by this means almost anywhere—we struck at once for the highest peak, over a mile or more of comparatively open land, still very gradually ascending the while. Here it fell to my lot, as the oldest mountain climber, to take the lead. So, scanning the woody side of the mountain, which lay still at an indefinite distance, stretched out some seven or eight miles in length before us, we determined to steer directly for the base of the highest peak, leaving a large slide, by which, as I have since learned, some of our predecessors ascended, on our left. This course would lead us parallel to a dark seam in the forest, which marked the bed of a torrent, and over a slight spur, which extended southward from the main mountain, from whose bare summit we could get an outlook over the country, and climb directly up the peak, which would then be close at hand. Seen from this

---

[1] Mount Katahdin, elevation 5,268 feet, the highest point in the state of Maine.

point, a bare ridge at the extremity of the open land, Ktaadn presented a different aspect from any mountain I have seen, there being a greater proportion of naked rock rising abruptly from the forest; and we looked up at this blue barrier as if it were some fragment of a wall which anciently bounded the earth in that direction. Setting the compass for a northeast course, which was the bearing of the southern base of the highest peak, we were soon buried in the woods.

We soon began to meet with traces of bears and moose, and those of rabbits were everywhere visible. The tracks of moose, more or less recent, to speak literally, covered every square rod on the sides of the mountain; and these animals are probably more numerous there now than ever before, being driven into this wilderness, from all sides, by the settlements. The track of a full-grown moose is like that of a cow, or larger, and of the young, like that of a calf. Sometimes we found ourselves travelling in faint paths, which they had made, like cow-paths in the woods, only far more indistinct, being rather openings, affording imperfect vistas through the dense underwood, than trodden paths; and everywhere the twigs had been browsed by them, clipped as smoothly as if by a knife. The bark of trees was stripped up by them to the height of eight or nine feet, in long, narrow strips, an inch wide, still showing the distinct marks of their teeth. We expected nothing less than to meet a herd of them every moment, and our Nimrod[2] held his shooting-iron in readiness; but we did not go out of our way to look for them, and, though numerous, they are so wary that the unskillful hunter might range the forest a long time before he could get the very clouds, as though a waterspout had just burst over the mountain. Leaving this at last, I began to work my way, scarcely less arduous than Satan's anciently through Chaos,[3] up the nearest though not the highest peak, at first scrambling on all fours over the tops of ancient black spruce trees (*Abies nigra*), old as the flood, from two to ten or twelve feet in height, their tops flat and spreading, and their foliage blue, and nipped with cold, as if for centuries they had ceased growing upward against the bleak sky, the solid cold. I walked some good rods erect upon the tops of these trees, which were overgrown with moss and mountain cranberries. It seemed that in the course of time they had filled up the intervals between the huge rocks, and the cold wind had uniformly levelled all over. Here the principle of vegetation was hard put to it. There was apparently a belt of this kind running quite round the mountain, though, perhaps, nowhere so remarkable as here. Once, slumping through, I looked down ten feet, into a dark and cavernous region, and saw the stem of a spruce, on whose top I stood, as on a mass of coarse basket-work, fully nine inches in diameter at the ground. These holes were bears' dens, and the bears were even then at home. This was the sort of garden I made my way *over*, for an eighth of a mile, at the risk, it is true, of treading on some of the plants, not seeing any path *through* it—certainly the most treacherous and porous country I ever travelled.

---

[2] In Genesis 10.8–9, Nimrod is a mighty hunter, the great-grandson of Noah.

[3] In Milton's *Paradise Lost*, Satan travels through the realm of Chaos on his way to Earth. Thoreau further develops this theme with two quotations from *Paradise Lost* (see following notes).

"Nigh foundered on he fares,
Treading the crude consistence, half on foot,
Half flying."[4]

But nothing could exceed the toughness of the twigs—not one snapped under my weight, for they had slowly grown. Having slumped, scrambled, rolled, bounced, and walked, by turns, over this scraggy country, I arrived upon a side hill, or rather side mountain, where rocks, gray, silent rocks, were the flocks and herds that pastured, chewing a rocky cud at sunset. They looked at me with hard gray eyes, without a bleat or a low. This brought me to the skirt of a cloud, and bounded my walk that night. But I had already seen that Maine country when I turned about, waving, flowing, rippling, down below.

When I returned to my companions, they had selected a camping-ground on the torrent's edge, and were resting on the ground; one was on the sick list, rolled in a blanket, on a damp shelf of rock. It was a savage and dreary scenery enough, so wildly rough, that they looked long to find a level and open space for the tent. We could not well camp higher, for want of fuel; and the trees here seemed so evergreen and sappy, that we almost doubted if they would acknowledge the influence of fire; but fire prevailed at last, and blazed here, too, like a good citizen of the world. Even at this height we met with frequent traces of moose, as well as of bears. As here was no cedar, we made our bed of coarser feathered spruce; but at any rate the feathers were plucked from the live tree. It was, perhaps, even a more grand and desolate place for a night's lodging than the summit would have been, being in the neighborhood of those wild trees, and of the torrent. Some more aerial and finer-spirited winds rushed and roared through the ravine all night, from time to time arousing our fire, and dispersing the embers about. It was as if we lay in the very nest of a young whirl-wind. At midnight, one of my bed-fellows, being startled in his dreams by the sudden blazing up to its top of a fir tree, whose green boughs were dried by the heat, sprang up, with a cry, from his bed, thinking the world on fire, and drew the whole camp after him.

In the morning, after whetting our appetite on some raw pork, a wafer of hard-bread, and a dipper of condensed cloud or waterspout, we all together began to make our way up the falls, which I have described; this time choosing the right hand, or highest peak, which was not the one I had approached before. But soon my companions were lost to my sight behind the mountain ridge in my rear, which still seemed ever retreating before me, and I climbed alone over huge rocks, loosely poised, a mile or more, still edging toward the clouds; for though the day was clear elsewhere, the summit was concealed by mist. The mountain seemed a vast aggregation of loose rocks, as if some time it had rained rocks, and they lay as they fell on the mountain sides, nowhere fairly at rest, but leaning on each other, all rocking stones, with cavities between, but scarcely any soil or smoother shelf. They were the raw materials of a planet dropped from an unseen

[4] Milton, *Paradise Lost*, 2:940–42.

quarry, which the vast chemistry of nature would anon work up, or work down, into the smiling and verdant plains and valleys of earth. This was an undone extremity of the globe; as in lignite we see coal in the process of formation.

At length I entered within the skirts of the cloud which seemed forever drifting over the summit, and yet would never be gone, but was generated out of that pure air as fast as it flowed away; and when, a quarter of a mile farther, I reached the summit of the ridge, which those who have seen it in clearer weather say is about five miles long, and contains a thousand acres of table-land, I was deep within the hostile ranks of clouds, and all objects were obscured by them. Now the wind would blow me out a yard of clear sunlight, wherein I stood; then a gray, dawning light was all it could accomplish, the cloud-line ever rising and falling with the wind's intensity. Sometimes it seemed as if the summit would be cleared in a few moments, and smile in sunshine; but what was gained on one side was lost on another. It was like sitting in a chimney and waiting for the smoke to blow away. It was, in fact, a cloud-factory—these were the cloud-works, and the wind turned them off done from the cool, bare rocks. Occasionally, when the windy columns broke in to me, I caught sight of a dark, damp crag to the right or left; the mist driving ceaselessly between it and me. It reminded me of the creations of the old epic and dramatic poets, of Atlas, Vulcan, the Cyclops, and Prometheus.[5] Such was Caucasus and the rock where Prometheus was bound. Aeschylus[6] had no doubt visited such scenery as this. It was vast, Titanic, and such as man never inhabits. Some part of the beholder, even some vital part, seems to escape through the loose grating of his ribs as he ascends. He is more lone than you can imagine. There is less of substantial thought and fair understanding in him than in the plains where men inhabit. His reason is dispersed and shadowy, more thin and subtile, like the air. Vast, Titanic, inhuman Nature has got him at disadvantage, caught him alone, and pilfers him of some of his divine faculty. She does not smile on him as in the plains. She seems to say sternly, Why came ye here before your time. This ground is not prepared for you. Is it not enough that I smile in the valleys? I have never made this soil for thy feet, this air for thy breathing, these rocks for thy neighbors. I cannot pity nor fondle thee here, but forever relentlessly drive thee hence to where I *am* kind. Why seek me where I have not called thee, and then complain because you find me but a stepmother? Shouldst thou freeze or starve, or shudder thy life away, here is no shrine, nor altar, nor any access to my ear.

> "Chaos and ancient Night, I come no spy
> With purpose to explore or to disturb
> The secrets of your realm, but . . .

[5] In Greek mythology, Atlas and Prometheus were Titans, the most ancient race of gods. The Titans deposed their father, Uranus, and ruled the universe until they were defeated by Zeus. The Greek god Hephaestus (identified with the Roman god Vulcan) was, in some versions of the myth, lamed by Zeus and thrown down into Hades. The Cyclopes were primeval giants who assisted Zeus in his battle against the Titans. All of these mythical references relate to the general theme of warfare in heaven.

[6] In his tragedy, *Prometheus Bound*, the Greek dramatist Aeschylus relates how Zeus chained Prometheus to a rock in the Caucasus Mountains, to punish him for stealing fire from the gods.

. . . . . . as my way

Lies through your spacious empire up to light."[7]

The tops of mountains are among the unfinished parts of the globe, whither it is a slight insult to the gods to climb and pry into their secrets, and try their effect on our humanity. Only daring and insolent men, perchance, go there. Simple races, as savages, do not climb mountains—their tops are sacred and mysterious tracts never visited by them. Pomola[8] is always angry with those who climb to the summit of Ktaadn.

According to Jackson, who, in his capacity of geological surveyor of the State, has accurately measured it, the altitude of Ktaadn is 5300 feet, or a little more than one mile above the level of the sea, and he adds, "It is then evidently the highest point in the State of Maine, and is the most abrupt granite mountain in New England." The peculiarities of that spacious table-land on which I was standing, as well as the remarkable semicircular precipice or basin on the eastern side, were all concealed by the mist. I had brought my whole pack to the top, not knowing but I should have to make my descent to the river, and possibly to the settled portion of the State alone, and by some other route, and wishing to have a complete outfit with me. But at length fearing that my companions would be anxious to reach the river before night, and knowing that the clouds might rest on the mountain for days, I was compelled to descend. Occasionally, as I came down, the wind would blow me a vista open, through which I could see the country eastward, boundless forests, and lakes, and streams, gleaming in the sun, some of them emptying into the East Branch. There were also new mountains in sight in that direction. Now and then some small bird of the sparrow family would flit away before me, unable to command its course, like a fragment of the gray rock blown off by the wind.

I found my companions where I had left them, on the side of the peak, gathering the mountain cranberries, which filled every crevice between the rocks, together with blueberries, which had a spicier flavor the higher up they grew, but were not the less agreeable to our palates. When the country is settled, and roads are made, these cranberries will perhaps become an article of commerce. From this elevation, just on the skirts of the clouds, we could overlook the country, west and south, for a hundred miles. There it was, the State of Maine, which we had seen on the map, but not much like that—immeasurable forest for the sun to shine on, that eastern *stuff* we hear of in Massachusetts. No clearing, no house. It did not look as if a solitary traveller had cut so much as a walking-stick there. Countless lakes—Moosehead in the southwest, forty miles long by ten wide, like a gleaming silver platter at the end of the table; Chesuncook, eighteen long by three wide, without an island; Millinocket, on the south, with its hundred islands; and a hundred others without a name; and mountains, also, whose names, for the most part, are known only to the Indians. The forest looked like a firm grass sward, and the effect of these lakes in its midst has been well com-

---

[7] Milton, *Paradise Lost*, 2:970–74.

[8] In Wabanaki myth, Pomola was a birdlike creature that lived on Katahdin and resented intrusion by humans. For this reason, Native Americans considered Katahdin forbidden territory.

pared, by one who has since visited this same spot, to that of a "mirror broken into a thousand fragments, and wildly scattered over the grass, reflecting the full blaze of the sun." It was a large farm for somebody, when cleared. According to the Gazetteer, which was printed before the boundary question was settled, this single Penobscot County, in which we were, was larger than the whole State of Vermont, with its fourteen counties; and this was only a part of the wild lands of Maine. We are concerned now, however, about natural, not political limits. We were about eighty miles, as the bird flies, from Bangor, or one hundred and fifteen, as we had ridden, and walked, and paddled. We had to console ourselves with the reflection that this view was probably as good as that from the peak, as far as it went; and what were a mountain without its attendant clouds and mists? Like ourselves, neither Bailey nor Jackson had obtained a clear view from the summit.

Setting out on our return to the river, still at an early hour in the day, we decided to follow the course of the torrent, which we supposed to be Murch Brook, as long as it would not lead us too far out of our way. We thus travelled about four miles in the very torrent itself, continually crossing and recrossing it, leaping from rock to rock, and jumping with the stream down falls of seven or eight feet, or sometimes sliding down on our backs in a thin sheet of water. This ravine had been the scene of an extraordinary freshet in the spring, apparently accompanied by a slide from the mountain. It must have been filled with a stream of stones and water, at least twenty feet above the present level of the torrent. For a rod or two, on either side of its channel, the trees were barked and splintered up to their tops, the birches bent over, twisted, and sometimes finely split, like a stable broom; some, a foot in diameter, snapped off, and whole clumps of trees bent over with the weight of rocks piled on them. In one place we noticed a rock, two or three feet in diameter, lodged nearly twenty feet high in the crotch of a tree. For the whole four miles we saw but one rill emptying in, and the volume of water did not seem to be increased from the first. We travelled thus very rapidly with a downward impetus, and grew remarkably expert at leaping from rock to rock, for leap we must, and leap we did, whether there was any rock at the right distance or not. It was a pleasant picture when the foremost turned about and looked up the winding ravine, walled in with rocks and the green forest, to see, at intervals of a rod or two, a red-shirted or green-jacketed mountaineer against the white torrent, leaping down the channel with his pack on his back, or pausing upon a convenient rock in the midst of the torrent to mend a rent in his clothes, or unstrap the dipper at his belt to take a draught of the water. At one place we were startled by seeing, on a little sandy shelf by the side of the stream, the fresh print of a man's foot, and for a moment realized how Robinson Crusoe felt in a similar case; but at last we remembered that we had struck this stream on our way up, though we could not have told where, and one had descended into the ravine for a drink. The cool air above and the continual bathing of our bodies in mountain water, alternate foot, sitz, douche, and plunge baths, made this walk exceedingly refreshing, and we had travelled only a mile or two, after leaving the torrent, before every thread of our clothes was as dry as usual, owing perhaps to a peculiar quality in the atmosphere.

After leaving the torrent, being in doubt about our course, Tom threw down his pack at the foot of the loftiest spruce tree at hand, and shinned up the bare trunk some twenty feet, and then climbed through the green tower, lost to our sight, until he held the topmost spray in his hand. McCauslin, in his younger days, had marched through the wilderness with a body of troops, under General Somebody, and with one other man did all the scouting and spying service. The General's word was, "Throw down the top of that tree," and there was no tree in the Maine woods so high that it did not lose its top in such a case. I have heard a story of two men being lost once in these woods, nearer to the settlements than this, who climbed the loftiest pine they could find, some six feet in diameter at the ground, from whose top they discovered a solitary clearing and its smoke. When at this height, some two hundred feet from the ground, one of them became dizzy, and fainted in his companion's arms, and the latter had to accomplish the descent with him, alternately fainting and reviving, as best he could. To Tom we cried, "Where away does the summit bear? where the burnt lands?" The last he could only conjecture; he descried, however, a little meadow and pond, lying probably in our course, which we concluded to steer for. On reaching this secluded meadow, we found fresh tracks of moose on the shore of the pond, and the water was still unsettled as if they had fled before us. A little farther, in a dense thicket, we seemed to be still on their trail. It was a small meadow, of a few acres, on the mountain-side, concealed by the forest, and perhaps never seen by a white man before, where one would think that the moose might browse and bathe, and rest in peace. Pursuing this course, we soon reached the open land, which went sloping down some miles toward the Penobscot.

Perhaps I most fully realized that this was primeval, untamed, and forever untamable *Nature*, or whatever else men call it, while coming down this part of the mountain. We were passing over "Burnt Lands," burnt by lightning, perchance, though they showed no recent marks of fire, hardly so much as a charred stump, but looked rather like a natural pasture for the moose and deer, exceedingly wild and desolate, with occasional strips of timber crossing them, and low poplars springing up, and patches of blueberries here and there. I found myself traversing them familiarly, like some pasture run to waste, or partially reclaimed by man; but when I reflected what man, what brother or sister or kinsman of our race made it and claimed it, I expected the proprietor to rise up and dispute my passage. It is difficult to conceive of a region uninhabited by man. We habitually presume his presence and influence everywhere. And yet we have not seen pure Nature, unless we have seen her thus vast and drear and unhuman, though in the midst of cities. Nature was here something savage and awful, though beautiful. I looked with awe at the ground I trod on, to see what the Powers had made there, the form and fashion and material of their work. This was that Earth of which we have heard, made out of Chaos and Old Night. Here was no man's garden, but the unhandselled globe. It was not lawn, nor pasture, nor mead, nor woodland, nor lea, nor arable, nor waste land. It was the fresh and natural surface of the planet Earth, as it was made forever and ever—to be the dwelling of man, we say—so Nature made it, and man may use it if he can. Man was not to be associated with it. It was Matter, vast, terrific—not his Mother Earth that we have heard of, not for him to tread on, or be buried in—no, it were being too familiar even to let his bones lie there—the home, this, of Necessity and Fate. There was clearly felt the presence of a force not bound to be kind to man. It was a place for heathenism and superstitious rites—to be inhabited by men nearer of kin to the rocks and to wild animals than we. We walked over it with a certain awe, stopping, from time to time, to pick the blueberries which grew there, and had a smart and spicy taste. Perchance where *our* wild pines stand, and leaves lie on their forest floor, in Concord, there were once reapers, and husbandmen planted grain; but here not even the surface had been scarred by man, but it was a specimen of what God saw fit to make this world. What is it to be admitted to a museum, to see a myriad of particular things, compared with being shown some star's surface, some hard matter in its home! I stand in awe of my body, this matter to which I am bound has become so strange to me. I fear not spirits, ghosts, of which I am one—*that* my body might—but I fear bodies, I tremble to meet them. What is this Titan that has possession of me? Talk of mysteries! Think of our life in nature—daily to be shown matter, to come in contact with it—rocks, trees, wind on our cheeks! the *solid* earth! the *actual* world! the *common sense! Contact! Contact! Who* are we? *where* are we?

Emily Brontë (1818–1848)

When Emily Brontë and her sisters Charlotte and Anne first published their work, they did so under the androgynous pseudonyms of Ellis, Currer, and Acton Bell, respectively. Such a strategy makes sense considering that the Victorian reading public no doubt would have scorned Emily's honest, passionate poetry and prose as "unladylike." The daughter of a poor clergyman, Emily grew up in Haworth parsonage in Yorkshire, in a landscape of moors she was to immortalize in her novel Wuthering Heights. *Her mother died when she was two, and her two oldest sisters died as a result of illness contracted during a brief period in which the four eldest Brontë girls were sent to a boarding school (the inhuman conditions of that school are detailed in Charlotte Brontë's novel* Jane Eyre). *She had a very close relationship with her remaining siblings, Charlotte, her younger sister, Anne, and their brother, Branwell, and all four were afterwards kept at home and profited by their father's library and by their own imaginative play. They collaborated on creating the story of a fantastical kingdom called Gondal. The sagas the children wrote about Gondal have been identified as the source of much of Emily Brontë's poetry. Emily and Charlotte left home again briefly in 1835 and 1837 to work as schoolteachers, and in 1842 the two traveled to Belgium to study languages so that they might be qualified to open their own school. Emily returned before the year was out and never left home again, devoting herself to her writing and to the care of her family.*

The sisters together first published a collection of their poems in 1846. Despite negligible sales, they each next put forth novels. Wuthering Heights *was Emily Brontë's effort. As in her poems, the natural world represented in the novel is imbued with mystery and mythology. Heathcliff, the novel's Byronic hero, and the headstrong Catherine*

Earnshaw, seem only to make sense in the bleak and dramatic setting of the moors. When they are displaced to the more civilized landscape of the Linton family's garden park at Thrushcross Grange, the characters' own natural wildness becomes even more striking, for they seem only to thrive in their original natural habitat. Catherine Earnshaw is so connected to the moors that she haunts them after her death. Emily Brontë's own relationship to the natural world might be summed up by the concluding lines of one of her poems:

What have those lonely mountains worth revealing?
   More glory and more grief than I can tell:
The earth that wakes *one* human heart to feeling
   Can center both the worlds of Heaven and Hell.

For Brontë, as for her characters, nature was a source of solace and a reminder of her own limited condition. She died at her home, of tuberculosis, at the age of thirty.

Loud without the wind was roaring

Loud without the wind was roaring
   Through the waned autumnal sky;
Drenching wet, the cold rain pouring
   Spoke of stormy winters nigh.

All too like that dreary eve   5
Sighed within repining grief;
Sighed at first, but sighed not long—
Sweet—How softly sweet it came!
Wild words of an ancient song,
Undefined, without a name.   10

"It was spring, for the skylark was singing."
   Those words, they awakened a spell—
They unlocked a deep fountain whose springing
   Nor Absence nor Distance can quell.

In the gloom of a cloudy November,   15
   They uttered the music of May;
They kindled the perishing ember
   Into fervour that could not decay.

Awaken on all my dear moorlands
   The wind in its glory and pride!   20
O call me from valleys and highlands
   To walk by the hill-river's side!

It is swelled with the first snowy weather;
   The rocks they are icy and hoar

And darker waves round the long heather   25
And the fern leaves are sunny no more.

There are no yellow stars on the mountain,
The blue-bells have long died away
From the brink of the moss-bedded fountain,
From the side of the wintery brae—   30

But lovelier than corn-fields all waving
In emerald and scarlet and gold
Are the slopes where the north-wind is raving,
And the glens where I wandered of old.

"It was morning; the bright sun was beaming."   35
How sweetly that brought back to me
The time when nor labour nor dreaming
Broke the sleep of the happy and free.

But blithely we rose as the dusk heaven
Was melting to amber and blue;   40
And swift were the wings to our feet given
While we traversed the meadows of dew,

For the moors, for the moors where the short grass
Like velvet beneath us should lie!
For the moors, for the moors where each high pass   45
Rose sunny against the clear sky!

For the moors where the linnet was trilling
Its song on the old granite stone;
Where the lark—the wild skylark was filling
Every breast with delight like its own.   50

What language can utter the feeling
That rose when, in exile afar,
On the brow of a lonely hill kneeling
I saw the brown heath growing there.

It was scattered and stunted, and told me   55
That soon even that would be gone;
Its whispered, "The grim walls enfold me;
I have bloomed in my last summer's sun."

But not the loved music whose waking
Makes the soul of the Swiss die away   60
Has a spell more adored and heart-breaking
Than in its half-blighted bells lay.

The spirit that bent 'neath its power,
How it longed, how it burned to be free!

If I could have wept in that hour   65
Those tears had been heaven to me.

Well, well, the sad minutes are moving
Though loaded with trouble and pain;
And sometime the loved and the loving
Shall meet on the mountains again.   70

The Night-Wind

In summer's mellow midnight,
A cloudless moon shone through
Our open parlour window
And rosetrees wet with dew.

I sat in silent musing,   5
The soft wind waved my hair:
It told me Heaven was glorious,
And sleeping Earth was fair.

I needed not its breathing
To bring such thoughts to me,   10
But still it whispered lowly,
"How dark the woods will be!

"The thick leaves in my murmur
Are rustling like a dream,
And all their myriad voices   15
Instinct with spirit seem."

I said, "Go, gentle singer,
Thy wooing voice is kind,
But do not think its music
Has power to reach my mind.   20

"Play with the scented flower,
The young tree's supple bough,
And leave my human feelings
In their own course to flow."

The wanderer would not leave me;   25
Its kiss grew warmer still—
"O come," it sighed so sweetly,
"I'll win thee 'gainst thy will.

"Have we not been from childhood friends?
Have I not loved thee long?   30

As long as thou hast loved the night
Whose silence wakes my song.

"And when thy heart is laid at rest
Beneath the church-yard stone
I shall have time enough to mourn   35
And thou to be alone."

Shall Earth no more inspire thee

Shall Earth no more inspire thee,
Thou lonely dreamer now?
Since passion may not fire thee
Shall Nature cease to bow?

Thy mind is ever moving   5
In regions dark to thee;
Recall its useless roving—
Come back and dwell with me.

I know my mountain breezes
Enchant and soothe thee still—   10
I know my sunshine pleases
Despite thy wayward will.

When day with evening blending
Sinks from the summer sky,
I've seen thy spirit bending   15
In fond idolatry.

I've watched thee every hour;
I know my mighty sway,
I know my magic power
To drive thy griefs away.   20

Few hearts to mortals given
On earth so wildly pine;
Yet none would ask a Heaven
More like this Earth than thine.

Then let my winds caress thee;   25
Thy comrade let me be—
Since nought beside can bless thee,
Return and dwell with me.

Ah! why, because the dazzling sun

Ah! why, because the dazzling sun
Restored my earth to joy
Have you departed, every one,
And left a desert sky?

All through the night, your glorious eyes   5
Were gazing down in mine,
And with a full heart's thankful sighs
I blessed that watch divine!

I was at peace, and drank your beams
As they were life to me   10
And revelled in my changeful dreams
Like petrel on the sea.

Thought followed thought—star followed star
Through boundless regions on,
While one sweet influence, near and far,   15
Thrilled through and proved us one.

Why did the morning rise to break
So great, so pure a spell,
And scorch with fire the tranquil cheek
Where your cool radiance fell?   20

Blood-red he rose, and arrow-straight
His fierce beams struck my brow:
The soul of Nature sprang elate,
But mine sank sad and low!

My lids closed down—yet through their veil   25
I saw him blazing still;
And bathe in gold the misty dale,
And flash upon the hill.

I turned me to the pillow then
To call back Night, and see   30
Your worlds of solemn light, again
Throb with my heart and me!

It would not do—the pillow glowed
And glowed both roof and floor,
And birds sang loudly in the wood,   35
And fresh winds shook the door.

The curtains waved, the wakened flies
Were murmuring round my room,

Imprisoned there, till I should rise
And give them leave to roam.   40

O Stars and Dreams and Gentle Night;
O Night and Stars return!
And hide me from the hostile light
That does not warm, but burn—

That drains the blood of suffering men;   45
Drinks tears, instead of dew:
Let me sleep through his blinding reign,
And only wake with you!

A.E. and R.C.

Heavy hangs the raindrop
From the burdened spray;
Heavy broods the damp mist
On uplands far away;

Heavy looms the dull sky,   5
Heavy rolls the sea—
And heavy beats the young heart
Beneath that lonely tree.

Never has a blue streak
Cleft the clouds since morn—   10
Never has his grim Fate
Smiled since he was born.

Frowning on the infant,
Shadowing childhood's joy,
Guardian angel knows not   15
That melancholy boy.

Day is passing swiftly
Its sad and sombre prime;
Youth is fast invading
Sterner manhood's time.   20

All the flowers are praying
For sun before they close,
And he prays too, unknowing,
That sunless human rose!

Blossoms, that the west wind   25
Has never wooed to blow,
Scentless are your petals,
Your dew as cold as snow.

Soul, where kindred kindness
No early promise woke,   30
Barren is your beauty
As weed upon the rock.

Wither, Brothers, wither,
You were vainly given—
Earth reserves no blessing   35
For the unblessed of Heaven!

🖋 *John Ruskin* (1819–1900)

The Storm-Cloud of the Nineteenth Century *(1884) is one of the first, and one of the most impassioned, protests against the effects of industrial pollution. However, its author was an art critic, not a scientist. John Ruskin's objections to pollution were primarily aesthetic: It destroyed the beauty of the landscape. Ruskin's concern with beauty, both natural and contrived, dominates his work and forms the basis of his powerful social and cultural critique. Born of middle-class parents and raised in London, Ruskin had a strict and sheltered upbringing, although he did enjoy trips around rural England and in Europe with his father. On these trips, he discovered an intense love for the splendors of the natural environment. He attended Oxford and began his writing career by publishing some poetry and essays on architecture and the visual arts in popular magazines. In 1843 Ruskin produced the first of what would become the five volumes of his work* Modern Painters *(1843–60). Although the project began as a discussion of English landscape artist J. M. W. Turner, its scope expanded, and by the time of its completion in 1860, the treatise touched as well on issues of politics, economics, and religion. In all of his subsequent works, Ruskin treated a society's attitude toward art as a measure of its overall health, and this analysis underpins numerous works in which he linked aesthetic appreciation with a culture's underlying morality. He wrote prodigiously and shared his work publicly in popular lectures, which he gave at Oxford and in London. Some of his best-known works, including* The Storm-Cloud of the Nineteenth Century, *began as lectures, and their tone gives an indication of the power and persuasiveness of Ruskin's style. His early published work includes* The Seven Lamps of Architecture *(1849),* The Stones of Venice *(1851–53),* Lectures on Architecture and Painting *(1854), and* The Political Economy of Art *(1857). This last book, together with the final volume of* Modern Painters *(1860), moved Ruskin to a more profoundly radical stance. He condemned capitalist society for its detrimental effect on the spiritual—and hence the aesthetic—sensibilities of modern individuals. And although Ruskin allied himself with working-class political organizations, his vision of the ideal society looked backward rather than forward. He cherished the Christian feudal society that produced Gothic architecture, and he deplored the dehumanizing tendencies of modern technologies of mass production.*

In 1870, Ruskin became a professor of art at Oxford. He continued, however, to give and publish lectures to the public on a wide variety of topics. His political views were unpopular with university officials and led to his temporary retirement from his post in 1878 and permanent resignation in 1885. The Storm-Cloud *was one of the lectures given during his last year at Oxford. Although he had great success and influence as a writer and a critic, his personal life was troubled. His marriage to Euphemia (Effie) Gray ended in annulment; later in his life, he fell in love with a nine-year-old girl, although he did not propose to her until she was eighteen. In his final years, he was overtaken with mental illness. One of his last publications was a moving autobiography,* Praeterita, *written between 1885 and 1889.*

From The Storm-Cloud of the Nineteenth Century

From Lecture 1

1.   Let me first assure my audience that I have no *arrière pensée*[1] in the title chosen for this lecture. I might, indeed, have meant, and it would have been only too like me to mean, any number of things by such a title;—but, tonight, I mean simply what I have said, and propose to bring to your notice a series of cloud phenomena, which, so far as I can weigh existing evidence, are peculiar to our own times; yet which have not hitherto received any special notice or description from meteorologists.

2.   So far as the existing evidence, I say, of former literature can be interpreted, the storm-cloud—or more accurately plague-cloud, for it is not always stormy—which I am about to describe to you, never was seen but by now living, or *lately* living eyes. It is not yet twenty years that this—I may well call it, wonderful—cloud has been, in its essence, recognizable. There is no description of it, so far as I have read, by any ancient observer. Neither Homer nor Virgil, neither Aristophanes nor Horace, acknowledge any such clouds among those compelled by Jove.[2] Chaucer has no word of them, nor Dante; Milton none, nor Thomson. In modern times, Scott, Wordsworth, and Byron are alike unconscious of them; and the most observant and descriptive of scientific men, De Saussure, is utterly silent concerning them. Taking up the traditions of air from the year before Scott's[3] death, I am able, by my own constant and close observation, to certify you that in the forty following years (1831 to 1871 approximately—for the phenomena in question came on gradually) —no such clouds as these are, and are now often for months without intermission, were ever seen in the skies of England, France, or Italy.

3.   In those old days, when weather was fine, it was luxuriously fine; when it was bad—it was often abominably bad, but it had its fit of temper and was done with it—it didn't sulk for three months without letting you see the sun,—nor

---

[1] Literally, thought behind; or, a hidden agenda.

[2] Jove is the classical god of thunder; Homer and Aristophanes are classical Greek, and Virgil and Horace are Roman, authors.

[3] Sir Walter Scott (1771–1832), British novelist and poet.

send you one cyclone inside out, every Saturday afternoon, and another outside in, every Monday morning.

In fine weather the sky was either blue or clear in its light; the clouds, either white or golden, adding to, not abating, the lustre of the sky. In wet weather, there were two different species of clouds,—those of beneficent rain, which for distinction's sake I will call the nonelectric rain-cloud, and those of storm, usually charged highly with electricity. The beneficent rain-cloud was indeed often extremely dull and grey for days together, but gracious nevertheless, felt to be doing good, and often to be delightful after drought; capable also of the most exquisite colouring, under certain conditions; and continually traversed in clearing by the rainbow:—and, secondly, the storm-cloud, always majestic, often dazzlingly beautiful, and felt also to be beneficent in its own way, affecting the mass of the air with vital agitation, and purging it from the impurity of all morbific elements.

4.   In the entire system of the Firmament, thus seen and understood, there appeared to be, to all the thinkers of those ages, the incontrovertible and unmistakable evidence of a Divine Power in creation, which had fitted, as the air for human breath, so the clouds for human sight and nourishment;—the Father who was in heaven feeding day by day the souls of His children with marvels, and satisfying them with bread, and so filling their hearts with food and gladness.

Their *hearts*, you will observe, it is said, not merely their bellies,—or indeed not at all, in this sense, their bellies—but the heart itself, with its blood for this life, and its faith for the next. The opposition between this idea and the notions of our own time may be more accurately expressed by modification of the Greek than of the English sentence. The old Greek is—

ἐμπιπλῶν   τροφῆς   καὶ   εὐφροσύνης   τὰς   καρδίας   ἡμῶν.

filling with meat, and cheerfulness, our hearts.

The modern Greek should be—

ἐμπιπλῶν   ἀνέμου   καὶ   ἀφροσύνης   τὰς   γαστέρας   ἡμῶν.

filling with wind, and foolishness, our stomachs.

.   .

29.   The first time I recognized the clouds brought by the plague-wind as distinct in character was in walking back from Oxford, after a hard day's work, to Abingdon,[4] in the early spring of 1871: it would take too long to give you any account this evening of the particulars which drew my attention to them; but during the following months I had too frequent opportunities of verifying my first thoughts of them, and on the first of July in that year wrote the description of them which begins the *Fors Clavigera*[5] of August, thus:—

[4] Where Ruskin was living at the time.

[5] Published between 1871 and 1878, *Fors Clavigera* were public letters that Ruskin wrote to laborers. In this series of letters, he often took up the subject of air and water pollution.

It is the first of July, and I sit down to write by the dismallest light that ever yet I wrote by; namely, the light of this midsummer morning, in mid-England (Matlock, Derbyshire), in the year 1871.

For the sky is covered with grey cloud;—not rain-cloud, but a dry black veil, which no ray of sunshine can pierce; partly diffused in mist, feeble mist, enough to make distant objects unintelligible, yet without any substance, or wreathing, or colour of its own. And everywhere the leaves of the trees are shaking fitfully, as they do before a thunderstorm; only not violently, but enough to show the passing to and fro of a strange, bitter, blighting wind. Dismal enough, had it been the first morning of its kind that summer had sent. But during all this spring, in London, and at Oxford, through meagre March, through changelessly sullen April, through despondent May, and darkened June, morning after morning has come grey-shrouded thus.

And it is a new thing to me, and a very dreadful one. I am fifty years old, and more; and since I was five, have gleaned the best hours of my life in the sun of spring and summer mornings; and I never saw such as these, till now.

And the scientific men are busy as ants, examining the sun and the moon, and the seven stars, and can tell me all about *them*, I believe, by this time; and how they move, and what they are made of.

And I do not care, for my part, two copper spangles how they move, nor what they are made of. I can't move them any other way than they go, nor make them of anything else, better than they are made. But I would care much and give much, if I could be told where this bitter wind comes from, and what *it* is made of.

For, perhaps, with forethought, and fine laboratory science, one might make it of something else.

It looks partly as if it were made of poisonous smoke; very possibly it may be: there are at least two hundred furnace chimneys in a square of two miles on every side of me. But mere smoke would not blow to and fro in that wild way. It looks more to me as if it were made of dead men's souls—such of them as are not gone yet where they have to go, and may be flitting hither and thither, doubting, themselves, of the fittest place for them.

You know, if there *are* such things as souls, and if ever any of them haunt places where they have been hurt, there must be many above us, just now, displeased enough!

The last sentence refers of course to the battles of the Franco-German campaign, which was especially horrible to me, in its digging, as the Germans should have known, a moat flooded with waters of death between the two nations for a century to come.

30. Since that Midsummer day, my attention, however otherwise occupied, has never relaxed in its record of the phenomena characteristic of the plague-wind; and I now define for you, as briefly as possible, the essential signs of it.

(1.) It is a wind of darkness,—all the former conditions of tormenting winds, whether from the north or east, were more or less capable of co-existing with sunlight, and often with steady and bright sunlight; but whenever, and wherever the plague-wind blows, be it but for ten minutes, the sky is darkened instantly.

31.   (2.) It is a malignant *quality* of wind, unconnected with any one quarter of the compass; it blows indifferently from all, attaching its own bitterness and malice to the worst characters of the proper winds of each quarter. It will blow either with drenching rain, or dry rage, from the south, —with ruinous blasts from the west,—with bitterest chills from the north,—and with venomous blight from the east.

Its own favourite quarter, however, is the southwest, so that it is distinguished in its malignity equally from the Bise of Provence, which is a north wind always, and from our own old friend, the east.

32.   (3.) It always blows *tremulously*, making the leaves of the trees shudder as if they were all aspens, but with a peculiar fitfulness which gives them—and I watch them this moment as I write—an expression of anger as well as of fear and distress. You may see the kind of quivering, and hear the ominous whimpering, in the gusts that precede a great thunderstorm; but plague-wind is more panic-struck, and feverish; and its sound is a hiss instead of a wail.

When I was last at Avallon, in South France, I went to see *Faust* played at the little country theatre: it was done with scarcely any means of pictorial effect, except a few old curtains, and a blue light or two. But the night on the Brocken was nevertheless extremely appalling to me,—a strange ghastliness being obtained in some of the witch scenes merely by fine management of gesture and drapery; and in the phantom scenes, by the half-palsied, half-furious, faltering or fluttering past of phantoms stumbling as into graves; as if of not only soulless, but senseless, Dead, moving with the very action, the rage, the decrepitude, and the trembling of the plague-wind.

33.   (4.) Not only tremulous at every moment, it is also *intermittent* with a rapidity quite unexampled in former weather. There are, indeed, days—and weeks, on which it blows without cessation, and is as inevitable as the Gulf Stream; but also there are days when it is contending with healthy weather, and on such days it will remit for half an hour, and the sun will begin to show itself, and then the wind will come back and cover the whole sky with clouds in ten minutes; and so on, every half-hour, through the whole day; so that it is often impossible to go on with any kind of drawing in colour, the light being never for two seconds the same from morning till evening.

34.   (5.) It degrades, while it intensifies, ordinary storm; but before I read you any description of its efforts in this kind, I must correct an impression which has got abroad through the papers, that I speak as if the plague-wind blew now always, and there were no more any natural weather. On the contrary, the winter of 1878–9 was one of the most healthy and lovely I ever saw ice in;—Coniston lake shone under the calm clear frost in one marble field, as strong as the floor of Milan Cathedral, half a mile across and four miles down; and the first entries in my diary which I read you shall be from the 22nd to 26th June, 1876, of perfectly lovely and natural weather:—

Sunday, 25th June, 1876.

Yesterday, an entirely glorious sunset, unmatched in beauty since that at Abbeville,—deep scarlet, and purest rose, on purple grey, in bars; and stationary, plumy, sweeping filaments above in upper sky, like *"using up the brush,"* said Joanie; remaining in glory, every moment best, changing from one good into another, (but only in colour or light—*form steady*,) for half an hour full, and the clouds afterwards fading into the grey against amber twilight, *stationary in the same form for about two hours*, at least. The darkening rose tint remained till half-past ten, the grand time being at nine.

The day had been fine,—exquisite green light on afternoon hills.

Monday, 26th June, 1876.

Yesterday an entirely perfect summer light on the Old Man; Lancaster Bay all clear; Ingleborough and the great Pennine fault as on a map. Divine beauty of western colour on thyme and rose,—then twilight of clearest *warm* amber far into night, of *pale* amber all night long; hills dark-clear against it.

And so it continued, only growing more intense in blue and sunlight, all day. After breakfast, I came in from the well under strawberry bed, to say I had never seen anything like it, so pure or intense, in Italy; and so it went glowing on, cloudless, with soft north wind, all day.

16th July.

The sunset almost too bright *through the blinds* for me to read Humboldt at tea by,—finally, new moon like a lime-light, reflected on breeze-struck water; traces, across dark calm, of reflected hills.

35.   These extracts are, I hope, enough to guard you against the absurdity of supposing that it all only means that I am myself soured, or doting, in my old age, and always in an ill humour. Depend upon it, when old men are worth anything, they are better-humoured than young ones; and have learned to see what good there is, and pleasantness, in the world they are likely so soon to have orders to quit.

Now then—take the following sequences of accurate description of thunderstorm, *with* plague-wind.

22nd June, 1876.

Thunderstorm; pitch dark, with no *blackness*,—but deep, high, *filthiness* of lurid, yet not sublimely lurid, smoke-cloud; dense manufacturing mist; fearful squalls of shivery wind, making Mr. Severn's sail quiver like a man in a fever fit—all about four, afternoon—but only two or three claps of thunder, and feeble, though near, flashes. I never saw such a dirty, weak, foul storm. It cleared suddenly after raining all afternoon, at half-past eight to nine, into pure, natural weather,—low rain-clouds on quite clear, green, wet hills.

Brantwood, 13th August, 1879.

The most terrific and horrible thunderstorm, this morning, I ever remember. It waked me at six, or a little before—then rolling incessantly, like railway luggage trains, quite ghastly in its mockery of them—the air one loathsome mass of sultry and foul fog, like smoke; scarcely raining at all, but increasing to heavier rollings, with flashes quivering vaguely through all the air, and at last terrific double streams of reddish-violet fire, not forked or zigzag, but rippled rivulets—two at the same instant some twenty to thirty degrees apart, and lasting on the eye at least half a second, with grand artillery-peals following; not rattling crashes, or irregular cracklings, but delivered volleys. It lasted an hour, then passed off, clearing a little, without rain to speak of,—not a glimpse of blue,—and now, half-past seven, seems settling down again into Manchester devil's darkness.

Quarter to eight, morning.—Thunder returned, all the air collapsed into one black fog, the hills invisible, and scarcely visible the opposite shore; heavy rain in short fits, and frequent, though less formidable, flashes, and shorter thunder. While I have written this sentence the cloud has again dissolved itself, like a nasty solution in a bottle, with miraculous and unnatural rapidity, and the hills are in sight again; a double-forked flash—rippled, I mean, like the others—starts into its frightful ladder of light between me and Wetherlam, as I raise my eyes. All black above, a rugged spray cloud on the Eaglet. (The "Eaglet" is my own name for the bold and elevated crag to the west of the little lake above Coniston mines. It had no name among the country people, and is one of the most conspicuous features of the mountain chain, as seen from Brantwood.)

Half-past eight.—Three times light and three times dark since last I wrote, and the darkness seeming each time as it settles more loathsome, at last stopping my reading in mere blindness. One lurid gleam of white cumulus in upper lead-blue sky, seen for half a minute through the sulphurous chimney-pot vomit of blackguardly cloud beneath, where its rags were thinnest.

Thursday, 22nd Feb. 1883.

Yesterday a fearfully dark mist all afternoon, with steady, south plague-wind of the bitterest, nastiest, poisonous blight, and fretful flutter. I could scarcely stay in the wood for the horror of it. Today, really rather bright blue, and bright semi-cumuli, with the frantic Old Man blowing sheaves of lancets and chisels across the lake—not in strength enough, or whirl enough, to raise it in spray, but tracing every squall's outline in black on the silver grey waves, and whistling meanly, and as if on a flute made of a file.

Sunday, 17th August, 1879.

Raining in foul drizzle, slow and steady; sky pitch-dark, and I just get a little light by sitting in the bow-window; diabolic clouds over everything: and looking over my kitchen garden yesterday, I found it one miserable mass of weeds gone to seed, the roses in the higher garden putrefied into brown sponges, feeling like dead snails; and the half-ripe strawberries all rotten at the stalks.

36.   (6.) And now I come to the most important sign of the plague-wind and the plague-cloud: that in bringing on their peculiar darkness, they *blanch* the sun instead of reddening it. And here I must note briefly to you the uselessness of observation by instruments, or machines, instead of eyes. In the first year when I had begun to notice the specialty of the plague-wind, I went of course to the Oxford observatory to consult its registrars. They have their anemometer always on the twirl, and can tell you the force, or at least the pace, of a gale, by day or night. But the anemometer can only record for you how often it has been driven round, not at all whether it went round *steadily*, or went round *trembling*. And on that point depends the entire question whether it is a plague breeze or a healthy one: and what's the use of telling you whether the wind's strong or not, when it can't tell you whether it's a strong medicine, or a strong poison?

But again—you have your *sun*-measure, and can tell exactly at any moment how strong, or how weak, or how wanting, the sun is. But the sun-measurer can't tell you whether the rays are stopped by a dense *shallow* cloud, or a thin *deep* one. In healthy weather, the sun is hidden behind a cloud, as it is behind a tree; and, when the cloud is past, it comes out again, as bright as before. But in plague-wind, the sun is choked out of the whole heaven, all day long, by a cloud which may be a thousand miles square and five miles deep.

And yet observe: that thin, scraggy, filthy, mangy, miserable cloud, for all the depth of it, can't turn the sun red, as a good, business-like fog does with a hundred feet or so of itself. By the plague-wind every breath of air you draw is polluted, half round the world; in a London fog the air itself is pure, though you choose to mix up dirt with it, and choke yourself with your own nastiness.

.   .   .

Blanched Sun,—blighted grass,—blinded man.—If, in conclusion, you ask me for any conceivable cause or meaning of these things—I can tell you none, according to your modern beliefs; but I can tell you what meaning it would have borne to the men of old time. Remember, for the last twenty years, England, and all foreign nations, either tempting her, or following her, have blasphemed the name of God deliberately and openly; and have done iniquity by proclamation, every man doing as much injustice to his brother as it is in his power to do. Of states in such moral gloom every seer of old predicted the physical gloom, saying, "The light shall be darkened in the heavens thereof, and the stars shall withdraw their shining."[6] All Greek, all Christian, all Jewish prophecy insists on the same truth through a thousand myths; but of all the chief, to former thought, was the fable of the Jewish warrior and prophet, for whom the sun hasted not to go down,[7] with which I leave you to compare at leisure the physical result of your own wars and prophecies, as declared by your own elect journal not four-

---

[6] Reference to the Bible, Joel 2:10.

[7] A reference to a story from the Bible, in Joshua 10:13.

teen days ago,—that the Empire of England, on which formerly the sun never set, has become one on which he never rises.

39. What is best to be done, do you ask me? The answer is plain. Whether you can affect the signs of the sky or not, you *can* the signs of the times. Whether you can bring the *sun* back or not, you can assuredly bring back your own cheerfulness, and your own honesty. You may not be able to say to the winds, "Peace; be still," but you can cease from the insolence of your own lips, and the troubling of your own passions. And all *that* it would be extremely well to do, even though the day *were* coming when the sun should be as darkness, and the moon as blood. But, the paths of rectitude and piety once regained, who shall say that the promise of old time would not be found to hold for us also?— "Bring ye all the tithes into my storehouse, and prove me now herewith, saith the Lord God, if I will not open you the windows of heaven, and pour you out a blessing, that there shall not be room enough to receive it."[8]

[8] This paragraph is heavily laden with allusions to apocalyptic passages from the Bible, including Matthew 16:8, Mark 4:39, Job 3:17, Joel 2:31, and Malachi 3:10.

✒ *Walt Whitman* (1819–1892)

Walt Whitman was born on Long Island and raised in Brooklyn, New York, where he went to school and worked briefly as printer's apprentice. From 1838 to 1848, he worked as a writer and editor for several New York and Brooklyn journals. In 1848 he and his brother Jeff went to New Orleans, where his eyes were opened to a more extravagant and permissive lifestyle; he is rumored to have had a mistress and fathered a child out of wedlock. Returning to New York, Whitman edited a Brooklyn paper and worked inter-mittently as a carpenter, while privately he was engaged in composing a collection of twelve poems, Leaves of Grass, *which he published at his own expense in 1855. This groundbreaking volume was largely ignored by critics, but it was noticed by some leading intellectuals, most notably Emerson, who wrote a warm personal letter of commendation. An enlarged second edition in 1856 was attacked by critics for its unconventional subject matter and its bold new metrical form: long lines of rhythmic, incantatory free verse.* Leaves of Grass *revealed its author as a mystic, a pantheist, and a lover of all humankind. He celebrated the democratic spirit of America, the splendor of the American landscape, and the beauty of the human body. As an advocate of sexual freedom, Whitman shocked many of his contemporaries. Yet he is regarded today as one of the leading voices in the history of American poetry, remarkable for his innovations in poetic form and memorable for the encompassing scope of his subject matter.*

Whitman continued to revise and expand Leaves of Grass *through many successive editions, adding new poems and dramatically reshaping his earlier work, until the final edition of 1892. During the Civil War, he cared for his wounded brother in Virginia and served as an unofficial nurse in Union military hospitals. The assassination of President Abraham Lincoln called forth two of his best-known poems, "When Lilacs Last in the Dooryard Bloomed" and "O Captain! My Captain!" Whitman applauded the west-*

ward expansion of the frontier in "Pioneers! O Pioneers!" and he evoked the awesome immensity of the newly discovered sequoias in "Song of the Redwood Tree." Although Whitman never achieved the popular readership that he desired, his poetry had enormous influence on subsequent writers, validating the American vernacular as an medium for poetry and revealing the expressive possibilities of the vast American landscape.

Pioneers! O Pioneers!

    Come my tan-faced children,
Follow well in order, get your weapons ready,
Have you your pistols? have you your sharp-edged axes?
    Pioneers! O pioneers!

    For we cannot tarry here,   5
We must march my darlings, we must bear the brunt of danger,
We the youthful sinewy races, all the rest on us depend,
    Pioneers! O pioneers!

    O you youths, Western youths,
So impatient, full of action, full of manly pride and friendship,   10
Plain I see you Western youths, see you tramping with the foremost,
    Pioneers! O pioneers!

    Have the elder races halted?
Do they droop and end their lesson, wearied over there beyond the seas?
We take up the task eternal, and the burden and the lesson,   15
    Pioneers! O pioneers!

    All the past we leave behind,
We debouch upon a newer mightier world, varied world,
Fresh and strong the world we seize, world of labor and the march,
    Pioneers! O pioneers!   20

    We detachments steady throwing,
Down the edges, through the passes, up the mountains steep,
Conquering, holding, daring, venturing as we go the unknown ways,
    Pioneers! O pioneers!

    We primeval forests felling,   25
We the rivers stemming, vexing we and piercing deep the mines within,
We the surface broad surveying, we the virgin soil upheaving,
    Pioneers! O pioneers!

    Colorado men are we,
From the peaks gigantic, from the great sierras and the high plateaus,   30
From the mine and from the gully, from the hunting trail we come,
    Pioneers! O pioneers!

From Nebraska, from Arkansas,
Central inland race are we, from Missouri, with the continental blood
    intervEined,
All the hands of comrades clasping, all the Southern, all the Northern,   35
    Pioneers! O pioneers!

O resistless restless race!
O beloved race in all! O my breast aches with tender love for all!
O I mourn and yet exult, I am rapt with love for all,
    Pioneers! O pioneers!   40

Raise the mighty mother mistress,
Waving high the delicate mistress, over all the starry mistress, (bend your heads all,)
Raise the fanged and warlike mistress, stern, impassive, weaponed mistress,
    Pioneers! O pioneers!

See my children, resolute children,   45
By those swarms upon our rear we must never yield or falter,
Ages back in ghostly millions frowning there behind us urging,
    Pioneers! O pioneers!

On and on the compact ranks,
With accessions ever waiting, with the places of the dead quickly filled,   50
Through the battle, through defeat, moving yet and never stopping,
    Pioneers! O pioneers!

O to die advancing on!
Are there some of us to droop and die? has the hour come?
Then upon the march we fittest die, soon and sure the gap is filled,   55
    Pioneers! O pioneers!

All the pulses of the world,
Falling in they beat for us, with the Western movement beat,
Holding single or together, steady moving to the front, all for us,
    Pioneers! O pioneers!   60

Life's involved and varied pageants,
All the forms and shows, all the workmen at their work,
All the seamen and the landsmen, all the masters with their slaves,
    Pioneers! O pioneers!

All the hapless silent lovers,   65
All the prisoners in the prisons, all the righteous and the wicked,
All the joyous, all the sorrowing, all the living, all the dying,
    Pioneers! O pioneers!

I too with my soul and body,
We, a curious trio, picking, wandering on our way,   70
Through these shores amid the shadows, with the apparitions pressing,
    Pioneers! O pioneers!

Lo, the darting bowling orb!
Lo, the brother orbs around, all the clustering suns and planets,
All the dazzling days, all the mystic nights with dreams,   75
    Pioneers! O pioneers!

These are of us, they are with us,
All for primal needed work, while the followers there in embryo wait behind,
We today's procession heading, we the route for travel clearing,
    Pioneers! O pioneers!   80

O you daughters of the West!
O you young and elder daughters! O you mothers and you wives!
Never must you be divided, in our ranks you move united,
    Pioneers! O pioneers!

Minstrels latent on the prairies!   85
(Shrouded bards of other lands, you may rest, you have done your work,)
Soon I hear you coming warbling, soon you rise and tramp amid us,
    Pioneers! O pioneers!

Not for delectations sweet,
Not the cushion and the slipper, not the peaceful and the studious,   90
Not the riches safe and palling, not for us the tame enjoyment,
    Pioneers! O pioneers!

Do the feasters gluttonous feast?
Do the corpulent sleepers sleep? have they locked and bolted doors?
Still be ours the diet hard, and the blanket on the ground,   95
    Pioneers! O pioneers!

Has the night descended?
Was the road of late so toilsome? did we stop discouraged nodding on our way?
Yet a passing hour I yield you in your tracks to pause oblivious,
    Pioneers! O pioneers!   100

Till with sound of trumpet,
Far, far off the daybreak call—hark! how loud and clear I hear it wind,
Swift! to the head of the army!—swift! spring to your places,
    Pioneers! O pioneers!

Song of the Redwood Tree

I

A California song,
A prophecy and indirection, a thought impalpable to breathe as air,
A chorus of dryads, fading, departing, or hamadryads departing,

A murmuring, fateful, giant voice, out of the earth and sky,
Voice of a mighty dying tree in the redwood forest dense.

Farewell my brethren,
Farewell O earth and sky, farewell ye neighboring waters,
My time has ended, my term has come.

Along the northern coast,
Just back from the rock-bound shore and the caves,
In the saline air from the sea in the Mendocino country,
With the surge for base and accompaniment low and hoarse,
With crackling blows of axes sounding musically driven by strong arms,
Riven deep by the sharp tongues of the axes, there in the redwood forest
    dense,
I heard the mighty tree its death-chant chanting.

The choppers heard not, the camp shanties echoed not,
The quick-eared teamsters and chain and jack-screw men heard not,
As the wood spirits came from their haunts of a thousand years to join
    the refrain,
But in my soul I plainly heard.
Murmuring out of its myriad leaves,
Down from its lofty top rising two hundred feet high,
Out of its stalwart trunk and limbs, out of its foot-thick bark,
That chant of the seasons and time, chant not of the past only but the
    future.

You untold life of me,
And all you venerable and innocent joys,
Perennial hardy life of me with joys 'mid rain and many a summer sun,
And the white snows and night and the wild winds;
O the great patient rugged joys, my soul's strong joys unrecked by man,
(For know I bear the soul befitting me, I too have consciousness, identity,
And all the rocks and mountains have, and all the earth,)
Joys of the life befitting me and brothers mine,
Our time, our term has come.

Nor yield we mournfully majestic brothers,
We who have grandly filled our time;
With Nature's calm content, with tacit huge delight,
We welcome what we wrought for through the past,
And leave the field for them.
For them predicted long,
For a superber race, they too to grandly fill their time,
For them we abdicate, in them ourselves ye forest kings!
In them these skies and airs, these mountain peaks, Shasta, Nevadas,
These huge precipitous cliffs, this amplitude, these valleys, far Yosemite,
To be in them absorbed, assimilated.

Then to a loftier strain,
Still prouder, more ecstatic rose the chant,   45
As if the heirs, the deities of the West,
Joining with master tongue bore part.

Not wan from Asia's fetiches,
Nor red from Europe's old dynastic slaughter-house,
(Area of murder plots of thrones, with scent left yet of wars and scaffolds
*   everywhere,)*   50
But come from Nature's long and harmless throes, peacefully builded thence,
These virgin lands, lands of the Western shore,
To the new culminating man, to you, the empire new,
You promised long, we pledge, we dedicate.

You occult deep volitions,   55
You average spiritual manhood, purpose of all, poised on yourself, giving not
*   taking law,*
You womanhood divine, mistress and source of all, whence life and love and
*   aught that comes from life and love,*
You unseen moral essence of all the vast materials of America, (age upon age
*   working in death the same as life,)*
You that, sometimes known, oftener unknown, really shape and mold the New
*   World, adjusting it to Time and Space,*
You hidden national will lying in your abysms, concealed but ever alert,   60
You past and present purposes tenaciously pursued, maybe unconscious of
*   yourselves,*
Unswerved by all the passing errors, perturbations of the surface;
You vital, universal, deathless germs, beneath all creeds, arts, statutes,
*   literatures,*
Here build your homes for good, establish here, these areas entire, lands of the
*   Western shore,*
We pledge, we dedicate to you.   65

For man of you, your characteristic race,
Here may be hardy, sweet, gigantic grow, here tower proportionate to Nature,
Here climb the vast pure spaces unconfined, unchecked by wall or roof,
Here laugh with storm or sun, here joy, here patiently inure,
Here heed himself, unfold himself, (not others' formulas heed,) here fill his time,   70
To duly fall, to aid, unrecked at last,
To disappear, to serve.

Thus on the northern coast,
In the echo of teamsters' calls and the clinking chains, and the music of
    choppers' axes,
The falling trunk and limbs, the crash, the muffled shriek, the groan,   75
Such words combined from the redwood tree, as of voices ecstatic,
    ancient and rustling,

The century-lasting, unseen dryads, singing, withdrawing,
All their recesses of forests and mountains leaving,
From the Cascade range to the Wasatch, or Idaho far, or Utah,
To the deities of the modern henceforth yielding,   80
The chorus and indications, the vistas of coming humanity, the
    settlements, features all,
In the Mendocino woods I caught.

2

The flashing and golden pageant of California,
The sudden and gorgeous drama, the sunny and ample lands,
The long and varied stretch from Puget sound to Colorado south,   85
Lands bathed in sweeter, rarer, healthier air, valleys and mountain cliffs,
The fields of Nature long prepared and fallow, the silent, cyclic chemistry,
The slow and steady ages plodding, the unoccupied surface ripening, the
    rich ores forming beneath;
At last the New arriving, assuming, taking possession,
A swarming and busy race settling and organizing everywhere,   90
Ships coming in from the whole round world, and going out to the
    whole world,
To India and China and Australia and the thousand island paradises of
    the Pacific,
Populous cities, the latest inventions, the steamers on the rivers, the
    railroads, with many a thrifty farm, with machinery,
And wood and wheat and the grape, and diggings of yellow gold.   95

3

But more in you than these, lands of the Western shore,
(These but the means, the implements, the standing-ground,)
I see in you, certain to come, the promise of thousands of years, till now
    deferred,
Promised to be fulfilled, our common kind, the race.

The new society at last, proportionate to Nature,   100
In man of you, more than your mountain peaks or stalwart trees imperial,
In woman more, far more, than all your gold or vines, or even vital air.

Fresh come, to a new world indeed, yet long prepared,
I see the genius of the modern, child of the real and ideal,
Clearing the ground for broad humanity, the true America, heir of the
    past so grand,   105
To build a grander future.

The Dalliance of the Eagles

Skirting the river road, (my forenoon walk, my rest,)
Skyward in air a sudden muffled sound, the dalliance of the eagles,
The rushing amorous contact high in space together,
The clinching interlocking claws, a living, fierce, gyrating wheel,
Four beating wings, two beaks, a swirling mass tight grappling,   5
In tumbling turning clustering loops, straight downward falling,
Till o'er the river poised, the twain yet one, a moment's lull,
A motionless still balance in the air, then parting, talons loosing,
Upward again on slow-firm pinions slanting, their separate diverse flight,
She hers, he his, pursuing.   10

Herman Melville (1819–1891)

*Born and raised in New York City, Herman Melville spent his early childhood in pros-
perous circumstances. However, his father's dry-goods business failed, and when he suddenly died, the family was left virtually penniless and dependent on the charity of relatives. Melville spent his teenage years in poverty; he dropped out of school at age twelve to
work at various odd jobs: a clerk in a bank, laborer on a farm, clerk in his brother's fur-
cap store. At the age of twenty, he signed on for a voyage to Liverpool and back, and
then, in January 1841, at age twenty-one, he embarked on the whaler* Acushnet *for an
eighteen-month voyage as a sailor. He rounded Cape Horn and visited Peru, but working conditions were so intolerable that, with a companion, he escaped from the ship in the
Marquesas Islands. The two men were captured by the Typees, an indigenous people
whose alleged cannibalism did not prevent them from treating their American captives
with great friendship and hospitality. After a month on the island, Melville was rescued
by an Australian whaler and put ashore at Tahiti. He greatly enjoyed the climate of the
South Pacific and spent two years island-hopping, getting as far as the remote Galapagos
Islands, previously visited, in 1835, by Charles Darwin on the voyage of the* Beagle.
*Melville's perception of these islands was in stark contrast to that of Darwin; as he subse-
quently described them in* The Encantadas, or Enchanted Isles *(1854), they are desolate "heaps of cinders," inhabited only by reptiles, castaways, and eccentrics. Yet the Galapagos tortoises that fascinated Darwin also kindle Melville's imagination, as he ponders
the self-sufficiency of these strange creatures, lurking in "that impregnable armor of
their living mail."*

*After spending some time in Hawaii, Melville shipped home from Honolulu on a
U.S. naval vessel and was discharged in Boston in 1844. From his years of seafaring ad-
venture, he wrote his most popular books:* Typee: A Peep at Polynesian Life *(1846);*
Omoo: A Narrative of Adventures in the South Seas *(1847);* Mardi and a Voyage
Thither *(1849);* White-Jacket; or, the World in a Man-of-War *(1850); and his
greatest work,* Moby-Dick; or, The Whale *(1851). Of these books, only* Typee *was
an unqualified popular success, entrancing readers with its idyllic depiction of island life.
Melville's readers grew impatient with his metaphysical digressions in later works, espe-*

cially in Mardi; Moby-Dick *was greeted by uniformly negative reviews. His later works, including the satirical novels* Pierre; or, the Ambiguities *(1852) and* The Confidence-Man *(1857), sold poorly and were virtually unnoticed by contemporary reviewers. Married in 1847, Melville lived most of his life in poverty and died in obscurity. Only in the twentieth century has his work received the thoughtful attention that it deserves.*

From The Encantadas, or Enchanted Isles

Sketch First. The Isles at Large

— That may not be, said then the ferryman,
Least we unweeting hap to be fordonne;
For those same islands seeming now and than,
Are not firme land, nor any certein wonne,
But stragling plots which to and fro do ronne
In the wide waters; therefore are they hight
The Wandering Islands; therefore do them shonne;
For they have oft drawne many a wand'ring wight
Into most deadly daunger and distressed plight;
For whosoever once hath fastened
His foot thereon may never it secure
But wandreth evermore uncertein and unsure.

.   .   .   .

Darke, dolefull, dreary, like a greedy grave,
That still for carrion carcasses doth crave;
On top whereof ay dwelt the ghastly owl,
Shrieking his balefull note, which ever drave
Far from that haunt all other cheerful fowl,
And all about it wand'ring ghosts did wayle and howl.[1]

Take five-and-twenty heaps of cinders dumped here and there in an outside city lot; imagine some of them magnified into mountains, and the vacant lot the sea; and you will have a fit idea of the general aspect of the Encantadas, or Enchanted Isles. A group rather of extinct volcanoes than of isles; looking much as the world at large might, after a penal conflagration.

It is to be doubted whether any spot of earth can, in desolateness, furnish a parallel to this group. Abandoned cemeteries of long ago, old cities by piecemeal tumbling to their ruin, these are melancholy enough; but, like all else which has but once been associated with humanity, they still awaken in us some thoughts of sympathy, however sad. Hence, even the Dead Sea, along with whatever other emotions it may at times inspire, does not fail to touch in the pilgrim some of his less unpleasurable feelings.

---

[1] From Edmund Spenser's *The Faerie Queene* 2.12.11 and the concluding lines of stanza 12; also from 1.9.33.

And as for solitariness; the great forests of the north, the expanses of unnavigated waters, the Greenland ice-fields, are the profoundest of solitudes to a human observer; still the magic of their changeable tides and seasons mitigates their terror; because, though unvisited by men, those forests are visited by the May; the remotest seas reflect familiar stars even as Lake Erie does; and in the clear air of a fine Polar day, the irradiated, azure ice shows beautifully as malachite.

But the special curse, as one may call it, of the Encantadas, that which exalts them in desolation above Idumea[2] and the Pole, is, that to them change never comes; neither the change of seasons nor of sorrows. Cut by the Equator, they know not autumn, and they know not spring; while already reduced to the lees of fire, ruin itself can work little more upon them. The showers refresh the deserts; but in these isles, rain never falls. Like split Syrian gourds left withering in the sun, they are cracked by an everlasting drought beneath a torrid sky. "Have mercy upon me," the wailing spirit of the Encantadas seems to cry, "and send Lazarus that he may dip the tip of his finger in water and cool my tongue, for I am tormented in this flame."[3]

Another feature in these isles is their emphatic uninhabitableness. It is deemed a fit type of all-forsaken overthrow, that the jackal should den in the wastes of weedy Babylon; but the Encantadas refuse to harbor even the outcasts of the beasts. Man and wolf alike disown them. Little but reptile life is here found: tortoises, lizards, immense spiders, snakes, and that strangest anomaly of outlandish nature, the *aguano*.[4] No voice, no low, no howl is heard; the chief sound of life here is a hiss.

On most of the isles where vegetation is found at all, it is more ungrateful than the blankness of Aracama.[5] Tangled thickets of wiry bushes, without fruit and without a name, springing up among deep fissures of calcined rock, and treacherously masking them; or a parched growth of distorted cactus trees.

In many places the coast is rock-bound, or, more properly, clinker-bound; tumbled masses of blackish or greenish stuff like the dross of an iron-furnace, forming dark clefts and caves here and there, into which a ceaseless sea pours a fury of foam; overhanging them with a swirl of gray, haggard mist, amidst which sail screaming flights of unearthly birds heightening the dismal din. However calm the sea without, there is no rest for these swells and those rocks; they lash and are lashed, even when the outer ocean is most at peace with itself. On the oppressive, clouded days, such as are peculiar to this part of the watery Equator, the dark, vitrified masses, many of which raise themselves among white whirlpools and breakers in detached and perilous places off the shore, present a most Plutonian[6] sight. In no world but a fallen one could such lands exist.

[2] Wasteland near the Dead Sea, where the Israelites spent a part of their exodus from Egypt, according to Hebrew Scripture.

[3] Allusion to Luke 16.24 and the story of Dives and Lazarus.

[4] A lizard of the region that can grow to six feet in length.

[5] Desert in South America.

[6] Hellish. Pluto was the Roman name for the ancient god of the underworld.

Those parts of the strand free from the marks of fire, stretch away in wide level beaches of multitudinous dead shells, with here and there decayed bits of sugar-cane, bamboos, and cocoanuts, washed upon this other and darker world from the charming palm isles to the westward and southward; all the way from Paradise to Tartarus;[7] while mixed with the relics of distant beauty you will sometimes see fragments of charred wood and moldering ribs of wrecks. Neither will any one be surprised at meeting these last, after observing the conflicting currents which eddy throughout nearly all the wide channels of the entire group. The capriciousness of the tides of air sympathizes with those of the sea. Nowhere is the wind so light, baffling, and every way unreliable, and so given to perplexing calms, as at the Encantadas. Nigh a month has been spent by a ship going from one isle to another, though but ninety miles between; for owing to the force of the current, the boats employed to tow barely suffice to keep the craft from sweeping upon the cliffs, but do nothing towards accelerating her voyage. Sometimes it is impossible for a vessel from afar to fetch up with the group itself, unless large allowances for prospective lee-way have been made ere its coming in sight. And yet, at other times, there is a mysterious indraft, which irresistibly draws a passing vessel among the isles, though not bound to them.

True, at one period, as to some extent at the present day, large fleets of whalemen cruised for spermaceti[8] upon what some seamen call the Enchanted Ground. But this, as in due place will be described, was off the great outer isle of Albemarle, away from the intricacies of the smaller isles, where there is plenty of sea-room; and hence, to that vicinity, the above remarks do not altogether apply; though even there the current runs at times with singular force, shifting, too, with as singular a caprice.

Indeed, there are seasons when currents quite unaccountable prevail for a great distance round about the total group, and are so strong and irregular as to change a vessel's course against the helm, though sailing at the rate of four or five miles the hour. The difference in the reckonings of navigators, produced by these causes, along with the light and variable winds, long nourished a persuasion, that there existed two distinct clusters of isles in the parallel of the Encantadas, about a hundred leagues apart. Such was the idea of their earlier visitors, the Buccaneers; and as late as 1750, the charts of that part of the Pacific accorded with the strange delusion. And this apparent fleetingness and unreality of the locality of the isles was most probably one reason for the Spaniards calling them the Encantada, or Enchanted Group.

But not uninfluenced by their character, as they now confessedly exist, the modern voyager will be inclined to fancy that the bestowal of this name might have in part originated in that air of spell-bound desertness which so significantly invests the isles. Nothing can better suggest the aspect of once living things malignly crumbled from ruddiness into ashes. Apples of Sodom,[9] after touching, seem these isles.

---

[7] The mythological depths of the classical underworld, reserved for the most evil of the dead.

[8] Sperm whales.

[9] According to classical authors, these were visually attractive but turned to ash and smoke when taken off the tree.

However wavering their place may seem by reason of the currents, they themselves, at least to one upon the shore, appear invariably the same: fixed, cast, glued into the very body of cadaverous death.

Nor would the appellation, enchanted, seem misapplied in still another sense. For concerning the peculiar reptile inhabitant of these wilds—whose presence gives the group its second Spanish name, Gallipagos—concerning the tortoises found here, most mariners have long cherished a superstition, not more frightful than grotesque. They earnestly believe that all wicked sea-officers, more especially commodores and captains, are at death (and, in some cases, before death) transformed into tortoises; thenceforth dwelling upon these hot aridities, sole solitary lords of Asphaltum.[10]

Doubtless, so quaintly dolorous a thought was originally inspired by the woe-begone landscape itself; but more particularly, perhaps, by the tortoises. For, apart from their strictly physical features, there is something strangely self-condemned in the appearance of these creatures. Lasting sorrow and penal hopelessness are in no animal form so suppliantly expressed as in theirs; while the thought of their wonderful longevity does not fail to enhance the impression.

Nor even at the risk of meriting the charge of absurdly believing in enchantments, can I restrain the admission that sometimes, even now, when leaving the crowded city to wander out July and August among the Adirondack Mountains, far from the influences of towns and proportionally nigh to the mysterious ones of nature; when at such times I sit me down in the mossy head of some deep-wooded gorge, surrounded by prostrate trunks of blasted pines and recall, as in a dream, my other and far-distant rovings in the baked heart of the charmed isles; and remember the sudden glimpses of dusky shells, and long languid necks protruded from the leafless thickets; and again have beheld the vitreous inland rocks worn down and grooved into deep ruts by ages and ages of the slow draggings of tortoises in quest of pools of scanty water; I can hardly resist the feeling that in my time I have indeed slept upon evilly enchanted ground.

Nay, such is the vividness of my memory, or the magic of my fancy, that I know not whether I am not the occasional victim of optical delusion concerning the Gallipagos. For, often in scenes of social merriment, and especially at revels held by candle-light in old-fashioned mansions, so that shadows are thrown into the further recesses of an angular and spacious room, making them put on a look of haunted undergrowth of lonely woods, I have drawn the attention of my comrades by my fixed gaze and sudden change of air, as I have seemed to see, slowly emerging from those imagined solitudes, and heavily crawling along the floor, the ghost of a gigantic tortoise, with "Memento * * * * *"[11] burning in live letters upon his back.

[10] Asphalt, a stone which melts when heated.

[11] I.e., *memento mori*, Latin for "remember that you must die"; any warning of death.

Sketch Second. Two Sides to a Tortoise

Most ugly shapes and horrible aspects,
Such as Dame Nature selfe mote feare to see,
Or shame, that ever should so fowle defects
From her most cunning hand escaped bee;
All dreadfull pourtraicts of deformitee.
Ne wonder if these do a man appall;
For all that here at home we dreadfull hold
Be but as bugs to fearen babes withall
Compared to the creatures in these isles' entrall

.   .   .   .

Fear naught, then said the palmer, well avized,
For these same monsters are not there indeed,
But are into these fearful shapes disguized.

.   .   .   .

And lifting up his vertuous staffe on high,
Then all that dreadful armie fast gan flye
Into great Zethy's bosom, where they hidden lye.[1]

In view of the description given, may one be gay upon the Encantadas? Yes: that is, find one the gayety, and he will be gay. And, indeed, sackcloth and ashes as they are, the isles are not perhaps unmitigated gloom. For while no spectator can deny their claims to a most solemn and superstitious consideration, no more than my firmest resolutions can decline to behold the spectre-tortoise when emerging from its shadowy recess; yet even the tortoise, dark and melancholy as it is up the back, still possesses a bright side; its calipee or breast-plate being sometimes of a faint yellowish or golden tinge. Moreover, every one knows that tortoises as well as turtles are of such a make, that if you but put them on their backs you thereby expose their bright sides without the possibility of their recovering themselves, and turning into view the other. But after you have done this, and because you have done this, you should not swear that the tortoise has no dark side. Enjoy the bright, keep it turned up perpetually if you can, but be honest, and don't deny the black. Neither should he, who cannot turn the tortoise from its natural position so as to hide the darker and expose his livelier aspect, like a great October pumpkin in the sun, for that cause declare the creature to be one total inky blot. The tortoise is both black and bright. But let us to particulars.

Some months before my first stepping ashore upon the group, my ship was cruising in its close vicinity. One noon we found ourselves off the South Head of

---

[1] From Edmund Spenser's *The Faerie Queene* 2.12.23 and 25 and 26.

Albemarle, and not very far from the land. Partly by way of freak, and partly by way of spying out so strange a country, a boat's crew was sent ashore, with orders to see all they could, and besides, bring back whatever tortoises they could conveniently transport.

It was after sunset, when the adventurers returned. I looked down over the ship's high side as if looking down over the curb of a well, and dimly saw the damp boat deep in the sea with some unwonted weight. Ropes were dropt over, and presently three huge antediluvian-looking tortoises, after much straining, were landed on deck. They seemed hardly of the seed of earth. We had been broad upon the waters for five long months, a period amply sufficient to make all things of the land wear a fabulous hue to the dreamy mind. Had three Spanish custom-house officers boarded us then, it is not unlikely that I should have curiously stared at them, felt of them, and stroked them much as savages serve civilized guests. But instead of three custom-house officers, behold these really wondrous tortoises—none of your schoolboy mud turtles—but black as widower's weeds, heavy as chests of plate, with vast shells medallioned and orbed like shields, and dented and blistered like shields that have breasted a battle, shaggy, too, here and there, with dark green moss, and slimy with the spray of the sea. These mystic creatures, suddenly translated by night from unutterable solitudes to our peopled deck, affected me in a manner not easy to unfold. They seemed newly crawled forth from beneath the foundations of the world. Yea, they seemed the identical tortoises whereon the Hindoo plants this total sphere. With a lantern I inspected them more closely. Such worshipful venerableness of aspect! Such furry greenness mantling the rude peelings and healing the fissures of their shattered shells. I no more saw three tortoises. They expanded—became transfigured. I seemed to see three Roman Coliseums in magnificent decay.

Ye oldest inhabitants of this, or any other isle, said I, pray, give me the freedom of your three-walled towns.

The great feeling inspired by these creatures was that of age:—dateless, indefinite endurance. And in fact that any other creature can live and breathe as long as the tortoise of the Encantadas, I will not readily believe. Not to hint of their known capacity of sustaining life, while going without food for an entire year, consider that impregnable armor of their living mail. What other bodily being possesses such a citadel wherein to resist the assaults of Time?

As, lantern in hand, I scraped among the moss and beheld the ancient scars of bruises received in many a sullen fall among the marly mountains of the isle— scars strangely widened, swollen, half obliterate, and yet distorted like those sometimes found in the bark of very hoary trees, I seemed an antiquary of a geologist, studying the bird-tracks and ciphers upon the exhumed slates trod by incredible creatures whose very ghosts are now defunct.

As I lay in my hammock that night, overhead I heard the slow weary draggings of the three ponderous strangers along the encumbered deck. Their stupidity or their resolution was so great, that they never went aside for any impediment. One ceased his movements altogether just before the mid-watch. At sunrise I found him butted like a battering-ram against the immovable foot of the foremast, and still striving, tooth and nail, to force the impossible passage.

That these tortoises are the victims of a penal, or malignant, or perhaps a down-right diabolical enchanter, seems in nothing more likely than in that strange in-fatuation of hopeless toil which so often possesses them. I have known them in their journeyings ram themselves heroically against rocks, and long abide there, nudging, wriggling, wedging, in order to displace them, and so hold on their in-flexible path. Their crowning curse is their drudging impulse to straightforward-ness in a belittered world.

Meeting with no such hinderance as their companion did, the other tortoises merely fell foul of small stumbling-blocks—buckets, blocks, and coils of rig-ging—and at times in the act of crawling over them would slip with an astound-ing rattle to the deck. Listening to these draggings and concussions, I thought me of the haunt from which they came; an isle full of metallic ravines and gulches, sunk bottomlessly into the hearts of splintered mountains, and covered for many miles with inextricable thickets. I then pictured these three straightfor-ward monsters, century after century, writhing through the shades, grim as blacksmiths; crawling so slowly and ponderously, that not only did toad-stools and all fungus things grow beneath their feet, but a sooty moss sprouted upon their backs. With them I lost myself in volcanic mazes; brushed away endless boughs of rotting thickets; till finally in a dream I found myself sitting cross-legged upon the foremost, a Brahmin similarly mounted upon either side, form-ing a tripod of foreheads which upheld the universal cope.

Such was the wild nightmare begot by my first impression of the Encantadas tortoise. But next evening, strange to say, I sat down with my shipmates, and made a merry repast from tortoise steaks and tortoise stews; and supper over, out knife, and helped convert the three mighty concave shells into three fanciful soup-tureens, and polished the three flat yellowish calipees into three gorgeous salvers.

⧉ *Emily Dickinson* (*1830–1886*)

Although in her lifetime Emily Dickinson published only a handful of the nearly 1,800 poems she wrote, she is nevertheless recognized as one of the greatest American authors of the nineteenth century. Dickinson's poetic style is at once unmistakable but difficult to re-produce; terse, emphatic, elliptical, her elegantly written lines are as intellectually chal-lenging as they are emotionally breathtaking. Her poems are intensely visual yet simul-taneously enigmatic. The author of such unique work, known to a wider public only after her death, cannot help but inspire curiosity, and such curiosity is further provoked by the mysterious uneventfulness of her life. Dickinson is closely associated with the town of Amherst, Massachusetts. She was born there and, but for a few trips on the East Coast, remained there her entire life. Her family was well-to-do and encouraged her artistic and educational pursuits. She studied one year at the Mount Holyoke Female Seminary (later Mount Holyoke College, one of the first institutions of higher learning available to women), but returned home for what some scholars presume was a dislike of the religious climate or, as others speculate, simply because she wished to be back with her family. This incident, like many in Dickinson's life, leaves readers to ponder over her motivations. Although many have turned to her poetry to explicate her biography, there too the reader is often left with more questions than answers.

Perhaps the most enduring mystery about Dickinson was her choice, during the later part of her life, to remain increasingly reclusive, eventually not even leaving her room. Explanations for her choice range from the psychological (intense agoraphobia) to the artistic (she was so committed to her art that she did not want the least interference to hinder her dedication) to the political (she was protesting the oppression of women by refusing to participate in patriarchal society). Whatever her reasons, such biographical details are perhaps irrelevant to an appreciation of the intensity in all of Dickinson's poetry, and in particular, her poetry about nature. Like Emily Brontë, whom she read and admired, Dickinson refused any "ladylike" sentimentalization of nature. In her vision of the natural world, she defied conventions of all kind—in style and in subject matter. Instead of celebrating the signs of springtime, for example, the speaker in one of her poems dreads it. Moreover, Dickinson understood that decay and death were essential parts of the natural world and frequently made them the focus of her poetry. Her poems are equally striking because they present an image of the natural world that often seems to stand apart from human morality, religion, or psychology, thus marking Dickinson's important departure from the work of Neoclassical or Romantic poets. The world of nature that she writes about is often one in which birds, flowers, or butterflies simply are, without any "higher" philosophical justification. The influence of Dickinson's vision on twentieth-century poetry is incalculable. Just as significantly, Dickinson's work marks a turning point in the tradition of women writing about the environment.

285

The Robin's my Criterion for Tune—
Because I grow—where Robins do—
But, were I Cuckoo born—
I'd swear by him—
The ode familiar—rules the Noon—   5
The Buttercup's, my Whim for Bloom—
Because, we're Orchard sprung—
But, were I Britain born,
I'd Daisies spurn—
None but the Nut—October fit—   10
Because, through dropping it,
The Seasons flit—I'm taught—
Without the Snow's Tableau
Winter, were lie—to me—
Because I see—New Englandly—   15
The Queen, discerns like me—
Provincially—

314

Nature—sometimes sears a Sapling—
Sometimes—scalps a Tree—
Her Green People recollect it
When they do not die—

Fainter Leaves—to Further Seasons—   5
Dumbly testify—
We—who have the Souls—
Die oftener—Not so vitally—

328

A Bird came down the Walk—
He did not know I saw—
He bit an Angleworm in halves
And ate the fellow, raw,

And then he drank a Dew   5
From a convenient Grass—
And then hopped sidewise to the Wall
To let a Beetle pass—

He glanced with rapid eyes
That hurried all around—   10
They looked like frightened Beads, I thought—
He stirred his Velvet Head

Like one in danger, Cautious,
I offered him a Crumb
And he unrolled his feathers   15
And rowed him softer home—

Than Oars divide the Ocean,
Too silver for a seam—
Or Butterflies, off Banks of Noon
Leap, plashless as they swim.   20

333

The Grass so little has to do—
A Sphere of simple Green—
With only Butterflies to brood
And Bees to entertain—

And stir all day to pretty Tunes   5
The Breezes fetch along—
And hold the Sunshine in its lap
And bow to everything—

And thread the Dews, all night, like Pearls—
And make itself so fine   10
A Duchess were too common
For such a noticing—

And even when it dies—to pass
In Odors so divine—
Like Lowly spices, lain to sleep—   15
Or Spikenards, perishing—

And then, in Sovereign Barns to dwell—
And dream the Days away,
The Grass so little has to do
I wish I were a Hay—   20

348

I dreaded that first Robin, so,
But He is mastered, now,
I'm some accustomed to Him grown,
He hurts a little, though—

I thought if I could only live   5
Till that first Shout got by—
Not all Pianos in the Woods
Had power to mangle me—

I dared not meet the Daffodils—
For fear their Yellow Gown   10
Would pierce me with a fashion
So foreign to my own—

I wished the Grass would hurry—
So—when 'twas time to see—
He'd be too tall, the tallest one   15
Could stretch—to look at me—

I could not bear the Bees should come,
I wished they'd stay away
In those dim countries where they go,
What word had they, for me?   20

They're here, though; not a creature failed—
No Blossom stayed away

In gentle deference to me—
The Queen of Calvary[1]—

Each one salutes me, as he goes,   25
And I, my childish Plumes,
Lift, in bereaved acknowledgment
Of their unthinking Drums—

392

Through the Dark Sod—as Education—
The Lily passes sure—
Feels her white foot—no trepidation—
Her faith—no fear—

Afterward—in the Meadow—   5
Swinging her Beryl Bell—
The Mold-life—all forgotten—now—
In Ecstasy—and Dell—

520

I started Early—Took my Dog—
And visited the Sea—
The Mermaids in the Basement
Came out to look at me—

And Frigates—in the Upper Floor   5
Extended Hempen Hands—
Presuming Me to be a Mouse—
Aground—upon the Sands—

But no Man moved Me—till the Tide
Went past my simple Shoe—   10
And past my Apron—and my Belt
And past my Bodice—too—

And made as He would eat me up—
As wholly as a Dew
Upon a Dandelion's Sleeve—   15
And then—I started—too—

And He—He followed—close behind—
I felt His Silver Heel

---

[1] Calvary is the name of the hill near Jerusalem where Christ was crucified; perhaps a reference to Christ's mother, Mary.

Upon my Ankle—Then my Shoes
Would overflow with Pearl—   20

Until We met the Solid Town—
No One He seemed to know—
And bowing—with a Mighty look—
At me—The Sea withdrew—

585

I like to see it lap the Miles—
And lick the Valleys up—
And stop to feed itself at Tanks—
And then—prodigious step

Around a Pile of Mountains—   5
And supercilious peer
In Shanties—by the sides of Roads—
And then a Quarry pare

To fit its Ribs
And crawl between   10
Complaining all the while
In horrid—hooting stanza—
Then chase itself down Hill—

And neigh like Boanerges[2]—
Then—punctual as a Star   15
Stop—docile and omnipotent
At its own stable door—

668

"Nature" is what we see—
The Hill—the Afternoon—
Squirrel—Eclipse—the Bumble bee—
Nay—Nature is Heaven—
Nature is what we hear—   5
The Bobolink[3]—the Sea—
Thunder—the Cricket—
Nay—Nature is Harmony—
Nature is what we know—
Yet have no art to say—   10

[2] From the Greek meaning "sons of thunder"; a loud preacher or speaker.
[3] A migratory songbird.

So impotent Our Wisdom is
To her Simplicity.

742

Four Trees—upon a solitary Acre—
Without Design
Or Order, or Apparent Action—
Maintain—

The Sun—upon a Morning meets them—   5
The Wind—
No nearer Neighbor—have they—
But God—

The Acre gives them—Place—
They—Him—Attention of Passer by—   10
Of Shadow, or of Squirrel, haply—
Or Boy—

What Deed is Theirs unto the General Nature—
What Plan
They severally—retard—or further—   15
Unknown—

790

Nature—the Gentlest Mother is,
Impatient of no Child—
The feeblest—or the waywardest—
Her Admonition mild—

In Forest—and the Hill—   5
By Traveller—be heard—
Restraining Rampant Squirrel—
Or too impetuous Bird—

How fair Her Conversation—
A Summer Afternoon—   10
Her Household—Her Assembly—
And when the Sun go down—

Her Voice among the Aisles
Incite the timid prayer
Of the minutest Cricket—   15
The most unworthy Flower—

When all the Children sleep—
She turns as long away

As will suffice to light Her lamps—
Then bending from the Sky—   20

With infinite Affection—
And infiniter Care—

978

It bloomed and dropt, a Single Noon—
The Flower—distinct and Red—
I, passing, thought another Noon
Another in its stead

Will equal glow, and thought no More   5
But came another Day
To find the Species disappeared—
The Same Locality—

The Sun in place—no other fraud
On Nature's perfect Sum—   10
Had I but lingered Yesterday—
Was my retrieveless blame—

Much Flowers of this and further Zones
Have perished in my Hands
For seeking its Resemblance—   15
But unapproached it stands—

The single Flower of the Earth
That I, in passing by
Unconscious was—Great Nature's Face
Passed infinite by Me—   20

986

A narrow Fellow in the Grass
Occasionally rides—
You may have met Him—did you not
His notice sudden is—

The Grass divides as with a Comb—   5
A spotted shaft is seen—
And then it closes at your feet
And opens further on—

He likes a Boggy Acre
A Floor too cool for Corn—   10

Yet when a Boy, and Barefoot—
I more than once at Noon
Have passed, I thought, a Whip lash
Unbraiding in the Sun
When stooping to secure it   15
It wrinkled, and was gone—

Several of Nature's People
I know, and they know me—
I feel for them a transport
Of cordiality—   20

But never met this Fellow
Attended, or alone
Without a tighter breathing
And Zero at the Bone—

1084

At Half past Three, a single Bird
Unto a silent Sky
Propounded but a single term
Of cautious melody.

At Half past Four, Experiment   5
Had subjugated test
And lo, Her silver Principle
Supplanted all the rest.

At Half past Seven, Element
Nor Implement, be seen—   10
And Place was where the Presence was
Circumference between.

1670

In Winter in my Room
I came upon a Worm—
Pink, lank and warm—
But as he was a worm
And worms presume   5
Not quite with him at home—
Secured him by a string
To something neighboring
And went along.

A Trifle afterward   10
A thing occurred
I'd not believe it if I heard
But state with creeping blood—
A snake with mottles rare
Surveyed my chamber floor   15
In feature as the worm before
But ringed with power—
The very string with which
I tied him—too
When he was mean and new   20
That string was there—

I shrank—"How fair you are"!
Propitiation's claw—
"Afraid," he hissed
"Of me"?   25
"No cordiality"—
He fathomed me—
Then to a Rhythm *Slim*
Secreted in his Form
As Patterns swim   30
Projected him.

That time I flew
Both eyes his way
Lest he pursue
Nor ever ceased to run   35
Till in a distant Town
Towns on from mine
I set me down
This was a dream.

🎜 *Christina Rossetti* (1830–1894)

Christina Rossetti's biography bears some significant similarities to those of Emily Dickinson and Emily Brontë. All three of these Victorian women lived what would appear to be uneventful lives, yet each produced passionate, beautifully crafted, and frequently enigmatic and ambiguous poetry. Rossetti's father was an Italian émigré who left his native country because of his political associations; her mother was of Anglo-Italian heritage. She and her siblings were raised in a bilingual household and were encouraged to study the great works of both the Italian and the English literary and artistic traditions. Like the Brontë family, the Rossetti children engaged in collaborative creative projects while they were growing up, and they all went on to become noted intellectuals and artists. Christina Rossetti's brother, Dante Gabriel Rossetti, a painter, poet, and one of the founders of the Pre-Raphaelite Brotherhood, is perhaps the best known of her family members. The family had planned for her to become a governess, a career which she successfully resisted through her claims to fragile health. While Christina Rossetti never married, she led an active social life, surrounded by many of the leading artists and authors of the Victorian age, including Robert Browning, John Ruskin, and Lewis Carroll, among others. She was also dedicated to serving those less fortunate than herself and was actively involved in several charitable endeavors.

Rossetti first published her poetry privately at the age of seventeen. But it was not until 1862 that her work appeared publicly with Goblin Market, and Other Poems, *followed by* The Prince's Progress, and Other Poems *(1865). Both collections were favorably received and established her reputation as an accomplished author. While the poems are often emotionally expressive, they are also artistically sophisticated. Her vision of the natural world, much like Emily Brontë's, is overlaid with mythical and magical associations, evident in her best-known poem "Goblin Market." Rossetti's association with the Pre-Raphaelites is palpable in the sensuality of her representation of the countryside, a feature which the Pre-Raphaelites inherited from Keats. The sensuality of these poems is in striking contrast with what is known about Rossetti's own religiously grounded self-denial. Recent critics have read poems such as "Goblin Market" as explorations of Rossetti's own struggles with expressing her desires—desires which were inappropriate for Victorian women to articulate. Her strict Anglican beliefs came to dominate her writing in the 1870s, as she produced numerous devotional essays along with poems and stories for children and works of literary criticism. Rossetti continued to write and reissue her works, even despite increasingly poor health, until her death from cancer.*

Goblin Market

Morning and evening
Maids heard the goblins cry:
"Come buy our orchard fruits,
Come buy, come buy:
Apples and quinces,   5
Lemons and oranges,
Plump unpecked cherries,
Melons and raspberries,
Bloom-down-cheeked peaches,
Swart-headed mulberries,   10
Wild free-born cranberries,
Crab apples, dewberries,
Pine-apples, blackberries,
Apricots, strawberries;—
All ripe together   15
In summer weather,—
Morns that pass by,
Fair eves that fly;

Come buy, come buy:
Our grapes fresh from the vine,   20
Pomegranates full and fine,
Dates and sharp bullaces,
Rare pears and greengages,
Damsons and bilberries,
Taste them and try: 25
Currants and gooseberries,
Bright-fire-like barberries,
Figs to fill your mouth,
Citrons from the South,
Sweet to tongue and sound to eye;   30
Come buy, come buy."
Evening by evening
Among the brookside rushes,
Laura bowed her head to hear,
Lizzie veiled her blushes: 35
Crouching close together
In the cooling weather,
With clasping arms and cautioning lips,
With tingling cheeks and finger tips.
"Lie close," Laura said,   40
Pricking up her golden head:
"We must not look at goblin men,
We must not buy their fruits:
Who knows upon what soil they fed
Their hungry thirsty roots?"   45
"Come buy," call the goblins
Hobbling down the glen.
"Oh," cried Lizzie, "Laura, Laura,
You should not peep at goblin men."
Lizzie covered up her eyes,   50
Covered close lest they should look;
Laura reared her glossy head,
And whispered like the restless brook:
"Look, Lizzie, look, Lizzie,
Down the glen tramp little men.   55
One hauls a basket,
One bears a plate,
One lugs a golden dish
Of many pounds' weight.
How fair the vine must grow   60
Whose grapes are so luscious
How warm the wind must blow
Through those fruit bushes."
"No," said Lizzie: "No, no, no;

Their offers should not charm us, 65
Their evil gifts would harm us."
She thrust a dimpled finger
In each ear, shut eyes and ran:
Curious Laura chose to linger
Wondering at each merchant man. 70
One had a cat's face,
One whisked a tail,
One tramped at a rat's pace,
One crawled like a snail,
One like a wombat prowled obtuse and furry, 75
One like a ratel[1] tumbled hurry-skurry.
She heard a voice like voice of doves
Cooing all together:
They sounded kind and full of loves
In the pleasant weather. 80

Laura stretched her gleaming neck
Like a rush-imbedded swan,
Like a lily from the beck,[2]
Like a moonlit poplar branch,
Like a vessel at the launch 85
When its last restraint is gone.

Backwards up the mossy glen
Turned and trooped the goblin men,
With their shrill repeated cry,
"Come buy, come buy." 90
When they reached where Laura was
They stood stock still upon the moss,
Leering at each other,
Brother with queer brother;
Signalling each other, 95
Brother with sly brother.
One set his basket down,
One reared his plate;
One began to weave a crown
Of tendrils, leaves, and rough nuts brown 100
(Men sell not such in any town);
One heaved the golden weight
Of dish and fruit to offer her:
"Come buy, come buy," was still their cry.
Laura stared but did not stir, 105
Longed but had no money.

[1] A badgerlike animal.

[2] Stream or brook.

The whisk-tailed merchant bade her taste
In tones as smooth as honey,
The cat-faced purred,
The rat-paced spoke a word   110
Of welcome, and the snail-paced even was heard;
One parrot-voiced and jolly
Cried "Pretty Goblin" still for "Pretty Polly";
One whistled like a bird.

But sweet-tooth Laura spoke in haste: 115
"Good Folk, I have no coin;
To take were to purloin:
I have no copper in my purse,
I have no silver either,
And all my gold is on the furze   120
That shakes in windy weather
Above the rusty heather."
"You have much gold upon your head,"
They answered all together:
"Buy from us with a golden curl."   125
She clipped a precious golden lock,
She dropped a tear more rare than pearl,
Then sucked their fruit globes fair or red.
Sweeter than honey from the rock,
Stronger than man-rejoicing wine,   130
Clearer than water flowed that juice;
She never tasted such before,
How should it cloy with length of use?
She sucked and sucked and sucked the more
Fruits which that unknown orchard bore;   135
She sucked until her lips were sore;
Then flung the emptied rinds away
But gathered up one kernel stone,
And knew not was it night or day
As she turned home alone.   140

Lizzie met her at the gate
Full of wise upbraidings:
"Dear, you should not stay so late,
Twilight is not good for maidens;
Should not loiter in the glen   145
In the haunts of goblin men.
Do you not remember Jeanie,
How she met them in the moonlight,
Took their gifts both choice and many,
Ate their fruits and wore their flowers   150
Plucked from bowers

Where summer ripens at all hours?
But ever in the noonlight
She pined and pined away;
Sought them by night and day,   155
Found them no more, but dwindled and grew grey;
Then fell with the first snow,
While to this day no grass will grow
Where she lies low:
I planted daisies there a year ago   160
That never blow.
You should not loiter so."
"Nay, hush," said Laura:
"Nay, hush, my sister:
I ate and ate my fill,   165
Yet my mouth waters still:
Tomorrow night I will
Buy more;" and kissed her.
"Have done with sorrow;
I'll bring you plums tomorrow   170
Fresh on their mother twigs,
Cherries worth getting;
You cannot think what figs
My teeth have met in,
What melons icy-cold   175
Piled on a dish of gold
Too huge for me to hold,
What peaches with a velvet nap,
Pellucid grapes without one seed:
Odorous indeed must be the mead   180
Whereon they grow, and pure the wave they drink
With lilies at the brink,
And sugar-sweet their sap."

Golden head by golden head,
Like two pigeons in one nest   185
Folded in each other's wings,
They lay down in their curtained bed:
Like two blossoms on one stem,
Like two flakes of new-fallen snow,
Like two wands of ivory   190
Tipped with gold for awful kings.
Moon and stars gazed in at them,
Wind sang to them lullaby,
Lumbering owls forebore to fly,
Not a bat flapped to and fro   195
Round their nest:

Cheek to cheek and breast to breast
Locked together in one nest.

Early in the morning
When the first cock crowed his warning,   200
Neat like bees, as sweet and busy,
Laura rose with Lizzie:
Fetched in honey, milked the cows,
Aired and set to rights the house,
Kneaded cakes of whitest wheat,   205
Cakes for dainty mouths to eat,
Next churned butter, whipped up cream,
Fed their poultry, sat and sewed;
Talked as modest maidens should:
Lizzie with an open heart,   210
Laura in an absent dream,
One content, one sick in part;
One warbling for the mere bright day's delight,
One longing for the night.

At length slow evening came: 215
They went with pitchers to the reedy brook;
Lizzie most placid in her look,
Laura most like a leaping flame.
They drew the gurgling water from its deep.
Lizzie plucked purple and rich golden flags,   220
Then turning homeward said: "The sunset flushes
Those furthest loftiest crags;
Come, Laura, not another maiden lags.
No wilful squirrel wags,
The beasts and birds are fast asleep."   225
But Laura loitered still among the rushes,
And said the bank was steep.

And said the hour was early still,
The dew not fallen, the wind not chill;
Listening ever, but not catching   230
The customary cry,
"Come buy, come buy,"
With its iterated jingle
Of sugar-baited words:
Not for all her watching   235
Once discerning even one goblin
Racing, whisking, tumbling, hobbling—
Let alone the herds
That used to tramp along the glen,
In groups or single,   240
Of brisk fruit-merchant men.

Till Lizzie urged, "O Laura, come;
I hear the fruit-call, but I dare not look:
You should not loiter longer at this brook:
Come with me home.
The stars rise, the moon bends her arc,   245
Each glow-worm winks her spark,
Let us get home before the night grows dark:
For clouds may gather
Though this is summer weather,   250
Put out the lights and drench us through;
Then if we lost our way what should we do?"

Laura turned cold as stone
To find her sister heard that cry alone,
That goblin cry,   255
"Come buy our fruits, come buy."
Must she then buy no more such dainty fruit?
Must she no more such succous pasture find,
Gone deaf and blind?
Her tree of life drooped from the root: 260
She said not one word in her heart's sore ache:
But peering through the dimness, nought discerning,
Trudged home, her pitcher dripping all the way;
So crept to bed, and lay
Silent till Lizzie slept;   265
Then sat up in a passionate yearning,
And gnashed her teeth for balked desire, and wept
As if her heart would break.

Day after day, night after night,
Laura kept watch in vain   270
In sullen silence of exceeding pain.
She never caught again the goblin cry,
"Come buy, come buy;"—
She never spied the goblin men
Hawking their fruits along the glen: 275
But when the noon waxed bright
Her hair grew thin and grey;
She dwindled, as the fair full moon doth turn
To swift decay and burn
Her fire away.   280

One day remembering her kernel-stone
She set it by a wall that faced the south;
Dewed it with tears, hoped for a root,
Watched for a waxing shoot,
But there came none.   285
It never saw the sun,

It never felt the trickling moisture run:
While with sunk eyes and faded mouth
She dreamed of melons, as a traveller sees
False waves in desert drouth   290
With shade of leaf-crowned trees,
And burns the thirstier in the sandful breeze.

She no more swept the house,
Tended the fowls or cows,
Fetched honey, kneaded cakes of wheat,   295
Brought water from the brook:
But sat down listless in the chimney-nook
And would not eat.

Tender Lizzie could not bear
To watch her sister's cankerous care,   300
Yet not to share.
She night and morning
Caught the goblins' cry:
"Come buy our orchard fruits,
Come buy, come buy:"—   305
Beside the brook, along the glen,
She heard the tramp of goblin men,
The voice and stir
Poor Laura could not hear;
Longed to buy fruit to comfort her,   310
But feared to pay too dear.
She thought of Jeanie in her grave,
Who should have been a bride;
But who for joys brides hope to have
Fell sick and died   315
In her gay prime,
In earliest winter time,
With the first glazing rime,
With the first snow-fall of crisp winter time.

Till Laura dwindling   320
Seemed knocking at Death's door.
Then Lizzie weighed no more
Better and worse;
But put a silver penny in her purse,
Kissed Laura, crossed the heath with clumps of furze   325
At twilight, halted by the brook:
And for the first time in her life
Began to listen and look.

Laughed every goblin
When they spied her peeping: 330

Came towards her hobbling,
Flying, running, leaping,
Puffing and blowing,
Chuckling, clapping, crowing,
Clucking and gobbling,   335
Mopping and mowing,
Full of airs and graces,
Pulling wry faces,
Demure grimaces,
Cat-like and rat-like,   340
Ratel- and wombat-like,
Snail-paced in a hurry,
Parrot-voiced and whistler,
Helter-skelter, hurry-skurry,
Chattering like magpies,   345
Fluttering like pigeons,
Gliding like fishes,—
Hugged her and kissed her:
Squeezed and caressed her:
Stretched up their dishes,   350
Panniers, and plates:
"Look at our apples
Russet and dun,
Bob at our cherries,
Bite at our peaches,   355
Citrons and dates,
Grapes for the asking,
Pears red with basking
Out in the sun,
Plums on their twigs;   360
Pluck them and suck them,—
Pomegranates, figs."

"Good folk," said Lizzie,
Mindful of Jeanie:
"Give me much and many:"   365
Held out her apron,
Tossed them her penny.
"Nay, take a seat with us,
Honour and eat with us,"
They answered grinning: 370
"Our feast is but beginning.
Night yet is early,
Warm and dew-pearly,
Wakeful and starry:
Such fruits as these   375
No man can carry;

Half their bloom would fly,
Half their dew would dry,
Half their flavour would pass by.
Sit down and feast with us,   380
Be welcome guest with us,
Cheer you and rest with us."—
"Thank you," said Lizzie: "But one waits
At home alone for me:
So without further parleying,   385
If you will not sell me any
Of your fruits though much and many,
Give me back my silver penny
I tossed you for a fee."—
They began to scratch their pates,   390
No longer wagging, purring,
But visibly demurring,
Grunting and snarling.
One called her proud,
Cross-grained, uncivil;   395
Their tones waxed loud,
Their looks were evil.
Lashing their tails
They trod and hustled her,
Elbowed and jostled her,   400
Clawed with their nails,
Barking, mewing, hissing, mocking,
Tore her gown and soiled her stocking,
Twitched her hair out by the roots,
Stamped upon her tender feet,   405
Held her hands and squeezed their fruits
Against her mouth to make her eat.

White and golden Lizzie stood,
Like a lily in a flood,—
Like a rock of blue-veined stone   410
Lashed by tides obstreperously,—
Like a beacon left alone
In a hoary roaring sea,
Sending up a golden fire,—
Like a fruit-crowned orange tree   415
White with blossoms honey-sweet
Sore beset by wasp and bee,—
Like a royal virgin town
Topped with gilded dome and spire
Close beleaguered by a fleet   420
Mad to tug her standard down.

One may lead a horse to water,
Twenty cannot make him drink.
Though the goblins cuffed and caught her,
Coaxed and fought her,　　　　　　　　　　　　　　　425
Bullied and besought her,
Scratched her, pinched her black as ink,
Kicked and knocked her,
Mauled and mocked her,
Lizzie uttered not a word;　　　　　　　　　　　　　430
Would not open lip from lip
Lest they should cram a mouthful in:
But laughed in heart to feel the drip
Of juice that syruped all her face,
And lodged in dimples of her chin,　　　　　　　　　435
And streaked her neck which quaked like curd.
At last the evil people,
Worn out by her resistance,
Flung back her penny, kicked their fruit
Along whichever road they took,　　　　　　　　　　440
Not leaving root or stone or shoot;
Some writhed into the ground,
Some dived into the brook
With ring and ripple,
Some scudded on the gale without a sound,　　　445
Some vanished in the distance.

In a smart, ache, tingle,
Lizzie went her way;
Knew not was it night or day;
Sprang up the bank, tore through the furze,　　　450
Threaded copse and dingle,
And heard her penny jingle
Bouncing in her purse, —
Its bounce was music to her ear.
She ran and ran　　　　　　　　　　　　　　　455
As if she feared some goblin man
Dogged her with gibe or curse
Or something worse:
But not one goblin skurried after,
Nor was she pricked by fear;　　　　　　　　　　460
The kind heart made her windy-paced
That urged her home quite out of breath with haste
And inward laughter.

She cried, "Laura," up the garden,
"Did you miss me?　　　　　　　　　　　　　　465
Come and kiss me.

Never mind my bruises,
Hug me, kiss me, suck my juices
Squeezed from goblin fruits for you,
Goblin pulp and goblin dew.   470
Eat me, drink me, love me;
Laura, make much of me;
For your sake I have braved the glen
And had to do with goblin merchant men."

Laura started from her chair,   475
Flung her arms up in the air,
Clutched her hair:
"Lizzie, Lizzie, have you tasted
For my sake the fruit forbidden?
Must your light like mine be hidden,   480
Your young life like mine be wasted,
Undone in mine undoing,
And ruined in my ruin,
Thirsty, cankered, goblin-ridden?" —
She clung about her sister,   485
Kissed and kissed and kissed her:
Tears once again
Refreshed her shrunken eyes,
Dropping like rain
After long sultry drouth;   490
Shaking with aguish fear, and pain,
She kissed and kissed her with a hungry mouth.

Her lips began to scorch,
That juice was wormwood to her tongue,
She loathed the feast: 495
Writhing as one possessed she leaped and sung,
Rent all her robe, and wrung
Her hands in lamentable haste,
And beat her breast.
Her locks streamed like the torch   500
Borne by a racer at full speed,
Or like the mane of horses in their flight,
Or like an eagle when she stems the light
Straight toward the sun,
Or like a caged thing freed,   505
Or like a flying flag when armies run.

Swift fire spread through her veins, knocked at her heart,
Met the fire smouldering there
And overbore its lesser flame;

She gorged on bitterness without a name: 510
Ah fool, to choose such part
Of soul-consuming care!
Sense failed in the mortal strife:
Like the watch-tower of a town
Which an earthquake shatters down,   515
Like a lightning-stricken mast,
Like a wind-uprooted tree
Spun about,
Like a foam-topped waterspout
Cast down headlong in the sea,   520
She fell at last;
Pleasure past and anguish past,
Is it death or is it life?

Life out of death.
That night long Lizzie watched by her,   525
Counted her pulse's flagging stir,
Felt for her breath,
Held water to her lips, and cooled her face
With tears and fanning leaves.
But when the first birds chirped about their eaves,   530
And early reapers plodded to the place
Of golden sheaves,
And dew-wet grass
Bowed in the morning winds so brisk to pass,
And new buds with new day   535
Opened of cup-like lilies on the stream,
Laura awoke as from a dream,
Laughed in the innocent old way,
Hugged Lizzie but not twice or thrice;
Her gleaming locks showed not one thread of grey,   540
Her breath was sweet as May,
And light danced in her eyes.

Days, weeks, months, years
Afterwards, when both were wives
With children of their own;   545
Their mother-hearts beset with fears,
Their lives bound up in tender lives;
Laura would call the little ones
And tell them of her early prime,
Those pleasant days long gone   550
Of not-returning time:
Would talk about the haunted glen,
The wicked quaint fruit-merchant men,

Their fruits like honey to the throat
But poison in the blood   555
(Men sell not such in any town):
Would tell them how her sister stood
In deadly peril to do her good,
And win the fiery antidote:
Then joining hands to little hands   560
Would bid them cling together,—
"For there is no friend like a sister
In calm or stormy weather;
To cheer one on the tedious way,
To fetch one if one goes astray,   565
To lift one if one totters down,
To strengthen whilst one stands."

Sonnet 17

Something this foggy day, a something which
    Is neither of this fog nor of today,
    Has set me dreaming of the winds that play
Past certain cliffs, along one certain beach,
    And turn the topmost edge of waves to spray: 5
    Ah pleasant pebbly strand so far away,
So out of reach while quite within my reach,
    As out of reach as India or Cathay!
I am sick of where I am and where I am not,
    I am sick of foresight and of memory,   10
    I am sick of all I have and all I see,
    I am sick of self, and there is nothing new;
Oh weary impatient patience of my lot!—
    Thus with myself: how fares it, Friends, with you?

Sonnet 18

So late in Autumn half the world's asleep,
    And half the wakeful world looks pinched and pale;
    For dampness now, not freshness, rides the gale;
And cold and colourless comes ashore the deep
With tides that bluster or with tides that creep;   5
    Now veiled uncouthness wears an uncouth veil
    Of fog, not sultry haze; and blight and bale
Have done their worst, and leaves rot on the heap.

So late in Autumn one forgets the Spring,
    Forgets the Summer with its opulence,   10
The callow birds that long have found a wing,
    The swallows that more lately gat them hence:
Will anything like Spring, will anything
    Like Summer, rouse one day the slumbering sense?

Sonnet 19

Here now is Winter. Winter, after all,
    Is not so drear as was my boding dream
    While Autumn gleamed its latest watery gleam
On sapless leafage too inert to fall.
Still leaves and berries clothe my garden wall   5
    Where ivy thrives on scantiest sunny beam;
    Still here a bud and there a blossom seem
Hopeful, and robin still is musical.
Leaves, flowers, and fruit, and one delightful song,
    Remain; these days are short, but now the nights,   10
    Intense and long, hang out their utmost lights;
Such starry nights are long, yet not too long;
Frost nips the weak, while strengthening still the strong
    Against that day when Spring sets all to rights.

Sonnet 20

A hundred thousand birds salute the day: —
    One solitary bird salutes the night:
Its mellow grieving wiles our grief away,
    And tunes our weary watches to delight;
It seems to sing the thoughts we cannot say,   5
    To know and sing them, and to set them right;
Until we feel once more that May is May,
    And hope some buds may bloom without a blight.
This solitary bird outweighs, outvies,
    The hundred thousand merry-making birds;   10
Whose innocent warblings yet might make us wise,
Would we but follow when they bid us rise,
    Would we but set their notes of praise to words
And launch our hearts up with them to the skies.

Sonnet 21

A host of things I take on trust: I take
　　The nightingales on trust, for few and far
　　Between those actual summer moments are
When I have heard what melody they make.
So chanced it once at Como on the Lake:　　　　　　　　　　5
　　But all things, then, waxed musical; each star
　　Sang on its course, each breeze sang on its car,
All harmonies sang to senses wide awake.
All things in tune, myself not out of tune,
　　Those nightingales were nightingales indeed:　　　　　　10
　　Yet truly an owl had satisfied my need,
And wrought a rapture underneath that moon,
　　Or simple sparrow chirping from a reed;
For June that night glowed like a doubled June.

Sonnet 22

The mountains in their overwhelming might
　　Moved me to sadness when I saw them first,
And afterwards they moved me to delight;
　　Struck harmonies from silent chords which burst
　　Out into song, a song by memory nursed;　　　　　　　5
For ever unrenewed by touch or sight
Sleeps the keen magic of each day or night,
　　In pleasure and in wonder then immersed.
All Switzerland behind us on the ascent,
All Italy before us, we plunged down　　　　　　　　　　10
　　St. Gothard, garden of forget-me-not:
　　Yet why should such a flower choose such a spot?
Could we forget that way which once we went
　　Though not one flower had bloomed to weave its crown?

Sonnet 23

Beyond the seas we know stretch seas unknown,
　　Blue and bright-coloured for our dim and green;
　　Beyond the lands we see stretch lands unseen
With many-tinted tangle overgrown;
And icebound seas there are like seas of stone,　　　　　5
　　Serenely stormless as death lies serene;
　　And lifeless tracts of sand, which intervene
Betwixt the lands where living flowers are blown.

This dead and living world befits our case
   Who live and die: we live in wearied hope,   10
We die in hope not dead; we run a race
Today, and find no present halting-place;
   All things we see lie far within our scope,
And still we peer beyond with craving face.

Winter: My Secret

I tell my secret? No indeed, not I:
Perhaps some day, who knows?
But not today; it froze, and blows, and snows,
And you're too curious: fie!
You want to hear it? well: 5
Only, my secret's mine, and I won't tell.

Or, after all, perhaps there's none:
Suppose there is no secret after all,
But only just my fun.
Today's a nipping day, a biting day;   10
In which one wants a shawl,
A veil, a cloak, and other wraps:
I cannot ope to every one who taps,
And let the draughts come whistling through my hall;
Come bounding and surrounding me,   15
Come buffeting, astounding me,
Nipping and clipping through my wraps and all.
I wear my mask for warmth: who ever shows
His nose to Russian snows
To be pecked at by every wind that blows?   20
You would not peck? I thank you for good will,
Believe, but leave that truth untested still.

Spring's an expansive time: yet I don't trust
March with its peck of dust,
Nor April with its rainbow-crowned brief showers,   25
Nor even May, whose flowers
One frost may wither through the sunless hours.

Perhaps some languid summer day,
When drowsy birds sing less and less,
And golden fruit is ripening to excess,   30
If there's not too much sun nor too much cloud,
And the warm wind is neither still nor loud,
Perhaps my secret I may say,
Or you may guess.

🦢 *William Morris* (1834–1896)

William Morris's art was intimately connected with a political critique of his era. Morris deplored the ugliness that resulted from the rapid pace of industrialization in England in the nineteenth century as much as the critic John Ruskin. Even more so than Ruskin, however, Morris idealized the world of the Middle Ages. Medieval styles and values dominate all of Morris's art, from his poetry to the furniture he designed. He attended Oxford and began training for a career as an architect. After graduation, he associated with members of the Pre-Raphaelite Brotherhood, and he became particularly close to Christina Rossetti's brother, Dante Gabriel. The Defence of Guenevere, *his first collection of poetry, appeared in 1858 and, as with his subsequent early poetry, was set in the distant past of Arthurian legends. His most popular work,* The Earthly Paradise *(1868–70), continued his exploration of medieval themes and subjects.*

An admired narrative poet, Morris also distinguished himself as a designer of household furnishings. One of the founders of the revolutionary English Arts and Crafts movement, Morris emphasized simplicity and quality in his designs for wallpaper, tapestries, furniture, stained glass, and textiles. In his design work as with his writing, he found inspiration in medieval styles and, in fact, attempted to bestow on this work the care exercised by an artisan of the Middle Ages. Morris not only aspired to reinvigorate a medieval aesthetic in the Victorian age, he also worked to preserve the past in historical buildings throughout England. A man of diverse talents, including a devotion to translating Icelandic poetry, Morris's disgust with the culture of bourgeois capitalism that he saw around him led him to become increasingly involved with the fledgling Socialist movement in Britain. His literary work in the 1880s and 1890s had primarily a political aim, such as his Poems of the Way *(1891) and* Chants for Socialists *(1884–5). During the last years of his life, he continued to blend his nostalgized vision of and love for a medieval communitarian past with his political hopes for the future in the utopian fiction he produced in such novels as* News from Nowhere *(1891).*

Winter Weather

We rode together
In the winter weather
   To the broad mead under the hill;
Though the skies did shiver
With the cold, the river 5
   Ran, and was never still.

No cloud did darken
The night; we did hearken
   The hound's bark far away. 10
It was solemn midnight
In that dread, dread night,
   In the years that have passed for aye.

Two rode beside me,
My banner did hide me,
 As it drooped adown from my lance; 15
With its deep blue trapping,
The mail over-lapping,
 My gallant horse did prance.

So ever together
In the sparkling weather 20
 Moved my banner and lance;
And its laurel trapping,
The steel over-lapping,
 The stars saw quiver and dance.

We met together 25
In the winter weather
 By the town walls under the hill;
His mail-rings came clinking,
They broke on my thinking,
 For the night was hushed and still. 30

Two rode beside him,
His banner did hide him,
 As it drooped down straight from his lance;
With its blood-red trapping,
The mail over-lapping, 35
 His mighty horse did prance.

And ever together
In the solemn weather
 Moved his banner and lance;
And the holly trapping, 40
The steel overlapping,
 Did shimmer and shiver, and dance.

Back reined the squires
Till they saw the spires
 Over the city wall; 45
Ten fathoms between us,
No dames could have seen us,
 Tilt from the city wall.

There we sat upright
Till the full midnight 50
 Should be told from the city chimes:
Sharp from the towers
Leapt forth the showers
 Of the many clanging rhymes.

'Twas the midnight hour,   55
Deep from the tower
   Boomed the following bell;
Down go our lances,
Shout for the lances!
   The last toll was his knell.   60

There he lay, dying;
He had, for his lying,
   A spear in his traitorous mouth;
A false tale made he
Of my true, true lady;   65
   But the spear went through his mouth.

In the winter weather
We rode back together
   From the broad mead under the hill;
And the cock sung his warning   70
As it grew toward morning,
   But the far-off hound was still.

Black grew his tower
As we rode down lower,
   Black from the barren hill;   75
And our horses strode
Up the winding road
   To the gateway dim and still.

At the gate of his tower,
In the quiet hour,   80
   We laid his body there;
But his helmet broken,
We took as a token;
   Shout for my lady fair!

We rode back together   85
In the winter weather
   From the broad mead under the hill;
No cloud did darken
The night; we did hearken
   How the hound bayed from the hill.   90

The Haystack in the Floods

Had she come all the way for this,
To part at last without a kiss?
Yea, had she borne the dirt and rain

That her own eyes might see him slain
Beside the haystack in the floods?   5

Along the dripping leafless woods,
The stirrup touching either shoe,
She rode astride as troopers do;
With kirtle[1] kilted to her knee,
To which the mud splashed wretchedly;   10
And the wet dripped from every tree
Upon her head and heavy hair,
And on her eyelids broad and fair;
The tears and rain ran down her face.
By fits and starts they rode apace,   15
And very often was his place
Far off from her; he had to ride
Ahead, to see what might betide
When the roads crossed; and sometimes, when
There rose a murmuring from his men,   20
Had to turn back with promises;
Ah me! she had but little ease;
And often for pure doubt and dread
She sobbed, made giddy in the head
By the swift riding; while, for cold,   25
Her slender fingers scarce could hold
The wet reins; yea, and scarcely, too,
She felt the foot within her shoe
Against the stirrup: all for this,
To part at last without a kiss   30
Beside the haystack in the floods.

For when they neared that old soaked hay,
They saw across the only way
That Judas, Godmar, and the three
Red running lions dismally   35
Grinned from his pennon, under which,
In one straight line along the ditch,
They counted thirty heads.

                    So then,
While Robert turned round to his men,
She saw at once the wretched end,   40
And, stooping down, tried hard to rend
Her coif the wrong way from her head,
And hid her eyes; while Robert said:
"Nay, love, 'tis scarcely two to one,

---

[1] Skirt.

At Poitiers[2] where we made them run   45
So fast—why, sweet my love, good cheer.
The Gascon frontier is so near,
Nought after this."

            But, "O," she said,
"My God! my God! I have to tread
The long way back without you;[3] then   50
The court at Paris; those six men;
The gratings of the Chatelet;
The swift Seine on some rainy day
Like this, and people standing by,
And laughing, while my weak hands try   55
To recollect how strong men swim.
All this, or else a life with him,
For which I should be damned at last,
Would God that this next hour were past!"

He answered not, but cried his cry,   60
"St. George for Marny!" cheerily;
And laid his hand upon her rein.
Alas! no man of all his train
Gave back that cheery cry again;
And, while for rage his thumb beat fast   65
Upon his sword hilts, some one cast
About his neck a kerchief long,
And bound him.

          Then they went along
To Godmar; who said: "Now, Jehane,
Your lover's life is on the wane   70

So fast, that, if this very hour
You yield not as my paramour,
He will not see the rain leave off—
Nay, keep your tongue from gibe and scoff,
Sir Robert, or I slay you now."   75

She laid her hand upon her brow,
Then gazed upon the palm, as though
She thought her forehead bled, and—"No."
She said, and turned her head away,
As there were nothing else to say,   80
And everything were settled: red

---

[2] The English soldiers described in the poem were part of the army that was defeated by the French at Poitiers in 1356. They are traveling to Gascony to rejoin the English troops.

[3] Jehane, Sir Robert's mistress, is French and cannot return to England with him. In this stanza, she worries about her punishment for involvement with the enemy.

Grew Godmar's face from chin to head:
"Jehane, on yonder hill there stands
My castle, guarding well my lands:
What hinders me from taking you,   85
And doing that I list to do
To your fair wilful body, while
Your knight lies dead?"

    A wicked smile
Wrinkled her face, her lips grew thin,
A long way out she thrust her chin: 90
"You know that I should strangle you
While you were sleeping; or bite through
Your throat, by God's help—ah!" she said,
"Lord Jesus, pity your poor maid!
For in such wise they hem me in,   95
I cannot choose but sin and sin,
Whatever happens: yet I think
They could not make me eat or drink,
And so should I just reach my rest."
"Nay, if you do not my behest,   100
O Jehane! though I love you well,"
Said Godmar, "would I fail to tell
All that I know." "Foul lies," she said.
"Eh? lies my Jehane? by God's head,
At Paris folks would deem them true!   105
Do you know, Jehane, they cry for you,
'Jehane the brown! Jehane the brown!
Give us Jehane to burn or drown!'—
Eh—gag me Robert!—sweet my friend,
This were indeed a piteous end   110
For those long fingers, and long feet,
And long neck, and smooth shoulders sweet;
An end that few men would forget
That saw it—So, an hour yet:
Consider, Jehane, which to take   115
Of life or death!"

    So, scarce awake,
Dismounting, did she leave that place,
And totter some yards: with her face
Turned upward to the sky she lay,
Her head on a wet heap of hay,   120
And fell asleep: and while she slept,
And did not dream, the minutes crept
Round to the twelve again; but she,
Being waked at last, sighed quietly,

And strangely childlike came, and said: 125
"I will not." Straightway Godmar's head,
As though it hung on strong wires, turned
Most sharply round, and his face burned.

For Robert—both his eyes were dry,
He could not weep, but gloomily   130
He seemed to watch the rain; yea, too,
His lips were firm; he tried once more
To touch her lips; she reached out, sore
And vain desire so tortured them,
The poor grey lips, and now the hem   135
Of his sleeve brushed them.

                         With a start
Up Godmar rose, thrust them apart;
From Robert's throat he loosed the bands
Of silk and mail; with empty hands
Held out, she stood and gazed, and saw,   140
The long bright blade without a flaw
Glide out from Godmar's sheath, his hand
In Robert's hair; she saw him bend
Back Robert's head; she saw him send
The thin steel down; the blow told well,   145
Right backward the knight Robert fell,
And moaned as dogs do, being half dead,
Unwitting, as I deem: so then
Godmar turned grinning to his men,
Who ran, some five or six, and beat   150
His head to pieces at their feet.

Then Godmar turned again and said:
"So, Jehane, the first fitte[4] is read!
Take note, my lady, that your way
Lies backward to the Chatelet!"   155
She shook her head and gazed awhile
At her cold hands with a rueful smile,
As though this thing had made her mad.

This was the parting that they had
Beside the haystack in the floods.   160

[4] *Fitte*: canto or section of poetry.

✒ *Samuel Langhorne Clemens (Mark Twain)*
(1835–1910)

Samuel Langhorne Clemens, renowned as the author Mark Twain, was born in a two-room clapboard house in Florida, Missouri, the fifth of six children. This childhood home in Missouri still stands and is very close to the store that was owned by his uncle, John Quarles, who is a significant character in Mark Twain's Autobiography *(1924) and* Life on the Mississippi *(1883). The family soon moved to Hannibal, about thirty miles away, and it was there that Clemens's fascination with the Missouri River and its steamboats began. It was his childhood dream to become a steamboatman. He would fulfill that dream from 1857 to 1861, working at a profession he described as the most fulfilling of his life.*

Having come from such a poor background, Samuel Clemens was never quite comfortable with the idea of being rich. This was a reality he had to face at the age of twelve upon the death of his father, who bequeathed some 70,000 acres in Tennessee to the family. Clemens was convinced that he would fail to manage such wealth and the family's circumstances would eventually revert to poverty. For this reason, he commenced his wanderings. The young Clemens spent several years as a drifter and itinerant printer, living in New York, St. Louis, and Philadelphia. In 1856, he decided that South America was his next stop, there to make his fortune in cocoa. However, he was sidetracked when he met Horace Bixby, who made him into a steamboat pilot, his great ambition. The Civil War ended the steamboat traffic on the Missouri River and Clemens's career as a pilot. He then served briefly as a volunteer in the Confederate ranks. He rode west in 1861 in a stagecoach with his brother Orion who was the secretary to the governor of the Nevada Territory. This journey was later recounted in Roughing It *(1872). In 1875 in the magazine* Atlantic Monthly, *and already having established the nom de plume Mark Twain, he began a series of seven installments that recounted his experiences as a steamboat pilot. Eight years later, these articles became the basis for* Life on the Mississippi, *which dealt with the author's return to the river after the Civil War and the advent of railroads, the mode of transport that led to the demise of the grand, ornate steamboats.*

Mark Twain, more than any other writer of his time, made humor an acceptable, even indispensable, part of American literature. Arguably America's greatest humorist, he gave the genre credibility by blending folksy common sense with a rough mix of optimism and underlying satirical pessimism. In so doing, he helped shape the American vernacular of his time.

From Life on the Mississippi

It turned out to be true. The face of the water, in time, became a wonderful book—a book that was a dead language to the uneducated passenger, but which told its mind to me without reserve, delivering its most cherished secrets as clearly as if it uttered them with a voice. And it was not a book to be read once and thrown aside, for it had a new story to tell every day. Throughout the long twelve hundred miles there was never a page that was void of interest, never one that you could leave unread without loss, never one that you would want to skip, thinking you could find higher enjoyment in some other thing. There never was so wonderful a book written by man; never one whose interest was so absorbing, so unflagging, so sparklingly renewed with every reperusal. The passenger who could not read it was charmed with a peculiar sort of faint dimple on its surface (on the rare occasions when he did not overlook it altogether); but to the pilot that was an *italicized* passage; indeed, it was more than that, it was a legend of the largest capitals, with a string of shouting exclamation points at the end of it, for it meant that a wreck or a rock was buried there that could tear the life out of the strongest vessel that ever floated. It is the faintest and simplest expression the water ever makes, and the most hideous to a pilot's eye. In truth, the passenger who could not read this book saw nothing but all manner of pretty pictures in it, painted by the sun and shaded by the clouds, whereas to the trained eye these were not pictures at all, but the grimmest and most dead-earnest of reading matter.

Now when I had mastered the language of this water, and had come to know every trifling feature that bordered the great river as familiarly as I knew the letters of the alphabet, I had made a valuable acquisition. But I had lost something, too. I had lost something which could never be restored to me while I lived. All the grace, the beauty, the poetry, had gone out of the majestic river! I still kept in mind a certain wonderful sunset which I witnessed when steamboating was new to me. A broad expanse of the river was turned to blood; in the middle distance the red hue brightened into gold, through which a solitary log came floating, black and conspicuous; in one place a long, slanting mark lay sparkling upon the water; in another the surface was broken by boiling, tumbling rings, that were as many-tinted as an opal; where the ruddy flush was faintest, was a smooth spot that was covered with graceful circles and radiating lines, ever so delicately traced; the shore on our left was densely wooded, and the somber shadow that fell from this forest was broken in one place by a long, ruffled trail that shone like silver; and high above the forest wall a clean-stemmed dead tree waved a single leafy bough that glowed like a flame in the unobstructed splendor that was flowing from the sun. There were graceful curves, reflected images, woody heights, soft distances; and over the whole scene, far and near, the dissolving lights drifted steadily, enriching it every passing moment with new marvels of coloring.

I stood like one bewitched. I drank it in, in a speechless rapture. The world was new to me, and I had never seen anything like this at home. But as I have said, a day came when I began to cease from noting the glories and the charms which the moon and the sun and the twilight wrought upon the river's face; another day came when I ceased altogether to note them. Then, if that sunset scene had been repeated, I should have looked upon it without rapture, and should have commented upon it, inwardly, after this fashion: "This sun means that we are going to have wind tomorrow; that floating log means that the river is rising, small thanks to it; that slanting mark on the water refers to a bluff reef which is going to kill somebody's steamboat one of these nights, if it keeps on stretching out like that; those tumbling 'boils' show a dissolving bar and a changing channel there; the lines and circles in the slick water over yonder are a warning that that troublesome place is shoaling up dangerously; that silver streak in the shadow of the forest is the 'break' from a new snag, and he has located himself in the very best place he could have found to fish for steamboats; that tall dead tree, with a single living branch, is not going to last long, and then how is a body ever going to get through this blind place at night without the friendly old landmark?"

No, the romance and beauty were all gone from the river. All the value any feature of it had for me now was the amount of usefulness it could furnish toward compassing the safe piloting of a steamboat. Since those days, I have pitied doctors from my heart. What does the lovely flush in a beauty's cheek mean to a doctor but a "break" that ripples above some deadly disease? Are not all her visible charms sown thick with what are to him the signs and symbols of hidden decay? Does he ever see her beauty at all, or doesn't he simply view her professionally, and comment upon her unwholesome condition all to himself? And doesn't he sometimes wonder whether he has gained most or lost most by learning his trade?

🦢 *Algernon Charles Swinburne* (1837–1909)

Algernon Charles Swinburne is remembered today as one of the most daring and unconventional lyricists ever to write in English. His reputation rests upon two volumes that he published before he reached the age of thirty: Atalanta in Calydon *(1865), a lyrical drama that recalls Aeschylean tragedy, and* Poems and Ballads *(1866), which shocked the Victorian public with its atheism and eroticism. Swinburne harks back to the English Romantic poets, particularly Byron and Shelley, in his use of erotic imagery in nature poetry, particularly when the speaker is overwhelmed by the fierce, elemental forces of the sea, wind, and sun. Swinburne's passionate response to the natural world was fostered during his early childhood on the Isle of Wight, where he rode horses with reckless abandon and spent endless hours exploring the island's windswept shores and frolicking in the waves. He recalled how, when he was a young boy, his father brandished him naked in midair, then flung him "shouting and laughing with delight, head foremost into the coming wave." This childhood memory evokes the intensity of the sensual delight that Swinburne found in his early encounters with the raw, elemental energies of nature. Much of Swinburne's poetry celebrates an exuberant paganism and proclaims an unabashed eroticism, deeply disturbing to many Victorian readers.*

Swinburne was a precocious reader, enjoying Shakespeare at age six, and by age twelve, he was fluent in French and Italian. He attended Eton for four years, then matriculated at Oxford University, but left without taking a degree. He soon settled in London, where he mingled with the Pre-Raphaelite circle of artists and writers, and in 1862 he shared a communal household with Dante Gabriel Rossetti. The two bachelors devoted themselves to a bohemian lifestyle, keeping a pet wombat and engaging in rowdy, drunken escapades. Swinburne eventually became a chronic alcoholic. John Ruskin described him as a "demoniac boy," and his public image as a depraved reprobate was en-

hanced in 1866 by the publication of his Poems and Ballads, *denounced by contemporary reviewers as "prurient trash." Yet these poems break new ground in their metrical form. Swinburne creates unusual effects by rejecting the familiar iambic line and exploring the imitative possibilities of the dactyl and anapest, echoing the thunder of waves in a storm or evoking the lisp of leaves in an autumn wind. "The Garden of Proserpine" exemplifies the lush imagery and innovative metrical forms of this collection. By 1879, Swinburne's alcoholism had affected his health, and he was obliged to place himself in the care of a friend who kept him secluded in the countryside. Swinburne continued to write, publishing over fifty books of poetry and criticism during the course of his lifetime. The best of his later poetry, such as "A Forsaken Garden" (1878) and "The Palace of Pan" (1893), displays an exuberant paganism and a lush profusion of imagery.*

The Garden of Proserpine*

Here, where the world is quiet,
   Here, where all trouble seems
Dead winds' and spent waves' riot
   In doubtful dreams of dreams;
I watch the green field growing   5
For reaping folk and sowing,
For harvest time and mowing,
   A sleepy world of streams.

I am tired of tears and laughter,
   And men that laugh and weep;   10
Of what may come hereafter
   For men that sow to reap:
I am weary of days and hours,
Blown buds of barren flowers,
Desires and dreams and powers   15
   And everything but sleep.

Here life has death for neighbor,
   And far from eye or ear
Wan waves and wet winds labor,
   Weak ships and spirits steer;   20
They drive adrift, and whither
They wot not who make thither;
But no such winds blow hither,
   And no such things grow here.

---

* Or Persephone. According to classical mythology, she was the daughter of Demeter (or Ceres, Roman) the goddess of the harvest and of agriculture. Hades (or Pluto), the god of the underworld, abducted her, but Demeter persuaded him to release her for eight months of the year. She would have to return for four months each year because she had eaten four pomegranate seeds while with Hades. When she left the earth, all the plants died, but came to life again upon her annual return. The story provides a mythic basis for the origin of the seasons.

No growth of moor or coppice,
    No heather-flower or vine,
But bloomless buds of poppies,
    Green grapes of Proserpine,
Pale beds of blowing rushes
Where no leaf blooms or blushes,
Save this whereout she crushes
    For dead men deadly wine.

Pale, without name or number,
    In fruitless fields of corn,
They bow themselves and slumber
    All night till light is born;
And like a soul belated,
In hell and heaven unmated,
By cloud and mist abated
    Comes out of darkness morn.

Though one were strong as seven,
    He too with death shall dwell,
Nor wake with wings in heaven,
    Nor weep for pains in hell;
Though one were fair as roses,
His beauty clouds and closes;
And well though love reposes,
    In the end it is not well.

Pale, beyond porch and portal,
    Crowned with calm leaves, she stands
Who gathers all things mortal
    With cold immortal hands;
Her languid lips are sweeter
Than love's who fears to greet her
To men that mix and meet her
    From many times and lands.

She waits for each and other,
    She waits for all men born;
Forgets the earth her mother,
    The life of fruits and corn;
And spring and seed and swallow
Take wing for her and follow
Where summer song rings hollow
    And flowers are put to scorn.

There go the loves that wither,
    The old loves with wearier wings;
And all dead years draw thither,

And all disastrous things;
Dead dreams of days forsaken
Blind buds that snows have shaken,   70
Wild leaves that winds have taken,
    Red strays of ruined springs.

We are not sure of sorrow,
    And joy was never sure;
Today will die tomorrow;   75
    Time stoops to no man's lure;
And love, grown faint and fretful
With lips but half regretful
Sighs, and with eyes forgetful
    Weeps that no loves endure.   80

From too much love of living,
    From hope and fear set free,
We thank with brief thanksgiving
    Whatever gods may be
That no life lives for ever;   85
That dead men rise up never;
That even the weariest river
    Winds somewhere safe to sea.

Then star nor sun shall waken,
    Nor any change of light: 90
Nor sound of waters shaken
    Nor any sound or sight:
Nor wintry leaves nor vernal,
Nor days nor things diurnal;
Only the sleep eternal   95
    In an eternal night.

Chorus

When the hounds of spring are on winter's traces,
    The mother of months in meadow or plain
Fills the shadows and windy places
    With lisp of leaves and ripple of rain;   5
And the brown bright nightingale amorous
Is half assuaged for Itylus,[1]
For the Thracian ships and the foreign faces,
    The tongueless vigil, and all the pain.

---

[1] According to ancient Greek legend, the son of Tereus and Procne, who was killed by his mother and Philomela. Tereus had cut out Philomela's tongue, and to avenge herself she killed Itylus and fed him to his father. Before Tereus could punish her, the gods turned her into a nightingale.

Come with bows bent and with emptying of quivers, 10
    Maiden most perfect, lady of light,
With a noise of winds and many rivers,
    With a clamor of waters, and with might;
Bind on thy sandals, O thou most fleet,
Over the splendor and speed of thy feet; 15
For the faint east quickens, the wan west shivers,
    Round the feet of the day and the feet of the night.

Where shall we find her, how shall we sing to her,
    Fold our hands round her knees, and cling?
O that man's heart were as fire and could spring to her, 20
    Fire, or the strength of the streams that spring!
For the stars and the winds are unto her
As raiment, as songs of the harp-player;
For the risen stars and the fallen cling to her,
    And the southwest wind and the west wind sing. 25

For winter's rains and ruins are over,
    And all the season of snows and sins;
The days dividing lover and lover,
    The light that loses, the night that wins;
And time remembered is grief forgotten, 30
And frosts are slain and flowers begotten,
And in green underwood and cover
    Blossom by blossom the spring begins.

The full streams feed on flower of rushes,
    Ripe grasses trammel a travelling foot, 35
The faint fresh flame of the young year flushes
    From leaf to flower and flower to fruit;
And fruit and leaf are as gold and fire,
And the oat is heard above the lyre,
And the hoofèd heel of a satyr crushes 40
    The chestnut husk at the chestnut root.

And Pan[2] by noon and Bacchus[3] by night,
    Fleeter of foot than the fleet-foot kid,
Follows with dancing and fills with delight
    The Maenad and the Bassarid;[4] 45
And soft as lips that laugh and hide
The laughing leaves of the trees divide,
And screen from seeing and leave in sight
    The god pursuing, the maiden hid

[2] Pan is the classical god of shepherds.

[3] Bacchus is the god of wine and of fertility.

[4] Maenads were female followers of Bacchus whose mode of worship entailed working themselves into an ecstatic frenzy; Bassarids were other followers of Bacchus.

The ivy falls with the Bacchanal's[5] hair   50
    Over her eyebrows hiding her eyes;
The wild vine slipping down leaves bare
    Her bright breast shortening into sighs;
The wild vine slips with the weight of its leaves,
But the berried ivy catches and cleaves   55
To the limbs that glitter, the feet that scare
    The wolf that follows, the fawn that flies.

A Forsaken Garden

In a coign of the cliff between lowland and highland,
    At the sea-down's edge between windward and lee,
Walled round with rocks as an inland island,
    The ghost of a garden fronts the sea.
A girdle of brushwood and thorn encloses   5
    The steep square slope of the blossomless bed
Where the weeds that grew green from the graves of its roses
        Now lie dead.

The fields fall southward, abrupt and broken,
    To the low last edge of the long lone land.
If a step should sound or a word be spoken,   10
    Would a ghost not rise at the strange guest's hand?
So long have the gray bare walks lain guestless,
    Through branches and briers if a man make way,
He shall find no life but the sea-wind's, restless   15
        Night and day.

The dense hard passage is blind and stifled
    That crawls by a track none turn to climb
To the strait waste place that the years have rifled
    Of all but the thorns that are touched not of time.   20
The thorns he spares when the rose is taken;
    The rocks are left when he wastes the plain.
The wind that wanders, the weeds wind-shaken,
        These remain.

Not a flower to be prest of the foot that falls not;   25
    As the heart of a dead man the seed plots are dry;
From the thicket of thorns whence the nightingale calls not,
    Could she call, there were never a rose to reply.
Over the meadows that blossom and wither

---

[5] Someone celebrating the worship of Bacchus.

Rings but the note of a sea-bird's song; 30
Only the sun and the rain come hither
    All year long.

The sun burns sere and the rain dishevels
  One gaunt bleak blossom of scentless breath.
Only the wind here hovers and revels 35
  In a round where life seems barren as death.
Here there was laughing of old, there was weeping,
Haply, of lovers none ever will know,
  Whose eyes went seaward a hundred sleeping
    Years ago. 40

Heart handfast in heart as they stood, "Look thither,"
  Did he whisper! "Look forth from the flowers to the sea;
For the foam-flowers endure when the rose blossoms wither,
  And men that love lightly may die—but we?"
And the same wind sang and the same waves whitened, 45
  And or ever the garden's last petals were shed,
In the lips that had whispered, the eyes that had lightened,
    Love was dead.

Or they loved their life through, and then went whither?
  And were one to the end—but what end who knows? 50
Love deep as the sea as a rose must wither,
  As the rose-red seaweed that mocks the rose.
Shall the dead take thought for the dead to love them?
  What love was ever as deep as a grave?
They are loveless now as the grass above them 55
    Or the wave.

All are at one now, roses and lovers,
  Not known of the cliffs and the fields and the sea.
Not a breath of the time that has been hovers
  In the air now soft with a summer to be. 60
Not a breath shall there sweeten the seasons hereafter
  Of the flowers or the lovers that laugh now or weep,
When as they that are free now of weeping and laughter,
    We shall sleep.

Here death may deal not again forever; 65
  Here change may come not till all change end.
From the graves they have made they shall rise up never,
  Who have left nought living to ravage and rend.
Earth, stones, and thorns of the wild ground growing,
  While the sun and the rain live, these shall be; 70
Till a last wind's breath upon all these blowing
    Roll the sea.

Till the slow sea rise and the sheer cliff crumble,
    Till terrace and meadow the deep gulfs drink,
Till the strength of the waves of the high tides humble   75
    The fields that lessen, the rocks that shrink,
Here now in his triumph where all things falter,
    Stretched out on the spoils that his own hand spread,
As a god self-slain on his own strange altar,
        Death lies dead.   80

The Palace of Pan

Inscribed to my Mother

September, all glorious with gold, as a king
    In the radiance of triumph attired,
Outlightening the summer, outsweetening the spring,
Broods wide on the woodlands with limitless wing,
    A presence of all men desired.   5

Far eastward and westward the sun-colored lands
    Smile warm as the light on them smiles;
And statelier than temples upbuilded with hands,
Tall column by column, the sanctuary stands
    Of the pine-forest's infinite aisles.   10

Mute worship, too fervent for praise or for prayer,
    Possesses the spirit with peace,
Fulfilled with the breath of the luminous air,
The fragrance, the silence, the shadows as fair
    As the rays that recede or increase.   15

Ridged pillars that redden aloft and aloof,
    With never a branch for a nest,
Sustain the sublime indivisible roof,
To the storm and the sun in his majesty proof,
    And awful as waters at rest.   20

Man's hand hath not measured the height of them, thought
    May measure not, awe may not know;
In its shadow the woofs of the woodland are wrought;
As a bird is the sun in the toils of them caught,
    And the flakes of it scattered as snow.   25

As the shreds of a plumage of gold on the ground
    The sun-flakes by multitudes lie,
Shed loose as the petals of roses discrowned
On the floors of the forest engilt and embrowned
    And reddened afar and anigh.   30

Dim centuries with darkling inscrutable hands
    Have reared and secluded the shrine
For gods that we know not, and kindled as brands
On the altar the years that are dust, and their sand
    Time's glass has forgotten for sign.   35

A temple whose transepts are measured by miles,
    Whose chancel has morning for priest,
Whose floor-work the foot of no spoiler defiles,
Whose musical silence no music beguiles,
    No festivals limit its feast.   40

The noon's ministration, the night's and the dawn's,
    Conceals not, reveals not for man,
On the slopes of the herbless and blossomless lawns,
Some track of a nymph's or some trail of a faun's
    To the place of the slumber of Pan.   45

Thought, kindled and quickened by worship and wonder
    To rapture too sacred for fear
On the ways that unite or divide them in sunder,
Alone may discern if about them or under
    Be token or trace of him here.   50

With passionate awe that is deeper than panic
    The spirit subdued and unshaken
Takes heed of the godhead terrene and Titanic
Whose footfall is felt on the breach of volcanic
    Sharp steeps that their fire has forsaken.   55

By a spell more serene than the dim necromantic
    Dead charms of the past and the night,
Or the terror that lurked in the noon to make frantic
Where Etna takes shape from the limbs of gigantic
    Dead gods disanointed of might,   60

The spirit made one with the spirit whose breath
    Makes noon in the woodland sublime
Abides as entranced in a presence that saith
Things loftier than life and serener than death,
    Triumphant and silent as time.   65

ﻌ *John Muir* (*1838–1914*)

Born in Dunbar, Scotland, John Muir came to the United States with his family in 1849, settling on a Wisconsin farm. His father was a strict Calvinist, and Muir came of age in an atmosphere of austerity, strict discipline, and hard work. He attended the Uni-

versity of Wisconsin, becoming an adept student of the natural sciences, particularly chemistry, geology, and botany. In 1864, seeking to avoid military service in the Civil War, Muir vanished into the wilds of northern Michigan and Canada, where he wandered for several months in utter solitude. He found solace in the sight of a rare orchid, Calypso borealis, *blooming far from the presence of any human being. From this experience, Muir gained his first insight into the complete self-sufficiency and intrinsic self-worth of all living things. Returning to Wisconsin, Muir worked in a rake factory, impressing his employer with his skill in devising new machinery. An industrial accident in 1867 nearly resulted in the loss of sight in one eye, and during his recovery from this injury, Muir renounced the "gobble gobble school of economics" and resolved to follow a less materialistic way of life.*

Inspired by the South American travels of the great naturalists Alexander von Humboldt and Charles Darwin, Muir set forth to explore the Amazon River to its source. After a thousand-mile walk to Florida, camping in swamps and botanizing along the way, Muir fell desperately ill with malaria and abandoned his South American journey. But he still felt the lure of unknown wilderness, and in 1868 he traveled by ship to California. Working as a shepherd, Muir climbed into the Sierra Nevada, where he was astonished by the beauty of the "Range of Light," particularly the awesome crags of Yosemite Valley. For several years, he made these mountains his home. Muir's first book, The Mountains of California *(1894), established him as a leading advocate for the preservation of wilderness, and he later became the founder and first president of the Sierra Club. In a chapter from this book, "A Wind-Storm in the Forests" (excerpted below), Muir combines hard-edged scientific observation with a more exalted conception of nature that harks back to the American Transcendentalists in its intensity of vision and exuberance of detail. Muir was personally acquainted with Emerson, who visited him in Yosemite in 1871, and he was familiar with the works of Thoreau.*

In his later years, Muir explored wilderness areas throughout the United States, and he became a tireless defender of the national park system. He published numerous books, including My First Summer in the Sierra *(1911),* The Story of My Boyhood and Youth *(1913),* Travels in Alaska *(1915), and* A Thousand-Mile Walk to the Gulf *(1916). Muir's career came sadly to an end with the damming of Hetch Hetchy Valley in Yosemite National Park, an ecological disaster that Muir denounced with prophetic fury, but to no avail. His twelve-year struggle to save Hetch Hetchy was lost in 1913; Muir died in the following year.*

From The Mountains of California

Chapter 10. A Wind-Storm in the Forests

The mountain winds, like the dew and rain, sunshine and snow, are measured and bestowed with love on the forests to develop their strength and beauty. However restricted the scope of other forest influences, that of the winds is universal. The snow bends and trims the upper forests every winter, the lightning strikes a single tree here and there, while avalanches mow down thousands at a swoop as a gardener trims out a bed of flowers. But the winds go to every tree, fingering every leaf and branch and furrowed bole; not one is forgotten; the mountain pine towering with outstretched arms on the rugged buttresses of the icy peaks, the lowliest and most retiring tenant of the dells; they seek and find them all, caressing them tenderly, bending them in lusty exercise, stimulating their growth, plucking off a leaf or limb as required, or removing an entire tree or grove, now whispering and cooing through the branches like a sleepy child, now roaring like the ocean; the winds blessing the forests, the forests the winds, with ineffable beauty and harmony as the sure result.

After one has seen pines six feet in diameter bending like grasses before a mountain gale, and ever and anon some giant falling with a crash that shakes the hills, it seems astonishing that any, save the lowest thickset trees, could ever have found a period sufficiently stormless to establish themselves; or, once established, that they should not, sooner or later, have been blown down. But when the storm is over, and we behold the same forests tranquil again, towering fresh and unscathed in erect majesty, and consider what centuries of storms have fallen upon them since they were first planted,—hail, to break the tender seedlings; lightning, to scorch and shatter; snow, winds, and avalanches, to crush and over-whelm,—while the manifest result of all this wild storm-culture is the glorious perfection we behold; then faith in Nature's forestry is established, and we cease to deplore the violence of her most destructive gales, or of any other storm-im-plement whatsoever.

There are two trees in the Sierra forests that are never blown down, so long as they continue in sound health. These are the juniper and the dwarf pine of the summit peaks. Their stiff, crooked roots grip the storm-beaten ledges like eagles' claws, while their lithe, cord-like branches bend round compliantly, offering but slight holds for winds, however violent. The other alpine conifers—the needle pine, mountain pine, two-leaved pine, and hemlock spruce—are never thinned out by this agent to any destructive extent, on account of their admirable tough-ness and the closeness of their growth. In general the same is true of the giants of the lower zones. The kingly sugar pine, towering aloft to a height of more than two hundred feet, offers a fine mark to storm-winds; but it is not densely foliaged, and its long, horizontal arms swing round compliantly in the blast, like tresses of green, fluent algae in a brook; while the silver firs in most places keep their ranks well together in united strength. The yellow or silver pine is more frequently overturned than any other tree on the Sierra, because its leaves and branches form a larger mass in proportion to its height, while in many places it is planted sparsely, leaving open lanes through which storms may enter with full force. Furthermore, because it is distributed along the lower portion of the range, which was the first to be left bare on the breaking up of the ice sheet at the close of the glacial winter, the soil it is growing upon has been longer ex-posed to postglacial weathering, and consequently is in a more crumbling, de-cayed condition that the fresher soils farther up the range, and therefore offers a less secure anchorage for the roots.

While exploring the forest zones of Mount Shasta, I discovered the path of a hurricane strewn with thousands of pines of this species. Great and small had been uprooted or wrenched off by sheer force, making a clean gap, like that made by a snow avalanche. But hurricanes capable of doing this class of work are rare in the Sierra, and when we have explored the forests from one extremity of the range to the other, we are compelled to believe that they are the most beautiful on the face of the earth, however we may regard the agents that have made them so.

There is always something deeply exciting; not only in the sounds of winds in the woods, which exert more or less influence over every mind, but in their varied waterlike flow as manifested by the movements of the trees, especially those of the conifers. By no other trees are they rendered so extensively and impressively visible, not even by the lordly tropic palms or tree ferns responsive to the gentlest breeze. The waving of a forest of the giant sequoias is indescribably impressive and sublime, but the pines seem to me the best interpreters of winds. They are mighty waving goldenrods, ever in tune, singing and writing wind-music all their long century lives. Little, however, of this noble tree-waving and tree-music will you see or hear in the strictly alpine portion of the forests. The burly juniper, whose girth sometimes more than equals its height, is about as rigid as the rocks on which it grows. The slender, lash-like sprays of the dwarf pine stream out in wavering ripples, but the tallest and slenderest are far too unyielding to wave even in the heaviest gales. They only shake in quick, short vibrations. The hemlock spruce, however, and the mountain pine, and some of the tallest thickets of the two-leaved species bow in storms with considerable scope and gracefulness. But it is only in the lower and middle zones that the meeting of winds and woods is to be seen in all its grandeur.

One of the most beautiful and exhilarating storms I ever enjoyed in the Sierra occurred in December, 1874, when I happened to be exploring one of the tributary valleys of the Yuba River. The sky and the ground and the trees had been thoroughly rain-washed and were dry again. The day was intensely pure, one of those incomparable bits of California winter, warm and balmy and full of white sparkling sunshine, redolent of all the purest influences of the spring, and at the same time enlivened with one of the most bracing wind-storms conceivable. Instead of camping out, as I usually do, I then chanced to be stopping at the house of a friend. But when the storm began to sound, I lost no time in pushing out into the woods to enjoy it. For on such occasions Nature has always something rare to show us, and the danger to life and limb is hardly greater than one would experience crouching deprecatingly beneath a roof.

It was still early morning when I found myself fairly adrift. Delicious sunshine came pouring over the hills, lighting the tops of the pines, and setting free a steam of summery fragrance that contrasted strangely with the wild tones of the storm. The air was mottled with pine tassels and bright green plumes, that went flashing past in the sunlight like birds pursued. But there was not the slightest dustiness, nothing less pure than leaves, and ripe pollen, and flecks of withered bracken and moss. I heard trees falling for hours at the rate of one every two or three minutes; some uprooted, partly on account of the loose, water-soaked condition of the ground; others broken straight across, where some weakness caused by fire had determined the spot. The gestures of the various trees made a delightful study. Young sugar pines, light and feathery as squirrel tails, were bowing almost to the ground; while the grand old patriarchs, whose massive boles had where they bloom white in falls, glide in crystal plumes, surge gray and foam-filled in boulder-choked gorges, and slip through the woods in long, tranquil reaches—after thus learning their language and forms in detail, we may at length hear them chanting all together in one grand anthem, and comprehend them all in clear inner vision, covering the range like lace. But even this spectacle is far less sublime and not a whit more substantial than what we may behold of these storm-streams of air in the mountain woods.

We all travel the milky way together, trees and men; but it never occurred to me until this storm-day, while swinging in the wind, that trees are travelers, in the ordinary sense. They make many journeys, not extensive ones, it is true; but our own little journeys, away and back again, are only little more than tree-wavings—many of them not so much.

When the storm began to abate, I dismounted and sauntered down through the calming woods. The storm-tones died away, and, turning toward the east, I beheld the countless hosts of the forests hushed and tranquil, towering above one another on the slopes of the hills like a devout audience. The setting sun filled them with amber light, and seemed to say, while they listened, "My peace I give unto you."

As I gazed on the impressive scene, all the so-called ruin of the storm was forgotten, and never before did these noble woods appear so fresh, so joyous, so immortal.

🦢 Thomas Hardy (1840–1928)

Thomas Hardy was born near Dorchester, in the southwest part of England known in his novels as "Wessex." He was apprenticed to a church architect for six years, but he aspired to become a professional writer, and in 1871 his first novel, Desperate Remedies, *was published anonymously. He found even greater success with his next two novels,* Under the Greenwood Tree *(1872) and* Far From the Madding Crowd *(1874). Hardy then embarked upon his Wessex novels, which he classified as novels of character and environment.* The Return of the Native *(1878),* The Mayor of Casterbridge *(1886),* The Woodlanders *(1887),* Tess of the D'Urbervilles *(1891), and* Jude the Obscure *(1896) are now generally considered his finest works. However, contemporary reviewers were harsh in their criticism, particularly of the last two novels, which were denounced as indecent, immoral, and corrupting in their influence on British youth. Perplexed and disgusted by such insensitive treatment of his work, Hardy abandoned novel writing entirely after 1896 and devoted himself instead to writing poetry.*

Wessex Poems was published in 1898, followed by Poems of the Past and the Present *(1901) and a lyric drama,* The Dynasts *(1904–8). The drama, first intended to be an epic poem on the Napoleonic era, gradually evolved into a compendious vehicle for Hardy's meditations on human society, nature, and the inscrutable supernatural force that governs the universe. Hardy published several more volumes of lyric poetry in the remaining years of his life, including* Satires of Circumstance *(1914),* Moments of Vision *(1917), and the posthumous* Winter Words *(1928).*

been tried in a hundred storms, waved solemnly above them, their long, arching branches streaming fluently on the gale, and every needle thrilling and ringing and shedding off keen lances of light like a diamond. The Douglas spruces, with long sprays drawn out in level tresses, and needles massed in a gray, shimmering glow, presented a most striking appearance as they stood in bold relief along the hilltops. The madroños[1] in the dells, with their red bark and large glossy leaves tilted every way, reflected the sunshine in throbbing spangles like those one so often sees on the rippled surface of a glacier lake. But the silver pines were now the most impressively beautiful of all. Colossal spires two hundred feet in height waved like supple goldenrods chanting and bowing low as if in worship, while the whole mass of their long, tremulous foliage was kindled into one continuous blaze of white sun-fire. The force of the gale was such that the most steadfast monarch of them all rocked down to its roots with a motion plainly perceptible when one leaned against it. Nature was holding high festival, and every fiber of the most rigid giants thrilled with glad excitement.

I drifted on through the midst of this passionate music and motion, across many a glen, from ridge to ridge; often halting in the lee of a rock for shelter, or to gaze and listen. Even when the grand anthem had swelled to its highest pitch, I could distinctly hear the varying tones of individual trees,—spruce, and fir, and pine, and leafless oak,—and even the infinitely gentle rustle of the withered grasses at my feet. Each was expressing itself in its own way,—singing its own song, and making its own peculiar gestures,—manifesting a richness of variety to be found in no other forest I have yet seen. The coniferous woods of Canada, and the Carolinas, and Florida, are made up of trees that resemble one another about as nearly as blades of grass, and grow close together in much the same way. Coniferous trees, in general, seldom possess individual character, such as is manifest among oaks and elms. But the California forests are made up of a greater number of distinct species than any other in the world. And in them we find, not only a marked differentiation into special groups, but also a marked individuality in almost every tree, giving rise to storm effects indescribably glorious.

Toward midday, after a long, tingling scramble through copses of hazel and ceanothus, I gained the summit of the highest ridge in the neighborhood; and then it occurred to me that it would be a fine thing to climb one of the trees to obtain a wider outlook and get my ear close to the Aeolian[2] music of its topmost needles. But under the circumstances the choice of a tree was a serious matter. One whose instep was not very strong seemed in danger of being blown down, or of being struck by others in case they should fall; another was branchless to a considerable height above the ground, and at the same time too large to be grasped with arms and legs in climbing; while others were not favorably situated for clear views. After cautiously casting about, I made choice of the tallest of a group of Douglas spruces that were growing close together like a tuft of grass, no one of which seemed likely to fall unless all the rest fell with it. Though com-

---

[1] An evergreen tree native to Pacific North America, with leathery leaves and edible red berries (American Spanish).

[2] Relating to Aeolus, god of the winds. Muir probably envisions the tree as an Aeolian harp, a favorite Romantic image for poetic inspiration. See Coleridge, "The Eolian Harp," page 463.

paratively young, they were about one hundred feet high, and their lithe, brushy tops were rocking and swirling in wild ecstasy. Being accustomed to climb trees in making botanical studies, I experienced no difficulty in reaching the top of this one, and never before did I enjoy so noble an exhilaration of motion. The slender tops fairly flapped and swished in the passionate torrent, bending and swirling backward and forward, round and round, tracing indescribable combinations of vertical and horizontal curves, while I clung with muscles firm braced, like a bobolink on a reed.

In its widest sweeps my tree-top described an arc of from twenty to thirty degrees, but I felt sure of its elastic temper, having seen others of the same species still more severely tried—bent almost to the ground indeed, in heavy snows—without breaking a fiber. I was therefore safe, and free to take the wind into my pulses and enjoy the excited forest from my superb outlook. The view from here must be extremely beautiful in any weather. Now my eye roved over the piny hills and dales as over fields of waving grain, and felt the light running in ripples and broad swelling undulations across the valleys from ridge to ridge, as the shining foliage was stirred by corresponding waves of air. Oftentimes these waves of reflected light would break up suddenly into a kind of beaten foam, and again, after chasing one another in regular order, they would seem to bend forward in concentric curves, and disappear on some hillside, like sea waves on a shelving shore. The quantity of light reflected from the bent needles was so great as to make whole groves appear as if covered with snow, while the black shadows beneath the trees greatly enhanced the effect of the silvery splendor.

Excepting only the shadows there was nothing somber in all this wild sea of pines. On the contrary, notwithstanding this was the winter season, the colors were remarkably beautiful. The shafts of the pine and libocedrus were brown and purple, and most of the foliage was well tinged with yellow; the laurel groves, with the pale undersides of their leaves turned upward, made masses of gray; and then there was many a dash of chocolate color from clumps of manzanita, and jet of vivid crimson from the bark of the madroños, while the ground on the hillsides, appearing here and there through openings between the groves, displayed masses of pale purple and brown.

The sounds of the storm corresponded gloriously with this wild exuberance of light and motion. The profound bass of the naked branches and boles booming like waterfalls; the quick, tense vibrations of the pine needles, now rising to a shrill, whistling hiss, now falling to a silky murmur; the rustling of laurel groves in the dells, and the keen, metallic click of leaf on leaf—all this was heard in easy analysis when the attention was calmly bent.

The varied gestures of the multitude were seen to fine advantage, so that one could recognize the different species at a distance of several miles by this means alone, as well as by their forms and colors, and the way they reflected the light. All seemed strong and comfortable, as if really enjoying the storm, while responding to its most enthusiastic greetings. We hear much nowadays concerning the universal struggle for existence,[3] but no struggle in the common meaning of the word was manifest here; no recognition of danger by any tree; no deprecation; but rather an invincible gladness as remote from exultation as from fear.

I kept my lofty perch for hours, frequently closing my eyes to enjoy the music by itself, or to feast quietly on the delicious fragrance that was streaming past. The fragrance of the woods was less marked than that produced during warm rain, when so many balsamic buds and leaves are steeped like tea; but, from the chafing of resiny branches against each other, and the incessant attrition of myriads of needles, the gale was spiced to a very tonic degree. And besides the fragrance from these local sources there were traces of scents brought from afar. For this wind came first from the sea, rubbing against its fresh, briny waves, then distilled through the redwoods, threading rich, ferny gulches, and spreading itself in broad, undulating currents over many a flower-enameled ridge of the coast mountains, then across the golden plains, up the purple foothills, and into these piny woods with the varied incense gathered by the way.

Winds are advertisements of all they touch, however much or little we may be able to read them; telling their wanderings even by their scents alone. Mariners detect the flowery perfume of land winds far at sea, and sea winds carry the fragrance of dulse[4] and tangle far inland, where it is quickly recognized, though mingled with the scents of a thousand land flowers. As an illustration of this, I may tell here that I breathed sea air on the Firth of Forth, in Scotland, while a boy; then was taken to Wisconsin, where I remained nineteen years; then, without in all this time having breathed one breath of the sea, I walked quietly, alone, from the middle of the Mississippi Valley to the Gulf of Mexico, on a botanical excursion, and while in Florida, far from the coast, my attention wholly bent on the splendid tropical vegetation about me, I suddenly recognized a sea breeze, as it came sifting through the palmettos and blooming vine tangles, which at once awakened and set free a thousand dormant associations, and made me a boy again in Scotland, as if all the intervening years had been annihilated.

Most people like to look at mountain rivers, and bear them in mind; but few care to look at the winds, though far more beautiful and sublime, and though they become at times about as visible as flowing water. When the north winds in winter are making upward sweeps over the curving summits of the High Sierra, the fact is sometimes published with flying snow-banners a mile long. Those portions of the winds thus embodied can scarce be wholly invisible, even to the darkest imagination. And when we look around over an agitated forest, we may see something of the wind that stirs it, by its effects upon the trees. Yonder it descends in a rush of water-like ripples, and sweeps over the bending pines from hill to hill. Nearer, we see detached plumes and leaves, now speeding by on level currents, now whirling in eddies, or, escaping over the edges of the whirls, soaring aloft on grand, upswelling domes of air, or tossing on flame-like crests. Smooth, deep currents, cascades, falls, and swirling eddies, sing around every tree and leaf, and overall the varied topography of the region with telling changes of form, like mountain rivers conforming to the features of their channels.

After tracing the Sierra streams from their fountains to the plains, marking

---

[3] Alludes to Charles Darwin's theory of natural selection in *On the Origin of Species* (1859).

[4] Edible red algae that grows on rocky seashores (a word of Scots Gaelic origin).

All of Hardy's writing is concerned with the way that human lives are shaped by the visible and invisible forces of nature. In his lyric poetry, Hardy presents brief anecdotes that illustrate the interconnectedness of human beings and the natural world that surrounds them. In some cases, the influence of nature is entirely benevolent, as in "Under the Waterfall"; but often the natural world seems grimly foreboding, as in "Neutral Tones" and "The Darkling Thrush." In such poems as "By the Earth's Corpse," the tone is positively apocalyptic, as the Lord reflects ruefully upon the world He has created and destroyed. Hardy's gloomy outlook must be understood in its historical context. Having lived through the brutal conflicts of the Boer War and the First World War, Hardy anticipated nothing but increased human suffering and environmental destruction as the inevitable consequence of advanced technology in the twentieth century. Unfortunately for us, he was entirely correct in this prediction.

Neutral Tones

We stood by a pond that winter day,
And the sun was white, as though chidden of God,
And a few leaves lay on the starving sod,
   — They had fallen from an ash, and were gray.

Your eyes on me were as eyes that rove   5
Over tedious riddles solved years ago;
And words played between us to and fro—
   On which lost the more by our love.

The smile on your mouth was the deadest thing
Alive enough to have strength to die;   10
And a grin of bitterness swept thereby
   Like an ominous bird a-wing. . . .

Since then, keen lessons that love deceives,
And wrings with wrong, have shaped to me
Your face, and the God-curst sun, and a tree,   15
   And a pond edged with grayish leaves.

Nature's Questioning

When I look forth at dawning, pool,
      Field, flock, and lonely tree,
      All seem to gaze at me
Like chastened children sitting silent in a school;

      Their faces dulled, constrained, and worn,   5
         As though the master's way

Through the long teaching day
Had cowed them till their early zest was overborne.

And on them stirs, in lippings mere,[1]
    (As if once clear in call,
    But now scarce breathed at all) —   10
"We wonder, ever wonder, why we find us here!

"Has some Vast Imbecility,
    Mighty to build and blend,
    But impotent to tend,   15
Framed us in jest, and left us now to hazardry?[2]

"Or come we of an Automaton
    Unconscious of our pains? . . .
    Or are we live remains
Of Godhead dying downwards, brain and eye now gone?   20

"Or is it that some high Plan betides,[3]
    As yet not understood,
    Of Evil stormed by Good,
We the Forlorn Hope over which Achievement strides?"

Thus things around. No answerer I. . . .   25
    Meanwhile the winds, and rains,
    And Earth's old glooms and pains
Are still the same, and Life and Death are neighbours nigh.

[1] Silently moving the lips.
[2] Chance, luck.
[3] Takes place; occurs.

By the Earth's Corpse

I

"O Lord, why grievest Thou? —
    Since Life has ceased to be
Upon this globe, now cold
    As lunar land and sea,
And humankind, and fowl, and fur   5
    Are gone eternally,
All is the same to Thee as ere
    They knew mortality."

2

"O Time," replied the Lord,
    "Thou read'st me ill, I ween;   10

Were all *the same*, I should not grieve
    At that late earthly scene,
Now blestly past—though planned by me
    With interest close and keen!—
Nay, nay: things now are *not* the same   15
    As they have earlier been.

3

    "Written indelibly
    On my eternal mind
    Are all the wrongs endured
    By Earth's poor patient kind,   20
Which my too oft unconscious hand
    Let enter undesigned.
No god can cancel deeds foredone,
    Or thy old coils unwind!

4

    "As when, in Noë's[1] days,   25
    I whelmed the plains with sea,
    So at this last, when flesh
    And herb but fossils be,
And, all extinct, their piteous dust
    Revolves obliviously,   30
That I made Earth, and life, and man,
    It still repenteth me!"[2]

[1] Noah.

[2] Alludes to Genesis 6.7: "The Lord said, I will destroy man whom I have created from the face of the earth . . . for it repenteth me that I have made them."

The Last Chrysanthemum

    Why should this flower delay so long
        To show its tremulous plumes?
Now is the time of plaintive robin song,
        When flowers are in their tombs.

    Through the slow summer, when the sun   5
        Called to each frond and whorl
That all he could for flowers was being done,
        Why did it not uncurl?

    It must have felt that fervid call
        Although it took no heed,   10

Waking but now, when leaves like corpses fall,
    And saps all retrocede.[1]

    Too late its beauty, lonely thing,
        The season's shine is spent,
Nothing remains for it but shivering   15
        In tempests turbulent.

    Had it a reason for delay,
        Dreaming in witlessness
That for a bloom so delicately gay
        Winter would stay its stress?   20

    —I talk as if the thing were born
        With sense to work its mind;
Yet it is but one mask of many worn
        By the Great Face behind.

[1] Go back (down into the roots).

The Darkling Thrush

I leant upon a coppice gate[1]
    When Frost was spectre-gray,
And Winter's dregs made desolate
    The weakening eye of day.
The tangled bine-stems scored the sky   5
    Like strings of broken lyres,
And all mankind that haunted nigh
    Had sought their household fires.

The land's sharp features seemed to be
    The Century's corpse outleant,[2]   10
His crypt the cloudy canopy,
    The wind his death-lament.
The ancient pulse of germ and birth
    Was shrunken hard and dry,
And every spirit upon earth   15
    Seemed fervourless as I.

At once a voice arose among
    The bleak twigs overhead
In a full-hearted evensong
    Of joy illimited;   20

[1] The gate to a thicket or grove of small trees.
[2] Leaning out (of its coffin). This poem was written on the last day of the nineteenth century, December 31, 1900.

been tried in a hundred storms, waved solemnly above them, their long, arching branches streaming fluently on the gale, and every needle thrilling and ringing and shedding off keen lances of light like a diamond. The Douglas spruces, with long sprays drawn out in level tresses, and needles massed in a gray, shimmering glow, presented a most striking appearance as they stood in bold relief along the hilltops. The madroños[1] in the dells, with their red bark and large glossy leaves tilted every way, reflected the sunshine in throbbing spangles like those one so often sees on the rippled surface of a glacier lake. But the silver pines were now the most impressively beautiful of all. Colossal spires two hundred feet in height waved like supple goldenrods chanting and bowing low as if in worship, while the whole mass of their long, tremulous foliage was kindled into one continuous blaze of white sun-fire. The force of the gale was such that the most steadfast monarch of them all rocked down to its roots with a motion plainly perceptible when one leaned against it. Nature was holding high festival, and every fiber of the most rigid giants thrilled with glad excitement.

I drifted on through the midst of this passionate music and motion, across many a glen, from ridge to ridge; often halting in the lee of a rock for shelter, or to gaze and listen. Even when the grand anthem had swelled to its highest pitch, I could distinctly hear the varying tones of individual trees,—spruce, and fir, and pine, and leafless oak,—and even the infinitely gentle rustle of the withered grasses at my feet. Each was expressing itself in its own way,—singing its own song, and making its own peculiar gestures,—manifesting a richness of variety to be found in no other forest I have yet seen. The coniferous woods of Canada, and the Carolinas, and Florida, are made up of trees that resemble one another about as nearly as blades of grass, and grow close together in much the same way. Coniferous trees, in general, seldom possess individual character, such as is manifest among oaks and elms. But the California forests are made up of a greater number of distinct species than any other in the world. And in them we find, not only a marked differentiation into special groups, but also a marked individuality in almost every tree, giving rise to storm effects indescribably glorious.

Toward midday, after a long, tingling scramble through copses of hazel and ceanothus, I gained the summit of the highest ridge in the neighborhood; and then it occurred to me that it would be a fine thing to climb one of the trees to obtain a wider outlook and get my ear close to the Aeolian[2] music of its topmost needles. But under the circumstances the choice of a tree was a serious matter. One whose instep was not very strong seemed in danger of being blown down, or of being struck by others in case they should fall; another was branchless to a considerable height above the ground, and at the same time too large to be grasped with arms and legs in climbing; while others were not favorably situated for clear views. After cautiously casting about, I made choice of the tallest of a group of Douglas spruces that were growing close together like a tuft of grass, no one of which seemed likely to fall unless all the rest fell with it. Though com-

---

[1] An evergreen tree native to Pacific North America, with leathery leaves and edible red berries (American Spanish).

[2] Relating to Aeolus, god of the winds. Muir probably envisions the tree as an Aeolian harp, a favorite Romantic image for poetic inspiration. See Coleridge, "The Eolian Harp," page 463.

746 The Nineteenth Century: All Creatures Great and Small

paratively young, they were about one hundred feet high, and their lithe, brushy tops were rocking and swirling in wild ecstasy. Being accustomed to climb trees in making botanical studies, I experienced no difficulty in reaching the top of this one, and never before did I enjoy so noble an exhilaration of motion. The slender tops fairly flapped and swished in the passionate torrent, bending and swirling backward and forward, round and round, tracing indescribable combinations of vertical and horizontal curves, while I clung with muscles firm braced, like a bobolink on a reed.

In its widest sweeps my tree-top described an arc of from twenty to thirty degrees, but I felt sure of its elastic temper, having seen others of the same species still more severely tried—bent almost to the ground indeed, in heavy snows—without breaking a fiber. I was therefore safe, and free to take the wind into my pulses and enjoy the excited forest from my superb outlook. The view from here must be extremely beautiful in any weather. Now my eye roved over the piny hills and dales as over fields of waving grain, and felt the light running in ripples and broad swelling undulations across the valleys from ridge to ridge, as the shining foliage was stirred by corresponding waves of air. Oftentimes these waves of reflected light would break up suddenly into a kind of beaten foam, and again, after chasing one another in regular order, they would seem to bend forward in concentric curves, and disappear on some hillside, like sea waves on a shelving shore. The quantity of light reflected from the bent needles was so great as to make whole groves appear as if covered with snow, while the black shadows beneath the trees greatly enhanced the effect of the silvery splendor.

Excepting only the shadows there was nothing somber in all this wild sea of pines. On the contrary, notwithstanding this was the winter season, the colors were remarkably beautiful. The shafts of the pine and libocedrus were brown and purple, and most of the foliage was well tinged with yellow; the laurel groves, with the pale undersides of their leaves turned upward, made masses of gray; and then there was many a dash of chocolate color from clumps of manzanita, and jet of vivid crimson from the bark of the madroños, while the ground on the hillsides, appearing here and there through openings between the groves, displayed masses of pale purple and brown.

The sounds of the storm corresponded gloriously with this wild exuberance of light and motion. The profound bass of the naked branches and boles booming like waterfalls; the quick, tense vibrations of the pine needles, now rising to a shrill, whistling hiss, now falling to a silky murmur; the rustling of laurel groves in the dells, and the keen, metallic click of leaf on leaf—all this was heard in easy analysis when the attention was calmly bent.

The varied gestures of the multitude were seen to fine advantage, so that one could recognize the different species at a distance of several miles by this means alone, as well as by their forms and colors, and the way they reflected the light. All seemed strong and comfortable, as if really enjoying the storm, while responding to its most enthusiastic greetings. We hear much nowadays concerning the universal struggle for existence,[3] but no struggle in the common meaning of

---

[3] Alludes to Charles Darwin's theory of natural selection in *On the Origin of Species* (1859).

the word was manifest here; no recognition of danger by any tree; no deprecation; but rather an invincible gladness as remote from exultation as from fear.

I kept my lofty perch for hours, frequently closing my eyes to enjoy the music by itself, or to feast quietly on the delicious fragrance that was streaming past. The fragrance of the woods was less marked than that produced during warm rain, when so many balsamic buds and leaves are steeped like tea; but, from the chafing of resiny branches against each other, and the incessant attrition of myriads of needles, the gale was spiced to a very tonic degree. And besides the fragrance from these local sources there were traces of scents brought from afar. For this wind came first from the sea, rubbing against its fresh, briny waves, then distilled through the redwoods, threading rich, ferny gulches, and spreading itself in broad, undulating currents over many a flower-enameled ridge of the coast mountains, then across the golden plains, up the purple foothills, and into these piny woods with the varied incense gathered by the way.

Winds are advertisements of all they touch, however much or little we may be able to read them; telling their wanderings even by their scents alone. Mariners detect the flowery perfume of land winds far at sea, and sea winds carry the fragrance of dulse[4] and tangle far inland, where it is quickly recognized, though mingled with the scents of a thousand land flowers. As an illustration of this, I may tell here that I breathed sea air on the Firth of Forth, in Scotland, while a boy; then was taken to Wisconsin, where I remained nineteen years; then, without in all this time having breathed one breath of the sea, I walked quietly, alone, from the middle of the Mississippi Valley to the Gulf of Mexico, on a botanical excursion, and while in Florida, far from the coast, my attention wholly bent on the splendid tropical vegetation about me, I suddenly recognized a sea breeze, as it came sifting through the palmettos and blooming vine tangles, which at once awakened and set free a thousand dormant associations, and made me a boy again in Scotland, as if all the intervening years had been annihilated.

Most people like to look at mountain rivers, and bear them in mind; but few care to look at the winds, though far more beautiful and sublime, and though they become at times about as visible as flowing water. When the north winds in winter are making upward sweeps over the curving summits of the High Sierra, the fact is sometimes published with flying snow-banners a mile long. Those portions of the winds thus embodied can scarce be wholly invisible, even to the darkest imagination. And when we look around over an agitated forest, we may see something of the wind that stirs it, by its effects upon the trees. Yonder it descends in a rush of water-like ripples, and sweeps over the bending pines from hill to hill. Nearer, we see detached plumes and leaves, now speeding by on level currents, now whirling in eddies, or, escaping over the edges of the whirls, soaring aloft on grand, upswelling domes of air, or tossing on flame-like crests. Smooth, deep currents, cascades, falls, and swirling eddies, sing around every tree and leaf, and overall the varied topography of the region with telling changes of form, like mountain rivers conforming to the features of their channels.

After tracing the Sierra streams from their fountains to the plains, marking

---

[4] Edible red algae that grows on rocky seashores (a word of Scots Gaelic origin).

where they bloom white in falls, glide in crystal plumes, surge gray and foam-filled in boulder-choked gorges, and slip through the woods in long, tranquil reaches—after thus learning their language and forms in detail, we may at length hear them chanting all together in one grand anthem, and comprehend them all in clear inner vision, covering the range like lace. But even this spectacle is far less sublime and not a whit more substantial than what we may behold of these storm-streams of air in the mountain woods.

We all travel the milky way together, trees and men; but it never occurred to me until this storm-day, while swinging in the wind, that trees are travelers, in the ordinary sense. They make many journeys, not extensive ones, it is true; but our own little journeys, away and back again, are only little more than tree-wavings—many of them not so much.

When the storm began to abate, I dismounted and sauntered down through the calming woods. The storm-tones died away, and, turning toward the east, I beheld the countless hosts of the forests hushed and tranquil, towering above one another on the slopes of the hills like a devout audience. The setting sun filled them with amber light, and seemed to say, while they listened, "My peace I give unto you."

As I gazed on the impressive scene, all the so-called ruin of the storm was forgotten, and never before did these noble woods appear so fresh, so joyous, so immortal.

◈ *Thomas Hardy* (1840–1928)

Thomas Hardy was born near Dorchester, in the southwest part of England known in his novels as "Wessex." He was apprenticed to a church architect for six years, but he aspired to become a professional writer, and in 1871 his first novel, Desperate Remedies, *was published anonymously. He found even greater success with his next two novels,* Under the Greenwood Tree *(1872) and* Far From the Madding Crowd *(1874). Hardy then embarked upon his Wessex novels, which he classified as novels of character and environment.* The Return of the Native *(1878),* The Mayor of Casterbridge *(1886),* The Woodlanders *(1887),* Tess of the D'Urbervilles *(1891), and* Jude the Obscure *(1896) are now generally considered his finest works. However, contemporary reviewers were harsh in their criticism, particularly of the last two novels, which were denounced as indecent, immoral, and corrupting in their influence on British youth. Perplexed and disgusted by such insensitive treatment of his work, Hardy abandoned novel writing entirely after 1896 and devoted himself instead to writing poetry.*

Wessex Poems was published in 1898, followed by Poems of the Past and the Present *(1901) and a lyric drama,* The Dynasts *(1904–8). The drama, first intended to be an epic poem on the Napoleonic era, gradually evolved into a compendious vehicle for Hardy's meditations on human society, nature, and the inscrutable supernatural force that governs the universe. Hardy published several more volumes of lyric poetry in the remaining years of his life, including* Satires of Circumstance *(1914),* Moments of Vision *(1917), and the posthumous* Winter Words *(1928).*

All of Hardy's writing is concerned with the way that human lives are shaped by the visible and invisible forces of nature. In his lyric poetry, Hardy presents brief anecdotes that illustrate the interconnectedness of human beings and the natural world that surrounds them. In some cases, the influence of nature is entirely benevolent, as in "Under the Waterfall"; but often the natural world seems grimly foreboding, as in "Neutral Tones" and "The Darkling Thrush." In such poems as "By the Earth's Corpse," the tone is positively apocalyptic, as the Lord reflects ruefully upon the world He has created and destroyed. Hardy's gloomy outlook must be understood in its historical context. Having lived through the brutal conflicts of the Boer War and the First World War, Hardy anticipated nothing but increased human suffering and environmental destruction as the inevitable consequence of advanced technology in the twentieth century. Unfortunately for us, he was entirely correct in this prediction.

Neutral Tones

We stood by a pond that winter day,
And the sun was white, as though chidden of God,
And a few leaves lay on the starving sod,
   —They had fallen from an ash, and were gray.

Your eyes on me were as eyes that rove   5
Over tedious riddles solved years ago;
And words played between us to and fro—
   On which lost the more by our love.

The smile on your mouth was the deadest thing
Alive enough to have strength to die;   10
And a grin of bitterness swept thereby
   Like an ominous bird a-wing. . . .

Since then, keen lessons that love deceives,
And wrings with wrong, have shaped to me
Your face, and the God-curst sun, and a tree,   15
   And a pond edged with grayish leaves.

Nature's Questioning

When I look forth at dawning, pool,
      Field, flock, and lonely tree,
      All seem to gaze at me
Like chastened children sitting silent in a school;

      Their faces dulled, constrained, and worn,   5
         As though the master's way

Through the long teaching day
Had cowed them till their early zest was overborne.

And on them stirs, in lippings mere,[1]
 (As if once clear in call,
 But now scarce breathed at all)—
"We wonder, ever wonder, why we find us here!

 "Has some Vast Imbecility,
  Mighty to build and blend,
  But impotent to tend,
Framed us in jest, and left us now to hazardry?[2]

 "Or come we of an Automaton
  Unconscious of our pains? . . .
  Or are we live remains
Of Godhead dying downwards, brain and eye now gone?

 "Or is it that some high Plan betides,[3]
  As yet not understood,
  Of Evil stormed by Good,
We the Forlorn Hope over which Achievement strides?"

 Thus things around. No answerer I. . . .
  Meanwhile the winds, and rains,
  And Earth's old glooms and pains
Are still the same, and Life and Death are neighbours nigh.

[1] Silently moving the lips.
[2] Chance, luck.
[3] Takes place; occurs.

By the Earth's Corpse

I

"O Lord, why grievest Thou?—
 Since Life has ceased to be
Upon this globe, now cold
 As lunar land and sea,
And humankind, and fowl, and fur
 Are gone eternally,
All is the same to Thee as ere
 They knew mortality."

2

"O Time," replied the Lord,
 "Thou read'st me ill, I ween;

Were all *the same*, I should not grieve
    At that late earthly scene,
Now blestly past—though planned by me
    With interest close and keen! —
Nay, nay: things now are *not* the same   15
    As they have earlier been.

3

    "Written indelibly
    On my eternal mind
    Are all the wrongs endured
    By Earth's poor patient kind,   20
Which my too oft unconscious hand
    Let enter undesigned.
No god can cancel deeds foredone,
    Or thy old coils unwind!

4

    "As when, in Noë's[1] days,   25
    I whelmed the plains with sea,
    So at this last, when flesh
    And herb but fossils be,
And, all extinct, their piteous dust
    Revolves obliviously,   30
That I made Earth, and life, and man,
    It still repenteth me!"[2]

[1] Noah.

[2] Alludes to Genesis 6.7: "The Lord said, I will destroy man whom I have created from the face of the earth . . . for it repenteth me that I have made them."

The Last Chrysanthemum

    Why should this flower delay so long
        To show its tremulous plumes?
Now is the time of plaintive robin song,
        When flowers are in their tombs.

    Through the slow summer, when the sun   5
        Called to each frond and whorl
That all he could for flowers was being done,
        Why did it not uncurl?

    It must have felt that fervid call
        Although it took no heed,   10

Waking but now, when leaves like corpses fall,
    And saps all retrocede.[1]

    Too late its beauty, lonely thing,
      The season's shine is spent,
Nothing remains for it but shivering   15
      In tempests turbulent.

    Had it a reason for delay,
      Dreaming in witlessness
That for a bloom so delicately gay
      Winter would stay its stress?   20

    —I talk as if the thing were born
      With sense to work its mind;
Yet it is but one mask of many worn
      By the Great Face behind.

[1] Go back (down into the roots).

The Darkling Thrush

I leant upon a coppice gate[1]
    When Frost was spectre-gray,
And Winter's dregs made desolate
    The weakening eye of day.
The tangled bine-stems scored the sky   5
    Like strings of broken lyres,
And all mankind that haunted nigh
    Had sought their household fires.

The land's sharp features seemed to be
    The Century's corpse outleant,[2]   10
His crypt the cloudy canopy,
    The wind his death-lament.
The ancient pulse of germ and birth
    Was shrunken hard and dry,
And every spirit upon earth   15
    Seemed fervourless as I.

At once a voice arose among
    The bleak twigs overhead
In a full-hearted evensong
    Of joy illimited;   20

[1] The gate to a thicket or grove of small trees.
[2] Leaning out (of its coffin). This poem was written on the last day of the nineteenth century, December 31, 1900.

An aged thrush, frail, gaunt, and small,
    In blast-beruffled plume,
Had chosen thus to fling his soul
    Upon the growing gloom.

So little cause for carollings   25
    Of such ecstatic sound
Was written on terrestrial things
    Afar or nigh around,
That I could think there trembled through
    His happy good-night air   30
Some blessed Hope, whereof he knew
    And I was unaware.

In Tenebris* I

    Wintertime nighs;
But my bereavement-pain
It cannot bring again:
    Twice no one dies.

    Flower-petals flee;   5
But, since it once hath been,
No more that severing scene
    Can harrow me.

    Birds faint in dread:
I shall not lose old strength   10
In the lone frost's black length:
    Strength long since fled!

    Leaves freeze to dun;
But friends can not turn cold
This season as of old   15
    For him with none.

    Tempests may scath;
But love can not make smart
Again this year his heart
    Who no heart hath.   20

    Black is night's cope;
But death will not appal
One who, past doubtings all,
    Waits in unhope.

* "In the Darkness" (Latin).

In Tenebris II

When the clouds' swoln bosoms echo back the shouts of the many
    and strong
That things are all as they best may be, save a few to be right ere long,
And my eyes have not the vision in them to discern what to these is
    so clear,
The blot seems straightway in me alone; one better he were not here.

The stout upstanders chime, All's well with us: ruers have nought to rue!   5
And what the potent so often say, can it fail to be somewhat true?
Breezily go they, breezily come; their dust smokes around their career,
Till I think I am one born out of due time, who has no calling here.

Their dawns bring lusty joys, it seems; their evenings all that is sweet;
Our times are blessed times, they cry: Life shapes it as is most meet,   10
And nothing is much the matter; there are many smiles to a tear;
Then what is the matter is I, I say. Why should such an one be here?. . .

Let him in whose ears the low-voiced Best is killed by the clash of
    the First,
Who holds that if way to the Better there be, it exacts a full look at
    the Worst,
Who feels that delight is a delicate growth cramped by crookedness,   15
    custom, and fear,
Get him up and be gone as one shaped awry; he disturbs the order here.

In Tenebris III

There have been times when I well might have passed and the ending
    have come—
Points in my path when the dark might have stolen on me, artless,
    unrueing—
Ere I had learnt that the world was a welter of futile doing:
Such had been times when I well might have passed, and the ending
    have come!

Say, on the noon when the half-sunny hours told that April was nigh,   5
And I upgathered and cast forth the snow from the crocus-border,
Fashioned and furbished the soil into a summer-seeming order,
Glowing in gladsome faith that I quickened the year thereby.

Or on that loneliest of eves when afar and benighted we stood,
She who upheld me and I, in the midmost of Egdon[1] together,   10
Confident I in her watching and ward through the blackening heather,
Deeming her matchless in might and with measureless scope endued.

---

[1] Egdon Heath, a gloomy, desolate setting for several of Hardy's Wessex novels.

Or on that winter-wild night when, reclined by the chimney-nook quoin,[2]
Slowly a drowse overgat me, the smallest and feeblest of folk there,
Weak from my baptism of pain; when at times and anon I awoke there—   15
Heard of a world wheeling on, with no listing or longing to join.

Even then! while unweeting that vision could vex or that knowledge
   could numb,
That sweets to the mouth in the belly are bitter, and tart, and untoward,
Then, on some dim-coloured scene should my briefly raised curtain have
   lowered,
Then might the Voice that is law have said "Cease!" and the ending   20
   have come.

[2] Corner.

Under the Waterfall

"Whenever I plunge my arm, like this,
In a basin of water, I never miss
The sweet sharp sense of a fugitive day
Fetched back from its thickening shroud of gray.
            Hence the only prime   5
            And real love-rhyme
            That I know by heart,
            And that leaves no smart,
Is the purl[1] of a little valley fall
About three spans[2] wide and two spans tall   10
Over a table of solid rock,
And into a scoop of the self-same block;
The purl of a runlet that never ceases
In stir of kingdoms, in wars, in peaces;
With a hollow boiling voice it speaks   15
And has spoken since hills were turfless peaks."

"And why gives this the only prime
Idea to you of a real love-rhyme?
And why does plunging your arm in a bowl
Full of spring water, bring throbs to your soul?"   20

"Well, under the fall, in a crease of the stone,
Though where precisely none ever has known,
Jammed darkly, nothing to show how prized,

[1] Murmuring noise.
[2] A span is the breadth of an extended hand, about nine inches.

And by now with its smoothness opalized,[3]
<blockquote>
Is a drinking-glass: 25
For, down that pass
My lover and I
Walked under a sky
</blockquote>
Of blue with a leaf-wove awning of green,
In the burn of August, to paint the scene,   30
And we placed our basket of fruit and wine
By the runlet's rim, where we sat to dine;
And when we had drunk from the glass together,
Arched by the oak-copse from the weather,
I held the vessel to rinse in the fall,   35
Where it slipped, and sank, and was past recall,
Though we stooped and plumbed the little abyss
With long bared arms. There the glass still is.
And, as said, if I thrust my arm below
Cold water in basin or bowl, a throe[4]   40
From the past awakens a sense of that time,
And the glass we used, and the cascade's rhyme.
The basin seems the pool, and its edge
The hard smooth face of the brook-side ledge,
And the leafy pattern of china-ware   45
The hanging plants that were bathing there.

"By night, by day, when it shines or lours,[5]
There lies intact that chalice of ours,
And its presence adds to the rhyme of love
Persistently sung by the fall above.   50
No lip has touched it since his and mine
In turns therefrom sipped lovers' wine."

---

[3] Rendered milky and translucent (like an opal) by gradual erosion in the streambed.

[4] Spasm of pain.

[5] Looks dark and ominous.

✍ *Gerard Manley Hopkins* (1844–1889)

It was only after his death that Gerard Manley Hopkins, as with Emily Dickinson, gained acclaim for his unique vision and verse. Educated at Oxford, Hopkins studied with Victorian aesthetes Matthew Arnold and Walter Pater. But it was John Henry Newman who exerted the most lasting influence upon his life, inspiring him to convert to Roman Catholicism, despite his family's strong disapproval, in 1866. Already devout and fastidiously ascetic, Hopkins soon decided to enter the highly disciplined order of the Society of Jesus; he was ordained as a Jesuit priest in 1877. He had written poetry as a young man, but soon after he began studying for the priesthood, he burned all of his early work, feeling it necessary to deny himself the pleasure he found in composing poetry. Hopkins did not write again until 1875, and then only after having received the approval and encouragement of his superiors in the order. In 1884 he became a professor of classics at University College, Dublin.

Always in poor health, Hopkins was given to bouts of severe depression and frequently struggled with his faith. Yet in his poetry, we enter into a world wherein all creation is a reflection or manifestation of divine goodness and justice. All creation, in Hopkins's theology, exhibited what he called "inscape" or an "inner landscape": that is, the uniqueness of an object, its "thisness," the contemplation of which led one to the magnificence of the Creator. By definition, then, inscape was more than a simply visual phenomenon. The predominant way in which Hopkins attempted to express his perception of the inscape of nature in his poetry was through his style and versification. Hopkins's difficult but intensely musical style employs irregular syntax, with complex and eccentric wording that is rich in sonorous effects such as alliteration and assonance. Most significant in his poetry is his own system of poetic metrics, called "sprung rhythm." As with most metrical systems, there is a limited number of stressed syllables. However, the number and placement of the unaccented syllables varies in each line of every poem, as if to echo the uniqueness in all creation. When the world discovered Hopkins in 1918, his poems seemed to resemble the more experimental works of the Modernist movement, despite the religious sensibility expressed in their content. His poems about the natural world express his belief in the beauty of the inner dynamism and outer variety of all God's creation. As he writes in "Pied Beauty":

> All things counter, original, spare, strange;
>> Whatever is fickle, freckled (who knows how?)
>>> With swift, slow; sweet, sour; adazzle, dim;
> He fathers-forth whose beauty is past change:
>> Praise him.

The beauty of nature, in Hopkins's poetry, always leads us back to an appreciation not of nature itself, but of God.

God's Grandeur

The world is charged with the grandeur of God.
    It will flame out, like shining from shook foil;
    It gathers to a greatness, like the ooze of oil
Crushed. Why do men then now not reck his rod?
Generations have trod, have trod, have trod;   5
    And all is seared with trade; bleared, smeared with toil;
    And wears man's smudge and shares man's smell: the soil
Is bare now, nor can foot feel, being shod.

And for all this, nature is never spent;
    There lives the dearest freshness deep down things;   10

And though the last lights off the black West went
   Oh, morning, at the brown brink eastward, springs—
Because the Holy Ghost over the bent
   World broods with warm breast and with ah! bright wings.

Spring

Nothing is so beautiful as Spring—
   When weeds, in wheels, shoot long and lovely and lush;
   Thrush's eggs look little low heavens, and thrush
Through the echoing timber does so rinse and wring
The ear, it strikes like lightnings to hear him sing;   5
   The glassy peartree leaves and blooms, they brush
   The descending blue; that blue is all in a rush
With richness; the racing lambs too have fair their fling.

What is all this juice and all this joy?
   A strain of the earth's sweet being in the beginning   10
In Eden garden.—Have, get, before it cloy,
   Before it cloud, Christ, lord, and sour with sinning,
Innocent mind and Mayday in girl and boy,
   Most, O maid's child,[1] thy choice and worthy the winning.

[1] I.e., Jesus Christ, son of the Virgin Mary.

The Windhover

To Christ our Lord

I caught this morning morning's minion, king-
   dom of daylight's dauphin,[1] dapple-dawn-drawn Falcon, in his riding
   Of the rolling level underneath him steady air, and striding
High there, how he rung upon the rein of a wimpling wing
In his ecstasy! then off, off forth on swing,   5
   As a skate's heel sweeps smooth on a bow-bend: The hurl and gliding
   Rebuffed the big wind. My heart in hiding
Stirred for a bird,—the achieve of, the mastery of the thing!

Brute beauty and valour and act, oh, air, pride, plume, here
   Buckle! AND the fire that breaks from thee then, a billion   10
Times told lovelier, more dangerous. O my chevalier![2]

[1] French term for the prince who will inherit the throne.
[2] French for "knight."

No wonder of it: shéer plód makes plough down sillion[3]
Shine, and blue-bleak embers, ah my dear,
  Fall, gall themselves, and gash gold-vermilion.

[3] In a field, this is the raised area between two plowed furrows.

Pied Beauty

Glory be to God for dappled things—
    For skies of couple-colour as a brinded cow;
        For rose-moles all in stipple upon trout that swim;
Fresh-firecoal chestnut-falls; finches' wings;
    Landscape plotted and pieced—fold, fallow, and plough;   5
        And áll trádes, their gear and tackle and trim.

All things counter, original, spare, strange;
    Whatever is fickle, freckled (who knows how?)
        With swift, slow; sweet, sour; adazzle, dim;
He fathers-forth whose beauty is past change: 10
                                Praise him.

Binsey Poplars

felled 1879

My aspens dear, whose airy cages quelled,
Quelled or quenched in leaves the leaping sun,
All felled, felled, are all felled;
    Of a fresh and following folded rank
                Not spared, not one   5
            That dandled a sandalled
        Shadow that swam or sank
On meadow and river and wind-wandering
    weed-winding bank.

O if we but knew what we do   10
        When we delve or hew—
    Hack and rack the growing green!
        Since country is so tender
    To touch, her being só slender,
    That, like this sleek and seeing ball   15
    But a prick will make no eye at all,

> Where we, even where we mean
>   To mend her we end her,
>   When we hew or delve:
> After-comers cannot guess the beauty been.   20
>   Ten or twelve, only ten or twelve
>   Strokes of havoc únselve
>   The sweet especial scene,
>   Rural scene, a rural scene,
>   Sweet especial rural scene.   25

Spring and Fall

to a young child

Márgarét, áre you gríeving
Over Goldengrove unleaving?
Leáves líke the things of man, you
With your fresh thoughts care for, can you?
Ah! ás the heart grows older   5
It will come to such sights colder
By and by, nor spare a sigh
Though worlds of wanwood leafmeal lie;
And yet you will weep and know why.
Now no matter, child, the name: 10
Sórrow's spríngs áre the same.
Nor mouth had, no nor mind, expressed
What heart heard of, ghost guessed:
It ís the blight man was born for,
It is Margaret you mourn for.   15

Inversnaid

This darksome burn, horseback brown,
His rollrock highroad roaring down;
In coop and in comb the fleece of his foam
Flutes and low to the lake falls home.

A windpuff-bonnet of fáwn-fróth   5
Turns and twindles over the broth
Of a pool so pitchblack, féll-fRówning,
It rounds and rounds Despair to drowning.

Degged with dew, dappled with dew
Are the groins of the braes[1] that the brook treads through,   10
Wiry heathpacks, flitches of fern,
And the beadbonny ash that sits over the burn.

What would the world be, once bereft
Of wet and of wilderness? Let them be left,
O let them be left, wildness and wet;   15
Long live the weeds and the wilderness yet.

[1] A hillside or bank.

As kingfishers catch fire

As kingfishers catch fire, dragonflies draw flame;
As tumbled over rim in roundy wells
Stones ring; like each tucked string tells, each hung bell's
Bow swung finds tongue to fling out broad its name;
Each mortal thing does one thing and the same: 5
Deals out that being indoors each one dwells;
Selves—goes itself; *myself* it speaks and spells,
Crying *Whát I dó is me: for that I came.*

I say móre: the just man justices;
Keeps gráce: thát keeps all his goings graces;   10
Acts in God's eye what in God's eye he is—
Chríst—for Christ plays in ten thousand places,
Lovely in limbs, and lovely in eyes not his
To the Father through the features of men's faces.

🦢 *Sarah Orne Jewett* (*1849–1909*)

The rugged landscape of rural Maine is an essential ingredient in most of Sarah Orne Jewett's fiction. She captures the contours of this region with the same skill that she uses to reproduce the cadences of the dialect of its inhabitants. Born in South Berwick, Maine, she came to know the countryside and the people who lived there while she was a young girl, accompanying her father, a doctor, on his medical rounds. After finishing her schooling at Berwick Academy, she began writing professionally in 1865 and published her work in magazines such as Atlantic Monthly. *Her collection* A White Heron, and Other Stories *appeared in 1886, with another edition of short stories,* The King of Folly Island, *following in 1888. Although she felt her true gift was in short fiction, she also wrote novels, the best known of which remains* The Country of the Pointed Firs *(1896).*

Jewett is admired for the lyricism of her narratives, which rely less on action-driven plots and more upon the exploration of relationships, whether it is the relationship of the individual person to their natural environment or relationships between people. Jewett places special emphasis on friendships between women. Her attention to the question of gendered relationships to the environment is in the foreground in "A White Heron." The young heroine, Sylvia, is named for the woods—the Latin term for forest is sylva—which she inhabits and with which she is identified. She is transformed in her pivotal encounter with the hunter, for whom nature is merely an object to be conquered. The story plays out confrontations not just between the human and the natural but also between rural and urban and conventional female and male attitudes toward nature. Jewett's voice and woman-centered fictional world influenced subsequent women authors such as Kate Chopin and Willa Cather, who dedicated her novel O Pioneers! *to Jewett.*

A White Heron

I

The woods were already filled with shadows one June evening, just before eight o'clock, though a bright sunset still glimmered faintly among the trunks of the trees. A little girl was driving home her cow, a plodding, dilatory, provoking creature in her behavior, but a valued companion for all that. They were going away from the western light, and striking deep into the dark woods, but their feet were familiar with the path, and it was no matter whether their eyes could see it or not.

There was hardly a night the summer through when the old cow could be found waiting at the pasture bars; on the contrary, it was her greatest pleasure to hide herself away among the high huckleberry bushes, and though she wore a loud bell she had made the discovery that if one stood perfectly still it would not ring. So Sylvia had to hunt for her until she found her, and call Co'! Co'! with never an answering Moo, until her childish patience was quite spent. If the creature had not given good milk and plenty of it, the case would have seemed very different to her owners. Besides, Sylvia had all the time there was, and very little use to make of it. Sometimes in pleasant weather it was a consolation to look upon the cow's pranks as an intelligent attempt to play hide and seek, and as the child had no playmates she lent herself to this amusement with a good deal of zest. Though this chase had been so long that the wary animal herself had given an unusual signal of her whereabouts, Sylvia had only laughed when she came upon Mistress Moolly at the swamp-side, and urged her affectionately homeward with a twig of birch leaves. The old cow was not inclined to wander farther, she even turned in the right direction for once as they left the pasture, and stepped along the road at a good pace. She was quite ready to be milked now, and seldom stopped to browse. Sylvia wondered what her grandmother would say because they were so late. It was a great while since she had left home at half past five o'clock, but everybody knew the difficulty of making this errand a short one. Mrs. Tilley had chased the hornéd torment too many summer evenings herself to blame any one else for lingering, and was only thankful as she waited that she had Sylvia, nowadays, to give such valuable assistance. The good woman suspected that Sylvia loitered occasionally on her own account; there never was such a child for straying about out-of-doors since the world was made! Everybody said that it was a good change for a little maid who had tried to grow for eight years in a crowded manufacturing town, but, as for Sylvia herself, it seemed as if she never had been alive at all before she came to live at the farm. She thought often with wistful compassion of a wretched dry geranium that belonged to a town neighbor.

"'Afraid of folks,'" old Mrs. Tilley said to herself, with a smile, after she had made the unlikely choice of Sylvia from her daughter's houseful of children, and was returning to the farm. "'Afraid of folks,' they said! I guess she won't be troubled no great with 'em up to the old place!" When they reached the door of the lonely house and stopped to unlock it, and the cat came to purr loudly, and rub against them, a deserted pussy, indeed, but fat with young robins, Sylvia whispered that this was a beautiful place to live in, and she never should wish to go home.

The companions followed the shady wood-road, the cow taking slow steps, and the child very fast ones. The cow stopped long at the brook to drink, as if the pasture were not half a swamp, and Sylvia stood still and waited, letting her bare feet cool themselves in the shoal water, while the great twilight moths struck softly against her. She waded on through the brook as the cow moved away, and listened to the thrushes with a heart that beat fast with pleasure. There was a stirring in the great boughs overhead. They were full of little birds and beasts that seemed to be wide awake, and going about their world, or else saying goodnight to each other in sleepy twitters. Sylvia herself felt sleepy as she walked along. However, it was not much farther to the house, and the air was soft and sweet. She was not often in the woods so late as this, and it made her feel as if she were a part of the gray shadows and the moving leaves. She was just thinking how long it seemed since she first came to the farm a year ago, and wondering if everything went on in the noisy town just the same as when she was there; the thought of the great red-faced boy who used to chase and frighten her made her hurry along the path to escape from the shadow of the trees.

Suddenly this little woods-girl is horror-stricken to hear a clear whistle not very far away. Not a bird's whistle, which would have a sort of friendliness, but a boy's whistle, determined, and somewhat aggressive. Sylvia left the cow to whatever sad fate might await her, and stepped discreetly aside into the bushes, but she was just too late. The enemy had discovered her, and called out in a very cheerful and persuasive tone, "Halloa, little girl, how far is it to the road?" and trembling Sylvia answered almost inaudibly, "A good ways."

She did not dare to look boldly at the tall young man, who carried a gun over his shoulder, but she came out of her bush and again followed the cow, while he walked alongside.

"I have been hunting for some birds," the stranger said kindly, "and I have lost my way, and need a friend very much. Don't be afraid," he added gallantly. "Speak up and tell me what your name is, and whether you think I can spend the night at your house, and go out gunning early in the morning."

Sylvia was more alarmed than before. Would not her grandmother consider her much to blame? But who could have foreseen such an accident as this? It did not appear to be her fault, and she hung her head as if the stem of it were broken, but managed to answer "Sylvy," with much effort when her companion again asked her name.

Mrs. Tilley was standing in the doorway when the trio came into view. The cow gave a loud moo by way of explanation.

"Yes, you'd better speak up for yourself, you old trial! Where'd she tucked herself away this time, Sylvy?" Sylvia kept an awed silence; she knew by instinct that her grandmother did not comprehend the gravity of the situation. She must be mistaking the stranger for one of the farmer-lads of the region.

The young man stood his gun beside the door, and dropped a heavy game-bag beside it; then he bade Mrs. Tilley good-evening, and repeated his wayfarer's story, and asked if he could have a night's lodging.

"Put me anywhere you like," he said. "I must be off early in the morning, before day; but I am very hungry, indeed. You can give me some milk at any rate, that's plain."

"Dear sakes, yes," responded the hostess, whose long slumbering hospitality seemed to be easily awakened. "You might fare better if you went out on the main road a mile or so, but you're welcome to what we've got. I'll milk right off, and you make yourself at home. You can sleep on husks or feathers," she proffered graciously. "I raised them all myself. There's good pasturing for geese just below here towards the ma'sh. Now step round and set a plate for the gentleman, Sylvy!" And Sylvia promptly stepped. She was glad to have something to do, and she was hungry herself.

It was a surprise to find so clean and comfortable a little dwelling in this New England wilderness. The young man had known the horrors of its most primitive housekeeping, and the dreary squalor of that level of society which does not rebel at the companionship of hens. This was the best thrift of an old-fashioned farmstead, though on such a small scale that it seemed like a hermitage. He listened eagerly to the old woman's quaint talk, he watched Sylvia's pale face and shining gray eyes with ever growing enthusiasm, and insisted that this was the best supper he had eaten for a month; then afterward, the new-made friends sat down in the doorway together while the moon came up.

Soon it would be berry-time, and Sylvia was a great help at picking. The cow was a good milker, though a plaguy thing to keep track of, the hostess gossiped frankly, adding presently that she had buried four children, so that Sylvia's mother, and a son (who might be dead) in California were all the children she had left. "Dan, my boy, was a great hand to go gunning," she explained sadly. "I never wanted for pa'tridges or gray squer'ls while he was to home. He's been a great wand'rer, I expect, and he's no hand to write letters. There, I don't blame him, I'd ha' seen the world myself if it had been so I could.

"Sylvia takes after him," the grandmother continued affectionately, after a minute's pause. "There ain't a foot o' ground she don't know her way over, and the wild creatur's counts her one o' themselves. Squer'ls she'll tame to come an' feed right out o' her hands, and all sorts o' birds. Last winter she got the jay-birds to banging here, and I believe she'd 'a' scanted herself of her own meals to have plenty to throw out amongst 'em, if I hadn't kep' watch. Anything but crows, I tell her, I'm willin' to help support,—though Dan he went an' tamed one o' them that did seem to have reason same as folks. It was round here a good spell after he went away. Dan an' his father they didn't hitch,—but he never held up his head ag'in after Dan had dared him an' gone off."

The guest did not notice this hint of family sorrows in his eager interest in something else.

"So Sylvy knows all about birds, does she?" he exclaimed, as he looked round at the little girl who sat, very demure but increasingly sleepy, in the moonlight. "I am making a collection of birds myself. I have been at it ever since I was a boy." (Mrs. Tilley smiled.) "There are two or three very rare ones I have been hunting for these five years. I mean to get them on my own ground if they can be found."

"Do you cage 'em up?" asked Mrs. Tilley doubtfully, in response to this enthusiastic announcement.

"Oh, no, they're stuffed and preserved, dozens and dozens of them," said the ornithologist, "and I have shot or snared every one myself. I caught a glimpse of a white heron three miles from here on Saturday, and I have followed it in this direction. They have never been found in this district at all. The little white heron, it is," and he turned again to look at Sylvia with the hope of discovering that the rare bird was one of her acquaintances.

But Sylvia was watching a hop-toad in the narrow footpath.

"You would know the heron if you saw it," the stranger continued eagerly. "A queer tall white bird with soft feathers and long thin legs. And it would have a nest perhaps in the top of a high tree, made of sticks, something like a hawk's nest."

Sylvia's heart gave a wild beat; she knew that strange white bird, and had once stolen softly near where it stood in some bright green swamp grass, away over at the other side of the woods. There was an open place where the sunshine always seemed strangely yellow and hot, where tall, nodding rushes grew, and her grandmother had warned her that she might sink in the soft black mud underneath and never be heard of more. Not far beyond were the salt marshes and beyond those was the sea, the sea which Sylvia wondered and dreamed about, but never had looked upon, though its great voice could often be heard above the noise of the woods on stormy nights.

"I can't think of anything I should like so much as to find that heron's nest," the handsome stranger was saying. "I would give ten dollars to anybody who could show it to me," he added desperately, "and I mean to spend my whole vacation hunting for it if need be. Perhaps it was only migrating, or had been chased of out its own region by some bird of prey."

Mrs. Tilley gave amazed attention to all this, but Sylvia still watched the toad, not divining, as she might have done at some calmer time, that the creature wished to get to its hole under the doorstep, and was much hindered by the unusual spectators at that hour of the evening. No amount of thought, that night, could decide how many wished-for treasures the ten dollars, so lightly spoken of, would buy.

The next day the young sportsman hovered about the woods, and Sylvia kept him company, having lost her first fear of the friendly lad, who proved to be most kind and sympathetic. He told her many things about the birds and what they knew and where they lived and what they did with themselves. And he gave her a jack-knife, which she thought as great a treasure as if she were a desert islander. All day long he did not once make her troubled or afraid except when he brought down some unsuspecting singing creature from its bough. Sylvia would have liked him vastly better without his gun; she could not understand why he killed the very birds he seemed to like so much. But as the day waned, Sylvia still watched the young man with loving admiration. She had never seen anybody so charming and delightful; the woman's heart, asleep in the child, was vaguely thrilled by a dream of love. Some premonition of that great power stirred and swayed these young foresters who traversed the solemn woodlands with soft-footed silent care. They stopped to listen to a bird's song; they pressed forward again eagerly, parting the branches,—speaking to each other rarely and in whispers; the young man going first and Sylvia following, fascinated, a few steps behind, with her gray eyes dark with excitement.

She grieved because the longed-for white heron was elusive, but she did not lead the guest, she only followed, and there was no such thing as speaking first. The sound of her own unquestioned voice would have terrified her,—it was hard enough to answer yes or no when there was need of that. At last evening began to fall, and they drove the cow home together, and Sylvia smiled with pleasure when they came to the place where she heard the whistle and was afraid only the night before.

II

Half a mile from home, at the farther edge of the woods, where the land was highest, a great pine tree stood, the last of its generation. Whether it was left for a boundary mark, or for what reason, no one could say; the woodchoppers who had felled its mates were dead and gone long ago, and a whole forest of sturdy trees, pines and oaks and maples, had grown again. But the stately head of this old pine towered above them all and made a landmark for sea and shore miles and miles away. Sylvia knew it well. She had always believed that whoever climbed to the top of it could see the ocean; and the little girl had often laid her hand on the great rough trunk and looked up wistfully at those dark boughs that the wind always stirred, no matter how hot and still the air might be below. Now she thought of the tree with a new excitement, for why, if one climbed it at break of day, could not one see all the world, and easily discover whence the white heron flew, and mark the place, and find the hidden nest?

What a spirit of adventure, what wild ambition! What fancied triumph and delight and glory for the later morning when she could make known the secret! It was almost too real and too great for the childish heart to bear.

All night the door of the little house stood open, and the whippoorwills came and sang upon the very step. The young sportsman and his old hostess were sound asleep, but Sylvia's great design kept her broad awake and watching. She forgot to think of sleep. The short summer night seemed as long as the winter darkness, and at last when the whippoorwills ceased, and she was afraid the morning would after all come too soon, she stole out of the house and followed the pasture path through the woods, hastening toward the open ground beyond, listening with a sense of comfort and companionship to the drowsy twitter of a half-awakened bird, whose perch she had jarred in passing. Alas, if the great wave of human interest which flooded for the first time this dull little life should sweep away the satisfactions of an existence heart to heart with nature and the dumb life of the forest!

There was the huge tree asleep yet in the paling moonlight, and small and hopeful Sylvia began with utmost bravery to mount to the top of it, with tingling, eager blood coursing the channels of her whole frame, with her bare feet and fingers, that pinched and held like bird's claws to the monstrous ladder reaching up, up, almost to the sky itself. First she must mount the white oak tree that grew alongside, where she was almost lost among the dark branches and the green leaves heavy and wet with dew; a bird fluttered off its nest, and a red squirrel ran to and fro and scolded pettishly at the harmless housebreaker. Sylvia felt her way easily. She had often climbed there, and knew that higher still one of the oak's upper branches chafed against the pine trunk, just where its lower boughs were set close together. There, when she made the dangerous pass from one tree to the other, the great enterprise would really begin.

She crept out along the swaying oak limb at last, and took the daring step across into the old pine tree. The way was harder than she thought; she must reach far and hold fast, the sharp dry twigs caught and held her and scratched her like angry talons, the pitch made her thin little fingers clumsy and stiff as she went round and round the tree's great stem, higher and higher upward. The sparrows and robins in the woods below were beginning to wake and twitter to the dawn, yet it seemed much lighter there aloft in the pine tree, and the child knew that she must hurry if her project were to be of any use.

The tree seemed to lenghten itself out as she went up, and to reach farther and farther upward. It was like a great main-mast to the voyaging earth; it must truly have been amazed that morning through all its ponderous frame as it felt this determined spark of human spirit creeping and climbing from higher branch to branch. Who knows how steadily the least twigs held themselves to advantage this light, weak creature on her way! The old pine must have loved his new dependent. More than all the hawks, and bats, and moths, and even the sweet-voiced thrushes, was the brave, beating heart of the solitary gray-eyed child. And the tree stood still and held away the winds that June morning while the dawn grew bright in the east.

Sylvia's face was like a pale star, if one had seen it from the ground, when the last thorny bough was past, and she stood trembling and tired but wholly triumphant, high in the tree-top. Yes, there was the sea with the dawning sun making a golden dazzle over it, and toward that glorious east flew two hawks with slow-moving pinions. How low they looked in the air from that height when before one had only seen them far up, and dark against the blue sky. Their gray feathers were as soft as moths; they seemed only a little way from the tree, and

Sylvia felt as if she too could go flying away among the clouds. Westward, the woodlands and farms reached miles and miles into the distance; here and there were church steeples, and white villages; truly it was a vast and awesome world.

The birds sang louder and louder. At last the sun came up bewilderingly bright. Sylvia could see the white sails of ships out at sea, and the clouds that were purple and rose-colored and yellow at first began to fade away. Where was the white heron's nest in the sea of green branches, and was this wonderful sight and pageant of the world the only reward for having climbed to such a giddy height? Now look down again, Sylvia, where the green marsh is set among the shining birches and dark hemlocks; there where you saw the white heron once you will see him again; look, look! a white spot of him like a single floating feather comes up from the dead hemlock and grows larger, and rises, and comes close at last, and goes by the landmark pine with steady sweep of wing and out-stretched slender neck and crested head. And wait! wait! do not move a foot or a finger, little girl, do not send an arrow of light and consciousness from your two eager eyes, for the heron has perched on a pine bough not far beyond yours, and cries back to his mate on the nest, and plumes his feathers for the new day!

The child gives a long sigh a minute later when a company of shouting cat-birds comes also to the tree, and vexed by their fluttering and lawlessness the solemn heron goes away. She knows his secret now, the wild, light, slender bird that floats and wavers, and goes back like an arrow presently to his home in the green world beneath. Then Sylvia, well satisfied, makes her perilous way down again, not daring to look far below the branch she stands on, ready to cry some-times because her fingers ache and her lamed feet slip. Wondering over and over again what the stranger would say to her, and what he would think when she told him how to find his way straight to the heron's nest.

"Sylvy, Sylvy!" called the busy old grandmother again and again, but nobody an-swered, and the small husk bed was empty, and Sylvia had disappeared.

The guest waked from a dream, and remembering his day's pleasure hurried to dress himself that it might sooner begin. He was sure from the way the shy lit-tle girl looked once or twice yesterday that she had at least seen the white heron, and now she must really be persuaded to tell. Here she comes now, paler than ever, and her worn old frock is torn and tattered, and smeared with pine pitch. The grandmother and the sportsman stand in the door together and question her, and the splendid moment has come to speak of the dead hemlock tree by the green marsh.

But Sylvia does not speak after all, though the old grandmother fretfully re-bukes her, and the young man's kind appealing eyes are looking straight in her own. He can make them rich with money; he has promised it, and they are poor now. He is so well worth making happy, and he waits to hear the story she can tell.

No, she must keep silence! What is it that suddenly forbids her and makes her dumb? Has she been nine years growing, and now, when the great world for the first time puts out a hand to her, must she thrust it aside for a bird's sake? The murmur of the pine's green branches is in her ears, she remembers how the white heron came flying through the golden air and how they watched the sea and the morning together, and Sylvia cannot speak; she cannot tell the heron's secret and give its life away.

Dear loyalty, that suffered a sharp pang as the guest went away disappointed later in the day, that could have served and followed him and loved him as a dog loves! Many a night Sylvia heard the echo of his whistle haunting the pasture path as she came home with the loitering cow. She forgot even her sorrow at the sharp report of his gun and the piteous sight of thrushes and sparrows dropping silent to the ground, their songs hushed and their pretty feathers stained and wet with blood. Were the birds better friends than their hunter might have been,—who can tell? Whatever treasures were lost to her, woodlands and summer-time, remember! Bring your gifts and graces and tell your secrets to this lonely country child!

The Twentieth Century: The Web of Life

O ne of the most telling images to emerge into popular consciousness during the late twentieth century is a picture of Earth taken in 1969 by the
Apollo astronauts on their way to the Moon. Seen from that vantage
point, Earth was a distant blue globe fleeced by clouds, hanging silent in the
blackness of space, surrounded by stars. As never before, Earth appeared a small,
fragile place, unique in its ability to support life, especially when it rose above
the jagged and lifeless horizon of the Moon. This single image has been repro-
duced so many times in magazines, on television, and on posters and T-shirts
that it is now part of our common cultural heritage, and it reflects many ideas
that were emerging into public awareness during the mid-twentieth century
about the earth, the global environment, and the role of advanced technology,
both in sustaining human life and in threatening to destroy natural ecosystems.

The U.S. space program is itself a prime example of the enduring American
belief in technology, and the Apollo moon landing represented a culmination in
the development of several high-technology fields, including rocket propulsion,
astrophysics, metallurgy, and digital computers, without which the moon landing
could not have been successful. Indeed, ever since the dawn of the Industrial Revolution, both Britain and America have been at the forefront of new technological
developments, and the remarkable improvements in transportation and communication as well as dramatic increases in standards of living in the nineteenth and
twentieth centuries have occurred as the result of an astonishingly rapid pace of
scientific discovery and technological innovation. England was the cradle of the
Industrial Revolution, as James Watt's invention of the steam engine provided a
new power source for textile factories, steel mills, steamships, and railroads.
During the nineteenth century, both Britain and the United States witnessed the
rapid spread of railroads, which eventually linked the local economies of both

nations in a seamless web of national and international commerce. The process of industrialization continued to accelerate during the twentieth century; daily life was transformed for millions of people through the invention of new technologies of communication, mainly developed in America, including the telephone, the phonograph record, the motion picture, radio, television, and (most recently) the Internet. Over the course of the twentieth century, the automobile transformed daily life—and the design of the built landscape—even more dramatically than the railroad had done in the previous century. Automobiles became affordable to millions of people after 1920, when Henry Ford started mass-producing his Model T roadster, and an entirely new industrial infrastructure was built to accommodate the insatiable demand for larger and more powerful vehicles. In both Britain and America, the automobile radically changed the look of the landscape, as thousands of miles of highways were constructed, urban cores became congested with traffic, and the suburban way of life, with its bungalows, lawn mowers, gas stations, and shopping malls, came into being. Along with suburbanization came the consumer lifestyle, whereby one's social status and sense of self-worth were measured by the gross accumulation of mass-produced objects.

New technologies, and the new lifestyles they made possible, were met with attitudes ranging from ecstatic celebration to deep concern about the social and environmental consequences of unlimited industrial development. In 1900 Britain and the United States were the world's dominant military and industrial powers, and their prospects for continued economic growth seemed virtually unlimited. Many British and American writers applauded the onward march of technology and reflected the prevailing tone of optimism. But already at the turn of the century, several writers were expressing serious concern about the future of industrial capitalism, especially with regard to its effects on the rural landscape and the creatures that inhabit the earth's wild places. Thomas Hardy, in "The Darkling Thrush," surveys a desolate rural landscape in midwinter. Pondering the incongruously cheerful song of a thrush, Hardy can see no reason for optimism about the future of humankind. A similar note of gloom and fatalism creeps into the work of several American writers of the early twentieth century. Stephen Crane's story "The Open Boat" depicts human beings as pawns of an implacable fate, and their struggle for survival as ultimately meaningless. Jack London's story "To Build a Fire" describes a similar struggle for survival in the Arctic wilderness; ironically, a dog turns out to be much better adapted for survival in this harsh climate than even the most clever and well-equipped human. The human intellect, even when assisted by technology, is ultimately powerless to defeat nature. Both of these stories question American self-confidence and technological prowess.

As the twentieth century unfolded, many more writers began to question the value of the vast military-industrial enterprise that had come to involve the entire global economy. Two world wars resulted in a greater loss of human life than in all previous wars combined. The invention and widespread deployment of the atomic bomb meant that, for the first time, global annihilation was a distinct possibility. Meanwhile, the lethal consequences of industrial pollution, ozone depletion, and global warming became ever more apparent. In the latter half of the twentieth century, most people in the English-speaking world became fully aware of the adverse environmental consequences of global industrial development. Many of the writers represented in this anthology were instrumental in bringing about this dramatic change in public awareness. Rachel Carson sparked the formation of the modern environmental movement with the publication of her book *Silent Spring*, which describes the lethal effects of chemical pollutants in the air we breathe and the water we drink in chilling and scientifically accurate detail. Carson's previous nonfiction book, *The Edge of the Sea* (1955), brought a deep ecological understanding to its lyrical depiction of shoreline habitat, and this best-selling book likewise did a great deal to create an environmental sensibility among its readers. Aldo Leopold's influential essay "Thinking Like a Mountain" is another important instance of environmental advocacy that actually brought about a significant change in public awareness. Leopold's elegy for a dying wolf not only created a strong sense of outrage in its readers, it also kindled a desire to see his preservationist "land ethic" realized before America's last wild creatures were hunted to extinction. In the twentieth century, as never before, environmental writing has had a direct effect on public awareness and public policy. The passage of landmark environmental legislation, such as the Clean Water Act and the Endangered Species Act, owes much to the persistent and eloquent advocacy of writers like Carson and Leopold.

Several other nonfiction prose writers of the twentieth century have combined effective environmental advocacy with luminous, powerful modes of personal expression. Mary Hunter Austin, in *The Land of Little Rain*, penned an environmental classic in defense of the California desert and all of its native creatures, even such despised "vermin" as vultures and coyotes. Edward Abbey, in *Desert Solitaire*, also writes evocatively of a fragile desert landscape that is threatened with destruction by miners, developers, and the tourist industry. Gretel Ehrlich, in the gracefully written essay "On Water," describes her self-sufficient way of life on a Wyoming ranch. Barry Lopez, in *Arctic Dreams*, tells of his fleeting encounter with one of the world's most rare and elusive creatures: *Monodon monoceros*, the narwhal. All of these writers explore the boundless possibilities of natural description, environmental advocacy, and personal expression within the literary genre of the natural history essay.

While nonfiction prose, especially in the form of the natural history essay, has played a vital role in twentieth-century nature writing, a wide variety of other literary forms have continued to develop in significant ways. The personal essay has taken on a confessional tone in several writers of the twentieth century, from Luther Standing Bear's account of his initiation into buffalo hunting through Terry Tempest Williams's narrative reworking of traditional Native American tales of Bear. In the latter instance, the border between nonfiction and fiction seems especially porous and permeable, as Williams presents her dreamlike experience of identification with a powerful predator. Short stories, such as Wallace Stegner's "The Colt," may be regarded as approaching the confessional mode from another angle. While doubtless founded in part upon Stegner's knowledge of the difficult necessities of rural life, this story of the relationship between a boy and a horse suggests that an essential ingredient in coming of age is confronting the beauties and the cruelties of nature. The young protagonist's psychological development is intimately tied with his material surroundings, and, as often occurs in modern short fiction, the central character discovers something about himself and the world through a strenuous encounter with nature.

British and American poets of the twentieth century have used a wide variety of metrical forms to express their views of the natural world. In the first half of the century, the advent of literary Modernism was accompanied by the demise of virtually all fixed poetic forms and the advent of free verse, an unrhymed form in which the length of the line is quite variable, determined by the local cadence of particular phrases rather than by a set number of syllables. Walt Whitman used an expansive form of free verse in the mid-nineteenth century, but the new Modernist mode of poetry pioneered by Ezra Pound and T. S. Eliot tends to be much shorter in line length, clipped and spare. Few Modernist writers evinced any appreciation or fondness for the natural world, projecting instead a bleak and forbidding urban landscape, often devoid of human meaning or moral purpose. However, the Modernist poet H. D. (Hilda Doolittle) drew upon the French technique known as Imagism to create poems that celebrated the beauty of the natural world in terse, enigmatic lines. In such poems as "Sea Lily" and "Sheltered Garden," H. D. examines whether it is possible to represent natural objects purely and simply as they appear to our senses, thereby resisting the common Victorian tendency to explain or moralize the object. The poems of H. D. have been widely influential in Britain and America; her concise handling of imagery and her innovative use of free verse have found followers among many of the poets represented here, particularly D. H. Lawrence (who was a close friend of H. D. during the early years of her career), as well as Robinson Jeffers, Denise Levertov, and Mary Oliver. Because she was first "discovered" at age 15 by Ezra Pound, H. D. has generally been associated with the Modernist movement, but she later became acquainted with several leading figures of the Harlem Renaissance, and her influence is clearly apparent in the spare lines and evocative imagery of Langston Hughes. In poems such as "The Negro Speaks of Rivers," "Sun Song," and "Long Trip," Hughes deploys short lines and keen, clipped imagery to evoke rather than explain his meaning.

Free verse is only one of many metrical forms available to poets in the twentieth century, and some of the best nature poetry of this era has been written by poets who have chosen to explore the possibilities of more traditional verse forms, using rhyme and meter to convey their impressions of the natural world. Robert Frost is perhaps the best-known American poet of the twentieth century, and his preference for traditional verse forms, suffused with accessible images of natural phenomena, bespeaks his underlying democratic urge to communicate intelligibly to the common reader as well as his belief that poetry provides "a momentary stay against confusion," an island of order amid the terrifying entropy of the universe. Like a biological organism, the poem builds an orderly structure from the web of life that surrounds it, and it passes on its form to the next generation. Such a biological metaphor for the act of poetic creation is very much in the spirit of Frost's way of writing; for instance, his poem "Spring Pools" expresses an essentially ecological understanding of the dynamic relationship between different organisms: trees and flowers competing for scarce resources of light and water. Frost's dedication to the craft of writing poetry and his thoughtful attention to the way that plants and animals coexist in their natural habitat ensure that his work will continue to be influential among nature writers of the twenty-first century.

🦢 *William Butler Yeats* (1865–1939)

W. B. Yeats originally intended to follow in his father's footsteps and pursue a career as a visual artist. Early on, however, he decided to use words, not paint, as his medium. Yeats's long and varied writing career defies easy summary. His work bridges a gap between the dreamy visions of Pre-Raphaelite neo-Romanticism to the harsher and more abstract images of High Modernism. There are a few common threads that weave together the complex tapestry of Yeats's art. Perhaps the most significant is his relationship to Ireland. Although his parents were of English heritage, Yeats was born in Dublin and Irish culture and history shaped his personality and his poetry. In the early part of his career, Yeats turned to Irish mythology and pagan spirituality for figures and images. He also helped to found Irish literary societies in London and in Dublin, participating in efforts to help reinvigorate Irish culture and public appreciation for Irish cultural heritage. By the late 1890s, Yeats's interest expanded to include the theater. During his years with the Irish National Theatre, he drew, both in his plays and his poetry, from the legends of ancient Irish history and its heroes. He also helped produce the plays of other Irish dramatists and worked on critical studies and collections of Irish folklore. In the later years of his career, contemporary Irish politics often played a more direct role in Yeats's work, and he eventually served in the Irish government. His career coincided with a tumultuous period in Irish history, a period of uprising, revolution, and renewal, and Yeats's work was both shaped by and helped to shape that history.

Another thread that unites all of Yeats's literary efforts is the complex use of symbolism. Drawing from a variety of sources, including Neoplatonic philosophy, mystical religious systems, and classical mythology, Yeats worked continuously to build his own idiosyncratic and internally consistent system of symbols, which recur throughout his later poems. Although these symbols are often drawn from the natural world, they are colored over with layers of mythic, religious, historical, and personal significance, lending every poem an often vexing yet always evocative complexity. While a knowledge of Irish mythology and history, as well as of Yeats's own biography, can help the reader appreciate the poems, the powerful visual quality of even the most potentially abstruse images in them can provoke and sustain the reader's interest.

The Lake Isle of Innisfree*

I will arise and go now, and go to Innisfree,
And a small cabin build there, of clay and wattles[1] made:
Nine bean-rows will I have there, a hive for the honeybee,
And live alone in the bee-loud glade.

---

* An island in Lough Gill in County Sligo in Ireland.
[1] Interwoven branches and twigs.

And I shall have some peace there, for peace comes dropping slow, 5
Dropping from the veils of the morning to where the cricket sings;
There midnight's all a glimmer, and noon a purple glow,
And evening full of the linnet's wings.

I will arise and go now, for always night and day
I hear lake water lapping with low sounds by the shore; 10
While I stand on the roadway, or on the pavements grey,
I hear it in the deep heart's core.

The White Birds

I would that we were, my beloved, white birds on the foam of the sea!
We tire of the flame of the meteor, before it can fade and flee;
And the flame of the blue star of twilight, hung low on the rim of the sky,
Has awaked in our hearts, my beloved, a sadness that may not die.

A weariness comes from those dreamers, dew-dabbled, the lily and rose; 5
Ah, dream not of them, my beloved, the flame of the meteor that goes,
Or the flame of the blue star that lingers hung low in the fall of the dew:
For I would we were changed to white birds on the wandering foam:
    I and you!

I am haunted by numberless islands, and many a Danaan[1] shore,
Where Time would surely forget us, and Sorrow come near us no more; 10
Soon far from the rose and the lily and fret of the flames would we be,
Were we only white birds, my beloved, buoyed out on the foam of the
    sea!

[1] Location in Greek mythology.

The Wild Swans at Coole*

The trees are in their autumn beauty,
The woodland paths are dry,
Under the October twilight the water
Mirrors a still sky;
Upon the brimming water among the stones 5
Are nine-and-fifty swans.

The nineteenth autumn has come upon me
Since I first made my count;
I saw, before I had well finished,
All suddenly mount 10

*Coole Park was the estate of Yeats's friend, Lady Gregory.

And scatter wheeling in great broken rings
Upon their clamorous wings.

I have looked upon those brilliant creatures,
And now my heart is sore.
All's changed since I, hearing at twilight,   15
The first time on this shore,
The bell-beat of their wings above my head,
Trod with a lighter tread.

Unwearied still, lover by lover,
They paddle in the cold   20
Companionable streams or climb the air;
Their hearts have not grown old;
Passion or conquest, wander where they will,
Attend upon them still.

But now they drift on the still water,   25
Mysterious, beautiful;
Among what rushes will they build,
By what lake's edge or pool
Delight men's eyes when I awake some day
To find they have flown away?   30

Sailing to Byzantium

1

That is no country for old men. The young
In one another's arms, birds in the trees
—Those dying generations—at their song,
The salmon-falls, the mackerel-crowded seas,
Fish, flesh, or fowl, commend all summer long   5
Whatever is begotten, born, and dies.
Caught in that sensual music all neglect
Monuments of unageing intellect.

2

An aged man is but a paltry thing,
A tattered coat upon a stick, unless   10
Soul clap its hands and sing, and louder sing
For every tatter in its mortal dress,
Nor is there singing school but studying
Monuments of its own magnificence;
And therefore I have sailed the seas and come   15
To the holy city of Byzantium.

them into white culture. There, he was given the name Luther Standing Bear and for-bidden to speak his native language. Returning to the Dakotas, he worked in various ca-pacities as a teacher, a storekeeper, and a rancher on the Rosebud and the Pine Ridge reservations. He later became involved in show business, traveling the globe with Buffalo Bill's Wild West Show and eventually moving to Hollywood to act in films.

Standing Bear returned once again to his homeland in the late 1920s and early 1930s, and he was inspired to direct political activism in the face of the utter destitution and despair that confronted him on the reservations. His four books include My People, the Sioux *(1928),* My Indian Boyhood *(1931),* Land of the Spotted Eagle *(1933), and* Stories of the Sioux *(1934). These works blend autobiography, ethnography, and suggestions for governmental policy. The selection provided below recounts Standing Bear's personal memories of his boyhood training as a warrior in the days before the Lakota had been defeated and to a great extent assimilated by the hegemonic white culture.*

From My People, the Sioux

Chapter 5. My First Buffalo

Once we were camped between the White River and a place known as Crow Butte. As usual, every one in camp seemed to be having a good time. One day I observed a great many horses near our camp. They were such beautiful animals, sleek and fat. I asked my stepmother where the horses came from. She told me the Great Father at Washington had sent them to be given to us. I was very happy, thinking I should get one, as I was now regarded as a young man.

A chief from each band was chosen to distribute the horses to his own people. As the name of each chief was called, he was given as many small sticks as there were horses allotted to his band. My father was called, and he received his bunch of sticks. Then he told all the young men who wanted horses to come to his tipi. As each man came in, he was given a stick, which signified that he was to receive a horse from my father when the animals had been turned over to the camp.

After he had given out all the sticks, there were still two young men without horses. But Father did not let them go away disappointed. He picked up two sticks and gave one to each man. He then said he would give them each a horse from his own herd, as he had already allotted all the animals which the Govern-ment was to present them.

Although we had nice ponies in our band, they were nothing as compared to the horses the Government sent. My father would have liked one of them him-self, but he was a chief, and was obliged to look out for his people first. How dif-ferent from the methods of the "big man" among the whites of this day and age! Before he gets in office he is ready to promise anything and everything to those who can put him there by their votes. But do they keep their promises? Well, I should say not! After they are elected, the first thing they do is to feather their own nests and that of their own families.

But the Indian chief, without any education, was at least honest. When any-thing was sent to his band, they got it. His family did not come first. He received no salary. In case of war he was always found at the front, but when it came to receiving gifts, his place was in the rear. There was no hand-shaking, smiling, and "glad-handing" which meant nothing. The chief was dignified and sincere.

One day we boys heard some of the men talking about going to the agency. They said the Government had sent some spotted buffalo for the Indians. This was the name the Indians gave to the cows, there being no word in the Sioux tongue for the white man's cattle. Our own wild buffalo had been disappearing very rapidly, as the white people had been killing them as fast as possible. We were very happy to learn that we were to receive more meat, this being our main diet. We had heard about these spotted buffalo, but had never seen them.

So we got on our ponies and rode over to the agency with some of the men. What a terrible odor met us! It was awful! We had to hold our noses. Then I asked my father what was the matter around there, as the stench was more than I could stand. He told me it was the odor of the spotted buffalo. Then I asked him if we were going to be obliged to eat those terrible animals. "The white people eat them," was his reply.

Now we had several white people around us, but they were all bald-headed. I began to wonder if they got that way from eating those vile-smelling cattle. I then recalled that buzzards were bald-headed, and they lived on carrion, and I began to feel sorry for the white people who had to live on such stuff.

Each man was called to receive his cattle, and as they were driven out of the corral they were shot down. Here and there, all about, one could see cows lying where they had been shot down, as they did not care to drive them near their homes. They skinned the cow, cutting out the tenderest parts, and roasted it right there. This roasting killed most of the odor. Then they took the skin and traded it off for calicoes and paints. If they happened to cut the tail off while skinning the animal, and brought it to the trader later, he exchanged some candy for it, to give to the children. The Indians soon "wised up" to this, and thereafter demanded something for the tail, whether it was on the hide or off it.

Did you ever stop to think of the difference there is in meat that is killed while in a contented state, and meat that is carried in trains day after day on the hoof? Some of these poor animals stand so closely together in box cars that they have no room even to lie down and get rested, and if they do, they are poked in the ribs by men on the cars just for the purpose of keeping the animals on their feet. We knew the difference—which was the reason we could not eat this sort of meat when we first began to receive it.

In spite of the fact that we received plenty of beef and rations from the Government, we were hungry for buffalo meat, and we wanted the skins. So one day we left the agency without a permit. We were very independent in those days. We started for the northern part of Nebraska, as we knew that section to be good hunting-grounds.

I had been out with my father and grandfather many times on buffalo hunts, but they had always attended to the killing, and I had only assisted in the eating afterward. But this time I was going as a hunter. I was determined to try to kill a buffalo all by myself if possible. My father had made me a special bow and some steel-pointed arrows with which to kill big game, and this was to be my first chance to see what sort of hunter I was.

A scout had been sent out, and one morning, very early, he reported that there were some buffalo near. Everybody, including myself, began to get ready. While one of my stepmothers was helping me, she said, "Son, when you kill a buffalo, save me the kidney and the skin." I didn't know whether she was trying to poke fun at me or to give me encouragement. But it made me feel proud to have her talk like that to me.

But my father always talked to me as if I were a man. Of course I now felt that I was big enough to do a man's work. The night before the hunt, my father instructed me as follows:

"My son, the land on which these buffalo have been found is reported not to be rough, and you will not have to chase the buffalo into dangerous places, as the land is very level. Whatever you do, watch the buffalo closely. If the one you are after is running straight ahead and not turning, then you can get in very close, and you will stand a good chance to shoot it in the heart. But if you observe the buffalo to be looking at you from the corner of its eye, then look out! They are very quick and powerful. They can get their horns under your horse and toss him high in the air, and you might get killed.

"If you hit in the right spot, you may kill the buffalo with only one arrow, but if not, you will have to use more. If your pony is not fast enough to catch up with the buffalo, the best thing you can do is to shoot an arrow right behind the small ribs. Perhaps it will reach the heart. If the buffalo runs down a hill or into a bank, then you have another chance. Shoot at the joint of the hips, then your buffalo will sit down and you can take your time to kill it.

"Keep your eyes open! In the beginning there will be lots of dust, but after you pass through that, it will be clear, and you will be able to see where you are going."

This was the first time I was to go on a hunt after such large animals. I had killed several small animals, but a buffalo is far from being a small creature, and you can imagine that I was greatly excited.

Early the next morning every one was ready for the start. I carried my bow in my hand, as there was not room for it in my quiver where I kept my arrows. I rode a little black mare, a very fine runner that could cover the ground like a deer.

Two men on beautiful horses rode in front of us. This was for the purpose of keeping order in the party. There was no chance of one man getting ahead of the others and scaring the game. We all had to keep together and stay behind these men.

They rode to the top of a hill where they could get a good look at the herd and figure if there was any better place from which to approach it. We always got as close to the buffalo as possible, because it makes the meat tough to run an animal any farther than necessary.

After looking at the herd from various positions, they chose what was considered the most advantageous spot. Here they cautioned the hunters to change to their running-horses and be all ready. I did not have to make any change, as the little black mare was all the animal I had. I saw some of the men tying their two braids of hair back, and others, who wore shirts, began rolling up their sleeves. They wanted their arms free once they began shooting. They fixed their quivers on the side instead of carrying them on the back. Nobody wore any feathers or carried any spears or lances.

The extra horses were hobbled and left in the charge of an old man. When the two riders gave the command, everybody started right up. Of course I was right at the front with them. I wanted to do something brave. I depended a great deal on my pony, as I knew she was sure-footed and could run as I wanted her to.

At the top of the hill, all the hunters turned their horses loose, and the animals started in running like the wind! I whipped up my little black mare and nearly got ahead of the others. Soon I was mixed up in the dust and could see nothing ahead of me. All I could hear was the roar and rattle of the hoofs of the buffalo as they thundered along. My pony shied this way and that, and I had to hold on for dear life.

For a time I did not even try to pull an arrow from my quiver, as I had all I could do to take care of myself. I knew if my pony went down and one of those big animals stepped on me, it would be my last day on earth. I then realized how helpless I was there in all that dust and confusion, with those ponderous buffalo all around me. The sound of their hoofs was frightening. My pony ran like the wind, while I just clung to her mane; but presently we came out of the dust.

Then I observed what my father had told me previously. I was quite a bit ahead of the buffalo now, and when they caught sight of me, they started running in two different directions. When I looked at those big animals and thought of trying to kill one of them, I realized how small I was. I was really afraid of them. Then I thought about what my stepmother had said to me about bringing her a kidney and a skin, and the feeling that I was a man, after all, came back to me; so I turned my pony toward the bunch which was running north. There was no dust now, and I knew where I was going.

I was all alone, and I was determined to chase them, whether I killed one or not. By this time I could hear shots fired by some of the hunters who carried guns, and I knew they were killing some. So I rode on after this small bunch, and when I dashed behind them, I pulled out one of my arrows and shot into the middle of them. I did not even know where my arrow went, and was just thinking of quitting when I observed a young heifer running slower than the others.

This encouraged me, so I whipped up my pony again and took after her. As I came close, she stopped and turned. Then she started running in another direction, but I saw she was losing fast. She was not as big as the others, so I was not afraid. I made up my mind I was going to kill that buffalo if it took all the arrows in my quiver.

I rode right up alongside the buffalo, just as my father had instructed me. Drawing an arrow from my quiver, and holding to my pony with all the strength of my legs, I fitted the arrow and let drive with all my strength. I had expected to kill the buffalo right quick, but the arrow went into the neck—and I thought I had taken such good aim! But the buffalo only shook her head and kept on running. I again caught up with her, and let another arrow loose, which struck near the heart. Although it was not fired with sufficient strength to kill at once, I saw that she was fast weakening and running much slower. Then I pulled my third arrow and fired again. This went into the heart. I began to think that buffalo had all the nine lives of a cat, and was going to prove about as hard as a cat to kill, when I saw blood running from her nose. Then I knew she would have to drop pretty soon. I shot my fourth arrow into her, and she staggered and dropped over on her side, and was soon dead. So I had killed my first buffalo.

When I examined the fallen animal and noted that I had shot five arrows into her, I felt that this was too many arrows for just one buffalo. Then I recalled that my father had once killed two buffalo with only a single arrow. He knew he had hit the first one in the right spot, as the arrow penetrated very deeply and he simply rode up alongside, drew the arrow through, pulled it out again and used it to kill the second one.

As I stood there thinking of this, it made me feel ashamed of my marksmanship. I began to think of pulling all the arrows out but one. In fact, I had started to do this, when a remark that my father had once made to me came into my head. It was, "Son, always remember that a man who tells lies is never liked by anybody." So, instead of trying to cheat, I told the truth; and it made me feel happier.

I took all the arrows out and started in to skin the buffalo. I was doing splendidly until I tried to turn the animal over. Then I discovered that it was too heavy a task for me. As I had but one side skinned I began to think of removing the kidney and cutting out a nice piece of meat for my stepmother. Just then I heard some one call me. I got on my pony and rode to the top of the hill. There I saw my father, who had been looking for me. He called to me, but I just rode back to my buffalo. He knew something had happened, so came over, and then I pointed to the dead buffalo, lying there half-skinned.

He was so pleased that I had tried to do my best. Then I told him about the number of arrows I had had to use, and where each one had struck. I even told him how I had shot my first arrow into the whole bunch, not knowing where it had landed. He laughed, but he was proud of me. I guess it was because I had told the truth, and not tried to cheat or lie, even though I was just a youngster.

Then Father started in on my buffalo. He soon had it all skinned and butchered. He said he had been all ready to go home when he discovered I was missing. He had thought I was with my grandfather, while Grandfather thought I was with him. All that time I was having a hard job all by myself. When we reached home it made me very proud to be able to give my stepmother the skin and kidney. And she was pleased that I had done so well.

My father called the old man of the camp, who always acted as herald, to announce that "Ota Kte" (or "Plenty Kill") had shot his first buffalo, and that "Standing Bear," his father, was giving away a horse.

This was the first and last buffalo I ever killed, and it took five arrows to complete the job.

ᔰ *Mary Austin* (1868–1934)

Mary Hunter Austin was the author of thirty-four books and well over two hundred articles, essays, short stories, and poems on such diverse subjects as anthropology, folklore, politics, metaphysics, and poetics. She was an ardent feminist, championing women's suffrage and birth control, and a staunch environmental advocate, devoted to sustainable development, local control of natural resources, and the preservation of America's wild places. Born in Carlinville, Illinois, Austin attended Blackburn College and developed early a sense of vocation as a professional writer. Her first published essay, "One Hundred Miles on Horseback" (1887), describes her family's epic journey by covered wagon to a homestead in the remote valley of the Kern River in Southern California. Here she met her future husband, Wallace Stafford Austin, and moved with him to the high desert country of the Owens Valley, east of the Sierra Nevada. Her husband proved feckless and improvident, and their marriage failed after the birth of a daughter who was mentally disabled; but even as her marriage crumbled, Mary Austin fell in love with the stark beauty of the Owens Valley and the wild creatures that inhabited it. Austin's classic evocation of the California desert, The Land of Little Rain *(1903), is unsurpassed in its treatment of the harsh beauty of that landscape. Austin tempers the exuberant celebration of American wilderness (found in such writers as John Muir) by introducing a more austere depiction of the lives of desert creatures attempting to thrive in a permanent condition of scarcity. She also provides a sensitive characterization of the Paiute and Shoshone Indians, based on her intimate acquaintance with their folktales, material culture, and way of life.*

Mary Austin was actively engaged in the tragic struggle of the people of the Owens Valley to defend their water supply from acquisition by the City of Los Angeles. When this struggle failed, and the valley's ecosystem was slated for destruction, Austin left the region forever, moving to San Francisco, then to New York and on to London, and eventually settling in Santa Fe, New Mexico, where she wrote The Land of Journey's Ending *(1924) and other works about the American West. Austin's struggle for existence in a harsh land, complicated by a troubled relationship with her husband, resulted in a ecofeminist vision of the natural world that still serves as an influential model for contemporary environmental writers.*

The Land of Little Rain

East away from the Sierras, south from Panamint and Amargosa, east and south many an uncounted mile, is the Country of Lost Borders.

Ute, Paiute, Mojave, and Shoshone inhabit its frontiers, and as far into the heart of it as a man dare go. Not the law, but the land sets the limit. Desert is the name it wears upon the maps, but the Indian's is the better word. Desert is a loose term to indicate land that supports no man; whether the land can be bitted and broken to that purpose is not proven. Void of life it never is, however dry the air and villainous the soil.

This is the nature of that country. There are hills, rounded, blunt, burned, squeezed up out of chaos, chrome and vermilion painted, aspiring to the snow line. Between the hills lie high level-looking plains full of intolerable sun glare, or narrow valleys drowned in a blue haze. The hill surface is streaked with ash drift and black, unweathered lava flows. After rains water accumulates in the hollows of small closed valleys and, evaporating, leaves hard dry levels of pure desertness that get the local name of dry lakes. Where the mountains are steep and the rains heavy, the pool is never quite dry, but dark and bitter, rimmed about with the efflorescence of alkaline deposits. A thin crust of it lies along the marsh over the vegetating area, which has neither beauty nor freshness. In the broad wastes open to the wind the sand drifts in hummocks about the stubby shrubs, and between them the soil shows saline traces. The sculpture of the hills here is more wind than water work, though the quick storms do sometimes scar them past many a year's redeeming. In all the Western desert edges there are essays in miniature at the famed, terrible Grand Cañon, to which, if you keep on long enough in this country, you will come at last.

Since this is a hill country one expects to find springs, but not to depend upon them; for when found they are often brackish and unwholesome, or maddening, slow dribbles in a thirsty soil. Here you find the hot sink of Death Valley, or high rolling districts where the air has always a tang of frost. Here are the long heavy winds and breathless calms on the tilted mesas where dust devils dance, whirling up into a wide, pale sky. Here you have no rain when all the earth cries for it, or quick downpours called cloud-bursts for violence. A land of lost rivers, with little in it to love; yet a land that once visited must be come back to inevitably. If it were not so there would be little told of it.

This is the country of three seasons. From June on to November it lies hot, still, and unbearable, sick with violent unrelieving storms; then on until April, chill, quiescent, drinking its scant rain and scanter snows; from April to the hot season again, blossoming, radiant, and seductive. These months are only approximate; later or earlier the rain-laden wind may drift up the water gate of the Colorado from the Gulf, and the land sets its seasons by the rain.

The desert floras shame us with their cheerful adaptations to the seasonal limitations. Their whole duty is to flower and fruit, and they do it hardly, or with tropical luxuriance, as the rain admits. It is recorded in the report of the Death Valley expedition that after a year of abundant rains, on the Colorado desert was found a specimen of Amaranthus ten feet high. A year later the same species in the same place matured in the drought at four inches. One hopes the land may breed like qualities in her human offspring, not tritely to "try," but to do. Seldom does the desert herb attain the full stature of the type. Extreme aridity and extreme altitude have the same dwarfing effect, so that we find in the high Sierras and in Death Valley related species in miniature that reach a comely growth in mean temperatures. Very fertile are the desert plants in expedients to prevent evaporation, turning their foliage edgewise toward the sun, growing silky hairs, exuding viscid gum. The wind, which has a long sweep, harries and helps them. It rolls up dunes about the stocky stems, encompassing and protective, and above the dunes, which may be, as with the mesquite, three times as high as a man, the blossoming twigs flourish and bear fruit.

There are many areas in the desert where drinkable water lies within a few feet of the surface, indicated by the mesquite and the bunch grass (*Sporobolus airoides*). It is this nearness of unimagined help that makes the tragedy of desert deaths. It is related that the final breakdown of that hapless party that gave Death Valley its forbidding name occurred in a locality where shallow wells would have saved them. But how were they to know that? Properly equipped it is possible to go safely across that ghastly sink, yet every year it takes its toll of death, and yet men find there sun-dried mummies, of whom no trace or recollection is preserved. To underestimate one's thirst, to pass a given landmark to the right or left, to find a dry spring where one looked for running water—there is no help for any of these things.

Along springs and sunken watercourses one is surprised to find such water-loving plants as grow widely in moist ground, but the true desert breeds its own kind, each in its particular habitat. The angle of the slope, the frontage of a hill, the structure of the soil determines the plant. South-looking hills are nearly bare, and the lower tree line higher here by a thousand feet. Cañons running east and west will have one wall naked and one clothed. Around dry lakes and marshes the herbage preserves a set and orderly arrangement. Most species have well-defined areas of growth, the best index the voiceless land can give the traveler of his whereabouts.

If you have any doubt about it, know that the desert begins with the creosote. This immortal shrub spreads down into Death Valley and up to the lower timber-line, odorous and medicinal as you might guess from the name, wandlike, with shining fretted foliage. Its vivid green is grateful to the eye in a wilderness of gray and greenish white shrubs. In the spring it exudes a resinous gum which the Indians of those parts know how to use with pulverized rock for cementing arrow points to shafts. Trust Indians not to miss any virtues of the plant world!

Nothing the desert produces expresses it better than the unhappy growth of the tree yucca. Tormented, thin forests of it stalk drearily in the high mesas, particularly in that triangular slip that fans out eastward from the meeting of the Sierras and coastwise hills where the first swings across the southern end of the San Joaquin Valley. The yucca bristles with bayonet-pointed leaves, dull green, growing shaggy with age, tipped with panicles of fetid, greenish bloom. After death, which is slow, the ghostly hollow network of its woody skeleton, with hardly power to rot, makes the moonlight fearful. Before the yucca has come to flower, while yet its bloom is a creamy cone-shaped bud of the size of a small cabbage, full of sugary sap, the Indians twist it deftly out of its fence of daggers and roast it for their own delectation. So it is that in those parts where man inhabits one sees young plants of *Yucca arborensis* infrequently. Other yuccas, cacti, low herbs, a thousand sorts, one finds journeying east from the coastwise hills. There is neither poverty of soil nor species to account for the sparseness of desert growth, but simply that each plant requires more room. So much earth must be preempted to extract so much moisture. The real struggle for existence, the real brain of the plant, is underground; above there is room for a rounded perfect growth. In Death Valley, reputed the very core of desolation, are nearly two hundred identified species.

Above the lower tree line, which is also the snow line, mapped out abruptly by the sun, one finds spreading growth of piñon, juniper, branched nearly to the ground, lilac and sage, and scattering white pines.

There is no special preponderance of self-fertilized or wind-fertilized plants, but everywhere the demand for and evidence of insect life. Now where there are seeds and insects there will be birds and small mammals, and where these are, will come the slinking, sharp-toothed kind that prey on them. Go as far as you dare in the heart of a lonely land, you cannot go so far that life and death are not before you. Painted lizards slip in and out of rock crevices, and pant on the white hot sands. Birds, hummingbirds even, nest in the cactus scrub; woodpeckers befriend the demoniac yuccas; out of the stark, treeless waste rings the music of the night-singing mockingbird. If it be summer and the sun well down, there will be a burrowing owl to call. Strange, furry, tricksy things dart across the open places, or sit motionless in the conning towers of the creosote.The poet may have "named all the birds without a gun," but not the fairy-footed, ground-inhabiting, furtive, small folk of the rainless regions. They are too many and too swift; how many you would not believe without seeing the footprint tracings in the sand. They are nearly all night workers, finding the days too hot and white. In mid-desert where there are no cattle, there are no birds of carrion, but if you go far in that direction the chances are that you will find yourself shadowed by their tilted wings. Nothing so large as a man can move unspied upon in that country, and they know well how the land deals with strangers. There are hints to be had here of the way in which a land forces new habits on its dwellers. The quick increase of suns at the end of spring sometimes overtakes birds in their nesting and effects a reversal of the ordinary manner of incubation. It becomes necessary to keep eggs cool rather than warm. One hot, stifling spring in the Little Antelope I had occasion to pass and repass frequently the nest of a pair of meadowlarks, located unhappily in the shelter of a very slender weed. I never caught them sitting except near night, but at midday they stood, or drooped above it, half fainting with pitifully parted bills, between their treasure and the sun. Sometimes both of them together with wings spread and half lifted continued a spot of shade in a temperature that constrained me at last in a fellow feeling to spare them a bit of canvas for permanent shelter. There was a fence in that country shutting in a cattle range, and along its fifteen miles of posts one could be sure of finding a bird or two in every strip of shadow; sometimes the sparrow and the hawk, with wings trailed and beaks parted, drooping in the white truce of noon.

If one is inclined to wonder at first how so many dwellers came to be in the loneliest land that ever came out of God's hands, what they do there and why stay, one does not wonder so much after having lived there. None other than this long brown land lays such a hold on the affections. The rainbow hills, the tender bluish mists, the luminous radiance of the spring, have the lotus charm. They trick the sense of time, so that once inhabiting there you always mean to go away without quite realizing that you have not done it. Men who have lived there, miners and cattle-men, will tell you this, not so fluently, but emphatically, cursing the land and going back to it. For one thing there is the divinest, cleanest air to be breathed anywhere in God's world. Some day the world will understand that, and the little oases on the windy tops of hills will harbor for healing its ailing, house-weary broods. There is promise there of great wealth in ores and earths, which is no wealth by reason of being so far removed from water and workable conditions, but men are bewitched by it and tempted to try the impossible.

You should hear Salty Williams tell how he used to drive eighteen and twenty-mule teams from the borax marsh to Mojave, ninety miles, with the trail wagon full of water barrels. Hot days the mules would go so mad for drink that the clank of the water bucket set them into an uproar of hideous, maimed noises, and a tangle of harness chains, while Salty would sit on the high seat with the sun glare heavy in his eyes, dealing out curses of pacification in a level, uninterested voice until the clamor fell off from sheer exhaustion. There was a line of shallow graves along that road; they used to count on dropping a man or two of every new gang of coolies brought out in the hot season. But when he lost his swamper,[1] smitten without warning at the noon halt, Salty quit his job; he said it was "too durn hot." The swamper he buried by the way with stones upon him to keep the coyotes from digging him up, and seven years later I read the penciled lines on the pine headboard, still bright and unweathered.

But before that, driving up on the Mojave stage, I met Salty again crossing Indian Wells, his face from the high seat, tanned and ruddy as a harvest moon, looming through the golden dust above his eighteen mules. The land had called him.

The palpable sense of mystery in the desert air breeds fables, chiefly of lost treasure. Somewhere within its stark borders, if one believes report, is a hill strewn with nuggets; one seamed with virgin silver; an old clayey water-bed where Indians scooped up earth to make cooking pots and shaped them reeking with grains of pure gold. Old miners drifting about the desert edges, weathered into the semblance of the tawny hills, will tell you tales like these convincingly. After a little sojourn in that land you will believe them on their own account. It is a question whether it is not better to be bitten by the little horned snake of the desert that goes sidewise and strikes without coiling, than by the tradition of a lost mine.

And yet—and yet—is it not perhaps to satisfy expectation that one falls into the tragic key in writing of desertness? The more you wish of it the more you get, and in the meantime lose much of pleasantness. In that country which begins at the foot of the east slope of the Sierras and spreads out by less and less lofty hill ranges toward the Great Basin, it is possible to live with great zest, to have red blood and delicate joys, to pass and repass about one's daily performance an area that would make an Atlantic seaboard State, and that with no peril, and, according to our way of thought, no particular difficulty. At any rate, it was not people who went into the desert merely to write it up who invented the fabled Hassaympa, of whose waters, if any drink, they can no more see fact as naked fact, but all radiant with the color of romance. I, who must have drunk of it in my twice seven years' wanderings, am assured that it is worthwhile.

For all the toll the desert takes of a man it gives compensations, deep breaths, deep sleep, and the communion of the stars. It comes upon one with new force in the pauses of the night that the Chaldeans were a desert-bred people. It is hard to escape the sense of mastery as the stars move in the wide clear heavens to risings and settings unobscured. They look large and near and palpitant; as if they moved on some stately service not needful to declare. Wheeling to their stations in the sky, they make the poor world fret of no account. Of no account you who lie out there watching, nor the lean coyote that stands off in the scrub from you and howls and howls.

---

[1] Assistant to the muleskinner.

⤳ *Stephen Crane* (1871–1900)

Born in Newark, New Jersey, the son of a methodist minister, Stephen Crane was the youngest of fourteen children. Crane spent his boyhood in the small town of Port Jervis, New York. His father died when he was nine years old, and his family moved to the coastal resort of Asbury Park, New Jersey. Awkward and introverted, Crane did poorly in school and dropped out of Syracuse University after one semester. By 1891, he had started to write for newspapers, and he moved to New York City to attempt a career as a professional writer. His first book, Maggie: A Girl of the Streets *(1893), proved too harshly realistic for contemporary readers and sold very few copies. But his next novel,* The Red Badge of Courage *(1895), a gripping tale of a soldier under fire in the Civil War, was a best-seller that has become a classic of American literature.*

As a result of his popular success, Crane was hired by his publisher as a roving reporter in the American West and Mexico; then he was dispatched to cover an insurrection against the Spanish colonial government in Cuba. On his way south, in Jacksonville, Florida, he met Cora Howorth Taylor, the proprietor of a bordello called the Hotel de Dream. She and Crane became inseparable companions, and they lived together for the remaining three years of his life. He embarked on the steamship Commodore, *bound for Cuba; but the ship sank off the coast of Florida on January 2, 1897, leaving Crane and a few other survivors to struggle for their lives in an open lifeboat. Crane published a nonfictional account of this harrowing adventure in the New York* Press, *and he later revised that newspaper report into his classic short story, "The Open Boat" (1898), reprinted here. Avoiding cheap melodrama, Crane presents the events of the story in a detached, sardonic manner, examining how the character of each of the survivors is revealed as they contend with the grim, implacable forces of nature.*

In addition to his novels and journalistic writing, Crane published two collections of poems: The Black Riders and Other Lines *(1895) and* War is Kind *(1899). These experiments in epigrammatic free verse found few admirers in their own time but are regarded today as heralds of the Modernist movement in poetry. Disappointed by the lukewarm reception of his writing in America, Crane moved to England, where he became close friends with the writers Joseph Conrad, H. G. Wells, and Henry James. He died of tuberculosis at the age of twenty-eight.*

The Open Boat

A Tale Intended to Be After the Fact: Being the Experience of Four Men from the Sunk Steamer *Commodore*

I

None of them knew the color of the sky. Their eyes glanced level, and were fastened upon the waves that swept toward them. These waves were of the hue of slate, save for the tops, which were of foaming white, and all of the men knew the colors of the sea. The horizon narrowed and widened, and dipped and rose, and at all times its edge was jagged with waves that seemed thrust up in points like rocks.

Many a man ought to have a bathtub larger than the boat which here rode upon the sea. These waves were most wrongfully and barbarously abrupt and tall, and each froth-top was a problem in small-boat navigation.

The cook squatted in the bottom, and looked with both eyes at the six inches of gunwale which separated him from the ocean. His sleeves were rolled over his fat forearms, and the two flaps of his unbuttoned vest dangled as he bent to bail out the boat. Often he said, "Gawd! that was a narrow clip." As he remarked it he invariably gazed eastward over the broken sea.

The oiler, steering with one of the two oars in the boat, sometimes raised himself suddenly to keep clear of water that swirled in over the stern. It was a thin little oar, and it seemed often ready to snap.

The correspondent, pulling at the other oar, watched the waves and wondered why he was there.

The injured captain, lying in the bow, was at this time buried in that profound dejection and indifference which comes, temporarily at least, to even the bravest and most enduring when, willy-nilly, the firm fails, the army loses, the ship goes down. The mind of the master of a vessel is rooted deep in the timbers of her, though he command for a day or a decade; and this captain had on him the stern impression of a scene in the grays of dawn of seven turned faces, and later a stump of a topmast with a white ball on it, that slashed to and fro at the waves, went low and lower, and down. Thereafter there was something strange in his voice. Although steady, it was deep with mourning, and of a quality beyond oration or tears.

"Keep'er a little more south, Billie," said he.

"A little more south, sir," said the oiler in the stern.

A seat in this boat was not unlike a seat upon a bucking broncho, and by the same token a broncho is not much smaller. The craft pranced and reared and plunged like an animal. As each wave came, and she rose for it, she seemed like a horse making at a fence outrageously high. The manner of her scramble over these walls of water is a mystic thing, and, moreover, at the top of them were ordinarily these problems in white water, the foam racing down from the summit of each wave requiring a new leap, and a leap from the air. Then, after scornfully bumping a crest, she would slide and race and splash down a long incline, and arrive bobbing and nodding in front of the next menace.

A singular disadvantage of the sea lies in the fact that after successfully surmounting one wave you discover that there is another behind it just as important and just as nervously anxious to do something effective in the way of swamping boats. In a ten-foot dinghy one can get an idea of the resources of the sea in the line of waves that is not probable to the average experience, which is never at sea in a dinghy. As each slaty wall of water approached, it shut all else from the view of the men in the boat, and it was not difficult to imagine that this particular wave was the final outburst of the ocean, the last effort of the grim water. There was a terrible grace in the move of the waves, and they came in silence, save for the snarling of the crests.

In the wan light the faces of the men must have been gray. Their eyes must have glinted in strange ways as they gazed steadily astern. Viewed from a balcony, the whole thing would doubtless have been weirdly picturesque. But the men in the boat had no time to see it, and if they had had leisure, there were other things to occupy their minds. The sun swung steadily up the sky, and they knew it was broad day because the color of the sea changed from slate to emerald-green streaked with amber lights, and the foam was like tumbling snow. The process of the breaking day was unknown to them. They were aware only of this effect upon the color of the waves that rolled toward them.

In disjointed sentences the cook and the correspondent argued as to the difference between a life-saving station and a house of refuge. The cook had said: "There's a house of refuge just north of the Mosquito Inlet Light, and as soon as they see us they'll come off in their boat and pick us up."

"As soon as who see us?" said the correspondent.

"The crew," said the cook.

"Houses of refuge don't have crews," said the correspondent. "As I understand them, they are only places where clothes and grub are stored for the benefit of shipwrecked people. They don't carry crews."

"Oh, yes, they do," said the cook.

"No, they don't," said the correspondent.

"Well, we're not there yet, anyhow," said the oiler, in the stern.

"Well," said the cook, "perhaps it's not a house of refuge that I'm thinking of as being near Mosquito Inlet Light; perhaps it's a lifesaving station."

"We're not there yet," said the oiler in the stern.

II

As the boat bounced from the top of each wave the wind tore through the hair of the hatless men, and as the craft plopped her stern down again the spray slashed past them. The crest of each of these waves was a hill, from the top of which the men surveyed for a moment a broad tumultuous expanse, shining and wind-riven. It was probably splendid, it was probably glorious, this play of the free sea, wild with lights of emerald and white and amber.

"Bully good thing it's an onshore wind," said the cook. "If not, where would we be? Wouldn't have a show."

"That's right," said the correspondent.

The busy oiler nodded his assent.

Then the captain, in the bow, chuckled in a way that expressed humor, contempt, tragedy, all in one. "Do you think we've got much of a show now, boys?" said he.

Whereupon the three were silent, save for a trifle of hemming and hawing. To express any particular optimism at this time they felt to be childish and stupid, but they all doubtless possessed this sense of the situation in their minds. A young man thinks doggedly at such times. On the other hand, the ethics of their condition was decidedly against any open suggestion of hopelessness. So they were silent.

"Oh, well," said the captain, soothing his children, "we'll get ashore all right."

But there was that in his tone which made them think; so the oiler quoth, "Yes! if this wind holds."

The cook was bailing. "Yes! if we don't catch hell in the surf."

Canton-flannel gulls flew near and far. Sometimes they sat down on the sea, near patches of brown seaweed that rolled over the waves with a movement like carpets on a line in a gale. The birds sat comfortably in groups, and they were envied by some in the dinghy, for the wrath of the sea was no more to them than it was to a covey of prairie chickens a thousand miles inland. Often they came very close and stared at the men with black bead-like eyes. At these times they were uncanny and sinister in their unblinking scrutiny, and the men hooted angrily at them, telling them to be gone. One came, and evidently decided to alight on the top of the captain's head. The bird flew parallel to the boat and did not circle, but made short sidelong jumps in the air in chicken fashion. His black eyes were wistfully fixed upon the captain's head. "Ugly brute," said the oiler to the bird. "You look as if you were made with a jackknife." The cook and the correspondent swore darkly at the creature. The captain naturally wished to knock it away with the end of the heavy painter, but he did not dare do it, because anything resembling an emphatic gesture would have capsized this freighted boat; and so, with his open hand, the captain gently and carefully waved the gull away. After it had been discouraged from the pursuit the captain breathed easier on account of his hair, and others breathed easier because the bird struck their minds at this time as being somehow gruesome and ominous.

In the meantime the oiler and the correspondent rowed. And also they rowed. They sat together in the same seat, and each rowed an oar. Then the oiler took both oars; then the correspondent took both oars; then the oiler; then the correspondent. They rowed and they rowed. The very ticklish part of the business was when the time came for the reclining one in the stern to take his turn at the oars. By the very last star of truth, it is easier to steal eggs from under a hen than it was to change seats in the dinghy. First the man in the stern slid his hand along the thwart and moved with care, as if he were of Sèvres.[1] Then the man in the rowing-seat slid his hand along the other thwart. It was all done with the most extraordinary care. As the two sidled past each other, the whole party kept watchful eyes on the coming wave, and the captain cried: "Look out, now! Steady, there!"

The brown mats of seaweed that appeared from time to time were like islands, bits of earth. They were traveling, apparently, neither one way nor the other. They were, to all intents, stationary. They informed the men in the boat that it was making progress slowly toward the land.

The captain, rearing cautiously in the bow after the dinghy soared on a great swell, said that he had seen the lighthouse at Mosquito Inlet. Presently the cook remarked that he had seen it. The correspondent was at the oars then, and for some reason he too wished to look at the lighthouse; but his back was toward the far shore, and the waves were important, and for some time he could not seize an opportunity to turn his head. But at last there came a wave more gentle than the others, and when at the crest of it he swiftly scoured the western horizon.

"See it?" said the captain.

---

[1] A French china.

"No," said the correspondent, slowly; "I didn't see anything."

"Look again," said the captain. He pointed. "It's exactly in that direction."

At the top of another wave the correspondent did as he was bid, and this time his eyes chanced on a small, still thing on the edge of the swaying horizon. It was precisely like the point of a pin. It took an anxious eye to find a lighthouse so tiny.

"Think we'll make it, Captain?"

"If this wind holds and the boat don't swamp, we can't do much else," said the captain.

The little boat, lifted by each towering sea and splashed viciously by the crests, made progress that in the absence of seaweed was not apparent to those in her. She seemed just a wee thing wallowing, miraculously top up, at the mercy of five oceans. Occasionally a great spread of water, like white flames, swarmed into her.

"Bail her, cook," said the captain, serenely.

"All right, Captain," said the cheerful cook.

III

It would be difficult to describe the subtle brotherhood of men that was here established on the seas. No one said that it was so. No one mentioned it. But it dwelt in the boat, and each man felt it warm him. They were a captain, an oiler, a cook, and correspondent, and they were friends—friends in a more curiously ironbound degree than may be common. The hurt captain, lying against the water jar in the bow, spoke always in a low voice and calmly; but he could never command a more ready and swiftly obedient crew than the motley three of the dinghy. It was more than a mere recognition of what was best for the common safety. There was surely in it a quality that was personal and heartfelt. And after this devotion to the commander of the boat, there was this comradeship, that the correspondent, for instance, who had been taught to be cynical of men, knew even at the time was the best experience of his life. But no one said that it was so. No one mentioned it.

"I wish we had a sail," remarked the captain. "We might try my overcoat on the end of an oar, and give you two boys a chance to rest." So the cook and the correspondent held the mast and spread wide the overcoat; the oiler steered; and the little boat made good way with her new rig. Sometimes the oiler had to scull sharply to keep a sea from breaking into the boat, but otherwise sailing was a success.

Meanwhile the lighthouse had been growing slowly larger. It had now almost assumed color, and appeared like a little gray shadow on the sky. The man at the oars could not be prevented from turning his head rather often to try for a glimpse of this little gray shadow.

At last, from the top of each wave, the men in the tossing boat could see land. Even as the lighthouse was an upright shadow on the sky, this land seemed but a long black shadow on the sea. It certainly was thinner than paper. "We must be about opposite New Smyrna," said the cook, who had coasted this shore often in schooners. "Captain, by the way, I believe they abandoned that lifesaving station there about a year ago."

"Did they?" said the captain.

The wind slowly died away. The cook and the correspondent were not now obliged to slave in order to hold high the oar. But the waves continued their old impetuous swooping at the dinghy, and the little craft, no longer under way, struggled woundily over them. The oiler or the correspondent took the oars again.

Shipwrecks are *apropos* of nothing. If men could only train for them and have them occur when the men had reached pink condition, there would be less drowning at sea. Of the four in the dinghy none had slept any time worth mentioning for two days and two nights previous to embarking in the dinghy, and in the excitement of clambering about the deck of a foundering ship they had also forgotten to eat heartily.

For these reasons, and for others, neither the oiler nor the correspondent was fond of rowing at this time. The correspondent wondered ingenuously how in the name of all that was sane could there be people who thought it amusing to row a boat. It was not an amusement; it was a diabolical punishment, and even a genius of mental aberrations could never conclude that it was anything but a horror to the muscles and a crime against the back. He mentioned to the boat in general how the amusement of rowing struck him, and the weary-faced oiler smiled in full sympathy. Previously to the foundering, by the way, the oiler had worked a double watch in the engine room of the ship.

"Take her easy now, boys," said the captain. "Don't spend yourselves. If we have to run a surf you'll need all your strength, because we'll sure have to swim for it. Take your time."

Slowly the land arose from the sea. From a black line it became a line of black and a line of white—trees and sand. Finally the captain said that he could make out a house on the shore. "That's the house of refuge, sure," said the cook. "They'll see us before long, and come out after us."

The distant lighthouse reared high. "The keeper ought to be able to make us out now, if he's looking through a glass," said the captain. "He'll notify the lifesaving people."

"None of those other boats could have got ashore to give word of this wreck," said the oiler, in a low voice, "else the lifeboat would be out hunting us."

Slowly and beautifully the land loomed out of the sea. The wind came again. It had veered from the northeast to the southeast. Finally a new sound struck the ears of the men in the boat. It was the low thunder of the surf on the shore. "We'll never be able to make the lighthouse now," said the captain. "Swing her head a little more north, Billie."

"A little more north, sir," said the oiler.

Whereupon the little boat turned her nose once more down the wind, and all but the oarsman watched the shore grow. Under the influence of this expansion doubt and direful apprehension were leaving the minds of the men. The management of the boat was still most absorbing, but it could not prevent a quiet cheerfulness. In an hour, perhaps, they would be ashore.

Their backbones had become thoroughly used to balancing in the boat, and they now rode this wild colt of a dinghy like circus men. The correspondent thought that he had been drenched to the skin, but happening to feel in the top pocket of his coat, he found therein eight cigars. Four of them were soaked with seawater; four were perfectly scatheless. After a search, somebody produced three dry matches; and thereupon the four waifs rode impudently in their little boat and, with an assurance of an impending rescue shining in their eyes, puffed at the big cigars, and judged well and ill of all men. Everybody took a drink of water.

IV

"Cook," remarked the captain, "there don't seem to be any signs of life about your house of refuge."

"No," replied the cook. "Funny they don't see us!"

A broad stretch of lowly coast lay before the eyes of the men. It was of low dunes topped with dark vegetation. The roar of the surf was plain, and sometimes they could see the white lip of a wave as it spun up the beach. A tiny house was blocked out black upon the sky. Southward, the slim lighthouse lifted its little gray length.

Tide, wind, and waves were swinging the dinghy northward. "Funny they don't see us," said the men.

The surf's roar was here dulled, but its tone was nevertheless thunderous and mighty. As the boat swam over the great rollers the men sat listening to this roar. "We'll swamp sure," said everybody.

It is fair to say here that there was not a lifesaving station within twenty miles in either direction; but the men did not know this fact, and in consequence they made dark and opprobrious remarks concerning the eyesight of the nation's lifesavers. Four scowling men sat in the dinghy and surpassed records in the invention of epithets.

"Funny they don't see us."

The light-heartedness of a former time had completely faded. To their sharpened minds it was easy to conjure pictures of all kinds of incompetency and blindness and, indeed, cowardice. There was the shore of the populous land, and it was bitter and bitter to them that from it came no sign.

"Well," said the captain, ultimately, "I suppose we'll have to make a try for ourselves. If we stay out here too long, we'll none of us have strength left to swim after the boat swamps."

And so the oiler, who was at the oars, turned the boat straight for the shore. There was a sudden tightening of muscles. There was some thinking.

"If we don't all get ashore," said the captain—"if we don't all get ashore, I suppose you fellows know where to send news of my finish?"

They then briefly exchanged some addresses and admonitions. As for the reflections of the men, there was a great deal of rage in them. Perchance they might be formulated thus: "If I am going to be drowned—if I am going to be drowned—if I am going to be drowned, why, in the name of the seven mad gods who rule the sea, was I allowed to come thus far and contemplate sand and trees? Was I brought here merely to have my nose dragged away as I was about to nibble the sacred cheese of life? It is preposterous. If this old ninny-woman, Fate, cannot do better than this, she should be deprived of the management of men's fortunes. She is an old hen who knows not her intention. If she has decided to drown me, why did she not do it in the beginning and save me all this trouble? The whole affair is absurd. . . . But no; she cannot mean to drown me. She dare not drown me. She cannot drown me. Not after all this work." Afterward the man might have had an impulse to shake his fist at the clouds. "Just you drown me, now, and then hear what I call you!"

The billows that came at this time were more formidable. They seemed always just about to break and roll over the little boat in a turmoil of foam. There was a preparatory and long growl in the speech of them. No mind unused to the sea would have concluded that the dinghy could ascend these sheer heights in time. The shore was still afar. The oiler was a wily surfman. "Boys," he said swiftly, "she won't live three minutes more, and we're too far out to swim. Shall I take her to sea again, Captain?"

"Yes; go ahead!" said the captain.

This oiler, by a series of quick miracles and fast and steady oarsmanship, turned the boat in the middle of the surf and took her safely to sea again.

There was a considerable silence as the boat bumped over the furrowed sea to deeper water. Then somebody in gloom spoke: "Well, anyhow, they must have seen us from the shore by now."

The gulls went in slanting flight up the wind toward the gray, desolate east. A squall, marked by dingy clouds and clouds brick-red, like smoke from a burning building, appeared from the southeast.

"What do you think of those lifesaving people? Ain't they peaches?"

"Funny they haven't seen us."

"Maybe they think we're out here for sport! Maybe they think we're fishin'. Maybe they think we're damned fools."

It was a long afternoon. A changed tide tried to force them southward, but wind and wave said northward. Far ahead, where coastline, sea, and sky formed their mighty angle, there were little dots which seemed to indicate a city on the shore.

"St. Augustine?"

The captain shook his head. "Too near Mosquito Inlet."

And the oiler rowed, and then the correspondent rowed; then the oiler rowed. It was a weary business. The human back can become the seat of more aches and pains than are registered in books for the composite anatomy of a regiment. It is a limited area, but it can become the theater of innumerable muscular conflicts, tangles, wrenches, knots, and other comforts.

"Did you ever like to row, Billie?" asked the correspondent.

"No," said the oiler; "hang it!"

When one exchanged the rowing-seat for a place in the bottom of the boat, he suffered a bodily depression that caused him to be careless of everything save an obligation to wiggle one finger. There was cold seawater swashing to and fro in the boat, and he lay in it. His head, pillowed on a thwart, was within an inch of the swirl of a wave-crest, and sometimes a particularly obstreperous sea came inboard and drenched him once more. But these matters did not annoy him. It is almost certain that if the boat had capsized he would have tumbled comfortably out upon the ocean as if he felt sure that it was a great soft mattress.

"Look! There's a man on the shore?"

"Where?"

"There! See 'im? See 'im?"

"Yes, sure! He's walking along."

"Now he's stopped. Look! He's facing us!"

"He's waving at us!"

"So he is! By thunder!"

"Ah, now we're all right! Now we're all right! There'll be a boat out here for us in half an hour."

"He's going on. He's running. He's going up to that house there."

The remote beach seemed lower than the sea, and it required a searching glance to discern the little black figure. The captain saw a floating stick, and they rowed to it. A bath towel was by some weird chance in the boat, and, tying this on the stick, the captain waved it. The oarsman did not dare turn his head, so he was obliged to ask questions.

"What's he doing now?"

"He's standing still again. He's looking, I think. . . . There he goes again— toward the house. . . . Now he's stopped again."

"Is he waving at us?"

"No, not now; he was, though."

"Look! There comes another man!"

"He's running."

"Look at him go, would you!"

"Why, he's on a bicycle. Now he's met the other man. They're both waving at us. Look!"

"There comes something up the beach."

"What the devil is that thing?"

"Why, it looks like a boat."

"Why, certainly, it's a boat."

"No; it's on wheels."

"Yes, so it is. Well, that must be the lifeboat. They drag them along shore on a wagon."

"That's the lifeboat, sure."

"No, by God, it's—it's an omnibus."

"I tell you it's a lifeboat."

"It is not! It's an omnibus. I can see it plain. See? One of these big hotel omnibuses."

"By thunder, you're right. It's an omnibus, sure as fate. What do you suppose they are doing with an omnibus? Maybe they are going around collecting the life-crew, hey?"

"That's it, likely. Look! There's a fellow waving a little black flag. He's standing on the steps of the omnibus. There come those other two fellows. Now they're all talking together. Look at the fellow with the flag. Maybe he ain't waving it!"

"That ain't a flag, is it? That's his coat. Why, certainly, that's his coat."

"So it is; it's his coat. He's taken it off and is waving it around his head. But would you look at him swing it!"

"Oh, say, there isn't any lifesaving station there. That's just a winter resort hotel omnibus that has brought over some of the boarders to see us drown."

"What's that idiot with the coat mean? What's he signaling, anyhow?"

"It looks as if he were trying to tell us to go north. There must be a lifesaving station up there."

"No; he thinks we're fishing. Just giving us a merry hand. See? Ah, there, Willie!"

"Well, I wish I could make something out of those signals. What do you suppose he means?"

"He don't mean anything; he's just playing."

"Well, if he'd just signal us to try the surf again, or to go to sea and wait, or go north, or go south, or go to hell, there would be some reason in it. But look at him! He just stands there and keeps his coat revolving like a wheel. The ass!"

"There come more people."

"Now there's quite a mob. Look! Isn't that a boat?"

"Where? Oh, I see where you mean. No, that's no boat."

"That fellow is still waving his coat."

"He must think we like to see him do that. Why don't he quit it? It don't mean anything."

"I don't know. I think he is trying to make us go north. It must be that there's a lifesaving station there somewhere."

"Say, he ain't tired yet. Look at 'im wave!"

"Wonder how long he can keep that up. He's been revolving his coat ever since he caught sight of us. He's an idiot. Why aren't they getting men to bring a boat out? A fishing boat—one of those big yawls—could come out here all right. Why don't he do something?"

"Oh, it's all right now."

"They'll have a boat out here for us in less than no time, now that they've seen us."

A faint yellow tone came into the sky over the low land. The shadows on the sea slowly deepened. The wind bore coldness with it, and the men began to shiver.

"Holy smoke!" said one, allowing his voice to express his impious mood, "if we keep on monkeying out here! If we've got to flounder out here all night!"

"Oh, we'll never have to stay here all night! Don't you worry. They've seen us now, and it won't be long before they'll come chasing out after us."

The shore grew dusky. The man waving a coat blended gradually into this gloom, and it swallowed in the same manner the omnibus and the group of people. The spray, when it dashed uproariously over the sides made the voyagers shrink and swear like men who were being branded.

"I'd like to catch the chump who waved the coat. I feel like socking him one, just for luck."

"Why? What did he do?"

"Oh, nothing, but then he seemed so damned cheerful."

In the meantime the oiler rowed, and then the correspondent rowed, and then the oiler rowed. Gray-faced and bowed forward, they mechanically, turn by turn, plied the leaden oars. The form of the lighthouse had vanished from the southern horizon, but finally a pale star appeared, just lifting from the sea. The streaked saffron in the west passed before the all-merging darkness, and the sea to the east was black. The land had vanished, and was expressed only by the low and drear thunder of the surf.

"If I am going to be drowned—if I am going to be drowned—if I am going to be drowned, why, in the name of the seven mad gods who rule the sea, was I allowed to come thus far and contemplate sand and trees? Was I brought here merely to have my nose dragged away as I was about to nibble the sacred cheese of life?"

The patient captain, drooped over the water jar, was sometimes obliged to speak to the oarsman.

"Keep her head up! Keep her head up!"

"Keep her head up, sir." The voices were weary and low.

This was surely a quiet evening. All save the oarsman lay heavily and listlessly in the boat's bottom. As for him, his eyes were just capable of noting the tall black waves that swept forward in a most sinister silence, save for an occasional subdued growl of a crest.

The cook's head was on a thwart, and he looked without interest at the water under his nose. He was deep in other scenes. Finally he spoke. "Billie," he murmured, dreamfully, "what kind of pie do you like best?"

V

"Pie!" said the oiler and the correspondent, agitatedly. "Don't talk about those things, blast you!"

"Well," said the cook, "I was just thinking about ham sandwiches, and—"

A night on the sea in an open boat is a long night. As darkness settled finally, the shine of the light, lifting from the sea in the south, changed to full gold. On the northern horizon a new light appeared, a small bluish gleam on the edge of the waters. These two lights were the furniture of the world. Otherwise there was nothing but waves.

Two men huddled in the stern, and distances were so magnificent in the dinghy that the rower was enabled to keep his feet partly warm by thrusting them under his companions. Their legs indeed extended far under the rowing-seat until they touched the feet of the captain forward. Sometimes, despite the efforts of the tired oarsman, a wave came piling into the boat, an icy wave of the night, and the chilling water soaked them anew. They would twist their bodies for a moment and groan, and sleep the dead sleep once more, while the water in the boat gurgled about them as the craft rocked.

The plan of the oiler and the correspondent was for one to row until he lost the ability, and then arouse the other from his sea-water couch in the bottom of the boat.

The oiler plied the oars until his head drooped forward and the overpowering sleep blinded him; and he rowed yet afterward. Then he touched a man in the bottom of the boat, and called his name. "Will you spell me for a little while?" he said meekly.

"Sure, Billie," said the correspondent, awaking and dragging himself to a sitting position. They exchanged places carefully, and the oiler, cuddling down in the seawater at the cook's side, seemed to go to sleep instantly.

The particular violence of the sea had ceased. The waves came without snarling. The obligation of the man at the oars was to keep the boat headed so that the tilt of the rollers would not capsize her, and to preserve her from filling when the crests rushed past. The black waves were silent and hard to be seen in the darkness. Often one was almost upon the boat before the oarsman was aware.

In a low voice the correspondent addressed the captain. He was not sure that the captain was awake, although this iron man seemed to be always awake. "Captain, shall I keep her making for that light north, sir?"

The same steady voice answered him. "Yes. Keep it about two points off the port bow."

The cook had tied a lifebelt around himself in order to get even the warmth which this clumsy cork contrivance could donate, and he seemed almost stovelike when a rower, whose teeth invariably chattered wildly as soon as he ceased his labor, dropped down to sleep.

The correspondent, as he rowed, looked down at the two men sleeping underfoot. The cook's arm was around the oiler's shoulders, and, with their fragmentary clothing and haggard faces, they were the babes of the sea—a grotesque rendering of the old babes in the wood.

Later he must have grown stupid at his work, for suddenly there was a growling of water, and a crest came with a roar and a swash into the boat, and it was a wonder that it did not set the cook afloat in his lifebelt. The cook continued to sleep, but the oiler sat up, blinking his eyes and shaking with the new cold.

"Oh, I'm awful sorry, Billie," said the correspondent, contritely.

"That's all right, old boy," said the oiler, and lay down again and was asleep.

Presently it seemed that even the captain dozed, and the correspondent thought that he was the one man afloat on all the oceans. The wind had a voice as it came over the waves, and it was sadder than the end.

There was a long, loud swishing astern of the boat, and a gleaming trail of phosphorescence, like blue flame, was furrowed on the black waters. It might have been made by a monstrous knife.

Then there came a stillness, while the correspondent breathed with open mouth and looked at the sea.

Suddenly there was another swish and another long flash of bluish light, and this time it was alongside the boat, and might almost have been reached with an oar. The correspondent saw an enormous fin speed like a shadow through the water, hurling the crystalline spray and leaving the long glowing trail.

The correspondent looked over his shoulder at the captain. His face was hidden, and he seemed to be asleep. He looked at the babes of the sea. They certainly were asleep. So, being bereft of sympathy, he leaned a little way to one side and swore softly into the sea.

But the thing did not then leave the vicinity of the boat. Ahead or astern, on one side or the other, at intervals long or short, fled the long sparkling streak, and there was to be heard the *whirroo* of the dark fin. The speed and power of the thing was greatly to be admired. It cut the water like a gigantic and keen projectile.

The presence of this biding thing did not affect the man with the same horror that it would if he had been a picnicker. He simply looked at the sea dully and swore in an undertone.

Nevertheless, it is true that he did not wish to be alone with the thing. He wished one of his companions to awake by chance and keep him company with it. But the captain hung motionless over the water jar, and the oiler and the cook in the bottom of the boat were plunged in slumber.

VI

"If I am going to be drowned—if I am going to be drowned—if I am going to be drowned, why, in the name of the seven mad gods who rule the sea, was I allowed to come thus far and contemplate sand and trees?"

During this dismal night, it may be remarked that a man would conclude that it was really the intention of the seven mad gods to drown him, despite the abominable injustice of it. For it was certainly an abominable injustice to drown a man who had worked so hard, so hard. The man felt it would be a crime most unnatural. Other people had drowned at sea since galleys swarmed with painted sails, but still——

When it occurs to a man that nature does not regard him as important, and that she feels she would not maim the universe by disposing of him, he at first wishes to throw bricks at the temple, and he hates deeply the fact that there are no bricks and no temples. Any visible expression of nature would surely be pelleted with his jeers.

Then, if there be no tangible thing to hoot, he feels, perhaps, the desire to confront a personification and indulge in pleas, bowed to one knee, and with hands supplicant, saying, "Yes, but I love myself."

A high cold star on a winter's night is the word he feels that she says to him. Thereafter he knows the pathos of his situation.

The men in the dinghy had not discussed these matters, but each had, no doubt, reflected upon them in silence and according to his mind. There was seldom any expression upon their faces save the general one of complete weariness. Speech was devoted to the business of the boat.

To chime the notes of his emotion, a verse mysteriously entered the correspondent's head. He had even forgotten that he had forgotten this verse, but it suddenly was in his mind.

A soldier of the Legion lay dying in Algiers;
There was lack of woman's nursing, there was dearth of woman's tears;
But a comrade stood beside him, and he took that comrade's hand,
And he said, "I never more shall see my own, my native land."

In his childhood the correspondent had been made acquainted with the fact that a soldier of the Legion lay dying in Algiers, but he had never regarded the fact as important. Myriads of his schoolfellows had informed him of the soldier's plight, but the dinning had naturally ended by making him perfectly indifferent. He had never considered it his affair that a soldier of the Legion lay dying in Algiers, nor had it appeared to him as a matter for sorrow. It was less to him than the breaking of a pencil's point.

Now, however, it quaintly came to him as a human, living thing. It was no longer merely a picture of a few throes in the breast of a poet, meanwhile drinking tea and warming his feet at the grate; it was an actuality—stern, mournful, and fine.

The correspondent plainly saw the soldier. He lay on the sand with his feet out straight and still. While his pale left hand was upon his chest in an attempt to thwart the going of his life, the blood came between his fingers. In the far Algerian distance, a city of low square forms was set against a sky that was faint with the last sunset hues. The correspondent, plying the oars and dreaming of the slow and slower movements of the lips of the soldier, was moved by a profound and perfectly impersonal comprehension. He was sorry for the soldier of the Legion who lay dying in Algiers.

The thing which had followed the boat and waited had evidently grown bored at the delay. There was no longer to be heard the slash of the cut-water, and there was no longer the flame of the long trail. The light in the north still glimmered, but it was apparently no nearer to the boat. Sometimes the boom of the surf rang in the correspondent's ears, and he turned the craft seaward then and rowed harder. Southward, some one had evidently built a watch fire on the beach. It was too low and too far to be seen, but it made a shimmering, roseate reflection upon the bluff in back of it, and this could be discerned from the boat. The wind came stronger, and sometimes a wave suddenly raged out like a mountain cat, and there was to be seen the sheen and sparkle of a broken crest.

The captain, in the bow, moved on his water jar and sat erect. "Pretty long night," he observed to the correspondent. He looked at the shore. "Those life-saving people take their time."

"Did you see that shark playing around?"

"Yes, I saw him. He was a big fellow, all right."

"Wish I had known you were awake."

Later the correspondent spoke into the bottom of the boat. "Billie!" There was a slow and gradual disentanglement. "Billie, will you spell me?"

"Sure," said the oiler.

As soon as the correspondent touched the cold, comfortable seawater in the bottom of the boat and had huddled close to the cook's lifebelt he was deep in sleep, despite the fact that his teeth played all the popular airs. This sleep was so good to him that it was but a moment before he heard a voice call his name in a tone that demonstrated the last stages of exhaustion. "Will you spell me?"

"Sure, Billie."

The light in the north had mysteriously vanished, but the correspondent took his course from the wide-awake captain.

Later in the night they took the boat farther out to sea, and the captain directed the cook to take one oar at the stern and keep the boat facing the seas. He was to call out if he should hear the thunder of the surf. This plan enabled the oiler and the correspondent to get respite together. "We'll give those boys a chance to get into shape again," said the captain. They curled down and, after a few preliminary chatterings and trembles, slept once more the dead sleep. Neither knew they had bequeathed to the cook the company of another shark, or perhaps the same shark.

As the boat caroused on the waves, spray occasionally bumped over the side and gave them a fresh soaking, but this had no power to break their repose. The ominous slash of the wind and the water affected them as it would have affected mummies.

"Boys," said the cook, with the notes of every reluctance in his voice, "she's drifted in pretty close. I guess one of you had better take her to sea again." The correspondent, aroused, heard the crash of the toppled crests.

As he was rowing, the captain gave him some whiskey-and-water, and this steadied the chills out of him. "If I ever get ashore and anybody shows me even a photograph of an oar—"

At last there was a short conversation.

"Billie! . . . Billie, will you spell me?"

"Sure," said the oiler.

VII

When the correspondent again opened his eyes, the sea and the sky were each of the gray hue of the dawning. Later, carmine and gold was painted upon the waters. The morning appeared finally, in its splendor, with a sky of pure blue, and the sunlight flamed on the tips of the waves.

On the distant dunes were set many little black cottages, and a tall white windmill reared above them. No man, nor dog, nor bicycle appeared on the beach. The cottages might have formed a deserted village.

The voyagers scanned the shore. A conference was held in the boat. "Well," said the captain, "if no help is coming, we might better try a run through the surf right away. If we stay out here much longer we will be too weak to do anything for ourselves at all." The others silently acquiesced in this reasoning. The boat was headed for the beach. The correspondent wondered if none ever ascended the tall windtower, and if then they never looked seaward. This tower was a giant, standing with its back to the plight of the ants. It represented in a degree, to the correspondent, the serenity of nature amid the struggles of the individual—nature in the wind, and nature in the vision of men. She did not seem cruel to him then, nor beneficent, nor treacherous, nor wise. But she was indifferent, flatly indifferent. It is, perhaps, plausible that a man in this situation, impressed with the unconcern of the universe, should see the innumerable flaws of his life, and have them taste wickedly in his mind, and wish for another chance. A distinction between right and wrong seems absurdly clear to him, then, in this new ignorance of the grave-edge, and he understands that if he were given another opportunity he would mend his conduct and his words, and be better and brighter during an introduction or at a tea.

"Now, boys," said the captain, "she is going to swamp sure. All we can do is to work her in as far as possible, and then when she swamps, pile out and scramble for the beach. Keep cool now, and don't jump until she swamps sure."

The oiler took the oars. Over his shoulders he scanned the surf. "Captain," he said, "I think I'd better bring her about and keep her head-on to the seas and back her in."

"All right, Billie," said the captain. "Back her in." The oiler swung the boat then, and, seated in the stern, the cook and the correspondent were obliged to look over their shoulders to contemplate the lonely and indifferent shore.

The monstrous inshore rollers heaved the boat high until the men were again enabled to see the white sheets of water scudding up the slanted beach. "We won't get in very close," said the captain. Each time a man could wrest his attention from the rollers, he turned his glance toward the shore, and in the expression of the eyes during this contemplation there was a singular quality. The correspondent, observing the others, knew that they were not afraid, but the full meaning of their glances was shrouded.

As for himself, he was too tired to grapple fundamentally with the fact. He tried to coerce his mind into thinking of it, but the mind was dominated at this time by the muscles, and the muscles said they did not care. It merely occurred to him that if he should drown it would be a shame.

There were no hurried words, no pallor, no plain agitation. The men simply looked at the shore. "Now, remember to get well clear of the boat when you jump," said the captain.

Seaward the crest of a roller suddenly fell with a thunderous crash, and the long white comber came roaring down upon the boat.

"Steady now," said the captain. The men were silent. They turned their eyes from the shore to the comber and waited. The boat slid up the incline, leaped at the furious top, bounced over it, and swung down the long back of the wave. Some water had been shipped, and the cook bailed it out.

But the next crest crashed also. The tumbling, boiling flood of white water caught the boat and whirled it almost perpendicular. Water swarmed in from all sides. The correspondent had his hands on the gunwale at this time, and when the water entered at that place he swiftly withdrew his fingers, as if he objected to wetting them.

The little boat, drunken with this weight of water, reeled and snuggled deeper into the sea.

"Bail her out, cook! Bail her out!" said the captain.

"All right, Captain," said the cook.

"Now, boys, the next one will do for us sure," said the oiler. "Mind to jump clear of the boat."

The third wave moved forward, huge, furious, implacable. It fairly swallowed the dinghy, and almost simultaneously the men tumbled into the sea. A piece of lifebelt had lain in the bottom of the boat, and as the correspondent went over-board he held this to his chest with his left hand.

The January water was icy, and he reflected immediately that it was colder than he had expected to find it off the coast of Florida. This appeared to his dazed mind as a fact important enough to be noted at the time. The coldness of the water was sad; it was tragic. This fact was somehow mixed and confused with his opinion of his own situation, so that it seemed almost a proper reason for tears. The water was cold.

When he came to the surface he was conscious of little but the noisy water. Afterward he saw his companions in the sea. The oiler was ahead in the race. He was swimming strongly and rapidly. Off to the correspondent's left, the cook's great white and corked back bulged out of the water; and in the rear the captain was hanging with his one good hand to the heel of the overturned dinghy.

There is a certain immovable quality to a shore, and the correspondent won-dered at it amid the confusion of the sea.

It seemed also very attractive; but the correspondent knew that it was a long journey, and he paddled leisurely. The piece of life preserver lay under him, and sometimes he whirled down the incline of a wave as if he were on a hand-sled.

But finally he arrived at a place in the sea where travel was beset with difficulty. He did not pause swimming to inquire what manner of current had caught him, but there his progress ceased. The shore was set before him like a bit of scenery on a stage, and he looked at it and understood with his eyes each detail of it.

As the cook passed, much farther to the left, the captain was calling to him, "Turn over on your back, cook! Turn over on your back and use the oar."

"All right, sir." The cook turned on his back, and, paddling with an oar, went ahead as if he were a canoe.

Presently the boat also passed to the left of the correspondent, with the captain clinging with one hand to the keel. He would have appeared like a man raising himself to look over a board fence if it were not for the extraordinary gymnastics of the boat. The correspondent marveled that the captain could still hold to it.

They passed on nearer to shore—the oiler, the cook, the captain—and fol-lowing them went the water jar, bouncing gaily over the seas.

The correspondent remained in the grip of this strange new enemy—a current. The shore, with its white slope of sand and its green bluff topped with little silent cottages, was spread like a picture before him. It was very near to him then, but he was impressed as one who, in a gallery, looks at a scene from Brittany or Algiers.

He thought: "I am going to drown? Can it be possible? Can it be possible? Can it be possible?" Perhaps an individual must consider his own death to be the final phenomenon of nature.

But later a wave perhaps whirled him out of this small deadly current, for he found suddenly that he could again make progress toward the shore. Later still he was aware that the captain, clinging with one hand to the keel of the dinghy, had his face turned away from the shore and toward him, and was calling his name. "Come to the boat! Come to the boat!"

In his struggle to reach the captain and the boat, he reflected that when one gets properly wearied drowning must really be a comfortable arrangement—a cessation of hostilities accompanied by a large degree of relief; and he was glad of it, for the main thing in his mind for some moments had been horror of the temporary agony. He did not wish to be hurt.

Presently he saw a man running along the shore. He was undressing with most remarkable speed. Coat, trousers, shirt, everything flew magically off him.

"Come to the boat!" called the captain.

"All right, Captain." As the correspondent paddled, he saw the captain let himself down to bottom and leave the boat. Then the correspondent performed his one little marvel of the voyage. A large wave caught him and flung him with ease and supreme speed completely over the boat and far beyond it. It struck him even then as an event in gymnastics and a true miracle of the sea. An overturned boat in the surf is not a plaything to a swimming man.

The correspondent arrived in water that reached only to his waist, but his condition did not enable him to stand for more than a moment. Each wave knocked him into a heap, and the undertow pulled at him.

Then he saw the man who had been running and undressing, and undressing and running, come bounding into the water. He dragged ashore the cook, and then waded toward the captain; but the captain waved him away and sent him to the correspondent. He was naked—naked as a tree in winter; but a halo was about his head, and he shone like a saint. He gave a strong pull, and a long drag, and a bully heave at the correspondent's hand. The correspondent, schooled in the minor formulae, said, "Thanks, old man." But suddenly the man cried, "What's that?" He pointed a swift finger. The correspondent said, "Go."

In the shallows, face downward, lay the oiler. His forehead touched sand that was periodically, between each wave, clear of the sea.

The correspondent did not know all that transpired afterward. When he achieved safe ground he fell, striking the sand with each particular part of his body. It was as if he had dropped from a roof, but the thud was grateful to him.

It seems that instantly the beach was populated with men with blankets, clothes, and flasks, and women with coffeepots and all the remedies sacred to their minds. The welcome of the land to the men from the sea was warm and generous; but a still and dripping shape was carried slowly up the beach, and the land's welcome for it could only be the different and sinister hospitality of the grave.

When it came night, the white waves paced to and fro in the moonlight, and the wind brought the sound of the great sea's voice to the men on the shore, and they felt that they could then be interpreters.

🦢 Willa Cather (1873–1947)

Like many of the characters represented in her fiction, early in her life Willa Cather experienced the shock of being uprooted from one landscape and placed into another that was radically unfamiliar. Born in Virginia, she moved with her family to the flat, open prairies of southeastern Nebraska. There she encountered the pioneers and immigrants, mostly from northern Europe, who would later reappear as characters in her stories. She attended the University of Nebraska at Lincoln, where she first published her work in the school's literary magazine. Soon after graduation she began a journalistic career, which she would pursue until she was able to dedicate herself full-time to her creative writing in 1912. Cather worked for a year with the newspaper in Lincoln but then relocated to Pittsburgh, where she first served as a magazine editor and later worked as an arts reviewer for the local newspaper. She published a collection of poems, April Twilights, *in 1903 and a collection of short stories,* The Troll Garden, *in 1905. In 1906 Cather moved to New York City to work as an editor at* McClure's Magazine, *but she was able to resign when her first novel,* Alexander's Bridge *(1912), was published. Several of her best-known works, some of which had been drafted earlier, followed: O Pioneers! (1913);* The Song of the Lark *(1915);* My Antonia *(1918);* Coming, Aphrodite! *(1920);* One of Ours *(1922), for which she was awarded a Pulitzer Prize;* The Professor's House *(1925);* My Mortal Enemy *(1926);* Death Comes to the Archbishop *(1927);* Shadows in the Rock *(1931);* Lucy Gayheart *(1940); and her last novel,* Sapphira and the Slave Girl *(1940).*

After the success of her first novel, wherein Cather adopts a male voice and protagonist, she was urged by her good friend Sarah Orne Jewett to focus on representing women's lives and voices. Cather's response was to create such memorable women characters as Alexandra Bergson and Antonia Pavelka. Alexandra, who is featured in the selection from O Pioneers! *below, and whose name evokes that of the ancient warrior Alexander the Great, reverses the conventional American myth of the heroic male pioneer conquering the "virgin" wilderness. Here it is a female heroine who is responsible for the growth and flourishing of what had once been a harsh and untamed landscape. While Cather's evocative depiction of the richness and complexity of what for some appeared to be tedious sameness in the landscape of the Great Plains has made her generally regarded as a Western writer, her fiction is set in a wide variety of locales. She once wrote that she resisted focusing on only one geographical region: ". . . using one setting all the time is very like planting a field with corn season after season. I believe in rotation of crops." No matter the geographical setting, Cather frequently emphasizes her characters' important relationships to their physical environment as defining features of their identities. Alexandra Bergson, for example, transforms herself as she transforms the fields around her into farmland. Such a transformation of the natural world gives her a freedom and an independence that was rare for most pioneer women.*

From O Pioneers!

From Part 1, The Wild Land

2

On one of the ridges of that wintry waste stood the low log house in which John Bergson was dying. The Bergson homestead was easier to find than many another, because it overlooked Norway Creek, a shallow, muddy stream that sometimes flowed, and sometimes stood still, at the bottom of a winding ravine with steep, shelving sides overgrown with brush and cottonwoods and dwarf ash. This creek gave a sort of identity to the farms that bordered upon it. Of all the bewildering things about a new country, the absence of human landmarks is one of the most depressing and disheartening. The houses on the Divide were small and were usually tucked away in low places; you did not see them until you came directly upon them. Most of them were built of the sod itself, and were only the unescapable ground in another form. The roads were but faint tracks in the grass, and the fields were scarcely noticeable. The record of the plow was insignificant, like the feeble scratches on stone left by prehistoric races, so indeterminate that they may, after all, be only the markings of glaciers, and not a record of human strivings.

In eleven long years John Bergson had made but little impression upon the wild land he had come to tame. It was still a wild thing that had its ugly moods; and no one knew when they were likely to come, or why. Mischance hung over it. Its Genius was unfriendly to man. The sick man was feeling this as he lay looking out of the window, after the doctor had left him, on the day following Alexandra's trip to town. There it lay outside his door, the same land, the same lead-colored miles. He knew every ridge and draw and gully between him and the horizon. To the south, his plowed fields; to the east, the sod stables, the cattle corral, the pond,—and then the grass.

Bergson went over in his mind the things that had held him back. One winter his cattle had perished in a blizzard. The next summer one of his plow horses broke its leg in a prairie-dog hole and had to be shot. Another summer he lost his hogs from cholera, and a valuable stallion died from a rattlesnake bite. Time and again his crops had failed. He had lost two children, boys, that came between Lou and Emil, and there had been the cost of sickness and death. Now, when he had at last struggled out of debt, he was going to die himself. He was only forty-six, and had, of course, counted upon more time.

Bergson had spent his first five years on the Divide getting into debt, and the last six getting out. He had paid off his mortgages and had ended pretty much where he began, with the land. He owned exactly six hundred and forty acres of what stretched outside his door; his own original homestead and timber claim, making three hundred and twenty acres, and the half-section adjoining, the homestead of a younger brother who had given up the fight, gone back to Chicago to work in a fancy bakery and distinguish himself in a Swedish athletic club. So far John had not attempted to cultivate the second half-section, but used it for pasture land, and one of his sons rode herd there in open weather.

John Bergson had the Old-World belief that land, in itself, is desirable. But this land was an enigma. It was like a horse that no one knows how to break to harness, that runs wild and kicks things to pieces. He had an idea that no one understood how to farm it properly, and this he often discussed with Alexandra. Their neighbors, certainly, knew even less about farming than he did. Many of them had never worked on a farm until they took up their homesteads. They had been *handwerkers* at home; tailors, locksmiths, joiners, cigar-makers, etc. Bergson himself had worked in a shipyard.

For weeks, John Bergson had been thinking about these things. His bed stood in the sitting-room, next to the kitchen. Through the day, while the baking and washing and ironing were going on, the father lay and looked up at the roof beams that he himself had hewn, or out at the cattle in the corral. He counted the cattle over and over. It diverted him to speculate as to how much weight each of the steers would probably put on by spring. He often called his daughter in to talk to her about this. Before Alexandra was twelve years old she had begun to be a help to him, and as she grew older he had come to depend more and more upon her resourcefulness and good judgment. His boys were willing enough to work, but when he talked with them they usually irritated him. It was Alexandra who read the papers and followed the markets, and who learned by the mistakes of their neighbors. It was Alexandra who could always tell about what it had cost to fatten each steer, and who could guess the weight of a hog before it went on the scales closer than John Bergson himself. Lou and Oscar were industrious, but he could never teach them to use their heads about their work.

Alexandra, her father often said to himself, was like her grandfather; which was his way of saying that she was intelligent. John Bergson's father had been a shipbuilder, a man of considerable force and of some fortune. Late in life he married a second time, a Stockholm woman of questionable character, much younger than he, who goaded him into every sort of extravagance. On the shipbuilder's part, this marriage was an infatuation, the despairing folly of a powerful man who cannot bear to grow old. In a few years his unprincipled wife warped the probity of a lifetime. He speculated, lost his own fortune and funds entrusted to him by poor seafaring men, and died disgraced, leaving his children nothing. But when all was said, he had come up from the sea himself, had built up a proud little business with no capital but his own skill and foresight, and had proved himself a man. In his daughter, John Bergson recognized the strength of will, and the simple direct way of thinking things out, that had characterized his father in his better days. He would much rather, of course, have seen this likeness in one of his sons, but it was not a question of choice. As he lay there day after day he had to accept the situation as it was, and to be thankful that there was one among his children to whom he could entrust the future of his family and the possibilities of his hard-won land.

The winter twilight was fading. The sick man heard his wife strike a match in the kitchen, and the light of a lamp glimmered through the cracks of the door. It seemed like a light shining far away. He turned painfully in his bed and looked at his white hands, with all the work gone out of them. He was ready to give up, he felt. He did not know how it had come about, but he was quite willing to go deep under his fields and rest, where the plow could not find him. He was tired of making mistakes. He was content to leave the tangle to other hands; he thought of his Alexandra's strong ones.

"*Dotter*," he called feebly, "*dotter!*" He heard her quick step and saw her tall figure appear in the doorway, with the light of the lamp behind her. He felt her youth and strength, how easily she moved and stooped and lifted. But he would not have had it again if he could, not he! He knew the end too well to wish to begin again. He knew where it all went to, what it all became.

His daughter came and lifted him up on his pillows. She called him by an old Swedish name that she used to call him when she was little and took his dinner to him in the shipyard.

"Tell the boys to come here, daughter. I want to speak to them."

"They are feeding the horses, father. They have just come back from the Blue. Shall I call them?"

He sighed. "No, no. Wait until they come in. Alexandra, you will have to do the best you can for your brothers. Everything will come on you."

"I will do all I can, father."

"Don't let them get discouraged and go off like Uncle Otto. I want them to keep the land."

"We will, father. We will never lose the land."

There was a sound of heavy feet in the kitchen. Alexandra went to the door and beckoned to her brothers, two strapping boys of seventeen and nineteen. They came in and stood at the foot of the bed. Their father looked at them searchingly, though it was too dark to see their faces; they were just the same boys, he told himself, he had not been mistaken in them. The square head and heavy shoulders belonged to Oscar, the elder. The younger boy was quicker, but vacillating.

"Boys," said the father wearily, "I want you to keep the land together and to be guided by your sister. I have talked to her since I have been sick, and she knows all my wishes. I want no quarrels among my children, and so long as there is one house there must be one head. Alexandra is the oldest, and she knows my wishes. She will do the best she can. If she makes mistakes, she will not make so many as I have made. When you marry, and want a house of your own, the land will be divided fairly, according to the courts. But for the next few years you will have it hard, and you must all keep together. Alexandra will manage the best she can."

Oscar, who was usually the last to speak, replied because he was the older, "Yes, father. It would be so anyway, without your speaking. We will all work the place together."

"And you will be guided by your sister, boys, and be good brothers to her, and good sons to your mother? That is good. And Alexandra must not work in the fields any more. There is no necessity now. Hire a man when you need help. She can make much more with her eggs and butter than the wages of a man. It was one of my mistakes that I did not find that out sooner. Try to break a little more land every year; sod corn is good for fodder. Keep turning the land, and always put up more hay than you need. Don't grudge your mother a little time for plowing her garden and setting out fruit trees, even if it comes in a busy season. She has been a good mother to you, and she has always missed the old country."

When they went back to the kitchen the boys sat down silently at the table. Throughout the meal they looked down at their plates and did not lift their red eyes. They did not eat much, although they had been working in the cold all day, and there was a rabbit stewed in gravy for supper, and prune pies.

John Bergson had married beneath him, but he had married a good housewife. Mrs. Bergson was a fair-skinned, corpulent woman, heavy and placid like her son, Oscar, but there was something comfortable about her; perhaps it was her own love of comfort. For eleven years she had worthily striven to maintain some semblance of household order amid conditions that made order very difficult. Habit was very strong with Mrs. Bergson, and her unremitting efforts to repeat the routine of her old life among new surroundings had done a great deal to keep the family from disintegrating morally and getting careless in their ways. The Bergsons had a log house, for instance, only because Mrs. Bergson would not live in a sod house. She missed the fish diet of her own country, and twice every summer she sent the boys to the river, twenty miles to the southward, to fish for channel cat. When the children were little she used to load them all into the wagon, the baby in its crib, and go fishing herself.

Alexandra often said that if her mother were cast upon a desert island, she would thank God for her deliverance, make a garden, and find something to preserve. Preserving was almost a mania with Mrs. Bergson. Stout as she was, she roamed the scrubby banks of Norway Creek looking for fox grapes and goose plums, like a wild creature in search of prey. She made a yellow jam of the insipid ground-cherries that grew on the prairie, flavoring it with lemon peel; and she made a sticky dark conserve of garden tomatoes. She had experimented even with the rank buffalo-pea, and she could not see a fine bronze cluster of them without shaking her head and murmuring, "What a pity!" When there was nothing more to preserve, she began to pickle. The amount of sugar she used in these processes was sometimes a serious drain upon the family resources. She was a good mother, but she was glad when her children were old enough not to be in her way in the kitchen. She had never quite forgiven John Bergson for bringing her to the end of the earth; but, now that she was there, she wanted to be let alone to reconstruct her old life in so far as that was possible. She could still take some comfort in the world if she had bacon in the cave, glass jars on the shelves, and sheets in the press. She disapproved of all her neighbors because of their slovenly housekeeping, and the women thought her very proud. Once when Mrs. Bergson, on her way to Norway Creek, stopped to see old Mrs. Lee, the old woman hid in the haymow "for fear Mis' Bergson would catch her barefoot."

.　.　.

5

Alexandra and Emil spent five days down among the river farms, driving up and down the valley. Alexandra talked to the men about their crops and to the women about their poultry. She spent a whole day with one young farmer who had been away at school, and who was experimenting with a new kind of clover hay. She learned a great deal. As they drove along, she and Emil talked and planned. At last, on the sixth day, Alexandra turned Brigham's head northward and left the river behind.

"There's nothing in it for us down there, Emil. There are a few fine farms, but they are owned by the rich men in town, and couldn't be bought. Most of the land is rough and hilly. They can always scrape along down there, but they can never do anything big. Down there they have a little certainty, but up with us there is a big chance. We must have faith in the high land, Emil. I want to hold on harder than ever, and when you're a man you'll thank me." She urged Brigham forward.

When the road began to climb the first long swells of the Divide, Alexandra hummed an old Swedish hymn, and Emil wondered why his sister looked so happy. Her face was so radiant that he felt shy about asking her. For the first time, perhaps, since that land emerged from the waters of geologic ages, a human face was set toward it with love and yearning. It seemed beautiful to her, rich and strong and glorious. Her eyes drank in the breadth of it, until her tears blinded her. Then the Genius of the Divide, the great, free spirit which breathes across it, must have bent lower than it ever bent to a human will before. The history of every country begins in the heart of a man or a woman.

Alexandra reached home in the afternoon. That evening she held a family council and told her brothers all that she had seen and heard.

"I want you boys to go down yourselves and look it over. Nothing will convince you like seeing with your own eyes. The river land was settled before this, and so they are a few years ahead of us, and have learned more about farming. The land sells for three times as much as this, but in five years we will double it. The rich men down there own all the best land, and they are buying all they can get. The thing to do is to sell our cattle and what little old corn we have, and buy the Linstrum place. Then the next thing to do is to take out two loans on our half-sections, and buy Peter Crow's place; raise every dollar we can, and buy every acre we can."

"Mortgage the homestead again?" Lou cried. He sprang up and began to wind the clock furiously. "I won't slave to pay off another mortgage. I'll never do it. You'd just as soon kill us all, Alexandra, to carry out some scheme!"

Oscar rubbed his high, pale forehead. "How do you propose to pay off your mortgages?"

Alexandra looked from one to the other and bit her lip. They had never seen her so nervous. "See here," she brought out at last. "We borrow the money for six years. Well, with the money we buy a half-section from Linstrum and a half from Crow, and a quarter from Struble, maybe. That will give us upwards of fourteen hundred acres, won't it? You won't have to pay off your mortgages for six years. By that time, any of this land will be worth thirty dollars an acre—it will be worth fifty, but we'll say thirty; then you can sell a garden patch anywhere, and pay off a debt of sixteen hundred dollars. It's not the principal I'm worried about, it's the interest and taxes. We'll have to strain to meet the payments. But as sure as we are sitting here tonight, we can sit down here ten years from now independent landowners, not struggling farmers any longer. The chance that father was always looking for has come."

Lou was pacing the floor. "But how do you *know* that land is going to go up enough to pay the mortgages and—"

"And make us rich besides?" Alexandra put in firmly. "I can't explain that, Lou. You'll have to take my word for it. I *know*, that's all. When you drive about over the country you can feel it coming."

Oscar had been sitting with his head lowered, his hands hanging between his knees. "But we can't work so much land," he said dully, as if he were talking to himself. "We can't even try. It would just lie there and we'd work ourselves to death." He sighed, and laid his calloused fist on the table.

Alexandra's eyes filled with tears. She put her hand on his shoulder. "You poor boy, you won't have to work it. The men in town who are buying up other people's land don't try to farm it. They are the men to watch, in a new country. Let's try to do like the shrewd ones, and not like these stupid fellows. I don't want you boys always to have to work like this. I want you to be independent, and Emil to go to school."

Lou held his head as if it were splitting. "Everybody will say we are crazy. It must be crazy, or everybody would be doing it."

"If they were, we wouldn't have much chance. No, Lou, I was talking about that with the smart young man who is raising the new kind of clover. He says the right thing is usually just what everybody don't do. Why are we better fixed than any of our neighbors? Because father had more brains. Our people were better people than these in the old country. We *ought* to do more than they do, and see further ahead. Yes, mother, I'm going to clear the table now."

Alexandra rose. The boys went to the stable to see to the stock, and they were gone a long while. When they came back Lou played on his *dragharmonika* and Oscar sat figuring at his father's secretary all evening. They said nothing more about Alexandra's project, but she felt sure now that they would consent to it. Just before bedtime Oscar went out for a pail of water. When he did not come back, Alexandra threw a shawl over her head and ran down the path to the windmill. She found him sitting there with his head in his hands, and she sat down beside him.

"Don't do anything you don't want to do, Oscar," she whispered. She waited a moment, but he did not stir. "I won't say any more about it, if you'd rather not. What makes you so discouraged?"

"I dread signing my name to them pieces of paper," he said slowly. "All the time I was a boy we had a mortgage hanging over us."

"Then don't sign one. I don't want you to, if you feel that way."

Oscar shook his head. "No, I can see there's a chance that way. I've thought a good while there might be. We're in so deep now, we might as well go deeper. But it's hard work pulling out of debt. Like pulling a threshing-machine out of the mud; breaks your back. Me and Lou's worked hard, and I can't see it's got us ahead much."

"Nobody knows about that as well as I do, Oscar. That's why I want to try an easier way. I don't want you to have to grub for every dollar."

"Yes, I know what you mean. Maybe it'll come out right. But signing papers is signing papers. There ain't no maybe about that." He took his pail and trudged up the path to the house.

Alexandra drew her shawl closer about her and stood leaning against the frame of the mill, looking at the stars which glittered so keenly through the frosty autumn air. She always loved to watch them, to think of their vastness and distance, and of their ordered march. It fortified her to reflect upon the great operations of nature, and when she thought of the law that lay behind them, she felt a sense of personal security. That night she had a new consciousness of the country, felt almost a new relation to it. Even her talk with the boys had not taken away the feeling that had overwhelmed her when she drove back to the Divide that afternoon. She had never known before how much the country meant to her. The chirping of the insects down in the long grass had been like the sweetest music. She had felt as if her heart were hiding down there, some-where, with the quail and the plover and all the little wild things that crooned or buzzed in the sun. Under the long shaggy ridges, she felt the future stirring.

Robert Frost (1874–1963)

With their plain-speaking diction, their emphasis on the value of rugged individualism, and their rural setting, the poems of Robert Frost are synonymous with the traditional culture of New England. Yet Frost himself was not necessarily identical to the poor-but-honest-farmer persona he cultivated in those poems. He was born in San Francisco and moved back to his family's hometown of Lawrence, Massachusetts, while he was a boy. Lawrence was primarily a mill town, and Frost spent some time working in the mills. He briefly attended both Dartmouth and Harvard, taking degrees from neither institu-tion. Although he moved to a farm in Derry, New Hampshire, in 1900, severe allergies limited Frost's ability to work outdoors, and he instead supported his family with teach-ing jobs at the Pinkerton Academy and at a teacher's college in Plymouth, New Hamp-shire. He sold the farm in 1911 and shortly thereafter moved to England and began writing poetry full-time.

Ironically, this quintessentially American poet published his first two collections of po-etry in England before they were ever brought out in America: A Boy's Will *(1913) and* North of Boston *(1914). He returned to the United States in 1915, and his repu-tation as a poet continued to grow. Some of Frost's subsequent books include* Mountain Interval *(1916),* New Hampshire *(1923),* Collected Poems *(1930),* A Further Range *(1936), and* A Witness Tree *(1942). He was awarded the Pulitzer Prize on four separate occasions (1924, 1931, 1937, and 1943). Although his family purchased another farm in New Hampshire, Frost also had several special academic appointments at different colleges and universities. His status as a great American poet was cemented when he read at President John F. Kennedy's inauguration in 1961.*

As a writer, Frost has little in common with the more experimental poets of the early twentieth century. He is by no means a Modernist in his aesthetic, preferring traditional verse forms and homespun imagery; his conservatism was political as well as artistic. Al-though Frost has much in common with American Transcendentalists from the nine-teenth century, such as Emerson or Thoreau, his poetry offers less challenge to the status quo, instead reaffirming a simpler, old-fashioned, rural set of values while addressing an urbanized, highly educated modern reading audience. Frost is justifiably renowned for his depictions of the sights and rhythms of country life, but the description of nature is not his main object. In an interview in which he commented on the glut of writing about na-ture, he asserted: "There must be a human foreground to supplement this background of nature. There are beautiful stage settings in the theater but few people would go to see them if there were no actors and actresses." Despite the fact that Frost sets the natural "background" of his poems almost always in New England, he has escaped being classified as strictly a regional writer. He once claimed that his regionalism was essential to his poems' wider appeal: "You can't be universal without being provincial, can you? It's like trying to embrace the wind."

The Pasture

I'm going out to clean the pasture spring;
I'll only stop to rake the leaves away
(And wait to watch the water clear, I may)
I sha'n't be gone long.—You come too.

I'm going out to fetch the little calf   5
That's standing by the mother. It's so young
It totters when she licks it with her tongue.
I sha'n't be gone long.—You come too.

The Exposed Nest

You were forever finding some new play.
So when I saw you down on hands and knees
In the meadow, busy with the new-cut hay,
Trying, I thought, to set it up on end,
I went to show you how to make it stay,   5
If that was your idea, against the breeze,
And, if you asked me, even help pretend
To make it root again and grow afresh.
But 'twas no make-believe with you today,
Nor was the grass itself your real concern,   10
Though I found your hand full of wilted fern,
Steel-bright June-grass, and blackening heads of clover.
'Twas a nest full of young birds on the ground
The cutter bar had just gone champing over
(Miraculously without tasting flesh)   15
And left defenseless to the heat and light.
You wanted to restore them to their right
Of something interposed between their sight
And too much world at once—could means be found.
The way the nest-full every time we stirred   20
Stood up to us as to a mother-bird
Whose coming home has been too long deferred,
Made me ask would the mother-bird return
And care for them in such a change of scene

And might our meddling make her more afraid.   25
That was a thing we could not wait to learn.
We saw the risk we took in doing good,
But dared not spare to do the best we could
Though harm should come of it; so built the screen
You had begun, and gave them back their shade.   30
All this to prove we cared. Why is there then
No more to tell? We turned to other things.
I haven't any memory—have you?—
Of ever coming to the place again
To see if the birds lived the first night through,   35
And so at last to learn to use their wings.

The Oven Bird

There is a singer everyone has heard,
Loud, a mid-summer and a mid-wood bird,
Who makes the solid tree trunks sound again.
He says that leaves are old and that for flowers
Mid-summer is to spring as one to ten.   5
He says the early petal-fall is past
When pear and cherry bloom went down in showers
On sunny days a moment overcast;
And comes that other fall we name the fall.
He says the highway dust is over all.   10
The bird would cease and be as other birds
But that he knows in singing not to sing.
The question that he frames in all but words
Is what to make of a diminished thing.

Birches

When I see birches bend to left and right
Across the lines of straighter darker trees,
I like to think some boy's been swinging them.
But swinging doesn't bend them down to stay
As ice storms do. Often you must have seen them   5
Loaded with ice a sunny winter morning
After a rain. They click upon themselves
As the breeze rises, and turn many-colored
As the stir cracks and crazes their enamel.
Soon the sun's warmth makes them shed crystal shells   10
Shattering and avalanching on the snow crust—

Such heaps of broken glass to sweep away
You'd think the inner dome of heaven had fallen.
They are dragged to the withered bracken by the load,
And they seem not to break; though once they are bowed   15
So low for long, they never right themselves:
You may see their trunks arching in the woods
Years afterwards, trailing their leaves on the ground
Like girls on hands and knees that throw their hair
Before them over their heads to dry in the sun.   20
But I was going to say when Truth broke in
With all her matter-of-fact about the ice storm
I should prefer to have some boy bend them
As he went out and in to fetch the cows—
Some boy too far from town to learn baseball,   25
Whose only play was what he found himself,
Summer or winter, and could play alone.
One by one he subdued his father's trees
By riding them down over and over again
Until he took the stiffness out of them,   30
And not one but hung limp, not one was left
For him to conquer. He learned all there was
To learn about not launching out too soon
And so not carrying the tree away
Clear to the ground. He always kept his poise   35
To the top branches, climbing carefully
With the same pains you use to fill a cup
Up to the brim, and even above the brim.
Then he flung outward, feet first, with a swish,
Kicking his way down through the air to the ground.   40
So was I once myself a swinger of birches.
And so I dream of going back to be.
It's when I'm weary of considerations,
And life is too much like a pathless wood
Where your face burns and tickles with the cobwebs   45
Broken across it, and one eye is weeping
From a twig's having lashed across it open.
I'd like to get away from earth awhile
And then come back to it and begin over.
May no fate willfully misunderstand me   50
And half grant what I wish and snatch me away
Not to return. Earth's the right place for love:
I don't know where it's likely to go better.
I'd like to go by climbing a birch tree,
And climb black branches up a snow-white trunk   55
Toward heaven, till the tree could bear no more,
But dipped its top and set me down again.

That would be good both going and coming back.
One could do worse than be a swinger of birches.

Spring Pools

These pools that, though in forests, still reflect
The total sky almost without defect,
And like the flowers beside them, chill and shiver,
Will like the flowers beside them soon be gone,
And yet not out by any brook or river,   5
But up by roots to bring dark foliage on.

The trees that have it in their pent-up buds
To darken nature and be summer woods—
Let them think twice before they use their powers
To blot out and drink up and sweep away   10
These flowery waters and these watery flowers
From snow that melted only yesterday.

Design

I found a dimpled spider, fat and white,
On a white heal-all, holding up a moth
Like a white piece of rigid satin cloth—
Assorted characters of death and blight
Mixed ready to begin the morning right,   5
Like the ingredients of a witches' broth—
A snow-drop spider, a flower like a froth,
And dead wings carried like a paper kite.

What had that flower to do with being white,
The wayside blue and innocent heal-all?   10
What brought the kindred spider to that height,
Then steered the white moth thither in the night?
What but design of darkness to appall?—
If design govern in a thing so small.

The Most of It

He thought he kept the universe alone;
For all the voice in answer he could wake
Was but the mocking echo of his own

From some tree-hidden cliff across the lake.
Some morning from the boulder-broken beach   5
He would cry out on life, that what it wants
Is not its own love back in copy speech,
But counter-love, original response.
And nothing ever came of what he cried
Unless it was the embodiment that crashed   10
In the cliff's talus on the other side,
And then in the far distant water splashed,
But after a time allowed for it to swim,
Instead of proving human when it neared
And someone else additional to him,   15
As a great buck it powerfully appeared,
Pushing the crumpled water up ahead,
And landed pouring like a waterfall,
And stumbled through the rocks with horny tread,
And forced the underbrush—and that was all.   20

🖎 *Jack London* (1876–1916)

Jack London's body of work consists of over fifty books, four hundred nonfiction pieces, and two hundred short stories. Even more astonishing is the fact that London accomplished this literary output in less than twenty years. If it is true that writers do their best work when they draw from personal experience, then it is easy to understand London's ability to write so articulately on a variety of subjects. He was a crusader for social causes, a global traveler, a sailor, a hobo, and a self-made millionaire.

London was born in San Francisco to a single mother. It is believed that his father was William Henry Chaney, an astrologer, although Chaney disputed his paternity and left London's mother, Flora Wellman, before London was born. Wellman was Chaney's common-law wife and she named the child John Griffith Chaney. In the late summer of 1876, she married John London, a widower whose two daughters, Eliza and Ida, had been sent to live in an orphanage so that he could work as a carpenter. Thereafter, London's stepfather worked itinerantly as a door-to-door salesman, a contractor, and a shopkeeper, and the family moved often. The financially insecure young London found stability and solace in books, but as a poor child, also always had a variety of jobs: He delivered newspapers, swept floors, and was a pinsetter in a bowling alley, among other more dangerous occupations, such as oyster pirate.

In high school, London discovered the writings of Charles Darwin and Karl Marx and quickly became known as an activist and a socialist. He was accepted into the University of California at Berkeley only to have to leave after one semester for financial reasons. London began to work at various manual labor jobs, but he left in 1897 for the Klondike in the Yukon Territory with his brother-in-law, there to make their fortune in the gold rush. His best-known novel, The Call of the Wild *(1903), emerged from his encounters with wolves in the Far North. His 1907 book,* The Cruise of the Snark, *was inspired by his adventures in the South Pacific.*

One of London's most famous short stories is "To Build a Fire," which was undoubtedly based upon his experiences in the Klondike. Like many of his short stories, it shows the beauty and the wonder of nature, as well as the unforgiving and destructive power that lurks within that beauty.

To Build a Fire

Day had broken cold and gray, exceedingly cold and gray, when the man turned aside from the main Yukon trail and climbed the high earth-bank, where a dim and little-travelled trail led eastward through the fat spruce timberland. It was a steep bank, and he paused for breath at the top, excusing the act to himself by looking at his watch. It was nine o'clock. There was no sun nor hint of sun, though there was not a cloud in the sky. It was a clear day, and yet there seemed an intangible pall over the face of things, a subtle gloom that made the day dark, and that was due to the absence of sun. This fact did not worry the man. He was used to the lack of sun. It had been days since he had seen the sun, and he knew that a few more days must pass before that cheerful orb, due south, would just peep above the sky-line and dip immediately from view.

The man flung a look back along the way he had come. The Yukon lay a mile wide and hidden under three feet of ice. On top of this ice were as many feet of snow. It was all pure white, rolling in gentle undulations where the ice jams of the freeze-up had formed. North and south, as far as his eye could see, it was unbroken white, save for a dark hair-line that curved and twisted from around the spruce-covered island to the south, and that curved and twisted away into the north, where it disappeared behind another spruce-covered island. This dark hair-line was the trail—the main trail—that led south five hundred miles to the Chilcoot Pass, Dyea, and salt water; and that led north seventy miles to Dawson, and still on to the north a thousand miles to Nulato, and finally to St. Michael on Bering Sea, a thousand miles and half a thousand more.

But all this—the mysterious, far-reaching hair-line trail, the absence of sun from the sky, the tremendous cold, and the strangeness and weirdness of it all—made no impression on the man. It was not because he was long used to it. He was a newcomer in the land, a *chechaquo*, and this was his first winter. The trouble with him was that he was without imagination. He was quick and alert in the things of life, but only in the things, and not in the significances. Fifty degrees below zero meant eighty-odd degrees of frost. Such fact impressed him as being cold and uncomfortable, and that was all. It did not lead him to meditate upon his frailty as a creature of temperature, and upon man's frailty in general, able only to live within certain narrow limits of heat and cold; and from there on it did not lead him to the conjectural field of immortality and man's place in the universe. Fifty degrees below zero stood for a bite of frost that hurt and that must be guarded against by the use of mittens, ear-flaps, warm moccasins, and thick socks. Fifty degrees below zero was to him just precisely fifty degrees below zero. That there should be anything more to it than that was a thought that never entered his head.

As he turned to go on, he spat speculatively. There was a sharp, explosive crackle that startled him. He spat again. And again, in the air, before it could fall to the snow, the spittle crackled. He knew that at fifty below spittle crackled on the snow, but this spittle had crackled in the air. Undoubtedly it was colder than fifty below—how much colder he did not know. But the temperature did not matter. He was bound for the old claim on the left fork of Henderson Creek, where the boys were already. They had come over across the divide from the Indian Creek country, while he had come the roundabout way to take a look at the possibilities of getting out logs in the spring from the islands in the Yukon. He would be in to camp by six o'clock; a bit after dark, it was true, but the boys would be there, a fire would be going, and a hot supper would be ready. As for lunch, he pressed his hand against the protruding bundle under his jacket. It was also under his shirt, wrapped up in a handkerchief and lying against the naked skin. It was the only way to keep the biscuits from freezing. He smiled agreeably to himself as he thought of those biscuits, each cut open and sopped in bacon grease, and each enclosing a generous slice of fried bacon.

He plunged in among the big spruce trees. The trail was faint. A foot of snow had fallen since the last sled had passed over, and he was glad he was without a sled, travelling light. In fact he carried nothing but the lunch wrapped in the handkerchief. He was surprised, however, at the cold. It certainly was cold, he concluded, as he rubbed his numb nose and cheek-bones with his mittened hand. He was a warm-whiskered man, but the hair on his face did not protect the high cheek-bones and the eager nose that thrust itself aggressively into the frosty air.

At the man's heels trotted a dog, a big native husky, the proper wolf-dog, gray-coated and without any visible or temperamental difference from its brother, the wild wolf. The animal was depressed by the tremendous cold. It knew that it was no time for traveling. Its instinct told it a truer tale than was told to the man by the man's judgment. In reality, it was not merely colder than fifty below zero; it was colder than sixty below, than seventy below. It was seventy-five below zero. Since the freezing point is thirty-two above zero, it meant that one hundred and seven degrees of frost obtained. The dog did not know anything about thermometers. Possibly in its brain there was no sharp consciousness of a condition of very cold such as was in the man's brain. But the brute had its instinct. It experienced a vague but menacing apprehension that subdued it and made it slink along at the man's heels, and that made it question eagerly every unwonted movement of the man as if expecting him to go into camp or to seek shelter somewhere and build a fire. The dog had learned fire, and it wanted fire, or else to burrow under the snow and cuddle its warmth away from the air.

The frozen moisture of its breathing had settled on its fur in a fine powder of frost, and especially were its jowls, muzzle, and eyelashes whitened by its crystalled breath. The man's red beard and mustache were likewise frosted, but more solidly, the deposit taking the form of ice and increasing with every warm, moist breath he exhaled. Also, the man was chewing tobacco, and the muzzle of ice held his lips so rigidly that he was unable to clear his chin when he expelled the juice. The result was that a crystal beard of the color and solidity of amber was increasing its length on his chin. If he fell down it would shatter itself, like glass, into brittle fragments. But he did not mind the appendage. It was the penalty all tobacco-chewers paid in that country, and he had been out before in two cold snaps. They had not been so cold as this, he knew, but by the spirit thermometer at Sixty Mile he knew they had been registered at fifty below and at fifty-five.

He held on through the level stretch of woods for several miles, crossed a wide flat of nigger-heads,[1] and dropped down a bank to the frozen bed of a small stream. This was Henderson Creek, and he knew he was ten miles from the forks. He looked at his watch. It was ten o'clock. He was making four miles an hour, and he calculated that he would arrive at the forks at half-past twelve. He decided to celebrate that event by eating his lunch there.

The dog dropped in again at his heels, with a tail drooping discouragement, as the man swung along the creek bed. The furrow of the old sled trail was plainly visible, but a dozen inches of snow covered the marks of the last runners. In a month no man had come up or down that silent creek. The man held steadily on. He was not much given to thinking, and just then particularly he had nothing to think about save that he would eat lunch at the forks and that at six o'clock he would be in camp with the boys. There was nobody to talk to; and, had there been, speech would have been impossible because of the ice-muzzle on his mouth. So he continued monotonously to chew tobacco and to increase the length of his amber beard.

Once in a while the thought reiterated itself that it was very cold and that he had never experienced such cold. As he walked along he rubbed his cheek-bones and nose with the back of his mittened hand. He did this automatically, now and again changing hands. But rub as he would, the instant he stopped his cheek-bones went numb, and the following instant the end of his nose went numb. He was sure to frost his cheeks; he knew that, and experienced a pang of regret that he had not devised a nose-strap of the sort Bud wore in cold snaps. Such a strap passed across the cheeks, as well, and saved them. But it didn't matter much, after all. What were frosted cheeks? A bit painful, that was all; they were never serious.

Empty as the man's mind was of thoughts, he was keenly observant, and he noticed the changes in the creek, the curves and bends and timber-jams, and always he sharply noted where he placed his feet. Once, coming around a bend, he shied abruptly, like a startled horse, curved away from the place where he had been walking, and retreated several paces back along the trail. The creek he knew was frozen clear to the bottom,—no creek could contain water in that arctic winter,—but he knew also that there were springs that bubbled out from the hillsides and ran along under the snow and on top the ice of the creek. He knew that the coldest snaps never froze these springs, and he knew likewise their danger. They were traps. They hid pools of water under the snow that might be three inches deep, or three feet. Sometimes a skin of ice half an inch thick covered them, and in turn was covered by the snow. Sometimes there were alternate

---

[1] Round, flat boulders.

layers of water and ice-skin, so that when one broke through he kept on breaking through for a while, sometimes wetting himself to the waist.

That was why he had shied in such panic. He had felt the give under his feet and heard the crackle of a snow-hidden ice-skin. And to get his feet wet in such a temperature meant trouble and danger. At the very least it meant delay, for he would be forced to stop and build a fire, and under its protection to bare his feet while he dried his socks and moccasins. He stood and studied the creek bed and its banks, and decided that the flow of water came from the right. He reflected awhile, rubbing his nose and cheeks, then skirted to the left, stepping gingerly and testing the footing for each step. Once clear of the danger, he took a fresh chew of tobacco and swung along at his four-mile gait.

In the course of the next two hours he came upon several similar traps. Usually the snow above the hidden pools had a sunken, candied appearance that advertised the danger. Once, again, however, he had a close call; and once, suspecting danger, he compelled the dog to go on in front. The dog did not want to go. It hung back until the man shoved it forward, and then it went quickly across the white, unbroken surface. Suddenly it broke through, floundered to one side, and got away to firmer footing. It had wet its forefeet and legs, and almost immediately, the water that clung to it turned to ice. It made quick efforts to lick the ice off its legs, then dropped down in the snow and began to bite out the ice that had formed between the toes. This was a matter of instinct. To permit the ice to remain would mean sore feet. It did not know this. It merely obeyed the mysterious prompting that arose from the deep crypts of its being. But the man knew, having achieved a judgment on the subject, and he removed the mitten from his right hand and helped tear out the ice particles. He did not expose his fingers more than a minute, and was astonished at the swift numbness that smote them. It certainly was cold. He pulled on the mitten hastily, and beat the hand savagely across his chest.

At twelve o'clock the day was at its brightest. Yet the sun was too far south on its winter journey to clear the horizon. The bulge of the earth intervened between it and Henderson Creek, where the man walked under a clear sky at noon and cast no shadow. At half-past twelve, to the minute, he arrived at the forks of the creek. He was pleased at the speed he had made. If he kept it up, he would certainly be with the boys by six. He unbuttoned his jacket and shirt and drew forth his lunch. The action consumed no more than a quarter of a minute, yet in that brief moment the numbness laid hold of the exposed fingers. He did not put the mitten on, but, instead, struck the fingers a dozen sharp smashes against his leg. Then he sat down on a snow-covered log to eat. The sting that followed upon the striking of his fingers against his leg ceased so quickly that he was startled. He had no chance to take a bite of biscuit. He struck the fingers repeatedly and returned them to the mitten, baring the other hand for the purpose of eating. He tried to take a mouthful, but the ice-muzzle prevented. He had forgotten to build a fire and thaw out. He chuckled at his foolishness, and as he chuckled he noted the numbness creeping into the exposed fingers. Also, he noted that the stinging which had first come to his toes when he sat down was already passing away. He wondered whether the toes were warm or numb. He moved them inside the moccasins and decided that they were numb.

He pulled the mitten on hurriedly and stood up. He was a bit frightened. He stamped up and down until the stinging returned into the feet. It certainly was cold, was his thought. That man from Sulphur Creek had spoken the truth when telling how cold it sometimes got in the country. And he had laughed at him at the time! That showed one must not be too sure of things. There was no mistake about it, it *was* cold. He strode up and down, stamping his feet and threshing his arms, until reassured by the returning warmth. Then he got out matches and proceeded to make a fire. From the undergrowth where high water of the previous spring had lodged a supply of seasoned twigs, he got his fire-wood. Working carefully from a small beginning, he soon had a roaring fire, over which he thawed the ice from his face and in the protection of which he ate his biscuits. For the moment the cold of space was outwitted. The dog took satisfaction in the fire stretching out close enough for warmth and far enough away to escape being singed.

When the man had finished, he filled his pipe and took his comfortable time over a smoke. Then he pulled on his mittens, settled the ear-flaps of his cap firmly about his ears, and took the creek trail up the left fork. The dog was disappointed and yearned back toward the fire. This man did not know cold. Possibly all the generations of his ancestry had been ignorant of cold, of real cold, of cold one hundred and seven degrees below freezing point. But the dog knew; all its ancestry knew, and it had inherited the knowledge. And it knew that it was not good to walk abroad in such fearful cold. It was the time to lie snug in a hole in the snow and wait for a curtain of cloud to be drawn across the face of outer space whence this cold came. On the other hand, there was no keen intimacy between the dog and the man. The one was the toil-slave of the other, and the only caresses it had ever received were the caresses of the whip-lash and of harsh and menacing throat sounds that threatened the whip-lash. So the dog made no effort to communicate its apprehension to the man. It was not concerned in the welfare of the man; it was for its own sake that it yearned back toward the fire. But the man whistled, and spoke to it with the sound of whip-lashes, and the dog swung in at the man's heels and followed after.

The man took a chew of tobacco and proceeded to start a new amber beard. Also, his moist breath quickly powdered with white his mustache, eyebrows, and lashes. There did not seem to be so many springs on the left fork of the Henderson, and for half an hour the man saw no signs of any. And then it happened. At a place where there were no signs, where the soft, unbroken snow seemed to advertise solidity beneath, the man broke through. It was not deep. He wet himself halfway to the knees before he floundered out to the firm crust.

He was angry, and cursed his luck aloud. He had hoped to get into camp with the boys at six o'clock, and this would delay him an hour, for he would have to build a fire and dry out his foot-gear. This was imperative at that low temperature—he knew that much; and he turned aside to the bank, which he climbed. On top, tangled in the underbrush about the trunks of several small spruce trees, was a high-water deposit of dry fire-wood—sticks and twigs, principally, but also larger portions of seasoned branches and fine, dry, last year's grasses. He threw down several large pieces on top of the snow. This served for a foundation and prevented the young flame from drowning itself in the snow it otherwise would melt. The flame he got by touching a match to a small shred of birch-bark that he took from his pocket. This burned even more readily than paper. Placing it on the foundation, he fed the young flame with wisps of dry grass and with the tiniest dry twigs.

He worked slowly and carefully, keenly aware of his danger. Gradually, as the flame grew stronger, he increased the size of the twigs with which he fed it. He squatted in the snow, pulling the twigs out from their entanglement in the brush and feeding directly to the flame. He knew there must be no failure. When it is seventy-five below zero, a man must not fail in his first attempt to build a fire—that is, if his feet are wet. If his feet are dry, and he fails, he can run along the trail for half a mile and restore his circulation. But the circulation of wet and freezing feet cannot be restored by running when it is seventy-five below. No matter how fast he runs, the wet feet will freeze the harder.

All this the man knew. The old-timer on Sulphur Creek had told him about it the previous fall, and now he was appreciating the advice. Already all sensation had gone out of his feet. To build the fire he had been forced to remove his mittens, and the fingers had quickly gone numb. His pace of four miles an hour had kept his heart pumping blood to the surface of his body and to all the extremities. But the instant he stopped, the action of the pump eased down. The cold of space smote the unprotected tip of the planet, and he, being on that unprotected tip, received the full force of the blow. The blood of his body recoiled before it. The blood was alive, like the dog, and like the dog it wanted to hide away and cover itself up from the fearful cold. So long as he walked four miles an hour, he pumped that blood, willy-nilly, to the surface; but now it ebbed away and sank down into the recesses of his body. The extremities were the first to feel its absence. His wet feet froze the faster, and his exposed fingers numbed the faster, though they had not yet begun to freeze. Nose and cheeks were already freezing, while the skin of all his body chilled as it lost its blood.

But he was safe. Toes and nose and cheeks would be only touched by the frost, for the fire was beginning to burn with strength. He was feeding it with twigs the size of his finger. In another minute he would be able to feed it with branches the size of his wrist, and then he could remove his wet foot-gear and, while it dried, he could keep his naked feet warm by the fire, rubbing them at first, of course, with snow. The fire was a success. He was safe. He remembered the advice of the old-timer on Sulphur Creek, and smiled. The old-timer had been very serious in laying down the law that no man must travel alone in the Klondike after fifty below. Well, here he was; he had had the accident; he was alone; and he had saved himself. Those old-timers were rather womanish, some of them, he thought. All a man had to do was to keep his head, and he was all right. Any man who was a man could travel alone. But it was surprising, the rapidity with which his cheeks and nose were freezing. And he had not thought his fingers could go lifeless in so short a time. Lifeless they were, for he could scarcely make them move together to grip a twig, and they seemed remote from his body and from him. When he touched a twig, he had to look and see whether or not he had hold of it. The wires were pretty well down between him and his finger-ends.

All of which counted for little. There was the fire, snapping and crackling and promising life with every dancing flame. He started to untie his moccasins. They were coated with ice; the thick German socks were like sheaths of iron halfway to the knees; and the moccasin strings were like rods of steel all twisted and knotted as by some conflagration. For a moment he tugged with his numb fingers, then, realizing the folly of it, he drew his sheath-knife.

But before he could cut the strings, it happened. It was his own fault or, rather, his mistake. He should not have built the fire under the spruce tree. He should have built it in the open. But it had been easier to pull the twigs from the brush and drop them directly on the fire. Now the tree under which he had done this carried a weight of snow on its boughs. No wind had blown for weeks, and each bough was fully freighted. Each time he had pulled a twig he had communicated a slight agitation to the tree—an imperceptible agitation, so far as he was concerned, but an agitation sufficient to bring about the disaster. High up in the tree one bough capsized its load of snow. This fell on the boughs beneath, capsizing them. This process continued spreading out and involving the whole tree. It grew like an avalanche, and it descended without warning upon the man and the fire, and the fire was blotted out! Where it had burned was a mantle of fresh and disordered snow.

The man was shocked. It was as though he had just heard his own sentence of death. For a moment he sat and stared at the spot where the fire had been. Then he grew very calm. Perhaps the old-timer on Sulphur Creek was right. If he had only a trail-mate he would have been in no danger now. The trail-mate could have built the fire. Well, it was up to him to build the fire over again, and this second time there must be no failure. Even if he succeeded, he would most likely lose some toes. His feet must be badly frozen by now, and there would be some time before the second fire was ready.

Such were his thoughts, but he did not sit and think them. He was busy all the time they were passing through his mind. He made a new foundation for a fire, this time in the open, where no treacherous tree could blot it out. Next, he gathered dry grasses and tiny twigs from the high-water flotsam. He could not bring his fingers together to pull them out, but he was able to gather them by the handful. In this way he got many rotten twigs and bits of green moss that were undesirable, but it was the best he could do. He worked methodically, even collecting an armful of the larger branches to be used later when the fire gathered strength. And all the while the dog sat and watched him, a certain yearning wistfulness in its eyes, for it looked upon him as the fire-provider, and the fire was slow in coming.

When all was ready, the man reached in his pocket for a second piece of birch-bark. He knew the bark was there, and, though he could not feel it with his fingers, he could hear its crisp rustling as he fumbled for it. Try as he would, he could not clutch hold of it. And all the time, in his consciousness, was the knowledge that each instant his feet were freezing. This thought tended to put him in a panic, but he fought against it and kept calm. He pulled on his mittens with his teeth, and threshed his arms back and forth, beating his hands with all his might against his sides. He did this sitting down, and he stood up to do it; and all the while the dog sat in the snow, its wolf-brush of a tail curled around warmly over its forefeet, its sharp wolf-ears pricked forward intently as it watched the man. And the man, as he beat and threshed with his arms and hands felt a great surge of envy as he regarded the creature that was warm and secure in its natural covering.

After a time he was aware of the first far-away signals of sensation in his beaten fingers. The faint tingling grew stronger till it evolved into a stinging ache that was excruciating, but which the man hailed with satisfaction. He stripped the mitten from his right hand and fetched forth the birch-bark. The exposed fingers were quickly going numb again. Next he brought out his bunch of sulphur matches. But the tremendous cold had already driven the life out of his fingers. In his effort to separate one match from the others, the whole bunch fell in the snow. He tried to pick it out of the snow, but failed. The dead fingers could neither touch nor clutch. He was very careful. He drove the thought of his freezing feet, and nose, and cheeks out of his mind, devoting his whole soul to the matches. He watched, using the sense of vision in place of that of touch, and when he saw his fingers on each side the bunch, he closed them—that is, he willed to close them, for the wires were down, and the fingers did not obey. He pulled the mitten on the right hand, and beat it fiercely against his knee. Then, with both mittened hands, he scooped the bunch of matches, along with much snow, into his lap. Yet he was no better off.

After some manipulation he managed to get the bunch between the heels of his mittened hands. In this fashion he carried it to his mouth. The ice crackled and snapped when by a violent effort he opened his mouth. He drew the lower jaw in, curled the upper lip out of the way, and scraped the bunch with his upper teeth in order to separate a match. He succeeded in getting one, which he dropped on his lap. He was no better off. He could not pick it up. Then he devised a way. He picked it up in his teeth and scratched it on his leg. Twenty times he scratched before he succeeded in lighting it. As it flamed he held it with his teeth to the birch-bark. But the burning brimstone went up his nostrils and into his lungs, causing him to cough spasmodically. The match fell into the snow and went out.

The old-timer on Sulphur Creek was right, he thought in the moment of controlled despair that ensued: after fifty below, a man should travel with a partner. He beat his hands, but failed in exciting any sensation. Suddenly he bared both hands, removing the mittens with his teeth. He caught the whole bunch between the heels of his hands. His arm muscles not being frozen enabled him to press the hand-heels tightly against the matches. Then he scratched the bunch along his leg. It flared into flame, seventy sulphur matches at once! There was no wind to blow them out. He kept his head to one side to escape the strangling fumes, and held the blazing bunch to the birch-bark. As he so held it, he became aware of sensation in his hand. His flesh was burning. He could smell it. Deep down below the surface he could feel it. The sensation developed into pain that grew acute. And still he endured it, holding the flame of the matches clumsily to the bark that would not light readily because his own burning hands were in the way, absorbing most of the flame.

At last, when he could endure no more, he jerked his hands apart. The blazing matches fell sizzling into the snow, but the birch-bark was alight. He began laying dry grasses and the tiniest twigs on the flame. He could not pick and choose, for he had to lift the fuel between the heels of his hands. Small pieces of rotten wood and green moss clung to the twigs, and he bit them off as well as he could with his teeth. He cherished the flame carefully and awkwardly. It meant life, and it must not perish. The withdrawal of blood from the surface of his body now made him begin to shiver, and he grew more awkward. A large piece of green moss fell squarely on the little fire. He tried to poke it out with his fingers, but his shivering frame made him poke too far, and he disrupted the nucleus of the little fire, the burning grasses and tiny twigs separating and scattering. He tried to poke them together again, but in spite of the tenseness of the effort, his shivering got away with him, and the twigs were hopelessly scattered. Each twig gushed a puff of smoke and went out. The fire-provider had failed. As he looked apathetically about him, his eyes chanced on the dog, sitting across the ruins of the fire from him, in the snow, making restless, hunching movements, slightly lifting one forefoot and then the other, shifting its weight back and forth on them with wistful eagerness.

The sight of the dog put a wild idea into his head. He remembered the tale of the man, caught in a blizzard, who killed a steer and crawled inside the carcass, and so was saved. He would kill the dog and bury his hands in the warm body until the numbness went out of them. Then he could build another fire. He spoke to the dog, calling it to him; but in his voice was a strange note of fear that frightened the animal, who had never known the man to speak in such way before. Something was the matter, and its suspicious nature sensed danger—it knew not what danger, but somewhere, somehow, in its brain arose an apprehension of the man. It flattened its ears down at the sound of the man's voice, and its restless, hunching movements and the liftings and shiftings of its forefeet became more pronounced; but it would not come to the man. He got on his hands and knees and crawled toward the dog. This unusual posture again excited suspicion, and the animal sidled mincingly away.

The man sat up in the snow for a moment and struggled for calmness. Then he pulled on his mittens, by means of his teeth, and got upon his feet. He glanced down at first in order to assure himself that he was really standing up, for the absence of sensation in his feet left him unrelated to the earth. His erect position in itself started to drive the webs of suspicion from the dog's mind; and when he spoke peremptorily, with the sound of whip-lashes in his voice, the dog rendered its customary allegiance and came to him. As it came within reaching distance, the man lost his control. His arms flashed out to the dog, and he experienced genuine surprise when he discovered that his hands could not clutch, that there was neither bend nor feeling in the fingers. He had forgotten for the moment that they were frozen and that they were freezing more and more. All this happened quickly, and before the animal could get away, he encircled its body with his arms. He sat down in the snow, and in this fashion held the dog, while it snarled and whined and struggled.

But it was all he could do, hold its body encircled in his arms and sit there. He realized that he could not kill the dog. There was no way to do it. With his helpless hands he could neither draw nor hold his sheath-knife nor throttle the animal. He released it, and it plunged wildly away, with tail between its legs, and still snarling. It halted forty feet away and surveyed him curiously, with ears sharply pricked forward. The man looked down at his hands in order to locate them, and found them hanging on the ends of his arms. It struck him as curious that one should have to use his eyes in order to find out where his hands were. He began threshing his arms back and forth, beating the mittened hands against his sides. He did this for five minutes, violently, and his heart pumped enough blood up to the surface to put a stop to his shivering. But no sensation was aroused in the hands. He had an impression that they hung like weights on the ends of his arms, but when he tried to run the impression down, he could not find it.

A certain fear of death, dull and oppressive, came to him. This fear quickly became poignant as he realized that it was no longer a mere matter of freezing his fingers and toes, or of losing his hands and feet, but that it was a matter of life and death with the chances against him. This threw him into a panic, and he turned and ran up the creek bed along the old, dim trail. The dog joined in behind and kept up with him. He ran blindly, without intention, in fear such as he had never known in his life. Slowly, as he ploughed and floundered through the snow, he began to see things again,—the banks of the creek, the old timberjams, the leafless aspens, and the sky. The running made him feel better. He did not shiver. Maybe, if he ran on, his feet would thaw out; and, anyway, if he ran far enough, he would reach camp and the boys. Without doubt he would lose some fingers and toes and some of his face; but the boys would take care of him, and save the rest of him when he got there. And at the same time there was another thought in his mind that said he would never get to the camp and the boys; that it was too many miles away, that the freezing had too great a start on him, and that he would soon be stiff and dead. This thought he kept in the background and refused to consider. Sometimes it pushed itself forward and demanded to be heard, but he thrust it back and strove to think of other things.

It struck him as curious that he could run at all on feet so frozen that he could not feel them when they struck the earth and took the weight of his body. He seemed to himself to skim along above the surface, and to have no connection with the earth. Somewhere he had once seen a winged Mercury, and he wondered if Mercury felt as he felt when skimming over the earth.

His theory of running until he reached camp and the boys had one flaw in it: he lacked the endurance. Several times he stumbled, and finally he tottered, crumpled up, and fell. When he tried to rise, he failed. He must sit and rest, he decided, and next time he would merely walk and keep on going. As he sat and regained his breath, he noted that he was feeling quite warm and comfortable. He was not shivering, and it even seemed that a warm glow had come to his chest and trunk. And yet, when he touched his nose or cheeks, there was no sensation. Running would not thaw them out. Nor would it thaw out his hands and feet. Then the thought came to him that the frozen portions of his body must be extending. He tried to keep this thought down, to forget it, to think of something else; he was aware of the panicky feeling that it caused, and he was afraid of the panic. But the thought asserted itself, and persisted, until it produced a vision of his body totally frozen. This was too much, and he made another wild run along the trail. Once he slowed down to a walk, but the thought of the freezing extending itself made him run again.

And all the time the dog ran with him, at his heels. When he fell down a second time, it curled its tail over its forefeet and sat in front of him, facing him, curiously eager and intent. The warmth and security of the animal angered him, and he cursed it till it flattened down its ears appeasingly. This time the shivering came more quickly upon the man. He was losing in his battle with the frost. It was creeping into his body from all sides. The thought of it drove him on, but he ran no more than a hundred feet, when he staggered and pitched headlong. It was his last panic. When he had recovered his breath and control, he sat up and entertained in his mind the conception of meeting death with dignity. However, the conception did not come to him in such terms. His idea of it was that he had been making a fool of himself, running around like a chicken with its head cut off—such was the simile that occurred to him. Well, he was bound to freeze anyway, and he might as well take it decently. With this new-found peace of mind came the first glimmerings of drowsiness. A good idea, he thought, to sleep off to death. It was like taking an anaesthetic. Freezing was not so bad as people thought. There were lots worse ways to die.

He pictured the boys finding his body next day. Suddenly he found himself with them, coming along the trail and looking for himself. And, still with them, he came around a turn in the trail and found himself lying in the snow. He did not belong with himself any more, for even then he was out of himself, standing with the boys and looking at himself in the snow. It certainly was cold, was his thought. When he got back to the States he could tell the folks what real cold was. He drifted on from this to a vision of the old-timer on Sulphur Creek. He could see him quite clearly, warm and comfortable, and smoking a pipe.

"You were right, old hoss; you were right," the man mumbled to the old-timer of Sulphur Creek.

Then the man drowsed off into what seemed to him the most comfortable and satisfying sleep he had ever known. The dog sat facing him and waiting. The brief day drew to a close in a long, slow twilight. There were no signs of a fire to be made, and, besides, never in the dog's experience had it known a man to sit like that in the snow and make no fire. As the twilight drew on, its eager yearning for the fire mastered it, and with a great lifting and shifting of forefeet, it whined softly, then flattened its ears down in anticipation of being chidden by the man. But the man remained silent. Later, the dog whined loudly. And still later it crept close to the man and caught the scent of death. This made the animal bristle and back away. A little longer it delayed, howling under the stars that leaped and danced and shone brightly in the cold sky. Then it turned and trotted up the trail in the direction of the camp it knew, where were the other food-providers and fire-providers.

✍ *Wallace Stevens* (1879-1955)

Born in Reading, Pennsylvania, Wallace Stevens was educated at Harvard University and New York Law School. From 1916 onward, he was employed by the Hartford Accident and Indemnity Company; in 1934 he was appointed its vice president. His first book of poetry, Harmonium, *appeared in 1923. Subsequent volumes included* Ideas of Order *(1936),* The Man with a Blue Guitar *(1937),* Parts of a World *(1942),* Transport to Summer *(1947), and* Auroras of Autumn *(1950). Playful and elegant, sonorous and philosophical, his poetry reveals a fascination with abstract ideas at the same time that it presents bold, colorful images drawn from his personal experience of the natural world.*

As a counterpoint to the snowy winter fields of Connecticut, presented in "The Snow Man," Stevens often employs the lush tropical landscape of Florida, which he regularly visited on business, as a touchstone for his poetic imagery. In poems such as "The Green Plant" (from the later Collected Poems*), for instance, the "legend of the maroon and olive forest," suggesting a garish tropical luxuriance of vegetation, is contrasted with the bleak, barren trees of autumn in New England. "Anecdote of the Jar" presents a somewhat analogous contrast between the "slovenly wilderness" of Tennessee, brimming with disorderly vegetation, and the rounded aesthetic wholeness of the jar. Deeper intimations about the complementarity of civilization and wilderness are shadowed forth in these resonant images, but never quite made fully explicit. Stevens's best poetry works through such elliptical patterns of imagery, keyed to specific geographical places that serve as emblems for intangible states of mind. "The Poems of Our Climate" (from* Parts of a World*) further elaborates this meditation on the relation of poetry to place, perhaps suggesting an underlying dissatisfaction with the quiet conformity that was expected of Stevens in his all-too-predictable life as an insurance executive. Harking back to a classic theme of American nature writing since Thoreau, Stevens extols the wildness that he found in the disorderly tangle of tropical jungles: "The imperfect is our paradise." Stevens's great accomplishment as a nature poet is his investment of that wildness in the form of language itself, "in flawed words and stubborn sounds."*

The Snow Man

One must have a mind of winter
To regard the frost and the boughs
Of the pine trees crusted with snow;

And have been cold a long time
To behold the junipers shagged with ice,   5
The spruces rough in the distant glitter

Of the January sun; and not to think
Of any misery in the sound of the wind,
In the sound of a few leaves,

Which is the sound of the land   10
Full of the same wind
That is blowing in the same bare place

For the listener, who listens in the snow,
And, nothing himself, beholds
Nothing that is not there and the nothing that is.   15

Anecdote of the Jar

I placed a jar in Tennessee,
And round it was, upon a hill.
It made the slovenly wilderness
Surround that hill.

The wilderness rose up to it,   5
And sprawled around, no longer wild.
The jar was round upon the ground
And tall and of a port in air.

It took dominion everywhere.
The jar was gray and bare.   10
It did not give of bird or bush,
Like nothing else in Tennessee.

Thirteen Ways of Looking at a Blackbird

I

Among twenty snowy mountains,
The only moving thing
Was the eye of the blackbird.

2

I was of three minds,
Like a tree   5
In which there are three blackbirds.

3

The blackbird whirled in the autumn winds.
It was a small part of the pantomime.

4

A man and a woman
Are one.   10
A man and a woman and a blackbird
Are one.

5

I do not know which to prefer,
The beauty of inflections
Or the beauty of innuendoes,   15
The blackbird whistling
Or just after.

6

Icicles filled the long window
With barbaric glass.
The shadow of the blackbird   20
Crossed it, to and fro.
The mood
Traced in the shadow
An indecipherable cause.

7

O thin men of Haddam,[1]
Why do you imagine golden birds?   25
Do you not see how the blackbird
Walks around the feet
Of the women about you?

8

I know noble accents
And lucid, inescapable rhythms;   30
But I know, too,
That the blackbird is involved
In what I know.

9

When the blackbird flew out of sight,   35
It marked the edge
Of one of many circles.

[1]A town in Connecticut, settled in 1662.

10

At the sight of blackbirds
Flying in a green light,
Even the bawds of euphony   40
Would cry out sharply.

11

He rode over Connecticut
In a glass coach.
Once, a fear pierced him,
In that he mistook   45
The shadow of his equipage
For blackbirds.

12

The river is moving.
The blackbird must be flying.

13

It was evening all afternoon.   50
It was snowing
And it was going to snow.
The blackbird sat
In the cedar-limbs.

The Plain Sense of Things

After the leaves have fallen, we return
To a plain sense of things. It is as if
We had come to an end of the imagination,
Inanimate in an inert savoir.[1]

It is difficult even to choose the adjective   5
For this blank cold, this sadness without cause.
The great structure has become a minor house.
No turban walks across the lessened floors.

The greenhouse never so badly needed paint.
The chimney is fifty years old and slants to one side.   10
A fantastic effort has failed, a repetition
In a repetitiousness of men and flies.

---

[1]The French verb meaning "to know," referring specifically to intellectual knowledge.

Yet the absence of the imagination had
Itself to be imagined. The great pond,
The plain sense of it, without reflections, leaves, 15
Mud, water like dirty glass, expressing silence

Of a sort, silence of a rat come out to see,
The great pond and its waste of the lilies, all this
Had to be imagined as an inevitable knowledge,
Required, as a necessity requires. 20

The Planet on the Table

Ariel was glad he had written his poems.
They were of a remembered time
Or of something seen that he liked.

Other makings of the sun
Were waste and welter 5
And the ripe shrub writhed.

His self and the sun were one
And his poems, although makings of his self,
Were no less makings of the sun.

It was not important that they survive. 10
What mattered was that they should bear
Some lineament or character,

Some affluence, if only half-perceived,
In the poverty of their words,
Of the planet of which they were part. 15

The River of Rivers in Connecticut

There is a great river this side of Stygia,[1]
Before one comes to the first black cataracts
And trees that lack the intelligence of trees.

In that river, far this side of Stygia,
The mere flowing of the water is a gayety, 5
Flashing and flashing in the sun. On its banks,

---

[1] An allusion to the river Styx; in ancient Greek mythology, it is one of the five rivers over which dead souls were ferried.

No shadow walks. The river is fateful,
Like the last one. But there is no ferryman.
He could not bend against its propelling force.

It is not to be seen beneath the appearances   10
That tell of it. The steeple at Farmington
Stands glistening and Haddam shines and sways.

It is the third commonness with light and air,
A curriculum, a vigor, a local abstraction . . .
Call it, once more, a river, an unnamed flowing,   15

Space-filled, reflecting the seasons, the folklore
Of each of the senses; call it, again and again,
The river that flows nowhere, like a sea.

☙ *Virginia Woolf* (1882–1941)

*As a an intellectual woman and a feminist writing during the early years of the twenti-
eth century, Virginia Woolf faced many challenges. Her education was superior to many
other young women of her class, as her father, Leslie Stephen, was an important writer
and editor and was able to introduce her to some of the leading minds of the late Victorian age. Nonetheless, as she recounts in her famous essay on the difficulties of being a
woman writer,* A Room of One's Own *(1929), she was still denied access to the
higher education available to her brothers. It was only after her father's death in 1904
that she felt liberated enough to begin her own literary career in earnest. With her
brothers and her sister, Vanessa, she turned the family's home in London into a center
for a group of intellectuals and artists known as the Bloomsbury Group, in reference to
the Square on which the house was located. In 1912, she married another group member, Leonard Woolf, and in 1915 she published her first novel,* The Voyage Out. *In
addition to pursuing her literary work, Woolf was active in the feminist movement, a
concern that is evident in the emphasis on women's lives and women's perspectives that
is a part of her creative as well as her critical writing. Her second novel,* Night and
Day, *appeared in 1919; however, it was in the 1920s that Woolf began to develop and
refine the fluid style and the technique of multiple narrative perspectives that distinguish her work. Although it might loosely be described as "stream of consciousness," such
an epithet scarcely captures the complexity and versatility of Woolf's literary innovations. The growth of her style can be traced from novel to novel, beginning with* Jacob's
Room *(1922) to* Mrs. Dalloway *(1925) to* To the Lighthouse *(1927) and, finally,
to its apogee in* The Waves *(1931). Woolf also wrote important essays.* A Room of
One's Own, *which challenged the male-dominated literary canon, remains one of the
essential texts of feminist history.* Three Guineas *(1938) sustains Woolf's commitment
to women's rights. Because she herself was always an outsider, Woolf writes sympath-*

etically and intensely of alterity in all its manifestations, as can be seen in "The Death of the Moth" (1942). Troubled all her life by depression and mental illness, Woolf drowned herself in 1941.

The Death of the Moth

Moths that fly by day are not properly to be called moths; they do not excite that pleasant sense of dark autumn nights and ivy-blossom which the commonest yellow-underwing asleep in the shadow of the curtain never fails to rouse in us. They are hybrid creatures, neither gay like butterflies nor sombre like their own species. Nevertheless the present specimen, with his narrow hay-coloured wings, fringed with a tassel of the same colour, seemed to be content with life. It was a pleasant morning, mid-September, mild, benignant, yet with a keener breath than that of the summer months. The plough was already scoring the field opposite the window, and where the share had been, the earth was pressed flat and gleamed with moisture. Such vigour came rolling in from the fields and the down beyond that it was difficult to keep the eyes strictly turned upon the book. The rooks too were keeping one of their annual festivities; soaring round the tree tops until it looked as if a vast net with thousands of black knots in it had been cast up into the air; which, after a few moments sank slowly down upon the trees until every twig seemed to have a knot at the end of it. Then, suddenly, the net would be thrown into the air again in a wider circle this time, with the utmost clamour and vociferation, as though to be thrown into the air and settle slowly down upon the tree tops were a tremendously exciting experience.

The same energy which inspired the rooks, the ploughmen, the horses, and even, it seemed, the lean bare-backed downs, sent the moth fluttering from side to side of his square of the window-pane. One could not help watching him. One was, indeed, conscious of a queer feeling of pity for him. The possibilities of pleasure seemed that morning so enormous and so various that to have only a moth's part in life, and a day moth's at that, appeared a hard fate, and his zest in enjoying his meagre opportunities to the full, pathetic. He flew vigorously to one corner of his compartment, and, after waiting there a second, flew across to the other. What remained for him but to fly to a third corner and then to a fourth? That was all he could do, in spite of the size of the downs, the width of the sky, the far-off smoke of houses, and the romantic voice, now and then, of a steamer out at sea. What he could do he did. Watching him, it seemed as if a fibre, very thin but pure, of the enormous energy of the world had been thrust into his frail and diminutive body. As often as he crossed the pane, I could fancy that a thread of vital light became visible. He was little or nothing but life.

Yet, because he was so small, and so simple a form of the energy that was rolling in at the open window and driving its way through so many narrow and intricate corridors in my own brain and in those of other human beings, there was something marvellous as well as pathetic about him. It was as if someone had taken a tiny bead of pure life and decking it as lightly as possible with down and feathers, had set it dancing and zigzagging to show us the true nature of life. Thus displayed one could not get over the strangeness of it. One is apt to forget all about life, seeing it humped and bossed and garnished and cumbered so that it has to move with the greatest circumspection and dignity. Again, the thought of all that life might have been had he been born in any other shape caused one to view his simple activities with a kind of pity.

After a time, tired by his dancing apparently, he settled on the window ledge in the sun, and, the queer spectacle being at an end, I forgot about him. Then, looking up, my eye was caught by him. He was trying to resume his dancing, but seemed either so stiff or so awkward that he could only flutter to the bottom of the window-pane; and when he tried to fly across it he failed. Being intent on other matters I watched these futile attempts for a time without thinking, unconsciously waiting for him to resume his flight, as one waits for a machine, that has stopped momentarily, to start again without considering the reason of its failure. After perhaps a seventh attempt he slipped from the wooden ledge and fell, fluttering his wings, on to his back on the window sill. The helplessness of his attitude roused me. It flashed upon me that he was in difficulties; he could no longer raise himself; his legs struggled vainly. But, as I stretched out a pencil, meaning to help him to right himself, it came over me that the failure and awkwardness were the approach of death. I laid the pencil down again.

The legs agitated themselves once more. I looked as if for the enemy against which he struggled. I looked out of doors. What had happened there? Presumably it was mid-day, and work in the fields had stopped. Stillness and quiet had replaced the previous animation. The birds had taken themselves off to feed in the brooks. The horses stood still. Yet the power was there all the same, massed outside indifferent, impersonal, not attending to anything in particular. Somehow it was opposed to the little hay-coloured moth. It was useless to try to do anything. One could only watch the extraordinary efforts made by those tiny legs against an oncoming doom which could, had it chosen, have submerged an entire city, not merely a city, but masses of human beings; nothing, I knew had any chance against death. Nevertheless after a pause of exhaustion the legs fluttered again. It was superb this last protest, and so frantic that he succeeded at last in righting himself. One's sympathies, of course, were all on the side of life. Also, when there was nobody to care or to know, this gigantic effort on the part of an insignificant little moth, against a power of such magnitude, to retain what no one else valued or desired to keep, moved one strangely. Again, somehow, one saw life, a pure bead. I lifted the pencil again, useless though I knew it to be. But even as I did so, the unmistakable tokens of death showed themselves. The body relaxed, and instantly grew stiff. The struggle was over. The insignificant little creature now knew death. As I looked at the dead moth, this minute wayside triumph of so great a force over so mean an antagonist filled me with wonder. Just as life had been strange a few minutes before, so death was now as strange. The moth having righted himself now lay most decently and uncomplainingly composed. O yes, he seemed to say, death is stronger than I am.

✍ *D. H. Lawrence* (1885–1930)

The son of a Nottingham coal miner, David Herbert Lawrence grew up with a confused sense of identity and a deeply divided loyalty to both the coarse, loutish, and sometimes drunken behavior of his father and the more delicate, refined sensibility of his mother. She had high educational aspirations for her son; she encouraged Lawrence to attend high school, then to obtain a teacher's certificate from Nottingham University College. From 1908 to 1912, he taught school in the southern suburbs of London, but he quit this job after falling scandalously in love with Frieda von Richthofen, the wife of a professor of French at Nottingham. They eloped to Germany and were married in 1914, after Frieda had obtained a divorce from her first husband. They returned to England at the start of World War I, but Frieda's German origins, and Lawrence's radical pacifism, got them in trouble with the authorities. When his experimental novel The Rainbow *was banned for indecency, Lawrence came to feel that the whole repressive civilization of Western Europe was bearing down upon them.*

Increasingly dissatisfied with the genteel culture that he had acquired from his mother, Lawrence attempted in his fiction to show how men and women can connect with deep natural and instinctive forces that will bring them happiness. He sought to uncover and express these instinctive forces by writing of transgressive and passionate episodes in the lives of ordinary people, in which they are transformed through contact with the "blood self," a tangle of primitive urges that lurks just below the surface of consciousness in even the most normal, well-adjusted person. He drew upon Freudian and Jungian psychoanalysis, theosophy, history, and archaeology in composing his novels and poetry, all transmuted by his unusual personality into a unique literary synthesis. Lawrence's novels include Sons and Lovers *(1913),* The Rainbow *(1915),* Women in Love *(1920),* The Plumed Serpent *(1926), and* Lady Chatterley's Lover *(1928). He wrote lyric poems that address several of the same themes as his novels, while also exploring the natural world from a deliberately nonhuman point of view. These poems seek to discover what it feels like, from the inside, to be a slithering snake, or a great whale. An eclectic artist in many different genres, Lawrence also wrote short stories, a play, and numerous essays, and he exhibited his paintings in London in 1929. From an early age, Lawrence had a sickly constitution, and he spent much of his life seeking healthful climates, especially in Italy, New Mexico, and Mexico. He died of tuberculosis in southern France at the age of forty-five.*

Moonrise

And who has seen the moon, who has not seen
Her rise from out the chamber of the deep,
Flushed and grand and naked, as from the chamber
Of finished bridegroom, seen her rise and throw
Confession of delight upon the wave,   5
Littering the waves with her own superscription

Of bliss, till all her lambent beauty shakes toward us
Spread out and known at last, and we are sure
That beauty is a thing beyond the grave,
That perfect, bright experience never falls   10
To nothingness, and time will dim the moon
Sooner than our full consummation here
In this odd life will tarnish or pass away.

Green

The dawn was apple-green,
    The sky was green wine held up in the sun,
The moon was a golden petal between.
She opened her eyes, and green
    They shone, clear like flowers undone   5
For the first time, now for the first time seen.

Snake

A snake came to my water-trough
On a hot, hot day, and I in pyjamas for the heat,
To drink there.

In the deep, strange-scented shade of the great dark carob tree
I came down the steps with my pitcher   5
And must wait, must stand and wait, for there he was at the trough
    before me.

He reached down from a fissure in the earth-wall in the gloom
And trailed his yellow-brown slackness soft-bellied down, over the edge
    of the stone trough
And rested his throat upon the stone bottom,
And where the water had dripped from the tap, in a small clearness,   10
He sipped with his straight mouth,
Softly drank through his straight gums, into his slack long body,
Silently.

Someone was before me at my water-trough,
And I, like a second comer, waiting.   15

He lifted his head from his drinking, like cattle do,
And looked at me vaguely, as drinking cattle do,
And flickered his two-forked tongue from his lips, and mused a moment,
And stooped and drank a little more,

Being earth-brown, earth-golden from the burning bowels of the earth   20
On the day of Sicilian July, with Etna smoking.

The voice of my education said to me
He must be killed,
For in Sicily the black, black snakes are innocent, the gold are venomous.

And voices in me said, If you were a man   25
You would take a stick and break him now, and finish him off.

But I must confess how I liked him,
How glad I was he had come like a guest in quiet, to drink at my
      water-trough
And depart peaceful, pacified, and thankless,
Into the burning bowels of this earth.   30

Was it cowardice, that I dared not kill him?
Was it perversity, that I longed to talk to him?
Was it humility, to feel so honoured?
I felt so honoured.

And yet those voices: 35
If you were not afraid, you would kill him!

And truly I was afraid, I was most afraid,
But even so, honoured still more
That he should seek my hospitality
From out the dark door of the secret earth.   40

He drank enough
And lifted his head, dreamily, as one who has drunken,
And flickered his tongue like a forked night on the air, so black,
Seeming to lick his lips,
And looking around like a god, unseeing, into the air,   45
And slowly turned his head,
And slowly, very slowly, as if thrice adream,
Proceeded to draw his slow length curving round
And climb again the broken bank of my wall-face.

And as he put his head into that dreadful hole,   50
And as he slowly drew up, snake-easing his shoulders, and entered farther,
A sort of horror, a sort of protest against his withdrawing into that horrid
      black hole,
Deliberately going into the blackness, and slowly drawing himself after,
Overcame me now his back was turned.

I looked around, I put down my pitcher,   55
I picked up a clumsy log
And threw it at the water-trough with a clatter.

I think I did not hit him,
But suddenly that part of him that was left behind convulsed in
   undignified haste,
Writhed like lightning, and was gone   60
Into the black hole, the earth-lipped fissure in the wall-front,
At which, in the intense still noon, I stared with fascination.

And immediately I regretted it.
I thought how paltry, how vulgar, what a mean act!
I despised myself and the voices of my accursed human education.   65

And I thought of the albatross,
And I wished he would come back, my snake.

For he seemed to me again like a king,
Like a king in exile, uncrowned in the underworld,
Now due to be crowned again.   70

And so, I missed my chance with one of the lords
Of life.
And I have something to expiate;
A pettiness.

Whales Weep Not!

They say the sea is cold, but the sea contains
the hottest blood of all, and the wildest, the most urgent.

All the whales in the wider deeps, hot are they, as they urge
on and on, and dive beneath the ice-bergs.

The right whales, the sperm whales, the hammer-heads, the killers   5
there they blow, there they blow, hot wild white breath out of the sea!

And they rock and they rock, through the sensual ageless ages
on the depths of the seven seas,
and through the salt they reel with drunk delight
and in the tropics tremble they with love   10
and roll with massive, strong desire, like gods.
Then the great bull lies up against his bride
in the blue deep of the sea
as mountain pressing on mountain, in the zest of life:
and out of the inward roaring of the inner red ocean of whale blood   15
the long tip reaches strong, intense, like a maelstrom-tip, and comes
   to rest
in the clasp and the soft, wild clutch of a she-whale's fathomless body.

And over the bridge of the whale's strong phallus, linking the wonder
    of whales
the burning archangels under the sea keep passing, back and forth,
keep passing archangels of bliss   20
from him to her, from her to him, great Cherubim
that wait on whales in mid-ocean, suspended in the waves of the sea
great heaven of whales in the waters, old hierarchies.
And enormous mother whales lie dreaming suckling their whale-tender
    young
and dreaming with strange whale eyes wide open in the waters of the
    beginning and the end.   25

And bull whales gather their women and whale calves in a ring
when danger threatens, on the surface of the ceaseless flood
and range themselves like great fierce Seraphim facing the threat
encircling their huddled monsters of love.
and all this happiness in the sea, in the salt   30
where God is also love, but without words:
and Aphrodite is the wife of whales
most happy, happy she!

and Venus among the fishes skips and is a she-dolphin
she is the gay, delighted porpoise sporting with love and the sea   35
she is the female tunny-fish, round and happy among the males
and dense with happy blood, dark rainbow bliss in the sea.

H. D. (Hilda Doolittle) (1886–1961)

Hilda Doolittle was born in the smoky steel-manufacturing town of Bethlehem, Pennsylvania, and educated at Bryn Mawr College. At the age of fifteen she met Ezra Pound, who was then a student at the University of Pennsylvania. Pound was impressed by her talents, and he first aroused her interest in poetry as a vocation. The two were briefly engaged, and in 1911 she moved to London to join the bohemian clique that was then in the process of inventing literary Modernism. She soon became one of the best known of the Modernist poets, with many of her early poems appearing in the pages of Poetry *magazine under the pseudonym "H. D., Imagiste." Her first book of verse,* Sea Garden *(1916), was followed by* Hymen *(1921),* Heliodora and Other Poems *(1924), and* Red Shoes for Bronze *(1929). Exploiting the French technique known as Imagism, the poems celebrate the beauty of the natural world in terse, enigmatic lines. In such works as "Sea Lily" and "Sheltered Garden," H. D. presents natural objects purely and simply as they appear to our senses, without embedding them in any kind of explanatory narrative or logical argument. Her concise handling of imagery and her innovative use of free verse have been influential in both Britain and America.*

In 1913 she married Richard Aldington, a fellow American poet, but their marriage did not succeed, and they separated in 1919. For a few months, H. D. enjoyed an intimate friendship with D. H. Lawrence. She eventually found long-term affection and stability in a relationship with Winifred Ellerman, a wealthy young Englishwoman known by the pen name Bryher. With Bryher's assistance, H. D. settled in Switzerland, where she raised her daughter Perdita (born out of wedlock) and pursued her poetic career. In 1933 and 1934, she traveled to Vienna, where she underwent psychoanalysis with Sigmund Freud and became fascinated by his theory of the unconscious, partly as a way of justifying the nonrational sequence of imagery in her best poems. During the 1930s, she became acquainted with the writers of the Harlem Renaissance, particularly Langston Hughes, whose early poetry reveals an Imagist tendency. H. D.'s later work explores the expressive possibilities of longer poetic forms, later gathered in a collection entitled Trilogy (1973), *an extended response to the terrible years of World War II.*

Sea Lily

Reed,
slashed and torn
but doubly rich —
such great heads as yours
drift upon temple steps,   5
but you are shattered
in the wind.

Myrtle-bark
is flecked from you,
scales are dashed   10
from your stem,
sand cuts your petal,
furrows it with hard edge,
like flint
on a bright stone.   15

Yet though the whole wind
slash at your bark,
you are lifted up,
aye — though it hiss
to cover you with froth.   20

Sheltered Garden

I have had enough.
I gasp for breath.

Every way ends, every road,
every foot-path leads at last
to the hill-crest—
then you retrace your steps,   5
or find the same slope on the other side,
precipitate.

I have had enough—
border-pinks, clove-pinks, wax-lilies,
herbs, sweet-cress.   10

O for some sharp swish of a branch—
there is no scent of resin
in this place,
no taste of bark, of coarse weeds,
aromatic, astringent—   15
only border on border of scented pinks.

Have you seen fruit under cover
that wanted light—
pears wadded in cloth,
protected from the frost,   20
melons, almost ripe,
smothered in straw?

Why not let the pears cling
to the empty branch?
All your coaxing will only make   25
a bitter fruit—
let them cling, ripen of themselves,
test their own worth,
nipped, shrivelled by the frost,   30
to fall at last but fair
with a russet coat.

Or the melon—
let it bleach yellow
in the winter light,
even tart to the taste—   35
it is better to taste of frost—
the exquisite frost—
than of wadding and of dead grass.

For this beauty,   40
beauty without strength,
chokes out life.
I want wind to break,
scatter these pink-stalks,
snap off their spiced heads,   45

fling them about with dead leaves—
spread the paths with twigs,
limbs broken off,
trail great pine branches,
hurled from some far wood   50
right across the melon patch,
break pear and quince—
leave half-trees, torn, twisted
but showing the fight was valiant.

O to blot out this garden   55
to forget, to find a new beauty
in some terrible
wind-tortured place.

Sea Violet

The white violet
is scented on its stalk,
the sea violet
fragile as agate,
lies fronting all the wind   5
among the torn shells
on the sand-bank.

The greater blue violets
flutter on the hill,
but who would change for these   10
who would change for these
one root of the white sort?

Violet
your grasp is frail
on the edge of the sand-hill,   15
but you catch the light—
frost, a star edges with its fire.

Robinson Jeffers (1887–1962)

*Born in Pittsburgh, Pennsylvania, Robinson Jeffers graduated from Occidental College,
Los Angeles, in 1905. He went on to study medicine at the University of Southern California, literature and history at the University of Zurich, and forestry at the University
of Washington. In 1905 he met Una Kall Custer, and although she was a married
woman, their deep sense of commitment to each other endured for eight years until she*

was able to obtain a divorce; they married in 1913. The couple enjoyed a deeply satisfying marriage, with three surviving children, and lived happily together until Una's death in 1950. They spent their entire lives in Carmel, California, dwelling in a home that Jeffers helped build in the summer of 1919. Constructed entirely by hand from rough-hewn blocks of granite, Tor House and the nearby Hawk Tower came to embody Jeffers's rugged sense of personal identity, standing aloof on the craggy California coast, far removed from the daily distractions, literary fashions, and false dilemmas of contemporary society.

In 1912 Jeffers received an inheritance of $9,500 that freed him to embark upon a career as a professional poet. His first publication, Flagons and Apples *(1912), an insipid collection of love poems, disappeared without a trace. He achieved a much higher level of originality and critical acclaim with his next two books:* Tamar and Other Poems *(1924) and* Roan Stallion *(1925). These were followed by* The Women at Point Sur *(1927),* Dear Judas *(1929),* Give Your Heart to the Hawks *(1933),* Solstice *(1935), and several other volumes of poetry and plays. Jeffers uses Greek myth and Old Testament narrative to convey his two central themes: the narcissistic introversion of modern society and its consequent detachment from the reality of nature. His poems are deeply pessimistic in tone, recalling the gloomy outlook of Thomas Hardy, but without Hardy's sense that the universe is a cruel joke played by a fickle God. There is no such external agency, either cruel or kind, at work in Jeffers's universe; he portrays a hard, granitic world, in which humans themselves represent the highest stage yet attained in a cosmic progression toward full consciousness. Jeffers affirms that the material world itself is God, and in such poems as "Hurt Hawks" he shows how "the wild God of the world" is revealed to our awareness in moments of extreme crisis. Animals play a vital role in many of his poems. Their awareness is more akin to ours than we imagine, and their quiet dignity, even in suffering, can teach us important lessons. In his deep affection for all birds and beasts, and in his cosmic sense of identity with the world that he inhabits, Jeffers harks back to the deep ecological sensibility of John Clare, a poet he greatly admired.*

Hurt Hawks

I

The broken pillar of the wing jags from the clotted shoulder,
The wing trails like a banner in defeat,
No more to use the sky forever but live with famine
And pain a few days: cat nor coyote
Will shorten the week of waiting for death, there is game without talons.   5
He stands under the oak-bush and waits
The lame feet of salvation; at night he remembers freedom
And flies in a dream, the dawns ruin it.
He is strong and pain is worse to the strong, incapacity is worse.
The curs of the day come and torment him   10
At distance, no one but death the redeemer will humble that head,
The intrepid readiness, the terrible eyes.
The wild God of the world is sometimes merciful to those

That ask mercy, not often to the arrogant.
You do not know him, you communal people, or you have forgotten him;   15
Intemperate and savage, the hawk remembers him;
Beautiful and wild, the hawks, and men that are dying, remember him.

2

I'd sooner, except the penalties, kill a man than a hawk; but the
    great redtail
Had nothing left but unable misery
From the bone too shattered for mending, the wing that trailed under
    his talons when he moved.   20
We had fed him six weeks, I gave him freedom,
He wandered over the foreland hill and returned in evening, asking
    for death,
Not like a beggar, still eyed with the old
Implacable arrogance. I gave him the lead gift in twilight. What fell
    was relaxed,
Owl-downy, soft feminine feathers; but what   25
Soared: the fierce rush: the night-herons by the flooded river cried fear
    at its rising
Before it was quite unsheathed from reality.

Animals

At dawn a knot of sea lions lies off the shore
In the slow swell between the rock and the cliff,
Sharp flippers lifted, or great-eyed heads, as they roll in the sea,
Bigger than draft horses, and barking like dogs
Their all-night song. It makes me wonder a little   5
That life near kin to human, intelligent, hot-blooded, idle and singing,
    can float at ease
In the ice-cold midwinter water. Then, yellow dawn
Colors the south, I think about the rapid and furious lives in the sun:
They have little to do with ours; they have nothing to do with oxygen
    and salted water; they would look monstrous
If we could see them: the beautiful passionate bodies of living flame,
    batlike flapping and screaming,   10
Tortured with burning lust and acute awareness, that ride the storm-tides
Of the great fire-globe. They are animals, as we are.
    There are many other chemistries of animal life
Besides the slow oxidation of carbohydrates and amino acids.

Carmel Point

The extraordinary patience of things!
This beautiful place defaced with a crop of surburban houses—
How beautiful when we first beheld it,
Unbroken field of poppy and lupin walled with clean cliffs;
No intrusion but two or three horses pasturing,   5
Or a few milch cows rubbing their flanks on the outcrop rockheads—
Now the spoiler has come: does it care?
Not faintly. It has all time. It knows the people are a tide
That swells and in time will ebb, and all
Their works dissolve. Meanwhile the image of the pristine beauty   10
Lives in the very grain of the granite,
Safe as the endless ocean that climbs our cliff. —As for us:
We must uncenter our minds from ourselves;
We must unhumanize our views a little, and become confident
As the rock and ocean that we were made from.   15

Vulture

I had walked since dawn and lay down to rest on a bare hillside
Above the ocean. I saw through half-shut eyelids a vulture wheeling high
    up in heaven,
And presently it passed again, but lower and nearer, its orbit narrowing,
    I understood then
That I was under inspection. I lay death-still and heard the flight-feathers
Whistle above me and make their circle and come nearer.   5
I could see the naked red head between the great wings
Bear downward staring. I said, "My dear bird, we are wasting time here.
These old bones will still work; they are not for you."
    But how beautiful he looked, gliding down
On those great sails; how beautiful he looked, veering away in the
    sea-light over the precipice. I tell you solemnly   10
That I was sorry to have disappointed him. To be eaten by that beak
    and become part of him, to share those wings and those eyes—
What a sublime end of one's body, what an enskyment;
    What a life after death.

✒ *Aldo Leopold* (1888–1948)

Born in Burlington, Iowa, Aldo Leopold is best known for his advocacy of a "land ethic," in which humans regard themselves as part of a larger community of living things. After graduating from Yale University in 1905, he received a master's degree from the Yale Forest School in 1909. Leopold spent most of his career as a professional forester working for the U.S. Forest Service. In the early twentieth century, the duties of a forester included the extermination of supposedly "harmful" predators. One of Leopold's most poignant essays, "Thinking Like a Mountain," describes how his killing of a wolf, and seeing "a fierce green fire dying in her eyes," brought him suddenly to realize the need to conserve all wildlife species, since all are essential to the ecological well-being of a region. In his later years, Leopold taught wildlife management at the University of Wisconsin, and he was one of the founders of the Wilderness Society. In 1924 he successfully advocated the establishment of the Gila National Forest in New Mexico, the first officially designated Wilderness Area in the United States. He is best known today as the author of A Sand County Almanac *(1949), published shortly after he died while fighting a forest fire. One of the most seminal works of twentieth-century nature writing,* A Sand County Almanac *provided a vital impetus to the formation of the U.S. environmental movement.*

Leopold's writing is quiet and observant in tone, not strident or polemical. He perceptively describes the goings and comings of chickadees, the growth of pine seedlings, and the annual return of whooping cranes to the great northern marshland. Meditative and elegiac, Leopold bears witness to a rapidly vanishing American wilderness.

From A Sand County Almanac

Wisconsin

Marshland Elegy

A dawn wind stirs on the great marsh. With almost imperceptible slowness it rolls a bank of fog across the wide morass. Like the white ghost of a glacier the mists advance, riding over phalanxes of tamarack, sliding across bog-meadows heavy with dew. A single silence hangs from horizon to horizon.

Out of some far recess of the sky a tinkling of little bells falls soft upon the listening land. Then again silence. Now comes a baying of some sweet-throated hound, soon the clamor of a responding pack. Then a far clear blast of hunting horns, out of the sky into the fog.

High horns, low horns, silence, and finally a pandemonium of trumpets, rattles, croaks, and cries that almost shakes the bog with its nearness, but without yet disclosing whence it comes. At last a glint of sun reveals the approach of a great echelon of birds. On motionless wing they emerge from the lifting mists, sweep a final arc of sky, and settle in clangorous descending spirals to their feeding grounds. A new day has begun on the crane marsh.

*   *   *

A sense of time lies thick and heavy on such a place. Yearly since the ice age it has awakened each spring to the clangor of cranes. The peat layers that comprise the bog are laid down in the basin of an ancient lake. The cranes stand, as it were, upon the sodden pages of their own history. These peats are the compressed remains of the mosses that clogged the pools, of the tamaracks that spread over the moss, of the cranes that bugled over the tamaracks since the retreat of the ice sheet. An endless caravan of generations has built of its own bones this bridge into the future, this habitat where the oncoming host again may live and breed and die.

To what end? Out on the bog a crane, gulping some luckless frog, springs his ungainly hulk into the air and flails the morning sun with mighty wings. The tamaracks re-echo with his bugled certitude. He seems to know.

*　　*　　*

Our ability to perceive quality in nature begins, as in art, with the pretty. It expands through successive stages of the beautiful to values as yet uncaptured by language. The quality of cranes lies, I think, in this higher gamut, as yet beyond the reach of words.

This much, though, can be said: our appreciation of the crane grows with the slow unraveling of earthly history. His tribe, we now know, stems out of the remote Eocene. The other members of the fauna in which he originated are long since entombed within the hills. When we hear his call we hear no mere bird. We hear the trumpet in the orchestra of evolution. He is the symbol of our untamable past, of that incredible sweep of millennia which underlies and conditions the daily affairs of birds and men.

And so they live and have their being—these cranes—not in the constricted present, but in the wider reaches of evolutionary time. Their annual return is the ticking of the geologic clock. Upon the place of their return they confer a peculiar distinction. Amid the endless mediocrity of the commonplace, a crane marsh holds a paleontological patent of nobility, won in the march of aeons, and revocable only by shotgun. The sadness discernible in some marshes arises, perhaps, from their once having harbored cranes. Now they stand humbled, adrift in history.

Some sense of this quality in cranes seems to have been felt by sportsmen and ornithologists of all ages. Upon such quarry as this the Holy Roman Emperor Frederick loosed his gyrfalcons. Upon such quarry as this once swooped the hawks of Kublai Khan. Marco Polo tells us: "He derives the highest amusement from sporting with gyrfalcons and hawks. At Changanor the Khan has a great Palace surrounded by a fine plain where are found cranes in great numbers. He causes millet and other grains to be sown in order that the birds may not want."

The ornithologist Bengt Berg, seeing cranes as a boy upon the Swedish heaths, forthwith made them his life work. He followed them to Africa and discovered their winter retreat on the White Nile. He says of his first encounter: "It was a spectacle which eclipsed the flight of the roc in the Thousand and One Nights."

*　　*　　*

When the glacier came down out of the north, crunching hills and gouging valleys, some adventuring rampart of the ice climbed the Baraboo Hills and fell back into the outlet gorge of the Wisconsin River. The swollen waters backed up and formed a lake half as long as the state, bordered on the east by cliffs of ice, and fed by the torrents that fell from melting mountains. The shorelines of this old lake are still visible; its bottom is the bottom of the great marsh.

The lake rose through the centuries, finally spilling over east of the Baraboo range. There it cut a new channel for the river, and thus drained itself. To the residual lagoons came the cranes, bugling the defeat of the retreating winter, summoning the on-creeping host of living things to their collective task of marsh-building. Floating bogs of sphagnum moss clogged the lowered waters, filled them. Sedge and leatherleaf, tamarack and spruce successively advanced over the bog, anchoring it by their root fabric, sucking out its water, making peat. The lagoons disappeared, but not the cranes. To the moss meadows that replaced the ancient waterways they returned each spring to dance and bugle and rear their gangling sorrel-colored young. These, albeit birds, are not properly called chicks, but *colts*. I cannot explain why. On some dewy June morning watch them gambol over their ancestral pastures at the heels of the roan mare, and you will see for yourself.

One year not long ago a French trapper in buckskins pushed his canoe up one of the moss-clogged creeks that thread the great marsh. At this attempt to invade their miry stronghold the cranes gave vent to loud and ribald laughter. A century or two later Englishmen came in covered wagons. They chopped clearings in the timbered moraines that border the marsh, and in them planted corn and buckwheat. They did not intend, like the Great Khan at Changanor, to feed the cranes. But the cranes do not question the intent of glaciers, emperors, or pioneers. They ate the grain, and when some irate farmer failed to concede their usufruct in his corn, they trumpeted a warning and sailed across the marsh to another farm.

There was no alfalfa in those days, and the hill-farms made poor hay land, especially in dry years. One dry year someone set a fire in the tamaracks. The burn grew up quickly to bluejoint grass, which, when cleared of dead trees, made a dependable hay meadow. After that, each August, men appeared to cut hay. In winter, after the cranes had gone South, they drove wagons over the frozen bogs and hauled the hay to their farms in the hills. Yearly they plied the marsh with fire and axe, and in two short decades hay meadows dotted the whole expanse.

Each August when the haymakers came to pitch their camps, singing and drinking and lashing their teams with whip and tongue, the cranes whinnied to their colts and retreated to the far fastnesses. "Red shitepokes" the haymakers called them, from the rusty hue which at that season often stains the battleship-gray of crane plumage. After the hay was stacked and the marsh again their own, the cranes returned, to call down out of October skies the migrant flocks from Canada. Together they wheeled over the new-cut stubbles and raided the corn until frosts gave the signal for the winter exodus.

These hay-meadow days were the Arcadian age for marsh dwellers. Man and beast, plant and soil lived on and with each other in mutual toleration, to the mutual benefit of all. The marsh might have kept on producing hay and prairie chickens, deer and muskrat, crane-music and cranberries forever.

The new overlords did not understand this. They did not include soil, plants, or birds in their ideas of mutuality. The dividends of such a balanced economy were too modest. They envisaged farms not only around, but *in* the marsh. An epidemic of ditch-digging and land-booming set in. The marsh was gridironed with drainage canals, speckled with new fields and farmsteads.

But crops were poor and beset by frosts, to which the expensive ditches added an aftermath of debt. Farmers moved out. Peat beds dried, shrank, caught fire. Sun-energy out of the Pleistocene shrouded the countryside in acrid smoke. No man raised his voice against the waste, only his nose against the smell. After a dry summer not even the winter snows could extinguish the smoldering marsh. Great pockmarks were burned into field and meadow, the scars reaching down to the sands of the old lake, peat-covered these hundred centuries. Rank weeds sprang out of the ashes, to be followed after a year or two by aspen scrub. The cranes were hard put, their numbers shrinking with the remnants of unburned meadow. For them, the song of the power shovel came near being an elegy. The high priests of progress knew nothing of cranes, and cared less. What is a species more or less among engineers? What good is an undrained marsh anyhow?

For a decade or two crops grew poorer, fires deeper, wood-fields larger, and cranes scarcer, year by year. Only reflooding, it appeared, could keep the peat from burning. Meanwhile cranberry growers had, by plugging drainage ditches, reflooded a few spots and obtained good yields. Distant politicians bugled about marginal land, overproduction, unemployment relief, conservation. Economists and planners came to look at the marsh. Surveyors, technicians, CCC's,[1] buzzed about. A counter-epidemic of reflooding set in. Government bought land, resettled farmers, plugged ditches wholesale. Slowly the bogs are re-wetting. The fire-pocks become ponds. Grass fires still burn, but they can no longer burn the wetted soil.

All this, once the CCC camps were gone, was good for cranes, but not so the thickets of scrub popple that spread inexorably over the old burns, and still less the maze of new roads that inevitably follow governmental conservation. To build a road is so much simpler than to think of what the country really needs. A roadless marsh is seemingly as worthless to the alphabetical conservationist as an undrained one was to the empire-builders. Solitude, the one natural resource still undowered of alphabets, is so far recognized as valuable only by ornithologists and cranes.

Thus always does history, whether of marsh or market place, end in paradox. The ultimate value in these marshes is wildness, and the crane is wildness incarnate. But all conservation of wildness is self-defeating, for to cherish we must see and fondle, and when enough have seen and fondled, there is no wilderness left to cherish.

*   *   *

Some day, perhaps in the very process of our benefactions, perhaps in the fullness of geologic time, the last crane will trumpet his farewell and spiral skyward from the great marsh. High out of the clouds will fall the sound of hunting horns, the

---

[1] CCC is the acronym for the Civilian Conservation Corps (1933–43), a New Deal agency.

baying of the phantom pack, the tinkle of little bells, and then a silence never to be broken, unless perchance in some far pasture of the Milky Way.

.   .   .

On a Monument to the Pigeon[1]

We have erected a monument to commemorate the funeral of a species. It symbolizes our sorrow. We grieve because no living man will see again the onrushing phalanx of victorious birds, sweeping a path for spring across the March skies, chasing the defeated winter from all the woods and prairies of Wisconsin.

Men still live who, in their youth, remember pigeons. Trees still live who, in their youth, were shaken by a living wind. But a decade hence only the oldest oaks will remember, and at long last only the hills will know.

There will always be pigeons in books and in museums, but these are effigies and images, dead to all hardships and to all delights. Book-pigeons cannot dive out of a cloud to make the deer run for cover, or clap their wings in thunderous applause of mast-laden woods. Book-pigeons cannot breakfast on new-mown wheat in Minnesota, and dine on blueberries in Canada. They know no urge of seasons; they feel no kiss of sun, no lash of wind and weather. They live forever by not living at all.

Our grandfathers were less well-housed, well-fed, well-clothed than we are. The strivings by which they bettered their lot are also those which deprived us of pigeons. Perhaps we now grieve because we are not sure, in our hearts, that we have gained by the exchange. The gadgets of industry bring us more comforts than the pigeons did, but do they add as much to the glory of the spring?

It is a century now since Darwin gave us the first glimpse of the origin of species. We know now what was unknown to all the preceding caravan of generations: that men are only fellow voyagers with other creatures in the odyssey of evolution. This new knowledge should have given us, by this time, a sense of kinship with fellow creatures; a wish to live and let live; a sense of wonder over the magnitude and duration of the biotic enterprise.

Above all we should, in the century since Darwin, have come to know that man, while now captain of the adventuring ship, is hardly the sole object of its quest, and that his prior assumptions to this effect arose from the simple necessity of whistling in the dark.

These things, I say, should have come to us. I fear they have not come to many.

For one species to mourn the death of another is a new thing under the sun. The Cro-Magnon who slew the last mammoth thought only of steaks. The sportsman who shot the last pigeon thought only of his prowess. The sailor who clubbed the last auk thought of nothing at all. But we, who have lost our pigeons, mourn the loss. Had the funeral been ours, the pigeons would hardly have mourned us. In this fact, rather than in Mr. DuPont's nylons or Mr. Vannevar Bush's bombs, lies objective evidence of our superiority over the beasts.

*   *   *

[1] The monument to the Passenger Pigeon, placed in Wyalusing State Park, Wisconsin, by the Wisconsin Society for Ornithology. Dedicated 11 May 1947.

This monument, perched like a duckhawk on this cliff, will scan this wide valley, watching through the days and years. For many a March it will watch the geese go by, telling the river about clearer, colder, lonelier waters on the tundra. For many an April it will see the redbuds come and go, and for many a May the flush of oak-blooms on a thousand hills. Questing wood ducks will search these basswoods for hollow limbs; golden prothonotaries will shake golden pollen from the river willows. Egrets will pose on these sloughs in August; plovers will whistle from September skies. Hickory nuts will plop into October leaves, and hail will rattle in November woods. But no pigeons will pass, for there are no pigeons, save only this flightless one, graven in bronze on this rock. Tourists will read this inscription, but their thoughts will not take wing.

We are told by economic moralists that to mourn the pigeon is mere nostalgia; that if the pigeoners had not done away with him, the farmers would ultimately have been obliged, in self-defense, to do so.

This is one of those peculiar truths that are valid, but not for the reasons alleged.

The pigeon was a biological storm. He was the lightning that played between two opposing potentials of intolerable intensity: the fat of the land and the oxygen of the air. Yearly the feathered tempest roared up, down, and across the continent, sucking up the laden fruits of forest and prairie, burning them in a traveling blast of life. Like any other chain reaction, the pigeon could survive no diminution of his own furious intensity. When the pigeoners subtracted from his numbers, and the pioneers chopped gaps in the continuity of his fuel, his flame guttered out with hardly a sputter or even a wisp of smoke.

Today the oaks still flaunt their burden at the sky, but the feathered lightning is no more. Worm and weevil must now perform slowly and silently the biological task that once drew thunder from the firmament.

The wonder is not that the pigeon went out, but that he ever survived through all the millennia of pre-Babbittian[2] time.

*   *   *

The pigeon loved his land: he lived by the intensity of his desire for clustered grape and bursting beechnut, and by his contempt of miles and seasons. Whatever Wisconsin did not offer him gratis today, he sought and found tomorrow in Michigan, or Labrador, or Tennessee. His love was for present things, and these things were present somewhere; to find them required only the free sky, and the will to ply his wings.

To love what *was* is a new thing under the sun, unknown to most people and to all pigeons. To see America as history, to conceive of destiny as a becoming, to smell a hickory tree through the still lapse of ages—all these things are possible for us, and to achieve them takes only the free sky, and the will to ply our wings. In these things, and not in Mr. Bush's bombs and Mr. DuPont's nylons, lies objective evidence of our superiority over the beasts.

·   ·   ·

[2] Irving Babbitt (1865–1933), a professor and harsh critic of Romantic views of nature.

Thinking Like a Mountain

A deep chesty bawl echoes from rimrock to rimrock, rolls down the mountain, and fades into the far blackness of the night. It is an outburst of wild defiant sorrow, and of contempt for all the adversities of the world.

Every living thing (and perhaps many a dead one as well) pays heed to that call. To the deer it is a reminder of the way of all flesh, to the pine a forecast of midnight scuffles and of blood upon the snow, to the coyote a promise of gleanings to come, to the cowman a threat of red ink at the bank, to the hunter a challenge of fang against bullet. Yet behind these obvious and immediate hopes and fears there lies a deeper meaning, known only to the mountain itself. Only the mountain has lived long enough to listen objectively to the howl of a wolf.

Those unable to decipher the hidden meaning know nevertheless that it is there, for it is felt in all wolf country, and distinguishes that country from all other land. It tingles in the spine of all who hear wolves by night, or who scan their tracks by day. Even without sight or sound of wolf, it is implicit in a hundred small events: the midnight whinny of a pack horse, the rattle of rolling rocks, the bound of a fleeing deer, the way shadows lie under the spruces. Only the ineducable tyro can fail to sense the presence or absence of wolves, or the fact that mountains have a secret opinion about them.

My own conviction on this score dates from the day I saw a wolf die. We were eating lunch on a high rimrock, at the foot of which a turbulent river elbowed its way. We saw what we thought was a doe fording the torrent, her breast awash in white water. When she climbed the bank toward us and shook out her tail, we realized our error: it was a wolf. A half-dozen others, evidently grown pups, sprang from the willows and all joined in a welcoming mêlée of wagging tails and playful maulings. What was literally a pile of wolves writhed and tumbled in the center of an open flat at the foot of our rimrock.

In those days we had never heard of passing up a chance to kill a wolf. In a second we were pumping lead into the pack, but with more excitement than accuracy: how to aim a steep downhill shot is always confusing. When our rifles were empty, the old wolf was down, and a pup was dragging a leg into impassable slide-rocks.

We reached the old wolf in time to watch a fierce green fire dying in her eyes. I realized then, and have known ever since, that there was something new to me in those eyes—something known only to her and to the mountain. I was young then, and full of trigger-itch; I thought that because fewer wolves meant more deer, that no wolves would mean hunters' paradise. But after seeing the green fire die, I sensed that neither the wolf nor the mountain agreed with such a view.

*   *   *

Since then I have lived to see state after state extirpate its wolves. I have watched the face of many a newly wolfless mountain, and seen the south-facing slopes wrinkle with a maze of new deer trails. I have seen every edible bush and seedling browsed, first to anaemic desuetude, and then to death. I have seen every edible tree defoliated to the height of a saddlehorn. Such a mountain looks as if someone had given God a new pruning shears, and forbidden Him all other exercise. In the end the starved bones of the hoped-for deer herd, dead of its own too-much, bleach with the bones of the dead sage, or molder under the high-lined junipers.

I now suspect that just as a deer herd lives in mortal fear of its wolves, so does a mountain live in mortal fear of its deer. And perhaps with better cause, for while a buck pulled down by wolves can be replaced in two or three years, a range pulled down by too many deer may fail of replacement in as many decades.

So also with cows. The cowman who cleans his range of wolves does not realize that he is taking over the wolf's job of trimming the herd to fit the range. He has not learned to think like a mountain. Hence we have dustbowls, and rivers washing the future into the sea.

*   *   *

We all strive for safety, prosperity, comfort, long life, and dullness. The deer strives with his supple legs, the cowman with trap and poison, the statesman with pen, the most of us with machines, votes, and dollars, but it all comes to the same thing: peace in our time. A measure of success in this is all well enough, and perhaps is a requisite to objective thinking, but too much safety seems to yield only danger in the long run. Perhaps this is behind Thoreau's dictum: In wildness is the salvation of the world. Perhaps this is the hidden meaning in the howl of the wolf, long known among mountains, but seldom perceived among men.

Zora Neale Hurston (1891–1960)

Zora Neale Hurston was born in 1891 in Notasulga, Alabama, although she claimed throughout her adult life that she was born ten years later in Eatonville, Florida, where her family moved when she was an infant. Hurston's mother was a former schoolteacher who died when Hurston was very young, and her father was a Baptist preacher, mayor, sharecropper, and carpenter. When Hurston left home, she worked for a theater company, and later supported herself as a manicurist, secretary, drama coach, anthropologist, and Guggenheim Fellow, among other occupations. After Hurston began her studies at Howard University in 1920 and had published her first short works, she was encouraged by her editors to move to New York City. There, she became an active member of the Harlem Renaissance, at the time called the New Negro Movement, which led to social and professional relationships with several prominent literary figures. For example, she collaborated with Langston Hughes to write the play The Mule Bone *(1931), as a reaction against African American stereotypes. In 1926, after studying anthropology at Barnard College, Hurston began working for the renowned anthropologist Frank Boas. The anthropological fieldwork she did would prove very influential to her later writings, which are heavily dependent on her studies of Southern folklore and voodoo.*

Hurston gained a reputation for behavior that was considered quite outlandish at the time—not only was she a diversely educated, politically devoted black woman, she was also liberated sexually, smoked in public, and wore eye-catching clothes. Sadly, Hurston's life was frequently marked by tragedy: She spent much time dejected and lonely. She became seriously depressed for a period of one and a half years after she was falsely accused of molesting a little boy. She died of heart disease in a welfare home in 1960.

Hurston's collection and utilization of Southern folklore introduced a uniquely historical voice to American literature in a socially conscious manner similar to the movement precipitated by the Grimm brothers' collection of folklore in Germany. Her establishment of a drama school devoted specifically to African American expression utilized the same political conduit as did Lady Gregory's and W. B. Yeats's Irish National Theatre in Dublin. Hurston resisted racial stereotypes and retold history from a Black perspective in works such as "Cudjo's Own Story of the Last African Slaver" (1927), "How It Feels to Be Colored Me" (1928), Moses, Man of the Mountain *(1929), and "Story in Harlem Slang" (1942). These concerns with history and voice, together with her contention that "There is no single face in nature, because every eye that looks upon it sees it from its own angle," validated the voices and identities of marginalized authors and readers. Hurston continues to have a profound influence on American letters. Alice Walker, who has written extensively on Hurston, placed a memorial on Hurston's unmarked grave, and fifty years after her death, Hurston's books continue to be read in great numbers, as new generations of readers discover her original and engaging voice. The selection included below is from her well-known novel,* Their Eyes Were Watching God *(1937). Hurston is one of the first authors to represent the relationship of an African American woman to the natural world.*

From Their Eyes Were Watching God

Since Tea Cake and Janie had friended with the Bahaman workers in the 'Glades, they, the "Saws," had been gradually drawn into the American crowd. They quit hiding out to hold their dances when they found that their American friends didn't laugh at them as they feared. Many of the Americans learned to jump and liked it as much as the "Saws." So they began to hold dances night after night in the quarters, usually behind Tea Cake's house. Often now, Tea Cake and Janie stayed up so late at the fire dances that Tea Cake would not let her go with him to the field. He wanted her to get her rest.

So she was home by herself one afternoon when she saw a band of Seminoles passing by. The men walking in front and the laden, stolid women following them like burros. She had seen Indians several times in the 'Glades, in twos and threes, but this was a large party. They were headed towards the Palm Beach road and kept moving steadily. About an hour later another party appeared and went the same way. Then another just before sundown. This time she asked where they were all going and at last one of the men answered her.

"Going to high ground. Saw-grass bloom. Hurricane coming."

Everybody was talking about it that night. But nobody was worried. The fire dance kept up till nearly dawn. The next day, more Indians moved east, unhurried but steady. Still a blue sky and fair weather. Beans running fine and prices good, so the Indians could be, *must* be, wrong. You couldn't have a hurricane when you're making seven and eight dollars a day picking beans. Indians are dumb anyhow, always were. Another night of Stew Beef making dynamic subtleties with his drum and living, sculptural, grotesques in the dance. Next day, no Indians passed at all. It was hot and sultry and Janie left the field and went home.

Morning came without motion. The winds, to the tiniest, lisping baby breath had left the earth. Even before the sun gave light, dead day was creeping from bush to bush watching man.

Some rabbits scurried through the quarters going east. Some possums slunk by and their route was definite. One or two at a time, then more. By the time the people left the fields the procession was constant. Snakes, rattlesnakes began to cross the quarters. The men killed a few, but they could not be missed from the crawling horde. People stayed indoors until daylight. Several times during the night Janie heard the snort of big animals like deer. Once the muted voice of a panther. Going east and east. That night the palm and banana trees began that long distance talk with rain. Several people took fright and picked up and went in to Palm Beach anyway. A thousand buzzards held a flying meet and then went above the clouds and stayed.

One of the Bahaman boys stopped by Tea Cake's house in a car and hollered. Tea Cake came out throwin' laughter over his shoulder into the house.

"Hello Tea Cake."

"Hello 'Lias. You leavin', Ah see."

"Yeah man. You and Janie wanta go? Ah wouldn't give nobody else uh chawnce at uh seat till Ah found out if you all had any way tuh go."

"Thank yuh ever so much, 'Lias. But we 'bout decided tuh stay."

"De crow gahn up, man."

"Dat ain't nothin'. You ain't seen de bossman go up, is yuh? Well all right now. Man, de money's too good on de muck. It's liable tuh fair off by tuhmorrer. Ah wouldn't leave if Ah wuz you."

"Mah uncle come for me. He say hurricane warning out in Palm Beach. Not so bad dere, but man, dis muck is too low and dat big lake is liable tuh bust."

"Ah naw, man. Some boys in dere now talkin' 'bout it. Some of 'em been in de 'Glades fuh years. 'Tain't nothin' but uh lil blow. You'll lose de whole day tuh-morrer tryin' tuh git back out heah."

"De Indians gahn east, man. It's dangerous."

"Dey don't always know. Indians don't know much uh nothin', tuh tell de truth. Else dey'd own dis country still. De white folks ain't gone nowhere. Dey oughta know if it's dangerous. You better stay heah, man. Big jumpin' dance tuh-night right heah, when it fair off."

'Lias hesitated and started to climb out, but his uncle wouldn't let him. "Dis time tuhmorrer you gointuh wish you follow crow," he snorted and drove off. 'Lias waved back to them gaily.

"If Ah never see you no mo' on earth, Ah'll meet you in Africa."

Others hurried east like the Indians and rabbits and snakes and coons. But the majority sat around laughing and waiting for the sun to get friendly again.

Several men collected at Tea Cake's house and sat around stuffing courage into each other's ears. Janie baked a big pan of beans and something she called sweet biscuits and they all managed to be happy enough.

Most of the great flame-throwers were there and naturally, handling Big John de Conquer and his works. How he had done everything big on earth, then went up tuh heben without dying atall. Went up there picking a guitar and got all de angels doing the ring-shout round and round de throne. Then everybody but God and Old Peter flew off on a flying race to Jericho and back and John de Conquer won the race; went on down to hell, beat the old devil and passed out ice water to everybody down there. Somebody tried to say that it was a mouth organ harp that John was playing, but the rest of them would not hear that. Don't care how good anybody could play a harp, God would rather to hear a guitar. That brought them back to Tea Cake. How come he couldn't hit that box a lick or two? Well, all right now, make us know it.

When it got good to everybody, Muck-Boy woke up and began to chant with the rhythm and everybody bore down on the last word of the line:

> Yo' mama don't wear no Draws
> Ah seen her when she took 'em Off
> She soaked 'em in alcoHol
> She sold 'em tuh de Santy Claus
> He told her 'twas aginst de Law
> To wear dem dirty Draws

Then Muck-Boy went crazy through the feet and danced himself and everybody else crazy. When he finished he sat back down on the floor and went to sleep again. Then they got to playing Florida flip and coon-can. Then it was dice. Not for money. This was a show-off game. Everybody posing his fancy shots. As always it broiled down to Tea Cake and Motor Boat. Tea Cake with his shy grin and Motor Boat with his face like a little black cherubim just from a church tower doing amazing things with anybody's dice. The others forgot the work and the weather watching them throw. It was art. A thousand dollars a throw in Madison Square Garden wouldn't have gotten any more breathless suspense. It would have just been more people holding in.

After a while somebody looked out and said, "It ain't gitting no fairer out dere. B'lieve Ah'll git on over tuh mah shack." Motor Boat and Tea Cake were still playing so everybody left them at it.

Sometime that night the winds came back. Everything in the world had a strong rattle, sharp and short like Stew Beef vibrating the drum head near the edge with his fingers. By morning Gabriel was playing the deep tones in the center of the drum. So when Janie looked out of her door she saw the drifting mists gathered in the west—that cloud field of the sky—to arm themselves with thunders and march forth against the world. Louder and higher and lower and wider the sound and motion spread, mounting, sinking, darking.

It woke up old Okechobee and the monster began to roll in his bed. Began to roll and complain like a peevish world on a grumble. The folks in the quarters and the people in the big houses further around the shore heard the big lake and wondered. The people felt uncomfortable but safe because there were the sea-walls to chain the senseless monster in his bed. The folks let the people do the thinking. If the castles thought themselves secure, the cabins needn't worry. Their decision was already made as always. Chink up your cracks, shiver in your wet beds and wait on the mercy of the Lord. The bossman might have the thing stopped before morning anyway. It is so easy to be hopeful in the day time when you can see the things you wish on. But it was night, it stayed night. Night was striding across nothingness with the whole round world in his hands.

A big burst of thunder and lightning that trampled over the roof of the house. So Tea Cake and Motor stopped playing. Motor looked up in his angel-looking way and said, "Big Massa draw him chair upstairs."

"Ah'm glad y'all stop dat crap-shootin' even if it wasn't for money," Janie said. "Ole Massa is doin' *His* work now. Us oughta keep quiet."

They huddled closer and stared at the door. They just didn't use another part of their bodies, and they didn't look at anything but the door. The time was past for asking the white folks what to look for through that door. Six eyes were questioning God.

Through the screaming wind they heard things crashing and things hurtling and dashing with unbelievable velocity. A baby rabbit, terror ridden, squirmed through a hole in the floor and squatted off there in the shadows against the wall, seeming to know that nobody wanted its flesh at such a time. And the lake got madder and madder with only its dikes between them and him.

In a little wind-lull, Tea Cake touched Janie and said, "Ah reckon you wish now you had of stayed in yo' big house 'way from such as dis, don't yuh?"

"Naw."

"Naw?"

"Yeah, naw. People don't die till dey time come nohow, don't keer where you at. Ah'm wid mah husband in uh storm, dat's all."

"Thanky, Ma'am. But 'sposing you wuz thu die, now. You wouldn't git mad at me for draggin' yuh heah?"

"Naw. We been tuhgether round two years. If you kin see de light at daybreak, you don't keer if you die at dusk. It's so many people never seen de light at all. Ah wuz fumblin' round and God opened de door."

He dropped to the floor and put his head in her lap. "Well then, Janie, you meant whut you didn't say, 'cause Ah never *knowed* you wuz so satisfied wid me lak dat. Ah kinda thought —"

The wind came back with triple fury, and put out the light for the last time. They sat in company with the others in other shanties, their eyes straining against crude walls and their souls asking if He meant to measure their puny might against His. They seemed to be staring at the dark, but their eyes were watching God.

As soon as Tea Cake went out pushing wind in front of him, he saw that the wind and water had given life to lots of things that folks think of as dead and given death to so much that had been living things. Water everywhere. Stray fish swimming in the yard. Three inches more and the water would be in the house. Already in some. He decided to try to find a car to take them out of the 'Glades before worse things happened. He turned back to tell Janie about it so she could be ready to go.

"Git our insurance papers tuhgether, Janie. Ah'll tote mah box mahself and things lak dat."

"You got all de money out de dresser drawer, already?"

"Naw, git it quick and cut uh piece off de tablecloth tuh wrap it up in. Us liable tuh git wet tuh our necks. Cut uh piece uh dat oilcloth quick fuh our papers. We got tuh go, if it ain't too late. De dish can't bear it out no longer."

He snatched the oilcloth off the table and took out his knife. Janie held it straight while he slashed off a strip.

"But Tea Cake, it's too awful out dere. Maybe it's better tuh stay heah in de wet than it is tuh try tuh —"

He stunned the argument with half a word. "Fix," he said and fought his way outside. He had seen more than Janie had.

Janie took a big needle and ran up a longish sack. Found some newspaper and wrapped up the paper money and papers and thrust them in and whipped over the open end with her needle. Before she could get it thoroughly hidden in the pocket of her overalls, Tea Cake burst in again.

" 'Tain't no cars, Janie."

"Ah thought not! Whut we gointuh do now?"

"We got tuh walk."

"In all dis weather, Tea Cake? Ah don't b'lieve Ah could make it out de quarters."

"Oh yeah you kin. Me and you and Motor Boat kin all lock arms and hold one 'nother down. Eh, Motor?"

"He's sleep on de bed in yonder," Janie said. Tea Cake called without moving.

"Motor Boat! You better git up from dere! Hell done broke loose in Georgy. Dis minute! How kin you sleep at uh time lak dis? Water knee deep in de yard."

They stepped out in water almost to their buttocks and managed to turn east. Tea Cake had to throw his box away, and Janie saw how it hurt him. Dodging flying missiles, floating dangers, avoiding stepping in holes and warmed on the wind now at their backs until they gained comparatively dry land. They had to fight to keep from being pushed the wrong way and to hold together. They saw other people like themselves struggling along. A house down, here and there, frightened cattle. But above all the drive of the wind and the water. And the lake. Under its multiplied roar could be heard a mighty sound of grinding rock and timber and a wail. They looked back. Saw people trying to run in raging waters and screaming when they found they couldn't. A huge barrier of the makings of the dike to which the cabins had been added was rolling and tumbling forward. Ten feet higher and as far as they could see the muttering wall advanced before the braced-up waters like a road crusher on a cosmic scale. The monstropolous beast had left his bed. The two hundred miles an hour wind had loosed his chains. He seized hold of his dikes and ran forward until he met the quarters; up-rooted them like grass and rushed on after his supposed-to-be conquerors, rolling the dikes, rolling the houses, rolling the people in the houses along with other timbers. The sea was walking the earth with a heavy heel.

"De lake is comin'!" Tea Cake gasped.

"De lake!" In amazed horror from Motor Boat, "De lake!"

"It's comin' behind us!" Janie shuddered. "Us can't fly."

"But we still kin run," Tea Cake shouted and they ran. The gushing water ran faster. The great body was held back, but rivers spouted through fissures in the rolling wall and broke like day. The three fugitives ran past another line of shanties that topped a slight rise and gained a little. They cried out as best they could, "De lake is comin'!" and barred doors flew open and others joined them in flight crying the same as they went. "De lake is comin'!" and the pursuing waters growled and shouted ahead, "Yes, Ah'm comin'!" and those who could fled on.

They made it to a tall house on a hump of ground and Janie said, "Less stop heah. Ah can't make it no further. Ah'm done give out."

"All of us is done give out," Tea Cake corrected. "We'se goin' inside out dis weather, kill or cure." He knocked with the handle of his knife, while they leaned their faces and shoulders against the wall. He knocked once more then he and Motor Boat went round to the back and forced a door. Nobody there.

"Dese people had mo' sense than Ah did," Tea Cake said as they dropped to the floor and lay there panting. "Us oughta went on wid 'Lias lak he ast me."

"You didn't know," Janie contended. "And when yuh don't know, yuh just don't know. De storms might not of come sho nuff."

They went to sleep promptly but Janie woke up first. She heard the sound of rushing water and sat up.

"Tea Cake! Motor Boat! De lake is comin'!"

The lake was coming on. Slower and wider, but coming. It had trampled on most of its supporting wall and lowered its front by spreading. But it came muttering and grumbling onward like a tired mammoth just the same.

"Dis is uh high tall house. Maybe it won't reach heah at all," Janie counselled. "And if it do, maybe it won't reach tuh de upstairs part."

"Janie, Lake Okechobee is forty miles wide and sixty miles long. Dat's uh whole heap uh water. If dis wind is shovin' dat whole lake disa way, dis house ain't nothin' tuh swaller. Us better go. Motor Boat!"

"Whut you want, man?"

"De lake is comin'!"

"Aw, naw it 'tain't."

"Yes, it is so comin'! Listen! You kin hear it way off."

"It kin jus' come on. Ah'll wait right here."

"Aw, get up, Motor Boat! Less make it tuh de Palm Beach road. Dat's on uh fill. We'se pretty safe dere."

"Ah'm safe here, man. Go ahead if yuh wants to. Ah'm sleepy."

"What you gointuh do if de lake reach heah?"

"Go upstairs."

"S'posing it come up dere?"

"Swim, man. Dat's all."

"Well, uh, good bye, Motor Boat. Everything is pretty bad, yuh know. Us might git missed of one 'nother. You sho is a grand friend fuh uh man tuh have."

"Good bye, Tea Cake. Y'all oughta stay here and sleep, man. No use in goin' off and leavin' me lak dis."

"We don't wanta. Come on wid us. It might be night time when de water hem you up in heah. Dat's how come Ah won't stay. Come on, man."

"Tea Cake Ah got tuh have mah sleep. Definitely."

"Good bye, then, Motor. Ah wish you all de luck. Goin' over tuh Nassau fuh dat visit widja when all dis is over."

"Definitely, Tea Cake. Mah mama's house is yours."

Tea Cake and Janie were some distance from the house before they struck serious water. Then they had to swim a distance, and Janie could not hold up more than a few strokes at a time, so Tea Cake bore her up till finally they hit a ridge that led on towards the fill. It seemed to him the wind was weakening a little so he kept looking for a place to rest and catch his breath. His wind was gone. Janie was tired and limping but she had not had to do that hard swimming in the turbulent waters, so Tea Cake was much worse off. But they couldn't stop. Gaining the fill was something but it was no guarantee. The lake was coming. They had to reach the six-mile bridge. It was high and safe perhaps.

Everybody was walking the fill. Hurrying, dragging, falling, crying, calling out names hopefully and hopelessly. Wind and rain beating on old folks and beating on babies. Tea Cake stumbled once or twice in his weariness and Janie held him up. So they reached the bridge at Six Mile Bend and thought to rest.

But it was crowded. White people had pre-empted that point of elevation and there was no more room. They could climb up one of its high sides and down the other, that was all. Miles further on, still no rest.

They passed a dead man in a sitting position on a hummock, entirely surrounded by wild animals and snakes. Common danger made common friends. Nothing sought a conquest over the other.

Another man clung to a cypress tree on a tiny island. A tin roof of a building hung from the branches by electric wires and the wind swung it back and forth like a mighty ax. The man dared not move a step to his right lest this crushing blade split him open. He dared not step left for a large rattlesnake was stretched full length with his head in the wind. There was a strip of water between the island and the fill, and the man clung to the tree and cried for help.

"De snake won't bite yuh," Tea Cake yelled to him. "He skeered tuh go intuh uh coil. Skeered he'll be blowed away. Step round dat side and swim off!"

Soon after that Tea Cake felt he couldn't walk anymore. Not right away. So he stretched long side of the road to rest. Janie spread herself between him and the wind and he closed his eyes and let the tiredness seep out of his limbs. On each side of the fill was a great expanse of water like lakes—water full of things living and dead. Things that didn't belong in water. As far as the eye could reach, water and wind playing upon it in fury. A large piece of tar-paper roofing sailed through the air and scudded along the fill until it hung against a tree. Janie saw it with joy. That was the very thing to cover Tea Cake with. She could lean against it and hold it down. The wind wasn't quite so bad as it was anyway. The very thing. Poor Tea Cake!

She crept on hands and knees to the piece of roofing and caught hold of it by either side. Immediately the wind lifted both of them and she saw herself sailing off the fill to the right, out and out over the lashing water. She screamed terribly and released the roofing which sailed away as she plunged downward into the water.

"Tea Cake!" He heard her and sprang up. Janie was trying to swim but fighting water too hard. He saw a cow swimming slowly towards the fill in an oblique line. A massive built dog was sitting on her shoulders and shivering and growling. The cow was approaching Janie. A few strokes would bring her there.

"Make it tuh de cow and grab hold of her tail! Don't use yo' feet. Jus' yo' hands is enough. Dat's right, come on!"

Janie achieved the tail of the cow and lifted her head up along the cow's rump, as far as she could above water. The cow sunk a little with the added load and thrashed a moment in terror. Thought she was being pulled down by a gator. Then she continued on. The dog stood up and growled like a lion, stiff-standing hackles, stiff muscles, teeth uncovered as he lashed up his fury for the charge. Tea Cake split the water like an otter, opening his knife as he dived. The dog raced down the backbone of the cow to the attack and Janie screamed and slipped far back on the tail of the cow, just out of reach of the dog's angry jaws. He wanted to plunge in after her but dreaded the water, somehow. Tea Cake rose out of the water at the cow's rump and seized the dog by the neck. But he was a powerful dog and Tea Cake was overtired. So he didn't kill the dog with one stroke as he had intended. But the dog couldn't free himself either. They fought and somehow he managed to bite Tea Cake high up on his cheek-bone once. Then Tea Cake finished him and sent him to the bottom to stay there. The cow relieved of a great weight was landing on the fill with Janie before Tea Cake stroked in and crawled weakly upon the fill again.

Janie began to fuss around his face where the dog had bitten him but he said it didn't amount to anything. "He'd uh raised hell though if he had uh grabbed me uh inch higher and bit me in mah eye. Yuh can't buy eyes in de store, yuh know." He flopped to the edge of the fill as if the storm wasn't going on at all. "Lemme rest awhile, then us got tuh make it on intuh town somehow."

It was next day by the sun and the clock when they reached Palm Beach. It was years later by their bodies. Winters and winters of hardship and suffering. The wheel kept turning round and round. Hope, hopelessness and despair. But the storm blew itself out as they approached the city of refuge.

Havoc was there with her mouth wide open. Back in the Everglades the wind had romped among lakes and trees. In the city it had raged among houses and men. Tea Cake and Janie stood on the edge of things and looked over the desolation.

"How kin Ah find uh doctor fuh yo' face in all dis mess?" Janie wailed.

"Ain't got de damn doctor tuh study 'bout. Us needs uh place tuh rest."

A great deal of their money and perseverance and they found a place to sleep. It was just that. No place to live at all. Just sleep. Tea Cake looked all around and sat heavily on the side of the bed.

"Well," he said humbly, "reckon you never 'spected tuh come tuh dis when you took up wid me, didja?"

"Once upon uh time, Ah never 'spected nothin' Tea Cake but bein' dead from the standin' still and trying' tuh laugh. But you come 'long and made somethin' outa me. So Ah'm thankful fuh anything we come through together."

"Thanky, Ma'am."

"You was twice noble tuh save me from dat dawg. Tea Cake, Ah don't speck you seen his eyes lak Ah did. He didn't aim fuh jus' bite me, Tea Cake. He aimed tuh kill me stone dead. Ah'm never tuh fuhgit dem eyes. He wuzn't nothin' all over but pure hate. Wonder where he come from?"

"Yeah, Ah did see 'im too. It wuz frightenin'. Ah didn't mean tuh take his hate neither. He had tuh die uh me one. Mah switch blade said it wuz him."

"Po' me, he'd tore me tuh pieces, if it wuzn't fuh you, honey."

"You don't have tuh say, if it wuzn't fuh me, baby, cause Ah'm *heah*, and then Ah want yuh tuh know it's uh man heah."

❧ Jean Toomer (1894–1967)

Although he is best known for his work Cane *(1923) which evocatively presents life in rural Georgia, Jean Toomer came from an upper-class African American family in Washington, D.C. His grandfather, Pinckney Pinchback, a free black, had been an officer in the Union army and later served as governor of Louisiana during Reconstruction. Toomer held a variety of jobs, but it was his work as a school principal in Sparta, Georgia, that took him to the South and the setting that inspired his first work. Toomer's approach is unique and heralds the later innovations of the authors of the Harlem Renaissance. While depicting the lives of rural African Americans, Toomer's style is distinctively experimental, mixing the modes of fiction and poetry. Although the first edition of* Cane *sold only five hundred copies, the work was hailed by avant-garde critics and its audience soon spread beyond intellectuals and inspired a generation of African American writers, including Langston Hughes and Zora Neale Hurston. After* Cane, *Toomer's commitment to writing about issues of race was quickly overshadowed by his interest in spirituality, which he felt transcended racial boundaries. He became deeply involved with the Russian mystic Georges I. Gurdjieff, and dedicated himself during the 1930s to touring and lecturing on his behalf. He later turned to Quakerism. His other works include* Essentials *(1931),* An Interpretation of Friends' Worship *(1947),* The Flavor of Man *(1949), and a posthumous collection,* The Wayward and the Seeking *(1980).*

November Cotton Flower

Boll-weevil's coming, and the winter's cold,
Made cotton-stalks look rusty, seasons old,
And cotton, scarce as any southern snow,
Was vanishing; the branch, so pinched and slow,
Failed in its function as the autumn rake;   5
Drouth fighting soil had caused the soil to take
All water from the streams; dead birds were found
In wells a hundred feet below the ground—
Such was the season when the flower bloomed.
Old folks were startled, and it soon assumed   10
Significance. Superstition saw
Something it had never seen before:
Brown eyes that loved without a trace of fear,
Beauty so sudden for that time of year.

Storm Ending

Thunder blossoms gorgeously above our heads,
Great, hollow, bell-like flowers,

Rumbling in the wind,
Stretching clappers to strike our ears . .
Full-lipped flowers   5
Bitten by the sun
Bleeding rain
Dripping rain like golden honey—
And the sweet earth flying from the thunder.

✍ *William Faulkner* (1897–1962)

Nobel Prize–winning novelist and short story writer William Faulkner was born in New Albany but spent most of his life in Oxford, Mississippi. His great-grandfather, a plantation owner, had been a colonel in the Confederate army and would inspire some of Faulkner's most memorable characters. Though he was a mediocre student, dropping out of high school in the tenth grade, he began his writing career at a young age as a poet. He published his first poem, "L'Après-Midi d'un Faune," at the age of twenty-two, in The New Republic. *At the outbreak of World War I, he was greatly disappointed to be turned down for active service and so enlisted in the Canadian Royal Air Force. After the war, he enrolled at the University of Mississippi, where he earned a C in Freshman English and dropped out after a year.*

The decade of the 1930s was his most productive period, during which he wrote most of his major novels: As I Lay Dying *(1930),* Sanctuary *(1931),* Light in August *(1932),* Absalom, Absalom! *(1936), and* The Unvanquished *(1938). For most of his career, Faulkner wrote and published without receiving critical or popular attention. He had to support himself with other jobs, including stints as a screenwriter in Hollywood. It was not until he received the Nobel Prize in Literature in 1949 that he found national and international acclaim. Ironically, when he was awarded the prize, none of his books were in print. All that changed after the Nobel Prize, and Faulkner became a much sought-after speaker, even representing the U.S. State Department as a goodwill ambassador in foreign countries. After his acclaim, he wrote and published more than ever, though none of the later books would achieve the polish and power of his work from the thirties. In 1962 he was injured in a fall from a horse; he later died of a heart attack in the hospital, possibly in consequence of chronic alcoholism.*

Faulkner's chief interest is time, which he explores through generations of characters who struggle with their own personal history and the history of their region, the American South. He shows characters desperately trying to resist change, clinging to a past by which they once defined themselves but that now no longer seems to work. The land itself becomes part of the struggle, especially in Absalom, Absalom!, *a novel in which the characters try to come to terms with events unfolding on the same plot of land and their effects on the place, the time, and the people. This interest in time is reflected even in the writing of the novels and stories, which are often structured according to many layers of time and different points of view.* The Sound and the Fury *is a good example: In this story, Faulkner shows how one childhood incident reverberates through the lives of several family members as they tell and retell the incident and its consequences in their own voices. The story below, from 1940, not only represents the struggle of the protagonist to accept and understand his own aging in relationship to the island where he has gone hunting all of his life, it also subtly explores the racial tensions which, like the lush landscape, are intrinsic to life in the rural American South.*

Delta Autumn

Soon now they would enter the Delta. The sensation was familiar to old Isaac McCaslin. It had been renewed like this each last week in November for more than fifty years—the last hill, at the foot of which the rich unbroken alluvial flatness began as the sea began at the base of its cliffs, dissolving away beneath the unhurried November rain as the sea itself would dissolve away.

At first they had come in wagons: the guns, the bedding, the dogs, the food, the whiskey, the keen heart-lifting anticipation of hunting; the young men who could drive all night and all the following day in the cold rain and pitch a camp in the rain and sleep in the wet blankets and rise at daylight the next morning and hunt. There had been bear then. A man shot a doe or a fawn as quickly as he did a buck, and in the afternoons they shot wild turkey with pistols to test their stalking skill and marksmanship, feeding all but the breast to the dogs. But that time was gone now. Now they went in cars, driving faster and faster each year because the roads were better and they had farther and farther to drive, the territory in which game still existed drawing yearly inward as his life was drawing inward, until now he was the last of those who had once made the journey in wagons without feeling it and now those who accompanied him were the sons and even grandsons of the men who had ridden for twenty-four hours in the rain or sleet behind the steaming mules. They called him "Uncle Ike" now, and he no longer told anyone how near eighty he actually was because he knew as well as they did that he no longer had any business making such expeditions, even by car.

In fact, each time now, on that first night in camp, lying aching and sleepless in the harsh blankets, his blood only faintly warmed by the single thin whiskey-and-water which he allowed himself, he would tell himself that this would be his last. But he would stand that trip—he still shot almost as well as he ever had, still killed almost as much of the game he saw as he ever killed; he no longer even knew how many deer had fallen before his gun—and the fierce long heat of the next summer would renew him. Then November would come again, and again in the car with two of the sons of his old companions, whom he had taught not only how to distinguish between the prints left by a buck or a doe but between the sound they made in moving, he would look ahead past the jerking arc of the windshield wiper and see the land flatten suddenly and swoop, dissolving away beneath the rain as the sea itself would dissolve, and he would say, "Well, boys, there it is again."

This time though, he didn't have time to speak. The driver of the car stopped it, slamming it to a skidding halt on the greasy pavement without warning, actually flinging the two passengers forward until they caught themselves with their braced hands against the dash. "What the hell, Roth!" the man in the middle said. "Can't you whistle first when you do that? Hurt you, Uncle Ike?"

"No," the old man said. "What's the matter?" The driver didn't answer. Still leaning forward, the old man looked sharply past the face of the man between them, at the face of his kinsman. It was the youngest face of them all, aquiline, saturnine, a little ruthless, the face of his ancestor too, tempered a little, altered a little, staring somberly through the streaming windshield across which the twin wipers flicked and flicked.

"I didn't intend to come back in here this time," he said suddenly and harshly.

"You said that back in Jefferson last week," the old man said. "Then you changed your mind. Have you changed it again? This ain't a very good time to——"

"Oh, Roth's coming," the man in the middle said. His name was Legate. He seemed to be speaking to no one, as he was looking at neither of them. "If it was just a buck he was coming all this distance for, now. But he's got a doe in here. Of course a old man like Uncle Ike can't be interested in no doe, not one that walks on two legs—when she's standing up, that is. Pretty light-colored, too. The one he was after them nights last fall when he said he was coon-hunting, Uncle Ike. The one I figured maybe he was still running when he was gone all that month last January. But of course a old man like Uncle Ike ain't got no interest in nothing like that." He chortled, still looking at no one, not completely jeering.

"What?" the old man said. "What's that?" But he had not even so much as glanced at Legate. He was still watching his kinsman's face. The eyes behind the spectacles were the blurred eyes of an old man, but they were quite sharp too; eyes which could still see a gun-barrel and what ran beyond it as well as any of them could. He was remembering himself now: how last year, during the final stage by motor boat in to where they camped, a box of food had been lost overboard and how on the next day his kinsman had gone back to the nearest town for supplies and had been gone overnight. And when he did return, something had happened to him. He would go into the woods with his rifle each dawn when the others went, but the old man, watching him, knew that he was not hunting. "All right," he said. "Take me and Will on to shelter where we can wait for the truck, and you can go on back."

"I'm going in," the other said harshly. "Don't worry. Because this will be the last of it."

"The last of deer hunting, or of doe hunting?" Legate said. This time the old man paid no attention to him even by speech. He still watched the young man's savage and brooding face.

"Why?" he said.

"After Hitler gets through with it? Or Smith or Jones or Roosevelt or Willkie or whatever he will call himself in this country?"

"We'll stop him in this country," Legate said. "Even if he calls himself George Washington."

"How?" Edmonds said. "By singing 'God Bless America' in bars at midnight and wearing dime-store flags in our lapels?"

"So that's what's worrying you," the old man said. "I ain't noticed this country being short of defenders yet, when it needed them. You did some of it yourself twenty-odd years ago, before you were a grown man even. This country is a little mite stronger than any one man or group of men, outside of it or even inside of it either. I reckon, when the time comes and some of you have done got tired of hollering we are whipped if we don't go to war and some more are hollering we are whipped if we do, it will cope with one Austrian paperhanger, no matter what he will be calling himself. My pappy and some other better men than any of them you named tried once to tear it in two with a war, and they failed."

"And what have you got left?" the other said. "Half the people without jobs and half the factories closed by strikes. Half the people on public dole that won't work and half that couldn't work even if they would. Too much cotton and corn and hogs, and not enough for people to eat and wear. The country full of people to tell a man how he can't raise his own cotton whether he will or won't, and Sally Rand with a sergeant's stripes and not even the fan couldn't fill the army rolls. Too much not-butter and not even the guns——"

"We got a deer camp—if we ever get to it," Legate said. "Not to mention does."

"It's a good time to mention does," the old man said. "Does and fawns both. The only fighting anywhere that ever had anything of God's blessing on it has been when men fought to protect does and fawns. If it's going to come to fighting, that's a good thing to mention and remember too."

"Haven't you discovered in—how many years more than seventy is it?—that women and children are one thing there's never any scarcity of?" Edmonds said.

"Maybe that's why all I am worrying about right now is that ten miles of river we still have got to run before we can make camp," the old man said. "So let's get on."

They went on. Soon they were going fast again, as Edmonds always drove, consulting neither of them about the speed just as he had given neither of them any warning when he slammed the car to stop. The old man relaxed again. He watched, as he did each recurrent November while more than sixty of them passed, the land which he had seen change. At first there had been only the old towns along the River and the old towns along the hills, from each of which the planters with their gangs of slaves and then of hired laborers had wrested from the impenetrable jungle of water-standing cane and cypress, gum and holly and oak and ash, cotton patches which, as the years passed, became fields and then plantations. The paths made by deer and bear became roads and then highways, with towns in turn springing up along them and along the rivers Tallahatchie and Sunflower which joined and became the Yazoo, the River of the Dead of the Choctaws—the thick, slow, black, unsunned streams almost without current, which once each year ceased to flow at all and then reversed, spreading, drowning the rich land and subsiding again, leaving it still richer.

Most of that was gone now. Now a man drove two hundred miles from Jefferson before he found wilderness to hunt in. Now the land lay open from the cradling hills on the east to the rampart of levee on the west, standing horseman-tall with cotton for the world's looms—the rich black land, imponderable and vast, fecund up to the very doorsteps of the Negroes who worked it and of the white men who owned it; which exhausted the hunting life of a dog in one year, the working life of a mule in five and of a man in twenty—the land in which neon flashed past them from the little countless towns, and countless shining this-year's automobiles sped past them on the broad plumb-ruled highways, yet in which the only permanent mark of man's occupation seemed to be the tremendous gins, constructed in sections of sheet iron and in a week's time though they were, since no man, millionaire though he be, would build more than a roof and walls to shelter the camping equipment he lived from, when he knew that once each ten years or so his house would be flooded to the second storey and all within it ruined;—the land across which there came now no scream of panther but instead the long hooting of locomotives: trains of incredible length and drawn by a single engine, since there was no gradient anywhere and no elevation save those raised by forgotten aboriginal hands as refuges from the yearly water and used by their Indian successors to sepulchre their fathers' bones, and all that remained of that old time were the Indian names on the little towns and usually pertaining to water—Aluschaskuna, Tillatoba, Homochitto, Yazoo.

By early afternoon, they were on water. At the last little Indian-named town at the end of pavement they waited until the other car and the two trucks—the one carrying the bedding and tents and food, the other the horses—overtook them. They left the concrete and, after another mile or so, the gravel too. In caravan they ground on through the ceaselessly dissolving afternoon, with skid-chains on the wheels now, lurching and splashing and sliding among the ruts, until presently it seemed to him that the retrograde of his remembering had gained an inverse velocity from their own slow progress, that the land had retreated not in minutes from the last spread of gravel but in years, decades, back toward what it had been when he first knew it: the road they now followed once more the ancient pathway of bear and deer, the diminishing fields they now passed once more scooped punily and terrifically by axe and saw and mule-drawn plow from the wilderness' flank, out of the brooding and immemorial tangle, in place of ruthless mile-wide parallelograms wrought by ditching the dyking machinery.

They reached the river landing and unloaded, the horses to go overland downstream to a point opposite the camp and swim the river, themselves and the bedding and food and dogs and guns in the motor launch. It was himself, though no horseman, no farmer, not even a countryman save by his distant birth and boyhood, who coaxed and soothed the two horses, drawing them by his own single frail hand until, backing, filling, trembling a little, they surged, halted, then sprang scrambling down from the truck, possessing no affinity for them as creatures, beasts, but being merely insulated by his years and time from the corruption of steel and oiled moving parts which tainted the others.

Then, his old hammer double gun which was only twelve years younger than he standing between his knees, he watched even the last puny marks of man—cabin, clearing, the small and irregular fields which a year ago were jungle and in which the skeleton stalks of this year's cotton stood almost as tall and rank as the old cane had stood, as if man had had to marry his planting to the wilderness in order to conquer it—fall away and vanish. The twin banks marched with wilderness as he remembered it—the tangle of brier and cane impenetrable even to sight twenty feet away, the tall tremendous soaring of oak and gum and ash and hickory which had rung to no axe save the hunter's, had echoed to no machinery save the beat of old-time steam boats traversing it or to the snarling of launches like their own of people going into it to dwell for a week or two weeks because it was still wilderness. There was some of it left, although now it was two hundred miles from Jefferson when once it had been thirty. He had watched it, not being conquered, destroyed, so much as retreating since its purpose was served now and its time an outmoded time, retreating southward through this inverted-apex, this ∇-shaped section of earth between hills and River until what was left of it seemed now to be gathered and for the time arrested in one tremendous density of brooding and inscrutable impenetrability at the ultimate funnelling tip.

They reached the site of their last-year's camp with still two hours left of light. "You go on over under that driest tree and set down," Legate told him. "—if you can find it. Me and these other young boys will do this." He did neither. He was not tired yet. That would come later. *Maybe it won't come at all this time,* he thought, as he had thought at this point each November for the last five or six of them. *Maybe I will go out on stand in the morning too;* knowing that he would not, not even if he took the advice and sat down under the driest shelter and did nothing until camp was made and supper cooked. Because it would not be the fatigue. It would be because he would not sleep tonight but would lie instead wakeful and peaceful on the cot amid the tent-filling snoring and the rain's whisper as he always did on the first night in camp; peaceful, without regret or fretting, telling himself that was all right too, who didn't have so many of them left as to waste one sleeping.

In his slicker he directed the unloading of the boat—the tents, the stove, the bedding, the food for themselves and the dogs until there should be meat in camp. He sent two of the Negroes to cut firewood; he had the cook-tent raised and the stove up and a fire going and supper cooking while the big tent was still being staked down. Then in the beginning of dusk he crossed in the boat to where the horses waited, backing and snorting at the water. He took the lead-ropes and with no more weight than that and his voice, he drew them down into the water and held them beside the boat with only their heads above the surface, as though they actually were suspended from his frail and strengthless old man's hands, while the boat recrossed and each horse in turn lay prone in the shallows, panting and trembling, its eyes rolling in the dusk, until the same weightless hand and unraised voice gathered it surging upward, splashing and thrashing up the bank.

Then the meal was ready. The last of light was gone now save the thin stain of it snared somewhere between the river's surface and the rain. He had the single glass of thin whiskey-and-water, then, standing in the churned mud beneath the stretched tarpaulin, he said grace over the fried slabs of pork, the hot soft shapeless bread, the canned beans and molasses and coffee in iron plates and cups,—the town food, brought along with them—then covered himself again, the others following. "Eat," he said. "Eat it all up. I don't want a piece of town meat in camp after breakfast tomorrow. Then you boys will hunt. You'll have to. When I first started hunting in this bottom sixty years ago with old General Compson and Major de Spain and Roth's grandfather and Will Legate's too, Major de Spain wouldn't allow but two pieces of foreign grub in his camp. That was one side of pork and one ham of beef. And not to eat for the first supper and breakfast neither. It was to save until along toward the end of camp when everybody was so sick of bear meat and coon and venison that we couldn't even look at it."

"I thought Uncle Ike was going to say the pork and beef was for the dogs," Legate said, chewing. "But that's right; I remember. You just shot the dogs a mess of wild turkey every evening when they got tired of deer guts."

"Times are different now," another said. "There was game here then."

"Yes," the old man said quietly. "There was game here then."

"Besides, they shot does then too," Legate said. "As it is now, we ain't got but one doe-hunter in——"

"And better men hunted it," Edmonds said. He stood at the end of the rough plank table, eating rapidly and steadily as the others ate. But again the old man looked sharply across at the sullen, handsome, brooding face which appeared now darker and more sullen still in the light of the smoky lantern. "Go on. Say it."

"I didn't say that," the old man said. "There are good men everywhere, at all times. Most men are. Some are just unlucky, because most men are a little better than their circumstances give them a chance to be. And I've known some that even the circumstances couldn't stop."

"Well, I wouldn't say—" Legate said.

"So you've lived almost eighty years," Edmonds said, "and that's what you finally learned about the other animals you lived among. I suppose the question to ask you is, where have you been all the time you were dead?"

There was a silence; for the instant even Legate's jaw stopped chewing while he gaped at Edmonds. "Well, by God, Roth—" the third speaker said. But it was the old man who spoke, his voice still peaceful and untroubled and merely grave:

"Maybe so," he said. "But if being what you call alive would have learned me any different, I reckon I'm satisfied, wherever it was I've been."

"Well, I wouldn't say that Roth—" Legate said.

The third speaker was still leaning forward a little over the table, looking at Edmonds. "Meaning that it's only because folks happen to be watching him that a man behaves at all," he said. "Is that it?"

"Yes," Edmonds said. "A man in a blue coat, with a badge on it watching him. Maybe just the badge."

"I deny that," the old man said. "I don't——"

The other two paid no attention to him. Even Legate was listening to them for the moment, his mouth still full of food and still open a little, his knife with another lump of something balanced on the tip of the blade arrested halfway to his mouth. "I'm glad I don't have your opinion of folks," the third speaker said. "I take it you include yourself."

"I see," Edmonds said. "You prefer Uncle Ike's opinion of circumstances. All right. Who makes the circumstances?"

"Luck," the third said. "Chance. Happen-so. I see what you are getting at. But that's just what Uncle Ike said: that now and then, maybe most of the time, man is a little better than the net result of his and his neighbors' doings, when he gets the chance to be."

This time Legate swallowed first. He was not to be stopped this time. "Well, I wouldn't say that Roth Edmonds can hunt one doe every day and night for two weeks and was a poor hunter or a unlucky one neither. A man that still have the same doe left to hunt on again next year——"

"Have some meat," the man next to him said.

"——ain't so unlucky—What?" Legate said.

"Have some meat." The other offered the dish.

"I got some," Legate said.

"Have some more," the third speaker said. "You and Roth Edmonds both. Have a heap of it. Clapping your jaws together that way with nothing to break the shock." Someone chortled. Then they all laughed, with relief, the tension broken. But the old man was speaking, even into the laughter, in that peaceful and still untroubled voice:

"I still believe. I see proof everywhere. I grant that man made a heap of his circumstances, him and his living neighbors between them. He even inherited some of them already made, already almost ruined even. A while ago Henry Wyatt there said how there used to be more game here. There was. So much that we even killed does. I seem to remember Will Legate mentioning that too——" Someone laughed, a single guffaw, stillborn. It ceased and they all listened, gravely, looking down at their plates. Edmonds was drinking his coffee, sullen, brooding, inattentive.

"Some folks still kill does," Wyatt said. "There won't be just one buck hanging in this bottom tomorrow night without any head to fit it."

"I didn't say all men," the old man said. "I said most men. And not just because there is a man with a badge to watch us. We probably won't even see him unless maybe he will stop here about noon tomorrow and eat dinner with us and check our licenses——"

"We don't kill does because if we did kill does in a few years there wouldn't even be any bucks left to kill, Uncle Ike," Wyatt said.

"According to Roth yonder, that's one thing we won't never have to worry about," the old man said. "He said on the way here this morning that does and fawns—I believe he said women and children—are two things this world ain't ever lacked. But that ain't all of it," he said. "That's just the mind's reason a man has to give himself because the heart don't always have time to bother with thinking up words that fit together. God created man and He created the world for him to live in and I reckon He created the kind of world He would have wanted to live in if He had been a man—the ground to walk on, the big woods, the trees and the water, and the game to live in it. And maybe He didn't put the desire to hunt and kill game in man but I reckon He knew it was going to be there, that man was going to teach it to himself, since he wasn't quite God himself yet——"

"When will he be?" Wyatt said.

"I think that every man and woman, at the instant when it don't even matter whether they marry or not, I think that whether they marry then or afterward or don't never, at that instant the two of them together were God."

"Then there are some Gods in this world I wouldn't want to touch, and with a damn long stick," Edmonds said. He set his coffee cup down and looked at Wyatt. "And that includes myself, if that's what you want to know. I'm going to bed." He was gone. There was a general movement among the others. But it ceased and they stood again about the table, not looking at the old man, apparently held there yet by his quiet and peaceful voice as the heads of the swimming horses had been held above the water by his weightless hand. The three Negroes—the cook and his helper and old Isham—were sitting quietly in the entrance of the kitchen tent, listening too, the three faces dark and motionless and musing.

"He put them both here: man, and the game he would follow and kill, foreknowing it. I believe He said, 'So be it.' I reckon He even foreknew the end. But He said, 'I will give him his chance. I will give him warning and foreknowledge too, along with the desire to follow and the power to slay. The woods and fields he ravages and the game he devastates will be the consequence and signature of his crime and guilt, and his punishment.'— Bed time," he said. His voice and inflection did not change at all. "Breakfast at four o'clock, Isham. We want meat on the ground by sunup time."

There was a good fire in the sheet-iron heater; the tent was warm and was beginning to dry out, except for the mud underfoot. Edmonds was already rolled into his blankets, motionless, his face to the wall. Isham had made up his bed too—the strong, battered iron cot, the stained mattress which was not quite soft enough, the worn, often-washed blankets which as the years passed were less and less warm enough. But the tent was warm; presently, when the kitchen was cleaned up and readied for breakfast, the young Negro would come in to lie down before the heater, where he could be roused to put fresh wood into it from time to time. And then, he knew now he would not sleep tonight anyway; he no longer needed to tell himself that perhaps he would. But it was all right now. The day was ended now and night faced him, but alarmless, empty of fret. *Maybe I came for this*, he thought: *Not to hunt, but for this. I would come anyway, even if only to go back home tomorrow.* Wearing only his bagging woolen underwear, his spectacles folded away in the worn case beneath the pillow where he could reach them readily and his lean body fitted easily into the old worn groove of mattress and blankets, he lay on his back, his hands crossed on his breast and his eyes closed while the others undressed and went to bed and the last of the sporadic talking died into snoring. Then he opened his eyes and lay peaceful and quiet as a child, looking up at the motionless belly of rain-murmured canvas upon which the glow of the heater was dying slowly away and would fade still further until the young Negro, lying on two planks before it, would sit up and stoke it and lie back down again.

They had a house once. That was sixty years ago, when the Big Bottom was only thirty miles from Jefferson and old Major de Spain, who had been his father's cavalry commander in '61 and '2 and '3 and '4, and his cousin (his older brother; his father too) had taken him into the woods for the first time. Old Sam Fathers was alive then, born in slavery, son of a Negro slave and a Chickasaw chief, who had taught him how to shoot, not only when to shoot but when not to; such a November dawn as tomorrow would be and the old man led him straight to the great cypress and he had known the buck would pass exactly there because there was something running in Sam Fathers' veins which ran in the veins of the buck too, and they stood there against the tremendous trunk, the old man of seventy and the boy of twelve, and there was nothing save the dawn until suddenly the buck was there, smoke-colored out of nothing, magnificent with speed: and Sam Fathers said, 'Now. Shoot quick and shoot slow:' and the gun levelled rapidly without haste and crashed and he walked to the buck lying still intact and still in the shape of that magnificent speed and bled it with Sam's knife and Sam dipped his hands into the hot blood and marked his face forever while he stood trying not to tremble, humbly and with pride too though the boy of twelve had been unable to phrase it then: *I slew you; my bearing must not shame your quitting life. My conduct forever onward must become your death;* marking him for that and for more than that: that day and himself and McCaslin juxtaposed, not against the wilderness but against the tamed land, the old wrong and shame itself, in repudiation and denial at least of the land and the wrong and shame, even if he couldn't cure the wrong and eradicate the shame, who at fourteen when he learned of it had believed he could do both when he became competent, and when at twenty-one he became competent he knew that he could do neither but at least he could repudiate the wrong and shame, at least in principle, and at least the land itself in fact, for his son at least: and did, thought he had: then (married then) in a rented cubicle in a back-street stock-traders' boardinghouse, the first and last time he ever saw her naked body, himself and his wife juxtaposed in their turn against that same land, that same wrong and shame from whose regret and grief he would at least save and free his son and, saving and freeing his son, lost him.

They had the house then. That roof, the two weeks of each November which they spent under it, had become his home. Although since that time they had lived during the two fall weeks in tents and not always in the same place two years in succession and now his companions were the sons and even the grandsons of them with whom he had lived in the house, and for almost fifty years now the house itself had not even existed, the conviction, the sense and feeling of home, had been merely transferred into the canvas. He owned a house in Jefferson, a good house though small, where he had had a wife and lived with her and lost her, ay, lost her even though he had lost her in the rented cubicle before he and his old clever dipsomaniac partner had finished the house for them to move into it: but lost her, because she loved him. But women hope for so much. They never live too long to still believe that anything within the scope of their passionate wanting is likewise within the range of their passionate hope: and it was still kept for him by his dead wife's widowed niece and her children, and he was comfortable in it, his wants and needs and even the small trying harmless crochets of an old man looked after by blood at least related to the blood which he had elected out of all the earth to cherish. But he spent the time within those walls waiting for November, because even this tent with its muddy floor and the bed which was not wide enough nor soft enough nor even warm enough, was his home and these men, some of whom he only saw during these two November weeks and not one of whom even bore any name he used to know—De Spain and Compson and Ewell and Hogganbeck—were more his kin than any. Because this was his land——

The shadow of the youngest Negro loomed. It soared, blotting the heater's dying glow from the ceiling, the wood billets thumping into the iron maw until the glow, the flame, leaped high and bright across the canvas. But the Negro's shadow still remained, by its length and breadth, standing, since it covered most of the ceiling, until after a moment he raised himself on one elbow to look. It was not the Negro, it was his kinsman; when he spoke the other turned sharp against the red firelight the sullen and ruthless profile.

"Nothing," Edmonds said. "Go on back to sleep."

"Since Will Legate mentioned it," McCaslin said, "I remember you had some trouble sleeping in here last fall too. Only you called it coon-hunting then. Or was it Will Legate called it that?" The other didn't answer. Then he turned and went back to his bed. McCaslin, still propped on his elbow, watched until the other's shadow sank down the wall and vanished, became one with the mass of sleeping shadows. "That's right," he said. "Try to get some sleep. We must have meat in camp tomorrow. You can do all the setting up you want to after that." He lay down again, his hands crossed again on his breast, watching the glow of the heater on the canvas ceiling. It was steady again now, the fresh wood accepted, being assimilated; soon it would begin to fade again, taking with it the last echo of that sudden upflare of a young man's passion and unrest. Let him lie awake for a little while, he thought; He will lie still some day for a long time without even dissatisfaction to disturb him. And lying awake here, in these surroundings, would soothe him if anything could, if anything could soothe a man just forty years old. Yes, he thought; Forty years old or thirty, or even the trembling and sleepless ardor of a boy; already the tent, the rain-murmured canvas globe, was once more filled with it. He lay on his back, his eyes closed, his breathing quiet and peaceful as a child's, listening to it—that silence which was never silence but was myriad. He could almost see it, tremendous, primeval, looming, musing downward upon this puny, evanescent clutter of human sojourn which after a single brief week would vanish and in another week would be completely healed, traceless in the unmarked solitude. Because it was his land, although he had never owned a foot of it. He had never wanted to, not even after he saw plain its ultimate doom, watching it retreat year by year before the onslaught of axe and saw and log-lines and then dynamite and tractor plows, because it belonged to no man. It belonged to all; they had only to use it well, humbly and with pride. Then suddenly he knew why he had never wanted to own any of it, arrest at least that much of what people called progress, measure his longevity at least against that much of its ultimate fate. It was because there was just exactly enough of it. He seemed to see the two of them—himself and the wilderness—as coevals, his own span as a hunter, a woodsman, not contemporary with his first breath but transmitted to him gladly, humbly, with joy and pride, from that old Major de Spain and that old Sam Fathers who had taught him to hunt, the two spans running out together, not toward oblivion, nothingness, but into a dimension free of both time and space, where once more the untreed land warped and wrung to mathematical squares of rank cotton for the frantic old-world people to turn into shells to shoot at one another, would find ample room for both—the names, the faces of the old men he had known and loved and for a little while outlived, moving again among the shades of tall unaxed trees and sightless brakes where the wild strong immortal game ran forever before the tireless belling immortal hounds, falling and rising phoenix-like to the soundless guns.

He had been asleep. The lantern was lighted now. Outside in the darkness the oldest Negro, Isham, was beating a spoon against the bottom of a tin pan and crying, "Raise up and get yo foa clock coffy. Raise up and get yo foa clock coffy," and the tent was full of low talk and of men dressing, and Legate's voice, repeating: "Get out of here now and let Uncle Ike sleep. If you wake him up, he'll go out with us. And he ain't got any business in the woods this morning."

So he didn't move. He lay with his eyes closed, his breathing gentle and peaceful, and heard them one by one leave the tent. He listened to the breakfast sounds from the table beneath the tarpaulin and heard them depart—the horses, the dogs, the last voice until it died away and there was only the sounds of the Negroes clearing breakfast away. After a while he might possibly even hear the first faint clear cry of the first hound ring through the wet woods from where the buck had bedded, then he would go back to sleep again— The tent-flap swung in and fell. Something jarred sharply against the end of the cot and a hand grasped his knee through the blanket before he could open his eyes. It was Edmonds, carrying a shotgun in place of his rifle. He spoke in a harsh, rapid voice:

"Sorry to wake you. There will be a——"

"I was awake," McCaslin said. "Are you going to shoot that shotgun today?"

"You just told me last night you want meat," Edmonds said. "There will be a——"

"Since when did you start having trouble getting meat with your rifle?"

"All right," the other said, with that harsh, restrained, furious impatience. Then McCaslin saw in his hand a thick oblong: an envelope. "There will be a message here some time this morning, looking for me. Maybe it won't come. If it does, give the messenger this and tell h— say I said No."

"A what?" McCaslin said. "Tell who?" He half rose onto his elbow as Edmonds jerked the envelope onto the blanket, already turning toward the entrance, the envelope striking solid and heavy and without noise and already sliding from the bed until McCaslin caught it, divining by feel through the paper as instantaneously and conclusively as if he had opened the envelope and looked, the thick sheaf of banknotes. "Wait," he said. "Wait:"—more than the blood kinsman, more even than the senior in years, so that the other paused, the canvas lifted, looking back, and McCaslin saw that outside it was already day. "Tell her No," he said. "Tell her." They stared at one another—the old face, wan, sleepraddled above the tumbled bed, the dark and sullen younger one at once furious and cold. "Will Legate was right. This is what you called coon-hunting. And now this." He didn't raise the envelope. He made no motion, no gesture to indicate it. "What did you promise her that you haven't the courage to face her and retract?"

"Nothing!" the other said. "Nothing! This is all of it. Tell her I said No." He was gone. The tent flap lifted on an in-waft of faint light and the constant murmur of rain, and fell again, leaving the old man still half-raised onto one elbow, the envelope clutched in the other shaking hand. Afterward it seemed to him that he had begun to hear the approaching boat almost immediately, before the other could have got out of sight even. It seemed to him that there had been no interval whatever: the tent flap falling on the same out-waft of faint and rain-filled light like the suspiration and expiration of the same breath and then in the next second lifted again—the mounting snarl of the outboard engine, increasing, nearer and nearer and louder and louder then cut short off, ceasing with the absolute instantaneity of a blown-out candle, into the lap and plop of water under the bows as the skiff slid in to the bank, the youngest Negro, the youth, raising the tent flap beyond which for that instant he saw the boat—a small skiff with a Negro man sitting in the stern beside the upslanted motor—then the woman entering, in a man's hat and a man's slicker and rubber boots, carrying the blanket-swaddled bundle on one arm and holding the edge of the unbuttoned raincoat over it with the other hand: and bringing something else, something intangible, an effluvium which he knew he would recognize in a moment because Isham had already told him, warned him, by sending the young Negro to the tent to announce the visitor instead of coming himself, the flap falling at last on the young Negro and they were alone—the face indistinct and as yet only young and with dark eyes, queerly colorless but not ill and not that of a country woman despite the garments she wore, looking down at him where he sat upright on the cot now, clutching the envelope, the soiled undergarment bagging about him and the twisted blankets huddled about his hips.

"Is that his?" he cried. "Don't lie to me!"

"Yes," she said. "He's gone."

"Yes. He's gone. You won't jump him here. Not this time. I don't reckon even you expected that. He left you this. Here." He fumbled at the envelope. It was not to pick it up, because it was still in his hand; he had never put it down. It was as if he had to fumble somehow to co-ordinate physically his heretofore obedient hand with what his brain was commanding of it, as if he had never performed such an action before, extending the envelope at last, saying again, "Here. Take it. Take it:" until he became aware of her eyes, or not the eyes so much as the look, the regard fixed now on his face with that immersed contemplation, that bottomless and intent candor, of a child. If she had ever seen either the envelope or his movement to extend it, she did not show it.

"You're Uncle Isaac," she said.

"Yes," he said. "But never mind that. Here. Take it. He said to tell you No." She looked at the envelope, then she took it. It was sealed and bore no superscription. Nevertheless, even after she glanced at the front of it, he watched her hold it in the one free hand and tear the corner off with her teeth and manage to rip it open and tilt the neat sheaf of bound notes onto the blanket without even glancing at them and look into the empty envelope and take the edge between her teeth and tear it completely open before she crumpled and dropped it.

"That's just money," she said.

"What did you expect? What else did you expect? You have known him long enough or at least often enough to have got that child, and you don't know him any better than that?"

"Not very often. Not very long. Just that week here last fall, and in January he sent for me and we went west, to New Mexico. We were there six weeks, where I could at least sleep in the same apartment where I cooked for him and looked after his clothes———"

"But not marriage," he said. "Not marriage. He didn't promise you that. Don't lie to me. He didn't have to."

"No. He didn't have to. I didn't ask him to. I knew what I was doing. I knew that to begin with, long before honor, I imagine he called it, told him the time had come to tell in so many words what his code, I suppose he would call it, would forbid him forever to do. And we agreed. Then we agreed again before he left New Mexico, to make sure. That that would be all of it. I believed him. No, I don't mean that; I mean I believed myself. I wasn't even listening to him any more by then because by that time it had been a long time since he had had anything else to tell me for me to have to hear. By then I wasn't even listening enough to ask him to please stop talking. I was listening to myself. And I believed it. I must have believed it. I don't see how I could have helped but believe it, because he was gone then as we had agreed and he didn't write as we had agreed, just the money came to the bank in Vicksburg in my name but coming from nobody as we had agreed. So I must have believed it. I even wrote him last month to make sure again and the letter came back unopened and I was sure. So I left the hospital and rented myself a room to live in until the deer season opened so I could make sure myself and I was waiting beside the road yesterday when your car passed and he saw me and so I was sure."

"Then what do you want?" he said. "What do you want? What do you expect?"

"Yes," she said. And while he glared at her, his white hair awry from the pillow and his eyes, lacking the spectacles to focus them, blurred and irisless and apparently pupilless, he saw again that grave, intent, speculative and detached fixity like a child watching him. "His great great— Wait a minute—great great *great* grandfather was your grandfather. McCaslin. Only it got to be Edmonds. Only it got to be more than that. Your cousin McCaslin was there that day when your father and Uncle Buddy won Tennie from Mr. Beauchamp for the one that had no name but Terrel so you called him Tomey's Terrel, to marry. But after that it got to be Edmonds." She regarded him, almost peacefully, with that unwinking and heatless fixity—the dark, wide, bottomless eyes in the face's dead and toneless pallor which to the old man looked anything but dead, but young and incredibly and even ineradicably alive—as though she were not only not looking at anything, she was not even speaking to anyone but herself. "I would have made a man of him. He's not a man yet. You spoiled him. You, and Uncle Lucas and Aunt Mollie. But mostly you."

"Me?" he said. "Me?"

"Yes. When you gave to his grandfather that land which didn't belong to him, not even half of it, by will or even law."

"And never mind that too," he said. "Never mind that too. You," he said. "You sound like you have been to college even. You sound almost like a Northerner even, not like the draggle-tailed women of these Delta peckerwoods. Yet you meet a man on the street one afternoon just because a box of groceries happened to fall out of a boat. And a month later you go off with him and live with him until he got a child on you: and then, by your own statement, you sat there while he took his hat and said goodbye and walked out. Even a Delta peckerwood would look after even a draggle-tail better than that. Haven't you got any folks at all?"

"Yes," she said. "I was living with one of them. My aunt, in Vicksburg. I came to live with her two years ago when my father died; we lived in Indianapolis then. But I got a job, teaching school here in Aluschaskuna, because my aunt was a widow, with a big family, taking in washing to sup——"

"Took in what?" he said. "Took in washing?" He sprang, still seated even, flinging himself backward onto one arm, awry-haired, glaring. Now he understood what it was she had brought into the tent with her, what old Isham had already told him by sending the youth to bring her in to him—the pale lips, the skin pallid and dead-looking yet not ill, the dark and tragic and foreknowing eyes. *Maybe in a thousand or two thousand years in America*, he thought. *But not now! Not now!* He cried, not loud, in a voice of amazement, pity, and outrage: "You're a nigger!"

"Yes," she said. "James Beauchamp—you called him Tennie's Jim though he had a name—was my grandfather. I said you were Uncle Isaac."

"And he knows?"

"No," she said. "What good would that have done?"

"But you did," he cried. "But you did. Then what do you expect here?"

"Nothing."

"Then why did you come here? You said you were waiting in Aluschaskuna yesterday and he saw you. Why did you come this morning?"

"I'm going back North. Back home. My cousin brought me up the day before yesterday in his boat. He's going to take me on to Leland to get the train."

"Then go," he said. Then he cried again in that thin not loud and grieving voice: "Get out of here! I can do nothing for you! Can't nobody do nothing for you!" She moved; she was not looking at him again, toward the entrance. "Wait," he said. She paused again, obediently still, turning. He took up the sheaf of banknotes and laid it on the blanket at the foot of the cot and drew his hand back beneath the blanket. "There," he said.

Now she looked at the money, for the first time, one brief blank glance, then away again. "I don't need it. He gave me money last winter. Besides the money he sent to Vicksburg. Provided. Honor and code too. That was all arranged."

"Take it," he said. His voice began to rise again, but he stopped it. "Take it out of my tent." She came back to the cot and took up the money; whereupon once more he said, "Wait:" although she had not turned, still stooping, and he put out his hand. But, sitting, he could not complete the reach until she moved her hand, the single hand which held the money, until he touched it. He didn't grasp it, he merely touched it—the gnarled, bloodless, bone-light, bone-dry old man's fingers touching for a second the smooth young flesh where the strong old blood ran after its long lost journey back to home. "Tennie's Jim," he said. "Tennie's Jim." He drew the hand back beneath the blanket again: he said harshly now: "It's a boy, I reckon. They usually are, except that one that was its own mother too."

"Yes," she said. "It's a boy." She stood for a moment longer, looking at him. Just for an instant her free hand moved as though she were about to lift the edge of the raincoat away from the child's face. But she did not. She turned again when once more he said Wait and moved beneath the blanket.

"Turn your back," he said. "I am going to get up. I ain't got my pants on." Then he could not get up. He sat in the huddled blanket, shaking, while again she turned and looked down at him in dark interrogation. "There," he said harshly, in the thin and shaking old man's voice. "On the nail there. The tent-pole."

"What?" she said.

"The horn!" he said harshly. "The horn." She went and got it, thrust the money into the slicker's side pocket as if it were a rag, a soiled handkerchief, and lifted down the horn, the one which General Compson had left him in his will, covered with the unbroken skin from a buck's shank and bound with silver.

"What?" she said.

"It's his. Take it."

"Oh," she said. "Yes. Thank you."

"Yes," he said, harshly, rapidly, but not so harsh now and soon not harsh at all but just rapid, urgent, until he knew that his voice was running away with him and he had neither intended it nor could stop it: "That's right. Go back North. Marry: a man in your own race. That's the only salvation for you—for a while yet, maybe a long while yet. We will have to wait. Marry a black man. You are young, handsome, almost white; you could find a black man who would see in you what it was you saw in him, who would ask nothing of you and expect less and get even still less than that, if it's revenge you want. Then you will forget all this, forget it ever happened, that he ever existed—" until he could stop it at last and did, sitting there in his huddle of blankets during the instant when, without moving at all, she blazed silently down at him. Then that was gone too. She stood in the gleaming and still dripping slicker, looking quietly down at him from under the sodden hat.

"Old man," she said, "have you lived so long and forgotten so much that you don't remember anything you ever knew or felt or even heard about love?"

Then she was gone too. The waft of light and the murmur of the constant rain flowed into the tent and then out again as the flap fell. Lying back once more, trembling, panting, the blanket huddled to his chin and his hands crossed on his breast, he listened to the pop and snarl, the mounting then fading whine of the motor until it died away and once again the tent held only silence and the sound of rain. And cold too: he lay shaking faintly and steadily in it, rigid save for the shaking. This Delta, he thought: This Delta. *This land which man has deswamped and denuded and derivered in two generations so that white men can own plantations and commute every night to Memphis and black men own plantations and ride in Jim Crow cars to Chicago to live in millionaires' mansions on Lake Shore Drive; where white men rent farms and live like niggers and niggers crop on shares and live like animals; where cotton is planted and grows man-tall in the very cracks of the sidewalks, and usuary and mortgage and bankruptcy and measureless wealth, Chinese and African and Aryan and Jew, all breed and spawn together until no man has time to say which one is which nor cares. . . .* No wonder the ruined woods I used to know don't cry for retribution! he thought: The people who have destroyed it will accomplish its revenge.

The tent flap jerked rapidly in and fell. He did not move save to turn his head and open his eyes. It was Legate. He went quickly to Edmonds' bed and stooped, rummaging hurriedly among the still-tumbled blankets.

"What is it?" he said.

"Looking for Roth's knife," Legate said. "I come back to get a horse. We got a deer on the ground." He rose, the knife in his hand, and hurried toward the entrance.

"Who killed it?" McCaslin said. "Was it Roth?"

"Yes," Legate said, raising the flap.

"Wait," McCaslin said. He moved, suddenly, onto his elbow. "What was it?" Legate paused for an instant beneath the lifted flap. He did not look back.

"Just a deer, Uncle Ike," he said impatiently. "Nothing extra." He was gone; again the flap fell behind him, wafting out of the tent again the faint light and the constant and grieving rain. McCaslin lay back down, the blanket once more drawn to his chin, his crossed hands once more weightless on his breast in the empty tent.

"It was a doe," he said.

Langston Hughes (1902–1967)

Langston Hughes was born in Joplin, Missouri, to a family with a history of political activism. His grandfather was the first African American to hold local public office. From an early age, Hughes displayed a talent for writing, but he decided (partly at his father's urging) to pursue engineering at Columbia University, hoping to build a more lucrative career. His interest in engineering didn't last, however, and he dropped out of college. He later received his degree from Lincoln University in Pennsylvania. Hughes's interest in writing remained a constant, and he began publishing his workings at a young age in the auspicious magazines Crisis, Opportunity, *and* The Nation. *Political and racial concerns were the frequent and compelling subjects of his writing, which included fiction, nonfiction, drama, and poetry.*

His political astuteness and literary talent thrust him to the forefront of the Harlem Renaissance, which allowed Hughes to work with some of the leading artists and intellectuals of his time. Hughes was a world traveler and a global thinker, and the recipient of an honorary doctorate and Guggenheim and Rosenwald fellowships. While his expository work and activism were responsible for much social change, his creative writing is an equally important legacy. Hughes has a concise yet descriptive style that utilizes the natural landscape as a symbol of the shared and mythic history of humankind.

Hughes wrote two autobiographical volumes, the first of which, The Big Sea, *was published in 1940. His literary works include* The Weary Blues *(1926),* The Dream Keeper *(1932),* Shakespeare in Harlem *(1942),* The First Book of Jazz *(1955), and* Selected Poems *(1959). Hughes also empowered other African American poets by editing several anthologies of African American writing. Hughes died of cancer in 1967.*

The Negro Speaks of Rivers

I've known rivers:
I've known rivers ancient as the world and older than the flow of human
    blood in human veins.

My soul has grown deep like the rivers.

I bathed in the Euphrates when dawns were young.
I built my hut near the Congo and it lulled me to sleep.   5
I looked upon the Nile and raised the pyramids above it.
I heard the singing of the Mississippi when Abe Lincoln went down to
    New Orleans, and I've seen its muddy bosom turn all golden in the
    sunset.

I've known rivers:
Ancient, dusky rivers.

My soul has grown deep like the rivers.   10

Sun Song

Sun and softness,
Sun and the beaten hardness of the earth,
Sun and the song of all the sun-stars
Gathered together—
Dark ones of Africa,   5
I bring you my songs
To sing on the Georgia roads.

Long Trip

The sea is a wilderness of waves,
A desert of water.
We dip and dive,
Rise and roll,
Hide and are hidden   5
On the sea.
    Day, night,
    Night, day,
The sea is a desert of waves,
A wilderness of water.   10

Fulfilment

The earth-meaning
Like the sky-meaning
Was fulfilled.

We got up
And went to the river,   5
Touched silver water,
Laughed and bathed
In the sunshine.

Day
Became a bright ball of light   10
For us to play with,
Sunset
A yellow curtain,
Night
A velvet screen.   15

The moon,
Like an old grandmother,
Blessed us with a kiss
And sleep
Took us both in   20
Laughing.

John Steinbeck (1902–1968)

The works of John Steinbeck are the products not only of his genius but also his personal experience. Born in Salinas, California, in 1902, he was from early childhood in love with nature. He also learned to love reading, particularly the works of Dostoyevsky, George Eliot, and John Milton. Perhaps most important, Steinbeck cultivated lifelong acquaintances with those about whom he wrote, from the paisanos of Pacific Grove, California, to the migrant workers from Oklahoma. He studied at Stanford University but never completed his degree, and then worked a variety of odd jobs before settling into a career as a novelist in the early 1930s. He spent the next few decades in California and New York and traveling extensively. Tortilla Flat *was published in 1935,* Of Mice and Men *in 1937, his collection of stories* The Long Valley *in 1938, and* The Grapes of Wrath *in 1939. During World War II, Steinbeck spent time as a correspondent in Italy and Northern Africa. He published* Cannery Row *in 1945,* East of Eden *in 1952, and, in 1957,* The Short Reign of Pippin IV. *Steinbeck was awarded the Nobel Prize in Literature in 1962. He continued to write until his death at Sag Harbor, New York, in 1968.*

Nature in Steinbeck's writing is not merely a scenic backdrop to the predominantly social themes of his work; on the contrary, his treatment of nature helps to elevate his work from working-class radicalism to a profound expression of human place in the world. Steinbeck depicts nature as both alien and sublime, and in this world human beings must cower beneath the hostile sun or unfriendly rain. Steinbeck's scenes of ants crawling through yards or of sunlight warping porches remind us at first that time is relentless and indifferent. But a more careful reading of Steinbeck's nature writing will reveal a surprising optimism and a tacit Marxist aesthetic of social realism. Steinbeck shows us how to find human fellowship in sensuality, and he shows us how, as human beings, we are intimately linked with nature. Steinbeck convinces us that the world is beautiful, and in being so convinced, we experience that fellowship which is the most important theme of his work.

The chapter below is excerpted from a nonfiction work, The Log from the Sea of Cortez *(1951), in which Steinbeck recounts a research trip in the Gulf of California that he took with a marine biologist, Ed Ricketts, who was also a close friend. Steinbeck's reflections on the nature of science, and on the science of nature, bespeak his deep insight into the "great tide pool" that provides a living context for all human experience.*

From The Log from the Sea of Cortez

March 31

The tide was very poor this morning, only two and a half to three feet below the uppermost line of barnacles. We started about ten o'clock and had a little collecting under water, but soon the wind got up and so ruffled the surface that we could not see what we were doing. To a certain extent this was a good thing. Not being able to get into the low littoral, where no doubt the spectacular spiny lobsters would have distracted us, we were able to make a more detailed survey of the upper region. One fact increasingly emerged: the sulphury-green and black cucumber[1] is the most ubiquitous shore animal of the Gulf of California, with *Heliaster*, the sun-star, a close second. These two are found nearly everywhere. In this region at San Carlos, Sally Lightfoot lives highest above the ordinary high tide, together with a few *Ligyda occidentalis*, a cockroach-like crustacean. Attached to the rocks and cliffsides, high up and fully exposed to this deadly sun, were barnacles and limpets, so placed that they must experience only occasional immersion, although they may be often dampened by spray. Under rocks and boulders, in the next association lower down, were the mussel-like ruffled clams and the brown chitons, many cucumbers, a few *Heliasters*, and only two species of brittle-stars—another common species, *Ophiothrix spiculata*, we did not find here although we had seen it everywhere else. In this zone verrucose anemones were growing under overhangs on the sides of rocks and in pits in the rocks. There were also a few starfish;[2] garbanzo clams were attached to the rock undersides by the thousands together with club urchins. Farther down in a new zone was a profusion of sponges of a number of species, including a beautiful blue sponge. There were octopi[3] here, and one species of chiton; there were many large purple urchins, although no specimens were taken, and heart-urchins in the sand and between the rocks. There were some sipunculids and a great many tunicates.

We found extremely large sponges, a yellow form (probably *Cliona*) superficially resembling the Monterey *Lissodendoryx noxiosa*, and a white one, *Steletta*, of the wicked spines. There were brilliant-orange nudibranchs, giant terebellid worms, some shell-less air-breathing (pulmonate) snails, a ribbon-worm, and a number of solitary corals. These were the common animals and the ones in which we were most interested, for while we took rarities when we came upon them in normal observation, our interest lay in the large groups and their associations—the word "association" implying a biological assemblage, all the animals in a given habitat.

It would seem that the commensal idea is a very elastic thing and can be extended to include more than host and guest; that certain kinds of animals are often found together for a number of reasons. One, because they do not eat one another; two, because these different species thrive best under identical conditions of wave-shock and bottom; three, because they take the same kinds of food, or different aspects of the same kinds of food; four, because in some cases the armor or weapons of some are protection to the others (for instance, the sharp spines of an urchin may protect a tide-pool johnny from a larger preying fish); five, because some actual commensal partition of activities may truly occur. Thus the commensal tie may be loose or very tight and some associations may partake of a real thigmotropism.

Indeed, as one watches the little animals, definite words describing them are likely to grow hazy and less definite, and as species merges into species, the whole idea of definite independent species begins to waver, and a scale-like concept of animal variations comes to take its place. The whole taxonomic method

---

[1] *Holothuria lubrica.*

[2] *Astrometis sertulifera.*

[3] *Octopus bimaculatus.*

in biology is clumsy and unwieldy, shot through with the jokes of naturalists and the egos of men who wished to have animals named after them.

Originally the descriptive method of naming was not so bad, for every observer knew Latin and Greek well and was able to make out the descriptions. Such knowledge is fairly rare now and not even requisite. How much easier if the animals bore numbers to which the names were auxiliary! Then, one knowing that the phylum Arthropoda was represented by the roman figure *VI*, the class Crustacea by a capital *B*, order by arabic figure *13*, and genus and species by a combination of small letters, would with little training be able to place the animals in his mind much more quickly and surely than he can now with the descriptive method tugged bodily from a discarded antiquity.

As we ascended the Gulf it became more sparsely inhabited; there were fewer of the little heat-struck *rancherias*, fewer canoes of fishing Indians. Above Santa Rosalia very few trading boats travel. One would be really cut off up here. And yet here and there on the beaches we found evidences of large parties of fishermen. On one beach there were fifteen or twenty large sea-turtle shells and the charcoal of a bonfire where the meat had been cooked or smoked. In this same place we found also a small iron harpoon which had been lost, probably the most valued possession of the man who had lost it. These Indians do not seem to have firearms; probably the cost of them is beyond even crazy dreaming. We have heard that in some of the houses are the treasured weapons of other times, muskets, flintlocks, old long muzzle-loaders kept from generation to generation. And one man told us of finding a piece of Spanish armor, a breastplate, in an Indian house.

There is little change here in the Gulf. We think it would be very difficult to astonish these people. A tank or a horseman armed cap-a-pie would elicit the same response—a mild and dwindling interest. Food is hard to get, and a man lives inward, closely related to time; a cousin of the sun, at feud with storm and sickness. Our products, the mechanical toys which take up so much of our time, preoccupy and astonish us so, would be considered what they are, rather clever toys but not related to very real things. It would be interesting to try to explain to one of these Indians our tremendous projects, our great drives, the fantastic production of goods that can't be sold, the clutter of possessions which enslave whole populations with debt, the worry and neuroses that go into the rearing and educating of neurotic children who find no place for themselves in this complicated world; the defense of the country against a frantic nation of conquerors, and the necessity for becoming frantic to do it; the spoilage and wastage and death necessary for the retention of the crazy thing; the science which labors to acquire knowledge, and the movement of people and goods contrary to the knowledge obtained. How could one make an Indian understand the medicine which labors to save a syphilitic, and the gas and bomb to kill him when he is well, the armies which build health so that death will be more active and violent. It is quite possible that to an ignorant Indian these might not be evidences of a great civilization, but rather of inconceivable nonsense.

It is not implied that this fishing Indian lives a perfect or even a very good life. A toothache may be to him a terrible thing, and a stomachache may kill him. Often he is hungry, but he does not kill himself over things which do not closely concern him.

A number of times we were asked, Why do you do this thing, this picking up and pickling of little animals? To our own people we could have said any one of a number of meaningless things, which by sanction have been accepted as meaningful. We could have said, "We wish to fill in certain gaps in the knowledge of the Gulf fauna." That would have satisfied our people, for knowledge is a sacred thing, not to be questioned or even inspected. But the Indian might say, "What good is this knowledge? Since you make a duty of it, what is its purpose?" We could have told our people the usual thing about the advancement of science, and again we would not have been questioned further. But the Indian might ask, "Is it advancing, and toward what? Or is it merely becoming complicated? You save the lives of children for a world that does not love them. It is our practice," the Indian might say, "to build a house before we move into it. We would not want a child to escape pneumonia, only to be hurt all its life." The lies we tell about our duty and our purposes, the meaningless words of science and philosophy, are walls that topple before a bewildered little "why." Finally, we learned to know why we did these things. The animals were very beautiful. Here was life from which we borrowed life and excitement. In other words, we did these things because it was pleasant to do them.

We do not wish to intimate in any way that this hypothetical Indian is a noble savage who lives in logic. His magics and his techniques and his teleologies are just as full of nonsense as ours. But when two people, coming from different social, racial, intellectual patterns, meet and wish to communicate, they must do so on a logical basis. Clavigero discusses what seems to our people a filthy practice of some of the Lower California Indians. They were always hungry, always partly starved. When they had meat, which was a rare thing, they tied pieces of string to each mouthful, then ate it, pulled it up and ate it again and again, often passing it from hand to hand. Clavigero found this a disgusting practice. It is rather like the Chinese being ridiculed for eating twenty-year-old eggs who said, "Your cheese is rotten milk. You like rotten milk—we like rotten eggs. We are both silly."

*   *   *

Costume on the *Western Flyer* had degenerated completely. Shirts were no longer worn, but the big straw hats were necessary. On board we went barefoot, clad only in hats and trunks. It was easy then to jump over the side to freshen up. Our clothes never got dry; the salt deposited in the fibers made them hygroscopic, always drawing the humidity. We washed the dishes in hot salt water, so that little crystals stuck to the plates. It seemed to us that the little salt adhering to the coffee pot made the coffee delicious. We ate fish nearly every day: bonito, dolphin, sierra, red snappers. We made thousands of big fat biscuits, hot and unhealthful. Twice a week Sparky created his magnificent spaghetti. Unbelievable amounts of coffee were consumed. One of our party made some lemon pies, but the quarreling grew bitter over them; the thievery, the suspicion of favoritism, the vulgar traits of selfishness and perfidy those pies brought out saddened all of us. And when one of us who, from being the most learned should have been the most self-controlled, took to hiding pie in his bed and munching it secretly when the lights were out, we decided there must be no more lemon pie. Character was crumbling, and the law of the fang was too close to us.

One thing had impressed us deeply on this little voyage: the great world dropped away very quickly. We lost the fear and fierceness and contagion of war and economic uncertainty. The matters of great importance we had left were not important. There must be an infective quality in these things. We had lost the virus, or it had been eaten by the antibodies of quiet. Our pace had slowed greatly; the hundred thousand small reactions of our daily world were reduced to very few. When the boat was moving we sat by the hour watching the pale, burned mountains slip by. A playful swordfish, jumping and spinning, absorbed us completely. There was time to observe the tremendous minutiae of the sea. When a school of fish went by, the gulls followed closely. Then the water was littered with feathers and the scum of oil. These fish were much too large for the gulls to kill and eat, but there is much more to a school of fish than the fish themselves. There is constant vomiting; there are the hurt and weak and old to cut out; the smaller prey on which the school feeds sometimes escape and die; a moving school is like a moving camp, and it leaves a camp-like debris behind it on which the gulls feed. The sloughing skins coat the surface of the water with oil.

At six P.M. we made anchorage at San Francisquito Bay. This cove-like bay is about one mile wide and points to the north. In the southern part of the bay there is a pretty little cove with a narrow entrance between two rocky points. A beach of white sand edges this cove, and on the edge of the beach there was a poor Indian house, and in front of it a blue canoe. No one came out of the house. Perhaps the inhabitants were away or sick or dead. We did not go near; indeed, we had a strong feeling of intruding, a feeling sharp enough even to prevent us from collecting on that little inner bay. The country hereabouts was stony and barren, and even the brush had thinned out. We anchored in four fathoms of water on the westerly side of the bay, then went ashore immediately and set up our tide stake at the water's edge, with a bandanna on it so we could see it from the boat. The wind was blowing and the water was painfully cold. The tide had dropped two feet below the highest line of barnacles. Three types of crabs[4] were common here. There were many barnacles and great limpets and two species of snails, *Tegula* and a small *Purpura*. There were many large smooth brown chitons, and a few bristle-chitons. Farther down under the rocks were great anastomosing masses of a tube-worm with rusty red gills,[5] some tunicates, *Astrometis*, and the usual holothurians.

Tiny found the shell of a fine big lobster,[6] newly cleaned by isopods. The isopods and amphipods in their millions do a beautiful job. It is common to let them clean skeletons designed for study. A dead fish is placed in a jar having a cap pierced with holes just large enough to permit the entrance of the isopods.

[4] *Pachygrapsus crassipes, Geograpsus lividus*, and, under the rocks, *Petrolisthes nigrunguiculatus*, a porcelain crab.

[5] *Salmacina*.

[6] Apparently the northern *Panulirus interruptus*.

This is lowered to the bottom of a tide pool, and in a very short time the skeleton is clean of every particle of flesh, and yet is articulated and perfect.

The wind blew so and the water was so cold and ruffled that we did not stay ashore for very long. On board, we put down the baited bottom nets as usual to see what manner of creatures were crawling about there. When we pulled up one of the nets, it seemed to be very heavy. Hanging to the bottom of it on the outside was a large horned shark.[7] He was not caught, but had gripped the bait through the net with a bulldog hold and he would not let go. We lifted him unstruggling out of the water and up onto the deck, and still he would not let go. This was at about eight o'clock in the evening. Wishing to preserve him, we did not kill him, thinking he would die quickly. His eyes were barred, rather like goat's eyes. He did not struggle at all, but lay quietly on the deck, seeming to look at us with a baleful, hating eye. The horn, by the dorsal fin, was clean and white. At long intervals his gill-slits opened and closed but he did not move. He lay there all night, not moving, only opening his gill-slits at great intervals. The next morning he was still alive, but all over his body spots of blood had appeared. By this time Sparky and Tiny were horrified by him. Fish out of water should die, and he didn't die. His eyes were wide and for some reason had not dried out, and he seemed to regard us with hatred. And still at intervals his gill-slits opened and closed. His sluggish tenacity had begun to affect all of us by this time. He was a baleful personality on the boat, a sluggish, gray length of hatred, and the blood spots on him did not make him more pleasant. At noon we put him into the formaldehyde tank, and only then did he struggle for a moment before he died. He had been out of the water for sixteen or seventeen hours, had never fought or flopped a bit. The fast and delicate fishes like the tunas and mackerels waste their lives out in a complete and sudden flurry and die quickly. But about this shark there was a frightful quality of stolid, sluggish endurance. He had come aboard because he had grimly fastened on the bait and would not release it, and he lived because he would not release life. In some earlier time he might have been the basis for one of those horrible myths which abound in the spoken literature of the sea. He had a definite and terrible personality which bothered all of us, and, as with the sea-turtle, Tiny was shocked and sick that he did not die. This fish, and all the family of the Heterodontidae, ordinarily live in shallow, warm lagoons, and, although we do not know it, the thought occurred to us that sometimes, perhaps fairly often, these fish may be left stranded by a receding tide so that they may have developed the ability to live through until the flowing tide comes back. The very sluggishness in that case would be a conservation of vital energy, whereas the beautiful and fragile tuna make one frantic rush to escape, conserving nothing and dying immediately.

Within our own species we have great variation between these two reactions. One man may beat his life away in furious assault on the barrier, where another simply waits for the tide to pick him up. Such variation is also observable among the higher vertebrates, particularly among domestic animals. It would be strange if it were not also true of the lower vertebrates, among the individualistic ones anyway. A fish, like the tuna or the sardine, which lives in a school, would be less

---

[7] *Gyropleurodus* of the Heterodontidae.

likely to vary than this lonely horned shark, for the school would impose a discipline of speed and uniformity, and those individuals which would not or could not meet the school's requirements would be killed or lost or left behind. The overfast would be eliminated by the school as readily as the overslow, until a standard somewhere between the fast and slow had been attained. Not intending a pun, we might note that our schools have to some extent the same tendency. A Harvard man, a Yale man, a Stanford man—that is, the ideal—is as easily recognized as a tuna, and he has, by a process of elimination, survived the tests against idiocy and brilliance. Even in physical matters the standard is maintained until it is impossible, from speech, clothing, haircuts, posture, or state of mind, to tell one of these units of his school from another. In this connection it would be interesting to know whether the general collectivization of human society might not have the same effect. Factory mass production, for example, requires that every man conform to the tempo of the whole. The slow must be speeded up or eliminated, the fast slowed down. In a thoroughly collectivized state, mediocre efficiency might be very great, but only through the complete elimination of the swift, the clever, and the intelligent, as well as the incompetent. Truly collective man might in fact abandon his versatility. Among school animals there is little defense technique except headlong flight. Such species depend for survival chiefly on tremendous reproduction. The great loss of eggs and young to predators is the safety of the school, for it depends for its existence on the law of probability that out of a great many which start some will finish.

It is interesting and probably not at all important to note that when a human state is attempting collectivization, one of the first steps is a frantic call by the leaders for an increased birth rate—replacement parts in a shoddy and mediocre machine.

Our interest had been from the first in the common animals and their associations, and we had not looked for rarities. But it was becoming apparent that we were taking a number of new and unknown species. Actually, more than fifty species undescribed at the time of capture will have been taken. These will later have been examined, classified, described, and named by specialists. Some of them may not be determined for years, for it is one of the little by-products of the war that scientific men are cut off from one another. A Danish specialist in one field is unable to correspond with his colleague in California. Thus some of these new animals may not be named for a long time. We have listed in the Appendix those already specified and indicated in so far as possible those which have not been worked on by specialists.

Dr. Rolph Bolin, ichthyologist at the Hopkins Marine Station, found in our collection what we thought to be a new species of commensal fish which lives in the anus of a cucumber, flipping in and out, possibly feeding on the feces of the host but more likely merely hiding in the anus from possible enemies. This fish later turned out to be an already named species, but, carrying on the ancient and disreputable tradition of biologists, we had hoped to call it by the euphemistic name *Proctophilus winchellii*.

There are some marine biologists whose chief interest is in the rarity, the seldom seen and unnamed animal. These are often wealthy amateurs, some of whom have been suspected of wishing to tack their names on unsuspecting and unresponsive invertebrates. The passion for immortality at the expense of a little beast must be very great. Such collectors should to a certain extent be regarded as in the same class with those philatelists who achieve a great emotional stimulation from an unusual number of perforations or a misprinted stamp. The rare animal may be of individual interest, but he is unlikely to be of much consequence in any ecological picture. The common, known, multitudinous animals, the red pelagic lobsters which litter the sea, the hermit crabs in their billions, scavengers of the tide pools, would by their removal affect the entire region in widening circles. The disappearance of plankton, although the components are microscopic, would probably in a short time eliminate every living thing in the sea and change the whole of man's life, if it did not through a seismic disturbance of balance eliminate all life on the globe. For these little animals, in their incalculable numbers, are probably the base food supply of the world. But the extinction of one of the rare animals, so avidly sought and caught and named, would probably go unnoticed in the cellular world.

Our own interest lay in relationships of animal to animal. If one observes in this relational sense, it seems apparent that species are only commas in a sentence, that each species is at once the point and the base of a pyramid, that all life is relational to the point where an Einsteinian relativity seems to emerge. And then not only the meaning but the feeling about species grows misty. One merges into another, groups melt into ecological groups until the time when what we know as life meets and enters what we think of as nonlife: barnacle and rock, rock and earth, earth and tree, tree and rain and air. And the units nestle into the whole and are inseparable from it. Then one can come back to the microscope and the tide pool and the aquarium. But the little animals are found to be changed, no longer set apart and alone. And it is a strange thing that most of the feeling we call religious, most of the mystical outcrying which is one of the most prized and used and desired reactions of our species, is really the understanding and the attempt to say that man is related to the whole thing, related inextricably to all reality, known and unknowable. This is a simple thing to say, but the profound feeling of it made a Jesus, a St. Augustine, a St. Francis, a Roger Bacon, a Charles Darwin, and an Einstein. Each of them in his own tempo and with his own voice discovered and reaffirmed with astonishment the knowledge that all things are one thing and that one thing is all things—plankton, a shimmering phosphorescence on the sea and the spinning planets and an expanding universe, all bound together by the elastic string of time. It is advisable to look from the tide pool to the stars and then back to the tide pool again.

✎ *Rachel Carson* (1907–1964)

Born in Springfield, Pennsylvania, Rachel Carson received her B.A. from Johns Hopkins University. She spent much of her career as a specialist in commercial fisheries at the Marine Biological Laboratories in Woods Hole, Massachusetts. Carson wrote three best-selling books on marine biology: Under the Sea Wind *(1941),* The Sea Around Us

(1951), and The Edge of the Sea *(1954). In 1962 she published the most famous of her books,* Silent Spring, *a revolutionary text that asked its readers to question their own lifestyle and consumer choices, particularly their ever-increasing use of synthetic chemicals with unknown toxic side effects. A classic of science writing in its careful explanation of chemical and biological processes,* Silent Spring *is also a masterful commentary on the state of the environment, in which Carson forcefully denounces the poisoning of wildlife, the contamination of groundwater, and the hidden hazards to human health that have resulted from the indiscriminate use of dangerous pesticides.* Silent Spring *sparked the growth of the modern environmental movement as a political force to be reckoned with.*

The historical importance of Silent Spring *has tended to overshadow Carson's earlier books and the lyrical presentation of scientific ideas that makes them so rewarding.* The Edge of the Sea *is particularly compelling in its exploration of the "marginal world" that forms the boundary between sea and land. Such boundary regions, known as "ecotones," have unique importance in the study of ecology because they contain an extremely rich variety of species, each one adapted to a special niche, and because they are highly dynamic, offering ever-changing possibilities of discovery to the scientific observer.*

From The Edge of the Sea

The Marginal World

The edge of the sea is a strange and beautiful place. All through the long history of Earth it has been an area of unrest where waves have broken heavily against the land, where the tides have pressed forward over the continents, receded, and then returned. For no two successive days is the shore line precisely the same. Not only do the tides advance and retreat in their eternal rhythms, but the level of the sea itself is never at rest. It rises or falls as the glaciers melt or grow, as the floor of the deep ocean basins shifts under its increasing load of sediments, or as the earth's crust along the continental margins warps up or down in adjustment to strain and tension. Today a little more land may belong to the sea, tomorrow a little less. Always the edge of the sea remains an elusive and indefinable boundary.

The shore has a dual nature, changing with the swing of the tides, belonging now to the land, now to the sea. On the ebb tide it knows the harsh extremes of the land world, being exposed to heat and cold, to wind, to rain and drying sun. On the flood tide it is a water world, returning briefly to the relative stability of the open sea.

Only the most hardy and adaptable can survive in a region so mutable, yet the area between the tide lines is crowded with plants and animals. In this difficult world of the shore, life displays its enormous toughness and vitality by occupying almost every conceivable niche. Visibly, it carpets the intertidal rocks; or half hidden, it descends into fissures and crevices, or hides under boulders, or lurks in the wet gloom of sea caves. Invisibly, where the casual observer would say there is no life, it lies deep in the sand, in burrows and tubes and passageways. It tunnels into solid rock and bores into peat and clay. It encrusts weeds or drifting spars or the hard, chitinous shell of a lobster. It exists minutely, as the film of bacteria that spreads over a rock surface or a wharf piling; as spheres of protozoa, small as pinpricks, sparkling at the surface of the sea; and as Lilliputian beings swimming through dark pools that lie between the grains of sand.

The shore is an ancient world, for as long as there has been an earth and sea there has been this place of the meeting of land and water. Yet it is a world that keeps alive the sense of continuing creation and of the relentless drive of life. Each time that I enter it, I gain some new awareness of its beauty and its deeper meanings, sensing that intricate fabric of life by which one creature is linked with another, and each with its surroundings.

In my thoughts of the shore, one place stands apart for its revelation of exquisite beauty. It is a pool hidden within a cave that one can visit only rarely and briefly when the lowest of the year's low tides fall below it, and perhaps from that very fact it acquires some of its special beauty. Choosing such a tide, I hoped for a glimpse of the pool. The ebb was to fall early in the morning. I knew that if the wind held from the northwest and no interfering swell ran in from a distant storm the level of the sea should drop below the entrance to the pool. There had been sudden ominous showers in the night, with rain like handfuls of gravel flung on the roof. When I looked out into the early morning the sky was full of a gray dawn light but the sun had not yet risen. Water and air were pallid. Across the bay the moon was a luminous disc in the western sky, suspended above the dim line of distant shore—the full August moon, drawing the tide to the low, low levels of the threshold of the alien sea world. As I watched, a gull flew by, above the spruces. Its breast was rosy with the light of the unrisen sun. The day was, after all, to be fair.

Later, as I stood above the tide near the entrance to the pool, the promise of that rosy light was sustained. From the base of the steep wall of rock on which I stood, a moss-covered ledge jutted seaward into deep water. In the surge at the rim of the ledge the dark fronds of oarweeds swayed, smooth and gleaming as leather. The projecting ledge was the path to the small hidden cave and its pool. Occasionally a swell, stronger than the rest, rolled smoothly over the rim and broke in foam against the cliff. But the intervals between such swells were long enough to admit me to the ledge and long enough for a glimpse of that fairy pool, so seldom and so briefly exposed.

And so I knelt on the wet carpet of sea moss and looked back into the dark cavern that held the pool in a shallow basin. The floor of the cave was only a few inches below the roof, and a mirror had been created in which all that grew on the ceiling was reflected in the still water below.

Under water that was clear as glass the pool was carpeted with green sponge. Gray patches of sea squirts glistened on the ceiling and colonies of soft coral were a pale apricot color. In the moment when I looked into the cave a little elfin starfish hung down, suspended by the merest thread, perhaps by only a single tube foot. It reached down to touch its own reflection, so perfectly delineated that there might have been, not one starfish, but two. The beauty of the reflected images and of the limpid pool itself was the poignant beauty of things that are ephemeral, existing only until the sea should return to fill the little cave.

Whenever I go down into this magical zone of the low water of the spring tides, I look for the most delicately beautiful of all the shore's inhabitants—flowers that are not plant but animal, blooming on the threshold of the deeper sea. In that fairy cave I was not disappointed. Hanging from its roof were the pendent flowers of the hydroid Tubularia, pale pink, fringed and delicate as the wind flower. Here were creatures so exquisitely fashioned that they seemed unreal, their beauty too fragile to exist in a world of crushing force. Yet every detail was functionally useful, every stalk and hydranth and petal-like tentacle fashioned for dealing with the realities of existence. I knew that they were merely waiting, in that moment of the tide's ebbing, for the return of the sea. Then in the rush of water, in the surge of surf and the pressure of the incoming tide, the delicate flower heads would stir with life. They would sway on their slender stalks, and their long tentacles would sweep the returning water, finding in it all that they needed for life.

And so in that enchanted place on the threshold of the sea the realities that possessed my mind were far from those of the land world I had left an hour before. In a different way the same sense of remoteness and of a world apart came to me in a twilight hour on a great beach on the coast of Georgia. I had come down after sunset and walked far out over sands that lay wet and gleaming, to the very edge of the retreating sea. Looking back across that immense flat, crossed by winding, water-filled gullies and here and there holding shallow pools left by the tide, I was filled with awareness that this intertidal area, although abandoned briefly and rhythmically by the sea, is always reclaimed by the rising tide. There at the edge of low water the beach with its reminders of the land seemed far away. The only sounds were those of the wind and the sea and the birds. There was one sound of wind moving over water, and another of water sliding over the sand and tumbling down the faces of its own wave forms. The flats were astir with birds, and the voice of the willet rang insistently. One of them stood at the edge of the water and gave its loud, urgent cry; an answer came from far up the beach and the two birds flew to join each other.

The flats took on a mysterious quality as dusk approached and the last evening light was reflected from the scattered pools and creeks. Then birds became only dark shadows, with no color discernible. Sanderlings scurried across the beach like little ghosts, and here and there the darker forms of the willets stood out. Often I could come very close to them before they would start up in alarm—the sanderlings running, the willets flying up, crying. Black skimmers flew along the ocean's edge silhouetted against the dull, metallic gleam, or they went flitting above the sand like large, dimly seen moths. Sometimes they "skimmed" the winding creeks of tidal water, where little spreading surface ripples marked the presence of small fish.

The shore at night is a different world, in which the very darkness that hides the distractions of daylight brings into sharper focus the elemental realities. Once, exploring the night beach, I surprised a small ghost crab in the searching beam of my torch. He was lying in a pit he had dug just above the surf, as though watching the sea and waiting. The blackness of the night possessed water, air, and beach. It was the darkness of an older world, before Man. There was no sound but the all-enveloping, primeval sounds of wind blowing over water and land, and of waves crashing on the beach. There was no other visible life—just one small crab near the sea. I have seen hundreds of ghost crabs in other settings, but suddenly I was filled with the odd sensation that for the first time I knew the creature in its own world—that I understood, as never before, the essence of its being. In that moment time was suspended; the world to which I belonged did not exist and I might have been an onlooker from outer space. The little crab alone with the sea became a symbol that stood for life itself—for the delicate, destructible, yet incredibly vital force that somehow holds its place amid the harsh realities of the inorganic world.

The sense of creation comes with memories of a southern coast, where the sea and the mangroves, working together, are building a wilderness of thousands of small islands off the southwestern coast of Florida, separated from each other by a tortuous pattern of bays, lagoons, and narrow waterways. I remember a winter day when the sky was blue and drenched with sunlight; though there was no wind one was conscious of flowing air like cold clear crystal. I had landed on the surf-washed tip of one of those islands, and then worked my way around to the sheltered bay side. There I found the tide far out, exposing the broad mud flat of a cove bordered by the mangroves with their twisted branches, their glossy leaves, and their long prop roots reaching down, grasping and holding the mud, building the land out a little more, then again a little more.

The mud flats were strewn with the shells of that small, exquisitely colored mollusk, the rose tellin, looking like scattered petals of pink roses. There must have been a colony nearby, living buried just under the surface of the mud. At first the only creature visible was a small heron in gray and rusty plumage—a reddish egret that waded across the flat with the stealthy, hesitant movements of its kind. But other land creatures had been there, for a line of fresh tracks wound in and out among the mangrove roots, marking the path of a raccoon feeding on the oysters that gripped the supporting roots with projections from their shells. Soon I found the tracks of a shore bird, probably a sanderling, and followed them a little; then they turned toward the water and were lost, for the tide had erased them and made them as though they had never been.

Looking out over the cove I felt a strong sense of the interchangeability of land and sea in this marginal world of the shore, and of the links between the life of the two. There was also an awareness of the past and of the continuing flow of time, obliterating much that had gone before, as the sea had that morning washed away the tracks of the bird.

The sequence and meaning of the drift of time were quietly summarized in the existence of hundreds of small snails—the mangrove periwinkles—browsing on the branches and roots of the trees. Once their ancestors had been sea dwellers, bound to the salt waters by every tie of their life processes. Little by little over the thousands and millions of years the ties had been broken, the snails had adjusted themselves to life out of water, and now today they were living many feet above the tide to which they only occasionally returned. And perhaps, who could say how many ages hence, there would be in their descendants not even this gesture of remembrance for the sea.

The spiral shells of other snails—these quite minute—left winding tracks on the mud as they moved about in search of food. They were horn shells, and when I saw them I had a nostalgic moment when I wished I might see what

Audubon saw, a century and more ago. For such little horn shells were the food of the flamingo, once so numerous on this coast, and when I half closed my eyes I could almost imagine a flock of these magnificent flame birds feeding in that cove, filling it with their color. It was a mere yesterday in the life of the earth that they were there; in nature, time and space are relative matters, perhaps most truly perceived subjectively in occasional flashes of insight, sparked by such a magical hour and place.

There is a common thread that links these scenes and memories—the spectacle of life in all its varied manifestations as it has appeared, evolved, and sometimes died out. Underlying the beauty of the spectacle there is meaning and significance. It is the elusiveness of that meaning that haunts us, that sends us again and again into the natural world where the key to the riddle is hidden. It sends us back to the edge of the sea, where the drama of life played its first scene on earth and perhaps even its prelude; where the forces of evolution are at work today, as they have been since the appearance of what we know as life; and where the spectacle of living creatures faced by the cosmic realities of their world is crystal clear.

✍ Loren Eiseley (1907–1977)

Born "at the turn of the century when the frontier was fading," Loren Eiseley lived for most of his first twenty-six years in Lincoln, Nebraska. His father worked as a hardware salesman and spent many evenings as an amateur Shakespearian actor. His mother, an untaught painter, had lost her hearing in childhood and communicated by thumping on the floor. There was not much happiness in the household, and Eiseley was considered brilliant but moody by his parents, from whom he felt increasingly alienated. As a child, one of the most influential books he read was The Home Aquarium: How to Care for It, *which led him to his lifelong interest in nature writing. His enthusiasm for collecting fish for his aquarium nearly resulted in his death, when he fell through the ice during one trip to the pond.*

Eiseley took part in several archaeological expeditions while a student at the University of Nebraska, where he earned a B.A. in English and anthropology. He would later earn advanced degrees in anthropology from the University of Pennsylvania. In his writing, Eiseley often celebrates the "wild innocence" of the untamed: "Some lands are flat and grass covered and smile so evenly up at the sun that they seem forever youthful, untouched by wind or time . . . a sunlit, timeless prairie over which nothing passed but an antelope or a wandering bird." Eiseley's lyrical and sensitive nonfiction makes science and scientific information and theories accessible to a wide audience. His most famous book is The Immense Journey *(1946), a collection of essays that look at biology, paleontology, and a number of other scientific topics from a deeply humane point of view. The selection below demonstrates Eiseley's gift for putting facts in perspective and revealing the relevance of seemingly abstract or distant natural phenomena to the realm of common experience. His other books include* The Firmament of Time *(1960),* The Mind as Nature *(1962),* The Unexpected Universe *(1969),* The Invisible Pyramid

(1970), and The Night Country *(1971). Eiseley was also a widely published poet. His writing demonstrates a particular gift for depicting the passage of time, the evolution of living things, and the relationships among organisms. Eiseley's concern about the potentially detrimental impact of technology led him to a pessimistic outlook in his later years. As he writes in his essay "The Winter of Man":*

> We have come now in this time to fear the water that we drink, the air we breathe, the insecticides that we have dusted over our giant fruits. Because of the substances we have poured into our contaminated rivers, we fear the food that comes to us from the sea . . . we fear the awesome powers we have lifted out of nature and cannot return to her. We fear the weapons we have made, the hatreds we have engendered . . . we have come to fear even the scientists and their gifts . . . we fear the end of man.

The Bird and the Machine

I suppose their little bones have years ago been lost among the stones and winds of those high glacial pastures. I suppose their feathers blew eventually into the piles of tumbleweed beneath the straggling cattle fences and rotted there in the mountain snows, along with dead steers and all the other things that drift to an end in the corners of the wire. I do not quite know why I should be thinking of birds over the *New York Times* at breakfast, particularly the birds of my youth half a continent away. It is a funny thing what the brain will do with memories and how it will treasure them and finally bring them into odd juxtapositions with other things, as though it wanted to make a design, or get some meaning out of them, whether you want it or not, or even see it.

It used to seem marvelous to me, but I read now that there are machines that can do these things in a small way, machines that can crawl about like animals, and that it may not be long now until they do more things—maybe even make themselves—I saw that piece in the *Times* just now. And then they will, maybe—well, who knows—but you read about it more and more with no one making any protest, and already they can add better than we and reach up and hear things through the dark and finger the guns over the night sky.

This is the new world that I read about at breakfast. This is the world that confronts me in my biological books and journals, until there are times when I sit quietly in my chair and try to hear the little purr of the cogs in my head and the tubes flaring and dying as the messages go through them and the circuits snap shut or open. This is the great age, make no mistake about it; the robot has been born somewhat appropriately along with the atom bomb, and the brain they say now is just another type of more complicated feedback system. The engineers have its basic principles worked out; it's mechanical, you know; nothing to get superstitious about; and man can always improve on nature once he gets the idea. Well, he's got it all right and that's why, I guess, that I sit here in my chair, with the article crunched in my hand, remembering those two birds and that blue mountain sunlight. There is another magazine article on my desk that reads "Machines Are Getting Smarter Every Day." I don't deny it, but I'll still stick with the birds. It's life I believe in, not machines.

Maybe you don't believe there is any difference. A skeleton is all joints and pulleys, I'll admit. And when man was in his simpler stages of machine building in the eighteenth century, he quickly saw the resemblances. "What," wrote Hobbes, "is the heart but a spring, and the nerves but so many strings, and the joints but so many wheels, giving motion to the whole body?" Tinkering about in their shops it was inevitable in the end that men would see the world as a huge machine "subdivided into an infinite number of lesser machines."

The idea took on with a vengeance. Little automatons toured the country—dolls controlled by clockwork. Clocks described as little worlds were taken on tours by their designers. They were made up of moving figures, shifting scenes and other remarkable devices. The life of the cell was unknown. Man, whether he was conceived as possessing a soul or not, moved and jerked about like these tiny puppets. A human being thought of himself in terms of his own tools and implements. He had been fashioned like the puppets he produced and was only a more clever model made by a greater designer.

Then in the nineteenth century, the cell was discovered, and the single machine in its turn was found to be the product of millions of infinitesimal machines—the cells. Now, finally, the cell itself dissolves away into an abstract chemical machine—and that into some intangible, inexpressible flow of energy. The secret seems to lurk all about, the wheels get smaller and smaller, and they turn more rapidly, but when you try to seize it the life is gone—and so, by popular definition, some would say that life was never there in the first place. The wheels and the cogs are the secret and we can make them better in time—machines that will run faster and more accurately than real mice to real cheese.

I have no doubt it can be done, though a mouse harvesting seeds on an autumn thistle is to me a fine sight and more complicated, I think, in his multiform activity, than a machine "mouse" running a maze. Also, I like to think of the possible shape of the future brooding in mice, just as it brooded once in a rather ordinary mousy insectivore who became a man. It leaves a nice fine indeterminate sense of wonder that even an electronic brain hasn't got, because you know perfectly well that if the electronic brain changes, it will be because of something man has done to it. But what man will do to himself he doesn't really know. A certain scale of time and a ghostly intangible thing called change are ticking in him. Powers and potentialities like the oak in the seed, or a red and awful ruin. Either way, it's impressive; and the mouse has it, too. Or those birds, I'll never forget those birds—yet before I measured their significance, I learned the lesson of time first of all. I was young then and left alone in a great desert—part of an expedition that had scattered its men over several hundred miles in order to carry on research more effectively. I learned there that time is a series of planes existing superficially in the same universe. The tempo is a human illusion, a subjective clock ticking in our own kind of protoplasm.

As the long months passed, I began to live on the slower planes and to observe more readily what passed for life there. I sauntered, I passed more and more slowly up and down the canyons in the dry baking heat of midsummer. I slumbered for long hours in the shade of huge brown boulders that had gathered in tilted companies out on the flats. I had forgotten the world of men and the world had forgotten me. Now and then I found a skull in the canyons, and these justified my remaining there. I took a serene cold interest in these discoveries. I had come, like many a naturalist before me, to view life with a wary and subdued attention. I had grown to take pleasure in the divested bone.

I sat once on a high ridge that fell away before me into a waste of sand dunes. I sat through hours of a long afternoon. Finally, as I glanced beside my boot an indistinct configuration caught my eye. It was a coiled rattlesnake, a big one. How long he had sat with me I do not know. I had not frightened him. We were both locked in the sleep-walking tempo of the earlier world, baking in the same high air and sunshine. Perhaps he had been there when I came. He slept on as I left, his coils, so ill discerned by me, dissolving once more among the stones and gravel from which I had barely made him out.

Another time I got on a higher ridge, among some tough little wind-warped pines half covered over with sand in a basin-like depression that caught everything carried by the air up to those heights. There were a few thin bones of birds, some cracked shells of indeterminable age, and the knotty fingers of pine roots bulged out of shape from their long and agonizing grasp upon the crevices of the rock. I lay under the pines in the sparse shade and went to sleep once more.

It grew cold finally, for autumn was in the air by then, and the few things that lived thereabouts were sinking down into an even chillier scale of time. In the moments between sleeping and waking I saw the roots about me and slowly, slowly, a foot in what seemed many centuries, I moved my sleep-stiffened hands over the scaling bark and lifted my numbed face after the vanishing sun. I was a great awkward thing of knots and aching limbs, trapped up there in some long, patient endurance that involved the necessity of putting living fingers into rock and by slow, aching expansion bursting those rocks asunder. I suppose, so thin and slow was the time of my pulse by then, that I might have stayed on to drift still deeper into the lower cadences of the frost, or the crystalline life that glistens pebbles, or shines in a snowflake, or dreams in the meteoric iron between the worlds.

It was a dim descent, but time was present in it. Somewhere far down in that scale the notion struck me that one might come the other way. Not many months thereafter I joined some colleagues heading higher into a remote windy tableland where huge bones were reputed to protrude like boulders from the turf. I had drowsed with reptiles and moved with the century-long pulse of trees; now, lethargically, I was climbing back up some invisible ladder of quickening hours. There had been talk of birds in connection with my duties. Birds are intense, fast-living creatures—reptiles, I suppose one might say, that have escaped out of the heavy sleep of time, transformed fairy creatures dancing over sunlit meadows. It is a youthful fancy, no doubt, but because of something that happened up there among the escarpments of that range, it remains with me a lifelong impression. I can never bear to see a bird imprisoned.

We came into that valley through the trailing mists of a spring night. It was a place that looked as though it might never have known the foot of man, but our scouts had been ahead of us and we knew all about the abandoned cabin of stone that lay far up on one hillside. It had been built in the land rush of the last century and then lost to the cattlemen again as the marginal soils failed to take to the plow.

There were spots like this all over that country. Lost graves marked by unlettered stones and old corroding rim-fire cartridge cases lying where somebody had made a stand among the boulders that rimmed the valley. They are all that remain of the range wars; the men are under the stones now. I could see our cavalcade winding in and out through the mist below us: torches, the reflection of the truck lights on our collecting tins, and the far-off bumping of a loose dinosaur thigh bone in the bottom of a trailer. I stood on a rock a moment looking down and thinking what it cost in money and equipment to capture the past.

We had, in addition, instructions to lay hands on the present. The word had come through to get them alive—birds, reptiles, anything. A zoo somewhere abroad needed restocking. It was one of those reciprocal matters in which science involves itself. Maybe our museum needed a stray ostrich egg and this was the payoff. Anyhow, my job was to help capture some birds and that was why I was there before the trucks.

The cabin had not been occupied for years. We intended to clean it out and live in it, but there were holes in the roof and the birds had come in and were roosting in the rafters. You could depend on it in a place like this where everything blew away, and even a bird needed some place out of the weather and away from coyotes. A cabin going back to nature in a wild place draws them till they come in, listening at the eaves, I imagine, pecking softly among the shingles till they find a hole and then suddenly the place is theirs and man is forgotten.

Sometimes of late years I find myself thinking the most beautiful sight in the world might be the birds taking over New York after the last man has run away to the hills. I will never live to see it, of course, but I know just how it will sound because I've lived up high and I know the sort of watch birds keep on us. I've listened to sparrows tapping tentatively on the outside of air conditioners when they thought no one was listening, and I know how other birds test the vibrations that come up to them through the television aerials.

"Is he gone?" they ask, and the vibrations come up from below, "Not yet, not yet."

Well, to come back, I got the door open softly and I had the spotlight all ready to turn on and blind whatever birds there were so they couldn't see to get out through the roof. I had a short piece of ladder to put against the far wall where there was a shelf on which I expected to make the biggest haul. I had all the information I needed just like any skilled assassin. I pushed the door open, the hinges squeaking only a little. A bird or two stirred—I could hear them— but nothing flew and there was a faint starlight through the holes in the roof.

I padded across the floor, got the ladder up and the light ready, and slithered up the ladder till my head and arms were over the shelf. Everything was dark as pitch except for the starlight at the little place back of the shelf near the eaves. With the light to blind them, they'd never make it. I had them. I reached my arm carefully over in order to be ready to seize whatever was there and I put the flash on the edge of the shelf where it would stand by itself when I turned it on. That way I'd be able to use both hands.

Everything worked perfectly except for one detail—I didn't know what kind of birds were there. I never thought about it at all, and it wouldn't have mattered if I had. My orders were to get something interesting. I snapped on the flash and sure enough there was a great beating and feathers flying, but instead of my having them, they, or rather he, had me. He had my hand, that is, and for a small hawk not much bigger than my fist he was doing all right. I heard him give one short metallic cry when the light went on and my hand descended on the bird beside him; after that he was busy with his claws and his beak was sunk in my thumb. In the struggle I knocked the lamp over on the shelf, and his mate got her sight back and whisked neatly through the hole in the roof and off among the stars outside. It all happened in fifteen seconds and you might think I would have fallen down the ladder, but no, I had a professional assassin's reputation to keep up, and the bird, of course, made the mistake of thinking the hand was the enemy and not the eyes behind it. He chewed my thumb up pretty effectively and lacerated my hand with his claws, but in the end I got him, having two hands to work with.

He was a sparrow hawk and a fine young male in the prime of life. I was sorry not to catch the pair of them, but as I dripped blood and folded his wings carefully, holding him by the back so that he couldn't strike again, I had to admit the two of them might have been more than I could have handled under the circumstances. The little fellow had saved his mate by diverting me, and that was that. He was born to it, and made no outcry now, resting in my hand hopelessly, but peering toward me in the shadows behind the lamp with a fierce, almost indifferent glance. He neither gave nor expected mercy and something out of the high air passed from him to me, stirring a faint embarrassment.

I quit looking into that eye and managed to get my huge carcass with its fist full of prey back down the ladder. I put the bird in a box too small to allow him to injure himself by struggle and walked out to welcome the arriving trucks. It had been a long day, and camp still to make in the darkness. In the morning that bird would be just another episode. He would go back with the bones in the truck to a small cage in a city where he would spend the rest of his life. And a good thing, too. I sucked my aching thumb and spat out some blood. An assassin has to get used to these things. I had a professional reputation to keep up.

In the morning, with the change that comes on suddenly in that high country, the mist that had hovered below us in the valley was gone. The sky was a deep blue, and one could see for miles over the high outcroppings of stone. I was up early and brought the box in which the little hawk was imprisoned out onto the grass where I was building a cage. A wind as cool as a mountain spring ran over the grass and stirred my hair. It was a fine day to be alive. I looked up and all around and at the hole in the cabin roof out of which the other little hawk had fled. There was no sign of her anywhere that I could see.

"Probably in the next county by now," I thought cynically, but before beginning work I decided I'd have a look at my last night's capture.

Secretively, I looked again all around the camp and up and down and opened the box. I got him right out in my hand with his wings folded properly and I was careful not to startle him. He lay limp in my grasp and I could feel his heart pound under the feathers but he only looked beyond me and up.

I saw him look that last look away beyond me into a sky so full of light that I could not follow his gaze. The little breeze flowed over me again, and nearby a mountain aspen shook all its tiny leaves. I suppose I must have had an idea then of what I was going to do, but I never let it come up into consciousness. I just reached over and laid the hawk on the grass.

He lay there a long minute without hope, unmoving, his eyes still fixed on that blue vault above him. It must have been that he was already so far away in heart that he never felt the release from my hand. He never even stood. He just lay with his breast against the grass.

In the next second after that long minute he was gone. Like a flicker of light, he had vanished with my eyes full on him, but without actually seeing even a premonitory wing beat. He was gone straight into that towering emptiness of light and crystal that my eyes could scarcely bear to penetrate. For another long moment there was silence. I could not see him. The light was too intense. Then from far up somewhere a cry came ringing down.

I was young then and had seen little of the world, but when I heard that cry my heart turned over. It was not the cry of the hawk I had captured; for, by shifting my position against the sun, I was now seeing further up. Straight out of the sun's eye, where she must have been soaring restlessly above us for untold hours, hurtled his mate. And from far up, ringing from peak to peak of the summits over us, came a cry of such unutterable and ecstatic joy that it sounds down across the years and tingles among the cups on my quiet breakfast table.

I saw them both now. He was rising fast to meet her. They met in a great soaring gyre that turned to a whirling circle and a dance of wings. Once more, just once, their two voices, joined in a harsh wild medley of question and response, struck and echoed against the pinnacles of the valley. Then they were gone forever somewhere into those upper regions beyond the eyes of men.

I am older now, and sleep less, and have seen most of what there is to see and am not very much impressed any more, I suppose, by anything. "What Next in the Attributes of Machines?" my morning headline runs. "It Might Be the Power to Reproduce Themselves."

I lay the paper down and across my mind a phrase floats insinuatingly: "It does not seem that there is anything in the construction, constituents, or behavior of the human being which it is essentially impossible for science to duplicate and synthesize. On the other hand . . ."

All over the city the cogs in the hard, bright mechanisms have begun to turn. Figures move through computers, names are spelled out, a thoughtful machine selects the fingerprints of a wanted criminal from an array of thousands. In the laboratory an electronic mouse runs swiftly through a maze toward the cheese it can neither taste nor enjoy. On the second run it does better than a living mouse.

"On the other hand . . ." Ah, my mind takes up, on the other hand the machine does not bleed, ache, hang for hours in the empty sky in a torment of hope to learn the fate of another machine, nor does it cry out with joy nor dance in the air with the fierce passion of a bird. Far off, over a distance greater than space, that remote cry from the heart of heaven makes a faint buzzing among my breakfast dishes and passes on and away.

✍ *Theodore Roethke* (1908–1963)

Born in Saginaw, Michigan, Theodore Roethke grew up in the world of nature. His father and uncle owned the largest greenhouse in North America—twenty-two acres under glass. He attended the University of Michigan and, briefly, Harvard. His first book, Open House *(1941), was well received by critics, who praised its chiseled lyrics and expressive irony. But at the prompting of his friend, literary critic Kenneth Burke, his next book,* The Lost Son *(1948), marked a change of direction, presenting the fierce sensuality of his father's greenhouse world in language that veers from high to low, from intellectual to primal, from deeply philosophical musings to baby talk. In 1954 he won a Pulitzer Prize for* The Waking *(1953). Over the course of his life, he received the Bollingen Prize, a Guggenheim fellowship, and the National Book Award (twice). He taught at Lafayette College, Michigan State University, Pennsylvania State University, Bennington College, and the University of Washington.*

Roethke's enduring subject is the essential mystery of the natural world, which he depicts in poetry that moves from tightly constructed formal verse to no-holds-barred free verse, relying heavily on preconscious imagery, rhythms, and sounds. His best work is highly realistic and sensual, with touches of surrealism. For Roethke, the writing of poetry was a dangerous journey—"the journey from I to otherwise"—through which what is at stake is nothing less than the poet's soul. An admirer of Wordsworth (the title of his collection Praise to the End! *(1951) is drawn from* The Prelude*), Roethke felt that nature is both a reflection of and a window upon the elemental forces of life. The poet also saw his lifelong battle with manic-depression as part of the fierce struggle to construct the self. A "poet's poet," Roethke was a mentor to a rich variety of contemporary poets of note, including Richard Hugo, Carolyn Kizer, David Wagoner, and James Wright.*

"Long Live the Weeds"

Hopkins

Long live the weeds that overwhelm
My narrow vegetable realm!
The bitter rock, the barren soil
That force the son of man to toil;
All things unholy, marred by curse,   5
The ugly of the universe.
The rough, the wicked, and the wild
That keep the spirit undefiled.

With these I match my little wit
And earn the right to stand or sit,   10
Hope, love, create, or drink and die:
These shape the creature that is I.

Cuttings

Sticks-in-a-drowse droop over sugary loam,
Their intricate stem-fur dries;
But still the delicate slips keep coaxing up water;
The small cells bulge;

One nub of growth   5
Nudges a sand-crumb loose,
Pokes through a musty sheath
Its pale tendrilous horn.

Cuttings

(later)

This urge, wrestle, resurrection of dry sticks,
Cut stems struggling to put down feet,
What saint strained so much,
Rose on such lopped limbs to a new life?

I can hear, underground, that sucking and sobbing,   5
In my veins, in my bones I feel it,—
The small waters seeping upward,
The tight grains parting at last.
When sprouts break out,
Slippery as fish,   10
I quail, lean to beginnings, sheath-wet.

Root Cellar

Nothing would sleep in that cellar, dank as a ditch,
Bulbs broke out of boxes hunting for chinks in the dark,
Shoots dangled and drooped,
Lolling obscenely from mildewed crates,
Hung down long yellow evil necks, like tropical snakes.   5
And what a congress of stinks!—

Roots ripe as old bait,
Pulpy stems, rank, silo-rich,
Leaf-mold, manure, lime, piled against slippery planks.
Nothing would give up life: 10
Even the dirt kept breathing a small breath.

Moss-Gathering

To loosen with all ten fingers held wide and limber
And lift up a patch, dark-green, the kind for lining cemetery baskets,
Thick and cushiony, like an old-fashioned doormat,
The crumbling small hollow sticks on the underside mixed with roots,
And wintergreen berries and leaves still stuck to the top,—   5
That was moss-gathering.
But something always went out of me when I dug loose those carpets
Of green, or plunged to my elbows in the spongy yellowish moss of the marshes:
And afterwards I always felt mean, jogging back over the logging road,
As if I had broken the natural order of things in that swampland;   10
Disturbed some rhythm, old and of vast importance,
By pulling off flesh from the living planet;
As if I had committed, against the whole scheme of life, a desecration.

The Minimal

I study the lives on a leaf: the little
Sleepers, numb nudgers in cold dimensions,
Beetles in caves, newts, stone-deaf fishes,
Lice tethered to long limp subterranean weeds,
Squirmers in bogs,   5
And bacterial creepers
Wriggling through wounds
Like elvers in ponds,
Their wan mouths kissing the warm sutures,
Cleaning and caressing,   10
Creeping and healing.

Slug

How I loved one like you when I was little!—
With his stripes of silver and his small house on his back,
Making a slow journey around the well-curb.

I longed to be like him, and was,
In my way, close cousin   5
To the dirt, my knees scrubbing
The gravel, my nose wetter than his.

When I slip, just slightly, in the dark,
I know it isn't a wet leaf,
But you, loose toe from the old life,   10
The cold slime come into being,
A fat, five-inch appendage
Creeping slowly over the wet grass,
Eating the heart out of my garden.

And you refuse to die decently!—   15
Flying upward through the knives of my lawnmower
Like pieces of smoked eel or raw oyster,
And I go faster in my rage to get done with it,
Until I'm scraping and scratching at you, on the doormat,
The small dead pieces sticking under an instep;   20
Or, poisoned, dragging a white skein of spittle over a path—
Beautiful, in its way, like quicksilver—
You shrink to something less,
A rain-drenched fly or spider.

I'm sure I've been a toad, one time or another.   25
With bats, weasels, worms—I rejoice in the kinship.
Even the caterpillar I can love, and the various vermin.
But as for you, most odious—
Would Blake call you holy?

≈ *Wallace Stegner* (*1909–1993*)

Born in Lake Mills, Iowa, Wallace Stegner would become one of the country's most enduring writers of fiction and nonfiction. Stegner was raised all over the West, in Utah, North Dakota, Washington, Montana, Wyoming, and the plains of Saskatchewan, in Canada, the setting for two of his most highly regarded novels, The Big Rock Candy Mountain *and* Wolf Willow. *In the latter work, he describes life in a place that some would describe as desolate and forbidding: "There was never a country that in its good moments was more beautiful. Even in drouth or dust storm or blizzard it is the reverse of monotonous, once you have submitted to it with all the senses. You don't get out of the wind, but learn to lean and squint against it. You don't escape sky and sun, but wear them in your eyeballs and on your back. You become acutely aware of yourself."*

Stegner graduated from the University of Utah in 1930, attended the University of Iowa for his graduate degrees, and then held academic posts at the University of Utah, the University of Wisconsin-Madison, and Harvard University. He later became a pro-

fessor of English at Stanford University, where he taught for twenty-six years. Believing that "talent can't be taught, but it can be awakened," Stegner founded the Stanford Creative Writing Program in 1946 and over the years had a major influence on a wide variety of contemporary American writers, including Robert Stone, Larry McMurtry, Tillie Olsen, Thomas McGuane, Ernest Gaines, Raymond Carver, Ken Kesey, Edward Abbey, Wendell Berry, and many others. In addition to a vigorous schedule of writing and teaching, Stegner became a relentless supporter of the conservation movement in the 1950s, when he began to speak out against the construction of the Green River Dam at Dinosaur National Monument. This led to his appointment as assistant to the Secretary of the Interior during the Kennedy administration. His Wilderness Letter *(1960), a work on the need to protect wild places, was used to introduce the federal bill that established the National Wilderness Preservation System. In 1992, troubled by the attack on the National Endowment for the Arts, he turned down the National Medal for the Arts. Stegner died at the age of 84 from injuries suffered in an auto accident in Santa Fe, New Mexico. In addition to his many achievements as a writer and teacher, he will be remembered most for his affecting writing about the American West. Writer Edward Abbey once described Stegner as "the only living American writer worthy of the Nobel."*

Stegner's thirty books, written over a long career, include the novels The Big Rock Candy Mountain *(1943),* Joe Hill *(1950),* All the Little Live Things *(1967),* Angle of Repose *(1972),* The Spectator Bird *(1977), and* Recapitulation *(1979) as well as short fiction* Crossing to Safety *(1987) and* Collected Stories *(1990). His nonfiction includes* Beyond the Hundredth Meridian *(1954),* Wolf Willow *(1962),* The Sound of Mountain Water *(1969), and* Where the Bluebird Sings to the Lemonade Springs: Living and Writing in the West *(1992). His awards include the National Book Award, the Guggenheim Memorial Fellowship (twice), the National Endowment for the Humanities Senior Fellowship, and a Pulitzer Prize.*

The Colt

It was the swift coming of spring that let things happen. It was spring, and the opening of the roads, that took his father out of town. It was spring that clogged the river with floodwater and ice pans, sent the dogs racing in wild aimless packs, ripped the railroad bridge out and scattered it down the river for exuberant townspeople to fish out piecemeal. It was spring that drove the whole town to the riverbank with pikepoles and coffeepots and boxes of sandwiches for an impromptu picnic, lifting their sober responsibilities out of them and making them whoop blessings on the Canadian Pacific Railway for a winter's firewood. Nothing might have gone wrong except for the coming of spring. Some of the neighbors might have noticed and let them know; Bruce might not have forgotten; his mother might have remembered and sent him out again after dark.

But the spring came, and the ice went out, and that night Bruce went to bed drunk and exhausted with excitement. In the restless sleep just before waking he dreamed of wolves and wild hunts, but when he awoke finally he realized that he had not been dreaming the noise. The window, wide open for the first time in months, let in a shivery draught of fresh, damp air, and he heard the faint yelping far down in the bend of the river.

He dressed and went downstairs, crowding his bottom into the warm oven, not because he was cold but because it had been a ritual for so long that not even the sight of the sun outside could convince him it wasn't necessary. The dogs were still yapping; he heard them through the open door.

"What's the matter with all the pooches?" he said. "Where's Spot?"

"He's out with them," his mother said. "They've probably got a porcupine treed. Dogs go crazy in the spring."

"It's dog days they go crazy."

"They go crazy in the spring, too." She hummed a little as she set the table. "You'd better go feed the horses. Breakfast won't be for ten minutes. And see if Daisy is all right."

Bruce stood perfectly still in the middle of the kitchen. "Oh my gosh!" he said. "I left Daisy picketed out all night!"

His mother's head jerked around. "Where?"

"Down in the bend."

"Where those dogs are?"

"Yes," he said, sick and afraid. "Maybe she's had her colt."

"She shouldn't for two or three days," his mother said. But just looking at her, he knew that it might be bad, that there was something to be afraid of. In another moment they were out the door, running.

But it couldn't be Daisy they were barking at, he thought as he raced around Chance's barn. He'd picketed her higher up, not clear down in the U where the dogs were. His eyes swept the brown, wet, close-cropped meadow, the edge of the brush where the river ran close under the north bench. The mare wasn't there! He opened his mouth and half turned, running, to shout at his mother coming behind him, and then sprinted for the deep curve of the bend.

As soon as he rounded the little clump of brush that fringed the cutbank behind Chance's he saw them. The mare stood planted, a bay spot against the gray brush, and in front of her, on the ground, was another smaller spot. Six or eight dogs were leaping around, barking, sitting. Even at that distance he recognized Spot and the Chapmans' Airedale.

He shouted and pumped on. At a gravelly patch he stooped and clawed and straightened, still running, with a handful of pebbles. In one pausing, straddling, aiming motion he let fly a rock at the distant pack. It fell far short, but they turned their heads, sat on their haunches, and let out defiant short barks. Their tongues lolled as if they had run far.

Bruce yelled and threw again, one eye on the dogs and the other on the chestnut colt in front of the mare's feet. The mare's ears were back, and as he ran Bruce saw the colt's head bob up and down. It was all right then. The colt was alive. He slowed and came up quietly. Never move fast or speak loud around an animal, Pa said.

The colt struggled again, raised its head with white eyeballs rolling, spraddled its white-stockinged legs and tried to stand. "Easy, boy," Bruce said. "Take it easy, old fella." His mother arrived, getting her breath, her hair half down, and he turned to her gleefully. "It's all right, Ma. They didn't hurt anything. Isn't he a beauty, Ma?"

He stroked Daisy's nose. She was heaving, her ears pricking forward and back; her flanks were lathered, and she trembled. Patting her gently, he watched the colt, sitting now like a dog on its haunches, and his happiness that nothing had really been hurt bubbled out of him. "Lookit, Ma," he said. "He's got four white socks. Can I call him Socks, Ma? He sure is a nice colt, isn't he? Aren't you, Socks, old boy?" He reached down to touch the chestnut's forelock, and the colt struggled, pulling away.

Then Bruce saw his mother's face. It was quiet, too quiet. She hadn't answered a word to all his jabber. Instead she knelt down, about ten feet from the squatting colt, and stared at it. The boy's eyes followed hers. There was something funny about . . .

"Ma!" he said. "What's the matter with its front feet?"

He left Daisy's head and came around, staring. The colt's pasterns looked bent—*were* bent, so that they flattened clear to the ground under its weight. Frightened by Bruce's movement, the chestnut flopped and floundered to its feet, pressing close to its mother. And it walked, Bruce saw, flat on its fetlocks, its hooves sticking out in front like a movie comedian's too-large shoes.

Bruce's mother pressed her lips together, shaking her head. She moved so gently that she got her hand on the colt's poll, and he bobbed against the pleasant scratching. "You poor broken-legged thing," she said with tears in her eyes. "You poor little friendly ruined thing!"

Still quietly, she turned toward the dogs, and for the first time in his life Bruce heard her curse. Quietly, almost in a whisper, she cursed them as they sat with hanging tongues just out of reach. "God damn you," she said. "God damn your wild hearts, chasing a mother and a poor little colt."

To Bruce, standing with trembling lip, she said, "Go get Jim Enich. Tell him to bring a wagon. And don't cry. It's not your fault."

His mouth tightened, a sob jerked in his chest. He bit his lip and drew his face down tight to keep from crying, but his eyes filled and ran over.

"It is too my fault!" he said, and turned and ran.

Later, as they came in the wagon up along the cutbank, the colt tied down in the wagon box with his head sometimes lifting, sometimes bumping on the boards, the mare trotting after with chuckling vibrations of solicitude in her throat, Bruce leaned far over and tried to touch the colt's haunch. "Gee whiz!" he said. "Poor old Socks."

His mother's arm was around him, keeping him from leaning over too far. He didn't watch where they were until he heard his mother say in surprise and relief, "Why, there's Pa!"

Instantly he was terrified. He had forgotten and left Daisy staked out all night. It was his fault, the whole thing. He slid back into the seat and crouched between Enich and his mother, watching from that narrow space like a gopher from its hole. He saw the Ford against the barn and his father's big body leaning into it, pulling out gunny sacks and straw. There was mud all over the car, mud on his father's pants. He crouched deeper into his crevice and watched his father's face while his mother was telling what had happened.

Then Pa and Jim Enich lifted and slid the colt down to the ground, and Pa stooped to feel its fetlocks. His face was still, red from windburn, and his big square hands were muddy. After a long examination he straightened up.

"Would've been a nice colt," he said. "Damn a pack of mangy mongrels, anyway." He brushed his pants and looked at Bruce's mother. "How come Daisy was out?"

"I told Bruce to take her out. The barn seems so cramped for her, and I thought it would do her good to stretch her legs. And then the ice went out, and the bridge with it, and there was a lot of excitement. . . ." She spoke very fast, and in her voice Bruce heard the echo of his own fear and guilt. She was trying to protect him, but in his mind he knew he was to blame.

"I didn't mean to leave her out, Pa," he said. His voice squeaked, and he swallowed. "I was going to bring her in before supper, only when the bridge . . ."

His father's somber eyes rested on him, and he stopped. But his father didn't fly into a rage. He just seemed tired. He looked at the colt and then at Enich. "Total loss?" he said.

Enich had a leathery, withered face, with two deep creases from beside his nose to the corner of his mouth. A brown mole hid in the left one, and it emerged and disappeared as he chewed a dry grass stem. "Hide," he said.

Bruce closed his dry mouth, swallowed. "Pa!" he said. "It won't have to be shot, will it?"

"What else can you do with it?" his father said. "A crippled horse is no good. It's just plain mercy to shoot it."

"Give it to me, Pa. I'll keep it lying down and heal it up."

"Yeah," his father said, without sarcasm and without mirth. "You could keep it lying down about one hour."

Bruce's mother came up next to him, as if the two of them were standing against the others. "Jim," she said quickly, "isn't there some kind of brace you could put on it? I remember my dad had a horse once that broke a leg below the knee, and he saved it that way."

"Not much chance," Enich said. "Both legs, like that." He plucked a weed and stripped the dry branches from the stalk. "You can't make a horse understand he has to keep still."

"But wouldn't it be worth trying?" she said. "Children's bones heal so fast, I should think a colt's would too."

"I don't know. There's an outside chance, maybe."

"Bo," she said to her husband, "why don't we try it? It seems such a shame, a lovely colt like that."

"I know it's a shame!" he said. "I don't like shooting colts any better than you do. But I never saw a broken-legged colt get well. It'd just be a lot of worry and trouble, and then you'd have to shoot it finally anyway."

"Please," she said. She nodded at him slightly, and then the eyes of both were on Bruce. He felt the tears coming up again, and turned to grope for the colt's ears. It tried to struggle to its feet, and Enich put his foot on its neck. The mare chuckled anxiously.

"How much this hobble brace kind of thing cost?" the father said finally. Bruce turned again, his mouth open with hope.

"Two-three dollars, is all," Enich said.

"You think it's got a chance?"

"One in a thousand, maybe."

"All right. Let's go see MacDonald."

"Oh, good!" Bruce's mother said, and put her arm around him tight.

"I don't know whether it's good or not," the father said. "We might wish we never did it." To Bruce he said, "It's your responsibility. You got to take complete care of it."

"I will!" Bruce said. He took his hand out of his pocket and rubbed below his eye with his knuckles. "I'll take care of it every day."

Big with contrition and shame and gratitude and the sudden sense of immense responsibility, he watched his father and Enich start for the house to get a tape measure. When they were thirty feet away he said loudly, "Thanks, Pa. Thanks an awful lot."

His father half turned, said something to Enich. Bruce stooped to stroke the colt, looked at his mother, started to laugh, and felt it turn horribly into a sob. When he turned away so that his mother wouldn't notice he saw his dog Spot looking inquiringly around the corner of the barn. Spot took three or four tentative steps and paused, wagging his tail. Very slowly (never speak loud or move fast around an animal) the boy bent and found a good-sized stone. He straightened casually, brought his arm back, and threw with all his might. The rock caught Spot squarely in the ribs. He yiped, tucked his tail, and scuttled around the barn, and Bruce chased him, throwing clods and stones and gravel, yelling, "Get out! Go on, get out of here or I'll kick you apart. Get out! Go on!"

So all that spring, while the world dried in the sun and the willows emerged from the floodwater and the mud left by the freshet hardened and caked among their roots, and the grass of the meadow greened and the river brush grew misty with tiny leaves and the dandelions spread yellow among the flats, Bruce tended his colt. While the other boys roamed the bench hills with .22's looking for gophers or rabbits or sage hens, he anxiously superintended the colt's nursing and watched it learn to nibble the grass. While his gang built a darkly secret hide-out in the deep brush beyond Hazard's, he was currying and brushing and trimming the chestnut mane. When packs of boys ran hare and hounds through the town and around the river's slow bends, he perched on the front porch with his slingshot and a can full of small round stones, waiting for stray dogs to appear. He waged a holy war on the dogs until they learned to detour widely around his house, and he never did completely forgive his own dog, Spot. His whole life was wrapped up in the hobbled, leg-ironed chestnut colt with the slow-motion lunging walk and the affectionate nibbling lips.

Every week or so Enich, who was now working out of town at the Half Diamond Bar, rode in and stopped. Always, with that expressionless quiet that was terrible to the boy, he stood and looked the colt over, bent to feel pastern and fetlock, stood back to watch the plunging walk when the boy held out a handful of grass. His expression said nothing; whatever he thought was hidden back of his leathery face as the dark mole was hidden in the crease beside his mouth. Bruce found himself watching that mole sometimes, as if revelation might lie there. But when he pressed Enich to tell him, when he said, "He's getting better, isn't he? He walks better, doesn't he, Mr. Enich? His ankles don't bend so much, do they?" the wrangler gave him little encouragement.

"Let him be awhile. He's growin', sure enough. Maybe give him another month."

May passed. The river was slow and clear again, and some of the boys were already swimming. School was almost over. And still Bruce paid attention to nothing but Socks. He willed so strongly that the colt should get well that he grew furious even at Daisy when she sometimes wouldn't let the colt suck as much as he wanted. He took a butcher knife and cut the long tender grass in the fence corners, where Socks could not reach, and fed it to his pet by the handful. He trained him to nuzzle for sugar-lumps in his pockets. And back in his mind was a fear: in the middle of June they would be going out to the homestead again, and if Socks weren't well by that time he might not be able to go.

"Pa," he said, a week before they planned to leave. "How much of a load are we going to have, going out to the homestead?"

"I don't know, wagonful, I suppose. Why?"

"I just wondered." He ran his fingers in a walking motion along the round edge of the dining table, and strayed into the other room. If they had a wagon load, then there was no way Socks could be loaded in and taken along. And he couldn't walk fifty miles. He'd get left behind before they got up on the bench, hobbling along like the little crippled boy in the Pied Piper, and they'd look back and see him trying to run, trying to keep up.

That picture was so painful that he cried over it in bed that night. But in the morning he dared to ask his father if they couldn't take Socks along to the farm. His father turned on him eyes as sober as Jim Enich's, and when he spoke it was with a kind of tired impatience. "How can he go? He couldn't walk it."

"But I want him to go, Pa!"

"Brucie," his mother said, "don't get your hopes up. You know we'd do it if we could, if it was possible."

"But, Ma . . ."

His father said, "What you want us to do, haul a broken-legged colt fifty miles?"

"He'd be well by the end of the summer, and he could walk back."

"Look," his father said. "Why can't you make up your mind to it? He isn't getting well. He isn't going to get well."

"He is too getting well!" Bruce shouted. He half stood up at the table, and his father looked at his mother and shrugged.

"Please, Bo," she said.

"Well, he's got to make up his mind to it sometime," he said.

Jim Enich's wagon pulled up on Saturday morning, and Bruce was out the door before his father could rise from his chair. "Hi, Mr. Enich," he said.

"Hello, Bub. How's your pony?"

"He's fine," Bruce said. "I think he's got a lot better since you saw him last."

"Uh-huh." Enich wrapped the lines around the whipstock and climbed down. "Tell me you're leaving next week."

"Yes," Bruce said. "Socks is in the back."

When they got into the back yard Bruce's father was there with his hands behind his back, studying the colt as it hobbled around. He looked at Enich. "What do you think?" he said. "The kid here thinks his colt can walk out to the homestead."

"Uh-huh," Enich said. "Well, I wouldn't say that." He inspected the chestnut, scratched between his ears. Socks bobbed, and snuffled at his pockets. "Kid's made quite a pet of him."

Bruce's father grunted. "That's just the damned trouble."

"I didn't think he could walk out," Bruce said. "I thought we could take him in the wagon, and then he'd be well enough to walk back in the fall."

"Uh," Enich said. "Let's take his braces off for a minute."

He unbuckled the triple straps on each leg, pulled the braces off, and stood back. The colt stood almost as flat on his fetlocks as he had the morning he was born. Even Bruce, watching with his whole mind tight and apprehensive, could see that. Enich shook his head.

"You see, Bruce?" his father said. "It's too bad, but he isn't getting better. You'll have to make up your mind. . . ."

"He will get better, though!" Bruce said. "It just takes a long time, is all." He looked at his father's face, at Enich's, and neither one had any hope in it. But when Bruce opened his mouth to say something else his father's eyebrows drew down in sudden, unaccountable anger, and his hand made an impatient sawing motion in the air.

"We shouldn't have tried this in the first place," he said. "It just tangles everything up." He patted his coat pockets, felt in his vest. "Run in and get me a couple cigars."

Bruce hesitated, his eyes on Enich. "Run!" his father said harshly.

Reluctantly he released the colt's halter rope and started for the house. At the door he looked back, and his father and Enich were talking together, so low that their words didn't carry to where he stood. He saw his father shake his head, and Enich bend to pluck a grass stem. They were both against him, they both were sure Socks would never get well. Well, he would! There was some way.

He found the cigars, came out, watched them both light up. Disappointment was a sickness in him, and mixed with the disappointment was a question. When he could stand their silence no more he burst out with it. "But what are we going to *do?* He's got to have some place to stay."

"Look, kiddo." His father sat down on a sawhorse and took him by the arm. His face was serious and his voice gentle. "We can't take him out there. He isn't well enough to walk, and we can't haul him. So Jim here has offered to buy him. He'll give you three dollars for him, and when you come back, if you want, you might be able to buy him back. That is, if he's well. It'll be better to leave him with Jim."

"Well . . ." Bruce studied the mole on Enich's cheek. "Can you get him better by fall, Mr. Enich?"

"I wouldn't expect it," Enich said. "He ain't got much of a show."

"If anybody can get him better, Jim can," his father said. "How's that deal sound to you?"

"Maybe when I come back he'll be all off his braces and running around like a house afire," Bruce said. "Maybe next time I see him I can ride him." The mole disappeared as Enich tongued his cigar.

"Well, all right then," Bruce said, bothered by their stony-eyed silence. "But I sure hate to leave you behind, Socks, old boy."

"It's the best way all around," his father said. He talked fast, as if he were in a hurry. "Can you take him along now?"

"Oh, gee!" Bruce said. "Today?"

"Come on," his father said. "Let's get it over with."

Bruce stood by while they trussed the colt and hoisted him into the wagon box, and when Jim climbed in he cried out, "Hey, we forgot to put his hobbles back on." Jim and his father looked at each other.

His father shrugged. "All right," he said, and started putting the braces back on the trussed front legs.

"He might hurt himself if they weren't on," Bruce said. He leaned over the endgate stroking the white blazed face, and as the wagon pulled away he stood with tears in his eyes and the three dollars in his hand, watching the terrified straining of the colt's neck, the bony head raised above the endgate and one white eye rolling.

Five days later, in the sun-slanting, dew-wet spring morning, they stood for the last time that summer on the front porch, the loaded wagon against the front fence. The father tossed the key in his hand and kicked the doorjamb. "Well, good-bye, Old Paint," he said. "See you in the fall."

As they went to the wagon Bruce sang loudly,

> *Good-bye, Old Paint, I'm leavin' Cheyenne,*
> *I'm leavin' Cheyenne, I'm goin' to Montana,*
> *Good-bye, Old Paint, I'm leavin' Cheyenne.*

"Turn it off," his father said. "You want to wake up the whole town?" He boosted Bruce into the back end, where he squirmed and wiggled his way neck-deep into the luggage. His mother, turning to see how he was settled, laughed at him. "You look like a baby owl in a nest," she said.

His father turned and winked at him. "Open your mouth and I'll drop in a mouse."

It was good to be leaving; the thought of the homestead was exciting. If he could have taken Socks along it would have been perfect, but he had to admit, looking around at the jammed wagon box, that there sure wasn't any room for him. He continued to sing softly as they rocked out into the road and turned east toward MacKenna's house, where they were leaving the keys.

At the low, sloughlike spot that had become the town's dump ground the road split, leaving the dump like an island in the middle. The boy sniffed at the old familiar smells of rust and tar-paper and ashes and refuse. He had collected a lot of old iron and tea lead and bottles and broken machinery and clocks, and once a perfectly good amberheaded cane, in that old dumpground. His father turned up the right fork, and as they passed the central part of the dump the wind, coming in from the northeast, brought a rotten, unbearable stench across them.

"Pee-you!" his mother said, and held her nose.

Bruce echoed her. "Pee-you! Pee-you-willy!" He clamped his nose shut and pretended to fall dead.

"Guess I better get to windward of that coming back," said his father.

They woke MacKenna up and left the key and started back. The things they passed were very sharp and clear to the boy. He was seeing them for the last time all summer. He noticed things he had never noticed so clearly before: how the hills came down into the river from the north like three folds in a blanket, how the stovepipe on the Chinaman's shack east of town had a little conical hat on it. He chanted at the things he saw. "Good-bye, old Chinaman. Good-bye, old Frenchman River. Good-bye, old Dumpground, good-bye."

"Hold your noses," his father said. He eased the wagon into the other fork around the dump. "Somebody sure dumped something rotten."

He stared ahead, bending a little, and Bruce heard him swear. He slapped the reins on the team till they trotted. "What?" the mother said. Bruce, half rising to see what caused the speed, saw her lips go flat over her teeth, and a look on her face like the woman he had seen in the traveling dentist's chair, when the dentist dug a living nerve out of her tooth and then got down on his knees to hunt for it, and she sat there half raised in her seat, her face lifted.

"For gosh sakes," he said. And then he saw.

He screamed at them. "Ma, it's Socks! Stop, Pa! It's Socks!"

His father drove grimly ahead, not turning, not speaking, and his mother shook her head without looking around. He screamed again, but neither of them turned. And when he dug down into the load, burrowing in and shaking with long smothered sobs, they still said nothing.

So they left town, and as they wound up the dugway to the south bench there was not a word among them except his father's low, "For Christ sakes, I thought he was going to take it out of town." None of them looked back at the view they had always admired, the flat river bottom green with spring, its village snuggled in the loops of river. Bruce's eyes, pressed against the coats and blankets under him until his sight was a red haze, could still see through it the bloated, skinned body of the colt, the chestnut hair left a little way above the hooves, the iron braces still on the broken front legs.

Eudora Welty (*born 1909*)

As a young child growing up in Jackson, Mississippi, Eudora Welty believed that books were a phenomenon of nature:

> It had been startling and disappointing to me to find out (at a young age) that story books had been written by people, that books were not natural wonders, coming up of themselves like grass. Yet regardless of where they came from, I cannot remember a time when I was not in love with them.

Welty's parents had great respect for books, making sure that their children always had a ready supply. As a child, she "listened for" stories, waiting and hoping for one to come out like a mouse from its hole. She recalls climbing into the car between her mother and a neighbor and, as the car pulled away, saying, "Now talk."

Welty was a published writer before her teenage years, writing for children's magazines. She would later attend the Mississippi State College for Women, the University of Wisconsin at Madison, and, briefly, Columbia University, where she studied advertising but spent a great deal of time taking advantage of New York City's cultural opportunities. She returned to Jackson in 1931 and began to work for a local radio station and newspaper. During Franklin Roosevelt's New Deal administration, she worked as a "junior publicity agent" for the Works Progress Administration. Her job was to travel throughout Mississippi taking photographs and writing news articles in order to promote the building of roads and factories in the poorer parts of the state. She credits this experience as an important influence on her writing.

Welty's first short story was published in 1936. Among her many books are A Curtain of Green *(1941),* The Robber Bridegroom *(1942),* The Wide Net *(1943),* The Ponder Heart *(1954), and* The Optimist's Daughter *(1972). Back problems, severe arthritis, and hearing loss have made writing difficult for her in recent years. She keeps mostly to her home, the house her father built in Jackson, Mississippi. Welty's autobiography,* One Writer's Beginnings *(1984), is a moving account of her development as a writer and as a human being. Since her days working for the WPA, Welty has been an avid photographer. Her work—both her fiction and her photography—is marked by especially intimate insights into human nature. Her characters are developed from the inside out, which is why she is so often drawn to first-person narrative—a way of letting characters tell their stories in their own words and revealing so much more about themselves in the process. Like other Southern writers, such as William Faulkner and Flannery O'Connor, Welty puts the still-wild landscape of the undeveloped American South at the forefront of stories like "At the Landing." Nature and natural disasters, as much as people, determine the course of events.*

At the Landing

The night that Jenny's grandfather died, he dreamed of high water.

He came in his dream and stood just outside the door of her room, his little chin that was like a chicken's clean breastbone tilting upwards.

"It has come," the old man said, and he made a complaint of it.

Jenny in her bed lay still, waking more still than in the sleep of a moment before.

"The river has come back. That Floyd came to tell me. The sun was shining full on the face of the church, and that Floyd came around it with his wrist hung with a great long catfish. 'It's coming,' he said. 'It's the river.' Oh, it came then! Like a head and arm. Like a horse. A mane of cedar trees tossing over the top. It has borne down, and it has closed us in. That Floyd was right."

He reached as if to lift an obstacle that he thought was stretched there—the bar that crossed the door in her mother's time. It seemed beyond his strength, she tried to cry out, and he came in through the doorway. The cord and tassel of his brocade robe—for he had put it on—seemed to weigh upon his fragile walking like a chain, and yet it could have been by inexorable will that he wore it, so set were his little steps, in such duty he dragged it.

"Like poor people who have learned to fly at last," he said, walking, dragging, the fine deprecation in his voice, "all the people in The Landing, all kinds and conditions of people, are gliding off and upward to darkness. The little mandolin that my daughter used to play—it's rising like a bubble, and filling with water."

"Grandpa!" cried Jenny, and then she was up and taking her grandfather by his tiny adamant shoulders. It was moonlight. She saw his open eyes. "Wake up, Grandpa!"

"That Floyd's catfish has gone loose and free," he said gently, as if breaking news to someone. "And all of a sudden, my dear—my dears, it took its river life back, and shining so brightly swam through the belfry of the church, and downstream." At that his mouth clamped tight shut.

She held out both arms and he fell trembling against her. With beating heart she carried him through the dark halls to his room and put him down into his bed. He lay there in the moonlight, which moved and crept across him as it would a little fallen withered leaf, and he never moved or spoke any more, but lay softly, as if he were floating, being carried away, drawn by the passing moon; and Jenny's heart beat on and on, sharp as birdsong in the night, under her breast, until day.

Under the shaggy bluff the bottomlands lay in a river of golden haze. The road dropped like a waterfall from the ridge to the town at its foot and came to a grassy end there. It was spring. One slowly moving figure that was a man with a fishing pole passed like a dreamer through the empty street and on through the trackless haze toward the river. The town was still called The Landing. The river had gone, three miles away, beyond sight and smell, beyond the dense trees. It came back only in flood, and boats ran over the houses.

Up the light-scattered hill, in the house with the galleries, the old man and his granddaughter had always lived. They were the people least seen in The Landing. The grandfather was too old, and the girl was too shy of the world, and they were both too good—the old ladies said—to come out, and so they stayed inside.

For all her life the shy Jenny could look, if she stayed in the parlor, back and forth between her mother's two paintings, "The Bird Fair" and "The Massacre at Fort Rosalie." Or if she went in the dining room she could walk around the table or sit on one after the other of eight needlepoint pieces, each slightly different, which her mother had worked and sewn to the chairs, or she could count the plates that stood on their rims in the closet. In the library she could circle an entirely bare floor and make up a dance to a song she made up, all silently, or gaze at the backs of the books without titles—books that had been on ships and in oxcarts and through fire and water, and were singed and bleached and swollen and shrunken, and arranged up high and nearly unreachable, like objects of beauty. Wherever she went she almost touched a prism. The house was full of prisms. They hung everywhere in the shadow of the halls and in the sunlight of the rooms, stirring under the hanging lights, dangling and circling where they were strung in the window curtains. They gave off the faintest of musical notes when air stirred in any room or when only herself passed by, and they touched. It was her way not to touch them herself, but to let the touch be magical, a stir of the curtain by the outer air, that would also make them rainbows. Vases with landscapes on them stood in the halls and were reflected endlessly rising in front of her when she passed quickly between the two mirrors. She might stop and touch all things, trace their little pictures with her finger, and put them back again; it was not forbidden; but her touch that dared not break would have been transparent as a spirit's on the objects. She was calm the way a child is calm, with never the calmness of a spirit. But like distant lightning that silently bathes a whole shimmering sky, one awareness was always trembling about her: one day she would be free to come and go. Nothing now held her in her own room, with the great wardrobe in which she had sometimes longed to hide, and the great box-like canopied bed and the little picture on the wall of her mother with up-turned eyes. Jenny could go from room to room, and out at the door. But at the door her grandfather would call her back, with his little murmur.

At sunset the old man and his granddaughter would take their supper in the pavilion on the knoll, that had been a gazebo when the river ran before it. There a little breeze came all the way from the river still. All about the pavilion was an ancient circling thorny rose, like the initial letter in a poetry book. The cook came out and served with exaggerated dignity, as though she scolded in the house. A little picture might be preserved then in all their heads. The old man and the young girl looked across the round table leaf-shadowed under the busy black hands, and smiled by long habit at each other. But her grandfather could not look at her without speculation in his eyes, and the gaze that went so fondly between them held and stretched tight the memory of Jenny's mother. It seemed strange that her mother had been dead now for so many years and yet the wild desire that had torn her seemed still fresh and still a small thing. It was a desire to get to Natchez. People said Natchez was a nice little town on Saturdays with a crowd filling it and moving around.

The grandfather stirred his black coffee and smiled at Jenny. He deprecated raving simply as raving, as a force of Nature and so beneath notice or mention. And yet—even now, too late—if Jenny could plead . . . ! In a heat wave one called the cook to bring a fan, and in his daughter's first raving he rang a bell and told the cook to take her off and sit by her until she had done with it, but in the end she died of it. But Jenny could not plead for her.

Her grandfather, frail as a little bird, would say when it was time to go in. He would rise slowly in the brocade gown he wore to study in, and put his weight, which was the terrifying weight of a claw, on Jenny's arm. Jenny was obedient to her grandfather and would have been obedient to anybody, to a stranger in the street if there could be one. She never performed any act, even a small act, for herself, she would not touch the prisms. It might seem that nothing began in her own heart.

Nothing ever happened, to be seen from the gazebo, except that Billy Floyd went through the town. He was almost unknown, and one to himself. If he came at all, he would come at this time of day. In the long shadows below they could see his figure with the gleaming fish he carried move clear as a candle over the road that he had to himself, and out to the blue distance. In The Landing, every person that moved was watched out of sight, and it made a little pause in every life. And if in each day a moment of hope must come, in Jenny's day the moment was when the rude wild Floyd walked through The Landing carrying the big fish he had caught.

Under the blue sky, skirting the ravine, a half-ring of twenty cedar trees stood leading to the cemetery, their bleached trunks the colors of red and white roses. Jenny, given permission, would walk up there to visit the grave of her mother.

The cemetery was a dark shelf above the town, on the site of the old landing place when the ships docked from across the world a hundred years ago, and its brink was marked by an old table-like grave with its top ajar where the woodbine grew. Everywhere there, the hanging moss and the upthrust stones were in that strange graveyard shade where, by the light they give, the moss seems made of stone, and the stone of moss.

On one of the days, while she sat there on a stile, Jenny looked across the ravine and there was Floyd, standing still in a sunny pasture. She could watch between the grapevines, which hung and held back like ropes on either side to clear her view. Floyd had a head of straight light-colored hair and it hung over his forehead, for he never was near a comb. He stood facing her in a tall squared posture of silence and rest, while a rusty-red horse that belonged to the Lockharts cropped loudly beside him in the wild-smelling pasture.

It was said by the old ladies that he slept all morning for he fished all night. Stiff and stern, Jenny sat there with her feet planted just so on the step below, in the posture of a child who is appalled at the stillness and unsurrender of the still and unsurrendering world.

At last she sighed, and when she took up her skirt to go, as if she were dreaming she saw Floyd coming across the pasture toward her. When he reached the ravine and leaped down into it with widespread arms as though he jumped into something dangerous, she stood still on the stile to watch. He moved up near to her now, his feet on the broken ferns at the spring. The wind whipped his hair, almost making a noise.

"Go back," she said. She wanted to watch him a while longer first, before he got to her.

He stopped and looked full at her, his strong neck bending to one side as if yielding in pleasure to the wind. His arms went down and his fists opened. But for her, his eyes were as bright and unconsumed as stars up in the sky. Then she wanted to catch him and see him close, but not to touch him. He stood watching her, though, as if to prevent it. They were as still and rigid as two mocking-birds that were about to strike their beaks and dance.

She waited, but he smiled, and then knelt and cupped both hands to his face in the spring water. He drank for a long time, while she stood there with her skirt whipping in the wind, and waited on him to see how long he could drink without lifting his face. When he had drunk that much, he went back to the field and threw himself yawning down into the grass. The grass was so deep there that she could see only the one arm flung out in the torn sleeve, straight, sun-blacked and motionless.

The day she watched him in the woods, she felt it come to her dimly that her innocence had left her, since she could watch his. She could only sink down onto the step of the stile, and lay her heavy forehead in her hand. But if innocence had left, she still did not know what was to come. She would wait and see him come awake.

But he slept and slept like the dead, and defeated her. She went to her grandfather and left Floyd sleeping.

Another day, they walked for a little near together, each picking some berry or leaf to hold in the mouth, on their opposite sides of the little spring. The pasture, the sun and the grazing horse were on his side, the graves on hers, and they each looked across at the other's. The whole world seemed filled with butterflies. At each step they took, two black butterflies over the flowers were whirring just alike, suspended in the air, one circling the other rhythmically, or both moving from side to side in a gentle wave-like way, one above the other. They were blue-black and moving their wings faster than Jenny's eye could follow, always together, like each other's shadows, beautiful each one with the other. Jenny could see to start with that no kiss had ever brought love tenderly enough from mouth to mouth.

Jenny and Floyd stopped and looked for a little while at all the butterflies and they never touched each other. When Jenny did touch Floyd, touch his sleeve, he started.

He went alert in the field like a listening animal. The horse came near and when he touched it, stood with lifted ears beside him, then broke away. But over all The Landing there was not a sound that she could hear. It could only be that Floyd missed nothing in the world, and could hear innumerable outward things. He suddenly flung up his head. She knew he was smiling. And a smile was always a barrier.

She said his name, for she was so close by. It was the first time.

He stayed motionless, and she knew that he lived apart in delight. That could make a strange glow fall over the field where he was, and the world go black for her, left behind. She felt terrified, as if at a pitiless thing.

Floyd lifted his foot and stamped on the ground, and held out his careless arms to catch the horse he had excited. Then he was jumping on its bare back and riding into a gallop, shouting to frighten and amaze whoever listened. She threw herself down into the grass. Never had she known that the Lockhart horse could run like that. Floyd went at a racing speed and he seemed somehow in his tattered shirt—as she watched from beneath her arm—to stream with the wind, and he circled the steep field three times, and with flying yellow hair and a diminishing shout rode up into the woods.

If she could have followed and found him then, she would have started on foot. But she knew what she would find when she would come to him. She would find him equally real with herself—and could not touch him then. As she was living and inviolate, so of course was he, and when that gave him delight, how could she bring a question to him? She walked in the woods and around the graves in it, and knew about love, how it would have a different story in the world if it could lose the moral knowledge of a mystery that is in the other heart. Nothing in Floyd frightened her that drew her near, but at once she had the knowledge come to her that a fragile mystery was in everyone and in herself, since there it was in Floyd, and that whatever she did, she would be bound to ride over and hurt, and the secrecy of life was the terror of it. When Floyd rode the red horse, she lay in the grass. He might even have jumped across her. But the vaunting and prostration of love told her nothing—nothing at all.

The very next day Jenny waited on the stile and she saw Floyd come walking up the road in the morning, with drenched hair. He might have come and found her, but he came to the Lockhart house first.

The Lockhart house stood between two of the empty stretches along the road. It was wide, low, and twisted. Its roof, held up at the corners by the two chimneys, sagged like a hammock, and was mended with bark and small colored signs. The black high-water mark made a belt around the house and that alone seemed to tighten it and hold it together. Floyd stood gazing in at the doorway, as if what might not come out? And it was a beautiful doorway to see, with its fanlight and its sidelights, though they were blind with silt. The door was shut and the squirrels were asleep on the floor of the long cage across the front wall. Under the forward-tilting porch the clay-colored hens were sitting in twos in the old rowboat. And while Floyd looked, out came Mag.

And the next thing, he was playing with Mag Lockhart, that was an albino. Mag's short white hair would stream out from her head when she crouched nodding over her flowers in the yard, tending them with a jack-knife all day, and she would give a splitting laugh to see anyone come. Jenny from the stile watched them wrestle and play. The treadmill ran under the squirrels' quick feet.

Mag's voice came a long distance through the still day. "You are not!" "It is not!" "I am not!" she would scream, and she would jump away.

Floyd would turn on his heel and whirl old Mag off the ground. Mag ran and she snapped at him, she struggled and she crackled like a green wood fire, and he laughed and caught her. She pointed and sent him for the water, and he went and clattered and banged the buckets for her at the well until she begged him to stop. He went straight off and old Mag sat down on her front steps with the hens and rubbed at her flame-pink arms.

And then suddenly Mag was gone.

Jenny put her hands over her forehead, and then rubbed at her own arms. She believed Mag had been there, because she had felt whatever Mag had felt. If this was a vision, it was the first. And it did not frighten her; she knew it only came because she had felt what was in another heart besides her own. But it had been Mag's heart that grew clear to her, while Floyd ran away.

She lay down in the grass, which whispered in her ear. If desperation were only a country, it would be at the bottom of the well. She wanted to get there, to arrive graceful and airy in some strange other country and walk along its level land beneath its secret sky. She thought she could see herself, fleet as a mirror-image, rising up in a breath of astonished farewell and walking to the well of old

Mag. It was built so that it had steps like a stile. She saw herself walk up them, stand on top, look about, and then go into the dark passage.

But my grandfather, she thought, even while she sank so deeply, will call me back. I will have to go back. He will ask me if I have put flowers on my mother's grave. And she looked over at the stone on the grave of her mother, with her married name of Lockhart cut into it.

She clutched the thing in her hand, a blade of grass, and held on. There she was, sitting up in the sun, with the blade of grass stretched between her thumbs and held to her mouth, for the calling back that was in the world. She blew on the grass. It made a thoughtless reedy sound, and she blew again.

II

The morning after her grandfather's death, Jenny put on a starched white dress and went down the hill into The Landing. A little crocheted bag hung by a ribbon over her wrist, and she had taken a nickel to put in it. Her good black strapped slippers moved lightly in the dust. She was going to tell the news of her grandfather, whom the old ladies had said would die suddenly—like *that*. And looking about with every step she took, she saw what a lonesome place it was for all of this to happen in.

She passed a house that only the mice inhabited. She passed a black boarded-up store where an owl used to live and maintain its nocturnal habits. And there, a young calf belonging to the Lockharts used to nose through the grassy rooms, before the walls were carried away by the Negroes and burned in a winter for firewood. In front of the row of Negro cabins was one long fence, made of lumber from old boats, built there to delay the river for one more moment when it came, the same as they would have delayed a giant bent on destruction by some foolish pretext.

Across the end of the road, crumbling under her eyes, was a two-story building with a remnant of gallery, and that was Jenny's destination. The store and the postoffice were in the one used room. Across the tin awning hung the moss icicles with which the postmaster had decorated for Christmas. Over the door was the shriveled mistletoe, and the gun that had shot it down still standing in the corner. Tipped back against the front wall sat five old men in their chairs, with one holding the white cat. On the step, Son Alford was playing his mandolin that had been Jenny's mother's and given away. He was singing his fast song.

> *"Ain't she cute*
> *Ain't she smart*
> *Don't look twice*
> *It'll break my heart*
> *Everybody loves my gal."*

All nodded to her, but they knew she was not supposed to speak to them.

She went inside, and the first thing she saw was Billy Floyd. He was standing in the back of the room with the postmaster saying to him, "Reckon we're going to have water this year?"

She had never seen the man between walls and under a roof and somehow it made him a different man after the one in the field. He stood in the dim and dingy store with a 10w of filmy glass lamps and a pair of boots behind his head, and there was something close, gathering-close, and used and worldly about him.

"That slime, that's just as slick! You know how a fish is, I expect," the postmaster was saying affably to them both, just as if they were in any way together. "That's the way a house is, been under water. It's a sight to see those niggers try to clean this place out, falling down to slide from here to the front door and back. You have to get the slime off right away too, or you never can. Sure would make the best paint in the world." He laughed.

There was something handled and used about Floyd, something strong as an odor, the odor of the old playing cards that the old men of The Landing shuffled every day over their table in the street.

"Reckon we're going to have water this year?" the postmaster asked again. He looked from one of them to the other.

Floyd said nothing, he only held a penny. For a moment Jenny thought he was going to drop his high head at being trapped in the confined place, with her between him and the door, which would be the same as telling it out, before a third person, that he could be known in time if he were caught and cornered in a little store.

"What would you like today, Miss Jenny?" asked the postmaster. "Posy seeds?"

But she could not think what she would like. She held her little bag quite still, the strings drawn tight.

All the time, Floyd was giving her a glaring look.

"Well, it makes you think sometimes, to see the water come over all the world," said the postmaster: "I took everything I could out of here last time. Then I come down from the hill and peeked in the door and what did I see? My showcases commencing to float loose. What a sight that did make! I wouldn't have thought I sold some of them things. Carried the showcases out on the hill, but nowhere much to take them. Could you believe I could carry everything out of my store in twenty minutes but my safe? Couldn't lift that. Left the door to it open and went off and left it. So as it wouldn't rust shut, Floyd, Miss Jenny. Took me a long time to scrape the river out of that thing."

All three waited a moment, and then the postmaster spoke again in a softer, intimate voice, smilingly. "Some stranger lost through here says, 'Why don't you all move away?' Move away?" He laughed, and pointed a finger at Jenny. "Did you hear that, Miss Jenny—why don't we move away? Because we live here, don't we, Miss Jenny?"

Then she knew it was a challenge Floyd made with his hard look, and she lost to him. She walked out and left him where he held his solid stand. And when the postmaster had pointed his finger at her, she remembered that she was never to speak to Billy Floyd, by the order of her grandfather.

Outside the door, she stopped still. The weight of the nickel swung in her little bag, and she felt as if she had forgotten Doomsday. She took a step back toward the challenging Floyd. Then in a kind of haste she whispered to the five old men, separately, and even to Son Alford, and each time nearer to tears for her grandfather that died in the night. Then they gathered round her, and hurried her to the old women, and so back home.

But Floyd's face glared before her eyes all the way, it was like something in her vision that kept her from seeing. It was brighter than the glare of death. He might have been buying a box of matches with his penny, which was what his going cost. He would go. The danger of flood was her grandfather's dream, and the postmaster's storekeeper wit. These were bright days and clear nights; and so Floyd would not wait long in The Landing. That was what the old ladies said, and asked that their words be marked.

But on a later day, Jenny took a walk and met Floyd by the little river that came out of the spring and went to the Mississippi beyond. She sat down and made a clover chain that would never get long because the cloverheads slipped out, and while she made it she kept looking with assuring looks into his illuminated eyes that went over the landscape and searched the sky for clouds. She could hold his look for a moment and then it would get away. She did not say a thing to him, for nobody can say, "It is a heavy heart that makes me clumsy." Nobody can say anything so true and apologetic. Nobody can say, "Forgive the heavy heart that loves more than the tongue can say or the hands can do. Look back at me every time I look at you and never feel pity, for what my heart holds this minute is better than what you offer the least bit less." Her eyes were telling him this but if he knew it or felt a threat in it, he never gave a sign. "My heart loves more than I can say or do, but feel no pity, only have a little vision too, of all clumsiness fallen away." She guessed that all grace belongs to the future. But he never had anything to say to her thought or her guess. He stood above her with his feet planted down and looked out over the landscape from within that moment. Level with him now, all The Landing spread under his eyes. Not knowing the world around, she could not know how The Landing looked set down in it. All she knew was that he would leave it when his patience gave out, and that this little staving moment by the river would reach its limit and go first.

Her eyes descended slowly, as if adorned with flowers, from his light blowing hair and his gathering brows down, down him, past his clever hands that caught and trapped so delicately away from her side, softly down to the ground that was a sandy shore. A hidden mussel was blowing bubbles like a spring through the sand where his boot was teasing the water. It was the little pulse of bubbles and not himself or herself that was the moment for her then; and he could have already departed and she could have already wept, and it would have been the same, as she stared at the little fountain rising so gently out of the shimmering sand. A clear love is *in the world*—this came to her as insistently as the mussel's bubbles through the water. There it was, existing there where they came and were beside it now. It is in the bubble in the water in the river, and it has its own changing and its mysteries of days and nights, and it does not care how we come and go.

But when the moment ended, he went. And as soon as he left The Landing, the rain began to fall.

Each day the storm clouds were opening like great purple flowers and pouring out their dark thunder. Each nightfall, the storm was laid down on their houses like a burden the day had carried. The noise of rain, of the gullies filling, of the little river leaping up and running in waves filled all The Landing.

And when at last the river came, it did come like a hand and arm, and pushed black trees before it, but it was at dawn. Jenny went with the others, behind Mag Lockhart, onto the hill and the water followed, whirling and bobbing the young dead animals around on its roaring breast. The clouds lowered and broke again and the rain put out the lanterns. Boat whistles began crying as faint as baby cries in that rainy dark.

Jenny had not spoken for a day and a night on the hill when she told someone that she was sleepy. It was Billy Floyd that she told it to. He put her in his boat, that she had never seen. Jenny looked in Floyd's shining eyes and saw how they held the whole flood, as the flood held its triumph in its whirlpools, and it was a vast and unsuspected thing.

It was on the high hill of the cemetery, when the water was at its peak. They came in Floyd's boat where the river lapped around the dark cedar tops, and monuments like pillars to bear them up scraped their passage, and she knew they rode over the grave of her grandfather and the grave of her mother. Muscadine vines spread under the water rippling their leaves like schools of fishes. It was always the same darkness. Fires burned somewhere, but in the distance, red and blue.

"I . . ." she began, and stopped.

He scowled.

She knew at once that there was nothing in her life past or even now in the flood that would make anything to tell. He already knew that he had saved her life, for that had taken up his time in the time of danger. Yet she might confess it. It came to her lips. He scowled on. Still, it was not any kind of confession that she would finally wish to make. She would like to tell him some strange beautiful thing, if she could speak at all, something to make him speak. Communication would be telling something that is all new, so as to have more of the new told back. The dream of that held her spellbound, with the things possible that hung in the air like clouds over the world, and she smiled in pure belief, for they were beautiful.

"I . . ." She looked softly at him as if from a distance down a little road or a little tether he sent her on.

He took hold of her, put her out of the boat into a little place he made that was dry and green and smelled good, and she went to sleep. After a time that could have been long or short, she thought she heard him say, "Wake up."

When her eyes were open and clear upon him, he violated her and still he was without care or demand and as gay as if he were still clanging the bucket at the well. With the same thoughtlessness of motion, that was a kind of grace, he next speared a side of wild meat from an animal he had killed and had ready in his boat, and cooked it over a fire he had burning on the ground. All the water lapped around. Over its sound she whispered something, but his movement and his task went on firmly about his leaping fire. People who had been there in other floods had put their initials on the tree. Her words came a little louder and in shyness she changed them from words of love to words of wishing, but still he did not look around. "I wish you and I could be far away. I wish for a little house." But ideas of any different thing from what was in his circle of fire might never have reached his ears, for all the attention he paid to her remarks.

He had fishes ready too, wrapped and cooking in a hole scooped in the ground. When she ate it was in obedience to him, though he did not say "Eat" or say anything, he only smiled at the fire, and for him it was all a taking freely of what was free. She knew from him nevertheless that what people ate in the world was earth, river, wildness and litheness, fire and ashes. People took the fresh death and the hot fire into their mouths and got their own life. She ate greedily as long as he ate, and took what he took. She ate eagerly, looking up at him while her teeth bit, to show him herself, her proud hunger, as if to please and flatter him with her original and now lost starvation. But she could make him neither sorry nor proud. When she was sick afterwards, he walked away and waited apart from her shame, as he had left her in his delight.

The dream of love, that made her hold as still in her life as if she heard music, had never carried her yet to the first country of which it told. But there was a country, as surely as there was herself. When she saw the moon come up that night and grow bright as it went above the flood and the boats in it, she was not as sorrowful as she might have been, now that they floated so high, that no threads hung down from the moon, no tender ladder all at once caught light and drifted down. There was a need in all dreams for something to stay far, far away, never to torment with the rest, and the bright moon now was that.

III

When the water was down, Jenny went back below and Floyd went down the river in his boat. They parted with the clumsiest of touches. Down through the exhausted and still dripping trees she made her way, again behind Mag, following the tracks and signs of others, and the mud sticking to her. Ashes sifted through the air and she saw them touch her skin but did not feel them. She came to the stile where she could look at the world below. The sun was going down and a wind blew following after the river, and the little town had turned the color of river water and the trees in their shame of refuse rattled like yellow pebbles and the houses sank below them scuffed and small. The smoky band of woods that lay in the distance toward the retreating river still seemed to waver and slide.

In The Landing the houses had turned a little, like people whose skirts are pulled. Where the front of the Lockhart house had been pulled away, the furniture, that had been carried out of the corners by the river and rocked about, stood in the middle of the floor and showed down its back the curly yellow grain, like its long hair. One old store had been carried clean away, after it was closed so long, and in its foundations were the old men standing around poking for money with little sticks. Money could have fallen through the cracks for many years. Fifteen cents and twenty cents and a Spanish piece were found, and the old fellows poking with their sticks were laughing like women.

Jenny came to her house. It stood as before, except that in the yellow and windy light it seemed to draw its galleries to itself, to return to its cave of night and trees, crouched like a child going backwards to the womb.

But once inside, she took one step and was into a whole new ecstasy, an ecstasy of cleaning, to wash the river out. She ran as if driven, carrying buckets and mops. She scrubbed and pried and shook the river away. Even the pages of books seemed to have been opened and written on again by muddy fingers. In the long days when she stretched and dried white curtains and sheets, rubbed the rust off knives and made them shine, and wiped the dark river from all the prisms, she forgot even love, to clean.

But the shock of love had brought a trembling to her fingers that made her drop what she touched, and made her stumble on the stair, though all the time she was driven on. And when the house was clean again she felt that there was no place to hide in it, not one room. She even opened the small door of her mother's last room, but when she looked in she thought of her mother who was kept guard on there, who struggled unweariedly and all in loneliness, and it was not a hiding place.

If in all The Landing she could have found a place to feel alone and out of sight, she would have gone there. One old lady or another would always call to her when she went by, to tell her something, and if she walked out in the road she brushed up against the old men sitting at their cards, and they spoke to her. She did not like to see faces, which were ugly, or flowers, which were beautiful and smelled sweet.

But at last the trembling left and dull strength came back, as if a wound had ceased to flow its blood. And then one day in summer she could look at a bird flying in the air, its tiny body like a fist opening and closing, and did not feel daze or pain, and then she was healed of the shock of love.

Then whenever she thought that Floyd was in the world, that his life lived and had this night and day, it was like discovery once more and again fresh to her, and if it was night and she lay stretched on her bed looking out at the dark, a great radiant energy spread intent upon her whole body and fastened her heart beneath its breath, and she would wonder almost aloud, "Ought I to sleep?" For it was love that might always be coming, and she must watch for it this time and clasp it back while it clasped, and while it held her never let it go.

Then the radiance touched at her heart and her brain, moving within her. Maybe some day she could become bright and shining all at once, as though at the very touch of another with herself. But now she was like a house with all its rooms dark from the beginning, and someone would have to go slowly from room to room, slowly and darkly, leaving each one lighted behind, before going to the next. It was not caution or distrust that was in herself, it was only a sense of journey, of something that might happen. She herself did not know what might lie ahead, she had never seen herself. She looked outward with the sense of rightful space and time within her, which must be traversed before she could be known at all. And what she would reveal in the end was not herself, but the way of the traveler.

In The Landing much was known about all kinds of love that had happened there, and wisdom traveled, when it left the porches, in the persons of three old women. The day the old women would come to see Jenny, it would be to celebrate her ruin that they trudged through the sun in their bonnets. They would come up the hill to say, "Why don't you run after him?" and to say, "Now you won't love him any more," for they always did pay a visit to say those words.

Now only Mag came sidling up, and brought a bouquet of amaryllis to present with blushes to Jenny. Jenny blushed too.

"Some people that don't speak to other people don't grow the prettiest flowers!" Mag cried victoriously as Jenny took them. Her baby hair blew down and her sharp smile cut back into her long dry cheek.

"I speak to you, Mag," said Jenny.

When she walked she heard them talk—the three old ladies. About her they said, "She'll follow her mother to her mother's grave." About Floyd they had more to say. They called him "the wild man" because they had never been told quite who he was or where he had come from. The sun had burned his skin dark and his hair light, till he was golden in the road, and they freely considered his walking by again, as if they could take his life up into their fingers with their sewing and sew it or snip it on their laps. They always went back to saying that at any rate he caught enormous fish wherever he fished in the river, and always had a long wet thing slung over his wrist when he went by, ugh! One old lady thought he was a Gipsy and had called "Gipsy!" after him when he went by her front porch once too often. One lady said she did not care what he was or if she ever knew what he was, and whether he lived or died it was all the same to her. But the third old lady had books, though she was the one that was a little crazy, and she waited till the others had done and then explained that Floyd had the blood of a Natchez Indian, though the Natchez might be supposed to be all gone, massacred. The Natchez, she said—and she nodded toward her books, "The Queen's Library," high on the shelf—were the people from the lost Atlantis, had they heard of that? and took their pride in the escape from that flood, when the island went under. And there was something all Indians knew, about never letting the last spark of fire go out. What did the other ladies think of that?

They were shocked. They had thought all the time he was really the bastard of one of the old checker-players, that had been let grow up away in the woods until he got big enough to come back and make trouble. They said he was half-wild like one family they could name, and half of the time he did not know what he was doing, like another family. All in his own right he could scent coming things like an animal and in some of his ways, just like all men, he was something of an animal. But they said it was the way he was.

"Why don't you run after him?"—"Now you won't love him any more."

Jenny wondered what more love would be like. Then of course she knew. More love would be quiet. She would never be so quiet as she wished until she was quiet with her love. In the center of everything, in the center of thunder, there was a precious piece of quiet, and into quiet her love would go. The Landing was filled with clangor, it seemed to her, until her love was filled with quiet. It seemed to her that she had been the same as in many places in the world, traveling and traveling, always with quiet to give. It had been enough to make her desperate in her heart, the long search for Billy Floyd to give quiet to.

But if Floyd had a search, what was it?

She was holding the amber beads they used to give her mother to play with. She looked at the lump of amber, and looked through to its core. Nobody could ever know about the difference between the radiance that was the surface and the radiance that was inside. There were the two worlds. There was no way at all to put a finger on the center of light. And if there were a mountain, the cloud over it could not touch its heart when it traveled over, and if there were an island out in the sea, the waves at its shore would never come over the place in the middle of the island. She looked in her very dreams at Floyd who had such clear eyes shining at her, and knew his heart lay clearer still, safe and deep in his innocence, safe and away from the outside, deeper than quiet. What she remembered was that when her hand started out to touch him in delight, he smiled and turned away—not from her, but toward something. . . .

Was it toward one thing, toward some one thing alone?

But it was when love was of the one for the one, that it seemed to hold all that was multitudinous and nothing was single any more. She had one love and that was all, but she dreamed that she lined up on both sides of the road to see her love come by in a procession. She herself was more people than there were people in The Landing, and her love was enough to pass through the whole night, never lifting the same face.

It was July when Jenny left The Landing. The grass was tall and gently ticking between the tracks of the road. The stupor of air, the quiet of the river that now went behind a veil, the sheen of heat and the gray sheen of summering trees, and the silence of day and night seemed all to touch, to bathe and administer to The Landing. The little town took a languor and a kind of beauty from the treatment of time and place. It stretched and swooned, and when two growing boys knelt in the road and caught the sun rays in a bit of glass and got fire, they seemed to tease a sleeper, and when they said "Hooray!" they sounded like adventurers in a dream.

Pears lying on the ground warmed and soured, bees gathered at the figs, birds put their little holes of possession in each single fruit in the world that they could fly to. The scent of lilies rolled sweetly from their heavy cornucopias and trickled down by shady paths to fill the golden air of the valley. The mourning dove called its three notes, kept its short silence—which was its mourning?—and called three more.

Jenny had known the most when she knew Floyd rode the horse in the field of butterflies while she was still; and she had known something when she watched him cook the meat and had eaten it for him under his eye; and now once more, in the dream of July, she knew very little, she was lost in wonder again. If she could find him now, or even find the place where he had last passed through, she would gain the next wisdom. It was a following after, now—it was too late to find any way alone.

The sun was going down when she went. The red eyes of the altheas were closing, and the lizards ran on the wall. The last lily buds hung green and glittering, pendulant in the heat. The crape-myrtle trees were beginning to fill with light for they drank the last of it every day, and gave off their white and flame in the evening that filled with the throb of cicadas. There was an old mimosa closing in the ravine—the ancient fern, as old as life, the tree that shrank from the touch, grotesque in its tenderness. All nearness and darkness affected it, even clouds going by, but for Jenny that left it no tree ever gave such allurement of fragrance anywhere.

She looked behind her for the last time as she went down under the trees. As if it were made of shells and pearls and treasures from the sea, the house glinted in the sunset, tinted with the drops of light that seemed to fall slowly through the vaguely stirring leaves. Tenderly as seaweed the long moss swayed. The chimney branched like coral in the upper blue.

Then green branches closed it over, and with her next step trumpet and mus-cadine vines and the great big-leaved vines made pillars about the trunks of the trees and arches and buttresses all among them. Passion flowers bloomed with their white and purple rays about her shoulders and under her feet. She walked on into the streaming hot shade of the wilderness, and put out her hands between the hanging vines. She feared the snakes in the sudden cool. Like thousands of sil-ver bells the frogs rang her through the swamp, which then closed behind her.

All at once the whole open sky could be seen—she had come to the river. A quiet fire burned on the bluff and moving as far outward as she could see was the cold blur of water. A great spiraled net lay on its side and its circles twinkled faintly on the sky. Veil behind veil of long drying nets hung on all sides, dropping softly and blue-colored in the low wind and the place was folded in by them. All things, river, sky, fire, and air, seemed the same color, the color that is seen behind the closed eyelids, the color of day when vision and despair are the same thing.

Some fishermen came around her and when she named Billy Floyd they nodded their heads. They said, what with the rains, they waited for the racing of the waters to slow down, but that he went out on them. They said he was out on them now, but would come back to the camp, if he did not turn over and drown first. She asked the fishermen to let her wait there with them, since it was to them that he would return. They said it did not matter to them how long she waited, or where.

She stood by the nets. A little distance away men and women were cooking and eating and she smelled the fish and the wild meat. The river went by immea-surable under the sky, moving and dimly catching and snagging itself, freeing it-self without effort, heavy with its great waves of drift, deep with stirring fish.

But after a certain length of time, the men that had been throwing knives at the tree by the last light put her inside a grounded houseboat on the plank of which chickens were standing. The willow branches hung down over and dragged softly back and forth across the roof. There were noises and fires all around. There were pigs in the wood.

One by one the men came in to her. She actually spoke to the first one that entered between the dozing chickens, for now she could speak to everyone, in a vague stir of welcome or in the humility that moved now deep in her spirit. About them all and closer to them than their own breath was the smell of trees that had bled to the knives they wore.

When she called out, she did not call any name; it was a cry with a rising sound, as if she said "Go back," or asked a question, and then at the last protested. A rude laugh covered her cry, and somehow both the harsh human sounds could easily have been heard as rejoicing, going out over the river in the dark night. By the fire, little boys were slapped crossly by their mothers—as if they knew that the original smile now crossed Jenny's face, and hung there no matter what was done to her, like a bit of color that kindles in the sky after the light has gone.

"Is she asleep? Is she in a spell? Or is she dead?" asked a little old bright-eyed woman who went and looked in the door, and crept up to the now meditating men outside. She was so precise in her question that she even held up three rheumatic fingers when she asked.

"She's waiting for Billy Floyd," they said.

The old woman nodded, and nodded out to the flowing river, with the firelight following her face and showing its dignity. The younger boys separated and took their turns throwing knives with a dull *pit* at the tree.

✍ *Elizabeth Bishop* (*1911–1979*)

Elizabeth Bishop's straightforward diction has much in common with her fellow New England poet Robert Frost, yet the influences on Bishop's emotionally powerful descriptive poetry range from the work of seventeenth-century author George Herbert to the works of Jesuit poet Gerard Manley Hopkins and American Transcendentalist Henry David Thoreau. Bishop spent the early years of her life shuttling back and forth between the two sets of grandparents who raised her, one pair in Nova Scotia, the other in her birthplace of Worcester, Massachusetts. Because she suffered from severe asthma, Bishop attended school only irregularly. She enrolled in Vassar College in 1930 and there began to discover her literary gifts. With her friends Muriel Rukeyser and Mary McCarthy she helped found a college literary magazine. She also published her stories and poems in national magazines and, while still at college, formed a lifelong friendship with poet Marianne Moore, who would become her mentor and who convinced her to devote herself to her writing.

After college, Bishop traveled extensively. From 1951 to 1966, she lived in Brazil. In the late 1960s she returned to the United States and held an academic position at the University of Washington. During the last two years of her life, she taught at Harvard. Her collections include North and South *(1946),* Questions of Travel *(1965), and* Geography III *(1976). Bishop was awarded a Pulitzer Prize in 1956. Although an ardent feminist, she refused to feature explicit political positions in her poems, believing that art should transcend questions of gender. Nonetheless, readers do see in her natural descriptions points of view or perspectives that might productively be labeled "feminine." Most of all, however, Bishop is known for her powerful, seemingly objective visual imagery, captured in poems such as "The Fish" which narrates an encounter between human and animal. As is typical of other Bishop efforts, there is more to the poem than sheer description; there is an inner moral transformation on the part of the beholder.*

The Fish

I caught a tremendous fish
and held him beside the boat
half out of water, with my hook

fast in a corner of his mouth.
He didn't fight.   5
He hadn't fought at all.
He hung a grunting weight,
battered and venerable
and homely. Here and there
his brown skin hung in strips   10
like ancient wallpaper,
and its pattern of darker brown
was like wallpaper:
shapes like full-blown roses
stained and lost through age.   15
He was speckled with barnacles,
fine rosettes of lime,
and infested
with tiny white sea-lice,
and underneath two or three   20
rags of green weed hung down.
While his gills were breathing in
the terrible oxygen
—the frightening gills,
fresh and crisp with blood,   25
that can cut so badly—
I thought of the coarse white flesh
packed in like feathers,
the big bones and the little bones,
the dramatic reds and blacks   30
of his shiny entrails,
and the pink swim-bladder
like a big peony.
I looked into his eyes
which were far larger than mine   35
but shallower, and yellowed,
the irises backed and packed
with tarnished tinfoil
seen through the lenses
of old scratched isinglass.[1]   40
They shifted a little, but not
to return my stare.
—It was more like the tipping
of an object toward the light.
I admired his sullen face,   45
the mechanism of his jaw,
and then I saw

---

[1] A semitransparent substance, made from fish, and often used in the past for window covering.

that from his lower lip
—if you could call it a lip—
grim, wet, and weaponlike,   50
hung five old pieces of fish-line,
or four and a wire leader
with the swivel still attached,
with all their five big hooks
grown firmly in his mouth.   55
A green line, frayed at the end
where he broke it, two heavier lines,
and a fine black thread
still crimped from the strain and snap
when it broke and he got away.   60
Like medals with their ribbons
frayed and wavering,
a five-haired beard of wisdom
trailing from his aching jaw.
I stared and stared   65
and victory filled up
the little rented boat,
from the pool of bilge
where oil had spread a rainbow
around the rusted engine   70
to the bailer rusted orange,
the sun-cracked thwarts,
the oarlocks on their strings,
the gunnels—until everything
was rainbow, rainbow, rainbow!   80
And I let the fish go.

The Moose

For Grace Bulmer Bowers

From narrow provinces
of fish and bread and tea,
home of the long tides
where the bay leaves the sea
twice a day and takes   5
the herrings long rides,

where if the river
enters or retreats
in a wall of brown foam
depends on if it meets   10

the bay coming in,
the bay not at home;

where, silted red,
sometimes the sun sets
facing a red sea,   15
and others, veins the flats'
lavender, rich mud
in burning rivulets;

on red, gravelly roads,
down rows of sugar maples,   20
past clapboard farmhouses
and neat, clapboard churches,
bleached, ridged as clamshells,
past twin silver birches,

through late afternoon   25
a bus journeys west,
the windshield flashing pink,
pink glancing off of metal,
brushing the dented flank
of blue, beat-up enamel;   30

down hollows, up rises,
and waits, patient, while
a lone traveller gives
kisses and embraces
to seven relatives   35
and a collie supervises.

Goodbye to the elms,
to the farm, to the dog.
The bus starts. The light
grows richer; the fog,   40
shifting, salty, thin,
comes closing in.

Its cold, round crystals
form and slide and settle
in the white hens' feathers,   45
in gray glazed cabbages,
on the cabbage roses
and lupins like apostles;

the sweet peas cling
to their wet white string   50
on the whitewashed fences;
bumblebees creep

inside the foxgloves,
and evening commences.

One stop at Bass River.   55
Then the Economies—
Lower, Middle, Upper;
Five Islands, Five Houses,
where a woman shakes a tablecloth
out after supper.   60

A pale flickering. Gone.
The Tantramar marshes
and the smell of salt hay.
An iron bridge trembles
and a loose plank rattles   65
but doesn't give way.

On the left, a red light
swims through the dark:
a ship's port lantern.
Two rubber boots show,   70
illuminated, solemn.
A dog gives one bark.

A woman climbs in
with two market bags,
brisk, freckled, elderly.   75
"A grand night. Yes, sir,
all the way to Boston."
She regards us amicably.

Moonlight as we enter
the New Brunswick woods,   80
hairy, scratchy, splintery;
moonlight and mist
caught in them like lamb's wool
on bushes in a pasture.

The passengers lie back.   85
Snores. Some long sighs.
A dreamy divagation
begins in the night,
a gentle, auditory,
slow hallucination. . . .   90

In the creakings and noises,
an old conversation
—not concerning us,
but recognizable, somewhere,

back in the bus: 95
Grandparents' voices

uninterruptedly
talking, in Eternity:
names being mentioned,
things cleared up finally;   100
what he said, what she said,
who got pensioned;

deaths, deaths and sicknesses;
the year he remarried;
the year (something) happened.   105
She died in childbirth.
That was the son lost
when the schooner foundered.

He took to drink. Yes.
She went to the bad.   110
When Amos began to pray
even in the store and
finally the family had
to put him away.

"Yes . . ." that peculiar   115
affirmative. "Yes . . ."
A sharp, indrawn breath,
half groan, half acceptance,
that means "Life's like that.
We know it (also death)."   120

Talking the way they talked
in the old featherbed,
peacefully, on and on,
dim lamplight in the hall,
down in the kitchen, the dog   125
tucked in her shawl.

Now, it's all right now
even to fall asleep
just as on all those nights.
— Suddenly the bus driver   130
stops with a jolt,
turns off his lights.

A moose has come out of
the impenetrable wood
and stands there, looms, rather,   135
in the middle of the road.

It approaches; it sniffs at
the bus's hot hood.

Towering, antlerless,
high as a church,   140
homely as a house
(or, safe as houses).
A man's voice assures us
"Perfectly harmless. . . ."

Some of the passengers   145
exclaim in whispers,
childishly, softly,
"Sure are big creatures."
"It's awful plain."
"Look! It's a she!"   150

Taking her time,
she looks the bus over,
grand, otherworldly.
Why, why do we feel
(we all feel) this sweet   155
sensation of joy?

"Curious creatures,"
says our quiet driver,
rolling his *r*'s.
"Look at that, would you."   160
Then he shifts gears.
For a moment longer,

by craning backward,
the moose can be seen
on the moonlit macadam;   165
then there's a dim
smell of moose, an acrid
smell of gasoline.

🐦 Dylan Thomas *(1914–1953)*

Dylan Thomas was born in Swansea, Wales, and became renowned at age twenty following the publication of his first book, 18 Poems *(1934), and his next,* Twenty-Five Poems *(1936). Before his early death, he had produced several more collections, including* The Map of Love *(1939),* Deaths and Entrances *(1946), and* Collected Poems *(1952). He also wrote the autobiography* Portrait of the Artist as a Young Dog *(1940) and the play* Under Milk Wood *(1954). During his lifetime, Thomas was a well-known figure, widely admired for his subtle, sonorous readings of his own poems as well as those of others, but generally notorious for his dissolute lifestyle, especially his irreverent public behavior and uncontrolled alcoholism, which contributed to his death at only age thirty-nine. Thomas's personal reputation probably accounts for the fact that his poetry is sometimes alleged to be loud and reckless, when in fact it is carefully structured.*

Thomas's poems are, like his own life, marked by violent contrasts. His works bear the unmistakable imprint of his puritanical upbringing; at the same time, they are overwhelmingly sensual and emotionally jarring. Often, he narrowly skirts outright blasphemy. In "This Bread I Break" for example, Thomas considers the Holy Communion along with the metabolic transformation of "oat and grape" into flesh and blood. Evidently his intention is either to invert the meaning of the sacrament or to show that its meaning is deeper, that it is a communion not only of man and God but also of the body and elemental nature. It is hard to say, however, which of these readings is correct.

Thomas often writes as if he is desperately afraid of forgetting some astounding truth. Two themes are predominant in his poetry: First, he is convinced of the unity of nature, that all things are common in their elements and impelled by the same forces. Second, he is fascinated by the transformations of individual organisms, and of nature as a whole, at certain times and seasons. He is so amazed by these transformations that he often suggests that they are magical or supernatural processes. In order to advance these ideas, Thomas uses shocking contrasts, free associations, and intense, brilliant images. Although his poetry is sometimes grandiloquent, he has nevertheless created some of the most emotionally intense and intellectually provocative poetry of the twentieth century.

The force that through the green fuse drives the flower

The force that through the green fuse drives the flower
Drives my green age; that blasts the roots of trees
Is my destroyer.
And I am dumb to tell the crooked rose
My youth is bent by the same wintry fever.   5

The force that drives the water through the rocks
Drives my red blood; that dries the mouthing streams
Turns mine to wax.
And I am dumb to mouth unto my veins
How at the mountain spring the same mouth sucks.   10

The hand that whirls the water in the pool
Stirs the quicksand; that ropes the blowing wind
Hauls my shroud sail.
And I am dumb to tell the hanging man
How of my clay is made the hangman's lime.   15

The lips of time leech to the fountain head;
Love drips and gathers, but the fallen blood
Shall calm her sores.
And I am dumb to tell a weather's wind
How time has ticked a heaven round the stars.   20

And I am dumb to tell the lover's tomb
How at my sheet goes the same crooked worm.

Fern Hill

Now as I was young and easy under the apple boughs
About the lilting house and happy as the grass was green,
    The night above the dingle starry,
        Time let me hail and climb
    Golden in the heydays of his eyes,   5
And honoured among wagons I was prince of the apple towns
And once below a time I lordly had the trees and leaves
        Trail with daisies and barley
    Down the rivers of the windfall light.

And as I was green and carefree, famous among the barns   10
About the happy yard and singing as the farm was home,
    In the sun that is young once only,
        Time let me play and be
    Golden in the mercy of his means,
And green and golden I was huntsman and herdsman, the calves   15
Sang to my horn, the foxes on the hills barked clear and cold,
        And the sabbath rang slowly
    In the pebbles of the holy streams.

All the sun long it was running, it was lovely, the hay
Fields high as the house, the tunes from the chimneys, it was air   20
    And playing, lovely and watery
        And fire green as grass.
    And nightly under the simple stars
As I rode to sleep the owls were bearing the farm away,
All the moon long I heard, blessed among stables, the nightjars   25
    Flying with the ricks, and the horses
        Flashing into the dark.

And then to awake, and the farm, like a wanderer white
With the dew, come back, the cock on his shoulder: it was all
    Shining, it was Adam and maiden,   30
        The sky gathered again
    And the sun grew round that very day.

So it must have been after the birth of the simple light
In the first, spinning place, the spellbound horses walking warm
   Out of the whinnying green stable   35
      On to the fields of praise.

And honoured among foxes and pheasants by the gay house
Under the new made clouds and happy as the heart was long,
   In the sun born over and over,
      I ran my heedless ways,   40
   My wishes raced through the house high hay
And nothing I cared, at my sky blue trades, that time allows
In all his tuneful turning so few and such morning songs
   Before the children green and golden
      Follow him out of grace,   45

Nothing I cared, in the lamb white days, that time would take me
Up to the swallow thronged loft by the shadow of my hand,
   In the moon that is always rising,
      Nor that riding to sleep
   I should hear him fly with the high fields   50
And wake to the farm forever fled from the childless land.
Oh as I was young and easy in the mercy of his means,
      Time held me green and dying
   Though I sang in my chains like the sea.

✒ *Howard Nemerov* (1920–1991)

*Born and raised in New York City, Howard Nemerov might have been expected to be-
come a stereotypical urban intellectual, with a distaste for nature. Instead, from an early
age he was attuned to even the most subtle appearances of the natural world, both as he
found them on walks through Central Park and as he encountered them on his family's
periodic excursions to the countryside. He attended Harvard University, graduating in
1941, and during World War II, he served as an officer in the Royal Canadian Air
Force and the U.S. Air Force. After the war, he taught at several distinguished institutions of higher learning: Hamilton College, Bennington College, Brandeis University,
the University of Minnesota, and Washington University in St. Louis. Throughout his
peripatetic teaching career, he was exposed to a cross section of American people and
places; his extended residence in rural areas of Vermont and Minnesota enlarged his understanding and appreciation of the wild.*

    *Nemerov published a great variety of fiction, poetry, and critical essays. His poetry
ranges in tone from witty repartee to deep philosophical reflection; his collections include*
Image and the Law *(1947),* The Salt Garden *(1955),* Mirrors and Windows
(1958), and Collected Poems *(1964), which won the Pulitzer Prize. Later collections
include* The Blue Swallows *(1964),* The Western Approaches *(1975),* Inside the
Onion *(1984), and* War Stories *(1987). In the year 1963–64 Nemerov served as Po-*

etry Consultant at the Library of Congress, and in 1988 he was Poet Laureate of the United States.

Nemerov's nature poetry is just one of many strands that emerge from the skein of his collected work. Particularly in his poems about fish, birds, and reptiles, his voice is distinctive in the respect that he pays to the enigmatic qualities of these nonhuman creatures. Wary of anthropomorphizing them, his poetry bears witness to their uncanny otherness. In "The Goose Fish," for example, a trysting pair of lovers suddenly notice the fish's "hugely grinning head," but "they knew not what he would express." The goose fish remains inscrutable to the end, like Melville's White Whale.

The Goose Fish

On the long shore, lit by the moon
To show them properly alone,
Two lovers suddenly embraced
So that their shadows were as one.
The ordinary night was graced   5
For them by the swift tide of blood
That silently they took at flood,
And for a little time they prized
    Themselves emparadised.

Then, as if shaken by stage-fright   10
Beneath the hard moon's bony light,
They stood together on the sand
Embarrassed in each other's sight
But still conspiring hand in hand,
Until they saw, there underfoot,   15
As though the world had found them out,
The goose fish turning up, though dead,
    His hugely grinning head.

There in the china light he lay,
Most ancient and corrupt and grey.   20
They hesitated at his smile,
Wondering what it seemed to say
To lovers who a little while
Before had thought to understand,
By violence upon the sand,   25
The only way that could be known
    To make a world their own.

It was a wide and moony grin
Together peaceful and obscene;
They knew not what he would express,   30
So finished a comedian

He might mean failure or success,
But took it for an emblem of
Their sudden, new and guilty love
To be observed by, when they kissed,   35
   That rigid optimist.

So he became their patriarch,
Dreadfully mild in the half-dark.
His throat that the sand seemed to choke,
His picket teeth, these left their mark   40
But never did explain the joke
That so amused him, lying there
While the moon went down to disappear
Along the still and tilted track.
   That bears the zodiac.   45

Sandpipers

In the small territory and time
Between one wave and the next, they run
Down the beach and back, eating things
Which seem, conveniently for them,
To surface only when the sand gets wet.   5
Small, dapper birds, they make me think
Of commuters seen, say, in an early movie
Where the rough screen wavers, where the light
Jerks and seems to rain; of clockwork dolls
Set going on the sidewalk, drawing a crowd   10
Beside the newsstand at five o'clock; their legs
Black toothpicks, their heads nodding at nothing.
But this comedy is based upon exact
Perceptions, and delicately balanced
Between starvation and the sea: 15
Though sometimes I have seen one slip and fall,
From either the undertow or greed,
And have to get up in the wave's open mouth,
Still eating, I have never seen
One caught; if necessary he spreads his wings,   20
With the white stripe, and flutters rather than flies
Out, to begin eating again at once.
Now they are over every outer beach,
Procrastinating steadily southwards
In endlessly local comings and goings.   25

Whenever a flock of them takes flight,
And flies with the beautiful unison

Of banners in the wind, they are
No longer funny. It is their courage,
Meaningless as the word is when compared   30
With their thoughtless precisions, which strikes
Me when I watch them hidden and revealed
Between two waves, lost in the sea's
Lost color as they distance me; flying
From winter already, while I   35
Am in August. When suddenly they turn
In unison, all their bellies shine
Like mirrors flashing white with signals
I cannot read, but I wish them well.

The Blue Swallows

Across the millstream below the bridge
Seven blue swallows divide the air
In shapes invisible and evanescent,
Kaleidoscopic beyond the mind's
Or memory's power to keep them there.   5

"History is where tensions were,"
"Form is the diagram of forces."
Thus, helplessly, there on the bridge,
While gazing down upon those birds—
How strange, to be above the birds!—   10
Thus helplessly the mind in its brain
Weaves up relation's spindrift web,
Seeing the swallow's tails as nibs
Dipped in invisible ink, writing . . .

Poor mind, what would you have them write?   15
Some cabalistic history
Whose authorship you might ascribe
To God? to Nature? Ah, poor ghost,
You've capitalized your Self enough.
That villainous William of Occam[1]   20
Cut out the feet from under that dream
Some seven centuries ago.
It's taken that long for the mind
To waken, yawn and stretch, to see
With opened eyes emptied of speech   25

[1] An English scholastic philosopher, who taught at Oxford in the early fourteenth century. He argued that abstract knowledge has no relation to reality and that intuitive knowledge provides our immediate knowledge of things and experiences.

The real world where the spelling mind
Imposes with its grammar book
Unreal relations on the blue
Swallows. Perhaps when you will have
Fully awakened, I shall show you   30
A new thing: even the water
Flowing away beneath those birds
Will fail to reflect their flying forms,
And the eyes that see become as stones
Whence never tears shall fall again.   35

O swallows, swallows, poems are not
The point. Finding again the world,
That is the point, where loveliness
Adorns intelligible things
Because the mind's eye lit the sun.   40

The Mud Turtle

Out of the earth beneath the water,
Dragging over the stubble field
Up to the hilltop in the sun
On his way from water to water,
He rests an hour in the garden,   5
His alien presence observed by all:
His lordly darkness decked in filth
Bearded with weed like a lady's favor,
He is a black planet, another world
Never till now appearing, even now   10
Not quite believably old and big,
Set in the summer morning's midst
A gloomy gemstone to the sun opposed.
Our measures of him do not matter,
He would be huge at any size;   15
And neither does the number of his years,
The time he comes from doesn't count.

When the boys tease him with sticks
He breaks the sticks, striking with
As great a suddenness as speed;   20
Fingers and toes would snap as soon,
Says one of us, and the others shudder.
Then when they turn him on his back
To see the belly heroically yellow,
He throws himself fiercely to his feet,   25
Brings down the whole weight of his shell,
Spreads out his claws and digs himself in

Immovably, invulnerably,
But for the front foot on the left,
Red-budded, with the toes torn off.   30
So over he goes again, and shows
Us where a swollen leech is fastened
Softly between plastron and shell.
Nobody wants to go close enough
To burn it loose; he can't be helped   35
Either, there is no help for him
As he makes it to his feet again
And drags away to the meadow's edge.
We see the tall grass open and wave
Around him, it closes, he is gone   40
Over the hill toward another water,
Bearing his hard and chambered hurt
Down, down, down, beneath the water,
Beneath the earth beneath. He takes
A secret wound out of the world.   45

The Consent

Late in November, on a single night
Not even near to freezing, the ginkgo trees
That stand along the walk drop all their leaves
In one consent, and neither to rain nor to wind
But as though to time alone: the golden and green   5
Leaves litter the lawn today, that yesterday
Had spread aloft their fluttering fans of light.

What signal from the stars? What senses took it in?
What in those wooden motives so decided
To strike their leaves, to down their leaves,   10
Rebellion or surrender? and if this
Can happen thus, what race shall be exempt?
What use to learn the lessons taught by time,
If a star at any time may tell us: *Now.*

✍ *James Dickey* (1923–1997)

James Dickey, one of the foremost American poets of the twentieth century, was born in Atlanta, Georgia. He was quite athletic and participated enthusiastically in sports while he was growing up. In the 1940s and 1950s, Dickey served in the U.S. Army Air Corps, participating in many bombing missions during World War II and the Korean War. These experiences taught him invaluable lessons about struggle and survival.

As a fiction writer, Dickey knew how to utilize his public's tastes to build a lucrative career. He turned his controversial novel Deliverance *(1970) into a popular screenplay for a successful movie. He was so skilled at catering to the public in his fiction that he once remarked that writing fiction for him was only a way "to pay the bills." In his personal life, Dickey was less successful; his intense view of the world as a theater for struggle and survival caused him much mental anguish, leading him to promiscuity, frequent lying, and alcoholism. In his poetry, however, Dickey knew how to subtly convey this turmoil, and he developed a strongly empathic and observant voice that, coupled with his masterful use of free verse, has made him one of the major poets of our time. Nature is a frequent subject of Dickey's poems, because it was the most suitable setting for his themes of competition, life, and death. It is in Dickey's nature poetry that his voice discovers its many tones: sometimes melancholy, often ecstatic, but always observant and fully engaged with the subject.*

Dickey's novels include Buckdancer's Choice *(1965),* Alnilam *(1987), and* To the White Sea *(1993). His collections of poetry include* Falling, May Day Sermon, and Other Poems *(1982),* The Eagle's Mile *(1990), and* The Whole Motion: Collected Poems *(1992).*

The Heaven of Animals

Here they are. The soft eyes open.
If they have lived in a wood
It is a wood.
If they have lived on plains
It is grass rolling   5
Under their feet forever.

Having no souls, they have come,
Anyway, beyond their knowing.
Their instincts wholly bloom
And they rise.   10
The soft eyes open.

To match them, the landscape flowers,
Outdoing, desperately
Outdoing what is required:
The richest wood,   15
The deepest field.

For some of these,
It could not be the place
It is, without blood.
These hunt, as they have done,   20
But with claws and teeth grown perfect,

More deadly than they can believe.
They stalk more silently,

And crouch on the limbs of trees,
And their descent   25
Upon the bright backs of their prey

May take years
In a sovereign floating of joy.
And those that are hunted
Know this as their life,   30
Their reward: to walk

Under such trees in full knowledge
Of what is in glory above them,
And to feel no fear,
But acceptance, compliance.   35
Fulfilling themselves without pain

At the cycle's center,
They tremble, they walk
Under the tree,
They fall, they are torn,   40
They rise, they walk again.

In the Tree House at Night

And now the green household is dark.
The half-moon completely is shining
On the earth-lighted tops of the trees.
To be dead, a house must be still.
The floor and the walls wave me slowly;   5
I am deep in them over my head.
The needles and pine cones about me

Are full of small birds at their roundest,
Their fists without mercy gripping
Hard down through the tree to the roots   10
To sing back at light when they feel it.
We lie here like angels in bodies,
My brothers and I, one dead,
The other asleep from much living,

In mid-air huddled beside me.   15
Dark climbed to us here as we climbed
Up the nails I have hammered all day
Through the sprained, comic rungs of the ladder
Of broom handles, crate slats, and laths
Foot by foot up the trunk to the branches   20
Where we came out at last over lakes

Of leaves, of fields disencumbered of earth
That move with the moves of the spirit.
Each nail that sustains us I set here;
Each nail in the house is now steadied   25
By my dead brother's huge, freckled hand.
Through the years, he has pointed his hammer
Up into these limbs, and told us

That we must ascend, and all lie here.
Step after step he has brought me,   30
Embracing the trunk as his body,
Shaking its limbs with my heartbeat,
Till the pine cones danced without wind
And fell from the branches like apples.
In the arm-slender forks of our dwelling   35

I breathe my live brother's light hair.
The blanket around us becomes
As solid as stone, and it sways.
With all my heart, I close
The blue, timeless eye of my mind.   40
Wind springs, as my dead brother smiles
And touches the tree at the root;

A shudder of joy runs up
The trunk; the needles tingle;
One bird uncontrollably cries.   45
The wind changes round, and I stir
Within another's life. Whose life?
Who is dead? Whose presence is living?
When may I fall strangely to earth,

Who am nailed to this branch by a spirit?   50
Can two bodies make up a third?
To sing, must I feel the world's light?
My green, graceful bones fill the air
With sleeping birds. Alone, alone
And with them I move gently.   55
I move at the heart of the world.

The Salt Marsh

Once you have let the first blade
Spring back behind you
To the way it has always been,
You no longer know where you are.

All you can see are the tall 5
Stalks of sawgrass, not sawing,
But each of them holding its tip
Exactly at the level where your hair

Begins to grow from your forehead.
Wherever you come to is 10
The same as before,
With the same blades of oversized grass,
And wherever you stop, the one
Blade just in front of you leans,
That one only, and touches you 15
At the place where your hair begins

To grow; at that predestined touch
Your spine tingles crystally, like salt,
And the image of a crane occurs,
Each flap of its wings creating 20
Its feathers anew, this time whiter,
As the sun destroys all points
Of the compass, refusing to move
From its chosen noon.

Where is the place you have come from 25
With your buried steps full of new roots?
You cannot leap up to look out,
Yet you do not sink,
But seem to grow, and the sound,
The oldest of sounds, is your breath 30
Sighing like acres.
If you stand as you are for long,

Green panic may finally give
Way to another sensation,
For when the embodying wind 35
Rises, the grasses begin to weave
A little, then all together,
Not bending enough for you
To see your way clear of the swaying,
But moving just the same, 40

And nothing prevents your bending
With them, helping their wave
Upon wave upon wave upon wave
By not opposing,
By willing your supple inclusion 45
Among fields without promise of harvest,
In their marvelous, spiritual walking
Everywhere, anywhere.

✑ *Denise Levertov* (*1923–1997*)

Although she is considered one of America's most important modern poets, Denise Levertov was born and grew up in England, just outside of London in Ilford, Essex. Levertov's youth was spent in the company of adults who engaged in various political causes, most notably in the opposition to fascism in Germany and Spain. This same circle of friends later gave shelter to political refugees during the Second World War. She studied ballet, was home-schooled by her mother until the age of twelve, and worked as a nurse in London during the war.

Levertov published her first book of poems, The Double Image, *in 1946. The poems emphasized nature and sexual love. But by the 1960s, with books such as* The Sorrow Dance *(1967) and* Relearning the Alphabet *(1970), Levertov's poetry became more political, protesting now as a resident of the United States the U.S. military's involvement in Vietnam and earning her the label of a "liberal." These works made her one of the leading poets of her generation. Through the late 1970s and the 1980s, Levertov underwent a conversion to Christianity and her poetry began to take on a voice that echoed biblical texts. Her 1982 book* Candles in Babylon *was a revisiting of the political ideals of her earlier works, combined with her newfound Christian faith. By 1993, in her book* Evening Train, *Levertov was weaving a unique style of Romantic natural imagery and political idealism in her poems, speaking out against the Persian Gulf War.*

For Levertov, nature is sometimes a backdrop for portraying the artist as craftsman. At other times, the desirability of nature itself is the focus. The beautiful English countryside of her youth helped to shape her poetic vision, and often presents a counterpoint to the landscape of war and nuclear destruction and environmental degradation that her work frequently protests. Influenced by such poets as William Carlos Williams and H. D., her style is notable for its directness and plainness of diction. However, despite her poems' linguistic simplicity, Levertov came to view her poetry as a spiritual vocation and as an outlet for her responsibility to reveal the inner sacredness of all things.

She is the author of numerous collections of poetry in addition to those already mentioned, including Jacob's Ladder *(1961),* O Taste and See *(1964),* The Freeing of the Dust *(1975), and* Breathing the Water *(1987). She has also published three collections of essays:* The Poet in the World *(1973),* Light Up the Cave *(1981), and* Tesserae: Memories and Suppositions *(1995). Levertov held a number of academic positions at universities such as M.I.T., Brandeis, Tufts, and Stanford, and she remained a highly committed social activist. She protested actively against American military actions of every sort and was a leading figure in the antinuclear and environmentalist movements.*

The Life Around Us

For David Mitchell and David Hass

Poplar and oak awake
all night. And through
all weathers of the days of the year.
There is a consciousness

undefined.   5
Yesterday's twilight, August
almost over, lasted, slowly changing,
until daybreak. Human sounds
were shut behind curtains.
No human saw the night in this garden,   10
sliding blue into morning.
Only the sightless trees,
without braincells, lived it
and wholly knew it.

Beginners

Dedicated to the memory of Karen Silkwood and Eliot Gralla

> *"From too much love of living,*
> *   Hope and desire set free,*
> *Even the weariest river*
> *   Winds somewhere to the sea—"*

But we have only begun
to love the earth.

We have only begun
to imagine the fulness of life.

How could we tire of hope?   5
—so much is in bud.

How can desire fail?
—we have only begun

to imagine justice and mercy,
only begun to envision   10

how it might be
to live as siblings with beast and flower,
not as oppressors.

Surely our river
cannot already be hastening   15
into the sea of nonbeing?

Surely it cannot
drag, in the silt,
all that is innocent?

Not yet, not yet—   20
there is too much broken
that must be mended,

too much hurt we have done to each other
that cannot yet be forgiven.

We have only begun to know   25
the power that is in us if we would join
our solitudes in the communion of struggle.

So much is unfolding that must
complete its gesture,

so much is in bud.   30

Brother Ivy

Between road and sidewalk, the broadleafed ivy,
unloved, dusty, littered, sanctuary of rats,
gets on with its life. New leaves shine gaily
among dogged older ones
that have lost their polish.   5
It does not require appreciation. The foliage
conceals a brown tangle of stems
thick as a mangrove swamp; the roots
are spread tenaciously. Unwatered
throughout the long droughts, it simply   10
grips the dry ground by the scruff of the neck.

I am not its steward.
If we are siblings, and I
my brother's keeper therefore,
the relation is reciprocal. The ivy   15
meets its obligation by pure
undoubtable being.

Mysterious Disappearance of May's Past Perfect

Even as the beaches blacken again with oil,
reporters tell us, "If the ship had had
a double hull, the spill
may not have occurred." And now a poet
writing of one who died some years ago   5
too young, recounts that had she been and done
otherwise than she was and did, it's thought she
"*may* have survived." The poet does not agree—
but this impoverished grammar, nonetheless,

places in doubt an undeniable death.   10
          Is it collective fear suppresses
might have, fear that causes do
produce effects? Does *may* still trail with it,
misused, a comforting openness, illusion
that what has already happened, after all   15
can be revoked, reversed?
                    Or, in these years
when from our mother-tongue some words
were carelessly tossed away, while others hastily
were being invented—chief among them, *overkill*—   20
has the other meaning, swollen as never before,
of *might* thrust out of memory its minor
homonym, so apt for the precise
nuance of elegy, for the hint of judgement,
reproachful clarities of tense and sense?   25

Tragic Error

The earth is the Lord's, we gabbled,
and the fullness thereof—
while we looted and pillaged, claiming indemnity:
the fullness thereof
given over to us, to our use—   5
while we preened ourselves, sure of our power,
wilful or ignorant, through the centuries.

Miswritten, misread, that charge:
subdue was the false, the misplaced word in the story.
Surely we were to have been   10
earth's mind, mirror, reflective source.
Surely our task
was to have been
to love the earth,
to *dress and keep it* like Eden's garden.   15

That would have been our *dominion:*
to be those cells of earth's body that could
perceive and imagine, could bring the planet
into the haven it is to be known,
(as the eye blesses the hand, perceiving   20
its form and the work it can do).

The Almost-Island

The woods which give me their silence,
their ancient Douglas firs and red cedars, their ferns,
are not the wilderness. They're contained
in the two-mile circumference of an almost-island,
a park in city limits. Pleasure-boats crowd at weekends   5
into the small bay. The veils hiding the mountain
are not always natural cloud. Eagle and heron
speak of solitude, but when you emerge from forest shade
the downtown skyline rears up, phantasmagoric but near,
across the water. Yet the woods, the lake,   10
the great-winged birds, the vast mountain at the horizon,
are Nature: metonymy of the spirit's understanding
knows them to be a concentrate
of all Thoreau or Wordsworth knew by that word,
Nature: "a never-failing principle   15
of joy and purest passion." Thoreau's own pond
was bounded by the railroad, punctuated
by the "telegraph trees" and their Aeolian wires.
All of my dread and all of my longing hope that Earth
may outwit the huge stupidity of its humans,   20
can find their signs and portents here, their recapitulations
of joy and awe. This fine, incised two inches
of goldsmith-work just drifted down, can speak
as well for *tree* as a thousand forest acres,
and tree means depth of roots, uprisen height, outreaching branches.   25
This musical speech of wavelets jounced against reeds
as a boat's wake tardily reaches the shore,
is *voice of the waters*, voice of all the blue
encircling the terrestrial globe
which as a child I loved to spin   30
slowly upon its creaking axis—blue globe
we have seen now, round, small as an apple,
afloat in the wilderness we name
so casually, as if we knew it
or ever could know it, "Space."   35

✒ Flannery O'Connor (1925–1964)

Mary Flannery O'Connor was born in Savannah, Georgia. She attended Georgia State College for Women (B.A., 1945) and the University of Iowa (M.F.A., 1947). From the publication of her first book, the novel Wise Blood *(1952), she established herself as— and remains—one of the most influential writers of fiction in the late twentieth century. Among her many awards are the National Institute of Arts and Letters grant in litera-*

ture, the National Book Award, and the O. Henry Award. Her other books include A Good Man Is Hard to Find *(1955),* The Violent Bear It Away *(1960), and* Everything That Rises Must Converge *(1965).*

Best known for her incisive short stories, O'Connor's subject is most often human weakness, which she writes about with darkly comic genius. Yet she is not a writer of satire or social criticism. In the world of her fiction, characters are forced to confront their limitations as human beings and to move somehow beyond them, to become the agents of their own salvation. It is a salvation, however, won at great price. O'Connor was a deeply religious writer, though the brand of Roman Catholicism embodied in her work has a strong Pentecostal strain. The God of her fiction is a cross between Sophocles and Monty Python, and nature, far from being a haven from suffering, is an unforgiving backdrop for the dark comedy of human life. In "A View of the Woods," O'Connor works with essential social dualisms (youth and age, male and female, rich and poor). The relationships between and among these terms are each complicated by one of the questions that drives the plot: whether or not land is improved through development. As in the fiction of William Faulkner, the landscape of the rural American South is much more a character in O'Connor's work than it is simply its setting. At age twenty-six, O'Connor contracted lupus erythematosus, the disease that took her father's life and that would cause her early death at thirty-nine, in Milledgeville, Georgia, on August 3, 1964.

A View of the Woods

The week before, Mary Fortune and the old man had spent every morning watching the machine that lifted out dirt and threw it in a pile. The construction was going on by the new lakeside on one of the lots that the old man had sold to somebody who was going to put up a fishing club. He and Mary Fortune drove down there every morning about ten o'clock and he parked his car, a battered mulberry-colored Cadillac, on the embankment that overlooked the spot where the work was going on. The red corrugated lake eased up to within fifty feet of the construction and was bordered on the other side by a black line of woods which appeared at both ends of the view to walk across the water and continue along the edge of the fields.

He sat on the bumper and Mary Fortune straddled the hood and they watched, sometimes for hours, while the machine systematically ate a square red hole in what had once been a cow pasture. It happened to be the only pasture that Pitts had succeeded in getting the bitterweed off and when the old man had sold it, Pitts had nearly had a stroke; and as far as Mr. Fortune was concerned, he could have gone on and had it.

"Any fool that would let a cow pasture interfere with progress is not on my books," he had said to Mary Fortune several times from his seat on the bumper, but the child did not have eyes for anything but the machine. She sat on the hood, looking down into the red pit, watching the big disembodied gullet gorge itself on the clay, then, with the sound of a deep sustained nausea and a slow mechanical revulsion, turn and spit it up. Her pale eyes behind her spectacles followed the repeated motion of it again and again and her face—a small replica of the old man's—never lost its look of complete absorption.

No one was particularly glad that Mary Fortune looked like her grandfather except the old man himself. He thought it added greatly to her attractiveness. He thought she was the smartest and the prettiest child he had ever seen and he let the rest of them know that if, IF that was, he left anything to anybody, it would be Mary Fortune he left it to. She was now nine, short and broad like himself, with his very light blue eyes, his wide prominent forehead, his steady penetrating scowl and his rich florid complexion; but she was like him on the inside too. She had, to a singular degree, his intelligence, his strong will, and his push and drive. Though there was seventy years' difference in their ages, the spiritual distance between them was slight. She was the only member of the family he had any respect for.

He didn't have any use for her mother, his third or fourth daughter (he could never remember which), though she considered that she took care of him. She considered—being careful not to say it, only to look it—that she was the one putting up with him in his old age and that she was the one he should leave the place to. She had married an idiot named Pitts and had had seven children, all likewise idiots except the youngest, Mary Fortune, who was a throwback to him. Pitts was the kind who couldn't keep his hands on a nickel and Mr. Fortune had allowed them, ten years ago, to move onto his place and farm it. What Pitts made went to Pitts but the land belonged to Fortune and he was careful to keep the fact before them. When the well had gone dry, he had not allowed Pitts to have a deep well drilled but had insisted that they pipe their water from the spring. He did not intend to pay for a drilled well himself and he knew that if he let Pitts pay for it, whenever he had occasion to say to Pitts, "It's my land you're sitting on," Pitts would be able to say to him, "Well, it's my pump that's pumping the water you're drinking."

Being there ten years, the Pittses had got to feel as if they owned the place. The daughter had been born and raised on it but the old man considered that when she married Pitts she showed that she preferred Pitts to home; and when she came back, she came back like any other tenant, though he would not allow them to pay rent for the same reason he would not allow them to drill a well. Anyone over sixty years of age is in an uneasy position unless he controls the greater interest and every now and then he gave the Pittses a practical lesson by selling off a lot. Nothing infuriated Pitts more than to see him sell off a piece of the property to an outsider, because Pitts wanted to buy it himself.

Pitts was a thin, long-jawed, irascible, sullen, sulking individual and his wife was the duty-proud kind: It's my duty to stay here and take care of Papa. Who would do it if I didn't? I do it knowing full well I'll get no reward for it. I do it because it's my duty.

The old man was not taken in by this for a minute. He knew they were waiting impatiently for the day when they could put him in a hole eight feet deep and cover him up with dirt. Then, even if he did not leave the place to them, they figured they would be able to buy it. Secretly he had made his will and left everything in trust to Mary Fortune, naming his lawyer and not Pitts as executor. When he died Mary Fortune could make the rest of them jump; and he didn't doubt for a minute that she would be able to do it.

Ten years ago they had announced that they were going to name the new baby Mark Fortune Pitts, after him, if it were a boy, and he had not delayed in telling them that if they coupled his name with the name Pitts he would put them off the place. When the baby came, a girl, and he had seen that even at the age of one day she bore his unmistakable likeness, he had relented and suggested himself that they name her Mary Fortune, after his beloved mother, who had died seventy years ago, bringing him into the world.

The Fortune place was in the country on a clay road that left the paved road fifteen miles away and he would never have been able to sell off any lots if it had not been for progress, which had always been his ally. He was not one of these old people who fight improvement, who object to everything new and cringe at every change. He wanted to see a paved highway in front of his house with plenty of new-model cars on it, he wanted to see a supermarket store across the road from him, he wanted to see a gas station, a motel, a drive-in picture-show within easy distance. Progress had suddenly set all this in motion. The electric power company had built a dam on the river and flooded great areas of the surrounding country and the lake that resulted touched his land along a half-mile stretch. Every Tom, Dick and Harry, every dog and his brother, wanted a lot on the lake. There was talk of their getting a telephone line. There was talk of paving the road that ran in front of the Fortune place. There was talk of an eventual town. He thought this should be called Fortune, Georgia. He was a man of advanced vision, even if he was seventy-nine years old.

The machine that drew up the dirt had stopped the day before and today they were watching the hole being smoothed out by two huge yellow bulldozers. His property had amounted to eight hundred acres before he began selling lots. He had sold five twenty-acre lots on the back of the place and every time he sold one, Pitts's blood pressure had gone up twenty points. "The Pittses are the kind that would let a cow pasture interfere with the future," he said to Mary Fortune, "but not you and me." The fact that Mary Fortune was a Pitts too was something he ignored, in a gentlemanly fashion, as if it were an affliction the child was not responsible for. He liked to think of her as being thoroughly of his clay. He sat on the bumper and she sat on the hood with her bare feet on his shoulders. One of the bulldozers had moved under them to shave the side of the embankment they were parked on. If he had moved his feet a few inches out, the old man could have dangled them over the edge.

"If you don't watch him," Mary Fortune shouted above the noise of the machine, "he'll cut off some of your dirt!"

"Yonder's the stob," the old man yelled. "He hasn't gone beyond the stob."

"Not YET he hasn't," she roared.

The bulldozer passed beneath them and went on to the far side. "Well you watch," he said. "Keep your eyes open and if he knocks that stob, I'll stop him. The Pittses are the kind that would let a cow pasture or a mule lot or a row of beans interfere with progress," he continued. "The people like you and me with heads on their shoulders know you can't stop the marcher time for a cow. . . ."

"He's shaking the stob on the other side!" she screamed and before he could stop her, she had jumped down from the hood and was running along the edge of the embankment, her little yellow dress billowing out behind.

"Don't run so near the edge," he yelled but she had already reached the stob and was squatting down by it to see how much it had been shaken. She leaned over the embankment and shook her fist at the man on the bulldozer. He waved at her and went on about his business. More sense in her little finger than all the rest of that tribe in their heads put together, the old man said to himself, and watched with pride as she started back to him.

She had a head of thick, very fine, sand-colored hair—the exact kind he had had when he had had any—that grew straight and was cut just above her eyes and down the sides of her cheeks to the tips of her ears so that it formed a kind of door opening onto the central part of her face. Her glasses were silver-rimmed like his and she even walked the way he did, stomach forward, with a careful abrupt gait, something between a rock and a shuffle. She was walking so close to the edge of the embankment that the outside of her right foot was flush with it.

"I said don't walk so close to the edge," he called; "you fall off there and you won't live to see the day this place gets built up." He was always very careful to see that she avoided dangers. He would not allow her to sit in snakey places or put her hands on bushes that might hide hornets.

She didn't move an inch. She had a habit of his of not hearing what she didn't want to hear and since this was a little trick he had taught her himself, he had to admire the way she practiced it. He foresaw that in her own old age it would serve her well. She reached the car and climbed back onto the hood without a word and put her feet back on his shoulders where she had had them before, as if he were no more than a part of the automobile. Her attention returned to the far bulldozer.

"Remember what you won't get if you don't mind," her grandfather remarked.

He was a strict disciplinarian but he had never whipped her. There were some children, like the first six Pittses, whom he thought should be whipped once a week on principle, but there were other ways to control intelligent children and he had never laid a rough hand on Mary Fortune. Furthermore, he had never allowed her mother or her brothers and sisters so much as to slap her. The elder Pitts was a different matter.

He was a man of a nasty temper and of ugly unreasonable resentments. Time and again, Mr. Fortune's heart had pounded to see him rise slowly from his place at the table—not the head, Mr. Fortune sat there, but from his place at the side—and abruptly, for no reason, with no explanation, jerk his head at Mary Fortune and say, "Come with me," and leave the room, unfastening his belt as he went. A look that was completely foreign to the child's face would appear on it. The old man could not define the look but it infuriated him. It was a look that was part terror and part respect and part something else, something very like cooperation. This look would appear on her face and she would get up and follow Pitts out. They would get in his truck and drive down the road out of earshot, where he would beat her.

Mr. Fortune knew for a fact that he beat her because he had followed them in his car and had seen it happen. He had watched from behind a boulder about a hundred feet away while the child clung to a pine tree and Pitts, as methodically as if he were whacking a bush with a sling blade, beat her around the ankles with his belt. All she had done was jump up and down as if she were standing on a hot stove and make a whimpering noise like a dog that was being peppered. Pitts had kept at it for about three minutes and then he had turned, without a word, and got back in his truck and left her there, and she had slid down under the tree and taken both feet in her hands and rocked back and forth. The old man had crept forward to catch her. Her face was contorted into a puzzle of small red lumps and her nose and eyes were running. He sprang on her and sputtered, "Why didn't you hit him back? Where's your spirit? Do you think I'd a let him beat me?"

She had jumped up and started backing away from him with her jaw stuck out. "Nobody beat me," she said.

"Didn't I see it with my own eyes?" he exploded.

"Nobody is here and nobody beat me," she said. "Nobody's ever beat me in my life and if anybody did, I'd kill him. You can see for yourself nobody is here."

"Do you call me a liar or a blindman!" he shouted. "I saw him with my own two eyes and you never did a thing but let him do it, you never did a thing but hang onto that tree and dance up and down a little and blubber and if it had been me, I'd a swung my fist in his face and . . ."

"Nobody was here and nobody beat me and if anybody did I'd kill him!" she yelled and then turned and dashed off through the woods.

"And I'm a Poland china pig and black is white!" he had roared after her and he had sat down on a small rock under the tree, disgusted and furious. This was Pitts's revenge on him. It was as if it were *he* that Pitts was driving down the road to beat and it was as if *he* were the one submitting to it. He had thought at first that he could stop him by saying that if he beat her, he would put them off the place but when he had tried that, Pitts had said, "Put me off and you put her off too. Go right ahead. She's mine to whip and I'll whip her every day of the year if it suits me."

Anytime he could make Pitts feel his hand he was determined to do it and at present he had a little scheme up his sleeve that was going to be a considerable blow to Pitts. He was thinking of it with relish when he told Mary Fortune to remember what she wouldn't get if she didn't mind, and he added, without waiting for an answer, that he might be selling another lot soon and that if he did, he might give her a bonus but not if she gave him any sass. He had frequent little verbal tilts with her but this was a sport like putting a mirror up in front of a rooster and watching him fight his reflection.

"I don't want no bonus," Mary Fortune said.

"I ain't ever seen you refuse one."

"You ain't ever seen me ask for one neither," she said.

"How much have you laid by?" he asked.

"Noner yer bidnis," she said and stamped his shoulders with her feet. "Don't be buttin into my bidnis."

"I bet you got it sewed up in your mattress," he said, "just like an old nigger woman. You ought to put it in the bank. I'm going to start you an account just as soon as I complete this deal. Won't anybody be able to check on it but me and you."

The bulldozer moved under them again and drowned out the rest of what he wanted to say. He waited and when the noise had passed, he could hold it in no longer. "I'm going to sell the lot right in front of the house for a gas station," he said. "Then we won't have to go down the road to get the car filled up, just step out the front door."

The Fortune house was set back about two hundred feet from the road and it was this two hundred feet that he intended to sell. It was the part that his daughter airily called "the lawn" though it was nothing but a field of weeds.

"You mean," Mary Fortune said after a minute, "the lawn?"

"Yes mam!" he said. "I mean the lawn," and he slapped his knee.

She did not say anything and he turned and looked up at her. There in the little rectangular opening of hair was his face looking back at him, but it was a reflection not of his present expression but of the darker one that indicated his displeasure. "That's where we play," she muttered.

"Well there's plenty of other places you can play," he said, irked by this lack of enthusiasm.

"We won't be able to see the woods across the road," she said.

The old man stared at her. "The woods across the road?" he repeated.

"We won't be able to see the view," she said.

"The view?" he repeated.

"The woods," she said; "we won't be able to see the woods from the porch."

"The woods from the porch?" he repeated.

Then she said, "My daddy grazes his calves on that lot."

The old man's wrath was delayed an instant by shock. Then it exploded in a roar. He jumped up and turned and slammed his fist on the hood of the car. "He can graze them somewheres else!"

"You fall off that embankment and you'll wish you hadn't," she said.

He moved from in front of the car around to the side, keeping his eye on her all the time. "Do you think I care where he grazes his calves! Do you think I'll let a calf interfere with my bidnis? Do you think I give a damn hoot where that fool grazes his calves?"

She sat, her red face darker than her hair, exactly reflecting his expression now. "He who calls his brother a fool is subject to hell fire," she said.

"Jedge not," he shouted, "lest ye be not jedged!" The tinge of his face was a shade more purple than hers. "You!" he said. "You let him beat you any time he wants to and don't do a thing but blubber a little and jump up and down!"

"He nor nobody else has ever touched me," she said, measuring off each word in a deadly flat tone. "Nobody's ever put a hand on me and if anybody did, I'd kill him."

"And black is white," the old man piped, "and night is day!"

The bulldozer passed below them. With their faces about a foot apart, each held the same expression until the noise had receded. Then the old man said, "Walk home by yourself. I refuse to ride a Jezebel!"

"And I refuse to ride with the Whore of Babylon," she said and slid off the other side of the car and started off through the pasture.

"A whore is a woman!" he roared. "That's how much you know!" But she did not deign to turn around and answer him back, and as he watched the small robust figure stalk across the yellow-dotted field toward the woods, his pride in her, as if it couldn't help itself, returned like the gentle little tide on the new lake—all except that part of it that had to do with her refusal to stand up to Pitts; that pulled back like an undertow. If he could have taught her to stand up to Pitts the way she stood up to him, she would have been a perfect child, as fearless and sturdy-minded as anyone could want; but it was her one failure of character. It was the one point on which she did not resemble him. He turned and looked away over the lake to the woods across it and told himself that in five years, instead of woods, there would be houses and stores and parking places, and that the credit for it could go largely to him.

He meant to teach the child spirit by example and since he had definitely made up his mind, he announced that noon at the dinner table that he was negotiating with a man named Tilman to sell the lot in front of the house for a gas station.

His daughter, sitting with her worn-out air at the foot of the table, let out a moan as if a dull knife were being turned slowly in her chest. "You mean the lawn!" she moaned and fell back in her chair and repeated in an almost inaudible voice, "He means the lawn."

The other six Pitts children began to bawl and pipe, "Where we play!" "Don't let him do that, Pa!" "We won't be able to see the road!" and similar idiocies. Mary Fortune did not say anything. She had a mulish reserved look as if she were planning some business of her own. Pitts had stopped eating and was staring in front of him. His plate was full but his fists sat motionless like two dark quartz stones on either side of it. His eyes began to move from child to child around the table as if he were hunting for one particular one of them. Finally they stopped on Mary Fortune sitting next to her grandfather. "You done this to us," he muttered.

"I didn't," she said but there was no assurance in her voice. It was only a quaver, the voice of a frightened child.

Pitts got up and said, "Come with me," and turned and walked out, loosening his belt as he went, and to the old man's complete despair, she slid away from the table and followed him, almost ran after him, out the door and into the truck behind him, and they drove off.

This cowardice affected Mr. Fortune as if it were his own. It made him physically sick. "He beats an innocent child," he said to his daughter, who was apparently still prostrate at the end of the table, "and not one of you lifts a hand to stop him."

"You ain't lifted yours neither," one of the boys said in an undertone and there was a general mutter from that chorus of frogs.

"I'm an old man with a heart condition," he said. "I can't stop an ox."

"She put you up to it," his daughter murmured in a languid listless tone, her head rolling back and forth on the rim of her chair. "She puts you up to everything."

"No child never put me up to nothing!" he yelled. "You're no kind of a mother! You're a disgrace! That child is an angel! A saint!" he shouted in a voice so high that it broke and he had to scurry out of the room.

The rest of the afternoon he had to lie on his bed. His heart, whenever he knew the child had been beaten, felt as if it were slightly too large for the space that was supposed to hold it. But now he was more determined than ever to see the filling station go up in front of the house, and if it gave Pitts a stroke, so much the better. If it gave him a stroke and paralyzed him, he would be served right and he would never be able to beat her again.

Mary Fortune was never angry with him for long, or seriously, and though he did not see her the rest of that day, when he woke up the next morning, she was sitting astride his chest ordering him to make haste so that they would not miss the concrete mixer.

The workmen were laying the foundation for the fishing club when they arrived and the concrete mixer was already in operation. It was about the size and color of a circus elephant; they stood and watched it churn for a half-hour or so. At eleven-thirty, the old man had an appointment with Tilman to discuss his transaction and they had to leave. He did not tell Mary Fortune where they were going but only that he had to see a man.

Tilman operated a combination country store, filling station, scrap-metal dump, used-car lot and dance hall five miles down the highway that connected with the dirt road that passed in front of the Fortune place. Since the dirt road would soon be paved, he wanted a good location on it for another such enterprise. He was an up-and-coming man—the kind, Mr. Fortune thought, who was never just in line with progress but always a little ahead of it so that he could be there to meet it when it arrived. Signs up and down the highway announced that Tilman's was only five miles away, only four, only three, only two, only one; "Watch out for Tilman's, Around this bend!" and finally, "Here it is, Friends, TILMAN's!" in dazzling red letters.

Tilman's was bordered on either side by a field of old used-car bodies, a kind of ward for incurable automobiles. He also sold outdoor ornaments, such as stone cranes and chickens, urns, jardinieres, whirligigs, and farther back from the road, so as not to depress his dance-hall customers, a line of tombstones and monuments. Most of his businesses went on out-of-doors, so that his store building itself had not involved excessive expense. It was a one-room wooden structure onto which he had added, behind, a long tin hall equipped for dancing. This was divided into two sections, Colored and White, each with its private nickelodeon. He had a barbecue pit and sold barbecued sandwiches and soft drinks.

As they drove up under the shed of Tilman's place, the old man glanced at the child sitting with her feet drawn up on the seat and her chin resting on her knees. He didn't know if she would remember that it was Tilman he was going to sell the lot to or not.

"What you going in here for?" she asked suddenly, with a sniffing look as if she scented an enemy.

"Noner yet bidnis," he said. "You just sit in the car and when I come out, I'll bring you something."

"Don'tcher bring me nothing," she said darkly, "because I won't be here."

"Haw!" he said. "Now you're here, it's nothing for you to do but wait," and he got out and without paying her any further attention, he entered the dark store where Tilman was waiting for him.

When he came out in half an hour, she was not in the car. Hiding, he decided. He started walking around the store to see if she was in the back. He looked in the doors of the two sections of the dance hall and walked on around by the tombstones. Then his eye roved over the field of sinking automobiles and he realized that she could be in or behind any one of two hundred of them. He came back out in front of the store. A Negro boy, drinking a purple drink, was sitting on the ground with his back against the sweating ice cooler.

"Where did that little girl go to, boy?" he asked.

"I ain't seen nair little girl," the boy said.

The old man irritably fished in his pocket and handed him a nickel and said, "A pretty little girl in a yeller cotton dress."

"If you speakin about a stout chile look lak you," the boy said, "she gone off in a truck with a white man."

"What kind of a truck, what kind of a white man?" he yelled.

"It were a green pick-up truck," the boy said smacking his lips, "and a white man she call 'daddy.' They gone thataway some time ago."

The old man, trembling, got in his car and started home. His feelings raced back and forth between fury and mortification. She had never left him before and certainly never for Pitts. Pitts had ordered her to get in the truck and she was afraid not to. But when he reached this conclusion he was more furious than ever. What was the matter with her that she couldn't stand up to Pitts? Why was there this one flaw in her character when he had trained her so well in everything else? It was an ugly mystery.

When he reached the house and climbed the front steps, there she was sitting in the swing, looking glum-faced in front of her across the field he was going to sell. Her eyes were puffy and pink-rimmed but he didn't see any red marks on her legs. He sat down in the swing beside her. He meant to make his voice severe but instead it came out crushed, as if it belonged to a suitor trying to reinstate himself.

"What did you leave me for? You ain't ever left me before," he said.

"Because I wanted to," she said, looking straight ahead.

"You never wanted to," he said. "He made you."

"I toljer I was going and I went," she said in a slow emphatic voice, not looking at him, "and now you can go on and lemme alone." There was something very final, in the sound of this, a tone that had not come up before in their disputes. She stared across the lot where there was nothing but a profusion of pink and yellow and purple weeds, and on across the red road, to the sullen line of black pine woods fringed on top with green. Behind that line was a narrow gray-blue line of more distant woods and beyond that nothing but the sky, entirely blank except for one or two threadbare clouds. She looked into this scene as if it were a person that she preferred to him.

"It's my lot, ain't it?" he asked. "Why are you so up-in-the-air about me selling my own lot?"

"Because it's the lawn," she said. Her nose and eyes began to run horribly but she held her face rigid and licked the water off as soon as it was in reach of her tongue. "We won't be able to see across the road," she said.

The old man looked across the road to assure himself again that there was nothing over there to see. "I never have seen you act in such a way before," he said in an incredulous voice. "There's not a thing over there but the woods."

"We won't be able to see 'um," she said, "and that's the *lawn* and my daddy grazes his calves on it."

At that the old man stood up. "You act more like a Pitts than a Fortune," he said. He had never made such an ugly remark to her before and he was sorry the instant he had said it. It hurt him more than it did her. He turned and went in the house and upstairs to his room.

Several times during the afternoon, he got up from his bed and looked out the window across the "lawn" to the line of woods she said they wouldn't be able to see any more. Every time he saw the same thing: woods—not a mountain, not a waterfall, not any kind of planted bush or flower, just woods. The sunlight was woven through them at that particular time of the afternoon so that every thin pine trunk stood out in all its nakedness. A pine trunk is a pine trunk, he said to himself, and anybody that wants to see one don't have to go far in this neighborhood. Every time he got up and looked out, he was reconvinced of his wisdom in selling the lot. The dissatisfaction it caused Pitts would be permanent, but he could make it up to Mary Fortune by buying her something. With grown people, a road led either to heaven or hell, but with children there were always stops along the way where their attention could be turned with a trifle.

The third time he got up to look at the woods, it was almost six o'clock and the gaunt trunks appeared to be raised in a pool of red light that gushed from the almost hidden sun setting behind them. The old man stared for some time, as if for a prolonged instant he were caught up out of the rattle of everything that led to the future and were held there in the midst of an uncomfortable mystery that he had not apprehended before. He saw it, in his hallucination, as if someone were wounded behind the woods and the trees were bathed in blood. After a few minutes this unpleasant vision was broken by the presence of Pitts's pick-up truck grinding to a halt below the window. He returned to his bed and shut his eyes and against the closed lids hellish red trunks rose up in a black wood.

At the supper table nobody addressed a word to him, including Mary Fortune. He ate quickly and returned again to his room and spent the evening pointing out to himself the advantages for the future of having an establishment like Tilman's so near. They would not have to go any distance for gas. Anytime they needed a loaf of bread, all they would have to do would be step out their front door into Tilman's back door. They could sell milk to Tilman. Tilman was a likable fellow. Tilman would draw other business. The road would soon be paved. Travelers from all over the country would stop at Tilman's. If his daughter thought she was better than Tilman, it would be well to take her down a little. All men were created free and equal. When this phrase sounded in his head, his patriotic sense triumphed and he realized that it was his duty to sell the lot, that he must insure the future. He looked out the window at the moon shining over the woods across the road and listened for a while to the hum of crickets and tree frogs, and beneath their racket, he could hear the throb of the future town of Fortune.

He went to bed certain that just as usual, he would wake up in the morning looking into a little red mirror framed in a door of fine hair. She would have forgotten all about the sale and after breakfast they would drive into town and get the legal papers from the courthouse. On the way back he would stop at Tilman's and close the deal.

When he opened his eyes in the morning, he opened them on the empty ceiling. He pulled himself up and looked around the room but she was not there. He hung over the edge of the bed and looked beneath it but she was not there either. He got up and dressed and went outside. She was sitting in the swing on the front porch, exactly the way she had been yesterday, looking across the lawn into the woods. The old man was very much irritated. Every morning since she had been able to climb, he had waked up to find her either on his bed or underneath it. It was apparent that this morning she preferred the sight of the woods. He decided to ignore her behavior for the present and then bring it up later when she was over her pique. He sat down in the swing beside her but she continued to look at the woods. "I thought you and me'd go into town and have us a look at the boats in the new boat store," he said.

She didn't turn her head but she asked suspiciously, in a loud voice. "What else are you going for?"

"Nothing else," he said.

After a pause she said, "If that's all, I'll go," but she did not bother to look at him.

"Well put on your shoes," he said. "I ain't going to the city with a barefoot woman." She did not bother to laugh at this joke.

The weather was as indifferent as her disposition. The sky did not look as if it were going to rain or as if it were not going to rain. It was an unpleasant gray and the sun had not troubled to come out. All the way into town, she sat looking at her feet, which stuck out in front of her, encased in heavy brown school shoes. The old man had often sneaked up on her and found her alone in conversation with her feet and he thought she was speaking with them silently now. Every now and then her lips moved but she said nothing to him and let all his remarks pass as if she had not heard them. He decided it was going to cost him considerable to buy her good humor again and that he had better do it with a boat, since he wanted one too. She had been talking boats ever since the water backed up onto his place. They went first to the boat store. "Show us the yachts for po' folks!" he shouted jovially to the clerk as they entered.

"They're all for po' folks!" the clerk said. "You'll be po' when you finish buying one!" He was a stout youth in a yellow shirt and blue pants and he had a ready wit. They exchanged several clever remarks in rapid-fire succession. Mr. Fortune looked at Mary Fortune to see if her face had brightened. She stood staring absently over the side of an outboard motor boat at the opposite wall.

"Ain't the lady innerested in boats?" the clerk asked.

She turned and wandered back out onto the sidewalk and got in the car again. The old man looked after her with amazement. He could not believe that a child of her intelligence could be acting this way over the mere sale of a field. "I think she must be coming down with something," he said. "We'll come back again," and he returned to the car.

"Let's go get us an ice-cream cone," he suggested, looking at her with concern.

"I don't want no ice-cream cone," she said.

His actual destination was the courthouse but he did not want to make this apparent. "How'd you like to visit the ten-cent store while I tend to a little bidnis of mine?" he asked. "You can buy yourself something with a quarter I brought along."

"I ain't got nothing to do in no ten-cent store," she said. "I don't want no quarter of yours."

If a boat was of no interest, he should not have thought a quarter would be and reproved himself for that stupidity. "Well what's the matter, sister?" he asked kindly. "Don't you feel good?"

She turned and looked him straight in the face and said with a slow concentrated ferocity, "It's the lawn. My daddy grazes his calves there. We won't be able to see the woods any more."

The old man had held his fury in as long as he could. "He beats you!" he shouted. "And you worry about where he's going to graze his calves!"

"Nobody's ever beat me in my life," she said, "and if anybody did, I'd kill him."

A man seventy-nine years of age cannot let himself be run over by a child of nine. His face set in a look that was just as determined as hers. "Are you a Fortune," he said, "or are you a Pitts? Make up your mind."

Her voice was loud and positive and belligerent. "I'm Mary—Fortune—Pitts," she said.

"Well I," he shouted, "am PURE Fortune!"

There was nothing she could say to this and she showed it. For an instant she looked completely defeated, and the old man saw with a disturbing clearness that this was the Pitts look. What he saw was the Pitts look, pure and simple, and he felt personally stained by it, as if it had been found on his own face. He turned in disgust and backed the car out and drove straight to the courthouse.

The courthouse was a red and white blaze-faced building set in the center of a square from which most of the grass had been worn off. He parked in front of it and said, "Stay here," in an imperious tone and got out and slammed the car door.

It took him a half-hour to get the deed and have the sale paper drawn up and when he returned to the car, she was sitting on the back seat in the corner. The expression on that part of her face that he could see was foreboding and withdrawn. The sky had darkened also and there was a hot sluggish tide in the air, the kind felt when a tornado is possible.

"We better get on before we get caught in a storm," he said and emphatically, "because I got one more place to stop at on the way home," but he might have been chauffeuring a small dead body for all the answer he got.

On the way to Tilman's he reviewed once more the many just reasons that were leading him to his present action and he could not locate a flaw in any of them. He decided that while this attitude of hers would not be permanent, he was permanently disappointed in her and that when she came around she would have to apologize; and that there would be no boat. He was coming to realize slowly that his trouble with her had always been that he had not shown enough firmness. He had been too generous. He was so occupied with these thoughts that he did not notice the signs that said how many miles to Tilman's until the last one exploded joyfully in his face: "Here it is, Friends, TILMAN's!" He pulled in under the shed.

He got out without so much as looking at Mary Fortune and entered the dark store where Tilman, leaning on the counter in front of a triple shelf of canned goods, was waiting for him.

Tilman was a man of quick action and few words. He sat habitually with his arms folded on the counter and his insignificant head weaving snake-fashion above them. He had a triangular-shaped face with the point at the bottom and the top of his skull was covered with a cap of freckles. His eyes were green and very narrow and his tongue was always exposed in his partly opened mouth. He had his checkbook handy and they got down to business at once. It did not take him long to look at the deed and sign the bill of sale. Then Mr. Fortune signed it and they grasped hands over the counter.

Mr. Fortune's sense of relief as he grasped Tilman's hand was extreme. What was done, he felt, was done and there could be no more argument, with her or with himself. He felt that he had acted on principle and that the future was assured.

Just as their hands loosened, an instant's change came over Tilman's face and he disappeared completely under the counter as if he had been snatched by the feet from below. A bottle crashed against the line of tinned goods behind where he had been. The old man whirled around. Mary Fortune was in the door, red-faced and wild-looking, with another bottle lifted to hurl. As he ducked, it broke behind him on the counter and she grabbed another from the crate. He sprang at her but she tore to the other side of the store, screaming something unintelligible and throwing everything within her reach. The old man pounced again and this time he caught her by the tail of her dress and pulled her backward out of the store. Then he got a better grip and lifted her, wheezing and whimpering but suddenly limp in his arms, the few feet to the car. He managed to get the door open and dump her inside. Then he ran around to the other side and got in himself and drove away as fast as he could.

His heart felt as if it were the size of the car and was racing forward, carrying him to some inevitable destination faster than he had ever been carried before. For the first five minutes he did not think but only sped forward as if he were being driven inside his own fury. Gradually the power of thought returned to him. Mary Fortune, rolled into a ball in the corner of the seat, was snuffling and heaving.

He had never seen a child behave in such a way in his life. Neither his own children nor anyone else's had ever displayed such temper in his presence, and he had never for an instant imagined that the child he had trained himself, the child who had been his constant companion for nine years, would embarrass him like this. The child he had never lifted a hand to!

Then he saw, with the sudden vision that sometimes comes with delayed recognition, that that had been his mistake.

She respected Pitts because, even with no just cause, he beat her; and if he—with his just cause—did not beat her now, he would have nobody to blame but himself if she turned out a hellion. He saw that the time had come, that he could no longer avoid whipping her, and as he turned off the highway onto the dirt road leading to home, he told himself that when he finished with her, she would never throw another bottle again.

He raced along the clay road until he came to the line where his own property began and then he turned off onto a side path, just wide enough for the automobile and bounced for a half a mile through the woods. He stopped the car at the exact spot where he had seen Pitts take his belt to her. It was a place where the road widened so that two cars could pass or one could turn around, an ugly red bald spot surrounded by long thin pines that appeared to be gathered there to witness anything that would take place in such a clearing. A few stones protruded from the clay.

"Get out," he said and reached across her and opened the door.

She got out without looking at him or asking what they were going to do and he got out on his side and came around the front of the car.

"Now I'm going to whip you!" he said and his voice was extra loud and hollow and had a vibrating quality that appeared to be taken up and passed through the tops of the pines. He did not want to get caught in a downpour while he was whipping her and he said, "Hurry up and get ready against that tree," and began to take off his belt.

What he had in mind to do appeared to come very slowly as if it had to penetrate a fog in her head. She did not move but gradually her confused expression began to clear. Where a few seconds before her face had been red and distorted and unorganized, it drained now of every vague line until nothing was left on it but positiveness, a look that went slowly past determination and reached certainty. "Nobody has ever beat me," she said, "and if anybody tries it, I'll kill him."

"I don't want no sass," he said and started toward her. His knees felt very unsteady, as if they might turn either backward or forward.

She moved exactly one step back and, keeping her eye on him steadily, removed her glasses and dropped them behind a small rock near the tree he had told her to get ready against. "Take off your glasses," she said.

"Don't give me orders!" he said in a high voice and slapped awkwardly at her ankles with his belt.

She was on him so quickly that he could not have recalled which blow he felt first, whether the weight of her whole solid body or the jabs of her feet or the pummeling of her fist on his chest. He flailed the belt in the air, not knowing where to hit but trying to get her off him until he could decide where to get a grip on her.

"Leggo!" he shouted. "Leggo I tell you!" But she seemed to be everywhere, coming at him from all directions at once. It was as if he were being attacked not by one child but by a pack of small demons all with stout brown school shoes and small rocklike fists. His glasses flew to the side.

"I toljer to take them off," she growled without pausing.

He caught his knee and danced on one foot and a rain of blows fell on his stomach. He felt five claws in the flesh of his upper arm where she was hanging from while her feet mechanically battered his knees and her free fist pounded him again and again in the chest. Then with horror he saw her face rise up in front of his, teeth exposed, and he roared like a bull as she bit the side of his jaw. He seemed to see his own face coming to bite him from several sides at once but he could not attend to it for he was being kicked indiscriminately, in the stomach and then in the crotch. Suddenly he threw himself on the ground and began to roll like a man on fire. She was on top of him at once, rolling with him and still kicking, and now with both fists free to batter his chest.

"I'm an old man!" he piped. "Leave me alone!" But she did not stop. She began a fresh assault on his jaw.

"Stop stop!" he wheezed. "I'm your grandfather!"

She paused, her face exactly on top of his. Pale identical eye looked into pale identical eye. "Have you had enough?" she asked.

The old man looked up into his own image. It was triumphant and hostile. "You been whipped," it said, "by me," and then it added, bearing down on each word, "and I'm PURE Pitts."

In the pause she loosened her grip and he got hold of her throat. With a sudden surge of strength, he managed to roll over and reverse their positions so that he was looking down into the face that was his own but had dared to call itself Pitts. With his hands still tight around her neck, he lifted her head and brought it down once hard against the rock that happened to be under it. Then he brought it down twice more. Then looking into the face in which the eyes, slowly rolling back, appeared to pay him not the slightest attention, he said, "There's not an ounce of Pitts in me."

He continued to stare at his conquered image until he perceived that though it was absolutely silent, there was no look of remorse on it. The eyes had rolled back down and were set in a fixed glare that did not take him in. "This ought to teach you a good lesson," he said in a voice that was edged with doubt.

He managed painfully to get up on his unsteady kicked legs and to take two steps, but the enlargement of his heart which had begun in the car was still going on. He turned his head and looked behind him for a long time at the little motionless figure with its head on the rock.

Then he fell on his back and looked up helplessly along the bare trunks into the tops of the pines and his heart expanded once more with a convulsive motion. It expanded so fast that the old man felt as if he were being pulled after it through the woods, felt as if he were running as fast as he could with the ugly pines toward the lake. He perceived that there would be a little opening there, a little place where he could escape and leave the woods behind him. He could see it in the distance already, a little opening where the white sky was reflected in the water. It grew as he ran toward it until suddenly the whole lake opened up before him, riding majestically in little corrugated folds toward his feet. He realized suddenly that he could not swim and that he had not bought the boat. On both sides of him he saw that the gaunt trees had thickened into mysterious dark files that were marching across the water and away into the distance. He looked around desperately for someone to help him but the place was deserted except for one huge yellow monster which sat to the side, as stationary as he was, gorging itself on clay.

🖎 *Maxine Kumin* (born 1925)

Maxine Kumin is a poet comfortable with the public image created by the persona who speaks through her poems. Although she has written fiction and children's books that have been very well received, she is best known for her numerous collections of poetry. Kumin is often likened to a female version of Robert Frost because her pastoral—and often georgic—poetry focuses largely on nature and the life of a farm. But Kumin also moves beyond Frost, who eschewed revealing personal details in his work, because of the straightforward and unabashed insertion of her own passionate interior life into the rural landscape. Kumin was born in Philadelphia, Pennsylvania, but has resided on a farm with her husband, Victor Montwid, in Warner, New Hampshire, since the end of the 1970s. When she is not writing or lecturing, she spends much of her time there training horses and raising vegetables.

Kumin published her first book of poetry, Halfway, *in 1961 at the age of thirty-six. The poems were written during a period in her life that Kumin describes as miserable. She had given up writing after one of her professors at Radcliffe College had scathingly dismissed her work, and for several years she devoted herself to her marriage and her three children. However, in the late 1950s, she began attending workshops at the Boston Center for Adult Education, and it was there that she met Anne Sexton. The two collaborated on four children's books and became mentors to one another, critiquing each other's writing and furthering their respective developments. The collaboration lasted until Sexton's suicide in 1974. Kumin would feel her friend's loss deeply.*

Kumin credits her poetry as the inspiration for her fiction. She says that the art of writing poetry involves such careful selection that much of what she desires to say gets left out. She has gone so far as to suggest that the process leaves her feeling cheated. Like many writers, she returns to these unused ideas. However, for Kumin, those lost words have been the foundation for four novels. This process of careful selection is best exemplified in her nature poetry and particularly in her attention to the details and nuances of a farm life in New England. "I particularly observe things in nature because they interest me, but I don't think of it as observing. What I'm always after is to get the facts: to be true to the actuality." Her published works of poetry include House, Bridge, Fountain, Gate *(1975),* Our Ground Time Here Will Be Brief *(1982),* The Long Approach *(1986),* Nurture *(1989),* Looking for Luck *(1992), and* Connecting the Dots *(1996). She was awarded the Pulitzer Prize for* Up Country: Poems of New England *in 1972.*

The Excrement Poem

It is done by us all, as God disposes, from
the least cast of worm to what must have been
in the case of the brontosaur, say, spoor
of considerable heft, something awesome.

We eat, we evacuate, survivors that we are.   5
I think these things each morning with shovel

and rake, drawing the risen brown buns
toward me, fresh from the horse oven, as it were,

or culling the alfalfa-green ones, expelled
in a state of ooze, through the sawdust bed   10
to take a serviceable form, as putty does,
so as to lift out entire from the stall.

And wheeling to it, storming up the slope,
I think of the angle of repose the manure
pile assumes, how sparrows come to pick   15
the redelivered grain, how inky-cap

coprinus mushrooms spring up in a downpour.
I think of what drops from us and must then
be moved to make way for the next and next.
However much we stain the world, spatter   20

it with our leavings, make stenches, defile
the great formal oceans with what leaks down,
trundling off today's last barrowful,
I honor shit for saying: We go on.

Territory

Mistaking him for a leaf, I cut a toad
in two with the power mower and he goes on
lopsidedly hopping until his motor runs out

his known universe a jungle of inch-high trees
the ferns by the granite ledge as immense   5
as sequoias, the stone a terrible Andes.

By the next pass there is no sign of my carnage.
Now I have cut a swath around the perimeter
declaring this far the grass is tamed.

I think of the wolf who marks his territory   10
with urine, and where there is wolf there is
the scientist who follows him, yellowing

the same pines at the same intervals
until the baffled creature, worn out
with producing urea, cedes his five acres.   15

We are not of it, but in it. We are
in it willynilly with our machinery
and measurements, and all for the good.

One rarely sees the blood of the toad.

Woodchucks

Gassing the woodchucks didn't turn out right.
The knockout bomb from the Feed and Grain Exchange
was featured as merciful, quick at the bone
and the case we had against them was airtight,
both exits shoehorned shut with puddingstone,   5
but they had a sub-sub-basement out of range.

Next morning they turned up again, no worse
for the cyanide than we for our cigarettes
and state-store Scotch, all of us up to scratch.
They brought down the marigolds as a matter of course   10
and then took over the vegetable patch
nipping the broccoli shoots, beheading the carrots.

The food from our mouths, I said, righteously thrilling
to the feel of the .22, the bullets' neat noses.
I, a lapsed pacifist fallen from grace   15
puffed with Darwinian pieties for killing,
now drew a bead on the littlest woodchuck's face.
He died down in the everbearing roses.

Ten minutes later I dropped the mother. She
flipflopped in the air and fell, her needle teeth   20
still hooked in a leaf of early Swiss chard.
Another baby next. O one-two-three
the murderer inside me rose up hard,
the hawkeye killer came on stage forthwith.

There's one chuck left. Old wily fellow, he keeps   25
me cocked and ready day after day after day.
All night I hunt his humped-up form. I dream
I sight along the barrel in my sleep.
If only they'd all consented to die unseen
gassed underground the quiet Nazi way.   30

An Insider's View of the Garden

How can I help but admire the ever perseverant
unquenchable dill
that sways like an unruly crowd at a soccer match
waving its lacy banners
where garlic belongs or slyly invading a hill   5
of Delicata squash—
how can I help but admire such ardor? I seek it

as bees the flower's core, hummingbirds
the concocted sugar water
that lures them to the feeder in the lilacs.   10
I praise the springy mane
of untamed tendrils asprawl on chicken wire
that promise to bring forth
peas to overflow a pillowcase.

Some days I adore my coltish broccolis,   15
the sketchbook beginnings
of their green heads still encauled, incipient trees
sprung from the Pleistocene.
Some days the leeks, that Buckingham Palace patrol
and the quarter-mile of beans   20
—green, yellow, soy, lima, bush and pole—

demand applause. As do dilatory parsnips,
a ferny dell of tops
regal as celery. Let me laud onion that erupts
slim as a grass stem   25
then spends the summer inventing its pungent tulip
and the army of brussels sprouts
extending its spoon-shaped leaves over dozens of armpits

that conceal what are now merely thoughts, mere nubbins
needing long ripening.   30
But let me lament my root-maggot-raddled radishes
my bony and bored red peppers
that drop their lower leaves like dancehall strippers
my cauliflowers that spit
out thimblesize heads in the heat and take beetles to bed.   35

O children, citizens, my wayward jungly dears
you are all to be celebrated
plucked, transplanted, tilled under, resurrected here
—even the lowly despised
purslane, chickweed, burdock, poke, wild poppies.   40
For all of you, whether eaten or extirpated
I plan to spend the rest of my life on my knees.

Almost Spring, Driving Home, Reciting Hopkins

"A devout but highly imaginative Jesuit,"
Untermeyer says in my yellowed
college omnibus of modern poets,
perhaps intending an oxymoron, but is it?
Shook foil, sharp rivers start to flow.   5
Landscape plotted and pieced, gray-blue, snow-pocked

begins to show its margins. Speeding back
down the interstate into my own hills
I see them *fickle, freckled,* mounded fully
and softened by millennia into pillows.   10
The priest's sprung metronome tick-tocks,
repeating how old winter is. It asks
each mile, snow fog battening the valleys,
what is all this juice and all this joy?

❧ Robert Bly *(born 1926)*

Robert Bly is a poet, writer, accomplished translator, and activist. He is best known today for his work as a leader of the emerging men's movement, given impetus by his book Iron John, *which was North America's best-selling nonfiction book in 1991. In* Iron John, *Bly calls for a return to "primal masculinity"; he debunks stereotypical conceptions of manhood, replacing them with a more emotional ideal. Bly has used his deep understanding of the American landscape as a means to restore this masculinity, hosting workshops nationwide in which men are encouraged to explore their connection to their natural, earth-based selves. His work has evolved from* Iron John *and the rediscovery of manhood to focus on balance between gender-identified attributes. In* The Maiden King *(1999), cowritten by Jungian psychoanalyst Marion Woodman, Bly advocates the reunion of masculine and feminine qualities in human nature. This balance is crucial, as Bly himself asserts: "[Men] cannot remain unbalanced . . . we need literature, poetry, the thought of each other and the mythology if we are going to live joyfully until we're 90 years old." A graduate of Harvard University, Bly studied mathematics before beginning his career as a writer. Today, he lives with his wife and three children on a farm in western Minnesota.*

A committed pacifist, Bly frequently uses poetry as a moral tool. His poems, which emphasize the intricacies of nature, rely on lush imagery to convey emotion. The ability to connect the poems with the reader's emotional life makes Bly effective as a writer and as an activist. He is a winner of the National Book Award, and his work has appeared in numerous magazines, including Poetry, The Nation, Paris Review, *and* Choice. *His books include* Silence in the Snowy Fields *(1962),* The Light Around the Body *(1967),* Sleepers Joining Hands *(1972),* The Man in the Black Coat Turns *(1981), and* Loving a Woman in Two Worlds *(1985).*

Solitude Late at Night in the Woods

I

The body is like a November birch facing the full moon
And reaching into the cold heavens.
In these trees there is no ambition, no sodden body, no leaves,
Nothing but bare trunks climbing like cold fire!

2

My last walk in the trees has come. At dawn   5
I must return to the trapped fields,
To the obedient earth.
The trees shall be reaching all the winter.

3

It is a joy to walk in the bare woods.
The moonlight is not broken by the heavy leaves.   10
The leaves are down, and touching the soaked earth,
Giving off the odor that partridges love.

Reading in Fall Rain

The fields are black once more.
The old restlessness is going.
I reach out with open arms
to pull in the black fields.

All morning rain has fallen   5
steadily on the roof.
I feel like a butterfly
joyful in its powerful cocoon.

* * *

I break off reading:
one of my bodies is gone!   10
It's outdoors, walking
swiftly away in the rain!

I get up and look out.
Sure enough, I see
the rooster lifting his legs   15
high in the wet grass.

The Starfish

It is low tide. Fog. I have climbed down the cliffs from Pierce Ranch
to the tide pools. Now the ecstasy of the low tide, kneeling down, alone.
In six inches of clear water I notice a purple starfish—with nineteen
arms! It is a delicate purple, the color of old carbon paper, or an attic
dress . . . at the webs between the arms sometimes a more intense   5

sunset red glows through. The fingers are relaxed . . . some curled up at the tips . . . with delicate rods . . . apparently globes on top of each, as at world's fairs, waving about. The starfish slowly moves up the groin of the rock . . . then back down . . . many of its arms rolled up now, lazily, like a puppy on its back. One arm is especially active and curves up over its own body as if a dinosaur were looking behind him.

How slowly and evenly it moves! The starfish is a glacier, going sixty miles a year! It moves over the pink rock, by means I cannot see . . . and into marvelously floating delicate brown weeds. It is about the size of the bottom of a pail. When I reach out to it, it tightens and then slowly relaxes. . . . I take an arm and quickly lift. The underside is a pale tan. . . . Gradually, as I watch, thousands of tiny tubes begin rising from all over the underside . . . hundreds in the mouth, hundreds along the nineteen underarms . . . all looking . . . feeling . . . like a man looking for a woman . . . tiny heads blindly feeling for a rock and finding only air. A purple rim runs along the underside of every arm, with paler tubes. Probably its moving-feet.

I put him back in. He unfolds—I had forgotten how purple he was— and slides down into his rock groin, the snail-like feelers waving as if nothing had happened, and nothing has.

The Dead Seal

I

Walking north toward the point, I come on a dead seal. From a few feet away, he looks like a brown log. The body is on its back, dead only a few hours. I stand and look at him. There's a quiver in the dead flesh: My God, he's still alive. And a shock goes through me, as if a wall of my room had fallen away.

His head is arched back, the small eyes closed; the whiskers sometimes rise and fall. He is dying. This is the oil. Here on its back is the oil that heats our houses so efficiently. Wind blows fine sand back toward the ocean. The flipper near me lies folded over the stomach, looking like an unfinished arm, lightly glazed with sand at the edges. The other flipper lies half underneath. And the seal's skin looks like an old overcoat, scratched here and there—by sharp mussel shells maybe.

I reach out and touch him. Suddenly he rears up, turns over. He gives three cries: Awaark! Awaark! Awaark!—like the cries from Christmas toys. He lunges toward me; I am terrified and leap back, though I know there can be no teeth in that jaw. He starts flopping toward the sea. But he falls over, on his face. He does not *want* to go back to the sea. He looks up at the sky, and he looks like an old lady who has lost her hair. He puts his chin back down on the sand, rearranges his flippers, and waits for me to go. I go.

2

The next day I go back to say goodbye. He's dead now. But he's not. 20
He's a quarter mile farther up the shore. Today he is thinner, squatting
on his stomach, head out. The ribs show more: each vertebra on the
back under the coat is visible, shiny. He breathes in and out.

A wave comes in, touches his nose. He turns and looks at me—the
eyes slanted; the crown of his head looks like a boy's leather jacket 25
bending over some bicycle bars. He is taking a long time to die. The
whiskers white as porcupine quills, the forehead slopes. . . . Goodbye,
brother; die in the sound of waves. Forgive us if we have killed you.
Long live your race, your inner-tube race, so uncomfortable on land, so
comfortable in the ocean. Be comfortable in death then, when the sand 30
will be out of your nostrils, and you can swim in long loops through the
pure death, ducking under as assassinations break above you. You don't
want to be touched by me. I climb the cliff and go home the other way.

Edward Abbey (1927–1989)

*A flamboyant and irreverent personality yet a passionate and sensitive author, Edward
Abbey was a nature writer who saw his mission as one of radical political activism—although he flippantly claimed, "In my case, saving the world was only a hobby." A committed anarchist, Abbey advocated ecodefense of the strongest order, including the acts of
environmental terrorism depicted in his popular novel* The Monkey Wrench Gang
*(1975). He once asserted that "The artist in our time has two chief responsibilities: (1)
art; and (2) sedition." Abbey identified himself with the desert regions of the American
Southwest, finding in that harsh and seemingly unwelcoming landscape the perfect home
for a rugged individualist such as himself. Like Thoreau (an author whom he admired),
Abbey's life was associated with his chosen place. As he wrote, "Why do I live in the
desert? Because the desert is the* locus Dei.*" Abbey objected to those—in particular, governmental officials—who saw the desert as wasteland, as merely a place in which to
build dams or to dump nuclear waste. In all his work, he mocked the vain belief that nature was in the service of humanity and advocated ecocentrism: "From the point of view
of a tapeworm, man was created by God to serve the appetite of the tapeworm."*

*Abbey was born and raised in rural Pennsylvania. From 1945 to 1947, he served in
the military, and afterward briefly attended Indiana University of Pennsylvania. He set
out to see the West in 1948, roughing it along the way, jumping trains and hitchhiking.
He later settled for a time in New Mexico, where he studied at the University of New
Mexico, eventually earning a masters degree, with a thesis entitled "Anarchism and the
Morality of Violence." For fifteen years, Abbey worked on and off as a part-time park
ranger and fire watcher in the national parks of the Southwest. The two summers he
spent at Arches National Park provided the material that would form one of his best-
loved nonfiction works,* Desert Solitaire *(1968). Abbey was a prolific writer of fiction,
nonfiction, and even poetry. His novels include* Jonathan Troy *(1954),* The Brave

Cowboy *(1956)*, Fire on the Mountain *(1962)*, Black Sun *(1971)*, Good News *(1980)*, The Fool's Progress *(1988)*, *and* Hayduke Lives! *(1989)*. *His nonfiction works include* Appalachian Wilderness *(1970)*, Slickrock *(1971)*, Cactus Country *(1973)*, The Journey Home *(1977)*, The Hidden Canyon *(1977)*, Abbey's Road *(1979)*, Desert Images *(1979)*, Down the River *(1982)*, In Praise of Mountain Lions *(1984)*, Beyond the Wall *(1984)*, One Life at a Time, Please *(1988)*, *and* A Voice Crying in the Wilderness *(1989)*. *He spent his later years at his home in Tucson, which he named "Fort Llatikcuf" (read it backwards). When he died, he had his remains buried at an unspecified locale in the desert, with the epitaph, "No Comment." He once wrote, "If my decomposing carcass helps nourish the roots of a juniper tree or the wings of a vulture—that is immortality enough for me. And as much as anyone deserves."*

From Desert Solitaire

Water

"This would be good country," a tourist says to me, "if only you had some water."

He's from Cleveland, Ohio.

"If we had water here," I reply, "this country would not be what it is. It would be like Ohio, wet and humid and hydrological, all covered with cabbage farms and golf courses. Instead of this lovely barren desert we would have only another blooming garden state, like New Jersey. You see what I mean?"

"If you had more water more people could live here."

"Yes sir. And where then would people go when they wanted to see something besides people?"

"I see what you mean. Still, I wouldn't want to live here. So dry and desolate. Nice for pictures but my God I'm glad I don't have to live here."

"I'm glad too, sir. We're in perfect agreement. You wouldn't want to live here, I wouldn't want to live in Cleveland. We're both satisfied with the arrangement as it is. Why change it?"

"Agreed."

We shake hands and the tourist from Ohio goes away pleased, as I am pleased, each of us thinking he has taught the other something new.

The air is so dry here I can hardly shave in the mornings. The water and soap dry on my face as I reach for the razor: aridity. It is the driest season of a dry country. In the afternoons of July and August we may get thundershowers but an hour after the storms pass the surface of the desert is again bone dry.

It seldom rains. The geography books credit this part of Utah with an annual precipitation of five to nine inches but that is merely a statistical average. Low enough, to be sure. And in fact the rainfall and snowfall vary widely from year to year and from place to place even within the Arches region. When a cloud bursts open above the Devil's Garden the sun is blazing down on my ramada. And wherever it rains in this land of unclothed rock the run-off is rapid down cliff and dome through the canyons to the Colorado.

Sometimes it rains and still fails to moisten the desert—the falling water evaporates halfway down between cloud and earth. Then you see curtains of blue rain dangling out of reach in the sky while the living things wither below for want of water. Torture by tantalizing, hope without fulfillment. And the clouds disperse and dissipate into nothingness.

Streambeds are usually dry. The dry wash, dry gulch, *arroyo seco*. Only after a storm do they carry water and then but briefly—a few minutes, a couple of hours. The spring-fed perennial stream is a rarity. In this area we have only two of them, Salt Creek and Onion Creek, the first too salty to drink and the second laced with arsenic and sulfur.

Permanent springs or waterholes are likewise few and far between though not so rare as the streams. They are secret places deep in the canyons, known only to the deer and the coyotes and the dragonflies and a few others. Water rises slowly from these springs and flows in little rills over bare rock, over and under sand, into miniature fens of wire grass, rushes, willow and tamarisk. The water does not flow very far before disappearing into the air and under the ground. The flow may reappear farther down the canyon, surfacing briefly for a second time, a third time, diminishing in force until it vanishes completely and for good.

Another type of spring may be found on canyon walls where water seeps out between horizontal formations through cracks thinner than paper to support small hanging gardens of orchids, monkeyflower, maidenhair fern, and ivy. In most of these places the water is so sparingly measured that it never reaches the canyon floor at all but is taken up entirely by the thirsty plant life and transformed into living tissue.

Long enough in the desert a man like other animals can learn to smell water. Can learn, at least, the smell of things associated with water—the unique and heartening odor of the cottonwood tree, for example, which in the canyonlands is the tree of life. In this wilderness of naked rock burnt to auburn or buff or red by ancient fires there is no vision more pleasing to the eyes and more gratifying to the heart than the translucent acid green (bright gold in autumn) of this venerable tree. It signifies water, and not only water but also shade, in a country where shelter from the sun is sometimes almost as precious as water.

Signifies water, which may or may not be on the surface, visible and available. If you have what is called a survival problem and try to dig for this water during the heat of the day the effort may cost you more in sweat than you will find to drink. A bad deal. Better to wait for nightfall when the cottonwoods and other plants along the streambed will release some of the water which they have absorbed during the day, perhaps enough to allow a potable trickle to rise to the surface of the sand. If the water still does not appear you may then wish to attempt to dig for it. Or you might do better by marching farther up the canyon. Sooner or later you should find a spring or at least a little seep on the canyon wall. On the other hand you could possibly find no water at all, anywhere. The desert is a land of surprises, some of them terrible surprises. Terrible as derived from terror.

When out for a walk carry water; not less than a gallon a day per person.

More surprises. In places you will find clear-flowing streams, such as Salt Creek near Turnbow Cabin, where the water looks beautifully drinkable but tastes like brine.

You might think, beginning to die of thirst, that any water however salty would be better than none at all. Not true. Small doses will not keep you going or alive and a deep drink will force your body to expend water in getting rid of the excess salt. This results in a net loss of bodily moisture and a hastening of the process of dehydration. Dehydration first enervates, then prostrates, then kills.

Nor is blood, your own or a companion's, any adequate substitute for water; blood is too salty. The same is true of urine.

If it's your truck or car which has failed you, you'd be advised to tap the radiator, unless it's full of Prestone. If this resource is not available and water cannot be found in the rocks or under the sand and you find yourself too tired and discouraged to go on, crawl into the shade and wait for help to find you. If no one is looking for you write your will in the sand and let the wind carry your last words and signature east to the borders of Colorado and south to the pillars of Monument Valley—someday, never fear, your bare elegant bones will be discovered and wondered and marveled at.

A great thirst is a great joy when quenched in time. On my first walk down into Havasupai Canyon, which is a branch of the Grand Canyon, never mind exactly where, I took with me only a quart of water, thinking that would be enough for a mere fourteen-mile downhill hike on a warm day in August. At Topocoba on the rim of the canyon the temperature was a tolerable ninety-six degrees but it rose about one degree for each mile on and downward. Like a fool I rationed my water, drank frugally, and could have died of the heatstroke. When late in the afternoon I finally stumbled—sun-dazed, blear-eyed, parched as an old bacon rind—upon that blue stream which flows like a miraculous mirage down the floor of the canyon I was too exhausted to pause and drink soberly from the bank. Dreamily, deliriously, I waded into the waist-deep water and fell on my face. Like a sponge I soaked up moisture through every pore, letting the current bear me along beneath a canopy of overhanging willow trees. I had no fear of drowning in the water—I intended to drink it all.

In the Needles country high above the inaccessible Colorado River there is a small spring hidden at the heart of a maze of fearfully arid grabens and crevasses. A very small spring: the water oozes from the grasp of moss to fall one drop at a time, one drop per second, over a lip of stone. One afternoon in June I squatted there for an hour—two hours? three?—filling my canteen. No other water within miles, the local gnat population fought me for every drop. To keep them out of the canteen I had to place a handkerchief over the opening as I filled it. Then they attacked my eyes, drawn irresistibly by the liquid shine of the human eyeball. Embittered little bastards. Never have I tasted better water.

Other springs, more surprises. Northeast of Moab in a region of gargoyles and hobgoblins, a landscape left over from the late Jurassic, is a peculiar little waterhole named Onion Spring. A few wild onions grow in the vicinity but more striking, in season, is the golden princess plume, an indicator of selenium, a mild poison often found in association with uranium, a poison not so mild. Approaching the spring you notice a sulfurous stink in the air though the water itself, neither warm nor cold, looks clear and drinkable.

Unlike most desert waterholes you will find around Onion Spring few traces of animal life. Nobody comes to drink. The reason is the very good one that the water of Onion Spring contains not only sulfur, and perhaps selenium, but also arsenic. When I was there I looked at the water and smelled it and ran my hands through it and after a while, since the sampling of desert water is in my line, I tasted it, carefully, and spat it out. Afterwards I rinsed my mouth with water from my canteen.

This poison spring is quite clear. The water is sterile, lifeless. There are no bugs, which in itself is a warning sign, in case the smell were not sufficient. When in doubt about drinking from an unknown spring look for life. If the water is scummed with algae, crawling with worms, grubs, larvae, spiders and liver flukes, be reassured, drink hearty, you'll get nothing worse than dysentery. But if it appears innocent and pure, beware. Onion Spring wears such a deceitful guise. Out of a tangle of poison-tolerant weeds the water drips into a basin of mud and sand, flows from there over sandstone and carries its potent solutions into the otherwise harmless waters of the creek.

There are a number of springs similar to this one in the American desert. Badwater pool in Death Valley, for example. And a few others in the canyonlands, usually in or below the Moenkopi and Shinarump formations—mudstone and shales. The prospector Vernon Pick found a poison spring at the source of the well-named Dirty Devil River, when he was searching for uranium over in the San Rafael Swell a few years ago. At the time he needed water; he *had* to have water; and in order to get a decent drink he made something like a colander out of his canteen, punching it full of nail holes, filling it with charcoal from his campfire and straining the water through the charcoal. How much this purified the water he had no means of measuring but he drank it anyway and although it made him sick he survived, and is still alive today to tell about it.

There are rumors that when dying of the thirst you can save your soul *and* body by extracting water from the barrel cactus. This is a dubious proposition and I don't know anyone who has made the experiment. It might be possible in the Sonoran desert where the barrel cactus grows tall as a man and fat as a keg of beer. In Utah, however, its nearest relative stands no more than a foot high and bristles with needles curved like fishhooks. To get even close to this devilish vegetable you need leather gloves and a machete. Slice off the top and you find inside not water but only the green pulpy core of the living plant. Carving the core into manageable chunks you might be able to wring a few drops of bitter liquid into your cup. The labor and the exasperation will make you sweat, will cost you dearly.

When you reach this point you are doomed. Far better to have stayed at home with the TV and a case of beer. If the happy thought arrives too late, crawl into the shade and contemplate the lonely sky. See those big black scrawny wings far above, waiting? Comfort yourself with the reflection that within a few hours, if all goes as planned, your human flesh will be working its way through the gizzard of a buzzard, your essence transfigured into the fierce greedy eyes and unimaginable consciousness of a turkey vulture. Whereupon you, too, will soar on motionless wings high over the ruck and rack of human suffering. For most of us a promotion in grade, for some the realization of an ideal.

In July and August on the high desert the thunderstorms come. Mornings begin clear and dazzling bright, the sky as blue as the Virgin's cloak, unflawed by a trace of cloud in all that emptiness bounded on the north by the Book Cliffs, on the east by Grand Mesa and the La Sal Mountains, on the south by the Blue Mountains and on the west by the dragon-tooth reef of the San Rafael. By noon, however, clouds begin to form over the mountains, coming it seems out of nowhere, out of nothing, a special creation.

The clouds multiply and merge, cumuli-nimbi piling up like whipped cream, like mashed potatoes, like sea foam, building upon one another into a second mountain range greater in magnitude than the terrestrial range below.

The massive forms jostle and grate, ions collide, and the sound of thunder is heard over the sun-drenched land. More clouds emerge from empty sky, anvil-headed giants with glints of lightning in their depths. An armada assembles and advances, floating on a plane of air that makes it appear, from below, as a fleet of ships must look to the fish in the sea.

At my observation point on a sandstone monolith the sun is blazing down as intensely as ever, the air crackling with dry heat. But the storm clouds continue to spread, gradually taking over more and more of the sky, and as they approach the battle breaks out.

Lightning streaks like gunfire through the clouds, volleys of thunder shake the air. A smell of ozone. While the clouds exchange their bolts with one another no rain falls, but now they begin bombarding the buttes and pinnacles below. Forks of lightning—illuminated nerves—join heaven and earth.

The wind is rising. For anyone with sense enough to get out of the rain now is the time to seek shelter. A lash of lightning flickers over Wilson Mesa, scorching the brush, splitting a pine tree. Northeast over the Yellowcat area rain is already sweeping down, falling not vertically but in a graceful curve, like a beaded curtain drawn lightly across the desert. Between the rain and the mountains, among the tumbled masses of vapor, floats a segment of a rainbow—sunlight divided. But where I stand the storm is only beginning.

Above me the clouds roll in, unfurling and smoking billows in malignant violet, dense as wool. Most of the sky is lidded over but the sun remains clear halfway down the west, shining in under the storm. Overhead the clouds thicken, then crack and split with a roar like that of cannonballs tumbling down a marble staircase; their bellies open—too late to run now—and the rain comes down.

Comes down: not softly not gently, with no quality of mercy but like heavy water in buckets, raindrops like pellets splattering on the rock, knocking the berries off the junipers, plastering my shirt to my back, drumming on my hat like hailstones and running in a waterfall off the brim.

The pinnacles, arches, balanced rocks, fins and elephant-backs of sandstone, glazed with water but still in sunlight, gleam like old gray silver and everything appears transfixed in the strange wild unholy light of the moment. The light that never was.

For five minutes the deluge continues under the barrage of thunder and lightning, then trails off quickly, diminishing to a shower, to a sprinkling, to nothing at all. The clouds move off and rumble for a while in the distance. A fresh golden light breaks through and now in the east, over the turrets and domes, stands the rainbow sign, a double rainbow with one foot in the canyon of the Colorado and the other far north in Salt Wash. Beyond the rainbow and framed within it I can see jags of lightning still playing in the stormy sky over Castle Valley.

The afternoon sun falls lower; above the mountains and the ragged black clouds hangs the new moon, pale fragment of what is to come; in another hour, at sundown, Venus too will be there, planet of love, to glow bright as chromium down on the western sky. The desert storm is over and through the pure sweet pellucid air the cliff swallows and the nighthawks plunge and swerve, making cries of hunger and warning and—who knows?—maybe of exultation.

Stranger than the storms, though not so grand and symphonic, are the flash floods that follow them, bursting with little warning out of the hills and canyons, sometimes an hour or more after the rain has stopped.

I have stood in the middle of a broad sandy wash with not a trickle of moisture to be seen anywhere, sunlight pouring down on me and on the flies and ants and lizards, the sky above perfectly clear, listening to a queer vibration in the air and in the ground under my feet—like a freight train coming down the grade, very fast—and looked up to see a wall of water tumble around a bend and surge toward me.

A wall of water. A poor image. For the flash flood of the desert poorly resembles water. It looks rather like a loose pudding or a thick dense soup, thick as gravy, dense with mud and sand, lathered with scuds of bloody froth, loaded on its crest with a tangle of weeds and shrubs and small trees ripped from their roots.

Surprised by delight, I stood there in the heat, the bright sun, the quiet afternoon, and watched the monster roll and roar toward me. It advanced in crescent shape with a sort of forelip about a foot high streaming in front, making hissing sucking noises like a giant amoeba, nosing to the right and nosing to the left as if on the spoor of something good to eat. Red as tomato soup or blood it came down on me about as fast as a man could run. I moved aside and watched it go by.

A flick of lightning to the north
where dun clouds grumble—
while here in the middle of the wash
black beetles tumble
and horned toads fumble
over sand as dry as bone
and hard-baked mud and glaring stone.

Nothing here suggests disaster
for the ants' shrewd play;
their busy commerce for tomorrow
shows no care for today;

but a mile away
and rolling closer in a scum of mud
comes the hissing lapping blind mouth of the flood.

Through the tamarisk whine the flies
in pure fat units of conceit
as if the sun and the afternoon
and blood and the smells and the heat
and something to eat
would be available forever, never die
beyond the fixed imagination of a fly.

The flood comes, crawls thickly by, roaring
with self-applause, a loud
spongy smothering liquid avalanche:
great ant-civilizations drown,
worlds go down,
trees go under, the mud bank breaks
and deep down underneath the bedrock shakes.

A few hours later the bulk of the flood was past and gone. The flow dwindled to a trickle over bars of quicksand. New swarms of insect life would soon come to recover the provinces of those swept away. Nothing had changed but the personnel, a normal turnover, and the contours of the watercourse, that not much.

Now we've mentioned quicksand. What is quicksand anyway? First of all, quicksand is *not* as many think a queer kind of sand which has the hideous power to draw men and animals down and down into a bottomless pit. There can be no quicksand without water. The scene of the sand-drowned camel boy in the movie *Lawrence of Arabia* is pure fakery. The truth about quicksand is that it is simply a combination of sand and water in which the upward force of the water is sufficient to neutralize the frictional strength of the particles of sand. The greater the force and saturation, the less weight the sand can bear.

Ordinarily it is possible for a man to walk across quicksand, if he keeps moving. But if he stops, funny things begin to happen. The surface of the quicksand, which may look as firm as the wet sand on an ocean beach, begins to liquefy beneath his feet. He finds himself sinking slowly into a jelly-like substance, soft and quivering, which clasps itself around his ankles with the suction power of any viscous fluid. Pulling out one foot, the other foot necessarily goes down deeper, and if a man waits too long, or cannot reach something solid beyond the quicksand, he may soon find himself trapped. The depth to which he finally sinks depends upon the depth and the fluidity of the quicksand, upon the nature of his efforts to extricate himself, and upon the ratio of body weight to volume of quicksand. Unless a man is extremely talented, he cannot work himself in more than waist-deep. The quicksand will not *pull* him down. But it will not let him go either. Therefore the conclusion is that while quicksand cannot drown its captive, it could possibly starve him to death. Whatever finally happens, the immediate effects are always interesting.

My friend Newcomb, for instance. He has only one good leg, used to wear a brace on the other, can't hike very well in rough country, tends to lag behind. We were exploring a deep dungeon-like defile off Glen Canyon one time (before the dam). The defile turned and twisted like a snake under overhanging and interlocking walls so high, so close, that for most of the way I could not see the sky. The floor of this cleft was irregular, wet, sandy, in places rather soupy, and I was soon far ahead and out of sight of Newcomb.

Finally I came to a place in the canyon so narrow and dark and wet and ghastly that I had no heart to go farther. Retracing my steps I heard, now and then, a faint and mournful wail, not human, which seemed to come from abysmal depths far back in the bowels of the plateau, from the underworld, from subterranean passageways better left forever unseen and unknown. I hurried on, the cries faded away. I was glad to be getting out of there. Then they came again, louder and as it seemed from all sides, out of the rock itself, surrounding me. A terrifying caterwauling it was, multiplied and amplified by echoes piled on echoes, overlapping and reinforcing one another. I looked back to see what was hunting me but there was only the naked canyon in the dim, bluish light that filtered down from far above. I thought of the Minotaur. Then I thought of Newcomb and began to run.

It wasn't bad. He was in only a little above the knees and sinking very slowly. As soon as he saw me he stopped hollering and relit his pipe. Help, he said, simply and quietly.

What was all the bellowing about? I wanted to know. I'm sorry, he said, but it's a horrible way to die. Get out of that mud, I said, and let's get out of here. It ain't just mud, he said. I don't care what it is, get out of there; you look like an idiot. I'm sinking, he said.

And he was. The stuff was now halfway up his thighs.

Don't you ever read any books? I said. Don't you have sense enough to know that when you get in quicksand you have to lie down flat? Why? he asked. So you'll live longer, I explained. Face down or face up? he asked next.

That stumped me. I couldn't remember the answer to that one. You wait here, I said, while I go back to Albuquerque and get the book.

He looked down for a moment. Still sinking, he said; please help?

I stepped as close to him as I could without getting bogged down myself but our extended hands did not quite meet. Lean forward, I said. I am, he said. All the way, I said; fall forward.

He did that and then I could reach him. He gripped my wrist and I gripped his and with a slow steady pull I got him out of there. The quicksand gurgled a little and made funny, gasping noises, reluctant to let him go, but when he was free the holes filled up at once, the liquid sand oozing into place, and everything looked as it had before, smooth and sleek and innocent as the surface of a pudding. It was in fact the same pool of quicksand that I had walked over myself only about an hour earlier.

Quicksand is more of a menace to cattle and horses, with their greater weight and smaller feet, than it is to men, and the four-legged beasts generally avoid it when they can. Sometimes, however, they are forced to cross quicksand to reach water, or are driven across, and then the cattleman may have an unpleasant chore on his hands. Motor vehicles, of course, cannot negotiate quicksand; even a four-wheel-drive jeep will bog down as hopelessly as anything else.

Although I hesitate to deprive quicksand of its sinister glamour I must confess that I have not yet heard of a case where a machine, an animal or a man has actually sunk *completely* out of sight in the stuff. But it may have happened; it may be happening to somebody at this very moment. I sometimes regret that I was unable to perform a satisfactory experiment with my friend Newcomb when the chance presented itself; such opportunities come but rarely. But I needed him; he was among other things a good camp cook.

After the storms pass and the flash floods have dumped their loads of silt into the Colorado, leaving the streambeds as arid as they were before, it is still possible to find rainwater in the desert. All over the slickrock country there are natural cisterns or potholes, tubs, tanks and basins sculptured in the soft sandstone by the erosive force of weathering, wind and sand. Many of them serve as little catchment basins during rain and a few may contain water for days or even weeks after a storm, the length of time depending on the shape and depth of the hole and the consequent rate of evaporation.

Often far from any spring, these temporary pools attract doves, ravens and other birds, and deer and coyotes; you, too, if you know where to look or find one by luck, can slake your thirst and fill your water gourd. Such pools may be found in what seem like the most improbable places: out on the desolate White Rim below Grandview Point, for example, or on top of the elephant-back dome above the Double Arch. At Toroweap in Grand Canyon I found a deep tank of clear sweet water almost over my head, countersunk in the summit of a sandstone bluff which overhung my campsite by a hundred feet. A week after rain there was still enough water there to fill my needs; hard to reach, it was well worth the effort. The Bedouin know what I mean.

The rain-filled potholes, set in naked rock, are usually devoid of visible plant life but not of animal life. In addition to the inevitable microscopic creatures there may be certain amphibians like the spadefoot toad. This little animal lives through dry spells in a state of estivation under the dried-up sediment in the bottom of a hole. When the rain comes, if it comes, he emerges from the mud singing madly in his fashion, mates with the handiest female and fills the pool with a swarm of tadpoles, most of them doomed to a most ephemeral existence. But a few survive, mature, become real toads, and when the pool dries up they dig into the sediment as their parents did before, making burrows which they seal with mucus in order to preserve that moisture necessary to life. There they wait, day after day, week after week, in patient spadefoot torpor, perhaps listening—we can imagine—for the sound of raindrops pattering at last on the earthen crust above their heads. If it comes in time the glorious cycle is repeated; if not, this particular colony of *Bufonidae* is reduced eventually to dust, a burden on the wind.

Rain and puddles bring out other amphibia, even in the desert. It's a strange, stirring, but not uncommon thing to come on a pool at night, after an evening of thunder and lightning and a bit of rainfall, and see the frogs clinging to the edge of their impermanent pond, bodies immersed in water but heads out, all croaking away in tricky counterpoint. They are windbags: with each croak the pouch under the frog's chin swells like a bubble, then collapses.

Why do they sing? What do they have to sing about? Somewhat apart from one another, separated by roughly equal distances, facing outward from the water, they clank and croak all through the night with tireless perseverance. To human ears their music has a bleak, dismal, tragic quality, dirgelike rather than jubilant. It may nevertheless be the case that these small beings are singing not only to claim their stake in the pond, not only to attract a mate, but also out of spontaneous love and joy, a contrapuntal choral celebration of the coolness and wetness after weeks of desert fire, for love of their own existence, however brief it may be, and for joy in the common life.

Has joy any survival value in the operations of evolution? I suspect that it does; I suspect that the morose and fearful are doomed to quick extinction. Where there is no joy there can be no courage; and without courage all other virtues are useless. Therefore the frogs, the toads, keep on singing even though we know, if they don't, that the sound of their uproar must surely be luring all the snakes and ringtail cats and kit foxes and coyotes and great horned owls toward the scene of their happiness.

What then? A few of the little amphibians will continue their metamorphosis by way of the nerves and tissues of one of the higher animals, in which process the joy of one becomes the contentment of the second. Nothing is lost, except an individual consciousness here and there, a trivial perhaps even illusory phenomenon. The rest survive, mate, multiply, burrow, estivate, dream, and rise again. The rains will come, the potholes shall be filled. Again. And again. And again.

More secure are those who live in and around the desert's few perennial waterholes, those magical hidden springs that are scattered so austerely through the barren vastness of the canyon country. Of these only a rare few are too hot or too briny or too poisonous to support life—the great majority of them swarm with living things. Here you will see the rushes and willows and cottonwoods, and four-winged dragonflies in green, blue, scarlet and gold, and schools of minnows in the water, moving from sunlight to shadow and back again. At night the mammals come—deer, bobcat, cougar, coyote, fox, jackrabbit, bighorn sheep, wild horse and feral burro—each in his turn and in unvarying order, under the declaration of a truce. They come to drink, not to kill or be killed.

Finally, in this discussion of water in the desert, I should make note of a distinctive human contribution, one which has become a part of the Southwestern landscape no less typical than the giant cactus, the juniper growing out of solid rock or the red walls of a Navajo canyon. I refer to the tiny oasis formed by the drilled well, its windmill and storage tank. The windmill with its skeleton tower and creaking vanes is an object of beauty as significant in its way as the cottonwood tree, and the open tank at its foot, big enough to swim in, is a thing of joy to man and beast, no less worthy of praise than the desert spring.

Water, water, water. . . . There is no shortage of water in the desert but exactly the right amount, a perfect ratio of water to rock, of water to sand, insuring that wide, free, open, generous spacing among plants and animals, homes and towns and cities, which makes the arid West so different from any other part of the nation. There is no lack of water here, unless you try to establish a city where no city should be.

The Developers, of course—the politicians, businessmen, bankers, administrators, engineers—they see it somewhat otherwise and complain most bitterly and interminably of a desperate water shortage, especially in the Southwest. They propose schemes of inspiring proportions for diverting water by the damful from the Columbia River, or even from the Yukon River, and channeling it overland down into Utah, Colorado, Arizona and New Mexico.

What for? "In anticipation of future needs, in order to provide for the continued industrial and population growth of the Southwest." And in such an answer we see that it's only the old numbers game again, the monomania of small and very simple minds in the grip of an obsession. They cannot see that growth for the sake of growth is a cancerous madness, that Phoenix and Albuquerque will not be better cities to live in when their populations are doubled again and again. They would never understand that an economic system which can only expand or expire must be false to all that is human.

So much by way of futile digression: the pattern is fixed and protest alone will not halt the iron glacier moving upon us.

No matter, it's of slight importance. Time and the winds will sooner or later bury the Seven Cities of Cibola and the ruins of the others, all of them, under dunes of glowing sand, over which blue-eyed Navajo bedouin will herd their sheep and horses, following the river in winter, the mountains in summer, and sometimes striking off across the desert toward the red canyons of Utah where great waterfalls plunge over silt-filled, ancient, mysterious dams.

Only the boldest among them, seeking visions, will camp for long in the strange country of the standing rock, far out where the spadefoot toads bellow madly in the moonlight on the edge of doomed rainpools, where the arsenic-selenium spring waits for the thirst-crazed wanderer, where the thunderstorms blast the pinnacles and cliffs, where the rust-brown floods roll down the barren washes, and where the community of the quiet deer walk at evening up glens of sandstone through tamarisk and sage toward the hidden springs of sweet, cool, still, clear, unfailing water.

James Wright (1927–1980)

James Wright was born in Martin's Ferry, Ohio, a steel-producing town on the Ohio River. His father was a steel worker. After serving in the United States Army, Wright went to Kenyon College, from which he graduated in 1952. He attended the University of Vienna in 1952 and 1953; he received both a master of arts degree in 1954 and a doctorate in 1959 from the University of Washington in Seattle, where he studied with Theodore Roethke. Wright taught at Macalester College in St. Paul, Minnesota, at the University of Minnesota, and at Hunter College of the City University of New York. While still a graduate student, Wright published three poems in Poetry *magazine, for which he received the Eunice Tietjens Memorial Prize in 1955. He went on to publish several books of poetry, including* The Green Wall *(1957),* Saint Judas *(1959),* The Branch Will Not Break *(1963), and* Shall We Gather at the River *(1968).*

Wright is endowed with keen senses and a dexterous command of language. The natural and artificial converge in his poems: Wright regards men and women, and the things they make, as if they were natural objects. Wright's poetry is noticeably less concerned with politics than that of many other nature poets. He seems much more interested in immediate sensual experience, in our acute sensory and emotional responses to physical nature. Wright is remarkably attuned to these things, and in his poems he gives them thoughtful, eloquent expression.

Depressed by a Book of Bad Poetry, I Walk Toward an Unused Pasture and Invite the Insects to Join Me

Relieved, I let the book fall behind a stone.
I climb a slight rise of grass.
I do not want to disturb the ants
Who are walking single file up the fence post,
Carrying small white petals,   5
Casting shadows so frail that I can see through them.
I close my eyes for a moment, and listen.
The old grasshoppers
Are tired, they leap heavily now,
Their thighs are burdened.   10
I want to hear them, they have clear sounds to make.
Then lovely, far off, a dark cricket begins
In the maple trees.

Two Horses Playing in the Orchard

Too soon, too soon, a man will come
To lock the gate, and drive them home.
Then, neighing softly through the night,
The mare will nurse her shoulder bite.
Now, lightly fair, through lock and mane   5
She gazes over the dusk again,
And sees her darkening stallion leap
In grass for apples, half asleep.

Lightly, lightly, on slender knees
He turns, lost in a dream of trees.   10
Apples are slow to find this day,
Someone has stolen the best away.

Still, some remain before the snow,
A few, trembling on boughs so low
A horse can reach them, small and sweet: 15
And some are tumbling to her feet.

Too soon, a man will scatter them,
Although I do not know his name,
His age, or how he came to own
A horse, an apple tree, a stone.   20
I let those horses in to steal
On principle, because I feel
Like half a horse myself, although
Too soon, too soon, already. Now.

Snowstorm in the Midwest

Though haunches of whales
Slope into whitecap doves,
It is hard to drown here.

Between two walls,
A fold of echoes,
A girl's voice walks naked.   5

I step into the water
Of two flakes.
The crowns of white birds rise
To my ankles,
To my knees,   10
To my face.

Escaping in silence
From locomotive and smoke,
I hunt the huge feathers of gulls   15
And the fountains of hills,
I hunt the sea, to walk on the waters.

A splayed starling
Follows me down a long stairway
Of white sand.   20

Milkweed

While I stood here, in the open, lost in myself,
I must have looked a long time

Down the corn rows, beyond grass,
The small house,
White walls, animals lumbering toward the barn.   5
I look down now. It is all changed.
Whatever it was I lost, whatever I wept for
Was a wild, gentle thing, the small dark eyes
Loving me in secret.
It is here. At a touch of my hand,   10
The air fills with delicate creatures
From the other world.

Late November in a Field

Today I am walking alone in a bare place,
And winter is here.
Two squirrels near a fence post
Are helping each other drag a branch
Toward a hiding place; it must be somewhere   5
Behind those ash trees.
They are still alive, they ought to save acorns
Against the cold.
Frail paws rifle the troughs between cornstalks when the moon
Is looking away.   10
The earth is hard now,
The soles of my shoes need repairs.
I have nothing to ask a blessing for,
Except these words.
I wish they were   15
Grass.

Galway Kinnell (*born 1927*)

Galway Kinnell earned a B.A. from Princeton in 1948 and an M.A. from the University of Rochester in 1949, and in the time since has authored numerous collections of poems. His many publications include First Poems 1946–1954 *(1971),* What a Kingdom It Was *(1960),* Flower Herding on Mount Monadnock *(1964),* The Book of Nightmares *(1971),* Selected Poems *(1982), and* Imperfect Thirst *(1994). He has also published two works of prose and several translations. He won both the National Book Award and the Pulitzer Prize for* Selected Poems *in 1982, and is currently the Erich Maria Remarque Professor of Creative Writing at New York University. He lives in Vermont and New York.*

In his poem "Saint Francis and the Sow," Kinnell writes, "sometimes it is necessary to reteach a thing its loveliness, / to put a hand on its brow and retell it in words and in touch it is lovely / until it flowers again from within, of self blessing." These lines aptly describe Kinnell's treatment of his subjects. Throughout his examination of diverse topics, which range from natural landscapes to war scenes and from infancy to the dying, Kinnell writes in a deeply personal voice that is always and unflinchingly determined to summon the beauty and the mystery from the world around him. Kinnell was born in 1927 in Rhode Island, around the same time that writers such as T. S. Eliot and Ezra Pound were elaborating the dominant Modernist aesthetic. In its rejection of the pessimism common in much Modernist poetry, in its embrace of the natural scenes and rich images comparable to those found in Robert Frost and Seamus Heaney, and in its socially conscious themes, Kinnell's work can be read as an innovative and eclectic response to much twentieth-century poetry. Kinnell once remarked during a public reading that was interrupted by a crying child, "The baby's voice is the tuning fork of the poet." His poems are always listening for this sound, the voice of uncorruptible humanity confronting the horrors, wonders, and mysteries of life and death.

To Christ Our Lord

The legs of the elk punctured the snow's crust
And wolves floated lightfooted on the land
Hunting Christmas elk living and frozen;
Inside snow melted in a basin, and a woman basted
A bird spread over coals by its wings and head.   5

Snow had sealed the windows; candles lit
The Christmas meal. The Christmas grace chilled
The cooked bird, being long-winded and the room cold.
During the words a boy thought, is it fitting
To eat this creature killed on the wing?   10

He had killed it himself, climbing out
Alone on snowshoes in the Christmas dawn,
The fallen snow swirling and the snowfall gone,
Heard its throat scream as the gunshot scattered,
Watched it drop, and fished from the snow the dead.   15

He had not wanted to shoot. The sound
Of wings beating into the hushed air
Had stirred his love, and his fingers
Froze in his gloves, and he wondered,
Famishing, could he fire? Then he fired.   20

Now the grace praised his wicked act. At its end
The bird on the plate
Stared at his stricken appetite.

There had been nothing to do but surrender,
To kill and to eat; he ate as he had killed, with wonder.   25

At night on snowshoes on the drifting field
He wondered again, for whom had love stirred?
The stars glittered on the snow and nothing answered.
Then the Swan spread her wings, cross of the cold north,
The pattern and mirror of the acts of earth.   30

Flower Herding on Mount Monadnock

1

I can support it no longer.
Laughing ruefully at myself
For all I claim to have suffered
I get up. Damned nightmarer!

It is New Hampshire out here,   5
It is nearly the dawn.
The song of the whippoorwill stops
And the dimension of depth seizes everything.

2

The song of a peabody bird goes overhead
Like a needle pushed five times through the air,   10
It enters the leaves, and comes out little changed.

The air is so still
That as they go off through the trees
The love songs of birds do not get any fainter.

3

The last memory I have   15
Is of a flower which cannot be touched,

Through the bloom of which, all day,
Fly crazed, missing bees.

4

As I climb sweat gets up my nostrils,
For an instant I think I am at the sea,   20

One summer off Cap Ferrat we watched a black seagull
Straining for the dawn, we stood in the surf,

Grasshoppers splash up where I step,
The mountain laurel crashes at my thighs.

5

There is something joyous in the elegies   25
Of birds. They seem
Caught up in a formal delight,
Though the mourning dove whistles of despair.

But at last in the thousand elegies
The dead rise in our hearts,   30
On the brink of our happiness we stop
Like someone on a drunk starting to weep.

6

I kneel at a pool,
I look through my face
At the bacteria I think   35
I see crawling through the moss.

My face sees me,
The water stirs, the face,
Looking preoccupied,
Gets knocked from its bones.   40

7

I weighed eleven pounds
At birth, having stayed on
Two extra weeks in the womb.
Tempted by room and fresh air
I came out big as a policeman   45
Blue-faced, with narrow red eyes.
It was eight days before the doctor
Would scare my mother with me.

Turning and craning in the vines
I can make out through the leaves   50
The old, shimmering nothingness, the sky.

8

Green, scaly moosewoods ascend,
Tenants of the shaken paradise,

At every wind last night's rain
Comes splattering from the leaves,   55

It drops in flurries and lies there,
The footsteps of some running start.

9

From a rock
A waterfall,
A single trickle like a strand of wire,   60
Breaks into beads halfway down.

I know
The birds fly off
But the hug of the earth wraps
With moss their graves and the giant boulders.   65

10

In the forest I discover a flower.

The invisible life of the thing
Goes up in flames that are invisible
Like cellophane burning in the sunlight.

It burns up. Its drift is to be nothing.   70

In its covertness it has a way
Of uttering itself in place of itself,
Its blossoms claim to float in the Empyrean,

A wrathful presence on the blur of the ground.

The appeal to heaven breaks off.   75
The petals begin to fall, in self-forgiveness.
It is a flower. On this mountainside it is dying.

The Porcupine

1

Fatted
on herbs, swollen on crabapples,
puffed up on bast and phloem, ballooned
on willow flowers, poplar catkins, first
leafs of aspen and larch,   5
the porcupine
drags and bounces his last meal through ice,
mud, roses and goldenrod, into the stubbly high fields.

2

In character
he resembles us in seven ways: 10
he puts his mark on outhouses,

he alchemizes by moonlight,
he shits on the run,
he uses his tail for climbing,
he chuckles softly to himself when scared,   15
he's overcrowded if there's more than one of him per five acres,
his eyes have their own inner redness.

3

Digger of
goings across floors, of hesitations
at thresholds, of   20
handprints of dread
at doorpost or window jamb, he would
gouge the world
empty of us, hack and crater
it   25
until it is nothing, if that
could rid it of all our sweat and pathos.

Adorer of axe
handles aflow with grain, of arms
of Morris chairs,[1] of hand   30
crafted objects
steeped in the juice of fingertips,
of surfaces wetted down
with fist grease and elbow oil,
of clothespins that have   35
grabbed our body-rags by underarm and crotch . . .

Unimpressed—bored—
by the whirl of the stars, by *these*
he's astonished, ultra-
Rilkean angel![2]   40

for whom the true
portion of the sweetness of earth
is one of those bottom-heavy, glittering, saccadic
bits
of salt water that splash down   45
the haunted ravines of a human face.

4

A farmer shot a porcupine three times
as it dozed on a tree limb. On

---

[1] Chairs made according to the designs of poet and artist, William Morris (whose poems are also included in this anthology).

[2] Rainer Maria Rilke (1875–1926), a German poet who used images of angels frequently. His angels were not like familiar Christian spirits, feathered and loving toward humanity, but more akin to the classical notion of the daemon.

the way down it tore open its belly
on a broken   50
branch, hooked its gut,
and went on falling. On the ground
it sprang to its feet, and
paying out gut heaved
and spartled through a hundred feet of goldenrod   55
before
the abrupt emptiness.

5

The Avesta[3]
puts porcupine killers
into hell for nine generations, sentencing them   60
to gnaw out
each other's hearts for the
salts of desire.

I roll
this way and that in the great bed, under   65
the quilt
that mimics this country of broken farms and woods,
the fatty sheath of the man
melting off,
the self-stabbing coil   70
of bristles reversing, blossoming outward—
a red-eyed, hard-toothed, arrow-stuck urchin
tossing up mattress feathers,
pricking the
woman beside me until she cries.   75

6

In my time I have
crouched, quills erected,
Saint
Sebastian[4] of the
scared heart, and been   80
beat dead with a locust club
on the bare snout.
And fallen from high places
I have fled, have
jogged   85
over fields of goldenrod,
terrified, seeking home,

---

[3] The sacred writings of the ancient Zoroastrian religion as well as of its modern form among the Parsees.

[4] A Christian saint, martyred by being shot through with arrows.

and among flowers
I have come to myself empty, the rope
strung out behind me   90
in the fall sun
suddenly glorified with all my blood.

7

And tonight I think I prowl broken
skulled or vacant as a
sucked egg in the wintry meadow, softly chuckling, blank   95
template of myself, dragging
a starved belly through the lichflowered acres,
where
burdock looses the ark of its seed
and thistle holds up its lost bloom   100
and rosebushes in the wind scrape their dead limbs
for the forced-fire
of roses.

The Bear

1

In late winter
I sometimes glimpse bits of steam
coming up from
some fault in the old snow
and bend close and see it is lung-colored   5
and put down my nose
and know
the chilly, enduring odor of bear.

2

I take a wolf's rib and whittle
it sharp at both ends   10
and coil it up
and freeze it in blubber and place it out
on the fairway of the bears.

And when it has vanished
I move out on the bear tracks,   15
roaming in circles
until I come to the first, tentative, dark
splash on the earth.

And I set out
running, following the splashes
of blood wandering over the world.   20
At the cut, gashed resting places
I stop and rest,
at the crawl-marks
where he lay out on his belly   25
to overpass some stretch of bauchy ice
I lie out
dragging myself forward with bear-knives in my fists.

3

On the third day I begin to starve,
at nightfall I bend down as I knew I would   30
at a turd sopped in blood,
and hesitate, and pick it up,
and thrust it in my mouth, and gnash it down,
and rise
and go on running.   35

4

On the seventh day,
living by now on bear blood alone,
I can see his upturned carcass far out ahead, a scraggled,
steamy hulk,   40
the heavy fur riffling in the wind.

I come up to him
and stare at the narrow-spaced, petty eyes,
the dismayed
face laid back on the shoulder, the nostrils
flared, catching   45
perhaps the first taint of me as he
died.

I hack
a ravine in his thigh, and eat and drink,
and tear him down his whole length   50
and open him and climb in
and close him up after me, against the wind,
and sleep.

5

And dream
of lumbering flatfooted   55
over the tundra,

stabbed twice from within,
splattering a trail behind me,
splattering it out no matter which way I lurch,
no matter which parabola of bear-transcendence,   60
which dance of solitude I attempt,
which gravity-clutched leap,
which trudge, which groan.

6

Until one day I totter and fall—
fall on this   65
stomach that has tried so hard to keep up,
to digest the blood as it leaked in,
to break up
and digest the bone itself: and now the breeze
blows over me, blows off   70
the hideous belches of ill-digested bear blood
and rotted stomach
and the ordinary, wretched odor of bear,

blows across
my sore, lolled tongue a song   75
or screech, until I think I must rise up
and dance. And I lie still.

7

I awaken I think. Marshlights
reappear, geese
come trailing again up the flyway.   80
In her ravine under old snow the dam-bear
lies, licking
lumps of smeared fur
and drizzly eyes into shapes
with her tongue. And one   85
hairy-soled trudge stuck out before me,
the next groaned out,
the next,
the next,
the rest of my days I spend   90
wandering: wondering
what, anyway,
was that sticky infusion, that rank flavor of blood, that
  poetry, by which I lived?

🦅 Gary Snyder *(born 1930)*

Described by some critics as America's greatest living nature poet, Gary Snyder was born in San Francisco and grew up in the Pacific Northwest on a series of small farms. He attended Reed College, where he studied literature and anthropology, and later studied Asian languages at the University of California at Berkeley and Rinzai Zen Buddhism for twelve years in Japan. He worked on the docks in San Francisco, the city where he would become one of the influential Beat poets of the 1950s and 1960s. Jack Kerouac's novel The Dharma Bums *(1958) is a loosely fictionalized account of Snyder's life, particularly his interest in mountain climbing ("a true path," he says, "always leads through a mountain"). While a young man, Snyder worked as a seaman, logger, and fire watcher, serving in the U.S. Forest Service in Washington and California. An avid hiker, mountain climber, and Zen practitioner, he was largely responsible for the interest in Zen Buddhism that swept the Beats and, to some extent, the generation of the 1960s. He is a staunch advocate for peace, environmental awareness, and the rights of indigenous peoples.*

For Snyder, it is important not only to be mindful of nature but also to recreate the organic relationship with nature that modern life has destroyed. He is an advocate for the wild in itself and not as a representation of something else. His poems often remind the reader to notice nature as it is, wherever it is:

> A cross street leads toward a river
> North goes to the woods
> South takes you fishing
> Peregrines nest at the thirty-fifth floor

Snyder has written, "As a poet I hold the most archaic values on earth. They go back to the late Paleolithic: the fertility of the soil, the magic of animals, the power-vision in solitude, the terrifying initiation and rebirth, the love and ecstasy of the dance, the common work of the tribe. I try to hold both history and wilderness in mind, that my poems may approach the true measure of things and stand against the unbalance and ignorance of our times."

Snyder is a professor of English at the University of California, Davis, and one of the founders of the Program in Nature and Culture, an interdisciplinary undergraduate program on society and the environment. He lives with his family on the San Juan Ridge of the northern Sierra foothills, where he was a founding member of the Ring of Bone zendo for Zen Buddhist practice. In 1998 he received the Buddhism Transmission Award from the Bukkyo Dendo Kyokai Foundation (Buddhist Awareness Foundation) of Japan. Snyder is the first American to receive this award, which honors scholars, artists, and monks for a lifetime body of work linking Zen and nature. His books include Riprap *(1959),* Earth House Hold *(1969),* Axe Handles *(1983),* Left Out in the Rain *(1986),* The Practice of the Wild *(1990),* No Nature *(1992), and* Mountains and Rivers Without End *(1997). Perhaps his most highly regarded collection is* Turtle Island *(1974), which won the Pulitzer Prize for poetry.*

Above Pate Valley

We finished clearing the last
Section of trail by noon,
High on the ridge-side
Two thousand feet above the creek
Reached the pass, went on   5
Beyond the white pine groves,
Granite shoulders, to a small
Green meadow watered by the snow,
Edged with Aspen—sun
Straight high and blazing   10
But the air was cool.
Ate a cold fried trout in the
Trembling shadows. I spied
A glitter, and found a flake
Black volcanic glass—obsidian—   15
By a flower. Hands and knees
Pushing the Bear grass, thousands
Of arrowhead leavings over a
Hundred yards. Not one good
Head, just razor flakes   20
On a hill snowed all but summer,
A land of fat summer deer,
They came to camp. On their
Own trails. I followed my own
Trail here. Picked up the cold-drill,   25
Pick, singlejack, and sack
Of dynamite.
Ten thousand years.

Marin-an

sun breaks over the eucalyptus
grove below the wet pasture,
water's about hot,
I sit in the open window
& roll a smoke.   5

distant dogs bark, a pair of
cawing crows; the twang
of a pygmy nuthatch high in a pine—
from behind the cypress windrow
the mare moves up, grazing.   10

a soft continuous roar
comes out of the far valley

of the six-lane highway—thousands
and thousands of cars
driving men to work.　　　　　　　　　　　　　　　15

Pine Tree Tops

in the blue night
frost haze, the sky glows
with the moon
pine tree tops
bend snow-blue, fade　　　　　　　　　　　　　　5
into sky, frost, starlight.
the creak of boots.
rabbit tracks, deer tracks,
what do we know.

For Nothing

Earth a flower
A phlox on the steep
slopes of light
hanging over the vast
solid spaces　　　　　　　　　　　　　　　　　5
small rotten crystals;
salts.

Earth a flower
by a gulf where a raven
flaps by once　　　　　　　　　　　　　　　　　10
a glimmer, a color
forgotten as all
falls away.

A flower
for nothing;
an offer;　　　　　　　　　　　　　　　　　　15
no taker;

Snow-trickle, feldspar, dirt.

Old Woman Nature

Old Woman Nature
naturally has a bag of bones
　　　　tucked away somewhere.
　　　　a whole room full of bones!

A scattering of hair and cartilage   5
    bits in the woods.

A fox scat with hair and a tooth in it.
    a shellmound
        a bone flake in a streambank.

A purring cat, crunching   10
    the mouse head first,
        eating on down toward the tail—

The sweet old woman
    calmly gathering firewood in the
        moon . . .   15

Don't be shocked,
She's heating you some soup.

VII 81, Seeing Ichikawa Ennosuke in
"Kurozuka"—"Demoness"—at the Kabuki-za in Tokyo

Ripples on the Surface

"Ripples on the surface of the water—
were silver salmon passing under—different
from the ripples caused by breezes"

A scudding plume on the wave—
a humpback whale is   5
breaking out in air up
gulping herring
      —Nature not a book, but a *performance*, a
high old culture

Ever-fresh events   10
scraped out, rubbed out, and used, used, again—
the braided channels of the rivers
hidden under fields of grass—

The vast wild
    the house, alone.   15
The little house in the wild,
    the wild in the house.
Both forgotten.

        No nature

    Both together, one big empty house.   20

🖎 *John McPhee* (born 1931)

John McPhee was born in Princeton, New Jersey. He studied at Princeton University, graduating in 1953, and he completed his graduate studies at Cambridge University. McPhee married Pryde Brown in 1957; after his first marriage ended, he wed Yolanda Whitman in 1972. He has four daughters from his first marriage, and several stepchildren from his second. McPhee's major works include A Sense of Where You Are *(1965),* The Headmaster *(1966),* Oranges *(1967),* The Deltoid Pumpkin Seed *(1973),* The Survival of the Bark Canoe *(1975),* Coming into the Country *(1977),* Rising from the Plains *(1986), and* The Control of Nature *(1989).*

McPhee has been employed as an editor for Time *magazine and as a staff writer for* The New Yorker, *and accordingly, his works read much like journalism. As a practice, McPhee tries to exclude any reference to himself in his writing, and one sometimes feels that the author or narrator is painfully absent from a McPhee story. He devotes painstaking attention to things, often overlooked or seemingly insignificant things, without betraying a trace of emotion or even any motivation for his attentiveness. A delightful example of this tendency is McPhee's book* Oranges, *a study of the fruit and its history, production, and consumption.*

McPhee writes about many subjects, including sports, food, history, and popular culture, but his skill as a writer emanates most impressively in his works on nature. It is in his nature writing that one can most easily see his sincere appreciation for, careful attention to, and delicate treatment of his subject. One of his best-known works, The Pine Barrens *(1968), is excerpted below. Virtually an unknown landscape to most Americans, although it is located close to a major metropolitan area, the Pine Barrens provide McPhee with an opportunity to exercise his powers of meticulous description with subtlety, wit, and insight into the lives of the people that dwell in this strange netherworld in northern New Jersey.*

From The Pine Barrens

The Woods from Hog Wallow

From the fire tower on Bear Swamp Hill, in Washington Township, Burlington County, New Jersey, the view usually extends about twelve miles. To the north, forest land reaches to the horizon. The trees are mainly oaks and pines, and the pines predominate. Occasionally, there are long, dark, serrated stands of Atlantic white cedars, so tall and so closely set that they seem to be spread against the sky on the ridges of hills, when in fact they grow along streams that flow through the forest. To the east, the view is similar, and few people who are not native to the region can discern essential differences from the high cabin of the fire tower, even though one difference is that huge areas out in this direction are covered with dwarf forests, where a man can stand among the trees and see for miles over their uppermost branches. To the south, the view is twice broken slightly—by a lake and by a cranberry bog—but otherwise it, too, goes to the horizon in forest. To the west, pines, oaks, and cedars continue all the way, and the western horizon includes the summit of another hill—Apple Pie Hill—and the outline of another fire tower, from which the view three hundred and sixty degrees around is virtually the same as the view from Bear Swamp Hill, where, in a moment's sweeping glance, a person can see hundreds of square miles of wilderness. The picture of New Jersey that most people hold in their minds is so different from this one that, considered beside it, the Pine Barrens, as they are called, become as incongruous as they are beautiful. West and north of the Pine Barrens is New Jersey's central transportation corridor, where traffic of freight and people is more concentrated than it is anywhere else in the world. The corridor is one great compression of industrial shapes, industrial sounds, industrial air, and thousands and thousands of houses webbing over the spaces between the factories. Railroads and magnificent highways traverse this crowded scene, and by 1985 New Jersey hopes to have added so many additional high-speed roads that the present New Jersey Turnpike will be quite closely neighbored by the equivalent of at least six other turnpikes, all going in the same direction. In and around the New Jersey corridor, towns indistinguishably abut one another. Of the great unbroken city that will one day reach at least from Boston to Richmond, this section is already built. New Jersey has nearly a thousand people per square mile—the greatest population density of any state in the Union. In parts of northern New Jersey, there are as many as forty thousand people per square mile. In the central area of the Pine Barrens—the forest land that is still so undeveloped that it can be called wilderness—there are only fifteen people per square mile. This area, which includes about six hundred and fifty thousand acres, is nearly as large as Yosemite National Park. It is almost identical in size with Grand Canyon National Park, and it is much larger than Sequoia National Park, Great Smoky Mountains National Park, or, for that matter, most of the national parks in the United States. The people who live in the Pine Barrens are concentrated mainly in small forest towns, so the region's uninhabited sections are quite large—twenty thousand acres here, thirty thousand acres there—and in one section of well over a hundred thousand acres there are only twenty-one people. The Pine Barrens are so close to New York that on a very clear night a bright light in the pines would be visible from the Empire State Building. A line ruled on a map from Boston to Richmond goes straight through the middle of the Pine Barrens. The halfway point between Boston and Richmond—the geographical epicenter of the developing megalopolis—is in the northern part of the woods, about twenty miles from Bear Swamp Hill.

Technically, the Pine Barrens are much larger than the thousand or so square miles of them that remain wild, and their original outline is formed by the boundaries of a thick layer of sand soils that covers much of central and southern New Jersey—down the coast from the outskirts of Asbury Park to the Cape May Peninsula, and inland more than halfway across the state. Settlers in the seventeenth and eighteenth centuries found these soils unpromising for farms, left the land uncleared, and began to refer to the region as the Pine Barrens. People in New Jersey still use the term, with variants such as "the pine belt," "the pinelands," and, most frequently, "the pines." Gradually, development of one kind or another has moved in over the edges of the forest, reducing the circumference of the wild land and creating a man-made boundary in place of the natural one. This transition line is often so abrupt that in many places on the periphery of the pines it is possible to be at one moment in farmland, or even in a residential development or an industrial zone, and in the next moment to be in the silence of a bewildering green country, where a journey of forty or fifty miles is necessary to get to the farms and factories on the other side. I don't know where the exact center of the pines may be, but in recent years I have spent considerable time there and have made outlines of the integral woodland on topographic maps and road maps, and from them I would judge that the heart of the pine country is in or near a place called Hog Wallow. There are twenty-five people in Hog Wallow. Some of them describe it, without any apparent intention to be clever, as a suburb of Jenkins, a town three miles away, which has forty-five people. One resident of Hog Wallow is Frederick Chambers Brown. I met him one summer morning when I stopped at his house to ask for water.

Fred Brown's house is on an unpaved road that curves along the edge of a wide cranberry bog. What attracted me to it was the pump that stands in his yard. It was something of a wonder that I noticed the pump, because there were, among other things, eight automobiles in the yard, two of them on their sides and one of them upside down, all ten years old or older. Around the cars were old refrigerators, vacuum cleaners, partly dismantled radios, cathode-ray tubes, a short wooden ski, a large wooden mallet, dozens of cranberry picker's boxes, many tires, an orange crate dated 1946, a cord or so of firewood, mandolins, engine heads, and maybe a thousand other things. The house itself, two stories high, was covered with tarpaper that was peeling away in some places, revealing its original shingles, made of Atlantic white cedar from the stream courses of the surrounding forest. I called out to ask if anyone was home, and a voice inside called back, "Come in. Come in. Come on the hell in."

I walked through a vestibule that had a dirt floor, stepped up into a kitchen, and went on into another room that had several overstuffed chairs in it and a porcelain-topped table, where Fred Brown was seated, eating a pork chop. He was dressed in a white sleeveless shirt, ankle-top shoes, and undershorts. He gave me a cheerful greeting and, without asking why I had come or what I wanted, picked up a pair of khaki trousers that had been tossed onto one of the overstuffed chairs and asked me to sit down. He set the trousers on another chair, and he apologized for being in the middle of his breakfast, explaining that he seldom drank much but the night before he had had a few drinks and this had caused his day to start slowly. "I don't know what's the matter with me, but there's got to be something the matter with me, because drink don't agree with me anymore," he said. He had a raw onion in one hand, and while he talked he shaved slices from the onion and ate them between bites of the chop. He was a muscular and well-built man, with short, bristly white hair, and he had bright, fast-moving eyes in a wide-open face. His legs were trim and strong, with large muscles in the calves. I guessed that he was about sixty, and for a man of sixty he seemed to be in remarkably good shape. He was actually seventy-nine. "My rule is: Never eat except when you're hungry," he said, and he ate another slice of the onion.

In a straight-backed chair near the doorway to the kitchen sat a young man with long black hair, who wore a visored red leather cap that had darkened with age. His shirt was coarse-woven and had eyelets down a V neck that was laced with a thong. His trousers were made of canvas, and he was wearing gum boots. His arms were folded, his legs were stretched out, he had one ankle over the other, and as he sat there he appeared to be sighting carefully past his feet, as if his toes were the outer frame of a gunsight and he could see some sort of target in the floor. When I had entered, I had said hello to him, and he had nodded without looking up. He had a long, straight nose and high cheekbones, in a deeply tanned face that was, somehow, gaunt. I had no idea whether he was shy or hostile. Eventually, when I came to know him, I found him to be as shy a person as I have ever had a chance to know. His name is Bill Wasovwich, and he lives alone in a cabin about half a mile from Fred. First his father, then his mother left him when he was a young boy, and he grew up depending on the help of various people in the pines. One of them, a cranberry grower, employs him and has given him some acreage, in which Bill is building a small cranberry bog of his own, "turfing it out" by hand. When he is not working in the bogs, he goes roaming, as he puts it, setting out cross-country on long, looping journeys, hiking about thirty miles in a typical day, in search of what he calls "events"— surprising a buck, or a gray fox, or perhaps a poacher or a man with a still. Almost no one who is not native to the pines could do this, for the woods have an undulating sameness, and the understory—huckleberries, sheep laurel, sweet fern, high-bush blueberry—is often so dense that a wanderer can walk in a fairly tight circle and think that he is moving in a straight line. State forest rangers spend a good part of their time finding hikers and hunters, some of whom have vanished for days. In his long, pathless journeys, Bill always emerges from the woods near his cabin—and about when he plans to. In the fall, when thousands of hunters come into the pines, he sometimes works as a guide. In the evenings, or in the daytime when he is not working or roaming, he goes to Fred Brown's house and sits there for hours. The old man is a widower whose seven children are long since gone from Hog Wallow, and he is as expansively talkative and worldly as the young one is withdrawn and wild. Although there are fifty-three years between their ages, it is obviously fortunate for each of them to be the other's neighbor.

That first morning, while Bill went on looking at his outstretched toes, Fred got up from the table, put on his pants, and said he was going to cook me a pork chop, because I looked hungry and ought to eat something. It was about noon, and I was even hungrier than I may have looked, so I gratefully accepted his offer, which was a considerable one. There are two or three small general stores in the pines, but for anything as fragile as a fresh pork chop it is necessary to make a round trip from Fred's place of about fifty miles. Fred went into the kitchen and dropped a chop into a frying pan that was crackling with hot grease. He has a fairly new four-burner stove that uses bottled gas. He keeps water in a large bowl on a table in the kitchen and ladles some when he wants it. While he cooked the meat, he looked out a window through a stand of pitch pines and into the cranberry bog. "I saw a big buck out here last night with velvet on his horns," he said.

"Them horns is soft when they're in velvet." On a nail high on one wall of the room that Bill and I were sitting in was a large meat cleaver. Next to it was a billy club. The wall itself was papered in a flower pattern, and the wallpaper continued out across the ceiling and down the three other walls, lending the room something of the appearance of the inside of a gift box. In some parts of the ceiling, the paper had come loose. "I didn't paper this year," Fred said. "For the last couple months, I've had sinus." The floor was covered with old rugs. They had been put down in random pieces, and in some places as many as six layers were stacked up. In winter, when the temperature approaches zero, the worst cold comes through the floor. The only source of heat in the house is a wood-burning stove in the main room. There were seven calendars on the walls, all current and none with pictures of nudes. Fading into pastel on one wall was a rotogravure photograph of President and Mrs. Eisenhower. A framed poem read:

> God hath not promised
> Sun without rain
> Joy without sorrow
> Peace without pain.

Noticing my interest in all this, Fred reached into a drawer and showed me what appeared to be a postcard. On it was a photograph of a woman, and Fred said with a straight face that she was his present girl, adding that he meets her regularly under a juniper tree on a road farther south in the pines. The woman, whose appearance suggested strongly that she had never been within a great many miles of the Pine Barrens, was wearing nothing at all.

I asked Fred what all those cars were doing in his yard, and he said that one of them was in running condition and the rest were its predecessors. The working vehicle was a 1956 Mercury. Each of the seven others had at one time or another been his best car, and each, in turn, had lain down like a sick animal and had died right there in the yard, unless it had been towed home after a mishap elsewhere in the pines. Fred recited, with affection, the history of each car. Of one old Ford, for example, he said, "I upset that up to Speedwell in the creek." And of an even older car, a station wagon, he said, "I busted that one up in the snow. I met a car on a little hill, and hit the brake, and hit a tree." One of the cars had met its end at a narrow bridge about four miles from Hog Wallow, where Fred had hit a state trooper, head on.

The pork was delicious and almost crisp. Fred gave me a potato with it, and a pitcher of melted grease from the frying pan to pour over the potato. He also handed me a loaf of bread and a dish of margarine, saying, "Here's your bread. You can have one piece or two. Whatever you want."

Fred apologized for not having a phone, after I asked where I would have to go to make a call, later on. He said, "I don't have no phone because I don't have no electric. If I had electric, I would have had a phone in here a long time ago." He uses a kerosene lamp, a propane lamp, and two flashlights.

He asked where I was going, and I said that I had no particular destination, explaining that I was in the pines because I found it hard to believe that so much unbroken forest could still exist so near the big Eastern cities, and I wanted to see it while it was still there. "Is that so?" he said, three times. Like many people in the pines, he often says things three times. "Is that so? Is *that* so?"

I asked him what he thought of a plan that has been developed by Burlington and Ocean Counties to create a supersonic jetport in the pines, connected by a spur of the Garden State Parkway to a new city of two hundred and fifty thousand people, also in the pines.

"They've been talking about that for three years, and they've never give up," Fred said.

"It'd be the end of these woods," Bill said. This was the first time I heard Bill speak. I had been there for an hour, and he had not said a word. Without looking up, he said again, "It'd be the end of these woods, I can tell you that."

Fred said, "They could build ten jetports around me. I wouldn't give a damn."

"You ain't going to be around very long," Bill said to him. "It would be the end of these woods."

Fred took that as a fact, and not as an insult. "Yes, it would be the end of these woods," he said. "But there'd be people here you could do business with."

Bill said, "There ain't no place like this left in the country, I don't believe— and I travelled around a little bit, too."

Eventually, I made the request I had intended to make when I walked in the door. "Could I have some water?" I said to Fred. "I have a jerry can and I'd like to fill it at the pump."

"Hell, yes," he said. "That isn't my water. That's God's water. That's God's water. That right, Bill?"

"I *guess* so," Bill said, without looking up. "It's good water, I can tell you that."

"That's God's water," Fred said again. "Take all you want."

Outside, on the pump housing, was a bright-blue coffee tin full of priming water. I primed the pump and, before filling the jerry can, cupped my hands and drank. The water of the Pine Barrens is soft and pure, and there is so much of it that, like the forest above it, it is an incongruity in place and time. In the sand under the pines is a natural reservoir of pure water that, in volume, is the equivalent of a lake seventy-five feet deep with a surface of a thousand square miles. If all the impounding reservoirs, storage reservoirs, and distribution reservoirs in the New York City water system were filled to capacity—from Neversink and Schoharie to the Croton basin and Central Park—the Pine Barrens aquifer would still contain thirty times as much water. So little of this water is used that it can be said to be untapped. Its constant temperature is fifty-four degrees, and, in the language of a hydrological report on the Pine Barrens prepared in 1966 for the United States Geological Survey, "it can be expected to be bacterially sterile, odorless, clear; its chemical purity approaches that of uncontaminated rain-water or melted glacier ice."

In the United States as a whole, only about thirty per cent of the rainfall gets into the ground; the rest is lost to surface runoff or to evaporation, transpiration from leaves, and similar interceptors. In the Pine Barrens, fully half of all precipitation makes its way into the great aquifer, for, as the government report put it, "the loose, sandy soil can imbibe as much as six inches of water per hour." The

Pine Barrens rank as one of the greatest natural recharging areas in the world. Thus, the City of New York, say, could take all its daily water requirements out of the pines without fear of diminishing the basic supply. New Jersey could sell the Pine Barrens' "annual ground-water discharge"—the part that at the moment is running off into the Atlantic Ocean—for about two hundred million dollars a year. However, New Jersey does not sell a drop, in part because the state has its own future needs to consider. In the eighteen-seventies, Joseph Wharton, the Philadelphia mineralogist and financier for whom the Wharton School of Finance and Commerce of the University of Pennsylvania is named, recognized the enormous potentiality of the Pine Barrens as a source of water for Philadelphia, and between 1876 and 1890 he gradually acquired nearly a hundred thousand contiguous acres of Pine Barrens land. Wharton's plan called for thirty-three shallow reservoirs in the pines, connected by a network of canals to one stupendous reservoir in Camden, from which an aqueduct would go under the Delaware River and into Philadelphia, where the pure waters of New Jersey would emerge from every tap, replacing a water supply that has been described as "dirty, bacterial soup." Wharton's plan was never executed, mainly because the New Jersey legislature drew itself together and passed prohibiting legislation. Wharton died in 1909. The Wharton Tract, as his immense New Jersey landholding was called, has remained undeveloped. It was considered as a site for the United States Air Force Academy. The state was slow in acquiring it in the public interest, but at last did so in 1955, and the whole of it is now Wharton State Forest.

All the major river systems in the United States are polluted, and so are most of the minor ones, but all the small rivers and streams in the Pine Barrens are potable. The pinelands have their own divide. The Pine Barrens rivers rise in the pines. Some flow west to the Delaware; most flow southeast directly into the sea. There are no through-flowing streams in the pines—no waters coming in from cities and towns on higher ground, as is the case almost everywhere else on the Atlantic coastal plain. I have spent many weekends on canoe trips in the Pine Barrens—on the Wading River, the Oswego, the Batsto, the Mullica. There is no white water in any of these rivers, but they move along fairly rapidly; they are so tortuous that every hundred yards or so brings a new scene—often one that is reminiscent of canoeing country in the northern states and in Canada. Even on bright days, the rivers can be dark and almost sunless under stands of white cedar, and then, all in a moment, they run into brilliant sunshine where the banks rise higher and the forest of oak and pine is less dense. One indication of the size of the water resource below the Pine Barrens is that the streams keep flowing without great declines in volume even in prolonged times of drought. When streams in other parts of New Jersey were reduced to near or total dryness in recent years, the rivers in the pines were virtually unaffected. The characteristic color of the water in the streams is the color of tea—a phenomenon, often called "cedar water," that is familiar in the Adirondacks, as in many other places where tannins and other organic waste from riparian cedar trees combine with iron from the ground water to give the rivers a deep color. In summer, the cedar water is ordinarily so dark that the riverbeds are obscured, and while drifting along one has a feeling of being afloat on a river of fast-moving potable ink. For a few days after a long rain, however, the water is almost colorless. At these times, one can look down into it from a canoe and see the white sand bottom, ten or twelve feet below, and it is as clear as an image in the lens of a camera, with sunken timbers now and again coming into view and receding rapidly, at the speed of the river. Every strand of subsurface grass and every contour of the bottom sand is so sharply defined that the deep water above it seems, and is, irresistibly pure. Sea captains once took the cedar water of the Pine Barrens rivers with them on voyages, because cedar water would remain sweet and potable longer than any other water they could find.

According to the government report, "The Pine Barrens have no equal in the northeastern United States not only for magnitude of water in storage and availability of recharge, but also for the ease and economy with which a large volume of water could be withdrawn." Typically, a pipe less than two inches in diameter driven thirty feet into the ground will produce fifty-five gallons a minute, and a twelve-inch pipe could bring up a million gallons a day. But, with all this, the vulnerability of the Pine Barrens aquifer is disturbing to contemplate. The water table is shallow in the pines, and the aquifer is extremely sensitive to contamination. The sand soil, which is so superior as a catcher of rain, is not good at filtering out or immobilizing wastes. Pollutants, if they happen to get into the water, can travel long distances. Industry or even extensive residential development in the central pinelands could spread contaminants widely through the underground reservoir.

When I had finished filling the jerry can from Fred Brown's pump, I took another drink, and I said to him, "You're lucky to live over such good water."

"You're telling me," he said. "You can put this water in a jug and put it away for a year and it will still be the same. Water from outside of these woods would stink. Outside of these woods, some water stinks when you pump it out of the ground. The people that has dug deep around here claims that there are streams of water under this earth that runs all the time."

In the weeks that followed, I stopped in many times to see Fred, and saw nearly as much of Bill. They rode with me through the woods, in my car, for five and six hours at a time. In the evenings, we returned to Fred's place with food from some peripheral town. It is possible to cross the pines on half a dozen state or federal roads, but very little of interest is visible from them. Several county roads—old crown roads with uneven macadam surfaces—connect the pine communities, but it is necessary to get off the paved roads altogether in order to see much of the forest. The areas are spacious—fifty, sixty, and seventy-five thousand acres—through which run no paved roads of any kind. There are many hundreds of miles of unpaved roads through the pines—two tracks in the sand, with underbrush growing up between them. Hunters use them, and foresters, firefighters, and woodcutters. A number of these sand roads have been there, and have remained unchanged, since before the American Revolution. They developed, for the most part, as Colonial stage routes, trails to charcoal pits, pulpwood-and-lumber roads, and connecting roads between communities that have disappeared from the world. In a place called Washington, five of these roads converge in the forest, as if from star points, and they suggest the former importance of Washington, but all that is left of the town is a single fragment of a stone structure. The sand roads are marked on topographic maps with parallel dotted lines, and driving on them can be something of a sport. It is possible to drive all day on the sand roads, and more than halfway across the state, but most people need to stop fairly often to study the topographic maps, for the roads sometimes come together in fantastic ganglia, and even when they are straight and apparently uncomplicated they constantly fork, presenting unclear choices between the main chance and culs-de-sac, of which there are many hundreds. No matter where we were—far up near Mt. Misery, in the northern part of the pines, or over in the western extremities of the Wharton Tract, or down in the southeast, near the Bass River—Fred kept calling out directions. He always knew exactly where he was going. Fred was nearly forty when the first paved roads were built in the pines. Once, not far from the Godfrey Bridge on the Wading River, he said, "Look at these big pines. You would never think that I was as old as these big pines, would you? I seen all of these big pines grow. I remember this when it was all cut down for charcoal." A short distance away, he pointed into a high stand of pitch pines and scarlet oaks, and he said, "That's the old Joe Holloway field. Holloway had a water-powered sawmill." In another part of the woods, we passed a small bald area, and he said, "That's the Dan Dillett field, where Dan made charcoal." As the car kept moving, bouncing in the undulations of the sand and scraping against blueberry bushes and scrub-oak boughs, Fred kept narrating, picking fragments of the past out of the forest, in moments separated by miles: "Right here in this piece of woods is more rattlesnakes than anyplace else in the State of New Jersey. They had a sawmill in there. They used to kill three or four rattlesnakes when they was watering their horses at noon. Rattlesnakes like water. . . . See that fire tower over there? The man in that tower— you take him fifty yards away from that tower and he's lost. He don't know the woods. He don't know the woods. He don't know the woods. He don't know nothing. He can't even fry a hamburger. . . . I've gunned this part of the woods since I was ten years old. I know every foot of it here. . . . Apple Pie Hill is a thunderstriking high hill. You don't realize how high until you get up here. It's the long slope of a hill that makes a high one. . . . See that open spot in there? A group of girls used to keep a house in there. It was called Noah's Ark. . . . I worked this piece of cedar off here. . . . I worked this bog for Joe Wharton once. My father used to work for Joe Wharton, too. He used to come and stay with my father. Joe Wharton was the nicest man you ever seen. That is, if you didn't lie to him. He was quiet. He didn't smile very often. I don't know as I ever heard him laugh out loud. . . . These are the Hocken Lowlands." The Hocken Lowlands surround the headwaters of Tulpehocken Creek, about five miles northwest of Hog Wallow, and are not identified on maps, not even on the large-scale topographic maps. As we moved along, Fred had a name for almost every rise and dip in the land. "This is Sandy Ridge," he said. "That road once went into a bog. Houses were there. Now there's nothing there. . . . This is Bony's Hole. A man named Bony used to water his horse here." Every so often, Fred would reach into his pocket and touch up his day with a minimal sip from a half pint of whiskey. He merely touched the bottle to his lips, then put it away. He did this at irregular intervals, and one day, when he had a new half pint, he took more than five hours to reduce the level of the whiskey from the neck to the shoulders of the bottle. At an intersection of two sand roads in the Wharton Tract, he pointed to a depression in the ground and said, "That hole in the ground was the cellar of an old jug tavern. That cellar was where they kept the jugs. There was a town here called Mount. That tavern is where my grandpop got drunk the last time he got drunk in his life. Grandmother went up to get him. When she came in, he said, 'Mary, what are you doing here?' He was so ashamed to see her there—and his daughter with her. He left a jug of whiskey right on the table, and his wife took one of his hands and his daughter the other and they led him out of there and past Washington Field and home to Jenkins Neck. He lived fifty years. He lived fifty years, and growed cranberries. He lived fifty years more, and he was never drunk again."

One evening, when it was almost dark and we were about five miles from Fred's place, he told me to stop, and he said, "See that upland red cedar? I helped set that out." Red cedar is not native in the Pine Barrens, and this one stood alone among the taller oaks and pines, in a part of the forest that seemed particularly remote. "I went to school there, by that red cedar," Fred said. "There was twenty-five of us in the school. We all walked. We wore leather boots in the winter that got soaked through and your feet froze. When you got home, you had to pull off your boots on a bootjack. In the summer, when I was a boy, if you wanted to go anywhere you rolled up your pantlegs, put your shoes on your shoulder, and you walked wherever you was going. The pigs and cows was everywhere. There was wild bulls, wild cows, wild boars. That's how Hog Wallow got its name. They call them the good old days. What do you think of that, Bill?"

"I wish I was back there, I can tell you that," Bill said.

✒ *Ted Hughes* (1930–1998)

Like Emily Brontë's, Ted Hughes's poetry was shaped by the landscape of the Yorkshire moors in which he was born and raised. He started writing poems at the age of eleven. Hughes enrolled at Cambridge University in 1951, intending to study literature, but he discovered that this stifled his creativity and he switched to archaeology and anthropology. After graduation, he held a number of jobs, including teacher and zookeeper. In 1956 he and several friends started a literary journal, The St. Botolph's Review, *and it was at a party for the review's debut that he met fellow poet Sylvia Plath. The two were married later that year. Hughes's first collection,* The Hawk in the Rain *(1957), appeared soon after. During the late 1950s, Hughes began a long and lucrative career as the author of books for children. He and Plath traveled to America, first holding teaching jobs at Smith College and then the University of Massachusetts-Amherst, living for a time in Boston and traveling across the United States. They returned to England in 1959 and settled in London. Hughes published* Lupercal *in 1960 and continued to write works for children.*

In 1963 Plath committed suicide, and Hughes gave up writing poetry for a time, choosing instead to write reviews and criticism, do editorial work, and continue composing poems and plays for children. He returned to writing poetry for adults in the late 1960s. After the suicide of his companion Assia Wevill, Hughes married Carol Orchard and with her bought a farm in Yorkshire, where he spent a good part of the rest of his life, writing and devoting himself to farm labor and animal husbandry. Along with his own poetry, Hughes continued his work in the theater, collaborating with such well-known directors as Peter Brook, and he also continued to edit and translate the works of other poets, including Shakespeare, Coleridge, and Ovid. He edited the work of Sylvia Plath, and, with Seamus Heaney, an anthology of poems for children entitled The Rattle Bag. *His later collections of poems include* Moortown Elegies *(1979), relating to life on the farm;* Under the North Star *(1981), a collection of poems on the animals of the arctic region; and* Wolfwatching *(1989).*

His poetry is deeply influenced by the English rural landscape, and Hughes has a particular interest in poetry about animals. Hughes served, in the footsteps of Wordsworth and Tennyson, as the poet laureate of England. Although he had long been criticized for his handling of Sylvia Plath's literary estate (he was rumored to have burned many of her manuscripts after her death), Hughes broke his silence about the relationship shortly before his death and published The Birthday Letters *in 1998.*

Relic

I found this jawbone at the sea's edge:
There, crabs, dogfish, broken by the breakers or tossed
To flap for half an hour and turn to a crust
Continue the beginning. The deeps are cold:
In that darkness camaraderie does not hold: 5
Nothing touches but, clutching, devours. And the jaws,
Before they are satisfied or their stretched purpose
Slacken, go down jaws; go gnawn bare. Jaws
Eat and are finished and the jawbone comes to the beach:
This is the sea's achievement; with shells,   10
Vertebrae, claws, carapaces, skulls.

Time in the sea eats its tail, thrives, casts these
Indigestibles, the spars of purposes
That failed far from the surface. None grow rich
In the sea. This curved jawbone did not laugh   15
But gripped, gripped and is now a cenotaph.[1]

[1]An empty tomb erected as a memorial.

An Otter

I

   Underwater eyes, an eel's
Oil of water body, neither fish nor beast is the otter:

Four-legged yet water-gifted, to outfish fish;
　　With webbed feet and long ruddering tail
　　And a round head like an old tomcat.   5

　　Brings the legend of himself
From before wars or burials, in spite of hounds and
　　　　　　　　　　　　　　　　　vermin-poles;
　　Does not take root like the badger. Wanders, cries;
　　Gallops along land he no longer belongs to;   10
　　Re-enters the water by melting.

　　Of neither water nor land. Seeking
Some world lost when first he dived, that he cannot
　　　　　　　　　　　　　　　come at since,
　　Takes his changed body into the holes of lakes;   15
　　As if blind, cleaves the stream's push till he licks
　　The pebbles of the source; from sea

　　To sea crosses in three nights
Like a king in hiding. Crying to the old shape of the
　　　　　　　　　　　　　　　starlit land,   20
　　Over sunken farms where the bats go round,
　　Without answer. Till light and birdsong come
　　Walloping up roads with the milk wagon.

2

The hunt's lost him. Pads on mud,
Among sedges, nostrils a surface bead,   25
The otter remains, hours. The air,
Circling the globe, tainted and necessary,

Mingling tobacco-smoke, hounds and parsley,
Comes carefully to the sunk lungs.
So the self under the eye lies,   30
Attendant and withdrawn. The otter belongs

In double robbery and concealment—
From water that nourishes and drowns, and from land
That gave him his length and the mouth of the hound.
He keeps fat in the limpid integument   35

Reflections live on. The heart beats thick,
Big trout muscle out of the dead cold;
Blood is the belly of logic; he will lick
The fishbone bare. And can take stolen hold

On a bitch otter in a field full   40
Of nervous horses, but linger nowhere.
Yanked above hounds, reverts to nothing at all,
To this long pelt over the back of a chair.

Two Tortoiseshell Butterflies

Mid-May—after May frosts that killed the Camellias,
After May snow. After a winter
Worst in human memory, a freeze
Killing the hundred-year-old Bay Tree,
And the ten-year-old Bay Tree—suddenly 5
A warm limpness. A blue heaven just veiled
With the sweatings of earth
And with the sweatings-out of winter
Feverish under the piled
Maywear of the lawn.
               Now two 10
Tortoiseshell butterflies, finding themselves alive,
She drunk with the earth-sweat, and he
Drunk with her, float in eddies
Over the Daisies' quilt. She prefers Dandelions,
Settling to nod her long spring tongue down 15
Into the nestling pleats, into the flower's
Thick-folded throat, her wings high-folded.
He settling behind her, among plain glistenings
Of the new grass, edging and twitching
To nearly touch—pulsing and convulsing 20
Wings wide open to tight-closed to flat open
Quivering to keep her so near, almost reaching
To stroke her abdomen with his antennae—
Then she's up and away, and he startlingly
Swallowlike overtaking, crowding her, heading her 25
Off any escape. She turns that
To her purpose, and veers down
Onto another Dandelion, attaching
Her weightless yacht to its crest.
Wobbles to stronger hold, to deeper, sweeter 30
Penetration, her wings tight shut above her,
A sealed book, absorbed in itself.
She ignores him
Where he edges to left and to right, flitting
His wings open, titillating her fur 35
With his perfumed draughts, spasming his patterns,
His tropical, pheasant appeals of folk-art,
Venturing closer, grass-blade by grass-blade,
Trembling with inhibition, nearly touching—
And again she's away, dithering blackly. He swoops 40
On an elastic to settle accurately
Under her tail again as she clamps to
This time a Daisy. She's been chosen,

Courtship has claimed her. And he's been conscripted
To what's required   45
Of the splitting bud, of the talented robin
That performs piercings
Out of the still-bare ash,
The whole air just like him, just breathing
Over the still-turned-inward earth, the first   50
Caresses of the wedding coming, the earth
Opening its petals, the whole sky
Opening a flower
Of unfathomably-patterned pollen.

The Honey Bee

The Honey Bee
Brilliant as Einstein's idea
Can't be taught a thing.
Like the sun, she's on course forever.

As if nothing else at all existed   5
Except her flowers.
No mountains, no cows, no beaches, no shops.
Only the rainbow waves of her flowers

A tremor in emptiness

A flying carpet of flowers   10

                         —a pattern
Coming and going—very loosely woven—
Out of which she works her solutions.

Furry goblin midgets
(The beekeeper's thoughts) clamber stickily   15
Over the sun's face—gloves of shadow.

But the Honey Bee
Cannot imagine him, in her brilliance,

Though he's a stowaway on her carpet of colour-waves
And drinks her sums.   20

The River

Fallen from heaven, lies across
The lap of his mother, broken by world.

But water will go on
Issuing from heaven

In dumbness uttering spirit brightness   5
Through its broken mouth.

Scattered in a million pieces and buried
Its dry tombs will split, at a sign in the sky,

At a rending of veils.
It will rise, in a time after times,   10

After swallowing death and the pit
It will return stainless

For the delivery of this world.
So the river is a god

Knee-deep among reeds, watching men,   15
Or hung by the heels down the door of a dam

It is a god, and inviolable.
Immortal. And will wash itself of all deaths.

✒ Sylvia Plath (*1932–1963*)

*Because so much of her work is autobiographical in origin, it is useful to have some
knowledge of Sylvia Plath's life when reading her works, and Plath did not hesitate to
make the facts of her life known to readers in her autobiographical novel* The Bell Jar
*(1963). But as a poet, Plath also transforms her life's story and speaks about it in a pow-
erful, often angry voice that distinguishes the literary creation from the historical facts.
Her emotionally charged and visually brilliant depictions of the natural world, however,
can stand alone as recordings of the interaction between a sensitive woman and her environment. Plath's father, who died when she was eight years old, was a professor of ento-
mology at Boston University, and an expert on bees. This fact gives her poems on bees
and bee-keeping added psychological dimensions and meaning. Plath began writing
early, and by the time she had enrolled in Smith College in 1950, she had already published in national magazines such as* Seventeen.

*In the summer of 1953, she won a contest to travel to New York City to be a guest ed-
itor at* Mademoiselle *magazine. Her exposure to the fashion world and its expectations
of women partially contributed to a mental breakdown and a suicide attempt the following fall. Institutionalized for a year, and made to undergo violent shock-therapy treat-
ments, Plath was able to return to Smith and graduate* summa cum laude. *Always an
exceptional student, Plath won a prestigious Fulbright grant to pursue a graduate degree
at Cambridge University in England. It was there, in 1956, that she met and married
Ted Hughes. The first years of their marriage were happy and productive, with the couple traveling and teaching in the United States and returning to England in 1959. Also*

in 1960, Plath published her first collection, Colossus. *By early 1962, and after two children, the marriage fell apart. Although during the last year of her life she was immensely prolific, she was also under increasing emotional stress, which led her to take her own life in 1963.*

Plath's tragic death, which some readers assert they can forecast from her poems (in particular the poems included in her posthumous 1965 collection, Ariel*), has made her a problematic figure, especially for feminist critics. Plath's poetry is highly critical of the victimization of women (and of nature) by patriarchal oppressors. Yet her suicide suggests either a personal weakness or invites the dangerous position of seeing suicide as a political act. Nonetheless, the facts of Plath's life and death should not cloud her accomplishment as an original poet whose keen eye and powerful empathetic abilities make her one of the finest nature writers of the late twentieth century.*

Point Shirley

From Water-Tower Hill to the brick prison
The shingle booms, bickering under
The sea's collapse.
Snowcakes break and welter. This year
The gritted wave leaps   5
The seawall and drops onto a bier
Of quahog chips,
Leaving a salty mash of ice to whiten

In my grandmother's sand yard. She is dead,
Whose laundry snapped and froze here, who   10
Kept house against
What the sluttish, rutted sea could do.
Squall waves once danced
Ship timbers in through the cellar window;
A thresh-tailed, lanced   15
Shark littered in the geranium bed—

Such collusion of mulish elements
She wore her broom straws to the nub.
Twenty years out
Of her hand, the house still hugs in each drab   20
Stucco socket
The purple egg-stones: from Great Head's knob
To the filled-in Gut
The sea in its cold gizzard ground those rounds.

Nobody wintering now behind   25
The planked-up windows where she set
Her wheat loaves
And apple cakes to cool. What is it

Survives, grieves
So, over this battered, obstinate spit   30
Of gravel? The waves'
Spewed relics clicker masses in the wind,

Grey waves the stub-necked eiders ride.
A labor of love, and that labor lost.
Steadily the sea   35
Eats at Point Shirley: She died blessed,
And I come by
Bones, bones only, pawed and tossed,
A dog-faced sea.
The sun sinks under Boston, bloody red.   40

I would get from these dry-papped stones
The milk your love instilled in them.
The black ducks dive.
And though your graciousness might stream,
And I contrive,   45
Grandmother, stones are nothing of home
To that spumiest dove.
Against both bar and tower the black sea runs.

Mushrooms

Overnight, very
Whitely, discreetly,
Very quietly

Our toes, our noses
Take hold on the loam,   5
Acquire the air.

Nobody sees us,
Stops us, betrays us;
The small grains make room.

Soft fists insist on   10
Heaving the needles,
The leafy bedding,

Even the paving.
Our hammers, our rams,
Earless and eyeless,   15

Perfectly voiceless,
Widen the crannies,
Shoulder through holes. We

Diet on water,
On crumbs of shadow,   20
Bland-mannered, asking

Little or nothing.
So many of us!
So many of us!

We are shelves, we are   25
Tables, we are meek,
We are edible,

Nudgers and shovers
In spite of ourselves.
Our kind multiplies: 30

We shall by morning
Inherit the earth.
Our foot's in the door.

Tulips

The tulips are too excitable, it is winter here.
Look how white everything is, how quiet, how snowed-in.
I am learning peacefulness, lying by myself quietly
As the light lies on these white walls, this bed, these hands.
I am nobody; I have nothing to do with explosions.   5
I have given my name and my day-clothes up to the nurses
And my history to the anesthetist and my body to surgeons.

They have propped my head between the pillow and the sheet-cuff
Like an eye between two white lids that will not shut.
Stupid pupil, it has to take everything in.   10
The nurses pass and pass, they are no trouble,
They pass the way gulls pass inland in their white caps,
Doing things with their hands, one just the same as another,
So it is impossible to tell how many there are.

My body is a pebble to them, they tend it as water   15
Tends to the pebbles it must run over, smoothing them gently.
They bring me numbness in their bright needles, they bring me sleep.
Now I have lost myself I am sick of baggage——
My patent leather overnight case like a black pillbox,
My husband and child smiling out of the family photo;   20
Their smiles catch onto my skin, little smiling hooks.

I have let things slip, a thirty-year-old cargo boat
Stubbornly hanging on to my name and address.

They have swabbed me clear of my loving associations.
Scared and bare on the green plastic-pillowed trolley   25
I watched my teaset, my bureaus of linen, my books
Sink out of sight, and the water went over my head.
I am a nun now, I have never been so pure.

I didn't want any flowers, I only wanted
To lie with my hands turned up and be utterly empty.   30
How free it is, you have no idea how free——
The peacefulness is so big it dazes you,
And it asks nothing, a name tag, a few trinkets.
It is what the dead close on, finally; I imagine them
Shutting their mouths on it, like a Communion tablet.   35

The tulips are too red in the first place, they hurt me.
Even through the gift paper I could hear them breathe
Lightly, through their white swaddlings, like an awful baby.
Their redness talks to my wound, it corresponds.
They are subtle: they seem to float, though they weigh me down,   40
Upsetting me with their sudden tongues and their color,
A dozen red lead sinkers round my neck.

Nobody watched me before, now I am watched.
The tulips turn to me, and the window behind me
Where once a day the light slowly widens and slowly thins,   45
And I see myself, flat, ridiculous, a cut-paper shadow
Between the eye of the sun and the eyes of the tulips,
And I have no face, I have wanted to efface myself.
The vivid tulips eat my oxygen.

Before they came the air was calm enough,   50
Coming and going, breath by breath, without any fuss.
Then the tulips filled it up like a loud noise.
Now the air snags and eddies round them the way a river
Snags and eddies round a sunken rust-red engine.
They concentrate my attention, that was happy   55
Playing and resting without committing itself.

The walls, also, seem to be warming themselves.
The tulips should be behind bars like dangerous animals;
They are opening like the mouth of some great African cat,
And I am aware of my heart: it opens and closes   60
Its bowl of red blooms out of sheer love of me.
The water I taste is warm and salt, like the sea,
And comes from a country far away as health.

Stings

Bare-handed, I hand the combs.
The man in white smiles, bare-handed,
Our cheesecloth gauntlets neat and sweet,
The throats of our wrists brave lilies.
He and I   5

Have a thousand clean cells between us,
Eight combs of yellow cups,
And the hive itself a teacup,
White with pink flowers on it,
With excessive love I enameled it   10

Thinking "Sweetness, sweetness."
Brood cells gray as the fossils of shells
Terrify me, they seem so old.
What am I buying, wormy mahogany?
Is there any queen at all in it?   15

If there is, she is old,
Her wings torn shawls, her long body
Rubbed of its plush——
Poor and bare and unqueenly and even shameful.
I stand in a column   20

Of winged, unmiraculous women,
Honey-drudgers.
I am no drudge
Though for years I have eaten dust
And dried plates with my dense hair.   25

And seen my strangeness evaporate,
Blue dew from dangerous skin.
Will they hate me,
These women who only scurry,
Whose news is the open cherry, the open clover?   30

It is almost over.
I am in control.
Here is my honey-machine,
It will work without thinking,
Opening, in spring, like an industrious virgin   35

To scour the creaming crests
As the moon, for its ivory powders, scours the sea.
A third person is watching.
He has nothing to do with the bee-seller or with me.
Now he is gone   40

In eight great bounds, a great scapegoat.
Here is his slipper, here is another,
And here the square of white linen
He wore instead of a hat.
He was sweet,   45

The sweat of his efforts a rain
Tugging the world to fruit.
The bees found him out,
Molding onto his lips like lies,
Complicating his features.   50

They thought death was worth it, but I
Have a self to recover, a queen.
Is she dead, is she sleeping?
Where has she been,
With her lion-red body, her wings of glass?   55

Now she is flying
More terrible than she ever was, red
Scar in the sky, red comet
Over the engine that killed her——
The mausoleum, the wax house.   60

Wintering

This is the easy time, there is nothing doing.
I have whirled the midwife's extractor,
I have my honey,
Six jars of it,
Six cat's eyes in the wine cellar,   5

Wintering in a dark without window
At the heart of the house
Next to the last tenant's rancid jam
And the bottles of empty glitters——
Sir So-and-so's gin.   10

This is the room I have never been in.
This is the room I could never breathe in.
The black bunched in there like a bat,
No light
But the torch and its faint   15

Chinese yellow on appalling objects——
Black asininity. Decay.
Possession.

It is they who own me.
Neither cruel nor indifferent,   20

Only ignorant.
This is the time of hanging on for the bees—the bees
So slow I hardly know them,
Filing like soldiers
To the syrup tin   25

To make up for the honey I've taken.
Tate and Lyle[1] keeps them going,
The refined snow.
It is Tate and Lyle they live on, instead of flowers.
They take it. The cold sets in.   30

Now they ball in a mass,
Black
Mind against all that white.
The smile of the snow is white.
It spreads itself out, a mile-long body of Meissen,[2]   35

Into which, on warm days,
They can only carry their dead.
The bees are all women,
Maids and the long royal lady.
They have got rid of the men,[3]   40

The blunt, clumsy stumblers, the boors.
Winter is for women——
The woman, still at her knitting,
At the cradle of Spanish walnut,
Her body a bulb in the cold and too dumb to think.   45

Will the hive survive, will the gladiolas
Succeed in banking their fires
To enter another year?
What will they taste of, the Christmas roses?
The bees are flying. They taste the spring.   50

---

[1] A brand name for syrup.

[2] A porcelain manufactured in Germany.

[3] During the winter, beehives do not have any male drones.

🐾 *Edward Hoagland* *(born 1932)*

Although Edward Hoagland writes primarily about the wilderness, he has spent much of his life in cities. Born in New York City, he has worked mainly at urban universities, including the City University of New York and Columbia University. Hoagland's rather surprising preoccupation with wild nature rather than urban life is perhaps due to a sense of social isolation that he has felt since childhood. Hoagland developed a severe stutter as a young child, which may have steered him toward a quiet communion with animals. Throughout his writing, he certainly seems to prefer the company of animals over that of people. Hoagland has said that he wrote his first childhood poem about a frog that lived in a creek near his grandfather's house.

Hoagland served in the U.S. Army from 1955 to 1957. In 1960 he married Amy Ferrara, whom he later divorced; he was remarried to Marion Magid in 1968. In the 1950s and 1960s, Hoagland wrote several novels, including Catman *(1956),* The Circle Home *(1960), and* The Peacock's Tail *(1965). He was a widely acclaimed writer by the late 1960s, when his concentration shifted to nonfiction. His nonfiction works include, among many others,* The Courage of Turtles *(1971),* The Moose on the Wall *(1974), and* African Calliope *(1979).* The Final Fate of the Alligators, *a collection of short stories, was published in 1992.*

In all of his writing, Hoagland comes across as an extremely thoughtful and meticulous observer. His stories and essays are also characterized by self-consciousness and an intelligent sentimentality. He is amazed by the inscrutable beauty of life, and he recognizes an obligation to respect it. For the most part, he is one of those people instinctively inclined to fulfill such an obligation. But there is also in his stories an underlying conflict: Hoagland is aware that caring for, or even about, every living thing is excruciatingly impractical. Human beings, in being able to discern the immaculate perfection in nature and the true value of living things, must assume the peculiar responsibility of being devoted to and caring for all of them. This is nearly impossible, and anyone who really dedicated himself to the task would lack good sense. We are all charged with a burden which none of us can really bear. Nevertheless, Hoagland does not dwell on his own predicament. His works are most importantly about living things other than himself: They are perceptive and insightful pictures of the animals he knows, respects, and adores.

Howling Back at the Wolves

Wolves have marvelous legs. The first thing one notices about them is how high they are set on their skinny legs, and the instant, blurred gait these can switch into, bicycling away, carrying them as much as forty miles in a day. With brindled coats in smoky shades, brushy tails, light-filled eyes, intense sharp faces which are more focused than an intelligent dog's but also less various, they are electric on first sighting, bending that bushy head around to look back as they run. In captivity when they are quarreling in a cage, the snarls sound guttural and their jaws chop, but scientists watching pet wolves in the woods speak of their flowing joy, of such a delight in running that they melt into the woods like sunlight, like running water.

The modern study of American wildlife may be said to have begun with Adolph Murie, who, writing about the wolves of Mount McKinley in 1944, realized there was not much point in a scientist's shooting them; so few wolves were left that this would be killing the goose laying the golden eggs. In those days even the biologists dealing with animals which weren't considered varmints mainly just boiled the flesh off their heads to examine the knobs on their skulls, or opened their stomachs to see what they ate. The scrutiny of skulls had resulted in a listing of eighty-six species and subspecies of the grizzly bear, for example (it's now considered that there were a maximum of only two), and twenty-seven specified New World wolves (again, now revised down to two). Murie, in the field and looking at scats, could do a more thorough investigation of diet than the autopsy fellows, who, as it was, knew almost nothing else about the life of wolves.

Murie and Ian McTaggart Cowan in Canada were the best of the bedroll scientists. They could travel with dogs all winter in the snow or camp alone on a gravel bar in a valley for the summer, go about quietly on foot and record everything that they saw. No amount of bush-plane maneuvering and electronic technology can quite replace these methods, by which the totality of a wilderness community can be observed and absorbed. Young scientists such as L. David Mech, who has been the salvation of wolves in Minnesota, which is practically the only place in the lower forty-eight states where they still occur, try to combine the current reliance on radiotelemetry with some of that old bedroll faithfulness to the five senses shared by a man with the animals he is studying.

Big game, like elk and caribou, and big glamorous predators have naturally received first attention, people being as they are, so that much more is known about wolves than about the grasshopper mouse, though the grasshopper mouse is a wolf among mice, trailing, gorging upon small mammals and insects; in fact, with nose pointed skyward, it even "howls." On lists of endangered species you occasionally find little beasts that wouldn't excite much attention on a picnic outing, but despite all the talk about saving the fruits of two billion years' worth of evolution, the funds available go to help those animals that tend to remind us of ourselves—rhinos, whales, falcons—and there aren't many lists of endangered plants.

So it is that the predator specialists are predatory. A hawk man drops out of the sky for a visit; he has radios attached to assorted raptors and albatrosses and swans, and flies around the world to track their migrations. During his chat about perfecting antennas it is obvious that he is full of what in an animal he would call "displaced aggression." The scientist Albert Erickson, who has worked on grizzlies in the north and leopard seals in Antarctica, was known as "Wild Man Erickson" when he studied black bears in Michigan. The Craighead brothers, Frank and John—territorial, secretive and competitive—have been working on a definitive study of grizzlies (which are also territorial, secretive and competitive) for umpteen years, scrapping with the National Park Service at Yellowstone and embargoing many of their own findings in the meantime. Maurice Hornocker, who is now the definitive mountain-lion man and who trained with them, is just as close-mouthed—as close-mouthed as a mountain lion, indeed. Down in Grand Chenier, Louisiana, Ted Joanen, the state's alligator expert, is equally able and reserved. One doesn't understand right away why he happens to be devoting his life to learning more about alligators than anybody else, rather than ibises or chimney swifts or pelicans, until he gets to describing how alligators can catch a swimming deer, pull it under the water, drown it and tear its leg off by spinning like a lathe, and then points to one's own twitching leg.

Wolves *would* be more of a loss to us than some exotic mouse, because they epitomize the American wilderness as no other animal does, and fill both the folklore of childhood and that of the woods—folklore that would wither away if they all were to die, and may do so in any case. We know that the folklore was exaggerated, that generally they don't attack man, which is a relief, but we treasure the stories nonetheless, wanting the woods to be woods. In the contiguous states the gray wolf's range is less than one percent of what it used to be, and that patch of Minnesota wilderness, twelve thousand square miles where they live in much the same density as in primeval times, is greatly enriched by the presence of wolves.

Wisconsin didn't get around to granting its wolves protection until they had become extinct, but Mech got the Minnesota bounty removed and almost single-handedly turned local thinking around, until there is talk of declaring the wolf a "state animal" and establishing a sanctuary for it in the Boundary Waters Canoe Area. Mech is a swift-thinking, urbane, amused man, bald, round-faced, not a bit wolflike in appearance, although he is sharp in his rivalry with other scientists. As an advocate he knows how to generate "spontaneous" nationwide letter-writing campaigns and can gather financial support from the National Geographic Society and the New York Zoological Society, from Minneapolis industrialists and the federal government. He has a soul-stirring howl, more real than reality, that triggers the wolves into howling back when he is afoot trying to locate them, but his ears have begun to dim from a decade or more of flying all winter in flimsy planes to spot them against the snow. Sometimes he needs an assistant along to hear whether a pack at a distance is answering him.

That wolves do readily answer even bad imitations of their howl may have a good deal of significance. Observers have noticed the similarities between the intricate life of a wolf pack and the most primitive grouping of man, the family-sized band. Often there is a "peripheral wolf," for instance, which is tolerated but picked on, and as though the collective psyche of the pack required a scapegoat, if the peripheral wolf disappears another pack member may slip down the social ladder and assume the role, or a stray that otherwise might have been driven off will be adopted. The strays, or "lone wolves," not being bound by territorial considerations, range much farther and frequently eat better than pack wolves do, but are always seeking to enroll themselves.

What seems so uncanny and moving about the experience of howling to wolves, then hearing them answer, may be the enveloping sense of déjà vu, perhaps partly subliminal, that goes right to one's roots—band replying to band, each on its own ground, gazing across a few hundred yards of meadow or bog at the same screen of trees. The listener rises right up on his toes, looking about happily at his human companions.

Wolf pups make a frothy ribbon of sound like fat bubbling, a shiny, witchy, fluttery yapping, while the adults siren less excitably, without those tremulous, flexible yips, although they sometimes do break pitch into a yodel. The senior wolf permits the response, if one is made, introducing it with his own note after a pause—which is sometimes lengthy—before the others join in. Ordinarily pups left alone will not answer unless the adult closest to them does so, as he or she returns to protect them. Wolves howl for only a half-minute or so, though they may respond again and again after a cautious intermission, if no danger is indicated from their having already betrayed their position. Each wolf has a tone, or series of tones, of its own that blends into an iridescent harmony with the others, and people who howl regularly at a wolf rendezvous soon acquire vocal personalities too, as well as a kind of choral sequence in which they join together—cupping their mouths to the shape of a muzzle on cue.

I went out with a student of Mech's, Fred Harrington, who records and voice-prints wolf howls. His wife was along, doing the puppy trills, and so was the trap-line crew, who attach radio-collars to the wolves they catch. We stood at the edge of a cutover jack-pine flat, with a few tall spruces where the wolves were. The sun was setting, the moon was rising, squirrels and birds were chitting close by, and we knew that a radio-collared bear was digging its winter den just over the rise. Howling is not a hunting cry and does not frighten other animals. The wolves howled as if for their own edification, as a pleasurable thing, a popular, general occasion set off by our calls to them, replying to us but not led by our emphasis or interpretation. If they had been actively scouting us they would have kept silent, as they do in the spring when the pups are too young to travel. To us, their chorus sounded isolated, vulnerable, the more so because obviously they were having fun, and we all felt the urge to run toward them; but they didn't share that feeling. A pack needs at least ten square miles for each member, as well as a deer every eighteen days for that individual, or a deer every three days for a pack of six. The figure for moose is one every three days for a pack of fifteen, Mech has calculated. Thus, howling between packs does not serve the function of calling them to confabulate. Instead, it seems to keep them apart, defining rough boundaries for their separate ranges, providing them mutually with a roster of strength, though by howling, mates in a pack do find one another and find solidarity.

In Algonquin Provincial Park in Ontario thousands of people howl with the wolves in the early autumn. Whether or not it is a high point for the wolves, it certainly is for the people. I've gone to one of the favorite locations, where the ground is littered with cigarette butts, and tried, except the day was rainy and the wolves couldn't hear me. Nobody who has had the experience will fail to root for the beasts ever after. Glacier National Park in Montana is next to Canada, like Mech's country, and they may manage to become reestablished there; Yellowstone Park has a small vanguard. In East Texas a few hundred survive, hiding in the coastal marshes. These are red wolves—relic relations of the gray wolf that inhabited the Southeast and lower Mississippi Valley and are probably now doomed, pushed up against the sea, with no reservoir such as the wildlands of Canada provide from which to replenish their numbers.

Apparently a special relationship can exist between men and wolves which is unlike that between men and any of the bears or big cats. One might have to look to the other primates for a link that is closer. It's not just a matter of howling; owls with their hoots and loons with their laughter also interact with wolves. Nor is it limited to the mystery of why dogs, about fifteen thousand years back, which is very recent as such events go, cut themselves away from other wolves by a gradual, at first "voluntary" process to become subservient to human beings as no other domestic creature is, running with man in packs in which *he* calls the tune. Another paradox is that the wolves which remained wolves, though they are large predators that might legitimately regard a man-shaped item as prey, don't seem to look upon him as such; don't even challenge him in the woods in quite the same way that they will accost a trespassing cougar or grizzly.

In the campaign to rescue the wolf from Red Ridinghood status, some scientists, including Mech, have overdone their testimonials as to its liberal behavior, becoming so categorical that they doubt that any North American wolf not rabid has ever attacked a human being. This does violence to scientific method, as well as to the good name of countless frontiersmen who knew more about the habits of wilderness animals than it is possible to learn today. (What these scientists really mean is that none of their Ph.D. candidates doing field work has been attacked by a wolf so far.) Such propaganda also pigeonholes the wolf in a disparaging way, as if it were a knee-jerk creature without any options, like a blowfish or hog-nosed snake.

But the link with man remains. Douglas H. Pimlott, who is Canada's wolf expert, explores this matter in *The World of the Wolf.* He mentions behavioral patterns that are shared by man and wolf, and by indirection might have come to influence wolves. Both hunt cooperatively in groups and are nearly unique in that respect; both have lived in complex bands in which the adults of either sex care for the young. He mentions the likelihood that there are subconscious attributes of the human mind that may affect wolves. After all, the bonds between a man and dog penetrate far beyond the awe of the one for the other—are more compulsive, more telepathic than awe—and cannot be fully explained under the heading of love. Wolves, like dogs, says Pimlott, are excellent readers of signs because of their social makeup and their cruising system of hunting, which does not depend as much on surprise as the habits of most other predators do: "They instinctively recognize aggression, fear, and other qualities of mind which are evidenced in subtle ways by our expressions and actions. . . . In hunting we stalk deliberately, quietly . . . in winter we move through the woods and across lakes and streams deliberately, as a wolf does in traveling over his range, hunting for prey."

These movements indicate to wolves that we are superior predators—superior wolves—and not prey. It could be added that wolves, like dogs, take a remarkable delight in submissive ritual, ingratiating themselves, placating a bigger, more daring beast—this part of their adaptation through the millennia to life in a pack, in which usually only one or two members are really capable of killing the sizable game that will feed many mouths; the rest dance attendance upon them. Of course not only the fellow prowling in the woods is predatory. In the city, when much more driving and successful men emerge on the street for a business lunch, their straight-line strides and manner, "bright-eyed and bushy-tailed," would bowl over any wolf.

N. Scott Momaday (born 1934)

Native American novelist, poet, and artist N. Scott Momaday was born on the Kiowa reservation in Lawton, Oklahoma, where his father was born and raised. His tribal name is Tsoai-talee ("Rock Tree Boy"), after the Kiowa name for Devils Tower, in Wyoming. When he was only a year old, his family moved to Arizona to work among the Navajo, Apache, and Jemez Indians for what was then called the Indian Service, now the Bureau of Indian Affairs. His mother is of English and Cherokee descent, and therefore by blood and by culture, Momaday himself is a reflection of the mixed heritage that he often writes about: "I had a Pan-Indian experience before I knew what that term meant." His work is strongly influenced by classical models of Western culture and by Kiowa customs and beliefs, especially the Native American oral tradition. He states in a recent interview: "The more I understand about storytelling, the more I realize that there is always a part of the story which leaves us wondering about this or that. Many things are not given us, and for the Western man this jars a little bit because we want to know. We expect to be told. We don't expect loose ends in a story. But in Indian traditions, it's not that way at all. There are always loose ends, and that is what you'd expect in a story."

Momaday is an eloquent spokesperson for the Native American tradition of respect for nature and an outspoken critic of modern technological threats to the environment. In another interview he notes: "We haven't done a very good job in protecting our planet. We have failed to recognize the spiritual life of the earth. I feel a sense of futility, because I think there's not much I can do about it, but I will, to the best of my ability, try to change that. I'm not at all confident that I can, but if I make the effort, that will mean something."

He holds an M.A. and a Ph.D. from Stanford University and received the Pulitzer Prize for his first novel, House Made of Dawn *(1968). His other books include the autobiographical work* The Way to Rainy Mountain *(1969),* The Ancient Child *(1989), and* In the Presence of the Sun: Stories and Poems, 1961–1991 *(1991). He is a Regents' Professor of English at the University of Arizona in Tucson, and a member of the Gourd Dance Society, the ancient fraternal organization of the Kiowa nation.*

The Bear

What ruse of vision,
escarping the wall of leaves,

    rending incision
into countless surfaces,

    would cull and color
his somnolence, whose old age
    has outworn valor,
all but the fact of courage?   5

    Seen, he does not come,
move, but seems forever there,
    dimensionless, dumb,
in the windless noon's hot glare.   10

    More scarred than others
these years since the trap maimed him,
    pain slants his withers,
drawing up the crooked limb.   15

    Then he is gone, whole,
without urgency, from sight,
    as buzzards control,
imperceptibly, their flight.   20

Plainview: 3

The sun appearing: a pendant
of clear cutbeads, flashing;
a drift of pollen and glitter
lapping and overlapping night;
a prairie fire.   5

The Delight Song of Tsoai-talee

I am a feather on the bright sky
I am the blue horse that runs in the plain
I am the fish that rolls, shining, in the water
I am the shadow that follows a child
I am the evening light, the lustre of meadows   5
I am an eagle playing with the wind
I am a cluster of bright beads
I am the farthest star
I am the cold of the dawn
I am the roaring of the rain   10
I am the glitter on the crust of the snow

I am the long track of the moon in a lake
I am a flame of four colors
I am a deer standing away in the dusk
I am a field of sumac and the pomme blanche   15
I am an angle of geese in the winter sky
I am the hunger of a young wolf
I am the whole dream of these things

You see, I am alive, I am alive
I stand in good relation to the earth   20
I stand in good relation to the gods
I stand in good relation to all that is beautiful
I stand in good relation to the daughter of Tsen-tainte
You see, I am alive, I am alive

Angle of Geese

   How shall we adorn
Recognition with our speech? —
   Now the dead firstborn
Will lag in the wake of words.

   Custom intervenes;   5
We are civil, something more:
   More than language means,
The mute presence mulls and marks.

   Almost of a mind,
We take measure of the loss;   10
   I am slow to find
The mere margin of repose.

   And one November
It was longer in the watch,
   As if forever,   15
Of the huge ancestral goose.

   So much symmetry! —
Like the pale angle of time
   And eternity.
The great shape labored and fell.   20

   Quit of hope and hurt,
It held a motionless gaze
   Wide of time, alert,
On the dark distant flurry.

Crows in a Winter Composition

This morning the snow,
The soft distances
Beyond the trees
In which nothing appeared—
Nothing appeared.   5
The several silences,
Imposed one upon another,
Were unintelligible.

I was therefore ill at ease
When the crows came down,   10
Whirling down and calling,
Into the yard below
And stood in a mindless manner
On the gray, luminous crust,
Altogether definite, composed,   15
In the bright enmity of my regard,
In the hard nature of crows.

A First American Views His Land

First Man
behold:
the earth
glitters
with leaves:
the sky
glistens
with rain.
Pollen
is borne
on winds
that low
and lean
upon
mountains.
Cedars
blacken
the slopes—
and pines.

One hundred centuries ago. There is a wide, irregular landscape in what is now
northern New Mexico. The sun is a dull white disk, low in the south; it is a perfect mystery, a deity whose coming and going are inexorable. The gray sky is

curdled, and it bears very close upon the earth. A cold wind runs along the ground, dips and spins, flaking drift from a pond in the bottom of a ravine. Beyond the wind the silence is acute. A man crouches in the ravine, in the darkness there, scarcely visible. He moves not a muscle; only the wind lifts a lock of his hair and lays it back along his neck. He wears skins and carries a spear. These things in particular mark his human intelligence and distinguish him as the lord of the universe. And for him the universe is especially *this* landscape; for him the landscape is an element like the air. The vast, virgin wilderness is by and large his whole context. For him there is no possibility of existence elsewhere.

Directly there is a blowing, a rumble of breath deeper than the wind, above him, where some of the hard clay of the bank is broken off and the clods roll down into the water. At the same time there appears on the skyline the massive head of a long-horned bison, then the hump, then the whole beast, huge and black on the sky, standing to a height of seven feet at the hump, with horns that extend six feet across the shaggy crown. For a moment it is poised there; then it lumbers obliquely down the bank to the pond. Still the man does not move, though the beast is now only a few steps upwind. There is no sign of what is about to happen; the beast meanders; the man is frozen in repose.

Then the scene explodes. In one and the same instant the man springs to his feet and bolts forward, his arm cocked and the spear held high, and the huge animal lunges in panic, bellowing, its whole weight thrown violently into the bank, its hooves churning and chipping earth into the air, its eyes gone wide and wild and white. There is a moment in which its awful, frenzied motion is wasted, and it is mired and helpless in its fear, and the man hurls the spear with his whole strength, and the point is driven into the deep, vital flesh, and the bison in its agony staggers and crashes down and dies.

This ancient drama of the hunt is enacted again and again in the landscape. The man is preeminently a predator, the most dangerous of all. He hunts in order to survive; his very existence is simply, squarely established upon that basis. But he hunts also because he can, because he has the means; he has the ultimate weapon of his age, and his prey is plentiful. His relationship to the land has not yet become a moral equation.

But in time he will come to understand that there is an intimate, vital link between the earth and himself, a link that implies an intricate network of rights and responsibilities. In some unimagined future he will understand that he has the ability to devastate and perhaps destroy his environment. That moment will be one of extreme crisis in his evolution.

The weapon is deadly and efficient. The hunter has taken great care in its manufacture, especially in the shaping of the flint point, which is an extraordinary thing. A larger flake has been removed from each face, a groove that extends from the base nearly to the tip. Several hundred pounds of pressure, expertly applied, were required to make these grooves. The hunter, then, is an artisan. His skill, manifest in the manufacture of this artifact, is unsurpassed for its time and purpose. By means of this weapon is the Paleo-Indian hunter eminently able to exploit his environment.

Thousands of years later, about the time that Columbus begins his first voyage to the New World, another man, in the region of the Great Lakes, stands in the forest shade on the edge of a sunlit brake. In a while a deer enters into the pool of light. Silently the man fits an arrow to a bow, draws aim, and shoots. The arrow zips across the distance and strikes home. The deer leaps and falls dead.

But this latter-day man, unlike his ancient predecessor, is only incidentally a hunter; he is also a fisherman, a husbandman, even a physician. He fells trees and builds canoes; he grows corn, squash, and beans, and he gathers fruits and nuts; he uses hundreds of species of wild plants for food, medicine, teas, and dyes. Instead of one animal, or two or three, he hunts many, none to extinction as the Paleo-Indian may have done. He has fitted himself far more precisely into the patterns of the wilderness than did his ancient predecessor. He lives on the land; he takes his living from it; but he does not destroy it. This distinction supports the fundamental ethic that we call conservation today. In principle, if not yet in name, this man is a conservationist.

These two hunting sketches are far less important in themselves than is the long distance between them, the whole possibility within the dimension of time. I believe that in that interim, there grew up in the mind of man an idea of land as sacred.

> *At dawn*
> *eagles*
> *hie and*
> *hover*
> *above*
> *the plain*
> *where light*
> *gathers*
> *in pools.*
> *Grasses*
> *shimmer*
> *and shine.*
> *Shadows*
> *withdraw*
> *and lie*
> *away*
> *like smoke.*

"The earth is our mother. The sky is our father." This concept of nature, which is at the center of the Native American worldview, is familiar to us all. But it may well be that we do not understand entirely what the concept is in its ethical and philosophical implications.

I tell my students that the American Indian has a unique investment in the American landscape. It is an investment that represents perhaps thirty thousand years of habitation. That tenure has to be worth something in itself—a great deal, in fact. The Indian has been here a long time; he is at home here. That simple and obvious trust is one of the most important realities of the Indian world, and it is integral in the Indian mind and spirit.

How does such a concept evolve? Where does it begin? Perhaps it begins with the recognition of beauty, the realization that the physical world *is* beautiful. We don't know much about the ancient hunter's sensitivities. It isn't likely that he had leisure in his life for the elaboration of an aesthetic ideal. And yet the weapon he made was beautiful as well as functional. It has been suggested that much of the minute chipping along the edges of his weapon served no purpose but that of aesthetic satisfaction.

A good deal more is known concerning that man of the central forests. He made beautiful boxes and dishes out of elm and birch bark, for example. His canoes were marvelous, delicate works of art: And this aesthetic perception was a principle of the whole Indian world of his time, as indeed it is of our time. The contemporary Native American is a man whose strong aesthetic perceptions are clearly evident in his arts and crafts, in his religious ceremonies, and in the stories and songs of his rich oral tradition. This, in view of the pressures that have been brought to bear upon the Indian world and the drastic changes that have been effected in its landscape, is a blessing and an irony.

Consider for example the Navajos of the Four Corners area where four states converge. In recent years an extensive coal-mining operation has mutilated some of their most sacred land. A large power plant in that same region spews a contamination into the sky that is visible for many miles. And yet, as much as any people of whom I have heard, the Navajos perceive and celebrate the beauty of the physical world.

There is a Navajo ceremonial song that celebrates the sounds that are made in the natural world, the particular voices that beautify the earth:

> *Voice above,*
> *voice of thunder,*
> *speak from the*
> *dark of clouds:*
> *voice below,*
> *grasshopper voice,*
> *speak from the*
> *green of plants;*
> *so may the earth*
> *be beautiful.*

There is in the motion and meaning of this song a comprehension of the world that is peculiarly native, I believe, that is integral in the Native American mentality. Consider: the singer stands at the center of the natural world, at the source of its sound, of its motion, of its life. Nothing of that world is inaccessible to him or lost upon him. His song is filled with reverence, with wonder and delight, and with confidence as well. He knows something about himself and about the things around him—and he knows that he knows. I am interested in what he sees and hears; I am interested in the range and force of his perception. Our immediate impression may be that his perception is narrow and deep—vertical. After all, "voice above . . . voice below," he sings. But is it vertical only? At each level of his expression there is an extension of his awareness across the whole landscape. The voice above is the voice of thunder, and thunder rolls. Moreover, it issues from the impalpable dark clouds and runs upon their horizontal range. It is a sound that integrates the whole of the atmosphere. And even so, the voice below, that of the grasshopper, issues from the broad plain and multiplicity of plants. And of course the singer is mindful of much more than thunder and insects; we are given in his song the wide angle of his vision and his hearing—and we are given the testimony of his dignity, his trust, and his deep belief.

This comprehension of the earth and air is surely a matter of morality, for it brings into account not only man's instinctive reaction to his environment but the full realization of his humanity as well, the achievement of his intellectual and spiritual development as an individual and as a race.

In my own experience I have seen numerous examples of this regard for nature. My grandfather Mammedaty was a farmer in his mature years; his grandfather was a buffalo hunter on the southern plains. It was not easy for Mammedaty to be a farmer; he was a Kiowa, and the Kiowas never had an agrarian tradition. Yet he had to make his living, even if the old, beloved life of roaming the plains and hunting the buffalo was gone forever. So, as much as any man before him, he fitted his mind and will and spirit to the land; there was nothing else. He could not have conceived of living apart from the land.

In *The Way to Rainy Mountain* I set down a small narrative that belongs in the oral tradition of my family. It indicates something essential about the Native American attitude toward the land:

> East of my grandmother's house, south of the pecan grove, there is buried a woman in a beautiful dress. Mammedaty used to know where she is buried, but now no one knows. If you stand on the front porch of the house and look eastward toward Carnegie, you know that the woman is buried somewhere within the range of your vision. But her grave is unmarked. She was buried in a cabinet, and she wore a beautiful dress. How beautiful it was! It was one of those fine buckskin dresses, and it was decorated with elk's teeth and beadwork. That dress is still there, under the ground.

It seems to me that this statement is primarily a declaration of love for the land, in which the several elements—the woman, the dress, and this plain—are at last become one reality, one expression of the beautiful in nature. Moreover, it seems to me a peculiarly Native American expression in this sense: that the concentration of things that are explicitly remembered—the general landscape, the simple, almost abstract nature of the burial, above all the beautiful dress, which is wholly singular (in kind as well as in its function within the narrative)—is especially Indian in character. The things that are *not* explicitly remembered—the woman's name, the exact location of her grave—are the things that matter least in the special view of the storyteller. What matters here is the translation of the woman into the landscape, a translation particularly signified by means of the beautiful and distinctive dress, an *Indian* dress.

In the late 1940s and early 1950s, when I was a boy, I lived for several years at Jemez Pueblo, New Mexico. The Pueblo Indians are perhaps more obviously invested in the land than are other people. Their whole life is predicated upon a thorough perception of the physical world and its myriad aspects. When I first went there to live, the cacique, or chief, of the Pueblos was a venerable old man with long, gray hair and bright, deep-set eyes. He was entirely dignified and imposing—and rather formidable in the eyes of a boy. He excited my imagination a good deal. I was told that this old man kept the calendar of the tribe, that each morning he stood on a certain spot of ground near the center of the town and watched to see where the sun appeared on the skyline. By means of this solar calendar did he know and announce to his people when it was time to plant, to harvest, to perform this or that ceremony. This image of him in my mind's eye—the old man gazing each morning after the ranging sun—came to represent for me the epitome of that real harmony between man and the land that signifies the Indian world.

One day when I was riding my horse along the Jemez River, I looked up to see a long caravan of wagons and people on horseback and on foot. Men, women, and children were crossing the river ahead of me, moving out to the west, where most of the cultivated fields were, the farmland of the town. It was a wonderful sight to see, this long procession, and I was immediately deeply curious. I wanted to investigate, but it was not in me to do so at once, for that racial reserve, that sense of propriety that is deep-seated in Native American culture, stayed me, held me up. Then I saw someone coming toward me on horseback, galloping. It was a friend of mine, a boy of my own age. "Come on," he said. "Come with us." "Where are you going?" I asked casually. But he would not tell me. He simply laughed and urged me to come along, and of course I was very glad to do so. It was a bright spring morning, and I had a good horse under me, and the prospect of adventure was delicious. We moved far out across the eroded plain to the farthest fields at the foot of a great red mesa, and there we planted two large fields of corn. And afterward, on the edge of the fields, we sat on blankets and ate a feast in the shade of a cottonwood grove.

Later I learned it was the cacique's fields we planted. This is an ancient tradition at Jemez. The people of the town plant and tend and harvest the cacique's fields, and in the winter the hunters give him a portion of the meat they bring home from the mountains. It is as if the cacique is himself the translation of man, every man, into the landscape.

I have not forgotten that day, nor shall I forget it. I remember the warm earth of the fields, the smooth texture of seeds in my hands, and the brown water moving slowly and irresistibly among the rows. Above all I remember the spirit in which the procession was made, the work was done, and the feasting was enjoyed. It was a spirit of communion, of the life of each man in relation to the life of the planet and of the infinite distance and silence in which it moves. We made, in concert, an appropriate expression of that spirit.

One afternoon an old Kiowa woman talked to me, telling me of the place in Oklahoma in which she had lived for a hundred years. It was the place in which my grandparents lived, too; and it is the place where I was born. And she told me of a time even further back, when the Kiowas came down from the north and centered their culture in the red earth of the southern plains. She told wonderful stories, and as I listened, I began to feel more and more sure that her voice proceeded from the land itself. I asked her many things concerning the Kiowas, for I wanted to understand all that I could of my heritage. I told the old woman that I had come there to learn from her and from people like her, those in whom the old ways were preserved. And she said simply, "It is good that you have come here." I believe that her word *good* meant many things; for one thing it meant "right," or "appropriate." And indeed it was appropriate that she should speak of the land. She was eminently qualified to do so. She had a great reverence for the land, and an ancient perception of it, a perception that is acquired only in the course of many generations.

It is this notion of the appropriate, along with that of the beautiful, that forms the Native American perspective on the land. In a sense these considerations are indivisible; Native American oral tradition is rich with songs and tales that celebrate natural beauty, the beauty of the natural world. What is more appropriate to our world than that which is beautiful?

> *At noon*
> *turtles*
> *enter*
> *slowly*
> *into*
> *the warm*
> *dark loam.*
> *Bees hold*
> *the swarm.*
> *Meadows*
> *recede*
> *through planes*
> *of heat*
> *and pure*
> *distance.*

Very old in the Native American worldview is the conviction that the earth is vital, that there is a spiritual dimension to it, a dimension in which man rightly exists. It follows logically that there are ethical imperatives in this matter. I think. Inasmuch as I am in the land, it is appropriate that I should affirm myself in the spirit of the land. I shall celebrate my life in the world and the world in my life. In the natural order man invests himself in the landscape and at the same time incorporates the landscape into his own most fundamental experience. This trust is sacred.

The process of investment and appropriation is, I believe, preeminently a function of the imagination. It is accomplished by means of an act of the imagination that is especially ethical in kind. We are what we imagine ourselves to be.

The Native American is someone who thinks of himself, imagines himself in a particular way. By virtue of his experience, his idea of himself comprehends his relationship to the land.

And the quality of this imagining is determined as well by racial and cultural experience. The Native American's attitudes toward this landscape have been formulated over a long period of time, a span that reaches back to the end of the Ice Age. The land, *this* land, is secure in his racial memory.

In our society as a whole we conceive of the land in terms of ownership and use. It is a lifeless medium of exchange; it has for most of us, I suspect, no more spirituality than has an automobile, say, or a refrigerator. And our laws confirm us in this view, for we can buy and sell the land, we can exclude each other from it, and in the context of ownership we can use it as we will. Ownership implies use, and use implies consumption.

But this way of thinking of the land is alien to the Indian. His cultural intelligence is opposed to these concepts; indeed, for him they are all but inconceivable quantities. This fundamental distinction is easier to understand with respect to ownership than to use, perhaps. For obviously the Indian does use, and has always used, the land and the available resources in it. The point is that *use* does not indicate in any real way his idea of the land. *Use* is neither his word nor his idea. As an Indian I think, "You say that I use the land, and I reply, yes, it is true; but it is not the first truth. The first truth is that I *love* the land; I see that it is beautiful; I delight in it; I am alive in it."

In the long course of his journey from Asia and in the realization of himself in the New World, the Indian has assumed a deep ethical regard for the earth and sky, a reverence for the natural world that is antipodal to the strange tenet of modern civilization which seemingly has it that man must destroy his environment. It is this ancient ethic of the Native American that must shape our efforts to preserve the earth and the life upon and within it.

> *At dusk*
> *the gray*
> *foxes*
> *stiffen*
> *in cold;*
> *blackbirds*
> *are fixed*
> *in the*
> *branches.*
> *Rivers*
> *follow*
> *the moon,*
> *the long*
> *white track*
> *of the*
> *full moon.*

✍ Mary Oliver *(born 1935)*

The luminous simplicity of Mary Oliver's poetry masks the deep complexity of the questions that her work poses. Perhaps the most important issue, stated in one way or another in each breathtaking poem, is described in "Starfish," where the poet tells of her own "reaching / into the darkness, learning / little by little to love / our only world." Mary Oliver's love for the world—and all living things—resonates in each carefully chosen word and in each tender but unwaveringly honest image. Born in Ohio, Oliver briefly attended the Ohio State University and Vassar College. Although she did not graduate from college, she has held numerous academic posts as a teacher of creative writing, including stints at Case Western Reserve, Bucknell, Sweet Briar, and Duke. Oliver is currently the Catharine Osgood Foster Chair for Distinguished Teaching at Bennington College, where she teaches courses on poets such as Gerard Manley Hopkins, Robert Frost, Elizabeth Bishop, and Linda Hogan. Her recent collections of poetry include Dream Work *(1986),* House of Light *(1992),* White Pine: Poems and Prose Poems *(1994),* Twelve Moons *(1997),* West Wind: Poems and Prose Poems *(1998), and* Winter Hours *(1999). She has also published a collection of nonfiction prose writing on nature,* Blue Pastures, *in 1995. Along with numerous other recognitions, Oliver was awarded the Pulitzer Prize for poetry in 1984 for her collection* American Primitive.*

Field Near Linden, Alabama

For hours
they float in the distance—
finally they drift down
like black shingles
from some old temple of the sun,   5
so I know, somewhere in the world
the terrible cleansing
has begun.
Once, across a field,
a dozen of them sat in a tree.   10
I stopped the car and walked toward them
until they were above me,
huge and shifty,
in their leather wings,
and what was below them, in the grass,   15
was clearly dead.
The story about Jesus in the cave
is a good one,
but when is it ever like that,
as sharp as lightning   20
or even the way the green sea does everything—
quickly,
and with such grace?

Clumsy and slow,
the birds clattered down, and huddled—   25
their beaks were soft as spoons,
but they bent to their labor
with a will, until
their bellies swelled,
they could hardly climb back into the air   30
and go flapping away.
A year later
I cross the field again, and in that hot place
the grass rises thick and clean, it
shines like the sea.   35

Whelks

Here are the perfect
fans of the scallops,
quahogs, and weedy mussels
still holding their orange fruit—
and here are the whelks—   5
whirlwinds,
each the size of a fist,
but always cracked and broken—
clearly they have been traveling
under the sky-blue waves   10
for a long time.
All my life
I have been restless—
I have felt there is something
more wonderful than gloss—   15
than wholeness—
than staying at home.
I have not been sure what it is.
But every morning on the wide shore
I pass what is perfect and shining   20
to look for the whelks, whose edges
have rubbed so long against the world
they have snapped and crumbled—
they have almost vanished,
with the last relinquishing   25
of their unrepeatable energy,
back into everything else.
When I find one
I hold it in my hand,
I look out over that shaking fire,   30

I shut my eyes. Not often,
but now and again there's a moment
when the heart cries aloud:
yes, I am willing to be
that wild darkness,   35
that long, blue body of light.

White Flowers

Last night
in the fields
I lay down in the darkness
to think about death,
but instead I fell asleep,   5
as if in a vast and sloping room
filled with those white flowers
that open all summer,
sticky and untidy,
in the warm fields.   10
When I woke
the morning light was just slipping
in front of the stars,
and I was covered
with blossoms.   15
I don't know
how it happened—
I don't know
if my body went diving down
under the sugary vines   20
in some sleep-sharpened affinity
with the depths, or whether
that green energy
rose like a wave
and curled over me, claiming me   25
in its husky arms.
I pushed them away, but I didn't rise.
Never in my life had I felt so plush,
or so slippery,
or so resplendently empty.   30
Never in my life
had I felt myself so near
that porous line
where my own body was done with
and the roots and the stems and the flowers   35
began.

Spring

Somewhere
   a black bear
      has just risen from sleep
         and is staring

down the mountain.   5
   All night
      in the brisk and shallow restlessness
         of early spring

I think of her,
   her four black fists   10
      flicking the gravel,
         her tongue

like a red fire
   touching the grass,
      the cold water.   15
         There is only one question:

how to love this world.
   I think of her
      rising
         like a black and leafy ledge   20

to sharpen her claws against
   the silence
      of the trees.
         Whatever else

my life is   25
   with its poems
      and its music
         and its glass cities,

it is also this dazzling darkness
   coming   30
      down the mountain,
         breathing and tasting;

all day I think of her—
   her white teeth,
      her wordlessness,   35
         her perfect love.

Nature

All night
  in and out the slippery shadows
    the owl hunted,
      the beads of blood

scarcely dry on the hooked beak before   5
  hunger again seized him
    and he fell, snipping
      the life from some plush breather,

and floated away
  into the crooked branches   10
    of the trees, that all night
      went on lapping

the sunken rain, and growing,
  bristling life
    spreading through all their branches   15
      as one by one

they tossed the white moon upward
  on its slow way
    to another morning
      in which nothing new   20

would ever happen,
  which is the true gift of nature,
    which is the reason
      we love it.

Forgive me.   25
  For hours I had tried to sleep
    and failed;
      restless and wild,

I could settle on nothing
  and fell, in envy   30
    of the things of darkness
      following their sleepy course—

the root and branch, the bloodied beak—
  even the screams from the cold leaves
    were as red songs that rose and fell   35
      in their accustomed place.

The Summer Day

Who made the world?
Who made the swan, and the black bear?
Who made the grasshopper?
This grasshopper, I mean —
the one who has flung herself out of the grass,   5
the one who is eating sugar out of my hand,
who is moving her jaws back and forth instead of up and down —
who is gazing around with her enormous and complicated eyes.
Now she lifts her pale forearms and thoroughly washes her face.
Now she snaps her wings open, and floats away.   10
I don't know exactly what a prayer is.
I do know how to pay attention, how to fall down
into the grass, how to kneel down in the grass,
how to be idle and blessed, how to stroll through the fields,
which is what I have been doing all day.   15
Tell me, what else should I have done?
Doesn't everything die at last, and too soon?
Tell me, what is it you plan to do
with your one wild and precious life?

✍ Seamus Heaney (born 1939)

Winner of the Nobel Prize in Literature in 1995, Seamus Heaney was born on a potato farm, Mossbawn, in County Derry in Northern Ireland. The landscape of rural Ireland remains even today "the country of the mind" and the setting and inspiration of many of Heaney's poems. As he writes in his essay on his poetic process, "Feeling into Words," he has found fruitful connections between the acts of agricultural labor and writing. His early poem "Digging" captures what Heaney states is the first time his "feeling had gotten into words," by equating the acts of unearthing potatoes and composing poetry, the pen acting as a spade. Heaney's Irish Catholic family's farm was situated directly next to a manicured estate, which belonged to an Anglo-Irish Protestant family. Thus, from a very early age, Heaney was aware of the ways in which landscape could also be inflected with the religious and political tensions that continue to define Northern Ireland.

Educated at Queen's University in Belfast, where he later returned as a teacher, Heaney's earliest collections, including Death of a Naturalist *(1966) and* Door into the Dark *(1969), are deeply influenced by the physical environment of his youth. Yet his work also addressed the Irish political climate, as in* North *(1975) and* Field Work *(1979). Called Ireland's greatest poet since Yeats, Heaney's work reveals a variety of influences, including the works of William Wordsworth, John Clare, Thomas Hardy,*

Gerard Manley Hopkins, Robert Frost, and Ted Hughes. Other collections of poetry include Sweeney Astray *(1984),* Station Island *(1985),* The Haw Lantern *(1987), and* Seeing Things *(1991). Heaney has also published essays and critical writing, including the collections* Preoccupations *(1980),* The Government of the Tongue *(1989), and* The Redress of Poetry *(1995). Although he lives in Dublin, Heaney is Professor of Poetry at Oxford University and he is Boylston Professor of Rhetoric at Harvard University, where he teaches for part of the year.*

Death of a Naturalist

All year the flax-dam festered in the heart
Of the townland; green and heavy-headed
Flax had rotted there, weighted down by huge sods.
Daily it sweltered in the punishing sun.
Bubbles gargled delicately, bluebottles   5
Wove a strong gauze of sound around the smell.
There were dragonflies, spotted butterflies,
But best of all was the warm thick slobber
Of frogspawn that grew like clotted water
In the shade of the banks. Here, every spring   10
I would fill jampotfuls of the jellied
Specks to range on window-sills at home,
On shelves at school, and wait and watch until
The fattening dots burst into nimble-
Swimming tadpoles. Miss Walls would tell us how   15
The daddy frog was called a bullfrog
And how he croaked and how the mammy frog
Laid hundreds of little eggs and this was
Frogspawn. You could tell the weather by frogs too
For they were yellow in the sun and brown   20
In rain.

    Then one hot day when fields were rank
With cowdung in the grass the angry frogs
Invaded the flax-dam; I ducked through hedges
To a coarse croaking that I had not heard   25
Before. The air was thick with a bass chorus.
Right down the dam gross-bellied frogs were cocked
On sods; their loose necks pulsed like sails. Some hopped:
The slap and plop were obscene threats. Some sat
Poised like mud grenades, their blunt heads farting.   30
I sickened, turned, and ran. The great slime kings
Were gathered there for vengeance and I knew
That if I dipped my hand the spawn would clutch it.

Bogland

For T. P. Flanagan

We have no prairies
To slice a big sun at evening—
Everywhere the eye concedes to
Encroaching horizon,

Is wooed into the cyclops' eye   5
Of a tarn. Our unfenced country
Is bog that keeps crusting
Between the sights of the sun.

They've taken the skeleton
Of the Great Irish Elk   10
Out of the peat, set it up,
An astounding crate full of air.

Butter sunk under
More than a hundred years
Was recovered salty and white.   15
The ground itself is kind, black butter

Melting and opening underfoot,
Missing its last definition
By millions of years.
They'll never dig coal here,   20

Only the waterlogged trunks
Of great firs, soft as pulp.
Our pioneers keep striking
Inwards and downwards,

Every layer they strip   25
Seems camped on before.
The bogholes might be Atlantic seepage.
The wet centre is bottomless.

Nesting-Ground

The sandmartins' nests were loopholes of darkness in the riverbank. He
could imagine his arm going in to the armpit, sleeved and straitened,
but because he had once felt the cold prick of a dead robin's claw and
the surprising density of its tiny beak he only gazed.

  He heard cheeping far in but because the men had once shown him a   5
rat's nest in the butt of a stack where chaff and powdered cornstalks
adhered to the moist pink necks and backs he only listened.

As he stood sentry, gazing, waiting, he thought of putting his ear to one of the abandoned holes and listening for the silence under the ground.   10

Badgers

When the badger glimmered away
into another garden
you stood, half-lit with whiskey,
sensing you had disturbed
some soft returning.   5

The murdered dead,
you thought.
But could it not have been
some violent shattered boy
nosing out what got mislaid   10
between the cradle and the explosion,
evenings when windows stood open
and the compost smoked down the backs?

Visitations are taken for signs.
At a second house I listened   15
for duntings under the laurels
and heard intimations whispered
about being vaguely honoured.

And to read even by carcasses
the badgers have come back.   20
One that grew notorious
lay untouched in the roadside.
Last night one had me braking
but more in fear than in honour.

Cool from the sett and redolent   25
of his runs under the night,
the bogey of fern country
broke cover in me
for what he is:
pig family   30
and not at all what he's painted.

How perilous is it to choose
not to love the life we're shown?
His sturdy dirty body
and interloping grovel.   35
The intelligence in his bone.
The unquestionable houseboy's shoulders
that could have been my own.

✎ *Angela Carter* (1940–1992)

Born in London, Angela Carter (whose maiden name was Stalker) claimed to be descended from a long line of witches, and much of her work focuses on the feminine spiritual and supernatural power that many associate with witchcraft. Educated at the University of Bristol, Carter published her first novel, Shadowdance, *in 1965. Her lifelong interest in fairy tales and folk legends influenced the many books she wrote for children and for adults. In many of her most powerful stories, such as "The Company of Wolves" included below, she takes a child's tale and rewrites it for a more adult audience. Such revisions of traditional stories, a technique Carter would use often, reveal the disturbing violence toward women that many of the old narratives contain. By reversing some of the characterizations and the plots, Carter is able to reclaim these tales so that they express female desire and female power, instead of female victimization.*

The role of nature is important to Carter's efforts to reassert women's strength. Like women, nature too has been seen as an object of oppression in the patriarchal culture that the conventional versions of these tales uphold. By linking the power of nature with the power of the feminine, Carter is able to write stories that blend fantasy and the techniques of magical realism together with a politically meaningful message. Carter has written numerous novels, including Several Perceptions *(1968),* Heroes and Villains *(1969),* Love *(1971),* The Infernal Desire Machine of Dr. Hoffman *(1972),* The Passion of New Eve *(1977),* Nights at the Circus *(1985), and* Wise Children *(1991). Her short story collections include* Fireworks: Nine Profane Pieces *(1974),* The Bloody Chamber *(1979),* Black Venus *(1985), and the posthumous* Burning Your Boats: Collected Short Stories *(1995). She has also written nonfiction essays, including a feminist study of the Marquis de Sade, and served as editor to numerous collections of fairy tales. She taught at the University of Sheffield and at the Iowa Writers' Workshop.*

The Company of Wolves

One beast and only one howls in the woods by night.

The wolf is carnivore incarnate and he's as cunning as he is ferocious; once he's had a taste of flesh then nothing else will do.

At night, the eyes of wolves shine like candle flames, yellowish, reddish, but that is because the pupils of their eyes fatten on darkness and catch the light from your lantern to flash it back to you—red for danger; if a wolf's eyes reflect only moonlight, then they gleam a cold and unnatural green, a mineral, a piercing colour. If the benighted traveller spies those luminous, terrible sequins stitched suddenly on the black thickets, then he knows he must run, if fear has not struck him stock-still.

But those eyes are all you will be able to glimpse of the forest assassins as they cluster invisibly round your smell of meat as you go through the wood unwisely late. They will be like shadows, they will be like wraiths, grey members of a congregation of nightmare; hark! his long, wavering howl . . . an aria of fear made audible.

The wolfsong is the sound of the rending you will suffer, in itself a murdering.

It is winter and cold weather. In this region of mountain and forest, there is now nothing for the wolves to eat. Goats and sheep are locked up in the byre, the deer departed for the remaining pasturage on the southern slopes—wolves grow lean and famished. There is so little flesh on them that you could count the starveling ribs through their pelts, if they gave you time before they pounced. Those slavering jaws; the lolling tongue; the rime of saliva on the grizzled chops—of all the teeming perils of the night and the forest, ghosts, hobgoblins, ogres that grill babies upon gridirons, witches that fatten their captives in cages for cannibal tables, the wolf is worst for he cannot listen to reason.

You are always in danger in the forest, where no people are. Step between the portals of the great pines where the shaggy branches tangle about you, trapping the unwary traveller in nets as if the vegetation itself were in a plot with the wolves who live there, as though the wicked trees go fishing on behalf of their friends—step between the gateposts of the forest with the greatest trepidation and infinite precautions, for if you stray from the path for one instant, the wolves will eat you. They are grey as famine, they are as unkind as plague.

The grave-eyed children of the sparse villages always carry knives with them when they go to tend the little flocks of goats that provide the homesteads with acrid milk and rank, maggoty cheese. Their knives are half as big as they are, the blades are sharpened daily.

But the wolves have ways of arriving at your own hearthside. We try and try but sometimes we cannot keep them out. There is no winter's night the cottager does not fear to see a lean, grey, famished snout questing under the door, and there was a woman once bitten in her own kitchen as she was straining the macaroni.

Fear and flee the wolf; for, worst of all, the wolf may be more than he seems.

There was a hunter once, near here, that trapped a wolf in a pit. This wolf had massacred the sheep and goats; eaten up a mad old man who used to live by himself in a hut halfway up the mountain and sing to Jesus all day; pounced on a girl looking after the sheep, but she made such a commotion that men came with rifles and scared him away and tried to track him to the forest but he was cunning and easily gave them the slip. So this hunter dug a pit and put a duck in it, for bait, all alive-oh; and he covered the pit with straw smeared with wolf dung. Quack, quack! went the duck and a wolf came slinking out of the forest, a big one, a heavy one, he weighed as much as a grown man and the straw gave way beneath him—into the pit he tumbled. The hunter jumped down after him, slit his throat, cut off all his paws for a trophy.

And then no wolf at all lay in front of the hunter but the bloody trunk of a man, headless, footless, dying, dead.

A witch from up the valley once turned an entire wedding party into wolves because the groom had settled on another girl. She use to order them to visit her, at night, from spite, and they would sit and howl around her cottage for her, serenading her with their misery.

Not so very long ago, a young woman in our village married a man who vanished clean away on her wedding night. The bed was made with new sheets and the bride lay down in it; the groom said, he was going out to relieve himself, insisted on it, for the sake of decency, and she drew the coverlet up to her chin and lay there. And she waited and she waited and then she waited again—surely he's been gone a long time? Until she jumps up in bed and shrieks to hear a howling, coming on the wind from the forest.

That long-drawn, wavering howl has, for all its fearful resonance, some inherent sadness in it, as if the beasts would love to be less beastly if only they knew how and never cease to mourn their own condition. There is a vast melancholy in the canticles of the wolves, melancholy infinite as the forest, endless as these long nights of winter and yet that ghastly sadness, that mourning for their own, irremediable appetites, can never move the heart for not one phrase in it hints at the possibility of redemption; grace could not come to the wolf from its own despair, only through some external mediator, so that, sometimes, the beast will look as if he half welcomes the knife that dispatches him.

The young woman's brothers searched the outhouses and the haystacks but never found any remains so the sensible girl dried her eyes and found herself another husband not too shy to piss into a pot who spent the nights indoors. She gave him a pair of bonny babies and all went right as a trivet until, one freezing night, the night of the solstice, the hinge of the year when things do not fit together as well as they should, the longest night, her first good man came home again.

A great thump on the door announced him as she was stirring the soup for the father of her children and she knew him the moment she lifted the latch to him although it was years since she'd worn black for him and now he was in rags and his hair hung down his back and never saw a comb, alive with lice.

"Here I am again, missus," he said. "Get me my bowl of cabbage and be quick about it."

Then her second husband came in with wood for the fire and when the first one saw she'd slept with another man and, worse, clapped his red eyes on her little children who'd crept into the kitchen to see what all the din was about, he shouted: "I wish I were a wolf again, to teach this whore a lesson!" So a wolf he instantly became and tore off the eldest boy's left foot before he was chopped by the hatchet they used for chopping logs. But when the wolf lay bleeding and gasping its last, the pelt peeled off again and he was just as he had been, years ago, when he ran away from his marriage bed, so that she wept and her second husband beat her.

They say there's an ointment the Devil gives you that turns you into a wolf the minute you rub it on. Or, that he was born feet first and had a wolf for his father and his torso is a man's but his legs and genitals are a wolf's. And he has a wolf's heart.

Seven years is a werewolf's natural span but if you burn his human clothes you condemn him to wolfishness for the rest of his life, so old wives hereabouts think it some protection to throw a hat or an apron at the werewolf, as if clothes made the man. Yet by the eyes, those phosphorescent eyes, you know him in all his shapes; the eyes alone unchanged by metamorphosis.

Before he can become a wolf, the lycanthrope[1] strips stark naked. If you spy a naked man among the pines, you must run as if the Devil were after you.

It is midwinter and the robin, the friend of man, sits on the handle of the gardener's spade and sings. It is the worst time in all the year for wolves but this strong-minded child insists she will go off through the wood. She is quite sure the wild beasts cannot harm her although, well-warned, she lays a carving knife in the basket her mother has packed with cheeses. There is a bottle of harsh liquor distilled from brambles; a batch of flat oatcakes baked on the heathstone; a pot or two of jam. The girl will take these delicious gifts to a reclusive grandmother so old the burden of her years is crushing her to death. Granny lives two hours' trudge through the winter woods; the child wraps herself up in her thick shawl, draws it over her head. She steps into her stout wooden shoes; she is dressed and ready and it is Christmas Eve. The malign door of the solstice still swings upon its hinges but she has been too much loved ever to feel scared.

Children do not stay young for long in this savage country. There are no toys for them to play with so they work hard and grow wise but this one, so pretty and the youngest of her family, a little late-comer, had been indulged by her mother and the grandmother who'd knitted her the red shawl that, today, has the ominous if brilliant look of blood on snow. Her breasts have just begun to swell; her hair is like lint, so fair it hardly makes a shadow on her pale forehead; her cheeks are an emblematic scarlet and white and she has just started her woman's bleeding, the clock inside her that will strike, henceforward, once a month.

She stands and moves within the invisible pentacle of her own virginity. She is an unbroken egg; she is a sealed vessel; she has inside her a magic space the entrance to which is shut tight with a plug of membrane; she is a closed system; she does not know how to shiver. She has her knife and she is afraid of nothing.

Her father might forbid her, if he were home, but he is away in the forest, gathering wood, and her mother cannot deny her.

The forest closed upon her like a pair of jaws.

There is always something to look at in the forest, even in the middle of winter—the huddled mounds of birds, succumbed to the lethargy of the season, heaped on the creaking boughs and too forlorn to sing; the bright frills of the winter fungi on the blotched trunks of the trees; the cuneiform slots of rabbits and deer, the herringbone tracks of the birds, a hare as lean as a rasher of bacon streaking across the path where the thin sunlight dapples the russet brakes of last year's bracken.

When she heard the freezing howl of a distant wolf, her practised hand sprang to the handle of her knife, but she saw no sign of a wolf at all, nor of a naked man, neither, but then she heard a clattering among the brushwood and there sprang on to the path a fully clothed one, a very handsome young one, in the green coat and wideawake hat of a hunter, laden with carcasses of game birds. She had her hand on her knife at the first rustle of twigs but he laughed with a flash of white teeth when he saw her and made her a comic yet flattering little bow; she'd

---

[1] A werewolf, or a human who transforms into a wolf, usually during the full moon.

never seen such a fine fellow before, not among the rustic clowns of her native village. So on they went, through the thickening light of the afternoon.

Soon they were laughing and joking like old friends. When he offered to carry her basket, she gave it to him although her knife was in it because he told her his rifle would protect them. As the day darkened, it began to snow again; she felt the first flakes settle on her eyelashes but now there was only half a mile to go and there would be a fire, and hot tea, and a welcome, a warm one surely, for the dashing huntsman as well as for herself.

This young man had a remarkable object in his pocket. It was a compass. She looked at the little round glassface in the palm of his hand and watched the wavering needle with a vague wonder. He assured her this compass had taken him safely through the wood on his hunting trip because the needle always told him with perfect accuracy where the north was. She did not believe it; she knew she should never leave the path on the way through the wood or else she would be lost instantly. He laughed at her again; gleaming trails of spittle clung to his teeth. He said, if he plunged off the path into the forest that surrounded them, he would guarantee to arrive at her grandmother's house a good quarter of an hour before she did, plotting his way through the undergrowth with his compass, while she trudged the long way, along the winding path.

I don't believe you. Besides, aren't you afraid of the wolves?

He only tapped the gleaming butt of his rifle and grinned.

Is it a bet? he asked her. Shall we make a game of it? What will you give me if I get to your grandmother's house before you?

What would you like? she asked disingenuously.

A kiss.

Commonplaces of a rustic seduction; she lowered her eyes and blushed.

He went through the undergrowth and took her basket with him but she forgot to be afraid of the beasts, although now the moon was rising, for she wanted to dawdle on her way to make sure the handsome gentleman would win his wager.

Grandmother's house stood by itself a little way out of the village. The freshly falling snow blew in eddies about the kitchen garden and the young man stepped delicately up the snowy path to the door as if he were reluctant to get his feet wet, swinging his bundle of game and the girl's basket and humming a little tune to himself.

There is a faint trace of blood on his chin; he has been snacking on his catch.

He rapped upon the panels with his knuckles.

Aged and frail, granny is three-quarters succumbed to the mortality the ache in her bones promises her and almost ready to give in entirely. A boy came out from the village to build up her hearth for the night an hour ago and the kitchen crackles with busy firelight. She has her Bible for company, she is a pious old woman. She is propped up on several pillows in the bed set into the wall peasant-fashion, wrapped up in the patchwork quilt she made before she was married, more years ago than she cares to remember. Two china spaniels with liver-coloured blotches on their coats and black noses sit on either side of the fireplace. There is a bright rug of woven rags on the pantiles. The grandfather clock ticks away her eroding time.

We keep the wolves outside by living well.

He rapped upon the panels with his hairy knuckles.

It is your granddaughter, he mimicked in a high soprano.

Lift up the latch and walk in, my darling.

You can tell them by their eyes, eyes of a beast of prey, nocturnal, devastating eyes as red as a wound; you can hurl your Bible at him and your apron after, granny, you thought that was a sure prophylactic against these infernal vermin . . . now call on Christ and his mother and all the angels in heaven to protect you but it won't do you any good.

His feral muzzle is sharp as a knife; he drops his golden burden of gnawed pheasant on the table and puts down your dear girl's basket, too. Oh, my God, what have you done with her?

Off with his disguise, that coat of forest-coloured cloth, the hat with the feather tucked into the ribbon; his matted hair streams down his white shirt and she can see the lice moving in it. The sticks in the hearth shift and hiss; night and the forest has come into the kitchen with darkness tangled in its hair.

He strips off his shirt. His skin is the colour and texture of vellum. A crisp stripe of hair runs down his belly, his nipples are ripe and dark as poison fruit but he's so thin you could count the ribs under his skin if only he gave you the time. He strips off his trousers and she can see how hairy his legs are. His genitals, huge. Ah! huge.

The last thing the old lady saw in all this world was a young man, eyes like cinders, naked as a stone, approaching her bed.

The wolf is carnivore incarnate.

When he had finished with her, he licked his chops and quickly dressed himself again, until he was just as he had been when he came through her door. He burned the inedible hair in the fireplace and wrapped the bones up in a napkin that he hid away under the bed in the wooden chest in which he found a clean pair of sheets. These he carefully put on the bed instead of the tell-tale stained ones he stowed away in the laundry basket. He plumped up the pillows and shook out the patchwork quilt, he picked up the Bible from the floor, closed it and laid it on the table. All was as it had been before except that grandmother was gone. The sticks twitched in the grate, the clock ticked and the young man sat patiently, deceitfully beside the bed in granny's nightcap.

Rat-a-tap-tap.

Who's there, he quavers in granny's antique falsetto.

Only your granddaughter.

So she came in, bringing with her a flurry of snow that melted in tears on the tiles, and perhaps she was a little disappointed to see only her grandmother sitting beside the fire. But then he flung off the blanket and sprang to the door, pressing his back against it so that she could not get out again.

The girl looked round the room and saw there was not even the indentation of a head on the smooth cheek of the pillow and how, for the first time she'd seen it so, the Bible lay closed on the table. The tick of the clock cracked like a whip. She wanted her knife from her basket but she did not dare to reach for it because his eyes were fixed upon her—huge eyes that now seemed to shine with a unique, interior light, eyes the size of saucers, saucers full of Greek fire, diabolic phosphorescence.

What big eyes you have.

All the better to see you with.

No trace at all of the old woman except for a tuft of white hair that had caught in the bark of an unburned log. When the girl saw that, she knew she was in danger of death.

Where is my grandmother?

There's nobody here but we two, my darling.

Now a great howling rose up all around them, near, very near as close as the kitchen garden, the howling of a multitude of wolves; she knew the worst wolves are hairy on the inside and she shivered, in spite of the scarlet shawl she pulled more closely round herself as if it could protect her although it was as red as the blood she must spill.

Who has come to sing us carols, she said.

Those are the voices of my brothers, darling; I love the company of wolves. Look out of the window and you'll see them.

Snow half-caked the lattice and she opened it to look into the garden. It was a white night of moon and snow; the blizzard whirled round the gaunt, grey beasts who squatted on their haunches among the rows of winter cabbage, pointing their sharp snouts to the moon and howling as if their hearts would break. Ten wolves; twenty wolves—so many wolves she could not count them, howling in concert as if demented or deranged. Their eyes reflected the light from the kitchen and shone like a hundred candles.

It is very cold, poor things, she said; no wonder they howl so.

She closed the window on the wolves' threnody and took off her scarlet shawl, the colour of poppies, the colour of sacrifices, the colour of her menses, and, since her fear did her no good, she ceased to be afraid.

What shall I do with my shawl?

Throw it on the fire, dear one. You won't need it again.

She bundled up her shawl and threw it on the blaze, which instantly consumed it. Then she drew her blouse over her head; her small breasts gleamed as if the snow had invaded the room.

What shall I do with my blouse?

Into the fire with it, too, my pet.

The thin muslin went flaring up the chimney like a magic bird and now off came her skirt, her woollen stockings, her shoes, and on to the fire they went, too, and were gone for good. The firelight shone through the edges of her skin; now she was clothed only in her untouched integument of flesh. This dazzling, naked she combed out her hair with her fingers; her hair looked white as the snow outside. Then went directly to the man with red eyes in whose unkempt mane the lice moved; she stood up on tiptoe and unbuttoned the collar of his shirt.

What big arms you have.

All the better to hug you with.

Every wolf in the world now howled a prothalamion[2] outside the window as she freely gave him the kiss she owed him.

---

[2] A song in celebration of a marriage.

What big teeth you have!

She saw how his jaw began to slaver and the room was full of the clamour of the forest's *Liebestod*[3] but the wise child never flinched, even as he answered: All the better to eat you with.

The girl burst out laughing; she knew she was nobody's meat. She laughed at him full in the face, she ripped off his shirt for him and flung it into the fire, in the fiery wake of her own discarded clothing. The flames danced like dead souls on Walpurgisnacht[4] and the old bones under the bed set up a terrible clattering but she did not pay them any heed.

Carnivore incarnate, only immaculate flesh appeases him.

She will lay his fearful head on her lap and she will pick out the lice from his pelt and perhaps she will put the lice into her mouth and eat them, as he will bid her, as she would do in a savage marriage ceremony.

The blizzard will die down.

The blizzard died down, leaving the mountains as randomly covered with snow as if a blind woman had thrown a sheet over them, the upper branches of the forest pines limed, creaking, swollen with the fall.

Snowlight, moonlight, a confusion of paw-prints.

All silent, all silent.

Midnight; and the clock strikes. It is Christmas day, the werewolves' birthday, the door of the solstice stands wide open; let them all sink through.

See! sweet and sound she sleeps in granny's bed, between the paws of the tender wolf.

---

[3] German for "death song."

[4] April 30, presumed to be the time when witches gather for a celebration; any kind of witches' Sabbath.

🖎 Annie Dillard (born 1945)

Calling herself "a wanderer with a background in theology," Annie Dillard writes in the American Transcendentalist tradition of Emerson and Thoreau. Like them, she is at once a naturalist and a mystic. While she analyzes and writes about her environment — both its beauty and its savagery — with an almost microscopic precision, she is also constantly searching for signs of the divine within the natural. Although she was raised as a Presbyterian, she converted to Catholicism later in her life. Her interest in world religions and in spirituality in general informs all of her writing.

Born Annie Doak in Pittsburgh, Pennsylvania, she enjoyed a relatively happy childhood with her affluent family. In her teens, however, she began to reject her family's upper-middle-class values and turned to writers such as Emerson and C. S. Lewis for alternatives. She attended Hollins College in Virginia, where she received both a B.A. and an M.A. in English, writing her masters thesis on Thoreau's Walden, *a work she would later emulate in her own writings. She married her writing teacher at Hollins, Richard Dillard, and in 1971, like Thoreau, she retreated to the wilderness near Tinker Creek to live for a year. From the detailed journals she kept, she fashioned* Pilgrim at Tinker

Creek, *a collection of essays on nature and on theology, published in 1974 and awarded a Pulitzer Prize in 1975. Dillard has also written poetry and fiction.*

Her publications include Tickets for a Prayer Wheel *(1974),* Holy the Firm *(1977),* Teaching a Stone to Talk: Expeditions and Encounters *(1982),* An American Childhood *(1988),* The Writing Life *(1990),* The Living *(1993),* Mornings Like This: Found Poems *(1996), and* For the Time Being *(1999). She has taught at Western Washington University and currently teaches at Wesleyan University in Connecticut.*

From Pilgrim at Tinker Creek

Untying the Knot

Yesterday I set out to catch the new season, and instead I found an old snakeskin. I was in the sunny February woods by the quarry; the snakeskin was lying in a heap of leaves right next to an aquarium someone had thrown away. I don't know why that someone hauled the aquarium deep into the woods to get rid of it; it had only one broken glass side. The snake found it handy, I imagine; snakes like to rub against something rigid to help them out of their skins, and the broken aquarium looked like the nearest likely object. Together the snakeskin and the aquarium made an interesting scene on the forest floor. It looked like an exhibit at a trial—circumstantial evidence—of a wild scene, as though a snake had burst through the broken side of the aquarium, burst through his ugly old skin, and disappeared, perhaps straight up in the air, in a rush of freedom and beauty.

The snakeskin had unkeeled scales, so it belonged to a nonpoisonous snake. It was roughly five feet long by the yardstick, but I'm not sure because it was very wrinkled and dry, and every time I tried to stretch it flat it broke. I ended up with seven or eight pieces of it all over the kitchen table in a fine film of forest dust.

The point I want to make about the snakeskin is that, when I found it, it was whole and tied in a knot. Now there have been stories told, even by reputable scientists, of snakes that have deliberately tied themselves in a knot to prevent larger snakes from trying to swallow them—but I couldn't imagine any way that throwing itself into a half hitch would help a snake trying to escape its skin. Still, ever cautious, I figured that one of the neighborhood boys could possibly have tied it in a knot in the fall, for some whimsical boyish reason, and left it there, where it dried and gathered dust. So I carried the skin along thoughtlessly as I walked, snagging it sure enough on a low branch and ripping it in two for the first of many times. I saw that thick ice still lay on the quarry pond and that the skunk cabbage was already out in the clearings, and then I came home and looked at the skin and its knot.

The knot had no beginning. Idly I turned it around in my hand, searching for a place to untie; I came to with a start when I realized I must have turned the thing around fully ten times. Intently, then, I traced the knot's lump around with a finger: it was continuous. I couldn't untie it any more than I could untie a doughnut; it was a loop without beginning or end. These snakes *are* magic, I thought for a second, and then of course I reasoned what must have happened. The skin had been pulled inside-out like a peeled sock for several inches; then an inch or so of the inside-out part—a piece whose length was coincidentally equal to the diameter of the skin—had somehow been turned right-side out again, making a thick lump whose edges were lost in wrinkles, looking exactly like a knot.

So. I have been thinking about the change of seasons. I don't want to miss spring this year. I want to distinguish the last winter frost from the out-of-season one, the frost of spring. I want to be there on the spot the moment the grass turns green. I always miss this radical revolution; I see it the next day from a window, the yard so suddenly green and lush I could envy Nebuchadnezzar[1] down on all fours eating grass. This year I want to stick a net into time and say "now," as men plant flags on the ice and snow and say, "here." But it occurred to me that I could no more catch spring by the tip of the tail than I could untie the apparent knot in the snakeskin; there are no edges to grasp. Both are continuous loops.

I wonder how long it would take you to notice the regular recurrence of the seasons if you were the first man on earth. What would it be like to live in open-ended time broken only by days and nights? You could say, "it's cold again; it was cold before," but you couldn't make the key connection and say, "it was cold this time last year," because the notion of "year" is precisely the one you lack. Assuming that you hadn't yet noticed any orderly progression of heavenly bodies, how long would you have to live on earth before you could feel with any assurance that any one particular long period of cold would, in fact, end? "While the earth remaineth, seedtime and harvest, and cold and heat, and summer and winter, and day and night shall not cease": God makes this guarantee very early in Genesis to a people whose fears on this point had perhaps not been completely allayed.

It must have been fantastically important, at the real beginnings of human culture, to conserve and relay this vital seasonal information, so that the people could anticipate dry or cold seasons, and not huddle on some November rock hoping pathetically that spring was just around the corner. We still very much stress the simple fact of four seasons to schoolchildren; even the most modern of modern new teachers, who don't seem to care if their charges can read or write or name two products of Peru, will still muster some seasonal chitchat and set the kids to making paper pumpkins, or tulips, for the walls. "The people," wrote Van Gogh in a letter, "are very sensitive to the changing seasons." That we are "very sensitive to the changing seasons" is, incidentally, one of the few good reasons to shun travel. If I stay at home I preserve the illusion that what is happening on Tinker Creek is the very newest thing, that I'm at the very vanguard and cutting edge of each new season. I don't want the same season twice in a row; I don't want to know I'm getting last week's weather, used weather, weather broadcast up and down the coast, old-hat weather.

But there's always unseasonable weather. What we think of the weather and behavior of life on the planet at any given season is really all a matter of statistical probabilities; at any given point, anything might happen. There is a bit of

---

[1] In Hebrew Scripture, the king of Babylon.

every season in each season. Green plants—deciduous green leaves—grow everywhere, all winter long, and small shoots come up pale and new in every season. Leaves die on the tree in May, turn brown, and fall into the creek. The calendar, the weather, and the behavior of wild creatures have the slimmest of connections. Everything overlaps smoothly for only a few weeks each season, and then it all tangles up again. The temperature, of course, lags far behind the calendar seasons, since the earth absorbs and releases heat slowly, like a leviathan breathing. Migrating birds head south in what appears to be dire panic, leaving mild weather and fields full of insects and seeds; they reappear as if in all eagerness in January, and poke about morosely in the snow. Several years ago our October woods would have made a dismal colored photograph for a sadist's calendar: a killing frost came before the leaves had even begun to brown; they drooped from every tree like crepe, blackened and limp. It's all a chancy, jumbled affair at best, as things seem to be below the stars.

Time is the continuous loop, the snakeskin with scales endlessly overlapping without beginning or end, or time is an ascending spiral if you will, like a child's toy Slinky. Of course we have no idea which arc on the loop is our time, let alone where the loop itself is, so to speak, or down whose lofty flight of stairs the Slinky so uncannily walks.

The power we seek, too, seems to be a continuous loop. I have always been sympathetic with the early notion of a divine power that exists in a particular place, or that travels about over the face of the earth as a man might wander— and when he is "there" he is surely not here. You can shake the hand of a man you meet in the woods; but the spirit seems to roll along like the mythical hoop snake with its tail in its mouth. There are no hands to shake or edges to untie. It rolls along the mountain ridges like a fireball, shooting off a spray of sparks at random, and will not be trapped, slowed, grasped, fetched, peeled, or aimed. "As for the wheels, it was cried unto them in my hearing, O wheel." This is the hoop of flame that shoots the rapids in the creek or spins across the dizzy meadows; this is the arsonist of the sunny woods: catch it if you can.

≥ Barry Lopez (born 1945)

Barry Holstun Lopez spent his childhood in California, where he was raised by his single mother. There, he developed a fondness for the natural world and began his lifelong devotion to the study of natural history. Lopez became painfully aware of his attachment to nature when, at the age of eleven, his mother moved the family to Manhattan, where Lopez felt alienated.

After hearing a reading of The Odyssey *as a young man, Lopez was so inspired that he felt an immediate calling to the profession of writing. Indeed,* The Odyssey's *treatment of nature as a primal and personified character would greatly influence Lopez's work; and like the Greek poets, Lopez demonstrates a strong sense of obligation to his community. Lopez writes not merely to entertain but to remind his readers of their relationship to the natural world and their responsibility to ensure its survival.*

Lopez has traveled throughout the world to explore wild places. He has spent considerable time in the extreme north of Canada and has traveled to Antarctica, Australia, Asia, and Africa in order to chronicle the wild beauty that he considers of essential importance to human life. His world travels, love of nature, and precise, descriptive style align him with such American nature writers as Ernest Hemingway. Unlike Hemingway, however, Lopez does not seek to overcome nature but to behold and adore it, to conserve rather than conquer the rugged world around him. In order to articulate such a balanced relationship with the wild, Lopez has written many works of nonfiction, such as Of Wolves and Men *(1978), which have done much to educate the American public about the necessity of conservation. Lopez claims that the writer's duty is to "be the one who recognizes the patterns that remind us of our obligations and our dreams."*

Lopez is particularly concerned with recognizing the validity of subjective human experiences and memories and how they are shaped by natural surroundings. His books also include About This Life: Journeys on the Threshold of Memory *(1998);* Lessons from the Wolverine *(1997);* Apologia, *an elegy about animals killed on American roads (1998); and* Arctic Dreams: Imagination and Desire in a Northern Landscape *(1986), based on five years of experience in the arctic wilderness and winner of the National Book Award. In the excerpt printed below, Lopez tells of his fleeting encounter with one of the world's most rare and elusive creatures:* Monodon monoceros, *the narwhal.*

From Arctic Dreams

From Lancaster Sound
Monodon monoceros

I am standing at the margin of the sea ice called the floe edge at the mouth of Admiralty Inlet, northern Baffin Island, three or four miles out to sea. The firmness beneath my feet belies the ordinary sense of the phrase "out to sea." Several Eskimo camps stand here along the white and black edge of ice and water. All of us have come from another place—Nuvua, 30 miles to the south at the tip of Uluksan Peninsula. We are here to hunt narwhals. They are out there in the open water of Lancaster Sound somewhere, waiting for this last ice barrier to break up so they can enter their summer feeding grounds in Admiralty Inlet.

As I walk along the floe edge—the light is brilliant, the ceaseless light of July; but after so many weeks I am weary of it; I stare at the few shadows on the ice with a kind of hunger—as I walk along here I am aware of both fear and elation, a mix that comes in remote regions with the realization that you are exposed and the weather can be capricious, and fatal. The wind is light and from the north—I can see its corrugation on the surface of the water. Should it swing around and come from the south, the ice behind us would begin to open up. Traverse cracks across the inlet, only a few inches wide yesterday, would begin to widen. We would have difficulty getting back to Nuvua, even if we left at the first sign of a wind shift.

A few days ago one of these men was caught like that. A distant explosion, like dynamite, told him what a compass bearing he quickly took on Borden Peninsula confirmed—that the five-square-mile sheet of floe ice he had camped on was being swept out of Admiralty Inlet toward open water in Lancaster Sound. He and his companion, knowing the set of local currents, struck out immediately to the east. Twelve hours later, near exhaustion, they came to a place where the ice floe was grounded in shallow coastal water, making a huge, slow turn in the current before breaking loose into Lancaster Sound. They leaped and plunged across broken ice cakes for the firm shore.

I am not so much thinking of these things, however, as I am feeling the exuberance of birds around me. Black-legged kittiwakes, northern fulmars, and black guillemots are wheeling and hovering in weightless acrobatics over the streams and lenses of life in the water—zooplankton and arctic cod—into which they plunge repeatedly for their sustenance. Out on the ice, at piles of offal from the narwhal hunt, glaucous and Thayer's gulls stake a rough-tempered claim to some piece of flesh, brash, shouldering birds alongside the more reticent and rarer ivory gulls.

Birds fly across these waters in numbers that encourage you to simply flip your pencil in the air. Certain species end their northward migration here and nest. Others fly on to Devon and Ellesmere islands or to northwest Greenland. From where I now stand I can study some that stay, nesting in an unbroken line for 10 miles on a cliff between Baillarge Bay and Elwin Inlet, a rugged wall of sedimentary and volcanic rock pocked with indentations and ledges, rising at an angle of 80° from the water. More than 50,000 northern fulmars. At other such rookeries around Lancaster Sound, guillemots, murres, and kittiwakes congregate in tens and even hundreds of thousands to nest and feed during the short summer. Gulls, arctic terns, snow geese, eiders, red-breasted mergansers, and dovekies have passed through in droves already. Of the dovekies—a small, stocky seabird with a black head and bright white underside—something on the order of a third of the northwest Greenland population of 30 *million* passes over Lancaster Sound in May and June.

On the white-as-eggshell ice plain where we are camped, with the mottled browns and ochers of Borden Peninsula to the east and the dark cliffs of Brodeur Peninsula obscured in haze to the west, the adroit movements of the birds above the water give the landscape an immediate, vivid dimension: the eye, drawn far out to pale hues on the horizon, comes back smartly to the black water, where, *plunk*, a guillemot disappears in a dive.

The outcry of birds, the bullet-whirr of their passing wings, the splashing of water, is, like the falling light, unending. Lancaster Sound is a rare arctic marine sanctuary, a place where creatures are concentrated in the sort of densities one finds in the Antarctic Ocean, the richest sea waters in the world. Marine ecologists are not certain why Lancaster Sound teems so with life, but local upwelling currents and a supply of nutrients from glacial runoff on Devon Island seem critical.[1]

[1] Lancaster Sound has been proposed as a world biological reserve by the International Biological Programme and singled out by the United Nations as a Natural Site of World Heritage Quality. The stability of this ecosystem is currently threatened by offshore oil development and increased shipping traffic. David Nettleship, an arctic ornithologist with preeminent experience here, has written that such economic development "should be strictly controlled in order to prevent the destruction of a uniquely rich high arctic oasis. To harm it would go far towards making a desert of arctic waters."

Three million colonial seabirds, mostly northern fulmars, kittiwakes, and guillemots, nest and feed here in the summer. It is no longer the haunt of 10,000 or so bowhead whales, but it remains a summering ground for more than 30 percent of the belukha whale population of North America, and more than three-quarters of the world's population of narwhals. No one is sure how many harp, bearded, and ringed seals are here—probably more than a quarter of a million. In addition there are thousands of Atlantic walrus. The coastal regions are a denning area for polar bear and home to thousands of arctic fox in the summer.

I am concerned, as I walk, however, more with what is immediate to my senses—the ternlike whiffle and spin of birds over the water, the chicken-cackling of northern fulmars, and cool air full of the breath of sea life. This community of creatures, including all those invisible in the water, constitutes a unique overlap of land, water, and air. This is a special meeting ground, like that of a forest's edge with a clearing; or where the fresh waters of an estuary meet the saline tides of the sea; or at a river's riparian edge. The mingling of animals from different ecosystems charges such border zones with evolutionary potential. Flying creatures here at Admiralty Inlet walk on ice. They break the pane of water with their dives to feed. Marine mammals break the pane of water coming the other way to breathe.

The edges of any landscape—horizons, the lip of a valley, the bend of a river around a canyon wall—quicken an observer's expectations. That attraction to borders, to the earth's twilit places, is part of the shape of human curiosity. And the edges that cause excitement are like these where I now walk, sensing the birds toying with gravity; or like those in quantum mechanics, where what is critical straddles a border between being a wave and being a particle, between being what it is and becoming something else, occupying an edge of time that defeats our geometries. In biology these transitional areas between two different communities are called ecotones.

The ecotone at the Admiralty Inlet floe edge extends in two planes. In order to pass under the ice from the open sea, an animal must be free of a need for atmospheric oxygen; the floe edge, therefore, is a barrier to the horizontal migration of whales. In the vertical plane, no bird can penetrate the ice and birds like gulls can't go below water with guillemots to feed on schools of fish. Sunlight, too, is halted at these borders.

To stand at the edge of this four-foot-thick ice platform, however, is to find yourself in a rich biological crease. Species of alga grow on the bottom of the sea ice, turning it golden brown with a patchwork of life. These tiny diatoms feed zooplankton moving through the upper layers of water in vast clouds—underwater galaxies of copepods, amphipods, and mysids. These in turn feed the streaming schools of cod. The cod feed the birds. And the narwhals. And also the ringed seal, which feeds the polar bear, and eventually the fox. The algae at the bottom of this food web are called "epontic" algae, the algae of the sea ice. (Ringed seals, ivory gulls, and other birds and mammals whose lives are ice-oriented are called "pagophylic.") It is the ice, however, that holds this life together. For ice-associated seals, vulnerable on a beach, it is a place offshore to rest, directly over their feeding grounds. It provides algae with a surface to grow on. It shelters arctic cod from hunting seabirds and herds of narwhals, and it shelters the narwhal from the predatory orca. It is the bear's highway over the sea. And it gives me a place to stand on the ocean, and wonder.

I walk here intent on the birds, half aware of the biological mysteries in these placid, depthless waters in which I catch fleeting silver glimpses of cod. I feel blessed. I draw in the salt air and feel the warmth of sunlight on my face. I recall a childhood of summer days on the beaches of California. I feel the wealth to be had in life in an aimless walk like this, through woods or over a prairie or down a beach.

It is not all benign and ethereal at the ice edge, however. You cannot—I cannot—lose completely the sense of how far from land this is. And I am wary of walrus. A male walrus is a huge animal, approaching the size of a small car. At close range in the water its agility and speed are intimidating. Walruses normally eat only bottom-dwelling organisms like clams, worms, and crabs, but there is an unusual sort of walrus—almost always a male, a loner, that deliberately hunts and kills seals. Its ivory tusks are crosshatched with the claw marks of seals fighting for their lives. (It is called *angeyegbaq* by the Eskimos on Saint Lawrence Island, who are familiar with its unusual behavior.) This rare carnivore will charge off an ice floe to attack a small boat, and actively pursue and try to kill people in the water. A friend of mine was once standing with an Eskimo friend at an ice edge when the man cautioned him to step back. They retreated 15 or 20 feet. Less than a minute later a walrus surfaced in an explosion of water where they had been standing. A polar bear trick.

When I walk along the floe edge I think of that story. I have no ear educated as was his companion's to anticipate the arrival of the walrus. A native ear. Experience. I walk here susceptible as any traveler to the unknown.

I stood still occasionally to listen. I heard only the claver of birds. Then there was something else. I had never heard the sound before, but when it came, plosive and gurgling, I knew instinctively what it was, even as everyone in camp jumped. I strained to see them, to spot the vapor of their breath, a warm mist against the soft horizon, or the white tip of a tusk breaking the surface of the water, a dark pattern that retained its shape against the dark, shifting patterns of the water. Somewhere out there in the ice fragments. Gone. Gone now. Others had heard the breathing. Human figures in a camp off to the west, dark lines on the blinding white ice, gesture toward us with upraised arms.

The first narwhals I ever saw lived far from here, in Bering Strait. The day I saw them I knew that no element of the earth's natural history had ever before brought me so far, so suddenly. It was as though something from a bestiary had taken shape, a creature strange as a giraffe. It was as if the testimony of someone I had no reason to doubt, yet could not quite believe, a story too farfetched, had been verified at a glance.

I was with a bowhead whale biologist named Don Ljungblad, flying search transects over Bering Sea. It was May, and the first bowheads of spring were slowly working their way north through Bering Strait toward their summer feeding grounds in the Chukchi and Beaufort seas. Each day as we flew these transects we would pass over belukha whale and walrus, ringed, spotted, and ribbon seals, bearded seals, and flocks of birds migrating to Siberia. I know of no other region in North America where animals can be met with in such numbers. Bering Sea itself is probably the richest of all the northern seas, as rich as Chesapeake Bay or the Grand Banks at the time of their discovery. Its bounty of crabs, pollock, cod, sole, herring, clams, and salmon is set down in wild numbers, the rambling digits of guesswork. The numbers of birds and marine mammals feeding here, to a person familiar with anything but the Serengeti or life at the Antarctic convergence, are magical. At the height of migration in the spring, the testament of life in Bering Sea is absolutely stilling in its dimensions.

The two weeks I spent flying with Ljungblad, with so many thousands of creatures moving through the water and the air, were a heady experience. Herds of belukha whale glided in silent shoals beneath transparent sheets of young ice. Squadrons of fast-flying sea ducks flashed beneath us as they banked away. We passed ice floes stained red in a hundred places with the afterbirths of walrus. Staring all day into the bright light reflected from the ice and water, however, and the compression in time of these extraordinary events, left me dazed some evenings.

Aspects of the arctic landscape that had become salient for me—its real and temporal borders; a rare, rich oasis of life surrounded by vast stretches of deserted land; the upending of conventional kinds of time; biological vulnerability made poignant by the forgiving light of summer—all of this was evoked over Bering Sea.

The day we saw the narwhals we were flying south, low over Bering Strait. The ice in Chukchi Sea behind us was so close it did not seem possible that bowheads could have penetrated this far; but it is good to check, because they can make headway in ice as heavy as this and they are able to come a long way north undetected in lighter ice on the Russian side. I was daydreaming about two bowheads we had seen that morning. They had been floating side by side in a broad lane of unusually clear water between a shelf of shorefast ice and the pack ice—the flaw lead. As we passed over, they made a single movement together, a slow, rolling turn and graceful glide, like figure skaters pushing off, these 50-ton leviathans. Ljungblad shouted in my earphones: "Waiting." They were waiting for the ice in the strait to open up. Ljungblad saw nearly 300 bowheads waiting calmly like this one year, some on their backs, some with their chins resting on the ice.

The narwhals appeared in the middle of this reverie. Two males, with ivory tusks spiraling out of their foreheads, the image of the unicorn with which history has confused them. They were close to the same size and light-colored, and were lying parallel and motionless in a long, straight lead in the ice. My eye was drawn to them before my conscious mind, let alone my voice, could catch up. I stared dumbfounded while someone else shouted. Not just to see the narwhals, but *here*, a few miles northwest of King Island in Bering Sea. In all the years scientists have kept records for these waters, no one had ever seen a narwhal alive in Bering Sea. Judging from the heaviness of the ice around them, they must have spent the winter here.[2] They were either residents, a wondrous thought, or

---

[2] The narwhal is not nearly as forceful in the ice as the bowhead. It can break through only about 6 inches of ice with its head. A bowhead, using its brow or on occasion its more formidable chin, can break through as much as 18 inches of sea ice.

they had come from the nearest population centers the previous fall, from waters north of Siberia or from northeastern Canada.

The appearance of these animals was highly provocative. We made circle after circle above them, until they swam away under the ice and were gone. Then we looked at each other. Who could say what this was, really?

Because you have seen something doesn't mean you can explain it. Differing interpretations will always abound, even when good minds come to bear. The kernel of indisputable information is a dot in space; interpretations grow out of the desire to make this point a line, to give it a direction. The directions in which it can be sent, the uses to which it can be put by a culturally, profession-ally, and geographically diverse society, are almost without limit. The possibili-ties make good scientists chary. In a region like the Arctic, tense with a hunger for wealth, with fears of plunder, interpretation can quickly get beyond a scien-tist's control. When asked to assess the meaning of a biological event—What were those animals doing out there? Where do they belong?—they hedge. They are sometimes reluctant to elaborate on what they saw, because they cannot say what it means, and they are suspicious of those who say they know. Some even distrust the motives behind the questions.

I think along these lines in this instance because of the animal. No large mammal in the Northern Hemisphere comes as close as the narwhal to having its very existence doubted. For some, the possibility that this creature might ac-tually live in the threatened waters of Bering Sea is portentous, a significant ap-parition on the eve of an era of disruptive oil exploration there. For others, those with the leases to search for oil and gas in Navarin and Norton basins, the possi-bility that narwhals may live there is a complicating environmental nuisance. Hardly anyone marvels solely at the fact that on the afternoon of April 16, 1982, five people saw two narwhals in a place so unexpected that they were flabber-gasted. They remained speechless, circling over the animals in a state of wonder. In those moments the animals did not have to mean anything at all.

✍ *Gretel Ehrlich* (born 1946)

Born in Santa Barbara, California, Gretel Ehrlich was educated at Bennington College in Vermont and then at the University of California, Los Angeles (UCLA) film school. It was while making a film that she first traveled to Wyoming. Ehrlich moved there per-manently in 1976, devoting herself to sheep and cattle ranching while also pursuing her writing. She began publishing as a poet with two collections, Geode, Rock Body *(1970) and* To Touch the Water *(1979). Her prose exhibits a lyricism and an eye for powerful images that one typically associates with poetry, and she continues to write in several genres.* The Solace of Open Spaces *(1984), a portion of which is selected be-low, is part memoir, part natural history, part philosophical and theological speculation. Other works include a collection of short stories,* Drinking Dry Clouds *(1985); a novel,* Heart Mountain *(1987); a collection of essays,* Islands, the Universe, Home *(1991);*

a volume of poetry, Arctic Heart *(1991); a memoir about her experience being struck by lightning,* A Match to the Heart *(1994); and work of travel writing,* Yellowstone, Land of Fire and Ice *(1995). She publishes frequently in popular magazines such as* Harper's, Atlantic, *and* Outside. *Her awards include fellowships from the National Endowment for the Arts and the Guggenheim Foundation. She lives part-time in California, in Wyoming, and in Vermont, where she is a professor at Bennington College.*

From The Solace of Open Spaces

On Water

Frank Hinckley, a neighboring rancher in his seventies, would rather irrigate than ride a horse. He started spreading water on his father's hay- and grainfields when he was nine, and his long-term enthusiasm for what's thought of disdainfully by cowboys as "farmers' work" is an example of how a discipline—a daily chore—can grow into a fidelity. When I saw Frank in May he was standing in a dry irrigation ditch looking toward the mountains. The orange tarp dams, hung like curtains from ten-foot-long poles, fluttered in the wind like prayer flags. In Wyoming we are supplicants, waiting all spring for the water to come down, for the snow pack to melt and fill the creeks from which we irrigate. Fall and spring rains amount to less than eight inches a year, while above our ranches, the mountains hold their snows like a secret: no one knows when they will melt or how fast. When the water does come, it floods through the state as if the peaks were silver pitchers tipped forward by mistake. When I looked in, the ditch water had begun dripping over Frank's feet. Then we heard a sound that might have been wind in a steep patch of pines. "Jumpin' Jesus, here it comes," he said, as a head of water, brown and foamy as beer, snaked toward us. He set five dams, digging the bright edges of plastic into silt. Water filled them the way wind fattens a sail, and from three notches cut in the ditch above each dam, water coursed out over a hundred acres of hayfield. When he finished, and the beadwork wetness had spread through the grass, he lowered himself to the ditch and rubbed his face with water.

A season of irrigating here lasts four months. Twenty, thirty, or as many as two hundred dams are changed every twelve hours, ditches are repaired and head gates adjusted to match the inconsistencies of water flow. By September it's over: all but the major Wyoming rivers dry up. Running water is so seasonal it's thought of as a mark on the calendar—a vague wet spot—rather than a geographical site. In May, June, July, and August, water is the sacristy at which we kneel; it equates time going by too fast.

Waiting for water is just one of the ways Wyoming ranchers find themselves at the mercy of weather. The hay they irrigate, for example, has to be cut when it's dry but baled with a little dew on it to preserve the leaf. Three days after Frank's water came down, a storm dumped three feet of snow on his alfalfa and the creeks froze up again. His wife, "Mike," who grew up in the arid Powder River country, and I rode to the headwaters of our creeks. The elk we startled had been licking ice in a draw. A snow squall rose up from behind a bare ridge and engulfed us. We built a twig fire behind a rock to warm ourselves, then rode home. The creeks didn't thaw completely until June.

Despite the freak snow, April was the second driest in a century; in the lower elevations there had been no precipitation at all. Brisk winds forwarded thunderclouds into local skies—commuters from other states—but the streamers of rain they let down evaporated before touching us. All month farmers and ranchers burned their irrigation ditches to clear them of obstacles and weeds—optimistic that water would soon come. Shell Valley resembled a battlefield: lines of blue smoke banded every horizon and the cottonwoods that had caught fire by mistake, their outstretched branches blazing, looked human. April, the cruelest month, the month of dry storms.

Six years ago, when I lived on a large sheep ranch, a drought threatened. Every water hole on 100,000 acres of grazing land went dry. We hauled water in clumsy beet-harvest trucks forty miles to spring range, and when we emptied them into a circle of stock tanks, the sheep ran toward us. They pushed to get at the water, trampling lambs in the process, then drank it all in one collective gulp. Other Aprils have brought too much moisture in the form of deadly storms. When a ground blizzard hit one friend's herd in the flatter, eastern part of the state, he knew he had to keep his cattle drifting. If they hit a fence line and had to face the storm, snow would blow into their noses and they'd drown. "We cut wire all the way to Nebraska," he told me. During the same storm another cowboy found his cattle too late: they were buried in a draw under a fifteen-foot drift.

High water comes in June when the runoff peaks, and it's another bugaboo for the ranchers. The otherwise amiable thirty-foot-wide creeks swell and change courses so that when we cross them with livestock, the water is belly-deep or more. Cowboys in the 1800s who rode with the trail herds from Texas often worked in the big rivers on horseback for a week just to cross a thousand head of longhorn steers, losing half of them in the process. On a less-grand scale we have drownings and near drownings here each spring. When we crossed a creek this year the swift current toppled a horse and carried the rider under a log. A cowboy who happened to look back saw her head go under, dove in from horseback, and saved her. At Trapper Creek, where Owen Wister spent several summers in the 1920s and entertained Mr. Hemingway, a cloudburst slapped down on us like a black eye. Scraps of rainbow moved in vertical sweeps of rain that broke apart and disappeared behind a ridge. The creek flooded, taking out a house and a field of corn. We saw one resident walking in a flattened alfalfa field where the river had flowed briefly. "Want to go fishing?" he yelled to us as we rode by. The fish he was throwing into a white bucket were trout that had been "beached" by the flood.

Westerners are ambivalent about water because they've never seen what it can create except havoc and mud. They've never walked through a forest of wild orchids or witnessed the unfurling of five-foot-high ferns. "The only way I like my water is if there's whiskey in it," one rancher told me as we weaned calves in a driving rainstorm. That day we spent twelve hours on horseback in the rain. Despite protective layers of clothing: wool union suits, chaps, ankle-length yellow slickers, neck scarves and hats, we were drenched. Water drips off hat brims into your crotch; boots and gloves soak through. But to stay home out of the storm is deemed by some as a worse fate: "Hell, my wife had me cannin' beans for a week," one cowboy complained. "I'd rather drown like a muskrat out there."

Dryness is the common denominator in Wyoming. We're drenched more often in dust than in water; it is the scalpel and the suit of armor that make westerners what they are. Dry air presses a stockman's insides outward. The secret, inner self is worn not on the sleeve but in the skin. It's an unlubricated condition: there's not enough moisture in the air to keep the whole emotional machinery oiled and working. "What you see is what you get, but you have to learn to look to see all that's there," one young rancher told me. He was physically reckless when coming to see me or leaving. That was his way of saying he had and would miss me, and in the clean, broad sweeps of passion between us, there was no heaviness, no muddy residue. Cowboys have learned not to waste words from not having wasted water, as if verbosity would create a thirst too extreme to bear. If voices are raspy, it's because vocal cords are coated with dust. When I helped ship seven thousand head of steers one fall, the dust in the big, roomy sorting corrals churned as deeply and sensually as water. We wore scarves over our noses and mouths; the rest of our faces blackened with dirt so we looked like raccoons or coal miners. The westerner's face is stiff and dark red as jerky. It gives no clues beyond the discerning look that says, "You've been observed." Perhaps the too-early lines of aging that pull across these ranchers' necks are really cracks in a wall through which we might see the contradictory signs of their character: a complacency, a restlessness, a shy, boyish pride.

I knew a sheepherder who had the words "hard luck" tattooed across his knuckles. "That's for all the times I've been dry," he explained. "And when you've been as thirsty as I've been, you don't forget how something tastes." That's how he mapped out the big ranch he worked for: from thirst to thirst, whiskey to whiskey. To follow the water courses in Wyoming—seven rivers and a network of good-sized creeks—is to trace the history of settlement here. After a few bad winters the early ranchers quickly discovered the necessity of raising feed for livestock. Long strips of land on both sides of the creeks and rivers were grabbed up in the 1870s and '80s before Wyoming was a state. Land was cheap and relatively easy to accumulate, but control of water was crucial. The early ranches such as the Swan Land & Cattle Company, the Budd Ranch, the M-L, the Bug Ranch, and the Pitchfork took up land along the Chugwater, Green, Greybull, Big Horn, and Shoshone rivers. It was not long before feuds over water began. The old law of "full and undiminished flow" to those who owned land along a creek was changed to one that adjudicated and allocated water by the acre foot to specified pieces of land. By 1890 residents had to file claims for the right to use the water that flowed through their ranches. These rights were, and still are, awarded according to the date a ranch was established regardless of ownership changes. This solved the increasing problem of upstream-downstream disputes, enabling the first ranch established on a creek to maintain the first water right, regardless of how many newer settlements occurred upstream.

Land through which no water flowed posed another problem. Frank's father was one of the Mormon colonists sent by Brigham Young to settle and put under cultivation the arid Big Horn Basin. The twenty thousand acres they claimed were barren and waterless. To remedy this problem they dug a canal thirty-seven miles long, twenty-seven feet across, and sixteen feet deep by hand. The project took four years to complete. Along the way a huge boulder gave the canal diggers trouble: it couldn't be moved. As a last resort the Mormon men held hands around the rock and prayed. The next morning the boulder rolled out of the way.

Piousness was not always the rule. Feuds over water became venomous as the population of the state grew. Ditch riders—so called because they monitored on horseback the flow and use of water—often found themselves on the wrong end of an irrigating shovel. Frank remembers when the ditch rider in his district was hit over the head so hard by the rancher whose water he was turning off that he fell unconscious into the canal, floating on his back until he bumped into the next head gate.

With the completion of the canal, the Mormons built churches, schools, and houses communally, working in unison as if taking their cue from the water that snaked by them. "It was a socialistic sonofabitch from the beginning," Frank recalls, "a beautiful damned thing. These 'western individualists' forget how things got done around here and not so damned many years ago at that."

Frank is the opposite of the strapping, conservative western man. Sturdy, but small-boned, he has an awkward, knock-kneed gait that adds to his chronic amiability. Though he's made his life close to home, he has a natural, panoramic vision as if he had upped-periscope through the Basin's dust clouds and had a good look around. Frank's generosity runs like water: it follows the path of least resistance and, tumbling downhill, takes on a fullness so replete and indiscriminate as to sometimes appear absurd. "You can't cheat an honest man," he'll tell you and laugh at the paradox implied. His wide face and forehead indicate the breadth of his unruly fair-mindedness—one that includes not just local affections but the whole human community.

When Frank started irrigating there were no tarp dams. "We plugged up those ditches with any old thing we had—rags, bones, car parts, sod." Though he could afford to hire an irrigator now he prefers to do the work himself, and when I'm away he turns my water as well, then mows my lawn. "Irrigating is a contemptible damned job. I've been fighting water all my life. Mother Nature is a bitter old bitch, isn't she? But we have to have that challenge. We crave it and I'll be goddamned if I know why. I feel sorry for these damned rich ranchers with their pumps and sprinkler systems and gated pipe because they're missing out on something. When I go to change my water at dawn and just before dark, it's peaceful out there, away from everybody. I love the fragrances—grass growing, wild rose on the ditch bank—and hearing the damned old birds twittering away. How can we live without that?"

Two thousand years before the Sidon Canal was built in Wyoming, the Hohokam, a people who lived in what became Arizona, used digging sticks to channel water from the Salt and Gila rivers to dry land. Theirs was the most extensive irrigation system in aboriginal North America. Water was brought thirty miles to spread over fields of corn, beans, and pumpkins—crops inherited from tribes in South and Central America. "It's a primitive damned thing," Frank said about the business of using water. "The change from a digging stick to a shovel isn't much of an evolution. Playing with water is something all kids have done, whether it's in creeks or in front of fire hydrants. Maybe that's how agriculture got started in the first place."

Romans applied their insoluble cement to waterways as if it could arrest the flux and impermanence they knew water to signify. Of the fourteen aqueducts that brought water from mountains and lakes to Rome, several are still in use today. On a Roman latifundium—their equivalent of a ranch—they grew alfalfa, a hot-weather crop introduced by way of Persia and Greece around the fifth century B.C., and fed it to their horses as we do here. Feuds over water were common: Nero was reprimanded for bathing in the canal that carried the city's drinking water, the brothels tapped aqueducts on the sly until once the whole city went dry. The Empire's staying power began to collapse when the waterways fell into disrepair. Crops dried up and the water that had carried life to the great cities stagnated and became breeding grounds for mosquitoes until malaria, not water, flowed into the heart of Rome.

There is nothing in nature that can't be taken as a sign of both mortality and invigoration. Cascading water equates loss followed by loss, a momentum of things falling in the direction of death, then life. In Conrad's *Heart of Darkness*, the river is a redundancy flowing through rain forest, a channel of solitude, a solid thing, a trap. Hemingway's Big Two-Hearted River is the opposite: it's an accepting, restorative place. Water can stand for what is unconscious, instinctive, and sexual in us, for the creative swill in which we fish for ideas. It carries, weightlessly, the imponderable things in our lives: death and creation. We can drown in it or else stay buoyant, quench our thirst, stay alive.

In Navajo mythology, rain is the sun's sperm coming down. A Crow woman I met on a plane told me that. She wore a flowered dess, a man's wool jacket with a package of Vantages stuck in one pocket, and calf-high moccasins held together with two paper clips. "Traditional Crow think water is medicinal," she said as we flew over the Yellowstone River which runs through the tribal land where she lives. "The old tribal crier used to call out every morning for our people to drink all they could, to make water touch their bodies. 'Water is your body,' they used to say." Looking down on the seared landscape below, it wasn't difficult to understand the real and imagined potency of water. "All that would be a big death yard," she said with a sweep of her arm. That's how the drought would come: one sweep and all moisture would be banished. Bluebunch and June grass would wither. Elk and deer would trample sidehills into sand. Draws would fill up with dead horses and cows. Tucked under ledges of shale, dens of rattlesnakes would grow into city-states of snakes. The roots of trees would rise to the surface and flail through dust in search of water.

Everything in nature invites us constantly to be what we are. We are often like rivers: careless and forceful, timid and dangerous, lucid and muddied, eddying, gleaming, still. Lovers, farmers, and artists have one thing in common, at least—a fear of "dry spells," dormant periods in which we do no blooming, internal droughts only the waters of imagination and psychic release can civilize. All such matters are delicate of course. But a good irrigator knows this: too little water brings on the weeds while too much degrades the soil the way too much easy money can trivialize a person's initiative. In his journal Thoreau wrote, "A man's life should be as fresh as a river. It should be the same channel but a new water every instant."

This morning I walked the length of a narrow, dry wash. Slabs of stone, broken off in great squares, lay propped against the banks like blank mirrors. A sagebrush had drilled a hole through one of these rocks. The roots fanned out and down like hooked noses. Farther up, a quarry of red rock bore the fossilized marks of rippling water. Just yesterday, a cloudburst sent a skinny stream beneath these frozen undulations. Its passage carved the same kind of watery ridges into the sand at my feet. Even in this dry country, where internal and external droughts always threaten, water is self-registering no matter how ancient, recent, or brief.

🦢 Linda Hogan (born 1947)

A member of the Chickasaw nation, Linda Hogan was born in Denver. She was raised apart from the immediate influence of tribal culture in Colorado and in Oklahoma, however, because she was a part of a military family. Hogan was educated at University of Colorado at Boulder, where she is currently on the faculty in the English Department. Hogan draws on her Native American background and emphasizes how that culture, in particular, teaches a reverence for the natural world and the important web of connections among all living things. A versatile writer, Hogan publishes in a variety of genres. She is also politically active in the antinuclear and environmentalist movements. Her collections of poetry include Calling Myself Home *(1979),* Daughters, I Love You *(1981),* Savings *(1988), and* The Book of Medicines *(1993). She has also written several novels:* Mean Spirit *(1990),* Solar Storms *(1995), and* Power *(1998). In addition, she writes essays and nonfiction prose specifically dedicated to exploring the human relationship to nature, collected in* Dwellings: Reflections on the Natural World *(1995) and* Intimate Nature *(1998). Hogan is the recipient of numerous awards for her work, including a Guggenheim Memorial Fellowship.*

Elk Song

We give thanks
to deer, otter,
the great fish
and birds that fly over
and are our bones and skin.   5
Even the yelping dog at our heels
is a hungry crow
picking bones wolf left behind.
And thanks to the corn and trees.
The earth   10
is a rich table
and a slaughterhouse
for humans as well.

But this is for the elk,
the red running one   15
like thunder over hills,
a saint with its holy hoof dance
an old woman whose night song
we try not to hear.

This song is for the elk   20
with its throat whistling
and antlers
above head and great hooves
rattling earth.

One spring night, elk   25
ran across me
while I slept on earth
and every hoof missed
my shaking bones.

That other time, I heard elk run   30
on earth's tight skin,
the time I was an enemy
from the other side of the forest.
Didn't I say the earth is a slaughterhouse
for humans as well?   35

Some nights in town's cold winter,
earth shakes.
People say it's a train full of danger
or the plane-broken barriers of sound,
but out there   40
behind the dark trunks of trees

the gone elk have pulled the hide of earth
tight and they are drumming
back the woodland,
tall grass and days we were equal   45
and strong.

Rain

Rain's story
falls to earth.
It tells corn
and wheat such tales
they believe   5
and rise up thin air.

This falling water is Africa rising.
Unfold the maps.
In all towns rain has fallen
life surged up   10
and turned to bones again.

Rain passes on
stories of people.
Some are loved in deep green jungles.
Some are tortured in mesquite hills.   15
In this town a man
was given something sharp to swallow
and no water. Rain said,
drink me.

Here they tell us, do not sing,   20
do not speak the name of rain
with its revolutionary
brewing of life
in death's harvest time.
Forget what has happened   25
in the round world.

Rain is banished
for making life
and carrying songs
and secrets   30
over state lines.
So tell this
from behind bars,
and the living rooms of homes,

from underground   35
where springs are flowing.

Tell your children
and mothers
rain beats on roofs,
men are forced to swallow sharpness,   40
flour sacks are pilfered by the full.
Lord have mercy.
Rain is falling.
It wants to touch our hair and skin,
wants to touch us,   45
and everyone knows
the stories of rain
and where it came from,
that's why they go inside
and bolt the door   50
and turn buttons of machines
off and on
even though the grass is growing back again
and everything we swallow
is the rain   55
and birth waters
are breaking down
the sturdy legs of sky.

Map

This is the world
so vast and lonely
without end, with mountains
named for men
who brought hunger   5
from other lands,
and fear
of the thick, dark forest of trees
that held each other up,
knowing fire dreamed of swallowing them   10
and spoke an older tongue,
and the tongue of the nation of wolves
was the wind around them.
Even ice was not silent.   15
It cried its broken self
back to warmth.
But they called it

ice, wolf, forest of sticks,
as if words would make it something
they could hold in gloved hands,   20
open, plot a way
and follow.

This is the map of the forsaken world.
This is the world without end
where forests have been cut away from their trees.   25
These are the lines wolf could not pass over.
This is what I know from science:
that a grain of dust dwells at the center
of every flake of snow,
that ice can have its way with land,   30
that wolves live inside a circle
of their own beginning.
This is what I know from blood:
the first language is not our own.
There are names each thing has for itself,   35
and beneath us the other order already moves.
It is burning.
It is dreaming.
It is waking up.

Chambered Nautilus

It's from before the spin of human fire,
before the dreaming that grew out of itself,
before there were people who ate the brains
of the dead,
before wind was leaving through a hole in the sky,   5
before zero and powers of ten,
before nets drifting the empty miles of water,
from when moon was the only tyrant that ruled the sea
and was the god shells rose to at night,
the builder of chambers,   10
the geometry of light, even infinity
is shaped this way
and the curve of sea lives in it,
the unwritten laws of water,
and it still rises   15
to the surface of darkness,
the country of drifting,
seeking a new kind of light to live inside,
from when we were less savage than now,

when shells were barter for corn 20
and cloth, and mirrors,
and we built dwellings of stone.
We were strong.
We were full.
Europeans did not powder our bones 25
and drink them, believing their powers
would grow
and there were no torturers leaving stone prisons
at night to buy bread and sugar
for their wives. 30
It was before there were bear-slayers
and slayers of women and land
and belief. We knew earth was a turtle
swimming between stars
and everything that was savage in us 35
fought to the quick
because everything that lived had radiance
like the curve of water and shell
of whatever animal
still inside 40
that has brought me here.

Leslie Marmon Silko *(born 1948)*

Although her origins are Pueblo, Laguna, Mexican, and Anglo, Leslie Marmon Silko has committed herself to writing for and about Native American culture. Born in Albuquerque, New Mexico, and raised on a Laguna reservation, Silko attended the University of New Mexico. She published her first work, "Tony's Story," in 1969. Her first book was a collection of poetry, Laguna Women Poems *(1974), but Silko is a versatile writer and works in several genres. Her debut novel,* Ceremony *(1977), received tremendous critical acclaim and established her as a leading voice among Native American writers of the late twentieth century. In all her works, whether poetry, fiction, or essays, Silko emphasizes the importance of storytelling to the integrity and continuity of Native American culture. She is also highly critical of white racism against Native Americans and of the United States government's Native American policies. Her works include* Western Stories *(1980),* Storyteller *(1981),* Almanac of the Dead *(1991),* Sacred Water: Narratives and Pictures *(1993),* Yellow Woman *(1993),* Yellow Woman and a Beauty of the Spirit *(1996),* Love Poem and Slim Man Canyon *(1996), and* Gardens in the Dunes *(1999). In her exploration of the continuing impact of Pueblo myths and legends, Silko highlights the essential aspects of Native American spirituality, which sees nature as inseparable from divinity. Moreover, in stories such as "Lullaby," below, she gives particular attention to a woman's perspective on the disjunctions between traditional Pueblo and more modern, westernized ways of life. Silko has taught at the University of New Mexico and has been the recipient of a highly prestigious MacArthur Foundation grant.*

Lullaby

The sun had gone down but the snow in the wind gave off its own light. It came in thick tufts like new wool—washed before the weaver spins it. Ayah reached out for it like her own babies had, and she smiled when she remembered how she had laughed at them. She was an old woman now, and her life had become memories. She sat down with her back against the wide cottonwood tree, feeling the rough bark on her back bones; she faced east and listened to the wind and snow sing a high-pitched Yeibechei song. Out of the wind she felt warmer, and she could watch the wide fluffy snow fill in her tracks, steadily, until the direction she had come from was gone. By the light of the snow she could see the dark outline of the big arroyo a few feet away. She was sitting on the edge of Cebolleta Creek, where in the springtime the thin cows would graze on grass already chewed flat to the ground. In the wide deep creek bed where only a trickle of water flowed in the summer, the skinny cows would wander, looking for new grass along winding paths splashed with manure.

Ayah pulled the old Army blanket over her head like a shawl. Jimmie's blanket—the one he had sent to her. That was a long time ago and the green wool was faded, and it was unraveling on the edges. She did not want to think about Jimmie. So she thought about the weaving and the way her mother had done it. On the tall wooden loom set into the sand under a tamarack tree for shade. She could see it clearly. She had been only a little girl when her grandma gave her the wooden combs to pull the twigs and burrs from the raw, freshly washed wool. And while she combed the wool, her grandma sat beside her, spinning a silvery strand of yarn around the smooth cedar spindle. Her mother worked at the loom with yarns dyed bright yellow and red and gold. She watched them dye the yarn in boiling black pots full of beeweed petals, juniper berries, and sage. The blankets her mother made were soft and woven so tight that rain rolled off them like birds' feathers. Ayah remembered sleeping warm on cold windy nights, wrapped in her mother's blankets on the hogan's sandy floor.

The snow drifted now, with the northwest wind hurling it in gusts. It drifted up around her black overshoes—old ones with little metal buckles. She smiled at the snow which was trying to cover her little by little. She could remember when they had no black rubber overshoes; only the high buckskin leggings that they wrapped over their elkhide moccasins. If the snow was dry or frozen, a person could walk all day and not get wet; and in the evenings the beams of the ceiling would hang with lengths of pale buckskin leggings, drying out slowly.

She felt peaceful remembering. She didn't feel cold any more. Jimmie's blanket seemed warmer than it had ever been. And she could remember the morning he was born. She could remember whispering to her mother, who was sleeping on the other side of the hogan, to tell her it was time now. She did not want to wake the others. The second time she called to her, her mother stood up and pulled on her shoes; she knew. They walked to the old stone hogan together, Ayah walking a step behind her mother. She waited alone, learning the rhythms of the pains while her mother went to call the old woman to help them. The morning was already warm even before dawn and Ayah smelled the bee flowers blooming and the young willow growing at the springs. She could remember that so clearly, but his birth merged into the births of the other children and to her it became all the same birth. They named him for the summer morning and in English they called him Jimmie.

It wasn't like Jimmie died. He just never came back, and one day a dark blue sedan with white writing on its doors pulled up in front of the boxcar shack where the rancher let the Indians live. A man in a khaki uniform trimmed in gold gave them a yellow piece of paper and told them that Jimmie was dead. He said the Army would try to get the body back and then it would be shipped to them; but it wasn't likely because the helicopter had burned after it crashed. All of this was told to Chato because he could understand English. She stood inside the doorway holding the baby while Chato listened. Chato spoke English like a white man and he spoke Spanish too. He was taller than the white man and he stood straighter too. Chato didn't explain why; he just told the military man they could keep the body if they found it. The white man looked bewildered; he nodded his head and he left. Then Chato looked at her and shook his head, and then he told her, "Jimmie isn't coming home anymore," and when he spoke, he used the words to speak of the dead. She didn't cry then, but she hurt inside with anger. And she mourned him as the years passed, when a horse fell with Chato and broke his leg, and the white rancher told them he wouldn't pay Chato until he could work again. She mourned Jimmie because he would have worked for his father then; he would have saddled the big bay horse and ridden the fence lines each day, with wire cutters and heavy gloves, fixing the breaks in the barbed wire and putting the stray cattle back inside again.

She mourned him after the white doctors came to take Danny and Ella away. She was at the shack alone that day they came. It was back in the days before they hired Navajo women to go with them as interpreters. She recognized one of the doctors. She had seen him at the children's clinic at Cañoncito about a month ago. They were wearing khaki uniforms and they waved papers at her and a black ball-point pen, trying to make her understand their English words. She was frightened by the way they looked at the children, like the lizard watches the fly. Danny was swinging on the tire swing on the elm tree behind the rancher's house, and Ella was toddling around the front door, dragging the broomstick horse Chato made for her. Ayah could see they wanted her to sign the papers, and Chato had taught her to sign her name. It was something she was proud of. She only wanted them to go, and to take their eyes away from her children.

She took the pen from the man without looking at his face and she signed the papers in three different places he pointed to. She stared at the ground by their feet and waited for them to leave. But they stood there and began to point and gesture at the children. Danny stopped swinging. Ayah could see his fear. She moved suddenly and grabbed Ella into her arms; the child squirmed, trying to get back to her toys. Ayah ran with the baby toward Danny; she screamed for him to run and then she grabbed him around his chest and carried him too. She ran south into the foothills of juniper trees and black lava rock. Behind her she heard the doctors running, but they had been taken by surprise, and as the hills became steeper and the cholla cactus were thicker, they stopped. When she reached the top of the hill, she stopped to listen in case they were circling around her. But in a few minutes she heard a car engine start and they drove away. The children had been too surprised to cry while she ran with them. Danny was shaking and Ella's little fingers were gripping Ayah's blouse.

She stayed up in the hills for the rest of the day, sitting on a black lava boulder in the sunshine where she could see for miles all around her. The sky was light blue and cloudless, and it was warm for late April. The sun warmth relaxed her and took the fear and anger away. She lay back on the rock and watched the sky. It seemed to her that she could walk into the sky, stepping through clouds endlessly. Danny played with little pebbles and stones, pretending they were birds eggs and then little rabbits. Ella sat at her feet and dropped fistfuls of dirt into the breeze, watching the dust and particles of sand intently. Ayah watched a hawk soar high above them, dark wings gliding; hunting or only watching, she did not know. The hawk was patient and he circled all afternoon before he disappeared around the high volcanic peak the Mexicans called Guadalupe.

Late in the afternoon, Ayah looked down at the gray boxcar shack with the paint all peeled from the wood; the stove pipe on the roof was rusted and crooked. The fire she had built that morning in the oil drum stove had burned out. Ella was asleep in her lap now and Danny sat close to her, complaining that he was hungry; he asked when they would go to the house. "We will stay up here until your father comes," she told him, "because those white men were chasing us." The boy remembered then and he nodded at her silently.

If Jimmie had been there he could have read those papers and explained to her what they said. Ayah would have known then, never to sign them. The doctors came back the next day and they brought a BIA policeman with them. They told Chato they had her signature and that was all they needed. Except for the kids. She listened to Chato sullenly; she hated him when he told her it was the old woman who died in the winter, spitting blood; it was her old grandma who had given the children this disease. "They don't spit blood," she said coldly. "The whites lie." She held Ella and Danny close to her, ready to run to the hills again. "I want a medicine man first," she said to Chato, not looking at him. He shook his head. "It's too late now. The policeman is with them. You signed the paper." His voice was gentle.

It was worse than if they had died: to lose the children and to know that somewhere, in a place called Colorado, in a place full of sick and dying strangers, her children were without her. There had been babies that died soon after they were born, and one that died before he could walk. She had carried them herself, up to the boulders and great pieces of the cliff that long ago crashed down from Long Mesa; she laid them in the crevices of sandstone and buried them in fine brown sand with round quartz pebbles that washed down the hills in the rain. She had endured it because they had been with her. But she could not bear this pain. She did not sleep for a long time after they took her children. She stayed on the hill where they had fled the first time, and she slept rolled up in the blanket Jimmie had sent her. She carried the pain in her belly and it was fed by everything she saw: the blue sky of their last day together and the dust and pebbles they played with; the swing in the elm tree and broomstick horse choked life from her. The pain filled her stomach and there was no room for food or for her lungs to fill with air. The air and the food would have been theirs.

She hated Chato, not because he let the policeman and doctors put the screaming children in the government car, but because he had taught her to sign her name. Because it was like the old ones always told her about learning their language or any of their ways: it endangered you. She slept alone on the hill until the middle of November when the first snows came. Then she made a bed for herself where the children had slept. She did not lie down beside Chato again until many years later, when he was sick and shivering and only her body could keep him warm. The illness came after the white rancher told Chato he was too old to work for him anymore, and Chato and his old woman should be out of the shack by the next afternoon because the rancher had hired new people to work there. That had satisfied her. To see how the white man repaid Chato's years of loyalty and work. All of Chato's fine-sounding English talk didn't change things.

It snowed steadily and the luminous light from the snow gradually diminished into the darkness. Somewhere in Cebolleta a dog barked and other village dogs joined with it. Ayah looked in the direction she had come, from the bar where Chato was buying the wine. Sometimes he told her to go on ahead and wait; and then he never came. And when she finally went back looking for him, she would find him passed out at the bottom of the wooden steps to Azzie's Bar. All the wine would be gone and most of the money too, from the pale blue check that came to them once a month in a government envelope. It was then that she would look at his face and his hands, scarred by ropes and the barbed wire of all those years, and she would think, this man is a stranger; for forty years she had smiled at him and cooked his food, but he remained a stranger. She stood up again, with the snow almost to her knees, and she walked back to find Chato.

It was hard to walk in the deep snow and she felt the air burn in her lungs. She stopped a short distance from the bar to rest and readjust the blanket. But this time he wasn't waiting for her on the bottom step with his old Stetson hat pulled down and his shoulders hunched up in his long wool overcoat.

She was careful not to slip on the wooden steps. When she pushed the door open, warm air and cigarette smoke hit her face. She looked around slowly and deliberately, in every corner, in every dark place that the old man might find to sleep. The bar owner didn't like Indians in there, especially Navajos, but he let Chato come in because he could talk Spanish like he was one of them. The men at the bar stared at her, and the bartender saw that she left the door open wide. Snowflakes were flying inside like moths and melting into a puddle on the oiled wood floor. He motioned to her to close the door, but she did not see him. She held herself straight and walked across the room slowly, searching the room with every step. The snow in her hair melted and she could feel it on her forehead. At the far corner of the room, she saw red flames at the mica window of the old stove door; she looked behind the stove just to make sure. The bar got quiet except for the Spanish polka music playing on the jukebox. She stood by the stove and shook the snow from her blanket and held it near the stove to dry. The wet wool smell reminded her of new-born goats in early March, brought inside to warm near the fire. She felt calm.

In past years they would have told her to get out. But her hair was white now and her face was wrinkled. They looked at her like she was a spider crawling slowly across the room. They were afraid; she could feel the fear. She looked at their faces steadily. They reminded her of the first time the white people brought her children back to her that winter. Danny had been shy and hid behind the thin white woman who brought them. And the baby had not known her until Ayah took her into her arms, and then Ella had nuzzled close to her as she had when she was nursing. The blonde woman was nervous and kept looking at a dainty gold watch on her wrist. She sat on the bench near the small window and watched the dark snow clouds gather around the mountains; she was worrying about the unpaved road. She was frightened by what she saw inside too: the strips of venison drying on a rope across the ceiling and the children jabbering excitedly in a language she did not know. So they stayed for only a few hours. Ayah watched the government car disappear down the road and she knew they were already being weaned from these lava hills and from this sky. The last time they came was in early June, and Ella stared at her the way the men in the bar were now staring. Ayah did not try to pick her up; she smiled at her instead and spoke cheerfully to Danny. When he tried to answer her, he could not seem to remember and he spoke English words with the Navajo. But he gave her a scrap of paper that he had found somewhere and carried in his pocket; it was folded in half, and he shyly looked up at her and said it was a bird. She asked Chato if they were home for good this time. He spoke to the white woman and she shook her head. "How much longer?" he asked, and she said she didn't know; but Chato saw how she stared at the boxcar shack. Ayah turned away then. She did not say good-bye.

She felt satisfied that the men in the bar feared her. Maybe it was her face and the way she held her mouth with teeth clenched tight, like there was nothing anyone could do to her now. She walked north down the road, searching for the old man. She did this because she had the blanket, and there would be no place for him except with her and the blanket in the old adobe barn near the arroyo. They always slept there when they came to Cebolleta. If the money and the wine were gone, she would be relieved because then they could go home again; back to the old hogan with a dirt roof and rock walls where she herself had been born. And the next day the old man could go back to the few sheep they still had, to follow along behind them, guiding them, into dry sandy arroyos where sparse grass grew. She knew he did not like walking behind old ewes when for so many years he rode big quarter horses and worked with cattle. But she wasn't sorry for him; he should have known all along what would happen.

There had not been enough rain for their garden in five years; and that was when Chato finally hitched a ride into the town and brought back brown boxes of rice and sugar and big tin cans of welfare peaches. After that, at the first of the month they went to Cebolleta to ask the postmaster for the check; and then Chato would go to the bar and cash it. They did this as they planted the garden every May, not because anything would survive the summer dust, but because it was time to do this. The journey passed the days that smelled silent and dry like the caves above the canyon with yellow painted buffaloes on their walls.

He was walking along the pavement when she found him. He did not stop or turn around when he heard her behind him. She walked beside him and she noticed how slowly he moved now. He smelled strong of woodsmoke and urine. Lately he had been forgetting. Sometimes he called her by his sister's name and she had been gone for a long time. Once she had found him wandering on the road to the white man's ranch, and she asked him why he was going that way; he laughed at her and said, "You know they can't run that ranch without me," and he walked on determined, limping on the leg that had been crushed many years before. Now he looked at her curiously, as if for the first time, but he kept shuffling along, moving slowly along the side of the highway. His gray hair had grown long and spread out on the shoulders of the long overcoat. He wore the old felt hat pulled down over his ears. His boots were worn out at the toes and he had stuffed pieces of an old red shirt in the holes. The rags made his feet look like little animals up to their ears in snow. She laughed at his feet; the snow muffled the sound of her laugh. He stopped and looked at her again. The wind had quit blowing and the snow was falling straight down; the southeast sky was beginning to clear and Ayah could see a star.

"Let's rest awhile," she said to him. They walked away from the road and up the slope to the giant boulders that had tumbled down from the red sandrock mesa throughout the centuries of rainstorms and earth tremors. In a place where the boulders shut out the wind, they sat down with their backs against the rock. She offered half of the blanket to him and they sat wrapped together.

The storm passed swiftly. The clouds moved east. They were massive and full, crowding together across the sky. She watched them with the feeling of horses—steely blue-gray horses startled across the sky. The powerful haunches pushed into the distances and the tail hairs streamed white mist behind them. The sky cleared. Ayah saw that there was nothing between her and the stars. The light was crystalline. There was no shimmer, no distortion through earth haze. She breathed the clarity of the night sky; she smelled the purity of the half moon and the stars. He was lying on his side with his knees pulled up near his belly for warmth. His eyes were closed now, and in the light from the stars and the moon, he looked young again.

She could see it descend out of the night sky: an icy stillness from the edge of the thin moon. She recognized the freezing. It came gradually, sinking snowflake by snowflake until the crust was heavy and deep. It had the strength of the stars in Orion, and its journey was endless. Ayah knew that with the wine he would sleep. He would not feel it. She tucked the blanket around him, remembering how it was when Ella had been with her; and she felt the rush so big inside her heart for the babies. And she sang the only song she knew to sing for babies. She could not remember if she had ever sung it to her children, but she knew that her grandmother had sung it and her mother had sung it:

> The earth is your mother,
>   she holds you.
> The sky is your father,
>   he protects you.
> Sleep,
> sleep.
> Rainbow is your sister,
>   she loves you.
> The winds are your brothers,
>   they sing to you.
> Sleep,
> sleep.
> We are together always
> We are together always
> There never was a time
> when this
> was not so.

❧ Joy Harjo (born 1951)

Born in Tulsa, Oklahoma, Joy Harjo is a writer whose work reflects her heritage as a member of the Muskogee Creek nation, in incorporating Native American myths, images, and the landscape of the Southwest. But first and foremost, Harjo is a poet of witness whose subject is the precarious place of the Native American—and of all of us—in the modern world. Nature, "the oldest story in the world," is the central subject of Secrets from the Center of the World *(1989), in which each poem is printed next to a photograph of the Southwest, suggesting the complex interrelationship between the personal and the universal. As Harjo remarked in an interview, "Sacred space—I call it a place of grace, or the place in which we're most human—the place in which there's a unity of human-ness with wolf-ness, with hummingbird-ness, with Sandia Mountain-ness, with rain cloud-ness . . . It's that place in which we understand there is no separation between worlds. It has everything to do with the way we live. The land is responsible for the clothes you have on, for my saxophone, for the paper that I write these things on, for our bodies. It's responsible for everything." The interconnectedness of all things is an especially strong theme in her most recent work, in which she combines Muskogee tribal song and storytelling, Navajo and Hawaiian philosophies, and the music of the Middle East.*

Harjo earned a B.A. from the University of New Mexico and the M.F.A. from the University of Iowa Writers' Workshop. She also studied filmmaking at the Anthropology Film Center. Harjo has been honored with many awards, among them the National Endowment for the Arts Fellowship, the American Indian Distinguished Achievement Award, the Josephine Miles Award, the William Carlos Williams Award, and the American Book Award. In addition to her writing, Harjo is also a musician who performs her poetry and plays the saxophone with her band, Poetic Justice. Her books of poetry also include The Last Song (1975), What Moon Drove Me to This? (1980), She Had Some Horses (1983), Thunder's Mouth (1983), In Mad Love and War (1990), The Woman Who Fell from the Sky (1996), and A Map to the Next World (1999). She has also collected the work of Native American writers in two anthologies, A Circle of Nations: Voices and Visions of American Indians (1993) and Reinventing the Enemy's Language: Contemporary Native Women's Writing of North America (1997).

Grace

(For Wind and Jim Welch)

I think of Wind and her wild ways the year we had nothing to lose
and lost it anyway in the cursed country of the fox. We still talk
about that winter, how the cold froze imaginary buffalo on the stuffed
horizon of snowbanks. The haunting voices of the starved and mutilated
broke fences, crashed our thermostat dreams, and we couldn't stand it   5
one more time. So once again we lost a winter in stubborn memory,
walked through cheap apartment walls, skated through fields of ghosts
into a town that never wanted us, in the epic search for grace.

Like Coyote, like Rabbit,[1] we could not contain our terror and clowned
our way through a season of false midnights. We had to swallow   10
that town with laughter, so it would go down easy as honey. And one
morning as the sun struggled to break ice, and our dreams had found us
with coffee and pancakes in a truck stop along Highway 80,
we found grace.

I could say grace was a woman with time on her hands, or a white   15
buffalo escaped from memory. But in that dingy light it was a promise
of balance. We once again understood the talk of animals, and spring
was lean and hungry with the hope of children and corn.

I would like to say, with grace, we picked ourselves up and walked
into the spring thaw. We didn't; the next season was worse. You went   20
home to Leech Lake to work with the tribe and I went south. And, Wind,
I am still crazy. I know there is something larger than the memory
of a dispossessed people. We have seen it.

[1]Coyote and Rabbit are Native American trickster figures.

Trickster

Crow, in the new snow.
You caw, caw
      like crazy.

Laugh.
Because you know I'm a fool   5
too, like you
skimming over the thin ice
to the war going on
all over the world.

Deer Ghost

1

I hear a deer outside; her glass voice of the invisible
calls my heart to stand up and weep in this fragile city.
The season changed once more, as if my childhood
was forced from me, stolen during the dream of the lion
fleeing the old-style houses my people used to make of mud   5
and straw to mother the source of burning. The skeleton
of stars encircling this misty world stares through the roof;
there is no hiding any more, and mystery is a skin that will never
quite fit. This is a night ghosts wander, and in this place
they are as nameless as the nightmare the muscles in my   10
left hand remember.

2

I have failed once more and let the fire go out. I misunderstood
and left my world on your musk angel wings. Your fire scorched
my lips, but it was sweet, a bitter poetry. I can taste you
now as I squat on the earth floor of this home I abandoned   15
for you. On this street named for a warrior people, a street
named after bravery, I am lighting the fire that crawls from my spine
to the gods with a coal from my sister's flame. This is what names
me in the ways of my people, who have called me back.
The deer knows what it is doing wandering the streets of this   20
city; it has never forgotten the songs.

3

I don't care what you say. The deer is no imaginary tale
I have created to fill this house because you left me.
There is more to this world than I have ever let on
to you, or anyone.   25

Eagle Poem

To pray you open your whole self
To sky, to earth, to sun, to moon

To one whole voice that is you.
And know there is more
That you can't see, can't hear,   5
Can't know except in moments
Steadily growing, and in languages
That aren't always sound but other
Circles of motion.
Like eagle that Sunday morning   10
Over Salt River. Circled in blue sky
In wind, swept our hearts clean
With sacred wings.
We see you, see ourselves and know
That we must take the utmost care   15
And kindness in all things.
Breathe in, knowing we are made of
All this, and breathe, knowing
We are truly blessed because we
Were born, and die soon within a   20
True circle of motion,
Like eagle rounding out the morning
Inside us.
We pray that it will be done
In beauty.   25
In beauty.

✍ *Rita Dove* *(born 1952)*

Born in Akron, Ohio, Rita Dove was encouraged by her parents to read anything and everything, leading her from Shakespeare's plays to Superman comic books. The library was the one place she was allowed to go without asking permission. From there, she would go on to write stories and plays, urging her classmates to perform them. She remarked in an interview, "My parents instilled in us the feeling that learning was the most exciting thing that could happen to you, and it never ends, and isn't that great." From 1993 to 1995 she served as Poet Laureate of the United States and Consultant in Poetry to the Library of Congress, the first African American, the first African American woman, and the youngest person ever to receive this honor. Throughout and beyond her tenure as Poet Laureate, she served as a tireless spokesperson for poetry and literacy, lecturing and appearing on popular television and radio shows such as Sesame Street, Prairie Home Companion, *and* The Today Show. *These appearances were part of her project to build a greater readership for poetry and "to bring poetry into everyday discourse . . . to make it much more of a household word."*

Dove holds a B.A. from Miami University of Ohio and an M.F.A. from the University of Iowa Writers' Workshop. She first won critical attention for The Yellow House on the Corner *(1980), a collection of poems arising from her middle-class life in Akron and from her awareness of the history of slavery. In 1987 she won the Pulitzer Prize for* Thomas and Beulah *(1986), a collection of poems about the quiet drama of her grandparents' lives, from early in the century until their deaths in the 1960s. She has also received two National Endowment for the Arts fellowships and a Guggenheim fellowship, among other awards.*

Marked by rich imagery, her poetry ranges from the personal subjects to matters of family history to poems of social awareness, always embodying a strong sense of story and an acute consciousness of American history and politics. In all her work, Dove is able to find the personal significance in broader themes and to make those themes immediate and real. In the poem "Afield," for example, Dove reworks the Persephone myth to explore issues of death and rebirth. Her books also include Selected Poems *(1993),* Mother Love *(1995), and* On the Bus with Rosa Parks *(1999). Dove is also an accomplished writer of fiction, with a collection of short stories,* Fifth Sunday *(1985), and a novel,* Through the Ivory Gate *(1992). In addition, she has written several plays and verse dramas, including* The Darker Face of the Earth *(1994). She is Commonwealth Professor of English at the University of Virginia, where she teaches creative writing.*

Daystar

She wanted a little room for thinking:
but she saw diapers steaming on the line,
a doll slumped behind the door.

So she lugged a chair behind the garage
to sit out the children's naps.   5

Sometimes there were things to watch—
the pinched armor of a vanished cricket,
a floating maple leaf. Other days
she stared until she was assured
when she closed her eyes   10
she'd see only her own vivid blood.

She had an hour, at best, before Liza appeared
pouting from the top of the stairs.
And just *what* was mother doing
out back with the field mice? Why,   15

building a palace. Later
that night when Thomas rolled over and
lurched into her, she would open her eyes
and think of the place that was hers
for an hour—where   20
she was nothing,
pure nothing, in the middle of the day.

Afield

Out where crows dip to their kill
under the clouds' languid white oars
she wanders, hands pocketed, hair combed tight
so she won't feel the breeze quickening—
as if she were trying to get back to him,   5
find the breach in the green
that would let her slip through,
then tug meadow over the wound like a sheet.

I've walked there, too: he can't give
you up, so you give in until you can't live   10
without him. Like these blossoms, white sores
burst upon earth's ignorant flesh, at first sight
everything is innocence—
then it's itch, scratch, putrescence.

✌ *Terry Tempest Williams* (born 1955)

Terry Tempest Williams's ancestors followed Brigham Young to Utah in the nineteenth century. Her family has stayed in the state ever since, and Williams claims that this connection to place not only provides the substance of her writings but is also a human necessity that everyone should enjoy. During an interview, she once said, "I think the whole idea of home is central to who we are as human beings." Her devotion to the West's rugged landscape and all of its inhabitants, human and otherwise, has pressured the otherwise shy writer to publish numerous books on conservation and to protest repeatedly against that which threatens the place and creatures she loves. Williams was very active in the 1980s when the radioactive residues of atmospheric nuclear testing in Nevada allegedly caused damage to human health and wildlife near her home outside Salt Lake City.

To Williams, the fate of humanity is inseparably bound to the wilderness, and her writings are a testament to her belief that responsible progress and conservation should be humankind's foremost concern. At a reading at the University of California at Davis, Williams once remarked, "What if we extend our notion of community to include all life forms? Perhaps that is our unspoken hunger." Williams's writings include The Clan of One-Breasted Women *(1991),* Refuge: An Unnatural History of Family and Place *(1992), and* An Unspoken Hunger: Stories from the Field *(1995).*

The Architecture of a Soul

Pink murex. *Melongena corona.* Cowry. Conch. Mussel. Left-sided whelk. Lightning whelk. True-heart cockle. Olivella. Pribilof lora. Angel wings.

These are the names of shells, the shells my grandmother and I catalogued together during the winter of 1963. I was eight years old.

With field guides all around us, we thumbed through plates of photographs, identifying each shell. Mimi would read the descriptions out loud to be certain our classifications were correct. Then, with a blue ballpoint pen, we would write the appropriate name on white adhesive tape and stick it on the corresponding shell.

"It's important to have a hobby," Mimi said, "something to possess you in your private hours."

My grandmother's hobby was spending time at the ocean, walking along the beach, picking up shells.

For a desert child, there was nothing more beautiful than shells. I loved their shapes, their colors. I cherished the way they felt in the palm of my hand—and they held the voice of the sea, a primal sound imprinted on me as a baby.

"Your mother and I took you to the beach shortly after you were born," Mimi said. "As you got older, you played in the sand by the hour."

I played with these shells in the bathtub. The pufferfish was my favorite animal. I knew it was dead, dried out, and hollow, but somehow when it floated in the hot water next to my small, pink body, it came to life—a spiny globe with eyes.

Mimi would knock on the bathroom door.

"Come in," I would say.

She surveyed my watery world. I handed her the puffer, wet.

"When I die," she said smiling, "these shells will be your inheritance."

Thirty years later, these shells—the same shells my grandmother collected on her solitary walks along the beach, the shells we spread out on the turquoise carpet of her study, the shells we catalogued, the shells I bathed with—now rest in a basket on a shelf in my study. They remind me of my natural history, that I was tutored by a woman who courted solitude and made pilgrimages to the edges of our continent in the name of her own pleasure, that beauty, awe, and curiosity were values illuminated in our own home.

My grandmother's contemplation of shells has become my own. Each shell is a whorl of creative expression, an architecture of a soul. I can hold *Melongena corona* to my ear and hear not only the ocean's voice, but the whisperings of my beloved teacher.

Undressing the Bear

He came home from the war and shot a bear. He had been part of the Tenth Mountain Division that fought on Mount Belvedere in Italy during World War II. When he returned home to Wyoming, he could hardly wait to get back to the wilderness. It was fall, the hunting season. He would enact the ritual of man against animal once again. A black bear crossed the meadow. The man fixed his scope on the bear and pulled the trigger. The bear screamed. He brought down his rifle and found himself shaking. This had never happened before. He walked over to the warm beast, now dead, and placed his hand on its shoulder. Setting his gun down, he pulled out his buck knife and began skinning the bear that he would pack out on his horse. As he pulled the fur coat away from the muscle, down the breasts and over the swell of the hips, he suddenly stopped. This was not a bear. It was a woman.

Another bear story: There is a woman who travels by sled dogs in Alaska. On one of her journeys through the interior, she stopped to visit an old friend, a Koyukon man. They spoke for some time about the old ways of his people. She listened until it was time for her to go. As she was harnessing her dogs, he offered one piece of advice.

"If you should run into Bear, lift up your parka and show him you are a woman."

And another: I have a friend who manages a bookstore. A regular customer dropped by to browse. They began sharing stories, which led to a discussion of dreams. My friend shared hers.

"I dreamt I was in Yellowstone. A grizzly, upright, was walking toward me. Frightened at first, I began to pull away, when suddenly a mantle of calm came over me. I walked toward the bear and we embraced."

The man across the counter listened, and then said matter-of-factly, "Get over it."

* * *

Why? Why should we give up the dream of embracing the bear? For me, it has everything to do with undressing, exposing, and embracing the Feminine.

I see the Feminine defined as a reconnection to the Self, a commitment to the wildness within—our instincts, our capacity to create and destroy; our hunger for connection as well as sovereignty, interdependence and independence, at once. We are taught not to trust our own experience.

The Feminine teaches us experience is our way back home, the psychic bridge that spans rational and intuitive waters. To embrace the Feminine is to embrace paradox. Paradox preserves mystery, and mystery inspires belief.

I believe in the power of Bear.

The Feminine has long been linked to the bear through mythology. The Greek goddess Artemis, whose name means "bear," embodies the wisdom of the wild. Christine Downing, in her book *The Goddess: Mythological Images of the Feminine*, describes her as "the one who knows each tree by its bark or leaf or fruit, each beast by its footprint or spoor, each bird by its plumage or call or nest."

It is Artemis, perhaps originally a Cretan goddess of fertility, who denounces the world of patriarchy, demanding chastity from her female attendants. Callisto, having violated her virginity and become pregnant, is transformed into the She-Bear of the night sky by Artemis. Other mythical accounts credit Artemis herself as Ursa Major, ruler of the heavens and protectress of the Pole Star or *axis mundi*.

I saw Ursa Major presiding over Dark Canyon in the remote corner of south-eastern Utah. She climbed the desert sky as a jeweled bear following her tracks around the North Star, as she does year after year, honoring the power of seasonal renewal.

At dawn, the sky bear disappeared and I found myself walking down-canyon. Three years ago, the pilgrimage had been aborted. I fell. Head to stone, I rolled down the steep talus slope stopped only by the grace of an old juniper tree precariously perched at a forty-five-degree angle. When I stood up, it was a bloody red landscape. Placing my hand on my forehead, I felt along the three-inch tear of skin down to the bony plate of my skull. I had opened my third eye. Unknowingly, this was what I had come for. It had been only a few months since the death of my mother. I had been unable to cry. On this day, I did.

Now scarred by experience, I returned to Dark Canyon determined to complete my descent into the heart of the desert. Although I had fears of falling again, a different woman inhabited my body. There had been a deepening of self through time. My mother's death had become part of me. She had always worn a small silver bear fetish around her neck to keep her safe. Before she died, she took off the bear and placed it in my hand. I wore it on this trip.

In canyon country, you pick your own path. Walking in wilderness becomes a meditation. I followed a small drainage up one of the benches. Lithic scatter was everywhere, evidence of Anasazi culture, a thousand years past. I believed the flakes of chert and obsidian would lead me to ruins. I walked intuitively. A smell of cut wood seized me. I looked up. Before me stood a lightning-struck tree blown apart by the force of the bolt. A fallout of wood chips littered the land in a hundred-foot radius. The piñon pine was still smoldering.

My companion, who came to the burning tree by way of another route, picked up a piece of the charred wood, sacred to the Hopi, and began carving a bull-roarer. As he whirled it above our heads on twisted cordage, it wailed in low, deep tones. Rain began — female rain falling gently, softly, as a fine mist over the desert.

Hours later, we made camp. All at once, we heard a roar up-canyon. Thunder? Too sustained. Jets overhead? A clear sky above. A peculiar organic smell reached us on the wind. We got the message. Flushed with fear, we ran to higher ground. Suddenly, a ten-foot wall of water came storming down the canyon, filling the empty streambed. If the flood had struck earlier, when we were hiking in the narrows, we would have been swept away like the cottonwood trees it was now carrying. We watched the muddy river as though it were a parade, continually inching back as the water eroded the earth beneath our feet.

That night, a lunar rainbow arched over Dark Canyon like a pathway of souls. I had heard the Navajos speak of them for years, never knowing if such magic could exist. It was a sweep of stardust within pastel bands of light — pink, lavender, yellow, and blue. And I felt the presence of angels, even my mother, her wings spread above me like a hovering dove.

In these moments, I felt innocent and wild, privy to secrets and gifts exchanged only in nature. I was the tree, split open by change. I was the flood, bursting through grief. I was the rainbow at night, dancing in darkness. Hands on the earth, I closed my eyes and remembered where the source of my power lies. My connection to the natural world is my connection to self—erotic, mysterious, and whole.

The next morning, I walked to the edge of the wash, shed my clothes, and bathed in pumpkin-colored water. It was to be one of the last warm days of autumn. Standing naked in the sand, I noticed bear tracks. Bending down, I gently placed my right hand inside the fresh paw print.

Women and bears.

Marian Engel, in her novel *Bear*, portrays a woman and a bear in an erotics of place. It doesn't matter whether the bear is seen as male or female. The relationship between the two is sensual, wild.

The woman says, "Bear, take me to the bottom of the ocean with you, Bear, swim with me, Bear, put your arms around me, enclose me, swim, down, down, down, with me."

"Bear," she says suddenly, "come dance with me."

They make love. Afterward, "She felt pain, but it was a dear sweet pain that belonged not to mental suffering, but to the earth."

I have felt the pain that arises from a recognition of beauty, pain we hold when we remember what we are connected to and the delicacy of our relations. It is this tenderness born out of a connection to place that fuels my writing. Writing becomes an act of compassion toward life, the life we so often refuse to see because if we look too closely or feel too deeply, there may be no end to our suffering. But words empower us, move us beyond our suffering, and set us free. This is the sorcery of literature. We are healed by our stories.

By undressing, exposing, and embracing the bear, we undress, expose, and embrace our authentic selves. Stripped free from society's oughts and shoulds, we emerge as emancipated beings. The bear is free to roam.

If we choose to follow the bear, we will be saved from a distractive and domesticated life. The bear becomes our mentor. We must journey out, so that we might journey in. The bear mother enters the earth before snowfall and dreams herself through winter, emerging in spring with young by her side. She not only survives the barren months, she gives birth. She is the caretaker of the unseen world. As a writer and a woman with obligations to both family and community, I have tried to adopt this ritual in the balancing of a public and private life. We are at home in the deserts and mountains, as well as in our dens. Above ground in the abundance of spring and summer, I am available. Below ground in the deepening of autumn and winter, I am not. I need hibernation in order to create.

We are creatures of paradox, women and bears, two animals that are enormously unpredictable, hence our mystery. Perhaps the fear of bears and the fear of women lies in our refusal to be tamed, the impulses we arouse and the forces we represent.

Last spring, our family was in Yellowstone. We were hiking along Pelican Creek, which separated us from an island of lodgepole pines. All at once, a dark form stood in front of the forest on a patch of snow. It was a grizzly, and behind her, two cubs. Suddenly, the sow turned and bolted through the trees. A female elk crashed through the timber to the other side of the clearing, stopped, and swung back toward the bear. Within seconds, the grizzly emerged with an elk calf secure in the grip of her jaws. The sow shook the yearling violently by the nape of its neck, threw it down, clamped her claws on its shoulders, and began tearing the flesh back from the bones with her teeth. The cow elk, only a few feet away, watched the sow devour her calf. She pawed the earth desperately with her front hooves, but the bear was oblivious. Blood dripped from the sow's muzzle. The cubs stood by their mother, who eventually turned the carcass over to them. Two hours passed. The sow buried the calf for a later meal, she slept on top of the mound with a paw on each cub. It was not until then that the elk crossed the river in retreat.

We are capable of harboring both these responses to life in the relentless power of our love. As women connected to the earth, we are nurturing and we are fierce, we are wicked and we are sublime. The full range is ours. We hold the moon in our bellies and fire in our hearts. We bleed. We give milk. We are the mothers of first words. These words grow. They are our children. They are our stories and our poems.

By allowing ourselves to undress, expose, and embrace the Feminine, we commit our vulnerabilities not to fear but to courage—the courage that allows us to write on behalf of the earth, on behalf of ourselves.

Credits

Edward Abbey, "Water" from *Desert Solitaire: A Season in the Wilderness* (New York: McGraw-Hill, 1968). Copyright © 1968 by Edward Abbey. Reprinted with the permission of Harold Matson, Inc.

Elizabeth Bishop, "The Fish" and "The Moose" from *The Complete Poems 1927–1979*. Copyright © 1979, 1983 by Alice Helen Methfessel. Reprinted with the permission of Farrar, Straus & Giroux, LLC.

Robert Bly, "Solitude Late at Night in the Woods," "Reading in Fall Rain," "The Starfish," and "The Dead Seal" from *Selected Poems*. Copyright © 1986 by Robert Bly. Reprinted with the permission of HarperCollins Publishers, Inc.

Rachel Carson, "The Marginal World" from *The Edge of the Sea*. Copyright © 1955 by Rachel L. Carson. Reprinted with the permission of Houghton Mifflin Company. All rights reserved.

Angela Carter, "The Company of Wolves" from *The Bloody Chamber and Other Adult Tales* (New York: HarperCollins Publishers, 1979). Copyright © 1979 by Angela Carter. Reprinted with the permission of the estate of the author, c/o Rodgers, Coleridge & White, 20 Powis Mews, London W11 1JN.

James Dickey, "The Heaven of Animals," "In the Tree House at Night," and "The Salt Marsh" from *Poems 1957–1967*. Copyright © 1958, 1959, 1960, 1961, 1962, 1963, 1964, 1965, 1966, 1967 by James Dickey. Reprinted with the permission of University Press of New England, Hanover, NH.

Emily Dickinson, poems from *The Complete Poems of Emily Dickinson*, edited by Thomas H. Johnson. Copyright © 1998 by the President and Fellows of Harvard College. Copyright 1929, 1935 by Martha Dickinson Bianchi, renewed © 1957, 1963 by Mary L. Hampson. Reprinted with the permission of The Belknap Press of Harvard University Press.

Annie Dillard, "Untying the Knot" from *Pilgrim at Tinker Creek*. Copyright © 1974 by Annie Dillard. Reprinted with the permission of HarperCollins Publishers, Inc.

H. D. (Hilda Doolittle), "Sheltered Garden" and "Sea Violet" from *Collected Poems 1912–1944*. Copyright © 1982 by The Estate of Hilda Doolittle. Reprinted with the permission of New Directions Publishing Corporation.

Rita Dove, "Daystar" from *Thomas and Beulah* (Pittsburgh, PA: Carnegie Mellon University Press, 1986). Copyright © 1986 by Rita Dove. Reprinted with the permission of the author. "Afield" from *Mother Love*. Copyright © 1995 by Rita Dove. Reprinted with the permission of the author and W. W. Norton & Company, Inc.

Loren Eiseley, "The Bird and the Machine" from *The Immense Journey*. Copyright © 1956 by Loren Eiseley. Reprinted with the permission of Random House, Inc.

Gretel Erlich, "On Water" from *The Solace of Open Spaces*. Copyright © 1985 by Gretel Erlich. Reprinted with the permission of Viking Penguin, a division of Penguin Putnam Inc.

William Faulkner, "Delta Autumn" from *Uncollected Stories*. Copyright 1942 by William Faulkner. Reprinted with the permission of Random House, Inc.

Robert Frost, "The Pasture," "The Exposed Nest," "The Oven Bird," "Birches," "Spring Pools," "Design," and "The Most of It" from *Complete Poems of Robert Frost*. Copyright

Index